we call "civilization" is relatively recent, indeed, with the first permanent settlements occurring in the Middle East a scant 12 000 years ago. But the written record of our species' existence extends back only half this long, to the time humans invented writing and first farmed with animal-driven plows some 5000 years BP.

Sociology came into being in the wake of the many changes to society wrought by the Industrial Revolution over the last few centuries—just the blink of an eye in evolutionary perspective. The lower timeline provides a close-up look at the events and trends that have defined **The Modern Era**, most of which are discussed in this text. Innovations in technology are charted in the beige panel below the line and provide a useful backdrop for viewing the milestones of social progress highlighted in the blue panel above the line. Major contributions to the development of sociological thought are traced along the very bottom of this timeline.

sociology

This book is offered to teachers of sociology in the hope that it will help our students understand their place in today's society and in tomorrow's world.

sociology

JOHN J. MACIONIS

Kenyon College

LINDA M. GERBER

University of Guelph

FIFTH CANADIAN EDITION

@Ryerson.ca
Sept. 2006

PEARSON

Prentice
Hall

Toronto

National Library of Canada Cataloguing in Publication

Macionis, John J.
   Sociology / John J. Macionis, Linda M. Gerber. — 5th Canadian ed.

 Includes bibliographical references and index.
ISBN 0-13-121753-4

   1. Sociology. I. Gerber, Linda Marie, 1944– II. Title.

HM586.M32 2005   301   C2003-905894-8

ISBN 0-13-121753-4

Vice President, Editorial Director: Michael J. Young
Executive Acquisitions Editor: Jessica Mosher
Executive Marketing Manager: Judith Allen
Developmental Editor: John Polanszky
Editorial Coordinator: Söğüt Y. Güleç
Copy Editor: Lesley Mann
Proofreader: Kathleen Richards
Production Manager: Wendy Moran
Page Layout: Hermia Chung
Permissions and Photo Research: Amanda McCormick
Art Director: Julia Hall
Interior Design: Dave McKay
Cover Design: Julia Hall
Cover Image: Photonica

Statistics Canada information is used with the permission of the Minister of Industry, as Minister responsible for Statistics Canada. Information on the availability of the wide range of data from Statistics Canada can be obtained from Statistics Canada's Regional Offices, its World Wide Web site at http://www.statcan.ca, and its toll-free access number 1-800-263-1136.

 4 5   09 08 07 06

Printed and bound in the USA.

BRIEF CONTENTS

PART I
THE FOUNDATIONS OF SOCIOLOGY

1 THE SOCIOLOGICAL PERSPECTIVE 2
2 SOCIOLOGICAL INVESTIGATION 26

the 1st Semester

PART II
THE FOUNDATIONS OF SOCIETY

3 CULTURE 54
4 SOCIETY 82
5 SOCIALIZATION 106
6 SOCIAL INTERACTION IN EVERYDAY LIFE 130
7 GROUPS AND ORGANIZATIONS 154
8 SEXUALITY 182
9 DEVIANCE 206

the 2nd Semester

PART III
SOCIAL INEQUALITY

10 SOCIAL STRATIFICATION 234
11 SOCIAL CLASS IN CANADA 258
12 GLOBAL STRATIFICATION 282
13 GENDER STRATIFICATION 308
14 RACE AND ETHNICITY 334
15 AGING AND THE ELDERLY 360

the 3rd Semester

PART IV
SOCIAL INSTITUTIONS

16 THE ECONOMY AND WORK 382
17 POLITICS AND GOVERNMENT 410
18 FAMILY 444
19 RELIGION 470
20 EDUCATION 494
21 HEALTH AND MEDICINE 518

the 4th Semester

PART V
SOCIAL CHANGE

22 POPULATION, URBANIZATION, AND THE ENVIRONMENT 542
23 COLLECTIVE BEHAVIOUR AND SOCIAL MOVEMENTS 574
24 SOCIAL CHANGE: TRADITIONAL, MODERN, AND POSTMODERN SOCIETIES 596

CONTENTS

Boxes   xix
Maps   xxiii
Preface   xxv
About the Authors   xxxi

PART I
THE FOUNDATIONS OF SOCIOLOGY

1 THE SOCIOLOGICAL PERSPECTIVE   2

THE SOCIOLOGICAL PERSPECTIVE   3

Seeing the General in the Particular   3
Seeing the Strange in the Familiar   5
Individuality in Social Context   6

THE IMPORTANCE OF GLOBAL PERSPECTIVE   6

APPLYING THE SOCIOLOGICAL PERSPECTIVE   6

Sociology and Social Marginality   10
Sociology and Social Crisis   10
Benefits of the Sociological Perspective   10
Applied Sociology   11

THE ORIGINS OF SOCIOLOGY   12

Science and Sociology   12
Social Change and Sociology   13
Marginal Voices   14
Canadian Sociology: Distinctive Touches   15

SOCIOLOGICAL THEORY   16

The Structural-Functional Paradigm   16
The Social-Conflict Paradigm   18
The Symbolic-Interaction Paradigm   19

The Feminist Paradigm   20
The Postmodernist Paradigm   20
Applying the Perspectives: The Sociology of Sport   21

*Summary   24   Critical-Thinking Questions   24
Applications and Exercises   24   Sites to See   25
Investigate with ContentSelect   25*

2 SOCIOLOGICAL INVESTIGATION   26

THE BASICS OF SOCIOLOGICAL INVESTIGATION   28

Science as One Form of "Truth"   28
Common Sense Versus Scientific Evidence   29

SCIENCE: BASIC ELEMENTS AND LIMITATIONS   30

Concepts, Variables, and Measurement   30
The Ideal of Objectivity   32
Some Limitations of Scientific Sociology (Positivism)   34
A Second Framework: Interpretive Sociology   35
A Third Framework: Critical Sociology   35
Gender and Research   37
Women as Methodologists   38
Research Ethics   39

THE METHODS OF SOCIOLOGICAL RESEARCH   40

Testing a Hypothesis: The Experiment   40
Asking Questions: Survey Research   42
In the Field: Participant Observation   45
Using Available Data: Secondary and Historical Analysis   47
Technology and Research   48
The Interplay of Theory and Method   49

PUTTING IT ALL TOGETHER: TEN STEPS IN SOCIOLOGICAL INVESTIGATION   50

*Summary   51   Critical-Thinking Questions   52
Applications and Exercises   52   Sites to See   52
Investigate with ContentSelect   53*

PART II
THE FOUNDATIONS OF SOCIETY

3 CULTURE 54

WHAT IS CULTURE? 55
Culture and Human Intelligence 56
Culture, Nation, State, and Society 58

THE COMPONENTS OF CULTURE 58
Symbols 58
Language 59
Values and Beliefs 62
Norms 64
"Ideal" and "Real" Culture 65
Material Culture and Technology 65
New Information Technology and Culture 66

CULTURAL DIVERSITY: MANY WAYS OF
LIFE IN ONE WORLD 66
High Culture and Popular Culture 66
Subculture 67
Multiculturalism 68
Counterculture 70
Cultural Change 70
Ethnocentrism and Cultural Relativity 71
A Global Culture? 72

THEORETICAL ANALYSIS OF CULTURE 73
Structural-Functional Analysis 73
Social-Conflict Analysis 74
Cultural Materialism 75
Sociobiology 76
Culture as Constraint 77
Culture as Freedom 77

*Summary 78 Critical-Thinking Questions 80
Applications and Exercises 80 Sites To See 80
Investigate with ContentSelect 81*

4 SOCIETY 82

GERHARD AND JEAN LENSKI:
SOCIETY AND TECHNOLOGY 83

Hunting-and-Gathering Societies 84
Horticultural and Pastoral Societies 85
Agrarian Societies 86
Industrial Societies 87
Post-industrial Societies 88
The Limits of Technology 89

KARL MARX: SOCIETY AND CONFLICT 89
Society and Production 89
Conflict in History 91
Capitalism and Class Conflict 92
Capitalism and Alienation 93
Revolution 94

MAX WEBER: THE RATIONALIZATION OF
SOCIETY 94
Two World Views: Tradition and
    Rationality 95
Is Capitalism Rational? 95
Weber's Great Thesis: Protestantism and
    Capitalism 95
Rational Social Organization 96

EMILE DURKHEIM: SOCIETY AND
FUNCTION 99
Structure: Society Beyond Ourselves 99
Function: Society as System 99
Personality: Society in Ourselves 99
Evolving Societies: The Division of Labour 100

CRITICAL EVALUATION: FOUR VISIONS
OF SOCIETY 101

*Summary 102 Critical-Thinking Questions 104
Applications and Exercises 104 Sites to See 104
Investigate with ContentSelect 105*

5 SOCIALIZATION 106

SOCIAL EXPERIENCE: THE KEY TO
OUR HUMANITY 107
Human Development: Nature and Nurture 107
Social Isolation 109

UNDERSTANDING THE SOCIALIZATION
PROCESS 110
Sigmund Freud: The Elements of
    Personality 110
Jean Piaget: Cognitive Development 111
Lawrence Kohlberg: Moral Development 113
Carol Gilligan: Bringing in Gender 113
George Herbert Mead: The Social Self 113
Erik H. Erikson: Eight Stages of Development
    116

AGENTS OF SOCIALIZATION   117
The Family   117
Schooling   117
The Peer Group   118
The Mass Media   119

SOCIALIZATION AND THE LIFE
COURSE   122
Childhood   122
Adolescence   122
Adulthood   123
Old Age   125
Dying   125
The Life Course: An Overview   126

RESOCIALIZATION:
TOTAL INSTITUTIONS   126

Summary   128   Critical-Thinking Questions   128
Applications and Exercises   129   Sites to See   129
Investigate with ContentSelect   129

6 SOCIAL INTERACTION IN
EVERYDAY LIFE   130
SOCIAL STRUCTURE: A GUIDE TO
EVERYDAY LIVING   131
Status   131
Status Set   132
Ascribed and Achieved Status   132
Master Status   132

ROLE   133
Role Set   133
Role Conflict and Role Strain   133
Role Exit   134

THE SOCIAL CONSTRUCTION OF
REALITY   135
The Thomas Theorem   136
Ethnomethodology   136
Reality Building: Some Broader
   Considerations   137

DRAMATURGICAL ANALYSIS:
"THE PRESENTATION OF SELF"   138
Performances   138
Nonverbal Communication   139
Gender and Personal Performances   141
Idealization   143
Embarrassment and Tact   143

INTERACTION IN EVERYDAY LIFE:
TWO ILLUSTRATIONS   145
Language: The Gender Issue   145

Humour: Playing with Reality   146

Summary   150   Critical-Thinking Questions   152
Applications and Exercises   152   Sites to See   153
Investigate with ContentSelect   153

7 GROUPS AND
ORGANIZATIONS   154
SOCIAL GROUPS   155
Groups, Categories, and Crowds   156
Primary and Secondary Groups   156
Group Leadership   157
Group Conformity   158
Reference Groups   160
Group Size   161
Social Diversity   162
Networks   163

FORMAL ORGANIZATIONS   164
Types of Formal Organizations   165
Origins of Bureaucracy   167
Characteristics of Bureaucracy   167
Organizational Size   168
The Informal Side of Bureaucracy   168
Problems of Bureaucracy   169
Gender and Race in Organizations   172
Beyond Bureaucracy: Humanizing
   Organizations   173
Self-Managed Work Teams   174
Organizational Environment   174
The McDonaldization of Society   174
Formal Organizations in Japan   176

GROUPS AND ORGANIZATIONS IN
GLOBAL PERSPECTIVE   178

Summary   180   Critical-Thinking Questions   180
Applications and Exercises   180   Sites to See   181
Investigate with ContentSelect   181

8 SEXUALITY   182
UNDERSTANDING SEXUALITY   183
Sex: A Biological Issue   183
Sex and the Body   184
Sex: A Cultural Issue   185
The Incest Taboo   186

SEXUAL ATTITUDES   187
The Sexual Revolution   187
The Sexual Counterrevolution   188
Premarital Sex   189

Sex Among Adults 189
Extramarital Sex 190

SEXUAL ORIENTATION 190

What Gives Us a Sexual Orientation? 191
How many gay people? 192
The Gay Rights Movement 192

SEXUAL CONTROVERSIES 193

Teen Pregnancy 193
Pornography 194
Prostitution 195
Sexual Violence 196

THEORETICAL ANALYSIS OF
SEXUALITY 196

Structural-Functional Analysis 198
Symbolic-Interaction Analysis 200
Social-Conflict Analysis 201

*Summary 203 Critical-Thinking Questions 204
Applications and Exercises 204 Sites to See 204
Investigate with ContentSelect 205*

9 DEVIANCE 206

WHAT IS DEVIANCE? 207

Social Control 208
The Biological Context 208
Personality Factors 209
The Social Foundations of Deviance 209

STRUCTURAL-FUNCTIONAL ANALYSIS 210

Emile Durkheim: The Functions of
Deviance 210
Merton's Strain Theory 211
Deviant Subcultures 212

SYMBOLIC-INTERACTION ANALYSIS 213

Labelling Theory 213
The Medicalization of Deviance 214
Sutherland's Differential Association Theory
214
Hirschi's Control Theory 214

SOCIAL-CONFLICT ANALYSIS 215

Deviance and Power 216
Deviance and Capitalism 216

DEVIANCE AND SOCIAL DIVERSITY 218

Deviance and Gender 218

CRIME 219

The Components of Crime 219
The "Street" Criminal: A Profile 219

THE CRIMINAL JUSTICE SYSTEM 225

Police 225
Courts 227
Punishment 228

*Summary 231 Critical-Thinking Questions 231
Applications and Exercises 231 Sites to See 232
Investigate with ContentSelect 232*

PART III
SOCIAL INEQUALITY

10 SOCIAL STRATIFICATION 234

WHAT IS SOCIAL STRATIFICATION? 235

CASTE AND CLASS SYSTEMS 236

The Caste System 236
The Class System 237
Caste and Class Together:
The United Kingdon 240
Another Example: Japan 241
The Former Soviet Union 242
Ideology: The "Staying Power" of
Stratification 244

THE FUNCTIONS OF SOCIAL
STRATIFICATION 245

The Davis-Moore Thesis 245
Meritocracy 246

STRATIFICATION AND CONFLICT 248

Karl Marx: Class and Conflict 248
Why No Marxist Revolution? 248
Max Weber: Class, Status, and Power 250

STRATIFICATION AND TECHNOLOGY IN
GLOBAL PERSPECTIVE 251

Hunting-and-Gathering Societies 251
Horticultural, Pastoral, and Agrarian Societies
251
Industrial Societies 251
The Kuznets Curve 252

SOCIAL STRATIFICATION:
FACTS AND VALUES 252

Summary 255 Critical-Thinking Questions 256
Applications And Exercises 256 Sites to See 256
Investigate with ContentSelect 257

11 SOCIAL CLASS IN CANADA 258
DIMENSIONS OF SOCIAL INEQUALITY 259
Income 260
Wealth 261
Power 261
Occupational Prestige 261
Schooling 262
ASCRIPTION AND SOCIAL
STRATIFICATION 263
Ancestry 263
Gender 263
Race and Ethnicity 263
SOCIAL CLASSES IN CANADA 264
The Upper Class 265
The Middle Clas 267
The Working Class 269
The Lower Class 269
Class, Family, and Gender 269
SOCIAL MOBILITY 270
Myth Versus Reality 271
POVERTY IN CANADA 272
The Extent of Canadian Poverty 272
Who Are the Poor? 272
Explaining Poverty 274
Homelessness 276
Class and Welfare, Politics and Values 277

Summary 277 Critical-Thinking Questions 279
Applications and Exercises 280 Sites to See 280
Investigate with ContentSelect 280

12 GLOBAL STRATIFICATION 282
GLOBAL INEQUALITY: AN OVERVIEW 284
A Word About Terminology 284
High-Income Countries 285
Middle-Income Countries 285
Low-Income Countries 286
GLOBAL WEALTH AND POVERTY 287
The Severity of Poverty 288
The Extent of Poverty 289

Poverty and Children 290
Poverty and Women 290
Slavery 290
Correlates of Global Poverty 292
GLOBAL INEQUALITY: THEORETICAL
ANALYSIS 293
Modernization Theory 293
Dependency Theory 297
GLOBAL INEQUALITY: LOOKING
AHEAD 301

Summary 305 Critical-Thinking Questions 305
Applications and Exercises 306 Sites to See 306
Investigate with ContentSelect 307

13 GENDER STRATIFICATION 308
GENDER AND INEQUALITY 309
Male–Female Differences 309
Gender in Global Perspective 310
Patriarchy and Sexism 311
GENDER SOCIALIZATION 313
Gender and the Family 314
Gender and the Peer Group 314
Gender and Schooling 314
Gender and the Mass Media 315
GENDER STRATIFICATION 315
Working Men and Women 315
Housework: Women's "Second Shift" 318
Gender, Income, and Wealth 318
Gender and Education 321
Gender and Politics 322
Are Women a Minority? 322
Minority Women 323
Violence Against Women 323
THEORETICAL ANALYSIS OF GENDER 326
Structural-Functional Analysis 326
Social-Conflict Analysis 327
FEMINISM 328
Basic Feminist Ideas 328
Variations Within Feminism 329
LOOKING AHEAD: GENDER IN THE
TWENTY-FIRST CENTURY 331

Summary 332 Critical-Thinking Questions 332
Applications and Exercises 332 Sites to See 333
Investigate with ContentSelect 333

14 RACE AND ETHNICITY 334

THE SOCIAL SIGNIFICANCE OF RACE AND ETHNICITY 335

Race 335
Racial Typology 336
Ethnicity 337
Minorities 337

PREJUDICE 338

Stereotypes 338
Racism 338
Theories of Prejudice 339

DISCRIMINATION 342

Institutional Prejudice and Discrimination 342
Prejudice and Discrimination: The Vicious Cycle 342

MAJORITY AND MINORITY: PATTERNS OF INTERACTION 342

Pluralism 343
Assimilation 344
Segregation 344
Genocide 345

RACE AND ETHNICITY IN CANADA 345

Social Standing 348

SPECIAL-STATUS SOCIETIES 350

Native Peoples 350
The Québécois 352

IMMIGRATION TO CANADA: A HUNDRED-YEAR PERSPECTIVE 353

RACE AND ETHNICITY: PAST AND FUTURE 356

*Summary 357   Critical-Thinking Questions 358
Applications and Exercises 358   Sites to See 358
Investigate with ContentSelect 359*

15 AGING AND THE ELDERLY 360

THE GREYING OF CANADA 362

LIFE EXPECTANCY: GOING UP 362

An Aging Society: Cultural Change 363
The "Young Old" and the "Old Old" 364

GROWING OLD: BIOLOGY AND CULTURE 365

Biological Changes 365
Psychological Changes 366
Aging and Culture 366
Age Stratification: A Global Assessment 366

TRANSITIONS AND PROBLEMS OF AGING 370

Finding Meaning 370
Social Isolation 371
Retirement 371
Aging and Income 372
Abuse of the Elderly 372

AGEISM 372

The Elderly: A Minority? 373

THEORETICAL ANALYSIS OF AGING 374

Structural-Functional Analysis: Aging and Disengagement 374
Symbolic-Interaction Analysis: Aging and Activity 374
Social-Conflict Analysis: Aging and Inequality 375

DEATH AND DYING 375

Historical Patterns of Death 376
The Modern Separation of Life and Death 376
Ethical Issues: Confronting Death 376
Bereavement 377

LOOKING AHEAD: AGING IN THE TWENTY-FIRST CENTURY 379

*Summary 380   Critical-Thinking Questions 380
Applications and Exercises 380   Sites to See 381
Investigate with ContentSelect 381*

PART IV
SOCIAL INSTITUTIONS

16 THE ECONOMY AND WORK 382

THE ECONOMY: HISTORICAL OVERVIEW 383

The Agricultural Revolution 384
The Industrial Revolution 384
The Information Revolution and the Post-industrial Society 384
Sectors of the Economy 386

The Global Economy 387
COMPARATIVE ECONOMIC SYSTEMS 387
Capitalism 387
Socialism 389
Welfare Capitalism and State Capitalism 390
Relative Advantages of Capitalism and
    Socialism 390
Changes in Socialist Countries 391
WORK IN THE POST-INDUSTRIAL
ECONOMY 391
The Decline of Agricultural Work 392
The Dual Labour Market 392
Labour Unions 392
Professions 393
Self-Employment 394
Underemployment 394
Unemployment 395
The Underground Economy 396
New Information Technology and Work 397
Economic Concentration 398
Foreign Ownership 398
Conglomerates And Corporate Linkages 400
Corporations and the Global Economy 403
THE ECONOMY OF THE TWENTY-FIRST
CENTURY 404

Summary 407 Critical-Thinking Questions 408
Applications and Exercises 408 Sites to See 409
Investigate with ContentSelect 409

17 POLITICS AND GOVERNMENT 410
POWER AND AUTHORITY 411
Traditional Authority 412
Rational-Legal Authority 412
Charismatic Authority 412
POLITICS IN GLOBAL PERSPECTIVE 413
Monarchy 413
Democracy 413
Authoritarianism 414
Totalitarianism 416
A Global Political System? 417
POLITICS IN CANADA 417
Culture, Economics, and Politics 418
Political Parties 419
Politics and the Individual 424
THEORETICAL ANALYSIS OF POWER IN
SOCIETY 428
The Pluralist Model 429

The Power-Elite Model 429
The Marxist Model: Bias in the System
    Itself 431
POWER BEYOND THE RULES 432
Revolution 432
Terrorism 433
WAR AND PEACE 435
The Causes of War 436
Terrorism: A New Kind of War? 437
The Costs and Causes of Militarism 437
Nuclear Weapons 437
Information Warfare 438
The Pursuit of Peace 438
LOOKING AHEAD: POLITICS IN THE
TWENTY-FIRST CENTURY 439

Summary 440 Critical-Thinking Questions 442
Applications and Exercises 442 Sites to See 442
Investigate with ContentSelect 443

18 FAMILY 444
THE FAMILY: BASIC CONCEPTS 446
The Family: Global Variety 446
Marriage Patterns 447
Residential Patterns 449
Patterns of Descent 449
Patterns of Authority 449
THEORETICAL ANALYSIS OF THE
FAMILY 449
Functions of the Family: Structural-Functional
    Analysis 449
Inequality and the Family: Social-Conflict
    Analysis 450
Constructing Family Life: Micro-Level
    Analysis 450
STAGES OF FAMILY LIFE 451
Courtship 451
Settling In: Ideal and Real Marriage 452
Child Rearing 453
The Family in Later Life 454
CANADIAN FAMILIES: CLASS, RACE,
AND GENDER 455
Social Class 456
Ethnicity and Race 456
Gender 457
TRANSITION AND PROBLEMS IN
FAMILY LIFE 458
Divorce 458

Remarriage   460
Family Violence   461

ALTERNATIVE FAMILY FORMS   463

One-Parent Families   463
Cohabitation   463
Gay And Lesbian Couples   464
Singlehood   464

NEW REPRODUCTIVE TECHNOLOGY AND
THE FAMILY   464

LOOKING AHEAD: FAMILY IN THE
TWENTY-FIRST CENTURY   466

Summary   467   *Critical-Thinking Questions*   468
Applications and Exercises   468   *Sites to See*   469
Investigate with ContentSelect   469

19   RELIGION   470

RELIGION: BASIC CONCEPTS   471

Religion and Sociology   472

THEORETICAL ANALYSIS OF
RELIGION   472

Functions of Religion: Structural-Functional
    Analysis   472
Constructing the Sacred: Symbolic-Interaction
    Analysis   473
Inequality and Religion: Social-Conflict
    Analysis   474

RELIGION AND SOCIAL CHANGE   475

Max Weber: Protestantism and Capitalism   476
Liberation Theology   476

TYPES OF RELIGIOUS
ORGANIZATION   476

Church and Sect   476
Cult   477

RELIGION IN HISTORY   478

Religion in Pre-industrial Societies   478
Religion in Industrial Societies   478

WORLD RELIGIONS   478

Christianity   478
Islam   479
Judaism   480
Hinduism   481
Buddhism   482
Confucianism   483
Religion: East and West   484

RELIGION IN CANADA   484

Religious Affiliation   484
Religiosity   484
Religion and Social Stratification   486

RELIGION IN A CHANGING SOCIETY   486

Secularization   487
Civil Religion   488
Religious Revival   488
Religious Fundamentalism   488

LOOKING AHEAD: RELIGION IN THE
TWENTY-FIRST CENTURY   489

Summary   490   *Critical-Thinking Questions*   492
Applications and Exercises   492   *Sites to See*   493
Investigate with ContentSelect   493

20   EDUCATION   494

EDUCATION: A GLOBAL SURVEY   495

Schooling and Economic Development   495
Schooling in India   497
Schooling in Japan   497
Schooling in Great Britain   498
Schooling in Canada   498

THE FUNCTIONS OF SCHOOLING   500

Socialization   500
Cultural Innovation   500
Social Integration   500
Social Placement   502
Latent Functions of Schooling   502

SCHOOLING AND
SOCIAL INEQUALITY   502

Social Control   503
Testing and Social Inequality   504
Streaming And Social Inequality   504
Unequal Access to Higher Education   504
Credentialism   508
Privilege and Personal Merit   508

PROBLEMS IN THE SCHOOLS   508

School Discipline   508
Dropping Out   510
Value for Our Money   511
Academic Standards   511
Education and the World of Work   513

EDUCATION FOR TOMORROW   515

Summary   516   *Critical-Thinking Questions*   516
Applications and Exercises   517   *Sites To See*   517
Investigate with ContentSelect   517

21 HEALTH AND MEDICINE   518

WHAT IS HEALTH?   519
Health and Society   519

HEALTH: A GLOBAL SURVEY   520
Health in History   520
Health in Low-Income Countries   520
Health in High-Income Countries   521

HEALTH IN CANADA   521
Social Epidemiology: The Distribution of
   Health   522
Health and Society: Three Examples   524
Ethical Issues: Confronting Death   529

THE MEDICAL ESTABLISHMENT   530
The Rise of Scientific Medicine   530
Holistic Medicine   531
Paying For Health: A Global Survey   531
Medicine in Canada   533

THEORETICAL ANALYSIS OF HEALTH
AND MEDICINE   534
Structural-Functional Analysis   534
Symbolic-Interaction Analysis   535
Social-Conflict Analysis   537

LOOKING AHEAD: HEALTH IN THE
TWENTY-FIRST CENTURY   539

Summary   539   Critical-Thinking Questions   540
Applications and Exercises   540   Sites to See   540
Investigate with Content Select   541

Part V
SOCIAL CHANGE

22 POPULATION, URBANIZATION,
AND THE ENVIRONMENT   542

DEMOGRAPHY: THE STUDY OF
POPULATION   543
Fertility   544
Mortality   545
Population Growth   546
Population Composition   547

HISTORY AND THEORY OF POPULATION
GROWTH   548
Malthusian Theory   548
Demographic Transition Theory   549
Global Population Today: A Brief Survey   550

URBANIZATION: THE GROWTH OF
CITIES   552
The Evolution of Cities   552
The Growth of North American Cities   553
Suburbs and Central Cities   554
Inter-Regional Population Movement   555

URBANISM AS A WAY OF LIFE   556
Ferdinand Tönnies: *Gemeinschaft* and
   Gesellschaft   556
Emile Durkheim: Mechanical and Organic
   Solidarity   556
Georg Simmel: The Blasé Urbanite   557
Observing the City: The Chicago School   557
Urban Ecology   557
Urban Political Economy   558

URBANIZATION IN POOR SOCIETIES   560

ENVIRONMENT AND SOCIETY   560
The Global Dimension   561
Technology and the Environmental Deficit   561
Culture: Growth and Limits   562
Solid Waste: The Disposable Society   563
Water and Air   564
The Rain Forests   567
Environmental Racism   569

LOOKING AHEAD: TOWARDS A
SUSTAINABLE WORLD   569

Summary   571   Critical-Thinking Questions   572
Applications and Exercises   572   Sites to See   573
Investigate with Content Select   573

23 COLLECTIVE BEHAVIOUR AND
SOCIAL MOVEMENTS   574

STUDYING COLLECTIVE BEHAVIOUR   576
Localized Collectivities: Crowds   577
Mobs and Riots   577
Crowds, Mobs, and Social Change   578
Explaining Crowd Behaviour   579

DISPERSED COLLECTIVITIES:
MASS BEHAVIOUR   580

Rumour and Gossip   581
Public Opinion and Propaganda   581
Panic and Mass Hysteria   582
Fashions and Fads   582

SOCIAL MOVEMENTS   583

Types of Social Movements   584
Explaining Social Movements   585
Gender and Social Movements   589
Stages in Social Movements   589
Social Movements and Social Change   591

LOOKING AHEAD: SOCIAL MOVEMENTS
IN THE TWENTY-FIRST CENTURY   593

Summary   593   Critical-Thinking Questions   594
Applications and Exercises   594   Sites to See   594
Investigate with ContentSelect   595

24 SOCIAL CHANGE: TRADITIONAL,
MODERN, AND POSTMODERN
SOCIETIES   596

WHAT IS SOCIAL CHANGE?   598

CAUSES OF SOCIAL CHANGE   598

Culture and Change   599
Conflict and Change   599
Ideas and Change   599
The Natural Environment And Change   600
Demographic Change   600

MODERNITY   600

Key Dimensions of Modernization   600
Ferdinand Tönnies: The Loss of
   Community   601
Emile Durkheim: The Division of Labour   602
Max Weber: Rationalization   603
Karl Marx: Capitalism   604

THEORETICAL ANALYSIS OF
MODERNITY   604

Structural-Functional Theory: Modernity as
   Mass Society   605
Social-Conflict Theory: Modernity As Class
   Society   607
Modernity and the Individual   608
Modernity and Progress   610
Modernity: Global Variation   610

POSTMODERNITY   611

LOOKING AHEAD: MODERNIZATION AND
OUR GLOBAL FUTURE   611

Summary   613   Critical-Thinking Questions   616
Applications and Exercises   616   Sites to See   616
Investigate with ContentSelect   617

Glossary   618
References   625
Credits   647
Name Index   650
Subject Index   657

A Great Way to Learn and Instruct Online

The Pearson Education Canada Companion Website is easy to navigate and is organized to correspond to the chapters in this textbook. Whether you are a student in the classroom or a distance learner you will discover helpful resources for in-depth study and research that empower you in your quest for greater knowledge and maximize your potential for success in the course.

[www.pearsoned.ca/macionis]

PEARSON Prentice Hall

Jump to...   http://www.pearsoned.ca/macionis   Home   Search   Help   Profile

Companion Website

Home >

Companion Website

Sociology, Fifth Canadian Edition, by Macionis and Gerber

Student Resources

The modules in this section provide students with tools for learning course material. These modules include:

- Chapter Overview
- Multiple-Choice Questions
- Key Terms Quiz
- True/False Questions
- Critical Evaluation
- Destinations
- Controversy and Debate
- Key Words

In the quiz modules students can send answers to the grader and receive instant feedback on their progress through the Results Reporter. Coaching comments and references to the textbook may be available to ensure that students take advantage of all available resources to enhance their learning experience.

BOXES

APPLYING SOCIOLOGY

Reining In the Cowboys in Outer Space   18
Feminist Research: Critical and Interpretive Examples   36
Aboriginal Languages in Danger of Extinction   61
Can Sociology Help Us Design a Better Society?   92
Gentle, Nurturing Women; Aggressive, Violent Men   114
Hide Those Lyin' Eyes: Can You Do It?   142
Double Take: Real Headlines That Make People Laugh   149
Virtual Community: Reaching Out through Cyberspace   164
Date Rape: Exposing Dangerous Myths   198
Suicide among Aboriginal People   219
Is Spanking Allowed in Canada?   228
How Wealthy Are the World's Richest Women?   245
Social Class and Native People   268
Seeking Livelihood Sustainability for Yucatán Farmers   301
The Pink Ghetto and the Gender Gap in Income   319
Visible Minorities: Toronto, Vancouver, and Montreal   349
Native Elders: Cultural Custodians   368
The Brain Drain   405
Canada and the United States: Two Snapshots of Politics   426
Cohabitation among Canadians   465
Are Children Going to Religious Services?   487
Explaining Educational Attainment   510
"Hi... How Are You?"   536
Environmentally Friendly Canada, Eh!   566
The Rumour Mill: Paul Is Dead!   580

DIVERSITY: RACE, CLASS, AND GENDER

Conducting Research with Aboriginal Peoples   40
Canadians and Americans: What Makes Us Different?   63
How Do the Media Portray Minorities?   121
Physical Disability as Master Status   134
The Boy Who Was Raised as a Girl   185
Same-Sex Marriage in Canada   194
The Titanic: Personal and Canadian Connections   238
Middle-Class Stampede?   270
Pretty Is as Pretty Does: The Beauty Myth   316
Canadian Women in Hockey: Going for Gold   324
Does Race Affect Intelligence?   340
Black Citizens of Canada: A History Ignored   346
The French Canadians of Manchester, New Hampshire   385

Regional Economic Disparities   400
The Irving Empire   402
Native Self-Government   420
Child Discipline, Child Abuse?   455
Religion and Patriarchy: Does God Favour Males?   474
"An Education of Oppression": Canada's Indian Residential Schools   506
Functional Illiteracy: Must We Rethink Education?   514

EXPLORING CYBER-SOCIETY

From Card Punching to Number Crunching: Technological Advances in Research   49
Here Comes Virtual Culture!   67
The Information Revolution: What Would Durkheim, Weber, and Marx Think?   101
Social Interaction: Reaching across Cyberspace   144
The Internet: Welcome to Cyberspace!   166
Computers and Social Class   266
Working through Cyberspace   399
Who Decides? The Impacts of Modern Communication—and Now the Courts   430
The Cyber-Church: Logging On to Religion   490
Welcome to Cyber-School   512
The Canadian Revolution through the Information Revolution: The Point of No Return   614

GLOBAL SOCIOLOGY

The Global Village: A Social Snapshot of Our World   8
Travellers Beware! The Meaning of Gestures in Other Societies   74
Emotions in Global Perspective: Do We All Feel the Same?   140
The Japanese Model: Does It Work in North America?   177
Race as Caste: A Report from South Africa   239
"God Made Me to Be a Slave"   293
Modernization and Women: A Report from Rural Bangladesh   296
Growing (Very) Old: A Report from Abkhasia   369
Death on Demand: A Report from the Netherlands   377
"Soft Authoritarianism" or Planned Prosperity? A Report from Singapore   416
International Adoption   447
Early to Wed: A Report from Rural India   452
Killer Poverty: A Report from Africa   522
Empowering Women: The Key to Controlling Population Growth   551

CONTROVERSY & DEBATE

Is Sociology Nothing More Than Stereotypes? 23
Can People Lie with Statistics? 50
The Paparazzi: Villains or Our Eyes to the World? 78
Is Our Society Getting Better or Worse? 103
Ontario's First Boot Camp as a Total Institution 127
Is Technology Changing Our Reality? 151
Are Large Organizations a Threat to Personal Privacy? 178
The Abortion Controversy 202
What Can Be Done about Crime? 227
Salaries: Are the Rich Worth What They Earn? 246
The Bell Curve Debate: Are Rich People Really Smarter? 254
The Welfare Dilemma 278
Will the World Starve? 304
Men's Rights! Are Men Really So Privileged? 330
Distinct Societies and National Unity 356
Setting Limits: Must We "Pull the Plug" on Old Age? 378
The Market: Does the "Invisible Hand" Serve Our Interests or Pick Our Pockets? 406
After 9/11: Managing Our Relationship with the United States 434
Reforming Canada's Political System: Throwing Out the Baby with the Bathwater 440
The New Reproductive Technologies 467
Does Science Threaten Religion? 491
Is Political Correctness Undermining Education? 515
SARS, West Nile, and One Mad Cow 528
Two-Tiered Health Care: Threat, Fact, or Fiction? 538
Will People Overwhelm the Earth? The Environmental Challenge 570
Are You Willing to Take a Stand? 592
The United States: A Nation in Decline? Will Canada Follow? 612

MAPS

GLOBAL MAPS: WINDOW ON THE WORLD

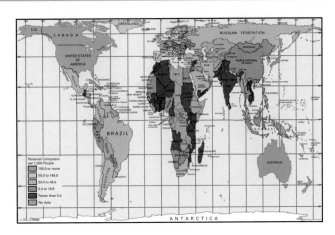

1–1	Women's Childbearing in Global Perspective	9
3–1	Language in Global Perspective	60
4–1	High Technology in Global Perspective	97
5–1	Child Labour in Global Perspective	124
7–1	Access to the Internet in Global Perspective	165
8–1	Prostitution in Global Perspective	197
9–1	Capital Punishment in Global Perspective	226
10–1	Income Disparity in Global Perspective	253
12–1	Median Age at Death in Global Perspective	291
12–2	Prosperity and Stagnation in Global Perspective	303
13–1	Women's Power in Global Perspective	313
13–2	Women's Paid Employment in Global Perspective	317
13–3	Housework in Global Perspective	320
15–1	The Elderly in Global Perspective, 2020	364
15–2	Life Expectancy in Global Perspective	367
16–1	Agricultural Employment in Global Perspective	388
16–2	Service-Sector Employment in Global Perspective	388
17–1	Political Freedom in Global Perspective	415
18–1	Marital Form in Global Perspective	448
19–1	Christianity in Global Perspective	480
19–2	Islam in Global Perspective	480
19–3	Hinduism in Global Perspective	482
19–4	Buddhism in Global Perspective	482
20–1	Illiteracy in Global Perspective	496
21–1	The Availability of Physicians in Global Perspective	523
22–1	Population Growth in Global Perspective	546
22–2	Water Consumption in Global Perspective	564

7–1   Employment in Government Service, 2001: Percentage by Province and Territory   171

9–1   Homicide Rates for Canada, Provinces and Territories, 1997–2001 (Five-Year Averages, Rates per 100 000 People)   221

11–1   Median Incomes by Province, Territory, and Census Subdivision, 2000   262

14–1   Percentage of Population Foreign-Born for Canada, the Provinces, Territories, and Census Subdivision, 2001   355

15–1   Percentage of the Population Age 65 and Over for Canada, the Provinces, Territories, and Census Subdivision, 2001   363

16–1   Unemployment Rates by Province, Territory, and Census Subdivision, 2000   397

18–1   Population Aged 15 Years and Older That Is Divorced (Percentage, by Province and Territory), 2001   461

19–1   Canadians Claiming "No Religion" (by Province, Territory, and Census Subdivision), 2001   486

20–1   Population 15 Years or Older with University Degree (Percentages by Province, Territory, and Census Subdivision) 2001   503

21–1   Percentage of the Population 12 Years and Over Smoking Cigarettes Daily, 2000–01   524

22–1   Birth Rates per 1000 Population, by Province and Territory, 2002–2003 (July 1–June 30)   544

PREFACE

Since the writing of the previous edition of *Sociology*, the tragic events of September 11, 2001, and related global developments have had a profound effect on the lives of many people around the world. The increased international concern over terrorism has greatly affected Canadian society and prompted us to re-examine so many dimensions of our everyday lives, including Canada's role within the world community.

More generally, these events force us to confront the question of what kind of world we live in and what kind of world we want for ourselves and for our children. It is here that readers of this book will discover the importance of the discipline of sociology.

The daily email we receive from students in Canada, the United States, and around the world stands as testimony to the power of sociology to help people understand their world and, often, to transform people's lives. All instructors know well the deep satisfaction that comes from making a difference in the lives of our students. Indeed, there is no greater reward for our work, and no better reason for constantly striving to improve each new edition of *Sociology*, the discipline's most popular text.

We hope you will find *Sociology* to be authoritative, comprehensive, stimulating, and—as so many students testify—plain fun to read. In addition to the book, every new copy of the Fifth Canadian Edition of *Sociology* comes with a second learning tool, a *HandsOnSociology* CD-ROM customized for this text, that provides a wealth of additional material including animated sociology tutorials, 2001 Census modules, flash cards, and interactive figures and maps.

Each new textbook also comes packaged with a booklet called the *PH Guide to Evaluating Online Resources with Research Navigator*™ accompanied by an access code to three exclusive online databases of high-quality source material: the ContentSelect™ Academic Journal Database, *The New York Times* Search-by-Subject™ Archive, and Link Library, a collection of editorially selected websites for sociology.

The final part of the learning package is a full-featured open-access website at **www.pearsoned.ca/macionis**. From the main page, users simply click on the cover of the text and select a chapter to find chapter summaries, learning objectives, critical-thinking and applying sociology exercises, links to additional online resources, and a variety of self-test quizzes that the server will immediately grade. Faculty will find a full complement of resources as well, including the syllabus manager system that allows posting a course syllabus to the Internet without having to learn hypertext markup language (HTML).

The textbook, the *HandsOnSociology* CD-ROM, Research Navigator™, and the Companion Website form a comprehensive multimedia package that is the foundation for sound learning in this new information age. We invite you to examine all these elements.

ORGANIZATION OF THIS TEXT

Part I of the textbook introduces the foundations of sociology. Underlying the discipline is the *sociological perspective*—the focus of Chapter 1, which explains how this invigorating point of view brings the world to life in a new and instructive way. Chapter 2 spotlights *sociological investigation*, or the "doing of sociology." This chapter explains the scientific, interpretive, and critical orientations of the discipline, and illustrates major research strategies with actual, well-known sociological work.

Part II surveys the foundations of social life. Chapter 3 focuses on the central concept of *culture*, emphasizing the cultural diversity that makes up our society and world. The focus of Chapter 4 is the concept of *society*, presenting four time-honoured models for understanding the structure and dynamics of social organization. This unique chapter provides introductory students with the background to understand the ideas of important thinkers—including Karl Marx, Max Weber, Emile Durkheim, and Gerhard Lenski—that appear in subsequent chapters. Chapter 5 turns to *socialization*, exploring how we gain our humanity as we learn to participate in society. Chapter 6 provides a micro-level look at the patterns of *social interaction* that make up our everyday lives. Chapter 7 offers full-chapter coverage of *groups and organizations*, explaining the importance of group life and investigating how and why large organizations have come to dominate our way of life. Chapter 8 explains the social foundations of *human sexuality*. This chapter surveys sexual patterns in Canada and also explores variations in sexual practices through history and around the world today. Chapter 9 explains how the operation of society generates both *deviance and conformity*, and also surveys the operation of the criminal justice system.

Part III offers unparalleled discussion of social inequality, beginning with three chapters on *social stratification*. Chapter 10 introduces major concepts and presents theoretical explanations of social inequality. This chapter richly illustrates historical changes in stratification and how patterns of inequality vary in today's world. Chapter 11 surveys *social inequality in Canada*, confronting common perceptions of inequality and assessing how well they square with research findings. Chapter 12 extends analysis with a look at *global stratification*, revealing the disparities in wealth and power that separate rich and poor nations. Both Chapters 11 and 12 pay special attention to how global developments affect stratification in Canada just as they explore our society's role in global inequality.

Chapter 13, *Gender Stratification*, explains how gender is a central element in social stratification in Canada, as it is worldwide. *Race and ethnicity*, additional important dimensions of social inequality that often intersect with differences based on class and gender, are detailed in Chapter 14. *Aging and the elderly*, a topic of increasing concern to "greying" societies such as our own, is addressed in Chapter 15.

Part IV includes a full chapter on each social institution. Leading off is Chapter 16, *The Economy and Work*, because most sociologists recognize the economy as having the greatest impact on all other institutions. This chapter traces the rise and fall of industrial production and the emergence of a global economy, and explains what such transformations mean for the Canadian labour force. Chapter 17, *Politics and Government*, analyzes the distribution of power in Canadian society as well as surveying political systems around the world. In addition, this chapter includes a new discussion of terrorism and its impact on global social structures. Chapter 18, *Family*, explains the central importance of families to social organization, and underscores the diversity of family life both here and in other societies. Chapter 19, *Religion*, addresses the timeless human search for ultimate purpose and meaning, introduces major world religions, and explains how religious beliefs are linked to other dimensions of social life. Chapter 20, *Education*, analyzes the expansion of schooling in industrial societies. Here again, schooling in Canada comes to life through contrasts with educational patterns in other countries. Chapter 21, *Health and Medicine*, reveals health to be a social issue just as much as it is a matter of biological processes. This chapter traces the historical emergence of medicine, analyzes current medical issues, and compares Canadian patterns in health care to those found in other countries.

Part V examines important dimensions of global social change. Chapter 22 highlights the impact of *population growth and urbanization* in Canada and throughout the world with special attention to the *natural environment*. Chapter 23 explores forms of *collective behaviour* and explains how people seek or resist social change by joining *social movements*. Chapter 24 concludes the text with an overview of *social change* that contrasts *traditional*, *modern*, and *postmodern societies*. This chapter rounds out the text by explaining how and why world societies change and by critically analyzing the benefits and liabilities of traditional, modern, and postmodern ways of life.

CONTINUITY: ESTABLISHED FEATURES OF SOCIOLOGY

Everyone knows that introductory sociology texts have some things in common, but differences run deep. The extraordinary success of *Sociology*—far and away the most widely adopted text of its kind—results from a combination of the following distinctive features.

The best writing style. Most important, this text offers a writing style widely praised by students and faculty alike as elegant and inviting. *Sociology* is an enjoyable text that encourages students to read—even beyond their assignments.

A global perspective. *Sociology* has taken a leading role in expanding the horizons of our discipline beyond Canada. *Sociology* was the first text to mainstream global content, introduce global maps, and offer coverage of global topics such as stratification and the environment. Each chapter explores global social diversity as well as explaining why social trends in Canada—from musical tastes, to the price of wheat, to Quebec separatism—are influenced by what happens elsewhere. Furthermore, students will learn ways in which social patterns and policies in Canada affect poor nations around the world.

A focus on social diversity. *Sociology* invites students from all social backgrounds to discover fresh and exciting ways to see the world and understand themselves. Readers will find in the text the diversity of Canadian society—people of African, Asian, European, and Aboriginal ancestry, as well as women and men of various classes—in all parts of the country, and at all points in life. Just as importantly, without flinching from the problems that marginalized people confront, this text does not treat minorities as social problems but notes their achievements.

Emphasis on critical thinking. Critical-thinking skills include the ability to challenge common assumptions by formulating questions, identify and weigh appropriate evidence, and reach reasoned conclusions. This text not only teaches but encourages students to discover on their own.

The broadest coverage so that instructors have a choice. No other text matches *Sociology*'s twenty-four-chapter coverage of the field. We offer such breadth—at no greater cost—knowing that few instructors will assign every chapter, but with the goal of supporting instructors as they choose exactly what they wish to teach.

Engaging and instructive chapter openings. One of the most popular features of earlier editions of *Sociology* has been the inviting vignettes that begin each chapter. These openings—for instance, using the tragic sinking of the *Titanic* to illustrate the life-and-death consequences of social inequality, or entering the world of lesbian mothers trying to gain custody of their children—spark the interest of readers as they introduce important themes. This revision retains this engrossing feature.

Inclusive focus on women and men. Beyond devoting two full chapters to the important concepts of sex and gender, *Sociology* mainstreams gender into *every* chapter, showing how the topic at hand affects women and men differently and explaining how gender operates as a basic dimension of social organization.

Theoretically clear and balanced. *Sociology* makes theory easy. Chapter 1 introduces the discipline's major theoretical approaches, which are used in all the chapters that follow. The text highlights not only the social-conflict, structural-functional, and symbolic-interaction paradigms, but incorporates feminist theory, postmodernist theory, social-exchange analysis, ethnomethodology, cultural ecology, and sociobiology.

Chapter 4—unique to this text—provides students with an easy-to-understand introduction to important social theorists *before* they encounter their work in later chapters. The ideas of Max Weber, Karl Marx, and Emile Durkheim, as well as Gerhard Lenski's historical overview of human societies, appear in distinct sections that instructors may assign together or refer to separately at different points in the course.

Recent research and the latest data. *Sociology* blends classical sociological statements with the latest research as reported in the leading publications in the field. Some 250 new studies inform this revision, and about half of the 1500 pieces of research cited throughout the book were published since 1995. From chapter to chapter, the text's statistical data are the most recent available and include the results of the 2001 Census.

Learning aids. This text has many features to help students learn. In each chapter, **Key Concepts** are identified by boldfaced type; following each is *a precise, italicized definition*. A complete **Glossary** is found at the end of the book. Each chapter also contains a numbered **Summary** and four **Critical-Thinking Questions** that help students review material and assess their understanding. Following these are a number of **Applications and Exercises**, which provide students with activities to do on or near campus. Each chapter also includes an annotated list of worthwhile **Sites to See** on the Internet, and more sites are provided in the form of **weblinks** at relevant points in the chapter.

Outstanding images: Photography and fine art. This book offers the finest and most extensive program of photography and artwork available in a sociology textbook. The Fifth Canadian Edition of *Sociology* displays many examples of fine art as well as hundreds of colour photographs. Each of these images is carefully selected by the author and appears with an insightful caption. Moreover, both photographs and artwork present people of various social backgrounds and historical periods. For example, alongside works by well-known international artists such as Vincent Van Gogh and George Tooker are paintings by Canadians such as Alex Colville, William Kurelek, Emily Carr, and Christiane Pflug.

Thought-provoking theme boxes. Although boxed material is common to introductory texts, *Sociology* provides a wealth of uncommonly good boxes. Each chapter typically contains a variety of boxes, which fall into five types that amplify central themes of the text. **Global Sociology** boxes provoke readers to think about their own way of life by examining the fascinating social diversity that characterizes our world. **Diversity: Race, Class, and Gender** boxes focus on multicultural issues, regionalism, or class distinctions and amplify voices of women and visible minorities. **Applying Sociology** boxes show the value of the sociological perspective to understanding the world around us. **Exploring Cyber-Society** boxes explore how rapidly changing information technologies are altering our lives. **Controversy & Debate** boxes complete each chapter by presenting several points of view on an issue of contemporary importance. *Continue the debate* questions conclude each debate box and are sure to stimulate spirited class discussion.

Sociology, Fifth Canadian Edition, contains over ninety boxes, many of which are brand new to this edition or have been heavily updated and revised. A complete list of the boxes in this text can be found following the table of contents.

A matchless program of global and national maps. This is the text that pioneered the use of global and national maps.

Window on the World Global Maps are truly sociological maps, offering a comparative look at global economic development, favoured languages and religions, the extent of worldwide prostitution, women's power, Internet access, permitted marriage forms, and a host of other issues. The global maps use non-Eurocentric projection devised by cartographer Arno Peters that accurately portrays the relative size of all continents. A complete listing of the **Window on the World Global Maps** follows the table of contents.

Seeing Ourselves National Maps help illuminate the social diversity of Canada. These maps highlight homicide rates, household income, foreign-born populations, birth rates, unemployment rates, and other measures of Canada's population. A complete listing of the **Seeing Ourselves National Maps** follows the table of contents.

INNOVATION: CHANGES IN THE FIFTH CANADIAN EDITION

Each edition of *Sociology* has broken new ground, one reason that the popularity of this text keeps growing. A revision raises high expectations, but, after several years of planning and hard work, we are pleased to offer a text that is better than ever. Here is a brief overview of the innovations that define *Sociology*, Fifth Canadian Edition:

Improved high-tech! For this edition, the *HandsOn-Sociology* CD-ROM features a wealth of additional material, including more than a dozen animated sociology tutorials, several 2001 Census modules, flash cards to help students review key concepts, and a variety of special interactive figures and maps.

Students also have access to an updated Companion Website at **www.pearsoned.ca/macionis**. At the site, students will find a full range of study materials, including computer-graded practice tests.

Linking technology to the text. At four or five points in each chapter, the text directs students to visit carefully selected websites. These sites provide biographical material about sociologists, useful data, online multimedia resources that present additional coverage of issues, or information about an organization that deals with the topic at hand.

A more integrated learning package. In addition to the *HandsOnSociology* CD-ROM, each new textbook comes with *The PH Guide to Evaluating Online Resources*, which includes an access code for Research Navigator™ with ContentSelect, a database of academic journals including Canadian publications. Students are guided on methods to search the Web effectively, evaluate material critically, and to cite sources properly.

The latest statistical data. Instructors count on this text for including the very latest statistical data. The Fifth Canadian Edition comes through again, incorporating data from the 2001 Census and making use of data from the Internet as well as from conventional bound publications of various government and private organizations. Wherever possible, tables, figures, charts, and maps have been updated using the new data.

Updated and improved maps. While all of the Seeing Ourselves National Maps have been updated using the most current statistical data, a majority of the maps now also display data on a census division level. These highly detailed maps reflect subtle regional differences and help paint a more accurate picture of Canadian diversity.

Expanded coverage of theory. This new edition of *Sociology* offers improved coverage of the major sociological perspectives, including the more recent feminist and postmodernist paradigms. Chapter 1 provides a comprehensive but accessible overview of these theories, which are then tied in to a number of different chapter topics throughout the text.

New topics. In the years since the last edition of *Sociology*, many events have occurred in Canada and abroad that have had a significant social impact on our lives. From September 11 and the war in Iraq to the same-sex marriage debate and the changing relationship between Canada and the United States, this text explores these topics within the sociological context.

SUPPLEMENTS

Sociology, Fifth Canadian Edition, is the heart of a learning package that includes a wide range of proven instructional aids. As the authors of the text, we maintain a keen interest in all of the supplements to ensure their quality and integration with the text. Supplements for this revision have been thoroughly updated, improved, and expanded.

FOR THE INSTRUCTOR

Instructor's Resource Manual. The *Instructor's Resource Manual* provides more than detailed chapter outlines and discussion questions; it contains statistical profiles of Canada and other nations, summaries of important developments and significant research, and supplemental lecture material for every chapter of the text.

Test Item File. A completely revised *Test Item File* is available in both Word and TestGenerator versions. The file contains 2400 items—100 per chapter—in multiple-choice, true-false, and essay formats. Questions are identified as simple "recall" items or as more complex "inferential" issues. The answers to all questions are page-referenced to the text. TestGen is a highly flexible testing program that allows for the creation of personalized exams and is compatible with both Windows and Mac platforms.

Introductory Sociology PowerPoint Slides. This Power-Point slide set combines graphics and text in a colourful format to help you convey sociological principles in a new and exciting way. This set contains more than 300 slides that cover the entire text and can be incorporated into lecture-specific PowerPoint presentations.

Instructor's Resource CD-ROM. Digital files of all of the above instructor supplements are now available on one convenient CD-ROM.

Instructor Central Website. This website provides password-protected access to all of the instructor supplements described above. Your Pearson representative can provide a password, or you can register online at **www.pearsoned.ca/instructor** to receive your password within a few hours, and download the supplements.

Pearson's Sociology Video Library 2004. Adopters of this text may receive a set of four VHS cassettes or two DVDs containing more than four hours of video clips for classroom use as well as an *Instructor's Manual and Video Guide*. Ask your Pearson representative for details.

MEDIA SUPPLEMENTS

HandsOnSociology CD-ROM. This interactive CD-ROM has been customized to complement the new edition of *Sociology*. In addition to a variety of self-paced, animated tutorials designed to refresh students' knowledge of core concepts and ideas, this CD-ROM features several 2001 Census modules, key concept flash cards, and interactive figures and maps. The CD-ROM is available free with all new copies of *Sociology*, Fifth Canadian Edition.

Companion Website™. In tandem with the text, students and professors can now take full advantage of the Internet to enrich their study of sociology. The *Sociology* Companion Website™ continues to lead the way in providing students with avenues for delving deeper into topics covered in the text. Features of the Companion Website™ include chapter objectives, study questions, and faculty resources, as well as links to interesting material and information from other sites on the Web that will reinforce and enhance the content of each chapter. To enter, simply visit the site at **www/pearsoned.ca/macionis** and click on the cover of the Fifth Canadian Edition.

Research Navigator™. The goal of Research Navigator™ is to help students understand the steps in the research process so they can more confidently and efficiently complete research assignments. In addition, Research Navigator™ offers students three exclusive databases of credible and reliable source content to help focus their research efforts and get the research process started.

Students and faculty can access Research Navigator™ through an access code found in the front of the *Evaluating Online Resources* guide. Each new edition of *Sociology* comes packaged with *Evaluating Online Resources* at no additional cost.

Research Navigator™ includes three databases of credible and reliable source material:

- **EBSCO's ContentSelect™ Academic Journal Database**, organized by subject, contains fifty to one hundred of the leading academic journals for each discipline. Instructors and students can search these online journals by keyword, topic, or multiple topics. Articles come complete with abstract and citation information and can be cut, pasted, emailed, or saved for later use.
- The *New York Times* **Search-by-Subject™ Archive** specific to sociology is searchable by single or multiple keywords. Instructors and students can view full-text articles from the world's leading journalists at the *New York Times*.
- **Link Library** offers editorially selected "Best of the Web" sites for sociology. Link Libraries are continually scanned and updated in order to provide the most relevant and accurate links for research assignments.

Online Learning Solutions. Pearson Education Canada supports instructors interested in using online course management systems. We provide text-related content in WebCT, Blackboard, and CourseCompass, our own private-label version of Blackboard. To find out more about creating an online course using Pearson content in one of these platforms, contact your local Pearson Education Canada representative.

FOR THE STUDENT

In addition to the media supplements mentioned above, students can also make use of the following learning aid.

Study Guide. This complete guide helps students review and reflect on the material presented in *Sociology*. Each of the twenty-four chapters in the *Study Guide* provides an overview of the corresponding chapter in the student text, summarizes its major topics and concepts, offers applied exercises, and features end-of-chapter tests with solutions.

IN APPRECIATION

The conventional practice of designating just two authors obscures the efforts of dozens of women and men that have resulted in *Sociology*, Fifth Canadian Edition. We would like to express our thanks to the Pearson Education Canada editorial team, including Jessica Mosher, John Polanszky, and Söğüt Y. Güleç.

We also have a large debt to Judith Allen for directing our marketing campaign, and the members of the sales staff, the men and women who have given this text such remarkable support over the years.

Thanks, too, to Laura Gardner and Julia Hall for providing the book's interior design and to Kathleen Richards for proofreading assistance. We are also grateful to Gerald V. Booth, Heather E. Metcalfe, Harry W. Rosenbaum, S. Mac Nelson, Keith Christopher Hampson, and Edward G. Thompson for preparing the supplements to this edition.

It goes without saying that every colleague knows more about some topics covered in this book than the authors do. For that reason, we are grateful to the hundreds of faculty and students who have written to offer comments and suggestions. More formally, we are grateful to the following people, who have reviewed the previous edition and the Fifth Canadian Edition manuscript:

Gerald V. Booth, University of Windsor
Philippe Couton, University of Ottawa
Christine Elsey, University College of the Fraser Valley
Ed Janzen, University of Waterloo, Conrad Grebel University College
John Manzo, University of Calgary
Alice Propper, York University
Harry Rosenbaum, University of Winnipeg
Kate Tilleczek, Laurentian University
Robert Wood, University of Lethbridge

Special thanks go to copy editor Lesley Mann whose passion for trivia sent Linda Gerber looking for more recent data in the most unlikely places. The text is richer for Lesley's prodding. The new-format maps were made possible by Carol Perry, who produced the data, and Robyn McMullen who converted the raw data into maps. Their contribution is greatly appreciated.

Without the support, encouragement, and patience of Linda Gerber's family—Gerhard and Martin Gerber, Laura Gerber and Glen Herbert, and Elsie Kojola—the Canadian revisions would not have been possible.

John Macionis
Linda Gerber

ABOUT THE AUTHORS

JOHN J. MACIONIS

John J. Macionis (pronounced ma-SHOW-nis) was born and raised in Philadelphia, Pennsylvania. He received his bachelor's degree from Cornell University and his doctorate in sociology from the University of Pennsylvania. His publications are wide-ranging, focusing on community life in the United States, interpersonal intimacy in families, effective teaching, humour, new information technology, and the importance of global education. He and Nijole V. Benokraitis have edited the companion volume to this text, *Seeing Ourselves: Classic, Contemporary, and Cross-Cultural Readings in Sociology*. Macionis has also authored *Society: The Basics*, the leading brief text in the field, and he collaborates on international editions of the texts: *Sociology: Canadian Edition* (with Linda M. Gerber, from Pearson Education Canada), *Society: The Basics, Canadian Edition* (with Mikael Jansson and Cecilia Benoit, also from Pearson Education Canada), and *Sociology: A Global Introduction* (with Ken Plummer, published by Prentice Hall Europe). *Sociology* is also available in various international and foreign language editions. In addition, Macionis and Vincent Parrillo have written the urban studies text, *Cities and Urban Life* (Prentice Hall). Macionis's most recent new text is *Social Problems* (Prentice Hall), which is the first text to take a social-constructioist approach to the study of social problems and public policy. The latest on all the Macionis textbooks, as well as news, information, and dozens of Internet links of interest to students and faculty in sociology, can be found at the author's personal Web site, http://www.macionis.com or http://www.TheSociologyPage.com.

John Macionis is Professor and Prentice Hall Distinguished Scholar of Sociology at Kenyon College in Gambier, Ohio. During a career of almost twenty-five years at Kenyon, he has chaired the Anthropology-Sociology Department, directed the college's multidisciplinary program in humane studies, and presided over the campus senate and also the college's faculty.

In 1998, the North Central Sociological Association named Macionis recipient of the Award for Distinguished Contribution to Teaching, citing his work with textbooks and his pioneering use of new technology in sociology.

Professor Macionis has been active in academic programs in other countries, having travelled to some fifty nations. In the fall of 1994, he directed the global education course for the University of Pittsburgh's Semester at Sea program, teaching 400 students on a floating campus that visited twelve countries as it circled the globe.

Macionis writes, "I am an ambitious traveller, eager to learn and, through the texts, to share much of what I discover with students, many of whom know so little about the rest of the world. For me, travelling and writing are all dimensions of teaching. First and foremost, I am a teacher—a passion for teaching animates everything I do." At Kenyon, Macionis offers a wide range of upper-level courses, but his favourite course is Introduction to Sociology, which he schedules every semester. He enjoys extensive contact with students and each term invites his students to enjoy a home-cooked meal.

The Macionis family—John, Amy, and children McLean and Whitney—live on a farm in rural Ohio. Their home serves as a popular bed and breakfast where they enjoy visiting with old friends and making new ones. In his free time, John enjoys bicycling through the Ohio countryside, swimming, sailing, and playing oldies rock and roll on his guitar. He is currently learning to play the Scottish bagpipes.

Professor Macionis welcomes (and responds to) comments and suggestions about this book from faculty and students. Write to the Sociology Department, Palme House, Kenyon College, Gambier, Ohio 43022, or direct e-mail to: MACIONIS@KENYON.EDU

LINDA M. GERBER

Linda M. Gerber was born in Toronto (to Finnish parents) and raised in Thornhill (just north of Toronto). Finnish was her first language and she remains sufficiently fluent to speak the language with scores of relatives on regular trips to Finland.

After graduating from the Nightingale School of Nursing (in Toronto), she toured Europe on a Eurailpass over the summer and spent the next year nursing in Helsinki, Finland. Upon her return, she completed a degree in nursing at the University of Toronto—before switching to sociology at the MA and PhD levels.

While still an undergraduate in nursing, she married Gerhard Gerber, whose family had escaped from East Germany just before the Berlin Wall was built. Contact with his parents and extended family ensured that she would come to understand German conversation quite well.

As a graduate student, she was a consultant in highway planning doing socio-economic impact assessment for a range of highway-building projects in southern Ontario. She also taught Canadian Native Peoples at York University's Glendon Campus.

On completion of their PhDs (in sociology and biochemistry) and the birth of their daughter, the Gerbers moved to Boston, Massachusetts, for continued study. Dr. Gerber spent three years there as a research associate at Harvard's Center for Population Studies before accepting a position in the Sociology and Anthropology Department at the University of Guelph. Over 26 years at Guelph, she has taught a wide range of courses at the undergraduate and graduate levels: most recently she has been teaching introductory sociology, political sociology, Native peoples, and Canadian society.

Professor Gerber's research has focused upon Canada's Native peoples, Canadian politics, and ethnic relations, but she has a broader interest in Canadian society (its demographic processes, its identity, and its regional tensions). Her publications are in the areas of Native studies, voting behaviour, gerontology, ethnic relations, and Quebec separatism.

The Gerber family now includes Martin (an 18-year old engineering student at the University of Toronto), Laura (the new pediatrician in town), Laura's husband, Glen Herbert, and come September, 2004, the first grandchild.

sociology

CHAPTER

1

John Sloan (1871–1951, American)
Traveling Carnival, Santa Fe, 1924

Oil on canvas, 76.5 × 91.6 cm. Smithsonian American Art Museum, Washington, D.C./Art Resource, N.Y.

THE SOCIOLOGICAL PERSPECTIVE

Imagine that you are walking along and have just taken the hand of a member of the opposite sex. Now stop and take a close look at what has just happened. If you are a man, it is almost certain that you will be holding your partner's hand from the front; if you are a woman, you will be holding hands from behind. Was this hypothesis supported in your case?

If you want to do a little experiment, try this. As you are about to clasp hands, stop, reconsider, and take your partner's hand opposite to the way you normally would. Now check for reactions in each of you. Are there any signs that this feels unnatural? Both of you are likely to feel uncomfortable with the new arrangement, and signs of this discomfort will be obvious.

So what does this reaction mean? Why does holding hands this way feel awkward? Since holding hands is a highly personal or individual act, people should be able to hold hands one way or

the other, as a matter of choice. Surely there are no unwritten rules about how males and females are to hold hands. Assuming an absence of hand-holding rules, it is worth noting that the vast majority of us *conform* to predictable patterns of behaviour. If, on the other hand, there *are* rules underlying this conformity, how do we learn about them? And why is it the man's hand that is in front? Is it a matter of height differences, leadership, or power and dominance?

Understanding *society* is a much more difficult task than understanding hand-holding behaviour, but this example suggests that people act in highly predictable ways; life does not unfold on the basis of sheer chance or complete free will. The essential wisdom of sociology is that society guides our actions and shapes our values; knowledge of the social forces at work allows sociologists to understand and predict the behaviour of individuals, groups, or categories of people.

THE SOCIOLOGICAL PERSPECTIVE

Formally, the discipline of **sociology** is *the systematic study of human society*. At the heart of sociology is a distinctive point of view.

SEEING THE GENERAL IN THE PARTICULAR

Peter Berger (1963) described the sociological perspective as *seeing the general in the particular*. He meant that sociologists identify general patterns in the behaviour of particular individuals. While acknowledging that each individual is unique, sociologists recognize that society acts differently on various *categories* of people (say, children compared to adults, women versus men,

the rich as opposed to the poor). We think sociologically when we realize how the general categories into which we happen to fall shape our particular life experiences.

At a 1997 Toronto conference, sociology professor Donna Winslow illustrated this perspective in her report on a study commissioned by the federal government. Her 400-page tome, *The Canadian Airborne Regiment: A Socio-Cultural Inquiry*, attempts to explain the atrocities committed by Canadian peacekeepers in Somalia—not in terms of the characteristics of the individual soldiers who brutally murdered a Somali civilian, but in terms of the combat or warrior culture within which they functioned. The culture of the Airborne regiment, which focused on war-making, was enhanced

We can easily grasp the power of society over the individual by imagining how different our world would be had we been born in place of any of these children from (top left reading clockwise) Guatemala, Sri Lanka, South Africa, El Salvador, People's Republic of China, and Botswana.

by recruitment, the chain of command, training, and even the nature of weapons at hand. Training for the peacekeeping role, in the areas of ethics and technique, was minimal: soldiers were unprepared in terms of recruitment, attitude, skill, or equipment to engage in problem solving, negotiation, or dealing with high-stress civilian situations with milder force (perhaps riot gear and dogs) (Winslow, 1997). Despite Canada's commitment to peacekeeping, our military has continued to prepare soldiers for war instead of peace, thereby setting the scene for violence towards civilians (Skelton, 1997). The explanation lies in the position within a structural and cultural environment, not in individual personality.

Each chapter of this text illustrates the general impact of society on the actions, thoughts, and feelings of particular people. For instance, the differences that distinguish children from adults reflect more than biological maturity: by attaching meaning to age, society shapes our experience into distinct stages of life. Following age-scripts, our society expects children to be "dependent," adults to behave "responsibly," and

elders to experience diminished standing and withdrawal from earlier routines.

How do we know that society (and not simply biology) is at work here? Looking back in time or around the world, we see that societies define the stages of life quite differently. The Hopi (an Arizona Pueblo people) confer surprising independence on children, while in Abkhazia (part of the Russian Federation) elderly people enjoy tremendous social clout and esteem. Through storytelling, the Inuit elders of northern Canada have been responsible for transmitting historical knowledge, traditional culture, and legends to the younger members of their society.

A sociological look around us reveals the power of class as well. Chapters 10 and 11 ("Social Stratification" and "Social Class in Canada") show that *how* we live and even *how long* we live are determined by our ranking in societal hierarchies.

Seeing the world sociologically also makes us aware of the importance of gender. As Chapter 13 ("Gender Stratification") points out, every society attaches meaning to being one sex or the other, according women and men different kinds of work and family responsibilities. Individuals experience the workings of society in the advantages and opportunities characteristic of each sex.

SEEING THE STRANGE IN THE FAMILIAR

Especially at the beginning, using the sociological perspective amounts to *seeing the strange in the familiar*. This does not mean that sociologists focus on the bizarre elements of society. Rather, observing sociologically requires giving up the familiar idea that human behaviour is simply a matter of what people decide to do in favour of the initially strange notion that society guides our thoughts and deeds.

For individualistic North Americans, learning to "see" how society affects us may take a bit of practice. Asked why you "chose" to enrol at your particular university or college, you might offer any of the following reasons: to stay near home, to ensure a good job, to be with old friends on campus, or because you were not accepted in a preferred program elsewhere.

Such responses are certainly grounded in reality for the people expressing them. But do they tell the whole story? The sociological perspective provides additional insights that may not be readily apparent.

Thinking sociologically about university and college attendance, we might first realize that for young people throughout most of the world, post-secondary education is all but out of reach. Moreover, had we lived a century ago, the "choice" to go to university or college probably would not have been an option. But even now, a look around your classroom suggests that social forces still have much to do with whether or not one pursues higher education. Typically, university and college students are relatively young—between eighteen and twenty-four years of age. Why? Because in our society university and college attendance is associated with this period of life. But more than age is involved, because the majority of university-age people in Canada are not enrolled in university.

Race is also involved. As Chapter 14 ("Race and Ethnicity") will point out, people of differing racial backgrounds vary in their likelihood of obtaining a post-secondary certificate. Moreover, the distinctions among racial or ethnic groups are great. For example, in Canada, adults of British and French origin are twice as likely to have achieved post-secondary certification as their Aboriginal counterparts. However, people of Black[1] and especially Asian origin are more likely to have achieved post-secondary certification than British- or French-origin individuals.

Whenever we come upon people whose habits differ from our own, we become more aware of social patterns. This is why travel is an excellent way to stimulate the sociological perspective. But even within Canada there is striking cultural diversity, which prompts us to become conscious of our social surroundings.

Another factor is the cost of higher education, so that university students (particularly those enrolled in professional programs such as medicine) tend to come from families with above-average incomes (Guppy and Arai, 1993).

Since, in Canada, college and university expenses are paid for by students and their families, those with modest means are likely to choose community colleges over universities. As a result, people from the upper-middle class or above tend to be overrepresented at universities (Levin, 1993)—although a recent study based on the General Social Survey (Statistics Canada, 2003f) reveals that young people from low-income families are actually closing the participation gap relative to those from middle-income families. Older students with job and family responsibilities also favour community colleges, taking advantage not only of lower costs but also of part-time and evening programs. Universities are typically the choice of younger, more affluent students who are able to study full time. Although it initially may seem strange to explain personal choices in terms of social forces, the sociological perspective empowers us as we come to understand how our own experiences—including the opportunities and barriers we face—are linked to

 For a closer look at post-secondary attendance by family income, go to www.statcan.ca/Daily/English/ 031003/d031003b.htm

where we are placed in the vast society around us.

---

[1]The labelling of people is a highly charged political issue. We use "Black" as that is the designation used by Statistics Canada.

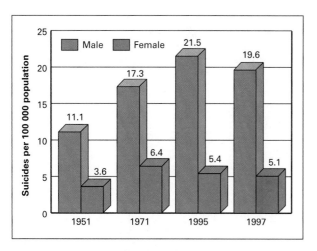

FIGURE 1–1 Suicide Rates by Sex, 1951, 1971, 1995, 1997

Source: Colombo (1992:61); Statistics Canada, 1999.

INDIVIDUALITY IN SOCIAL CONTEXT

To see the power of society to shape individual choices, consider the number of children born per woman. In Canada, as shown in Global Map 1–1 on page 9, the average woman has fewer than two children during her lifetime. In India, however, the average is about three; in South Africa, about four; in Cambodia, about five; in Saudi Arabia, about six; and in Niger, about seven.

Why these striking differences? As later chapters explain, women in poor countries have less schooling and fewer economic opportunities, are more likely to remain in the home, and are less likely to use contraception. Clearly, society has much to do with the decisions women and men make about childbearing.

Another illustration of the power of society to shape even our most private choices comes from the study of suicide. What could be more personal than the decision to take one's own life? Emile Durkheim (1858–1917), one of sociology's pioneers, showed that social forces are at work even in this apparently isolated act of self-destruction.

Examining official records in his native France, Durkheim found that some categories of people were more likely than others to take their own lives. Men, Protestants, wealthy people, and the unmarried each had significantly higher suicide rates than women, Catholics and Jews, the poor, and married people. Durkheim explained these differences in terms of social integration: categories of people with strong social ties had low suicide rates, whereas more socially isolated or individualistic people had higher suicide rates.

In the male-dominated society studied by Durkheim, men certainly had more autonomy than did women. Whatever freedom's advantages for men, concluded Durkheim, autonomy means lower social integration, which contributes to a higher male suicide rate. Likewise, more individualistic Protestants were more prone to suicide than Catholics and Jews, whose rituals foster stronger social ties. The wealthy clearly have much more freedom of action than the poor but, once again, at the cost of a higher suicide rate. Single people, with weaker social ties than married people, are also at greater risk of suicide. Finally, and importantly, rapid social change weakens the norms and values that define and stabilize the position of the individual within a social context.

A century later, statistical evidence continues to support Durkheim's analysis. Figure 1–1 shows the suicide rates for males and females from 1951 to 1997: the rates are consistently higher for men than for women. This male–female difference is apparent across all age groups and throughout the provinces and territories of Canada (Statistics Canada, 1999). Following Durkheim's argument, we can conclude that the higher suicide rate among men is due to their greater affluence and autonomy in Canadian society. Interestingly, male suicide rates are highest (30 per 100 000 population) in Quebec and the Northwest Territories, where marriage rates are the lowest, as well as in the Yukon (62 per 100 000 population), where the divorce rate is the highest. In addition, these areas are still undergoing substantial social change. Over the past decade or so, young people in Canada's First Nation communities have had suicide rates five or more times higher than those of other Canadians (as reported in *Acting on What We Know: Preventing Youth Suicide in First Nations*, Advisory Council on Suicide Prevention, 2003). Aboriginal communities are still experiencing massive social change and upheaval, which, Durkheim would have argued, affect levels of social integration by putting norms and values into a state of flux.

Thus, we observe general social patterns in even the most personal actions of individuals. Social forces are complex, of course, but we can see that linked to gender, they produce patterns with regard to suicide. Gender operates consistently: men are more prone to suicide than are women. The rates may change over time and across space, but even in the case of suicide we are able to see the impact of social conditions.

THE IMPORTANCE OF GLOBAL PERSPECTIVE

In recent years, as even the farthest reaches of the earth have become more easily accessible through advances in technology, many academic disciplines have incorporated a **global perspective**, *the study of the larger world and our society's place in it.* How does a global perspective enhance sociology?

Global awareness is a logical extension of the sociological perspective. Sociology's basic insight is that our positions in our society profoundly affect our individual experiences. It stands to reason that the position of our society in the larger world system, in turn, affects everyone in Canada. The "Global Sociology" box provides a brief sketch of our "global village," indicating that people the world over are far from equal in terms of quality of life.

Quality of life is determined, to a great extent, by variations in economic development of the world's countries. The world's **high-income countries** are *industrialized nations in which most people enjoy material abundance*.[2] High-income countries include Canada and the United States, most of Western Europe, Israel, Japan, and Australia. Taken together, the forty high-income societies generate most of the world's goods and services and control most of the planet's wealth. On average, individuals in these countries live well, not because they are particularly bright or exceptionally hard working, but because they had the good fortune to be born in an affluent region of the world.

The world's **middle-income countries** are *nations characterized by limited industrialization and moderate personal income*. Individuals living in any of the roughly ninety nations at this level of economic development—which include the countries of Eastern Europe and most of Latin America—are more likely to live in rural areas than in cities; to walk or ride bicycles, scooters, or animals rather than drive automobiles; and to receive only a few years of schooling. Most middle-income countries also have marked social inequality, so that while some people are extremely rich (the sheiks of oil-producing nations in the Middle East, for example), many more lack safe housing and adequate nutrition.

Finally, about half of the world's people live in the sixty **low-income countries**, which are *nations with little industrialization in which severe poverty is the rule*. Most of the poorest societies in the world are in Africa and Asia. Here, again, a small number of people in each of these nations are rich, but the majority barely get by with poor housing, unsafe water, too little food, little or no sanitation, and, perhaps most seriously of all, little chance to improve their lives.

The disparity between the "haves" and "have-nots" in the world is presented in another way in Table 1–1, which lists the ten best countries in which to live when ranked according to the United Nations' Human Development Index, formulated by the United Nations Development Programme in 1990. This controversial standard measures the quality of life in a country by factoring together measurements such as income, life expectancy, literacy, and school enrolment. Canada

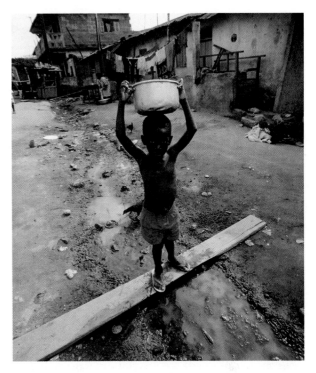

One important reason to gain a global understanding is that, living in a high-income society, we scarcely can appreciate the suffering that goes on in much of the world. This boy is growing up in the African nation of Ghana, where he carries water for cooking and drinking from a public faucet and sewage flows freely over unpaved streets. In poor nations like this, children have only a fifty-fifty chance of growing to adulthood.

ranked at the top of the list for many years before dropping to third place in 2001 and eighth place in 2003.

Chapter 12 ("Global Stratification") explores the causes and consequences of global wealth and poverty in detail. But every chapter of this text highlights life in the world beyond our own borders. Why? Here are three reasons for the prominence of global thinking in the sociological perspective.

1. **Societies the world over are increasingly interconnected.** Historically, Canadians have been relatively isolated from the rest of the world: separated from Europe and Asia by vast oceans, we have been influenced most clearly by our immediate neighbour to the south (the United States). In recent decades, however, Canada and the rest of the world have become linked as never before. People are whisked across continents or oceans in hours, and new electronic devices transmit pictures, sounds, and written documents around the globe in seconds. Email and Internet chat groups have freed social interaction from the constraints of geography.

---

[2]The text uses this terminology as opposed to the traditional, but outdated, terms "First World," "Second World," and "Third World." Chapter 12 ("Global Stratification") delves into the reasons for this shift.

The Global Village: A Social Snapshot of Our World

The earth is home to 6.2 billion people who live in the cities and villages of 192 nations. To grasp the social shape of the world, imagine for a moment that the planet's population is reduced to a single settlement of 1000 people. In this "global village," more than half (610) of the inhabitants are Asian, including 210 citizens of the People's Republic of China. Next, in terms of numbers, we would find 130 Africans, 120 Europeans, 85 people from Latin America and the Caribbean, 5 from Australia and the South Pacific, and just 50 North Americans, including 5 people from Canada.

A study of the settlement's ways of life would reveal some startling facts:

The village is a rich place, with a seemingly endless array of goods and services for sale. Yet most of the inhabitants only dream about such treasures because 80 percent of the village's total income is earned by just 200 people.

For the majority, the greatest problem is getting enough food. Every year, village workers produce more than enough to feed everyone; even so, half the village's people, including most of the children, do not get enough to eat, and many fall asleep hungry. The worst-off 200 residents (who, together, have less money than the richest person in the village) lack both clean drinking water and safe shelter. Weak and unable to work, some of them fall victim to life-threatening diseases every day.

Villagers boast of their community's many schools, including a fine university. About 50 inhabitants have completed a university degree, but almost half of the village's people can neither read nor write.

We in Canada, on average, would be among the richest people in this global village. Although we tend to credit ourselves for living well, the sociological perspective reminds us that our achievements are largely products of the privileged position our nation holds in the worldwide social system.

Source: Calculations by John J. Macionis based on data from United Nations and Population Reference Bureau publications.

Economic, social, and cultural contact is instantaneous, intense, and global.

One consequence of this new technology is that people all over the world now share many tastes in music, clothing, and food. With their economic clout, high-income nations—especially the United States—cast a global shadow, influencing members of other societies who eagerly embrace Coke and McDonald's hamburgers, rock-and-roll music, and even the English language, which dominates in business, science, and entertainment.

As the North American way of life is projected onto much of the world, the larger world, too, has its impact on Canada. Each year over most of the past decade, 200 000 or more immigrants have arrived here, adding to the historical flow of immigration that has built our country. In response, Canada has adopted many of the favourite sights, sounds, and tastes of its new members. The enhanced ethnic and cultural diversity of this country is apparent in our streets, our festivals, our grocery stores, and the media.

Commerce across national borders has created a global economy. Large corporations manufacture and market goods worldwide, just as global financial markets linked by satellite now operate around the clock. Today, no stock trader in Toronto dares to ignore what happens in the financial markets in New York, Tokyo, and Hong Kong, just as no wheat farmer in Manitoba can afford to overlook the price of grain in the former Soviet republic of Georgia. Because many new Canadian jobs involve international trade, gaining greater global understanding has never been more critical.

2. **A global perspective enables us to see that many human problems we face in Canada are far more serious elsewhere.** Poverty is certainly a serious problem in Canada, but, as Chapter 12 ("Global Stratification") explains, poverty is more widespread and more severe throughout Latin America, Africa, and Asia. Similarly, the social standing of women is especially low in the poor countries of the world.

3. **Thinking globally is an excellent way to learn more about ourselves.** Walking the streets of a foreign city makes us keenly aware of what it means to live in Canada and provides unexpected lessons. For instance, there is a garbage dump in Manila, the Philippines, that serves as a home for thousands of people. There, despite a desperate lack of basic material goods,

GLOBAL MAP 1-1 Women's Childbearing in Global Perspective

Is childbearing simply a matter of personal choice? A look around the world shows that it is not. In general, women living in poor countries have many more children than women in rich nations. Can you point to some of the reasons for this global disparity? In simple terms, such disparities mean that had you been born into another society (whether you are female or male), your life would have been quite different.

Source: Data from Mackay (2000).

people thrive in the love and support of family members. Why then is poverty in Canada so often associated with isolation and anger? Are material comforts—so crucial to our definition of "the good life"—the best way to gauge human well-being?

In sum, in an increasingly interconnected world, we fully know ourselves only to the extent that we understand others.

APPLYING THE SOCIOLOGICAL PERSPECTIVE

It is easy to apply the sociological perspective when we encounter people who differ from ourselves because they remind us of the power of social forces to shape our lives. But two other kinds of situations stimulate a sociological outlook, even before we take a first course in sociology.

TABLE 1-1	The Ten Best Places to Live in the World According to the United Nations Human Development Index (HDI)	
1997	**2001**	**2003**
Canada	Norway	Norway
Norway	Australia	Iceland
United States	Canada	Sweden
Australia	Sweden	Australia
Iceland	Belgium	Netherlands
Sweden	United States	Belgium
Belgium	Iceland	United States
Netherlands	Netherlands	Canada
Japan	Japan	Japan
United Kingdom	Finland	Switzerland

Source: United Nations Development Programme (2003).

SOCIOLOGY AND SOCIAL MARGINALITY

From time to time we all feel like "outsiders." For some categories of people, however, being an outsider is part of daily life. The more acute people's social marginality, the more likely they are to be keenly aware of their surroundings and to embrace the sociological perspective.

An Aboriginal person soon learns how much race or visible minority status affects personal experience. But white people, as the dominant majority, think about race only occasionally and often fail to recognize its impact; if they do acknowledge that race has consequences, they may imagine that race affects only people of colour—not themselves.

Much the same is true of women, gay people, people with disabilities, and the very old. All those relegated to the margins of social life typically become aware of social patterns others take for granted. This means that one develops a sociological perspective by stepping back from familiar routines and looking at one's life with new awareness and curiosity.

SOCIOLOGY AND SOCIAL CRISIS

Periods of massive social change or social crisis throw everyone a little off balance, and this, too, stimulates sociological vision. C. Wright Mills (1959), a noted U.S. sociologist, illustrated this principle by recalling the Great Depression of the 1930s. As the unemployment rate soared to 25 percent, people out of work could not help but see general social forces at work in their lives. Rather than personalizing their plight by claiming, "Something is wrong with me; I can't find a job," they took a more sociological approach, observing, "The economy has collapsed; there are no jobs to be found!"

Conversely, sociological thinking often fosters social change. The more we learn about the operation of

"the system," the more we may wish to change it in some way. As we confront the power of gender, for example, many of us actively try to reduce the traditional differences that distinguish men and women.

In short, an introduction to sociology is an invitation to learn new ways of looking at familiar patterns of social life. But is this invitation worth accepting? In other words, what are the benefits of applying the sociological perspective?

BENEFITS OF THE SOCIOLOGICAL PERSPECTIVE

Applying the sociological perspective in our daily lives benefits us in four ways.

1. **The sociological perspective challenges familiar understandings of ourselves and of others, so that we can critically assess the truth of commonly held assumptions.** Thinking sociologically, we may realize that ideas we have taken for granted are not always true. A good example of a widespread but misleading "truth" is that Canada is populated with "autonomous individuals" who are personally responsible for their lives. Thinking this way, we are sometimes too quick to praise particularly successful people as superior to others whose more modest achievements mark them as personally deficient. A sociological approach prompts us to ask whether these beliefs are actually true and, to the extent that they are not, why they are so widely held.

2. **The sociological perspective enables us to assess both the opportunities and the constraints in our lives.** Sociological thinking leads us to see that, in the game of life, we may decide how to play our cards, but it is society that deals us the hands. The more we understand the game, the better players we will be. Sociology helps us "size up" our world so that we can pursue our goals most effectively.

3. **The sociological perspective empowers us to be active participants in our society.** Without an awareness of how society operates, we are likely to accept the status quo. The greater our understanding of the operation of society, however, the more we can take an active part in shaping social life. Some people will embrace society as it is; others will attempt to change the world in some way. The discipline of sociology advocates no one particular political orientation, and sociologists themselves weigh in at many points across the political spectrum. But evaluating any aspect of social life—whatever one's eventual goal—depends on the ability to identify social forces and to assess their consequences.

Some forty years ago, C. Wright Mills (1959) wrote that the "sociological imagination," an understanding of the interplay between the individual and society, is a key source of change. By thinking sociologically, Mills maintained, people recognize that many others grapple with the same problems that they do. In this way, people can join together, turning personal problems into political issues.

4. **The sociological perspective helps us to recognize human diversity and to confront the challenges of living in a diverse world.** Sociological thinking highlights our world's remarkable social variety, revealing that the vast majority of our fellow human beings live in societies dramatically different from our own. While we tend to define our own way of life as proper and "natural" and to dismiss the lifestyles of those who differ from ourselves, the sociological perspective encourages us to think critically about the relative strengths and weaknesses of all ways of life—including our own.

APPLIED SOCIOLOGY

The benefits of sociology go well beyond intellectual growth. Indeed, sociology is sound training for literally hundreds of jobs in various fields, including advertising, banking, criminal justice, education, government, health care, public relations, and research (Billson and Huber, 1993).

Sociology has played an important role in the development of Canadian social policy. For example, the medicare system arose out of the Royal Commission on Health Services (1964–65), which was strongly influenced by sociological research. Other royal commissions, including the Royal Commission on Bilingualism and Biculturalism (1963–69) and the Royal Commission on the Status of Women in Canada (1967–70), were also based, in part, on the findings of sociologists. In Quebec, La Commission d'enquête sur l'enseignement au Québec (1963–66) drastically altered the educational system in that province. Aboriginal peoples hope that the Royal Commission on Aboriginal Affairs (1997) will have positive effects on public policy. Many sociologists have done policy-relevant work outside the context of royal commissions: Raymond Breton (University of Toronto professor emeritus and former director of Montreal's Institute for Research on Public Policy) has done influential work in the areas of ethnicity, cultural boundaries, Quebec nationalism, regionalism, and constitutional change.

Currently, most men and women who continue beyond a bachelor's degree to pursue advanced training in sociology go on to careers in teaching and research. But an increasing proportion of professional

Here we see Copernicus, the sixteenth-century astronomer, taking careful measurements of the world. Just as Copernicus challenged the common sense of his day, sociologists such as Auguste Comte later argued that society is neither fixed by God's will nor set by human nature. On the contrary, Comte claimed, society is a system we can study scientifically and, based on what we learn, we can act intentionally to improve our lives.

sociologists works in all sorts of applied fields. Evaluation research constitutes one type of applied sociology. In today's cost-conscious political climate, Canada's government and corporate administrators must evaluate the effectiveness of virtually every kind of program and policy. Sociologists—especially those with advanced research skills—are in high demand for this kind of work. Our criminal justice system employs numerous sociologists, as do the firms that engage in polling of opinion and voting intent. Journalists, in print or on screen, often produce good sociology

 All users of this book are invited to make use of videos, biographies, and dozens of links at www.TheSociologyPage.com. See the Video Gallery for a short video in which John Macionis offers a personal response to the question "Why would someone want to be a sociologist?"

while serving as Canada's "eyes" to the world: they are involved in data gathering, analysis, and presentation of results to a wide public.

THE ORIGINS OF SOCIOLOGY

Like the "choices" made by individuals, major historical events rarely just happen. They are typically products of powerful social forces that are always complex and only partly predictable. So it was with the emergence of sociology itself. Having described the discipline's distinct perspective and surveyed some of its benefits, we can now consider how and why sociology emerged in the first place.

Although human beings have mused about society since the beginning of our history, sociology is of relatively recent origin. It is among the youngest academic disciplines—newer than history, physics, or economics, for example. Only in 1838 did the French social thinker Auguste Comte coin the term *sociology* to describe a new way of looking at the world. Comte (1798–1857) grew up in the wake of the French Revolution, through the turbulent period that brought a sweeping transformation to his country. He felt that knowledge of how society operates, through what he called sociology ("the study of society"), would allow people to build a better future for themselves.

SCIENCE AND SOCIOLOGY

The nature of society was a major topic of inquiry for virtually all the brilliant thinkers of the ancient world, including the Chinese philosopher K'ung Fu-tzu, also known as Confucius (551–479 B.C.E.), and the Greek philosophers Plato (c. 427–347 B.C.E.) and Aristotle (384–322 B.C.E.).[3] Similarly, the Roman emperor Marcus Aurelius (121–180 C.E.), the medieval thinkers St. Thomas Aquinas (c. 1225–74) and Christine de Pisan (c. 1363–1431), and the English playwright William Shakespeare (1564–1616) all examined the state of human society. Yet, as Emile Durkheim noted almost a century ago, none of these social thinkers approached society from a sociological point of view.

> Looking back in history . . . we find that no philosophers ever viewed matters [[from a sociological perspective]] until quite recently. . . . It seemed to them sufficient to ascertain what the human will should strive for and what it should avoid in established societies. . . . Their aim was not to offer us as valid a description of nature as possible, but to present us with the idea of a perfect society, a model to be imitated. (1972:57; orig. 1918)

What sets sociology apart from earlier social thought? Prior to the birth of sociology, philosophers and theologians mostly focused on imagining the ideal society. None attempted to analyze society as it really was. Pioneers of the discipline such as Auguste Comte and Emile Durkheim reversed these priorities. Although they were certainly concerned with how human society could be improved, their major goal was to understand how society actually operates.

The key to achieving this objective, according to Comte, was to look at society scientifically. But, Comte added, a scientific outlook is a recent development—the last of three distinct stages of history (1975; orig. 1851–54). The earliest era, extending from the beginning of human history through Europe's medieval period (until roughly 1350 C.E.), he termed the *theological stage*. During this period, thinking was guided by religion. More specifically, people regarded society as an expression of God's will—at least insofar as humans were capable of fulfilling a divine plan.

With the Renaissance, the theological approach to society gradually gave way to what Comte called the *metaphysical stage*. During this period, people came to understand society as a natural, rather than supernatural, phenomenon. Human nature figured heavily in metaphysical visions of society: the English philosopher Thomas Hobbes (1588–1679), for example, posited that society reflected not the perfection of God as much as the failings of a rather selfish human nature.

What Comte heralded as the final, scientific stage in the long quest to understand society was propelled by scientists such as the Polish astronomer Copernicus (1473–1543), the Italian astronomer and physicist Galileo[4] (1564–1642), and the English physicist and mathematician Isaac Newton (1642–1727). Comte's contribution came in applying this scientific approach—first used to study the physical world—to the study of society.

 For a biographical sketch of Comte, go to the Gallery of Sociologists at www.TheSociologyPage.com

Comte was thus a proponent of **positivism**, defined as *a means to understand the world based on science*. As a positivist, Comte believed that society conforms to invariable laws, much as the physical world operates according to gravity and other laws of nature.

Sociology emerged as an academic discipline in North America at the beginning of the twentieth century, with early sociologists such as the American Lester Ward (1841–1913) pursuing Comte's vision of a scientific sociology. Even today, most sociologists agree that science plays a crucial role in sociology. But,

---

[3]Throughout this text, the abbreviation B.C.E. denotes "before the common era." We use this terminology in place of the traditional B.C. ("before Christ") in recognition of the religious plurality of our society. Similarly, in place of the traditional A.D. ("anno Domini," or "in the year of our Lord"), we employ the abbreviation C.E. ("common era").

[4]Illustrating Comte's stages, the ancient Greeks and Romans viewed the planets as gods, while Renaissance metaphysical thinkers saw them as astral influences (giving rise to astrology). By the time of Galileo, scientists understood planets as natural objects behaving in orderly ways.

The birth of sociology was prompted by rapid social change. The discipline developed in those regions of Europe where the Industrial Revolution most disrupted traditional ways of life, drawing people from isolated villages to rapidly growing industrial cities.

as Chapter 2 ("Sociological Investigation") explains, we now realize that human behaviour is often far more complex than natural phenomena. Human beings are creatures with considerable imagination and spontaneity, so that our behaviour can never be fully explained by any rigid "laws of society."

SOCIAL CHANGE AND SOCIOLOGY

Striking transformations in eighteenth- and nineteenth-century Europe drove the development of sociology. As the social ground trembled under their feet, people understandably focused their attention on society.

First came scientific discoveries and technological advances that produced a factory-based industrial economy. Second, factories drew millions of people from the countryside, causing an explosive growth of cities. Third, people in these burgeoning industrial cities soon entertained new ideas about democracy and political rights. We shall briefly describe each of these three changes.

A New Industrial Economy

During the European Middle Ages, most people tilled fields near their homes or engaged in small-scale *manufacturing* (a word derived from Latin meaning "to make by hand"). But by the end of the eighteenth century, inventors had applied new sources of energy—water power, then steam power—to the operation of large machines, giving birth to factories. Instead of labouring at home, workers became part of a large and anonymous industrial workforce, toiling for strangers

who owned the factories. This drastic change in the system of production weakened families and eroded traditions that had guided members of small communities for centuries.

The Growth of Cities

Factories sprouting across much of Europe became magnets attracting people in need of work. This "pull" of the new industrialized labour force was accentuated by an additional "push" as landowners fenced off more property, turning farms into grazing land for sheep—the source of wool for the thriving textile mills. This so-called enclosure movement forced countless tenant farmers from the countryside towards cities in search of work in the new factories.

Many villages were soon abandoned; at the same time, however, factory towns swelled rapidly into large cities. Such urban growth dramatically changed people's lives. Cities churned with strangers, in numbers that overwhelmed available housing. Widespread social problems—including poverty, disease, pollution, crime, and homelessness—were the order of the day. Such social crises further stimulated development of the sociological perspective.

Political Change

During the Middle Ages, as Comte noted, most people thought of society as the expression of God's will. Royalty claimed to rule by "divine right," and each person up and down the social hierarchy had some other part in the holy plan. This theological view of society is captured in lines from the old Anglican hymn "All Things Bright and Beautiful":

The rich man in his castle,
The poor man at his gate,
God made them high and lowly
And ordered their estate.

With economic development and the rapid growth of cities, changes in political thought were inevitable. Starting in the seventeenth century, every kind of tradition came under spirited attack. In the writings of Thomas Hobbes (1588–1679), John Locke (1632–1704), and Adam Smith (1723–90), we see a distinct shift in focus: no longer was it people's moral obligation to remain loyal to their rulers; rather, these thinkers contended, society is the product of individual self-interest. The key phrases in the new political climate, therefore, were *individual liberty* and *individual rights*. Echoing the thoughts of Locke, the Canadian constitution asserts that each individual has certain rights, freedoms, and protections. As section 2, "Fundamental Freedoms," puts it,

Everyone has the following fundamental freedoms:

(a) freedom of conscience and religion;

(b) freedom of thought, belief, opinion and expression, including freedom of the press and other media of communication;

(c) freedom of peaceful assembly; and

(d) freedom of association.

(The Canadian Charter of Rights and Freedoms, 1982)

The political revolution in France that began in 1789 constituted an even more dramatic break with political and social traditions. As the French social analyst Alexis de Tocqueville (1805–59) surveyed his society after the French Revolution, he exaggerated only slightly when he asserted that the changes we have described amounted to "nothing short of the regeneration of the whole human race" (1955:13; orig. 1856). In this context, it is easy to see why Auguste Comte and other pioneers of sociology soon developed the new discipline. Sociology flowered in precisely those societies—France, Germany, and England—where change was greatest.

Various sociologists reacted differently to the new social order then, just as they respond differently to society today. Some, including Auguste Comte, feared that people would be uprooted from long-established local communities and overpowered by change. So, in a conservative approach, Comte sought to shore up the family and traditional morality.

Taking a different view of these massive changes, the German social critic Karl Marx (1818–83) worried little about the loss of tradition, which he detested. But he could not condone the way industrial technology concentrated its great wealth in the hands of a small elite, while so many others faced hunger and misery. We examine his ideas in Chapter 4 ("Society").

Comte and Marx advanced radically different prescriptions for the problems of modernity, yet they shared the conviction that society rests on much more than individual choice. The sociological perspective animates the work of each, revealing that people's individual lives are framed by the broader society in which they live. This lesson, of course, remains as true today as it was a century ago.

 In subsequent chapters of this book, we delve into the major issues that concern sociologists. These pivotal social forces include culture, social class, race, ethnicity, gender, the economy, and the family. They all involve ways in which individuals are guided, united, and divided in the larger arena of society.

MARGINAL VOICES

Auguste Comte and Karl Marx stand among the giants of sociology. But, especially in recent years, sociologists have come to recognize the important contribution that others—pushed to the margins because they were women living in a male-dominated society—have made to their discipline.

Harriet Martineau (1802–76), born to a rich English family, first gained fame in 1832 when she published a monthly series, *Illustrations of Political Economy*. In 1853, she translated Auguste Comte's *Positive Philosophy* from the French. Soon afterwards, she established her own reputation as a sociologist with studies of slavery, factory laws, and women's rights. She wrote a controversial sociological analysis of the United States, *Society in America* (1837), and a book on social science methodology called *How to Observe Morals and Manners* (1838). She also found time to write novels, travel widely, and pursue a full-time career as a journalist. She accomplished all this in spite of recurrent ill health and deafness (McDonald, 1994:164–75).

In the United States, Jane Addams (1860–1935) was a pioneer in sociology who studied immigrants and provided assistance to immigrant families by founding a settlement house in Chicago. William Edward Burghardt Du Bois (1868–1963), the first person of colour to earn a doctorate at Harvard University, studied the Black community, spoke out against racial inequality, and was a founding member of the National Association for the Advancement of Coloured People (NAACP). Addams and Du Bois shared the belief that sociologists should try to solve social problems.

At that time, widespread belief in the social inferiority of women and of Blacks kept people like Martineau, Addams, and Du Bois at the margins of the discipline, causing many "established" sociologists to ignore their writings. Looking back with a sociological

Harold A. Innis (left) was best known as a political economist and a pioneer in communication studies—analyzing the impact of modes of communication on social development. He was a member of the University of Toronto's political economy department from 1920 to his death in 1952. His first major work, The Fur Trade in Canada *(1930), introduced the staples thesis of development and established his reputation.*

John Porter (centre left), a graduate of the London School of Economics, spent most of his career in Ottawa at Carleton University, as a faculty member, department chair, dean, and academic vice-president. He profoundly influenced his students, many of whom are important sociologists today (Vallee, 1988).

Marshall McLuhan (centre right) was a controversial figure who achieved international recognition in the 1960s and 1970s. His work fell out of favour for a while, but it is being revisited as social scientists acknowledge the revolutionary impact of the electronic media. Trained in literature at Cambridge, McLuhan became a rather unconventional professor of English at the University of Toronto, where he simultaneously enthralled and enraged his students.

Erving Goffman, born in Alberta in 1922, received his bachelor's degree from the University of Toronto before going on to his master's and doctorate at the University of Chicago. His immensely influential books include The Presentation of Self in Everyday Life *(1959),* Asylums: Essays on the Social Situation of Mental Patients and Other Inmates *(1961), and* Stigma: Notes on the Management of Spoiled Identity *(1963). He taught at the University of California at Berkeley and at the University of Pennsylvania and was the president of the American Sociological Association prior to his death in 1982. See page 138 for more details about his work.*

eye, we can see in their marginal standing how the forces of society were at work shaping even the history of sociology itself.

CANADIAN SOCIOLOGY: DISTINCTIVE TOUCHES

Canadian sociology arose from different traditions and continues to be, in many ways, distinct from U.S. sociology. As a discipline that reflects a country with two major cultures and linguistic communities, Canadian sociology includes a unique francophone component.

Sociology began in Canada, as in the United States, in the early part of the twentieth century. By 1920, sociology courses were being offered in a number of disciplines, including theology. During this period the Canadian Political Science Association, formed in 1913, accepted sociologists as members. Teaching and research in sociology were undertaken earlier in Quebec—at Laval, the University of Montreal, and then later at the University of Quebec—than in the rest of the country.

French-Canadian sociology was influenced, initially, by the Roman Catholic Church and, in the longer term, by developments in Europe and France, where sociologists tended to investigate and compare economic and political trends. English-Canadian sociology began both at McGill, following the U.S. tradition, and at the University of Toronto, following the British tradition.

Sociology did not have its own department at the University of Toronto until the 1960s. Before that time, social thinkers of the sociological cast worked out of the department of political economy. Sociology at the University of Toronto differed from the American-influenced social issues and community study approach that characterized studies at McGill. Modelled on British sociology, the University of Toronto's approach tackled questions of political and economic history. The person who most influenced sociology in the early years was Harold A. Innis. His emphasis on the way Canadian economic development depended on resource extraction and exportation (known as the staples thesis) formed the backdrop to the development of the sociological perspective in Canada. This perspective focused on economic developments in the country, particularly the branch-plant nature of the Canadian economy. Innis noted the role of communications and communications technology in the development of Canadian society.

The approach of the structural-functional paradigm is conveyed by the painting St. Regis Indian Reservation *by Amy Jones (1937). Here we see society composed of major rounds of life, each serving a particular purpose that contributes to the operation of the entire system.*

Amy Jones, *St. Regis Indian Reservation*, 1937. Photo courtesy Janet Marqusee Fine Arts Ltd.

Marshall McLuhan gained world renown for his insights into the impact of electronic communication on culture, politics, and personal identities. In reality a social theorist, he provoked Canadians with his musings on the interplay of the media (the electronic media in particular) with human thought, behaviour, and the shape of society. He had Canadians chew on tidbits such as "the medium is the message" and "global village" while his thinking laid the groundwork for our understanding of the current concepts of cyberspace and virtual reality and their impact on social cohesion and identity (Benedetti and DeHart, 1996; Goyder, 1997). Thirty years ahead of his time, McLuhan would have been very comfortable with the concepts of "cyberspace," "virtual reality," and "real time."

John Porter, in many minds, is Canada's leading sociologist. His book *The Vertical Mosaic* (1965) laid the groundwork for the focus on Canadian society in the context of development and underdevelopment (particularly as compared to the United States), inequality and inequity, elites, French–English relations, and bureaucratic structures.

Canada's massive size, its sparse but diverse population, its proximity to the United States, and its global situation (economic, cultural, and political) ensure that Canadian sociology will be concerned with questions of unity, political movements, economic development and inequality, regionalism, environment, identity, communications, and diversity, as well as cultural expression and survival (Helmes-Hayes, 1988; Whyte and Vallee, 1988; and Brym and Fox, 1989).

SOCIOLOGICAL THEORY

The task of weaving isolated observations into understanding brings us to another dimension of sociology: theory. A **theory** is *a statement of how and why specific facts are related*. Recall that Emile Durkheim observed that certain categories of people (men, Protestants,

the wealthy, and the unmarried) have higher suicide rates than others (women, Catholics and Jews, the poor, and the married). He explained these observations by creating a theory: a high risk of suicide stems from a low level of social integration.

Of course, as Durkheim pondered the issue of suicide, he considered any number of possible theories. But merely linking facts is no guarantee that a theory is correct. To evaluate a theory, as the next chapter explains, sociologists use scientific-research methods to gather evidence. Facts allow sociologists to confirm some theories while rejecting or modifying others. As a scientist, Durkheim was not content merely to identify a plausible cause of suicide: he set about collecting data to see precisely which categories of people committed suicide with the highest frequency. Poring over his data, Durkheim settled on a theory that best squared with all available evidence.

In building theory, sociologists face two basic questions: What issues should we study? How should we connect the facts? In making their decisions, sociologists are guided by one or more theoretical "road maps" or paradigms (Kuhn, 1970). For them, a **theoretical paradigm** is *a basic image of society that guides thinking and research*. These differences in perspective have contributed to the development of three major paradigms in sociology: the structural-functional paradigm, the social-conflict paradigm, and the symbolic interaction paradigm.

THE STRUCTURAL-FUNCTIONAL PARADIGM

The **structural-functional paradigm** is a framework for building theory that sees society as a complex system whose parts work together to promote solidarity and stability. As its name suggests, this paradigm begins by recognizing that our lives are guided by **social structure**, or relatively stable patterns of social behaviour. Social structure is what gives shape to the family, directs people to exchange greetings on the street, or steers events in a college classroom. Furthermore, this paradigm leads us to understand social structure in terms of its **social functions**, or consequences for the operation of society. All social structure—from family life to corporate organization—contributes to the operation of society, at least in its present form.

The structural-functional paradigm owes much to the ideas of Auguste Comte, who, as we have already explained, sought to promote social integration during a time of tumultuous change. A second architect of this theoretical approach was the influential English sociologist Herbert Spencer (1820–1903). Spencer compared society to the human body. Just as the structural parts of the human body—the skeleton, the muscles, and various internal organs—function independently to ensure survival, social structures work together to preserve society. Thus, the structural-functional paradigm organizes sociological observations, by identifying various structures of society and investigating their functions.

 The Gallery of Sociologists includes a biography of Herbert Spencer. Go to www.TheSociologyPage.com

In France, several decades after Comte's death, Emile Durkheim continued the development of sociology. Durkheim was primarily concerned with the issue of social solidarity, how societies "hang together." This concern of Durkheim (and Spencer) was taken up by Talcott Parsons (1902–79). The major U.S. proponent of the structural-functional paradigm, Parsons treated society as a system, identifying the basic tasks any and all societies must perform to survive and the ways they accomplish these tasks.

Robert K. Merton has expanded our understanding of the concept of social function in novel ways. Merton (1968) explains, first, that the consequences of any social pattern are likely to differ for various members of a society. For example, conventional families may provide crucial support for the development of children, but they also confer privileges on men while limiting the opportunities of women.

Second, Merton notes, people rarely perceive all the functions of a particular social structure. He described as **manifest functions** *the recognized and intended consequences of any social pattern*. By contrast, **latent functions** are *consequences that are largely unrecognized and unintended*. To illustrate, the obvious functions of our system of higher education include providing young people with the information and skills they need to perform jobs effectively. Perhaps just as important, although rarely acknowledged, is the way universities and colleges function as marriage brokers, bringing together people of similar social backgrounds in a social scene that operates as an ongoing setting for courtship. Another latent function of higher education is delaying the entry of millions of young people into the labour market, where many of them would fail to find jobs.

The painting Furnishings, *by Paul Marcus, presents the essential wisdom of social-conflict theory: society operates in a way that conveys wealth, power, and privilege to some at the expense of others. In the painting, what are most of the people doing? What do you make of the head hanging on the wall? The classical scene between the drapes? What categories of people does the artist suggest are disadvantaged?*

© Paul Marcus, *Furnishings*, oil on canvas, 163 × 122 cm. Studio SPM, Inc.

Merton also points out that some effects of any social structure may be negative. **Social dysfunctions** are *the undesirable consequences of any social pattern for the operation of society*. And, to make matters still more complex, people may well disagree about what is useful or harmful. Some critics from the political right have criticized universities for promoting left-wing thinking that threatens traditional values. Critics on the left of the political spectrum have argued that higher education is dysfunctional because it confers further privileges on the wealthy while remaining beyond the reach of individuals from lower-income families.

Critical evaluation. The most salient characteristic of the structural-functional paradigm is its vision of society as comprehensible, orderly, and stable. Sociologists typically couple this approach with scientific methods of research aimed at learning "what makes society tick."

APPLYING SOCIOLOGY

Reining In the Cowboys in Outer Space

Dr. Judith Lapierre wants to be an astronaut. This Canadian nurse has earned a PhD in public health and social medicine and studied space sociology as well: as a scientist and social scientist combined, she seems to be the ideal candidate for the job.

Under the sponsorship of the Canadian Space Agency, Dr. Lapierre participated in a simulated space mission at the Institute for Biomedical Problems in Moscow, spending 110 days in a mock space station that consisted of two linked capsules, each the size of a railway car. The space program mixed a "potent human cocktail," combining one woman, seven men, five cultures, and copious amounts of vodka for the duration of the mission. The results included frequent conflict, bloody fist-fights, and, for Judith Lapierre, sexual harassment when she was forcibly kissed by an amorous Russian colleague emboldened by the vodka.

Not surprisingly, the sexual harassment codes of our Canadian workplaces fail to apply in this international setting, but surely the highly trained and dedicated scientists who were carefully screened for the mission should know how to behave—whatever the context. Not so! There are no accepted guidelines for intercultural and gender relations within a mock space station, and it takes considerable time for sustained interaction to bring about the emergence of norms and shared understandings.

In the absence of naturally emergent rules for behaviour, the agencies that are preparing for the proposed International Space Station will have to resort to a strict, bureaucratically devised code of conduct—but creating a code that is acceptable to the different nations that are involved will not be easy. They will also have to spend more than the six hours that were allotted for Dr. Lapierre's colleagues to discuss topics such as team building, cultural and sensitivity awareness, and conflict resolution.

As Sandra remarks in her article about the incident, "Space may be the last frontier, but it's clearly time to set aside the old cowboy stereotypes of the rugged individual, and remember there's a place out there behind the beyond for social science as well as science" (p. R2).

Source: Based on Martin, 2000.

In the mid-1900s, the structural-functional paradigm dominated sociology; in recent decades, however, its influence has waned. How can we assume that society has a "natural" order, critics ask, when social patterns vary from place to place and change over time? Further, by emphasizing social integration, structural-functionalism tends to gloss over inequality based on social class, race, ethnicity, and gender—divisions that may generate considerable tension and conflict. This focus on stability at the expense of conflict and change gives the structural-functional paradigm a conservative character. As a critical response to this approach, sociologists have developed another theoretical orientation: the social-conflict paradigm.

THE SOCIAL-CONFLICT PARADIGM

The **social-conflict paradigm** is *a framework for building theory that envisions society as an arena of inequality generating conflict and change.* This approach contrasts with that of the structural-functional paradigm by highlighting not solidarity, but division based on inequality. Guided by this paradigm, sociologists investigate how factors such as social class, race, ethnicity, sex, and age are linked to unequal distribution of money, power, education, and social prestige. Conflict analysis points out that, rather than promot-ing the operation of society as a whole, social structure typically benefits some people while depriving others.

Working within the social-conflict paradigm, sociologists spotlight ongoing conflict between dominant and disadvantaged categories of people—the rich in relation to the poor, white people as opposed to visible minorities, men versus women. Typically, those on top strive to protect their privileges; the disadvantaged counter by attempting to gain more resources for themselves.

To illustrate, a conflict analysis of our educational system might highlight how schooling perpetuates inequality by helping to reproduce the class structure in every new generation. The process begins as secondary schools assign some students to university-preparatory programs while they provide vocational training for others. From a functional point of view, such "streaming" may benefit all of society because, ideally, students receive the training appropriate to their academic abilities. But conflict analysis counters that streaming often has less to do with talent than with a student's social background, as well-to-do students are placed in higher streams and poor students end up in the lower ones.

Through streaming, privileged families gain favoured treatment for their children from schools and, subsequently, universities. With the best schooling behind them, these young people leave university to pursue occupations that confer both prestige and high income. As Maxwell and Maxwell (1994) point out, private schools are an effective channelling device towards elite social status. Furthermore, the advantages of private schools for women are even greater than for men; women graduating from private girls' schools were to be the vanguard of women moving into high-status, male-dominated occupations. By contrast, the children of poor families are less prepared for university or college. So, like their parents before them, these young people typically move right from high school into low-paying jobs. In both cases, the social standing of one generation is passed on to another, with schools justifying the practice not in terms of privilege but in terms of individual merit.

Social conflict in Canada extends well beyond schools. Later chapters of this text highlight efforts by working people, women, and various racial and ethnic minorities to improve their lives. In each of these cases, the social-conflict paradigm helps us to see how inequality and the conflict it generates are rooted in the organization of society itself.

Finally, many sociologists who embrace the social-conflict paradigm attempt not just to understand society but to reduce social inequality. This was the goal of Karl Marx, the social thinker whose ideas underlie the social-conflict paradigm. Marx had little patience with those who sought merely to understand how society works. In a well-known declaration (inscribed on his monument in London's Highgate Cemetery), Marx asserted, "The philosophers have only interpreted the world, in various ways; the point, however, is to change it."

Critical evaluation. The social-conflict paradigm has developed rapidly in recent decades. Yet, like other approaches, it has come in for its share of criticism. Because this paradigm highlights inequality and division, it glosses over how shared values or interdependence generates unity among members of a society. For example, the shared values and economic or social bonds that link Quebecers to other Canadians might be overlooked. In addition, say critics, to the extent that the social-conflict approach explicitly pursues political goals, it relinquishes any claim to scientific objectivity. As Chapter 2 ("Sociological Investigation") explains in detail, conflict theorists are uneasy with the notion that science can be "objective." They contend, on the contrary, that the social-conflict paradigm and all theoretical approaches have political consequences, albeit different ones.

One additional criticism, which applies equally to both the structural-functional and social-conflict paradigms, is that these approaches envision society in very broad terms, describing our lives as a composite of "family," "social class," and so on. A third theoretical paradigm depicts society less in terms of abstract

To understand how the symbolic-interaction paradigm views society, consider Emil Bisttram's painting Domingo Chorus. *Society is never at rest; it is an ongoing process by which interacting individuals define and redefine reality.*

Emil Bisttram, American (1895–1976). *Domingo Chorus*, 1936, gouache and pencil on paper, 57.8 × 43.5 cm. Christie's Images/The Bridgeman Art Library.

generalizations and more in terms of people's everyday, situational experiences.

THE SYMBOLIC-INTERACTION PARADIGM

Both the structural-functional and social-conflict paradigms share a **macro-level orientation**, meaning *a focus on broad social structures that characterize society as a whole.* Macro-level sociology takes in the big picture, rather like observing a city from high above in a helicopter, noting the way highways carry traffic from place to place and the striking contrasts between rich and poor neighbourhoods. The symbolic-interaction paradigm takes another tack by providing a **micro-level orientation**, meaning *a focus on social interaction in specific situations.* Exploring urban life in this way occurs at street level, perhaps observing how friends interact in public parks or how pedestrians respond to homeless people. The **symbolic-interaction paradigm**, then, is *a theoretical framework that envisions society as the product of the everyday interactions of individuals.*

How does "society" result from the ongoing experiences of tens of millions of people? One answer, detailed in Chapter 6 ("Social Interaction in Everyday Life"), is that society arises as a shared reality, created by the interaction of its members. By attaching meaning to everything, we construct reality as we define our surroundings, our personal identities, and our obligations towards others.

How does power permeate social relations or society and change with circumstances? How do we understand societies or interpersonal relations while rejecting the theories and methods of the social sciences and our assumptions about human nature?

Of course, this process of definition varies a great deal from person to person. On a city street, for example, one person may define a homeless man as "just a bum looking for a handout" and ignore him. Another, however, may define him as a "fellow human being in need" and offer assistance. In the same way, one pedestrian may feel a sense of security passing by a police officer walking the beat, while another may be seized by a sense of nervous anxiety. Sociologists guided by the symbolic-interaction approach, therefore, view society as a mosaic of subjective meanings and variable responses.

The symbolic-interaction paradigm rests, in part, on the ideas of German sociologist Max Weber (1864–1920), who tried to understand settings from the perspectives of the people in them. Weber's approach is presented at length in Chapter 4 ("Society").

On this foundation, others have devised their own micro-level approaches to understanding social life. Chapter 5 ("Socialization") examines the ideas of U.S. sociologist George Herbert Mead (1863–1931), who looked at how we build our personalities over time based on social experience. Chapter 6 ("Social Interaction in Everyday Life") presents the work of Canadian sociologist Erving Goffman (1922–82), whose dramaturgical analysis emphasizes how we resemble actors on a stage as we play out our various roles before others. (See the photo on page 15.) Ethnomethodology is another micro-level analysis of the ways that people, as members of society, make sense of their social lives in order to carry out activities. Harold Garfinkel (1967), the founder of this perspective, showed how background understandings or assumptions are fundamental to the practice of social life through methods such as conversation analysis.

Other contemporary sociologists, including George Homans and Peter Blau, have developed social-exchange analysis. In their view, social interaction amounts to negotiation in which individuals are guided by what they stand to gain and lose from others (Molm, 1997). In the ritual of courtship, for example, people typically seek mates who offer at least as much—in terms of physical attractiveness, intelligence, and social background—as they provide in return.

Critical evaluation. The symbolic-interaction paradigm helps to correct for a bias inherent in all macro-level approaches to understanding society. Without denying the usefulness of abstract social structures such as "the family" and "social class," we must bear in mind that society basically amounts to people interacting. Put another way, this micro-level approach helps convey more of how individuals actually experience society.

However, by focusing on day-to-day interactions, the symbolic-interaction paradigm ignores larger social structures. Highlighting unique social settings risks downplaying the widespread effects of our culture, as well as factors such as class, gender, and race.

THE FEMINIST PARADIGM

Feminist sociology encompasses both the micro and the macro levels of analysis. Both levels focus on women's lives. The micro level examines the "re-production" of gender through such things as talk, body language, and emotion management. The macro level examines the myriad of constraints and forms of resistance in women's lives in such institutional realms as politics, economics, schooling, religion, and the family. The macro level of analysis has documented the patriarchal nature of the structure of societies, which characterizes virtually all realms of life.

In the past several decades, feminist sociology has been challenging the male-dominated discipline with critiques of methodology, theory, and all the substantive areas of the field. Feminist sociology, along with feminist analysis in other areas of academic life, has established a new field called *women's studies*. There are now women's studies programs in universities and colleges across Canada.

THE POSTMODERNIST PARADIGM

Postmodernism, at its core, is both anti-theory and anti-methods as applied by the social sciences: human sciences, it proposes, cannot be scientific because of human subjectivity, which makes it impossible to discover objective truth. Proponents argue that they are not trying to create systematic new knowledge, but are writing so as to permit multiple interpretations by their readers.

Postmodernists seek to observe other societies without applying the conceptual baggage of their own. They observe with the goal of achieving understanding and a vision rather than data collection. Deconstruction (taking apart) of existing text allows them to demystify (uncover or identify) the assumptions, hierarchies of knowledge, and ideological motivation of the social sciences.

Michel Foucault (1926–84), a French philosopher and one of the most influential postmodernists, would agree with Weber that scientific rationality is a means

TABLE 1–2 Theoretical Paradigms: A Summary

Classical Paradigm	Orientation	Image of Society	Illustrative Questions
Structural-functional	Macro-level	A system of interrelated parts that is relatively stable, based on widespread consensus as to what is morally desirable; each part has functional consequences for the operation of society as a whole.	How is society integrated? What are the major parts of society? How are these parts interrelated? What are the consequences of each for the operation of society?
Social-conflict	Macro-level	A system characterized by social inequality; any part of society benefits some categories of people more than others; conflict-based social inequality promotes social change.	How is society divided? What are major patterns of social inequality? How do some categories of people attempt to protect their privileges? How do other categories of people challenge the status quo?
Symbolic-interaction	Micro-level	An ongoing process of social interaction in specific settings, based on symbolic communications; individual perceptions of reality are variable and changing.	How is society experienced? How do human beings interact to create, sustain, and change social patterns? How do individuals attempt to shape the reality perceived by others? How does individual behaviour change from one situation to another?
Recent Paradigms			
Feminist	Micro/macro	A gender-based hierarchy where men dominate women in all realms of social life, including knowledge, the polity, the economy, education, etc.	Why is there a gender hierarchy? What have been the effects of male dominance on men and women? How can such a structure be overturned?
Postmodernist	Micro/macro	Shifting patterns of social order, institutions, and personal relations about which basic truths and assumptions are subject to change.	How does power permeate social relations or society and change with circumstances? How do we understand societies or interpersonal relations while rejecting the theories and methods of the social sciences and our assumptions about human nature?

to an end that tells us nothing about the values that should guide our lives. Furthermore, his treatment of power, which for him permeates all of society, takes it out of the exclusive hands of capitalists, males, or any other category of people.

Table 1–2 summarizes the important characteristics of our classical and recent paradigms: structural-functional, social-conflict, symbolic-interaction, feminist, and postmodernist. As we have explained, each paradigm is especially helpful in answering particular kinds of questions. By and large, however, the fullest understanding of society comes from linking multiple sociological perspectives, as we shall now illustrate with an analysis of sports in Canada and the United States.

APPLYING THE PERSPECTIVES: THE SOCIOLOGY OF SPORT

To people in North America, sports seem indispensable. Almost everyone has engaged in some type of sport, and athletics has evolved into a multibillion-dollar industry. In Canada, about 45 percent of those aged fifteen and over indicate regular participation in

some kind of sport; the number reaches a high of 53 percent in British Columbia and dips to 36 percent in Newfoundland (Corbeil, 2000a). What sociological insights about this familiar element of life can we derive from the three theoretical paradigms?

The Functions of Sports

A structural-functional approach directs attention to the ways sports help society to operate. The manifest functions include providing recreation, physical conditioning, and a relatively harmless way to let off steam. Sports have important latent functions as well, from fostering social relationships and teaching teamwork skills to generating tens of thousands of jobs. Perhaps most importantly, sports encourage competition and the pursuit of success, both of which are central to our way of life.

Sports also have dysfunctional consequences, of course. For example, North American colleges and universities intent on fielding winning teams sometimes recruit students for their athletic ability rather than their academic aptitude. Doing so can pull down the academic standards of a school and may short-change the athletes themselves, as coaches denigrate

Mike Weir, of Bright's Grove, ON, looks at his trophy after winning the Canadian Masters golf tournament in 1997.

academic endeavours so that student athletes will concentrate all their energies on sport.

Sports and Conflict

A social-conflict analysis begins by pointing out that sports are closely linked to social inequality. Some sports—including tennis, golf, and skiing—are expensive, so participation is largely limited to the well-to-do. By contrast, football, baseball, and basketball are accessible to people of all income levels. In short, the games people play are not simply a matter of choice but also reflect their social standing.

In Canada and the United States, sports are oriented primarily towards males. The first modern Olympic Games held in 1896, for example, excluded women from competition; until recently, moreover, even little league teams in most parts of Canada barred girls from the playing field. Such male-only practices have been defended by unfounded notions that girls and women lack the ability to engage in sports or risk losing their femininity if they do so. Thus, our society encourages men to be athletes and expects women to be attentive observers and cheerleaders. More women now play professional sports than ever before—in women's hockey, Canada won gold at the 2002 Winter Olympics at Salt Lake City, Utah—yet they continue to take a back seat to men, particularly in sports that yield the greatest earnings and social prestige.

Although North American society long excluded people of colour from "big league" sports, the opportunity to earn high incomes in professional sports has expanded in recent decades. Organized baseball first admitted African-American players when Jackie Robinson broke the "colour line" in 1946, playing for the Montreal Royals before moving to Major League Baseball in the United States. Willie O'Ree, originally from Fredericton, New Brunswick, was the first Black player in the National Hockey League when he was brought up from the minor leagues to play for the Boston Bruins in 1958. By 1993, African-Americans—12 percent of the U.S. population—accounted for 17 percent of Major League Baseball players, 68 percent of National Football League players, and 77 percent of

 For a look at how professional sports rank in their racial and gender integration, go to www.sportinsociety.org/rgrc2001.html

National Basketball Association players (Center for the Study of Sport in Society, 1998).

One reason for the increasing proportion of Black people in professional sports is the fact that precisely measured athletic performances cannot be diminished by white prejudice. There's no disputing the gold-medal Olympic performances of Canada's Donovan Bailey and the men's 4 × 100 metre relay team (1996), Daniel Igali in wrestling (2000), or Jarome Iginla as a dominant member of the men's hockey team (2002). Recently in North America, Black athletes have earned higher salaries, on average, than white players, and Tiger Woods and Venus and Serena Williams have achieved outstanding success in the traditionally elitist sports of professional golf and tennis. But racial discrimination still taints professional sports: Black athletes figure prominently in only a handful of sports (baseball, basketball, football, boxing, and

 For a look at racial "stacking" in professional baseball, go to www.sportinsociety.org/rgrc2001.html

track), and almost all managers, head coaches, and owners are white.

Taking a wider view, who gains the greatest benefits from professional sports? Although millions of fans follow their teams, the vast numbers of dollars teams take in are controlled by the small number of people (predominantly white men) for whom teams are income-generating property. In sum, sports in North America are bound up with inequalities based on gender, race, and economic power.

Sports as Interaction

At a micro level, a sporting event is a complex drama of face-to-face interaction. In part, play is guided by the players' assigned positions and, of course, by the rules of the game. But players are also spontaneous and unpredictable. Informed by the symbolic-interaction paradigm, then, we see sports less as a system than as an ongoing process.

Is Sociology Nothing More Than Stereotypes?

"Protestants are the ones who commit suicide!"

"People in Canada? They're dull as dishwater and won't stand up for themselves!"

"Everyone knows that you have to be Black to play professional basketball!"

It can't be denied that sociologists make generalizations about categories of people. Recognizing this fact, some students who begin the study of sociology may wonder whether statements like those above are sociological insights or simply stereotypes. What, exactly, is the difference between the two?

All three statements at the top of this page illustrate the *stereotype*—an exaggerated description that one applies to all people in a given category. Rather than describing averages, each statement paints every individual in a category with the same brush. Further, each ignores facts and distorts reality (even though each contains some element of truth), and each sounds more like a "put down" than an unbiased assertion.

Crafting a sociological insight, by contrast, does involve making generalizations, but with these important conditions. Instead of indiscriminately applying these generalizations to individuals, we ensure that a generalization squares with available facts. We also offer a generalization fair-mindedly, with an interest in getting at the truth.

Recall that the sociological perspective reveals "the general in the particular"; therefore, a sociological insight is a generalization about some category of people. An example is the assertion, made earlier in this chapter, that the suicide rate among Protestants is higher than that among Catholics or Jews. However, the way the statement above is phrased—"Protestants are the ones who commit suicide!"—is unreasonable because the vast majority of Protestants do no such thing.

Sociologists base their generalizations on available facts. A more factual and accurate version of the second statement above would be that historically Canadians have placed a high value on the role of consensus in decision making, both among themselves and in their dealings with other nations.

Lastly, sociologists strive to be fair-minded; that is, they are motivated by a passion for learning and for truth. The third statement above about Black athletes and basketball fails as good sociology not only because it doesn't square with the facts, but because it seems motivated by bias rather than truth-seeking or understanding.

Good sociology, then, stands apart from stereotyping. One of the most valuable aspects of a sociology course is that, through it, we learn how to collect the factual information that we need to assess the truth of popular wisdom.

Continue the debate . . .

1. *Are there stereotypes in sociology? What are they? Are they valid?*

2. *Do you think taking a sociology course erodes people's stereotypes? Does it generate new ones?*

3. *Can you cite a stereotype of your own that sociology challenges?*

From this point of view, too, we expect each player to understand the game a little differently. Some thrive in a setting of stiff competition while, for others, love[5] of the game may hold greater rewards than the thrill of victory.

Beyond different attitudes towards competition, team members will also shape their particular realities according to the various prejudices, jealousies, and ambitions they bring to the field. Then, too, the behaviour of any single player also changes over time. A rookie in professional baseball, for example, may feel quite self-conscious during his first few games in the big leagues. In time, however, a comfortable sense of fitting in with the team usually emerges. Coming to feel at home on the field was slow and painful for Jackie Robinson, who was initially all too aware that many white players, and millions of white fans, resented his presence in Major League Baseball (Tygiel, 1983). In time, however, his outstanding ability and his confident and cooperative manner won him widespread respect.

The three classical paradigms certainly offer different insights, but none is more correct than the others. Applied to any issue, each paradigm generates its own interpretations so that, to fully appreciate the power of the sociological perspective, you should become familiar with all three. Together, they stimulate fascinating debates and controversies, many of which are presented in the chapters that follow.

---

[5]The ancient Romans recognized this fact, evident in the word *amateur*, literally, "lover," which designates someone who engages in an activity for the sheer love of it.

SUMMARY

1. The sociological perspective reveals "the general in the particular," or the power of society to shape our lives.

2. Because people tend to think in terms of individual choice, recognizing the impact of society on our lives initially seems like "seeing the strange in the familiar."

3. Emile Durkheim's research demonstrating that suicide rates are higher among some categories of people than others shows that society affects even the most personal of our actions.

4. Global awareness enhances the sociological perspective because societies of the world are becoming more and more interconnected; many social problems are most serious beyond Canada's borders; and recognizing how others live helps us to better understand ourselves.

5. Socially marginal people are more likely than others to perceive the effects of society. For everyone, periods of social crisis or social change foster sociological thinking.

6. There are four general benefits to using the sociological perspective: (1) it challenges our familiar understandings of the world, helping us to separate fact from fiction; (2) it helps us appreciate the opportunities and constraints that frame our lives; (3) it encourages more active participation in society; and (4) it increases our awareness of social diversity in the world as a whole.

7. Auguste Comte gave sociology its name in 1838. Whereas previous social thought had focused on what society ought to be, Comte's new discipline of sociology used scientific methods to understand society as it is.

8. Sociology emerged as a reaction to the rapid transformation of Europe during the eighteenth and nineteenth centuries. Three dimensions of change—the rise of an industrial economy, the explosive growth of cities, and the emergence of new political ideas—focused people's attention on the operation of society.

9. Building theory involves linking insights to gain understanding. Various theoretical paradigms guide sociologists as they construct theories.

10. The structural-functional paradigm is a framework for exploring how social structures promote the stability and integration of society. This approach minimizes the importance of social inequality, conflict, and change.

11. The social-conflict paradigm highlights social inequality, conflict, and change. At the same time, this approach downplays the extent of society's integration and stability.

12. In contrast to these broad, macro-level approaches, the symbolic-interaction paradigm is a micro-level theoretical framework that focuses on face-to-face interaction in specific settings.

13. Feminist sociology analyzes the lives of women in terms of the definition of gender and the constraints placed upon them by the patriarchal, male-dominated structures of society.

14. Postmodernists seek to observe societies without applying their own conceptual baggage (e.g., theories and methods) in order to reveal the hidden assumptions and ideological underpinnings of the social sciences themselves.

15. Sociological thinking involves generalizations. But, unlike a stereotype, a sociological statement (a) is not applied indiscriminately to individuals, (b) is supported by facts, and (c) is put forward in the fair-minded pursuit of truth.

CRITICAL-THINKING QUESTIONS

1. In what ways does using the sociological perspective make us seem less in control of our lives? In what ways does it give us greater power over our surroundings?

2. Consider this statement: sociology would not have arisen if human behaviour were biologically programmed (like that of, say, ants); nor could sociology exist if our behaviour were utterly chaotic. Sociology thrives because human social life falls in a middle ground—as thinking people, we create social patterns, but those patterns are variable and changeable.

3. Why did sociology develop where and when it did?

4. Guided by the discipline's three major theoretical paradigms, what kinds of questions might a sociologist ask about (a) television, (b) war, (c) humour, and (d) universities and colleges?

APPLICATIONS AND EXERCISES

1. Spend several hours moving around your local community. Are there clear residential patterns? That is, does each neighbourhood contain certain categories of people? As best you can, identify who lives where. What social forces explain such patterns?

2. During a class, carefully observe the behaviour of the instructor and other students. What patterns do you see regarding use of space? Who speaks? What categories of people are in the classroom in the first place?

3. Observe a campus sporting event in sociological perspective. What functions do sports serve for your university or college? What patterns of inequality do they reflect and reinforce?

4. Think back to the 2002 Winter Olympics at Salt Lake City, Utah. Do you remember the controversy over judging when Salé and Pelletier were awarded silver, then gold, in pairs figure skating? When the Canadian men's and women's hockey teams won gold? What are the functions of the Olympic Games for Canada and for the international community? Can you apply the structural-functional, social-conflict, and symbolic-interaction perspectives to the Olympic Games?

 ## SITES TO SEE

www.macionis.com
or
www.TheSociologyPage.com
You can find more than fifty weblinks to sociological journals and other sources of data and information by visiting the Links Library at this website.

www.ccsd.ca/index.html
The Canadian Council on Social Development is a national, not-for-profit organization that focuses on the research and analysis of social and economic trends and their effects on the lives of Canadians.

www.solon.org
Canadian Constitutional Documents: A Legal History contains an extensive collection of constitutional documents, from the *Constitution Act* (1867) to the *Canada Act* (1982), in-cluding subsequent Acts and amendments, plus relevant documents predating Confederation.

www.sosig.ac.uk/welcome.html
A menu of worldwide sociology resources is provided at the *Social Science Information Gateway* (SOSIG), including an array of mailing lists, journals, associations, organizations, and archives.

www.nationalgeographic.com
and
http://atlas.gc.ca/
These two websites provide a number of maps showing patterns and trends of interest to sociologists.

www.countrywatch.com
This website offers a range of data about all 192 nations in the world.

 ## STUDY TOOLS

For more study tools to help you with your next exam, be sure to check out the Companion Website at **www. pearsoned. ca/macionis**, as well as Chapter 1 in your Study Guide.

 ## INVESTIGATE WITH CONTENTSELECT

To begin researching using ContentSelect™ and other resources associated with our new online research tool, Research Navigator,™ please find the access code located in the *Guide to Evaluating Online Resources* that may have been packaged with this textbook. (If your book did not come with this printed guide, you can purchase one through your college bookstore.) Visit our Research Navigator™ website at **www.researchnavigator.com**.

Once at the site, click on REGISTER and enter your access code to create a personal LOGIN ID and Password. When returning to the site, please use your LOGIN ID and Password. Enter keywords such as "sociology," "August Comte," and "sports," and the search engine will supply relevant and recent scholarly and popular press publications.

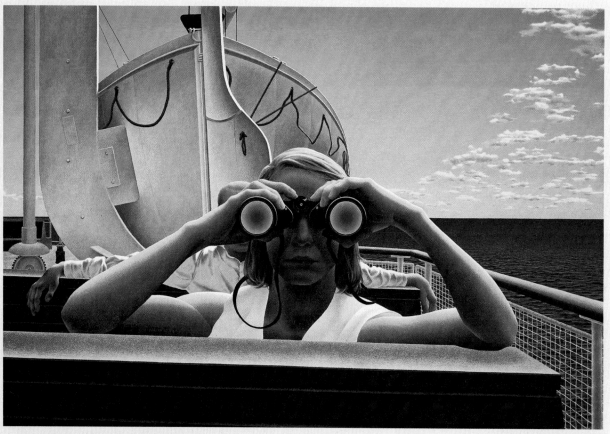

Alex Colville (1920– , Canadian)
To Prince Edward Island, 1965

Acrylic emulsion on masonite, 61.9 × 92.5 cm. National Gallery of Canada, Ottawa. © NGC/MBAC.

SOCIOLOGICAL INVESTIGATION

Students in Linda Gerber's political sociology course are busily engaged in *real* research. Each student is responsible for collecting census and election data for ten of Canada's 301 federal electoral districts (ridings). By comparing notes on socioeconomic characteristics and 1997 or 2000 election outcomes, these students are trying to explain voting behaviour in their assigned ridings. What riding characteristics, they ask, are associated with more or less support for the candidates of the major federal parties—Reform (now Canadian Alliance), Progressive Conservative, Liberal, Bloc Québécois, and New Democrat?

Each student, armed with a coding sheet, collects specific items of information from the census (on CD-ROM) and the Report of the Chief Electoral Officer for each of his or her ten electoral districts. The census data are then converted into percentages so that we know what proportions of the ridings' populations are, for example, immigrant, university educated,

francophone, bilingual, or employed in unionized occupations. We can then compare findings around the room, asking if Quebec ridings that are largely francophone are the ones most likely to vote for the Bloc Québécois—or if the proportion of immigrants across Canada's ridings is related to the proportion of the vote going to the Liberals.

By looking separately at patterns in specific regions, the class begins to understand the impact of riding characteristics and *region* on support for specific parties—for example, Reform (Canadian Alliance) had the greatest support in the western provinces, while the Bloc Québécois dominated in Quebec. The one-time surge in Atlantic Canada's support for the New Democratic Party in the 1997 election further illustrates the interplay of riding characteristics and regional circumstances.

Students come out of this process with a clear understanding of the ways in which 308 mini-elections, at the riding level, determine the outcome of a Canadian federal election.

Many people think that scientists work only in laboratories, carefully taking measurements using complex equipment. But, as this chapter explains, sociologists also conduct scientific research in the familiar terrain of neighbourhood streets, in homes, at workplaces, and in prisons, as well as in unfamiliar locales throughout the world—in short, wherever people can be found. The opening example illustrates the basics of scientific analysis—existing data or official statistics are used to determine the characteristics and actions of people.

There are, of course, many other approaches to sociological research, as illustrated by the work of

Reginald Bibby (a professor of sociology at the University of Lethbridge). For almost thirty years, Bibby measured changes in Canadians' attitudes towards a wide range of issues. Every five years from 1975 to 1995, Bibby mailed out a self-administered questionnaire to a representative sample of about 1100 adult Canadians. These questionnaires measured changes in attitudes towards a wide range of variables, including religion, sex, family, career, the economy, intergroup relations (and intermarriage), health, and happiness.

Along with his surveys of adult Canadians, Bibby has conducted a series dealing specifically with

TABLE 2-1 Correlates of Piercings and Tattoos

	Piercings		Tattoos	
	Yes	No	Yes	No
Self-image				
I am well liked	94%	93%	94%	93%
I am a good person	93	96	92	96
I am good-looking	79	76	80	76
I can do most things very well	78	83	82	83
I have lots of confidence	67	71	69	71
Behaviour/Values				
Engage in sex	71	45	82	45
Highly value concern for others	68	62	61	62
Use marijuana	61	33	65	33
Would return $10 in erroneous change	29	37	23	37
Attend services weekly-plus	12	23	10	23

Source: Bibby (2001):73.

teenagers. His most recent teen survey, in the fall of 2000, involved 3500 young people, aged 15 to 19, from 150 high-school classes chosen randomly across the country. One of his reasons for studying young people is that parents worry and fret about their attitudes and behaviours. His research shows that many—though not all—of those parental fears are unfounded.

Table 2-1 reveals that teens with body piercings and tattoos are similar to their peers in some respects, while differing in others. Bibby finds minor differences in self-image among teens with and without piercings or tattoos: regardless of body ornamentation, the teens are almost equally likely to feel that they are well-liked, good people, good-looking, capable, and confident. When he turns to behaviours and values, he finds that piercings and tattoos are associated with no difference in "concern for others"; but those *with* these ornamentations are more likely to engage in sex and use marijuana—and less likely to return a $10 bill erroneously given as change or attend religious services at least weekly. While this may suggest that you *can* judge a book by its cover, Bibby is careful to point out that there are many young people with piercings or tattoos who do *not* engage in sex or smoke marijuana (29 and 39 percent respectively, compared to 49 and 63 percent of the national sample).

In this case, the individual teenager is the unit of analysis, as opposed to the electoral district in the opening example. The latter illustrates analysis at the aggregate level; here, the analysis is carried out at the individual level. Nonetheless, both studies are consistent with the positivist approach outlined below.

This chapter highlights the range of methods that sociologists use to conduct research. Along the way, we shall see that sociological research involves not just procedures for gathering information but controversies about whether that research should strive to be objec-

tive or to offer a bold prescription for change. After all, some sociological research has important policy implications. We shall tackle questions of values after addressing the basics of sociological investigation.

THE BASICS OF SOCIOLOGICAL INVESTIGATION

Sociological investigation begins with two simple requirements. The first was the focus of Chapter 1: *to look at the world using the sociological perspective.* Suddenly, from this point of view, we see all around us intriguing patterns of behaviour that call out for further study—bringing us to the second requirement for sociological investigation: to be curious and ask questions. These two requirements—seeing the world sociologically and asking questions—are fundamental to sociological investigation. Yet they are only the beginning. They draw us into the social world, stimulating our curiosity. But then we face the challenging task of finding answers to our questions. To understand the kind of insights sociology offers, we need to realize that there are various kinds of "truth."

SCIENCE AS ONE FORM OF "TRUTH"

When we say we "know" something, we can mean any number of things. Most members of our society, a substantial 81 percent, in fact, claim to believe in the existence of God (Bibby, 1995). Few would assert that they have direct contact with God, but they are believers all the same. We call this kind of knowing "belief" or "faith." A second kind of truth rests on the pronouncement of some recognized expert. Parents with questions about raising their children, for example, often consult child psychologists or other experts

Myths as well as scientific facts are an important dimension of human existence. In his painting The Creation of the Earth, *Mexican painter Diego Rivera (1886–1957) offers a mythic account of human origins. A myth (from the Greek, meaning "story" or "word") may or may not be factual in the literal sense. Yet it conveys some basic truth about the meaning and purpose of life. Indeed, it is science, rather than art, that has no power to address such questions of meaning.*

Diego Rivera, Mexican (1886–1957). *The Creation of the Earth* page from Popol Vuh, watercolour on paper. Museo Casa Diego Rivera (INBA), Guanajuato, Mexico. Index/The Bridgeman Art Library. © 2003 Banco de Mexico Diego Rivera and Frida Kahlo Museums Trust.

about which practices are "right." A third type of truth is based on simple agreement among ordinary people. We come to "know" that, say, adult-child sex is wrong, because virtually everyone in our society says it is.

People's "truths" differ the world over, and we often encounter "facts" at odds with our own. Imagine being a CUSO volunteer just arriving in a small, traditional village in Latin America. With the job of helping the local people to grow more food, you take to the fields, observing a curious practice: farmers carefully plant seeds and then place a dead fish directly on top of each one. In response to your question, they reply that the fish is a gift to the god of the harvest. A local elder adds sternly that the harvest was poor one year when no fish were offered as gifts.

From that society's point of view, using fish as gifts to the harvest god makes sense. The people believe in it, their experts endorse it, and everyone seems to agree that the system works. But, with scientific training in agriculture, you have to shake your head and wonder. The scientific "truth" in this situation is something entirely different: the decomposing fish fertilize the ground, producing a better crop.

Science, then, represents a fourth way of knowing. **Science** is *a logical system that bases knowledge on direct, systematic observation.* Standing apart from faith, the wisdom of "experts," and general agreement, scientific knowledge rests on **empirical evidence**, meaning *information we can verify with our senses.*

Our CUSO example does not mean that people in traditional villages ignore what their senses tell them, or that members of technologically advanced societies reject nonscientific ways of knowing. A medical researcher using science to seek an effective treatment for cancer, for example, may still practise her religion as a matter of faith. She may turn to experts when making financial decisions, and she may derive political opinions from family and friends. In short, we all embrace various kinds of truths at the same time. Postmodernists, on the other hand, would argue that such "objective" truths are an impossibility.

COMMON SENSE VERSUS SCIENTIFIC EVIDENCE

Scientific evidence sometimes challenges our common sense. Here are six statements that many North Americans assume are "true," even though each is at least partly contradicted by scientific research.

1. **Poor people are far more likely than rich people to break the law.** Watching a television show such as *Cops*, one might well conclude that police arrest only people from "bad" neighbourhoods. As Chapter 9 ("Deviance") explains, poor people are arrested in disproportionate numbers. But research also reveals that police and prosecutors are likely to treat apparent wrongdoing by well-to-do people more leniently. Further, some researchers argue that our society adopts laws that reduce the risk of affluent people being criminalized.

2. **Canada is a middle-class society in which most people are more or less equal.** However, in 2000, 4.8 million Canadians or 16 percent of the population had incomes below the poverty line (or what Statistics Canada calls the low-income cut-off). In 2003, in any given month, about 750 000 Canadians were using Canada's 635+ food banks to feed themselves and their children. We may all be equal, but some, it seems, are much "more equal" than others.

Common sense suggests that, in a world of possibilities, people fall in love with that "special someone." Sociological research reveals that the vast majority of people select partners who are very similar in social background to themselves, as may be true of this couple from Alberta.

3. **Poor people ignore opportunities to work.** Research included in Chapter 11 ("Social Class in Canada") suggests that this is true of some but certainly not all or even most of the poor. Substantial majorities of the following categories are poor: unattached women and men over sixty-five, single-parent mothers with children, and *employed* people who work for low or minimum wages. These are not people who are simply avoiding work.

4. **Differences in the behaviour of females and males reflect human nature.** Much of what we call "human nature" is created by the society in which we are raised, as Chapter 3 ("Culture") details. Further, as argued in Chapter 8 ("Sexuality") and Chapter 13 ("Gender Stratification"), the world's numerous societies define "feminine" and "masculine" very differently.

5. **People change as they grow old, losing their former interests while focusing on their health.** Chapter 15 ("Aging and the Elderly") reports that aging actually changes our personalities very little. Problems of health increase in old age but, by and large, elderly people retain their distinctive personalities.

6. **Most people marry because they are in love.** To members of our society, few statements are so self-evident. But as surprising as it may seem, research shows that, in most societies, getting married has very little to do with love. Chapter 18 ("Family") explains why.

These examples confirm the old saying, "It's not what we don't know that gets us into trouble as much as things we do know that just aren't so." We have all been brought up believing conventional truths, bombarded by expert advice, and pressured to accept the opinions of people around us. As adults, we must learn to critically evaluate what we see, read, and hear, and sociology can help us to do that. Like any way of knowing, sociology has limitations, as we shall see. But scientific sociology gives us the tools to assess many kinds of information.

 To see how sociology deals with some of the most complex issues of the day, go to "Publications for the Public" at www.asanet.org/public/public.html

SCIENCE: BASIC ELEMENTS AND LIMITATIONS

In Chapter 1, we explained how early sociologists such as Auguste Comte and Emile Durkheim applied science to the study of society, just as natural scientists investigate the physical world. This approach to knowing, called *positivism*, assumes that an objective reality exists "out there." The job of the scientist is to discover this reality by gathering empirical evidence—facts we can verify with our senses.

In this chapter, we shall begin by introducing the major elements of scientific sociology. Then we shall discuss some limitations of scientific (or positivist) sociology and present alternative approaches to positivism.

CONCEPTS, VARIABLES, AND MEASUREMENT

A crucial element of science is the **concept**, *a mental construct that represents some part of the world, inevitably in a simplified form.* "Society" is itself a concept, as are the structural parts of societies, including "the family" and "the economy." Sociologists also use concepts to describe individuals, by noting, for example, their "sex," "race," "marital status," "sexual orientation," "education," "age," or "social class."

A **variable** is *a concept whose value changes from case to case.* The familiar variable "price," for example, changes from item to item in a supermarket. Similarly, people use the concept "social class" to evaluate people as "upper class," "middle class," "working class," or "lower class."

The use of variables depends on **measurement**, *the process of determining the value of a variable in a specific case*. Some variables—such as income—are easy to measure, but measuring others can be far more difficult. For example, how would you measure a person's "social class"? You might be tempted to look at clothing, listen to patterns of speech, or note a home address. In the interests of greater accuracy, you might ask about income, occupation, and education.

Researchers know that almost any variable can be measured in more than one way. Having a very high income might qualify a person as "upper class." But what if the income is derived from selling automobiles, an occupation most people think of as "middle class"? And would having only a grade 8 education make the person "lower class"? To resolve such a dilemma, sociologists sensibly (if somewhat arbitrarily) combine these three measures—income, occupation, and education—into a single composite assessment of social class, called *socioeconomic status*, which is described in Chapter 10 ("Social Stratification") and Chapter 11 ("Social Class in Canada").

Sociologists also face the challenge of describing thousands or even millions of people according to some variable of interest such as income. Reporting an interminable stream of numbers would carry little meaning and tell us nothing about the people as a whole. Thus, sociologists use *statistical measures* (such as a mean or average) to describe people collectively.

Measurement is always a bit arbitrary since the value of any variable depends, in part, on how one defines it. **Operationalizing a variable** means *specifying exactly what one intends to measure in assigning a value to a variable*—or translating concepts into tools of measurement. If we were measuring people's social class, for example, we would have to decide if we were going to measure income, occupational prestige, education, or something else and, if we measured more than one of these, how we would combine the scores. When reporting their results, researchers should specify how they operationalized each variable, so that readers can evaluate the research and fully understand the conclusions.

Reliability and Validity of Measurement

Useful measurement involves two further considerations. **Reliability** is *the quality of consistent measurement*. For a measure to be reliable, in other words, repeating the process should yield the same result. But consistency is no guarantee of **validity**, which is *the quality of measuring precisely what one intends to measure*. Valid measurement, in other words, means more than getting the same result time and again—it means obtaining a correct measurement.

To illustrate the difficulty of valid measurement, say you want to investigate how religious people are. A reasonable strategy would be to ask how often they attend religious services. But in trying to gauge religiosity in this way, what you are actually measuring is attendance at services, which may or may not amount to the same thing. Generally, religious people do attend services more frequently, but people also participate in religious rituals out of habit or a sense of duty. Moreover, some devout believers shun organized religion altogether. Thus, even when a measurement yields consistent results (making it reliable), it can still miss the real, intended target (and lack validity). In sum, sociological research is no better than the quality of its measurement.

Relationships among Variables

Once they achieve valid measurement, investigators can pursue the real payoff, which is determining how variables are related. The scientific ideal is **cause and effect**, *a relationship in which we know that change in one variable causes change in another*. A familiar cause-and-effect relationship occurs when a girl teases her brother until he becomes angry. *The variable that causes the change* (in this case, the teasing) is called the **independent variable**. *The variable that changes* (the behaviour of the brother) is known as the **dependent variable**. The value of one variable, in other words, is dependent on the value of another. Why is linking variables in terms of cause and effect important? Because doing so allows researchers to *predict*, that is, to use what they do know to predict what they don't know.

Because science puts a premium on prediction, people may be tempted to think that a cause-and-effect relationship is present any time variables change together. Consider, for instance, that the marriage rate tends to fall to its lowest point in January, exactly the same month in which the death rate peaks. This hardly means that people die because they fail to marry (or that they don't marry because they die). In fact, it is the dreary weather during January (and perhaps also the post-holiday blahs) that causes both a low marriage rate and a high death rate. The flip side holds as well: the warmer and sunnier summer months have the highest marriage rate and the lowest death rate. Thus, researchers often have to untangle cause-and-effect relationships that are not readily apparent.

Consider another example: sociologists have long recognized that juvenile delinquency is more common among young people who live in crowded housing. Say we operationalize the variable "juvenile delinquency" as the number of times (if any) a person under the age of eighteen has been arrested, and assess "crowded housing" by looking at the total square metres of living space per person in a home. We would find the variables related; that is, delinquency rates are, indeed, high in densely populated neighbourhoods. But should we conclude that crowding in the

Young people who live in the crowded inner city are more likely than those who live in the spacious suburbs to have trouble with the police. But does this mean that crowding causes delinquency? Researchers know that crowding and arrest rates do vary together, but they have demonstrated that the connection is spurious: both factors rise in relation to a third factor—declining income.

home (the independent variable) is what causes delinquency (the dependent variable)?

Not necessarily. **Correlation** is *a relationship by which two (or more) variables change together*. We know that density and delinquency are correlated because they change together, as shown in Part (a) of Figure 2–1. This relationship may mean that crowding causes misconduct, but often some third factor is at work, causing change in both variables under observation. To see how, think what kind of people live in crowded housing: people with less money, power, and choice—the poor. Poor children are also more likely to end up with police records. Thus, crowded housing and juvenile delinquency are found together because both are caused by a third factor—poverty—as shown in Part (b) of Figure 2–1. In other words, the apparent connection between crowding and delinquency is "explained away" by a third variable—low income—that causes them both to change. So our original connection turns out to be a **spurious correlation**, *an apparent, although false, association between two (or more) variables caused by some other variable*.

Unmasking a correlation as spurious requires a bit of detective work, assisted by a technique called

control, *holding constant all relevant variables except one in order to clearly see its effect*. In the example above, we suspect that income level may be behind a spurious connection between housing density and delinquency. To check, we control for income (that is, we hold it constant) by using as research subjects only young people of a single income level and looking again for a correlation between density and delinquency. If, by doing this, a correlation between density and delinquency remains (that is, if young people living in more crowded housing show higher rates of delinquency than young people with the same income in less crowded housing), we gain confidence that crowding does, in fact, cause delinquency. But if the relationship disappears when we control for income, as shown in Part (c) of Figure 2–1, we confirm that we have been dealing with a spurious correlation. Research has, in fact, shown that virtually all correlation between crowding and delinquency disappears if income is controlled (Fischer, 1984). So we have now sorted out the relationship among the three variables, as illustrated in Part (d) of Figure 2–1. Housing density and juvenile delinquency have a spurious correlation: evidence shows that both variables rise or fall according to people's income.

To sum up, correlation means only that two (or more) variables change together. Cause and effect rests on three conditions: (1) that there is a demonstrated correlation, (2) that the independent (or causal) variable precedes the dependent variable in time, and (3) that no third variable is responsible for a spurious correlation between the two.

Natural scientists identify cause-and-effect relationships more easily than do social scientists because the laboratories used for study of the physical world allow control of many variables at one time. The sociologist, carrying out research in a workplace or on the streets, faces a much more difficult task. Since human behaviour is highly complex, involving dozens of causal variables at any one time, sociologists often must be satisfied with demonstrating only correlation.

THE IDEAL OF OBJECTIVITY

Assume that ten writers who work for a magazine in Vancouver are collaborating on a story about that city's best restaurants. With their editor picking up the tab, they head out on the town for a week of fine dining. Later, they get together to compare notes. Do you think one restaurant would be everyone's clear favourite? That hardly seems likely.

In scientific terms, each of the ten reporters probably operationalizes the concept "best restaurant" differently. For one, it might be a place that serves delicious steaks at reasonable prices; for another, it might be the one with a rooftop view of the city; for yet another, stunning decor and attentive service might be the deciding factors. The best restaurant, it seems, turns out to be mostly a matter of individual taste.

Personal values are fine when recommending restaurants, but they pose a challenge to scientific research. On the one hand, every scientist has personal opinions about the world. On the other hand, science endorses the goal of **objectivity**, *a state of personal neutrality in conducting research*. Objectivity in research depends on careful adherence to scientific procedures in order not to bias the results. Scientific objectivity is an ideal rather than a reality, of course, since complete impartiality is virtually impossible to achieve. Even the subject a researcher selects to study and the framing of the questions are likely to grow out of personal interest. For example, ask your professor how his or her personal experiences have affected the choice of research question. Personal interest notwithstanding, scientists cultivate detachment and follow specific methods to minimize conscious or unconscious biases that distort their work. As an additional safeguard, researchers should try to identify and report their personal leanings to help readers evaluate their conclusions in the proper context.

Max Weber: Value-Free Research

The influential German sociologist Max Weber expected personal beliefs to play a part in a sociologist's selection of research topic. Why, after all, would one person study world hunger, another investigate the effects of racism, and still another examine one-parent families? But Weber (1958b; orig. 1918) admonished researchers that even though they select topics that are *value-relevant*, they should conduct research that is *value-free* in their pursuit of conclusions. Only by being dispassionate in their work (as we expect any professional to be) can researchers study the world as *it is* rather than tell others how they think *it should be*. In Weber's view, this detachment is a crucial element of science that sets it apart from politics. Politicians, in other words, are committed to a particular outcome, but scientists try to maintain an open-minded readiness to accept the results of their investigations, whatever they may be.

Most sociologists accept Weber's argument, while conceding that we can never be completely value-free or even aware of all our biases (Demerath, 1996). Moreover, sociologists are not "average" people: most are white, highly educated, and more politically liberal than the population as a whole (Wilson, 1979). Sociologists need to remember that they, too, are affected by their own social backgrounds: they must be careful to avoid bias arising from those backgrounds.

One strategy for limiting distortion caused by personal values is **replication**, *repetition of research by other investigators*. If other researchers repeat a study

(a)

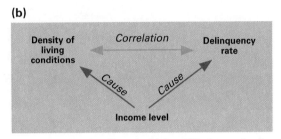

If two variables vary together, they are said to be correlated. In this example, density of living conditions and juvenile delinquency increase and decrease together.

(b)

Here we consider the effect of a third variable: income level. Low income level may cause *both* high-density living conditions *and* a high delinquency rate. In other words, as income level decreases, both density of living conditions and the delinquency rate increase.

(c)

If we control income level—that is, examine only cases with the same income level—do those with higher-density living conditions still have a higher delinquency rate? The answer is *no*. There is no longer a correlation between these two variables.

(d)

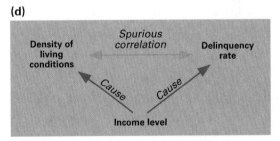

This finding leads us to conclude that income level is a cause of both density of living conditions and the delinquency rate. The original two variables (density of living conditions and delinquency rate) are thus correlated, but neither one causes the other. Their correlation is therefore *spurious*.

FIGURE 2–1 Correlation and Cause: An Example

using the same procedures and obtain the same results, they gain confidence that the original research (as well as their own) was conducted objectively. The

A basic lesson of sociological research is that being observed affects how people behave. Researchers can never be certain precisely how this will occur; while some people resent public attention, others become highly animated when they think they have an audience.

need for replication in scientific investigation is probably the reason that the search for knowledge is called research in the first place.

The values and beliefs of the scholar are not the only potential sources of bias in the research processes. Bias—which inhibits impartial judgment—is inherent in various research and sampling methods. Take the question of employment among Black Canadians, for example. Census-based analyses reported throughout this text, which compare British, French, Asian, Black, and Native populations, indicate that Blacks in Canada are relatively well educated and the most active in the labour force (with the highest levels of employment, including full-time employment). Nonetheless, Black *incomes* are relatively low. A very different picture of Black labour force involvement emerges if one goes to the Jane and Finch area of Toronto to do intensive community-based interviews. Bias enters each of these studies—it enters the first because the very poor and the homeless are not reliably included in the census, and the second because Blacks living in affluent communities throughout the country are excluded. The "findings" of these studies, though equally systematic, will paint very different pictures of reality.

It is important to keep in mind that the logic and methodology of science hold out no guarantee that we will grasp objective, absolute truth. What science offers is an approach to knowledge that is self-correcting so that, in the long run, researchers stand the best chance of overcoming their own biases and achieving greater understanding. Objectivity and truth, then, lie not in any particular research method, but in the scientific process itself.

SOME LIMITATIONS OF SCIENTIFIC SOCIOLOGY (POSITIVISM)

The first scientists probed the operation of the natural world. Contemporary sociologists use science to study the social world; however, this application of the scientific method to sociological investigation has several important limitations.

1. **Human behaviour is too complex to allow sociologists to predict precisely any individual's actions.** Astronomers calculate the movement of planets with remarkable precision, announcing years in advance when a comet will next pass near the earth. But planets and comets are unthinking objects; humans, by contrast, have minds of their own. Because no two people react to any event in exactly the same way, the best sociologists can do is show that categories of people typically act in one way or another. This is no failing of sociology; it is simply consistent with the nature of our mission—studying creative, spontaneous people.

2. **Because humans respond to their surroundings, the mere presence of a researcher may affect the behaviour being studied.** An astronomer gazing at the moon has no effect whatsoever on that celestial body. But people usually react to being observed. Some may become anxious, angry, or defensive; others may try to "help" by providing the answers or actions they think researchers expect of them.

3. **Social patterns change constantly; what is true in one time or place may not hold true in another.** The laws of physics apply tomorrow as

well as today, holding true around the world. But human behaviour is too variable for us to set down immutable sociological laws. In fact, some of the most interesting sociological research focuses on social diversity and social change.

4. **Because sociologists are part of the social world they study, being value-free when conducting social research can be difficult.** Barring a laboratory mishap, chemists are rarely personally affected by what goes on in test tubes. But sociologists live in their "test tubes"—the societies they study. Therefore, social scientists face a greater challenge in controlling—or even recognizing—personal values that may distort their work.

A SECOND FRAMEWORK: INTERPRETIVE SOCIOLOGY

All sociologists agree that studying social behaviour scientifically presents some real challenges; others go further, suggesting that science as it is used to study the natural world misses a vital part of the social world—and that is *meaning*.

Human beings do not simply act: they engage in meaningful action. Max Weber, who pioneered this framework, incorporated that insight, arguing that the proper focus of sociology is *interpretation*, or understanding the meanings involved in everyday life. **Interpretive sociology** is *the study of society that focuses on the meanings people attach to their social world*.

Interpretive sociology differs from scientific, or positivist, sociology in three ways. First, scientific sociology focuses on action, or what people do, whereas interpretive sociology deals with the meaning attached to behaviour. Second, while scientific sociology sees an objective reality "out there," interpretive sociology sees reality as being constructed by people themselves in the course of their everyday lives. Third, while scientific sociology tends to make use of *quantitative data*, interpretive sociology relies on *qualitative data*.

In sum, the scientific or positivist approach is well suited to research in a laboratory, where investigators observe while taking careful measurements. The interpretive approach is better suited to research in a natural setting where investigators interact with people, learning how they make sense of their everyday lives.

Max Weber combined the best of both the scientific and interpretive approaches—the positivism of Auguste Comte and the interpretive emphasis of Wilhelm Dilthey (1833–1911), who might accurately be called the founder of interpretive sociology (Bakker, 1999). Weber believed that one of the keys to the interpretive component lay in *Verstehen*—the German word for "understanding." That concept, in turn, can be attributed to Dilthey.

It is the interpretive sociologist's job not just to observe *what* people do but to share in their world of meaning and come to appreciate *why* they act as they do. Subjective thoughts and feelings—which science tends to dismiss as "bias"—now become the focus of the researcher (Berger and Kellner, 1981; Neuman, 2000).

Robert Prus of the University of Waterloo argues that George Herbert Mead forged the unique interpretive tradition of *symbolic interaction*. For Mead, *language* is absolutely fundamental to the human experience, to shared symbols and understandings, and to social life and interaction. To understand group life, one must get inside the minds of the individual actors through close and sustained contact. One must achieve intimate familiarity by relying on "three sources of data: *observation, participant-observation*, and *interviews*" (Prus, 1994:21).

In an attempt to understand how Canadian university students approach studying in preparation for exams, Albas and Albas (1994) relied on interviews, observations, and logs that, over their twenty years of teaching, they had students keep. Students, they found, came to identify themselves as *aces, moderates*, or *bombers* (the terminology may differ from year to year). Their identities determined their approaches to studying, their relationships with other students in each of the categories, their friendship choices, their leisure activities, their levels of procrastination, and their expectations with respect to grades.

Shared perspectives and patterns of behaviour were apparent within each of the categories, but almost all students sought to wear "the cloak of coolness"—the appearance of getting good grades with the minimum of effort. Since it is uncool to "work your butt off," serious studying—even among aces—was done out of sight or behind closed doors. Clearly, this type of interpretive understanding requires systematic analysis based on sustained personal contact with students themselves.

A THIRD FRAMEWORK: CRITICAL SOCIOLOGY

There is a third methodological approach to sociology. Like the interpretive approach, critical sociology developed in reaction to scientific research; however, this time, the issue is the scientific goal of "objectivity."

Scientific sociology holds that reality exists, and the researcher's task is to study and document this reality. Karl Marx, who founded the critical approach, rejected the notion that society exists as a "natural" system with a fixed order, arguing that this assumption leads to the conclusion that society cannot be changed—in effect, supporting the status quo.

Critical sociology, in contrast, is *the study of society that focuses on the need for social change*. Instead of asking the scientific question, "How does society work?"

Feminist Research: Critical and Interpretive Examples

How are women's lives affected by a capitalist and patriarchal social order? Canadian sociologists Dorothy Smith, Meg Luxton, and Susan Wendell have done sociological research to describe and analyze this question.

In a series of essays (1977, 1979, 1983), Dorothy Smith notes the ways in which relations between men and women depend on economic conditions. Her argument begins with the idea that in the early homesteading period, the division of labour between the sexes was fairly evenly split. Men and women depended on one another for house building, clearing land, growing and harvesting gardens, caring for livestock, and preserving food for winter. This situation of approximate equality changed as farmers moved towards cash production. As land speculation led to increased prices and expensive mortgages on houses and machinery, families had to produce more than they themselves needed for their own subsistence. They needed profits to pay off bank loans and to buy equipment and other goods. But, legally, only men could own property and borrow money at the bank. The labour of wives earned them nothing: the benefits went to their husbands. The result was drudgery and a loss of power for the women. As late as 1973, the powerlessness of the farm wife was underscored in the Supreme Court decision regarding Irene Murdoch. Murdoch had worked on the family farm for twenty-five years. When she and her husband divorced, the court decided that she had no right to any of the farm property. Women's organizations in Canada ral-

lied to protest this injustice; Murdoch took her case to the Supreme Court—and lost. Her case, however, was important. During the 1970s, province after province began to define marriage as a partnership of equals whose assets should be divided equally upon divorce (Anderson, 1991). By the late 1980s, Rosa Becker had won the right to the financial assets of a twenty-five-year common-law partnership.

Women's work is still undervalued, and women continue to play a subservient role to men in their homes and in corporations. Their services maintain the labour power of their husbands and children. Meg Luxton's book *More Than a Labour of Love* (1980) describes the process whereby women work to "re-produce" labour power for a corporation in a single-industry mining town in Flin Flon, Manitoba. She describes the way in which the lives of the women are constrained by the requirements of the corporations. The rhythms of women's lives and the lives of their children revolve around the husbands' need for sleep, food, rest, and relaxation, all in the interest of maintaining their employment. Luxton also documents the ways in which the husbands' frustrations at work are carried home to be vented on the wives. In extreme cases, wives contend not only with surplus anger and frustration but become the victims of violence, as their husbands act out their frustrations with the corporation.

Susan Wendell (1995), a woman who was suddenly stricken with a disabling chronic illness, uses her own experience, along with those of other disabled individuals, to develop what

she calls a "feminist theory of disability." Central to her interpretation is the assumption that disabled women are oppressed both as women in male-dominated societies and as the disabled in a world dominated by the able-bodied. But, she argues, "much of what is *disabling* about our physical conditions is also a consequence of social arrangements" (p. 457). Because we idealize the human body—in terms of appearance, strength, energy, and control—the disabled are marginalized. Furthermore, in a society that values independence, dependence on others is humiliating and damaging to one's self-esteem; as a result, profound alienation from one's body is a common experience of the disabled. The physical limitations imposed by disabilities are made more problematic by the social arrangements that designate the disabled as "other," or as marginal to normal human life; being a disabled *woman* compounds the difficulties.

Smith, Luxton, and Wendell are not concerned with the operationalization of concepts into quantitative variables. Causality is not determined mathematically on the basis of numerical measurements of variables, but instead is elicited from a subjective or interpretive analysis of the situation. In their view, exploitation and injustice in power, gender, class, and race characterize social relations, and changes in these relations over time and place need to be explained. Since change towards justice is the ultimate goal, sociology, in this tradition, differs greatly from positivist sociology.

---

critical sociologists ask moral and political questions—especially "Should society exist in its present form?" Their answer, typically, is that it should not. For Marx (1972:109; orig. 1845), the point is not to study the world as it is—the point is to *change* it. In making value

judgments about the ways in which society should be improved, critical sociology rejects Weber's goal that researchers be value free.

Sociologists using the critical approach seek to change not only society but the character of research

TABLE 2–2 Three Methodological Approaches in Sociology

	Scientific	Interpretive	Critical
What Is Reality?	Society is an orderly system; reality is "out there."	Society is ongoing interaction; reality is socially constructed meanings.	Society is patterns of inequality; reality is that some dominate others.
How Do We Conduct Research?	Gather empirical data—ideally, quantitative; researcher tries to be an objective observer.	Develop a qualitative account of the subjective sense people make of their world; researcher is a participant.	Research is a strategy to bring about desired change; researcher is an activist.
Corresponding Theoretical Paradigm	Structural-functional paradigm	Symbolic-interaction paradigm	Social-conflict paradigm

itself. They think of their research subjects as equals and encourage their participation in deciding what to study and how to do it. Often, their goal is to use their findings to provide a voice for less powerful people and advance the goal of a more equal society (Reinharz, 1992; Wolf, 1996; Hess, 1999). Sometimes, the political goals apply for specific categories of people such as Aboriginal women (Silman, 1987) or disabled women (Wendell, 1995). The "Applying Sociology" box provides examples of feminist research that illustrate the critical sociology approach.

Scientific sociologists object to taking sides in this way, charging that critical sociology (whether feminist, Marxist, or postmodern) is political and gives up any claim to objectivity. Critical sociologists respond that all research is political in that it either calls for change or does not. Sociologists thus have no choice about their work being political, but they can choose *which* positions to support. Critical sociology, therefore, is an activist approach tying knowledge to action—seeking not just to understand the world but also to improve it. Generally, scientific sociology tends to appeal to researchers with more conservative political views, whereas critical sociology appeals to those on the left of the political spectrum.

What about the link between methodological approaches and theory? In fact, each of the three methodological approaches is related to one of the classical theoretical paradigms presented in Chapter 1 ("The Sociological Perspective"). The scientific approach is most clearly linked to the structural-functional paradigm, the interpretive approach to the symbolic-interaction paradigm, and the critical approach to the social-conflict paradigm. Table 2–2 summarizes the differences among the three methodological approaches. Sociologists often favour one approach over another; however, most make some use of all three (Gamson, 1999).

GENDER AND RESEARCH

One political dimension of research involves **gender**, *the significance members of a society attach to being female or male.* Sociologists have come to realize that gender often plays a significant part in their work. Margrit Eichler (1988) identifies five threats to sound research that relate to gender.

1. **Androcentricity.** Androcentricity (*andro* is the Greek word for "male"; *centricity* means "being centred on") refers to approaching an issue from a male perspective. Sometimes researchers act as if only men's activities are important, ignoring those of women. For years, for example, researchers studying occupations focused on the paid work of men while overlooking the housework and child care traditionally performed by women (Counts, 1925; Hodge et al., 1966). When Matthews (1976) sought to understand the attitudes and values of three small Newfoundland communities that were being considered for relocation, he limited his interviews to a random sample of male household heads and all of the community leaders (who were also male). *Gynocentricity*—seeing the world from a female perspective—is equally limiting to sociological investigation. However, in our male-dominated society, this narrowness of vision arises much less frequently.

2. **Overgeneralizing.** This problem occurs when researchers use data drawn from only people of one sex to support conclusions about "humanity" or "society." For example, in an investigation of child-rearing practices, collecting data only from women would allow researchers to draw conclusions about "motherhood" but not about the more general issue of "parenthood."

3. **Gender blindness.** Failure to consider gender at all—gender blindness—is common, despite the fact that the lives of men and women differ in countless ways. A study of growing old in Canada that overlooked the fact that while most elderly men live with spouses, elderly women generally live alone, would be weakened by its gender blindness.

4. **Double standards.** Researchers must be careful not to distort what they study by applying different standards to men and women. For example, a family researcher who labels a couple as "man

Feminist research is a form of critical sociology. It is concerned not only with studying the social standing of women, but it also transforms research, putting the investigator on a more equal footing with subjects so that they can work together to solve their common problems.

and wife" may define the man as the "head of household" and treat him accordingly, while assuming that the woman simply engages in family "support work."

5. **Interference.** In this case, gender distorts a study because a subject reacts to the sex of the researcher in ways that interfere with the research operation. While studying a small community in Sicily, for instance, Maureen Giovannini (1992) found that many men responded to her as a woman rather than as a researcher, compromising her research efforts. Gender dynamics precluded her from certain activities, such as private conversations with men, that were deemed inappropriate for single women. In addition, local residents denied Giovannini access to places considered off-limits to women.

There is nothing wrong with focusing research on one sex or the other. But all sociologists, as well as people who read their work, should be aware of the effects of gender on sociological investigation.

WOMEN AS METHODOLOGISTS

Sociology's attention to men in the past has prompted some contemporary researchers to make special efforts to investigate the lives of women. Feminist researchers embrace two key tenets: (1) their research should focus on the condition of women in society, and (2) their research must be grounded in the assumption that women generally experience subordination. Thus, feminist research rejects Weber's value-free orientation in favour of being overtly political—doing research in pursuit of gender equality.

There is no single feminist research strategy. On the contrary, feminists employ any and all conventional scientific techniques, including all of those described in this chapter. But some go further, claiming that feminist research must transform science itself, which they see as a masculine form of knowledge. Mainstream methodology, in the eyes of many modern feminists, is simply "malestream" methodology that supports patriarchy and the status quo (McDonald, 1994:4). Whereas traditional notions about science demand detachment, feminists seek connections: a sympathetic understanding between investigator and subject. Moreover, conventional scientists take charge of the research agenda, deciding in advance what issues to raise and how to study them. Feminist researchers, by contrast, favour a more egalitarian approach that allows participants a chance to voice their needs and interests in their own words (Stanley and Wise, 1983; Nielsen, 1990; Stanley, 1990; Reinharz, 1992; Wolf, 1996).

Such alterations in research premises and methods have led more conventional sociologists to charge that feminist research is less science than simple political activism. Feminists respond that research and politics should not—indeed cannot—be distinct. Therefore, traditional notions that placed politics and science in separate spheres have now given way to some new thinking that merges these two dimensions.

University of Guelph professor Lynn McDonald (1994) has shaken up mainstream sociologists and feminists alike with her analysis of the role of women in the early development of sociology—and social science methodology in particular. McDonald argues that the feminists who reject empirical or scientific research and quantitative analysis—as serving the interests of men—are rejecting methodologies that women helped to develop in order to further their causes. Among the many women whose contributions are outlined in *The Women Founders of the Social Sciences* (McDonald, 1994) are Harriet Martineau (1802–76) and Florence Nightingale (1820–1910).

Martineau made her living as a writer and an investigative journalist, producing more than fifty books and 1600 feature articles on a wide range of issues. She also dealt with methodology in "Essays on the Art of Thinking" and an 1838 book entitled *How to Observe Morals and Manners*. Her *Society in America*, which appeared in 1837, made her the first to tackle comparative analysis, applying an explicitly sociological approach. Martineau, an activist, supported the anti-slavery movement and worked for women's rights to education, divorce, occupations, the franchise (the right to vote), and freedom from violence.

The name Florence Nightingale is familiar to all of us. She was "the lady with the lamp," the humble nurse from a wealthy background who ministered to the needs of soldiers wounded in Crimea. McDonald (1994) reveals a Nightingale of such methodological

Many women contributed to the emergence of sociology, although their achievements have long been unrecognized. Harriet Martineau (left) established her reputation as a sociologist with studies of slavery, factory laws, and women's rights. She also found time to write novels, travel widely, and pursue a full-time career as a journalist, in spite of recurrent ill health and deafness. Florence Nightingale (right) not only revolutionized the practice of nursing in the nineteenth century, but was also one of the first to use statistics and probability theory to reform public health laws.

and theoretical sophistication that one wonders if Durkheim was intellectually indebted to her. She was a "passionate statistician" who gathered data—often presented in pie charts that simultaneously compared data cross-sectionally and over time. She used her statistics to show that improved sanitation would reduce mortality in Crimean hospitals, in childbirth, and in British hospitals and would be cost-effective at the same time. Her application of statistics to more general issues of public administration led her to "describe the laws of social science as God's laws for the right operation of the world" (p. 186). She noted that crime, suicide, mortality, accident, marriage, and poverty levels could be predicted with exact precision, despite individual free will. As an activist who believed that social and individual conditions could be changed, Nightingale sought to improve a wide range of laws, policies, and administrative practices.

 For details about a Canadian project to publish the complete works of Florence Nightingale, go to www.sociology. uoguelph.ca/fnightingale/

RESEARCH ETHICS

Like all investigators, sociologists must be aware that research can harm as well as help subjects or communities. For this reason, the American Sociological Association—the major professional association of sociologists in North America—has established formal guidelines for the conduct of research (1997), as have the various bodies that fund social research in Canada (e.g., Canada's Social Sciences and Humanities Research Council).

 To read ethics guidelines from the American Sociological Association and Canada's Social Sciences and Humanities Research Council, go to www.asanet.org/members/ ecoderev.html and www.sshrc.ca/web/about/ policies/policy_list_e.asp

The prime directive is that sociologists strive to be both technically competent and fair-minded in conducting their research. Sociologists must disclose all their findings, without omitting significant data, and they are ethically bound to make their results available to other sociologists, some of whom may wish to replicate the research.

Sociologists also must strive to ensure the safety of subjects taking part in a research project. Should research develop in a manner that threatens the well-being of participants, investigators must terminate their work immediately. Furthermore, professional guidelines direct researchers to protect the privacy of anyone involved in a research project. Yet this is a promise that may be difficult to keep, since researchers sometimes come under pressure (say, from the police or courts) to disclose information. Therefore, researchers must think carefully about their responsibility to protect subjects, and they should discuss this issue with those who take part in research. An important principle in ethical research is obtaining the informed consent of participants, which means that subjects understand the responsibilities and risks that the research involves and agree—before the work begins—to take part.

Another important guideline concerns funding. Sociologists must include in their published results the sources of any and all financial support. Furthermore, sociologists must seek to avoid any conflicts of interest (or even the appearance of such conflicts) that may compromise the integrity of their work. For example, researchers must never accept funding from any organization that seeks to influence the research results for its own purposes.

Ethical concerns extend well beyond the issues raised here and address the role of sociologists as teachers, administrators, and clinical practitioners. At the broadest level, there are also global dimensions to research ethics. Before beginning research in other countries, investigators must become familiar enough with those societies to understand what people there are likely to perceive as a violation of privacy or as a source of personal danger. In a multicultural society such as ours, the same rule applies to studying people whose cultural backgrounds differ from our own. The "Diversity: Race, Class, and Gender" box offers some tips about how outsiders can effectively and sensitively study Aboriginal communities.

DIVERSITY: RACE, CLASS, AND GENDER

Conducting Research with Aboriginal Peoples

A Royal Commission on Aboriginal Peoples was announced in 1991 with a mandate to do extensive research and provide baseline data on the lives of Aboriginal peoples living in Canada. The ethical guidelines for the conduct of this research were published in the *Northern Health Research Bulletin*. As well as the standard principles for the conduct of ethical research, the royal commission established new guidelines with respect to the benefits of research to the community. As stated under the heading "Community Benefit,"

- In setting research priorities and objectives for community-based research, the Commission and the researchers it engages shall give serious and due consideration to the benefit of the community concerned.

- In assessing community benefit, regard shall be given to the widest possible range of community interest, whether the groups in question be Aboriginal or non-Aboriginal, and also to the impact of research at the

local, regional or national level. Wherever possible, conflicts between interests within the community should be identified and resolved in advance of commencing the project. Researchers should be equipped to draw on a range of problem-solving strategies to resolve such conflicts as may arise in the course of research.

- Whenever possible, research should support the transfer of skills to individuals and increase the capacity of the community to manage its own research.

The final, five-volume report of the royal commission covers every conceivable issue related to Aboriginal peoples—constitutional, political, social, medical, economic, demographic, and cultural. The report was based on the information acquired by the commission in meetings and hearings across the country, as well as from over 400 reports prepared by various organizations and individuals (Aboriginal and non-Aboriginal); sociologists and other social scientists were among those who

submitted these reports. The report is also available on CD-ROM under the title *For Seven Generations: An Information Legacy of the Royal Commission on Aboriginal Peoples*. The CD-ROM has an elaborate search capacity (by subject, for example) that greatly increases access to the contents of the report. Thus, social scientists, politicians, and Aboriginal communities can do research on the report itself.

Source: Based on Canada, The Royal Commission on Aboriginal Peoples, "Ethical Guidelines for Research," *Northern Health Bulletin*, 1993.

THE METHODS OF SOCIOLOGICAL RESEARCH

A **research method** is *a systematic plan for conducting research*. The remainder of this chapter introduces four commonly used methods of sociological investigation. None is inherently better or worse than any other. Rather, in the same way that a carpenter selects a particular tool for a specific task, researchers choose a method according to whom they choose to study and what they wish to learn.

TESTING A HYPOTHESIS: THE EXPERIMENT

The logic of science is most clearly expressed in the **experiment**, *a research method for investigating cause and effect under highly controlled conditions*. Experimental research is explanatory, meaning that it asks not just what happens but why. Typically, researchers turn to

an experiment to test a specific **hypothesis**, *an unverified statement of a relationship between variables*.

The ideal experiment consists of three steps: (1) the experimenter measures the dependent variable (the "effect"); (2) the investigator exposes the dependent variable to the independent variable (the "cause" or "treatment"); and (3) the researcher again measures the dependent variable to see if the predicted change took place. If the expected change did occur, the experiment lends support to the hypothesis; if not, the hypothesis is discounted.

However, a change in the dependent variable may be due to something other than the assumed cause. In order to identify the correct cause, researchers carefully control other factors that might intrude into the experiment and affect what is being measured. Such control is most easily accomplished in a laboratory, an artificial setting designed for research purposes. Another strategy for neutralizing outside influences is the random assignment of subjects into an *experimental group* and a *control group*. At the outset, the researcher measures the dependent variable for subjects in both groups but exposes only the experimental group to the independent variable or treatment (the control group typically gets a *placebo*, an apparently comparable treatment known to have no experimental effect). Then the investigator measures the dependent variable for the subjects in both groups again. It is assumed that any factor (such as some news event) occurring during the course of the research that influences people in the experimental group would do the same to the control group subjects, thus neutralizing the factor. In short, the use of a control group "washes out" many extraneous factors; comparing before and after measurements of the two groups, a researcher is able to assess how much of the observed change is due only to the independent variable.

The Hawthorne Effect

Subjects may alter their behaviour simply in response to a researcher's attention, as one classic experiment revealed. In the late 1930s, the Western Electric Company hired researchers to investigate worker productivity in its Hawthorne factory near Chicago (Roethlisberger and Dickson, 1939). One experiment examined whether increasing the available lighting would raise worker output. To test this idea, researchers measured initial productivity (the dependent variable); then they increased the lighting (the independent variable); and finally, they measured productivity a second time. Productivity increased, supporting the hypothesis. But when the research team subsequently reduced the lighting, productivity again increased, contradicting the initial hypothesis. In time, the researchers realized that the employees were working harder (even if they could not see as well) simply because people were paying attention to them. From this research, social scientists coined the term **Hawthorne effect** to refer to *a change in a subject's behaviour caused simply by the awareness of being studied.*

An Illustration: The Stanford County Prison

Prisons are often violent institutions, but does the prison setting itself play a part in generating violence and disorder? This question prompted Philip Zimbardo to devise a fascinating experiment to investigate the See www.prisonexp.org/ for a closer look at Zimbardo's Stanford County Prison experiment. causes of prison violence (Zimbardo, 1972; Haney et al., 1973).

Zimbardo's hypothesis was simple: prison violence is caused not so much by anti-social prisoners or guards as by the nature of prison itself. In other words, Zimbardo suspected that, once inside a prison, even emotionally healthy people become prone to violence.

Six inmates of the Prison for Women in Kingston, Ontario, turned on their guards in what became four days of violence. They were finally subdued by a male riot squad, which strip-searched the female inmates. A federal inquiry investigating the incident heard inmates' rights activists criticize the repressive, brutal actions of the male riot squad. The Prison for Women was closed in 1995.

Thus, Zimbardo treated the prison setting as the independent variable capable of causing violence, the dependent variable.

To test this hypothesis, Zimbardo's research team first constructed a realistic, artificial prison in the basement of the psychology building on the campus of Stanford University. Then they placed an ad in a Palo Alto newspaper, offering to pay young men for their help with a two-week research project. To each of the seventy men who responded they administered a series of physical and psychological tests, selecting the healthiest twenty-four for their experiment.

The next step was randomly designating half the men as "prisoners" and half as "guards." The plan called for the guards and prisoners to spend the next two weeks in the "Stanford County Prison." The "prisoners" began their part of the experiment soon afterwards when the Palo Alto police "arrested" them at their homes. After searching and handcuffing the men, the police took them to the local police station to be fingerprinted. Then they transported their captives to the Stanford "prison" where Zimbardo had the "guards" ready to secure them behind bars; video cameras would then record developments.

The experiment quickly degenerated beyond anyone's expectations, for both guards and prisoners soon became embittered and hostile towards one another. Guards humiliated the prisoners by assigning them tasks such as cleaning toilets with their bare hands. The prisoners, for their part, resisted and insulted the guards. Within four days, the researchers removed five prisoners who displayed "extreme emotional depression, crying, rage and acute anxiety" (Haney et al., 1973:81). By the end of one week, the situation had deteriorated so much that the researchers called off the experiment entirely. Zimbardo explains (1972:4): "The ugliest, most base, pathological side of human nature surfaced. We were horrified because we saw some boys (guards) treat others as if they were despicable animals, taking pleasure in cruelty, while other boys (prisoners) became servile, dehumanized robots who thought only of escape, of their own individual survival and of their mounting hatred for the guards."

The unfolding events in the "Stanford County Prison" supported Zimbardo's hypothesis that prison violence is rooted in the social character of jails themselves, rather than in the personalities of guards and prisoners. This finding raises questions about how and why our society operates prisons, suggesting the need for basic reform. But also note how this experiment reveals the potential of research to threaten the physical and mental well-being of subjects. Such dangers are not always as obvious as they were in this case. Therefore, researchers must carefully consider the potential harm to subjects at all stages of their work and end any study, as Zimbardo responsibly did, if subjects may suffer harm of any kind.

ASKING QUESTIONS: SURVEY RESEARCH

A **survey** is *a research method in which subjects respond to a series of items in a questionnaire or an interview*. The most widely used of all research methods, surveys are particularly well suited to studying attitudes that investigators cannot observe directly, including political and religious beliefs or the subjective effects of racism. Although surveys can shed light on cause and effect, most often they yield descriptive findings—snapshots of responses at one point in time.

Population and Sample

A survey targets a **population**—*the people who are the focus of research*. For example, in order to predict election results, political pollsters conduct surveys that treat every voting-age adult in Canada as the population.

Obviously, contacting millions of people would overwhelm even the most well-funded and patient researcher. Fortunately, there is an easier way to get accurate results: researchers collect data from a **sample**, *a part of a population that represents the whole*.

Although the term may be new to you, you use the logic of sampling all the time. You look around the classroom, notice five or six heads nodding off, and conclude that the class finds that day's lecture dull. That conclusion involves making an inference about all of the people (the "population") from observing some of the people (the "sample"). But how do we know if a sample actually represents the entire population?

One way to ensure representativeness is through *random sampling*, in which researchers draw a sample from the population in such a way that every element in the population has the same chance of ending up in the sample. If this is the case, the mathematical laws of probability dictate that the sample selected will, in the vast majority of cases, represent the population with a minimal amount of error. Seasoned researchers use special computer programs to generate random samples. Novice researchers, however, sometimes make the mistake of assuming that "randomly" walking up to people on the street produces a sample representative of an entire city. But such a strategy does not give every person an equal chance to be included in the sample. Any street—whether in a rich neighbourhood or a university town—contains more of some kinds of people than others. Furthermore, any researcher will find some people more approachable than others, again introducing bias.

Although good sampling is no simple task, it offers considerable savings in time and expense. We are spared the tedious work of contacting everyone in a

 For a discussion of the use of polls in political campaigns, go to http://faculty.vassar.edu/lowry/polls.html

population, while obtaining reliable results.

Questionnaires and Interviews

Selecting subjects is only the first step in carrying out a survey. Also needed is a plan for asking questions and recording answers. Surveys fall into two general categories: questionnaires and interviews.

A **questionnaire** is *a series of written questions a researcher supplies to subjects requesting their responses*. One type of questionnaire provides not only the questions but a series of fixed responses (similar to a multiple-choice examination). This *closed-ended format* makes the task of analyzing the results relatively easy, yet it narrows the range of responses in a way that might distort the findings. By contrast, a second type of questionnaire, using an *open-ended format*, allows subjects to respond freely, expressing various shades of opinion. The drawback of this approach is that the researcher later has to make sense out of what can be a bewildering array of answers.

Choosing a method of presenting questions is another part of the research strategy. Most often, researchers employ a *self-administered survey*, in which they mail questionnaires to respondents with a request to complete and mail back the form. Since no researcher is present when subjects read the questionnaire, it must be both inviting and clearly written. Pretesting a self-administered questionnaire with a small number of people before sending it to the entire sample can preclude the costly problem of finding out, too late, that instructions or questions are confusing.

Using the mail (or, more recently, email) has the advantage of allowing a researcher to contact a large number of people over a wide geographical area at minimal expense. But many people treat such questionnaires as "junk mail"; typically, no more than half are completed and returned. Researchers often send out follow-up mailings to coax reluctant subjects to fill out the questionnaire.

Finally, it is important to keep in mind that many people are not capable of completing a questionnaire on their own. Young children obviously cannot, nor can many hospital patients; in addition, a surprising number of adults simply lack the reading and writing skills needed to wade through a comprehensive questionnaire.

An **interview** is *a series of questions a researcher administers personally to respondents.* In a closed-ended format, researchers read a question or statement and then ask the subject to select one of several responses. Other interviews are open-ended so that subjects can respond in whatever way they choose and researchers can probe with follow-up questions. In the ensuing conversation, however, the researcher must guard against influencing a subject, a problem that can creep in through such subtle gestures as raising an eyebrow when a person begins to answer.

Experienced investigators know that a subject is more likely to complete a survey if contacted personally by the researcher. Yet interviews have some disadvantages: tracking people down and personally interrogating them is costly and time-consuming, especially if all subjects do not live in the same area. And while telephone interviews clearly allow far greater "reach," the impersonality of "cold calls" by telephone may result in a low completion rate.

In both questionnaires and interviews, the wording of questions may significantly affect answers. For instance, emotionally loaded language can easily sway subjects: the term "welfare mothers," as opposed to "women who receive public assistance," injects an emotional element into a survey and encourages respondents to answer more negatively. In still other cases, the wording of questions may hint at what other people think, thereby steering subjects. For example, people are more likely to respond positively to the question "Do you *agree* that the police force is doing a good job?" than to the similar question "Do you *think* that the police force is doing a good job?" Similarly, respondents are more likely to endorse a statement to "not allow" something (say, public speeches against the government) than a statement to "forbid" the same activity (Rademacher, 1992).

Finally, researchers may inadvertently confuse respondents by asking double questions such as "Do you think that the government should cut spending and raise taxes to reduce the deficit?" The problem here is that a subject could very well agree with one part of the question but reject the other, so that responding yes or no to the two-part question distorts the person's true opinion.

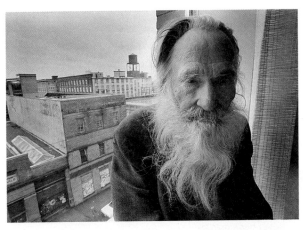

Most census data are obtained from questionnaires that officials send and receive back through the mail or deliver and pick up by hand. Although this strategy is generally quite efficient, it is likely to undercount the homeless or others who lack a customary street address. Olaf Solheim (above) was evicted from a rooming house in Vancouver's West End to make room for tourist housing for Expo '86. Less than six weeks later, Solheim was dead. Modern sociologists are committed to research that does not rely solely on government statistics, but that also allows voices like Solheim's to be heard.

Surveys at Work: The Case of Anti-Semitism in Quebec

On September 17, 1991, Mordecai Richler, a prominent Canadian novelist with an international reputation (and a Jew), wrote an article on French-Canadian nationalism in *The New Yorker* in which he alleged that French Canadians are anti-Semitic. His statements were the beginning of passionately felt and argued controversy. Are French Canadians anti-Semitic? If so, are they more anti-Semitic than English Canadians? If they are more anti-Semitic, what is the explanation? A team of sociologists headed by Paul Sniderman attempted to answer these questions.

Sniderman used the data from an existing survey entitled the *Charter of Rights Study Survey*, carried out in 1993. The study used random digit dialing (RDD) of a random sample (2084 people) of the 97 percent of Canadian households that have telephones. The Quebec sampling strategy was specifically designed to yield a representative sample of the province. Care was taken that the Quebec response rate was equal to that in the rest of the country, and that respondents filled the same demographic categories as those in the rest of Canada. In other words, the survey was designed to include the right proportions of male and female, older and younger, urban dwellers and rural dwellers, and so on, in order to reflect the total population of both the country and Quebec. The accuracy of this method is demonstrated by the similarities between the sample and the population of Canada, as

	1986 Census of Canada[*]	Charter	1986 Census Quebec Only	Charter Sample Quebec Only
Mean age of respondents	42	43	42	41
Highest level of schooling				
High-school graduation or less	55%	56%	58%	59%
College, technical school, some university, etc.	35%	28%	31%	30%
University degree(s)	10%	15%	9%	11%
Sex				
Female	51%	51%	52%	52%
Male	49%	49%	48%	48%
Marital status				
Married (living with partner)	65%	66%	64%	66%
Never been married	22%	23%	24%	22%
Separated, divorced, widowed	13%	11%	12%	12%
Employment status				
Employed	62%	63%	57%	55%
Not in labour force	31%	29%	35%	37%
Unemployed	7%	8%	8%	8%

[*]Statistics Canada Public Use Sample Tapes.

Source: Sniderman et al. (1993:246).

portrayed in Table 2–3. Notice, for example, that the average age of Canadian respondents in the 1986 census was forty-two years, while the average age of the *Charter* sample was forty-three years.

A review of the literature on explanations for prejudice identified several common bases for prejudicial attitudes. These included

1. **Personality type of the individual.** Apparently, people with authoritarian personalities are more likely to express prejudice.

2. **Normative prejudice.** This is prejudice widely taken for granted as acceptable—as in South Africa, where prejudice was legislated into what until the 1990s were the policies of apartheid.

3. **Normative conformity.** Conformity itself is seen as an important norm.

4. **Nationalism.** One of the consequences of Quebec nationalism may be the derogation of other ethnic groups.

The questionnaire was designed to identify not only whether French-speaking Quebecers held more anti-Semitic views than English-speaking Canadians (the dependent variable), but also which of these factors was the underlying cause of those views (the independent variable). The five questions used to measure anti-Semitism were as follows (Sniderman et al., 1993:247):

> We realize no statement is true of all people in a group, but generally speaking, please tell me whether you agree or disagree with the following statements. Would

you say you agree strongly, agree somewhat, disagree somewhat or disagree with this statement?

> Most Jews don't care what happens to people who aren't Jewish.

> Most Jews are pushy.

> Jews have made an important contribution to the cultural life of Canada.

> Jews are more willing than others to use shady practices to get ahead.

> Most Jews are warm and friendly people.

Note the carefully worded introduction, which was designed to make respondents feel comfortable expressing their views candidly by qualifying the responses. Given the sensitive nature of the topic, this qualification was deemed necessary in order to combat what sociologists refer to as the *social desirability effect*, whereby respondents are unwilling to commit themselves to an opinion that might place them outside the "normal" range of opinion. By acknowledging that the statements could not be applied to all Jews, the researchers allowed respondents freer rein in expressing their attitudes. Even if respondents agreed strongly with one of the negative statements, they could rest assured that they fell within "acceptable norms," since the response was not going to be taken as a blanket condemnation of all Jews.

Findings. The researchers found that French-speaking Quebecers were, in fact, more anti-Semitic than English-speaking Canadians. While the personality basis for anti-Semitism was conspicuously weak, the cultural basis for anti-Semitism was strong and related more to the high value placed on conformity in Quebec (normative conformity) than on nationalist sentiment, as had been suggested by some commentators. French-speaking Quebecers were significantly more likely than English-speaking Canadians to express support for conformity as a value. "They place a greater priority on people learning to fit in and get along with others" and on the larger society being "a unified body pursuing a common goal" (Sniderman et al., 1993:264). They are therefore more likely to distrust and dislike those whom they perceive as different or for whom cultural diversity is a more important value than cultural conformity.

Conclusions. The authors make the point that while francophone Quebecers, overall, are more anti-Semitic than other Canadians, most are not anti-Semitic at all. Moreover, on every test but one, a majority expressed positive sentiments regarding Jews. "Quebeckers differ from other Canadians not so much in their readiness to submit to the full syndrome of anti-Semitic ideas but rather in their willingness to accept one or two negative characterizations of Jews" (p. 265). Québécois were as tolerant as English-speaking Canadians and were as willing as anglophones to support such things as the rights of groups with unpopular points of view to hold public rallies, and the need for restrictions on the rights of Canada's security service to wiretap. Lastly, recognition of slightly more anti-Semitism in Quebec does nothing to negate its existence in the rest of Canada.

IN THE FIELD: PARTICIPANT OBSERVATION

Sociological investigation takes place not only in laboratories but "in the field"—or where people carry on their everyday lives. The most widely used strategy for field study is **participant observation**, *a method in which researchers systematically observe people while joining in their routine activities.*

Researchers choose participant observation in order to gain an inside look at social life in settings ranging from night clubs to religious seminaries. Cultural anthropologists commonly employ participant observation (which they call *fieldwork*) to study communities in other societies. They term their descriptions of unfamiliar cultures *ethnographies*; sociologists prefer to describe their accounts of people in particular settings as *case studies.*

At the outset of a field study, social scientists typically have only a vague idea of what they will encounter. Thus, most field research is *exploratory* and *descriptive*. Researchers might have hypotheses in mind, but just as likely they may not yet realize what the important questions will turn out to be.

As its name suggests, participant observation has two facets. On the one hand, gaining an "insider's" look depends on becoming a participant in the setting—"hanging out" with others, attempting to act, think, and even feel the way they do. Compared to experiments and survey research, then, participant observation has fewer hard-and-fast rules. But it is precisely this flexibility that allows investigators to explore the unfamiliar and to adapt to the unexpected.

Unlike other research methods, participant observation requires a researcher to become immersed in the setting, not for a week or two, but for months or even years. For the duration of the study, however, the researcher must maintain some distance as an "observer," mentally stepping back to record field notes and, eventually, make sense of the action. The tension inherent in this method comes through in the name: by playing the participant, the researcher gains acceptance and access to people's lives; yet playing the observer affords the distance and perspective needed for thoughtful analysis. The twin roles of "insider" participant and "outside observer," then, often come down to a series of careful compromises.

Most sociologists carry out participant observation alone, so they must remain mindful that results depend on the interpretations of a single individual. Participant observation is typically **qualitative research**, meaning *investigation in which a researcher gathers impressionistic, not numerical, data.* Unlike experiments or surveys, participant observation usually involves little **quantitative research**, *investigation in which a researcher collects numerical data.* Some scientists disparage a "soft" method such as participant observation as lacking in scientific rigour. Yet its personal approach—relying so heavily on personal impressions—is also a strength: while a highly visible team of sociologists attempting to administer formal surveys would disrupt many social settings, a sensitive participant-observer can often gain considerable insight into people's natural, day-to-day behaviour.

An Illustration: Street Corner Society

In the late 1930s, a young graduate student at Harvard University named William Foote Whyte became fascinated by the lively street life of a nearby, rather run-down section of Boston. His curiosity led him to carry out four years of participant observation in this neighbourhood, which he called "Cornerville," producing a sociological classic in the process.

At the time, Cornerville was home to first- and second-generation Italian immigrants. Many were poor and lived economically precarious lives, quite unlike the more affluent Bostonians familiar to Whyte. Popular wisdom in Boston held that Cornerville was a place to avoid: a poor, chaotic slum inhabited by racketeers. Unwilling to accept easy stereotypes, Whyte set out to discover for himself exactly what kind of life went on inside this community. His celebrated book, *Street Corner Society* (1981; orig. 1943), describes

Anthropologists and photographers Angela Fisher and Carol Beckwith have documented fascinating rituals around the world. As part of their fieldwork, they lived for months with the Himba in Namibia, in order to gain their acceptance and trust. During this time, a village man was killed by a lion. Later, his wives fell under the control of a lion spirit, apparently sent by the husband to bring these women to him in the afterlife.

Cornerville as a highly organized community with a distinctive code of values, complex social patterns, and particular social conflicts.

Whyte considered a range of research methods. He might have taken a pile of questionnaires to one of Cornerville's community centres and asked local people to fill them out, or he could have asked members of the community to come to his Harvard office for interviews. But it is easy to see that such formal strategies would have prompted little cooperation from the local people and yielded few insights. Whyte decided, therefore, to ease into Cornerville life and patiently seek out the keys to understanding this rather mysterious place.

Soon enough, Whyte discovered the challenges of just getting started in field research. After all, an upper-middle-class Anglo-Saxon graduate student from Harvard did not exactly "fit in" to Cornerville life. And, as Whyte quickly found out, even what he intended as a friendly overture could seem pushy and rude to others. Early on, Whyte dropped in at a local bar, hoping to buy a woman a drink and encourage her to talk about Cornerville. He looked around the room, but could find no woman alone. Presently, he thought he might have an opportunity when a fellow sat down with two women. He gamely remarked, "Pardon me. Would you mind if I joined you?" Instantly, he realized his miscalculation:

> There was a moment of silence while the man stared at me. Then he offered to throw me down the stairs. I as-

sured him that this would not be necessary, and demonstrated as much by walking right out of there without any assistance. (1981:289)

As this incident suggests, gaining entrée to a community—that is, becoming a participant—is the crucial (and sometimes hazardous) first step in this type of research. "Breaking in" typically depends on patience, ingenuity, and a little luck. For Whyte, a big break came when he met a young man named "Doc." Listening to Whyte's account of his bungled efforts to make friends in Cornerville, Doc sympathetically took Whyte under his wing and introduced him to others in the community. With Doc's help, Whyte soon became a "regular" in the neighbourhood.

Whyte's friendship with Doc illustrates the importance of a key informant in field research. Such people not only introduce a researcher to a community but often continue to be sources of help and information on a host of issues. But using a key informant also has its risks. Because any person has a particular circle of friends, a key informant's guidance is certain to introduce bias into the study. Moreover, in the eyes of others the reputation of the key informant—for better or worse—usually rubs off on the investigator. In sum, while relying on a key informant at the outset, a participant-observer soon must seek a broader range of contacts.

Having entered the Cornerville world, Whyte began his work in earnest. He soon realized that the careful field researcher needs to know when to speak up and when to simply listen, look, and learn. One evening, he joined a Cornerville group engaged in a discussion of neighbourhood gambling. Wanting to get the facts straight, Whyte asked naively, "I suppose the cops were all paid off?"

> The gambler's jaw dropped. He glared at me. Then he denied vehemently that any policeman had been paid off and immediately switched the conversation to another subject. For the rest of that evening I felt very uncomfortable.

The next day, Doc offered some sound advice:

> "Go easy on that 'who,' 'what,' 'why,' 'when,' 'where' stuff, Bill. You ask those questions and people will clam up on you. If people accept you, you can just hang around, and you'll learn the answers in the long run without even having to ask the questions." (1981:303)

In the months and years that followed, Whyte became familiar with life in Cornerville and married a woman from the community. In the process, he learned that this neighbourhood was hardly the stereotypical slum. On the contrary, most immigrants were working hard, many had earned considerable success, and some could boast of having sent children to college. In short, his book makes for fascinating reading about the dreams, deeds, and disappointments of one ethnic community, and it contains a richness of detail that only long-term participant observation can provide.

In Whyte's work, we also see that participant observation is a method rife with tensions and contrasts. Its flexibility helps a researcher respond to an unfamiliar setting but makes replication difficult for others. Insight depends on getting close to others, while scientific observation demands detachment. Participant observation calls for little expense, since no elaborate equipment or laboratory is needed, but a comprehensive community study does take time—typically a year or more. Perhaps this long-term commitment explains why participant observation is used less often than other methods described in this chapter. Yet the depth of understanding gained through interpretive research of this kind has greatly enriched our knowledge of many types of human communities.

USING AVAILABLE DATA: SECONDARY AND HISTORICAL ANALYSIS

Not all research requires investigators to collect their own data. In many cases, sociologists engage in **secondary analysis**, *a research method in which a researcher utilizes data collected by others.*

The most widely used statistics in social science are gathered by government agencies. Statistics Canada continually updates information about the Canadian population and offers much of interest to sociologists. Comparable data on the United States are available from the Bureau of the Census, a branch of the U.S. government. Global investigations benefit from various publications of the United Nations and the World Bank. In short, a wide range of data about the whole world is as close as the Internet. Since using available data—whether government statistics or the findings of individual researchers—saves researchers time and money, this approach holds special appeal to sociologists with low budgets. The quality of government data is generally better than that of any data even well-funded researchers could hope to obtain on their own.

Still, secondary analysis has inherent problems. For one thing, available data may not exist in precisely the form one might wish; further, there are always questions about the meaning and accuracy of work done by others. For example, in his classic study of suicide, Emile Durkheim realized that he could not be sure that a death classified as an "accident" was not, in reality, a "suicide," and vice versa. He also knew that various agencies used different procedures and categories in collecting data, making comparisons difficult. Thus, using second-hand data is a little like shopping for a used car: bargains are plentiful, but you have to be careful to avoid being stuck with a lemon.

Content Analysis

Another type of secondary analysis is called *content analysis*. This entails the counting or coding of the content of written, aural, or visual materials, such as television and radio programming, novels, magazines, and advertisements. Content analysis has a long tradition in sociology. One of the best-known early content analyses of this century in North America is *The Polish Peasant in Europe and America* by Thomas and Znaniecki (1971; orig. 1919), which used diaries and letters written to and from Polish immigrants in America to describe the adjustment processes of new American immigrants. A 1977 study by the Montreal YWCA Women's Centre of gender roles in thirty-eight grade 1 readers used in Montreal's anglophone schools is another example of the use of content research. The study found that gender stereotypes were mirrored in the books. Males were portrayed as central characters and as active, competitive problem-solvers. Females were less often included, and when they were included they tended to be portrayed in passive, domestic roles and occupations. Males were shown in seventy-eight different occupations; most females were housewives, and those who weren't were described as nurses, librarians, teachers, or cooks (Mackie, 1983). Research by Nancarrow Clarke (1991) on media "treatment" of cancer, heart disease, and AIDS (see Chapter 3, "Culture") provides another example of content analysis.

Historical Research: Open for Business

Since we are all trapped in the present, secondary analysis provides a key to investigating the past. Gordon Laxer's book *Open for Business: The Roots of Foreign Ownership in Canada* (1989) is an important contribution to the age-old Canadian debate about the reasons for the Canadian economy's high level of dependence on the United States and other foreign owners. Laxer rejected what have become the conventional explanations: geographical closeness to a powerful and expanding economy, our relative lack of technological development, the influence of merchant and banking elites, and a reliance on the export of raw materials. Focusing on forces beyond our control, he pointed out, tends to make Canadian failure to develop independently seem inevitable. Instead, Laxer chose to examine the internal social and political forces that have shaped Canada's development policies, by comparing Canada with other "late-followers" such as Germany, Japan, Sweden, and Russia (countries that were behind the United States and Great Britain in their economic development).

Laxer points out that at the turn of the century, Canada was the eighth-largest manufacturing country in the world, a fact that was particularly surprising, given its relatively small population. Early economic development was not due to American investment;

TABLE 2–4 Four Research Methods: A Summary

Method	Application	Advantages	Limitations
Experiment	For explanatory research that specifies relationships among variables; generates quantitative data	Provides greatest ability to specify cause-and-effect relationships; replication of research is relatively easy	Laboratory settings have artificial quality; unless research environment is carefully controlled, results may be biased
Survey	For gathering information about issues that cannot be directly observed, such as attitudes and values; useful for descriptive and explanatory research; generates quantitative or qualitative data	Sampling allows surveys to large populations using questionnaires; interviews provide in-depth responses	Questionnaires must be carefully prepared and may produce a low return rate; interviews are expensive and time-consuming
Participant observation	For exploratory and descriptive study of people in a "natural" setting; generates qualitative data	Allows study of "natural" behaviour; usually inexpensive	Time-consuming; replication of research is difficult; researcher must balance roles of participant and observer
Secondary analysis	For exploratory, descriptive, or explanatory research whenever suitable data are available	Saves time and expense of data collection; makes historical research possible	Researcher has no control over possible bias in data; data may not be suitable for current research needs

rather, it was Canada's already developed industry, the nature of its labour force, and its standard of living that attracted American companies. Before Canada became a "branch-plant" economy, Canadians were exporting sophisticated industrial goods, developed and made by Canadian-owned businesses, to such markets as Britain, France, and Germany.

An important cause of the demise of Canadian economic independence, Laxer found, was the weakness of the organized farmers' movements from before Confederation to World War I. (Agrarian movements, because of their attachment to the land, were important in protecting countries against economic penetration and the exploitation of the land and natural resources by foreign capitalists.) The weakness of the agrarian movements resulted from loyalty to Britain and from internal divisions (e.g., French–English, Protestant–Catholic, and class divisions). As a result, banks did not encourage Canadians to invest in their own country. Because of weak agrarian policies, the development of the West was delayed about twenty years, which in turn slowed the pace and scale of Canadian industrial development in the period immediately preceding the first major invasion of American branch plants. Finally, the weakness of agrarian and populist nationalism allowed open-door policies with regard to foreign investment.

Laxer concludes his book by warning Canadians that internal problems (anglophone–francophone tensions, regionalism, and ethnic, religious, and other divisions) must be solved on an equitable basis of mutual respect, so that Canadians form a united front for strong economic development. Looking at history, Laxer suggests, provides us with clues to the future development of the Canadian economy.

Table 2–4 summarizes the four major methods of sociological investigation. We now turn to some final considerations: the impact of technology on research and how to relate the specific facts, culled through sociological investigation, to theory.

TECHNOLOGY AND RESEARCH

In recent decades, new information technology has changed our lives considerably, and this applies to the practice of research as well. Personal computers—which have only been on the scene since the early 1980s—now give individual sociologists remarkable technical ability to randomly select samples, perform complex statistical analysis, and prepare written reports efficiently. Today's average office computer is far more powerful than even the massive mainframe devices that filled entire rooms on university campuses a generation ago.

The development of the Internet (the so-called electronic superhighway) is certain to further enhance our research capabilities in the years to come. The Internet now links some 670 million people throughout the world, allowing for an unprecedented level of communication. Contemporary sociologists are capable of building networks across the country and around the globe, which will facilitate collaboration and prompt comparative research. Both faculty and students can readily access rapidly increasing amounts of statistical information on the Internet. Statistics Canada opened a website on the Internet in 1994. Such developments—and other as-yet-unimagined forms of technological change—promise to transform

 To view the Statistics Canada website, go to www.statcan.ca/

From Card Punching to Number Crunching: Technological Advances in Research

How have technological advances changed research? One of the authors of this text, Linda Gerber, began the research for her PhD thesis—dealing with out-migration from First Nations communities—around 1970, which in technological terms was the dinosaur era. She had to laboriously code about eighty variables for more than 600 Aboriginal communities and then punch these coded data onto several thousand cards that had to be manually fed into the University of Toronto's huge mainframe computers for every new piece of analysis.

Towards the end of the research period, these cards were read onto magnetic tape, which made the final analyses—"one more run, just one more run"—considerably less labour-intensive. Several drafts of that thesis were hammered out on a manual typewriter: since whiteout was not allowed, mistakes on any of the 313 pages of the final document (Gerber, 1976) required that the entire page in question be re-typed. Subsequent papers submitted to journals in hopes of publication were produced in the same plodding way.

By the mid-1980s, the Canadian census was arriving at the University of Guelph's library on paper and on magnetic tape. The tapes made secondary analysis infinitely easier for anyone who analyzed census data. In addition, the development and improvement of word processors made "keyboarding" (males do not "type") of manuscripts a breeze. Journal articles were submitted on paper for consideration by reviewers, but by the early 1990s the final copy of an "accepted" paper would be sent to most of the major journals on a disk.

Today, data must still be coded, but the process is a lot less labour-intensive. Those who analyze census data pull the data directly off the Internet or a CD-ROM. The data are transferred onto microcomputer or mainframe files, where they can be recoded and subjected to all kinds of sophisticated analysis using statistical software packages. Word processing produces "papers," which might never see anything but electronic form until they appear in the journals destined for our libraries.

Increasingly, established journals are making the articles from their paper-based publications available on the Internet as well, with members paying for the right to read and print copies of the various papers. By 1996 a number of new sociology journals started appearing on the Internet and on the Internet alone. These journals have no paper copy available anywhere! Submission of papers to these journals is done electronically.

Familiarity with computers is far more common among younger members of our society than older generations. Today's young people will find computers a natural and indispensable part of day-to-day living.

Just think of the implications for a moment. It is now possible to "collect" data, conduct sophisticated analysis, write a "paper," submit the paper, and have it "published" with instantaneous access around the world. All of this is accomplished electronically without ever putting ink or laser imprint to paper. Communications theorist Marshall McLuhan would have been quick to point out the revolutionary impact of these developments.

---

sociological investigation as we enter the next century (Morton, 1995).

THE INTERPLAY OF THEORY AND METHOD

There are, of course, some research tasks that remain unaffected by technological change. No matter how we gather data, sociologists must ultimately transform facts into meaning by building theory.

Actually, sociological investigators move back and forth between facts and theory. **Inductive logical thought** is *reasoning that transforms specific observations into general theory*. In this mode, a researcher's thinking runs from the specific to the general, something like this: "I have some interesting data here; what are the data saying about human behaviour?"

A second type of logical thought works "downwards," in the opposite direction. **Deductive logical thought** is *reasoning that transforms general theory into specific hypotheses suitable for scientific testing*. This time, the researcher's thinking goes from the general to the specific: "I have this hunch about human behaviour; let's put it in a form we can test, collect some data, and see if it is correct." Working deductively, the researcher

Can People Lie with Statistics?

Is scientific research always as objective and "factual" as we think? Not according to the great English politician Benjamin Disraeli, who once noted wryly, "There are three kinds of lies: lies, damned lies, and statistics!" In a world that bombards us with numbers—often in the form of "scientific facts" and "official figures"—it is well worth pausing to consider that "statistical evidence" is not synonymous with truth. Every method of data collection is prone to error; furthermore, since data do not speak for themselves, someone has to interpret them to provide meaning. Some analysts may "dress up" their data almost the way politicians whip up a campaign speech—with an eye more to winning you over than to getting at the truth.

The best way to ferret out statistical manipulation is to understand how these tricks are performed. Here are three ways people can lie with statistics.

1. **People select their data.** Many times, the data we confront are not wrong—they just do not tell the whole story. Let's say someone claims that television is ruining our way of life and, as evidence, offers statistics indicating that we watch more TV today than a generation ago and that standard mathematics and reading scores have fallen during that time. Such data are actually correct, but they are selectively chosen. Another person could just as correctly counter that Canadians spend much more on books today than we did a generation ago, suggesting that there is no cultural crisis at all. In short, people on all sides of a political debate can find statistics to bolster their arguments.

2. **People interpret their data.** Another way people manipulate statistics is to "package" them inside a ready-made interpretation, as if to say, "Here are the numbers, and this is what they mean." Usually several different slants can be put on any particular set of data. For example, using average income as a measure, one can show irrefutably that Native people are poor relative to other Canadians. Looking at distribution across income categories reveals, just as truthfully, that there are many Native individuals in the upper income categories (say, $75 000 and over). The inferences based on these two measures of income are very different.

3. **People use graphs to "spin" the "truth."** Especially in newspapers and other popular media, we find graphic representations of statistical data. While graphs make comprehending data easy (showing, for example, an upward or downward trend), they also provide the designer with the opportunity to "spin" data in various ways. One common technique for casting data in a particular light involves compressing or expanding the graph's time frame. A graph of the crime rate over the last several years would reveal a downward trend: shifting the time frame to the last few decades would show a sharp increase.

Continue the debate . . .

1. *Why do you think people are so quick to accept "statistics" as true?*

2. *Can you cite a piece of research that you think presented biased data or conclusions? What are the biases?*

---

first states the theory in the form of a hypothesis and then selects a method by which to test it. To the extent that the data support the hypothesis, we conclude that the theory is correct; data that refute the hypothesis alert the researcher that the theory should be revised or perhaps rejected entirely.

Philip Zimbardo's Stanford County Prison experiment illustrates how this model operates. Zimbardo began with the general idea that prisons alter human behaviour. He then fashioned a specific, testable hypothesis: placed in a prison setting, even emotionally well-balanced young men would exhibit violent behaviour. Violence erupted soon after his experiment began, supporting this hypothesis. Had his experiment produced amicable behaviour between "prisoners" and "guards," his original theory would clearly have required reformulation.

Just as researchers commonly employ several methods over the course of one study, so they typically make use of both types of logical thought.

PUTTING IT ALL TOGETHER: TEN STEPS IN SOCIOLOGICAL INVESTIGATION

We can draw the material in this chapter together by outlining ten steps of sociological investigation. Each step is represented by an important question:

1. **What is your topic?** Being curious and looking at the world sociologically can generate ideas for social research anywhere. The topic you choose is likely to have some personal significance.

2. **What is known already?** You are probably not the first person to develop an interest in a particular issue. Visit the library to see what theories and methods researchers have applied to your topic in the past. In reviewing existing research, note problems that have come up.

3. **What, exactly, are your questions?** Are you seeking to explore an unfamiliar social setting, to describe some category of people, or to investigate cause and effect among variables? If your study is exploratory, or descriptive, identify whom you wish to study, the setting, and what kinds of issues you want to explore. If it is explanatory, you must state the hypothesis to be tested and operationalize each variable.

4. **What will you need to carry out the research?** How much time and money will you need? What special equipment or skills are necessary? Can you do the work yourself? What sources of funding are available to support the research? You should answer all these questions early in the research process.

5. **Are there ethical concerns?** Not all research raises serious ethical issues, but you must be sensitive to the possibility. Could the research cause harm or threaten anyone's privacy? How might you design the study to minimize the chances of injury? Will you promise anonymity to the subjects? If so, how will you ensure that anonymity will be maintained?

6. **What method(s) will you use?** Consider all major research strategies—as well as combinations of approaches. Keep in mind that the appropriate method depends on the kind of questions you are asking as well as on the resources available to you.

7. **How will you record your data?** The way you collect data depends on the research method you choose. Record all information in a way that will make sense later (it may be some time before you write up the results of your work). Watch for bias that may creep into your research.

8. **What do the data tell you?** Study the data in terms of answers to your initial questions. If your study involves a specific hypothesis, your data should allow you to confirm, reject, or modify the hypothesis. Keep in mind that different theoretical paradigms may suggest several ways to interpret the results of your study.

9. **What are your conclusions?** As you write your final report, specify conclusions supported by the data. Consider the significance of your work both for sociological theory and for research methods. Finally, evaluate your own work, noting problems that arose and questions that were left unanswered.

10. **How can you share what you have learned?** Submit your research paper to a professional journal, or present it at a meeting of professional sociologists. If the general public would be interested in your research, submit an article to a newspaper or magazine. The point is to share and let others respond to your work.

SUMMARY

1. Science provides the logical foundation of sociological research and, more broadly, helps us to critically evaluate information we encounter every day.

2. Two basic requirements for sociological investigation are (1) viewing the world from a sociological perspective, and (2) being curious and asking questions about society.

3. Measurement is the process of determining the value of a variable in any specific case. Sound measurement is both reliable and valid.

4. A goal of science is discovering how variables are related. Correlation means that two or more variables change value together. Knowledge about cause-and-effect relationships is more powerful, however, because a researcher can use an independent variable to predict change in a dependent variable.

5. Although investigators select topics according to their personal interests, the scientific ideal of objectivity demands that they try to suspend personal values and biases as they conduct research.

6. Human curiosity and imagination must infuse the scientific method; moreover, researchers must always bring their data to life through interpretation.

7. Investigators should avoid examining issues from the point of view of only one sex or basing generalizations about humanity on data collected from only men or women.

8. Three major methodological frameworks are scientific sociology (concerned with measurement, cause, and effect), interpretive sociology (which deals with meaning) and critical sociology (which promotes social change).

9. Because sociological research has the potential to cause discomfort and harm to subjects, sociological investigators are bound by ethical guidelines.

10. Experiments, which are performed under controlled conditions, attempt to specify causal relationships between two (or more) variables.

11. Surveys, which gather people's responses to statements or questions, may employ questionnaires or interviews.

12. Through participant observation, a form of field research, sociologists directly observe a social setting while participating in it for an extended period of time.

13. Secondary analysis, or making use of available data, is often preferable to collecting one's own data; it is also essential in the study of historical questions.

14. Theory and research are linked through two kinds of thinking. Deductive thought transforms general ideas into specific hypotheses suitable for testing. Inductive thought organizes specific observations into general ideas.

CRITICAL-THINKING QUESTIONS

1. What does it mean to state that there are various kinds of truth? What is the basic rationale for relying on science as a way of knowing?

2. How does scientific sociology differ from interpretive or critical sociology? Which methodological approach best describes the work of Emile Durkheim, Max Weber, and Karl Marx?

3. What are the differences between "hard" research (such as scientific experiments) and "soft" research (such as participant observations)?

4. What considerations lead a sociologist to select one method of research over another?

APPLICATIONS AND EXERCISES

1. Imagine that you are observing your instructor in an effort to assess that individual's skills as a teacher. Operationalize "good teaching." What kinds of behaviours might you note as relevant to this task? Do you think you can evaluate a teacher after observing a single class?

2. Drop by to see at least three sociology instructors (or other social science instructors) during their office hours. Ask each the extent to which sociology is an objective science. Do they agree about the character of their discipline? Why or why not?

3. Conduct a practice interview with a roommate or friend on the general topic of "What is the advantage of a university education?" Before the actual interview, prepare a list of specific questions or issues you think are relevant. Give some thought to why carrying out an effective interview is much harder than it may initially seem.

 ## SITES TO SEE

www.macionis.com
or
www.TheSociologyPage.com

You can find more than fifty weblinks to sociological journals and other sources of data and information by visiting the Links Library at this website.

sewww.d.umn.edu/cla/faculty/jhamlin/1400/ weber.html

The Max Weber site contains a brief biography and an overview of Weber's sociological theories and methodology.

129.97.58.10/discipline/sociology/research.html

Maintained by the University of Waterloo library, Doing Research in Sociology contains links to information sources on how to conduct research in sociology, including searching CD-ROM databases, citing electronic sources, and doing effective library research.

www.sociology.org/

The *Electronic Journal of Sociology* has been publishing full-text articles online since September 1994 and provides a keyword search function to help readers locate references to specific topics.

www.statcan.ca/

Statistics Canada offers a variety of resources, including *The Daily* (latest news from Statistics Canada), results from the 2001 Census, Canadian statistics, community profiles, and links to other Canadian and international statistical websites.

minerva.acc.virginia.edu/surveys/code.htm

The Code of Ethics at the University of Virginia's Center for Survey Research includes guidelines for dealing responsibly with survey subjects.

www.ascusc.org/jcmc/vol3/issue1/smith.html

Christine B. Smith looks at self-administered surveys conducted by email or web-based methods.

www.ropercenter.uconn.edu

To learn more about public opinion research, visit the Roper Center's website.

http://quickfacts.census.gov/qfd/

Data for any county in the United States are available from this U.S. Census Bureau website.

http://assda.anu.edu.au/

Visit this website to explore social science data for Australia.

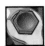 ## STUDY TOOLS

For more study tools to help you with your next exam, be sure to check out the Companion Website at **www.pearsoned. ca/macionis**, as well as Chapter 2 in your Study Guide.

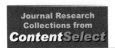 ## INVESTIGATE WITH CONTENTSELECT

Follow the instructions found on page 25 of this textbook to access ContentSelect™ at the Research Navigator™ website. Once at the site, enter your LOGINID and Password. Then enter keywords such as "science" and "objectivity," and the search engine will help you become an effective researcher.

CHAPTER

3

Emily Carr (1871–1945, Canadian)
Gitwangak, Queen Charlotte Islands, 1912
Oil on canvas, 13 × 13.8 cm. Courtesy of Kenneth R. Thomson, personal collection.

CULTURE

"*Mush!*" the hunter cried into the wind. Through the rising vapour of a northern Manitoba February, so crisp, so dry, the snow creaked underfoot, the caribou hunter Abraham Okimasis drove his sled and team of eight grey huskies through the orange-rose-tinted dusk. His left hand gripping handlebar of sled, his right snapping moose-hide whip above his head, Abraham Okimasis was urging his huskies forward . . .

He had sworn to his dear wife, Mariesis Okimasis, on pain of separation and divorce, unthinkable for a Roman Catholic in the year of our Lord 1951, that he would win the world championship just for her: the silver cup, that holy chalice was to be his twenty-first-anniversary gift to her . . .

"Please, please, God in heaven, let me win this race, and I will thank you with every deed, every touch, every breath for the rest of my long life, for hallowed be thy name" . . .

"Boom," the voice went, "boom, boom." Something about "Abraham Okimasis, forty-three years old, caribou hunter, fur trapper, fisherman, boom, boom." Something about "Abraham Okimasis, musher from the Eemanapiteepitat Indian reserve, northwestern Manitoba, boom." Something having to do with "Abraham Okimasis, first Indian to win this grueling race in its twenty-eight-year history . . ." The syllables became one vast, rolling rumble.

Source: Excerpted from *Kiss of the Fur Queen* by Tomson Highway (1999:3–6).

The 6.2 billion people on earth today are members of a single biological species: *Homo sapiens*. Even so, the differences among people the world over can delight, puzzle, disturb, and sometimes even overwhelm us. Some differences in lifestyles are simply matters of convention—the Chinese, for example, wear white at funerals, while people in Canada prefer black. Similarly, Chinese people associate the number four with bad luck, in the same way that Canadians think of the number thirteen. Or take the practice of kissing: most people in Canada kiss in public at times, whereas most Chinese kiss only in private; the French kiss publicly twice (once on each cheek), while Belgians kiss three times (starting on either cheek); for their part, most Nigerians don't kiss at all. At weddings, moreover, Canadian couples kiss, Koreans bow, and a Cambodian groom touches his nose to the bride's cheek.

Other cultural differences, however, are more profound. The world over, people wear much or little clothing, have many or few children, venerate or shunt aside the elderly, are peaceful or warlike, embrace different religious beliefs, and enjoy different kinds of art and music. In short, although we are all the same creatures biologically, the human beings on this planet have developed strikingly different ideas about what is pleasant and repulsive, polite and rude, beautiful and ugly, right and wrong. This capacity for startling difference is a wonder of our species: the expression of human culture.

WHAT IS CULTURE?

Sociologists define **culture** as *the values, beliefs, behaviour, and material objects that constitute a people's way of life*. Culture includes what we think, how we act, and what we own. But as our social heritage, culture is also a bridge to the past as well as a guide to the future.

To begin to understand all that culture entails, it is helpful to distinguish between thoughts and things. What sociologists call **nonmaterial culture** is *the intangible world of ideas created by members of a society* that spans a wide range, from altruism to Zen. **Material culture**, on the other hand, constitutes *the tangible*

Like so many elements of our lives, notions about kissing vary from place to place. People in Canada kiss in public; the Chinese do so only in private. Moreover, while we touch lips, the French kiss on the cheek, and New Zealand's Maoris, shown above, rub noses.

things created by members of a society; here, again, the range is vast, running from armaments to zippers.

Not only does culture shape what we do, it also helps form our personalities—what we commonly (yet inaccurately) describe as "human nature." The warlike Yąnomamö of the Brazilian rain forest look on aggression as natural in their children, just as, halfway around the world, the Semai of Malaysia expect their young to be peaceful and cooperative. The cultures of Canada and Japan both stress achievement and hard work, but we value individualism more than the Japanese, who place a stronger emphasis on tradition.

Given the extent of cultural differences in the world and our tendency to view our own way of life as "natural," it is no wonder that travellers commonly experience **culture shock**, *personal disorientation that comes from encountering an unfamiliar way of life.* People experience such disorientation when they immigrate to a new country or, to a lesser extent, when they move between social environments within their own countries.

 John Macionis offers a short video discussing the challenges and benefits of travel at www.TheSociologyPage.com

A young person moving from rural Newfoundland to attend university in Vancouver or Toronto knows the feeling of culture shock.

No cultural trait is inherently "natural" to humanity, even though most people around the world view their own way of life that way. What is natural to our species is the capacity to create culture in our collective lives. Every other form of life—from ants to zebras—behaves in uniform, species-specific ways. To a world traveller, the enormous diversity of human life stands out in contrast to the behaviour of, say, cats, which is the same everywhere. Most living creatures are guided by instincts, biological programming over which animals have no control. A few animals—notably chimpanzees and related primates—have the capacity for limited culture, as researchers have noted by observing them use tools and teach simple skills to their offspring. But the creative power of humans far exceeds that of any other form of life; in short, *only humans rely on culture rather than instinct to ensure the survival of their kind* (Harris, 1987).

To understand how this came to be, we must briefly review the history of our species on earth.

CULTURE AND HUMAN INTELLIGENCE

In a universe some 15 billion years old, our planet is a much younger 4.5 billion years of age (see the timelines inside the front cover of the text). Not for a billion years after the earth was formed did any life at all appear on our planet. Several billion more years went by before dinosaurs ruled the earth and then disappeared. And then, some 65 million years ago, our history took a crucial turn with the appearance of the creatures we call primates.

What sets primates apart is their intelligence, based on their large brains (relative to body size). As primates evolved, the human line diverged from that of our closest relatives, the great apes, about 12 million years ago. But our common lineage shows in the traits humans share with today's chimpanzees, gorillas, and orangutans: great sociability, affectionate and long-lasting bonds for child-rearing and mutual protection, the ability to walk upright (normal in humans, less common among other primates), and hands that manipulate objects with great precision.

Studying fossil records, scientists conclude that, about 2 million years ago, our distant ancestors grasped cultural fundamentals such as the use of fire, tools, and weapons, created simple shelters, and fashioned basic clothing. Although these Stone Age achievements may seem modest, they mark the point at which our ancestors embarked on a distinct evolutionary course, making culture the primary strategy for human survival.

To illustrate that human beings are wide-eyed infants in the larger scheme of things, Carl Sagan (1977) came up with the idea of superimposing the 15-billion-year history of our universe on a single calendar year. The life-giving atmosphere of the earth did not develop until the autumn, and the earliest beings who resembled humans did not appear until December 31— the last day of the year—at 10:30 at night! Yet not until 250 000 years ago, which is mere minutes before the end of Sagan's "year," did our own species finally

Human beings around the globe create diverse ways of life. Such differences begin with outward appearance: contrast the women shown here from Brazil, Kenya, New Guinea, and Morocco, and the men from Taiwan (Republic of China), India, Peru, and New Guinea. Less obvious, but of even greater importance, are internal differences, since culture also shapes our goals in life, our sense of justice, and even our innermost personal feelings.

emerge. These *Homo sapiens* (derived from Latin meaning "thinking person") have continued to evolve so that, about 40 000 years ago, humans who looked more or less like we do roamed the earth. With larger brains, these "modern" *Homo sapiens* produced culture at a rapid pace, as the wide range of tools and cave art from this period suggests.

Still, what we call "civilization," based on permanent settlements and specialized occupations, began in the Middle East (in what is today Iraq and Egypt) only about 12 000 years ago (Hamblin, 1973; Wenke, 1980). In terms of Sagan's "year," this cultural flowering occurred during the final seconds before midnight on New Year's Eve. And what of our modern, industrial way of life? Begun only 300 years ago, it amounts to a mere millisecond flash in Sagan's scheme.

Human culture, then, is very recent and was a long time in the making. As culture became a strategy for survival, our ancestors descended from the trees into the tall grasses of central Africa. There, walking upright, they discovered the advantages of hunting in groups. From this point on, the human brain grew larger, allowing for greater human capacity to create a way of life—as opposed to simply acting out biological imperatives. Gradually, culture pushed aside the biological forces we call instincts so that humans gained the mental power *to fashion the natural environment for ourselves.* Ever since, people have made and remade their worlds in countless ways, which explains today's extraordinary cultural diversity.

CULTURE, NATION, STATE, AND SOCIETY

At this point, we might well pause to clarify the proper use of several similar terms—"culture," "nation," "state," and "society." *Culture* refers to the ideas, values, and artifacts that make up a shared way of life. *Nation* is commonly used to refer to a political entity, a state or country; it also refers to a people who share a culture (including language), ancestry, and history. A *state* is a political entity in a territory with designated borders such as Argentina or Zimbabwe. *Society* refers to organized interaction of people in a nation, state, or other boundary. Although it is a controversial idea, Canada can be said to encompass several nations—including francophone Quebec, the First Nations (the term applied to themselves by status Indian communities), and the Inuit. When Canadians talk of nation-building, they refer to the attempt to create a sense of nationhood—at the federal level—that supersedes our multicultural and regional loyalties.

In the world as a whole, how many cultures are there? The number of cultures making up the human record is a matter of speculation. Experts have documented the existence of more than five thousand human languages, suggesting that at least this many cultures have existed on the earth (Durning, 1993; Crispell, 1997). High-technology communication, rising international migration, and the expanding global economy have combined to lessen the cultural diversity of the contemporary world. Even so, at least one thousand distinct cultures continue to flourish, and hundreds of them thrive in Canada.

The tally of world nations or states has risen and fallen throughout history as a result of political events. The dissolution of the former Soviet Union and the former Yugoslavia, for example, added nineteen nations to the count. There are now 192 politically independent nations in the world.

THE COMPONENTS OF CULTURE

Although the cultures found in all the world's nations differ in many ways, they are all built on five major components: symbols, language, values, norms, and material objects. We shall consider each in turn.

SYMBOLS

Human beings not only sense the surrounding world as other creatures do, we build a reality of *meaning.* Thus, humans transform elements of the world into **symbols**, *anything that carries a particular meaning recognized by people who share culture.* A whistle, a wall of graffiti, a flashing red light, and a fist raised in the air all serve as symbols. The human capacity to create and manipulate symbols is reflected in the very different meanings associated with the simple act of winking the eye. In some settings this action conveys interest; in others, understanding; in still others, insult.

We are so dependent on our culture's symbols that we take them for granted. Occasionally, however, we become keenly aware of a symbol when someone uses it in an unconventional way, as when political protesters in Brockville, Ontario, stomped on a Quebec flag in 1989. Entering an unfamiliar society also reminds us of the power of symbols: the resulting culture shock involves the inability to "read" meaning into one's surroundings. We feel lost and isolated, unsure of how to act, and sometimes frightened—a consequence of being outside the symbolic web of culture that joins individuals in meaningful social life.

Culture shock is a two-way process: it is something the traveller *experiences* when encountering people whose way of life is unfamiliar, and it is also what the traveller *inflicts* on others by acting in ways that may well offend them. For example, because North Americans consider dogs to be beloved household pets, travellers to northern regions of the People's Republic of China may be appalled to find people roasting dogs as a wintertime meal. On the other hand, a North American who orders a hamburger in an Indian restaurant causes offence to Hindus, who hold cows to be sacred and thus not available for human consumption.

Indeed, travel abroad provides almost endless opportunities for misunderstanding. When in an unfamiliar setting, we need to remember that even behaviour that seems innocent and quite normal to us may spark offence among others.

Then, too, symbolic meanings vary even within a single society. A fur coat, prized by one person as a luxurious symbol of success, may represent to another the inhumane treatment of animals. Similarly, the Canadian flag, which to many Canadians embodies national pride, to separatist Quebecers may symbolize oppression of the Québécois.

Cultural symbols also change over time. Blue jeans were created over a century ago as sturdy and inexpensive clothing for people engaged in physical labour. In the liberal political climate of the 1960s, this working-class aura made jeans popular among affluent students—many of whom wore them simply to look "different" or to identify with working people. A decade later, "designer jeans" emerged as high-priced status symbols that conveyed quite a different message. Today, everyday jeans remain as popular as ever, simply as comfortable apparel.

In sum, symbols allow people to make sense of their lives, and without them human existence would be meaningless. Manipulating symbols correctly allows us to readily engage others within our own cultural system. In a world of cultural diversity, however, the use of symbols may give rise to embarrassment and even conflict.

LANGUAGE

Helen Keller (1880–1968) became an international celebrity because she overcame the daunting disability of being blind and deaf from infancy. The loss of two key senses cut off this young girl from the symbolic world, greatly limiting her social development. Only when her teacher, Anne Mansfield Sullivan, broke through Helen Keller's isolation by teaching her sign language did she begin to realize her human potential. This remarkable woman, who later became a renowned educator herself, recalls

 To learn more about the life of Helen Keller, go to http://helen-keller.freeservers.com

the moment she grasped the concept of language.

We walked down the path to the well-house, attracted by the smell of honeysuckle with which it was covered. Someone was drawing water, and my teacher placed my hand under the spout. As the cool stream gushed over one hand, she spelled into the other the word water, first slowly, then rapidly. I stood still, my whole attention fixed upon the motions of her fingers. Suddenly I felt a misty consciousness as of something forgotten—a thrill of returning thought; and somehow the mystery of language was revealed to me. I knew then that "w-a-t-e-r" meant the wonderful cool something that was flowing over my hand. That living word awakened my soul; gave it light, hope, joy, set it free! (1903:21–24)

Language, the key to the world of culture, is *a system of symbols that allows members of a society to communicate with one another.* These symbols take the form of spoken and written words, which are culturally variable and composed of the various alphabets used around the world. Even conventions for writing differ: in general, people in Western societies write from left to right, people in northern Africa and western Asia write from right to left, and people in eastern Asia write from top to bottom.

Global Map 3–1 shows where in the world one finds the three most widely spoken languages. Chinese is the official language of 20 percent of humanity (about 1.2 billion people). English is the mother tongue of about 10 percent (600 million) of the world's people, with Spanish the official language of 6 percent

Behaviour people in one society consider routine can be chilling to members of another culture. In the Russian city of St. Petersburg, this young mother and her six-week-old son brave the –27°C temperature for a dip in a nearby lake. To Russians, this is something of a national pastime. To some members of our society, however, this practice may seem cruel or even dangerous.

(350 million). Notice, too, that one can travel virtually anywhere in the world other than much of western Africa and "get by" speaking English, which is fast becoming the favoured second language in most of the world and the international language of business and computer communication.

For people everywhere, language is the major means of **cultural transmission**, *the process by which one generation passes culture to the next.* Just as our bodies contain the genes of our ancestors, so our symbols carry our cultural heritage. Language gives us the power to gain access to centuries of accumulated wisdom. The "Applying Sociology" box makes just such an argument with respect to Canada's Aboriginal languages, most of which are threatened with extinction.

Canadians are very familiar with the importance of language to culture. Although Canada is officially bilingual, in practice it is geographically unilingual, with French-speaking majorities in Quebec and northern New Brunswick and English predominant elsewhere. Bill 101, which regulates the use of English in Quebec and made French the only official language of the province, was an attempt to preserve the distinctive Québécois culture. To many French-speaking Quebecers, Bill 101 is essential to their survival as a nation; to some English-speaking Canadians, the law seems like an infringement of the rights of the minority English-speaking Quebecers. The heated debates over

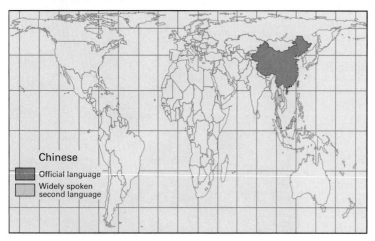

GLOBAL MAP 3–1
Language in Global Perspective

Chinese (including Mandarin, Cantonese, and dozens of other dialects) is the native tongue of 20 percent of the world's people, almost all of whom live in Asia. Although all Chinese people read and write with the same characters, they employ any of several dozen dialects. The "official" dialect, taught in schools throughout the People's Republic of China and the Republic of Taiwan, is Mandarin (the dialect of Beijing, China's historic capital city). Cantonese (the language of Canton, which differs in sound from Mandarin roughly the way French does from Spanish) is the second most common Chinese dialect.

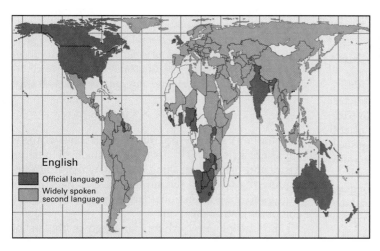

English is the native tongue or official language in several world regions and has become the preferred second language in most of the world.

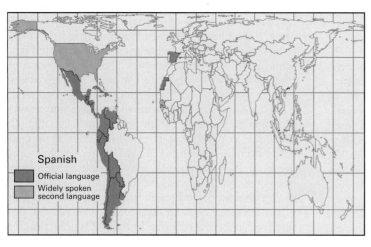

The largest concentration of Spanish speakers is in Latin America and, of course, in Spain. Spanish is also the preferred second language of the United States.

Source: *Peters Atlas of the World* (1990).

APPLYING SOCIOLOGY

Aboriginal Languages in Danger of Extinction

Of the sixty Aboriginal languages spoken across Canada a century ago, only four—namely, Cree, Inuktitut, Ojibwa, and Dakota—are not on the brink of extinction today. Some of Canada's Aboriginal languages are already extinct, and six others have fewer than ten known speakers. So serious is the linguistic hemorrhage that, in 1996, 71 percent of Native children had never spoken an Aboriginal language. According to Ron Ignace, Canada should be declaring a state of emergency, introducing legislation, and setting aside more than $100 million to fund Native language immersion programs across the country.

Ron Ignace is the chief of the Skeetchestn Reserve in British Columbia and chair of the Committee on Aboriginal Languages (Assembly of First Nations). His wife, Marianne Ignace, is an associate professor of First Nations Studies at Simon Fraser University. Mr. Ignace worries because he and his wife are the only parents in their community of 400 who are still speaking Shuswap to their children. When this happens, languages disappear.

"Canada is on the verge of losing precious jewels of its cultural heritage," says Mr. Ignace. "These languages represent vast reservoirs of intellectual knowledge stretching back thousands of years. The English language is an infant relative to our languages."

Their loss, he says, is one of the world's great ecological disasters.

The loss of Aboriginal languages in Canada can be attributed to residential schooling, English-language television and radio, migration to urban areas, and even intermarriage. The most secure languages are those spoken in the largest or most isolated communities.

The extinction of any language means serious loss to world culture: North America loses irreplaceable parts of its culture when the languages that evolved on this continent and embody its cultural heritage disappear.

Source: Based on Philp, 2000.

---

language that characterize Canadian (and especially Quebec) politics are evidence of how strongly people feel about their languages.

Throughout human history, people have transmitted culture through speech, a process sociologists call the *oral cultural tradition*. Only as recently as five thousand years ago did humans invent writing and, even then, just a favoured few ever learned to read and write. It was not until this century that nations (generally the industrial, high-income countries) have boasted of nearly universal literacy. However, the International Adult Literacy Survey of 1994 revealed that 48 percent of Canadians over sixteen years of age either have severe reading difficulties (22 percent) or are able to read only simple, well-laid-out materials (26 percent). Limited literacy skills range from a high of 54 percent in Quebec to 42 percent in the western provinces (National Literacy Secretariat, 1994). Clearly, many Canadians face almost insurmountable barriers to opportunity in a society that increasingly demands symbolic skills.

 For information about literacy in Canada, go to www.nald.ca/nls.htm

Language skills not only link us with others and with the past, they also set free the human imagination. Connecting symbols in new ways, we can conceive of an almost limitless range of future possibilities. Language—both spoken and written—distinguishes human beings as the only creatures who are self-conscious, mindful of our limitations and aware of our ultimate mortality. Yet our symbolic power also enables us to dream, to envision a better world, and to work to bring that world into being.

Is Language Uniquely Human?

Creatures great and small direct sounds, smells, and gestures towards one another. In most cases, these signals are instinctive. But research shows that some animals have at least a rudimentary ability to use symbols to communicate with one another and with humans.

Consider the remarkable achievement of a twelve-year-old pygmy chimp named Kanzi. Chimpanzees lack the physical ability to mimic human speech. But researcher E. Sue Savage-Rumbaugh discovered that Kanzi was able to learn language by listening and by observing people. Under Savage-Rumbaugh's supervision, Kanzi has amassed a vocabulary of several hundred words, and he has learned to "speak" by pointing to pictures on a special keyboard. Kanzi has correctly responded to requests like "Will you get a diaper for your sister?" or "Put the melon in the potty." More intriguing, Kanzi's abilities surpass mere rote learning because he can respond to requests he has not heard

Australian feminist artist Sally Swain alters a famous artist's painting to make fun of our culture's tendency to ignore the everyday lives of women. This spoof is entitled Mrs. Picasso Dusts the Mantelpiece.

before. In short, this fascinating animal has the language ability of a two-and-a-half-year-old human child (Eckholm, 1985; Linden, 1993).

Despite such accomplishments, the language skills of chimps, dolphins, and a few other animals are limited. And even specially trained animals cannot, on their own, teach language skills to others of their kind. But the demonstrated language skills of Kanzi and others caution us against assuming that humans alone can lay claim to culture.

Does Language Shape Reality?

Do the Japanese, who think in one language, experience the world differently from others who think in English, French, or Estonian? The answer is yes, since each language has its own distinct symbols serving as the building blocks of reality.

Edward Sapir (1929, 1949) and Benjamin Whorf (1956; orig. 1941), two anthropologists who specialized in linguistic studies, noted that each language has words or expressions with no precise counterparts in other tongues. Further, all languages fuse symbols with distinctive emotions. Thus, as multilingual people can attest, a single idea often "feels" different if spoken in, say, French rather than in English or Chinese (Falk, 1987).

Formally, then, what we now call the **Sapir-Whorf hypothesis** states that *people perceive the world through the cultural lens of language*. Using different symbolic systems, a Filipino, a Turk, a Brazilian, and, indeed, English and French Canadians actually experience "distinct worlds, not merely the same world with different labels attached" (Sapir, 1949:162).

The capacity to create and manipulate language gives humans everywhere the power to alter how they experience the world. For example, the use of Ms. rather than Mrs. or Miss means women can be introduced as women rather than as holders of a marital status. A system of language guides how we understand the world but does not preclude change.

VALUES AND BELIEFS

What accounts for the popularity of film characters such as James Bond, Dirty Harry, Rambo, and Ripley (Sigourney Weaver in the *Alien* movies)? Each is ruggedly individualistic, suspicious of "the system," and reliant on personal skill and savvy. In applauding such people, we celebrate a sturdy strain of individualism, traditionally for men but increasingly for women, too.

Sociologists call these judgments **values**, culturally defined standards by which people assess desirability, goodness, and beauty, and which serve as broad guidelines for social living. From the standpoint of a culture, values are statements about what ought to be.

Values are broad principles that underlie **beliefs**, specific statements that people hold to be true. While values are abstract standards of goodness, in other words, beliefs are particular matters that individuals consider to be true or false.

Cultural values and beliefs not only colour how we perceive our surroundings but they also form the core of our personalities. We learn from families, schools, and religious organizations to think and act according to approved principles, to pursue worthy goals, and to believe a host of cultural truths while rejecting alternatives as false. Particular values and beliefs thus operate as a form of "cultural capital" that can spark in some people the optimistic determination to pursue success and, in others, a sense of hopelessness that little will ever change (Sowell, 1996).

In a nation as large and diverse as Canada, of course, few cultural values and beliefs are shared by everyone. In fact, with a long history of immigration from the rest of the world, Canada has become a cultural mosaic. In this regard, we stand apart from many nations (especially China or Japan) that have more homogeneous cultural systems. Even so, there is a broad

Canadians and Americans: What Makes Us Different?

When asked about what it means to be Canadian or what factors contribute to a Canadian identity, the average person will shrug and say, "I don't really know." When pushed a little harder we might admit that we know we are Canadians because we are "not American." We share more attributes and attitudes with Americans than we realize, but there are significant differences as well, some of which are intriguing.

Seymour Martin Lipset argued in the 1950s that the traditional differences between Canadian and American values are rooted in the past. A central feature of U.S. history was the war of independence from Great Britain. In a sense, Canada separated formally from Britain only in the 1980s with the repatriation of the Constitution. This difference is pivotal, Lipset argues, for cultural distinctions between the United States and Canada.

Canada, in Lipset's view, sits somewhere between the United States and Great Britain with respect to values. Americans place great value on freedom, individual initiative, achievement, and success; Canadians, on the other hand, stress conformity and obedience to the law. In the American West, outlaws such as Jesse James and Billy the Kid were lionized; in Canada it was the Mountie—the policeman—who was admired.

Practically speaking, the Canadian tendency to emphasize the good of the collectivity over the good of the individual has resulted in social programs such as universal medical care. Until now, Americans have cherished the individual right to choose (and pay for) medical care as desired—with various sorts and levels of medical coverage for people with varying abilities to pay.

Roger Sauvé (a futurist and former journalist) gathered comparable data for the early 1990s on American and Canadian characteristics and attitudes, providing us with the following insights:

- Americans are more likely to think that Canadians and Americans are essentially or mainly the same (78 to Canada's 56 percent).

- Americans are more likely to favour Canada, becoming the fifty-first state (66 to our 14 percent).

- Canadians are more likely to turn out to vote in federal elections (73 to 54 percent).

- Americans believe in hell and the devil (60 and 52 percent) more than Canadians do (34 and 30 percent).

- Canadians are more inclined to allow gays in the military (67 to 57 percent).

- Canadians welcome more acceptance of sexual freedom (40 to 29 percent).

- Canadians are more likely than Americans to say that premarital sex is not wrong (70 to 54 percent).

- Canadians favour more restrictive gun laws (77 to 70 percent).

- Americans are more likely to own handguns (24 to 3 percent).

- Teenage girls in the United States have higher birth rates than Canadian teenagers (among 15- to 19-year-old girls 62 births per 1000 in the United States and 27 per 1000 in Canada).

- American marriages are more likely to end in divorce (43 to 28 percent).

- Americans aged 25 to 64 are more likely to be university graduates (25 to 17 percent).

- Canadians are more likely to rate local health care as excellent or good (71 to 59 percent).

- Americans are more likely to think their children will be better off than they are (41 to 35 percent).

Kevin Dowler puts their divergent views in a nutshell, noting that "Canadians are continually upset by American insensitivity to difference, and Americans are vexed by the fact that others are not like them."

Sources: Lipset (1985), Sauvé (1994), and Dowler (1999).

shape to our national life that may be described as "key values." The "Diversity: Race, Class, and Gender" box compares Canadian and U.S. values.

Values: Inconsistency and Conflict

Cultural values can be inconsistent and even outright contradictory (Lynd, 1967; Bellah et al., 1985). Living in Canada, we sometimes find ourselves torn between the "me first" attitude of an individualistic, success-at-all-costs way of life and the opposing need to belong and contribute to some larger community. Similarly, we affirm our belief in equality of opportunity only to turn around and promote or degrade others because of their race or sex.

Value inconsistency reflects the cultural diversity of Canadian society and the process of cultural change by which new trends supplant older traditions. One tradition that continues to be central to the Canadian winter and that elusive Canadian identity is hockey. The traditional hockey scene in Canada is being transformed by the arrival of women's hockey at

Standards of beauty—including the colour and design of everyday surroundings—vary significantly from one culture to another. These two Nankani women put the finishing touches on their lavishly decorated homes. Members of North America and European societies, by contrast, make far less use of bright colours and intricate detail so that their housing appears much more subdued.

the international level: young girls across the country now have women hockey players as *their* role models. So central to our identity is hockey that our failure to win gold at the 1998 Winter Olympics in Nagano, Japan, (a silver medal for the women and no medal at all for the men) unleashed anger, despair, and depressive slumps across the country. Fortunately, the double gold in men's and women's hockey in Salt Lake City (2002) restored our dignity and pride.

Whether based on the ethnic mix of Canadian society or changes in our way of life, today's value inconsistencies can lead to strain and awkward balancing acts. Sometimes we pursue one value at the expense of another, supporting the principle of equal opportunity, say, while opposing the acceptance of gays as elementary school teachers. Further, many Canadians feel that our values are too heavily influenced by the United States: 50 percent of Canadians believe that we should be doing more to develop a cultural identity separate from that of Americans; 52 percent feel that Canadian culture needs to be better protected from outside influence (Serrill, 1995).

NORMS

For most of our history, women and men in Canada generally held to the idea that sexual intercourse should occur only within the bounds of marriage. By the late 1960s, however, beliefs had changed so that sexual activity became widely viewed as a form of recreation, sometimes involving people who hardly knew each other. By the mid-1980s, however, the rules changed again. Amid growing fears of sexually transmitted diseases, especially the deadly acquired immune deficiency syndrome (AIDS), people began rethinking the wisdom of the "sexual revolution" (Smilgas, 1987).

Such patterns illustrate the operation of **norms**, *rules and expectations by which a society guides the behaviour of its members*. Some norms are *proscriptive*, mandating what we should *not* do, as when health officials warn us to avoid casual sex. *Prescriptive* norms, on the other hand, spell out what we *should* do. Practising "safe sex," for example, has become one such norm in recent years.

The most important norms apply virtually anywhere, any time. For example, parents expect obedience from children in any setting. Many normative conventions, by contrast, are situation-specific. We expect audience applause at the end of a musical performance; we accept (but do not expect) applause when a classroom lecture is over; we discourage applause when a priest or a rabbi finishes a sermon.

Mores and Folkways

William Graham Sumner (1959; orig. 1906), an early U.S. sociologist, recognized that some norms are more crucial to our lives than others. Sumner used the term **mores** (pronounced MORE-ays) to refer to *a society's standards of proper moral conduct*. Sumner counted among the mores all norms essential to maintaining a way of life; because of their importance, he contended that people develop an emotional attachment to mores and defend them publicly. In addition, mores apply to everyone, everywhere, all the time. Violation of mores—such as our society's prohibition against sexual relations between adults and children—typically brings a swift and strong reaction from others.

Sumner used the term **folkways** to designate *a society's customs for routine, casual interaction*. Folkways, with less moral significance than mores, include notions about proper dress, appropriate greetings, and common courtesy. In short, while mores distinguish between right and wrong, folkways draw a line between right and *rude*. Because folkways are less important than mores, societies grant a measure of personal discretion in matters involving folkways and punish infractions leniently. For example, a man who does not wear a tie to a formal dinner party is, at worst, guilty of a breach of etiquette. If, however, the man were to arrive at the dinner party wearing *only* a tie, he would be challenging social mores and inviting more serious sanctions.

Social Control

As participants in cultural systems, we learn to accept mores and many folkways as the basic rules of everyday life, typically responding to the behaviour of others with *sanctions*, which take the form of either reward or punishment. Conforming to norms provokes praise and approval from others, just as norm violations prompt avoidance, contempt, or even a formal response from the criminal justice system. Taken together, all kinds of sanctions form the heart of a culture's system of **social control**, *various means by which members of a society encourage conformity to norms.*

As we internalize cultural norms, we develop the capacity to respond critically to our own behaviour. "Doing wrong" (say, downloading a term paper from the Internet) can provoke not only *shame*—the painful sense that others disapprove of our actions—but also guilt, a negative judgment we make of ourselves. Only cultural creatures experience shame and guilt; this is probably what Mark Twain had in mind when he quipped that human beings "are the only animals that blush . . . or need to."

"IDEAL" AND "REAL" CULTURE

Societies devise values and norms as moral guidelines for their members. As such, these cultural elements do not describe actual behaviour as much as they tell us how we should behave. We must remember, then, that **ideal culture**, *social patterns mandated by cultural values and norms*, is not the same as **real culture**, *actual social patterns that only approximate cultural expectations.*

To illustrate, most of us acknowledge the importance of sexual fidelity in marriage. Even so, a 1994 *Maclean's* poll indicated that about 14 percent of married men and 7 percent of married women reported being sexually unfaithful to their spouses at some point in the marriage (Maclean's/CTV, 1994). Such discrepancies occur in all societies, since no one lives up to ideal standards all the time. But a culture's moral prodding is crucial to shaping the lives of individuals, calling to mind the old saying "Do as I say, not as I do."

MATERIAL CULTURE AND TECHNOLOGY

In addition to intangible elements such as values and norms, every culture encompasses a wide range of tangible (from Latin meaning "touchable") human creations that sociologists term *artifacts*. The Chinese eat with chopsticks rather than knives and forks, the Japanese place mats rather than rugs on the floor, many men and women in India prefer flowing robes to the tighter clothing common in Canada. An unfamiliar people's material culture may seem as strange to us as their language, values, and norms.

The artifacts common to a society typically reflect cultural values. The fact that poison-tipped arrows are

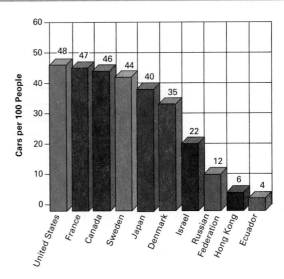

GLOBAL SNAPSHOT

FIGURE 3–1 Car Ownership in Global Perspective
Source: The World Bank (2001).

a prized possession of Yąnomamö males in the Amazon rain forest, for example, surely reflects the importance that society places on warfare and militaristic skills. Similarly, our own high regard for the automobile is rooted in cherished values of individuality and independence. Thousands of kilometres of highways crisscross Canada, and we own more than 13 million cars! Figure 3–1 shows that, even compared to other industrial societies, Canada stands out as a car-loving nation.

In addition to reflecting values, material culture reveals a society's **technology**, *knowledge that a society applies to the task of living in a physical environment*. In short, technology ties the world of nature to the world of culture. Among the most technologically simple people on earth, the Yąnomamö interfere little with the natural environment. They remain keenly aware of the cycles of rainfall and the movement of the animals they hunt for food. By contrast, technologically complex societies (such as those of North America) have an enormous impact on the natural world, reshaping the environment (for better or worse) according to their own interests and priorities.

Because we accord science such great importance and praise the sophisticated technology it has produced, members of our society tend to judge cultures with simpler technology as less advanced. Some facts would support such an assessment. For example, life expectancy for children born in Canada now exceeds seventy-five years; the lifespan of the Yąnomamö stands at only about forty years.

However, we must be careful not to make self-serving judgments about cultures that differ from our own. While our powerful and complex technology has produced work-reducing devices and seemingly miraculous forms of medical treatment, it has also contributed to unhealthy levels of stress, eroded the quality of the natural environment, and created weapons capable of destroying in a blinding flash everything that humankind has managed to achieve.

Finally, technology is another cultural element that varies substantially within Canada. Although many of us cannot imagine life without CD players, televisions, and the latest personal computers, many members of our society cannot afford such items, and others reject them on principle. The Old Order Mennonites, who live in small farming communities across southwestern Ontario, Alberta, and Manitoba, shun most modern conveniences as a matter of religious conviction. With their traditional black garb and horse-drawn buggies, the Old Order Mennonites may seem like a curious relic of the past. Yet their communities flourish, grounded in vibrant families and individuals with a strong sense of identity and purpose. And many of the thousands of outsiders who observe

 Go to http://grebel.uwaterloo.ca/mao/ for more information about Old Order Mennonites.

them each year come away with the suspicion that these simple, stable communities may well suggest an attractive alternative to modern materialism and competitiveness.

NEW INFORMATION TECHNOLOGY AND CULTURE

Many industrial societies, including Canada, are now entering a post-industrial phase in which production is based on computers and new information technology. In other words, while industrial production centres on factories and machinery generating material goods, post-industrial production centres on computers and other electronic devices that create, process, store, and apply information.

The emergence of an information economy thus changes the skills that dominate a way of life, from the mechanical abilities to make things to the symbolic abilities to speak, write, compute, design, and create images in art, advertising, and entertainment. This transformation is likely to bring major change to our culture. In short, new information technology offers our society the capacity to *generate culture* on an unprecedented scale. The "Exploring Cyber-Society" box takes a closer look.

CULTURAL DIVERSITY: MANY WAYS OF LIFE IN ONE WORLD

Canada is a nation of striking cultural diversity. Perhaps this can best be appreciated by contrasting

Canada with Japan, whose historic isolation has made it the most *monocultural* of all industrial nations. For Canada, on the other hand, heavy immigration over the past two centuries, especially over the last thirty years, has made it one of the most *multicultural* of all industrial nations.

The graph in Figure 3–2 gives some indication of our country's cultural diversity and reveals that *patterns* of immigration have changed over time. Before 1961, about 90 percent of immigrants to Canada hailed from Europe, especially the United Kingdom, and less than 5 percent came from countries in Asia and the Middle East. Since 1961, more and more immigrants have come from Asia and the Middle East. In the ten-year period between 1991 and 2001, European immigrants made up only 20 percent of all immigrants, while those from Asia and the Middle East made up 58 percent of the total. This change in pattern, which has greatly increased the cultural diversity of our country, has been the result of a deliberate change in immigration policy on the part of the federal government.

Given this diversity, sociologists sometimes call Canada a cultural mosaic. To understand the cultural diversity implied, we must move beyond the notion of overarching cultural patterns to consider cultural diversity.

HIGH CULTURE AND POPULAR CULTURE

Much cultural diversity has roots in social class. In fact, in everyday conversation we usually reserve the term "culture" for sophisticated art forms such as classical literature, music, dance, and painting. We praise symphony conductors, Shakespearean actors, and dance choreographers as "cultured" because they presumably appreciate the "finer things in life." The term "culture" itself has the same Latin root as the word "cultivate," suggesting that the "cultured" individual has cultivated or refined tastes.

In contrast, we speak less generously of ordinary people, assuming that everyday cultural patterns are somehow less worthy. In more concrete terms, we are tempted to judge the music of Mozart as "more cultured" than Motown, fine cuisine as better than fish sticks, and polo as more polished than ping-pong.

Such judgments imply that many cultural patterns are readily accessible to some but not all members of a society (Hall and Neitz, 1993). Sociologists use the shorthand term **high culture**[1] to refer to *cultural patterns that distinguish a society's elite*; **popular culture**, then, designates *cultural patterns that are widespread*

---

[1]The term "high culture" is derived from the more popular term "highbrow." Influenced by phrenology, the bogus nineteenth-century theory that personality was determined by the shape of the human skull, people a century ago contrasted the praiseworthy tastes of those they termed "highbrows" with the contemptible appetites of others they derided as "lowbrows."

Here Comes Virtual Culture!

The Information Revolution is now generating symbols—words, sounds, and images—at an unprecedented rate and rapidly spreading these symbols across the nation and around the world. What are the implications of new information technology for our way of life?

One key trend is that more and more of the cultural symbols that frame our lives are intentionally created. In the past, sociologists have described culture as a way of life transmitted over time from generation to generation. This traditional view envisions culture as a deeply rooted collective memory, a heritage passed along over the centuries and coming to us as something authentically our own because it belonged to our ancestors (Schwartz, 1996). But in the emerging cyber-society, more and more cultural symbols are new, intentionally generated by a small cultural elite of composers, writers, filmmakers, and others who work within the burgeoning information economy.

To comprehend this change, consider the changing character of cultural heroes, those people whose lives we celebrate and who represent an ideal we strive to live up to. In the early twentieth century, the commonly recognized heroes were real men and women who made a difference in the life of this nation—people such as Laura Secord, Alexander Graham Bell, Grey Owl, Nellie McClung, John A. Macdonald, Louis Riel, Banting and Best, Maurice Richard, Mary Pickford, Barbara Ann Scott, Billy Bishop, and Dr. Norman Bethune. Of course, when we make a hero of someone (almost always well after the person has died) we "clean up" the person's biography, highlighting the successes and overlooking the shortcomings. But, although idealized, these people were authentic parts of our society's history.

Today's youngsters, by contrast, are fed a steady diet of virtual culture, images that spring from the mind of a contemporary culture-maker and that reach us through a screen: television, movies, or computer cyberspace. More recent "heroes" include the almost entirely American Hank Hill, Homer Simpson, Teenage Mutant Ninja Turtles, Barney, Batman, Barbie, a continuous flow of Disney characters, Rambo, and the ever-smiling Ronald McDonald. No one doubts that many of these cultural icons embody at least some of the key cultural values that have shaped our way of life. But few of them have any historical reality and almost all of them have come into being for a single purpose: to make money.

What do you think?

1. *As the Information Revolution proceeds, do you think "virtual culture" will become ever more important? Why or why not?*

2. *Will virtual culture erode or enhance our cultural traditions? For better or worse?*

3. *What effect do you think the predominance of U.S. movies and television shows has on Canada's self-image and its image abroad?*

---

throughout society. The publication of *Mondo Canuck: A Canadian Pop Culture Odyssey* (Pevere and Dymond, 1996) is a refreshing celebration of Canada's eye-level cultural creativity: the book itself is pop culture.

Common sense may suggest that high culture is superior to popular culture. After all, history chronicles the lives of elites much more than those of ordinary women and men. But sociologists are uneasy with such a sweeping evaluation and generally use the term "culture" to refer to *all* elements of a society's way of life, even as they recognize that cultural patterns vary throughout a population (Gans, 1974).

We should resist quick judgments about the merits of high culture as opposed to popular culture for two key reasons. First, neither elites nor ordinary people have uniform tastes and interests; people in both categories differ in numerous ways. Second, it has been argued that we praise high culture not because it is inherently better than popular culture, but because its supporters have more money, power, and prestige. For example, there is no difference between a violin and a fiddle; however, we refer to the instrument as a violin when it is used to produce a type of music typically enjoyed by people of higher social position, and as a fiddle when the musician is playing for individuals with lower social standing.

SUBCULTURE

The term **subculture** refers to *cultural patterns that set apart some segment of a society's population.* Teenagers, Native Canadians living on a reserve, homeless people, race-car drivers, jazz musicians, and maybe even sociologists all display subcultural patterns.

It is easy—but often inaccurate—to place people in subcultural categories. Almost everyone participates simultaneously in numerous subcultures, and we often have little commitment to many of them.

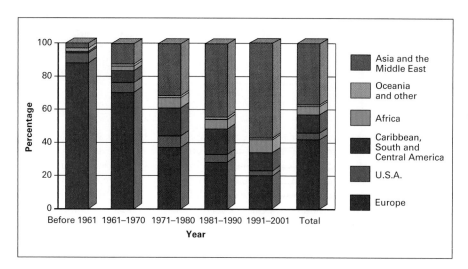

FIGURE 3–2
Immigrant Population by Place of Birth and Period of Immigration, 2001

Source: Calculations by Gerber based on Statistics Canada, Catalogue 11–008E and 2001 Census Tables, www.statcan.ca.

In some cases, however, important cultural traits such as ethnicity or religion do set off people from one another—sometimes with tragic results. Consider the former nation of Yugoslavia in southeastern Europe (now the five nations of Slovenia, Croatia, Macedonia, Bosnia and Herzegovina, and Serbia and Montenegro). The ongoing turmoil there is fuelled by astounding cultural diversity. This one small country (which, before its breakup, was about the size of the Maritime provinces, with a population of 25 million) made use of *two* alphabets, professed *three* religions, spoke *four* languages, was home to *five* major nationalities, was divided into *six* political republics, and absorbed the cultural influences of *seven* surrounding countries. The cultural conflict that plunged this nation into civil war reveals that subcultures are a source not only of pleasing variety but also of tensions and outright violence (cf. Sekulic et al., 1994).

Historically, we have been taught to view Canada as a "mosaic" with many nationalities contributing to a larger "Canadian" culture. But, considering the extent of our cultural diversity, how accurate is the "mosaic" description? One factor complicates this idealistic notion: cultural diversity involves not just *variety* but also *hierarchy*. Too often, what we view as "dominant" or "highbrow" cultural patterns are those favoured by powerful segments of the population, while we relegate the lives of the disadvantaged to the realm of "subculture." This dilemma has led some researchers to highlight the experiences of less powerful members of our society in a new approach called multiculturalism.

MULTICULTURALISM

As well as being bilingual, Canadian society is officially multicultural. **Multiculturalism** is embodied in *social policy designed to encourage ethnic or cultural heterogeneity*. Historically, our society downplayed cultural diversity, defining our way of life primarily in terms familiar to the English or French immigrants who have dominated Canada socially.

Historians highlighted the role of descendants of the English and French, described events from their point of view, and pushed to the side the perspectives and accomplishments of other immigrants and of Native peoples. The European way of life was set up as an ideal to which all should aspire and by which all should be judged. Multiculturalists describe this singular pattern in Canada as **Eurocentrism**, *the dominance of European cultural patterns*. The legacy of this practice is a spirited debate over whether we should continue to stress Western European, especially French and English, cultural contributions to the exclusion of those made by the Chinese, Caribbean, Ukrainian, and East Indian peoples to this country. An interesting example of the continued presence of Eurocentric ideas in Canada was the widespread opposition to the 1990 decision to allow a Sikh, Baltej Singh Dhillon, to wear a turban as part of his RCMP uniform.

Though few deny that our culture has multiple roots, multiculturalism has generated controversy because it requires us to rethink the norms and values at the core of our society. Not surprisingly, battles over how to describe our culture rage on many fronts.

One area of debate involves language. Although Canada is officially bilingual, the Canadian population is actually composed of people with many different mother tongues. Table 3–1 provides the distribution of Canadians by mother tongue. Despite the significant number of different languages spoken in this country, minority languages are not officially recognized. This oversight has led some critics to charge that multiculturalism has a mostly symbolic significance in Canada. By this statement they mean that multiculturalism allows minorities to maintain their cultures within their homes while forcing them to speak either French or English for any dealings out-

Whether visual expression in lines and colour is revered as "art," dismissed as "graffiti," or even condemned as "vandalism" depends on the social standing of the creator. How would you characterize images such as this one? Is this art? Why or why not?

side the home. Gradually, minorities will lose the use of their mother tongues, and with them many of their distinctive cultural practices.

On the other hand, some people point out that each minority actually makes up a very small part of the total population of Canada. They claim that trying to accommodate every minority in Canada would lead to a fractured society, one with no sense of commonality or cohesiveness. The debate still rages, and important questions have been left unresolved. To what extent should Canada encourage those who speak languages other than French or English to maintain their mother tongues? Should Canadian taxpayers support heritage language schools and courses?

An additional issue is how our schools—from the early grades through university—should teach about culture. It is among educators that the clash over multiculturalism has been most intense. Four basic positions have emerged from this discussion.

First, proponents defend multiculturalism as a way to capture a more accurate picture of our past. Proposed educational reforms seek, for example, to temper the simplistic praise directed at European explorers by realistically assessing the tragic impact of the European conquest on the Native peoples of this hemisphere. As detailed in Chapter 14 ("Race and Ethnicity"), from the point of view of the Native peoples of North America, contact with Europeans unleashed centuries of subordination and death from war and disease. In addition, a multicultural approach would recognize the achievements of many women and men whose cultural backgrounds up to now have kept them on the sidelines of history.

Second, proponents claim, multiculturalism is a means to come to terms with our country's even more

diverse present. Children born in the 1990s can expect that, during their lifetimes, immigration from African, Asian, and Hispanic countries will increase significantly. Third, proponents assert that multiculturalism is a way to strengthen the academic achievement of immigrant and visible minority children and others who find little personal relevance in traditional educational programs. Fourth, proponents see multiculturalism as worthwhile preparation for all people in Canada to live in a world that is increasingly interdependent. As various chapters of this book explain, social patterns in this country are becoming more closely linked to issues and events elsewhere in the world. Multiculturalism undermines nationalistic prejudices by pointing out global connectedness; it also makes Canadians more flexible in their international political and business dealings.

Although multiculturalism has found widespread favour in the last several years, it has provoked its share of criticism as well. The argument most commonly voiced by opponents is that any society remains cohesive only to the extent that its cultural patterns are widely shared. Multiculturalism, say critics, fuels the "politics of difference," encouraging divisiveness as individuals identify with their subculture rather than with Canada as a whole. Opponents also charge that multiculturalism erodes the claim to common truth by maintaining that ideas should be evaluated according to the race (and sex) of those who present them. Are we to conclude that there is no common humanity, in other words, but only an "Aboriginal experience," a "European experience," and so on? Furthermore, critics are skeptical that multiculturalism actually benefits minorities as claimed. Multiculturalism, critics argue, demands precisely the kind of racial

TABLE 3–1 Mother Tongues in Canada, 1996–2001		
Mother Tongue	**Percent of Population**	
	1996	**2001**
English	59.2	58.5
French	23.2	22.6
Chinese	2.5	2.8
Italian	1.7	1.6
German	1.6	1.5
Polish	0.7	0.7
Spanish	0.7	0.8
Portuguese	0.7	0.7
Punjabi	0.7	0.9
Ukrainian	0.6	0.5
Arabic	0.5	0.7
Dutch	0.5	0.4
Tagalog (Filipino)	0.5	0.6
Greek	0.4	0.4
Vietnamese	0.4	0.4
Cree	0.3	0.2
Inuktitut	0.1	0.1
Other nonofficial languages	4.2	5.1
Multiple languages	1.4	1.3

Source: Calculations by Gerber based on Statistics Canada 1996/2001 Census Tables, www.statcan.ca.

segregation that we claim to deplore. Furthermore, a heritage-centred curriculum may deny children a wide range of knowledge and skills by encouraging study from a more limited point of view.

Is there any common ground in this debate? Virtually everyone agrees that all people in Canada need to gain greater appreciation of the extent of our cultural diversity. Moreover, because visible minorities are an increasingly large component of our population, efforts in this direction are needed now. But precisely where the balance is to be struck is likely to remain a divisive issue for some time to come.

COUNTERCULTURE

Cultural diversity also includes outright rejection of conventional ideas or behaviour. **Counterculture** refers to *cultural patterns that strongly oppose those widely accepted within a society.*

In many societies, countercultures spring from adolescence (Spates, 1976b, 1983; Spates and Perkins, 1982). Most of us are familiar with the youth-oriented counterculture of the 1960s that rejected the cultural mainstream as overly competitive, self-centred, and materialistic. Instead, hippies and other counterculturalists favoured a cooperative lifestyle in which "being" took precedence over "doing" and the capacity for personal growth—or "expanded consciousness"—was prized over material possessions such as homes and cars. Such differences led some people at that time to "drop out" of the larger society.

Counterculture may involve not only distinctive values, but also unconventional behaviour (including dress and forms of greeting) and music. Many members of the 1960s counterculture, for instance, drew personal identity from long hair, headbands, and blue jeans; from displaying a peace sign rather than offering a handshake; and from drug use and the energy of ever-present rock-and-roll music.

Some countercultures, flourishing in North America, Europe, and beyond, seek to disrupt their societies. These highly significant countercultures may involve militaristic bands of men and women who are deeply suspicious of government and willing to resort to violence. Canada's FLQ (Front de libération du Québec), active through the 1960s and early 1970s, resorted to bombings, kidnapping, and murder in its quest for an independent socialist Quebec. More recently, counterculture extremists from the Earth Liberation Front (ELF) torched California Hummer dealerships and new construction sites in the summer of 2003 (Madigan, 2003).

CULTURAL CHANGE

Perhaps the most basic truth is that "All things shall pass." Even the dinosaurs, which dominated this planet for some 160 million years (see the time line), exist today only as fossils (and movie villains). Will humanity survive for millions of years to come? No one knows. All we can say with certainty is that, for as long as we do survive, the human record will be one of continuous cultural change.

Change in one dimension of a culture is usually associated with other transformations. For example, increased labour force participation among women occurs along with changing family patterns, including a later age at first marriage, a rising divorce rate, and increasing numbers of children being raised in households without fathers. Such connections illustrate the principle of **cultural integration**, *the close relationship among various elements of a cultural system.*

But all elements of a cultural system do not change at the same speed. William Ogburn (1964) observed that technology moves quickly, generating new elements of material culture (such as "test-tube babies") faster than nonmaterial culture (such as ideas about parenthood) can keep up with them. Ogburn called this inconsistency **cultural lag**, *cultural elements changing at different rates, causing various degrees of disruption in cultural systems.* In a culture with the technical ability to allow one woman to give birth to a child by using another woman's egg that has been fertilized in a laboratory with the sperm of a total stranger, how are we to apply the traditional notions of motherhood and fatherhood?

Cultural changes are set in motion in three ways. The first is *invention,* the process of creating new cultural elements. Invention has given us the telephone (1876), the airplane (1903), and the aerosol spray can (1941), all of which have had a tremendous impact on our way of life. The process of invention goes on constantly, as indicated by the numbers of applications submitted annually to the Canadian Patent Office.

Discovery, a second cause of cultural change, involves recognizing and understanding something not fully understood before—from a distant star, to the foods of another culture, to the athletic excellence of Canadian women like rower Silken Laumann and the members of our women's hockey team. Many discoveries result from scientific research. Yet discovery can also happen quite by accident, as when Marie Curie left a rock on a piece of photographic paper in 1898 and serendipitously discovered radium.

The third cause of cultural change is *diffusion*, the spread of cultural traits from one society to another. The technological ability to send information around the globe in seconds—by means of radio, television, facsimile, and computer—means that the level of cultural diffusion has never been greater than it is today. Insulin, developed first by Frederick Banting and Charles Best at the University of Toronto in the 1920s, and the telephone, conceived by Alexander Graham Bell in Brantford, Ontario, in 1874, have spread around the world.

Certainly our own society has contributed many significant cultural elements to the world. But diffusion works the other way as well, so that much of what we assume is inherently "Canadian" actually comes from other cultures. Ralph Linton (1937) explained that many commonplace elements of our way of life—most clothing and furniture, clocks, newspapers, money, and even the English language—are all derived from other cultures.

ETHNOCENTRISM AND CULTURAL RELATIVITY

North American travellers are among the world's greatest shoppers. They delight in surveying handwoven carpets in China, India, or Iran, inspecting finely crafted metals in Turkey, or collecting beautifully coloured porcelain tiles in Morocco. And, of course, all these items are wonderful bargains. But one major reason for the low cost is unsettling: many products from low- and middle-income countries of the world are produced by children, many as young as five or six, who work long days for extremely low wages.

We think of childhood as a time of innocence and freedom from adult burdens such as regular work. In poor countries throughout the world, however, families depend on income earned by children. So what people in one society think of as right and natural, people elsewhere find puzzling and even immoral. Perhaps the Chinese philosopher Confucius had it

Most people in affluent Canada take for granted that childhood should be a carefree time of life devoted to learning and play. In low-income societies of the world, however, poor families depend on the income earned by children, some of whom perform long days of heavy physical labour. We may not want to accept all cultural practices as "natural" just because they exist. But what universal standards can be used to judge social patterns as either right or wrong?

right when he noted that "All people are the same; it's only their habits that are different."

Just about every imaginable social habit is subject to at least some variation around the world, and such differences cause travellers excitement and distress in about equal measure. The tradition in Japan is to name intersections rather than streets, a practice that regularly confuses North Americans who do the opposite; Egyptians move very close to others in conversation, irritating North Americans used to maintaining several feet of "personal space."

Because a particular culture is the basis for everyone's reality, it is no wonder that people everywhere exhibit **ethnocentrism**, *the practice of judging another culture by the standards of one's own culture.* On one level, some ethnocentrism is inevitable if people are to be emotionally attached to a cultural system. On another level, however, ethnocentrism generates misunderstanding and sometimes conflict.

For example, take the seemingly trivial matter of people in North America referring to China as the

"Far East." Such a term, which has little meaning to the Chinese, is an ethnocentric expression for a region that is far east of Europe. For their part, the Chinese refer to their country with a word translated as "Middle Kingdom," suggesting that, like us, they see their society as the centre of the world.

Is there an alternative to ethnocentrism? The logical alternative is to imagine unfamiliar cultural traits from the point of view of them rather than us. The casual observer of an Old Order Mennonite farmer tilling his many hectares with a team of horses rather than a tractor might initially dismiss this practice as hopelessly backward and inefficient. But from the Old Order Mennonite point of view, hard work is a foundation of religious discipline. The Mennonites are well aware of tractors; they simply believe that using such machinery would be their undoing.

This alternative approach, called **cultural relativism**, is *the practice of judging a culture by its own standards*. Cultural relativism is a difficult attitude to adopt because it requires not only understanding the values and norms of another society but also suspending cultural standards we have known all our lives. But, as people of the world come into increasing contact with one another, we are confronting the need to more fully understand other cultures.

North American business is learning that success in the ever-expanding global economy depends on cultural sophistication. Trouble loomed when several corporations carelessly translated advertising slogans. When Hunt-Wesson introduced its "Big John" products into Quebec as "Gros Jos," little did they realize that they were using a slang term for "big breasts." Other errors involved English-to-Spanish translations. Coors' phrase "Turn It Loose" startled customers who read the claim that the beer would make you "Suffer from Diarrhea." Braniff airlines turned "Fly in Leather" into clumsy Spanish reading "Fly Naked." Eastern Airlines transformed its slogan "We Earn Our Wings Daily" into words customers read as "We Fly Daily to Heaven." Or how about "It Takes a Tough Man to Make a Tender Chicken" translated into Spanish as "It Takes a Sexually Excited Man to Make a Chicken Affectionate"?

 In two brief videos, John Macionis considers issues of cultural relativism. See www.TheSociologyPage.com

The world may need greater cultural understanding, but cultural relativity introduces problems of its own. Virtually any kind of behaviour is practised somewhere in the world, but does that mean that everything is equally right? Does the fact that Indian and Moroccan families benefit from having their children work long hours justify child labour?

Since we are all members of a single species, surely there must be some universal standards of proper conduct. But what are they? And, in trying to develop them, how can we avoid imposing our own standards of fair play on others? There are no simple answers. But here are some general guidelines to keep in mind when dealing with other cultures.

While cultural differences fascinate us, they can also be deeply disturbing. Be prepared to experience an emotional reaction when encountering the unfamiliar. Resist making snap judgments, so that you can observe unfamiliar cultural surroundings with an open mind. You might also imagine the issue from points of view other than your own. After careful thought, try to evaluate an unfamiliar custom; after all, there is no virtue in passively accepting every cultural practice. But in reaching a judgment, bear in mind that—despite your efforts—you can never really experience the world as others do. Finally, turn the argument around and think about your own way of life as others might see it, for what we gain most from studying others are insights into ourselves.

A GLOBAL CULTURE?

Today, more than ever before, we can observe many of the same cultural patterns the world over. Walking the streets of Seoul (South Korea), Kuala Lumpur (Malaysia), Madras (India), Cairo (Egypt), and Casablanca (Morocco), we find familiar forms of dress, hear well-known pop music, and see advertising for many of the same products we use at home. Just as importantly, as illustrated by Global Map 3–1 (page 60), English is rapidly emerging as the preferred second language of most of the world. So, are we witnessing the birth of a global culture?

The world is still divided into 192 states or countries and thousands of different cultural systems. Further, as recent violence in the former Soviet Union, the former Yugoslavia, the Middle East, Sri Lanka, and elsewhere attests, many people are intolerant of others whose cultures differ from their own. Yet, looking back through history, we see that societies around the world now have more contact with one another and enjoy more cooperation than ever before. These global connections involve the flow of goods, information, and people.

1. **The global economy: the flow of goods.** The extent of international trade has never been greater. The global economy has introduced many consumer goods (cars, TV shows, T-shirts) the world over. Canada's $745 billion in imports and exports (2001) suggests a complex web of production and distribution.

2. **Global communications: the flow of information.** A century ago, communication around the world depended on written messages delivered by boat, train, horse and wagon, or, occasionally, telegraph wire. Today's satellite-based communi-

cation system enables people to experience sights and sounds of events taking place thousands of kilometres away—often as they happen. When, in the 1960s, Marshall McLuhan conceived of "the global village" as a function of electronic (instantaneous) communication, we had only begun to scratch the surface of communications technology.

3. **Global migration: the flow of people.** Knowledge about the rest of the world motivates people to move where they imagine life will be better. Moreover, today's transportation technology—especially air travel—makes relocating easier than ever before. Canada, with one of the world's highest rates of immigration, has a population that is about 17 percent foreign-born. Travel, for business or pleasure, also contributes to interpersonal ties and global knowledge or awareness.

These global links have made the cultures of the world more similar at least in superficial respects. But there are three important limitations to the global culture thesis. First, the flow of goods, information, and people has been uneven throughout the world. Generally speaking, urban areas (centres of commerce, communication, and people) have stronger ties to one another, while rural villages remain more isolated. Then, too, the greater economic and military power of North America and Western Europe means that these regions influence the rest of the world more than the other way around.

Second, the global culture thesis assumes that people everywhere are able to afford various new goods and services. As Chapter 12 ("Global Stratification") explains, the grinding poverty in much of the world deprives millions of even the basic necessities of a safe and secure life.

Third, although many cultural traits are now found throughout the world, we should not conclude that people everywhere attach the same meanings to them (see the "Global Sociology" box). Do teenagers in Tokyo understand rap music the same way their counterparts in New York or Los Angeles do? Similarly, we mimic fashions from around the world with little knowledge of the lives of the people who first conceived them. In short, people everywhere look at the world through their own cultural "lenses" (Featherstone, 1990; Hall and Neitz, 1993).

THEORETICAL ANALYSIS OF CULTURE

Culture allows us to understand ourselves and the world around us. Sociologists and anthropologists, however, have the special task of understanding culture. They do so by using various theoretical paradigms.

STRUCTURAL-FUNCTIONAL ANALYSIS

Recall from Chapter 1 ("The Sociological Perspective") that structural-functional analysis sees society as a relatively stable system of integrated parts devised to meet human needs. Thus, various cultural traits each help to maintain the overall operation of society.

The stability of cultural systems is rooted in core values (Parsons, 1964; orig. 1951). In this way, structural-functionalism draws on the philosophical doctrine of *idealism*, the assertion that ideas (rather than material conditions) are the basis of human reality. Expressed in a wide range of everyday activities, core values serve to bind all members of a society together.

Using a structural-functional approach, let us reconsider the Old Order Mennonite farmer plowing his farm with a team of horses. Within the Old Order Mennonite cultural system, rejecting tractors, automobiles, and electricity makes sense because it ensures that there is plenty of hard work. Continuous labour—usually outside the home for men, inside for women—functions to maintain the Old Order Mennonite value of discipline, which shapes their way of life. Long days of work, along with meals and recreation at home, define Old Order Mennonite culture and bind family members together. Their rejection of modern technology also has the function of making them self-sufficient (Fretz, 1989).

Of course, cultural traits have both functional and dysfunctional consequences. The Old Order Mennonite trait of "shunning," by which people cease social contact with anyone judged to have violated Mennonite mores, generates conformity but also provokes tension and, at the extreme, can cause a serious rift in the community.

Because cultures are strategies to meet human needs, we would expect that cultures the world over would have many elements in common. The term **cultural universals** refers to *traits found in every culture of the world*. Comparing hundreds of cultures, George Murdock (1945) found dozens of traits common to them all. One cultural universal is the family, which functions everywhere to control sexual reproduction and to oversee the care and upbringing of children. Another cultural universal, funeral rites, serves as a tellingly human response to the reality of death. Jokes, too, are found in all cultures, acting as a relatively safe means of releasing social tensions.

Critical evaluation. The strength of the structural-functional paradigm is showing how culture operates as an integrated system for meeting human needs. Yet, by emphasizing cultural stability, it downplays the extent to which societies change. Similarly, functionalism's assertion that cultural values are embraced by all members of a society overlooks the range of cultural diversity. Finally, the cultural patterns favoured by powerful people often dominate a society, while other

Travellers Beware! The Meaning of Gestures in Other Societies

A young man from Manitoba is enjoying a summer trip through the German countryside. He stands by the side of a county road hoping for a lift and, as a beautiful sports car approaches, he raises his right hand to flash the "A-OK!" sign (see Figure C below). The horn blares as the car speeds past, the angry driver hurling a few colourful words back at the hapless traveller.

What has happened here? Are Germans hostile to hitchhikers? No, except that, like people everywhere, they don't take kindly to insults. What the young Canadian meant as a sign of approval, Germans see as an offensive gesture—a crude word meaning "rectum."

Since much human communication involves not words but gestures and body language—especially when we encounter people whose languages differ from our own—we need to be mindful that the innocent use of even a simple hand movement may provoke an angry response. Here are six bodily gestures that seem innocent enough to members of our society but that may evoke a stern response from people elsewhere.

Figures A and B would each offend members of Islamic societies. Since Muslims typically perform bathroom hygiene with the left hand, they recoil at the sight of a person eating with that

(A)

(B)

(C)

ways of life are pushed to the margins. Thus, cultures generate more conflict than structural-functional analysis leads us to believe.

SOCIAL-CONFLICT ANALYSIS

The social-conflict paradigm views culture in a very different light. To social-conflict theorists, culture forms a dynamic arena of conflict generated by social inequality. This paradigm draws attention to the ways in which cultural traits serve the needs of some members of society at the expense of others.

Social-conflict analysis critically questions why certain values dominate in a society. What forces generate one set of values rather than another? Who benefits from these social arrangements? Many using this paradigm, especially those influenced by Karl Marx,

argue that values are shaped by a society's system of economic production: it is social existence that shapes consciousness (1967; orig. 1867). This shows the social-conflict paradigm's link to the philosophical doctrine of *materialism*, the assertion that how people fashion their material world (for example, a capitalist economy) has a powerful effect on other dimensions of their culture. Such a materialist approach contrasts with the idealist leanings of structural-functionalism.

Social-conflict analysis ties the competitive and individualistic values of capitalist societies to their economies, which serve the interests of those who own factories and other businesses. The culture of capitalism further teaches us to believe that the rich and powerful have more talent and discipline than others and therefore deserve their wealth and privileges.

hand, illustrated in Figure A. Islam also holds that the sole of a shoe is unclean; therefore, any display of the bottom of the foot, as in Figure B, conveys insult. Figure C displays the common "A-OK" gesture by which people in North America express approval and pleasure. In France, however, this symbol imparts the snub "You're worth zero," while Germans interpret this gesture as a crude word for "rectum." Figure D shows the simple curling of a finger,

meaning "come here." Malaysians attach the same meaning to this gesture as we do, but they use it exclusively for calling animals; thus, they take no pleasure in being beckoned in this way. Figure E shows the familiar "thumbs up" gesture widely employed in North America to mean "Good job!" or "All right!" In Nigeria and also in Australia, flashing this gesture (especially with a slight upward motion) transmits the insulting message "Up yours!" Finally,

Figure F shows a gesture that members of our society read as "Stop!" or "No, thanks." But display this gesture to a motorist or street vendor anywhere in western Africa and you will probably have a fight on your hands. There it means "You have five fathers," or, more simply, "You bastard!"

Sources: Examples are drawn from Ekman et al. (1984) and Axtell (1991).

(D)

(E)

(F)

Viewing capitalism as somehow "natural," some people resist efforts to reduce economic disparity.

Eventually, however, the strains fostered by social inequality exert continuous pressure towards change. The Native rights movement and the women's movement exemplify the drive for change supported by disadvantaged segments of the Canadian population. Both, too, have encountered opposition from defenders of the status quo.

Critical evaluation. The strength of the social-conflict paradigm lies in showing that, if cultural systems address human needs, they do so unequally. Put another way, this orientation holds that cultural elements "function" to maintain the dominance of some people over others. This inequity, in turn, promotes change. Because the social-conflict paradigm stresses

the divisiveness of culture, however, this approach understates the ways in which cultural patterns integrate all members of society. Thus, we should consider both social-conflict and structural-functional insights to gain a fuller understanding of culture.

CULTURAL MATERIALISM

A third theoretical paradigm is derived from *ecology*, the natural science that delves into the relationship between a living organism and its environment. **Cultural materialism** (or cultural ecology), then, amounts to *a theoretical paradigm that explores the relationship of human culture to the physical environment.* This paradigm investigates how climate and the availability of food, water, and other natural resources shape cultural patterns.

Consider the case of India. This nation contends with widespread hunger and malnutrition, yet has cultural norms that prohibit the killing of cows. According to Hindu belief, cows are sacred animals. To North Americans who enjoy so much beef, this situation is puzzling. Why should Indians not consume beef to supplement their diet?

Investigating India's ecology, Marvin Harris (1975) concluded that the importance of cows greatly exceeds their value as a food source. Harris points out that cows cost little to raise, since they consume grasses of no interest to humans. And cows produce two valuable resources: oxen (the neutered offspring of cows) and manure. Unable to afford expensive farm machinery, Indian farmers rely on oxen to power their plows. For Indians, killing cows would be as clever as farmers in Canada destroying factories that build tractors. Furthermore, each year millions of tonnes of cow manure are processed into building material and burned as fuel (India has little oil, coal, or wood). To kill cows, then, would deprive Indians of homes and a source of heat. In short, there are sound ecological reasons to culturally protect the cow.

Critical evaluation. Cultural materialism expands our understanding of culture, highlighting its interplay with the environment, and revealing how cultural patterns arise in response to particular natural conditions. However, this paradigm has several limitations. We can only rarely draw simple or direct connections between the environment and culture because cultural and physical forces interact in subtle and complex ways. Further, this approach has less application to technologically sophisticated societies that extensively manipulate the natural world.

SOCIOBIOLOGY

We know culture is a human creation; but does our biological humanity influence how this process unfolds? A fourth multidisciplinary paradigm, standing with one leg in biology and one in sociology, attempts to answer this question. **Sociobiology**, then, is *a theoretical paradigm that explores ways in which our biology affects how humans create culture.*

Sociobiology rests on the logic of evolution. In his treatise *On the Origin of Species*, Charles Darwin (1859) asserted that living organisms change over long periods of time as a result of *natural selection*, a matter of four simple principles: (1) all living things seek to reproduce themselves; (2) the blueprint for reproduction lies in the genes—the basic units of life that carry traits of one generation into the next—while genetic variation allows a species to "try out" new life patterns in particular environments; (3) owing to genetic variation, some organisms are more likely than others to survive and to pass on their advantageous genes to their offspring; and (4) over thousands of generations,

specific genetic patterns that promote reproduction survive and become dominant. In this way, as biologists say, a species *adapts* to its environment, and dominant traits emerge as the "nature" of the organism.

In the case of humans, culture itself emerged as human nature. That is, rather than being biologically "wired" for specific behaviour, humans developed the intelligence and sociability to devise life patterns for themselves. Such flexibility has allowed our species to flourish all over the planet. Even so, sociobiologists point out, we are all one species—a fact evident in the large number of cultural universals.

Consider the fact that, as sex researcher Alfred Kinsey put it, "Among all people everywhere in the world, the male is more likely than the female to desire sex with a variety of partners" (quoted in Barash, 1981:49). What insights does sociobiology offer into the so-called double standard?

Though we know that children result from joining a woman's egg with a man's sperm, the significance of a single sperm or a single egg differs dramatically. For healthy men, sperm represent a "renewable resource" produced by the testes throughout most of life. A man releases hundreds of millions of sperm in a single ejaculation—technically, enough to fertilize every woman in North America (Barash, 1981). A newborn female's ovaries, however, contain her entire lifetime allotment of follicles or immature eggs; she commonly releases one mature egg cell each month. So, while a man is biologically capable of fathering thousands of offspring, a woman is able to bear only a relatively small number of children.

Given this biologically based difference, each sex is well served by a distinctive reproductive strategy. From a strictly biological perspective, a man reproduces his genes most efficiently by being promiscuous—readily engaging in sex. This scheme, however, opposes the reproductive interests of a woman, whose relatively few pregnancies demand that she carry the child for nine months, give birth, and provide care for long afterwards. Thus, efficient reproduction for woman depends on carefully selecting a mate whose qualities (beginning with the likelihood that he will stay around) will contribute to her child's survival (Remoff, 1984).

The double standard certainly involves more than biology and is tangled up with the historical domination of women by men (Barry, 1983). Sociobiology suggests that this cultural pattern has an underlying bio-logic. Simply put, it has developed around the world because women and men everywhere tend towards distinctive reproductive strategies.

Critical evaluation. Sociobiology has generated intriguing theories about the biological roots of some cultural patterns, especially those that are universal, but it remains controversial for several reasons.

Some critics fear that sociobiologists may revive biological arguments, common a century ago, touting

Using an evolutionary perspective, sociobiologists point to a double standard by which men treat women as sexual objects more than women treat men that way. While this may be so, many sociologists counter that behaviour—such as that shown in Ruth Orkin's photograph American Girl in Italy—is more correctly understood as resulting from a culture of male domination.

the superiority of one race or sex. But defenders counter that sociobiology rejects the past pseudoscience of racial superiority. On the contrary, they continue, sociobiology actually unites all of humanity by asserting that all people share a single evolutionary history. With regard to sex, sociobiology does rest on the assumption that men and women differ biologically in some ways that culture cannot overcome—if, in fact, any society intends to. But far from asserting that males are somehow more important than females, sociobiology emphasizes that both sexes are vital to human reproduction.

Furthermore, say the critics, sociobiologists have as yet amassed little evidence to support their theories. A generation ago, Edward O. Wilson (1975, 1978), generally credited as the founder of this field, optimistically claimed that sociobiology would reveal the biological roots of human culture. But research to date concludes that biological forces do not determine human behaviour in any rigid sense. Rather, abundant evidence supports the conclusion that human behaviour is learned within a cultural system. The contribution of sociobiology, then, lies in its explanation of why some cultural patterns seem "easier to learn" than others (Barash, 1981).

CULTURE AS CONSTRAINT

Over the long course of human evolution, culture became the human strategy for survival. Truly, we cannot live without culture, but the capacity for culture does have its drawbacks. We may be the only animals who name ourselves; yet, as symbolic beings, we alone experience alienation. Moreover, culture is largely a matter of habit, limiting our choices and driving us to

repeat troubling patterns, such as racial prejudice, in each new generation. And, in an electronic age, we may wonder at the extent to which the business-dominated media manipulate our cultural surroundings in pursuit of profits.

Moreover, while our society's insistence on competitive achievement urges us towards excellence, this same pattern also isolates us from one another. Material comforts improve our lives in many ways, yet our preoccupation with acquiring things distracts us from seeking the security and satisfaction of close relationships or cultivating spiritual strength. Our emphasis on personal freedom affords us privacy and autonomy, yet our culture often denies us the support of a human community in which to share life's problems (Slater, 1976; Bellah et al., 1985).

CULTURE AS FREEDOM

We may seem to be prisoners of culture, just as other animals are prisoners of biology, but careful thought about the ideas presented here reveals a crucial difference. Biological instinct operates in a ready-made world; culture, by contrast, gives us the responsibility to make and remake a world for ourselves.

Therefore, although culture seems at times to circumscribe our lives, it always embodies the human capacity for hope, creativity, and choice. There is no better evidence of this freedom than the fascinating cultural diversity of our own society and the far greater human variety of the larger world. Furthermore, far from being static, culture is ever-changing; it allows our imagination and inventiveness to come to the fore. The more we discover about the operation of our culture, the greater our capacity to use the freedom it offers us.

CONTROVERSY & DEBATE

The Paparazzi: Villains or Our Eyes to the World?

Dr. Esther Konigsberg, a family physician in Burlington, Ontario, responded to the death of Princess Diana with a crusade to get merchants to stop selling the tabloids that publish pictures taken by the paparazzi. She circulated a petition asking consumers, merchants, and advertisers to stop buying, selling, and advertising in the tabloids. Dr. Konigsberg found it personally unsettling to realize that she is "part of a society whose curiosity and fascination with public figures have contributed to the unfortunate events" that led to Diana's death (Whitnell, 1997).

Paparazzi! The word, which we heard repeatedly in the months following the tragic death of Princess Diana, is one that only then became part of our active vocabularies. The term comes from the classic film La Dolce Vita (1959), directed by Federico Fellini, in which the main character, a journalist, was named Paparazzo.

The paparazzi are freelance photojournalists who indulge our passion for intimate glimpses into the lives of celebrities by relentlessly stalking them: their goal is to capture private moments on camera. Many celebrities are pursued by the paparazzi, but Diana—the most photographed woman in the world—had experienced more than her share of their attentions. Some of the paparazzi had devoted their whole careers to "doing Di": taking rapid-fire pictures of her was referred to as "banging," "blitzing," "smudging," or "ripping" Di (Lyall and Pogrebin, 1997). The desperate quest for photos of Diana is understood better, perhaps, if one realizes that the right photo could be worth as much as a million dollars.

Princess Diana reached the heights of celebrity partly because of her am-bivalent relationship with the media, and the paparazzi in particular. The media propelled Diana—the beautiful, the vulnerable, the good, the irreverent—into the public eye, an outcome that she sometimes seemed to invite. For example, she used the media to present her own point of view, particularly concerning her relationship with Prince Charles and the rest of the royal family.

But at the same time, the media made her life a living hell. The cost of celebrity was the loss of her freedom and her privacy. She was stalked by the paparazzi, but it was through their work that we came to know her so well. When she died, mourner after mourner would say, "I really felt that I knew her!" This kind of intimacy, which was predicted by media theorist Marshall McLuhan.

Shortly after Diana's death the British tabloids collectively suggested their own code of ethics regarding the purchase of paparazzi photos. Princes William and Harry were to be off limits until they were adults, and other photos of the private lives of celebrities were to be obtained only with the permission of the subjects. As Prince William ap-

SUMMARY

1. Culture refers to a way of life shared by members of a society. Several species display a limited capacity for culture, but only human beings rely on culture for survival.

2. As the human brain evolved, the first elements of culture appeared some 3 million years ago; culture replaced biological instincts as our species' primary strategy for survival.

3. Culture relies on symbols. Language is the symbolic system by which one generation transmits culture to the next.

4. Values are culturally defined standards of what ought to be; beliefs are statements held to be true by people who share a culture.

5. Cultural norms guide human behaviour. Mores are of great moral significance; folkways are everyday matters of politeness.

6. High culture refers to patterns that distinguish a society's elites; popular culture refers to widespread social patterns.

7. Canada stands among the most culturally diverse societies in the world. Subculture refers to distinctive

proached his eighteenth birthday, Maclean's made this event its cover story (Came, 2000). Now he is known as "the reluctant prince" for his aversion to media attention and the perks of royalty.

The terrible accident that killed Princess Diana was the result of speed, alcohol, another car, bad judgment, and the actions of the pursuing paparazzi. There are many who would add that the mass media as a whole and the general public, worldwide, must share responsibility for creating the circumstances that hastened Diana's death. After all, we have a voracious collective appetite for information about celebrities—the more personal the information, the better. To some extent, the paparazzi were merely convenient scapegoats, soon forgotten when the public recovered from the initial shock over Diana's death.

There's a postmodernist explanation for the way in which a British royal was embraced as part of Canada's popular culture—as our "people's princess." Because she went public with her pain and vulnerability and resisted the domination of the royal family, she remained at the margins of royal and aristocratic privilege. Diana's story is

"an allegory of post-colonialism" in that her identity is compatible with English Canada's "post-colonial sense of itself as a nation that has emerged from the legacy of its inheritance from Britain and is now an autonomous player on the international stage" (Wilson, 1999:163).

It could be argued that celebrities need media exposure, and perhaps even the paparazzi, to keep them in the spotlight. If "the medium is the message," as Marshall McLuhan suggested, what does the existence of the paparazzi—and the media that support them—say about our culture?

Postscript: June 2, 2003: Fifty years since the coronation of Queen Elizabeth! Since live transatlantic broadcasting was impossible at the time of her coronation, the CBC flew a crew of three to London on a Royal Canadian Air Force jet—with the equipment to develop its film on the flight home. The CBC actually won the race to air its coronation footage against the better-funded American networks, NBC, ABC, and CBS.

Meanwhile in Canada, thousands of Canadians were buying their first televisions just so that they could watch the

coronation. This experience allowed them to see, up close, a Queen who previously had been so remote. Canadians formed a warm bond with their Queen as a result of this new and intimate involvement (Muhtadie, 2003).

Continue the debate . . .

1. Should the relevant governments take steps to restrain the activities of the paparazzi? What impact could this have on freedom of speech?

2. Why do we buy the magazines and tabloids that publish the paparazzi's pictures? Do we share responsibility for the activities of the paparazzi?

cultural patterns adopted by a segment of a population; counterculture means patterns strongly at odds with a conventional way of life. Multiculturalism is a social policy designed to enhance appreciation and acceptance of cultural diversity.

8. Invention, discovery, and diffusion all generate cultural change. When parts of a cultural system change more slowly than others, the result is cultural lag.

9. Ethnocentrism involves judging others by the standards of one's own culture; cultural relativism means judging another culture according to its own standards.

10. The structural-functional paradigm views culture as a relatively stable system built on core values. Cultural patterns function to maintain the overall system.

11. The social-conflict paradigm envisions culture as a dynamic arena of inequality and conflict. Cultural patterns typically benefit some categories of people more than others.

12. Sociobiology studies the influence of humanity's evolutionary past on present cultural patterns.

13. The cultural materialism model explores how climate and the availability of food, water, and other natural resources shapes cultural patterns.

14. Culture can constrain human needs and ambitions; yet as cultural creatures, we have the capacity to shape and reshape the world to meet our needs and pursue our dreams.

CRITICAL-THINKING QUESTIONS

1. What is the cultural significance of donuts? Are they a significant element of Canadian culture? Does their significance vary by region?

2. How does a schoolroom activity such as a "spelling bee" embody Canadian cultural values? What cultural values are expressed by children's stories such as "The Little Engine That Could" and popular board games such as Snakes and Ladders, Monopoly, and Risk?

3. Do you think Canadian cultural values are changing? If so, how and why?

4. Have there been protests in your province by Aboriginal peoples regarding land claims? What do you know about this issue, and what is the relationship between land claims and culture?

APPLICATIONS AND EXERCISES

1. Try to find someone on campus who has lived in another country. Ask for a chance to discuss how the culture of that other society differs from the way of life here. Try to identify ways in which the other person sees Canadian culture differently than most of us might.

2. Step back from your everyday thinking and look at several of your favourite television shows as you imagine someone from another country would. What cultural values do the shows reflect?

3. Play a game of Monopoly (Canadian edition) with several friends. As you play, comment to one another about what this popular game suggests about our way of life.

4. Take a look at your family tree. What does it tell you about the racial and ethnic mix in your background? What has happened to fertility over generations?

 SITES TO SEE

www.macionis.com
or
www.TheSociologyPage.com

You can find more than fifty weblinks to sociological journals and other sources of data and information by visiting the Links Library at this website.

www.geocities.com/Athens/Olympus/3808

This site puts you in touch with the Six Nations of the Grand River. You will learn about the community's history, cultural events, social services, and famous members such as actor Graham Greene.

www.civilization.ca/

Explore the Museum of Civilization (Hull, Quebec) with its wide range of displays and programs through the Virtual Museum.

www.symbols.com/

From ideograms carved in mammoth teeth by Cro-Magnon men to subway graffiti, *Symbols.com* contains more than 2500 Western signs, arranged according to their graphic characteristics, as well as 1600 articles about their histories, uses, and meanings.

www.nationalgeographic.com

Visit the website for the National Geographic Society. This site offers information on world cultures, including search engines and a library of maps.

www.gorilla.org

The Gorilla Foundation operates a website where you can follow the progress researchers are making in teaching a 200 kg gorilla named Koko to use sign language.

www.aaanet.org

Anthropologists study cultures all over the world. This is the website for the American Anthropological Association, where you can find out more about this discipline, which is closely related to sociology.

http://daphne.palomar.edu/mlane/SAGAN/sagan_mem.html

Scientific American's obituary for Carl Sagan—"A Pale Blue Planet Mourns the Passing of a Passionate Scientist"—contains links to many related sites on the Web, including earlier *Scientific American* articles.

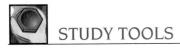 STUDY TOOLS

For more study tools to help you with your next exam, be sure to check out the Companion Website at **www.pearsoned. ca/macionis**, as well as Chapter 3 in your Study Guide.

 INVESTIGATE WITH CONTENTSELECT

Follow the instructions found on page 25 of this textbook to access ContentSelect™ at the Research Navigator™ website. Once at the site, enter your LOGINID and Password. Then, enter keywords such as "multiculturalism" and "immigration" and the search engine will supply relevant and recent scholarly and popular press publications.

CHAPTER
4

Tosa (attributed to, seventeenth century)
People Along the River

Detail from screen, representing the River Festival. Seventeenth century. Painting on paper. Photo: Arnaudet. Musée des Arts Asiatiques–Guimet, Paris, France. Réunion des Musées Nationaux/Art Resource, N.Y.

SOCIETY

What is it about Canadian society that is so intriguing? Is it the dilemmas and problems of a society created by wide open spaces? Is it the reality of being a relatively young society in spite of some longevity? Is it the search for common ground among a far-flung, diverse and changing population? Is it the sense of belonging together that persists in spite of crises that threaten to tear the society apart?

It may seem ironic indeed that even though the Canadian state is over one hundred and thirty years old, the precise nature of Canadian society and its existence as an entity are still in question. In fact, the stormy years after the centennial birthday in 1967 suggested more than ever that the concept of a Canadian society could not be taken for granted. While Quebec was contemplating what degree of distance from the rest of Canadian society was most appropriate, the Symons Report was concluding that Canadians knew little about their own society, and a federal Task Force on Canadian Unity was scouring the country for clues about ways to create a more integrated and cohesive society. More recently, the failure of the Meech Lake accord and the Charlottetown accord with their "distinct Quebec society" ideas, as well as the anxieties produced by two Quebec referendums (and now the threat of a third referendum), continued to point out the fragility of national unity. What kind of society is this that has been problematic for so long?

Source: Excerpted from *Canadian Society: A Macro Analysis* by Harry H. Hiller (2000:1–2).

Human societies have taken many forms throughout history, and remarkable diversity is still evident in the world today. But what is a society in the first place? What makes society "hang together"? How have societies changed over the course of human history? Why have they changed?

To begin, the concept of **society** refers to *people who interact in a defined territory and share culture*. In this chapter, we shall examine this deceptively simple term from four different angles. Gerhard Lenski and Jean Lenski describe the changing character of human society over the last ten thousand years. Focusing on how *technology* shapes social life, their analysis shows that a technological breakthrough often has revolutionary consequences for society as a whole. The remainder of the chapter presents classic visions of society developed by three of sociology's founders. Like the Lenskis, Karl Marx also understood human history as a long and complex process of social change. For Marx, however, the story of society spins around *social conflict*, which stems from inequality rooted in how people produce material goods. Max Weber rec-

ognized the importance of productive forces as well, but he sought to demonstrate the power of *ideas* to animate society. Weber was among the first to contrast the traditional thinking of many simple societies with the rational thought that animates our modern way of life. Finally, Emile Durkheim investigated patterns of *social solidarity*, noting that the bonds uniting traditional societies and their modern counterparts are strikingly different.

All four visions of society answer key questions: What makes other societies so different from the one familiar to us? How and why do societies change? What forces divide a society? What forces hold it together? Are societies getting better or worse?

GERHARD AND JEAN LENSKI: SOCIETY AND TECHNOLOGY

As people who take for granted schooling and medical care, and who enjoy rapid transportation and instant global communication, we must wonder at the nomads

In technologically simple societies, successful hunting wins men great praise. However, the gathering of vegetation by women is a more dependable and more easily available source of nutrition.

of the Sahara, who live as their ancestors did centuries ago. But sociologists who study the past (working with archaeologists and anthropologists) have learned quite a bit about our human heritage. Gerhard Lenski and Jean Lenski have chronicled the great differences among societies that have flourished and declined throughout human history. Just as importantly, the work of these researchers helps us better understand how we live today.

The Lenskis call the focus of their research **socio-cultural evolution**, *the process of change that results from a society's gaining new information, particularly technology* (Lenski et al., 1995:75). Rather like a biologist examining how a living species evolves over millennia, a sociologist employing this approach observes how societies change over centuries as they gain greater ability to manipulate their physical environments. Societies with rudimentary technology can support only a small number of people, who enjoy few choices about how to live. Technologically complex societies—while not necessarily "better" in any absolute sense—develop large populations characterized by diverse, highly specialized lives.

The Lenskis also explain that the greater the amount of technological information a society has in its grasp, the faster the rate at which it changes. Technologically simple societies, then, change very slowly; by contrast, industrial, high-technology societies change so quickly that people witness dramatic transformations during their lifetimes. Some familiar elements of North American culture would puzzle, delight, or even alarm people who lived just a few gen-

erations ago: beepers, phone sex, artificial hearts, the "information superhighway," laser surgery, test-tube babies, genetic engineering, email, fibre optics, smart bombs, the threat of nuclear holocaust, space shuttles, transsexualism, and "tell-all" talk shows.

As a society extends its technological reach, the effects ripple through the cultural system, generating countless repercussions. When our ancestors first harnessed the power of the wind by using a sail, they set the stage for building sailing ships, which took them to new lands, stimulated trade, and increased their power to make war. Consider, as a more recent example, the many ways modern life has been changed by the spread of computer technology.

Drawing on the Lenskis' work, we will describe five general types of societies distinguished by their technology: hunting-and-gathering societies, horticultural and pastoral societies, agrarian societies, industrial societies, and post-industrial societies.

HUNTING-AND-GATHERING SOCIETIES

Hunting and gathering refers to *simple technology for hunting animals and gathering vegetation*. From the emergence of our species until just ten thousand years ago, all humans were hunters and gatherers. Although hunting-and-gathering societies remained common several centuries ago, only a few persist today, including the Aka and Pygmies of central Africa, the Kung of the Kalahari, the Aborigines of Australia, and the Batek and Semai of Malaysia.

With scarcely any technology to make food production efficient, most members of these societies must search continually for game and edible plants. Only in lush areas where food is plentiful would hunters and gatherers have any leisure time. Moreover, foraging for food demands a large amount of land, so hunting-and-gathering societies comprise small bands of a few dozen people living at some distance from one another. These groups are also nomadic, moving on as they deplete vegetation in one area or in pursuit of migratory animals. Although periodically returning to favoured sites, they rarely form permanent settlements.

Hunting-and-gathering societies are based on kinship. The family obtains and distributes food, protects its members, and teaches the children. Most activities are common to everyone and centre on seeking their next meal; some specialization, however, corresponds to age and sex. The very young and the very old contribute only what they can, while healthy adults secure most of the food. The women gather vegetation—the more reliable food source—while men take on the less certain job of hunting. While the two sexes have somewhat different responsibilities, most hunters and gatherers probably accorded men and women comparable social importance (Leacock, 1978).

Pastoralism historically has flourished in regions of the world where arid soil does not support crops. Pastoral people still thrive in northern Africa, living today much as they did a thousand years ago.

Hunting-and-gathering societies have few formal leaders. Most recognize a *shaman*, or spiritual leader, who enjoys high prestige but receives no greater material rewards than other members of the society and must help procure food like everyone else. In short, hunting-and-gathering societies are relatively simple and egalitarian.

Hunting-and-gathering societies rarely use their simple, handcrafted weapons—the spear, the bow and arrow, and the stone knife—to wage war. Nonetheless, they are often ravaged by the forces of nature. Storms and droughts can easily destroy their food supply, and they stand vulnerable to accident and disease. Such risks encourage cooperation and sharing, a strategy that increases everyone's odds of survival. Nonetheless, many die in childhood, and many more perish before the age of twenty (Lenski et al., 1995:104).

During this century, technologically complex societies have slowly closed in on the few remaining hunters and gatherers, reducing their landholdings and depleting game and vegetation. The Lenskis predicted that the 1990s might well witness the end of hunting-and-gathering societies on earth. Fortunately, study of this way of life has already produced valuable information about human history and our fundamental ties to the natural world.

HORTICULTURAL AND PASTORAL SOCIETIES

Ten to twelve thousand years ago, a new technology began to change the lives of human beings (see the timeline on the inside front cover). **Horticulture** is *a technology based on using hand tools to cultivate plants*. The most important tools of horticulturalists are the hoe to work the soil and the digging stick to punch

holes in the ground for seeds. Humans first used these tools in fertile regions of the Middle East and later in Latin America and Asia. Cultural diffusion spread knowledge of horticulture throughout most of the world by about six thousand years ago.

Not all societies were quick to abandon hunting and gathering in favour of horticulture. Hunters and gatherers living amid plentiful vegetation and game probably saw little reason to embrace the new technology (Fisher, 1979). Then, too, people in particularly arid regions (such as the Sahara region of western Africa or the Middle East) or mountainous areas found horticulture to be of little value. Such people turned to a different strategy for survival, **pastoralism**, which is *technology based on the domestication of animals*. Still others combined horticulture and pastoralism to produce a variety of foods. Today, many horticultural-pastoral societies thrive in South America, Africa, and Asia.

The domestication of plants and animals greatly increased food production, enabling societies to support not dozens but hundreds of people. Pastoralists remained nomadic, leading their herds to fresh grazing lands; horticulturalists, by contrast, formed settlements, moving on only when they depleted the soil. These settlements, joined by trade, comprised multi-centred societies with overall populations often in the thousands.

Domesticating plants and animals generates a *material surplus*, more resources than necessary to sustain day-to-day living. A surplus frees some people from the job of securing food, allowing them to create crafts, engage in trade, cut hair, apply tattoos, or serve as priests. In comparison to hunting-and-gathering societies, then, horticultural and pastoral societies display more specialized and complex social arrangements.

Of Egypt's one hundred and thirty pyramids, the Great Pyramids at Giza are the largest. Each of the three major structures stands more than forty stories high and is composed of 3 million massive stone blocks. Some 4500 years ago, tens of thousands of people laboured to construct these pyramids so that one man, the pharaoh, might have a godlike monument for his tomb. Clearly, social inequality in this agrarian society was striking.

Hunters and gatherers recognize numerous spirits inhabiting the world. Horticulturalists practise ancestor worship and conceive of God as Creator. Pastoral societies carry this belief further, viewing God as directly involved in the well-being of the world. This view of God ("The Lord is my shepherd . . . ," Psalm 23) is widespread among members of our own society because Christianity, Islam, and Judaism originated as Middle Eastern, pastoral religions.

Expanding productive technology also intensifies social inequality. As some families produce more food than others, they assume positions of relative power and privilege. Forging alliances with other elite families ensures that social advantages endure over generations and a formal system of social inequality emerges. Along with social hierarchy, rudimentary government—backed by military force—is formed to shore up the power of elites. However, without the ability to communicate or to travel quickly, a ruler can control only a limited number of people, so empire-building proceeds on a small scale.

The domestication of plants and animals surely made simpler societies more productive. But advancing technology is never entirely beneficial. The Lenskis point out that, compared to hunters and gatherers, horticulturalists and pastoralists display more social inequality and, in many cases, engage in slavery and protracted warfare.

AGRARIAN SOCIETIES

About five thousand years ago, another technological revolution was underway in the Middle East and would eventually transform most of the world. This was the discovery of **agriculture**, *the technology of large-scale farming using plows harnessed to animals or, eventually, mechanical tractors.* The Lenskis state that the social significance of the animal-drawn plow, along with other technological innovations of the period—including irrigation, the wheel, writing, numbers, and the expanding use of metals—clearly qualifies this era as "the dawn of civilization" (Lenski et al., 1995:177).

Farmers with animal-drawn plows cultivated fields vastly larger than the garden-sized plots worked by horticulturalists. Plows have the additional advantage of turning, and thereby aerating, the soil to increase fertility. Such technology encouraged agrarian societies to farm the same land for decades, which, in turn, led to humanity's first permanent settlements. Large food surpluses, transported on animal-powered wagons, allowed agrarian societies to expand to unprecedented land area and population. As an extreme case, the Roman Empire at its height (about 100 C.E.) boasted a population of 70 million spread over some 5 million square kilometres (Stavrianos, 1983; Lenski et al., 1995).

As always, increasing production meant greater specialization. Tasks once performed by everyone, such as clearing land and securing food, became distinct occupations. Specialization made the early barter system obsolete and prompted the invention of money as a common standard of exchange. The appearance of money facilitated trade, sparking the growth of cities as economic centres with populations soaring into the millions.

Agrarian societies exhibit dramatic social inequality. In many cases, peasants or slaves constitute a significant share of the population and labour for elites: the seigneurial system of New France (part of Quebec) had its *habitants*, while slavery was practised coast to coast across what is now Canada from the 1750s through to the early 1800s. Thus freed from manual work, elites could devote their time to the study of philosophy, art, and literature. This phenomenon helps to explain the historical link between "high culture," as noted in Chapter 3 ("Culture"), and social privilege.

Among hunters and gatherers and also among horticulturalists, women are the primary providers of food. The development of agriculture, however, appears to have propelled men into a position of social dominance (Boulding, 1976; Fisher, 1979). Thus, social inequality also extended to the declining position of women in agrarian societies.

Religion reinforces the power of agricultural elites. Religious doctrine typically propounds the idea that people are morally obligated to perform whatever tasks correspond to their place in the social order. Many of the wonders of the ancient world, such as the Great Wall of China and the Great Pyramids of Egypt, were possible only because emperors and pharaohs wielded virtually absolute power to mobilize their people to endure a lifetime of labour without pay.

In agrarian societies, then, elites gain unparalleled power. To maintain control of large empires, leaders re-

 To see several wonders of the ancient world, all made primarily with muscle power, click on http://unmuseum. mus.pa.us/wonders.htm

quire the services of a wide range of administrators. Along with the growing economy, then, the political system becomes established as a distinct sphere of life.

In relation to the societies described so far, the Lenskis conclude, agrarian societies have greater specialization and more social inequality. Compared to horticultural and pastoral societies, agrarian societies are more diverse because advancing technology increases human control over the natural world.

INDUSTRIAL SOCIETIES

Industrialism, as found in Canada, the United States, and other rich nations of the world, is *technology that powers sophisticated machinery with advanced sources of energy.* Until the industrial era, the major source of energy was the muscles of humans and other animals. At the dawning of the *Industrial Revolution*, in about 1750, mills and factories relied on flowing water and then steam to power ever-larger and more efficient machinery.

Once industrial technology was at hand, societies began to change faster (see Figure 4–1). Industrial societies transformed themselves more in a century than they had in thousands of years before. As explained in Chapter 1 ("The Sociological Perspective"), this stunning change stimulated the birth of sociology itself. During the nineteenth century, railroads and steamships revolutionized transportation, and steel-framed skyscrapers recast the urban landscape, dwarfing the cathedrals that symbolized an earlier age.

As the twentieth century opened, automobiles reshaped Western societies, and electricity fast became the basis for countless "modern conveniences." Electronic communication, including the telephone, radio, and television, was mass-producing cultural patterns and gradually making a large world seem smaller

FIGURE 4–1 The Increasing Number of Technological Innovations

This figure illustrates the number of technological innovations in Western Europe after the beginning of the Industrial Revolution in the mid-eighteenth century. Technological innovation occurs at an accelerating rate because each innovation spins off existing cultural elements to produce many further innovations.

Source: Lenski et al. (1995).

and smaller. More recently, transportation technology gave humanity the capacity to fly faster than sound and even to break the bonds of earth. During the last generation, computers ushered in the *Information Revolution*, dramatically increasing humanity's capacity to process words and numbers.

Work, too, has changed. In agrarian societies, most men and women work in the home. Industrialization, however, creates factories near centralized machinery and energy sources. Lost in the process are close working relationships and strong kinship ties, as well as many of the traditional values, beliefs, and customs that guide agrarian life.

Occupational specialization, which expanded over the long course of sociocultural evolution, has become more pronounced than ever. Industrial people often size up one another in terms of their jobs rather than according to their kinship ties (as agrarian people do). Rapid change and movement from place to place also generate anonymity and cultural diversity, sparking the formation of numerous subcultures and counter-cultures, as described in Chapter 3 ("Culture").

Industrial technology recasts the family, too, diminishing its traditional significance as the centre of

Does advancing technology make society better? In some ways, perhaps. However, many films—including Frankenstein *(1931) and* Jurassic Park III *(2001)—have expressed the concern that new technology not only solves old problems but creates new ones. All the sociological theorists discussed in this chapter shared this ambivalent view of the modern world.*

social life. No longer does the family serve as the primary setting for economic production, learning, and religious worship. And, as Chapter 18 ("Family") explains in detail, technological change underlies the trend away from so-called traditional families to greater numbers of single people, divorced people, single-parent families, stepfamilies, and same-sex unions.

The Lenskis explain that early industrialization concentrated the benefits of advancing technology on a small segment of the population, with the majority living in poverty. In time, however, the material benefits of industrial productivity spread more widely. Poverty remains a serious problem in industrial societies, but compared to the situation a century ago, the standard of living has risen fivefold, and economic, social, and political inequality has declined. Some social levelling, detailed in Chapter 10 ("Social Stratification"), occurs because industrial societies demand an educated and skilled labour force. While most people in agrarian societies are illiterate, industrial societies provide state-funded schooling and confer numerous political rights on virtually everyone. Industrialization, in fact, intensifies demands for political participation, as seen recently in South Korea, Taiwan, the People's Republic of China, the former Soviet Union, and Eastern Europe.

POST-INDUSTRIAL SOCIETIES

Many industrial societies, including Canada, now appear to be entering yet another phase of technological development, to which we can extend the Lenskis' analysis. A generation ago sociologist Daniel Bell (1973) coined the term **post-industrialism** to refer to *technology that supports an information-based economy.* While production in industrial societies centres on factories and machinery generating material goods, post-industrial production focuses on computers and other electronic devices that create, process, store, and apply information. At the individual level, members of industrial societies concentrate on learning mechanical skills; people in post-industrial societies, however, work on honing information-based skills for work involving computers and other forms of high-technology communication.

As this shift in key skills indicates, the emergence of post-industrialism dramatically changes a society's occupational structure. Chapter 16 ("The Economy and Work") examines this process in detail, explaining that a post-industrial society uses more and more of its labour force for information-based production. As a result, the ranks of clerical workers, managers, and other people who process information (in fields ranging from academia and advertising to marketing and public relations) swell rapidly.

The Information Revolution is most pronounced in industrial, high-income societies, yet the reach of this new technology is so great that it is affecting the entire world. As explained in Chapter 3 ("Culture"), the unprecedented, worldwide flow of information originating in rich nations like our own has the predictable effect of tying far-flung societies together and fostering common patterns of global culture.

Another pivotal idea from Chapter 3—the concept of cultural lag—has an important application to post-industrial societies. Cultural lag refers to the process by which some cultural elements (especially technology) change faster than others (such as values and norms). Though *information* is fast replacing objects as the centre of our economy, our legal notions about property are still based on tangible things.

Consider, for example, the national practice by which government officials monitor the flow of property in and out of this country. Customs officers require travellers to declare all the property that they wish to carry with them when they arrive, and baggage is subject to physical search. Curiously, while people are lining up to discuss purchases of liquor, antiques, or oriental rugs, an individual in possession of valuable ideas or computer programs on a computer disk can easily and legally walk past customs officials and announce "Nothing to declare!" since our legal system has yet to fully recognize the value of nontangible property. In short, while recent decades have witnessed rapid technological change, many of our ways of thinking remain rooted in an earlier era.

Table 4–1 presents a summary of the contributions of technological innovation at various stages of sociocultural evolution.

THE LIMITS OF TECHNOLOGY

While technology remedies many human problems, by raising productivity, reducing infectious diseases, and sometimes simply relieving boredom, it provides no "quick fix" for many social problems. Poverty remains the plight of millions of women and men in this country (detailed in Chapter 11, "Social Class in Canada") and of 1 billion people worldwide (see Chapter 12, "Global Stratification"). Moreover, with the capacity to reshape the world, technology has created new problems that our ancestors could hardly imagine. Industrial societies provide more personal freedom, often at the cost of the sense of community that characterized pre-industrial life. Further, although the most powerful societies of today's world engage in all-out warfare infrequently, international conflict now poses unimaginable horrors. Should nations ever unleash even a fraction of their present stockpiles of nuclear weapons, human society would almost certainly regress to a technologically primitive state if, indeed, we survived at all.

Another stubborn social problem involves humanity's relation to the physical environment. Each stage in sociocultural evolution has introduced more powerful sources of energy and accelerated our appetite for the earth's resources at a rate even faster than that of population growth. We now face a vital question: can humanity continue to pursue material prosperity without subjecting the planet to damage and strains from which it will never recover?

In some ways, technological advances have improved life and brought the world's people closer together within a "global village," a term coined by Marshall McLuhan. Yet in technology's wake come daunting problems of establishing peace, ensuring justice, and sustaining a safe environment—problems that technology alone can never solve.

KARL MARX: SOCIETY AND CONFLICT

The first of our classic visions of society comes from Karl Marx (1818–83), one of the early giants of sociology. Few observed the industrial transformation of Europe as keenly as Marx, who spent most of his adult life in London, the centre of the vast British Empire. He was awed by the productive power of the new factories: not only were European societies producing more goods than ever before, but global commerce was funnelling resources from around the world through British factories at a dizzying rate.

 For biographical information about Karl Marx, go to www.TheSociologyPage.com and click on his name in the Gallery of Sociologists.

What astounded Marx even more was the concentration of industry's riches in the hands of a few. A walk almost anywhere in London revealed dramatic extremes of splendid affluence and wretched squalor. A handful of aristocrats and industrialists lived in fabulous mansions well staffed by servants, where they enjoyed luxury and privileges. Most people laboured long hours for low wages, living in slums or even sleeping in the streets, where many eventually succumbed to poor nutrition and infectious disease.

Throughout his life, Marx wrestled with a basic contradiction: the rich societies he observed contained too many who were desperately poor. How, Marx asked, could this situation be changed? Many people, no doubt, think of Karl Marx as a man determined to tear societies apart. But he was motivated by compassion for humanity and sought to help a society already badly divided forge what he hoped would be a new and just social order.

The key to Marx's thinking is the idea of **social conflict**, *struggle between segments of society over valued resources*. Social conflict can, of course, take many forms: individuals may quarrel, groups have long-standing rivalries, and nations sometimes go to war. For Marx, however, the most significant form of social conflict involved clashes between social classes arising from the way societies produce material goods.

SOCIETY AND PRODUCTION

Living in the nineteenth century, Marx observed the early stage of industrial capitalism in Europe. This economic system, Marx noted, transformed a small part of the population into **capitalists**, *people who own factories and other productive enterprises*. A capitalist's goal is

TABLE 4–1 Sociocultural Evolution: A Summary

Type of Society	Historical Period	Productive Technology	Population Size
Hunting-and-Gathering Societies	Only type of society until about 10 000 years ago; still common several centuries ago; the few examples remaining today are threatened with extinction	Primitive weapons	Twenty-five to forty people
Horticultural and Pastoral Societies	From about 10 000 years ago, with decreasing numbers after about 3000 B.C.E.	Horticultural societies use hand tools for cultivating plants; pastoral societies are based on the domestication of animals	Settlements of several hundred people, interconnected through trading ties to form societies of several thousand people
Agrarian Societies	From about 5000 years ago, with large but decreasing numbers today	Animal-drawn plow	Millions of people
Industrial Societies	From about 1750 to the present	Advanced sources of energy; mechanized production	Millions of people
Post-industrial Societies	Emerging in recent decades	Computers that support an information-based economy	Millions of people

profit, which results from selling a product for more than it costs to produce. Capitalism transforms most of the population into industrial workers, whom Marx called the **proletariat**, *people who provide labour necessary to operate factories and other productive enterprises.* Workers sell their labour for the wages they need to live. To Marx, an inevitable conflict between capitalists and workers has its roots in the productive process itself. To maximize profits, capitalists must minimize wages, generally their single greatest expense; yet workers want wages to be as high as possible. Since profits and wages come from the same pool of funds, ongoing conflict occurs. Marx argued that this conflict would end only when people overturned the capitalist system.

All societies are composed of **social institutions**, defined as *the major spheres of social life, or society's subsystems, organized to meet basic human needs.* In his analysis of society, Marx contended that one specific institution—the economy—dominates all others when it comes to steering the direction of a society. Drawing on the philosophical doctrine of *materialism*, which asserts that the way humans produce material goods shapes the rest of society, Marx claimed that all the other major social institutions—the political system, family, religion, and education—operated more or less to shore up a society's economy. The Lenskis' argument that technology shapes society echoes Marx's assertion that the economy is "the real foundation. . . . The mode of production in material life determines

the general character of the social, political, and spiritual processes of life" (1959:43; orig. 1859).

Marx therefore viewed the economic system as the social *infrastructure* (*infra* is Latin for "below"). Other social institutions, including the family, the political system, and religion, which are built on this foundation, form society's *superstructure*. These institutions extend economic principles into other areas of life, as illustrated in Figure 4–2. In practical terms, social institutions reinforce the domination of the capitalists, by legally protecting their wealth, for example, and by transferring property from one generation to the next through the family.

Generally, members of industrial-capitalist societies do not view their legal or family systems as hotbeds of social conflict. On the contrary, individuals come to see their rights to private property as "natural." We might think, for example, that affluent people have earned their wealth, whereas those who are poor or out of work lack skills or motivation. Marx rejected this kind of reasoning as rooted in a capitalist preoccupation with the "bottom line" that treats human well-being as a market commodity. Poverty and unemployment are not inevitable; as Marx saw it, grand wealth clashing with grinding poverty represents one set of human possibilities generated by capitalism (Cuff and Payne, 1979).

Marx rejected capitalist common sense, therefore, as **false consciousness**, *explanations of social problems*

Type of Society	Settlement Pattern	Social Organization	Examples
Hunting-and-Gathering Societies	Nomadic	Family-centred; specialization limited to age and sex; little social inequality	Pygmies of central Africa Kung of the Kalahari Aborigines of Australia Batek and Semai of Malaysia
Horticultural and Pastoral Societies	Horticulturalists form relatively small permanent settlements; pastoralists are nomadic	Family-centred; religious system begins to develop; moderate specialization; increased social inequality	Middle Eastern societies about 5000 B.C.E. Various societies today in New Guinea and other Pacific islands Yąnomamö today in South America
Agrarian Societies	Cities become common, though they generally contain only a small proportion of the population	Family loses significance as distinctive religious, political, and economic system emerge; extensive specialization; increased social inequality	Egypt during construction of the Great Pyramids Medieval Europe Numerous nonindustrial societies of the world today
Industrial Societies	Cities contain most of the population	Distinct religious, political, economic, educational, and family systems; highly specialized; marked social inequality persists, diminishing somewhat over time	Most societies today in Europe, North America, Australia, and Japan; these societies generate most of the world's industrial production
Post-industrial Societies	Population remains concentrated in cities	Similar to industrial societies with information processing and other service work gradually replacing industrial production	Industrial societies noted above are now entering post-industrial stage

grounded in the shortcomings of individuals rather than the flaws of society. Marx was saying, in effect, that industrial capitalism itself is responsible for many of the social problems he saw all around him. False consciousness, he maintained, victimizes people by obscuring the real cause of their problems and encouraging complacency.

CONFLICT IN HISTORY

Marx studied how societies have changed throughout history, noting that they often evolve gradually, although they sometimes change in rapid, revolutionary fashion. Marx observed (as do the Lenskis) that change is partly prompted by technological advance. But he steadfastly held that conflict between economic classes is the major engine of change.

To recast the Lenskis' analysis in Marxist terms, early hunters and gatherers formed primitive communist societies. The word *communism* refers to a social system in which the production of food and other material goods is a common effort shared more or less equally by all members of society. Because the resources of nature were available to all hunters and gatherers (rather than privately owned), and because everyone performed similar work (rather than dividing work into highly specialized tasks), there was little possibility for social conflict.

Horticulture, Marx noted, introduced significant social inequality. Among horticultural, pastoral, and early agrarian societies—which Marx lumped together as the "ancient world"—the victors in frequent warfare forced their captives into servitude. A small elite (the "masters") and their slaves were thus locked in an irreconcilable pattern of social conflict (Zeitlin, 1981).

Agriculture brought still more wealth to members of the elite, fuelling further social conflict. Agrarian serfs, occupying the lowest reaches of European feudalism from about the twelfth to the eighteenth centuries, were only slightly better off than slaves. In Marx's view, the power of both the church and the state defended feudal inequality by defining the existing social order as God's will. Thus, to Marx, feudalism amounted to little more than "exploitation, veiled by religious and political illusions" (Marx and Engels, 1972:337; orig. 1848).

Gradually, new productive forces undermined the feudal order. Commerce grew steadily throughout the Middle Ages as trade networks expanded and the power of guilds increased. Merchants and skilled craftsworkers in the cities formed a new social category, the *bourgeoisie* (a French word meaning "of the town"). Profits earned through expanding trade brought the bourgeoisie increasing wealth. After about 1800, with factories at their command, the bourgeoisie became true capitalists with power that soon rivalled that of the ancient, landed nobility. While the nobility regarded this upstart "commercial" class with disdain, their increasing wealth gradually

APPLYING SOCIOLOGY

Can Sociology Help Us Design a Better Society?

If sociology is of any value, it should help us to deal with social problems. Taking that thought further, sociology should allow us to design a better society. Karl Marx thought he knew how to create a classless society; various utopians have offered their versions of perfect societies. The trick, according to Ken Menzies, is designing a better society that will work—one that ultimately can reproduce or perpetuate itself without losing sight of its core values.

Applying theoretical and empirical knowledge of societal dynamics, Menzies is writing a book entitled *The People-Serving Society*. The result of a "thought experiment," the book fleshes out the design of a society based on liberal, social democratic values. The result is not a perfect society, because creating a society that *works* requires making com-

promises that detract from perfection. Also, one of the underlying values is that of providing freedom of choice—and, wherever there is choice, some people will choose evil or wrongdoing. (The political and legal framework of the society will have to discourage or prohibit some behaviours.)

Within the context of a liberal, social democratic society, the people-serving society will attempt to deliver freedom, equality, and justice to all citizens. To achieve this goal, the society's political, legal, educational and economic institutions must work together in relative harmony and equilibrium. This kind of total system approach is necessary because spot reduction of social problems does not work.

Menzies's society is based on an innovating or rapidly changing market

economy that embraces technology. The goal of his society is to make sure that everyone, on the basis of his or her skills or aptitudes, has access to appropriate opportunities. The educational institutions need to be flexible enough to provide access to initial education and training as well as regular upgrading for people who want to move up the occupational hierarchy.

Underlying this thought experiment is the assumption that only by making use of the theories and findings of modern social science—with its wide scope and complexity—can one come up with a credible vision of where we should be, as a society.

Source: Based on manuscript draft, *The People-Serving Society*, by Ken Menzies.

---

shifted control of European societies to the capitalists. To Marx's way of thinking, then, new technology was only part of the Industrial Revolution; it was also a class revolution by which capitalists overthrew the agrarian elite to preside over the new industrial economy.

Industrialization also fostered the development of the proletariat. English landowners converted fields once tilled by serfs into grazing land for sheep to secure wool for the prospering textile mills. Forced from the land, serfs migrated to cities to work in factories, where they joined the burgeoning industrial proletariat. Marx envisioned these workers one day joining hands across national boundaries to form a unified class, setting the stage for historic confrontation, this time between capitalists and the exploited workers.

CAPITALISM AND CLASS CONFLICT

Much of Marx's analysis centres on destructive aspects of industrial capitalism—especially on the ways it promotes class conflict and alienation. In examining his views on these topics, we will come to see why he advocated the overthrow of capitalist societies.

"The history of all hitherto existing society is the history of class struggles." With this declaration, Marx

and his collaborator Friedrich Engels began their best-known statement, the *Manifesto of the Communist Party* (1972:335; orig. 1848). The idea of social class suffuses Marx's critique of capitalist society. Industrial capitalism, like earlier types of society, contains two major social classes—the dominant and the oppressed—reflecting the two basic positions in the productive system. Capitalists and proletarians are the historical descendants of masters and slaves in the ancient world and nobles and serfs in feudal systems. In each case, one class controls the other as productive property. Marx used the term **class conflict** (and sometimes *class struggle*) to refer to *antagonism between entire classes over the distribution of wealth and power in society*.

Class conflict, then, dates back to civilizations long gone. What distinguishes the conflict in capitalist society, Marx pointed out, is how out into the open it has come. Agrarian nobles and serfs, for all their differences, were bound together by long-standing traditions and a host of mutual obligations. Industrial capitalism dissolved those ties so that pride and honour were replaced by "naked self-interest" and the pursuit of profit. With no personal ties to its oppressors, Marx believed that the proletariat had little reason to stand for its subjugation.

But though industrial capitalism brought class conflict out into the open, Marx realized that fundamental social change would not come easily. First, workers must *become aware* of their shared oppression and see capitalism as its true cause. Second, they must organize and act to address their problems. This means workers must replace false consciousness with **class consciousness**, *the recognition by workers of their unity as a class in opposition to capitalists and, ultimately, to capitalism itself*. Because the inhumanity of early capitalism was plain for him to see, Marx concluded that industrial workers would inevitably rise up en masse to destroy industrial capitalism.

And what of the workers' adversaries, the capitalists? The capitalists' formidable wealth and power, protected by the institutions of society, might seem invulnerable. But Marx saw a weakness in the capitalist armour. Motivated by a desire for personal gain, capitalists fear the competition of other capitalists. Thus, Marx thought that capitalists would be reluctant to band together, even though they, too, share common interests. Furthermore, he reasoned, capitalists keep employees' wages low in their drive to maximize profits. This strategy, in turn, bolsters the resolve of workers to forge an alliance against them. In the long run, Marx surmised, capitalists would only contribute to their own undoing.

CAPITALISM AND ALIENATION

Marx also condemned capitalism for producing **alienation**, *the experience of isolation resulting from powerlessness*. Dominated by capitalists and dehumanized by their jobs (especially monotonous and repetitive factory work), proletarians find little satisfaction and feel individually powerless to improve their situation. Herein lies another contradiction of capitalist society: as human beings devise technology to gain power over the world, the capitalist economy increasingly assumes power over human beings.

In practice, workers amount to only a commodity, a source of labour, bought by capitalists and discarded when no longer needed. Marx cited four ways in which capitalism alienates workers.

1. **Alienation from the act of working.** Ideally, people work both to meet immediate needs and to develop their long-range potential. Capitalism, however, tends to deny workers a say in what they produce or how they produce it. Furthermore, much work is tedious, involving countless repetitions of routine tasks. The modern-day replacement of human labour by machines would hardly have surprised Marx; as far as he was concerned, capitalism had turned human beings into machines long ago.

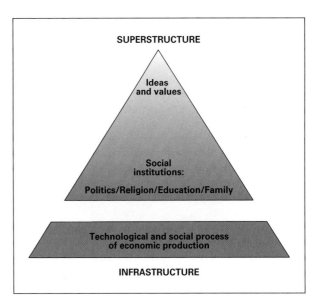

FIGURE 4–2 Karl Marx's Model of Society

This diagram illustrates Marx's materialist view that the process of economic production undergirds and shapes the entire society. Economic production involves both technology (industry, in the case of capitalism) and social relationships (for capitalism, the relationship between the capitalists, who control the process of economic production, and the workers, who are simply a source of labour). Upon this infrastructure, or foundation, are built the major social institutions as well as core cultural values and ideas. Taken together, these additional social elements represent the society's superstructure. Marx maintained that every part of a society operates in concert with the economic system.

2. **Alienation from the products of work.** The product of work belongs not to workers but to capitalists, who sell it for profit. Thus, Marx reasoned, the more workers invest of themselves in their work, the more they lose.

3. **Alienation from other workers.** Through work, Marx claimed, people build bonds of community. Industrial capitalism, however, renders work competitive rather than cooperative.

4. **Alienation from human potential.** Industrial capitalism alienates workers from their human potential. Marx argued that a worker "does not fulfill himself in his work but denies himself, has a feeling of misery rather than well-being, does not freely develop his physical and mental energies, but is physically exhausted and mentally debased. The worker, therefore, feels himself to be at home only during his leisure time, whereas at work he feels homeless" (1964a:124–25; orig. 1844). Industrial capitalism distorts work, which should express the best qualities in human beings, into a dull and dehumanizing experience.

Karl Marx, shown here at work on the Manifesto of the Communist Party *with his friend, benefactor, and collaborator Friedrich Engels, was surely the pioneering sociologist who had the greatest influence on the world as a whole. Through the second half of the last century, 1 billion people—nearly one-fifth of humanity—lived in societies organized on Marxist principles.*

Marx viewed alienation, in its various forms, as a barrier to social change. But he hoped that industrial workers would eventually overcome their alienation by uniting into a true social class, aware of the cause of their problems and galvanized to transform society.

REVOLUTION

The only way out of the trap of capitalism, contended Marx, was to deliberately refashion society. He envisioned a more humane and egalitarian productive system, one that would affirm rather than undermine our humanity. He called this system *socialism*. Marx knew well the obstacles to a socialist revolution; even so, he was disappointed that he never lived to see workers in England overthrow industrial capitalism. Still, convinced of the basic immorality of capitalist society, he was sure that, in time, the working majority would realize that they held the key to a better future in their own hands. This transformation would certainly be

revolutionary, perhaps even violent. What emerged from the workers' revolution, however, would be a co-operative socialist society intended to meet the needs of all.

The discussion of social stratification in Chapter 10 ("Social Stratification") reveals more about changes in industrial-capitalist societies since Marx's time and why the revolution he championed has not taken place. Later chapters also delve into why people in the societies of Eastern Europe recently revolted against established socialist governments. But, in his own time, Marx looked towards the future with hope (1972:362; orig. 1848): "The proletarians have nothing to lose but their chains. They have a world to win."

MAX WEBER:
THE RATIONALIZATION OF SOCIETY

With a broad understanding of law, economics, religion, and history, Max Weber (1864–1920) produced what many regard as the greatest individual contribution to sociology. This scholar, born to a prosperous family in Germany, generated ideas so wide ranging

 For biographical information about Max Weber, visit www.TheSociologyPage.com and click on his name in the Gallery of Sociologists. that we must limit ourselves to his vision of the evolution of modern society.

Weber's sociology reflects the philosophical approach known as *idealism*, which emphasizes how human ideas shape society. Weber understood the power of technology, and he shared many of Marx's ideas about social conflict. But he departed from Marx's materialist analysis, arguing that societies differ primarily in terms of the ways in which their members think about the world. For Weber, ideas—especially beliefs and values—are the keys to understanding society. Weber saw modern society as the product not just of new technology and capitalism, but of a new way of thinking. This emphasis on ideas contrasts with Marx's focus on material production, leading scholars to describe Weber's work as "a debate with the ghost of Karl Marx" (Cuff and Payne, 1979:73–74).

In all his work, Weber contrasted social patterns in different times and places. To sharpen comparisons, he relied on the **ideal type**, *an abstract statement of the essential characteristics of any social phenomenon*. He explored religion by contrasting the ideal "Protestant" with the ideal "Jew," "Hindu," and "Buddhist," knowing that these models precisely described no actual individuals. Note that Weber's use of the word *ideal* does not mean that something is "good" or "the best"; we could analyze "criminals" as well as "priests" as ideal types. We have already examined ideals, of course, in comparing "hunting-and-gathering societies" and "industrial societies," as well as "capitalism" and "socialism."

TWO WORLD VIEWS: TRADITION AND RATIONALITY

Rather than categorizing societies in terms of technology or productive systems, Max Weber highlighted differences in the ways people view the world, concluding that members of pre-industrial societies adhere to *tradition*, while people in industrial-capitalist societies endorse *rationality*.

By **tradition**, Weber meant *sentiments and beliefs passed from generation to generation*. Thus traditional societies are guided by the past. Their members evaluate particular actions as right and proper precisely because they have been accepted for so long.

People in modern societies take a different view of the world, argued Weber, embracing **rationality**, *deliberate, matter-of-fact calculation of the most efficient means to accomplish a particular goal*. Sentiment has no place in a rational world view, which treats tradition simply as one kind of information. Typically, modern people choose to think and act on the basis of present and future consequences, evaluating jobs, schooling, and even relationships in terms of what we put into them and what we expect to receive in return.

Weber viewed both the Industrial Revolution and capitalism as evidence of a historical surge of rationality. He used the phrase **rationalization of society** to denote *the historical change from tradition to rationality as the dominant mode of human thought*. Modern society, he concluded, has been "disenchanted," as scientific thinking and technology have swept away sentimental ties to the past.

The willingness to adopt the latest technology, then, is one good indicator of how rationalized a society is. Indicating the global pattern of rationalization, Global Map 4–1 shows where in the world personal computers are found. In general, the high-income countries of North America and Europe use these devices to the greatest degree, whereas they are quite rare in low-income nations.

Drawing on Weber's comparative perspective—and the data found in the map—we deduce that various societies place different values on technological advancement. What one society might herald as a breakthrough, another might deem unimportant, and a third might strongly oppose as a threat to tradition. In Canada today, for example, the Mennonites are guided by their traditions to staunchly oppose modern technology.

In Weber's view, technological innovation is promoted or hindered by the way people understand their world. He concluded that people in many societies have discovered keys to technological change, but only in the rational cultural climate of Western Europe did

Norbert Goenette's painting Pauper's Meal on a Winter's Day in Paris *suggests the numbing poverty common to migrants drawn to cities as the Industrial Revolution was getting underway. Karl Marx saw in such suffering a fundamental contradiction of modern society: industrial technology promises material plenty for all, but capitalism concentrates wealth in the hands of a few.*

people exploit these discoveries to spark the Industrial Revolution (1958a; orig. 1904–5).

IS CAPITALISM RATIONAL?

Is industrial capitalism a rational economic system? Here again, Weber and Marx came down on opposite sides of the issue. Weber considered industrial capitalism the essence of rationality, since capitalists pursue profit in eminently rational ways. Marx, however, dismissed capitalism as the antithesis of rationality, claiming that it failed to meet the basic needs of most of the people (Gerth and Mills, 1946).

WEBER'S GREAT THESIS: PROTESTANTISM AND CAPITALISM

But to look more closely at Weber's analysis, how did industrial capitalism emerge in the first place? Weber contended that industrial capitalism was the legacy of Calvinism—a Christian religious movement spawned by the Protestant Reformation. Calvinists,

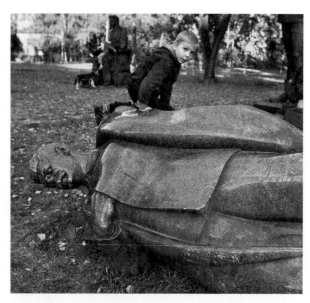

For years, the conventional wisdom in North America was that, once established, socialism stifled its opposition, rendering government immune to overthrow. But that notion collapsed along with the socialist regimes of Eastern Europe and the Soviet Union. The political transformation of this world region during the 1990s was symbolized, in city after city, by the removal of statues of Vladimir Lenin (1870–1924), architect of Soviet Marxism, and Josef Stalin (1879–1953), shown here.

Weber explained, approached life in a highly disciplined and rational way. Moreover, central to the religious doctrine of John Calvin (1509–64) was *predestination*, the idea that an all-knowing and all-powerful God has preordained some people for salvation and others for damnation. With everyone's fate set before birth, Calvinists believed that people could do nothing to alter their destiny. Nor could they even know what their future would be. Thus the lives of Calvinists were framed by hopeful visions of eternal salvation and anxious fears of unending damnation.

For such people, not knowing one's fate was intolerable. Calvinists gradually came to a resolution of sorts. Why shouldn't those chosen for glory in the next world, they reasoned, see signs of divine favour in this world? Such a conclusion prompted Calvinists to interpret worldly prosperity as a sign of God's grace. Anxious to acquire this reassurance, Calvinists threw themselves into a quest for success, applying rationality, discipline, and hard work to their tasks. This pursuit of riches was not for its own sake, of course, since self-indulgently spending money was clearly sinful. Calvinists also were little moved to share their wealth with the poor, because they saw poverty as a sign of God's rejection. Their duty was to carry forward what they held to be a personal calling from God.

As they reinvested their profits for greater success, Calvinists built the foundation of capitalism. They pi-

ously used wealth to generate more wealth, practised personal thrift, and eagerly embraced whatever technological advances would bolster their efforts.

These traits, Weber explained, distinguished Calvinism from other world religions. Catholicism, the traditional religion in most of Europe, gave rise to a passive, "otherworldly" view of life with hope of greater reward in the life to come. For Catholics, material wealth had none of the spiritual significance that so motivated Calvinists. And so it was, Weber concluded, that industrial capitalism became established primarily in areas of Europe where Calvinism had a strong hold.

Weber's study of Calvinism provides striking evidence of the power of ideas to shape society (versus Marx's contention that ideas merely reflect the process of economic production). But, always skeptical of simple explanations, Weber knew that industrial capitalism had many roots. In fact, one purpose of this research was to counter Marx's narrow explanation of modern society in strictly economic terms.

As religious fervour weakened among later generations of Calvinists, Weber concluded, success-seeking personal discipline remained strong. A *religious* ethic became simply a *work ethic*. From this point of view, industrial capitalism emerged as "disenchanted" religion, with wealth now valued for its own sake. It is revealing that "accounting," which to early Calvinists meant keeping a daily record of moral deeds, now refers simply to keeping track of money.

RATIONAL SOCIAL ORGANIZATION

Weber contended that by unleashing the Industrial Revolution and sparking the development of capitalism, rationality had defined the character of modern society. Rational social organization confers the following seven traits on today's social life.

1. **Distinctive social institutions.** Among hunters and gatherers, the family was the centre of virtually all activities. Gradually, however, other social institutions, including religious, political, and economic systems, broke away from family life. In modern societies, institutions of education and health care have also appeared. The separation of social institutions—each detailed in a later chapter—is a rational strategy to address human needs more efficiently.

2. **Large-scale organizations.** Modern rationality is exemplified by a proliferation of large-scale organizations. As early as the horticultural era, political officials oversaw religious observances, public works, and warfare. In medieval Europe, the Catholic Church grew larger still with thousands of officials. In modern, rational societies, government employees number in the millions and most people work for large organizations.

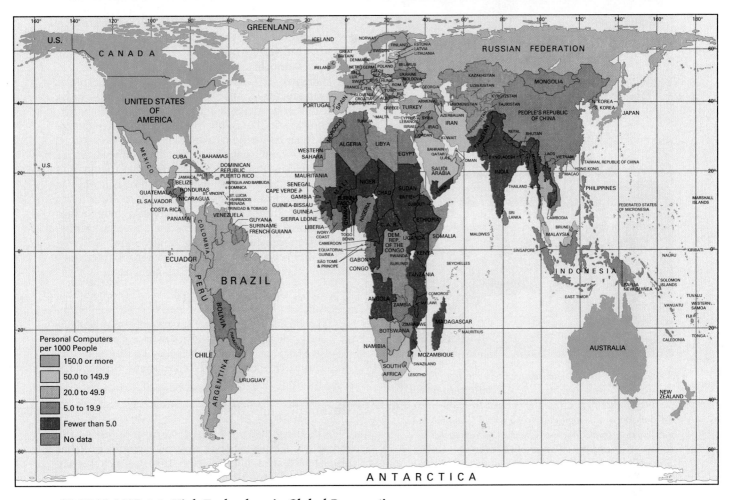

GLOBAL MAP 4–1 High Technology in Global Perspective

Countries with traditional cultures either cannot afford, ignore, or sometimes even resist technological innovation; nations with highly rationalized ways of life quickly embrace such changes. Personal computers, central to today's high technology, are numerous in high-income countries such as Canada and the United States. In low-income nations, by contrast, they are unknown to most people.

Source: *World Bank Atlas* by The World Bank. Copyright © 2001 by World Bank. Reproduced with permission of World Bank in textbook format via Copyright Clearance Center.

3. **Specialized tasks.** Unlike members of traditional societies, individuals in modern societies pursue a wide range of specialized activities. The enormous breadth of occupations can be seen in any city's Yellow Pages telephone directory.

4. **Personal discipline.** Modern society puts a premium on self-directed discipline. For early Calvinists, of course, such an approach to life was rooted in religious belief. Although now distanced

from its religious origins, discipline is still encouraged by cultural values such as achievement, success, and efficiency.

5. **Awareness of time.** In traditional societies, people measure time according to the rhythm of sun and seasons. Modern people, by contrast, schedule events precisely by the hour and minute. Interestingly, clocks began appearing in European cities some five hundred years ago just

A key element of North American culture has long been a "work ethic," with its roots in the Calvinist thinking that fascinated Max Weber. This Currier and Ives lithograph from 1875 makes a statement that people should shun the stock market, race track, lotteries, and even labour strikes as ways to improve their lives in favour of climbing the "Ladder of Fortune" based on personal virtue and individual effort.

as commerce was starting to expand; soon, people began to think (to borrow Benjamin Franklin's phrase) that "time is money."

6. **Technical competence.** Members of traditional societies evaluate one another largely on the basis of who they are—how they are joined to others in the web of kinship. Modern rationality, by contrast, prompts us to judge people according to what they are—that is, with an eye towards their skills and abilities.

7. **Impersonality.** Finally, in a rational society technical competence takes priority over close relationships, rendering the world impersonal. Modern social life can be viewed as the interplay of specialists concerned with particular tasks, rather than people broadly concerned with one another. Weber explained that we tend to devalue personal feelings and emotions as "irrational" because they often are difficult to control.

Rationality and Bureaucracy

Although the medieval church grew large, Weber argued that it remained largely traditional. Truly rational organizations, with the principal focus on efficiency, appeared only in the last few centuries. The organizational type Weber called *bureaucracy* became pronounced along with capitalism as an expression of modern rationality.

Chapter 7 ("Groups and Organizations") explains that bureaucracy is the model for modern businesses, government agencies, labour unions, and universities. For now, note that Weber considered this organizational form to be the clearest expression of a rational world view because its chief elements—offices, duties, and policies—are intended to achieve specific goals as efficiently as possible. By contrast, the inefficiency of traditional organization is reflected in its hostility to change. In short, Weber asserted that bureaucracy transformed all of society in the same way that industrialization transformed the economy.

Still, Weber emphasized that rational bureaucracy has a special affinity to capitalism. He wrote:

> Today, it is primarily the capitalist market economy that demands that the official business of public administration be discharged precisely, unambiguously, continuously, and with as much speed as possible. Normally, the very large capitalist enterprises are themselves unequalled models of strict bureaucratic organization. (1978:974; orig. 1921)

Rationality and Alienation

Max Weber joined with Karl Marx in recognizing the unparalleled efficiency of industrial capitalism. Weber also shared Marx's conclusion that modern society generates widespread alienation, although for different reasons. For Weber, the primary problem is not the economic inequality that so troubled Marx, but the stifling regulation and dehumanization that comes with expanding bureaucracy.

Bureaucracies, Weber warned, treat people as a series of cases rather than as unique individuals. In addition, working for large organizations demands highly specialized and often tedious routines. In the end, Weber envisioned modern society as a vast and growing system of rules seeking to regulate everything and threatening to crush the human spirit.

An irony found in the work of Marx reappears in Weber's thinking: rather than serving humanity, modern society turns on its creators and enslaves them. In language reminiscent of Marx's description of the human toll of industrial capitalism, Weber portrayed the modern individual as "only a small cog in a ceaselessly moving mechanism that prescribes to him an endlessly fixed routine of march" (1978:988; orig. 1921). Thus, although he could see the advantages of modern society, Weber ended his life deeply pessimistic. He feared that the rationalization of society would end up reducing people to robots.

EMILE DURKHEIM: SOCIETY AND FUNCTION

"To love society is to love something beyond us and something in ourselves." These are the words of Emile Durkheim (1858–1917), another founding architect of sociology. This curious phrase (1974:55; orig. 1924) condenses another highly influential vision of human society.

Durkheim is included in the Gallery of Sociologists at www.TheSociologyPage.com

STRUCTURE: SOCIETY BEYOND OURSELVES

Most significantly, Emile Durkheim recognized that society exists beyond ourselves. Society, as Durkheim saw it, is more than the individuals who compose it; society has a life of its own that stretches beyond our personal experiences. It was here long before we were born, it shapes us while we live, and it will remain long after we are gone. Patterns of human behaviour, Durkheim explained, are the basis of established *structures*: they are *social facts* that have an objective reality beyond the lives and perceptions of particular individuals. Cultural norms, values, religious beliefs—all endure as social facts.

Since society looms larger than individual lives, it has the power to shape our thoughts and actions, Durkheim noted. So studying individuals alone (as psychologists or biologists do) can never capture the essence of human experience. A classroom of first graders, a family sharing a meal, people milling about a country auction—all are examples of the countless situations that have an organization apart from any of the individuals who participate in them.

Once created by people, then, society takes on a momentum of its own, confronting its creators and demanding a measure of obedience. For our part, we experience society's influence as we come to see the order in our lives or as we face temptation and feel the tug of morality.

FUNCTION: SOCIETY AS SYSTEM

Having established that society has structure, Durkheim turned to the concept of *function*. The significance of any social fact, he explained, extends beyond individuals to how it helps society itself operate as a complex system.

To illustrate, consider crime. Most people think of lawbreaking as harmful acts that some individuals inflict on others. But, looking beyond individuals, Durkheim saw that crime has a vital function for the

Max Weber agreed with Karl Marx that modern society is alienating to the individual, but the two thinkers identified different causes of this estrangement. For Marx, economic inequality is the culprit; for Weber, the issue is pervasive and dehumanizing bureaucracy. George Tooker's painting Landscape *echoes Weber's sentiments.*

George Tooker, *Landscape with Figures*, 1963, egg tempera on gesso panel, 66 × 76 cm. Private collection.

ongoing life of society itself. As Chapter 9 ("Deviance") explains, only by recognizing and responding to acts as criminal do people construct and defend morality, which gives purpose and meaning to our collective life. For this reason, Durkheim rejected the common view of crime as "pathological." On the contrary, he concluded, crime is quite "normal" for the most basic of reasons: a society could not exist without it (1964a, orig. 1895; 1964b, orig. 1893).

PERSONALITY: SOCIETY IN OURSELVES

Durkheim contended that society is not only "beyond ourselves," it is also "in ourselves." Each of us, in short, builds a personality by internalizing social facts. How we act, think, and feel—our essential humanity—is drawn from the society that nurtures us. Moreover, Durkheim explained, society regulates human beings through moral discipline. Durkheim held that human beings are naturally insatiable and in constant danger of being overpowered by our own desires: "The more one has, the more one wants, since satisfactions received only stimulate instead of filling needs" (1966:248; orig. 1897). Having given us life, then, society must also rein us in.

Nowhere is the need for societal regulation better illustrated than in Durkheim's study of suicide (1966; orig. 1897), detailed in Chapter 1 ("The Sociological

Durkheim's observation that people with weak social bonds are prone to self-destructive behaviour stands as stark evidence of the power of society to shape individual lives. When rock-and-roll singers become famous, they are wrenched out of familiar life patterns and existing relationships, sometimes with deadly results. The history of rock and roll contains many tragic stories of this kind, including (from left) Janis Joplin's, Jimi Hendrix's, and Jim Morrison's deaths by drug overdose (1970–71) and Kurt Cobain's suicide (1994).

Perspective"). Why is it that, over the years, rock stars have been so vulnerable to self-destruction? Durkheim had the answer long before anyone made electric music: it is the least regulated categories of people that suffer the highest rates of suicide. The greater licence afforded to those who are young, rich, and famous exacts a high price in terms of the risk of suicide.

Modernity and Anomie

Compared to traditional societies, modern societies impose fewer restrictions on everyone. Durkheim acknowledged the advantages of modern freedom, but he warned of a rise in **anomie**, *a condition in which society provides little moral guidance to individuals*. What so many celebrities describe as "almost being destroyed by their fame," is one extreme example of the corrosive effects of anomie. Sudden fame or winning the lottery tears people away from their families and familiar routines, disrupting society's support and regulation of an individual, sometimes with fatal results. Durkheim instructs us, therefore, that the desires of the individual must be balanced by the claims and guidance of society—a balance that has become precarious in the modern world.

EVOLVING SOCIETIES: THE DIVISION OF LABOUR

Like Marx and Weber, Durkheim witnessed firsthand the rapid social transformation of Europe during the nineteenth century, noting sweeping evolution in the forms of social organization.

In pre-industrial societies, explained Durkheim, strong tradition operates as the social cement that binds people together. In fact, what he termed the *collective conscience* is so strong that the community moves quickly to punish anyone who dares to challenge con-

ventional ways of life. Durkheim called this system **mechanical solidarity**, meaning *social bonds, based on shared morality, that unite members of pre-industrial societies*. In practice, then, mechanical solidarity springs from likeness. Durkheim described these bonds as "mechanical" because people feel a more or less automatic sense of belonging together.

Durkheim considered the decline of mechanical solidarity to be a defining trait of modern society. But this does not mean that society dissolves; rather, modernity generates a new type of solidarity that rushes into the void left by discarded traditions. Durkheim called this new social integration **organic solidarity**, defined as *social bonds, based on specialization, that unite members of industrial societies*. Where solidarity was once rooted in likeness, in short, it now flows from differences among people who find that their specialized pursuits—as plumbers, midwives, or sociology instructors—make them rely on one another.

For Durkheim, then, the key dimension of change is a society's expanding **division of labour**, or *specialized economic activity*. As Max Weber explained, modern societies specialize in order to promote efficiency. Durkheim fills in the picture by showing us that members of modern societies count on the efforts of tens of thousands of others—most of them complete strangers—to secure the goods and services they need every day.

So modernity rests far less on *moral consensus* (the foundation of traditional societies) and far more on *functional interdependence*. That is, as members of modern societies, we depend more and more on people we trust less and less. Why, then, should we put our faith in people we hardly know and whose beliefs may differ radically from our own? Durkheim's answer: "Because we can't live without them." In a world in which morality sometimes seems like so much shifting sand, then, we confront what might be called "Durkheim's

The Information Revolution:
What Would Durkheim, Weber, and Marx Think?

Who can doubt that techno-logical change is now re-shaping society? If they were alive today, the founding sociologists discussed in this chapter would be eager observers of the current scene. Imagine for a moment the kinds of questions Emile Durkheim, Max Weber, and Karl Marx might ask about the societal effects of computer technology.

To Emile Durkheim, what stands out about modern society is its increasing division of labour, as people pursue a host of specialized occupations. Durkheim would be quick to wonder if new information technology is pushing specialization even further. And there is good reason to think that it is. Because electronic communication (say, a website home page) gives any individual a vast market (there are already more than 100 million computers that can access a home page), people can specialize far more than they would working in a limited geographical area. For example, while most small-town lawyers have a general practice, an information-age lawyer (living anywhere) could become a specialist in, say, prenuptial agree-

ments or electronic copyright law. Indeed, as the electronic age unfolds, there is already a rapidly increasing number of highly specialized "micro-businesses" in all fields, some of which end up becoming quite large!

Max Weber, of course, held that modern societies are distinctive because their members share a rational world view. And to Weber, nothing captured this way of thinking better than expanding bureaucracy. But will bureaucracy continue to dominate the social scene in the next century? Here is one reason to think it may not: while it may make sense for organizations to apply rules and regulations to workers performing the kinds of routine tasks that were common in the industrial era, more and more work in the post-industrial era involves imagination. Think, for instance, of work designing homes, composing music, or writing software. Certainly one cannot regulate creativity in the same way as, say, assembling automobiles on an assembly line. Perhaps this difficulty with regulation explains why many high-technology companies have done away with the dress codes and even the time clocks found in facto-

ries of the past. In short, the character of "rational organization" may well be changing along with the nature of work.

Finally, what might Karl Marx make of the Information Revolution? To Marx, you will recall, the earlier Industrial Revolution was really a class revolution, which soon allowed the owners of industry to dominate society. As we enter the Information Age, Marx would probably question whether a new symbolic elite is coming to dominate society. Some analysts point out, for example, that film and television writers, producers, and performers now enjoy enormous wealth, international prestige, and unprecedented power (Lichter et al., 1990). Similarly, just as those without industrial skills were held at the bottom of the class system in decades past, so people without symbolic skills are likely to become the new "underclass" in the next century.

Durkheim, Weber, and Marx greatly aided our understanding of industrial societies. As we move into the post-industrial age, there will be plenty of room for new generations of sociologists to carry on!

dilemma": the technological power and expansive personal freedom of modern society come only at the cost of receding morality and the ever-present danger of anomie.

Like Marx and Weber, Durkheim had misgivings about the direction society was taking. But of the three, Durkheim was the most optimistic. Confidence in the future sprang from his hope that we could enjoy greater freedom and privacy while creating for ourselves the social regulation that had once been forced on us by tradition.

Finally, how might Durkheim respond to the increasing importance of new information technology in today's world? The "Exploring Cyber-Society" box argues that Durkheim—and the other theorists we have

considered in this chapter—would probably have much to say about the Information Revolution.

CRITICAL EVALUATION: FOUR VISIONS OF SOCIETY

This chapter opened with several important queries about human societies. We will conclude by summarizing the answers provided by each of the four visions of society.

What Holds Societies Together?

How is something as complex as society possible? The Lenskis claim that members of a society are united by shared culture and that cultural patterns vary according to a society's level of technological development. But they note that inequality divides a society as technology becomes more complex; social stratification diminishes to some extent with the onset of industrialization. Marx spotlighted social division, not unity, treating class conflict as the hallmark of human societies throughout history. From his point of view, elites may force an uneasy peace between the classes, but true social unity would emerge only if production were to become a truly cooperative endeavour. To Weber, members of a society share a distinctive world view. Just as traditional beliefs joined people together in the past, so modern societies have created rational, large-scale organizations that fuse people's lives. Finally, Durkheim made solidarity the focus of his work, contrasting the morality-based mechanical solidarity of pre-industrial societies with modern society's organic solidarity based on specialization.

How Have Societies Changed?

According to the Lenski's model of sociocultural evolution, societies differ primarily in terms of changing technology. Modern society stands out in this regard because of its enormous productive power. Karl Marx also stressed historical differences in productive systems, yet he pointed to the persistence of social conflict throughout human history (except perhaps among simple hunters and gatherers). For Marx, modern society is distinctive only because it brings that conflict out into the open. Max Weber looked at this question from another perspective, tracing changes in the way people look at the world. Pre-industrial societies, he claimed, are guided by tradition, while modern societies espouse a rational world view. Finally, for Emile Durkheim, traditional societies are characterized by mechanical solidarity based on moral consensus. In industrial societies, mechanical solidarity gives way to organic solidarity based on productive specialization.

Why Do Societies Change?

As the Lenskis see it, social change is a matter of technological innovation that, over time, transforms an entire society. Marx's materialist approach pointed to the struggle between social classes as the "engine of history," pushing societies towards revolutionary reorganization. Weber's idealist view argued that modes of thought also contribute to social change. He demonstrated how a new world view—rational Calvinism—bolstered the Industrial Revolution and reshaped much of modern society. Finally, Durkheim pointed to an expanding division of labour as the key dimension of social change.

Like a kaleidoscope that shows us different patterns as we turn it, these four approaches reveal an array of insights into society. Yet no one approach is, in an absolute sense, right or wrong. Society is exceedingly complex, and we gain the richest understanding from using all of these visions, as we do in the "Controversy & Debate" box.

SUMMARY

Gerhard and Jean Lenski

1. Sociocultural evolution explores the societal consequences of technological advancements.
2. The earliest hunting-and-gathering societies were composed of a small number of family-centred nomads. Such societies have all but vanished from the earth.
3. Horticulture began some ten thousand years ago as people devised hand tools for the cultivation of crops. Pastoral societies domesticate animals and engage in extensive trade.
4. Agriculture, about five thousand years old, is large-scale cultivation using animal-drawn plows. This technology allows societies to expand into vast empires, characterized by higher productivity, greater specialization, and increasing social inequality.
5. Industrialization began 250 years ago in Europe, as people harnessed advanced energy sources to power sophisticated machinery.
6. In post-industrial societies, production shifts from material things to information: computers and other information-based technology replace the heavy machinery of the industrial era.

Karl Marx

7. Marx's materialist analysis pointed out historical and contemporary conflict between social classes.
8. Conflict in "ancient" societies involved masters and slaves; in agrarian societies, it places nobles and serfs in opposition; in industrial-capitalist societies, capitalists confront the proletariat.
9. Industrial capitalism alienates workers in four ways: from the act of working, from the products of work, from fellow workers, and from human potential.
10. Once workers had overcome their own false consciousness, Marx believed they would overthrow capitalists and the industrial-capitalist system.

Max Weber

11. Weber's idealist approach revealed that modes of thought have a powerful effect on society.

Is Our Society Getting Better or Worse?

Optimism has been a defining trait of Canadian society. As time goes on, life gets better—or so we thought. But a survey by Alberta sociologist Reginald Bibby suggests that optimism may be waning. Between 1975 and 1995, the proportion of people who believed that the "lot of the average person" is getting worse rose from 45 to 70 percent; the proportion who believed that racial and cultural minorities are experiencing discrimination increased from 55 percent in 1980 to 67 percent in 1995; and, in one decade (1985 to 1995), the proportion of respondents who agreed that "values in Canada have been changing for the worse" rose from 54 to 74 percent. In addition, when asked to identify their major concerns, Canadians placed the national debt, unemployment, and the economy at the top of their list—followed by crime, government incompetence, child abuse, AIDS, delinquency, family breakdown, and violence (Bibby, 1995). Clearly, in 1995, with the economy in a slump and Quebec coming close to voting "yes" on breaking up our country, Canadians were worried.

What's going on here? After all, there are good reasons for optimism about Canada. Since the beginning of this century, educational attainment has increased dramatically so that, proportionately, more of us are university and college graduates. In addition, after taking inflation into account, average Canadians have enjoyed higher incomes and greater buying power. Almost every household has a telephone, television, and refrigerator, and more than 80 percent have automobiles, VCRs, and microwaves. Most importantly, while people born in 1900

lived an average of forty-seven years, children born today can expect to live about thirty years longer.

But some trends of the last decade or two are troubling. Members of our society are less certain that hard work pays off. Despite an increase in two-income couples, family earnings have increased only slightly. At the same time, divorce rates are climbing while marriage rates are decreasing, and a perception of rising crime rates has undermined people's sense of personal safety, even in their own homes. For 46 percent of Canadians, crime is a "very serious" concern, and 87 percent think the courts should be tougher on law-breakers (Bibby, 1995). Our relative affluence, coupled with our capacity to move farther and faster than ever before, seems to have eroded our sense of responsibility for others, unleashing a wave of individualism accompanied by a dramatic move to the right of the political spectrum.

Despite recent trends, a large and slightly increasing majority of Canadians claim to be "very happy" or "pretty happy"—87 and 92 percent in 1975 and 1995—and even more claim to have marriages in the two "happy" categories—92 and 94 percent in 1975 and 1995 (Bibby, 1995:5). And since 9/11, Canada's economy has outperformed that of the United States: we have created hundreds of thousands of jobs, while the Americans have lost ground. Even our loonie has soared to unaccustomed heights. The stock market is finally recovering from the dot.com crash and real estate is booming. Things are looking good, eh!

So, which is it? Is Canadian society getting better or worse?

The theorists highlighted in this chapter shed some light on this question. It is easy to equate "high tech" with progress but, the Lenskis maintain, we should make such assumptions cautiously; history shows us that although advancing technology does offer real advantages, it is no guarantee of a "better" life. Marx, Weber, and Durkheim also acknowledged the growing affluence of societies over time, yet each offered a pointed criticism of modern society's dangerous tendency towards individualism. For Marx, capitalism is the culprit, elevating money to godlike status and fostering a culture of selfishness. Weber's analysis claims that the modern spirit of rationality wears away traditional ties of kinship and neighbourhood while expanding bureaucracy, which both manipulates and isolates people. In Durkheim's view, functional interdependence joins members of modern societies, who are less and less able to establish a common moral framework within which to judge right and wrong. Technological advances, it seems, are offset by the loss of human community. How well, one might ask, do the insights of these theorists describe Canadian society?

Continue the debate . . .

1. *Do you think life in Canada is getting better or worse? Why?*

2. *Under what conditions are we optimistic about the future of our country?*

3. *How optimistic are you and your peers about your personal futures? What factors determine your levels of optimism?*

---

12. Weber drew a sharp contrast between the tradition of pre-industrial societies and the rationality of modern, industrial societies.

13. Weber feared that rationality, embodied in efficiency-conscious bureaucratic organizations, would stifle human creativity.

Emile Durkheim

14. Durkheim explained that society has an objective existence apart from individuals.

15. His approach related social elements to the larger society through their functions.

16. Societies require solidarity: traditional societies are fused by mechanical solidarity based on moral consensus; modern societies depend on organic solidarity based on the division of labour or productive specialization.

CRITICAL-THINKING QUESTIONS

1. Present evidence that supports and contradicts the notion that technological advance amounts to "progress."

2. Contrast Marx's concept of materialism with Weber's idealism as general approaches to understanding society.

3. Both Marx and Weber were concerned with modern society's ability to alienate people. How are their approaches different? Contrast their notions of alienation with Durkheim's concept of anomie.

4. How do these visions of society explain the changing standing of women? What issues might be raised by a feminist critique of these theories?

APPLICATIONS AND EXERCISES

1. Hunting-and-gathering people mused over stars, and we still know the constellations in terms that were relevant to them—mostly animals and hunters. As a way of revealing what is important to our way of life, write a short paper imagining what meaning we would impose on the stars if we were beginning the process from scratch.

2. Look around your home for every device with a computer chip. How many did you find? Are you surprised?

3. Rent or watch on television an old *Tarzan* movie or another film that portrays technologically simpler people. How are they portrayed in the film?

4. Over the next few days, ask a dozen people over the age of twenty-five whether they think our society is getting better or worse, and why they hold their opinions. See how much agreement you find.

 ## SITES TO SEE

www.macionis.com
or
www.TheSociologyPage.com
Biographical sketches of Marx, Weber, Durkheim, and other social thinkers are found on this website, as well as more than fifty weblinks to sociological journals and other sources of data and information in the Links Library.

www2.pfeiffer.edu/~lridener/DSS/DEADSOC.HTML
Visit the Dead Sociologists Society to learn more about Marx, Weber, Durkheim, and other sociologists.

www.hewett.norfolk.sch.uk/curric/soc/durkheim/durk.htm
The *Durkheim Pages* contain a biography, critical summaries of his major works, some full texts, reviews, a glossary, a bibliography of primary and secondary sources, and more.

www.marxists.org/archive/marx/
http://csf.colorado.edu:80/psn/marx/index.html
These sites contain information on the collected works of Marx and Engels, biographical material, and letters of correspondence.

www2.pfeiffer.edu/~lridener/DSS/Weber/PECAP.HTML
In this long excerpt from *The Protestant Ethic and the Spirit of Capitalism*—one of many documents from the Dead Sociologists Society site—Max Weber attempts to define his concept of "the spirit of capitalism."

http://e-com.ic.gc.ca/english/fastfacts/435.html
Preparing Canada for a Digital World is the final report of the Information Highway Advisory Council, offering advice to policymakers on five key issues: economic growth, the Internet, access, Canadian content, and learning and the workplace.

www.fordham.edu/halsall/mod/modsbook14.html

This page explores the social, political, and technological dimensions of the Industrial Revolution and also features literary responses to these developments.

www.gwu.edu/~ccps/

Visit the website for the Communitarian Network, an organization concerned with balancing modern individuality with traditional social responsibility.

STUDY TOOLS

For more study tools to help you with your next exam, be sure to check out the Companion Website at **www.pearsoned.ca/macionis**, as well as Chapter 4 in your Study Guide.

INVESTIGATE WITH CONTENTSELECT

Follow the instructions found on page 25 of this textbook to access ContentSelect™ at the Research Navigator™ website. Once at the site, enter your LOGINID and Password. Then enter keywords such as "Karl Marx," "horticulture," and "Industrial Revolution," and the search engine will supply relevant and recent scholarly and popular press publications.

CHAPTER
5

Andrew Macara (1944– , English)
Footballers, Kos, 1993
Oil on canvas, 63.5 × 76.2 cm. Private Collection/The Bridgeman Art Library.

SOCIALIZATION

On a cold winter day in 1938, a social worker walked anxiously to the door of a rural Pennsylvania farmhouse. Investigating a case of possible child abuse, the social worker discovered a five-year-old girl hidden in a second-floor storage room. The child, whose name was Anna, was wedged into an old chair with her arms tied above her head so that she could not move. She was dressed in filthy garments, and her arms and legs—looking like matchsticks—were so frail that she could not use them.

Anna's situation can only be described as tragic. She was born in 1932 to an unmarried and mentally impaired woman of twenty-six who lived with her father. Enraged by his daughter's "illegitimate" motherhood, the grandfather did not even want the child in his house. Anna therefore spent her first six months

in various institutions. But her mother was unable to pay for such care, so Anna returned to the hostile home of her grandfather.

At this point, her ordeal intensified. To lessen the grandfather's anger, Anna's mother moved the child to the attic room, where she received little attention and just enough milk to keep her alive. There she stayed—day after day, month after month, with essentially no human contact—for five long years.

Upon learning of the discovery of Anna, sociologist Kingsley Davis (1940) travelled immediately to see the child. He found her at a county home, where local authorities had taken her. Davis was appalled by Anna's condition. She was emaciated and feeble. Unable to laugh, smile, speak, or even show anger, she was completely unresponsive, as if alone in an empty world.

SOCIAL EXPERIENCE: THE KEY TO OUR HUMANITY

Here is a deplorable but instructive case of a human being deprived of virtually all social contact. Although physically alive, Anna hardly seemed human. Her plight reveals that, isolated in this way, an individual develops scarcely any capacity for thought, emotion, and meaningful behaviour. In short, without social experience, an individual is more an object than a *person*.

This chapter explores what Anna was deprived of—the means by which we become fully human. This process is **socialization**, *the lifelong social experience by which individuals develop their human potential and learn patterns of their culture.* Unlike other living species whose behaviour is biologically set, human beings rely on social experience to learn the nuances of their culture in order to survive.

Social experience is also the foundation of **personality**, *a person's fairly consistent patterns of thinking,* *feeling, and acting.* We build a personality by internalizing our social surroundings. As personality develops, we participate in a culture while remaining, in some respects, distinct individuals. But in the absence of social experience, as the case of Anna shows, personality does not emerge at all.

Because societies exist beyond the life span of any person, each generation must teach something of its way of life to the next. Socialization, then, amounts to the ongoing process of cultural transmission. In short, social experience is the vital foundation of our lives—individually and collectively.

HUMAN DEVELOPMENT: NATURE AND NURTURE

Helpless at birth, human infants depend on others for care and nourishment as well as learning. Although Anna's short life makes this very clear, a century ago most people mistakenly believed that human behaviour was the product of biological imperatives.

Human infants display various reflexes—biologically based behaviour patterns that enhance survival. The sucking reflex, which actually begins before birth, enables the infant to obtain nourishment. The grasping reflex, triggered by placing a finger on the infant's palm and causing the hand to close, helps the infant maintain contact with a parent and, later on, grasp objects. The Moro reflex, activated by startling the infant, causes the infant to swing both arms outward and then bring them together across the chest. This action, which disappears after several months of life, probably developed among our evolutionary ancestors so that a falling infant could grasp the body hair of a parent.

Charles Darwin: The Role of Nature

Charles Darwin, whose groundbreaking theory of evolution is summarized in Chapter 3 ("Culture"), held that each species evolves over thousands of generations as genetic variations enhance survival and reproduction. Biologically rooted traits that enhance survival emerge as a species' "nature." As Darwin's fame grew, people assumed that humans, like other forms of life, had a fixed, instinctive "nature" as well.

Such notions are still with us. People sometimes claim, for example, that our economic system is a reflection of "instinctive human competitiveness" (known as social Darwinism), that some people are "born criminals," or that women are "naturally" more emotional while men are "inherently" more rational (Witkin-Lanoil, 1984). We often describe familiar personality traits as *human nature* as if people were born with them, just as we are born with five senses. More accurately, however, our human nature leads us to create and learn cultural traits, as we shall see.

People trying to understand cultural diversity also misconstrued Darwin's thinking. Centuries of world exploration and empire building taught Western Europeans that the behaviour of people around the world differs from their own. They attributed such contrasts to biology rather than to culture. It was easy to conclude that members of technologically simple societies were biologically less evolved and less human. Such self-serving and ethnocentric views helped justify colonial practices, including land seizures and slavery, since it is easier to exploit others if you are convinced that they are not truly human.

The Social Sciences: The Role of Nurture

In the twentieth century, social scientists launched a broad attack on biological explanations of human behaviour. Psychologist John B. Watson (1878–1958) devised a theory called *behaviourism*, which held that specific behaviour patterns are not instinctive but learned. Thus, people the world over have the same claim to humanity, Watson insisted; humans differ only in their cultural environment. For Watson, "human nature" was infinitely malleable:

> Give me a dozen healthy infants . . . and my own specified world to bring them up in, and I will guarantee to take any one at random and train him to become any type of specialist that I might select—doctor, lawyer, artist, merchant, chief, and yes, even beggar-man and thief—regardless of his talents, penchants, tendencies, abilities, vocations, and race of his ancestors. (1930:104)

Anthropologists weighed in on this debate as well, showing how variable the world's cultures are. An outspoken proponent of the "nurture" view, anthropologist Margaret Mead summed up the evidence: "The differences between individuals who are members of different cultures, like the differences between individuals within a culture, are almost entirely to be laid to differences in conditioning, especially during early childhood, and this conditioning is culturally determined" (1963:280; orig. 1935).

The research on the relationship between race and intelligence by Professor Philippe Rushton of the University of Western Ontario is an example of mod-

The personalities we develop depend largely on the environment in which we live. As William Kurelek shows in this painting, Prairie Childhood, *based on his childhood in the Alberta prairies, a young person's life on a farm is often characterized by periods of social isolation and backbreaking work. How would such a boy's personality be likely to differ from that of his wealthy cousin raised in Montreal?*

William Kurelek, *Prairie Childhood*, by permission of the Estate of William Kurelek, courtesy of the Isaacs Gallery of Toronto.

ern social Darwinism. In 1989 Rushton claimed to have demonstrated scientifically that "Orientals" (Rushton's term) were more intelligent than whites or Blacks, and that Blacks were the least intelligent of the three races. Widespread outrage in response to the publication of Rushton's work indicates the dramatic decline in the acceptance of social Darwinist theories today. Even the conceptualization of the hypothesis that there is a relationship between race and behaviour is seen today as racist.

Most social scientists are cautious about describing any type of behaviour as instinctive. Even sociobiology, examined in Chapter 3 ("Culture"), holds that human behaviour is primarily guided by the surrounding culture. Of course, this does not mean that biology plays *no* part in human behaviour. Human life, after all, depends on the functioning of the body. We also know that children share many biological traits with their parents, especially physical characteristics such as height, weight, hair and eye colour, and facial features. Intelligence and various personality characteristics (for example, how one reacts to stimulation or frustration) probably have some genetic component, as does the potential to excel in such activities as art and music. But the inherited potential depends on development of opportunity. Indeed, biologists point out that unless children *use* their brains in various ways in early life, the brain itself will not fully develop (Herrnstein, 1973; Plomin and Foch, 1980; Goldsmith, 1983; Begley, 1995).

In sum, without denying the importance of nature, the evidence shows that nurture is far more important in determining human behaviour. Rather than thinking of nature as opposing nurture, it is more correct to say that nurture—social experience and the creation of culture—is our nature. For humans, then, nature and nurture are inseparable.

SOCIAL ISOLATION

For obvious ethical reasons, researchers cannot subject human beings to experimental isolation. Consequently, much of what we know about this issue comes from rare cases of abused children like Anna. Researchers have, however, studied the impact of social isolation on animals.

Effects of Social Isolation on Nonhuman Primates

Psychologists Harry Harlow and Margaret Harlow (1962) conducted a classic investigation of the effects of social isolation on nonhuman primates. They observed the consequences of various conditions of isolation on rhesus monkeys, whose behaviour is in some ways remarkably similar to that of humans.

The Harlows found that complete social isolation for even six months (with adequate nutrition) seriously disturbed the monkeys' development. When these monkeys subsequently returned to their group, they were anxious, passive, and fearful.

The Harlows then isolated infant rhesus monkeys, but provided an artificial "mother" made of wire mesh with a wooden head and the nipple of a feeding tube where the breast would be. These monkeys survived but subsequently displayed emotional damage. When the artificial "mother" was covered with soft terry cloth, the infant monkeys would cling to it, apparently deriving emotional benefit from the closeness. Later on these monkeys revealed less emotional distress. The Harlows thus concluded that normal emotional development requires affectionate cradling as part of parent-infant interaction.

The Harlows made two other discoveries. As long as they were surrounded by other infants, monkeys were not adversely affected by the absence of a mother. This finding suggests that deprivation of social experience, rather than the absence of a specific parent, is what causes devastating effects. Furthermore, lesser periods of social isolation—up to about three months—caused emotional distress, but only temporarily. The damage of short-term isolation, then, can be overcome; longer-term isolation, however, appears to inflict on monkeys irreversible emotional and behavioural damage.

Effects of Social Isolation on Children

Unusual and tragic cases of children isolated by abusive family members demonstrate the catastrophic effects of depriving human beings of social experience. We will review three such cases.

Anna: The rest of the story. The case of Anna, described earlier, is the best-known instance of the extended social isolation of a human infant. After her discovery, Anna benefited from intense social contact and soon showed improvement. Visiting her ten days later, Kingsley Davis (1940) noted that she was more alert and even smiled with obvious pleasure. During the next year, Anna made slow but steady progress, showing greater interest in other people and gradually learning to walk. After a year and a half, she could feed herself and play with toys.

Consistent with the observations of the Harlows, however, it was becoming apparent that Anna's five years of social isolation had left her permanently damaged. At the age of eight her mental and social development was still less than that of a two-year-old. Not until she was almost ten did she begin to use words. Of course, since Anna's mother was mentally retarded, perhaps Anna was similarly disadvantaged. The riddle was never solved, because Anna died at age ten from a blood disorder, possibly related to her years of abuse (Davis, 1940, 1947).

Another case: Isabelle. A second, similar case involved another girl, found at about the same time as Anna and under strikingly similar circumstances. After more than six years of virtual isolation, this girl—known as Isabelle—displayed the same lack of human responsiveness. Unlike Anna, though, Isabelle benefited from a special learning program directed by psychologists. Within a week, Isabelle was attempting to speak, and a year and a half later, her vocabulary included nearly two thousand words. The psychologists concluded that intensive effort had propelled Isabelle through six years of normal development in only two

years. By the age of fourteen, Isabelle was attending sixth-grade classes, apparently on her way to an approximately normal life (Davis, 1947).

A third case: Genie. Yet another case of childhood isolation involved a thirteen-year-old California girl victimized in a host of ways by her parents from the age of two (Curtiss, 1977; Pines, 1981). Genie's ordeal included extended periods of being locked alone in a garage. Upon discovery, her condition was similar to that of Anna and Isabelle. Genie was emaciated (weighing only 26.8 kg) and had the mental development of a one-year-old. She could not walk, chew food, speak, or even control her bladder. She received intensive treatment by specialists and thrived physically.

 Read a transcript of the PBS *Nova* television program about the life of Genie at www.pbs.org/wgbh/nova/transcripts/2112gchild.html Yet even after years of care, her ability to use language remained that of a young child.

Conclusion. All the evidence points to the crucial role of social experience in personality development. Human beings are resilient creatures, sometimes able to recover from even the crushing experience of abuse and isolation. But there is a point—precisely when is unclear from the limited number of cases—at which social isolation or other abuse in infancy results in irreparable developmental damage.

UNDERSTANDING THE SOCIALIZATION PROCESS

Socialization is a complex, lifelong process. The following sections highlight the work of six men and women who have made lasting contributions to our understanding of human development.

SIGMUND FREUD: THE ELEMENTS OF PERSONALITY

Sigmund Freud (1856–1939) lived in Vienna at a time when most Europeans considered human behaviour to be biologically fixed. Trained as a physician, Freud gradually turned to the study of personality and eventually developed the celebrated theory of psychoanalysis. Many aspects of this work bear directly on our understanding of socialization.

 For a biographical sketch of Sigmund Freud, see the Gallery of Sociologists at www.TheSociologyPage.com

Basic Human Needs

Freud contended that biology plays an important part in social development, although not in terms of the simple instincts that guide other species. Humans,

Freud argued, respond to two general needs or drives. First, humans have a basic need for bonding, which he called the life instinct, or *eros* (from the Greek god of love). Second, opposing this need is an aggressive drive, which Freud termed the death instinct, or *thanatos* (from the Greek meaning "death"). Freud postulated that these opposing forces, operating primarily at the level of the unconscious mind, generate deeply rooted inner tensions.

Freud's Model of Personality

Freud incorporated basic drives and the influence of society into a model of personality with three parts: id, ego, and superego. The **id** represents *the human being's basic drives*, which are unconscious and demand immediate satisfaction. (The word *id* is Latin for "it," suggesting the tentative way in which Freud explored the unconscious mind.) Rooted in our biology, the id is present at birth, making a newborn a bundle of needs demanding attention, touch, and food. Since society does not tolerate such a self-centred orientation, one of the first words a child hears is "no."

To avoid frustration, the child learns to approach the world realistically. This accomplishment forms the second component of the personality, the **ego** (Latin for "I"), which is *a person's conscious efforts to balance innate, pleasure-seeking drives with the demands of society*. The ego arises as we gain awareness of our distinct existence; it reaches fruition as we come to understand that we cannot have everything we want.

Finally, the human personality develops the **superego** (Latin meaning "above" or "beyond" the ego), which is *the operation of culture within the individual in the form of internalized values and norms*. With the emergence of the superego, we can see why we cannot have everything we want. The superego consists of cultural values and norms—internalized in the form of conscience—that define moral limits. The superego emerges as children recognize parental control: it matures as they learn that their own behaviour—in fact, everyone's behaviour—reflects a broader system of cultural demands.

Personality Development

The id-centred child first encounters the world as a bewildering array of physical sensations. With gradual development of the superego, however, the child's comprehension extends beyond pleasure and pain to include the moral concepts of right and wrong. Initially, in other words, children can feel good only in the physical sense; but after three or four years, they feel good or bad as they evaluate their own behaviour according to cultural standards.

Conflict between id and superego is ongoing; however, in a well-adjusted person, these opposing forces are managed by the ego. Unresolved conflicts, especially during childhood, typically result in personality disorders later on.

As the source of superego, culture operates to control human drives, a process Freud termed *repression*. All culture involves repression, since any society must coerce people to look beyond themselves. Often the competing demands of self and society are resolved through compromise. This process, which Freud called *sublimation*, transforms fundamentally selfish drives into socially acceptable activities. Sexual urges, for example, may lead to marriage, just as aggression gives rise to competitive sports.

Critical evaluation. Freud's work sparked controversy in his own lifetime, and some of that controversy still smoulders today. The world he knew vigorously repressed human sexuality; thus, few of his contemporaries were prepared to concede that sex was a basic human need. More recently, Freud has come under fire for his depictions of humanity in allegedly male terms, thereby devaluing the lives of women (Donovan and Littenberg, 1982). But Freud provided a foundation that influenced virtually everyone who later studied the human personality. Of special importance to sociology is his notion that we internalize social norms and that childhood experiences have a lasting impact on socialization.

JEAN PIAGET: COGNITIVE DEVELOPMENT

Jean Piaget (1896–1980) is also among the foremost psychologists of the century. Much of his work centred on human *cognition*—how people think and understand. Early in his career, Piaget was fascinated by the behaviour of his three children, wondering not only *what* they knew but *how* they comprehended the world. He concluded that children's thinking undergoes dramatic and patterned changes as they mature biologically and gain social experience. Piaget identified four stages of cognitive development.

 For a closer look at Piaget and his work, go to www.piaget.org/

The Sensorimotor Stage

Piaget's first step is the **sensorimotor stage**, *the level of human development at which individuals experience the world only through sensory contact*. At this stage, roughly the first two years of life, the infant explores the world with the five senses: touching, tasting, smelling, looking, and listening. Because they are still unable to use symbols, "knowing" to infants amounts to direct, sensory experience.

The Preoperational Stage

The second plateau in Piaget's account of development is the **preoperational stage**, *the level of human development at which individuals first use language and*

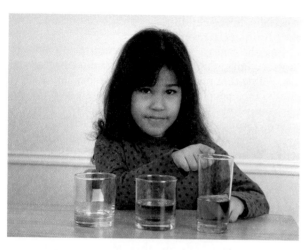

In a well-known experiment, Jean Piaget demonstrated that children over the age of seven had entered the concrete operational stage of development because they could recognize that the quantity of liquid remained the same when poured from a wide beaker into a tall one.

other symbols. At about age two, children begin to engage the world mentally: their capacity to *think* means reality moves beyond the senses. Children gain imagination and begin to appreciate the element of fantasy in fairy tales (Kohlberg and Gilligan, 1971; Skolnick, 1986). Children at this stage—roughly from age two to six—attach names and meanings only to specific things. They can describe a favourite toy, for example, but cannot explain what *kind* of toy appeals to them.

Without abstract concepts, a child also cannot judge size, weight, or volume. In one of his best-known experiments, Piaget placed two identical glasses containing equal amounts of water on a table. He asked several children aged five and six if the amount in each glass was the same. They nodded that it was. The children then watched Piaget take one of the glasses and pour its contents into a taller, narrower glass, raising the level of the water. He asked again if each glass held the same amount. The typical five- and six-year-old now insisted that the taller glass held more water. But children of seven or eight, who are able to think abstractly, could comprehend that the amount of water remained the same.

We have all seen young children place their hands in front of their faces and exclaim, "You can't see me!" They assume that if they cannot see you, then you are unable to see them. This behaviour reveals that preoperational children maintain an egocentric view of the world: they cannot perceive yet that any situation may appear different to another person.

The Concrete Operational Stage

Next comes the **concrete operational stage**, *the level of development at which individuals first perceive causal connections in their surroundings*. At this level, typically between ages seven and eleven, children begin to grasp how and why things happen, gaining a far greater ability to manipulate their environments.

In addition, girls and boys now can attach more than one symbol to a particular event or object. For instance, if you say to a girl of five, "Today is Wednesday," she might respond, "No, it's my birthday!" indicating the ability to use just one symbol at a time. Within a few years, however, she would be able to respond, "Yes, this Wednesday is my birthday!"

Also during the concrete operational stage, children transcend earlier egocentrism so that they can now imagine themselves as others see them. As we shall explain shortly, the ability to "stand in another's shoes" is the key to participating in complex social activities such as games.

The Formal Operational Stage

The final level in Piaget's model is the **formal operational stage**, *the level of human development at which individuals think abstractly and critically*. By about the age of twelve, children begin to reason in abstract terms rather than think only of concrete situations. If, for example, you were to ask a child of seven or eight, "What would you like to be when you grow up?" you might prompt a concrete response such as "A teacher." But a teenager might well respond abstractly, saying, "I would like a job that is exciting." At this point, young people's surging energy is matched by their creativity and imagination, sometimes evident in a passion for science fiction or poetry.

Also at this stage, children can comprehend metaphors. Hearing the phrase "a penny for your thoughts" might lead a young child to ask for a coin, but the adolescent (preteen or teenager) will recognize a gentle invitation to intimacy. Then, too, adolescents begin to evaluate the world "in principle," a trait widely evident in teenagers.

Critical evaluation. While Freud envisioned personality as an ongoing battle between opposing forces of biology and society, Piaget viewed the human mind as active and creative. Piaget's contribution to understanding socialization lies in showing that the capacity to engage the world unfolds predictably as the result of biological maturation and increasing social experience.

Some challenge Piaget's scheme by asking if people in every society progress through all four of the stages he identified. For instance, living in a slowly changing traditional society is likely to inhibit the capacity for abstract and critical thought. Even today, as many as 30 percent of adults may never reach the formal operational stage at all (Kohlberg and Gilligan, 1971:1065). People exposed to little creative and imaginative thinking do not generally develop this capacity on their own.

LAWRENCE KOHLBERG: MORAL DEVELOPMENT

Lawrence Kohlberg (1981) used Piaget's theory as a springboard for a study of moral reasoning—the ways in which individuals come to judge situations as right or wrong. Following Piaget's lead, Kohlberg argues that moral development proceeds in stages.

Young children who experience the world in terms of pain and pleasure (Piaget's sensorimotor stage) are at the *preconventional* level of moral development. At this early stage, in other words, "rightness" amounts to "what serves my needs" or "what feels good to me."

The *conventional* level of moral development, Kohlberg's second stage, begins to appear among teenagers (corresponding to Piaget's last, formal operational stage). At this point, young people shed some of their selfishness and begin to define right and wrong in terms of what pleases parents and what is consistent with broader cultural norms. In reaching moral judgments, individuals at this stage try to assess intention in addition to simply observing what others do.

A final stage of moral development, the *postconventional* level, moves individuals beyond the specific norms of their society to ponder more abstract ethical principles. At this level, people philosophically reflect on the meaning of liberty, freedom, or justice. Individuals are now capable of actively criticizing their own society and of arguing, for instance, that what is traditional or legal still may not be right.

Critical evaluation. Like the work of Piaget, Kohlberg's model explains that moral development occurs in more or less definable stages. Thus, some of the criticisms of Piaget's ideas also apply to Kohlberg's work. Whether this model applies to people in all societies, for example, remains unconfirmed. Then, too, many people apparently do not reach the postconventional level of moral reasoning, although exactly why is also, at present, an open question.

Another problem with Kohlberg's research is that his subjects were all boys. Kohlberg commits the research error, described in Chapter 2 ("Sociological Investigation"), of generalizing the results of male subjects to all of humanity. This problem prompted his colleague Carol Gilligan to investigate how gender affects moral reasoning.

CAROL GILLIGAN: BRINGING IN GENDER

Carol Gilligan, an educational psychologist at Harvard University, was disturbed that Kohlberg's research had overlooked girls. This narrow focus, as she sees it, is typical of much social science, which uses the behaviour of males as the norm for everyone.

Therefore, Gilligan (1982) set out to systematically compare the moral development of females and males. Simply put, her conclusion is that the two sexes make moral judgments in different ways. Males, she contends, have a *justice perspective*, relying on formal rules and abstract principles to define right and wrong. Girls, on the other hand, have a *care and responsibility perspective*, judging a situation with an eye towards personal relationships and loyalties. Stealing, as boys see it, is wrong because it breaks the law and violates common moral sentiments. Girls, however, are more likely to wonder why someone would steal, looking less severely upon an individual who felt forced to steal in order to, say, feed a hungry child.

Kohlberg treats the abstract male perspective as superior to the person-based female approach. Gilligan notes that impersonal rules have long dominated men's lives in the workplace. Concern for attachments, in contrast, has been more relevant to women's lives as wives, mothers, and caregivers. But, Gilligan asks, should we set male standards as the norms by which we evaluate everyone?

Gilligan's more recent work (1990) targets the issue of self-esteem. Her research team interviewed more than two thousand girls, ranging in age from six to eighteen years. Their responses made it clear that young girls start out with considerable confidence and self-esteem, only to find these vital resources slipping away as they pass through adolescence. An earlier Canadian survey by Bibby and Posterski (1985) had found that 35 percent of adolescent girls (compared to 23 percent of boys) said that they "felt inferior." Gilligan attributes the apparent lack of self-esteem among girls to our culture, which still defines the ideal woman as calm, controlled, and eager to please, and to the relative lack of women as teachers in later grades or as people in positions of authority.

Critical evaluation. Gilligan's work both sharpens our understanding of human development and highlights the problems related to gender in conducting and evaluating research. Is it nature or nurture that accounts for the observed differences between females and males? While it is impossible to rule out inherent differences between the sexes, Gilligan believes that these patterns reflect cultural conditioning.

GEORGE HERBERT MEAD: THE SOCIAL SELF

Our understanding of socialization stems in large part from the life work of George Herbert Mead (1863–1931), who described his approach as *social behaviourism* (1962; orig. 1934). While recognizing the power of the environment to shape human behaviour, Mead highlighted inward *thinking*, which he contended was humanity's defining trait.

 A short biography of George Herbert Mead is included in the Gallery of Sociologists at www.TheSociologyPage.com

Gentle, Nurturing Women; Aggressive, Violent Men

When we hear the words "domestic violence," most of us think "wife abuse"; rarely do we translate the term as "husband abuse." This tendency is explained in part by our beliefs about gender socialization and the nature/nurture debate. We believe that biological differences *and* socialization patterns underlie the cultural expectations that women be gentle, nurturing, emotional, and submissive and men rational, competitive, aggressive, and, sometimes, violent. We recoil in disbelief when we hear that teenage girls are involved in gangs that commit violent acts—such as the murder of Reena Virk in 1997. Similarly, we were slow to suspect and comprehend the role of Karla Homolka in the 1991 murders initially attributed to Paul Bernardo alone.

In light of our gender expectations, a study of family violence by Eugen Lupri (1992) is of particular interest. Based on data collected in 1987 from 1834 Canadians—who were or had ever been married or cohabiting—this study looks at the incidence of husband-to-wife and wife-to-husband violence. Respondents were asked how often, in the previous year, they had committed certain violent acts against their part-ners. The violent acts ranged from threatening to hit or throw something at the other to using a knife or gun on the other.

The scores on the Overall Violence Index were 17.8 and 23.3 percent for men and women respectively; the Severe Violence Index scores were 10.1 and 12.9 percent for men and women. We can draw two conclusions from these results: either women are more likely than men to commit violent acts against their partners, or women are more willing to *admit* to such acts, while men underreport their violent actions. Lupri reports the results but makes no comment about the fact that reported rates of spousal violence perpetrated by women are higher than those by men, even though gender socialization would lead us to predict the opposite. He examined family violence rates by education, income, age, and employment status, attributing them to structural stress and socialization that condones violence, by men or women, as a response to conflict, frustration, or anger. In pursuing his research on intimate violence, spousal abuse, and specifically male abuse, Lupri points out that there are at least thirty studies that have reported similar rates of as-sault by men and by women. His own research reveals a "consistent pattern of gender symmetry in woman-to-man and man-to-woman abuse" (2003:5).

While acknowledging the fact that women, too, are capable of violence, we need to know more about the context of or motivation for the female-to-male violence reported above—specifically, how much occurred in self-defence (DeKeseredy, 2001)? How serious were the resulting injuries relative to those inflicted by men on women? How would the inclusion of sexual assault—not measured in the Conflict Tactics Scale (CTS) used by Lupri—change the gender balance in violent behaviour?

Even if, controlling for all these factors, male-to-female abuse is more frequent and violent, we do need to question our assumptions about gender socialization and gentle women/violent men. Couple violence results in injury and psychological distress in both men and women (Grandin et al., 1998). There are good reasons for protecting women from violent or controlling men, but must we deny the fact that women are also capable of violence and inflicting physical and psychological harm on the males in their lives?

The Self

Mead's central concept is the **self**, *a dimension of personality composed of an individual's self-awareness and self-image*. Mead's genius lay in seeing that the self is inseparable from society, a connection explained in a series of steps.

First, Mead asserted, *the self develops over time*. The self is not part of the body that exists at birth. Mead rejected the position that personality is guided by biological drives (as Freud asserted) or biological maturation (as Piaget claimed). For Mead, the self develops only through social experience. In the absence of social interaction, as we see from the cases of isolated children, the body may grow but no self will emerge.

Second, Mead explained, *social experience is the exchange of symbols*. Using words, a wave of the hand, or a smile, people create meaning, which is a distinctively human experience. We use reward and punishment to train a dog, after all, but the dog attaches no meaning to these actions. Human beings, in contrast, make sense of actions by inferring people's underlying intentions. In short, a dog responds to *what you do*; a human responds to *what you have in mind as you do it*.

Return to our friendly dog for a moment. You can train a dog to walk to the porch and return with an umbrella. But the dog grasps no meaning in the act, no intention behind the command. Thus, if the dog cannot find the umbrella, it is incapable of the *human* response of looking for a raincoat instead.

Third, says Mead, *to understand intention, you must imagine the situation from another person's point of view.* Using symbols, we can imaginatively place ourselves in another person's shoes and thus see ourselves as that person does. This capacity allows us to anticipate how others will respond to us even before we act. A simple toss of a ball requires stepping outside ourselves to imagine how another will respond to our throw. Social interaction, then, involves seeing ourselves as others see us, a process that Mead called *taking the role of the other*.

The Looking-Glass Self

In social life, other people represent the *mirror* or *looking-glass* in which we perceive ourselves. Charles Horton Cooley (1864–1929), one of Mead's colleagues, used the phrase **looking-glass self** to designate *the image people have of themselves based on how they believe others perceive them* (1964; orig. 1902). Whether I think of myself as clever or clumsy, worthy or worthless, depends in large measure on what I think others think of me—i.e., my mirror image. This insight goes a long way towards explaining Carol Gilligan's finding that young women lose self-confidence as they come of age in a society that discourages women from being too assertive.

The I and the Me

Our capacity to see ourselves through others implies that the self has two components. As we initiate social action, *the self operates as a subject*. Humans are innately active and spontaneous, Mead claimed, dubbing this subjective element of the self the *I* (the subjective form of the personal pronoun). As we take the role of the other, *the self operates as an object*. Mead called this objective element of the self the *me* (the objective form of the personal pronoun). All social experience has both components: we initiate an action (the I-phase of self) and then we continue the action based on how others respond to us (the me-phase of self). Social experience is thus the interplay of the I and the me.

Mead stressed that thinking itself constitutes a social experience. Our thoughts are partly creative (representing the I), but in thought we also become objects to ourselves (representing the me) as we imagine how others will respond to our ideas.

Development of the Self

According to Mead, we gain a self as we learn to take the role of the other. Like Freud and Piaget, Mead regarded early childhood as the crucial time for this task, but the process goes on as long as we continue to have social experience.

Infants respond to others only in terms of *imitation*. They mimic behaviour without understanding underlying intentions. Without symbols (thus, unable to take the role of the other), infants have no self.

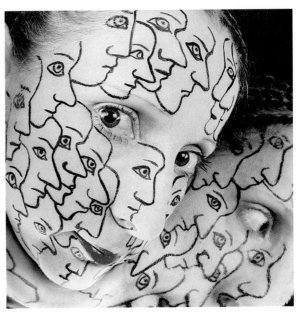

George Herbert Mead wrote: "No hard-and-fast line can be drawn between our own selves and the selves of others." The painting Manyness *by Rimma Gerlovina and Valeriy Gerlovin conveys this important truth. Although we tend to think of ourselves as unique individuals, each person's characteristics develop in an ongoing process of interaction with others.*

Rima Gerlovina and Valeriy Gerlovin, *Manyness*, 1990. © the artists, New City, N.C.

Children learn to use language and other symbols through *play*, especially role playing. Initially, they model themselves on key people in their lives—such as parents—whom we call *significant others*. Playing "mommy and daddy," for example, helps children imagine the world from their parents' point of view.

Gradually, children learn to take the roles of several others at once. This skill is the key to moving from simple play (say, playing catch) involving one other to complex *games* (such as baseball) involving many others. Only by the age of seven or eight have most children acquired sufficient social experience to engage in team sports that demand taking the role of numerous others simultaneously.

Figure 5–1 shows the logical progression from imitation to play to games. But a final stage in the development of the self remains. A game involves taking the role of others in just one situation. But members of a society also need to see themselves as others in general might. We recognize that people in any situation throughout society share cultural norms and values, and we begin to incorporate these general patterns into the self. Mead used the term **generalized other** to refer to *widespread cultural norms and values that we use as references in evaluating ourselves*.

Of course, the emergence of the self is not the end of socialization. Quite the contrary: Mead claimed

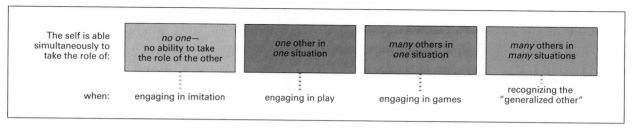

FIGURE 5–1 Building on Social Experience

George Herbert Mead described the development of the self as the process of gaining social experience. This development is largely a matter of taking the role of the other with increasing sophistication.

that socialization continues as long as we have social experience, so that changing circumstances can re-shape who we are. The self may change, for example, with divorce, disability, or unexpected wealth. And we retain some control over this process as we respond to events and circumstances and thereby play a part in our own socialization.

At times people develop multiple selves. This process may be related to the experience of extreme abuse in children. Sylvia Fraser, a Canadian novelist, describes her own experience of sexual abuse and the development of another personality as follows:

> When the conflict caused by my sexual relationship with my father became too acute to bear, I created a secret accomplice for my daddy by splitting my personality in two. Thus, somewhere around the age of seven, I acquired another self with memories and experiences separate from mine, whose existence was unknown to me. My loss of memory was retroactive. I did not remember my daddy ever having touched me sexually. I did not remember ever seeing my daddy naked. I did not remember my daddy ever seeing me naked. In future, whenever my daddy approached me sexually I turned into my other self, and afterwards I did not remember anything that had happened. (Fraser, 1987:15)

Critical evaluation. The strength of Mead's work lies in exploring the nature of social experience itself. He succeeded in explaining how our use of symbols is the key that makes possible both self and society.

Some critics disparage Mead's view as radically social because it acknowledges no biological element in the emergence of the self. In this position, he stands apart from Freud (who identified general drives within the organism) and Piaget (whose stages of development are tied to biological maturation).

Mead's concepts of the I and the me are often confused with Freud's concepts of the id and the superego. But Freud rooted the id in the biological organism, while Mead rejected any link between the self and biology (although he never specified the origin of the I). Freud's concept of the superego and Mead's concept of

the me both reflect the power of society to shape personality. But for Freud, superego and id are locked in continual combat. Mead, however, believed that the I and the me work closely and cooperatively together (Meltzer, 1978).

ERIK H. ERIKSON: EIGHT STAGES OF DEVELOPMENT

All of the thinkers we have discussed thus far highlight childhood as the crucial period during which personality emerges. Erik H. Erikson (1902–94) offered a broader view of socialization, claiming that personality changes throughout the life course as we face challenges linked to each stage of life. In Erikson's theory (1963; orig. 1950), life holds eight key challenges.

Stage 1—Infancy: The challenge of trust (versus mistrust). Erikson explains that the first of life's challenges, faced by infants up to about eighteen months of age, is to gain a sense of trust that their world is a safe place. Family members play a key role in how the child addresses this challenge.

Stage 2—Toddler: The challenge of autonomy (versus doubt and shame). Up to about three years of age, young children must gain the skills to cope with the world in a confident way. Gaining self-control is a key part of this challenge.

Stage 3—Preschooler: The challenge of initiative (versus guilt). Four- and five-year-olds must learn to engage their surroundings—including people outside the family—or experience guilt at having failed to meet the expectations of parents and others.

Stage 4—Preadolescent: The challenge of industriousness (versus inferiority). Between about age six and thirteen, children enter school, establish peer groups, and strike out on their own more and more. They soon gain pride in their accomplishments or fear that they do not measure up.

Stage 5—Adolescence: The challenge of gaining identity (versus confusion). During the teenage years, young people struggle to establish their own identity. In part, we identify with others close to us; in part, we identify ourselves as unique. Almost all teens experience some confusion as they struggle to meet this challenge.

Stage 6—Young adulthood: The challenge of intimacy (versus isolation). A key challenge for young adults is establishing and maintaining intimate relationships. Falling in love (or keeping close friendships and working relationships) involves balancing the need to bond and the need to maintain separate identities.

Stage 7—Middle adulthood: The challenge of making a difference (versus self-absorption). To Erikson, the key goal of middle age is contributing to the lives of others, in the family, at work, and in the larger world. Failing to do so, we become stagnant, caught up in our limited concerns.

Stage 8—Old age: The challenge of integrity (versus despair). As we near the end of our lives, Erikson explains, we hope to look back on what we have accomplished with a sense of integrity and satisfaction. For those who have been self-absorbed (one thinks of the character Scrooge in Dickens' classic *A Christmas Carol*), old age brings only a sense of despair at missed opportunities.

Critical evaluation. Erikson's theory suggests that personality formation is an ongoing process, beginning in childhood and continuing to old age. Further, his model suggests that success at one stage (say, an infant gaining trust) sets the stage for happily resolving the challenge of the next stage of life.

One problem with a rigid model of stages is that not everyone confronts these challenges in the precise order noted by Erikson. Nor is it clear that failure to meet the challenge of one stage of life—say, forming intimate relationships in young adulthood—precludes experiencing success in later life. A broader question, raised earlier in our discussion of Piaget's ideas, is whether people in other cultures and in other times in history would define a successful life in the same terms as Erikson does.

In short, then, Erikson's model helps us to make sense of the socialization process, but it may not be an actual description of how any of us experience the world. However, his model suggests the need to examine how the family, the school, and other settings shape us, as well as how we change over the life course. We turn now to take a close look at these issues.

AGENTS OF SOCIALIZATION

Every social experience we have affects us in at least some small way. In modern industrial societies, however, several familiar settings have special significance in the socialization process.

THE FAMILY

The family is the most important agent of socialization because it represents the centre of children's lives. As we have seen, infants are almost totally dependent on others, and the responsibility of meeting their needs almost always falls on parents and other family members. At least until the onset of schooling, the family also shoulders the task of teaching children cultural values and attitudes about themselves and others.

Family-based socialization is not all intentional. Children learn continuously from the kind of environment that adults create. Whether children learn to think of themselves as strong or weak, smart or stupid, loved or simply tolerated, and, as Erik Erikson suggests, whether they believe the world to be trustworthy or dangerous largely stem from this early environment.

Parenting styles aside, research points to the importance of parental *attention* in the social development of children. Physical contact, verbal stimulation, and responsiveness from parents and others all foster intellectual growth (Belsky et al., 1984).

The family also confers on children a social position; that is, parents not only bring children into the physical world but they also place them in society in terms of race, ethnicity, religion, and class. In time, all these elements become part of a child's self-concept. Of course, some aspects of social position may change later on, but social standing at birth affects us throughout our lives.

Interestingly, children are aware from a very early age of the accessories of class. Canadian sociologists Bernd Baldus and Verna Tribe (1978) presented children in grades 1, 3, and 6 with sets of pictures of two men (one who was "well-dressed" and one who was casually dressed), two houses (one from a high-income area of the city), two dining rooms, and two cars (again reflecting expensive taste and less expensive taste). Regardless of gender, school environment, or class background, the children's ability to match person and appropriate taste level increased with grade level. Furthermore, the children were able to give "character" descriptions of the two men. The well-dressed man was described as cheerful, nice, smart, and likeable, while the casually dressed man was described as tough, lazy, and likely to swear, steal, drink, or be uncaring about his family. Clearly, when children learn about class, they are actually learning to assign different values to different people. This ability, in return, can have an effect on how they value themselves—in short, on their self-esteem.

SCHOOLING

Schooling enlarges children's social worlds to include people with social backgrounds that differ from their own. As children confront social diversity, they learn the significance society attaches to people's race and sex and often act accordingly. Studies document the tendency of children to cluster together in play groups composed of one race and gender (Lever, 1978; Finkelstein and Haskins, 1983).

Formally, schooling teaches children a wide range of knowledge and skills. But schools convey a host of

Sociological research indicates that affluent parents tend to encourage creativity in their children while poor parents tend to foster conformity. While this general difference may be valid, parents at all class levels can and do provide loving support and guidance by simply involving themselves in their children's lives. Here father and daughter add a little fun to a practice session at a week-long Suzuki Institute workshop.

other lessons informally through what sociologists call the *hidden curriculum*. Activities such as spelling bees and sports teach children key cultural values such as competitive achievement and success. Children also receive countless formal and informal messages promoting their society's way of life as morally good.

Moving beyond the personal web of family life, children entering school soon discover that evaluations of skills such as reading and arithmetic are based on impersonal, standardized tests. Here, the emphasis shifts from *who* they are to *how* they perform. Of course, the confidence or anxiety that children develop at home can have a significant effect on how well they perform in school (Belsky et al., 1984).

School is also most children's first experience with rigid formality. The school day takes the form of a strict time schedule, subjecting children to impersonal regimentation and fostering punctuality. Perhaps not

surprisingly, these are the same traits expected by most of the organizations that will employ them later in life.

Finally, schools socialize children with regard to gender. Raphaela Best (1983) points out that, in primary school, boys engage in more physical activities and spend more time outdoors, while girls tend to be more sedentary, sometimes even helping the teacher with various housekeeping chores. Gender distinctions continue in the higher grades and persist right through college or university. Women still tend to select degrees in the arts or humanities, while men tend towards the physical sciences, mathematics, and engineering. This trend remains even though, in some of Canada's medical, veterinary medicine, and engineering programs, women are either a clear majority or a growing minority.

THE PEER GROUP

By the time they enter school, children have also discovered the **peer group**, *a social group whose members have interests, social position, and age in common*. A young child's peer group generally consists of neighbourhood playmates; later, peer groups are composed of friends from school or elsewhere.

Unlike the family and the school, the peer group allows young people to escape from the direct supervision of adults. With this newfound independence, members of peer groups gain valuable experience in forging social relationships on their own and developing a sense of themselves apart from their families. Peer groups also give young people the opportunity to discuss interests that may not be shared by adults (such as styles of dress and popular music) or tolerated comfortably by parents (such as drugs and sex).

For the young, the appeal of the peer group lies in the ever-present possibility of activity not condoned by adults. For the same reason, parents express concern about who their children's friends are. In a rapidly changing society, peer groups often rival parents in influence, as the attitudes of parents and children diverge along the lines of a "generation gap." The primacy of peer groups typically peaks during adolescence, as young people begin to break away from their families and think of themselves as responsible adults. At this stage of life, young people often display anxious conformity to peers because this new identity and sense of belonging eases some of the apprehension brought on by breaking away from the family.

The conflict between parents and peers may be more apparent than real, for even during adolescence children remain strongly influenced by their families. Peers may guide short-term concerns such as style of dress and musical taste, but parents retain greater sway over the long-term goals of their children. One study, for example, found that parents had more influence than even best friends on young people's educational aspirations (Davies and Kandel, 1981).

FIGURE 5–2 Television Viewing by Province, Fall 2001

Source: Calculations by Gerber based on Statistics Canada (2002e).

FIGURE 5–3 Television Viewing by Age and Sex, Fall 2003

Source: Calculations by Gerber based on Statistics Canada (2002c).

Finally, any neighbourhood or school operates as a social mosaic composed of numerous peer groups. As we will see in Chapter 7 ("Groups and Organizations"), members tend to perceive their own peer group in positive terms while discrediting others. Individuals are also influenced by peer groups they would like to join, a process sociologists call **anticipatory socialization**, *social learning directed towards gaining a desired position*. In school, for example, young people may mimic the styles and banter of the group they hope to join. Or, at a later point in life, a young lawyer who hopes to become a partner in her law firm may conform to the attitudes and behaviour of the firm's partners to ease her way into this rarefied group.

THE MASS MEDIA

The **mass media** are *impersonal communications directed to a vast audience*. The term *media* comes from Latin meaning "middle," suggesting that the media function to connect people. The development of mass media occurs as communications technologies (first newspapers, then radio and television, and now the Internet) disseminate information on a mass scale.

In Canada today, the mass media have an enormous effect on our attitudes and behaviour. For this reason, they are an important component of the socialization process. Television, introduced in 1939, has rapidly become the dominant medium in Canada. By 2001, 99.2 percent of Canadian households had colour televisions, 91.5 percent had VCRs, 19.8 had DVD players, and 68.3 had cable TV (Statistics Canada, 2002d). Rental spending on videos and DVDs is expected to reach $1.7 billion by 2007 (PricewaterhouseCoopers, 2003). Unfortunately, the vast majority of these expenditures will be on non-Canadian cultural products.

Just how "glued to the television" are we? The average Canadian watches twenty-one hours of television per week (see Figure 5–2). Years before children learn to read, watching television becomes a regular routine and, as they grow up, young girls and boys spend about fourteen hours per week in front of a television (see Figure 5–3). Indeed, television consumes as much of children's time as interacting with parents does. The extent of television viewing by children is a concern to researchers who have found that television renders children more passive and less likely to use their imaginations (Singer and Singer, 1983; APA, 1993; Fellman, 1995).

Virtually everyone in Canada watches television, but not to an equal degree. Figures 5–2 and 5–3 show variation in television watching by province, age, and gender. Furthermore, Canada has the second highest rate of television ownership among the industrial countries (see Figure 5–4).

Comedian Fred Allen once quipped that we call television a "medium" because it is rarely well done. For a variety of reasons, television (as well as all mass media) has provoked plenty of criticism. Some cite biases in television programming: liberal (or left-leaning) critics maintain that television shows mirror our society's patterns of inequality and rarely challenge the status quo. That is, TV shows have traditionally portrayed men and women according to cultural stereotypes, placing men in positions of power and relegating women to the roles of mothers or subordinates. Moreover, television shows have long portrayed well-to-do people favourably, while depicting less affluent individuals (Archie Bunker of *All in the Family* is

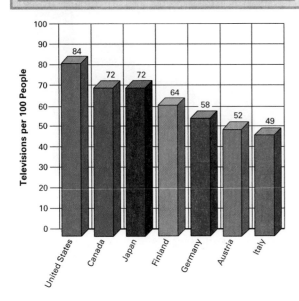

FIGURE 5–4 Television Ownership in Global Perspective

Source: The World Bank (2001).

the classic example) as ignorant and wrongheaded. And, although racial and ethnic minorities in the United States tend to watch more television than the white majority, until recent decades minorities have been all but absent from U.S. programming (Gans, 1980; Cantor and Pingree, 1983; Ang, 1985; Parenti, 1986; Brown, 1990). The "Diversity: Race, Class, and Gender" box discusses the characterization of minorities in television programming, much of which originates in the United States. In 2001, 61 percent of the television programs watched by Canadians were of foreign, mostly U.S., origin, whereas only 39 percent originated in Canada (Statistics Canada, 2002c). The CRTC requires that 60 percent of the programming on television, between 6 a.m. and midnight, is Canadian. Of course, television producers can provide Canadian content, but in the end the viewer operates the remote control.

On the other side of the fence, conservative critics charge that the television and film industries are dominated by a cultural elite that is far more liberal than the population as a whole. Especially in recent years, they maintain, the media have become increasingly "politically correct," advancing various socially liberal causes, including feminism, gay rights (Lichter et al., 1986; Woodward, 1992; Prindle, 1994; Prindle and Endersby, 1993; Rothman et al., 1993), and racial equality.

A final issue concerns violence and the mass media. In 1996, the American Medical Association

(AMA) expressed its concern that violence portrayed through the mass media—especially television and films—is a hazard to the public's well-being. An AMA survey (1996) found that three-fourths of American adults have either walked out of a movie or turned off a television program owing to objectionable levels of violence. A majority of parents also express concerns about sexual and violent content in popular music, in video games, and on the Internet.

Two similar neighbouring towns in British Columbia provided a unique opportunity to study the impact of television violence, as one of the towns had received television before the other. By measuring the level of aggressive behaviour in children in both communities, initially and two years after the arrival of television in the second town, Williams (1986) was able to demonstrate that, after the arrival of television, the children caught up—in terms of aggressiveness—to those in the neighbouring community who had had longer exposure.

The federal government turned its attention to the impact of television violence on the behaviour of children through a House of Commons committee. The committee concluded that the evidence of a link was inconclusive and contradictory; nonetheless, it recommended that legislation be implemented to control extremely violent forms of entertainment and that a classification system to help parents protect their children from exposure to television violence be developed (Canada, 1993).

The 1990s witnessed sustained activity on the part of the Canadian Radio-television and Telecommunications Commission (CRTC) regarding television violence. Two studies commissioned by the CRTC, reported in 1992, concluded that there is a link between violence on television and violence in society, though it is not one of direct cause and effect. The Action Group for Violence on Television (AGVOT) was set up with representatives from advertisers, producers, broadcasters, and cable companies. This committee developed classification guidelines and worked with other groups to regulate programming and broadcasting. They have worked closely with American legislators and producers on regulation and in the development of the V-chip, which allows parents to block unduly violent programming from their televisions. The Canadian Association of Broadcasters (CAB), deciding that *Mighty Morphin Power Rangers* violated its violence code, was instru-

 The CRTC website at www.crtc.gc.ca/ provides a detailed chronology of reports, regulations, and actions taken on television violence.

mental in getting YTV and Global to remove the program from their schedules in 1994.

Television and the other mass media have enriched our lives, generating a wide range of entertaining and educational programming. Moreover, the media increase our understanding of diverse cultures

How Do the Media Portray Minorities?

On an old *Saturday Night Live* sketch, Ron Howard tells comedian Eddie Murphy about a new film, *Night Shift*, in which two mortuary workers decide to open their own sideline business—a prostitution ring. Murphy asks whether any Black actors are in the film; Howard shakes his head "no." Murphy then thunders, "A story about two pimps and there wasn't no brothers in it? I don't know whether to thank you or punch you in the mouth, man!"

Murphy's ambivalence points up twin criticisms of the mass media. The first is that films and television portray minorities in stereotypical fashion; the second is that they are excluded altogether (Press, 1993). Certainly, at the beginning of the television age in the 1950s, minorities were almost nowhere to be found on television and in films. Even the wildly successful 1950s comedy *I Love Lucy* was originally turned down by every major television studio because it featured Desi Arnaz—a Cuban—in a starring role. While the early Westerns presented stereotypical images of cowboys and "Indians," at least one of them starred an authentic Canadian Aboriginal—Six Nations Jay Silverheels as Tonto, loyal sidekick of the Lone Ranger. Since then, the media have steadily included more minorities, so that the issue of visibility has declined in importance. Since a majority of the programming watched by Canadians is of U.S. origin, changes there have immediate impact here.

But the second issue is just as important: *how* the media portray minorities. The few African-Americans who managed to break into television in the 1950s (for example, the infamous Amos and Andy or Jack Benny's butler, Rochester) were confined to stereotypical roles portraying uneducated, low-status people. More recently, many television shows feature Black stars: some are situation comedies ("sitcoms") replete with crude humour and bumbling characters; others, though humorous, depict upper-status Black families; several soap operas (*The Young and the Restless, As the World Turns*) reveal Blacks as young professionals—among them, physicians, hospital administrators, lawyers, fashion photographers, successful models, and corporate vice-presidents. Oprah Winfrey, host of her own talk show, is very successful, very wealthy, and in a position of power or authority relative to that of her guests.

The portrayal of Aboriginal people has changed from the days when made-up white actors played "Indians" to American cowboys. Two Aboriginal performers from Canada, Chief Dan George (B.C.) and Graham Greene (Ontario), helped redefine the role of the Native in the major U.S. films *Little Big Man* and *Dances with Wolves*. Greene continues to appear in a wide range of film and television roles. In the meantime, singer/actor Buffy Sainte-Marie (Saskatchewan) provided early exposure to youngsters through her long-term involvement with *Sesame Street*. The popular Canadian production *North of 60* depicted Native people in the whole range of roles common to northern communities. Inuit singer Susan Aglukark (NWT) has changed the sound of Canadian music, just as Shania Twain (whose name means "on my way" in Ojibwa and who was raised for a time by an Ojibwa stepfather) has changed the sound of country music. Perhaps the best indicator of the stature of Aboriginal programming is the creation of APTN (the Aboriginal Peoples Television Network), which is broadcast to Canadian homes via cable or satellite.

Significant change has taken place in news reporting on the CBC and other U.S. and Canadian television channels. Representation of social diversity today is greater than it was even a decade ago. In large measure, this stems from deliberate personnel policies responding to demands for political correctness and the need to appeal to diverse audiences. Increasingly, the news is conveyed to us by women, by members of visible minorities, and, in Canada, by people with names that are neither English nor French. Even "white male" areas such as sports, stock market coverage, business analysis, and war zone activity increasingly are reported by women and visible minorities.

Certainly, the mass media in Canada and the United States can boast of improvement in the portrayal of minorities: the perpetuation of old stereotypes has given way to depiction of minority individuals (based on race, ethnicity, or gender) in a wide range of occupations and social classes. Some critics argue that depiction of minorities in high-status positions is unrealistic, as it masks the fact that minorities continue to face major barriers to full participation; on the other hand, such representation does reflect the fact that visible and ethnic minorities, as well as women, are to be found in the *real* world in all social class categories.

Finally, other spheres of life beyond those just described also play a part in social learning. For most people in Canada, these include religious organizations, the workplace, and social clubs. As a result, socialization inevitably proceeds inconsistently as we absorb different information from disparate sources. In the end, socialization is not a simple learning process; instead, it is a complex balancing act in which we encounter a wide range of ideas as we try to form our own distinctive personalities and world views.

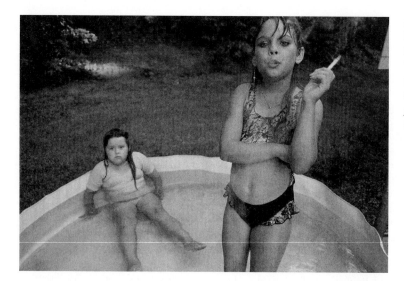

In recent decades, some analysts suggest that North American society is shortening childhood by pushing children to grow up faster and faster. What role do you think the mass media have in this process? What about the rising number of children left to fend for themselves while their parents work? What other factors are affecting the experience of childhood today?

and provoke discussion of current issues. At the same time, the power of the media—especially television—to shape how we think continues to fuel controversy on many fronts. Computers and the Internet complicate the picture further because governments cannot censor or otherwise control the flow of information into or out of their countries.

SOCIALIZATION AND THE LIFE COURSE

Although childhood is critical to the socialization process, learning continues throughout our lives. The following overview of the life course reveals that our society organizes human experience according to age, resulting in distinctive stages of life: childhood, adolescence, adulthood, and, finally, old age.

CHILDHOOD

Michael Jordan once came under fire for endorsing Nike athletic shoes because the sneakers are made in Taiwan and Indonesia by children who do not go to school but work full time for roughly fifty cents an hour. Such wages are typical for workers in poor countries, which include perhaps 200 million of the world's children (Gibbs, 1996).

Today, we think of *childhood*—roughly the first twelve years of life—as a time of freedom from the burdens of the adult world. But until about a century ago, children in Europe and North America shouldered burdens similar to those of adults. According to historian Philippe Ariès (1965), the whole idea of "childhood" is a fairly recent invention. Once children were able to survive without constant care, medieval Europeans expected them to assume the role of working adults. Although "child labour" is now prohibited in Canada, this historical pattern persists in poor soci-

 The Human Rights Watch webpage at www.hrw.org/ campaigns/crp/ reports on the state of children serving as soldiers around the world.

eties today, especially in Africa and Asia. Global Map 5–1 shows that work is commonplace for children in low-income nations of the world.

Our notion of childhood is grounded in important biological differences that set youngsters apart from adults, but as historical and global comparisons show, the concept of "childhood" is also rooted in culture. In rich countries, not everyone has to work: societies with sophisticated technology extend childhood so that young people have time to learn the many complex skills required for adult activities.

Some social scientists declare that our conception of childhood is changing again. High divorce rates, mothers and fathers absorbed into the workforce, and an increasing level of "adult" programming on television means that children are no longer protected from grown-up concerns as they were in the past. Rather, we are seeing the development of a "hurried child" syndrome, meaning that children have to grapple with sex, drugs, and violence as well as fend more and more for themselves (Elkind, 1981; Winn, 1983). Critics of this view counter that there is no convincing evidence yet of any dramatic shift in our society's conception of childhood. Further, the "hurried child" thesis overlooks the fact that children in the lower class have always assumed adult responsibilities sooner than their middle- and upper-class counterparts (Lynott and Logue, 1993).

ADOLESCENCE

As industrialization gradually framed childhood as a distinct stage of life, adolescence emerged as a buffer between childhood and adulthood. The preteen and teenage years comprise the stage of life when young people establish some independence and learn specialized skills required for adult life.

We generally associate adolescence with emotional and social turmoil: young people experience conflict with their parents and struggle to develop their own, separate identities. Since adolescence commonly begins at the onset of puberty, we may be tempted to attribute teenage turbulence to physiological changes. However, comparative research indicates that, like childhood, adolescence is a variable product of culture. Studying the Samoan Islanders in the 1920s, Margaret Mead (1961; orig. 1928) found little evidence of stress among teenagers; there, children appeared to move easily to adult standing. Our society, however, defines childhood and adulthood more in opposing terms, making the transition between the two stages of life more difficult.

Consider the ambivalence our society displays towards young people on the brink of adulthood. Eighteen-year-olds can vote and may face the prospect of going to war; yet in some provinces we deny them the privilege of drinking alcohol. We also present mixed messages when it comes to adolescent sexuality. The mass media often encourage sexual activity, while parents urge restraint; for their part, schools try to discourage casual sex even as they hand out condoms to students (Gibbs, 1993).

As is true of all stages of life, the experience of adolescence varies according to social background. Most young people from working-class families move directly from high school into the adult world of work and parenting. Wealthier teens, however, have the resources to attend university and perhaps graduate school, which may extend adolescence into their late twenties and even their thirties. For different reasons, of course, poverty may also extend adolescence. Especially in the inner cities, many young members of minority groups cannot attain full adult standing because jobs are not available.

ADULTHOOD

Adulthood is the period during which most of life's accomplishments typically occur, including pursuing careers and raising families. And, too, especially in later adulthood, people reflect on what they have been able to accomplish, perhaps with great satisfaction or with the sobering realization that many of the idealistic dreams of their youth will never come true.

Early Adulthood

By the onset of adulthood, personalities are largely formed. Even so, a marked shift in an individual's life situation—brought on by unemployment, divorce, or serious illness—can result in significant change to the self (Dannefer, 1984).

Early adulthood—from age twenty to about age forty—is generally a time of pursuing many goals set earlier in life. Young adults break free of parents and learn to manage for themselves a host of day-to-day responsibilities. With the birth of children, parents draw on experiences from their own upbringing, although, as children, they may have only vaguely perceived what adult life entailed. Typically, young adults try to master patterns of intimate living with another person who may have just as much to learn.

Early adulthood is also a period of juggling conflicting priorities: parents, partner, children, schooling, and work (Levinson et al., 1978). Women, especially, confront the difficulty of "doing it all," since our culture still confers on them primary responsibility for child-rearing and household chores, even if they have demanding occupations outside the home (Hochschild, 1989).

Middle Adulthood

Young adults usually cope optimistically with such tensions. But in middle adulthood—roughly age forty to age sixty—people begin to sense that marked improvements in life circumstances are less likely. The distinctive character of middle adulthood is the capacity to assess actual achievements in light of earlier expectations. At midlife, people also become more aware of the fragility of health, which the young typically take for granted.

Some women who have already spent many years raising a family find middle adulthood especially challenging. Children grow up and require less attention, husbands may become absorbed in their careers, leaving some women with spaces in their lives that they find difficult to fill. Women who divorce during middle adulthood may experience serious financial problems (Weitzman, 1985). For all these reasons, an increasing number of women mark middle adulthood by undertaking the challenge of returning to school and then launching careers.

Growing older means that both men and women face the reality of physical decline, but our society's traditional socialization has made this prospect more painful for women. Because good looks are defined as more important for women, wrinkles, weight gain, and loss of hair are more traumatic for them. Men have their own particular difficulties. Some confront limited achievement, knowing that their careers are unlikely to change for the better. Others, now realizing that the price of career success has been neglect of family or personal health, harbour uncertainties about their self-worth even as they bask in the praise of others (Farrell and Rosenberg, 1981). Women, too, who devote themselves single-mindedly to careers in early adulthood may experience regrets about what they have given up in pursuit of occupational success.

Constance Beresford-Howe, a Canadian novelist, often writes about people who make immense changes during adulthood. Her novel *A Serious Widow* begins with the funeral of Rowena Hill's husband of thirty years, and Rowena's discovery that he was a bigamist. Over the course of the novel, as Rowena re-edits her

Global Map 5–1 Child Labour in Global Perspective

Industrialization prolongs childhood and discourages children from engaging in work and other activities deemed suitable only for adults. Thus, child labour is relatively uncommon in Canada and other industrial societies. In less industrialized nations of the world, however, children serve as a vital economic asset, and they typically begin working as soon as they are able.

Source: The World Bank (2001) and estimates by John Macionis; map projection from *Peters Atlas of the World* (1990).

biography and the history of her marriage, she makes a number of surprising changes in her lifestyle and relationships. In the following scene, she reviews her wardrobe, finds it inadequate, and sews herself a new outfit:

> Refreshed by this encounter, I wrap myself in a towel and cross to the bedroom to dress. But a survey of the cupboard (half empty, now, with most of Edwin's things packed away) does nothing to encourage the idea of re-birth. My clothes are all depressing reminders of many things, in particular my dressmaking inadequacies. The brown checked skirt that never did hang quite straight.

The grey dress I made three years ago that looks even more boring whenever I try to brighten it up with a new scarf or belt. The beige skirt, baggy at the seat with age. Fretfully I push these dreary articles about on their hangers. Catching my eye in the mirror, it occurs to me that I look better in the bath towel pegged under my arms than in any of my clothes. The ruby colour and the soft pile are both pleasing. Turning first one way and then another, I look at my reflection thoughtfully. . . .

> Certainly it would take a bolder spirit than mine to wear such a rich red any place where other people could see it. But just to lounge around in at home. . . . The longer I look at myself the better I like the way that

ruby colour makes my hair look darker and my shoulders whiter.

After a minute, I pull the matching towels out of the linen cupboard. There is enough material for a wraparound skirt and a sort of tabard top. Half furtively I uncover the sewing machine and sit down. A few hours with scissors and thread. . . . Why not? It's not exactly fishing, Ethel, but maybe it's not far off. (Beresford-Howe, 1991:69–70)

Rowena Hill's midlife crisis may well have involved some of the personal transitions we have described. But her story also illustrates that the greatest productivity and personal satisfaction may occur after the middle of life. Socialization in our youth-oriented culture has convinced many people (especially the young) that life ends at forty. But as life expectancy in Canada has increased, such limiting notions have begun to dissolve.

 Major transformations may become less likely, but the potential for learning and new beginnings still infuses this stage of life with promise.

OLD AGE

Old age comprises the later years of adulthood and the final stage of life itself, beginning in about the mid-sixties. Here again, societies attach different meanings to a time of life. Pre-industrial people typically grant elders great influence and prestige. As explained in Chapter 15 ("Aging and the Elderly"), traditional societies confer on older people control of most of the land and other wealth; moreover, since their societies change slowly, older people amass a lifetime of wisdom, which earns them great respect (Sheehan, 1976; Hareven, 1982).

In industrial societies, however, most younger people work apart from the family, becoming more independent of their elders. Rapid change and our society's youth orientation combine to define what is older as unimportant or even obsolete. To younger people, then, the elderly are dismissed as unaware of new trends and fashions, and their knowledge and experience are often deemed irrelevant.

No doubt, however, this anti-elderly bias will diminish as the proportion of older people increases. The proportion of our population over sixty-five has almost tripled since the beginning of the twentieth century and life expectancy is still increasing. Most men and women in their mid-sixties (the "young elderly") can look forward to decades more of life. Statistics Canada expects the population aged eighty years old or more to reach an estimated 1.3 million by 2011, representing an increase of 43 percent from 2001 (Statistics Canada, 2002a).

This final phase of the life course differs in an important way from earlier stages. Growing up typically means entering new roles and assuming new responsibilities; growing old, in contrast, entails the opposite

Various categories of people experience the stages of the life course in distinctive ways. Most men, for example, pass through old age with the support of a partner. Women, who typically outlive men, endure much of their old age alone, a reality poignantly captured in G.G. Kopliak's painting Still Life.

G.G. Kopliak, *Still Life*, private collection, Superstock, Inc.

experience of leaving roles that provided both satisfaction and social identity. Retirement, for example, sometimes fits the common image of being a period of restful activity. But it may mean the loss of valued activity and even outright boredom. Like any life transition, retirement demands learning new and different patterns while simultaneously unlearning familiar routines. A nearly equal transition is required of the nonworking wife or husband, who must now accommodate a partner spending more time at home.

DYING

Through most of human history, death caused by disease or accident came at any age because of low living standards and primitive medical technology. Today, however, the average life span is seventy-nine years in Canada (seventy-six for males, eighty-three for females). Therefore, although most senior citizens can look forward to more than another decade of life, growing old cannot be separated from eventual physical decline and ultimate death.

As the proportion of women and men in old age increases, we can expect our culture to become more comfortable with the idea of death. In recent years, for example, people in Canada and elsewhere have been discussing death more openly than decades ago, and the trend is to view dying as preferable to painful or prolonged suffering in hospitals or at home. Moreover, more married couples now anticipate their own deaths with legal and financial planning. This openness may ease the disorientation that generally accompanies the death of a spouse—a greater problem for women, who usually outlive their husbands.

The demand by guards that new prisoners publicly disrobe is more than a matter of issuing new clothing. Such a degrading ritual is also the first stage in the process by which the staff in a total institution attempts to break down an individual's established social identity.

THE LIFE COURSE: AN OVERVIEW

This brief examination of the life course points to two major conclusions. Most importantly, although each stage of life is linked to the biological process of aging, the life course is largely a social construction—so that people in other societies may experience a stage of life quite differently, or not at all. Also, each stage of any society's life course presents characteristic problems and transitions that involve learning something new and unlearning familiar routines.

Note, too, that although societies organize human experience according to age, age cannot be isolated from the effects of other forces, such as class, race, ethnicity, and gender. Thus, the general patterns we have described are all subject to further modification as they apply to various categories of people.

Life experiences also vary depending on when, in the history of the society, people were born. A **cohort** is *a category of people with a common characteristic, usually age.* Age cohorts are likely to have been influenced by the same economic and cultural trends, so that members typically display similar attitudes and values (Riley et al., 1988). The lives of women and men born at mid-century, for example, were framed by economic expansion that gave them a sense of optimism uncommon among today's college and university students, who have grown up in an age of economic uncertainty.

RESOCIALIZATION: TOTAL INSTITUTIONS

A final type of socialization involves people being confined—often against their will—in prisons or mental hospitals. This is the special world of the **total institution**, *a setting in which people are isolated from the rest of society and manipulated by an administrative staff.*

According to Canadian sociologist Erving Goffman (1961), total institutions have three distinctive characteristics. First, staff members supervise all spheres of daily life, including where residents (often called "inmates") eat, sleep, and work. Second, a rigid system provides inmates with standardized food, sleeping quarters, and activities. Third, formal rules and daily schedules dictate when, where, and how inmates perform virtually every part of their daily routines.

Total institutions impose such regimentation with the goal of **resocialization**, *radically altering an inmate's personality through deliberate manipulation of the environment.* The power of a total institution to resocialize is also enhanced by its forcible segregation of inmates from the "outside" by means of physical barriers such as walls and fences topped with barbed wire and guard towers, barred windows, and locked doors. With inmates cut off in this way, their entire world can be manipulated by the administrative staff to produce lasting change—or at least immediate compliance—in the inmates.

Resocialization is a two-part process. First, the staff tries to erode the new inmate's autonomy and identity through what Goffman describes as "abasements, degradations, humiliations, and profanations of self" (1961:14). For example, inmates must surrender personal possessions, including clothing and grooming articles used to maintain their distinctive appearances. In their place, the staff provides standard-issue items that make everyone look alike. In addition, inmates all receive standard haircuts, so that, once again, what was personalized becomes uniform. The staff also subjects new inmates to "mortifications of self," including searches, medical examinations, and fingerprinting, and then assigns them a serial number. Once inside the walls, individuals surrender the right to privacy; guards may demand that inmates undress pub-

Ontario's First Boot Camp as a Total Institution

Resocialization in a total institution actually can change a human being, or so the theory goes. The rebuilding of the self is extremely difficult, however, and no two people are likely to respond to any program in precisely the same way. Resocialization is the goal of prisons, psychiatric hospitals, and, in this case, Operation Turnaround, Strict Discipline Facility—otherwise known as boot camp. The key to the operation of a total institution such as a boot camp is complete control of the environment so that only desired behaviours are permitted.

Staff members from military and social work backgrounds maintain discipline but are expected to treat inmates (called "cadets") with respect. In return, inmates are expected to refer to staff as "Sir" or "Ma'am" (they are made do push-ups if they forget). The atmosphere is stern, but not brutal: inmates do not experience physical punishment or abuse.

Upon arrival, young offenders get military-style brush cuts and learn to make their beds and tie their shoes the required way. They are introduced to discipline and plenty of it! Up at 6 a.m., lights out at 10 p.m., tidiness in austere surroundings, and lots of marching to wherever they otherwise might have sauntered.

Newly arrived cadets (in black) march in front of their guards at Operation Turnaround, a strict discipline facility, or "boot camp," in prime cottage country near Orillia, Ontario. The staff hopes that by the time inmates leave—in four to six months—they will have learned to respect discipline and structure. In theory, the thirty-two repeat offenders will leave the facility with greater self-esteem, new attitudes and values, and a reduced likelihood of returning to crime.

Other detention centres may allow inmates to play pool, watch television, play ping-pong or video games, and even select their own food. Idle moments also may be part of an inmate's day. However, none of these are on the agenda at the Strict Discipline Facility. Instead, plenty of military marching on the tarmac, more marching to and from various activities, calisthenics and some outdoor basketball and volleyball, three hours of school plus homework, and meals fill up the typical day. Towards the end of their terms, the inmates build cedar canoes and then take them, under staff supervision, on a wilderness adventure.

The program is designed, ultimately, to change cadet behaviour, attitudes, and values as well as to foster respect for themselves and for others. "Chins up. Look proud," they are told, in hopes that looking proud will make them feel proud. Those running the

program believe that young people who respect themselves will be less inclined to return to a life of crime.

Continue the debate . . .

1. *Do you feel that boot camp will actually turn around young offenders to the point where they will be less likely to reoffend?*

2. *Does the punishment fit the crime, or is it "cruel and unusual punishment" that occurs in this kind of setting?*

3. *If you were to be convicted of a crime, would you prefer to be sent to boot camp or to a conventional youth detention centre (or secure-custody facility)? Why?*

4. *Does resocialization necessitate the repudiation of prior socialization?*

Source: Based on Edwards (1997) and *About Turn (around) newsletter* [online, from www.encourageyouth.on.ca/main5.html; now discontinued].

---

licly as part of the admission procedure, and they routinely monitor inmates' living quarters.

The second part of the resocialization process includes efforts to systematically build a different self. The staff manipulates inmate behaviour through a system of rewards and punishments. The privilege of keeping a book, watching television, or making a telephone call may seem trivial to outsiders, but, in the rigid environment of the total institution, this can form a powerful motivation to conform. Bucking the system, on the other hand, means that privileges will be withdrawn or, in more serious cases, that the inmate will suffer further isolation or additional punishment. The duration of confinement in a prison or mental hospital also depends on an inmate's display of cooperation with official rules and regulations. Goffman emphasizes that the staff also seeks to win the hearts and minds of inmates and will punish even those who toe the line but have an "attitude problem."

In principle, total institutions can bring about considerable change in inmates. Yet the resocialization process is extremely complex, and no two people respond to such programs in precisely the same way (Irwin, 1980). While some inmates are deemed "rehabilitated" or "recovered," others display little change at all, and still others only become confused, hostile, or bitter. Over a long period of time, a rigidly controlled environment may destroy a person's capacity for independent living; such *institutionalized* personalities lose the capacity to deal with the demands of the outside world.

SUMMARY

1. For individuals, socialization is the process of building our humanity and particular identity through social experience. For society as a whole, socialization is the means by which one generation transmits culture to the next.

2. A century ago, people thought most human behaviour was guided by biological instinct. Today, the nature-nurture debate has tipped the other way as we understand human behaviour to be primarily the product of a social environment. But the two concepts are not entirely opposed, since it is human nature to nurture.

3. The permanently damaging effects of social isolation reveal the importance of social experience to human development.

4. Sigmund Freud envisioned the human personality as composed of three parts. The *id* represents general human drives (the life and death instincts), which Freud claimed were innate. The *superego* embodies cultural values and norms internalized by individuals. The *ego* operates to resolve competition between the demands of the id and the restraints of the superego.

5. Jean Piaget believed that human development reflects both biological maturation and increasing social experience. In his view, socialization proceeds through four major stages of development: sensorimotor, preoperational, concrete operational, and formal operational.

6. Carol Gilligan discovered that gender affects moral reasoning. Females, she asserts, look to the effect of decisions on relationships, while males rely more on abstract standards of rightness.

7. To George Herbert Mead, socialization is based on the emergence of the self, which is partly autonomous (the I) and partly guided by society (the me). Mead contended that, beginning with imitation, the self develops through play and games and eventually recognizes the "generalized other."

8. Charles Horton Cooley used the term "looking-glass self" to underscore that the self is influenced by how we think others respond to us.

9. Erik H. Erikson identified characteristic challenges that individuals face at each stage of life from childhood to old age.

10. Commonly the first setting of socialization, the family has the greatest influence on a child's attitudes and behaviour.

11. School exposes children to greater social diversity and the experience of impersonal evaluation. In addition to formal lessons, schools informally teach a wide range of cultural ideas, including attitudes about competition and achievement.

12. Members of youthful peer groups are less subject to adult supervision than they are in the family or in school. Peer groups take on great significance among adolescents.

13. The mass media, especially television, have a considerable impact on the socialization process. The average Canadian child now spends about 14.2 hours a week watching television.

14. As with each phase of the life course, the characteristics of childhood are socially constructed. Medieval Europeans scarcely recognized childhood as a stage of life. In rich, industrial nations such as Canada, people define childhood as very different from adulthood.

15. Adolescence, the transition between childhood and adulthood, is considered a difficult period in our society. This is not the case in all societies.

16. During early adulthood, socialization involves settling into careers and raising families. Later adulthood is marked by considerable reflection about initial goals in light of actual achievements.

17. In old age, people make many transitions, including retirement. While the elderly typically enjoy high prestige in pre-industrial societies, industrial and post-industrial societies tend to relegate older people to the sidelines.

18. Members of rich societies typically fend off death until old age. Adjustment to the death of a spouse (an experience more common to women) and acceptance of one's own death are part of socialization for the elderly.

19. Total institutions such as prisons and mental hospitals strive for resocialization—radically changing the inmate's personality.

20. Socialization demonstrates the power of society to shape our thoughts, feelings, and actions. Yet, as free humans, we also have the capacity to act on society to shape our lives and our world.

CRITICAL-THINKING QUESTIONS

1. What do cases of social isolation teach us about the importance of social experience to human development?

2. Describe the two sides of the nature–nurture debate. In what sense are human nature and nurture not opposed to one another?

3. What common themes are found in the theories of Freud, Piaget, Kohlberg, Gilligan, Mead, and Erikson? On what key points do they differ?

4. Television features far more physically attractive people, proportionately speaking, than exist in the population as a whole. Develop arguments for and against this practice. How does this practice affect the way we think about others—and ourselves?

APPLICATIONS AND EXERCISES

1. Along with several members of your sociology class, gather some data: each person should ask a variety of classmates to identify traits they assume are elements of "human nature." Get together later to compare notes and assess the extent to which the traits noted are the product of "nature" or "nurture."

2. See if you can find a copy of the video (or book) *Lord of the Flies*, a tale by William Golding based on a Freudian model of personality. Jack and his hunters represent the power of the id; Piggy consistently opposes them as the superego; Ralph stands between the two as the ego, the voice of reason. Golding wrote the book after participating in the carnage of the D-Day landing in France. Do you agree with his belief that the human proclivity for violence (as well as our capacity for cultural restraint) is basic to our

nature? Would his conclusions have been different if he had included girls among his characters?

3. Give some thought to your own personality. Think about the traits you believe characterize you and, if you have the courage, ask several others who know you well what they think of you. To what extent did you learn these traits?

4. Watch several hours of prime-time programming on television. Keep track of every time any element of violence is shown. For fun, assign each program a "YIP rating," for the number of Years in Prison a person would serve for committing all the violent acts you witness (Fobes, 1996). On the basis of observing this small (and unrepresentative) sample of programs, what are your conclusions?

 ## SITES TO SEE

www.macionis.com
or
www.TheSociologyPage.com

You can find brief biographies of George Herbert Mead, Charles Horton Cooley, and other sociologists discussed in this chapter, as well as more than fifty weblinks to sociological journals and other sources of data and information by visiting the Links Library at this website.

www.infidels.org/library/historical/charles_darwin/index.shtml

Fully searchable complete texts of Darwin's major works: *On the Origin of Species* (1859), *The Descent of Man* (1871), and *The Voyage of the Beagle* (1909).

www.freud-museum.at/

Visit the Sigmund Freud Museum of Vienna, Austria, at this site.

www.piaget.org/

The Jean Piaget Society hosts this website, which presents the work of this celebrated social psychologist.

www.nd.edu/~rbarger/kohlberg.html

This website is dedicated to the ideas and research of Lawrence Kohlberg.

http://spartan.ac.brocku.ca/~lward/mead/default.html

George's Page is a large, well-organized document repository for the work of George Herbert Mead, with resources to support research on his contribution to social psychology.

 ## STUDY TOOLS

For more study tools to help you with your next exam, be sure to check out the Companion Website at **www.pearsoned. ca/macionis**, as well as Chapter 5 in your Study Guide.

 ## INVESTIGATE WITH CONTENTSELECT

Follow the instructions found on page 25 of this textbook to access ContentSelect™ at the Research Navigator™ website. Once at the site, enter your LOGINID and Password. Then, enter keywords such as "Sigmund

Freud," "childhood," and "mass media", and the search engine will supply relevant and recent scholarly and popular press publications.

CHAPTER

6

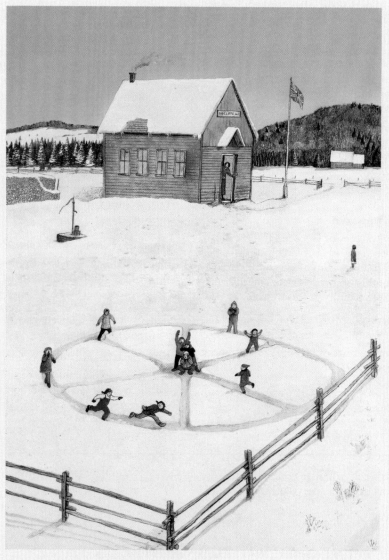

William Kurelek (1927–1977, Canadian)
The Game of Fox and Geese, from *They Sought a New World,* 1987
© 1985, The Estate of William Kurelek, published by Tundra Books.

SOCIAL INTERACTION IN EVERYDAY LIFE

Matt and Dianne are on their way to visit friends in an unfamiliar section of Calgary. They are now late because, for the last twenty minutes, they have been going in circles looking for Creek View Drive. Matt, gripping the wheel ever more tightly, is doing a slow burn. Dianne, sitting next to him, looks straight ahead, afraid to utter a word. Both realize the evening is off to a bad start.

Here we have a simple case of two people unable to locate the home of some friends. But Matt and Dianne are lost in more ways than one, since they fail to grasp why they are growing more and more angry with their situation and each other.

Consider the predicament from the man's point of view. Matt cannot tolerate getting lost—the longer he drives around, the more incompetent he feels. Dianne is seething, too, but for a different reason. She does not understand why Matt refuses to pull over and ask for directions

to Creek View Drive. If she were driving, she fumes to herself, they already would have arrived and would be comfortably settled with drinks in hand.

Why don't men ask for directions? Because men value their independence, they are uncomfortable asking for help (and also reluctant to accept it). To men, asking for assistance is an admission of inadequacy, a sure sign that others know something they don't. If it takes Matt a few more minutes to find Creek View Drive on his own—and to keep his self-respect in the process—he thinks the bargain is a good one.

If men pursue self-sufficiency and are sensitive to hierarchy, women are more attuned to others and strive for connectedness. Requesting directions seems as natural to Dianne as continuing to search on his own appears to Matt. But the two people will not resolve their situation as long as neither one understands the other's point of view.

Analyzing such examples of everyday life is the focus of this chapter. We begin by presenting many of the building blocks of common experience and then explore the almost magical way in which face-to-face interaction generates reality. The central concept is **social interaction**, *the process by which people act and react in relation to others*. Social interaction is the key to creating the reality we perceive. And we interact according to particular social guidelines.

SOCIAL STRUCTURE: A GUIDE TO EVERYDAY LIVING

Members of every society rely on social structure to make sense out of everyday situations. The world can be disorienting—even frightening—when cultural norms are unclear. So what, then, are the building blocks of our daily lives?

STATUS

One basic element of social structure is **status**, *a recognized social position that an individual occupies*. Notice that the sociological meaning of the term *status* differs from its everyday meaning of "prestige." In common usage, a university president has more "status" than a professor. Sociologically, however, both "president" and "professor" are statuses because they represent socially defined positions, even though one does confer more power and prestige than the other.

131

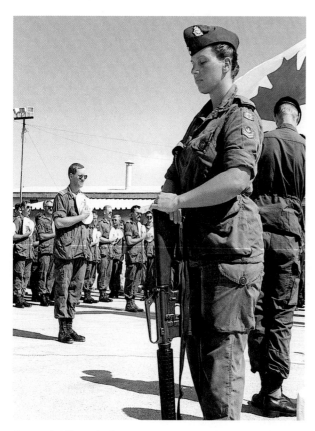

In any rigidly ranked setting, no interaction can proceed until people assess each other's social standing. Thus, military personnel such as these cadets at the Royal Military College in Kingston, Ontario, wear clear insignia to designate their level of authority. Don't we size up one another in much the same way in routine interaction, noting a person's rough age, quality of clothing, and manner for clues about social position?

Every status involves particular duties, rights, and expectations. The statuses people occupy thus guide their behaviour in any setting. In the university classroom, for example, professors and students have distinctive, well-defined responsibilities. Similarly, family interaction turns on the interplay of mother, father, daughters, sons, and others. In all these situations, statuses connect us to others, which is why, in the case of families, we commonly call others "relations." In short, a status defines who and what we are *in relation to* others.

Status is also a key component of social identity. Occupation, for example, is a major part of most self-concepts and is quickly offered as part of a social introduction. Long after retirement, people continue to identify themselves in terms of their life's work.

STATUS SET

Everyone occupies many statuses simultaneously. The term **status set** refers to *all the statuses a person holds at a given time*. A girl may be a *daughter* to her parents, a *sister* to her siblings, a *friend* to members of her social circle, and a *goalie* to others on her hockey team. Just as status sets branch out in many directions, so they also change over the life course. A child grows into an adult, a student becomes a lawyer, and people marry to become husbands and wives, sometimes becoming single again as a result of divorce or death. Joining an organization or finding a job enlarges our status set; withdrawing from activities diminishes it. Individuals gain and lose dozens of statuses over a lifetime.

ASCRIBED AND ACHIEVED STATUS

Sociologists classify statuses in terms of how people obtain them. An **ascribed status** is *a social position that someone receives at birth or assumes involuntarily later in life*. Examples of statuses that are generally ascribed include being a daughter, an Aboriginal person, a teenager, or a widower. Ascribed statuses are matters about which people have little or no choice.

In contrast, an **achieved status** refers to *a social position that someone assumes voluntarily and that reflects personal ability and effort*. Among achieved statuses in Canada are being an honour student, an Olympic athlete, a spouse, a computer programmer, a Rhodes Scholar, or a thief. In each case, the individual has at least some choice in the matter.

In practice, of course, most statuses involve some combination of ascription and achievement. That is, people's ascribed statuses influence the statuses they achieve. Adults who achieve the status of lawyer, for example, are likely to share the ascribed trait of being born into relatively privileged families. And any person of a privileged sex, race, ethnicity, or age has far more opportunity to realize desirable achieved statuses than does someone without such advantages. In contrast, many less desirable statuses such as being a criminal, a drug addict, or a welfare recipient are more easily "achieved" by people born into poverty.

MASTER STATUS

Some statuses matter more than others. A **master status** is *a status that has exceptional importance for social identity, often shaping a person's entire life*. For many people, occupation is a master status since it conveys a great deal about social background, education, and income. Family (of birth or marriage) can function this way, too. Being "an Eaton," "a McCain," "a Trudeau," "a Mulroney," or "a Stronach" is enough by itself to push an individual into the limelight. Most societies of the world also limit the opportunities of women, whatever their abilities, making gender, too, a master status, (cf. Webster and Hysom, 1998).

In a negative sense, serious disease also operates as a master status. Sometimes even lifelong friends shun cancer patients or people with AIDS simply because of their illness. Finally, we sometimes dehumanize people with physical disabilities by perceiving them only in terms of their disability. In the "Diversity: Race, Class, and Gender" box, two people with physical disabilities describe this problem.

ROLE

A second component of social interaction is **role**, *behaviour expected of someone who holds a particular status.* People *hold* a status and *perform* a role (Linton, 1937). The obligations and privileges of the status "student," for example, require you to perform a role by attending classes and completing assignments and, more generally, devoting much of your time to personal enrichment through academic study.

Both statuses and roles vary by culture. In Canada, the status "uncle" refers to a brother of either one's mother or father; in Vietnam, specific terms designate uncles on each side of the family, and responsibilities differ accordingly. In every society, actual role performance varies according to an individual's unique personality, although some societies permit more personal latitude than others do.

ROLE SET

Because we occupy many statuses simultaneously—a status set—everyday life is a mix of multiple roles. Robert Merton (1968) introduced the term **role set** to identify *a number of roles attached to a single status.*

Figure 6–1 illustrates the status set and corresponding role sets of one individual. Four statuses are presented, each linked to a different role set. As a professor, this woman interacts with students (the "teaching role"), as well as with other academics (the "colleague role"). She also holds the status of "mother," with routine responsibilities for her children (the "maternal role"), as well as obligations to their school and other organizations (the "civic role"). Her work as a researcher (the "laboratory role") generates the data she uses in her publications (the "author role"). In addition, she occupies the status of "wife," with corresponding roles in relation to her husband ("conjugal roles" such as confidante and sexual partner), with whom she would share a "domestic role" in terms of maintaining the household. Of course, Figure 6–1 lists only some of this person's status and role sets, since an individual generally occupies several dozen statuses at one time, each linked to a role set. This woman might be, additionally, a daughter caring for aging parents and a member of the city council.

ROLE CONFLICT AND ROLE STRAIN

Members of industrial societies routinely juggle a host of responsibilities demanded by their various statuses

Mike Myers poses with Lorne Michaels after the two unveiled their stars on the Canadian Walk of Fame in Toronto in 2003. Which qualities, do you think, make Mike Myers a role model for young people?

and roles. As most mothers can testify, parenting as well as working outside the home taxes both physical and emotional strength. Sociologists thus recognize **role conflict** as *incompatibility among roles corresponding to two or more statuses.*

We experience role conflict when we find ourselves pulled in various directions by the many statuses we hold. Some municipal or provincial politicians, for example, decide not to run for federal office because the demands of a campaign would impoverish family life; in other cases, ambitious people defer having children or choose to remain childless in order to stay on the "fast track" for career success.

Even the roles linked to a single status may make competing demands on us. The concept of **role strain** refers to *incompatibility among roles corresponding to a single status.* A plant supervisor may enjoy being friendly with other workers. At the same time, however, the supervisor's responsibility for everyone's performance requires maintaining some measure of personal distance from each employee. In short, performing the roles attached to even one status may involve something of a balancing act.

Another strategy for minimizing role conflict is "compartmentalizing" our lives so that we perform roles linked to one status at one time and place, and carry out roles corresponding to another status elsewhere at another time. A familiar example of this scheme is heading home while leaving the job "at work." Clearly, people who work from their homes—your professors, part of the time—would have considerable difficulty achieving this.

Physical Disability as Master Status

Following are some comments from two people with very different diseases, both of which may have profound effects on the whole round of life, including self-concept, primary relationships, acquaintance relationships, and work life.

The first is a person with cancer. Among strangers, neighbours, and acquaintances, the term "cancer" is mentioned with particular care. One woman told of her trips to the hairdresser, to whom she had been going for many years, during her chemotherapy treatment. "My hairdresser said to me, 'Your hair is falling out,' and I was too shocked and ashamed to tell her the truth. So I just said, 'Oh, I don't know what it could be.'" This woman stopped going to the hairdresser. She couldn't face this individual with her pain and shame. They had always had a good but distant professional relationship and she had had her hair done there for ten years. She had told her hairdresser the things of which she was proud. Her hairdresser knew that she had three children, knew their names and ages, and knew the name of her husband. The woman with cancer was surprised by her own reaction. She said,

I don't know why it is. Maybe it is something lacking in me. Maybe it's just my nature. I don't know. I'm not

that open. I don't know what it is, but I can't go around telling everybody. I just can't do it. It's not really that I'm trying to keep it a secret. Or maybe I am. I don't know what it is.

Notice that the diagnosis of cancer is thought to be so overwhelming as to diminish the person with the disease. The irony, then, is that it is assumed to be a status of such proportions that its very naming is problematic. The same woman had been trying to sell her home. When people learned from the real estate agent that she had cancer, they lost interest.

We just had to change real estate companies and agents. And this time, we didn't tell. Soon several people looked at the house and then we finally sold it. (Nancarrow Clarke, 1985:30)

The second person suffers from chronic fatigue syndrome (CFS), or myalgic encephalomyelitis (ME):

Well, when I first got diagnosed because there was such a stigma . . . you know, like it's a psychological thing and I felt embarrassed. I didn't really tell anybody other than my immediate family and my very closest friends, whereas now when I'm talking I'll just say what I have because how are

people going to learn if they don't know what it is and how it affects us? So in the beginning, I felt embarrassed. I cried . . . I mean I didn't cry when I had the growth as much as I cried when I got diagnosed with CFS because it was such a negative . . . I felt . . . you know, and I went to a support group and I said why do I feel like we're a group that has . . . you know, where we should be shipped on an island all by ourself. . . .

I mean I wouldn't even say half of my complaints because they were so weird . . . like my fingers hurt, my joints hurt or I feel like I have arthritis but I'm too young to have arthritis. You know, half the time you didn't even tell them because you felt like you were a hypochondriac. (Nancarrow Clarke, unpublished research)

Notice here how the disease is seen as a threat to the very self of the sufferer. She experiences social isolation, embarrassment, and stigma. There is continuing debate about whether CFS is just an excuse for a break among hard-driving, ambitious young people (hence its early nickname, the "Yuppie flu"), a psychosomatic disorder, or a biologically based, and therefore "real," disease. Those with the disease suffer from the current lack of clarity as to its cause and treatment.

ROLE EXIT

After she left the life of a Catholic nun to become a university sociologist, Helen Rose Fuchs Ebaugh (1988) began to study *role exit*, the process by which people disengage from important social roles. Studying a range of "exes," including ex-nuns, ex-doctors, ex-husbands, and ex-alcoholics, Ebaugh identified elements common to the process of "becoming an ex."

According to Ebaugh, people initiate the process of role exit by reflecting critically on their existing

lives and grappling with doubts about their ability or willingness to persist in a certain role. As they imagine alternative roles, they ultimately reach a point when they decide to pursue a new life.

Even at this point, however, a past role may continue to influence their lives. "Exes" retain a self-image shaped by an earlier role, which may interfere with the drive to build a new sense of self. An ex-nun, for example, may hesitate to wear stylish clothing and makeup.

"Exes" must also rebuild relationships with people who may have known them in their earlier lives and

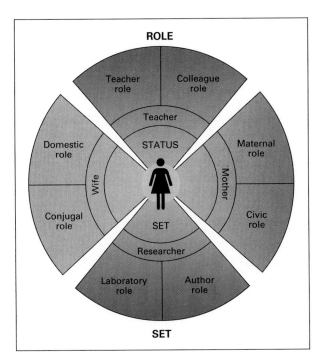

FIGURE 6–1 Status Set and Role Set

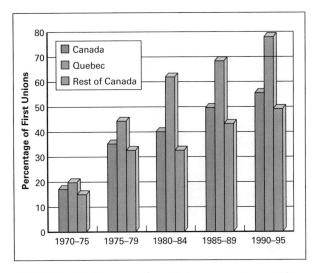

FIGURE 6-2 Common-law Unions as a Proportion of First Unions: Canada, Quebec, and Other Provinces

Source: Adapted by Linda Gerber from Turcotte and Bélanger (2000:106).

who may not realize just how new and unfamiliar their present role may be. And learning new social skills poses another challenge. For example, Ebaugh reports, ex-nuns who begin dating after decades in the church are often startled to learn that sexual norms are now vastly different from those they knew as teenagers.

THE SOCIAL CONSTRUCTION OF REALITY

While behaviour is guided by status and role, each human being has considerable ability to shape what happens moment to moment. "Reality," in other words, is not as fixed as we may think. The phrase **social construction of reality** identifies *the process by which people creatively shape reality through social interaction.* This idea stands at the foundation of sociology's symbolic-interaction paradigm, as described in earlier chapters.

Most everyday situations involve at least some agreement about what's going on, but participants perceive events differently to the extent that they are motivated by disparate interests and intentions. Social interaction, then, amounts to negotiating reality.

One area in which personal decisions have restructured social reality is that of family formation. Figure 6-2 reveals that since 1970 the proportion of Canadians forming first unions by common law has grown dramatically—from 17 to 57 percent by the

early 1990s (Turcotte and Bélanger, 2000:106). In Quebec, over the same two decades, the growth was from 21 to an astounding 80 percent. This means that, as Quebec couples negotiate the terms of their social interaction (i.e., their first unions), eight out of ten choose to cohabit rather than marry. The collective impact of these common-law unions, negotiated one at a time, on the institution of marriage is far greater than that of the gays and lesbians who will be affected by the federal government's decision in the summer of 2003 to change the definition of marriage to include same-sex couples. For the symbolic interactionist, the important elements in this restructuring of social life are the personal decisions made, in private, by individuals forming their first unions.

For another example of the social construction of reality, consider how this short excerpt from "True Trash," a short story by internationally renowned Canadian author Margaret Atwood, illustrates one way that names and clothing styles construct a certain "type" of person.

> Eleven years later Donny is walking along Yorkville Avenue, in Toronto, in the summer heat. He's no longer Donny. At some point, which even he can't remember exactly, he has changed into Don. He's wearing sandals, and a white Indian-style shirt over his cut-off jeans. He has longish hair and a beard. The beard has come out yellow, whereas the hair is brown. He likes the effect: WASP Jesus or Hollywood Viking, depending on his mood. He has a string of wooden beads around his neck.
>
> This is how he dresses on Saturdays, to go to Yorkville; to go there and just hang around, with the

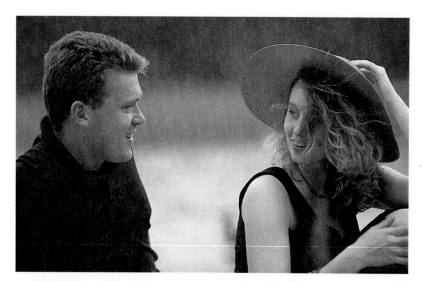

Flirting is an everyday experience in reality construction. Each person offers information to the other, and hints at romantic interest. Yet the interaction proceeds with a tentative and often humorous air so that either individual can withdraw at any time without further obligation.

crowds of others who are doing the same. Sometimes he gets high, on the pot that circulates as freely as cigarettes did once. He thinks he should be enjoying this experience more than he actually does.

During the rest of the week he has a job in his father's law office. He can get away with the beard there, just barely, as long as he balances it with a suit. (But even the older guys are growing their sideburns and wearing coloured shirts, and using words like "creative" more than they used to.) He doesn't tell the people he meets in Yorkville about this job, just as he doesn't tell the law office about his friends' acid trips. He's leading a double life. It feels precarious, and brave. (1991:30–31)

This situation reveals the drama—sometimes subtle, sometimes savage—by which human beings creatively build reality. There are limits, of course, to what even the most skilful and persuasive personality can achieve. And, of course, not everyone enters a negotiation with equal standing. The fact that Donny was the son of the lawyer in whose office he was working likely helped him bridge the two realities.

THE THOMAS THEOREM

Donny's impression management allowed him to be part of the Yorkville scene and his father's law office. W.I. Thomas (1966:301; orig. 1931) succinctly expressed this insight in what has come to be known as the **Thomas theorem**: *situations we define as real become real in their consequences.*

Applied to social interaction, Thomas's insight means that although reality is initially "soft" as it is fashioned, it can become "hard" in its effects. In the case of Donny, having succeeded as a member in two very different groups, he is able to lead a double life.

ETHNOMETHODOLOGY

Rather than assuming that reality is something "out there," the symbolic-interaction paradigm posits that reality is created by people in everyday encounters. But how, exactly, do we define reality for ourselves? Answering this question is the objective of ethnomethodology, a specialized approach within the symbolic-interaction paradigm.

The term itself has two parts: the Greek *ethno* refers to people and how they understand their surroundings; *methodology* designates a set of methods or principles. Combining them makes **ethnomethodology**, *the study of the way people make sense of their everyday lives.*

Ethnomethodology is largely the creation of Harold Garfinkel (1967), who challenged the then-dominant view of society as a broad, abstract "system" (recall the approach of Emile Durkheim, described in Chapter 4, "Society"). Garfinkel wanted to explore how we make sense of countless familiar situations. On the surface, we engage in intentional speech or action, but these efforts rest on deeper assumptions about the world that we usually take for granted.

Think, for a moment, about what we assume in asking someone the simple question "How are you?" Do we mean physically? Mentally? Spiritually? Financially? Are we even looking for an answer, or are we just being polite?

Ethnomethodology, then, delves into the sense-making process in any social encounter. Because so much of this process is ingrained, Garfinkel argues that the only effective way to expose how we make sense of events is to purposefully *break the rules.* Deliberately ignoring conventional rules and observing how people respond, he points out, allows us to tease out how people build a reality. Thus, Garfinkel (1967) directed his students to refuse to "play the game" in a wide range of situations. Some students living with their parents started acting as if they were boarders rather than children; others entered stores and insisted on bargaining for items; others recruited people into simple games (such as tic-tac-toe) only to intentionally flout the rules; still others initiated conversations while slowly moving closer and closer to the other person.

The students first noticed people's reactions. Typically, the "victims" of these rule violations became agitated. Attempts to identify exactly why people were disturbed led to insights about the unspoken agreements that underlie family life, shopping, fair play, and the like. As the hand-holding experiment suggests in the opener to Chapter 1, ethnomethodology succeeds in heightening awareness of many unnoticed patterns of everyday life.

REALITY BUILDING: SOME BROADER CONSIDERATIONS

Taking a broader view of reality construction, people do not build everyday experience out of thin air. In part, how we act or what we see in our surroundings depends on our interests. Scanning the night sky, for example, lovers discover romance, while scientists perceive the same stars as hydrogen atoms fusing into helium. Social background also directs our perceptions, since we build reality out of elements in the surrounding culture. For this reason, residents of, say, affluent Westmount in Montreal experience the city differently from those living in the city's east end, where the unemployment rate is one of the highest in Canada.

In global perspective, reality construction is even more variable. People waiting for a bus in London, England, typically "queue up" in a straight line; people in Quebec City wait in a much less orderly fashion. Constraints on the social experiences of women in Saudi Arabia would be incomprehensible to most Canadian women. Elvis lovers live in the rural and eastern regions of the United States, while Elvis loathers predominate throughout most of the western states. Though the birth rate is rising in Moscow, where women perceive increased economic security, it remains low in the rest of Russia, where economic turmoil persists.

From these examples, we conclude that people build reality from the surrounding culture. Chapter 3 ("Culture") explains how people the world over derive different meanings from specific gestures, so that travellers can find themselves building a most unexpected reality! Similarly, what we "see" in a book or a film also depends on the assumptions we make. JoEllen Shively (1992) screened "Western" films for men of European descent as well as Native-American men. Both categories claimed to enjoy the films, but for different reasons. White men interpreted the films as

Around the world, culture frames the reality people experience. Most people living in rich countries such as Canada rarely confront death. In contrast, these refugees in Rwanda—a poor nation shaken by violence and bloodshed— have been forced to accept death as a part of everyday life.

praising rugged people striking out for the west to impose their will on nature. Native-American men saw in the same films a celebration of land and nature apart from any human ambitions.

If people the world over inhabit different realities, are some happier than others? Figure 6–3 suggests that, when asked if they had recently felt themselves to be "on top of the world," people in Sweden, Canada, and the United States were much more likely to respond in the affirmative than those in India, Russia, and Japan. Significantly, when asked about their wants, Canadians put "happiness" first (see Figure 6–4), followed closely by "freedom" and "family life"—both of which might contribute to happiness.

A brief pause is in order here. Before taking Figure 6–3 at face value, we should revisit our earlier discussion of "cultural relativity" and the problems involved in translating advertisements. How, one might ask, does the concept or emotion of feeling "on top of the world" translate into different languages? Further, is the link between feeling "on top of the world" and "happiness" obvious in all cultural contexts? The World Values Survey, as you can see, faces some very complex translation problems.

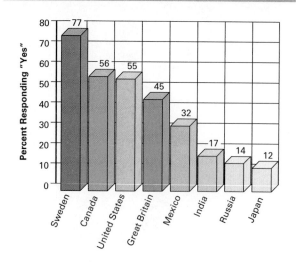

FIGURE 6–3 Global Happiness

Survey question: "We are interested in the way people are feeling these days. During the past few weeks, did you ever feel 'on top of the world,' feeling that life is wonderful?"

Source: World Values Survey (1994).

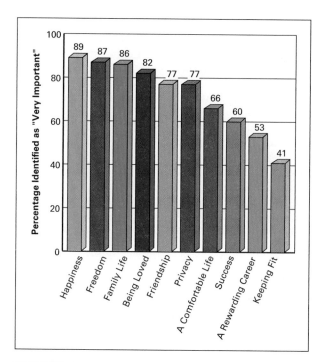

FIGURE 6–4 Top Ten Wants

What do Canadians want? This survey suggests that, more than anything, we want happiness. Does this strike you as a universal or a culturally specific trait?

Source: Bibby (1995:2).

DRAMATURGICAL ANALYSIS: "THE PRESENTATION OF SELF"

Erving Goffman (1922–82) enhanced the understanding of everyday life by noting that people interacting behave much like actors performing on a stage. By imagining ourselves as directors scrutinizing what goes on in some situational "theatre," we engage in what Goffman called **dramaturgical analysis**, *the investigation of social interaction in terms of theatrical performance.*

Dramaturgical analysis offers a fresh look at two familiar concepts. In theatrical terms, a status mirrors a part in a play, and a role serves as a script, supplying dialogue and action for each character. Moreover, in any setting, a person is both actor and audience. Goffman described each individual's "performance" as the **presentation of self**, *an individual's effort to create specific impressions in the minds of others.* Presentation of self, or impression management, contains several distinctive elements (Goffman, 1959, 1967).

PERFORMANCES

As we present ourselves in everyday situations, we convey information—consciously and unconsciously—to others. An individual's performance includes dress (costume), any objects carried along (props), and tone of voice and particular gestures (manner). In addition, people craft their performance according to the setting (stage). We may joke loudly on a sidewalk, for example, but assume a more reverent manner on entering a church. In addition, individuals design settings, such as a home or an office, to enhance a performance by invoking the desired reactions in others.

An Illustration: The Doctor's Office

Consider how a physician's office conveys information to an audience of patients. Physicians enjoy substantial prestige and power in Canada, a fact immediately grasped by patients upon entering a doctor's office. At first, the physician is nowhere to be seen. Instead, in what Goffman calls the "front region" of the setting, the patient encounters a receptionist who functions as a gatekeeper, deciding if and when the patient can meet the physician. Who waits to see whom is, of course, a power game. Observation of the doctor's waiting room, with patients (often impatiently) awaiting their call to the inner sanctum, leaves little doubt that the medical team controls events.

The physician's private office and examination room are the "back region" of the setting. Here the patient confronts a wide range of props (medical books, framed degrees), which reinforce the impression that the physician has the specialized knowledge necessary to call the shots. In the office, the physician remains seated behind a desk—the larger and grander the desk, the greater the statement of power—while the patient is provided with only a chair.

The physician's appearance and manner convey still more information. The usual costume of a white lab coat may have the practical function of keeping clothes from becoming soiled, but its social function is to let others know at a glance the physician's status. A stethoscope around the neck or a black medical bag in hand has the same purpose. A doctor's highly technical terminology—frequently mystifying—also emphasizes the hierarchy in the situation. The use of the title "Doctor" by patients who, in turn, are frequently addressed only by their first names also underscores the physician's dominant position. The overall message of a doctor's performance is clear: "I will help you only if you allow me to take charge."

NONVERBAL COMMUNICATION

Novelist William Sansom describes a fictional Mr. Preedy, an English vacationer on a beach in Spain:

> . . . He took care to avoid catching anyone's eye. First of all, he had to make it clear to those potential companions of his holiday that they were of no concern to him whatsoever. He stared through them, round them, over them—eyes lost in space. The beach might have been empty. If by chance a ball was thrown his way, he looked surprised; then let a smile of amusement lighten his face (Kindly Preedy), looked around dazed to see that there were people on the beach, tossed it back with a smile to himself and not a smile at the people. . . .
>
> [He] then gathered together his beach-wrap and bag into a neat sand-resistant pile (Methodical and Sensible Preedy), rose slowly to stretch at ease his huge frame (Big-Cat Preedy), and tossed aside his sandals (Carefree Preedy, after all). (*A Contest of Ladies*, 1956, 230–32, quoted in Goffman, 1959:4–5)

Through his conduct, Mr. Preedy offers a great deal of information about himself to anyone caring to observe him. Notice that he does so without uttering a single word. This illustrates the process of **nonverbal communication**, *communication using body movements, gestures, and facial expressions rather than speech.*

Virtually any part of the body can be used to transmit nonverbal communication. Facial expressions form the most significant element of "body language." As noted in the "Global Sociology" box, smiling and other facial gestures express basic emotions such as pleasure, surprise, and anger the world over. Further, people project particular shades of meaning with their faces. We distinguish, for example, between the delib-

When we enter the presence of others, we "construct" ourselves and begin a "presentation of self" that has much in common with a dramatic performance. Such a presentation involves clothing (costume), other objects (props), certain typical behaviour (script), and a particular setting (stage). No wonder the ancient Greeks, who understood the element of acting in everyday life, used the same word for "person" and "mask."

erate smile of Kindly Preedy on the beach, a spontaneous smile of joy at seeing a friend, a pained smile of embarrassment, and a full, unrestrained smile of self-satisfaction that we often associate with the "cat who ate the canary."

Eye contact is another crucial element of nonverbal communication. Generally, we use eye contact to initiate social interaction. Someone across the room "catches our eye," for example, sparking a conversation. Avoiding the eyes of another, on the other hand, discourages communication. Hands, too, speak for us. Common hand gestures in our culture convey, among other things, an insult, a request for a ride, an invitation for someone to join us, or a demand that others stop in their tracks. Gestures also supplement spoken words. Pointing in a menacing way at someone, for example, intensifies a word of warning, just as shrugging the shoulders adds an air of indifference to the phrase "I don't know," and rapidly waving the arms lends urgency to the single word "Hurry!"

Aboriginal people, in their encounters with Canada's justice system, are more likely than other Canadians to be arrested, indicted, convicted, and imprisoned (Frideres, 1998; Wotherspoon and Satzewich, 1993). Part of the explanation for the abysmal relationship between our justice system and Native individuals is cross-cultural miscommunication. Because they are dealing with a "foreign" and misunderstood legal system, Natives are particularly likely to plead guilty in court; however, even when they do not, they

Emotions in Global Perspective: Do We All Feel the Same?

On a Vancouver sidewalk, a woman reacts angrily to the skateboarder who zooms past her. Apart from a few choice words, her facial expression broadcasts a strong emotion that North Americans easily recognize. But would an observer from New Guinea be able to interpret her emotion? In other words, do people the world over share similar feelings, and do they express them in the same way?

Paul Ekman (1980b) and his colleagues studied emotions around the world, even among members of a small society in New Guinea. They concluded that people throughout the world experience six basic emotions: anger, fear, disgust, happiness, surprise, and sadness. Moreover, people everywhere recognize these feelings in the same distinctive facial gestures. To Ekman, this means that much of our emotional life is universal—rather than culturally variable—and that the display of emotion is biologically programmed in our facial features, muscles, and central nervous system.

But if the reality of emotions is rooted in our biology, Ekman and other researchers note three ways in which emotional life differs significantly in global perspective.

First, *what triggers an emotion varies from one society to another*. Whether people define a particular situation as an insult (causing anger), a loss (calling forth sadness), or a mystical event (provoking surprise and awe) depends on the cultural surroundings of the individual.

Second, *people display emotions according to the norms of their culture*. Every society has rules about when, where, and to whom an individual may exhibit certain emotions. People in Canada typically express emotions more freely in the home among family members than among colleagues in the workplace. Similarly, we expect children to express emotions to parents, although parents are taught to guard their emotions in front of children.

Third, *societies differ in terms of how people cope with emotions*. Some societies encourage the expression of feelings, while others belittle emotions and demand that their members suppress them. Societies also display significant gender differences in this regard. In Canada, most people regard emotional expression as feminine, expected of women but a sign of weakness in men. In other societies, however, this sex-typing of emotions is less pronounced or even reversed.

In sum, emotional life in global perspective has both common and variable elements. People around the world experience the same basic feelings. But what sparks a particular emotion, to whom someone expresses it, and whether people encourage or discourage the display of emotions are variable products of social learning.

Sources: Ekman (1980a, 1980b), Lutz and White (1986), and Lutz (1988).

---

are relatively likely to be convicted. Often, the reason is that body language and reluctance to establish eye contact with people in authority make them *look* guilty to those unfamiliar with Native cultural norms. The result is that nonverbal communication, indicating respect in many Native communities, suggests deceitfulness within the context of the dominant society.

Body Language and Deception

As any actor knows, the "perfect performance" is an elusive goal. In everyday performances, some element of body language often contradicts our intended meaning. A teenage boy offers an explanation for getting home late, for example, but his mother doubts his words because he avoids looking her in the eye. The movie star on a television talk show claims that her recent flop at the box office is "no big deal," but the nervous swing of her leg belies her casual denial. In practical terms, carefully observing nonverbal communication (most of which is not easily controlled) provides clues to deception, in much the same way that a lie detector records tell-tale changes in breathing, pulse rate, perspiration, and blood pressure.

Yet detecting lies is difficult, because no single bodily gesture directly indicates deceit the way, say, a smile indicates pleasure. Even so, because any performance involves so many expressions, few people can confidently lie without allowing some piece of contradictory information to slip through, arousing the suspicions of a careful observer. Therefore, the key to detecting deceit is to scan the whole performance with an eye for inconsistencies and discrepancies.

Lies are detectable, but training is the key to noticing relevant clues. Another key to spotting deception is knowing the other person well, the reason that parents can usually spot deceit in their children. Almost anyone can unmask deception when the liar is

To most people in Canada, these expressions convey anger, fear, disgust, happiness, surprise, and sadness. But do people elsewhere in the world define them in the same way? Research suggests that all human beings experience the same basic emotions and display them to others in the same basic ways. But culture plays a part by specifying the situations that trigger one emotion or another.

 Can you tell when Canadian actor Leslie Nielsen is acting? Test yourself with the Discovery Channel video at www.exn.ca/ Stories/2002/09/25/51.asp. For more information about facial expression and honesty, visit www.bbc.co.uk./science/ humanbody/humanface/ expertarticle_ekman.shtml

trying to cover up strong emotions. Check out the "Applying Sociology" box for further details on the detection of deceit.

GENDER AND PERSONAL PERFORMANCES

Because women are socialized to be less assertive than males, they tend to be especially sensitive to nonverbal communication. In fact, gender is a central element in personal performances. Based on the work of Nancy Henley, Mykol Hamilton, and Barrie Thorne (1992), we can extend the present discussion of personal performances to spotlight the importance of gender.

Demeanour

Demeanour—that is, general conduct or deportment—reflects a person's level of social power. Simply put, powerful people enjoy far greater personal discretion in how they act; subordinates act more formally and self-consciously. Off-colour remarks, swearing, or casually removing shoes and putting feet up on the desk may be acceptable behaviour for the boss, but it rarely is for employees. Similarly, people in positions of dominance can interrupt the performances of others with impunity, while others are expected to display deference by remaining silent (Smith-Lovin and Brody, 1989; Henley et al., 1992; Johnson, 1994).

Since women generally occupy positions of lesser power, demeanour is a gender issue as well. As Chapter 13 ("Gender Stratification") explains, about half of all working women in Canada hold clerical or service jobs that place them under the control of

Hide Those Lyin' Eyes: Can You Do It?

Poker players and police officers have long realized that a good liar has a real advantage. Deception is a common element of everyday interaction, if only because common politeness sometimes demands that we not say what we really think.

Can you tell when another person is trying to deceive you? Paul Ekman suggests paying close attention to four elements of a performance—words, voice, body language, and facial expression.

1. **Words.** Good liars mentally rehearse their lines, but they cannot always avoid a simple slip of the tongue—something the performer did not mean to say in quite that way. For example, a young man who is deceiving his parents by claiming that his roommate is a male friend rather than a female lover might mistakenly use the word "she" rather than "he" in conversation. The more complicated the de-

ception, the more likely a performer is to make a revealing mistake.

2. **Voice.** Tone and patterns of speech contain clues to deception because they are hard to control. Especially when trying to hide a powerful emotion, a person cannot easily prevent the voice from trembling or breaking. Similarly, the individual may speak more quickly (suggesting anger) or slowly (indicating sadness). Nervous laughter, inappropriate pauses between words, or nonwords, such as "ah" and "ummm," also hint at discomfort.

3. **Body language.** A "leak" from body language may tip off an observer to deception as well. Subtle body movements, for example, give the impression of nervousness, as does sudden swallowing or rapid breathing. These are especially good clues to deception because few people can control them. Sometimes, not using the body in the expected way—as when a person's body fails to confirm words that suggest excitement—also suggests deception.

4. **Facial expressions.** Because facial expressions, too, are hard to control, they give away many phony performances. Have you picked the lying face? It's the one on the right. While a real smile usually has a relaxed expression and lots of "laugh lines" around the eyes, a phony smile seems forced, with a less-open mouth and fewer wrinkles around the eyes.

Sources: Based on Ekman (1985) and Golden (1999).

---

supervisors, who are usually men. Women, then, craft their personal performances more carefully than men and display a greater degree of deference in everyday interaction.

Use of Space

How much space does a personal performance require? Here again, power plays a key role, since using more space conveys a nonverbal message of personal importance. Men typically command more space than women do, whether pacing back and forth before an audience or casually lounging on the beach. Why? Our culture traditionally has measured femininity by how little space women occupy—the standard of "daintiness"— while gauging masculinity by how much territory a man controls—the standard of "turf" (Henley et al., 1992).

The concept of **personal space** refers to *the surrounding area in which an individual makes some claim to privacy*. In Canada, people typically position themselves several feet apart when speaking; throughout the Middle East, in contrast, people stand much closer when they converse. Throughout the world, gender further modifies these patterns. In daily life, men commonly intrude on the personal space of women. A woman's encroachment into a man's personal space, however, is likely to be construed as a sexual overture. Here again, women have less power in everyday interaction than men do.

Staring, Smiling, and Touching

Eye contact encourages interaction. Typically, women employ eye contact to sustain conversation more than

Hand gestures vary widely from one culture to another. Yet people everywhere define a chuckle, grin, or smirk in response to someone's performance as an indication that one does not take another person seriously. Therefore, the world over, people who cannot restrain their mirth tactfully cover their faces.

men do. Men have their own distinctive brand of eye contact: staring. By making women the targets of stares, men are both making a claim of social dominance and defining women as sexual objects.

Although frequently signalling pleasure, *smiling* has a host of meanings. In a male-dominated world, women often smile to indicate appeasement or acceptance of submission. For this reason, women smile more than men; in extreme cases, smiling may reach the level of nervous habit (Henley et al., 1992).

Finally, *touching* constitutes an intriguing social pattern. Mutual touching generally conveys intimacy and caring. Apart from close relationships, however, touching is generally something men do to women (although rarely, in our culture, to other men). A male physician touches the shoulder of his female nurse as they examine a report, a young man touches the back of his woman friend as he guides her across the street, or a male skiing instructor looks for opportunities to touch his female students. In these examples—as well as many others—touching may evoke little response, so common is it in everyday life. But it amounts to a subtle ritual by which men express their dominant position in an assumed hierarchy that subordinates women.

IDEALIZATION

Complex motives underlie human behaviour. Even so, according to Goffman, we construct performances to idealize our intentions. We try to convince others (and maybe ourselves) that what we do reflects ideal cultural standards rather than selfish motives.

Idealization is easily illustrated by returning to the world of physicians and patients. In a hospital, physicians engage in a performance commonly described as "making rounds." Entering the room of a patient, the physician often stops at the foot of the bed and silently examines the patient's chart. Afterwards, physician and

patient converse briefly. In ideal terms, this routine involves a physician making a personal visit to inquire about a patient's condition.

In reality, something less exemplary is usually going on. A physician who sees several dozen patients a day may remember little about most of them. Reading the chart gives the physician the opportunity to rediscover the patient's identity and medical problems. Openly revealing the actual impersonality of much medical care would undermine the culturally ideal perception of the physician as deeply concerned about the welfare of others.

Idealization is woven into the fabric of everyday life in countless ways. Physicians, university professors, lawyers, and other professionals typically idealize their motives for entering their chosen careers. They describe their work as "making a contribution to science," "helping others," "answering a calling from God," or perhaps "serving the community." Rarely do such people concede the less honourable, although common, motives of seeking the income, power, prestige, and leisure these occupations confer.

 Taking a broader view, idealization underlies social civility, since we smile and make polite remarks to people we do not like. Such small hypocrisies ease our way through social interactions. Even when we suspect that others are putting on an act, rarely do we openly challenge their performance, for reasons we shall explain next.

EMBARRASSMENT AND TACT

The professor consistently mispronounces the dean's name; the visiting dignitary rises from the table to speak, unaware that a napkin still hangs from her neck; the prime minister becomes ill at a state dinner. Despite careful crafting of performances, slip-ups of all kinds occur. The result is *embarrassment*, which, in

Social Interaction: Reaching across Cyberspace

Whereas technology traditionally merely sustained human relationships already formed from face-to-face contact, an Internet relationship can be initiated technologically. Because they are so disembodied, so devoid of physical presence . . . divisions between man and woman, old and young, strong and weak, sick and healthy, cool dude and nerd begin to be bridged as in few other ways. (Goyder, 1997:186)

Social interaction based on electronic communication, and the Internet in particular, has become an increasingly important part of the experience of Canadians. While providing a new basis of interaction in ongoing relationships, this new medium has put us in contact with people around the world and given new meaning to the concept of social network. We are, in McLuhan's terms, disembodied and unconstrained in time and space to the point where we lose our old identities and become part of the world or global village (Benedetti and DeHart, 1996).

One of your authors, Linda Gerber, has students in second- and fourth-year Canadian society courses at the University of Guelph involved in computer conferencing. Students meet face-to-face in the classroom, but they also communicate electronically with the class as a whole and with smaller working groups as they report on their research activities, respond to current events, debate various issues, react to contributions by other group members, and prepare for class presentations. Since the conferencing begins early in each semester, most students "meet," or at least get to know, most of their classmates and study group members *first* via computer. Initially, one hears (and reads on the computer screen) rumblings of resistance and discontent as students complain about the impersonality of computer contact and try to arrange group meetings "in the flesh." Later, these same students are involved in intensive electronic communication—effective communication that reaches all group members without the need to juggle schedules for face-to-face meetings restricted by time and place.

Their task at hand might be rewriting the Canadian constitution (by groups representing Canada's provinces or regions), designing social or economic policies and programs (as "ministers" of government departments), researching special topics and preparing for group presentations—or simply sharing reactions to current events. The conferencing system allows students to reach the whole class or their research group by simply logging on, from home or the computer lab, at any time of the day or night.

Over the course of the semester, discussion—and sometimes even argument—can become quite intense.

Differences of opinion and interpersonal conflict are sorted out through computer conferences (as well as face-to-face contact). Some of the conference group members become almost "addicted," logging on several times a day with comments, references, or suggestions for areas to explore; others do the bare minimum. Comments on the conferences and in-course evaluations reveal that some students thoroughly enjoy the experience while others remain frustrated and unenthusiastic. Inevitably, at the end of the semester, conference messages turn to goodbyes and comment on the quality and emotional impact of the group work: "Let's keep in touch"; "I'm going to miss this"; "Hey, we really accomplished a lot!" One student noted, "I never thought I'd get emotionally attached to you all. This has been the best group experience I've had at university."

This experience with electronic communication is increasingly relevant to the world of work. Many people who work as teams through this medium may meet in person rarely or not at all. More and more people, including those highly placed in various corporations, are doing some or all of their work from home offices—electronically linked to their head offices and the rest of the world. Disembodied and unconstrained by time or place, students and workers alike are engaged in productive activity through cyberspace.

---

dramaturgical terms, means the discomfort that follows a spoiled performance. Goffman describes embarrassment simply as "losing face."

Embarrassment looms as an ever-present danger because, first, all performances typically contain some measure of deception. Second, most performances involve a complex array of elements, any one of which, in a thoughtless moment, may shatter the intended impression.

Interestingly, an audience usually overlooks flaws in a performance, thereby allowing an actor to avoid embarrassment. If we do point out a misstep ("Excuse me, but do you know that your fly is open?"), we do it discreetly and only to help someone avoid even greater loss of face. In Hans Christian Andersen's classic fable "The Emperor's New Clothes," the child who blurts out that the emperor is parading around naked is telling the truth, yet is scolded for being rude.

But members of an audience usually do more than ignore flaws in a performance, Goffman explains; typically, they help the performer recover from them. Tact, then, amounts to helping another person "save face." After hearing a supposed expert make an embarrassingly inaccurate remark, for example, people may tactfully ignore the comment as if it were never spoken at all. Alternatively, mild laughter may indicate that they wish to dismiss what they have heard as a joke. Or a listener may simply respond, "I'm sure you didn't mean that," acknowledging the statement but not allowing it to destroy the actor's performance.

Why is tact such a common response? Because embarrassment provokes discomfort not simply for one person but for *everyone*. As the entire audience feels uneasy when an actor forgets a line, people who observe awkward behaviour are reminded of how fragile their own performances often are. Socially constructed reality thus functions like a dam holding back chaos. If one person's performance springs a leak, others tactfully assist in making repairs. Everyone, after all, engages in building culture, and no one wants reality to be suddenly swept away.

In sum, Goffman's research shows that, while behaviour is spontaneous in some respects, it is more patterned than we like to think. Almost four hundred years ago, William Shakespeare captured this idea in memorable lines that still ring true:

> All the world's a stage,
> And all the men and women merely players:
> They have their exits and their entrances;
> And one man in his time plays many parts.
> (*As You Like It*, II.vii.139–42)

INTERACTION IN EVERYDAY LIFE: TWO ILLUSTRATIONS

We have now examined many elements of social interaction. The final sections of this chapter illustrate key lessons by focusing on two important, yet quite different, elements of everyday life.

LANGUAGE: THE GENDER ISSUE

Language is the thread that ties members of a society together in the symbolic web we call culture. In everyday life, language conveys meaning on more than one level. Besides the obvious message in what people say, a host of additional meanings is embedded in our language. One such message involves gender. Language defines men and women differently in at least three ways, involving control, value, and attention (Henley et al., 1992).[1]

[1]The following sections draw primarily on Henley et al. (1992). Additional material comes from Thorne et al. (1983) and others, as noted.

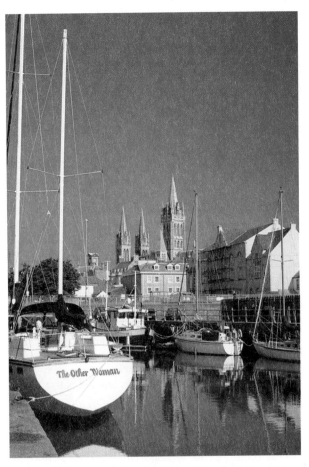

Why do we associate ownership with men and characterize what is owned as feminine? How easily can you imagine renaming this boat—The Other Woman—with the gender reversed?

Language and Control

A young man astride his new motorcycle rolls proudly into the gas station, and eagerly says to the attendant, "Isn't she a beauty?" On the surface, the question has little to do with gender. Yet, curiously, a common linguistic pattern confers the female "she," and never the male "he," on a man's prized possessions.

The language men use often reveals their concern with competence and control. In this case, a man attaches a female pronoun to a motorcycle (car, yacht, or other object) because it reflects ownership.

A more obvious control function of language relates to people's names. Traditionally in Canada, and in many other parts of the world, a woman takes the family name of the man she marries. While few people consider this an explicit statement of a man's ownership of a woman, many believe that it reflects male dominance. When Joe Clark became Canada's prime minister in 1979, he encountered hostility and resistance from some quarters because his wife, Maureen

McTeer, had retained her birth name: "If a man can't control his wife, how can he possibly run the country?" Over the years since McTeer was our prime minister's wife, an increasing proportion of married women have been retaining their own names or merging two family names. In Quebec, women are not merely encouraged to retain their original names: the law actually requires them to do so.

Language and Value

Language usually treats as masculine whatever has greater value, force, or significance. Although we may not notice it, this pattern is deeply rooted in the English language. For instance, the positive adjective *virtuous*, meaning "morally worthy" or "excellent," is derived from the Latin word *vir*, meaning "man"; the derogatory adjective *hysterical* is derived from the Greek word *hyster*, meaning "uterus."

In numerous, more familiar ways, language also confers different value on the two sexes. Traditional masculine terms such as "king" or "lord" have retained their positive meaning, while comparable terms such as "queen," "madam," or "dame" have acquired negative connotations in contemporary usage. Language thus both mirrors social attitudes and helps to perpetuate them.

Similarly, use of the suffixes "ette" and "ess" to denote femininity generally devalues the words to which they are added. For example, a "major" has higher standing than a "majorette," as does a "host" in relation to a "hostess." And, certainly, men's groups with names such as the Saskatchewan Roughriders carry more stature than women's groups with names such as the Radio City Music Hall Rockettes.

Language and Attention

Language also shapes reality by directing greater attention to masculine endeavours. Consider our use of personal pronouns. In the English language, the plural pronoun "they" is neutral, as it refers to both sexes. But the corresponding singular pronouns "he" and "she" specify gender. According to traditional grammatical practice, we use "he" along with the possessive "his" and the objective "him" to refer to all people. Thus, we assume that the bit of wisdom "He who hesitates is lost" refers to women as well as to men. But this practice also reflects the traditional cultural pattern of ignoring the lives of women. Some research suggests that people continue to respond to allegedly inclusive male pronouns as if only males were involved (MacKay, 1983). One old saying turns this understanding upside down: "Man, like other mammals, breast-feeds his young."

The English language has no gender-neutral, third-person-singular personal pronoun. Recently, however, the plural pronouns "they" and "them" have

gained currency as singular pronouns (e.g., "A person should do as they please"). This usage remains controversial because it violates grammatical rules. Yet there is no doubt that English is now evolving to accept such gender-neutral constructions.

Even as the English language changes in response to social imperatives, gender is likely to remain a source of miscommunication between women and men. A booklet entitled *Words that Count Women ~~Out~~ In* (Ontario Women's Directorate, 1992) examines some of the most common assumptions and barriers that have made the transition to gender-inclusive language troublesome. Some of their suggestions for bias-free wordings are included in Table 6–1.

The authors point out that sexist language is so prevalent that it can even be found in the one piece of music that all Canadians hear and sing thousands of times over in their lifetimes:

O Canada! Our home and native land!
True patriot love in all thy sons command.

Our national anthem, the symbol of our democratic spirit, excludes half the population—women—as well as immigrants who not native to Canada.

HUMOUR: PLAYING WITH REALITY

Some people think that comedy is Canada's greatest cultural export. Humour plays a vital part in everyday life. Comedians are among our favourite entertainers, most newspapers carry cartoons, and even professors and members of the clergy may include a joke or two in their performances. As with many aspects of social life, however, we largely take humour for granted. While everyone laughs at a joke, in other words, few people think about what makes something funny or why humans everywhere like to laugh. Many of the ideas developed in this chapter provide insights into the character of humour, as we shall now see.

The Foundations of Humour

Humour is a product of reality construction; stemming from the contrast between two, incongruous realities. Generally, one reality is *conventional*, corresponding to what people expect in a specific situation. The other reality is *unconventional*, representing a significant violation of cultural patterns. Humour, therefore, arises from contradiction, ambiguity, and "double meanings" generated by two differing definitions of the same situation. Note how this principle works in this Woody Allen line: "I'm not afraid to die; I just don't want to be there when it happens."

Here the first phrase represents a conventional notion; the second half, however, interjects an unconventional—even absurd—meaning that collides with what we are led to expect. This same simple pattern holds true for virtually all humour. Of course, there

TABLE 6–1 Examples of Bias and Bias-Free Words

Biased	Bias-Free	Biased	Bias-Free
The Work World		**Stereotypes**	
alderman	municipal councillor	femme fatale	seducer
anchorman	anchor	kingmaker	power behind the throne,
career girl, career woman	professional, manager, executive		éminence grise
cleaning lady	cleaner	lady luck	luck
engineman	engine operator	maiden voyage	first voyage
foreman	supervisor	man of letters	scholar, writer, literary figure
longshoreman	dockhand, shorehand	one-upmanship	upstaging, competitiveness
newsman	journalist, reporter, newshound	workmanship	quality construction, expertise
Word of Play		**Turns of Phrase**	
horseman, horsewoman	rider	All men are created equal.	We are all created equal.
sportsman	sports buff, sports enthusiast,	Boys will be boys.	Kids will be kids.
	athlete	A fool and his money are soon	Fools and their money are
		parted.	soon parted.
		Man does not live by bread	We don't live by bread
		alone.	alone.
Roles People Play		A man's home is his castle.	Your home is your castle.
alumni	graduates	no-man's-land territory	limbo, dead zone, unclaimed
boys in blue	armed forces	to a man	to a one, to a person, without
corporate wife	corporate spouse		exception
layman	layperson, uninitiated,		
	nonprofessional		
The Human Family		**Put-downs**	
brotherhood	kinship, community	fall guy	chump, dupe, scapegoat
common man	common person, average person	manhandle	abuse, mistreat
fatherland	native land	nervous Nellie	worrywart, worrier
fellowship	camaraderie	prodigal son	spendthrift, returned prodigal
sons of God	children of God	tomboy	rough-and-tumble child

Source: Adapted from Ontario Women's Directorate, 1992.

are countless ways to mix realities and thereby generate humour. Sometimes contrasting realities emerge simply from reordering syllables, as in the country song by Randy Hanzlick, "I'd Rather Have a Bottle in Front of Me Than a Frontal Lobotomy."

Of course, a joke can be built the other way around, so that the comic leads the audience to expect an unconventional answer but gives it a very ordinary one. When a reporter asked the famous desperado Willy Sutton why he robbed banks, for example, he replied dryly: "Because that's where the money is." However a joke is constructed, the greater the opposition or incongruity between the two definitions of reality, the greater the potential for humour.

The Dynamics of Humour: "Getting It"

If people fail to understand both the conventional and unconventional realities embedded in a joke, they usually say, with a puzzled expression, "I don't get it." To "get" humour, members of an audience must understand the two realities underlying the joke well enough to perceive their incongruity.

But getting a joke can be more challenging still, because comics may deliberately omit some of the information listeners must grasp. The audience, there-

fore, must pay attention to the stated elements of the joke, and then fill in the missing pieces on their own. As a simple case, consider the reflection of movie producer Hal Roach upon reaching his one-hundredth birthday:

If I had known I would live to be one hundred, I would have taken better care of myself!

Here, "getting" the joke depends on realizing that Roach must have taken pretty good care of himself to live to be one hundred in the first place. Or take one of W.C. Field's lines: "Some weasel took the cork out of my lunch." "Some lunch," we think to ourselves to "finish" the joke.

Of course, some jokes demand more mental effort than others. *The Globe and Mail* (August 2, 1997:A1), under "Your Morning Smile," published a submission by Torontonian Poly O'Keefe, who must have at least an introductory sociology course in her background:

What was the name of the first sociologist to study the impact of new communications technology on society? E-mail Durkheim.

To get this joke requires specialized knowledge about sociology. Of course, your recognition chuckle

Humorous treatment of shared experience is a way to express a common identity. On the TV program This Hour Has 22 Minutes, *controversial issues, politicians, and other public figures are satirized in a news broadcast format.*

would have been more spontaneous had you encountered this tidbit out of context in the newspaper.

Why would an audience be required to make this sort of effort in order to understand a joke? Simply because our enjoyment of a joke is heightened by the pleasure of having completed the puzzle necessary to "get it." In addition, once we understand a complex joke, we gain favoured status as an "insider" in the larger audience. These insights explain the frustration that accompanies not getting a joke: the fear of mental inadequacy coupled with a sense of being socially excluded from a pleasure shared by others. Not surprisingly, "outsiders" in such a situation may fake "getting" the joke; sometimes, too, others may tactfully explain a joke to end another's sense of being left out.

But, as the old saying goes, if a joke has to be explained, it won't be very funny. Besides taking the edge off the language and timing on which the punch depends, an explanation completely relieves the audience of any mental involvement, substantially reducing its pleasure.

The Topics of Humour

People throughout the world smile and laugh, signifying humour as a universal human trait. But, living in diverse cultures, the world's people differ in what they find funny, so humour does not travel well. John Macionis illustrates the difficulty of translating humour in his travel journal.

October 1, 1994, Kobe, Japan: Can you share a joke with people halfway around the world? At dinner, I ask two Japanese college women to tell a joke. "You know 'crayon'?" Asako asks. I nod. "How do you ask for a crayon in Japanese?" I respond that I have no idea. She laughs out loud as she says what sounds like "crayon crayon." Her companion Mayumi laughs too. Amy and I sit awkwardly straight-faced. Asako relieves some of our embarrassment by explaining that the Japanese word for "give me" is kureyo, which sounds like "crayon." I force a smile.

What is humorous to the Japanese, then, may be lost on the Chinese, Iraqis, or Canadians. To some degree, too, the social diversity of our own country means that people will find humour in different situations. Newfoundlanders, Québécois, and westerners have their own brands of humour, as do Italians and Inuit, fifteen- and forty-year-olds, Bay Street brokers and hardhat construction workers.

But for everyone, humour deals with topics that lend themselves to double meanings or *controversy*. For example, the first jokes many of us learned as children concerned the cultural taboo sex. The mere mention of "unmentionable acts" or even certain parts of the body can cause young faces to dissolve in laughter. Are there jokes that do break through the culture barrier? Yes, but they must touch upon universal human experiences such as turning on a friend.

[Journal entry continues] ... I try a number of jokes, to little effect. So

Double Take: Real Headlines That Make People Laugh

Humour is generated by mixing two distinct and opposing realities. Here are several actual headlines from real newspaper stories. Read each one and identify the conventional meaning intended by the writer as well as the unconventional interpretation that generates humour.

"Police Begin Campaign to Run Down Jaywalkers"

"Iraqi Head Seeks Arms"

"Panda Mating Fails: Veterinarian Takes Over"

"Squad Helps Dog Bite Victim"

"War Dims Hope for Peace"

"Drunk Gets Nine Months in Violin Case"

"Stud Tires Out"

"Soviet Virgin Lands Short of Goal Again"

"Miners Refuse to Work After Death"

"British Left Waffles on Falkland Islands"

"Survivor of Siamese Twins Joins Parents"

"Prostitutes Appeal to Pope"

"Teacher Strikes Idle Kids"

"Killer Sentenced to Die for Second Time in Ten Years"

"Stolen Painting Found by Tree"

Source: Thanks to Kay Fletcher (1977).

---

many of our jokes are ethnic, and the two Japanese women cannot connect. Inspiration: "Two fellows are walking in the woods and come upon a huge bear. One guy leans over and tightens up the laces on his running shoes. 'Jake,' says the other, 'what are you doing? You can't outrun this bear.' 'I don't have to outrun the bear' responds Jake. 'I just have to outrun you!'" Smiles all around.

The controversy inherent in humour often walks a fine line between what is funny and what is considered "sick." During the Middle Ages, the word *humours* (derived from the Latin *humidus*, meaning "moist") referred to a balance of bodily fluids that regulated a person's health. Today's researchers have provided scientific justification for the notion that "Laughter is the best medicine," because maintaining a sense of humour reduces a person's level of unhealthy stress (Robinson, 1983; Haig, 1988). At the extreme, however, people who always take conventional reality lightly risk being defined as deviant or even mentally ill (a common stereotype depicts insane people laughing uncontrollably, and we once dubbed psychiatric hospitals "funny farms").

And then there are certain topics that every social group declares to be too sensitive for humorous treatment. Of course, one can joke about such things,

 See www.cbc.ca/witness/ nokidding/laughlab.html for links to LaughLab, a British psychologist's quest to find the world's funniest joke.

but doing so courts criticism for telling a "sick" joke (or being sick). People's

religious beliefs, tragic accidents, or appalling crimes are the stuff of "sick" jokes.

The Functions of Humour

If humour is a cultural universal, it must make a significant contribution to social life. From a structural-functional perspective, humour serves as a social "safety valve," allowing people to release potentially disruptive sentiments safely. By means of humour, we can acceptably discuss a host of cultural taboos, from sex to prejudice to hostility towards parents.

Having strayed into controversy, an individual may also use humour to defuse the situation. Called to account for a remark an audience takes as offensive, a speaker may simply state, "I didn't mean anything by what I said; it was just a joke!" Likewise, an audience may use humour as a form of tact, smiling, as if to say, "We could take offence at what you said, but we'll assume you were only kidding."

As Canadians, we often use humour to express our common identity. By laughing at ourselves and putting ourselves down, we reinforce a sense of our common bond. In the following jokes, we are all being made fun of:

In a recent panel discussion at New York's 92nd Street Y called "Why Are Canadians So Funny?" moderator (and Vancouver native) Michael J. Fox mentioned a contest once sponsored by *Maclean's* magazine. *Maclean's*, which Fox identified as the "Canadian *Time*" (as is the Canadian comparative habit), once asked its readers to fill in the blank at the end of the phrase, "As Canadian as . . ." to counterbalance the motto "As American as apple pie." According to Fox, the winning entry was "As Canadian as . . . possible under the circumstances." (Vowell, 1999)

Canada's idea of a joke is spending a year debating a constitutional accord as if it were a matter of life and death, then changing the subject. "Canada is a nation without a punch line."

Both jokes play on Canadian insecurity about who we are. In the midst of the deep divisions caused by the constitutional discussions, the second joke reminds us that we have a common national identity. We are "insiders" to the joke, not only because we are familiar with the events being referred to, but also because we recognize in the situation as it is described a pattern that in some way characterizes our country. Because anglophones share constitutional angst with the Québécois, one can expect this joke to be funny in French translation. Would the joke seem as funny if the writer were an American?

Like theatre and art, humour allows us to challenge orthodox ideas and to explore alternatives to the status quo. In fact, humour may actually promote social change by loosening the grip of convention.

Humour and Conflict

If humour holds the potential to liberate those who laugh, it can also be used to oppress others. Men who tell jokes about feminists, for example, typically are voicing some measure of hostility towards them (Powell and Paton, 1988; Benokraitis and Feagin, 1995). Similarly, jokes at the expense of gay people reveal tensions surrounding sexual orientation. Humour may be a sign of real conflict in situations where one or both parties choose not to bring the conflict out into the open (Primeggia and Varacalli, 1990).

"Put-down" jokes may function to make one category of people feel good at the expense of another. After collecting and analyzing jokes from many societies, Christie Davies (1990) concluded that conflict among ethnic groups is one driving force behind humour virtually everywhere. In the typical ethnic joke, the jokester and the audience label some disadvantaged category of people as stupid or ridiculous, thereby imputing greater wisdom and skills to people like themselves. Given the Anglo-Saxon and French traditions of Canadian society, Poles and other ethnic and racial minorities have long been the butt of jokes, as have Newfoundlanders ("Newfies") in eastern

Canada, the Irish in England, Sikhs in India, Turks in Germany, and Kurds in Iraq.

At times, people in minority situations turn the joke on themselves. Peter Berger (1997) points out that Jews are so good at this that their jokes have become part of the larger American repertoire. This kind of humour often illustrates that "jokes can summarize an often complex situation in wondrously economical ways, simplifying and illuminating and definitely providing some cognitive benefit" (1997:137). One of Berger's examples reveals the feelings of the Québécois, who believe that theirs is an island of French in an English-speaking ocean:

> In a village in Quebec a little girl goes out to collect mushrooms when the Virgin Mary appears to her. The little girl sinks to her knees and says: "*Ah, vous êtes Notre Dame! Vous êtes si belle. Vous êtes magnifique. Je vous adore. Je vous aime.*"
> And the Virgin Mary replies: "I'm sorry. I don't speak French."

Aboriginal Canadians, who now have their own television channel (APTN), also create this kind of humour. The CBC radio program *Dead Dog Café* had the same effect of 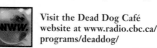 illuminating a certain culture—it was corny, satirical, and right on!

Visit the Dead Dog Café website at www.radio.cbc.ca/programs/deaddog/

Disadvantaged people, of course, also make fun of the powerful (although they usually do so discreetly). Women in North America have long joked about men, and poor people poke fun at the rich. Throughout the world, people target their leaders with humour, and officials in some countries take such jokes seriously enough to vigorously repress them. Political jokes are "subversive by definition" (Berger, 1997).

In sum, the significance of humour is much greater than first impressions suggest. Humour amounts to a means of mental escape from a conventional world that is not entirely to our liking (Flaherty, 1984, 1990; Yoels and Clair, 1995). With that in mind, it makes sense that a disproportionate number of North America's comedians come from among the ranks of oppressed people, including Jews and African-Americans. As long as we maintain a sense of humour, then, we assert our freedom and are never prisoners of reality. And, in doing so, we change the world and ourselves just a little.

SUMMARY

1. Social structure provides guidelines for behaviour, rendering everyday life understandable and predictable.

2. A major component of social structure is status. Within an entire status set, a master status has particular significance.

Is Technology Changing Our Reality?

Any technology tends to create a new human environment. . . . Technological environments are not merely passive containers of people but are active processes that reshape people and other technologies alike. In our time the sudden shift from the mechanical technology of the wheel to the technology of electric circuitry represents one of the major shifts of all historical time. (Marshall McLuhan, *The Gutenberg Galaxy*, 1969)

When Alexander Graham Bell invented the telephone in 1874 and made the first long-distance call between Brantford and Paris, Ontario, people were amazed that they had the ability to talk to others who were far away. People were just as astounded when Guglielmo Marconi received the first transatlantic wireless (radio) message on a hilltop at St. John's, Newfoundland (1901), or when the first airplane left the ground (1903), or when the first television signal was broadcast (1939).

Is today's new information technology once again restructuring reality? Absolutely. We can cite at least three reasons why. First, computers and other information technology have already altered the Canadian economy: the production of material goods (such as paper and steel) that defined the Industrial Age is steadily being replaced by the creation of ideas and images. This trend is changing not only the nature of work, but the skills needed to find employment, and even our legal definition of property.

Second, new information technology is eroding the importance of place in our lives. Bell's telephone was able to "reshape people"—to borrow McLuhan's phrase—by greatly extending their ears' "reach"; because sound travelled along wires, Bell knew exactly where the call was going. Telephones remained basically unchanged for a century after that. Today, cellular technology allows a person to key in a number and reach another person who could be, literally, anywhere on the continent, moving in a car, or flying twelve kilometres above the earth.

Similarly, technological advances are reconstructing the workplace so that "the new factory" is now any place one can position a computer terminal or fax machine, including one's home. Even the centuries-old concepts of national boundaries and citizenship have grown fuzzy under the influence of new technology. Consider an employee who logs on to a computer terminal in Vancouver and, over the information highway, connects to a U.S. bank in Manhattan where she processes transactions throughout the day. Is this "electronic immigrant" part of the labour force of Canada or the United States?

Third, there is no more basic foundation of our sense of reality than the timeless adage "Seeing is believing." But digital imagery now allows photographers to combine and manipulate pictures to show anything; computer animation enables movie producers to have humans interact with lifelike dinosaurs, and the technology of "virtual reality" means that, connected to computers, we can see, hear, and even feel the "touch" of another person thousands of kilometres away.

Finally, new information technology is reshaping the university and college scene. Historically, publishers have produced textbooks that augment the instruction of a classroom teacher. But books are becoming a smaller and smaller part of publishers' offerings, as we witness a proliferation of images on tape, film, and computer disk. In the years to come, textbooks themselves gradually will be replaced by CD-ROMs. In a world of interactive computer-based instruction, will students still need to travel to classrooms to learn? Indeed, will the university or college campus itself eventually become obsolete?

Continue the debate . . .

1. *More than thirty years ago, Canadian media theorist Marshall McLuhan predicted that nations and their boundaries would be unable to survive the new electronic technologies, with their power of "totally involving all people in all other people." Under the influence of border-jumping technologies such as the Internet, will Canada survive as a separate country? What is your own prediction?*

2. *As the "electronic age" unfolds, what changes would you predict in everyday routines involving school, recreation, entertainment, shopping, employment, and the economy?*

3. *If the university or college campus were to disappear, would the university or college as an institution disappear as well?*

---

3. Ascribed statuses are essentially involuntary, while achieved statuses are largely earned. In practice, however, many statuses incorporate elements of both ascription and achievement.

4. Role is the dynamic expression of a status. The incompatibility of roles corresponding to two or more statuses generates role conflict; likewise, incompatible roles linked to a single status produce role strain.

5. The phrase "social construction of reality" conveys the important idea that we all build the social world through our interaction.

6. The Thomas theorem states, "Situations defined as real become real in their consequences."

7. Ethnomethodology seeks to reveal the assumptions and understandings people have of their social world.

8. Dramaturgical analysis studies how people construct their personal behaviour. This approach casts everyday life in terms of theatrical performances, noting how people try to foster impressions in the minds of others, the settings of interaction, and how performers often idealize their intentions.

9. Social power affects performances; our society's general subordination of women causes them to craft their behaviour differently than men do.

10. Social behaviour carries the ever-present danger of embarrassment. Tact is a common response to "loss of face" by others.

11. Language is vital to the process of socially constructing reality. In various ways, language defines females and males differently, generally to the advantage of males.

12. Humour stems from the contrast between conventional and unconventional definitions of a situation. Because comedy is framed by a specific culture, people throughout the world find humour in very different situations.

CRITICAL-THINKING QUESTIONS

1. Consider ways in which a physical disability can serve as a master status. How do people commonly characterize, say, a person with the physical disability cerebral palsy with regard to mental ability? With regard to sexuality?

2. George Jean Nathan once quipped, "I only drink to make other people interesting." What does this mean in terms of reality construction? Identify the elements of humour within this statement.

3. How does modern communications technology alter social interaction?

4. Here is a joke about sociologists: "Question—How many sociologists does it take to change a light bulb? Answer—None, because there is nothing wrong with the light bulb; it's *the system* that needs to be changed!" What makes this joke funny? What sort of people are likely to "get it"? What kind of people probably won't? Why?

APPLICATIONS AND EXERCISES

1. Write down as many of your own statuses as you can. Do you consider any statuses to be a master status? To what extent are each of your statuses ascribed and achieved?

2. During the next twenty-four hours, every time people ask "How are you?" stop and actually tell them. What happens when you respond to a "polite" question in an unexpected way? (Watch people's body language as well as note what they say.) What does this experience suggest about everyday interactions?

3. This chapter illustrates Erving Goffman's ideas with a description of a physician's office. Investigate the offices of several professors in the same way. What furniture is there and how is it arranged? What "props" do professors use? How are the offices of physicians and professors different? Why are they different?

4. Spend an hour or two walking around the businesses of your town (or shops at a local mall). Observe the presence of women and men in each business. Based on your observations, would you conclude that physical space is "gendered"?

SITES TO SEE

www.macionis.com
or
www.TheSociologyPage.com

You can find more than fifty weblinks to sociological journals and other sources of data and information by visiting the Links Library at this website.

www.anu.edu.au/psychology/social/socident.htm

Social Psychology at ANU—Social Identity Page contains an essay that describes social identity as having to do with categorization, identification, and comparison. We identify with groups to which we feel we belong. Thinking of oneself as both a group member and as an individual is part of one's self-concept. This is an adaptation of a journal article.

http://people.brandeis.edu/~teuber/goffmanbio.html
and
http://ess.ntu.ac.uk/miller/cyberpsych/goffman.htm

Read more about the life and work of Erving Goffman at these sites. The second website, *Goffman on the Internet*, contains "The Presentation of Self in Electronic Life: Goffman on the Internet," a paper presented at the Embodied Knowledge and Virtual Space conference at the University of London in June 1995. Goffman's description of face-to-face interaction is discussed in relation to interpersonal communication on the Internet.

www.paulekman.com
and
http://mambo.ucsc.edu/psl/ekman.html

Discover more about Paul Ekman's research on human emotions.

www.aetherlumina.com/gnp/

Gender-Neutral Pronoun Frequently Asked Questions is a general information source for gender-free alternatives to gendered pronouns.

www.ai.mit.edu/projects/humanoid-robotics-group/kismet/kismet.html

Is it possible to build a machine capable of human interaction? That is the goal of robotics engineers at the Massachusetts Institute of Technology. Their website provides details and photographs. Look over their work and think about issues raised in this chapter. In what ways are machines able—and unable—to mimic human behaviour?

 ## STUDY TOOLS

For more study tools to help you with your next exam, be sure to check out the Companion Website at **www.pearsoned.ca/macionis**, as well as Chapter 6 in your Study Guide.

 ## INVESTIGATE WITH CONTENTSELECT

Follow the instructions found on page 25 of this textbook to access ContentSelect™ at the Research Navigator™ website. Once at the site, enter your LOGINID and Password. Then, enter keywords such as "social construction of reality," "ethnomethodology," "Goffman," and "emotions", and the search engine will supply relevant and recent scholarly and popular press publications.

CHAPTER

7

Colin William Moss (1914– , English)
Hunger Marchers, 1936
Oil on canvas, 64 × 76.5 cm. The Bridgeman Art Library.

GROUPS AND ORGANIZATIONS

Sixty years ago, the opening of a new restaurant in Pasadena, California, attracted little attention from the local community and went unnoticed by the nation as a whole. Yet this seemingly insignificant small business, owned and operated by Mac and Dick McDonald, would eventually spark a revolution in the restaurant industry and provide an organizational model that would be copied by countless other businesses of all kinds.

The basic formula the McDonald brothers put into place—which we now call "fast food"—was to serve good quality food quickly and inexpensively to large numbers of people. They trained employees to perform highly specialized jobs, so that one person grilled hamburgers while others "dressed" them, made French fries, whipped up milkshakes, and presented the food to the customers.

As the years went by, the McDonald brothers prospered and they moved their single restaurant from Pasadena to San Bernardino.

It was there, in 1954, that events took an unexpected turn when Ray Kroc, a travelling blender and mixer merchant, paid a visit to the McDonalds.

Kroc was fascinated by the brothers' efficient system and, almost immediately, saw the potential for a greatly expanded system of fast-food restaurants. Kroc launched his plans in partnership with the McDonald brothers. Soon, he bought out their interests and set out on his own to become one of the greatest success stories of all time. Today, about twenty-eight thousand McDonald's restaurants serve people in one hundred and twenty countries around the world.

From a sociological point of view, the success of McDonald's reveals much more than the popularity of hamburgers. As this chapter explains presently, the larger importance of this story lies in the extent to which the principles that guide the operation of McDonald's are coming to dominate social life in North America and elsewhere.

We begin by examining social groups, the clusters of people with whom we associate in much of our daily lives. As we shall see, the scope of group life has expanded greatly during this century. From a world built on the family, the local neighbourhood, and the small business, the structure of our society now turns on the operation of vast businesses and other bureaucracies that sociologists describe as formal organizations.

SOCIAL GROUPS

Virtually everyone moves through life with a sense of belonging; this is the experience of group life. A **social group** refers to *two or more people who identify and interact with one another*. Human beings continually come together to form couples, families, circles of friends, neighbourhoods, churches, businesses, clubs, and numerous large organizations. Whatever the form, groups encompass people with shared experiences,

155

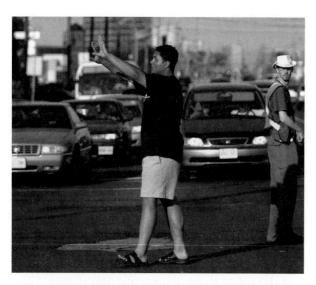

Volunteers help during the massive blackout that hit Ontario in August 2003. Extraordinary circumstances such as storms, floods, tornadoes, or accidents can turn a crowd into a group, and strangers into neighbours.

loyalties, and interests. In short, while maintaining their individuality, the members of social groups also think of themselves as a special "we."

GROUPS, CATEGORIES, AND CROWDS

People often use the term *group* imprecisely. Below, we distinguish the group from the similar concepts of category and crowd.

Category

A *category* refers to people who have some status in common. Women, single fathers, homeowners, and Roman Catholics are all examples of categories.

Why are categories not considered groups? Simply because, while the individuals involved are aware that they are not the only ones to hold that particular status, the vast majority are strangers to one another.

Crowd

A *crowd* refers to a temporary cluster of individuals who may or may not interact. Students sitting together in a lecture hall engage one another and share a common identity as college classmates; thus, such a crowd might be called a loosely formed group. In contrast, riders on a subway train or bathers enjoying a summer day at the beach pay little attention to one another and amount to an anonymous aggregate of people. In effect, crowds are too transitory and too impersonal to qualify as social groups.

Circumstances, however, can turn a crowd into a group. As Ontarians learned during the massive power

failure that occurred in August 2003, people quickly become keenly aware of their common plight and begin to help one another.. Such extraordinary experiences may become the basis for lasting relationships.

PRIMARY AND SECONDARY GROUPS

Acquaintances commonly greet one another with a smile and the simple phrase "Hi! How are you?" The response is usually a well-scripted "Just fine, thanks. How about you?" This answer, of course, is often more formal than truthful. In most cases, providing a detailed account of how you are *really* doing would prompt the other person to beat a hasty retreat.

Sociologists classify social groups by measuring them against two ideal types based on members' level of genuine personal concern. This variation is the key to distinguishing *primary* from *secondary* groups.

According to Charles Horton Cooley (1864–1929), who observed the effects of urbanization and industrialization on people's relationships over a century ago, a **primary group** is *a small social group whose members share personal and enduring relationships.* Bound together by *primary relationships,* individuals in these groups typically spend a great deal of time together, engage in a wide range of activities with one another, and feel that they know one another well. Although not without periodic conflict, members of primary groups display sincere concern for their mutual welfare. In every society, the family is the most important primary group.

Cooley characterized these personal and tightly integrated groups as *primary* because they are among the first groups we experience in life. In addition, the family and early play groups hold primary importance in the socialization process, shaping attitudes, behaviour, and social identity.

 For a biography of Charles Horton Cooley, go to the Gallery of Sociologists at www.TheSociologyPage.com

The strength of primary relationships gives people a comforting sense of security. In the familiar social circles of family or friends, people feel they can "be themselves" without constantly worrying about the impressions they are making.

Members of primary groups generally provide one another with economic and other forms of assistance as well. But, as important as primary ties are, people generally think of a primary group as an end in itself rather than as a means to other ends. In other words, we prefer to think that kinship or friendship links people who "belong together," rather than people who expect to benefit from each other. For this reason, we readily call on family members or close friends to help us move into a new apartment, without expecting to pay for their services. And we would do the same for them. A friend who never returns a favour, in contrast, is likely to leave us feeling "used" and questioning the depth of the friendship.

Moreover, this personal orientation means that members of a primary group view one another as unique and irreplaceable. We typically do not care who cashes our cheque at the bank or takes our money at the supermarket checkout. Yet in the primary group—especially in the family—we are bound to specific others by emotion and loyalty. So even though brothers and sisters do not always get along, they remain siblings.

In contrast to the primary group, the **secondary group** is *a large and impersonal social group whose members pursue specific interests or activities.* In most respects, secondary groups have precisely the opposite characteristics of primary groups. *Secondary relationships* usually involve weak emotional ties and little personal knowledge of one another. Secondary groups vary in duration, but they are frequently short-term, emerging and disappearing without particular significance. Students in a university or college course, for instance, who may not see one another after the year or semester ends, exemplify the secondary group.

Weaker social ties permit secondary groups to include many more people than primary groups do. For example, dozens or even hundreds of people may work together in the same office, yet most of them pay only passing attention to one another. Sometimes the passing of time will transform a group from secondary to primary, as with co-workers who share an office for many years. Generally, however, people in a secondary group only occasionally think of themselves as "we," and the boundary separating members of a secondary group from nonmembers is far less clear than it is in primary groups.

Secondary groups lack strong loyalties and emotions because members look to one another only to achieve limited ends. So while members of primary groups display a *personal orientation*, people in secondary groups reveal a *goal orientation*. Secondary ties need not be aloof or cold, of course. Social interactions among students or co-workers are often quite pleasant, even if they are rather impersonal.

In primary groups, members define one another according to *who* they are, that is, in terms of kinship or unique, personal qualities; members of secondary groups, however, look to one another for *what* they are or what they can do for one another. Thus, in secondary groups, we are always mindful of what we offer others and what we receive in return. For example, the people next door typically expect that a neighbourly favour will be reciprocated. Such "scorekeeping" comes through most clearly in business relationships, where exchange may be made explicit in contracts.

The goal orientation of secondary groups encourages individuals to craft their behaviour carefully. In these roles, we remain characteristically impersonal and polite. The secondary relationship, therefore, is one in which the question "How are you?" may be asked without really expecting a truthful answer.

Around the world, families are the most important primary group. In industrial societies, however, numerous friendship groups stand alongside families, joining individuals on the basis of shared interests rather than kinship.

Table 7–1 summarizes the characteristics that distinguish primary and secondary groups. Keep in mind that these traits define two types of social groups in ideal terms, whereas actual groups in our lives may contain elements of both. By placing these concepts at each end of a continuum, however, we devise a useful scheme for describing and analyzing group life.

In general, primary relationships predominate in low-income, pre-industrial societies throughout Latin America, Africa, and Asia in which people's lives revolve around families and local villages. In these countries, especially in rural areas, strangers stand out in the social landscape. In contrast, secondary ties take precedence in high-income, industrial societies, in which people assume highly specialized social roles. Most Canadians, especially in cities, routinely engage in impersonal, secondary contacts with virtual strangers—people about whom we know very little and whom we may never meet again (Wirth, 1938).

GROUP LEADERSHIP

How do groups operate? One important dimension of group dynamics is leadership. Groups vary in the extent to which members recognize leaders. Large, secondary groups generally place leaders in a formal chain of command; a small circle of friends may have no leader at all. Parents assume leadership roles in

TABLE 7–1 Primary Groups and Secondary Groups: A Summary

	Primary Group ⟷	Secondary Group
Quality of relationships	Personal orientation	Goal orientation
Duration of relationships	Usually long-term	Variable; often short-term
Breadth of relationships	Broad; usually involving many activities	Narrow; usually involving a few activities
Subjective perception of relationships	As an end in itself	As a means to an end
Typical examples	Families; close friendships	Co-workers; political organizations

families, although husband and wife may disagree about who is really in charge.

Two Leadership Roles

Groups typically benefit from two kinds of leadership (Bales, 1953; Bales and Slater, 1955). **Instrumental leadership** refers to *group leadership that emphasizes the completion of tasks*. Members look to instrumental leaders to get things done. **Expressive leadership**, in contrast, *focuses on collective well-being*. Expressive leaders take less of an interest in the performance goals of a group than in group morale and minimizing tension and conflict among members.

Concentrating on performance, instrumental leaders usually have formal, secondary relations with other group members: they give orders and reward or punish people according to their contributions to the group's efforts. Expressive leaders, on the other hand, cultivate more personal, primary ties. They offer sympathy to a member having a tough time, work to keep the group united, and lighten serious moments with humour. While successful instrumental leaders enjoy more distant *respect* from members, expressive leaders generally garner more personal *affection*.

In the traditional, North American family, this differentiation of leadership is linked to gender. Historically, cultural norms bestowed instrumental leadership on men so that, as fathers and husbands, they assume primary responsibility for earning income, making decisions, and disciplining children. In contrast, expressive leadership has been the traditional purview of women. Historically, mothers and wives have encouraged supportive and peaceful relationships among family members. This division of labour partly explains why many children have greater respect for their fathers but closer personal ties with their mothers (Parsons and Bales, 1955; Macionis, 1978a).

Of course, increasing equality between men and women has blurred this gender-based distinction between instrumental and expressive leadership. In more group settings, women and men now assume both of these leadership roles.

Three Leadership Styles

Sociologists also characterize group leadership in terms of three orientations to power. *Authoritarian leadership* stresses instrumental concerns, taking personal charge of decision making and demanding strict compliance from subordinates. Although this leadership style may win little affection from group members, a fast-acting authoritarian leader often earns praise in a crisis situation.

Democratic leadership has a more expressive focus, with concern for including everyone in the decision-making process. Democratic leaders generally draw on the ideas of all members to forge reflective and imaginative responses to the tasks at hand.

Laissez-faire leadership (from the French phrase meaning, roughly, "to leave alone") allows the group to function more or less on its own. This style typically is the least effective in promoting group goals (White and Lippitt, 1953; Ridgeway, 1983).

GROUP CONFORMITY

Canadians across the country were shocked by news from Vancouver Island in November 1997. A group of teenagers on a riverbank had brutally beaten fourteen-year-old Reena Virk, whose body was found in the water a week later. Perhaps the most shocking element in this story was the fact that the teenagers who viciously attacked their classmate were, with one exception, *girls*. An incident that began with accusations that Reena had been spreading rumours about one of the girls escalated into brutal violence after the girl stubbed a cigarette out on Reena's forehead. Seven girls and one boy proceeded to assault Reena, while ten others watched and did nothing to intervene. Actions that would not have been contemplated by the individuals involved became possible in the group context—in fact, the actions became part of the process of belonging to the group or conformity to group expectations.

The fact that teens are anxious to fit in surprises no one, although many people might be amazed at the lengths to which some will go to gain acceptance. Social scientists confirm the power of group pressure to shape human behaviour and report that it remains strong into adulthood.

Asch's Research

Solomon Asch (1952) conducted a classic investigation that revealed the power of group conformity.

Asch recruited students for an alleged study of visual perception. Before the actual experiment, however, he revealed to all but one member in each small group that their real purpose was to impose group pressure on the remaining subject. Placing all the students around a table, Asch asked each, in turn, to note the length of a "standard" line, as shown on Card 1 in Figure 7–1, and match it to one of three lines on Card 2.

Anyone with normal vision could easily see that the line marked "A" on Card 2 was the correct choice. Initially, as planned, everyone made the matches correctly. But then Asch's secret accomplices began answering incorrectly, making the naive subject (seated at the table in order to answer next to last) bewildered and uncomfortable.

What happened? Asch found that one-third of all subjects placed in this situation chose to conform to the others by answering incorrectly. His investigation indicates that many of us are willing to compromise our own judgment to avoid the discomfort of being different from others, even from people we do not know.

Milgram's Research

Stanley Milgram—a former student of Solomon Asch—conducted controversial conformity experiments of his own. In Milgram's initial study (1963, 1965; Miller, 1986), a researcher explained to male recruits that they were about to engage in a study of how punishment affects learning. One by one, he assigned them the role of "teacher" and placed another individual—an insider to the study—in a connecting room as the "learner."

The teacher saw the learner sit down in an ominous contraption resembling an electric chair. Before connecting an electrode attached to the learner's wrist, the researcher applied electrode paste to it, explaining that this would "prevent blisters and burns." The researcher explained to the teacher that leather straps holding the learner were "to prevent excessive movement while the learner was being shocked," and that, although the shocks would be painful, they would cause "no permanent tissue damage."

The researcher then led the teacher back into an adjoining room and explained that the "electric chair" was connected to a "shock generator," a bogus but forbidding piece of equipment (with a realistic-looking label that read "Shock Generator, Type ZLB, Dyson Instrument Company. Waltham, Mass."). Placed on a table in front of the teacher, this device included a shock switch and a dial marked to regulate electric current from 15 volts (labelled "slight shock") to 300 volts (marked "intense shock") to 450 volts (marked "Danger: Severe Shock" and "XXX").

Seated in front of the "shock generator," the teacher was told to begin reading aloud pairs of words.

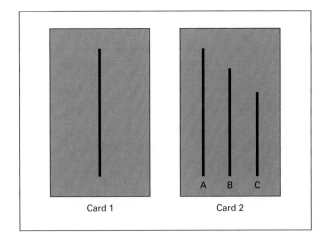

FIGURE 7–1 Cards Used in Asch's Experiment in Group Conformity

Source: Asch (1952).

Then, the teacher repeated the first word of each pair and waited for the learner to recall the second word of the pair. Whenever the learner failed to respond correctly, however, the teacher was instructed to apply an electric shock from the "shock generator."

The researcher directed the teacher to begin at the lowest level (15 volts), and to increase the shock by 15 volts every time the learner made a mistake. And so they did. At 75, 90, and 105 volts, the teacher heard audible moans from the learner; at 120 volts, shouts of pain; at 270 volts, screams; at 315 volts, pounding on the wall; after that, deathly silence.

The results show just how readily authority figures can obtain compliance from ordinary people. None of forty subjects assigned the role of teacher during the initial research even questioned the procedure before 300 volts had been applied, and twenty-six—almost two-thirds—went all the way to 450 volts.

Milgram (1964) then modified his research to see if Solomon Asch had documented such a high degree of group conformity only because the task of matching lines seemed trivial. What if groups pressured people to administer electrical shocks?

To investigate, he varied the experiment so that a group of three teachers, two of whom were his accomplices, made decisions jointly. Milgram's rule was that each of the three teachers would suggest a shock level when the learner made an error, and they would then administer the lowest of the three suggestions. This arrangement gave the naive subject the power to lessen the shock level regardless of the other two teachers' recommendations.

The accomplices called for increasing the shock level with each error, placing group pressure on the third member to do the same. Responding to this group pressure, subjects applied voltages three to four times higher than in control conditions in which subjects acted alone. Thus, Milgram's research suggests that people are surprisingly likely to follow the directions not only of "legitimate authority figures," but also of groups of ordinary individuals.

Janis's Research

Even the experts succumb to pressure for group conformity, according to Irving L. Janis (1972, 1989). Janis contends that a number of foreign policy errors made by the United States, including the failure to foresee the Japanese attack on Pearl Harbor in World War II, the disastrous U.S. invasion of Cuba's Bay of Pigs in 1961, and the ill-fated involvement in the Vietnam War, may have been the result of group conformity among the highest-ranking political leaders.

We often think that a group's "brainstorming" will improve decision making. However, Janis argues that group decision making sometimes backfires. Rather than examining a problem from many points of view, groups often seek consensus, thereby narrowing the range of options. Groups may develop a distinctive language, adopting terms that favour a single interpretation of events. Having settled on a position, members of the group may come to see anyone with another view as the "opposition." Janis called this process **groupthink**, *the tendency of group members to conform by adopting a narrow view of some issue.*

The effect of groupthink was apparent when federal and provincial leaders joined to campaign for the "Yes" side during the constitutional referendum battle of October 1992 and assumed that Canadians would obediently follow suit: they failed to explain why the Charlottetown Accord would be good for Canada, opting instead for a slick advertising campaign. Anyone who pointed out that the hard-sell approach might backfire was dismissed as talking nonsense. The use of the term "enemies of Canada" to describe opponents of the accord who carefully explained their objections and fears is also consistent with groupthink.

A more recent illustration of the groupthink phenomenon was the inability of the federal "No" forces to see that they were in difficulty in the Quebec sovereignty referendum of October 1995. Assuming that Quebecers would vote against sovereignty, Prime Minister Chrétien and his strategists appeared to have no plan for dealing with a victory by the "Yes" team. The dramatic takeover of the "Yes" forces by Bloc Québécois leader Lucien Bouchard, which took federal strategists by surprise, contributed to a razor-thin "No" victory (50.4 percent). Embarrassment and discomfort in the wake of the referendum led to attempts to assign or apportion blame. The Quebec Liberal leader and head of the provincial "No" camp, Daniel Johnson, became the convenient scapegoat.

REFERENCE GROUPS

How do we assess our own attitudes or behaviour? Frequently, we make use of a **reference group**, *a social group that serves as a point of reference in making evaluations or decisions.*

A young man who imagines his family's response to a woman he is dating uses his family as a reference group. Similarly, a banker who assesses her colleagues' reactions to a new loan policy uses her co-workers as a standard of reference. As these examples reveal, reference groups can be primary or secondary. In either case, the motivation to conform to a group means that the attitudes of others can greatly affect us.

We also use groups that we do not belong to for reference. People preparing for job interviews typically notice how those in the company they wish to join dress and act, adjusting their personal performances accordingly. The use of groups by nonmembers illustrates the process of anticipatory socialization, described in Chapter 5 ("Socialization"), by which individuals use conformity as a strategy to win acceptance by a particular group.

Stouffer's Research

Samuel A. Stouffer (1949) and his associates conducted a classic study of reference group dynamics during World War II. In a survey, researchers asked soldiers to evaluate the chances of promotion for a competent soldier in their branch of the service. One might guess that soldiers serving in outfits with a high promotion rate would be optimistic about their future advancement. Yet survey results supported the opposite conclusion: soldiers in branches of the service with low promotion rates were actually more optimistic about their own chances to move ahead.

The key to this paradox lies in sorting out the groups against which the soldiers measured their progress. Those in branches with low promotion rates looked around them and saw people making no more headway than they were. They had not been promoted, but neither had many others, so they did not feel unjustly deprived.

Soldiers in service branches with high promotion rates, however, could easily think of people who had been promoted sooner or more often than they had. With such people in mind, even soldiers who had been promoted themselves were likely to feel shortchanged. So, these were the soldiers who voiced more negative attitudes in their evaluations.

Stouffer's research demonstrates that we do not make judgments about ourselves in isolation, nor do we compare ourselves with just anyone. Instead, we use specific social groups as standards in developing individual attitudes. Whatever our situation in absolute terms, then, we assess our well-being subjectively, *relative* to some specific reference group (Merton, 1968; Mirowsky, 1987).

Ingroups and Outgroups

Differences among groups in political outlook, social prestige, or even manner of dress may lead us to embrace one group while avoiding others. Across North America, for example, students wear university or college jackets and place school decals on car windows to indicate that, to them, school serves as an important social group. Students attending another school may be targets of derision simply because they belong to a rival group. The deep-seated, "friendly" rivalry between Dalhousie and Saint Mary's or Guelph and Western undoubtedly is matched by other pairs of universities across the country.

This behaviour illustrates an important process of group dynamics: the opposition of ingroups and outgroups. An **ingroup** is *a social group commanding a member's esteem and loyalty.* An ingroup exists in relation to an **outgroup**, *a social group towards which one feels competition or opposition.* Many social groups follow this pattern. A sports team, the Montreal Canadiens, for example, is both an ingroup to its members and an outgroup for members of opposing teams such as the Calgary Flames. A town's active New Democrats are likely to think of themselves as an ingroup in relation to the local Tories. All ingroups and outgroups work on the principle that "we" have valued characteristics that "they" lack.

Tensions among groups often help to sharpen their boundaries and give people a clearer sense of social identity. However, this form of group dynamics also promotes self-serving distortions of reality. Specifically, research shows, members of ingroups construct overly positive views of themselves and hold unfairly negative views of various outgroups (Tajfel, 1982).

Power also guides intergroup relations. With greater power, members of one ingroup can define others as a lower-status outgroup; for their part, members of an outgroup may feel alienated from a system they feel victimizes them. For example, white people have historically viewed visible minorities in negative terms and subjected them to social, political, and economic disadvantages. Internalizing these negative attitudes, minorities often struggle to overcome negative self-images. In short, ingroups and outgroups foster loyalty but also generate tension and conflict.

GROUP SIZE

If you are the first person to arrive at a party, you are in a position to observe some fascinating group dynamics. Until about six people enter the room, everyone generally shares a single conversation. But as more people arrive, the group divides into two or more smaller clusters. It is apparent that size plays a crucial role in how group members interact.

To understand why, consider the mathematical connection between the number of people in a social

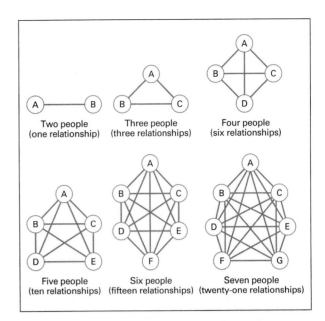

FIGURE 7–2 Group Size and Relationships

group and the number of relationships among them. As Figure 7–2 shows, two people form a single relationship; adding a third person generates three relationships; adding a fourth person yields six. Increasing the number of people one at a time, then, boosts the number of relationships much more rapidly since every new individual can interact with everyone already there. Thus, five people produce ten relationships and, by the time six people join one conversation fifteen "channels" connect them. This leaves too many people unable to speak, which is why the group usually divides at this point.

The Dyad

German sociologist Georg Simmel (1858–1918) explored the social dynamics in the smallest social groups. Simmel (1950; orig. 1902) used the term **dyad** to designate *a social group with two members.* Throughout the world, most love affairs, marriages, and close friendships are dyadic.

What makes the dyad a special relationship? As Simmel explained, social interaction in a dyad is typically more intense than in larger groups since, in a one-to-one relationship, neither member shares the other's attention with anyone else. Thus, dyads are the most meaningful of our social bonds.

Simmel also notes that dyads, like two-legged stools, have a characteristic instability. Both members of a dyad must actively sustain the relationship: if either one withdraws, the dyad collapses. Because the stability of marriage is important to society, the marital dyad is supported with legal, economic, and often religious ties. Since a large group, such as the United

The triad, illustrated by Jonathan Green's painting Friends, includes three people. A triad is more stable than a dyad because conflict between any two persons can be mediated by the third member. Even so, should the relationship between any two become more intense in a positive sense, those two are likely to exclude the third.

Jonathan Green, *Friends*, 1992. Oil on masonite. 35.6 × 27.9 cm.
© Jonathan Green, Naples, Florida. Collection of Patric McCoy.

Church women's auxiliary in Victoria, B.C., is inherently much more stable (as it can survive the loss of members), complex support mechanisms are not provided.

For more about Georg Simmel, see his biography in the Gallery of Sociologists at www.TheSociologyPage.com

Marriage in our society is dyadic: ideally, we expect powerful emotional ties to unite husbands and wives. As we shall see in Chapter 18 ("Family"), however, marriage in other societies may involve more than two people. In that case, the household usually is more stable, although the marital relationships themselves may be weaker.

The Triad

Simmel also probed the **triad**, *a social group with three members*. A triad encompasses three relationships, each uniting two of the three people. A triad is more stable than a dyad because, should the relationship between any two members become strained, the third can act as a mediator to restore the group's vitality. This bit of group dynamics helps explain why members of a dyad (say, a married couple) often seek out a third person (a counsellor) to air tensions between them.

Nonetheless, two of the three can form a coalition to press their views on the third, or two may intensify their relationship, leaving the other feeling like a "fifth wheel." For example, two members of a triad who develop a romantic interest in each other will understand the old saying "Two's company, three's a crowd": the potential for romance within a triad was the basis for much of the humour in the old TV sitcom *Three's Company*.

As groups grow beyond three members, they become progressively more stable because the loss of a few members does not threaten the group's existence. Increases in group size typically reduce the intense personal interaction possible only in the smallest groups. Larger groups are thus based less on personal attachments and more on formal rules and regulations. Such formality helps a large group persist over time, though the group is not immune to change. After all, their numerous members give large groups more contact with the outside world, opening the door to new attitudes and behaviour (Carley, 1991).

Does a social group have an ideal size? The answer depends on the group's purpose. A dyad offers unsurpassed emotional intensity, while a group of several dozen members is more stable, capable of accomplishing larger, more complex tasks, and better able to assimilate new members or ideas. People typically find more *personal pleasure* in smaller groups, while deriving *greater task satisfaction* in larger organizations (Slater, 1958; Ridgeway, 1983; Carley, 1991).

SOCIAL DIVERSITY

Social diversity affects group dynamics, especially the likelihood that members will interact with someone of another group. Peter Blau (1977; South and Messner, 1986) points out four ways in which the composition of social groups affects intergroup association.

1. **Large groups turn inward.** Extending Simmel's analysis of group size, Blau explains that the larger a group, the more likely its members are to maintain relationships exclusively among themselves. University of Toronto sociologist Raymond Breton (1964) studied this phenomenon among urban minorities, coining the term *institutional completeness* to account for the abilities of larger groups to meet their members' needs from within their own boundaries. In contrast, members of smaller groups reach beyond their immediate social circles. Generations ago, when the Montreal Jewish community was very small, young people could not find marriage partners

Today's university campuses value social diversity. One of the challenges of this movement is ensuring that all categories of students are fully integrated into campus life. This is not always easy. Following Blau's theory of group dynamics, as the number of minority students increases, these individuals are able to form a group unto themselves, perhaps interacting less with others.

from within; thus, many migrated to centres with larger Jewish populations (New York, for example) or married non-Jews, thus threatening the viability of the Montreal community.

2. **Heterogeneous groups turn outward.** The more internally heterogeneous a group is, the more likely its members are to interact with members of other groups. We would expect, for example, that campus groups that recruit members of both sexes and people of various ethnic and geographic backgrounds would experience more intergroup contact than those that choose members of only one social type.

3. **Social parity promotes contact.** An environment in which all groups have roughly equal standing encourages people of all social backgrounds to mingle and form social ties. Thus, whether groups insulate their members or not depends on whether the groups themselves are dispersed within a social hierarchy.

4. **Physical boundaries foster social boundaries.** Blau contends that physical space affects the chances of contact among groups. To the extent that a social group is physically segregated from others (by having its own dorm or dining area, for example), its members are less likely to interact with other people. The maintenance of social boundaries is enhanced by geographic separation as with First Nations reserves, Alberta's Hutterite colonies, or the province of Quebec.

NETWORKS

Formally, a **network** is *a web of social ties that links people who identify and interact little with one another*. Think of a network as a "fuzzy" group that brings people into

occasional contact without a group's sense of boundaries and belonging. Computer networks, or other high-technology links, now routinely connect people living all over the world. If we consider a group as a "circle of friends," then, we might describe a network as a "social web" expanding outward, often reaching great distances and including large numbers of people.

Some network contacts are regular, as among college friends who years later stay in touch by mail and telephone. More commonly, however, a network includes people we *know of*—or who *know of us*—but with whom we interact infrequently, if at all. As one woman with a widespread reputation as a community organizer explains, "I get calls at home, someone says, 'Are you Roseann Navarro? Somebody told me to call you. I have this problem . . .'" (quoted in Kaminer, 1984:94). For this reason, social networks amount to "clusters of weak ties" (Granovetter, 1973).

Network ties may be weak, but they serve as a significant resource. For example, many people rely on networks to find jobs. Even the scientific genius Albert Einstein needed a hand in landing his first job. After a year of unsuccessful interviewing, he found a job when the father of one of his classmates put him in touch with an office manager who hired him (Clark, 1971; cited in Fischer, 1977). This use of networks suggests that, as the saying goes, *who you know* is often just as important as *what you know*.

Networks are based on people's colleges, clubs, neighbourhoods, political parties, and personal interests. Some networks encompass people with considerably more wealth, power, and prestige than others do, which is the essence of describing someone as "well connected." And some people have denser networks than others—that is, they are connected to more people—which is also a valuable social resource. Typically, the most extensive social networks are

Virtual Community: Reaching Out through Cyberspace

Recently, young people have been turning to ICQ (or MSN) for intensive "conversation" with classmates who were involved in face-to-face communication hours, or minutes, earlier. Outside school hours, one can easily find ten or more of the members of this network (perhaps seventy-five in number) sharing information about some topic—or just chatting.

Darry Wellman and other prominent scholars have dedicated their careers to studying social networks and their role in the creation of community. Sociologists have long been concerned about the impact of urbanization and industrialization on traditional community bonds or solidarity. Every new technology that has lifted the individual from geographically defined community or neighbourhood—such as the telegraph, telephone, automobile, and airplane—has raised concerns about the demise of community. When social ties extend beyond the neighbourhood, sociologists have argued, surely they will be less meaningful and supportive.

In a book entitled *Networks in the Global Village*, Wellman has collected a number of articles on social networks in various settings around the world. Among these is an article by Wellman and Gulia entitled "Net-Surfers Don't Ride Alone: Virtual Communities as Communities."

The authors argue that instead of being "lost in cyberspace," people who establish contact over the Internet are able to build meaningful relationships and a sense of community. Although it is easy to create misunderstandings—and more difficult to repair them—in many ways, online relationships mimic those of the face-to-face world. Some relationships are weak; others are strong and broadly supportive. Some are short lived; others become more personal and intimate over time. While some online bonds are based on specialized interests, others are multifaceted. In many cases, online contact complements and enhances face-to-face relationships or maintains ties among old friends or relatives now separated by distance.

The authors conclude that although the Net does not *preclude* intimacy, the lack of social and physical cues allows individuals "to control the timing and content of self-disclosure" (p. 352) and thus the development of intimacy. Further, the Net fosters community diversity across the boundaries of geography, social class, gender, and race or ethnicity; thus, "cyberlinks between people become social links between groups that otherwise would be socially and physically dispersed" (p. 356).

Source: Based on Wellman and Gulia (1999).

---

maintained by people who are young, well educated, and living in urban areas. Finally, size of community also affects who falls within social networks: people who live in small communities have more kin in their networks than people who live in large settlements (Marsden, 1987; Markovsky et al., 1993; Kadushin, 1995; O'Brien et al., 1996).

In a study of "intimate networks" in East York (now part of amalgamated Toronto), Wellman (1979) found that almost everyone could name one to six intimates outside the home, only half of whom were kin. While most of their intimate contacts lived within Metropolitan Toronto, only 13 percent lived in the neighbourhood. In other words, Wellman's respondents felt close to people who were widely dispersed. Neither weak-tie networks nor the intimate variety are geographically bound. More recently, Wellman has turned his attention to Net-based social networks—as revealed in the "Applying Sociology" box.

New information technology has generated a global network of unprecedented size in the form of the Internet. The "Cyber-Society" box takes a closer look at the impacts of this twenty-first-century form of communication. Global Map 7–1 shows access to the Internet around the world.

FORMAL ORGANIZATIONS

Throughout human history, most people lived in small groups of family members and neighbours; this pattern was still widespread in Canada a century ago. Today, families and neighbourhoods persist, of course, but our lives revolve far more around **formal organizations**, *large, secondary groups that are organized to achieve their goals efficiently.*

Formal organizations, such as corporations or government agencies, differ from families and neighbourhoods because their greater size renders social re-

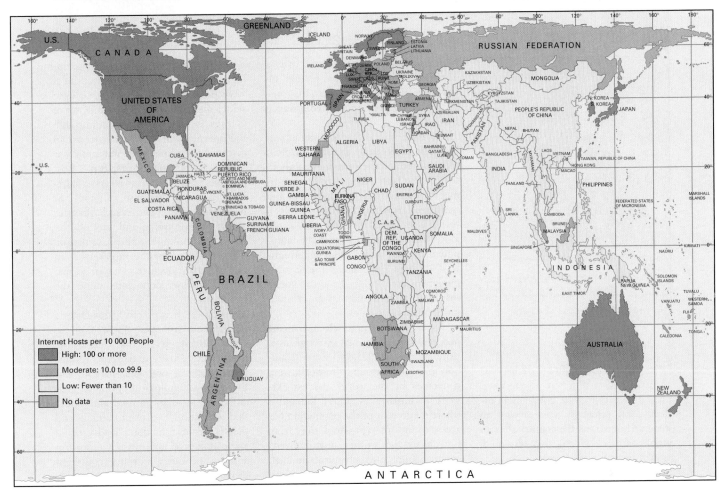

GLOBAL MAP 7-1 Access to the Internet in Global Perspective

This map shows access to the Internet around the world in terms of the number of Internet hosts for every 10 000 people. Most high-income countries and many middle-income nations are rated as having high Internet access. In contrast, about half the world's nations (mostly those with low average incomes) offer little access. What effect does this have on people's access to information? What are the likely consequences of this disparity for the future in terms of global inequality?

Source: The World Bank (2001).

lationships less personal and fosters a planned, formal atmosphere. In other words, they accomplish complex jobs rather than meet personal needs.

Organizing a society with 31 million members is a remarkable feat. Countless tasks are involved, from collecting taxes to delivering the mail. To meet most of these responsibilities, we rely on large, formal organizations. The Canadian government, our largest formal organization, employs about 1 million people in provincial, federal, and municipal government and the armed forces. Such vast organizations develop

lives and cultures of their own, so that as members come and go, the statuses they fill and the roles they perform remain unchanged.

TYPES OF FORMAL ORGANIZATIONS

Amitai Etzioni (1975) has identified three types of formal organizations, distinguished by why people participate—utilitarian organizations, normative organizations, and coercive organizations.

The Internet: Welcome to Cyberspace!

"On the Internet, nobody knows you're a dog."

Its origins seem right out of the 1963 Cold War film *Dr. Strangelove.* Three decades ago, government officials and scientists were trying to imagine how to run the country after an atomic attack, which, they assumed, would instantaneously eliminate telephones and television. The brilliant solution was to devise a communication system with no central headquarters, no one in charge, and no main power switch—in short, an electronic web that would link the country in one vast network.

The brain behind it all, 1980 Web creator Tim Berners-Lee, still runs the nonprofit World Wide Web Consortium from a small, barren office at the Massachusetts Institute of Technology, where he helps maintain technical standards. Unlike his associates, such as the founders of Microsoft and Netscape, Berners-Lee does not drive a Mercedes-Benz or see his picture on the cover of major magazines: this "unsung hero" drives an old Volkswagen Rabbit.

By 1985, the U.S. government was installing high-speed data lines around the country and the Internet was about to be born. Today, thousands of government offices, as well as universities and businesses around the world, are joined by the Internet. Many millions of other individuals connect their home computers to this "information superhighway" through a telephone-line or cable modem or use wireless devices to access the Internet from classrooms, restaurants, or trains.

No one knows precisely how many people use the Internet. A rough estimate is that, by 2003, at least 670 million individuals around the world were connected by the world's largest network in history. By 1997, Finland—where 60 percent of the population has access to the Internet—took over from Canada as the world's most "wired" country. Finns use the Internet to chat, do research, order postage stamps, bank, read newspapers, take university courses, and do their grocery shopping.

What is available on the Internet? There are now millions of sites—far more than anyone could ever list in a single directory. But popular "search engines" such as Yahoo! Canada (**www.yahoo.ca**) and Google (**www.google.com**) can provide site listings for just about any topic you can imagine. Other popular activities include electronic mail (start a cyber-romance with a pen pal, write to your textbook authors at macionis@kenyon.edu or lgerber@uoguelph.ca, check out sociological resources through our website at **www.pearsoned.ca/macionis**, or even send a message to the prime minister of Canada at **http://pm.gc.ca**). Through the Internet, you can also participate in discussion groups, visit museums for "virtual tours," locate data from a host of government agencies (a good starting point is Statistics Canada at **www.statcan.ca**), and search libraries across your campus and around the world for books or other information. The excitement of the Internet lies in the fact that, given the lack of formal rules for its use, its potential defies the imagination.

Ironically, it is precisely this chaotic quality that has many people up in arms. Pundits warn that "electronic democracy" may undermine established political practices, parents fear that their technologically sophisticated children can easily access "adult sites" that offer sexually explicit content, and purists bristle at the flood of advertising and commercial enterprise. Censorship and, at the other extreme, copyright protection will prove to be extremely difficult, if not impossible.

The "anything goes" character of the Internet only makes it more a virtual image of the real world. Not surprisingly, therefore, more and more users are now employing passwords, fees, and other "gates" to restrict access to subnetworks limited to people like themselves. As a result, a host of smaller social groups is emerging from the one vast network.

Sources: Elmer-DeWitt (1993, 1994), Hafner (1994), Ibrahim (1997), and Wright (1997).

Utilitarian Organizations

Just about everyone who works for income is a member of a *utilitarian organization*, which pays its members for their efforts. Large business enterprises, for example, generate profits for their owners and income for their employees. Joining utilitarian organizations is usually a matter of individual choice, although most people must join one to make a living.

Normative Organizations

People join *normative organizations* to pursue goals they consider morally worthwhile. Sometimes called *voluntary associations*, these include community service groups (such as the Lions Club or Kiwanis), political parties, churches, and other organizations concerned with specific social issues. Historically, women played a greater role than men in voluntary and charitable organizations, in part because of their more limited involvement in the paid labour force.

Americans have long been characterized as "joiners" and still are involved, disproportionately, as members of voluntary associations (Curtis et al., 1992). Figure 7–3 provides a comparative glance at membership in cultural or educational organizations for selected countries, and reveals that Canadians are not too far behind their American neighbours.

Coercive Organizations

In Etzioni's typology, *coercive organizations* are distinguished by involuntary membership. That is, people are forced to join the organization as a form of punishment (prisons) or treatment (psychiatric hospitals). Coercive organizations have extraordinary physical features, such as locked doors and barred windows, and are supervised by security personnel (Goffman, 1961). These settings segregate people as "inmates" or "patients" for a period of time and sometimes radically alter their attitudes and behaviour. Recall from Chapter 5 ("Socialization") the power of total institutions to transform a human being's overall sense of self.

From differing vantage points, any particular organization may fall into all of these categories. A psychiatric hospital, for example, serves as a coercive organization for a patient, a utilitarian organization for a psychiatrist, and a normative organization for a part-time hospital volunteer.

ORIGINS OF BUREAUCRACY

Formal organizations date back thousands of years. The rulers of early empires relied on government officials to extend their power over millions of people and vast geographic regions. Formal organization allowed them to collect taxes, undertake military campaigns, and construct monumental structures, from the Great Wall of China to the pyramids of Egypt.

The power of these early organizations was limited, however. This was not because elites lacked grandiose ambition, but because they lacked the technological means to communicate quickly, to travel over great distances, and to collect and store information. Early organizations existed within a traditional setting. In pre-industrial societies, cultural patterns placed greater importance on preserving the past or carrying out "God's will" than on organizational effi-

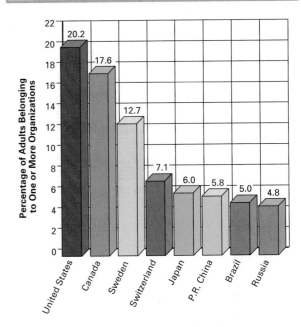

GLOBAL SNAPSHOT

FIGURE 7–3 Membership in Cultural or Educational Organizations

Source: World Values Survey (1994).

ciency. Only in the last few centuries did there emerge what Max Weber called a "rational world view," as described in Chapter 4 ("Society"). In the wake of the Industrial Revolution, the organizational structure called *bureaucracy* became commonplace in Europe and North America.

CHARACTERISTICS OF BUREAUCRACY

Bureaucracy is *an organizational model rationally designed to perform complex tasks efficiently.* In a bureaucratic business or government agency, officials deliberately enact and revise policy to make the organization as efficient as possible. To appreciate the power and scope of bureaucratic organization, consider that any one of more than 300 million phones in North America can connect you, within seconds, to any other phone—in homes, businesses, and automobiles, and even to a hiker on an Alberta mountain trail. Such instant communication was beyond the imagination of those who lived as recently as a century ago.

Of course, the telephone system depends on technological developments such as electricity, fibre optics, and computers. But neither could the system exist without the organizational capacity to keep track of every telephone call—noting which phone called

TABLE 7–2 Small Groups and Formal Organizations: A Comparison

	Small Groups	Formal Organizations
Activities	Members typically engage in many of the same activities	Members typically engage in various highly specialized activities
Hierarchy	Often informal or nonexistent	Clearly defined corresponding to offices
Norms	Informal application of general norms	Clearly defined rules and regulations
Criteria for membership	Variable, often based on personal affection or kinship	Technical competence to carry out assigned tasks
Relationships	Variable; typically primary	Typically secondary, with selective primary ties
Communications	Typically casual and face to face	Typically formal and in writing
Focus	Person-oriented	Task-oriented

which other phone, when, and for how long—and presenting all this information to many millions of telephone users in the form of monthly bills.

What specific traits promote organizational efficiency? Max Weber (1978; orig. 1921) identified six key elements of the ideal bureaucratic organization.

1. **Specialization.** Through most of human history, everyone pursued the basic goals of securing food and shelter. Bureaucracy, in contrast, assigns to individuals highly specialized duties.

2. **Hierarchy of offices.** Bureaucracies arrange personnel in a vertical hierarchy of offices. Each person is thus supervised by "higher-ups" in the organization while, in turn, supervising others in lower positions.

3. **Rules and regulations.** Cultural tradition holds scant sway in bureaucracy. Instead, operations are guided by rationally enacted rules and regulations. These rules control not only the organization's own functioning but, as much as possible, its larger environment. Ideally, a bureaucracy seeks to operate in a completely predictable fashion.

4. **Technical competence.** A bureaucratic organization expects officials to have the technical competence to carry out their official duties. Bureaucracies regularly monitor the performance of staff members. Such impersonal evaluation based on performance contrasts sharply with the custom, followed through most of human history,

of favouring relatives—whatever their talents—over strangers.

5. **Impersonality.** In bureaucratic organizations, rules take precedence over personal whim. This impersonality encourages uniform treatment for each client as well as other workers. From this detached approach stems the notion of the "faceless bureaucrat."

6. **Formal, written communications.** An old adage states that the heart of bureaucracy is not people but paperwork. Rather than casual, oral communication, bureaucracy relies on formal, written memos and reports. Over time, this correspondence accumulates into vast *files*. These files guide the subsequent operation of an organization in roughly the same way that social background shapes the life of an individual.

These traits represent a clear contrast to the more personal character of small groups. Bureaucratic organization promotes efficiency by carefully recruiting personnel and limiting the unpredictable effects of personal tastes and opinions. In smaller, informal groups, members allow one another considerable discretion in their behaviour; they respond to each other personally and regard everyone as more or less equal in rank. Table 7–2 summarizes the differences between small social groups and large formal organizations.

ORGANIZATIONAL SIZE

Just as the character of social groups differs according to their size, so does the nature of formal organizations. Analyzing organizations of various sizes, Arne L. Kalleberg and Mark E. Van Buren (1996) found that "bigger is better" when it comes to many employee rewards. Typically, large organizations provide their workers with higher salaries, more fringe benefits, and greater opportunities for promotion.

On the other hand, the researchers conclude, "small is beautiful" when it comes to autonomy. Small organizations usually give their employees more autonomy about how they perform their jobs.

THE INFORMAL SIDE OF BUREAUCRACY

Weber's ideal bureaucracy deliberately regulates every activity. In actual organizations, however, human beings have the creativity (or the stubbornness) to resist conforming to bureaucratic blueprints. Sometimes informality helps to meet a legitimate need overlooked by formal regulations. In other situations informality may amount to simply cutting corners in one's job (Scott, 1981).

In principle, power resides in offices, not with the people who occupy them. Nonetheless, the personalities of officials greatly affect patterns of leadership. For example, studies of corporations document that the

Although formal organization is vital to modern, industrial societies, it is far from new. Twenty-five centuries ago, the Chinese philosopher and teacher K'ung Fu-Tzu (known to Westerners as Confucius) endorsed the idea that government offices should be filled by the most talented young men. This led to what was probably the world's first system of civil service examinations. Here, would-be bureaucrats compose essays to demonstrate their knowledge of Confucian texts.

qualities and quirks of individuals—including personal charisma and interpersonal skills—have a tremendous impact on organizational outcomes (Halberstam, 1986). In Canada, the structure, operating style, and message of the former Reform Party were a reflection of one man—its founder, Preston Manning.

Authoritarian, democratic, and laissez-faire types of leadership—described earlier in this chapter—also reflect individual personality as much as any organizational plan. Then, too, in the "real world" of organizations, leaders and their cronies sometimes seek to benefit personally through abuse of organizational power. And perhaps even more commonly, leaders take credit for the efforts of their subordinates—many of them secretaries, who have far more authority and responsibility than their official job titles and salaries suggest. Some of those responsible secretaries have been promoted to newly created administrative or executive assistant positions.

Communication offers another example of how informality creeps into large organizations. Formally, memos and other written communications disseminate information through the hierarchy. Typically, however, individuals cultivate informal networks or "grapevines" that spread information much faster, if not always accurately. Grapevines—carried by informal social networks and email—are particularly important to subordinates because superiors often attempt to conceal important information from them.

Electronic mail is also inherently democratic, allowing even the lowest-ranking employee to bypass immediate superiors in order to communicate directly with the organization's president. Some leaders may find such "open-channel" communication unwelcome, of course. For this reason, Microsoft Corporation (whose leader, Bill Gates, has an "unlisted" address yet still receives hundreds of email messages a day) has developed filters that will allow messages only from approved people to reach a particular computer terminal (Gwynne and Dickerson, 1997).

PROBLEMS OF BUREAUCRACY

Despite our reliance on bureaucracy to manage countless dimensions of everyday life, many members of our society view it with ambivalence. The following sections review several of the problems associated with bureaucracy, ranging from its tendency to dehumanize and alienate individuals to the threats it poses to personal privacy and political democracy.

Bureaucratic Alienation

Max Weber touted bureaucracy as a model of productivity. Nonetheless, Weber was keenly aware of

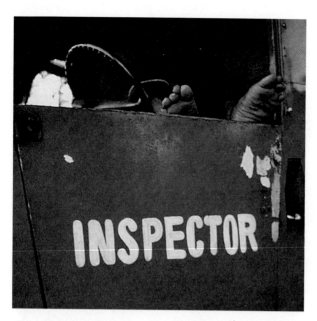

According to Max Weber, bureaucracy is an organizational strategy that promotes efficiency. Impersonality, however, also fosters alienation among employees, who may become indifferent to the formal goals of the organization. The behaviour of this municipal employee in Bombay, India, is understandable to members of formal organizations almost anywhere in the world.

bureaucracy's potential to *dehumanize* those it purports to serve. That is, the same impersonality that fosters efficiency simultaneously denies officials and clients the ability to respond to each other's unique, personal needs. On the contrary, officials must treat each client impersonally as a standard "case."

The impersonal bureaucratic environment, then, gives rise to *alienation*. Too often, Weber contended, formal organizations reduce the human being to "a small cog in a ceaselessly moving mechanism" (1978:988; orig. 1921). Thus, increasing formal organization left him deeply pessimistic about the future of humankind. Although formal organizations are designed to benefit humanity, he feared that humanity might well end up serving formal organizations.

Bureaucratic Inefficiency and Ritualism

Then there is the familiar problem of inefficiency, the failure of a bureaucratic organization to carry out the work that it allegedly exists to perform. Perhaps the greatest challenge to a large, formal organization is responding to special needs or circumstances. Anyone who has ever tried to replace a lost driver's licence or return defective merchandise to a discount store knows that bureaucracies sometimes can be maddeningly unresponsive.

The problem of inefficiency is captured in the concept of *red tape* (a phrase derived from the red tape used by eighteenth-century English administrators to wrap official parcels and records; Shipley, 1985). Red tape refers to a tedious preoccupation with organizational routines and procedures. Sociologist Robert Merton (1968) points out that red tape amounts to a new twist on the already-familiar concept of group conformity. He coined the term **bureaucratic ritualism** to designate *a preoccupation with rules and regulations to the point of thwarting an organization's goals.*

Ritualism impedes individual and organizational performance as it stifles creativity and imagination. In part, ritualism emerges because organizations, which pay modest, fixed salaries, give officials little or no financial stake in performing efficiently. Then, too, bureaucratic ritualism stands as another expression of the alienation that Weber feared would arise from bureaucratic rigidity (Whyte, 1957; Merton, 1968; Coleman, 1990; Kiser and Schneider, 1994).

Bureaucratic Inertia

If bureaucrats sometimes have little motivation to be efficient, they certainly have every reason to protect their jobs. Thus, officials typically strive to perpetuate their organization even when its purpose has been fulfilled. As Weber put it, "once fully established, bureaucracy is among the social structures which are hardest to destroy" (1978:987; orig. 1921).

Bureaucratic inertia refers to *the tendency of bureaucratic organizations to perpetuate themselves.* Formal organizations, in other words, tend to take on a life of their own beyond their formal objectives.

For example, as the need for service to veterans declined, Canadian War Amputations turned its attention to the needs of child amputees. Bureaucratic inertia usually leads formal organizations to devise new justifications for themselves after they have outlived their original purpose.

Oligarchy

Early in this century, Robert Michels (1876–1936) pointed out the link between bureaucracy and political **oligarchy**, *the rule of the many by the few* (1949; orig. 1911). According to what Michels called "the iron law of oligarchy," the pyramidlike structure of bureaucracy places a few leaders in charge of vast and powerful government organizations.

Pre-industrial societies did not possess the organizational means for even the most power-hungry ruler to control everyone. But the power of elites increased over the centuries with the steady expansion of formal organizations and the development of technology.

Max Weber credited bureaucracy's strict hierarchy of responsibility with increasing organizational efficiency. By applying Weber's thesis to the organization of government, Michels reveals that this hierarchical

19.9% and higher
10.7 to 19.8%
5.9 to 10.6%
Less than 5.9%

National Average: 6.2%

CANADA MAP 7-1
Employment in Government Service, 2001: Percentage by Province and Territory

Note: Employment at federal, provincial, and municipal levels is shown as a percentage of all employment.

Source: Calculations by Gerber based on data retrieved October 2003 from Statistics Canada online database, B2020, Profile Series.

structure concentrates power and thus endangers democracy. While the public expects organizational officials to subordinate personal interests to organizational goals, people who occupy powerful positions can—and often do—use their access to information and the media, plus numerous other advantages, to promote their personal interests.

Furthermore, bureaucracy also insulates officials from public accountability, whether in the form of a corporate president who is "unavailable for comment" to the local press or a national president seeking to control information by claiming "executive privilege." Oligarchy, then, thrives in the hierarchical structure of bureaucracy and undermines people's control over their elected leaders (Tolson, 1995).

Canada Map 7–1 illustrates the extent to which government bureaucracy permeates Canadian society. While 6.2 percent of Canada's labour force is employed in public administration (federal, provincial, and municipal), regional variation is clearly evident—with levels ranging from 4.8 percent in Alberta to 27.4 percent in Nunavut.

Parkinson's Law and the Peter Principle

Finally, and on a lighter note, we acknowledge two additional insights concerning the limitations of bureaucratic organizations. The concerns of C. Northcote Parkinson and Laurence J. Peter are familiar to anyone who has ever been a part of a formal organization.

Parkinson (1957) summed up his understanding of bureaucratic inefficiency with the assertion: "*Work expands to fill the time available for its completion.*" Enough truth underlies this tongue-in-cheek assertion that it is known today as Parkinson's Law. To illustrate, assume that a bureaucrat working for New Brunswick's Department of Transportation processes fifty driver's licence applications in an average day. If one day this worker had only twenty-five applications to examine, how much time would the task require? The logical answer is half a day. But Parkinson's Law suggests that if a full day is available to complete the work, a full day is how long it will take.

Because organizational employees have little personal involvement in their jobs, few are likely to seek extra work to fill their spare time. Bureaucrats do strive to appear busy, however, and their apparent activity often prompts organizations to take on more employees. The added time and expense required to hire, train, supervise, and evaluate a larger staff make everyone busier still, setting in motion a vicious cycle that results in *bureaucratic bloat*. Ironically, the larger organization may accomplish no more real work than it did before.

In the same light-hearted spirit as Parkinson, Laurence J. Peter (Peter and Hull, 1969) devised the Peter Principle: "*Bureaucrats rise to their level of incompetence.*" The logic here is simple: employees competent at one level of the organizational hierarchy are

George Tooker's painting Government Bureau *is a powerful statement about the human costs of bureaucracy. The artist depicts members of the public in monotonous similitude—reduced from human beings to mere "cases" to be disposed of as quickly as possible. Set apart from others by their positions, officials are "faceless bureaucrats" concerned more with numbers than with providing genuine assistance (notice that the artist places the fingers of the officials on calculators).*

George Tooker, *Government Bureau*, 1956. Egg tempera on gesso panel, 49.5 × 71.8 cm. The Metropolitan Museum of Art George A. Hearn Fund, 1956 (56.78). Photograph © 1984 The Metropolitan Museum of Art.

likely to earn promotion to higher positions. Eventually, however, they will reach a position where they are in over their heads; there, they perform poorly and thus are no longer eligible for promotions.

Reaching their level of incompetence dooms officials to a future of inefficiency. Adding to the problem, after years in the office they have almost certainly learned how to avoid demotion by hiding behind rules and regulations and taking credit for work actually performed by their more competent subordinates.

GENDER AND RACE IN ORGANIZATIONS

Rosabeth Moss Kanter, a professor of business administration at Harvard University, has analyzed how ascribed statuses such as gender and race figure in the power structure of bureaucratic hierarchies. To the extent that an organization has a dominant social composition, the gender- or race-based ingroup enjoys greater social acceptance, respect, credibility, and access to informal social networks.

As Figure 7–4 shows, much smaller proportions of women than men are in managerial occupations. Aboriginal and Black women have lower levels of representation than their British, French, and Asian counterparts, and the same holds true for men. Interestingly, though, if you consider the people employed at senior management level only (further calculations by Gerber), both Aboriginal men and women (1.9 percent and 0.9 percent, respectively) are more likely to be senior managers than are their British, French, or Asian counterparts.

A smaller representation in the workplace, argues Kanter, may leave women, people of colour, and those from economically disadvantaged backgrounds feeling like members of socially isolated outgroups. They are often uncomfortably visible, taken less seriously, and given fewer chances for promotion. Understandably, minority individuals may conclude that they must work twice as hard as those in dominant categories to maintain their present positions, let alone advance to higher ones (Kanter, 1977; Kanter and Stein, 1979). Bassett (1985) found a similar belief among Canadian career women and refers to this requirement as one of society's double standards.[1]

Kanter (1977) finds that providing a structure of unequal opportunities has important consequences for everyone's on-the-job performance. A company with many "dead-end" jobs, she explains, only encourages workers to become "zombies" with little aspiration, poor self-concept, and little loyalty to the organization. Widespread opportunity, in contrast, motivates employees, turning them into "fast-trackers" with higher aspirations, greater self-esteem, and stronger commitment to the organization.

In a corporate environment with wide-open opportunity for advancement, leaders value the input of subordinates and seek to bolster their morale and well-being. It is officials with no real power, Kanter maintains, who jealously guard their own privileges and rigidly ride herd over subordinates.

Organizational research in recent years has also spotlighted differences in management styles linked to gender. Deborah Tannen (1994) claims, for example, that women have a greater "information focus," and more readily ask questions in order to understand an issue. Men share an "image focus" that makes them

---

[1]Charlotte Whitton, the late mayor of Ottawa, put it as follows: "A woman has to be twice as good as a man to get ahead—fortunately, it's not difficult" (cited in Bassett, 1985:45).

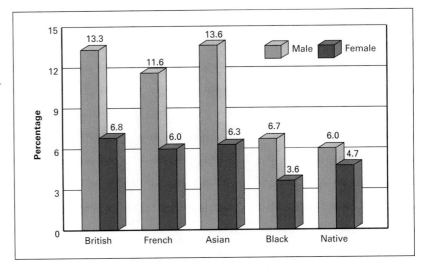

FIGURE 7–4 Representation in Management for Selected Categories, 1991

Percentage of employed population in managerial occupations.

Source: Calculations by Gerber based on 1991 Census Public Use Microdata Files, Statistics Canada, www.statcan.ca.

hesitate in the same situation, wondering what effect asking questions will have on their reputations.

In another study of women executives, Sally Helgesen (1990) notes three additional gender-linked patterns. First, claims Helgesen, women place greater value on communication skills and share information more than men do. Second, women are more flexible leaders who typically allow subordinates greater autonomy. Third, rather than emphasizing a narrow specialization, women are attentive to the interconnectedness of all organizational operations. Because many of today's leading business organizations operate more democratically and seek flexibility in order to contend with complex environments, Helgesen concludes that women bring a "female advantage" to the workplace.

One key conclusion drawn from recent research is that more open and adaptable organizations bring out the best in their employees. The flip side of this trend—in which women are playing a major part—is that, in more flexible environments, employees contribute the most to the organization.

BEYOND BUREAUCRACY: HUMANIZING ORGANIZATIONS

Humanizing organizations means *fostering a more democratic organizational atmosphere that recognizes and encourages the contributions of everyone.* Research by Kanter (1977, 1983, 1989; Kanter and Stein, 1980) and others (Peters and Waterman Jr., 1982) suggests that "humanizing" bureaucracy produces both happier employees and healthier profits. In the post-industrial era, in other words, organizations need to foster initiative and creativity among their members. Three paths to a more open and humane organizational structure are suggested here.

1. **Social inclusiveness.** The social composition of the organization should, ideally, make no one

feel "out of place" because of gender, race, or ethnicity. Everyone's performance will improve if no one is subject to social exclusion.

2. **Sharing of responsibilities.** Humanizing bureaucracy means reducing rigid oligarchical structures by spreading power and responsibility more widely. Managers cannot benefit from the ideas of employees who have no channels for expressing their opinions. Knowing that superiors are open to suggestions encourages all employees to think creatively, increasing organizational effectiveness.

3. **Expanding opportunities for advancement.** Expanding opportunity reduces the number of employees stuck in routine, dead-end jobs with little motivation to perform well. The organization should encourage employees at all levels to share ideas and try new approaches, defining everyone's job as the start of an upward career path.

Critical evaluation. Kanter's work takes a fresh look at the concept of bureaucracy and its application to business organizations. Rigid formality may have made sense in the past, when organizations hired unschooled workers primarily to perform physical labour. But today's educated workforce can contribute a wealth of ideas to bolster organizational efficiency—if the organization encourages and rewards innovation.

Many analysts agree that loosening up rigid organization is the key to improved performance. Companies that treat employees as a resource to be developed rather than as a group to be controlled stand out as more profitable. But some critics challenge Kanter's claim that social heterogeneity necessarily yields greater productivity. In controlled comparisons, they maintain, it is homogeneous work groups that typically produce more, while heterogeneous groups are better at generating a diversity of ideas and approaches. Optimal working groups appear

The recent trend is towards breaking down the rigid structure of conventional bureaucracy. One example of more flexible organizational form is the self-managed work team, whose members have the skills to carry out their tasks creatively and with minimal supervision.

to be those that strike a balance: team members offer a variety of backgrounds and perspectives in outlook and goals, yet are similar enough that they can effectively coordinate their efforts (Hackman, 1988; Yeatts, 1995).

SELF-MANAGED WORK TEAMS

At mid-century, formal organizations in North America typically were conventional bureaucracies, run from the top down according to a stern chain of command. Today, especially as these businesses face growing global competition, rigid structures are breaking down. One important element of this trend is the increasing use of the *self-managed work team*. Members of these small groups have the skills necessary to carry out tasks with minimal supervision. By allowing employees to operate within autonomous groups, organizations enhance worker involvement in the job, generate a broader understanding of operations, and raise employee morale.

Even though it is difficult to compare the performance of organizations with disparate goals and operations, research indicates that self-managed work teams do boost productivity while heading off some of the problems—including alienation—of the traditional bureaucratic model. In the business world, many companies have found that decentralizing re-

sponsibility in this way also raises product quality and lowers rates of employee absenteeism and turnover (Yeatts, 1991, 1995; Maddox, 1995).

ORGANIZATIONAL ENVIRONMENT

How any organization performs depends not only on its internal structure but also on the **organizational environment**, *a range of factors external to an organization that affect its operation.* Such factors include technology, politics, population patterns, and the economy, as well as other organizations.

For example, modern organizations are shaped by the *technology* of computers, telephone systems, and copiers. Computers give employees access to more information and people than ever before, while allowing executives to closely monitor the activities of workers (Markoff, 1991).

A second dimension of the organizational environment is *political and economic trends.* All organizations are buoyed or burdened by economic growth or recession, and no organization today can afford to overlook increasing competition from abroad. Similarly, changes in law—such as environmental regulations—can dramatically alter the way an organization operates. Canadian sociologist Kathryn Schellenberg studied small companies that go through periodic boom-and-bust cycles. She found that the repeated restructuring of their bureaucracies is costly in that it undermines trust in and commitment to the organization, often leading to the loss of valued employees (Schellenberg, 1996; Schellenberg and Miller, 1998).

Furthermore, *population patterns*—such as the size and composition of the surrounding populace—also affect organizations. The average age, typical education, and social diversity of a local community obviously shapes both the available workforce and the market for an organization's products or services.

Lastly, *other organizations* also contribute to the organizational environment. People who operate a hospital, for example, must be responsive not only to new government policies and regulations but also to the insurance industry and to organizations representing doctors, nurses, and other workers.

In sum, no organization operates in a social vacuum. But just as formal organizations are shaped by their environment, organizations themselves have an impact on the surrounding society.

THE MCDONALDIZATION OF SOCIETY

October 9, 1994, Macau. Here I am half way around the world in the Portuguese colony of Macau—a little nub jutting from the Chinese coast. Few people here speak English, and life on the streets seems a world apart from the urban rhythms of New York, Chicago, or Los Angeles. Then we turn the corner and stand face to face with (who else?) Ronald McDonald! After eating who-knows-what for so long, forgive our failure to resist the lure of the Big Mac! But the most amazing thing is that the food—the burgers, fries, and drinks—looks, smells, and tastes exactly the same as it does back home 16 000 kilometres away!

McDonald's has enjoyed enormous success. From a single store in the mid-1950s, McDonald's now operates more than thirty-one thousand restaurants in 119 countries, serving more than 46 million customers a day. As of October 2003, McDonald's Restaurants of Canada operated more than 1300 outlets in Canada. It was the Canadian branch that ventured into Moscow just as the Soviet Union crumbled, and its restaurant in Pushkin Square is the busiest McDonald's restaurant in the world. The appeal of the burger has placed McDonald's Restaurants of Canada near the top of Canadian companies ranked by revenues—number 102 in 2002 (*The Financial Post 500*, 2003) with $2.3 billion in revenues and 77 000 employees. (It is worth noting, however, that the value of McDonald's stock in Canada—but also in the United States—dropped precipitously when "mad cow" disease was found in one Alberta cow in May 2003. That financial setback, coupled with growing public concern about the relationship between fast-food consumption and obesity, led the company to initiate a worldwide marketing blitz to win back younger customers.)

McDonald's has become a symbol of the North American way of life, with polls suggesting that the gleeful clown Ronald McDonald is as much of a celebrity as Santa Claus. More importantly, the organizational principles that underlie McDonald's are beginning to dominate our entire society. Our culture is becoming "McDonaldized"—meaning that we model many aspects of our lives on the famous restaurant chain. Canadians, who love donuts more than Americans do, indulge their cravings at Tim Hortons or Country Style Donuts, where we know exactly what we'll get. We buy our household and automotive supplies at Canadian Tire, where inventory is continuously monitored for just-in-time replacement. More vacations take the form of resort and tour packages, television presents news in ten-second sound bites, and medical school applicants are screened on the basis of their MCAT results. The list goes on.

McDonaldization: Four Principles

What do all these developments have in common? According to George Ritzer (1993), the "McDonaldi-

Is McDonaldization becoming a global trend? Yes and no. The spread of McDonald's around the world has been dramatic and the company now earns most of its revenues from operations outside North America. But in some nations, McDonald's has altered its menu to take account of local cultural norms. For example, these women in a shopping mall in Dhahran, Saudi Arabia, are ordering food from a "ladies only" counter, which reflects the traditional gender norms of the nation.

zation of society" involves four basic organizational principles.

1. **Efficiency.** Ray Kroc, the marketing genius behind the expansion of McDonald's, set out with the goal of serving a hamburger, French fries, and a milkshake to a customer in fifty seconds. Today, one of the company's most popular items is the Egg McMuffin, an entire breakfast in a single sandwich. In the restaurant, customers bus their own trays or, better still, drive away from the pickup window, taking the packaging and whatever mess they make with them.

   Efficiency is now a value virtually without critics in our society. Almost everyone believes that anything that can be done quickly is, for that reason alone, good.

2. **Calculability.** The first McDonald's operating manual declared the weight of a regular raw hamburger to be 1.6 ounces (45 g), its size to be 3.875 inches (3.8 cm) across, and its fat content to be 19 percent. A slice of cheese weighs exactly half an ounce (14 g). Fries are cut $^9/_{32}$ of an inch (7 mm) thick.

Think about how many objects around the home, the workplace, or the campus are designed and mass-produced uniformly according to a calculated plan. Not just our environment but our life experiences—from travelling the nation's highways to sitting at home watching television—are now more deliberately planned than ever before.

3. **Uniformity and predictability.** An individual can walk into a McDonald's restaurant almost anywhere and receive the same sandwiches, drinks, and desserts prepared in precisely the same way. Predictability, of course, is the result of a highly rational system that specifies every course of action and leaves nothing to chance.

4. **Control through automation.** The most unreliable element in the McDonald's system is human beings. People, after all, have good and bad days, sometimes let their minds wander, or simply decide to try something a different way. To eliminate the unpredictable human element as much as possible, McDonald's has automated its equipment to cook food at fixed temperatures for set lengths of time. Even the cash register at a McDonald's is little more than pictures of the items so as to minimize the responsibility of the human being taking the customer's order.

The scope of McDonaldization is expanding. Automatic teller machines are replacing banks, highly automated bakeries now produce bread with scarcely any human intervention, and chickens and eggs (or is it eggs and chickens?) emerge from automated hatcheries. In supermarkets, laser scanners are phasing out the work of (less reliable) human cashiers. Most Canadian shopping now occurs in malls, in which everything from temperature and humidity to the kinds of stores and products are subject to continuous control and supervision (Ide and Cordell, 1994).

The mall—or, to some extent, a MacDonald's restaurant—can be seen as a postmodern phenomenon. Builders of malls "know very well how attractive and exciting a self-enclosed space may be" (Wilson, 1999:84). The initial step into a room or mall or McDonald's involves the decision to cross the threshold into strange and uncanny space; leaving the real world outside in the parking lot, you realize, with postmodern insight, that you are wrapped in a world of fakery, deception, and illusion. Wilson looks at the West Edmonton Mall, which is a physically isolated space offering a fantastic "total shopping-entertainment experience." But a McDonald's restaurant provides such an experience too: it is fun (the playroom and the colourful decor), comfortingly familiar, predictable (the menu), and based on fantasy or illusion. We see the friendly world of Ronald McDonald, comfort food, and moral goodness (signs of the various charities supported by the corporation); we do not see the vast, efficient corporate empire that works like a well-oiled, time-managed machine to change cattle, chickens, and field crops into *fast* food. Imagine visiting Bonn, Germany, looking at the spectacular cathedral, and turning to enter the McDonald's restaurant on your left. As you cross the threshold into a comfortingly familiar space, you might even breathe a sigh of relief.

Can Rationality Be Irrational?

No one would challenge the popularity or the efficiency of McDonald's and similar organizations. But there is another side to the story.

Max Weber viewed the increasing rationalization of the world with alarm, fearing that expanding control by formal organizations would cage our imaginations and crush the human spirit. As he saw it, rational systems were efficient, but at the terrible cost of dehumanization. Each of the four principles noted above depends on reining in human creativity, discretion, and autonomy. Moreover, as George Ritzer contends, McDonald's products are not particularly good for people or the natural environment. Echoing Weber's concern, he asserts that "the ultimate irrationality of McDonaldization is that people could lose control over the system and it would come to control us" (1993:145).

FORMAL ORGANIZATIONS IN JAPAN

We have described efforts to "humanize" formal organizations. Interestingly, however, organizations in some countries have long been more personal than ours. Those in Japan, a small nation that achieved remarkable economic success, prospered within a culture of strong collective identity and solidarity. While most members of our society prize rugged individualism, the Japanese maintain traditions of cooperation.

Because of Japan's social cohesiveness, formal organizations in that society approximate very large primary groups. William Ouchi (1981) highlights five distinctions between formal organizations in Japan and their counterparts in industrial societies of the West. In each case, the Japanese organization reflects that society's more collective orientation. The "Global Sociology" box looks at the application of these principles of Japanese organization in Canada, dealing as well with the strains that have forced Japan to restructure its economy.

1. **Hiring and advancement.** Organizations in North America hold out promotions and raises in salary as prizes won through individual competition. In Japanese organizations, however, companies hire new graduates together, and all employees of a particular age cohort receive the same salary and responsibilities. Only after several years is anyone likely to be singled out for individual advancement.

The Japanese Model: Does It Work in North America?

Economic competition from Asia, and increasingly from Europe, is forcing North American companies to reconsider long-held notions about how corporate organizations should operate. Although the Japanese economy has suffered setbacks in recent years, Canadian and American companies have continued to incorporate Japanese business principles.

Among the most interesting examples of new organizations are Japanese manufacturing plants built here in Canada and in the United States. By and large, these "transplants" have been quite successful in terms of productivity, demonstrating the adaptive ability of organizations. Yet some voices in this country—workers, union leaders, and managers—speak as bitterly about transplanting Japanese organizational techniques as they do about importing Japanese cars.

Manufacturing plants operated in Canada by Honda and Toyota (in Alliston, Ontario, and Cambridge, Ontario) and in the United States by Honda, Nissan, and Toyota have achieved the same degree of efficiency and quality that have won these companies praise in Japan. However, these organizations have had to struggle to win the support of many North Americans for some traditional Japanese practices, especially the idea of broad worker participation. Our corporate culture, with its rigid hierarchy, its heritage of individualism, and its history of labour–management conflict makes proposals to enhance worker participation highly controversial.

Many workers in this country dislike the concept of worker participation because they see it as increasing their workload. While still responsible for building cars, for instance, workers are now asked to worry about quality control, unit costs, and overall company efficiency—concerns usually shouldered by management. Some employees see the broad training favoured by the Japanese as a demanding routine of moving from job to job, always having to learn new skills. Many union leaders are also suspicious of new plans formulated by management, fearing an alliance between workers and managers may undermine union strength. Some managers, too, look cautiously on worker-participation programs. Sharing with employees the power to direct production and even schedule their own vacations does not come easily in light of past practices. Finally, North American corporations have a short-term outlook on profits, which discourages investing time and money in organizational restructuring.

Primarily owing to rising global competition, however, worker-participation programs are slowly changing the North American workplace. While the Honda and Toyota plants here in Canada brought with them the Japanese organizational and management package, many other firms are adopting components of that package and using them to modify their organizations. One of these approaches, Total Quality Management (TQM), has been adopted at Culinar (Montreal), Cadet Uniform Services (Toronto), Reimer Express Lines (Winnipeg), and General Electric (Bromont, Quebec). Culinar, the Canadian pioneer of TQM, has discontinued its effort, but the other three companies are very enthusiastic about the results in terms of worker involvement and morale, customer satisfaction, and profits. The second approach, called Continuous Improvement or CI (*kaizen* in Japanese), has been responsible for a major comeback at a Schneider food-processing plant in Kitchener, Ontario—the plant experienced improved efficiency, reduced waste, less absenteeism, and a dramatic increase in profits.

The successful implementation of either TQM or CI requires real commitment from senior management, a "friendly" or receptive corporate culture, highly motivated workers, willingness to change at all levels of the organization, and patience. The advantages go right to the bottom line: productivity and profits are usually higher when workers have a say in decision making. And most employees in worker-participation programs seem significantly happier about their jobs. Workers who have long used only their bodies are now enjoying the opportunity to use their minds as well.

While Canadian businesses have adopted Japanese management principles to their benefit, Japan has been reeling from the effects of a prolonged recession, reduced competitiveness and efficiency, downsizing, unprecedented levels of unemployment, and currency devaluation. The notion of lifelong bonds and loyalty between corporations and their employees suffered strain in some organizations and was abandoned in others. Despite what seemed to be superior business practices, Japan has joined the rest of the industrialized world in undergoing economic restructuring.

Sources: Hoerr (1989), Florida and Kenny (1991), Scott (1992), and Fife (1992).

---

2. **Lifetime security.** Employees in North America expect to move from one company to another to advance their careers. Companies, in turn, are quick to lay off employees when economic setbacks strike. In contrast, most Japanese firms hire employees for life, fostering strong, mutual

Are Large Organizations a Threat to Personal Privacy?

As he finishes dressing, Joe calls an 800 number to check the pollen count. As he listens to a recorded message, a Caller ID computer identifies Joe and pulls up his profile from a public records database. The profile, which now indicates that Joe suffers from allergies, is sold to a drug company, which sends Joe a free sample of a new allergy medication.

At a local department store, Nina uses her American Express card to buy an expensive new watch and some sleepwear. The store's computer adds Nina's name to its database of "buyers of expensive jewellery" and "sexy lingerie." The store trades its database with other companies. Within a month, Nina's mail includes four jewellery catalogues and a sex-videotape offer.

Are these cases of organizations providing consumers with interesting products, or are they violations of people's privacy? The answer, of course, is both: the same systems that help organizations operate predictably and efficiently

also empower them to invade our lives and manipulate us. So as bureaucracy has expanded in Canada, privacy has declined.

The problem reflects the enormous power of large organizations, their tendency to treat people impersonally, and their practice of collecting information. In recent decades, the danger to privacy has increased as organizations have acquired more and more computers and other new information technology that stores and shares information.

Consider some of the obvious ways in which organizations compile personal information. As they issue driver's licences, for example, provincial departments generate files that they can dispatch to police or other officials at the touch of a button. Similarly, Canada Customs and Revenue Agency, Health and Welfare, and government programs that benefit veterans, students, the poor, and the unemployed all collect extensive information.

Businesses in the private sector now do much the same thing, although, as

the examples above suggest, people may be unaware that their choices and activities end up in someone's database. Most people find the use of credit cards a great convenience (North Americans now average more than five per adult), but few people stop to think that credit card purchases automatically generate electronic records that can end up almost anywhere.

We also experience the erosion of privacy in the surveillance cameras that monitor more and more public places, along main streets, in the shopping malls, and even across campuses. And then there is the escalating amount of junk mail. Mailing lists for this material grow exponentially as one company sells names and addresses to others. Have you ever rented an X-rated video? Many video stores keep records of the movie preferences of customers and pass them along to other businesses whose advertising soon arrives in the mailbox.

Of particular concern to Canadians is the information stored in connection

---

loyalties among members. Japanese companies avoid layoffs by retraining expendable workers for new jobs in the organization.

3. **Holistic involvement.** North American workers tend to see the home and the workplace as distinct spheres. Japanese organizations, however, play a broad role in their employees' lives by providing home mortgages, sponsoring recreational activities, and scheduling social events. Interaction beyond the workplace strengthens collective identity and offers the respectful Japanese worker an opportunity to voice suggestions and criticisms informally.

4. **Broad-based training.** Bureaucratic organization in North America is based on specialization; many people spend an entire career at a single task. From the outset, a Japanese organization trains employees broadly in all phases of its operation, again with the idea that employees will remain with the organization for life.

5. **Collective decision making.** In our system, important decisions fall to key executives. Although

Japanese leaders also take responsibility for their organization's performance, they involve workers in "quality circles" that discuss any decision that affects them. A closer working relationship is also encouraged by greater economic equality between management and workers. The salary differential between executives and lower-ranking employees is about half that found in the United States.

These characteristics give the Japanese a strong sense of organizational loyalty. The cultural emphasis on *individual* achievement in our society finds its parallel in Japanese *groupism*. By tying their personal interests to those of their company, workers realize their ambitions through the organization.

GROUPS AND ORGANIZATIONS IN GLOBAL PERSPECTIVE

As this chapter has explained, formal organizations and their surrounding society interact, each influencwith our Social Insurance Numbers (SINs), which in some organizations have become employee identification numbers as well. The amount of personal information associated with one's SIN, the multiple uses of the number, and the possibility of merging massive files make SINs a particularly sensitive issue. Access by one government department or agency, such as the Canada Customs and Revenue Agency or the RCMP, to SIN-related data or Statistics Canada files would also be a worrisome invasion of privacy. It is possible, as well, for unauthorized users—from anywhere in the world, in fact—to gain access to and link the various files containing personal information about us.

In the spring of 2000, Human Resources Development Canada (HRDC) came under fire for compiling, into single files, data on individual Canadians from a variety of sources. So extreme was the public's reaction to the discovery that HRDC had up to 2000 items of information about every adult Canadian that the department was forced to destroy the files.

Similar concerns arise from the proliferation of multipurpose smart cards: simpler ones act as cash and allow access to all of one's accounts. Potentially, a single card—with a fingerprint—could act as driver's licence, cash card, health card, insurance record, and so on. The potential for information abuse here is high.

Concern about the erosion of privacy runs high. In response, privacy legislation has been enacted in Canada by the provinces and the federal government. The federal *Privacy Act* (1978; amended in 1982) permits citizens to examine and correct information contained about them in government files. Canadians also have access to information (e.g., consultants' reports) that contributes to the making of government decisions and policy. The *Personal Information Protection and Electronic Documents Act* (2001, with implementation by 2004) outlines corporate responsibilities and consumer rights when companies and other organizations collect information about individuals. But so many organizations now have information about us that current laws simply can't address the scope of the problem.

 See the website of Canada's privacy commissioner at www.privcom.gc.ca/ for more information about privacy legislation.

Continue the debate . . .

1. *Which do you think represents a larger threat to personal privacy, government or businesses? Why?*

2. *Internet search engines such as Yahoo! Canada (**www.yahoo.ca**) have "people search" programs that let you locate almost anyone. Do you think such programs are, on balance, helpful or threatening to the public?*

3. *Do you think the privacy problem will get worse or better? Why?*

Sources: Smith (1979), Rubin (1988), Miller (1991), and Bernstein (1997).

---

ing the other. Yet a global perspective reveals that bureaucracy does not take a consistent organizational form; formal organizations in Canada and Japan, for example, differ in a number of ways.

Organizations have also changed over time. Several centuries ago, most businesses in Europe and North America were small family enterprises. But the Industrial Revolution propelled large, impersonal organizations to the fore. Within this context, officials in the industrialized West came to define primary relationships at work (such as *nepotism*, favouritism shown to a family member) as an unethical barrier to organizational efficiency.

The development of formal organizations in Japan followed a different route. Historically, it was even more socially cohesive, organized according to family-based loyalties. As Japan industrialized, people there did not discard primary relationships as inefficient, as Westerners did. Rather, the Japanese modelled their businesses on the family, transferring traditional kinship loyalties to corporations.

From our point of view, then, Japan seems to be simultaneously modern and traditional, promoting organizational efficiency by cultivating personal ties. There are indications that Japanese workers are now becoming more individualistic. Yet the Japanese model still demonstrates that organizational life need not be so dehumanizing.

Economically challenged as never before, North American businesses are taking a closer look at organizational patterns elsewhere, especially in Japan. In fact, many efforts to humanize bureaucracy here are clear attempts to mimic the Japanese model.

Beyond the benefits for Western business organizations, there is another reason to study the Japanese approach carefully. Our society is less socially cohesive now than the more family-based society Weber knew. A rigidly bureaucratic form of organization only unravels the social fabric further. Perhaps by following the lead of the Japanese, our own formal organizations can promote—rather than diminish—a sense of collective identity and responsibility.

SUMMARY

1. Social groups—important building blocks of societies—foster personal development and common identity as well as performing various tasks.

2. Primary groups tend to be small and person-oriented; secondary groups are typically large and goal-oriented.

3. Instrumental leadership is concerned with realizing a group's goals; expressive leadership focuses on members' morale and well-being.

4. The process of group conformity is well documented. Because members seek consensus, work groups do not necessarily generate a wider range of ideas than do individuals working alone.

5. Reference groups—ingroups and outgroups—help individuals form attitudes and make decisions.

6. Georg Simmel characterized the dyad relationship as intense but unstable; a triad, he noted, can easily dissolve into a dyad by excluding one member.

7. Peter Blau explored how the size, internal homogeneity, social standing, and physical segregation of groups all affect members' behaviour.

8. Social networks are relational webs that link people who may have little common identity and limited interaction. The Internet links millions of users into networks.

9. Formal organizations are large, secondary groups that seek to perform complex tasks efficiently. According to their members' reasons for joining, formal organizations are classified as utilitarian, normative, or coercive.

10. Bureaucratic organization expands in modern societies to perform many complex tasks efficiently. Bureaucracy is based on specialization, hierarchy, rules and regulations, technical competence, impersonal interaction, and formal, written communications.

11. Bureaucracy may promote efficiency, but it also generates alienation and inefficiency, perpetuates itself beyond the achievement of its goals, and contributes to the erosion of privacy.

12. Formal organizations often mirror oligarchies: the concentration of power and opportunity in large corporations can compromise organizational effectiveness.

13. Humanizing bureaucracy means recognizing people as an organization's greatest resource. To develop human resources, organizations should spread responsibility and opportunity widely. One way to put this ideal into action is through self-managed work teams.

14. Technology, politics, population patterns, the economy, and other organizations combine to form the environment in which a particular organization must operate.

15. The trend towards the "McDonaldization of society" involves increasing automation, impersonality, and standardization.

16. Reflecting the collective spirit of Japanese culture, formal organizations in Japan are based on more personal ties than are their counterparts in North America.

CRITICAL-THINKING QUESTIONS

1. What are the key differences between primary and secondary groups? Identify examples of each in daily life.

2. What are some of the positive functions of group conformity (for example, fostering team spirit)? Note some of its dysfunctions.

3. According to Max Weber, what are the six characteristic traits of bureaucracy? How do Japanese organizations differ from those common to North America?

4. What does the "McDonaldization of society" mean? Cite familiar examples of this trend beyond those discussed in this chapter.

APPLICATIONS AND EXERCISES

1. Visit a large, public building with an elevator. Observe groups of people as they approach the elevator and, entering the elevator with them, watch what happens next. What happens to the conversations? Where do people fix their eyes? Can you account for these patterns?

2. Make a list of ingroups on your campus, and also identify outgroups. What traits account for groups falling into each category? Ask several other people to comment on your list to see if group hierarchy is a matter of agreement.

3. The next time you arrive at a social gathering early, note how many people share the conversation. What happens to the single group as more people arrive? What seems to be the typical size of a group for conversation?

4. Using available publications (and some assistance from an instructor), try to draw an "organizational pyramid" for your college or university showing the key offices and how they supervise and report to other offices.

 ## SITES TO SEE

www.macionis.com
or
www.TheSociologyPage.com
You can find more than fifty weblinks to sociological journals and other sources of data and information by visiting the Links Library at this website.

www.efc.ca/
Electronic Frontier Canada (EFC) was founded to ensure that the principles embodied in the *Canadian Charter of Rights and Freedoms* remain protected as new computing, communications, and information technologies are introduced into Canadian society.

www.airpower.au.af.mil/airchronicles/apj/apj94/waddell.html
Col. Donald E. Waddell, a professor of leadership studies at Air War College, writes about the art of leadership, a subject that may be studied more seriously in military schools than in civilian institutions, given the life-and-death nature of military business. He discusses the evolution of leadership theory and the application of the situational leadership model to military leadership and management.

www.mcspotlight.org/people/interviews/ritzer_george.html
This site features the transcript of a wide-ranging interview with George Ritzer, author of *The McDonaldization of Society*.

www.anderson.ucla.edu/research/japan/
Created to enhance North American understanding of Japanese culture and business practices, *Global Window: A Guide to Business Success—Japan* provides introductory essays on the Japanese economy, how to conduct business, legal considerations, and other useful topics, as well as a glossary, bibliography, and discussion forum.

www.georgetown.edu/faculty/tannend/
Here is the personal home page for Deborah Tannen, whose research in linguistics and communication is noted in the chapter.

www.cs.dal.ca/cam/univave.shtml
This website uses a camera placed at Halifax's University Avenue and Henry Street. Do you think Internet technology of this kind threatens people's privacy? Why or why not?

http://groups.yahoo.com/local/news.html
A number of websites, including this one, let people build their own social groups for chat or posting photos and other information. Take a look and see what you think about "virtual groups."

 ## STUDY TOOLS

For more study tools to help you with your next exam, be sure to check out the Companion Website at **www.pearsoned.ca/macionis**, as well as Chapter 7 in your Study Guide.

 ## INVESTIGATE WITH CONTENTSELECT

Follow the instructions found on page 25 of this textbook to access ContentSelect™ at the Research Navigator™ website. Once at the site, enter your LOGINID and Password. Then, enter keywords such as "Max Weber," "bureaucracy," "social network," and "McDonald's" and the search engine will supply relevant and recent scholarly and popular press publications.

CHAPTER

8

Andy Warhol (1928–1987, American)
Marilyn, 1967

SEXUALITY

Sergeant Sylvia Durand, in leopard-skin jacket and long auburn hair, is an example of recent profound change in the Canadian military: until recently she was Sergeant Sylvain Durand, a male communications specialist at the Department of National Defence in Ottawa. Her sex-change operation is significant enough in itself, but it has also become a historic event: the military was not just tolerant of the sex change, it actually paid the bill, at a Quebec clinic that draws clients from across North America.

Durand's partner, Cynthia Cousens, is a former Toronto police officer, Peter Cousens, who put in twenty-eight years of service in downtown's tough 14 Division—only to go to his retirement party dressed as a woman. Cousens had been a married man who loved his wife deeply and had two children, yet he felt compelled to deal with this deeply rooted thing within him.

Durand and Cousens met while they were undergoing

counselling and treatment prior to their sex-change operations, and went on to form a relationship that defies easy classification. They are not, as Sergeant Durand explains, in a traditional lesbian relationship. Nor are they gay. They are two transsexuals in transition who are very much in love.

Both Durand and Cousens realized, at about age five, that somehow they were not like other little boys. They grew up feeling that they were in the wrong bodies. The surgery, for Durand, was a miracle that left her feeling at peace with herself. Her "metamorphosis from he to she is a shining example of Canadian open-mindedness. She is the only soldier in the world to undergo a sex-change operation while serving in the military." That her transformation was accepted by her colleagues, with no ridicule or discrimination, speaks volumes about the change that has occurred in Canadian society and its military.

Source: Adapted from Peritz (2000).

UNDERSTANDING SEXUALITY

How much of the day goes by without your giving any thought at all to sexuality? If you are like most people, the answer is "not very much." That is because sexuality is not just about "having sex." Sexuality is a theme found throughout society, apparent on campus, in the workplace, and especially in the mass media. In addition, the sex industry—including pornography and prostitution—is a multibillion-dollar business in its own right. Since sexuality is an important part of how we think about ourselves and evaluate others, there are few areas of life in which sexuality does not play some part.

But in spite of its significance in life, few people understand sexuality. Through much of our history, sex has been a cultural taboo so that, at least in polite conversation, people did not talk about it. As a result, while sex can produce much pleasure, it also causes confusion, anxiety, and sometimes outright fear. Even scientists long considered sex off limits for research. It was not until the middle of the twentieth century that researchers turned attention to this pervasive dimension of social life. Since then, as this chapter reports, we have learned a great deal about human sexuality.

SEX: A BIOLOGICAL ISSUE

Sex refers to *the biological distinction between females and males.* From a biological point of view, sex is the means by which humans reproduce. A female ovum and a male sperm, each containing twenty-three chromosomes (biological codes that guide physical development), combine to form a fertilized embryo. One of

183

We claim that beauty is in the eye of the beholder, which suggests the importance of culture in setting standards of attractiveness. All of the people pictured here—from Morocco, South Africa, Nigeria, Myanmar (Burma), Japan, and Ecuador—are beautiful to members of their own societies. At the same time, sociobiologists point out that, in every society on earth, people are attracted to youthfulness. The reason is that, as sociobiologists see it, attractiveness underlies our choices about reproduction, which is most readily accomplished in early adulthood.

these chromosome pairs determines the child's sex. The mother contributes an X chromosome and the father contributes either an X or a Y. A second X from the father produces a female (XX) embryo; a Y from the father produces a male (XY). A child's sex, then, is determined at conception.

Within weeks, the sex of an embryo starts to guide its development. If the embryo is male, testicular tissue starts to produce testosterone, a hormone that triggers the development of male genitals. If no testosterone is present, the embryo develops female genitals. In developed countries, about 105 boys are born for every 100 girls, but a higher death rate among males makes females a slight majority by the time people reach their mid-twenties.

SEX AND THE BODY

What sets females and males apart are differences in the body. Right from birth, the two sexes have different **primary sex characteristics**, namely, *the genitals, organs used for reproduction*. At puberty, as individuals develop towards sexual maturity, additional sex differentiation takes place. At this point, individuals develop **secondary sex characteristics**, *bodily differences, apart from the genitals, that distinguish biologically mature females and males*. To allow for pregnancy, giving birth, and nurturing infants, mature females have wider hips, breasts, and soft fatty tissue that provides a reserve supply of nutrition for pregnancy and breast-feeding. Mature males typically develop more muscle in the upper body, more extensive body hair, and deeper voices. Of course, these are general differences, since some males are smaller and have less body hair and higher voices than some females.

Hermaphrodites

Sex is not always so clear-cut. In rare cases, a hormone imbalance before birth produces a **hermaphrodite** (a word derived from Hermaphroditus, the offspring of the mythological Greek gods Hermes and Aphrodite, who embodied both sexes), *a human being with some combination of female and male genitalia*.

The Boy Who Was Raised as a Girl

In 1963 a physician in a Canadian prairie town was performing a routine penis circumcision on seven-month-old identical twin boys. While using electrocautery (surgery with a heated needle), the physician accidentally burned off the penis of one boy. Understandably, the parents were horrified. After consulting with Dr. John Money of Johns Hopkins University, they decided to surgically change the boy's sex and to raise him as a girl.

The parents dressed Joan as a girl, let her hair grow long, and treated her according to cultural definitions of femininity. Meanwhile, the twin brother was raised as a boy.

In the initial reports, the researchers reported that because of their different socialization, each child adopted a distinctive **gender identity**, *traits that females and males, guided by their culture, incorporate into their personalities.* In this extraordinary case, it was reported, one child learned to think of himself in terms that our culture defines as masculine, while the other child—despite beginning life as a male—soon began to think of herself as feminine.

The girl's development did not proceed smoothly, however, suggesting that some biological forces were coming into play. While feminine in some respects, later researchers reported that she began to display some masculine

traits, including a desire to gain dominance among her peers. As she reached adolescence, she was showing signs of resisting her feminine gender identity (Diamond, 1982). By the spring of 1997, Diamond suggested that the gender reassignment had been much less successful than previously reported. By age fourteen, Joan (who had been teased mercilessly by other children for her boyish looks and behaviour) was suicidal and refused to continue living as a girl. When the father broke down and told Joan the truth, she was relieved, as she could finally understand herself. Since then, Joan has become John—undergoing a mastectomy, hormone treatment, and surgical reconstruction of male genitalia. Happy as a man, John has married and adopted his wife's children (Angier, 1997). This complex case reveals that while gender (a social construct) is the product of the social environment, cultural conditioning does not operate free from the influence of biology.

Joan/John was featured in a *Fifth Estate* documentary on gender reassignment (aired on September 23, 1997) in which he talked about the painful childhood he had endured because of rejection by his peers. His mother, who was interviewed as well, told of their experience from her perspective and, essentially, contradicted the statement

attributed to her by researchers Money and Ehrhardt concerning the "feminine" qualities of her child.

Several years later, John Colapinto, a reporter who had written an article for *Rolling Stone* on the story, came to Winnipeg to learn more about David Reimer (Joan/John's real current name). Colapinto convinced Reimer that it was time to put his experience into book form—but only if he was ready to reveal his true identity. The result, *As Nature Made Him: The Boy Who Was Raised as a Girl* (2000), was written by Colapinto with Reimer's cooperation. The book tells the story of David's struggle against his imposed girlhood, challenging Dr. John Money's contention that gender identity is determined by cultural conditioning rather than by genes.

What do you think?

1. *What should his parents have done when Reimer's penis was destroyed through botched circumcision?*

2. *Who has the right to "choose" the gender of a baby with damaged sex organs or indeterminate sex characteristics?*

3. *Is gender identity the function of nature or nurture?*

Source: Based on Colapinto (2000).

Because our culture is uneasy about sexual ambiguity, some people respond to hermaphrodites with confusion or even disgust. But other cultures lead people to respond quite differently: the Pokot of eastern Africa, for example, pay little attention to what they consider a simple biological error, and the Navajo look on hermaphrodites with awe, seeing in them the full potential of both the female and the male (Geertz, 1975).

Transsexuals

Some hermaphrodites undergo genital surgery to appear (and occasionally function as) a sexually normal

female or male. Other people, however, deliberately change their sex: **transsexuals** are *people who feel they are one sex even though biologically they are the other.* Tens of thousands of transsexuals in North America, like Durand and Cousens, as noted above, have surgically changed their genitals because they feel "trapped in the wrong body" (Restak, 1979, cited in Offir, 1982:146; Gagné et al., 1997).

SEX: A CULTURAL ISSUE

Sexuality has a biological foundation. But like all dimensions of human behaviour, sexuality is also very

The sexual revolution was well underway by the late 1960s, when the youth counterculture embraced the idea of "free love." This term is something of an exaggeration, but many people did enter into more casual sexual relationships.

much a cultural issue. Biology is sufficient to explain the strange mating ritual of scorpions, but humans have no similar biological program. Though there is a biological "sex drive" in the sense that people find sex pleasurable and may want to engage in sexual activity, our biology does not dictate specific ways of being sexual any more than our desire to eat dictates any particular foods or table manners.

Cultural Variation

Almost any sexual practice shows considerable variation from one society to another. In his pioneering study of sexuality in the United States, Alfred Kinsey (1948) found that most couples reported having intercourse face to face, with the woman on the bottom and the man on top. Halfway around the world, in the South Seas, most couples never have sex in this way. In fact, when people there learned of this practice from missionaries, they poked fun at it as the strange "missionary position."

As noted in Chapter 3 ("Culture"), even the practice of showing affection has extensive cultural variation, as kissing styles vary throughout the world.

Modesty, too, is a culturally variable matter. If a woman entering a bath is disturbed, what body parts does she cover? Helen Colton (1983) reports that an Islamic woman covers her face, a Laotian woman covers her breasts, a Samoan woman her navel, a Sumatran woman her knees, and a European woman covers her breasts with one hand and her genital area with the other.

Around the world, some societies tend to restrict sexuality, while others are more permissive. In China, for example, norms closely regulate sexuality so that few people have sexual intercourse before they marry. In Canada, however—at least in recent decades—intercourse prior to marriage has become the norm, and people may choose to have sex even when there is no strong commitment between them.

THE INCEST TABOO

Are any cultural views of sex the same everywhere? The answer is yes. One cultural universal—an element found in every society the world over—is the **incest taboo**, a *norm forbidding sexual relations or marriage between certain relatives.* In Canada, the law as well as cultural mores prohibit close relatives (including brothers and sisters, parents and children) from having sex or marrying. But exactly which family members are included in a society's incest taboo varies from one place to another. Some societies (such as the North American Navajo) apply incest taboos to the mother and others on her side of the family. There are also societies (including ancient Peru and Egypt) that have approved brother-sister marriages among the nobility (Murdock, 1965; orig. 1949).

Why does the incest taboo exist everywhere? Biology is part of the reason: reproduction between close relatives of any species risks offspring with mental or physical problems. But this fact does not explain why, of all living species, only humans observe an incest taboo. In other words, controlling sexuality among close relatives seems a necessary element of social organization. For one thing, the incest taboo limits sexual competition in families by restricting sex to spouses (ruling out, for example, sex between parent and child). Since family ties define people's rights and obligations towards each other, reproduction among close relatives would hopelessly confuse kinship (if a mother and son had a daughter, for example, what would the child's relation be to her parents?). Lastly, by requiring people to marry outside their immediate families, the incest taboo integrates the larger society as people look widely for partners to form new families.

The incest taboo has been an enduring sexual norm everywhere. But in Canada, other sexual norms have changed over time. During the twentieth century, as we now explain, our society experienced both a sexual revolution and, later, a sexual counterrevolution.

SEXUAL ATTITUDES

What do North Americans think about sex? Our cultural orientation towards sexuality has always been inconsistent. On the one hand, most of the Europeans who came to this continent held rigid notions about "correct" sexuality, which, ideally, meant that sex was only for the purpose of reproduction within marriage. As explained in Chapter 9 ("Deviance"), the Puritan settlers of New England demanded conformity in all attitudes and behaviour, and they imposed severe penalties for any misconduct—even if the sexual "misconduct" took place in the privacy of one's home. Efforts to regulate sexuality continued well into the twentieth century: it was not until 1969 that birth control or contraception was removed from Canada's Criminal Code. The same year, homosexual acts that take place in private between two consenting adults were decriminalized.

But this is just one side of the story of sexuality. As Chapter 3 ("Culture") explains, our culture is also individualistic, and many believe in giving people freedom to do pretty much as they wish, as long as they cause no direct harm to others. Such thinking—that what people do in the privacy of their own home is their business—makes sex a matter of individual freedom and personal choice.

So which is it? Is ours a restrictive or a permissive society when it comes to sexuality? The answer is that we are both. On the one hand, many Canadians still view sexual conduct as an important indicator of personal morality. On the other, sex is exploited and glorified everywhere in our culture—and strongly promoted by the mass media.

Table 8-1 reveals changes over time in our attitudes towards nonmarital sex (sex outside marriage), extramarital sex, and homosexuality. Bibby asked respondents to classify each as "not wrong at all," "sometimes wrong," "almost always wrong," or "always wrong." He found that Canadians became more accepting of nonmarital sex and homosexuality over the two decades in question: conversely, relative to 1975, we increasingly view extramarital sex as "always wrong" (an increase from 50 to 60 percent). Thus, we are more permissive with respect to nonmarital sex and homosexuality, but more restrictive with respect to extramarital sex (or adultery as it was commonly called).

Within this general framework, we turn now to changes in sexual attitudes and behaviour over the course of the twentieth century.

THE SEXUAL REVOLUTION

The last century witnessed profound changes in sexual attitudes and practices. The first indications of this change occurred in the 1920s, as millions from farms and small towns migrated to the rapidly growing

In December 1967, Pierre Elliott Trudeau shocked conservative Canada with the radical statement that "the state has no place in the nation's bedrooms"(Colombo, 1987:311). As justice minister, he had proposed to decriminalize homosexual acts carried out in private by two consenting adults—at a time when police actions and public opinion were still highly punitive of homosexuality (Kinsman, 1996).

cities. Living apart from their families and meeting in the workplace, young men and women enjoyed considerable sexual freedom. Indeed, this is one reason the decade became known as the "Roaring Twenties."

In the 1930s and 1940s, the Great Depression and World War II slowed the rate of change. But in the postwar period, after 1945, Alfred Kinsey set the stage for what later came to be known as the *sexual revolution.* Kinsey and his colleagues published their first study of sexuality in the United States in 1948, and it raised eyebrows everywhere. It was not so much what Kinsey said about sexual behaviour—although he did present some surprising results—but simply the fact that scientists were studying sex that set off an international conversation. At that time, after all, many people were uneasy talking about sex even privately at home.

But Kinsey's two books (1948 and 1953) became best-sellers because they revealed that people in the United States, on average, were far less conventional in sexual matters than most had thought. Thus, these books fostered a new openness towards sexuality, which helped move along the sexual revolution.

TABLE 8–1 Canadian Attitudes towards Nonmarital Sex, Extramarital Sex, and Homosexuality, 1975–95					
	Percentage Distribution of Responses				
	1975	1980	1985	1990	1995
Nonmarital sex					
Not wrong at all	39	46	50	55	57
Sometimes wrong	29	28	27	25	23
Almost always wrong	13	10	8	7	7
Always wrong	19	16	15	13	13
Extramarital sex					
Not wrong at all	5	4	3	3	3
Sometimes wrong	17	17	16	13	12
Almost always wrong	28	26	26	22	25
Always wrong	50	53	55	62	60
Homosexuality					
Not wrong at all	14	16	16	21	32
Sometimes wrong	14	14	13	13	16
Almost always wrong	10	8	9	7	7
Always wrong	62	62	62	59	45

Source: Adapted by Gerber from Bibby (1995:69, 72, 75).

In the late 1960s, the sexual revolution truly came of age. Youth culture dominated public life, and expressions like "if it feels good, do it" and "sex, drugs, and rock and roll" summed up a new freedom about sexuality. Some people were turned off by the idea of "turning on," of course, but the baby boom generation born between 1945 and 1960 became the first cohort to grow up with the idea that sex was part of everyone's life, married or not.

Technology, too, played a part in the sexual revolution. "The pill," introduced in 1960, not only prevented pregnancy, but it made sex more convenient. Unlike a condom or diaphragm, which has to be used at the time of intercourse, the birth control pill could be taken any time during the day. Now women as well as men could engage in sex without any special preparation.

The sexual revolution had special significance for women because, historically, women were subject to greater sexual regulation than men. According to the "double standard," society allows (and even encourages) men to be sexually active, while expecting women to remain chaste before marriage and faithful to their husbands afterwards. The survey data shown in Figure 8–1 support this conclusion. Among people born in the United States between 1933 and 1942 (that is, people in their mid-fifties to mid-sixties today), 56 percent of men but just 16 percent of women report having had two or more sexual partners by the time they were age twenty. Compare this wide gap to the pattern among the baby boomers born between 1953 and 1962 (people now in their forties and early fifties), who came of age after the sexual revolution. In this category, 62 percent of men and 48 per-

cent of women say they had two or more sexual partners by age twenty (Laumann et al., 1994:198). Thus, while the sexual revolution increased sexual activity overall, it changed behaviour among women more than among men.

THE SEXUAL COUNTERREVOLUTION

The sexual revolution made sex a topic of everyday discussion, and sexual activity more a matter of individual choice. But given that North Americans are of two minds about sex, the sexual revolution was also controversial. By 1980, the climate of sexual freedom that had marked the late 1960s and 1970s was criticized by some as evidence of moral decline. Thus the *sexual counterrevolution* began.

Politically speaking, the sexual counterrevolution was a conservative call for a return to "family values" by which sexual freedom was to be replaced by sexual responsibility. In practice, this meant moving sex back within marriage. Critics objected not just to the idea of "free love" but to trends such as cohabitation (living together) and having children out of wedlock.

Looking back, we can see that the sexual counterrevolution did not greatly change the idea that individuals should decide for themselves when and with whom to have a sexual relationship. What did happen is that more people began choosing to limit their number of sexual partners or to abstain from sex entirely. In many cases, such decisions are made on moral grounds. For others, however, the decision to limit sexual activity reflects a fear of sexually transmitted diseases (STDs). As Chapter 21 ("Health and Medicine") explains, although rates of most infectious diseases fell after 1960, rates of STDs rose sharply.

(a)   *(b)*   *(c)*   *(d)*   *(e)*

Contraception has a long history, beginning with the intrauterine device, or IUD, (a) in ancient times (originally, stones were used); by 1500, men employed condoms (b), more to prevent disease than pregnancy; the early 1600s saw the invention of the diaphragm (c), later used with spermicidal jelly; the birth control pill (d) came on the scene in 1960; sponges (e) were first licensed in 1983; the Norplant skin implant (f) debuted in 1990, followed by the female condom (g) in 1993.

(f)   *(g)*

Moreover, the fact that some STDs (such as genital herpes) are incurable and others (AIDS) are deadly has given individuals good reason to consider carefully their sexual choices.

PREMARITAL SEX

In light of the sexual revolution and the sexual counterrevolution, how much has sexual behaviour in North America really changed? One interesting trend involves premarital sex—the likelihood that young people will have sexual intercourse before marriage.

Table 8–2 shows attitudes towards premarital sex in Canada (1975 and 1995) and in the United States (1998). In Canada, attitudes towards premarital sex have changed dramatically between 1975 and 1995—in step with the sexual revolution. The proportion of Canadians who felt that premarital sex is "not wrong at all" increased from 39 to 57 percent, while the belief that it is "always wrong" decreased from 19 to 13 percent. Premarital sex, within Canada, has clearly gained in approval over this twenty-year period (Bibby, 1995:69). The table further suggests that Americans (in 1998) were less liberal than their Canadian counterparts: in fact, the U.S. figures for 1998 are similar to those for Canadians in 1975.

Now consider what young people *do* regarding premarital intercourse. For women, there has been marked change over time. The Kinsey studies (1948, 1953; see also Laumann et al., 1994) reported that for people born in the early 1900s, about 50 percent of men but just 6 percent of women had premarital sexual intercourse before age nineteen. Studies of baby boomers born after World War II show a slight in-

crease in premarital intercourse among men but a large increase—to about one-third—among women. Recent studies, targeting men and women born in the 1970s, show that 76 percent of men and 66 percent of women had premarital sexual intercourse by their senior year in high school (Laumann et al., 1994:323–24). Thus, although general public attitudes remain divided on premarital sex, this behaviour is broadly accepted among young people.

While the double standard (guys should, gals shouldn't) has been largely eliminated, male/female differences in the meaning attached to sex persist among Canadian university students. Among anglophone students, males are more likely than females (36.4 to 19.7 percent) to endorse the recreational or "fun" aspect of sex. Women, in contrast, adhere to a "love" standard more than men do (48.9 and 39.1 percent). Although the gender difference persists, francophone men and women are more likely to endorse the fun standard (51.9 and 37.1 percent) than are their anglophone peers; at the same time francophone men are slightly less likely (33.9 percent) to embrace the love standard (Nelson and Robinson, 1999:354).

SEX AMONG ADULTS

To hear the media tell it, Canadian adults are very active sexually. But do popular images exaggerate reality? Bibby (1995:65–67) found considerable variation in the frequency of sexual activity. The pattern breaks down as follows: 53 percent of Canadians have sex at least once a week; 23 percent are active one to three times per month; and 24 percent report sexual activity rarely or never. Quebecers report higher levels of

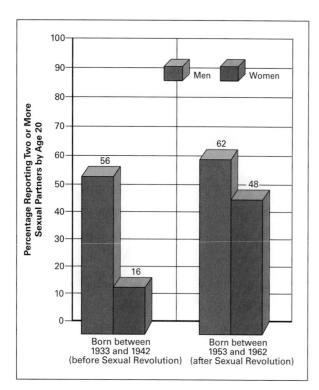

FIGURE 8–1 The Sexual Revolution: Closing the Double Standard

Source: Adapted from Laumann et al. (1994:198).

TABLE 8–2 How Canadians and Americans View Premarital Sex

	Canada 1975	Canada 1995	United States 1998
"Always wrong"	19%	13%	25%
"Not wrong at all"	39%	57%	42%

Sources: Bibby (1995) and NORC (1999).

sexual activity than Canadians on the whole, and activity peaks among thirty- to thirty-nine-year olds for both men and women, decreasing gradually into old age. Americans report lower levels of sexual activity than do Canadians (Laumann et al., 1994). The media, it seems, may be right!

EXTRAMARITAL SEX

What about married people having sex with people other than their marriage partners? What people commonly call "adultery" (sociologists prefer a more neutral-sounding term like "extramarital sex") is widely condemned. More than 85 and 90 percent, respectively, of Canadian and American adults consider extramarital sex to be "almost always wrong" or "always wrong." Thus, the norm of sexual fidelity within marriage has been and remains strongly supported in North American culture. In fact, this is one area in which we have become less liberal over the past few decades: the proportion of Canadians saying that extramarital sex is "always wrong" *increased* from 50 to 60 percent between 1975 and 1995 (see Table 8–1).

But, in terms of behaviour, the cultural ideal often differs from real life. It probably comes as no surprise that extramarital sexual activity is more common than people say it should be. At the same time, extramarital sex is not as frequent as many believe. Among Americans, about 25 percent of married men and 10 percent of married women have had at least one extramarital sexual experience (Laumann et al., 1994:214).

SEXUAL ORIENTATION

Over recent decades, public opinion about sexual orientation has changed remarkably. **Sexual orientation** refers to *a person's preference in terms of sexual partners: same sex, other sex, either sex, neither sex* (Lips, 1993). The norm in all human societies is **heterosexuality** (*hetero* is a Greek word meaning "the other of two"), meaning *sexual attraction to someone of the other sex*. Yet, in every society a significant share of people favour **homosexuality** (*homo* is the Greek word for "the same"), *sexual attraction to someone of the same sex*. When thinking about these categories, keep in mind that homosexuality and heterosexuality are not mutually exclusive. That is, people do not necessarily fall into one category or the other, but may have both sexual orientations to varying degrees. Figure 8–2 presents these two sexual orientations as a continuum, indicating that most people actually experience at least some degree of sexual attraction to people of both sexes.

The fact that sexual orientation is often not clear-cut points to the importance of a third category: **bisexuality**, which refers to *sexual attraction to people of both sexes*. Some bisexual people are equally attracted to males and females; many others, however, are more attracted to one sex over the other. Finally, one additional sexual orientation is **asexuality**, meaning *no sexual attraction to people of either sex*.

It is also important to note that sexual *attraction* is not the same thing as sexual *behaviour*. Though many people have experienced some attraction to someone of the same sex, fewer ever engage in same-sex behaviour, in large part because of cultural constraints on our actions.

 For a summary of recent research on sexual orientation, go to www.davidmyers.org/sexorient

Cultural systems do not accept all sexual orientations equally. Heterosexuality is the norm because, biologically speaking, heterosexual relations permit human reproduction. Even so, most societies tolerate homosexuality. In fact, among the ancient Greeks, upper-class men considered homosexuality the highest form of relationship, partly because they looked down on women as intellectually inferior. As men saw it, heterosexuality was necessary only so they could have children, and "real" men preferred homosexual relations (Kluckhohn, 1948; Ford and Beach, 1951; Greenberg, 1988).

WHAT GIVES US A SEXUAL ORIENTATION?

The question of *how* people come to have a sexual orientation in the first place is vigorously debated. But the arguments cluster into two general positions: first, sexual orientation is a product of society, and second, sexual orientation is a product of biology.

Sexual Orientation: A Product of Society

This approach argues that people in any society construct a set of meanings that lets them make sense of sexuality. Understandings of sexuality, therefore, differ from place to place and over time. For example, Michel Foucault (1978) points out that there was no distinct category of people called "homosexuals" until a century ago when scientists and, eventually, the public as a whole began labelling people that way. Through most of history, in other words, some people no doubt had what we would call "homosexual experiences." But neither they nor others saw in this behaviour the basis for any special identity.

In his influential postmodernist study, *The History of Sexuality*, Foucault argues that, in modern (i.e., capitalist) societies, sexuality and the language people use to describe it are subject to repression, prohibition, and censorship. The prohibition of all other forms of sexual expression (e.g., homosexuality, children's sexuality), except that between married couples for purposes of procreation, allows society "to ensure population, to reproduce labour capacity, (and) to perpetuate (its) form of social relations." The result is a sexuality that is socially constructed to be "economically useful and politically conservative" (1978:36–7).

Anthropologists provide further evidence that sexual orientation is socially constructed. Studies show that various kinds of homosexuality exist in different societies. In Siberia, for example, the Chukchi Eskimo have a ritual practice by which one man dresses like a female and does a woman's work. The Sambia, who dwell in the Eastern Highlands of New Guinea, have a ritual in which young boys perform oral sex on older men in the belief that ingesting semen will enhance their masculinity (Herdt, 1993). Such diverse patterns indicate that sexual orientation and sexual expression are socially constructed.

Sexual Orientation: A Product of Biology

The other view is that sexual orientation is innate, or rooted in human biology. Arguing this position, Simon LeVay (1993) links sexual orientation to the

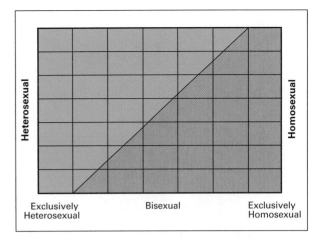

FIGURE 8–2 The Sexual Orientation Continuum

Source: Adapted from Kinsey et al. (1948).

structure of the human brain. LeVay studied the brains of both homosexual and heterosexual men and found a small but important difference in the size of the hypothalamus, a part of the brain that regulates hormones. Such an anatomical difference, some claim, plays a part in shaping sexual orientation.

Genetics, too, may influence sexual orientation. One study of forty-four pairs of brothers—all homosexual—found that thirty-three pairs had a distinctive genetic pattern involving the X chromosome. Moreover, the gay brothers had an unusually high number of gay male relatives—but only on their mother's side, the source of the X chromosome. Such evidence leads some researchers to think there may be a "gay gene" (Hamer and Copeland, 1994).

Critical evaluation. The best guess at present is that sexual orientation is derived from *both* society and biology (Gladue et al., 1984; Weinrich, 1987; Troiden, 1988; Isay, 1989; Puterbaugh, 1990; Angier, 1992; Gelman, 1992). But we need to bear in mind that sexual orientation is not a matter of neat categories. That is, most people who think of themselves as homosexual have had some heterosexual experiences, just as many people who think of themselves as heterosexual have had some homosexual experiences. Thus, the task of explaining sexual orientation is extremely complex.

 The American Psychological Association posts answers to commonly asked questions regarding sexual orientation at www.apa.org/pubinfo/answers.html

There is also a political issue here with great importance for gay men and lesbians. To the extent that sexual orientation is based in biology, homosexuality is not a matter of choice any more than, say, skin colour. If this is so, shouldn't gay men and lesbians expect the same legal protection from discrimination as other minorities (Herek, 1991)?

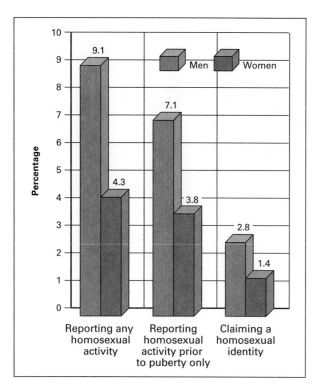

**FIGURE 8–3 Sexual Orientation in the United
States Survey Data**

Source: Adapted from Laumann et al. (1994).

HOW MANY GAY PEOPLE?

What share of the population is gay? This is a difficult question to answer because, as we have explained, sexual orientation is not a matter of neat categories. Moreover, people are not always willing to reveal their sexuality to strangers or even to family members. Pioneering sex researcher Alfred Kinsey (1948, 1953) estimated that about 4 percent of males and 2 percent of females have an exclusively same-sex orientation, although he thought that at least one-third of men and one-eighth of women have at least one homosexual experience leading to orgasm.

In light of the Kinsey studies, many social scientists put the gay share of the population at 10 percent. But a more recent national survey of sexuality in the United States indicates that how one operationalizes "homosexuality" makes a big difference in the results (Laumann et al., 1994). As Figure 8–3 shows, about 9 percent of U.S. men and about 4 percent of U.S. women aged between eighteen and fifty-nine reported homosexual activity *at some time* in their lives. The second set of numbers shows that a significant share of men (less so women) have a homosexual experience during childhood but not after puberty. And 2.8 percent of men and 1.4 percent of women define themselves as partly or entirely homosexual. A 2001 poll

indicated that 4.6 percent of the Canadian population had experienced same-sex attraction, while 2.6 percent of Canadians had had a sexual relationship with a person of the same sex (Canadian Press/Léger Marketing, 2003).

Finally, Kinsey treated sexual orientation as an "either/or" trait: to be more homosexual was, by definition, to be less heterosexual. But same-sex and other-sex attractions can operate independently. At one extreme, then, bisexual people feel strong attraction to people of both sexes; at the other, asexual people experience little sexual attraction to people of either sex.

In the U.S. survey noted above, less than 1 percent of adults described themselves as bisexual. But bisexual experiences appear to be fairly common (at least for a time) among younger people, especially on college campuses (Laumann et al., 1994; Leland, 1995). Many bisexuals, then, do not think of themselves as either gay or straight, and their behaviour reflects elements of both gay and straight living.

The Canadian census has never asked us about sexual orientation, but the census of 2001 changed that—under specific circumstances. Those individuals who claimed to be in a common-law relationship were asked to indicate if they were same-sex couples. The reason is that in Canada, same-sex couples are entitled to the same benefits as heterosexual couples involved in common-law relationships. The 2001 census counted 34 200 same-sex common-law couples, representing 0.5 percent of all couples (Statistics Canada, 2002c).

THE GAY RIGHTS MOVEMENT

In recent decades, the public has become increasingly accepting of homosexuality. In 1975, as shown in Figure 8–4, 72 percent of Americans and Canadians felt that homosexual relations were "always wrong" or "almost always wrong." From 1975 to 1990, Americans became slightly more intolerant before rapidly changing their attitudes, to the point where, in 1995, only 64 percent strongly disapproved of homosexuality (NORC, 1999:236). In Canada, the proportion of people who thought that homosexuality was very wrong dropped off sooner. By 1995, only 52 percent of Canadians were strongly disapproving, 45 percent saying that homosexuality is always wrong (Bibby, 1995:72). A poll in 2003 indicated 52 percent of Canadians agree there is nothing morally wrong about homosexuality (NFO Cfgroup, 2003).

In large measure, this change came about through the gay rights movement that arose in the mid-1900s (Chauncey, 1994). At that time, most people did not discuss homosexuality, and it was common for companies (including the federal government and the armed forces) to fire anyone who was thought to be gay. Mental health professionals, too, took a hard line, de-

FIGURE 8–4 Attitudes towards Homosexual Relations, 1975–95

Survey Question: "What about sexual relations between two adults of the same sex—do you think it is always wrong, almost always wrong, wrong only sometimes, or not wrong at all?"

Source: Bibby (1995) and NORC (1999).

scribing homosexuals as "sick," and sometimes placing them in mental hospitals, where, presumably, they might be cured.

In this climate of intolerance, most lesbians and gay men remained "in the closet"—closely guarding the secret of their sexual orientation. But the gay rights movement gained strength during the 1960s. In 1969, Canada removed homosexual activity that took place in private between consenting adults (aged twenty-one or over) from the Criminal Code. This limited reform was carried in the context of heated debate including talk of "gross indecency," "horror," and "sickness" (Kinsman, 1996). In 1974, the American Psychological Association declared that homosexuality was not an illness but simply a form of "sexual behaviour." By 1998, Canada had extended benefits to partners in same-sex relationships, but was careful to reiterate that *marriage* is defined as the union of a man and a woman—a definition reaffirmed in Bill C-23, which in June 2000 extended to same-sex couples in committed relationships both the *benefits* and *obligations* of other unions. But in June 2003, after the marriage laws were struck down by courts in Ontario, British Columbia, and Quebec, the federal government announced it would submit legislation allowing same-sex marriages to the Supreme Court for review. See the "Diversity: Race, Class, and Gender" box for details.

The gay rights movement began using the term **homophobia** to describe *the dread of close personal interaction with people thought to be gay, lesbian, or bisexual* (Weinberg, 1973). The concept of homophobia (liter-

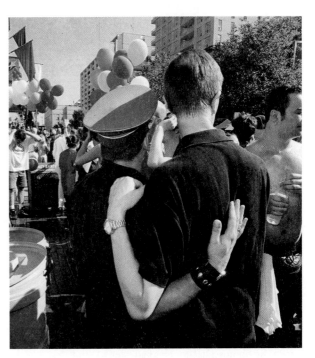

Halifax, Toronto, and Vancouver are among the North American and European cities that hold annual Gay Pride parades, like the one attended by this gay couple.

ally, "fear of sameness") turns the tables on society: instead of asking "What's wrong with gay people?" the question becomes "What's wrong with people who can't accept a different sexual orientation?"

SEXUAL CONTROVERSIES

Sexuality lies at the heart of a number of controversies. Here we take a look at four issues: teen pregnancy, pornography, prostitution, and sexual violence.

TEEN PREGNANCY

Being sexually active—especially having intercourse—demands a high level of responsibility, since pregnancy can result. Teenagers may be biologically mature, but many are not socially mature and may not appreciate all the consequences of their actions. Indeed, surveys indicate that while 1 million U.S. teens become pregnant each year—at rates of more than 100 pregnancies per 1000 teenage women—most do not intend to. Not only does pregnancy mean that many young women (and sometimes young fathers-to-be) cannot finish school, but they are at high risk of poverty.

Canada's rate of teen pregnancy is not as high as that of the United States—dropping from 50 pregnancies per 1000 women aged 15 to 19 in the early 1990s

DIVERSITY: RACE, CLASS, AND GENDER

Same-Sex Marriage in Canada

On January 14, 2001, Toronto made history, witnessing the world's first legal homosexual marriages since the Middle Ages—an event that attracted reporters from around the world. In Canada, legal marriage can be arranged through two routes: the first is through application for a marriage licence; the second involves the Christian tradition of the publication of banns on three Sundays prior to the marriage (giving members of the congregation opportunities to disclose legal impediments to the marriage). Applications for marriage licences by homosexual couples had been refused across Canada, but Toronto's Metropolitan Community Church published banns for Joe Varnell and Kevin Bourassa and for Anne and Elaine Vantour. Even though the Ontario government refused to register these marriages at that time, the marriages were legal—unless nullified by later court action (Humphreys, 2001). But much has changed since 2001.

In a judgment making same-sex marriage legal in Ontario in June 2003, the province's Court of Appeal said that the "exclusion of gays from the institution of marriage is illogical, offensive, and unjustifiable" (Makin, 2003). In doing so, the Ontario court joined those of British Columbia and Quebec in striking down marriage laws, but, unlike those of B.C. and Quebec, the Ontario court did not give the province a grace period to bring its laws into conformity with the Charter of Rights. As a result, Ontario acted immediately to give out marriage licences to gays and lesbians—the first among them being Joe Varnell and Kevin Bourassa, one of the two couples married by the Metropolitan Community Church in 2001.

Over the past decade or two, Canadians have become more and more tolerant and supportive of the alternative lifestyles of lesbians and gays. The extension of spousal rights—similar to those of heterosexual common-law couples—to same-sex couples was accepted by a majority of Canadians as just. A poll reported in the *Globe and Mail* (Makin, 2003) suggests that young adults 18 to 24 years of age are most supportive of same-sex marriage (61.2 percent of males, 69.2 percent of females); among those 35 to 54 years old, support comes in at 55 percent among males and 62.2 percent of females; while among the old folks over 55 years of age, support limps along at 24.6 percent among males and 37.6 percent among females. At a glance, it looks as if a large majority of Canadians is in favour of "extending the right to marry to same-sex couples," but if the results are weighted by the proportion of Canada's population (male and female) in each age category, one finds that 48.7 percent of adult males and 56.6 of adult females are in favour. A slightly later study carried out in August 2003 found that Canadians were evenly split between support for and opposition to the marriage of same-sex couples (49 per-

---

to 43 by 1997. In 1995, there were 19 724 babies born to teenage mothers and an additional 21 233 pregnancies that ended in abortion: in other words, more than half of Canada's teen pregnancies end in abortion. From a historical perspective, it is interesting to note that, between 1961 and 1991, the proportion of births to *unmarried* mothers that involved teens dropped from 38 to 19 percent because older women, in growing numbers, began to have children out of wedlock (Dryburgh, 2003; Belle and McQuillan, 2000).

 A global report from the Alan Guttmacher Institute discusses teenage sex and pregnancy: see www.guttmacher.org/pubs/ journals/ 3201400.html. Canadian data are available from Statistics Canada at www.statcan.ca/ english/kits/preg/preg3.htm

Concern about high rates of teenage pregnancy has led to sex education in the schools, but to some extent the focus has changed to concern about the problems of female-headed single-parent families—including those of teenage mothers.

PORNOGRAPHY

In general terms, **pornography** refers to *sexually explicit material that causes sexual arousal*. But what, exactly, is or is not pornographic has long been a matter of debate. In Canada, strictly speaking, pornography is legal. It is *obscenity* that is illegal, which involves the undue exploitation of sex and violation of community standards. Much of the debate in this area deals with the point at which pornography crosses the line from erotica to obscenity. Sex, combined with violence (even murder), bestiality, and the degradation or humiliation of women, qualifies as obscenity. But where exactly, in the continuum from *Playboy* to *snuff*, is that line crossed?

Definitions aside, pornography is surely popular in North America: X-rated videos, 1-900 telephone numbers for sexual conversations, and a host of sexually explicit movies and magazines together constitute roughly a $10-billion-a-year industry. The figure is cent each). This represented a slip from the 54 percent support recorded in early June (Ipsos-Reid, 2003).

While these figures reveal substantial support for same-sex marriage in principle, they do not reveal the extent of support for changing the *definition* of marriage. As recently as 1999, a motion to reaffirm the definition of marriage "as a union of one man and one woman to the exclusion of all others" was passed in Parliament with 216 votes for and 55 against (Lunman, 2003). A repeat motion to that effect, in the fall of 2003, was defeated by a very narrow margin.

Whatever the values and beliefs of our parliamentarians, recent court rulings—that the current laws discriminate against gays—mean that the government can no longer avoid dealing with this issue. And while the Canadian Alliance suggested that the issue should be put to a referendum so that all Canadians can vote on the matter, the federal government refused, saying that minority rights should not be dictated by majority rule. As a result, our justice department presented draft legislation that defines marriage as a union of two persons to the Supreme Court of Canada for its opinion on whether it is consistent with the Charter of Rights and the Constitution. Once the draft legislation is approved by the Supreme Court, it will be presented to the House of Commons, for debate and approval. Although it was the government of Jean Chrétien that referred the draft legislation to the Supreme Court, it has been left to the government of Paul Martin to see it through the legislative processes of the House of Commons and the Senate.

Once legislated by Parliament, Canada will join the Netherlands (April 2001) and Belgium (2002) as the first countries to allow same-sex marriage. Joe Varnell and Kevin Bourassa, because they rushed to have their marriage of January 2001 registered "legally" on June 11, 2003, have become the first gays to marry—not just in Canada, but in the world.

In August 2002, friends and family gathered on Algonquin Island (with the Toronto skyline in the background) for a commitment ceremony celebrating the love of this same-sex couple. On the first anniversary of this ceremony, the couple was able to marry legally, as the Court of Appeal had made same-sex marriage legal in Ontario.

rising as people buy more and more pornography from thousands of sites on the Web.

Traditionally, people have criticized pornography on *moral* grounds. U.S. surveys confirm that 60 percent of adults are concerned that "sexual materials lead to a breakdown of morals" (NORC, 1999:237). Today, however, pornography is also seen as a *power* issue because it depicts women as the sexual playthings of men (Nelson and Fleras, 1998).

Some critics also see pornography as a cause of violence against women. While it is difficult to document a scientific cause-and-effect relationship between what people view and how they act, research does support the idea that pornography makes men think of women as objects rather than as people. The public shares a concern about pornography and violence, with almost half of adults holding the opinion that pornography encourages people to commit rape (NORC, 1999:237). In fact, these are the kinds of concerns that informed Canada's obscenity legislation.

Though people everywhere object to sexual material they find offensive, many also value free speech and want to protect artistic expression. Thus, when we propose censorship of pornography in Canada, we need to balance our demands against our constitutionally protected rights of free expression.

PROSTITUTION

Prostitution is *the selling of sexual services*. Often called "the world's oldest profession," prostitution has always been widespread, and about one in five adult men in the United States reports having paid for sex on at least one occasion (NORC, 1999:996). Even so, to the extent that people think of sex as an expression of interpersonal intimacy, they find the idea of sex performed for money disturbing. As a result, prostitution is against the law almost everywhere in the United States. In Canada, prostitution among consenting adults is not a crime. Instead, our Criminal Code prohibits "those activities related to prostitution that are considered threatening to public order or offensive to public decency"—like soliciting or "communicating" for the purposes of prostitution in a public place (Wolff and Geissel, 2000).

Around the world, prostitution is greatest in poor countries where patriarchy is strong and traditional cultural norms limit women's ability to earn a living. Global Map 8–1 shows where in the world prostitution is most widespread.

Types of Prostitution

Most—but not all—prostitutes are women. Prostitutes (many prefer the morally neutral term "sex workers") fall into different categories. *Call girls* are elite prostitutes, typically women who are young, attractive, and well educated, and who arrange their own "dates" with clients by telephone. The classified pages of any large city newspaper contain numerous ads for "escort services," by which women (and sometimes men) offer both companionship and sex for a fee.

Members of a middle category of prostitutes work in "massage parlours" or brothels under the control of managers. These sex workers have less choice about their clients, receive less money for their services, and get to keep no more than half of what they make.

At the bottom of the sex-worker hierarchy are *street walkers*, women and men who "work the streets" of large cities. Female street walkers are often under the control of male pimps, who take most of their earnings. Many fall victim to violence from pimps and clients (Gordon and Snyder, 1989). Canadian homicide statistics further highlight the dangers associated with prostitution. In 1991 and 1992, twenty-two prostitutes were murdered, making up 5 percent of all the female murder victims sixteen years of age or older. Four of the twenty-two were sixteen and seventeen years of age (Wolff and Geissel, 2000).

Most, but not all, prostitutes offer heterosexual services. Gay prostitutes, too, trade sex for money. Researchers report that many gay prostitutes have suffered rejection by family and friends because of their sexual orientation (Weisberg, 1985; Boyer, 1989; Kruks, 1991).

A Victimless Crime?

Communicating for the purposes of prostitution is against the law in Canada, but many people consider it a victimless crime (see Chapter 9, "Deviance"). Thus, instead of enforcing prostitution laws all the time, police stage occasional crackdowns. Our society seems to want to control prostitution while assuming that nothing will eliminate it.

Is selling sex a victimless crime that hurts no one? Certainly, many people who take a "live and let live" attitude about prostitution would say it is. But this view overlooks the fact that prostitution subjects many

women to abuse and outright violence and plays a part in spreading sexually transmitted diseases, including AIDS. Also, many poor women become trapped in a life of selling sex, generally to the benefit of others, while putting their own lives at risk.

At the time this chapter was written in July 2003, British Columbia continued to be the scene of the most extensive murder probe in Canadian history—a probe into the disappearance of sixty-three women from Vancouver's skid row, most of whom were drug-addicted prostitutes. Since February 2002, hundreds of investigators, including fifty-two forensic anthropologists, had been searching every square inch of the farm of Robert Pickton and, more recently, a nearby piece of land along a highway near Mission, B.C. So far, the bodies of fifteen of the missing women have been found and identified and Pickton has been charged with fifteen counts of first-degree murder (Armstrong, 2003). Unfortunately, it took the disappearance of many prostitutes before the police clued in to the possibility of serial murder.

SEXUAL VIOLENCE

While sexual activity often occurs within a loving relationship, sex can be twisted by hate and violence. Sexual violence, which ranges from verbal abuse to rape and assault, is widespread in North America.

Rape

Although some people think rape is a form of sex, it is actually an expression of power—a violent act that uses sex to hurt, humiliate, or control another person. The U.S. Department of Justice reports that about 100 000 women are raped each year: since this number reflects only the reported cases, the actual number of rapes is several times higher (McCormick, 1994; U.S. Bureau of Justice Statistics, 1999).

In Canada, rape is officially recorded as *sexual assault*, with 27 100 cases reported in 2002. This represents 86 incidents per 100 000 population—an essentially steady rate for the past four years (Statistics Canada, 2003c). Victimization surveys in Canada lead to tremendous variation in estimates of sexual assault rates—for example, rates may vary from 6 to 29 per 1000 women, with only a fraction of cases showing up in official statistics (Johnson, 1996). U.S. rape statistics include only victims who are women, but men, too, are raped—in perhaps 10 percent of all cases. Most men who rape men are not homosexual. They are heterosexuals who are motivated by a desire not for sex but to dominate another person (Groth and Birnbaum, 1979; Gibbs, 1991a).

Date Rape

A common myth is that rape involves strangers. In reality, however, most rapes involve people who know

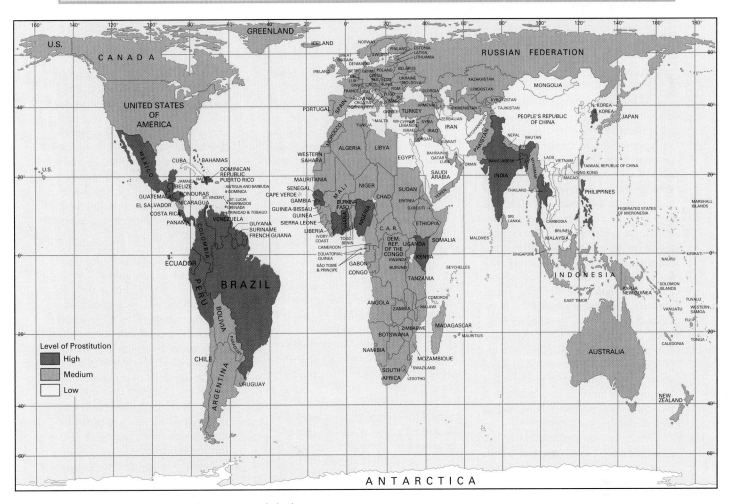

GLOBAL MAP 8–1 Prostitution in Global Perspective

Generally speaking, prostitution is widespread in societies where women have low standing. Officially, at least, the People's Republic of China boasts of gender equality, including the elimination of "vice," such as prostitution, which oppresses women. By contrast, in much of Latin America, where patriarchy is strong, prostitution is common. In many Islamic societies patriarchy is also strong, but religion is a counterbalance so prostitution is limited. Western, high-income nations have a moderate amount of prostitution.

Source: *Peters Atlas of the World* (1990) and Mackay (2000).

A new U.S. government report on the sexual victimization of college women is available at www.ojp.usdoj.gov/bjs/abstract/svcw.htm

one another, and they usually take place in familiar surroundings—especially the home. For this reason, the term *date rape* or *acquaintance rape* refers to forcible sexual violence against women by men they know.

Many victims of date rape do not report the crime. Some believe that because they know the offender, an attack could not have been rape. But the tide is turning, with more and more women speaking out. The "Applying Sociology" box takes a closer look.

THEORETICAL ANALYSIS OF SEXUALITY

We can better understand human sexuality by using sociology's various theoretical paradigms. In the following sections, we apply the three major paradigms in turn.

Date Rape: Exposing Dangerous Myths

Completing a day of work during a business trip to the courthouse in Tampa, Florida, thirty-two-year-old Sandra Abbott* pondered her return to her hotel. An attorney with whom she had been working—a pleasant enough man—made a kind offer of a lift. As his car threaded its way through the late afternoon traffic, their conversation was animated. "He was saying all the right things," Abbott recalled, "so I started to trust him." An invitation to join him for dinner was happily accepted. After lingering over an enjoyable meal, they walked together to the door of her hotel room. The new acquaintance angled for an invitation to come in, but Abbott hesitated, sensing that he might have something more on his mind. She explained that she was old-fashioned about relationships, but would allow him to come in for a little while with the understanding that talking was *all* they would do.

Sitting on the couch in the room, soon Abbott was overcome with drowsiness. Feeling comfortable in the presence of her new friend, she let her head fall gently onto his shoulder and, before she knew it, fell asleep. That's when the attack began. Abbott was startled back to consciousness as the man thrust himself sexually upon her. She shouted "No!" but he paid no heed. Abbott describes what happened next:

_____
*A pseudonym. The facts of this case are from Gibbs (1991a).

I didn't scream or run. All I could think of was my business contacts and what if they saw me run out of my room screaming rape. I thought it was my fault. I felt so filthy, I washed myself over and over in hot water. "Did he rape me?" I kept asking myself. I didn't consent.

But who's gonna believe me? I had a man in my hotel room after midnight. (Gibbs, 1991a:50)

Abbott knew that she had said "No!" and thus had been raped. She notified the police, who conducted an investigation and turned their findings over to the state attorney's office. But the authorities backed away. In the absence of evidence such as bruises, a medical examination, and torn clothes, they noted, there was little point in prosecuting.

The case of Sandra Abbott is all too typical. Even today, in most incidences of sexual attack, a victim files no police report, and no offender is arrested. So reluctant are the victims of such attacks to come forward that, in Canada, "somewhere between 60 and 90 percent of rapes go unreported" (DeKeseredy and Hinch, 1991:94). Where charges are not laid, the victim faces the bitter reality of simply trying as best she can to put a traumatic experience behind her.

The reason for such appalling inaction is that many people have a misguided understanding of rape. Three false notions about rape are so common that they might be called "rape myths."

Myth #1: Rape involves strangers. A sexual attack brings to mind young men lurking in the shadows who suddenly spring on their unsuspecting victims. But this pattern is the exception rather than the rule: experts report that only one in five rapes involves a stranger. For this reason, people have begun to speak more realistically about *acquaintance rape* or, more simply, *date rape*.

Myth #2: Women provoke their attackers. Surely, many people think, a woman claiming to have been raped must have done *something* to encourage the man, to lead him on, to make him think that she really wanted to have sex. In the case described above, didn't Sandra Abbott agree to have dinner with the man? Didn't she willingly admit him to her room? Such self-doubt often paralyzes victims. But having dinner with a man—or even inviting him into her hotel room—is hardly a woman's statement of consent to have sex with him any more than it is an invitation to have him beat her with a club.

Myth #3: Rape is simply sex. If there is no knife held to a woman's throat, or if she is not bound and gagged, then how can sex be a crime? The answer is that, under the law, forcing a woman to have sex without her consent is a *violent crime*. To accept the idea that rape is sex we would also have to see no

STRUCTURAL-FUNCTIONAL ANALYSIS

The structural-functional approach highlights the contribution of any social pattern to the overall operation of society. Because sexuality is an important dimension of social life, society regulates sexual behaviour.

The Need to Regulate Sexuality

From a biological point of view, sex allows our species to reproduce. But culture and social institutions regulate *with whom* and *when* people reproduce. For example, most societies condemn married people for having sex with people other than their spouses. To do other-difference between brutal combat and playful wrestling. "Having sex" implies intimacy, caring, and communication—none of which is present in cases of rape. Beyond the brutality of being physically violated, date rape also undermines a victim's sense of trust. This is especially serious in victims under eighteen, a significant percentage of whom are raped by their own fathers.

The more people believe these myths about rape, the more women will become victims of sexual violence. The ancient Babylonians stoned married women who became victims of rape, convinced that the women had committed adultery. Ideas about rape have not changed over thousands of years, which helps explain why, even today, most rapes go unreported to police and, even when authorities are notified, prosecutions and convictions are rare.

When women do report sexual attacks, police judgment as to whether or not a criminal act has occurred depends on the victim's reputation. When females referred to, by the Canadian police, as "women who can't be raped" or "open territory victims" filed complaints, 98 percent of the claims were dismissed as unfounded. "These women were prostitutes, known alcoholics, women who were drinking at the time of the offence, drug users, women on welfare, and unemployed women as well as women noted in police reports as 'idle'" (DeKeseredy and Hinch, 1991:66–67).

Nowhere has the issue of date rape been more widely discussed than at universities. The campus setting encourages trust, and young people often have much to learn about relationships and about themselves. While this open environment encourages communication, it also invites an alarming level of sexual violence. Studies in the United States estimate that one in six college women will be raped before she graduates. It is difficult to make estimates for Canada because of the limited amount of research on university rape done in this country. What is known is that university men who abuse their dates do so, quite often, with the support of male friends who encourage and legitimize female victimization (DeKeseredy and Hinch, 1991).

The extent of sexual assault as it affects students over eighteen is revealed by Statistics Canada's *Violence Against Women Survey*: while 12 percent of women in the larger population who are over eighteen years of age have experienced sexual assault by a date or boyfriend, this is true of 17 percent of female students. Considering the fact that these assaults are compressed into the short time span of the student years adds to the significance of the difference in rates and speaks volumes about the incidence of campus rape (Johnson, 1996).

To eliminate sexual violence we must begin by exposing the myths about rape. In addition, the campus must be transformed so that women and men interact with dignity and

Is a person who drinks alcohol to excess capable of making a responsible decision about having sex? What role does alcohol play in date rape on the campus?

equality. Serious questions surround the role of alcohol in campus social life and the effect of cultural patterns that define sex as a sport. To address the crisis of date rape, everyone needs to understand two simple truths: forcing sex without a woman's consent is rape, and when a woman says "No," she means just that.

Sources: DeKeseredy and Hinch (1991), Gibbs (1991a, 1991b), Gilbert (1992), and Johnson (1996).

---

wise—to give the forces of sexual passion free rein—would threaten family life and, especially, the raising of children.

Another example, discussed earlier in this chapter, is the incest taboo. The fact that this norm exists everywhere shows clearly that no society is willing to permit completely free choice in sexual partners.

Reproduction by family members other than married partners would break down the system of kinship and muddle relationships among people.

Historically, the social control of sexuality was strong, mostly because sex commonly led to childbirth. Moreover, offspring, as well as parents, were subject to these controls. We see this in the traditional

The control of women's sexuality is a common theme in human history. During the Middle Ages, Europeans devised the "chastity belt"—a metal device locked about a woman's groin that prevented sexual intercourse (and probably interfered with other bodily functions as well). While such devices are all but unknown today, the social control of sexuality continues. Can you point to examples?

distinction between "legitimate" reproduction (within marriage) and "illegitimate" reproduction (outside of marriage). But once a society can effectively control births, its norms become more permissive. This occurred in industrialized societies where, over the course of the twentieth century, sex moved beyond its basic reproductive function and became accepted as a form of intimacy and even recreation (Giddens, 1992).

Latent Functions: The Case of Prostitution

It is easy to see that prostitution is harmful because it spreads disease and exploits women. But are there latent functions that help explain why prostitution is widespread despite society's attempts to limit it? Definitely, explains Kingsley Davis (1971): prostitution performs several useful functions. It is one way to meet the sexual needs of a large number of people who do not have ready access to sex, including soldiers, travellers, and people who are not physically attractive, or who have trouble establishing relationships. Moreover, adds Davis, the availability of sex without commitment may even help to stabilize some loveless marriages that might otherwise collapse.

Critical evaluation. The structural-functional paradigm helps us to appreciate the role sexuality plays in how society is organized. With the incest taboo and other cultural norms, society pays attention to who has sex with whom and, especially, who reproduces with whom.

At the same time, this approach pays little attention to the great diversity of sexual ideas and practices found within every society. Moreover, sexual patterns change over time, just as they differ in remarkable ways around the world. To appreciate the varied and changeable character of sexuality, we turn to the symbolic-interaction paradigm.

SYMBOLIC-INTERACTION ANALYSIS

The symbolic-interaction paradigm highlights how, as people interact, they construct everyday reality. As Chapter 6 ("Social Interaction in Everyday Life") explains, the process of reality construction is highly variable, so that one group's or society's views of sexuality may well differ from another's. In the same way, how people understand sexuality can and does change over time.

The Social Construction of Sexuality

Almost all social patterns involving sexuality have seen considerable change over the course of the twentieth century. One good illustration is the changing importance of virginity. A century ago, our society's norm—for women, at least—was virginity before marriage. This norm was strong because there was no effective birth control, and virginity was the only assurance a man had that his bride-to-be was not carrying another man's child. Today, however, we have gone a long way towards separating sex from reproduction, and the virginity norm has weakened. Not surprisingly, premarital sex has increased in Canada to the point that, by 1992, 62 and 49 percent of teenage males and females, respectively, admitted to being sexually experienced; among university students, male and female, three-quarters were sexually experienced. These figures suggest a doubling of sexual activity levels among youth since the 1970s (Nelson and Robinson, 1999:354). Among single adults who have never been married, 87 percent say that they engage in sex—half of them at least weekly (Bibby, 1995:66). Very few, it seems adhere to the norm of virginity until marriage.

Another example of our society's construction of sexuality involves children. A century ago, childhood was a time of innocence in sexual matters. In recent decades, however, our thinking has changed. Though we expect them not to be sexually active, most people believe children should be educated about sex so that they can make intelligent choices about their own behaviour as they grow older.

Global Comparisons

The broader our view, the more variation we see in the meanings people attach to sexuality. In global perspective, differences can be striking, indeed. Anthropologists report that some cultures are far more accepting of childhood sexuality than people in the United States. Studying the Melanesian people of southeast New Guinea, anthropologist Ruth Benedict (1938) concluded that adults paid little attention when young children engaged in sexual experimentation with one another. Parents in Melanesia shrugged off such activity because, before puberty, sex cannot lead to reproduction.

Critical evaluation. The strength of the symbolic-interaction paradigm lies in revealing the constructed character of familiar social patterns. Understanding that people "construct" sexuality, we can better appreciate the variety of sexual practices found over the course of history and around the world.

One limitation of this approach, however, is that not everything is so variable. Throughout our own history—and around the world—men are more likely to see women in sexual terms than the other way around. If this pattern is widespread, some broader social structure must be at work, as we shall see in the next section.

SOCIAL-CONFLICT ANALYSIS

The social-conflict paradigm highlights dimensions of inequality. This approach, therefore, shows how sexuality both reflects patterns of social inequality and also helps create them.

Sexuality: Reflecting Social Inequality

Recall our discussion of prostitution, a practice outlawed almost everywhere. Even so, enforcement is uneven at best, especially when it comes to who is and is not likely to be arrested. Although two parties are involved, the record shows that police are far more likely to arrest (less powerful) female prostitutes than (more powerful) male clients. Similarly, of all women engaged in prostitution, it is street walkers—women with the least income and those most likely to be minorities—who face the highest risk of arrest (COYOTE, 2000). Then, too, we might wonder if so many women would be involved in prostitution at all if they had economic opportunities equal to those of men.

Sexuality: Creating Social Inequality

Social-conflict theorists, especially feminists, point to sexuality as being at the root of inequality between women and men. How can this be? Defining women in sexual terms amounts to devaluing them from full human beings into objects of men's interest and attention. Is it any wonder that the word *pornography* comes from the Greek word *porne*, meaning "a man's sexual slave"?

If men define women in sexual terms, it is easy to see why many people consider pornography—almost all of which is consumed by males—a power issue. Since most pornography depicts women seeking to please men, it supports the idea that men have power over women.

Some more radical critics doubt that this element of power can ever be removed from heterosexual relations (Dworkin, 1987). While most social-conflict theorists do not reject heterosexuality entirely, they do agree that sexuality can and does degrade women. Further, critics point out that our culture often depicts sexuality in terms of sport (men "scoring" with women) and also violence ("slamming," "banging," and "hitting on," for example, are verbs used for both fighting and sex).

Queer Theory

Finally, social-conflict theory has taken aim not only at men dominating women but also at heterosexuals dominating homosexuals. In recent years, just as many lesbians and gay men have come out in search of public acceptance, so have some sociologists tried to add a gay voice to their discipline. The term **queer theory** refers to *a growing body of knowledge that challenges an allegedly heterosexual bias in sociology.*

Queer theory begins with the assertion that our society is characterized by **heterosexism**, *a view stigmatizing anyone who is not heterosexual as "queer."* Our heterosexual culture victimizes a wide range of people, including gay men, lesbians, bisexuals, transsexuals, and even asexual people. Further, although most people agree that bias against women (sexism) and people of colour (racism) is wrong, heterosexism is widely tolerated and sometimes within the law.

Heterosexism also exists at a more subtle level in our everyday understanding of the world. When we describe something as "sexy," for example, do we not mean attractive to heterosexuals?

Critical evaluation. Applying the social-conflict paradigm shows how sexuality is both a cause and an effect of inequality. In particular, this paradigm helps us understand men's power over women and heterosexual people's domination of homosexual people.

At the same time, this approach overlooks the fact that sexuality is not a power issue for everyone: many couples enjoy a vital sexual relationship that deepens their commitment to one another. In addition, the social-conflict paradigm pays little attention to strides our society has made towards eliminating injustice. Men, in public at least, are less likely to describe

The Abortion Controversy

A van pulls up in front of the storefront in a busy section of the city. Two women get out of the front seat and cautiously scan the sidewalk. After a moment, one nods to the other and opens the rear door to let a third woman out of the van. Standing to the right and left of their charge, the two quickly whisk her inside the building.

This is an account of two clinic workers escorting a woman who has decided to have an abortion. Why should they be so cautious? Anyone who has read the papers in recent years knows about the heated confrontations at abortion clinics across North America. In fact, some opponents have even targeted and killed several doctors who perform abortions.

Abortion has been and still is a hotly contested and emotion-laden issue throughout North America, and especially in the United States.

There are about 1.3 million abortions performed in the United States each year. In Canada, about 60 000 therapeutic abortions were performed in hospitals each year from 1975 to 1985; others took place in doctors' offices or in abortion clinics like those run by Dr. Henry Morgentaler, an abortion advocate who performed abortions (and provided birth control to unmarried women) long before the liberalization of Canada's abortion laws.

Abortion was illegal in both Canada and the United States until the mid-1900s, driving abortion "underground," where many women—especially the poor—had little choice but to seek help from unlicensed "back alley" abortionists, sometimes with tragic results.

In 1969, under Prime Minister Trudeau, Canada's laws were liberalized to allow abortion in cases where three physicians certified that the mother's life or health was endangered. The law was not applied evenly across provinces or between large cities and rural areas because the definition of danger to the mother's life or health was not specified. If hospitals, many of them Catholic, simply refused to perform abortions, desperate women were forced to turn elsewhere.

In 1973, the U.S. Supreme Court rendered a landmark decision, striking down all state laws banning abortion—in effect, establishing a woman's legal access to abortion. It was not until 1988 that Canada's Supreme Court effectively left us without an abortion law by declaring the existing legislation unconstitutional.

While North American women now have legal access to abortion, the controversy has not abated. On one side are people who describe themselves as "pro-choice," who support a woman's right to choose; some of them are feminists who argue that women should have complete control of their sexuality and their bodies. On the other side are those who call themselves "pro-life," opposing abortion as morally wrong and defending life from the very moment of conception. The Canadian Alliance includes a pro-life faction that has feminists and liberals worried because of its stated aim of revisiting and perhaps re-establishing abortion laws.

How strong is the support for each side of the abortion controversy? About 40 percent of Canadians and Americans feel that women should have access to abortion, whatever their reasons. A vast majority of Americans and 95 percent of Canadians are in favour of abortion if a woman's health is in danger. The vast majority of Americans and 90 percent of Canadians would allow abortion if there were a strong chance of a serious defect in the baby or if the pregnancy were the result of rape. Only about 5 percent of Canadians would prohibit abortion under any circumstances.

Many anti-abortionists feel strongly that abortion is nothing more than killing unborn children. To them, people never have the right to end a life in this way. But pro-choice people are no less committed to their position. As they see it, the abortion debate is really about the standing of women in society.

Why? For the simple reason that women must have control over their own sexuality. If pregnancy dictates the course of women's lives, women will never be able to compete with men on equal terms, on campus or in the workplace. Thus, the pro-choice position concludes, women must have access to legal, safe abortion as a necessary condition to full participation in society.

Continue the debate . . .

1. *The more conservative anti-abortion people see abortion as a moral issue, while more liberal pro-choice people see abortion as a power issue. How does this relate to the way conservatives and liberals view the issue of pornography?*

2. *Surveys show that men and women have almost the same opinions about abortion. Does this surprise you? Why?*

3. *Why do you think the abortion controversy is often so bitter? Why have Canadians been unable to find a middle ground on which all can agree?*

Sources: Luker (1984), MacKenzie (1990), Tannahill (1992), Bibby (1995), and Nelson and Robinson (1999).

women as sex objects than a few decades ago; more-over, public concern about sexual harassment (see Chapter 13, "Gender Stratification") has had some effect in reducing sexuality in the workplace. Likewise, there is ample evidence that the gay rights movement has secured greater opportunities and social acceptance for gay people.

We bring this chapter to a close with a look at what is perhaps the most divisive sexuality issue of all: **abortion**, *the deliberate termination of a pregnancy*. Many people on both sides of this issue feel very strongly about abortion because, as we see in the "Controversy & Debate" box, it cuts to the heart of almost everyone's sense of justice.

SUMMARY

1. North American culture has long defined sex as a taboo topic. The Kinsey studies (1948, 1953) were among the first publications by social scientists on human sexuality.

2. Sex refers to the biological distinction between females and males, which is determined at conception as a male sperm joins a female ovum.

3. Males and females are distinguished not only by their genitals (primary sex characteristics) but also by bodily development as they mature (secondary characteristics). Hermaphrodites have some combination of both male and female genitalia. Transsexuals are people who feel they are one sex, although, biologically, they are the other.

4. For most species, sex is rigidly directed by biology; for human beings, sex is a matter of cultural definition as well as personal choice. Patterns of kissing, modesty, and beauty vary around the world, revealing the cultural foundation of sexual practices.

5. Historically, our society has held rigid attitudes towards sexuality, although these attitudes have become more permissive over time.

6. The sexual revolution, which has roots back to the 1920s but came of age in the 1960s and 1970s, brought a far greater openness in matters of sexuality. Research shows that changes in sexuality were greater for women than for men. By 1980, a sexual counter-revolution was taking form, condemning permissiveness and urging a return to more conservative "family values."

7. The share of Canadians who have premarital sexual intercourse increased over the last century. Research shows that by 1995 only 13 percent felt that premarital sex is always wrong.

8. The level of sexual activity varies among Canadian adults: 24 percent report having sex with a partner a few times a year or not at all; another 23 percent have sex one to three times a month; the remaining 53 percent have sex with a partner one or more times a week.

9. Extramarital sex is widely condemned, with 85 percent of Canadians saying it is always or almost always wrong.

10. Sexual orientation refers to people's preference in terms of sexual partners. Four major orientations are heterosexuality, homosexuality, bisexuality, and asexuality. Sexual orientation is caused by some combination of biological factors, cultural factors, and human choice.

11. The share of the population that is homosexual depends on how researchers define "homosexuality." About 9 percent of adult men and 4 percent of adult women report having some homosexual experience, compared with 2.8 percent of men and 1.4 percent of women who say they have a homosexual identity.

12. The gay rights movement has worked to gain greater acceptance for gay people. Largely owing to this movement, the share of Canadians condemning homosexuality as morally wrong has steadily decreased, while the share supporting gay rights and even gay marriage has increased.

13. Today, most pregnant teens are unmarried and, especially if they drop out of school, are at high risk of poverty. More than half of all pregnant teens in Canada choose abortion.

14. Although many people think of prostitution as a victimless crime, it victimizes women and spreads sexually transmitted diseases.

15. Some 27 100 sexual assaults are reported each year in Canada, but the actual number is likely much higher. Although many people think of sexual assault as a sexual act, it is really a violent expression of power. Most sexual assaults involve people who know one another.

16. Structural-functional theory highlights society's need to regulate sexual activity. A universal norm in this regard is the incest taboo that keeps kinship relations clear.

17. The symbolic-interaction paradigm points out how people attach various meanings to sexuality. Thus, societies differ from one another in terms of sexual attitudes and practices; similarly, sexual patterns change within any one society over time.

18. Social-conflict theory links sexuality to inequality. From this point of view, men dominate women in part by devaluing them as sexual objects.

CRITICAL-THINKING QUESTIONS

1. What do sociologists mean by the "sexual revolution"? What did the sexual revolution change? Can you suggest some of the reasons that these changes occurred?

2. What is sexual orientation? Why is this characteristic difficult for researchers to measure?

3. Do you think laws should regulate the portrayal of sex in books, in films, or on the Internet? Why or why not?

4. In what ways do societies regulate sexuality? In what ways does sexuality play a part in social inequality?

APPLICATIONS AND EXERCISES

1. Think for a moment about that factors that have shaped your attitudes towards homosexuality. Do you have a clear picture of what your older relatives, parents, and grandparents think about homosexuality? Among your contacts, do you detect increasing tolerance among younger cohorts?

2. Contact student services and ask about the extent of sexual violence on your campus. Do people report such incidents? What policies and programs on your campus are in place to deal with sexual violence?

3. Initiate conversations with friends to determine their attitudes about sex. Do males and females differ in their attitudes? Do they have different expectations of sex and definitions of rape? How do these differences reflect those of society at large?

 ## SITES TO SEE

www.macionis.com
or
www.TheSociologyPage.com
You can find more than fifty weblinks to sociological journals and other sources of data and information by visiting the Links Library at this website.

www.sieccan.org/
The Sex Information and Education Council of Canada (SIECCAN) is a national nonprofit educational organization established to promote public and professional education about human sexuality.

www.egale.ca/
Egale, Equality for Gays and Lesbians Everywhere, is a national organization that promotes equality and justice for lesbian, gay, bisexual, and transgendered people.

www.teenpregnancy.org
Visit the website of the National Campaign to Prevent Teen Pregnancy, a U.S. organization formed to guide teens towards responsible sexual behaviour. What are the key parts of this organization's program? How effective would you imagine it is? Why?

www.qrd.org
This website, the Queer Resource Directory, looks at a wide range of issues—including family, religion, education, and health—from a "queer theory" perspective. Visit this site to see in what ways various social institutions can be considered "heterosexist." Do you agree? Why?

www.gay.com
This is a search engine for all sorts of information on issues involving homosexuality.

 ## STUDY TOOLS

For more study tools to help you with your next exam, be sure to check out the Companion Website at **www.pearsoned. ca/macionis**, as well as Chapter 8 in your Study Guide.

Follow the instructions found on page 25 of this textbook to access ContentSelect™ at the Research Navigator™ website. Once at the site, enter your LOGINID and Password. Then, enter keywords such as "sexuality," "incest taboo," "transgender," and "abortion," and the search engine will supply relevant and recent scholarly and popular press publications.

CHAPTER
9

Emil Kazaz (1953– , Armenian-American)
Saratoga, 1998

Oil on linen, 152.4 × 182.9 cm. Collection of Rafael and Marina Akopian. Courtesy of Noah's Ark Fine Art.

DEVIANCE

Casablanca, Morocco, December 10, 1994. Casablanca! An exciting mix of African, European, and Middle Eastern cultures. Returning from a stroll through the medina, the medieval section of this coastal, north African city, we confront lines of police along one of Casablanca's breezy boulevards. Uniformed men stand between us and the harbour. Their presence has to do with the Islamic conference that has drawn many important leaders to one of the big hotels nearby. Are the streets closed? No one asks; people seem to halt at an invisible line some fifteen metres from the police officers. I play the brash urbanite and start across the street to inquire (in broken French) if I can pass by; but I stop cold as several officers draw a bead on me with their eyes. Their fingers nervously tap at the grips to their automatic weapons. This is no time to strike up a conversation.

Every society demands a certain measure of conformity from its members. Sometimes—in Canada and elsewhere—this process involves the use of armed officers. But in the vast majority of cases we conform to cultural patterns for the simple reason that they seem right and natural, part of the reality we inhabit.

This chapter explores many questions dealing with deviance and conformity: Why do societies create cultural norms, including laws, in the first place? Why are some people more likely than others to be accused of violations? To what extent does our country succeed in controlling crime? We begin our investigation by defining several basic concepts.

WHAT IS DEVIANCE?

Deviance is *the recognized violation of cultural norms.* Norms guide virtually all human action, so the concept of deviance covers a correspondingly broad spectrum. One distinct category of deviance is **crime**, *the violation of norms a society formally enacts into criminal law.* Even criminal deviance is extensive, ranging from certain traffic violations to serious offences such as murder. A subcategory of crime, **juvenile delinquency**, refers to *the violation of legal standards by the young.*

Some instances of deviance barely raise eyebrows; other cases command a swift and severe response. Members of our society pay little notice to mild nonconformity such as boastfulness or being a "nerd"; we take a dimmer view of reckless driving or dropping out of school, and we dispatch the police in response to a violent crime like armed robbery.

Not all deviance involves action or even choice. For some categories of individuals, just *existing* may be sufficient to provoke condemnation from others (think of the Palestinians and Israelis). To the young, elderly people sometimes seem hopelessly "out of it"; to whites who are in the majority, the mere presence of people of colour may cause discomfort. Able-bodied people often view people with disabilities as an outgroup. And affluent people may view the poor as disreputable to the extent that they fall short by conventional middle-class standards.

Most examples of nonconformity that come to mind are negative instances of rule breaking, such as stealing from a convenience store, abusing a child, or driving while intoxicated. But given our shortcomings, we also define especially righteous people—students who speak up too much in class or people who are enthusiastic about paying their taxes—as deviant, even if we accord them a measure of respect (Huls, 1987). What deviant actions or attitudes—whether negative

The kind of deviance people create reflects the moral values they embrace. The Berkeley campus of the University of California has long celebrated its open-minded tolerance of sexual diversity. Thus, in 1992, when Andrew Martinez decided to attend classes wearing virtually nothing, people were reluctant to accuse "The Naked Guy" of immoral conduct. However, in Berkeley's politically correct atmosphere, it was not long before school officials banned Martinez from campus—charging that his nudity constituted a form of sexual harassment.

or positive—have in common is some evaluation of difference that prompts us to regard another person as an "outsider" (Becker, 1966).

SOCIAL CONTROL

Members of a society try to influence one another with various kinds of social control. Much of this process is informal, as when parents praise or criticize children, or friends playfully comment on someone's latest romantic interest. Cases of serious deviance, however, provoke responses from the **criminal justice system**, *a formal response to alleged violations of law on the part of police, courts, and prison officials.*

In sum, deviance is much more than a matter of individual choice or personal failing. *How* a society defines deviance, *whom* individuals brand as deviant, and *what* people decide to do about nonconformity are all issues of social organization. Only gradually, however, have people recognized this basic truth.

THE BIOLOGICAL CONTEXT

Chapter 5 ("Socialization") explained that people a century ago understood—or, more correctly, misunderstood—human behaviour as an expression of biological instincts. Understandably, early interest in criminality emphasized biological causes as well. In 1876 Cesare Lombroso (1835–1909), an Italian physician who worked in prisons, characterized criminals as having a distinctive physique—low foreheads, prominent jaws and cheekbones, protruding ears, excessive hairiness, and unusually long arms, which, taken together, made them resemble the apelike ancestors of human beings.

But Lombroso's work was flawed. Had he looked beyond prison walls, he would have realized that the physical features he attributed exclusively to prisoners actually were found throughout the entire population. We now know that no physical attributes of the kind described by Lombroso distinguish criminals from noncriminals (Goring, 1972; orig. 1913).

William Sheldon (1949) took a different tack, positing that body structure might predict criminality. He categorized hundreds of young men in terms of body type and, checking for criminal history, concluded that delinquency occurred most frequently among boys with muscular, athletic builds. Glueck and Glueck (1950) confirmed Sheldon's conclusion, but cautioned that a powerful build does not necessarily cause or even predict criminality; they postulated that parents tend to be more distant from powerfully built males so that they, in turn, grow up less sensitive towards others. Moreover, in a self-fulfilling prophecy, people who expect muscular boys to act like bullies may provoke aggressive behaviour.

Recent genetics research continues to seek possible links between biology and crime. To date, no conclusive evidence connects criminality to any specific genetic flaw. Yet people's overall genetic composition, in combination with social influences, may account for some variation in criminality. In other words, biological factors probably have a real, if modest, effect on whether individuals engage in criminal activity (Rowe, 1983; Rowe and Osgood, 1984; Wilson and Herrnstein, 1985; Jencks, 1987).

Critical evaluation. At best, biological theories that try to explain crime in terms of specific physical traits explain only a small proportion of all crimes. Recent sociobiological research—noting, for example, that violent crime is overwhelmingly committed by males or that parents are more likely to abuse foster children than natural children—is promising, but, at this point, we know too little about the links between genes and human behaviour to draw any firm conclusions (Daly and Wilson, 1988).

Since the biological approach looks just at the individual, it offers no insight into how some kinds of behaviours come to be defined as deviant in the first place. While there is much to be learned about how human biology may affect behaviour, research currently places far greater emphasis on social influences (Gibbons and Krohn, 1986; Liska, 1991).

PERSONALITY FACTORS

Like biological theories, psychological explanations of deviance focus on cases of individual abnormality, this time involving personality. Some personality traits are hereditary, but most psychologists believe that temperament is shaped primarily by social experiences. Episodes of deviance, then, are viewed as the product of "unsuccessful" socialization.

The work of Reckless and Dinitz (1967) illustrates the psychological approach. These researchers began by asking teachers to categorize twelve-year-old boys as either likely or unlikely to become juvenile delinquents. Interviews with both categories of boys and their mothers allowed them to assess each boy's self-concept and how well he related to others. They concluded that the "good boys" displayed a strong conscience (or superego, in Sigmund Freud's terminology), coped well with frustration, and identified positively with cultural norms and values. The "bad boys," in contrast, had weaker consciences, showed little tolerance for frustration, and felt less in tune with conventional culture.

Furthermore, the researchers found that the "good boys" went on to have fewer contacts with the police than the "bad boys." Since all the boys studied lived in areas where delinquency was widespread, the investigators attributed the tendency to stay out of trouble to a personality that reined in impulses towards deviance. Based on this conclusion, Reckless and Dinitz call their analysis *containment theory*.

Critical evaluation. Psychologists have demonstrated that personality patterns have some connection to delinquency and other types of deviance. Nevertheless, this approach suffers from one key limitation: the vast majority of serious crimes are committed by people whose psychological profiles are *normal*.

In sum, both biological and psychological approaches view deviance as an individual attribute without exploring how conceptions of right and wrong initially arise, why people define some rule breakers but not others as deviant, and how social power shapes a society's system of social control. To explore these issues, we now turn to a sociological analysis of deviance.

THE SOCIAL FOUNDATIONS OF DEVIANCE

Although we tend to view deviance in terms of the free choice or personal failings of individuals, all behaviour—deviance as well as conformity—is shaped by

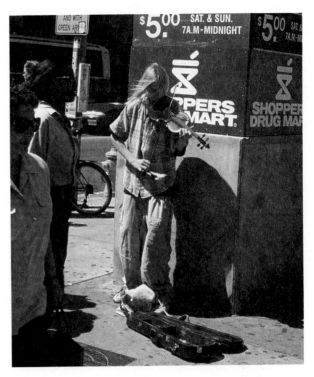

Artists have an important function in any society: to explore alternatives to conventional notions about how to live. For this reason, while we celebrate artists' creativity, we also accord them a mildly deviant identity. In today's more conservative political climate, some government officials have objected to art that seems to challenge traditional morality.

society. There are three social foundations of deviance, identified below.

1. **Deviance varies according to cultural norms.** No thought or action is inherently deviant; it becomes deviant only in relation to particular norms. The life patterns of rural Albertans, residents of Newfoundland fishing villages, and West Vancouverites differ in highly significant ways: as a result, their values and behavioural standards are different. Laws, too, differ from place to place. Quebecers can drink at a younger age than Ontarians and are able to purchase wine and beer at corner stores, whereas only beer with 0.5 percent alcohol can be found in Ontario grocery stores. Casinos are now legal in Ontario—even on Native reserves. They are also legal in Manitoba—but definitely not on Native reserves.[1] In other words, what is deviant or even criminal is not uniform across the country.

[1]In the 1990s, several reserve-based Native communities attempted to establish casinos, in part as a test of their sovereignty. While Manitoba closed down casinos that were opened illegally, Ontario gave its blessing to a casino on the Rama reserve near Orillia. Proceeds are shared with the other bands of Ontario.

In global context, deviance is even more diverse. Albania outlaws any public display of religious faith, such as crossing oneself; Cuba can prosecute its citizens for "consorting with foreigners"; police can arrest people in Singapore for selling chewing gum; and, in Iran, police can arrest a woman for wearing makeup.

2. **People become deviant as others define them that way.** Each of us violates cultural norms regularly, occasionally to the extent of breaking the law. For example, most of us have at some time walked around talking to ourselves, or have "borrowed" supplies, such as pens and paper, from the workplace. Whether such activities are sufficient to define us as mentally ill or criminal depends on how others perceive, define, and respond to any given situation.

3. **Both rule making and rule breaking involve social power.** The law, Karl Marx asserted, amounts to little more than a strategy by which powerful people protect their interests. For example, the owners of an unprofitable factory have a legal right to close their business, even if doing so throws thousands of people out of work. But if workers commit an act of vandalism that closes the same factory for a single day, they are subject to criminal prosecution.

Similarly, a homeless person who stands on a street corner denouncing the city government risks arrest for disturbing the peace; a mayoral candidate does exactly the same thing during an election campaign while receiving extensive police protection. In short, norms and their application are linked to social inequality.

STRUCTURAL-FUNCTIONAL ANALYSIS

We now turn to the structural-functional paradigm, which reveals how deviance contributes to the operation of society.

EMILE DURKHEIM: THE FUNCTIONS OF DEVIANCE

In his pioneering study of deviance, Emile Durkheim (1964a, orig. 1895; 1964b, orig. 1893) made the remarkable assertion that there is nothing abnormal about deviance; in fact, it supports the operation of society in four ways.

1. **Deviance affirms cultural values and norms.** Culture involves moral choices: unless our lives dissolve into chaos, people prefer some attitudes and behaviours to others. But any conception of virtue rests on an opposing notion of vice. Just as there can be no good without evil, so there can be no justice without crime. Deviance, in short, is indispensable to the process of generating and sustaining morality.

2. **Responding to deviance clarifies moral boundaries.** By defining people as deviant, people draw a social boundary between right and wrong. For example, universities mark the line between academic honesty and cheating by imposing disciplinary procedures on those who commit plagiarism.

3. **Responding to deviance promotes social unity.** People typically react to serious deviance with collective outrage. In doing so, Durkheim explained, they reaffirm the moral ties that bind them. For example, the murder of fourteen female engineering students at Montreal's L'École Polytechnique on December 6, 1989, was met with reactions of horror and profound grief in the larger community. The fact that anniversaries of the massacre are still commemorated indicates the depth of its impact.

4. **Deviance encourages social change.** Deviant people, Durkheim claimed, push a society's moral boundaries, suggesting alternatives to the status quo and encouraging change. Moreover, he declared, today's deviance sometimes becomes tomorrow's morality (1964a). In the 1950s, for example, many people denounced rock and roll as a threat to the morals of youth. Since then, however, rock and roll has been swept up in the musical mainstream, becoming a multibillion-dollar industry.

An Illustration: The Puritans of Massachusetts Bay

Kai Erikson's (1966) historical investigation of the early Puritans of Massachusetts Bay illustrates Durkheim's analysis. Erikson showed that even the Puritans—a disciplined and highly religious group—created deviance to clarify their moral boundaries. In fact, Durkheim might well have had the Puritans in mind when he wrote,

> Imagine a society of saints, a perfect cloister of exemplary individuals. Crimes, properly so called, will there be unknown; but faults which appear [insignificant] to the layman will create there the same scandal that the ordinary offence does in ordinary consciousness. . . . For the same reason, the perfect and upright man judges his smallest failings with a severity that the majority reserve for acts more truly in the nature of an offence. (1964a:68–69)

Deviance, in short, is not a matter of how good or bad individuals are; it is a necessary condition of "good" social living.

But the kind of deviance people generate depends on the moral issues they seek to clarify. Over time, the Puritans confronted a number of "crime waves." In responding to them, they sharpened their views on crucial moral quandaries. Thus, they answered questions about how much dissent to allow or what their religious goals should be by celebrating some of their members while branding others as deviants.

And, most fascinating of all, Erikson discovered that though the offences changed, the Puritans recognized a consistent proportion of their members as deviant over time. This stability, concludes Erikson, confirms Durkheim's contention that deviants serve as ethical markers, outlining a society's changing moral boundaries. By constantly defining a small number of people as deviant, the Puritans were able to maintain a certain "shape" to their society.

MERTON'S STRAIN THEORY

Some deviance may be necessary for a society to function, Robert Merton (1968) argues, but excessive violations arise from particular social arrangements. Specifically, the scope and character of deviance depend on how well a society makes cultural *goals* (such as financial success) accessible by providing the institutionalized *means* (such as schooling and job opportunities) to attain them.

The path to conformity, Merton begins, lies in pursuing conventional goals by approved means. The true success story, in other words, is someone who gains wealth and prestige through talent and hard work. But not everyone who desires conventional success has the opportunity to attain it. Children raised in poverty, for example, may see little hope of becoming successful if they play by the rules. As a result, they may seek wealth through crime—say, by dealing in drugs. Merton called this type of deviance *innovation*—the attempt to achieve a culturally approved goal (wealth) by unconventional means (drug sales). Figure 9–1 (page 212) characterizes innovation as accepting the goal of success while rejecting the conventional means of becoming rich.

According to Merton, the "strain" between our culture's emphasis on wealth and the limited opportunity to get rich gives rise, especially among the poor, to theft, the selling of illegal drugs, or other forms of street hustling. In some respects, a notorious gangster like Al Capone was quite conventional: he pursued the fame and fortune at the heart of the "American Dream." But finding the usual doors to success closed to minority members, he blazed his own trail to the top. In the meantime, a Canadian (with close ties to Capone) was establishing a parallel career.

When Prohibition outlawed the sale of liquor in Canada (1918), a young Hamilton, Ontario, grocer named Rocco Perri saw an opportunity to augment his income by selling bootleg liquor at the back of his store.

In Kosovo, as in Canada, young people (especially males) cut off from legitimate opportunity may form deviant subcultures as a strategy to gain the prestige denied them by the larger society.

By the time Prohibition was adopted in the United States (1920), "Perri had the organization and experience to take quick advantage of the opportunity. . . . Before long, he was a major supplier to gangsters like Al Capone" (Carrigan, 1991:174). He had become "King of the Bootleggers." In the wake of Prohibition, Rocco Perri's "formidable criminal organization" expanded its links to U.S. gangs through a wide range of activities, including gambling, prostitution, and extortion. Like Capone, Canada's innovator acquired wealth and power but never attained prestige in the larger society.

The inability to become successful by normative means may also prompt another type of deviance that Merton calls *ritualism* (see Figure 9–1). Ritualists resolve the strain of limited success by abandoning cultural goals in favour of almost compulsive efforts to live "respectably." In essence, they embrace the rules to the point where they lose sight of their larger goals. Lower-level bureaucrats often succumb to ritualism as a way of maintaining respectability.

A third response to the inability to succeed is *retreatism*—the rejection of both cultural goals and means so that one, in effect, drops out. Retreatists include some alcoholics and drug addicts, and some of the street people found in our cities. The deviance of retreatists lies in unconventional living and, perhaps more seriously, in accepting this situation.

The fourth response to failure is *rebellion*. Like retreatists, rebels reject both the cultural definition of success and the normative means of achieving it.

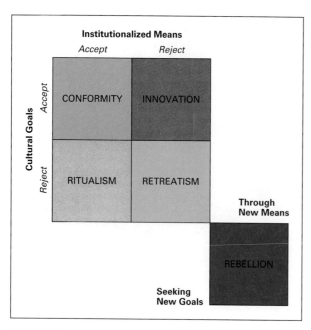

Institutionalized Means

	Accept	*Reject*
Accept	CONFORMITY	INNOVATION
Reject	RITUALISM	RETREATISM

Through New Means

REBELLION

Seeking New Goals

FIGURE 9–1 Merton's Strain Theory of Deviance

Source: Merton (1968).

Rebels, however, go one step further by advocating radical alternatives to the existing social order. Typically, they advocate a political or religious transformation of society, and often join a counterculture.

DEVIANT SUBCULTURES

Richard Cloward and Lloyd Ohlin (1966) extended Merton's theory in their investigation of delinquent youth. They maintain that criminal deviance results not simply from limited legitimate (legal) opportunity but also from available illegitimate (illegal) opportunity. In short, deviance or conformity grows out of the relative opportunity structure that frames our lives.

The life of Rocco Perri shows how an ambitious person denied legitimate opportunity could organize a criminal empire to meet the demand for alcohol during Prohibition. In other words, illegal opportunities foster the development of *criminal subcultures* that offer the knowledge, skills, and other resources needed to succeed in unconventional ways. Indeed, gangs may specialize in one or another form of criminality according to available opportunities and resources (Carrigan, 1991; Sheley et al., 1995).

But some poor, highly transient neighbourhoods may lack almost any form of opportunity—legal or illegal. Here, delinquency may surface in the form of *conflict subcultures* where violence is ignited by frustration and a desire for fame or respect. Conversely, those who fail to achieve success, even by criminal means, may sink into *retreatist subcultures*, dropping out through abuse of alcohol or other drugs.

Albert Cohen (1971; orig. 1955) asserts that delinquency is most pronounced among lower-class youths because it is they who contend with the least opportunity to achieve success in conventional ways. Sometimes those whom society neglects seek self-respect by building a deviant subculture that "defines as meritorious the characteristics they *do* possess, the kinds of conduct of which they *are* capable" (1971:66). A notorious street reputation may win no points with society as a whole, but it may satisfy a youth's gnawing desire to "be somebody."

Walter Miller (1970; orig. 1958) agrees that deviant subcultures typically develop among lower-class youths who encounter the least legitimate opportunity. He spotlights six focal concerns of these deviant subcultures: (1) *trouble*, arising from frequent conflict with teachers and police; (2) *toughness*, the value placed on physical size, strength, and athletic skills; (3) *smartness* ("street smarts"), the ability to out-think or "con" others, and to avoid being similarly taken advantage of; (4) *excitement*, the search for thrills, risk, or danger to escape from a daily routine that is predictable and unsatisfying; (5) *a preoccupation with fate*, derived from the lack of control these youths feel over their own lives; and (6) *autonomy*, a desire for freedom often expressed as resentment of authority figures.

Critical evaluation. Durkheim's pioneering work on the functions of deviance remains central to sociological thinking. Even so, recent critics point out that a community does not always come together in reaction to crime; sometimes fear of crime drives people to withdraw (Liska and Warner, 1991).

Derived from Durkheim's analysis, Merton's strain theory comes under criticism for explaining some kinds of deviance (theft, for example) far better than others (such as crimes of passion or mental illness). In addition, not everyone seeks success in conventional terms of wealth, as strain theory implies. As noted in Chapter 3 ("Culture"), members of our society embrace different cultural values and are motivated by various notions of personal success.

The general argument of Cloward and Ohlin, Cohen, and Miller—that deviance reflects the opportunity structure of society—has been confirmed by subsequent research (Allan and Steffensmeier, 1989). However, these theories fall short by assuming that everyone shares the same cultural standards for judging right and wrong. Also, we must be careful not to define deviance in ways that unfairly focus attention on poor people. If crime is defined to include stock fraud *and* street theft, offenders are more likely to include affluent individuals. Finally, all structural-functional theories imply that everyone who violates conventional cultural standards will be branded as deviant. Becoming deviant, however, is actually a highly complex process, as the next section explains.

SYMBOLIC-INTERACTION ANALYSIS

The symbolic-interaction paradigm analyzes the creation of deviance as a social process. From this point of view, definitions of deviance and conformity are surprisingly flexible.

LABELLING THEORY

The central contribution of symbolic-interaction analysis is **labelling theory**, *the assertion that deviance and conformity result not so much from what people do, as from how others respond to those actions*. Labelling theory stresses the relativity of deviance, arguing that all reality is socially constructed so that the same behaviour may be defined in any number of ways. Howard S. Becker claims that deviance is nothing more than "behaviour that people so label" (1966:9).

Consider these situations: a woman takes an article of clothing from a roommate; a married man at a convention far from home has sex with a prostitute; a member of Parliament drives home intoxicated after a party. In each case, "reality" depends on the response of others. Is the first situation a matter of borrowing, or is it theft? The consequences of the second case depend largely on whether news of the man's behaviour follows him back home. In the third case, is the MP an active socialite or a dangerous drunk? The social construction of reality, then, is a highly variable process of detection, definition, and response.

Primary and Secondary Deviance

Edwin Lemert (1951, 1972) notes that many episodes of norm violation—say, skipping school or underage drinking—provoke little reaction from others and have little effect on a person's self-concept. Lemert calls such passing episodes *primary deviance*.

But what happens if other people take notice of someone's deviance and make something of it? If, for example, people begin to describe a young man as a "boozer," and push him out of their social circle, he may become embittered, drink even more, and seek the company of others who condone his behaviour. So the response to initial deviance can set in motion *secondary deviance*, by which an individual engages in repeated norm violations and begins to take on a deviant identity. The development of secondary deviance is one application of the Thomas theorem, which states that situations defined as real become real in their consequences.

Stigma

The onset of secondary deviance marks the emergence of what Erving Goffman (1963) called a *deviant career*. As individuals develop a strong commitment to deviant behaviour, they typically acquire a **stigma**, *a powerfully*

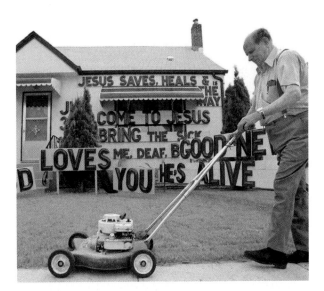

In Winnipeg, a born-again Christian gives visible expression to his faith. When the city council warned that his signs violated civic by-laws, the man vowed to challenge any charges in court.

negative social label that radically changes a person's self-concept and social identity.

Stigma operates as a master status (see Chapter 6, "Social Interaction in Everyday Life"), overpowering other dimensions of social identity so that an individual is diminished and discounted in the minds of others and, consequently, socially isolated. Sometimes an entire community formally stigmatizes individuals through what Harold Garfinkel (1956) calls a *degradation ceremony*. A criminal prosecution is one example, operating much like a high-school graduation except that people stand before the community to be labelled in a negative rather than positive way.

Labelling: Past and Future

Once people have stigmatized a person, they may engage in **retrospective labelling**, *the interpretation of someone's past consistent with present deviance* (Scheff, 1984). For example, after discovering that a priest has sexually molested a child, others may rethink his past, perhaps musing, "He always did want to be around young children." Retrospective labelling distorts a person's biography, in a highly selective and prejudicial way, guided more by the present stigma than by any attempt to be fair. This process often deepens a person's deviant identity.

People may also engage in *projective labelling* of a stigmatized person. In this case, an audience remains mindful of an individual's deviant identity when assessing any future action. The result, of course, is that people continue to find evidence of deviance in the future actions of a stigmatized individual.

Labelling and Mental Illness

Is a woman who believes that Jesus rides the bus to work with her every day seriously deluded or merely expressing her religious faith in a highly graphic way? Is a homeless woman who refuses to allow police to take her to a city shelter on a cold night mentally ill or simply trying to live independently?

Psychiatrist Thomas Szasz charges that people apply the label of insanity to what is only "difference." Such reasoning has led Szasz to the controversial conclusion that the notion of mental illness should be abandoned (1961, 1970, 1994, 1995). Illness, Szasz argues, is physical and afflicts only the body; mental illness, then, is a myth. The world is full of people whose "differences" in thought or action may irritate us, but difference is no grounds on which to define someone as sick. To do so, Szasz claims, simply enforces conformity to the standards of people powerful enough to impose their will on others.

Many of Szasz's colleagues reject the notion that all mental illness is a fiction. But some have hailed his work for pointing out the danger of abusing medical practice in the interest of promoting conformity. Most of us, after all, experience periods of extreme stress or other mental disability from time to time. Such episodes, although upsetting, are usually of passing importance. If, however, others respond with labelling that forms the basis of a social stigma, the long-term result may be further deviance as a self-fulfilling prophecy (Scheff, 1984).

THE MEDICALIZATION OF DEVIANCE

Labelling theory, particularly the ideas of Szasz and Goffman, helps to explain an important shift in the way our society understands deviance. Over the last fifty years, the growing influence of psychiatry and medicine in North America has encouraged the **medicalization of deviance**, *the transformation of moral and legal issues into medical matters*.

In essence, medicalization amounts to swapping one set of labels for another. In moral terms, we evaluate people or their behaviour as "bad" or "good." However, the scientific objectivity of modern medicine passes no moral judgment, using instead clinical diagnoses such as "ill" and "well."

To illustrate, until the mid-1900s, people generally viewed alcoholics as weak and morally deficient people easily tempted by the pleasure of drink. Gradually, however, medical specialists redefined alcoholism so that most people now consider it a disease, rendering individuals "sick" rather than "bad." Similarly, obesity, drug addiction, child abuse, promiscuity, and other behaviours that used to be moral matters are today widely defined as illnesses for which people need help rather than punishment.

The Significance of Labels

Whether we define deviance as a moral or medical issue has three profound consequences. First, it affects *who responds* to deviance. An offence against common morality typically provokes a reaction by ordinary people or the police. Applying medical labels, however, places the situation under the control of clinical specialists, including counsellors, psychiatrists, and physicians.

A second difference is *the response of people* to deviance. A moral approach defines the deviant as an "offender" subject to punishment. Medically, however, "patients" need treatment (for their own good, of course). Therefore, while punishment is designed to fit the crime, treatment programs are tailored to the patient and may involve virtually any therapy that a specialist thinks will prevent future deviance (von Hirsh, 1986).

Third, and most important, the two labels differ on the issue of *the personal competence of the deviant person*. Morally speaking, people take responsibility for their behaviour whether right or wrong. If we are sick, however, we are seen as lacking the capacity to control (or even comprehend) our behaviour. Those who are defined as incompetent are, in turn, subject to intense, often involuntary, treatment. For this reason alone, attempts to define deviance in medical terms should be made only with extreme caution.

SUTHERLAND'S DIFFERENTIAL ASSOCIATION THEORY

Learning any social pattern—whether conventional or deviant—is a process that takes place in groups. According to Edwin Sutherland (1940), any person's tendency towards conformity or deviance depends on the relative frequency of association with others who encourage conventional behaviour or norm violation. This is Sutherland's theory of *differential association*.

Sutherland's theory is illustrated by a study of drug and alcohol use among young adults at high-school and university levels (Akers et al., 1979; Nawaz, 1978). Researchers have discovered close links between the extent of alcohol and drug use and the extent to which peer groups engage in or encourage such activity. The investigators concluded that young people embrace delinquent patterns as they receive praise and other rewards for defining deviance rather than conformity in positive terms. At the extreme, differential association can make drug use, trafficking, and brutal violence (including murder) seem acceptable or "normal"—for example, if one's peer group is the biker gang Hell's Angels.

HIRSCHI'S CONTROL THEORY

In his *control theory*, Travis Hirschi (1969) claims that the essence of social control lies in people's anticipation of the consequences of their behaviour. Hirschi assumes that everyone finds at least some deviance tempting. Imagining condemnation from family or friends is sufficient to deter most people from temptation; concerns about career consequences of transgressions will give others pause. In contrast, individuals who have little to lose from deviance are most likely to become rule breakers.

Hirschi asserts that conformity arises from four types of social controls.

1. **Attachment.** Strong social attachments encourage conformity; weak relationships in the family, peer group, and school leave people freer to engage in deviance.

2. **Opportunity.** The higher one's commitment to legitimate opportunity, the greater the advantages of conformity. A university-bound young person, with good career prospects, has a high stake in conformity. In contrast, someone with little confidence in future success may drift towards deviance.

3. **Involvement.** Extensive involvement in legitimate activities—such as holding a job, going to school and completing homework, or pursuing hobbies—inhibits deviance. People with few such activities—who simply "hang out" waiting for something to happen—have time and energy for deviant activity.

4. **Belief.** Strong beliefs in conventional morality and respect for authority figures restrain tendencies towards deviance. In contrast, people with a weak conscience (and those who spend a great deal of time without an authority figure's supervision) are more vulnerable to temptation (Osgood et al., 1996).

Hirschi's analysis draws together a number of ideas presented earlier about the causes of deviant behaviour. Note that both relative social privilege and strength of moral character are crucial in generating a stake in conformity to conventional norms (Wiatrowski et al., 1981; Sampson and Laub, 1990; Free, 1992).

Critical evaluation. The various symbolic-interaction theories share a focus on deviance as process. Labelling theory links deviance not to *action* but to the *reaction* of others. Thus, some people come to be defined as deviant while others who think or behave in the same way are not. The concepts of stigma, secondary deviance, and deviant career demonstrate how people can incorporate the label of deviance into a lasting self-concept.

Yet labelling theory has several limitations. Because it takes a highly relative view of deviance, this theory glosses over the fact that some kinds of behaviour, such as murder, are condemned virtually everywhere (Wellford, 1980). Labelling theory is thus most

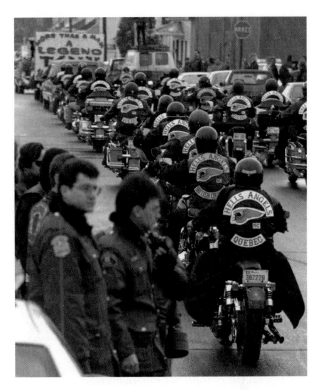

Many gangs constitute a peer group in which violence, drug use, and trafficking are "normal." Here, members of the Hell's Angels, identifiable by their hair and clothing, attend a funeral of one of their compatriots.

usefully applied to less serious deviance, such as sexual promiscuity or mental illness.

Furthermore, the consequences of deviant labelling are unclear. Research is inconclusive as to whether deviant labelling produces subsequent deviance or discourages further violations (Smith and Gartin, 1989; Sherman and Smith, 1992).

Lastly, not everyone resists the label of deviance; some people may actually relish being defined as deviant (Vold and Bernard, 1986). For example, individuals may engage in civil disobedience leading to arrest to call attention to social injustice.

Both Sutherland's differential association theory and Hirschi's control theory have had considerable influence in sociology. But they provide little insight into why society's norms and laws define certain kinds of activities as deviant in the first place. This important question is addressed by social-conflict analysis, the focus of the next section.

SOCIAL-CONFLICT ANALYSIS

The social-conflict paradigm demonstrates how deviance reflects social inequality. This approach holds that who or what is labelled as deviant depends on the relative power of categories of people.

Laws regulate the operation of businesses just as they direct the actions of individuals. But, as social-conflict analysis points out, powerful corporate leaders who face allegations of wrongdoing are rarely thought of as "criminals," and rarely are they subject to the punishment accorded to ordinary people.

DEVIANCE AND POWER

Alexander Liazos (1972) points out that everyday conceptions of deviants—"nuts, sluts, and 'perverts'"—are people who share the trait of powerlessness. Bag ladies (not corporate polluters) and unemployed men on street corners (not arms dealers) carry the stigma of deviance.

Social-conflict theory links deviance to power in three ways. First, the norms—and especially the laws—of any society generally reflect the interests of the rich and powerful. People who threaten the wealthy, either by seizing their property or by advocating a more egalitarian society, come to be tagged as "common thieves" or "political radicals." As noted in Chapter 4 ("Society"), Karl Marx argued that the law (and all other social institutions) tends to support the interests of the rich. Echoing Marx, Richard Quinney makes the point succinctly: "Capitalist justice is by the capitalist class, for the capitalist class, and against the working class" (1977:3).

Second, even if their behaviour is called into question, the powerful have the resources to resist deviant labels. Corporate executives who order the dumping of hazardous wastes are rarely held personally accountable for these acts. As the very public, televised O.J. Simpson trial made clear, even when charged with violent crimes, the rich have the resources to vigorously resist being labelled as criminal. While wealth can provide similar advantages in Canada, the absence of television cameras in the courtroom means that the drama is not enacted in our living rooms.

Third, the widespread belief that norms and laws are natural and good masks their political character. For this reason, we may condemn the unequal application of the law but give little thought to whether the *laws themselves* are inherently fair (Quinney, 1977).

DEVIANCE AND CAPITALISM

Following the Marxist tradition, Steven Spitzer (1980) argues that deviant labels are applied to people who impede the operation of capitalism. Because capitalism is based on private ownership of wealth, people who threaten the property of others—especially the poor who steal from the rich—are prime candidates for labelling as deviants. Conversely, the rich who exploit the poor are rarely called into question. Landlords, for example, who charge poor tenants high rents and evict those who cannot pay are not considered a threat to society; they are simply "doing business."

Since capitalism depends on productive labour, those who cannot or will not work risk deviant labelling. Many members of our society think of people out of work—even if through no fault of their own—as deviant.

Capitalism depends on respect for figures of authority, so people who resist authority are labelled as deviant. Examples are children who skip school or talk back to parents and teachers; adults who do not cooperate with employers or police; and anyone who opposes "the system."

Anyone who directly challenges the capitalist status quo is likely to be defined as deviant. Into this category fall antiwar activists, environmentalists, and labour organizers.

To turn the argument around, society offers positive labels to those who enhance the operation of capitalism. Thus, winning athletes have celebrity status because they express the values of individual achievement and competition vital to capitalism. Additionally, Spitzer notes, we condemn using drugs of escape (marijuana, crack, and ecstasy) as deviant, while espousing drugs that promote adjustment to the status quo (such as alcohol and caffeine).

The capitalist system also strives to control people who don't fit into the system. Those who are a "costly yet relatively harmless burden" on society, says Spitzer, include Robert Merton's retreatists (for example, those addicted to alcohol or other drugs), the elderly, and people with mental and/or physical disabilities. All are subject to control by social welfare agencies. But those who openly challenge the very underpinnings of the capitalist system, including the inner-city "underclass" and revolutionaries—Merton's innovators and rebels—come under the purview of the criminal justice system and, in times of crisis, military forces.

Prime Minister Pierre Trudeau invoked the *War Measures Act* in October 1970 to contain the threat posed by the Front de Libération du Québec (FLQ), which had planted numerous bombs and had kidnapped both the British trade commissioner, James Cross, and the Quebec labour and immigration minister, Pierre Laporte, who was subsequently murdered. Civil rights were suspended and 465 people were arrested because Trudeau perceived a threat to Canadian stability from the violent, revolutionary FLQ.

Note that both the social welfare and the criminal justice systems apply labels that blame individuals and not the system for the control they exert over people's lives. Welfare recipients are deemed unworthy freeloaders; poor people who vent rage at their powerlessness are labelled rioters; anyone who actively challenges the government is branded a radical or a communist; and those who attempt to gain illegally what they cannot otherwise acquire are called common thieves.

White-Collar Crime

"Reputable" Canadians have long been known to circumvent the law when doing so is likely to be immensely profitable (Carrigan, 1991:113–65). For example, during World War II, when consumer goods were being rationed in favour of the production of armaments, big and small businesses and helpful government officials were caught up in wartime racketeering, supplying illegal goods through the black market. More recently, Canada has had its share of stock and real estate fraud, bid-rigging, and tax evasion—activities that have cost taxpayers and consumers many millions of dollars. Many of these perpetrators never find themselves in the criminal courts.

One notorious Canadian example of 1997, the Bre-X case, may be the greatest gold hoax of all time. Investors, big and small alike, were scammed to the tune of over $3 billion by an upstart company that tampered with (or "salted") ore samples, thereby faking a massive gold find in Indonesia. The apparent suicide (?) of the chief geologist, Michael de Guzman, who "fell" from a helicopter into the jungle, and the complete collapse of Bre-X share prices brought the scam to an end. Proving criminal fraud requires that one shows "beyond a reasonable doubt that guilty parties intended to defraud," while fraud under "civil or securities laws (are) a different story" (Francis, 1997). Nonetheless, about $4 billion in lawsuits quickly piled up against the two Bre-X principals and the Guzman estate.

More recent American examples, Enron, WorldCom, and ImClone, brought corporate and white-collar crime into the limelight in a way that the

justice system could not ignore. Energy trading company Enron deceived its investors and employees by playing fast-and-loose with its accounts in order to enhance the value of its shares. The investigations and trials that followed Enron's bankruptcy were played out in public on CNN and other mass media. Its consulting accountant firm, Arthur Andersen, one of the largest in the United States, was put out of business. Among other banks, Canada's CIBC aided Enron with its deception by loaning it money ($205 million) while aware that Enron was concealing $22 billion in debt (Howlett et al., 2003). Executives at telecommunications giant WorldCom, including Canadian-born CEO Bernard Ebbers, were accused of securities fraud when the company fell $41 billion in debt. Because of the scale of their financial fraud, WorldCom and Enron rank first and second as the biggest companies to seek bankruptcy protection in American history (Waldie and Howlett, 2003). ImClone was a simpler case of insider trading, when company executives and friends sold their shares before bad news about the failure to gain FDA approval of one of their drugs became common knowledge. ImClone's CEO Sam Waksal was jailed. The trial of Waksal's friend Martha Stewart, charged with obstruction of justice, was ongoing at the time this book went to press, but the costs to her enterprise were immediate and devastating.

These cases exemplify **white-collar crime**, defined by Edwin Sutherland in 1940 as *crimes committed by persons of high social position in the course of their occupations* (Sutherland and Cressey, 1978:44). White-collar crime rarely involves uniformed police converging on a scene with drawn guns. Thus, it does not refer to crimes such as murder, assault, or sexual assault (rape) that happen to be carried out by people of high social position. Instead, white-collar crimes are acts by powerful people making use of their occupational positions to enrich themselves or others illegally, often causing significant public harm in the process (Hagan and Parker, 1985; Vold and Bernard, 1986). In short, white-collar offences that occur in government offices and corporate boardrooms are commonly dubbed *crime in the suites* rather than *crime in the streets*.

The public harm wreaked by false advertising, marketing of unsafe products, embezzlement, and bribery of public officials extends far beyond what most people realize. Some researchers contend that white-collar crime causes greater public harm than the more visible "street crime" (Reiman, 1990). The marketing of unsafe products and the failure to implement workplace safety regulations have been responsible for many deaths in Canada. Immeasurable sums of money are stolen every year through fraud. Since much of it goes undetected, and overburdened fraud units are unable to prosecute all known cases, it is difficult to estimate the dollar value of white-collar crime.

Until recently, elite deviance rarely resulted in criminal labelling of powerful people. Even when their

TABLE 9–1 Sociological Explanations of Deviance: A Summary	
Theoretical Paradigm	**Major Contributions**
Structural-functional analysis	While what is deviant may vary, deviance itself is found in all societies; deviance and the social response it provokes sustain the moral foundation of society; deviance may also guide social change.
Symbolic-interaction analysis	Nothing is inherently deviant but may become defined as such through the response of others; the reactions of others are highly variable; the label of deviance may lead to the emergence of secondary deviance and deviant careers.
Social-conflict analysis	Laws and other norms reflect the interest of powerful members of society; those who threaten the status quo are generally defined as deviant; social injury caused by powerful people is less likely to be considered criminal than social injury caused by people who have little social power.

actions lead to extensive public harm, officials are rarely prosecuted. And in the event that white-collar criminals do face the music, the odds are they will not go to jail. As well, Sutherland noted that the public is less concerned about white-collar crime than about street crime, partly because corporate crime victimizes everyone—and no one. White-collar criminals don't stick a gun in anyone's ribs, and the economic costs are usually spread throughout the population. However, the cases of Bre-X, Enron, WorldCom, and ImClone are changing the public perception of these costs.

As the "backbone of capitalism," corporations have immense power, influencing both the mass media and the political process. Corporate officials are frequently graduates of prestigious universities and professional schools, belong to exclusive social clubs, and have well-developed networks linking them to other powerful people in all walks of life. Many government officials, drawn from the ranks of corporate executives, regulate the very corporate enterprises in which they have spent most of their working lives. Not surprisingly, serious episodes of white-collar crime have made headlines only from time to time.

Critical evaluation. According to social-conflict theory, inequality in wealth and power guides the creation and application of laws and other norms. This approach asserts that criminal justice and social welfare act as political agents, controlling categories of people who threaten the capitalist system.

Like other analyses of deviance, however, social-conflict theory has its critics. This approach implies that laws and other cultural norms are created directly by the rich and powerful. At the very least, this assumption is an oversimplification, since many segments of our society influence, and benefit from, the political process. Laws also protect workers, consumers, and the environment, sometimes in opposition to the interests of the rich.

Furthermore, social-conflict analysis implies that criminality springs up only to the extent that a society treats its members unequally. However, as Durkheim noted, all societies generate deviance, whatever their economic systems.

The various sociological explanations for crime and other types of deviance are summarized in Table 9-1.

DEVIANCE AND SOCIAL DIVERSITY

The shape of deviance in a society has much to do with the relative power and privilege of different categories of people. The following section offers an example of how gender is linked to deviance. The "Applying Sociology" box deals with suicide among Aboriginal people.

DEVIANCE AND GENDER

Virtually every society in the world applies more stringent normative controls to women than to men. Historically, our society has restricted the role of women to the home. Despite considerable change, Canadian women still face limitations to their opportunities in the workplace, in athletics, in politics, and in the military. Elsewhere in the world, the normative constraints placed on women are much greater. In Saudi Arabia, for example, women cannot vote or legally operate motor vehicles; in Iran, women who dare to expose their hair or wear makeup in public can be whipped.

Given the importance of gender to the social construction of deviance, we need to pause a moment to see how gender figures in some of the theories we have already discussed. Robert Merton's strain theory, for example, has a masculine cast in that it defines cultural goals in terms of financial success. Traditionally at least, this goal has had more to do with the lives of men, while women have been socialized to view success in terms of relationships, particularly marriage and motherhood (Leonard, 1982). A more woman-focused theory might recognize the strain caused by the cultural ideals of equality clashing with the reality of gender-based inequality.

Labelling theory, the major approach in symbolic-interaction analysis, offers greater insight into ways in which gender influences how we define deviance. To the extent that we judge the behaviour of females and

Suicide among Aboriginal People

So serious is the problem of suicide among Aboriginal people—and youth in particular—that the Royal Commission on Aboriginal Peoples felt compelled to conduct a study of the problem. The result is a report entitled *Choosing Life: Special Report on Suicide among Aboriginal People* (1995).

The commission felt that suicide is a crucial issue not only because it is a matter of life and death, but also because it is an expression of the collective anguish that is "the cumulative effect of 300 years of colonial history: lands occupied, resources seized, beliefs and cultures ridiculed, children taken away, power concentrated in distant capitals, hopes for honourable co-existence dashed over and over again" (p. x). Note that the causes of suicide are attributed to social conditions rather than to individual troubles or idiosyncrasies.

The report points out that, year after year, Aboriginal suicide rates are two to three times higher than those of non-Aboriginal Canadians; rates among Aboriginal *youth* are five to six times

higher than among their non-Aboriginal peers. The problem is compounded by the ripple effect, whereby copycat suicides occur in related families and communities.

Looking for causes, the commission identifies four contributors: (1) psycho-biological factors; (2) life history or situational factors; (3) socioeconomic factors; and (4) cultural stress. Once again, social conditions loom large—particularly with respect to the last two categories. Cultural stress applies to "societies that have undergone massive, imposed or uncontrollable change" (p. 25).

The solutions suggested by the commission are varied. But among them are a number that relate to community solidarity or social integration: community development; self-determination (self-government or community control); cultural and spiritual revitalization; strengthened bonds of family and community; "holistic" (i.e., natural environment and community-based) health and healing programs; and involvement of the whole community.

If you think back to the discussion of Emile Durkheim's analysis of suicide in the opening pages of Chapter 1 ("The Sociological Perspective"), you will recall his conclusion that degree of *social integration* is the key to understanding suicide. High suicide rates are found among people who are more socially isolated and individualistic. The cultural and social dislocation experienced by Aboriginal peoples is the result of their colonial history—a history based on paternalism and compulsory residential schooling. A compounding factor contributing to weaker social ties is the phenomenal rate of social and economic change in recent decades.

It is likely that several members of the commission have had some exposure to sociology, but with or without such exposure, their report contains insights that mirror those of Durkheim's pioneering sociological analysis of a century ago.

Source: Based on Royal Commission on Aboriginal Peoples (1995).

---

males by different standards, the very process of labelling involves sex-linked biases. Because society generally places men in positions of power over women, men often escape direct responsibility for actions that victimize women. In the past, at least, men engaging in sexual harassment or other assaults against women have been tagged with only mildly deviant labels, if they have been punished at all.

In contrast, women who are victimized may have to convince an unsympathetic audience that they are not to blame for what happened. Research confirms an important truth: whether people define a situation as deviance—and, if so, whose deviance it is—depends on the sex of both the audience and the actors (King and Clayson, 1988). The issue of date rape provides one example of how such a double standard has proved harmful to women.

Ironically, social-conflict analysis—despite its focus on social inequality—virtually ignores the im-

portance of gender. If, as conflict theory suggests, economic disadvantage is a primary cause of crime, why do women (whose economic position is worse than that of men) commit far fewer crimes than men do? The following section on crime examines crime rates in Canada and addresses this question.

CRIME

Crime is the violation of statutes enacted into criminal law. In Canada, criminal law (collected in the *Criminal Code*) is enacted by the federal government, though implementation details may vary from province to province.

THE COMPONENTS OF CRIME

Technically, crime is composed of two elements: the *act* itself (or, in some cases, the failure to do what the

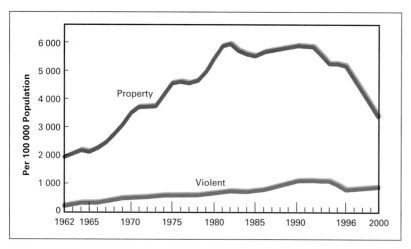

FIGURE 9–2 Violent and Property Crime Rates in Canada, 1962–2000

Source: Based on data from Statistics Canada, Catalogue Nos. 85-205 and 85-002-SPE, Vol. 17, No. 8, and Vol. 19, No. 9, Canadian Statistics, Justice and Crime, www.statcan.ca/english/Pgdb/legal12b.htm.

law requires) and *criminal intent* (in legal terminology, *mens rea*, or "guilty mind"). Intent is a matter of degree, ranging from wilful conduct to negligence in which a person does not deliberately set out to hurt anyone but acts (or fails to act) in a manner that may reasonably be expected to cause harm. Juries weigh the degree of intent in determining the seriousness of a crime and may find the person who kills another guilty of first-degree murder, second-degree murder, or manslaughter. In some cases (e.g., self-defence), homicide may be deemed justifiable.

 Selected data on crime in Canada are published by Statistics Canada at www.statcan.ca/english/Pgdb/justic.htm

Types of Crimes

In Canada, information on criminal offences is obtained from the Uniform Crime Reporting system and reported in a Statistics Canada publication called *Canadian Crime Statistics*. Violent crime and property crime are recorded separately.

Violent crimes, *crimes against people that involve violence or the threat of violence*, include murder, manslaughter, infanticide, assault, sexual assault, abduction, and robbery.

Property crimes encompass *crimes that involve theft of property belonging to others*, including breaking and entering, motor vehicle theft, theft over $5000 (changed from $1000 in 1995), theft of $5000 and under, possession of stolen goods, and fraud.

A third category of offences includes **victimless crimes**, *violations of law in which there are no readily apparent victims*—such as prostitution and gambling. There is also a separate category of *Narcotic Control Act* offences regarding the use of illegal drugs, including cannabis or marijuana. However, "victimless crime" is often a misnomer. How victimless is a crime when a young runaway is lured into prostitution and then made to believe that is her only way to live? And how

victimless is the crime if a young pregnant woman smoking crack causes the death of or permanent injury to her baby? In many cases, the people who commit such crimes are themselves both offenders and victims.

Criminal Statistics

Canada's crime statistics show steady increases in both violent and property crime rates from 1962 to 1992, followed by clear declines. Figure 9–2 illustrates these trends in violent and property crimes over the period in question.

Canadians often pride themselves on having a much less violent society than the United States. A comparison of homicide rates in the two countries suggests that this is indeed the case. Since the early 1960s, the U.S. homicide rate has been three to four times higher than that in Canada. Canada's homicide rate dropped from 2.7 per 100 000 population in 1992 to 2.1 in 1996 and to 1.8 in 2001.

Canada Map 9–1 suggests that homicide rates (per 100 000 population) differ not only between countries, but also among our own provinces. Note that the variation within Canada is greater than that between Canada and the United States. Nunavut's homicide rate is 11.5 times that of Newfoundland and Labrador; the American rate is three to four times that of Canada. Clearly, homicide rates in Canada increase from east to west and again to the north, roughly correlating with the level of gun ownership and the proportion of the population that is Aboriginal. Interestingly, the homicide rates in each province or territory are lower in the 1997–2001 period than they were in 1992–95 period—clear evidence of a gradual decline in homicide rates over the past decade.

Always read crime statistics with caution, since they include only crimes known to the police. The police learn about almost all homicides, but assaults—especially among acquaintances—are far less likely to be reported. The police record an even smaller

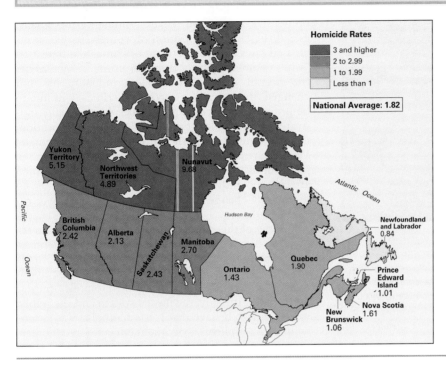

Homicide Rates

- 3 and higher
- 2 to 2.99
- 1 to 1.99
- Less than 1

National Average: 1.82

Yukon Territory 5.15

Northwest Territories 4.89

Nunavut 9.63

British Columbia 2.42

Alberta 2.13

Saskatchewan 2.43

Manitoba 2.70

Ontario 1.43

Quebec 1.90

Newfoundland and Labrador 0.84

Prince Edward Island 1.01

Nova Scotia 1.61

New Brunswick 1.06

Atlantic Ocean

Hudson Bay

Pacific Ocean

CANADA MAP 9–1
Homicide Rates for Canada, Provinces and Territories, 1997–2001 (Five-Year Averages, Rates per 100 000 People)

Note: The data for all of the provinces and the Yukon are based upon five-year averages; since Nunavut only became a territory in April 1999, the data for Nunavut and the Northwest Territories are based on three-year averages. Averages are compiled to even out the impacts of an unusual number of homicides in one year in a relatively small population—for example, the Yukon, where rates increased from 3.10 to 9.52 between 1997 and 1998.

Source: Adapted by Gerber from Statistics Canada, Canadian Statistics, Justice and Crime, www.statcan.ca/english/Pgdb/legal12b.htm.

---

proportion of property crimes, especially when losses are small. Some victims may not realize that a crime has occurred, or may assume they have little chance of recovering their property even if they notify the police. And reports of sexual assault still grossly understate the extent of this crime.

The University of Alberta's Health Information Page offers information about sexual assault and the law in Canada; see www.ualberta.ca/dept/health/public_html/healthinfo/sacan.htm

One way to evaluate official crime statistics is through a *victimization survey*, in which a researcher asks a representative sample of people about their experience with crime. People do not always respond fully or truthfully to such surveys, experts acknowledge, but the results of these surveys indicate that actual crime occurs at substantially higher rates than suggested by official reports. Canada's first national survey on violence against women (1993) found that half of Canadian women have experienced physical or sexual violence at least once since turning sixteen years of age. Among those who have been married or lived common-law, 29 percent have been physically or sexually assaulted by their partners. Victimization resulting from a wider range of criminal acts (measured by the General Social Survey) seems to have remained stable between 1988 and 1993, with 24 percent of the female population each year experiencing at least one in-

stance of criminal victimization (Statistics Canada, *Juristat*, 1994a).

The analysis above was based upon a "single-gender victimization survey" (Lupri, 2003), which implies that only women are subject to domestic abuse and ignores the fact that more than thirty studies in the 1970s and 1980s found "equal rates of assault by men *and* women." Research in the United States, New Zealand, and West Germany, along with some recent Canadian studies, suggests that men may suffer *more* partner abuse than women—including physical abuse, ranging from slapping or shoving to assault with a knife or gun, as well as emotional or psychological abuse. While more women report physical injury, both abused men and women suffer low levels of self-esteem, embarrassment, and shame. Whatever the direction of the abuse, Lupri argues, the impacts on children in the home are the same—behavioural effects like "aggression and delinquency," or psychological effects including "anxiety, depression, and low self-esteem." By focusing on the abuse of women and ignoring the abuse of men, society acknowledges only part of the problem.

THE "STREET" CRIMINAL: A PROFILE

Official statistics paint a broad-brush picture of people arrested for violent and property crimes. We now

Common sense suggests that the people we define as "criminal" are simply those who have broken the law. But the sociological perspective reveals that some categories of people are more likely than others to become entangled in the criminal justice system. As you read the remainder of this chapter, consider how our society places men, young people, and minorities at greater risk of becoming both offenders and victims of crime.

examine the breakdown of these arrest statistics by age, gender, social class, race, and ethnicity.

Age

Official crime rates rise sharply during adolescence and the early twenties, falling thereafter (Giffen, 1976; Hirschi and Gottfredson, 1983; Krisberg and Schwartz, 1983). Although people between the ages of twelve and twenty-four represent about 20 percent of the population, they account for about 60 percent of the people charged with property crimes and 35 percent of those charged with violent crimes. In contrast, those over forty-five years of age make up about 32 percent of the population but are responsible for only 5 percent of the property crimes and 10 percent of violent crimes. Not surprisingly, twenty- to thirty-four-year-olds make up 25 percent of the Canadian population and 62 percent of prison inmates.

Gender

Although each sex constitutes roughly half of the population in Canada, about 85 to 90 percent of arrests involve males, and about 97 percent of prison inmates are male. The proportion of females arrested is always low but varies considerably from one country to another: one study found Finland had a low of 6.7 percent, Canada had 9.8, the United States 13.7, and New Zealand 20.5 (Simon and Sharma, 1979).

Historically, the low levels and typical patterns of crime committed by women have been linked to their subordinate social and economic status. Alberta sociologist Helen Boritch (1997), in one of the first comprehensive analyses of female criminality in Canada, asks if the changing position of women has led to increased rates and new patterns of crime. She finds that "while women's participation in crime is increasing, the overall pattern of female criminality has not changed dramatically . . . women's crimes continue to be primarily non-violent in nature, economically motivated, or victimless crimes" (1997:20). Prostitution, drug offences, and shoplifting still predominate. Women are more involved in violent crime than in the past, but usually in low-level assault. Very few women are charged with homicide in Canada, and there is no discernible change in women's homicide rate over recent decades.

Some of this gender difference stems from the reluctance of law enforcement officials to define women as criminals (Scott, 1992; Cluff et al., 1998). Canada witnessed this reluctance to assume the worst about women as it watched the Bernardo-Homolka murder case unfold. Initially, the justice system and the public were ready to believe that Karla Homolka was an unwilling accomplice—a victim, in effect—forced to participate in abduction, rape, and murder by a husband she feared. Before the incriminating videotapes were found, Homolka was allowed to plea bargain (receiving a manslaughter conviction and a twelve-year sentence) in exchange for giving evidence against Paul Bernardo.

Social Class

Although people commonly associate criminality with poverty, sociological research suggests that rich and poor alike commit crimes, albeit somewhat different kinds of offences. People arrested for violent and property crimes in North America and elsewhere disproportionately have low social standing (Wolfgang et al., 1972; Clinard and Abbott, 1973; Elliot and Ageton, 1980; Braithwaite, 1981; Thornberry and Farnsworth, 1982; Wolfgang et al., 1987).

In part, this pattern reflects the historical tendency to view poor people as less worthy than those whose wealth and power confer "respectability" (Tittle and Villemez, 1977; Tittle et al., 1978; Elias, 1986). Even the strain theory discussed above contributes to the expectation that more lawbreakers will come from our less affluent neighbourhoods. Police officers, then, are conditioned to focus their search for crime and its perpetrators in the poor sections of town rather than in the pristine office towers of business and government where embezzlement, insider trading, and bid-rigging occur (as noted above).

The evidence also suggests that street crime disproportionately victimizes people of lower social position. Violent crime in particular is commonplace among the small number of chronically poor people living in inner-city neighbourhoods—or in isolated Native communities. But only a small proportion of less advantaged people are ever convicted of crimes; most crimes are committed by a relatively few hard-core offenders (Wolfgang et al., 1972; Elliot and Ageton, 1980; Wolfgang et al., 1987; Harries, 1990).

Moreover, the connection between social standing and criminality "depends entirely on what form of crime one is talking about" (Braithwaite, 1981:47). If the definition of crime is expanded beyond street crime to include white-collar crime, the average "common criminal" has a much higher social position.

Race and Ethnicity

Probing the relationship between race and criminality, we confront a raft of complex issues. Just as most people have long considered criminality the province of the poor, so they have also associated crime with people of colour—despite clear evidence that most crimes are committed by whites.

In Canada, Blacks and particularly Native people are arrested in disproportionate numbers. The effect is apparent in the racial composition of our prison inmates: in 1991, Black people represented roughly 1 percent of Canada's population but made up 3.8 percent of federal inmates. Aboriginals made up about 2 percent of the population but 11.3 percent of inmates. This pattern was even more pronounced among female prisoners, where 8.8 percent were Black and 15.4 percent were Aboriginal. More disturbing is the fact that in the Prairie provinces, where Natives made up about 6 percent of the population, 36 percent of male inmates and 47 percent of female inmates in federal prisons were Aboriginal. The overrepresentation of Native people in provincial prisons is even more pronounced.

By 1999, despite programs designed to divert them from prison, the proportion of Aboriginals in federal prisons had increased to 17.2 percent (Correctional Service Canada, **www.csc-scc.gc.ca/**). The figures for Aboriginal women and men were 21 and 17 percent respectively.

The report of the Commission on Systemic Racism in the Ontario Criminal Justice System (1996) revealed that the imprisonment of Blacks increased by 204 percent between 1986 and 1994, while the comparable figure for whites was 23 percent. The report argues that at every stage of their contact with the justice system—from arrest through trial to imprisonment—Blacks are treated more harshly.

To the degree that prejudice related to colour prompts police to arrest Natives and Blacks more readily than whites, and leads white citizens to more readily report members of these visible minorities to police as potential offenders, these two groups are overly criminalized. The same prejudices may work in the courtroom. In the long run, even small biases by law enforcement officials and the public substantially distort the official link between race and crime (Liska and Tausig, 1979; Unnever et al., 1980; Smith and Visher, 1981).

Race in Canada closely relates to social standing (Kallen, 2003:46–47; Li, 2003:104–14), which, as we have already shown, affects the likelihood of engaging in street crimes. Several researchers claim that membership in lower-class gangs promotes criminality. American sociologists Judith and Peter Blau (1982) take a different tack, suggesting that criminality—especially violent crime—is promoted by the sting of poverty in the midst of affluence. Suffering the hardships of poverty in a rich society encourages people to perceive society as unjust and to disregard its laws.

Crime statistics tend to be biased against reporting white-collar crimes. In the United States, these crimes are excluded from the official crime index. While Canadian statistics do include fraud and "theft over $5000" among property crimes, our society fails to recognize the range of white-collar crimes. Clearly, this omission contributes to the view of the typical criminal as not simply poor but a person of colour. If the examples of BreX, Enron, and ImClone noted earlier serve to broaden our definition of crime to include insider stock trading, toxic-waste dumping, embezzlement, bribery, and cheating on income tax returns, the proportion of white (and affluent) criminals will rise dramatically.

Crime: Canadian and American Perspectives

By world standards, the United States has a lot of crime. Global comparisons fall short because nations define crimes differently and not every country collects data with care, but rough comparisons suggest that the U.S. homicide rate stands four times higher than Canada's and five times higher than Europe's, and that the rape rate is 2.6 times higher than Canada's and seven times higher than Europe's. The United States contends with more crime than virtually any other country in the world (Kalish, 1988). New York City led all U.S. cities with 1182 murders in 1995, but lost its lead to Los Angeles by 2002, with only 575 murders in that year. In comparison, Canada as a whole, with almost four times the population of New York City, had 732 murders in 1995 and 582 in 2002 (Messing, 2003; Statistics Canada, 2003e).

Why are U.S. crime rates so high? Elliot Currie (1985) suggests that the problem stems from its cultural emphasis on individual economic success, frequently at the expense of family and community cohesion. Currie also notes that, unlike European nations, the United States neither guarantees families a minimum income nor publicly funds child-care

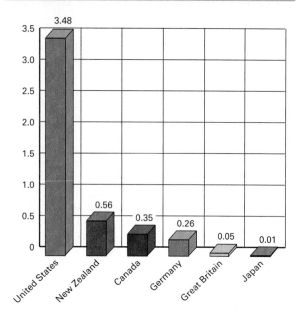

FIGURE 9–3 Handgun Deaths, Rate per 100 000 Population, 1996

Source: Adapted by Gerber from Handgun Control Inc. (1998).

programs. Such public policy decisions, he claims, erode the fabric of society, fuel frustration among society's have-nots, and thus encourage criminal behaviour. Furthermore, Currie asserts that the high level of unemployment and underemployment tolerated in the United States helps create a category of perpetually poor people whose opportunities to make money are often limited to criminal pursuits. The key to reducing crime, then, lies in social change, not in hiring more police and building more prisons. Canada falls between Europe and the United States in the provision of social services and income support, but in recent years our "safety nets" have become increasingly frayed. According to Currie's reasoning, we should have experienced rising crime rates. Instead, crime rates—in particular, violent crime rates—have declined in Canada, and in the United States (Macionis, 2003:208).

Another factor contributing to the relatively high level of violence in the United States is the widespread private ownership of guns. In any given year, roughly two-thirds of murder victims die from shootings, whereas in Canada, less than one-third of murder victims die in this way. Since the early 1900s, in Texas and several other southern states, shooting deaths have exceeded automobile-related fatalities. The fact that

there are as many guns in the hands of private individuals as there are people in the United States helps to account for its runaway leadership in handgun deaths among industrial nations (see Figure 9–3).

As critics of gun control point out, waiting periods and background checks at retail gun stores (mandated by the 1993 Brady Bill) are unlikely to affect criminals, who almost always obtain guns illegally (Wright, 1995). Moreover, we should be cautious about assuming gun control is a magic bullet in the war on crime. Currie notes that the number of Californians killed each year by knives alone exceeds the number of Canadians killed by weapons of all kinds. Most experts do think, however, that gun control will help lower the level of violence.

This is clearly the intent of the gun control legislation enacted in Canada in the fall of 1995. CAVEAT (Canadians Against Violence Everywhere Advocating its Termination) and other public-interest groups were instrumental in persuading the government to prohibit certain kinds of weapons and require the registration of others. As of 2000, all guns must be registered, and licences must be shown in order to purchase ammunition. Although very few urban Canadians have guns in their homes, collectors and rural people—including Aboriginals—mounted significant resistance to the new regulations. The gun registry has been an albatross around the neck of our Liberal government. Costs have ballooned to $1 billion as a result of technical problems and public resistance to registration—which, in many cases, amounts to blatant non-compliance. Registration "deadlines" have been moved several times.

Figure 9-4 shows Canadian firearm homicide rates, by type of firearm, from 1988 to 1998. Note the sharp decline in the rates since 1991 by all types of firearms except the "other" category. Interestingly, homicide rates have been declining in the United States over the same period. Still, in his controversial and provocative film *Bowling for Columbine*, an angry Michael Moore makes the case for gun control in the United States. He makes pointed comparisons between the United States and Canada—where, he says, people do not even lock their front doors.

As noted in earlier chapters, we are experiencing "globalization" on many fronts, including crime. Some types of crime have always been multinational, including terrorism, espionage, and arms dealing (Martin and Romano, 1992). Since the terrorist attack on New York's World Trade Center on September 11, 2001, the United States and Canada have become partners in the war on terror. However reluctantly, Canada has had to modify its approach to border and airport security in response to American fears. We even toyed, temporarily, with the idea of a national identity card with biometric data, like fingerprints or iris scans.

Another case in point is the illegal drug trade. In part, the proliferation of illegal drugs in North America stems from demand: there is a very profitable market for cocaine and other drugs, as well as legions of young people willing to risk arrest or even violent death by engaging in the lucrative drug trade. Montreal bikers the Hell's Angels, or "Les Hells," are involved in a murderous gang war as they manoeuvre for international domination of the illegal drug trade—much of which passes through Canada on its way to the United States. The Americans are concerned about our moves to decriminalize marijuana and to distribute it to certified medical users, fearing that these actions on our part will only increase the flow of Canadian-grown marijuana into the United States.

Countries have different strategies for dealing with crime. The use of the death penalty provides a case in point. Global Map 9–1 identifies countries that employ capital punishment in response to crime and those that do not. The global trend is towards abolition of the death penalty: according to Amnesty International (2000), since 1980 more than thirty nations have ended this practice. Canada abolished the death penalty in 1976. The United States still has the death penalty, though several states have abolished it.

THE CRIMINAL JUSTICE SYSTEM

The criminal justice system is a society's formal response to crime. In some countries, military police keep a tight rein on people's behaviour; in others, including Canada, police have more limited powers to respond to specific violations of criminal law. We shall briefly introduce the key elements of this scheme: police, the courts, and the punishment of convicted offenders.

POLICE

The police are the primary point of contact between the population and the criminal justice system. In principle, the police maintain public order by uniformly enforcing the law. Since Canada's police officers (1 per 523 people in 1995) cannot effectively monitor the activities of 30 million people, the police exercise considerable discretion about which situations warrant their attention and how to handle them.

How, then, do police carry out their duties? A study of police behaviour in five U.S. cities (Smith and Visher, 1981; Smith, 1987) concluded that, because they must respond swiftly, police make several quick assessments that guide their actions. First, *how serious is the alleged crime?* The more serious police perceive a situation to be, the more likely they are to make an arrest. Second, *what is the victim's preference?* Generally, if

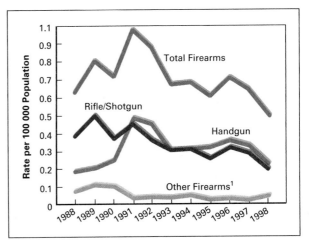

FIGURE 9–4 Firearm Homicide Rates by Type of Firearm, Canada 1988–98

[1]"Other firearms" includes sawed-off rifles/shotguns, fully automatic firearms, and other firearm-like weapons.

Source: Homicide Survey, Canadian Centre for Justice Statistics; Statistics Canada, Catalogue No. 85-002-XPE, Vol. 19, No. 10 (1998).

a victim demands that police make an arrest, they are likely to do so. Third, *is the suspect cooperative or not?* Resisting police efforts increases a suspect's chance of arrest. Fourth, *have they arrested the suspect before?* Police are more likely to take into custody anyone whom they have arrested before, presumably because previous arrest suggests guilt. Fifth, *are bystanders present?* According to Smith and Visher, the presence of observers prompts police to take stronger control of a situation; arrests also move the encounter from the street (the suspect's turf) to the police department (where law officers have the edge). Sixth, *what is the suspect's race?* All else being equal, Smith and Visher contend, police are more likely to arrest people of colour than whites.

Similarly, factors that affect police discretion have been examined in Ontario (Schellenberg, 1995). Police officers are more likely to apply the rules regarding traffic offences, leaving less room for leniency, when their actions are being recorded by mobile video camera. More generally, when the police are considering making arrests, they are less likely to check an individual's record—even when they have computer access in their patrol cars—if they know the individual in question or if they feel that the individual is trustworthy. Race and class can easily enter into the decision-making process at this point.

In Canada, people of colour are arrested and eventually imprisoned in disproportionate numbers, but this observation does not apply equally to all visible minorities. While Blacks and Aboriginals, respectively, are imprisoned at five and three times the rate for whites, those of Arab, East Indian, and Asian origin

GLOBAL MAP 9–1 Capital Punishment in Global Perspective

The map identifies eighty-six countries and territories in which the law provides for the death penalty for ordinary crimes; in fourteen more, the death penalty is reserved for exceptional crimes under military law or during times of war. The death penalty does not exist in seventy-five countries and territories; in twenty more, although the death penalty remains in law, no execution has taken place in more than a decade. Compare rich and poor nations: What general pattern do you see? In what way do the United States and Japan stand out?

Source: Amnesty International Website against the Death Penalty, www.web.amnesty.org/ (accessed September 20, 2001).

are imprisoned at two-thirds to half the rate for whites (Commission on Systemic Racism in the Ontario Criminal Justice System, 1996).

Finally, the greater numbers of police relative to population are found in areas with two key characteristics: high concentrations of minorities and large income disparities between rich and poor (Jacobs, 1979). Thus, the Northwest Territories and the Yukon have both the highest rates of violent crime, as indicated by

homicide (see Canada Map 9–1, page 221), and the largest numbers of police officers relative to their populations (one officer per 275 and 266 residents, respectively, in 1995). The higher crime rates in these areas may be partly alcohol-related and generated by underdevelopment or social disorganization; they may also reflect bias in police surveillance, arrests, and convictions, as well as an emphasis on crime control and law enforcement rather than crime prevention

What Can Be Done about Crime?

People across Canada are fearful of, and fed up with, crime. Guard dogs, special locks, and electronic security systems have never been more popular. By 1991, private security guards outnumbered police officers by more than two to one, and Canadians have begun, though slowly, to copy the American practice of building gated communities. Although, as revealed by the General Social Survey, overall levels of victimization changed little between 1988 and 1993, 46 percent of Canadians think that crime levels have increased in their neighbourhoods, and 27 percent (42 percent of women) are afraid to walk alone at night near their homes (Statistics Canada, 1994b). The perception that we are increasingly vulnerable to crime leads to questions of what we can do about it.

Travis Hirschi, sociologist and author of the well-known "control theory," has offered his own version of a "community approach" to crime. He begins by pointing out two key traits that define today's criminals. The first is age; specifically, most offenders are young. Crime rates are high in the late teens and early twenties, and they fall quickly thereafter. The second factor is the fact that most offenders take a short-term view of their lives. Lawbreakers, in Hirschi's words, are people "relatively unable to sustain a course of action towards some distant goal, whether that goal be education, friendship, employment, or criminal gain. In fact," he concludes, "the defining characteristic of offenders appears to be *low self-control.*"

These two factors, he continues, are clues that suggest why the criminal justice system, on its own, can never control crime. For one thing, going to jail is too uncertain (most crimes go unpunished) and too far removed in time (catching, putting on trial, and jailing criminals often takes a year or longer) to deter the typical offender. Thus, Hirschi explains, popular calls for "stiffer sentences" actually have little effect in suppressing crime. Moreover, by the time many offenders are sent packing to prison, they are already moving beyond the "crime years" simply because they are growing older. Statistically speaking, then, offenders aging in prison represent a crime threat already shrinking on its own.

Therefore, Hirschi argues that, rather than locking up adults, society needs to focus resources on younger people *before* they commit crimes. Hirschi calls for closer attention to teenagers—those at highest risk of criminal behaviour. Effective crime control, he explains, depends on keeping teens away from not only guns and drugs, but also alcohol, and, if necessary, cars and perhaps even each other.

A second suggestion comes even earlier in the life course. The most ef-fective way to control crime, Hirschi concludes, is for us to teach our children the key trait of *self-control.* This is a job ill suited to government, Hirschi continues, and so the responsibility must fall on parents. But government can help by targeting seriously dysfunctional families for assistance and through any other strategy that fosters strong—preferably two-parent—families. Simply "delaying pregnancy among teenage girls," he predicts, "would probably do more to affect long-term crime rates than all the criminal justice programs combined."

Continue the debate . . .

1. *Do you think limiting teenagers' freedom would reduce crime? What civil rights issues are raised by such a plan?*

2. *Do you think ensuring two-parent households would cut the crime rate? Can society realistically shape families in this way?*

3. *Would economic programs directed at reducing poverty diminish the crime problem? What specific programs would you suggest?*

Source: Based on Gottfredson and Hirschi (1995).

(LaPrairie, 1988; Depew, 1992). Thus, police form an imposing presence where a volatile mix of social forces encourages social disruption.

COURTS

After arrest, a court determines a suspect's guilt or innocence. In principle, our courts rely on an adversarial process involving attorneys—who represent the defendant on the one side and the Crown on the other—in the presence of a judge who monitors adherence to legal procedures. In practice, however, a large percentage of criminal cases are resolved prior to court appearance through **plea bargaining**, *a legal negotiation in which the prosecution reduces a defendant's charge in exchange for a guilty plea.* For example, a defendant charged with burglary may agree to plead guilty to the lesser charge of possession of burglary tools; another charged with selling cocaine may go along with pleading guilty to possession.

Is Spanking Allowed in Canada?

Over the past decade, we have been debating the acceptability and consequences of spanking—or, more generally, the use of corporal punishment by parents and teachers in their attempts to maintain discipline and control. Many critics view spanking as a kind of child abuse that, if unchecked, can lead to escalating violence against children. Furthermore, the child who is spanked is likely to spank or otherwise abuse his or her own child. Those who support spanking see it as a way of communicating "thou shalt not" to a child who is not yet amenable to reason or able to exercise judgment.

Tepperman and Blain (1999) point out that there is little cultural variation in the *practice* of corporal punishment, but that there is considerable diversity with respect to its *acceptance*. They note that North Americans generally practise and approve of physical punishment; at the same time, the authors

state, "Most economically developed, literate, and prosperous societies have rejected spanking and other corporal punishment as acceptable methods of child discipline" (p. 33). Is this the case?

The Canadian Centre for Studies of Children at Risk has pointed out that there are long-term, negative consequences of corporal punishment: people who were spanked as children are "more likely to develop a psychiatric illness or abuse drugs or alcohol" (Southworth, 2000). Nevertheless, according to Dawn Walker of the Canadian Institute of Child Health, as a result of section 43 of the Criminal Code, "Children are the only group in society that we are allowed to hit. You can't hit a spouse, but you can hit a child, the most vulnerable in society" (Southworth, 2000). Children's rights activists had hoped that Judge McCoombs of the Ontario Superior Court would recommend repealing section 43, the corporal-punishment

law, which allows parents some latitude with respect to child discipline. Instead, he ruled that although spanking does not violate the child's constitutional rights, we should develop "specific criteria to guide parents, teachers and law enforcement officials" (Southworth, 2000).

According to Canada's *Criminal Code*, section 43, teachers and parents are still justified in using reasonable force:

> Every schoolteacher, parent or person standing in the place of a parent is justified in using force by way of correction toward a pupil or child, as the case may be, who is under his care, if the force does not exceed what is reasonable under the circumstances.

Sources: Based on Tepperman and Blain (1999) and Southworth (2000).

Plea bargaining is widespread because it spares the judicial system the time and expense of court trials. A trial is usually unnecessary if there is little disagreement about the facts of the case. By selectively trying only a small proportion of the cases, the courts can also channel their resources into those deemed most important (Reid, 1991).

But this process pressures defendants (who are presumed innocent) to plead guilty. A person can exercise the right to a trial, but only at the risk of receiving a more severe sentence if found guilty. In essence, then, plea bargaining undercuts the rights of defendants as it circumvents the adversarial process. According to Abraham Blumberg (1970), defendants who have little understanding of the criminal justice system, as well as those unable to afford a good lawyer, are likely to suffer from this system of "bargain-counter justice." On the other hand, Canadians who felt that Karla Homolka got off too lightly asked to have her plea bargain reassessed. Her case was not reopened because doing so would have threatened the whole plea-bargaining system.

PUNISHMENT

Ever since differences in power and authority began to emerge in human groups, people have probably resorted to punishment as a means of discipline or control. Currently, punishments may range from "time out" or the spanking of children (see the "Applying Sociology" box) to imprisonment or capital punishment for the most serious of crimes.

In 1831, the officials in an English town hanged a nine-year-old boy who was found guilty of setting fire to a house (Kittrie, 1971:103). Canadians, today, would be appalled by this outcome for several reasons. We conducted our last execution in 1962 and abolished the death penalty in 1976—and have seen a general decline in homicide rates ever since. In addition, Canadians have decided that young people have a lower capacity for crime and deserve the special protections of the *Young Offenders Act* (replaced in 2003 by the *Youth Criminal Justice Act*).

 The history of Canadian legislation regarding youth crime is discussed at www.mapleleafweb.com/features/crime/youth-act/

Clearly, approaches to punishment have changed over time and vary from country to country. Debate about the appropriateness of specific punishments as applied to adults and juvenile offenders raises the question of how and why society should punish its wrongdoers. This leads us to consider four justifications for punishment.

Retribution stands as the oldest justification for punishment. During the Middle Ages, most people viewed crime as sin—an offence against God as well as society—that warranted a harsh response. Today, although critics charge that retribution does little to reform the offender, this principle retains widespread support.

A Toronto case illustrates the importance of the perceived appropriateness of the judicial response. In October 1997, Gordon Stuckless, the equipment manager of Maple Leaf Gardens, was sentenced to two years less a day for the sexual abuse of young boys over a period of twenty-odd years. Stuckless had traded sexual favours for tickets to hockey games or opportunities to meet players. After Martin Kruse came forward with allegations of sexual abuse, police received a stream of phone calls from other men who had had similar experiences. Shortly after Stuckless was sentenced, Kruse committed suicide. Other victims, their families, and many in the general public believed that the lenient sentence did not fit the crime; Kruse's family felt that the light sentence was one of the reasons for his suicide.

Deterrence

A second justification for punishment, **deterrence**, amounts to *the attempt to discourage criminality through punishment*. Deterrence reflects the eighteenth-century Enlightenment notion that, as calculating and rational creatures, humans will forgo deviance if they perceive that the pain of punishment outweighs the pleasure of mischief.

Deterrence emerged as reform directed at the harsh punishments based on retribution. Why put someone to death for stealing, critics asked, if theft can be discouraged with a prison sentence? As the concept of deterrence gained acceptance, execution and physical mutilation of criminals in most industrial societies were replaced by milder forms of punishment such as incarceration.

Punishment may deter crime in two ways. *Specific deterrence* demonstrates to an offender that crime does not pay. Through *general deterrence*, the punishment of one person serves as an example to others.

Rehabilitation

The third justification for punishment is **rehabilitation**, *a program for reforming the offender to preclude subsequent offences*. Rehabilitation paralleled the development of

TABLE 9–2 Four Justifications of Punishment: A Summary	
Retribution	The oldest justification for punishment still holds sway today. Punishment is atonement for a moral wrong by an individual; in principle, punishment should be comparable in severity to the deviance itself.
Deterrence	An early modern approach. Deviance is considered a social disruption, which society acts to control. People are viewed as rational and self-interested; for deterrence to work, the pains of punishment must outweigh the pleasures of deviance.
Rehabilitation	A modern approach linked to the development of the social sciences. Deviance is viewed as the product of social problems (such as poverty) or of personal problems (such as mental illness). Social conditions are improved and offenders are subjected to intervention appropriate to their condition.
Social protection	A modern approach easier to effect than rehabilitation. If society is unable or unwilling to rehabilitate offenders or reform social conditions, citizens are protected from further deviance by incarceration or execution of offenders.

the social sciences in the nineteenth century. According to sociologists of that time (and also since), crime and other deviance spring from an unfavourable environment marked by poverty or a lack of parental supervision. Logically, then, if offenders learn to be deviant, they can also learn to obey the rules—the key is controlling the environment. *Reformatories* or *houses of correction* served as a controlled setting to help people learn proper behaviour (recall the description of total institutions in Chapter 5, "Socialization").

Rehabilitation resembles deterrence in that both motivate the offender towards conformity. But rehabilitation emphasizes constructive improvement, while deterrence (like retribution) inflicts suffering on an offender. In addition, while retribution demands that the punishment fit the crime, rehabilitation tailors treatment to the offender. Thus, identical crimes would prompt similar acts of retribution but might call for different programs of rehabilitation.

Social Protection

A final justification for punishment, **social protection**, refers to *rendering an offender incapable of further offences either temporarily through incarceration or permanently by*

FIGURE 9–5 Incarceration Rates, 1995

Source: Mauer (2000).

execution. One of the concerns expressed by the Canadian public is that dangerous offenders are given "life" sentences and then released on parole. After the murder of her daughter Nina in Burlington, Ontario, Priscilla DeVilliers (who founded CAVEAT) involved herself in a massive campaign to restrict parole and bail for dangerous offenders. Her campaign touched a responsive cord in an apprehensive public that feels inadequately protected at present. When a dangerous man such as Clifford Olson is granted early release and kills eleven young people, as he did in British Columbia in 1980–81, people question the level of social protection afforded them.[2]

Table 9–2 (on page 229) summarizes these four justifications for punishment. Note, too, Figure 9–5, which shows that Russia and the United States incarcerate a larger share of their populations than most other countries in the world. Canada's rate, although the lowest shown here, is still well above those of most European countries.

---

[2]At the time of Olson's release in 1980, he was serving a prison sentence for murder. He is now serving the maximum sentence of twenty-five years without the possibility of parole. He can expect to be released in the year 2007, when he will be sixty-seven years old. Peter Worthington wrote about the 1980–81 murders of which Olson was convicted, as well as about many others he claims to have committed, in *Saturday Night* (July/August 1993).

Critical evaluation. We have identified four justifications for punishment. Assessing the actual consequences of punishment, however, is no simple task.

The value of retribution reminds us of Durkheim's contention that punishing the deviant person bolsters people's moral consciousness. To accomplish this objective, punishment was traditionally a public event. Public executions occurred in England until 1868; the last public execution in the United States took place in Kentucky in 1937. Even today, the American mass media ensure public awareness of executions carried out inside prison walls (Kittrie, 1971). Though executions no longer occur in Canada, we have television coverage when people like Paul Bernardo are taken away to prison.

Experts and the public as a whole agree that punishment deters some crime (Wright, 1994). Yet our society also has a high rate of **criminal recidivism**, *subsequent offences by people previously convicted of crimes.* Various studies of people released from prison show that substantial percentages have been rearrested and returned to prison within a few years, raising questions about the extent to which punishment actually deters crime. Then, too, only about one-third of all crimes are known to police, and of these, only about one in five results in an arrest. The old adage that "crime doesn't pay" rings rather hollow when we consider that such a small proportion of offences ever results in punishment.

General deterrence is even more difficult to investigate scientifically, since we have no way of knowing how people might act if they were unaware of punishments meted out to others. In the debate over capital punishment, critics of the practice point to research indicating that the death penalty has limited value as a general deterrent in the United States, which is the only Western, industrial society that routinely executes serious offenders (Sellin, 1980; van den Haag and Conrad, 1983; Archer and Gartner, 1987; Lester, 1987; Bailey and Peterson, 1989; Bailey, 1990; Bohm, 1991). Furthermore, an examination of the Canadian homicide rates compiled by Lenton (1989) from 1954 to 1986 reveals no sudden increase in homicide rates after 1962, when the last execution occurred, or after 1976, when capital punishment was abolished. In fact, the homicide rate went down for a few years after 1976.

Prisons accomplish short-term societal protection by keeping offenders off the streets, but they do little to reshape attitudes or behaviour in the long term (Carlson, 1976; Wright, 1994). Rehabilitation may be an unrealistic expectation, since, according to Sutherland's theory of differential association, locking someone up among criminals for months or years should simply strengthen criminal attitudes and skills. And because incarceration severs whatever social ties inmates may have in the outside world, individuals may be prone to further crime upon their release, consistent with Hirschi's control theory.

Ultimately, we should never assume that the criminal justice system—the police, courts, and prisons—can eliminate crime. The point, made strongly in the "Controversy & Debate" box, as it has been throughout this chapter, is simple: crime and all other deviance are more than simply the acts of "bad people"; they are inextricably bound up in the operation of society itself.

SUMMARY

1. Deviance refers to normative violations ranging from mild breaches of etiquette to serious violence.

2. Biological investigation, from Cesare Lombroso's nineteenth-century observations of convicts to recent research in human genetics, offers little insight into the causes of crime.

3. Psychological study links deviance to abnormal personality stemming from either biological or environmental causes. Psychological theories help to explain some kinds of deviance.

4. Deviance has societal rather than individual roots because it is related to (1) cultural norms, (2) situational processes of social definition, and (3) patterns of social power.

5. Using the structural-functional paradigm, Durkheim asserted that responding to deviance affirms values and norms, clarifies moral boundaries, promotes social unity, and encourages social change.

6. The symbolic-interaction paradigm is the basis of labelling theory, which holds that deviance arises in the reaction of others to a person's behaviour. Acquiring a stigma of deviance can lead to secondary deviance and the onset of a deviant career.

7. Following the approach of Karl Marx, social-conflict theory holds that laws and other norms reflect the interests of powerful members of society. Social-conflict theory also spotlights white-collar crimes, which cause extensive social harm even though the offenders are rarely branded as criminals.

8. Official statistics indicate that arrest rates peak in late adolescence, then drop steadily with advancing age. Three-fourths of those arrested for property crimes are males, as are almost nine of ten people charged with violent crimes.

9. People of lower social position commit more street crime than those with greater social privilege. When white-collar crimes are counted among criminal offences, however, this disparity in overall criminal activity diminishes.

10. More whites than Blacks are arrested for street crimes. However, Blacks are arrested more often than whites in proportion to their respective populations. Asian Canadians have lower than average rates of arrest.

11. The police exercise considerable discretion in their work. Research suggests that factors such as the seriousness of the offence, the presence of bystanders, and the accused being Black or Aboriginal make arrest more likely.

12. Although ideally an adversarial system, Canadian courts resolve many cases through plea bargaining. While efficient, this method nevertheless places less powerful people at a disadvantage.

13. Justifications for punishment include retribution, deterrence, rehabilitation, and societal protection. Because its consequences are difficult to evaluate scientifically, punishment—like deviance itself—sparks controversy among sociologists and the public as a whole.

CRITICAL-THINKING QUESTIONS

1. How does a sociological view of deviance differ from the common-sense notion that bad people do bad things?

2. Identify Durkheim's functions of deviance. From his point of view, could people create a society free from deviance? Why or why not?

3. How does social power affect deviant labelling? How do gender, race, and class figure in this process?

4. Why do you think crime rates have risen in Canada over the last fifty years? Do you agree or disagree with Travis Hirschi's prescription for crime control presented in the "Controversy & Debate" box? Why?

APPLICATIONS AND EXERCISES

1. Research the idea of computer crime. What new kinds of crime are emerging in the Information Age?

Is computer technology also generating new ways of tracking lawbreakers?

2. Watch an episode of the real-action police show *Cops*. From the perspective of the show, what kinds of people commit crimes?

3. Ask the security office for data about crime on your campus. How well does their view of campus crime square with your own?

SITES TO SEE

www.acjnet.org/

Access to Justice Network is a bilingual site for Canadian justice and legal information and services. These resources are organized under headings such as Aboriginal people, crime prevention, plain language, women, and youth.

www.crime-prevention.org/index.html

The National Crime Prevention Council is an independent, voluntary council whose mission is to develop strategies to empower individuals and their communities to improve their safety, security, and well-being. The site includes event listings, press releases, a publications archive, and links to crime prevention databases.

www.camh.net/

The Centre for Addiction and Mental Health is one of North America's pre-eminent facilities for research into alcohol, tobacco, and other drug problems. The Foundation's mission is to help prevent and reduce the harm associated with alcohol, tobacco, and other drugs in Ontario communities. The site includes journal articles, statistics, FAQs, and information about ARF, its library holdings, and training courses.

eserver.org/feminism/

This site publishes women's studies and feminist works, focusing on issues of sex, gender, sexual identity, and sexuality in cultural practices.

www.lawyers.ca/tgyad/

Canadian lawyers debate issues relating to the *Young Offenders Act* and its successor, the *Youth Criminal Justice Act*, at this website.

STUDY TOOLS

For more study tools to help you with your next exam, be sure to check out the Companion Website at **www.pearsoned.ca/macionis**, as well as Chapter 9 in your Study Guide.

INVESTIGATE WITH CONTENTSELECT

Follow the instructions found on page 25 of this textbook to access ContentSelect™ at the Research Navigator™ website. Once at the site, enter your LOGINID and Password. Then, enter keywords such as "deviance," "labelling," "rehabilitation," and "criminal recidivism" and the search engine will supply relevant and recent scholarly and popular press publications.

Paul Marcus (1953– , American)
Upstairs–Downstairs

© Paul Marcus, *Upstairs–Downstairs*
Studio SPM, Inc.

SOCIAL STRATIFICATION

On April 10, 1912, the ocean liner *Titanic* slipped away from the docks of Southampton, England, on its first voyage, across the North Atlantic to New York. A proud symbol of the new Industrial Age, the towering ship carried 2300 passengers, some enjoying more luxury than most travellers today could imagine. By contrast, poor immigrants crowded the lower decks, journeying to what they hoped would be a better life in North America.

Two days out, the crew received radio warnings of icebergs in the area but paid little notice. Then, near midnight, as the ship steamed swiftly and silently westward, a lookout was stunned to see a massive shape rising out of the dark ocean directly ahead. Moments later, the *Titanic* collided with a huge iceberg, almost as tall as the ship itself, which split open its starboard side as if the grand vessel were nothing more than a giant tin can.

Sea water surged into the ship's lower levels, and within twenty-five minutes people were rushing for the lifeboats. By 2:00 a.m., the bow of the *Titanic* was submerged and the

stern reared high above the water. Clinging to the deck, quietly observed by those in the lifeboats, hundreds of helpless passengers solemnly passed their final minutes before the ship disappeared into the frigid Atlantic (Lord, 1976).

The tragic loss of more than 1600 lives made news around the world. Looking back dispassionately at this terrible accident with a sociological eye, however, we see that some categories of passengers had much better odds of survival than others. In an age of conventional gallantry, women and children boarded the boats first, so that 80 percent of the casualties were men. Class, too, was at work. Of people holding first-class tickets, more than 60 percent were saved, primarily because they were on the upper decks, where warnings were sounded first and lifeboats were accessible. Only 36 percent of the second-class passengers survived, and of the third-class passengers on the lower decks, only 24 percent escaped drowning. On board the *Titanic*, class turned out to mean much more than the quality of accommodations: it was truly a matter of life or death.

The fate of the *Titanic* dramatically illustrates the consequences of social inequality for the ways people live—and sometimes whether they live at all. This chapter explores the important concept of social stratification. Chapter 11 ("Social Class in Canada") continues the story by highlighting social inequality in Canada, and Chapter 12 ("Global Stratification") examines how our country fits into a global system of wealth and poverty.

WHAT IS SOCIAL STRATIFICATION?

For tens of thousands of years, humans the world over lived in small hunting-and-gathering societies. Although

members of these bands might single out one person as being swifter, stronger, or more skilled in collecting food, everyone had more or less the same social standing. As societies became more complex—a process detailed in Chapter 4 ("Society")—a monumental change came about. The social system elevated entire categories of people above others, providing one segment of the population with more money, power, and schooling than others.

Sociologists use the concept of **social stratification** to refer to *a system by which a society ranks categories of people in a hierarchy*. Social stratification is a matter of four basic principles.

The personal experience of poverty is captured in Sebastiao Salgado's haunting photograph, which stands as a universal portrait of human suffering. The essential sociological insight is that, however strongly individuals feel its effects, our social standing is largely a consequence of the way in which a society (or a world of societies) structures opportunity and reward. To the core of our being, then, we are all the products of social stratification.

1. **Social stratification is a characteristic of society, not simply a reflection of individual differences.** Members of industrial societies consider social standing a reflection of personal talent and effort, although we typically exaggerate the extent to which people control their destinies. Children born into wealthy families are more likely than those born into poverty to enjoy health, achieve academically, succeed in their life's work, and live well into old age. Neither rich nor poor people are responsible for creating social stratification, yet this system shapes the lives of them all.

2. **Social stratification persists over generations.** To understand that stratification stems from society rather than from individual differences, note how inequality persists over time. In all societies, parents pass their social positions along to their children, so that patterns of inequality stay much the same from generation to generation.

   Especially in industrial societies, however, some individuals do experience **social mobility**, *change in a person's position in a social hierarchy*. Social mobility may be upward or downward. Our society celebrates the achievements of a Jean Chrétien, a Céline Dion, a Jim Carrey, or a Wayne Gretzky, all of whom rose to prominence from modest beginnings. But we also acknowledge that people move downward as a result of business setbacks, unemployment, or illness. More often, people move horizontally when they exchange one occupation for another that is com-

parable. For most people, however, social standing remains much the same over a lifetime.

3. **Social stratification is universal but variable.** Social stratification is found everywhere. At the same time, whatever the basis or extent of inequality, it varies from one society to another. Among the members of technologically simple societies, social differentiation is minimal and based mostly on age and sex. With the development of sophisticated technology for growing food, societies also forge complex and more rigid systems for distributing what people produce. As we shall see, industrialization has the effect of increasing social mobility and reducing at least some kinds of social inequality. On the other hand, there is evidence that, for the short term at least, the development of new information technology has had the opposite effect, increasing social inequality.

4. **Social stratification involves not just inequality but beliefs.** Any system of inequality not only gives some people more resources than others but defines certain arrangements as fair. Just as *what* is unequal differs from society to society, so too does the explanation of *why* people should be unequal. Furthermore, virtually everywhere, people with the greatest social privileges express the strongest support for their society's system of social stratification, while those with fewer social resources are more likely to seek change.

CASTE AND CLASS SYSTEMS

In describing social stratification in particular societies, sociologists often use two opposing standards: "closed" systems that allow little change in social position and "open" systems that permit considerable social mobility (Tumin, 1985).

THE CASTE SYSTEM

A **caste system** amounts to *social stratification based on ascription* (a social status received at birth, described in Chapter 6). A pure caste system, in other words, is "closed" so that birth alone determines one's social destiny with no opportunity for social mobility based on individual efforts. In caste systems, then, categories of people are ranked in a rigid hierarchy, and everyone is born, lives, and dies at the same social level.

Two Illustrations: India and South Africa

A number of the world's societies—most of them agrarian—approximate caste systems. One example is India, or India's traditional villages in which most people still live. The Indian system of castes (or *varna*, a Sanskrit word meaning "colour") is composed of

The traditional caste system still guides people's choice of work, especially in rural areas. Below the four basic castes are the Harijans, people defined as "outcasts" or "untouchables." These people perform jobs, such as turning leather into shoes, defined as unclean for others of higher social position.

four major categories: Brahmin, Kshatriya, Vaishya, and Shudra. On the local level, however, each is composed of hundreds of subcaste (or *jati*) groups.

Caste has also played a key role in the history of South Africa. In this nation's former policy of *apartheid*, the 5 million South Africans of European ancestry enjoyed a commanding share of wealth and power, dominating some 30 million Black South Africans. In a middle position were another 3 million mixed-race people, known as "coloureds," and about 1 million Asians. (See the "Global Sociology" box for a discussion of South Africa's caste system.)

In a caste system, birth determines the fundamental shape of people's lives in four crucial respects. First, traditional caste groups are linked to occupation, so that generations of a family perform the same type of work. In rural India, although some occupations (such as farming) are open to all, castes are identified with the work their members do (as priests, barbers, leather workers, street sweepers, and so on). In South Africa, whites still hold almost all the desirable jobs, while most Blacks are consigned to manual labour and other low-level service work.

No rigid social hierarchy could persist if people married outside their own categories; if they did, what rank would their children hold? To shore up the hierarchy, caste systems require that people marry others of the same rank. Sociologists call this pattern *endogamous* marriage (*endo* stems from Greek, meaning "within"). Traditionally, Indian parents select their children's marriage partners, often before the children reach their teens. Until 1985, South Africa banned marriage and even sex between the races.

As well, caste guides everyday life so that people remain in the company of "their own kind." Hindus in India enforce this segregation with the belief that a ritually "pure" person of a higher caste will be "polluted"

by contact with someone of lower standing. Apartheid in South Africa achieved much the same effect.

Finally, caste systems rest on powerful cultural beliefs. Indian culture is built on Hindu traditions that mandate accepting one's life work, whatever it may be, as a moral duty. And, although apartheid is no longer a matter of law, South Africans still cling to notions distinguishing "white jobs" from "Black jobs."

Caste and Agrarian Life

Caste systems are typical of agrarian societies, because the lifelong routines of agriculture depend on a rigid sense of duty and discipline. Thus, caste persists in rural India half a century after being formally outlawed, though its grip is easing in the nation's more industrial cities, where most people exercise greater choice about their work and marriage partners (Bahl, 1991). Similarly, the rapid industrialization of South Africa elevated the importance of personal choice and individual rights, making the abolition of apartheid only a matter of time. In Canada, although elements of caste survive, treating people categorically on the basis of their race or ethnicity is now widely denounced as unjust, inviting charges of racism.

Note, however, that the erosion of caste with all of its rigidities does not signal the end of social stratification. On the contrary, it simply marks a change in its character, as the next sections explain.

THE CLASS SYSTEM

Agrarian life relies on the discipline wrought by caste systems; industrial societies, in contrast, depend on developing specialized talents. Industrialization thus erodes caste in favour of a **class system**, *social stratification based on individual achievement.*

The *Titanic*: Personal and Canadian Connections

The grave of the Unknown Child in Halifax, recently identified as Eino Panula of Finland (second cousin of Linda Gerber).

In the spring of 1912, Maria Panula set off from Lapua, Finland, with five sons aged thirteen months to sixteen years. They boarded the magnificent new ship *Titanic* on its maiden voyage to the United States, where they were to join Juha Panula, who had gone on ahead to get established in America. Before leaving, Maria Panula had given an American silver dollar to her five-year-old godson and cousin

Viljo Kojola—the father of your author Linda Gerber.

The Panulas were among the third-class passengers, 76 percent of whom perished in the icy waters of the northern Atlantic. They must have been on the upper decks at the time disaster struck, for Maria made it onto a lifeboat with her infant son Eino. Survivors told her husband that when she realized her other children did not have places in the lifeboat, she got off with Eino in her arms to face certain death with the rest of her children.

After the shipwreck, the crew of the *Mackay-Bennett*, a Canadian ship, spotted a number of bodies floating in the water. Among them was "a young child, his blond hair and blue eyes poking through a grey coat trimmed with fur" (Humphreys, 2001). When no one claimed the child's body, the sailors resolved that he would have a proper burial. Thus, in a Halifax cemetery, you can find a tombstone that reads:

ERECTED TO THE MEMORY OF AN UNKNOWN CHILD WHOSE REMAINS WERE RECOVERED AFTER THE DISASTER TO THE 'TITANIC' APRIL 15TH 1912.

Thereafter, the grave was known, simply, as that of the Unknown Child.

In the mid-1990s, Ryan Parr, a professor at Lakehead University in Thunder Bay, and Alan Ruffman, a

Halifax oceanographer and historian, pulled together an international team of researchers who would use archives, genealogy, and cutting-edge DNA testing to determine the identity of the Unknown Child. Since there were six children of approximately the right age who went down with the *Titanic*, their task (still immensely complex) was limited to tracking down the families of those six children, getting blood samples from relatives on the maternal side of each family, and matching the mitochondrial DNA from the women with that of the tiny exhumed body. By early November 2002, the researchers had identified the child as Eino Panula.

The news hit the papers all over the world, but nowhere with as much impact as in Finland and Canada. Relatives had lived for ninety years with the story of Maria Panula, her children, and the *Titanic* tucked away in their memory banks. No one could have imagined that one day a nameless child buried in Halifax would be identified as one of our own kin. Had the Paleo-DNA Laboratory of Lakehead University not been capable of extracting and analyzing the ancient DNA from tiny bone fragments, and had Parr and Ruffman not dared to dream, none of this would have happened.

Source: Based on Humphreys (2002) and personal knowledge of Linda Gerber.

A class system is more "open," so that people who gain schooling and skills may experience some social mobility in relation to their parents and siblings. Mobility, in turn, blurs class distinctions. Social boundaries also break down as people immigrate from abroad or move from the country to the city, lured by greater opportunity for education and the promise of a brighter future (Lipset and Bendix, 1967; Cutright, 1968; Treiman, 1970). Typically, newcomers take low-paying jobs, thereby pushing

others up the social ladder (Clark, 1978; Tyree et al., 1979).

People in industrial societies come to think that everyone—not just someone of high social standing—is entitled to "rights." The principle of equal standing before the law gradually assumes a central place in the political culture of industrial class systems.

Class systems are no different from caste systems in one basic respect: people remain unequal. But social stratification now rests on personal talent and effort

Race as Caste: A Report from South Africa

At the southern tip of the African continent lies South Africa, a country about the size of Alaska and with a population of about 44 million in 2001. Long inhabited by Black people, the region attracted white Dutch traders and farmers in the mid-seventeenth century. Early in the nineteenth century, a second wave of colonization saw British immigrants push the Dutch inland. By the early 1900s, the British had taken over the country, proclaiming it the Union of South Africa. In 1961, the United Kingdom gave up control and recognized the independence of the Republic of South Africa.

But freedom was a reality only for the white minority. Years before, to ensure their political control over the Black majority, whites had instituted a policy of apartheid, or racial separation. Apartheid was made law in 1948, denying Blacks national citizenship, ownership of land, and any formal voice in the government. In effect, Black South Africans became a lower caste, receiving little schooling and performing menial, low-paying jobs. Under this system, even "middle-class" white households had at least one Black household servant.

The prosperous white minority defended apartheid, claiming that Blacks threatened their cultural traditions or, more simply, were inferior beings. But resistance to apartheid rose steadily, prompting whites to resort to brutal military repression to maintain their power.

Steady resistance—especially from younger Blacks, impatient for a political voice and economic opportunity—gradually forced change. Adding to the pressure was criticism from most other industrial nations, including Canada. By the mid-1980s, the tide began to turn as the South African government granted limited political rights to people of mixed race and Asian ancestry. Then came the right for all people to form labour unions, to enter occupations once restricted to whites, and to own property. Officials also began to dismantle the system of laws that separated the races in public places.

The rate of change increased in 1990 with Nelson Mandela's release from prison. In 1994, the first national election open to all people of all races elected Mandela the president, ending centuries of white minority rule.

Despite this dramatic political change, however, social stratification in South Africa is still based on race. Even with the right to own property, one-third of Black South Africans have no jobs, and the majority remain dirt poor. The worst off are some 7 million *ukuhleleleka*, which means "marginal people" in the Xhosa language. Soweto-by-the-Sea may sound like a summer getaway, but it is home to thousands of ukuhleleleka who live crammed into shacks made of packing cases, corrugated metal, cardboard, and other discarded materials. There is no electricity for lights or refrigeration. Without plumbing, people use buckets to haul sewage;

Nelson Mandela

women line up to take a turn at a single water tap that serves more than 1000 people. Any job is hard to come by, and those who do find work are lucky to earn $200 a month.

Thabo Mbeki, elected in 1999 as Mandela's successor, leads a nation still twisted by centuries of racial caste. Tourism is up and holds out promise of an economic boom in years to come. But the country can shed its past only by providing all its people with real opportunity.

Sources: Fredrickson (1981), Wren (1991), Hawthorne (1999), and Mabry and Masland (1999).

rather than the accident of birth. Careers and marriages are matters of individual choice.

Status Consistency

Status consistency refers to *the degree of consistency of a person's social standing across various dimensions of social inequality.* In a caste system, limited social mobility generates high status consistency so that the typical person has the same relative ranking with regard to wealth, power, and prestige. By contrast, the greater mobility of class systems allows for less status consistency. In industrial nations such as Canada, a university professor (with his or her Ph.D.) might enjoy high social prestige while receiving a comparatively modest income. Such status inconsistency contributes to the fact that *classes* are less clearly defined than *castes*.

CASTE AND CLASS TOGETHER: THE UNITED KINGDOM

There are no pure caste or class systems; social stratification everywhere involves some combination of these two forms. This mix is particularly striking in the United Kingdom, an industrial nation with a long agrarian history.

The Estate System

In the Middle Ages, social stratification in England (which, together with Wales, Scotland, and Northern Ireland constitutes today's United Kingdom of Great Britain and Northern Ireland) took the form of a caste-like system of three groups or "estates." A hereditary nobility, or first estate, was composed of 150 families, or barely 5 percent of the population (Laslett, 1984). These nobles exercised power and controlled wealth in the form of land. Typically, nobles had no formal occupation at all; to be "engaged in trade" or any other type of work for income was deemed "beneath" the aristocracy. Well tended by servants, many nobles used their leisure time to cultivate refined tastes in art, music, and literature.

The estate system depended on protecting vast landholdings from division by heirs. This was accomplished through the law of *primogeniture* (from Latin meaning "first born"), which mandated that a man's entire property be inherited by his eldest son or other nearest male relation. This process maintained a landed aristocracy, but primogeniture forced younger sons to seek out other sources of support. One possibility for such men was to enter the clergy—often dubbed the "second estate"—where spiritual power was supplemented by the church's extensive landholdings. Other young men of high birth became military officers or lawyers, or they took up other "honourable" professions set aside for "gentlemen."

And what of women? In an age when no woman could inherit her father's property and few women had the opportunity to earn a living on their own, the daughter of a noble family depended for her security on marrying well.

Below the nobility and the clergy, the vast majority of men and women formed the third estate, or "commoners." With little property, most commoners were serfs working plots of land belonging to nobles. The phrase "one's lot in life" literally describes the daily focus of commoners during the Middle Ages. Unlike the nobility and the clergy, most commoners had little access to schooling and remained illiterate.

As the Industrial Revolution steadily enlarged England's economy, some commoners living in cities gained enough wealth to rival the power of the nobility. The increasing importance of money, with the extension of schooling and legal rights to more and more people, blurred social rankings and gave rise to a class system. In a pointed illustration of how far the pendulum has swung, a descendant of nobility, working for a living as a writer, was asked in an interview if Britain's caste-like estates had finally broken down. Playfully she retorted, "Of course they have, or I wouldn't be here talking to someone like you!" (*New Haven Journal-Courier*, November 27, 1986).

The United Kingdom Today

Social stratification in the United Kingdom today is more of a class system, but one that retains the mark of a long, feudal past. At the top of the hierarchy, a small cluster of British families continues to enjoy inherited wealth, attends expensive schools, and wields political influence. Queen Elizabeth II, who traces her ancestry through a millennium of aristocracy, reigns as the United Kingdom's (and Canada's) head of state, while Parliament's House of Lords is composed of other "peers," most of noble birth. (Canadian newspaper tycoon Conrad Black had to give up his Canadian citizenship in 2001 in order to become Lord Black of Crossharbour; until then, Prime Minister Jean Chrétien blocked his appointment because the Nickle Resolution forbids Canadians from receiving foreign honours.) Actual control of government resides in the House of Commons, where the prime minister and other commoners gain their positions through achievement rather than by ascription. Looking beyond the government, most of the leading people in all sectors of British society today are individuals of extraordinary achievement rather than noble birth.

Moving down the hierarchy, roughly one-quarter of the population forms the British middle class. Some families are moderately wealthy, with high incomes from professions and business. These richer "commoners," along with the upper class, make up the 10 to 15 percent of Britons with significant financial holdings in the form of stocks and bonds. Most middle-class Britons, however, earn too little to accumulate substantial wealth.

Approximately half of all Britons think of themselves as "working class." As in Canada, members of the working class earn modest incomes, generally by performing manual labour. The decline of British industries such as coal mining and steel production has subjected many working-class families to chronic unemployment. Some have slipped into poverty, joining the remaining one-quarter of Britons who are socially and economically deprived. Lower-class people—or the poor—are heavily concentrated in the northern and western regions of the United Kingdom, which are plagued by economic decline.

Today's class system affords the British people some opportunity to move upward or downward. One legacy of the estate system, however, is that social mobility occurs less often in the United Kingdom than in Canada or the United States. Compared with

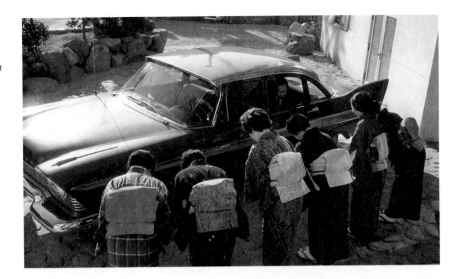

The traditional caste system, with its concern for people's different social rankings, is still evident in Japan today. Here, the women who work at a Japanese inn bow as a sign of respect to a male guest as he departs.

members of our society, therefore, Britons are relatively more resigned to remaining in the social position to which they were born (Snowman, 1977; Kerckhoff et al., 1985).

The greater rigidity of British stratification is exemplified in the importance of accent as a mark of social position. Distinctive patterns of speech develop in any society as people are segregated from one another over time. While people in North America treat accent as a matter of geography (there is little mistaking the Newfoundland lilt or the southern drawl), British accents identify one as a person of high birth (speaking the "Queen's English") or as someone of common ancestry. So different are these two accents that the British seem to be, as the saying goes, a single people divided by a common language, and there is some pressure to change one's accent to meet certain social expectations. For example, politician Margaret Thatcher took speech lessons so that her middle-class accent would sound more "posh," while middle-class Mick Jagger imitated the working-class accents of his bandmates to give him more street credibility.

ANOTHER EXAMPLE: JAPAN

Social stratification in Japan also mixes the traditional and the contemporary. Japan is at once the world's oldest continuously operating monarchy and a modern society in which wealth follows individual achievement.

Feudal Japan

As early as the fifth century B.C.E., Japan was an agrarian society with a rigid caste system composed of nobles and commoners and ruled by an "imperial family." Despite the widespread belief that the emperor ruled by divine right, limited government organization forced the emperor to delegate much authority to a network of regional nobles, or *shoguns*.

Below the nobility stood the *samurai*, or warrior caste. The word *samurai* means "to serve," indicating that this second rank of Japanese society comprised soldiers who cultivated elaborate martial skills and pledged their loyalty to the nobility. To set themselves off from the rest of the commoners, the samurai dressed and behaved according to a traditional code of honour.

As in Great Britain, the majority of people in Japan at this time in history were commoners who laboured to eke out a bare subsistence. Unlike their European counterparts, however, Japanese commoners were not the lowest in rank. The *burakumin*, or "outcasts," stood further down on that country's hierarchy, shunned by lord and commoner alike. Much like the lowest caste groups in India, "outcasts" lived apart from others, engaged in the most distasteful occupations, and, like everyone else, had no opportunity to change their standing.

Japan Today

Important changes in nineteenth-century Japan—industrialization, the growth of cities, and the opening of Japanese society to outside influences—combined to weaken the traditional caste structure. In 1871, the Japanese legally banned the social category of "outcast," although even today people look down on women and men who trace their lineage to this rank. After Japan's defeat in World War II, the nobility, too, lost legal standing, and, as the years have passed, fewer and fewer Japanese accept the notion that their emperor rules by divine right.

Thus, social stratification in contemporary Japan is a far cry from the rigid caste system in force centuries ago. Analysts describe the modern-day Japanese population in terms of social gradations, including "upper," "upper-middle," "lower-middle," and "lower." But since classes have no firm boundaries, they disagree

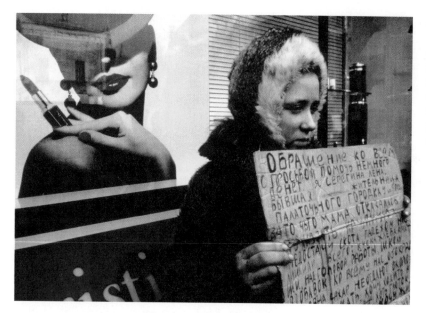

During the last decade, the former Soviet Union has moved towards a market economy. This process has made some people quite wealthy, while others have lost their jobs as old, inefficient factories closed. As a result, the problem of poverty is on the rise. This young woman was photographed begging for money in Moscow's Red Square.

about what proportion of the population falls into each category.

Today's Japanese class system also reveals this nation's fascinating ability to weave together tradition and modernity. Because many Japanese people revere the past, family background is never far from the surface in assessing someone's social standing. Despite legal reforms that assure everyone equal standing before the law and a modern culture that stresses individual achievement, the Japanese continue to perceive one another through the centuries-old lens of caste.

 For more information on Japanese society, visit www.library.pitt.edu/libraries/jic/jic.html

This dynamic mix echoes from the university campus to the corporate boardrooms. The most prestigious universities admit students with outstanding scores on rigorous entrance examinations. Even so, the highest achievers and business leaders in Japan are products of privilege, with noble or *samurai* background. At the other extreme, "outcasts" still live in isolated communities cut off from opportunities to better themselves (Hiroshi, 1974; Norbeck, 1983).

Finally, traditional ideas about gender still shape Japanese society. Despite legal reforms that confer formal equality on the sexes, women are clearly subordinate to men in most important respects. Japanese parents are more likely to push sons than daughters towards university, and the nation thus retains a significant "gender gap" in education (Brinton, 1988). As a consequence, women predominate in lower-level support positions in the corporate world, only rarely assuming leadership roles. In this sense, too, individual achievement in Japan's modern class system operates in the shadow of centuries of traditional privileges.

THE FORMER SOVIET UNION

The former Union of Soviet Socialist Republics (U.S.S.R.), which rivalled the United States as a military superpower through most of the twentieth century, was born out of revolution in 1917. The feudal estate system ruled by a hereditary nobility came to an abrupt end as the Russian Revolution transferred most farms, factories, and other productive property from private ownership to state control.

A Classless Society?

This transformation was guided by the ideas of Karl Marx, who asserted that private ownership of productive property was the basis of social classes (see Chapter 4, "Society"). As the state gained control of the economy, Soviet officials boasted that they had engineered a remarkable achievement: humanity's first classless society.

Analysts outside the Soviet Union were always skeptical about this claim of classlessness (Lane, 1984). The occupations of the people in the former Soviet Union, they pointed out, clustered into a four-level hierarchy. At the top were high government officials, or *apparatchiks*. Next came the Soviet intelligentsia, including lower government officials, university professors, scientists, physicians, and engineers. Below them stood the manual workers and, in the lowest stratum, the rural peasantry.

Since people in each of these categories enjoyed very different living standards—and levels of power— the former Soviet Union was never classless in the sense of having no social inequality. Nonetheless, placing factories, farms, universities, and hospitals under state control did rein in economic inequality to levels below those in capitalist societies such as the United States or Great Britain.

The Second Russian Revolution

After steady efforts to restructure Soviet society following the ideas of Karl Marx (and revolutionary Russian leader Vladimir Lenin), the Soviet Union underwent another sweeping transformation in the 1980s. Economic reforms accelerated when Mikhail Gorbachev came on the scene in 1985. His economic program, popularly known as *perestroika*, meaning "restructuring," sought to solve a dire problem. While the Soviet system had succeeded in minimizing economic inequality, everyone was relatively poor, and living standards lagged far behind those of other industrial nations. Simply put, Gorbachev hoped to stimulate economic expansion by reducing inefficient centralized control of the economy.

Gorbachev's reforms soon escalated into one of the most dramatic social movements in history as popular uprisings toppled one socialist government after another throughout Eastern Europe and, ultimately, brought down the Soviet system itself. In essence, people blamed their economic plight as well as their lack of basic freedoms on a repressive ruling class of Communist party officials.

From the founding of the Soviet Union in 1917 until its demise in 1991, the Communist party retained a monopoly of power, often brutally repressing any opposition. Near the end, 18 million party members (6 percent of the Soviet people) still made all the decisions about Soviet life while enjoying privileges such as vacation homes, chauffeured automobiles, and access to prized consumer goods and elite education for their children (Zaslavsky, 1982; Shipler, 1984; Theen, 1984). The second Soviet revolution, then, mirrors the first in that it was nothing less than the overthrow of the ruling class.

The rise and fall of the Soviet Union demonstrate that social inequality involves more than economic resources. But elite standing in the former Soviet Union was based on power rather than wealth. Though both Mikhail Gorbachev and his successor Boris Yeltsin earned far less than Western leaders, they wielded awesome power. The same may be said of current president Vladimir Putin.

And what about social mobility in the Soviet Union? Evidence indicates that during the past century there was more upward social mobility in the Soviet Union than in Great Britain, Japan, or Canada. Why? For one thing, Soviet society lacked the concentrated wealth that families elsewhere pass from one generation to the next. Even more importantly, industrialization and rapid bureaucratization pushed a large proportion of the working class and rural peasantry upward to occupations in industry and government.

Medieval Europeans accepted rigid social differences as part of a divine plan for the world. This fifteenth-century miniature from a Book of Hours by the Limbourg brothers shows nobles and high church officials well served by soldiers and servants.

Limbourg Brothers (Flemish, d. by 1416), *Les Trés Riches Heures: January.* 21 × 29 cm. By courtesy of The Board of Trustees of the Victoria & Albert Museum, London/Bridgeman Art Library, London/SuperStock.

Recently, however, the people of the Russian federation have experienced downward social mobility. A staggering fact is that, between 1990 and 1997, the average life span for Soviet men tumbled by eight years (two years in the case of women). Many factors are involved—including Russia's poor system of health care—but clearly the Russian people are suffering from a turbulent period of economic change (Róna-Tas, 1994; Specter, 1997a). Sociologists describe such upward and downward trends as **structural social mobility**, *a shift in the social position of large numbers of people owing more to changes in society itself than to individual efforts.* As we shall see in Chapter 11 ("Social Class in Canada"), much of the mobility of our society, too, follows from broad economic changes that took place over the course of the twentieth century.

IDEOLOGY: THE "STAYING POWER" OF STRATIFICATION

Looking around the world at the extent of social inequality, we might wonder how societies persist without distributing their resources more equally. Caste-like systems in Great Britain and Japan lasted for centuries, concentrating land and power in the hands of several hundred families. Even more strikingly, for two thousand years most people in India accepted the idea that they should be privileged or poor because of the accident of birth.

One key reason for the remarkable persistence of social hierarchies is that they are built on **ideology**, *cultural beliefs that serve to justify social stratification.* Any beliefs—for example, the claim that the rich are smart while the poor are lazy—are ideological in that they bolster the dominance of wealthy elites and suggest that the poor deserve their plight.

Plato and Marx on Ideology

The ancient Greek philosopher Plato (427–347 B.C.E.) defined justice as agreement about who should have what. Every society, Plato explained, teaches its members to view some stratification system as "fair." Karl Marx, too, understood this process, although he was far more critical of inequality than Plato was. Marx took capitalist societies to task for channelling wealth and power into the hands of a few, all the while defining the practice as simply "a law of the marketplace." Capitalist law, Marx continued, defines the right to own property as a bedrock principle. Then, laws of inheritance funnel money and privileges from one generation to the next. In short, Marx concluded, ideas as well as resources are controlled by a society's elite, which helps to explain why established hierarchies are so difficult to change.

Both Plato and Marx recognized that ideology is not a simple matter of privileged people conspiring to propound self-serving ideas about social inequality. In fact, ideology usually takes the form of cultural patterns that evolve over long periods of time. While embracing their society's conception of fairness, people may question the rightness of their own position without challenging the system itself.

Historical Patterns of Ideology

The ideas that shore up social stratification change along with a society's economy and technology. Early agrarian societies depended on slaves to perform burdensome manual labour. Aristotle (384–322 B.C.E.) defended the practice of slavery among the ancient Greeks, noting, for example, that some people with little intelligence deserve nothing better than life under the direction of their natural "betters."

Agrarian societies in Europe during the Middle Ages also required the daily farm labour of most people to support the small aristocracy. In this context, noble and serf learned to view occupation as rightfully determined by birth and any person's work as a matter of moral responsibility. In short, caste systems always rest on the assertion that social ranking is the product of a "natural" order.

The rise of industrial capitalism transformed wealth and power into prizes won by those who display the greatest talent and effort. Class systems celebrate individualism and achievement, so that social standing serves as a measure of personal worthiness. Thus, poverty, which called for charity under feudalism, was transformed under industrial capitalism into a scorned state of personal inadequacy. Nowhere was this harsh view more clearly stated than by Herbert Spencer, who applied the evolutionary model of Charles Darwin to the operation of society. That is, Spencer argued that society operates like a jungle, with the "fittest" people rising to wealth and power and the "deficient" gradually sinking to a state of miserable poverty.

Spencer's thinking was extremely popular among the rising industrialists a century ago as the new world of factories reached full speed. John D. Rockefeller (1839–1937), who made a vast fortune building the modern oil industry, often recited Spencer's "social gospel" to young children in Sunday school. As Rockefeller saw it, the growth of giant corporations—and the staggering wealth of their owners—was merely the "survival of the fittest," a basic fact of nature. Neither Spencer nor Rockefeller had any sympathy for the poor, viewing their plight as clear evidence of an inability or unwillingness to measure up in a competitive world.

Throughout human history, most people have regarded social stratification as unshakeable. Especially as traditions weaken, however, people begin to question cultural "truths" and to unmask their political foundations and consequences.

For example, historic notions of a "woman's place" seem far from natural today and are losing their power to deprive women of opportunities. For the present, however, the contemporary class system still subjects women to caste-like expectations that they perform traditional tasks out of altruism while men are financially rewarded for their efforts. To illustrate, most chefs are men who work for income, while most household cooks are women who perform this role as a household duty.

Yet, while gender differences persist in countries such as Canada, there is little doubt that women and men are becoming steadily more equal in important respects. (See the "Applying Sociology" box for a discussion of this change.) The continuing struggle for racial equality in South Africa also exemplifies widespread rejection of apartheid, which for decades shaped economic, political, and educational life in that nation. Apartheid, never widely accepted by Blacks, has lost its

How Wealthy Are the World's Richest Women?

Women have been gradually moving into occupations that were traditionally almost entirely male, in medicine, academia, and business. Women are increasingly entrepreneurial—in Germany, 60 percent of all businesses are owned by women—and moving in greater numbers into the boardroom and the CEO office of small and major corporations. Some of these women are now in control of immense wealth.

Kevin Cahill, wealth editor of *EuroBusiness Magazine*, compiled a list of the world's wealthiest women. Among the ten richest, nine inherited their wealth from fathers and husbands, but among the rest there are many who acquired their wealth on their own. Cahill foresees that over the next twenty years, women will increasingly be assuming executive roles:

> For most of the past century, there's clearly been a glass ceiling where females are shareholders, but men have very specifically kept them out. The fellas have held the executive roles, the chairmanships on behalf of their wives. I think that's going to die. Women are being treated as equals just as they should have been. (quoted in O'Reilly, 2000)

Interestingly, in Europe, the wealthy women tend to be in the retail business, whereas in Britain and the United States they excel in the media. The leading women in entertainment—Oprah Winfrey, Madonna, and Barbra Streisand—are all American.

The point is that a mere decade ago, Kevin Cahill would have compiled no such list. Since then, at least in the industrialized world, women have been achieving their *own* positions throughout the stratification hierarchy—rather than acquiring status through their fathers and husbands.

Source: Based on O'Reilly (2000).

TABLE 10–1 The World's Wealthiest Women

Five Wealthiest Women

1. Helen Walton (Wal-Mart), $64.9 billion* (USA)
2. Liliane Bettencourt (l'Oréal), $20.2 billion (France)
3. Barbara Anthony (Cox Enterprises), $13.37 billion (USA)
4. Alice Walton (Wal-Mart), $13.2 billion (USA)
5. Anne Chambers (Cox Enterprises), $12.8 billion (USA)

Others of Interest

Queen Elizabeth II, $4.4 billion (UK) #19 overall
Melinda Gates, $3.18 billion (USA) #29 overall
India James, $848 million (UK) #175 overall
Imelda Marcos, $1.1 billion (Philippines) #132 overall
Miuccia Prada, $3.1 billion (Italy) #30 overall

Wealthiest Female Entertainers

1. Oprah Winfrey, $1.15 billion
2. Madonna, $915 million
3. Barbra Streisand, $816.5 million
4. Nancy Sinatra, $795.4 million

Wealthiest Media Women

1. Barbara Anthony, $13.37 billion (USA)
2. Anne Chambers, $12.8 billion (USA)
3. Friede Springer, $11.7 billion (Germany)
4. Annielesco Brost, $3.3 billion (Germany)

Only Canadian

Lesley Thomson, $959.5 million, #159 overall and #23 out of 26 in media category

*All dollar figures are Canadian.

Source: *EuroBusiness Magazine* (July 10, 2000).

---

support as a "natural" system among whites who reject ideological racism (Friedrich, 1987; Contreras, 1992).

THE FUNCTIONS OF SOCIAL STRATIFICATION

Why are societies stratified at all? One answer, consistent with the structural-functional paradigm, is that social inequality plays a vital part in the operation of society. This influential—and controversial—argument was set forth some fifty years ago by Kingsley Davis and Wilbert Moore (1945).

THE DAVIS-MOORE THESIS

The **Davis-Moore thesis** is *the assertion that social stratification has beneficial consequences for the operation of a society*. How else, ask Davis and Moore, can we explain

CONTROVERSY & DEBATE

Salaries: Are the Rich Worth What They Earn?

For an hour of work, a Canadian child-care worker earns about $6, a police officer earns about $27, a miner earns about $28, a veterinarian earns about $32. The average worker—and even the prime minister and other high government officials—earns a salary that pales in comparison with those of popular athletes and entertainers.

In the United States, Barry Bonds garners about $40 000 per hour playing baseball for the San Francisco Giants. And what about the $100 000 Jim Carrey makes for every hour he spends making movies? Bill Cosby commands about $100 000 per hour to take the stage, and Oprah Winfrey earns about $200 000 for each hour she chats with guests before the television cameras. Mel Gibson landed a $25 million salary for filming *The Patriot*, and at the start of the 2003 TV season, the six actors in *Friends* were being paid $1.2 million

(U.S.) per episode (plus a percentage of profits). Many Canadians—among them Jim Carrey, Michael J. Fox, Mike Myers, Wayne Gretzky, Pamela Anderson, and William Shatner—have gone to the United States in search of greater opportunity and remuneration.

According to the Davis-Moore thesis, rewards reflect an occupation's value to society. But are the talents of Julia Louis-Dreyfus, who earned about $13 million a year as a sidekick on *Seinfeld*, worth almost as much as the efforts of all one hundred U.S. senators (who, unlike Canada's, are elected and accountable to their constituencies)? When Roger Clemens played for the Toronto Blue Jays, was he worth as much as thirty-five or forty of Canada's physicians or surgeons? In short, do earnings reflect the social importance of work?

Salaries in industrial-capitalist societies such as Canada are a product of

market forces. Defenders of the laws of supply and demand claim that the market impartially evaluates worth, rewarding each worker according to the supply of the talent in question and the public demand for it. According to this view, movie and television stars, top athletes, skilled professionals, and many business executives have rare talents that are much in demand; thus, they may earn hundreds of times more than the typical worker. Executive salaries in Canada in 2002 included $52 million to Frank Stronach of Magna Corporation, $12.5 million to Belinda Stronach of Magna, and $17 million to Travis Engen of Alcan (*Report on Business*, 2003:147). Are these and other Canadian CEOs really worth mega-million-dollar incomes?

Some critics claim that the market is not a good evaluator of occupational importance. Critics maintain that the economy is dominated by a small proportion of people who manipulate the

the fact that some form of social stratification has been found everywhere?

Davis and Moore describe our society as a complex system involving hundreds of occupational positions of varying importance. Certain jobs—say, changing spark plugs in a car—are fairly easy and can be performed by almost anyone. Other jobs—such as transplanting a human organ—are quite difficult and demand the scarce talents of people who have received extensive (and expensive) education. Positions of high day-to-day responsibility that demand special abilities are the most functionally significant.

In general, Davis and Moore explain, the greater the functional importance of a position, the more rewards a society offers. This strategy pays off, since rewarding important work with income, prestige, power, and leisure encourages people to enter these occupations. By distributing resources unequally, a society motivates each person to aspire to the most significant work possible, and to work better, harder, and longer. The overall effect of a system of unequal rewards—which is what social stratification amounts to—is a more productive society.

Davis and Moore concede that every society could be egalitarian. But, they caution, rewards can be equal only to the extent that people are willing to let anyone perform any job. Equality also demands that someone who carries out a job poorly be rewarded on a par with another who performs well. Logic dictates that such a system offers little incentive for people to make their best efforts, and thereby reduces a society's productive efficiency.

The Davis-Moore thesis points out why some form of stratification exists everywhere, but it does not endorse any *particular* system of inequality. Nor do Davis and Moore specify precisely what reward should be attached to any occupational position. They merely point out that positions a society deems crucial must yield sufficient rewards to draw talent.

MERITOCRACY

The Davis-Moore thesis implies that a productive society is a **meritocracy**, *a system of social stratification based on personal merit*. Such societies hold out rewards to develop the talents and encourage the efforts of system for their own benefit. In Canada, thirty-two of our wealthiest families play "monopoly with the money of average Canadians" (Francis, 1986). In 2003, forty-six of Canada's CEOs were compensated to the tune of $5 million to $52 million (*Report on Business*, 2003).

Corporate executives pay themselves multimillion-dollar salaries and bonuses whether their companies do well or not. Gilbert Amelio, CEO of Apple Computer, laid off more than 4000 employees during 1996 and his company's stock price tumbled by almost 40 percent, yet he still paid himself more than $23 million for his efforts. In Canada, Paul Stern of Northern Telecom Ltd. (now Nortel) was to have earned $5 million in 1992, despite serious mismanagement. His departure from the company, under a cloud, sent stock prices tumbling by almost 30 percent (Surtees, 1993). As noted by Newman (1996:183), these were "monumental pay-packets that had little connection with the success or failure of their enterprises."

A second problem with the idea that the market measures people's contributions to society is that many who make clear and significant contributions receive surprisingly little money. Tens of thousands of teachers, counsellors, and health-care workers enhance the welfare of others every day for little salary. The average teacher would have to work more than a thousand years to earn what Amelio received in one year.

Using salary to measure social worth only works to the extent that market forces actually gauge one's societal contribution. Some people view market forces as the most accurate measure of occupational worth; others contend that lucrative activities may or may not be socially valuable. Thus, the market system remains controversial.

Céline Dion is a multimillionaire who may earn as much as $85 million (U.S.) for her three-year concert deal in Las Vegas.

everyone. In pursuit of meritocracy, a society promotes equality of opportunity while, at the same time, mandating inequality of rewards. In other words, a pure class system would be a meritocracy, since it rewards everyone based on ability and effort. Such a society would have extensive social mobility, blurring social categories as individuals moved up or down in the social system depending on their performance.

To the extent that caste societies speak of "merit" (from Latin, meaning "worthy of praise"), they mean dutiful persistence in low-skill labour such as farming. Caste systems, in short, offer honour to those who remain "in their place."

Although caste systems waste human potential, they are quite orderly. And herein lies a clue to an important question: Why do modern industrial societies resist becoming pure meritocracies by retaining many caste-like qualities? Simply because, left unchecked, meritocracy erodes social structure such as kinship. No one, for example, evaluates family members solely on the basis of performance. Class systems in industrial societies, therefore, retain some caste elements to promote order and social cohesion.

Critical evaluation. By investigating the functions of social stratification, Davis and Moore made a lasting contribution to sociological analysis. Even so, critics point to several flaws in their thesis. Melvin Tumin (1953) wonders, first, whether functional importance really explains the high rewards that some people enjoy. Can one even measure functional importance? Perhaps, he suggests, the high rewards our society accords to physicians at least partly result from deliberate efforts by medical schools to limit the supply of physicians and increase the demand for their services.

If so, income and other rewards may have little to do with an individual's functional contribution to society. Before his retirement, Wayne Gretzky's hockey contract alone (apart from income earned through product endorsements) gave him twenty-one times the income of the prime minister, who earned a salary of $134 000 in 1996. What about the $65 million income reported for Céline Dion in 1997? Would anyone argue that, in societal significance, playing hockey or singing tops the responsibilities of the prime minister? The "Controversy & Debate" box takes a critical look at the link between pay and societal importance.

A second charge made by Tumin is that the Davis-Moore thesis exaggerates social stratification's role in developing individual talent. Our society does reward individual achievement, but we also allow families to transfer wealth and power from generation to generation in caste-like fashion. Additionally, for women, people of colour, and others with limited opportunities, stratification still raises barriers to personal accomplishment. In practice, Tumin concludes, social stratification functions to develop some people's abilities to the fullest while barring others from ever reaching their potential.

 Do corporate CEOs deserve their high salaries? The AFL-CIO offers a critical view at www.aflcio.org/corporateamerica/paywatch/

By contending that social stratification benefits all of society, the Davis-Moore thesis ignores how social inequality promotes conflict and even outright revolution. This assertion leads us to the social-conflict paradigm, which provides a very different explanation for the persistence of social hierarchy.

STRATIFICATION AND CONFLICT

Social-conflict analysis argues that rather than benefiting society as a whole, social stratification provides advantages to some people at the expense of others. This theoretical perspective draws heavily on the ideas of Karl Marx; additional contributions are drawn from Max Weber.

KARL MARX: CLASS AND CONFLICT

Karl Marx, whose approach to understanding social inequality is detailed in Chapter 4 ("Society"), identified two major social classes corresponding to the two basic relationships to the means of production: individuals either (1) own productive property or (2) labour for others. In medieval Europe, the nobility and the church owned the productive land; peasants toiled as farmers. Similarly, in industrial class systems, the capitalists (or the bourgeoisie) control factories, which depend on the labour of workers (the proletariat).

Marx noted great disparities in wealth and power arising from the industrial-capitalist productive system, which, he contended, made class conflict inevitable. In time, he believed, oppression and misery would drive the working majority to organize and ultimately to overthrow capitalism.

Marx's analysis was grounded in his observations of capitalism in the nineteenth century, when great industrialists dominated the economic scene. Andrew Carnegie, J.P. Morgan, and John Jacob Astor (one of the few very rich passengers to perish on the *Titanic*) lived in mansions filled with priceless art and staffed by dozens of servants. Their fortunes were staggering: Andrew Carnegie reportedly earned more than $20 million a year as the twentieth century began (worth close to $100 million in today's dollars)—at a time when wages paid to the average worker totalled roughly $500 a year (Baltzell, 1964; Pessen, 1990).

According to Marx, the capitalist elite draws its strength from more than the operation of the economy. Through the family, opportunity and wealth are passed down from generation to generation, while the legal system defends this practice through inheritance law. Also, exclusive schools bring children of the elite together, encouraging informal social ties that will benefit them throughout their lives. Overall, from Marx's point of view, capitalist society *reproduces the class structure in each new generation*.

Critical evaluation. Exploring how the capitalist economic system generates conflict between classes, Marx's analysis of social stratification has had enormous influence on sociological thinking in recent decades. Because it is revolutionary—calling for the overthrow of capitalist society—Marxism is also highly controversial.

One of the strongest criticisms of the Marxist approach is that it denies one of the central tenets of the Davis-Moore thesis: that motivating people to perform various social roles requires some system of unequal rewards. Marx separated rewards from performance, endorsing an egalitarian system based on the principle of "from each according to his abilities; to each according to his needs" (Marx and Engels, 1972:388; orig. 1848). Critics argue that severing rewards from performance is precisely the flaw that generated the low productivity characteristic of the former Soviet Union and other socialist economies around the world.

Defenders of Marx rebut this line of attack by pointing to considerable evidence supporting Marx's general view of humanity as inherently social rather than unflinchingly selfish (Clark, 1991; Fiske, 1991). They counter that we should not assume that individual rewards (much less monetary compensation alone) are the only way to motivate people.

In addition, although few doubt that capitalist society does perpetuate poverty and privilege as Marx asserted, the revolutionary developments he considered inevitable have failed to materialize. The next section explores why the socialist revolution Marx predicted and promoted has not occurred, at least in advanced capitalist societies.

WHY NO MARXIST REVOLUTION?

Despite Marx's prediction, capitalism is still thriving. Why have workers in Canada, the United States, and other industrial societies not overthrown capitalism? Ralf Dahrendorf (1959) pointed to four reasons.

1. **The fragmentation of the capitalist class.** First, the century since Marx's death has witnessed the fragmentation of the capitalist class in North America. A century ago, *single families* typically

owned large companies; today, *numerous stockholders* have assumed much of that ownership. Moreover, day-to-day operation of large corporations is now in the hands of a large managerial class, who may or may not be major stockholders. With stock more widely held, an increasing number of people have a direct stake in preserving the capitalist system (Wright et al., 1992; Wright, 1985). After all, most of our pension funds are invested in the stock market.

2. **A rising standard of living.** As Chapter 16 ("The Economy and Work") details, a century ago most workers laboured either on farms or in factories performing **blue-collar occupations**, *lower-prestige jobs involving mostly manual labour.* By contrast, most workers today hold **white-collar occupations**, *higher-prestige work involving mostly mental activity.* These occupations include positions in sales, management, and other service work, frequently in large, bureaucratic organizations.

   While many of today's white-collar workers perform repetitive tasks, most do not think of themselves as an "industrial proletariat." Just as important, workers' overall standard of living in North America rose fourfold over the course of the twentieth century in dollars controlled for inflation, even as the work week decreased. Is it any wonder, then, that most white-collar workers now perceive their social positions as higher than those of their blue-collar parents and grandparents? This structural mobility has cooled revolutionary aspirations among working people (Edwards, 1979; Gagliani, 1981; Wright and Martin, 1987).

3. **More extensive worker organization.** Employees have organizational strengths they lacked a century ago. Workers have won the right to organize into labour unions that can and do make demands of management backed by threats of work slowdowns and strikes. If not always peaceful, then, worker-management disputes are now institutionalized.

4. **More extensive legal protections.** During the twentieth century, the government extended laws to make the workplace safer and devised programs, such as employment insurance, disability protection, and social security, to provide workers with greater financial security.

   Taken together, these four developments mean that, despite persistent stratification, our society has smoothed out many of capitalism's rough edges.

A Counterpoint

Advocates of social-conflict analysis, however, counter that Marx's analysis of capitalism is still largely valid (Matthews, 1983; Brym, 1985; Smith, 1987; Clement, 1990; Wotherspoon and Satzewich, 1993). They offer this counterpoint:

1. **Wealth remains highly concentrated.** As Marx contended, wealth remains in the hands of the few. By the mid-1980s, Canada had six billionaire families, and another twenty-two worth $100 million or more, who control an inordinate amount of Canada's wealth (Francis, 1986). By 2003, Canada's Kenneth Thomson and his family ranked number 13 on *Forbes* magazine's list of the world's wealthiest people with an estimated worth of more than $14 billion (U.S.) (Forbes, 2003). In particular, the concentration of wealth and ownership of newspapers and cable TV (plus *Maclean's* magazine) by the Asper and Rogers families is a source of tremendous concern to critics of capitalist industrial society.

2. **White-collar work offers little to workers.** As contemporary Marxists see it, the white-collar revolution delivered little in the way of higher income or better working conditions over the factory jobs of a century ago. On the contrary, much white-collar work remains monotonous and routine, especially the low-level clerical jobs commonly held by women.

3. **Progress requires struggle.** Labour organizations may have advanced the interests of the workers over the last half-century, but regular negotiation between workers and management hardly signals the end of social conflict. In fact, many of the concessions won by workers came about precisely through the class conflict Marx described. Moreover, workers still strive to gain concessions from capitalists and struggle to hold on to the advances already achieved.

4. **The law still favours the rich.** Workers have gained some legal protections over the course of the past century. Even so, the law still defends the overall distribution of wealth in Canada and the United States. Just as importantly, "average" people cannot use the legal system to the same advantage as do the rich.

In sum, according to social-conflict theory, the fact that no socialist revolution has taken place in Canada or the United States hardly invalidates Marx's analysis of capitalism. As we shall see in Chapter 11 ("Social Class in Canada"), pronounced social inequality persists, as does social conflict—albeit less overtly and violently than in the nineteenth century.

Finally, some defenders of capitalism cite the collapse of communist regimes in Eastern Europe and the former Soviet Union as proof of the superiority of capitalism over socialism. Most analysts agree that socialism failed to meet the needs of the people it

TABLE 10–2 Two Explanations of Social Stratification: A Summary

Structural-Functional Paradigm	Social-Conflict Paradigm
Social stratification keeps society operating. The linkage of greater rewards to more important social positions benefits society as a whole.	Social stratification is the result of social conflict. Differences in social resources serve the interests of some and harm the interests of others.
Social stratification encourages a matching of talents and abilities to appropriate positions.	Social stratification ensures that much talent and ability within society will not be used at all.
Social stratification is both useful and inevitable.	Social stratification is useful to only some people; it is not inevitable.
The values and beliefs that legitimize social inequality are widely shared throughout society.	Values and beliefs tend to be ideological; they reflect the interests of the more powerful members of society.
Because systems of social stratification are useful to society as a whole and are supported by cultural values and beliefs, they are usually stable over time.	Because systems of social stratification reflect the interests of only part of the society, they are unlikely to remain stable over time.

Source: Adapted in part from Stinchcombe (October 1963):808.

purported to serve, either in terms of raising living standards or ensuring personal freedoms. But, to be fair, socialism's failings do not excuse flaws in capitalism. Many critics maintain that capitalism in North America has yet to demonstrate its ability to address problems of public education and desperate poverty, especially among the urban underclass (Uchitelle, 1991). Table 10–2 summarizes the contributions of the two contrasting sociological approaches to understanding social stratification.

MAX WEBER: CLASS, STATUS, AND POWER

Max Weber, whose approach to social analysis is described in Chapter 4 ("Society"), agreed with Karl Marx that social stratification sparks social conflict, but he thought Marx's two-class model was simplistic. Instead, he viewed social stratification as a more complex interplay of three distinct dimensions.

Weber took note of economic inequality—the issue so vital to Marx—which he termed *class position*. Weber's use of "class" refers not to crude categories but to a continuum on which anyone can be ranked from high to low. He also highlighted *status*, or social prestige, and emphasized the importance of *power* in a social hierarchy.

The Socioeconomic Status Hierarchy

Marx believed that social prestige and power derived from economic position; thus, he saw no reason to treat them as distinct dimensions of social inequality. Weber disagreed, recognizing that status consistency in modern societies is often quite low: a local government official, say, might wield considerable power, yet have little wealth or social prestige.

Weber's key contribution in this area, then, lies in showing that social stratification in industrial societies resembles a multidimensional ranking rather than clearly defined classes. Following Weber's thinking, sociologists often use the term **socioeconomic status (SES)** to refer to *a composite ranking based on various dimensions of social inequality*.

A population that varies widely in class, status, and power—Weber's three dimensions of inequality—creates a virtually infinite array of social categories, all of which pursue their own interests. Thus, unlike Marx, who focused on conflict between two distinct classes, Weber considered social conflict highly variable and complex.

Inequality in History

Weber also made a key historical observation, noting that each of his three dimensions of social inequality stands out at different points in the evolution of human societies. Agrarian societies, he maintained, emphasize status or social prestige, typically in the form of honour or symbolic purity. Members of these societies gain such status by conforming to cultural norms corresponding to their rank.

Industrialization and the development of capitalism level traditional rankings based on birth but generate striking material differences in the population. Thus, Weber argued, the crucial difference among people in industrial-capitalist societies lies in the economic dimension of class.

In time, industrial societies witness a surging growth of the bureaucratic state. This expansion of government, coupled with the proliferation of other types of formal organizations, means power gains importance in the stratification system. Power is also central to the organization of socialist societies, evident in their extensive government regulation of many aspects of life. The elite members of such societies are mostly high-ranking officials rather than rich people.

This historical analysis underlies a final disagreement between Weber and Marx. Looking to the future, Marx believed that social stratification could be largely eliminated by abolishing private ownership of productive property. Weber doubted that overthrowing capitalism would significantly diminish social stratification. It might lessen economic disparity, Weber reasoned, but socialism would simultaneously increase social inequality by expanding government and concentrating power in the hands of a political elite. Recent popular uprisings against entrenched bureaucracies in Eastern Europe and the former Soviet Union lend support to Weber's argument.

Critical evaluation. Weber's multidimensional analysis of social stratification retains enormous influence among sociologists. Some analysts (particularly those influenced by Marx's ideas) argue that while social class boundaries have blurred, striking patterns of social inequality persist in North America and elsewhere in the industrial world.

STRATIFICATION AND TECHNOLOGY IN GLOBAL PERSPECTIVE

We can weave together a number of observations made in this chapter by considering the relationship between a society's technology and its type of social stratification. This analysis draws on Gerhard Lenski and Jean Lenski's model of sociocultural evolution, detailed in Chapter 4 ("Society").

HUNTING-AND-GATHERING SOCIETIES

Simple technology limits the production of hunting-and-gathering societies to only what is necessary for day-to-day living. Although some individuals produce more than others, the group's survival depends on all sharing what they have. Thus, no categories of people emerge as better off than others. Until quite recently, this would have been an accurate description of stratification among the majority of Inuit communities across northern Canada.

HORTICULTURAL, PASTORAL, AND AGRARIAN SOCIETIES

Technological advances generate surplus production, while intensifying social inequality. In horticultural and pastoral societies, a small elite controls most of the surplus. Large-scale agriculture generates even greater abundance, but marked inequality—as great as any time in history—means various categories of people lead strikingly different lives. Agrarian nobility wield godlike power over the masses.

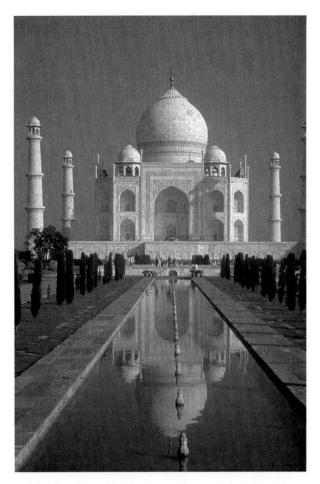

The extent of social inequality in agrarian systems is greater than that found in industrial society. One indication of the unchallenged power of rulers is the monumental structures built over years with the unpaid labour of common people. Although the Taj Mahal in India is among the world's most beautiful buildings, it is merely a tomb for a single individual—the Mughal Empress Mumtaz Mahal.

INDUSTRIAL SOCIETIES

Industrialization reverses the historical trend, nudging social inequality downward. Prompted by the need to develop individual talents, caste rankings gradually erode in favour of greater individual opportunity. Then, too, the increasing productivity of industrial technology steadily raises the living standards of the historically poor majority. Specialized work also demands the expansion of schooling, sharply reducing illiteracy. A literate population, in turn, tends to press for a greater voice in political decision making, further diminishing social inequality and reducing the domination of women by men.

The net effect is that, over time, even wealth becomes somewhat less concentrated (countering the trend predicted by Marx). Estimates suggest that the

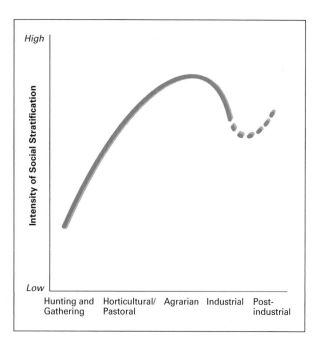

FIGURE 10–1 Social Stratification and Technological Development: The Kuznets Curve

The Kuznets curve reveals that greater technological sophistication is generally accompanied by more pronounced social stratification. The trend reverses itself, however, as industrial societies gradually become more egalitarian. Rigid caste-like distinctions are relaxed in favour of greater opportunity and equality under the law. Political rights are more widely extended, and there is even some levelling of economic differences. The Kuznets curve may also be usefully applied to the relative social standing of the two sexes.

Source: Created by John Macionis, based on Kuznets (1955).

proportion of all wealth controlled by the richest 1 percent of U.S. families peaked at about 36 percent just before the stock market crash in 1929, falling to about 30 percent by 1990 (Williamson and Lindert, 1980; Beeghley, 1989; *1991 Green Book*). Although, at one time, Canada appeared to have more billionaire families per capita than the United States—six compared to twelve (Francis, 1986)[1]—it is likely that our overall pattern in control of wealth is very similar to that of the United States.

THE KUZNETS CURVE

The trend described above can be distilled into the following statement: *in human history, technological progress first increases but then moderates the intensity of*

---

[1]By 1996 the number of billionaire families in Canada had increased to eight, according to *Financial Post Magazine* (Hamilton, 1996).

social stratification. So if greater inequality is functional for agrarian societies, then industrial societies benefit from a more egalitarian climate. This historical shift, recognized by Nobel Prize–winning economist Simon Kuznets (1955, 1966), is illustrated by the Kuznets curve, shown in Figure 10–1.

Current patterns of social inequality around the world generally square with the Kuznets curve. As shown in Global Map 10–1, industrial societies have somewhat less income inequality—one important measure of social stratification—than nations that remain predominantly agrarian. Specifically, mature industrial societies such as Canada, the United States, and the nations of Western Europe exhibit less income inequality than the less industrialized countries of Latin America, Africa, and Asia.

Yet income disparity reflects a host of factors beyond technology, especially political and economic priorities. Societies that have had socialist economic systems (including the People's Republic of China, the former Soviet Union, and the nations of Eastern Europe) display relatively little income inequality. Keep in mind, however, that an egalitarian society such as the People's Republic of China has an average income level that is quite low by world standards; further, on noneconomic dimensions such as political power, China's society reveals pronounced inequality.

And what of the future? We have extended the trend described by Kuznets (the broken line), showing an upturn in the intensity of inequality corresponding to the post-industrial era; as the Information Revolution has begun transforming Canada, we have experienced rising economic polarization (highlighted in the next chapter). In sum, the long-term pattern may diverge from that observed by Kuznets almost half a century ago (Nielsen and Alderson, 1997).

SOCIAL STRATIFICATION: FACTS AND VALUES

> The year was 2081 and everybody was finally equal. They weren't only equal before God and the law. They were equal every which way. Nobody was smarter than anybody else. Nobody was better looking than anybody else. Nobody was stronger or quicker than anybody else. All this equality was due to the 211th, 212th, and 213th Amendments to the Constitution and the unceasing vigilance of agents of the Handicapper General.

With these words, novelist Kurt Vonnegut, Jr. (1968; orig. 1961) begins the story "Harrison Bergeron," an imaginary account of a future United States in which social inequality has been totally abolished. While some people find equality appealing in principle, Vonnegut warns that it can be dangerous in practice. He describes a nightmare of social engi-

GLOBAL MAPS: WINDOW ON THE WORLD

GLOBAL MAP 10–1 Income Disparity in Global Perspective

Societies throughout the world differ in the rigidity and intensity of social stratification, as well as in overall standard of living. This map highlights income inequality. Generally speaking, countries that have had centralized, socialist economies (including the People's Republic of China, the former Soviet Union, and Cuba) display the least income inequality, although their standard of living is relatively low. Industrial societies with predominantly capitalist economies, including Canada, the United States, and most of Western Europe, have higher overall living standards, accompanied by severe income disparity. The low-income countries of Latin America and Africa (including Mexico, Brazil, and the Democratic Republic of the Congo), as well as the Russian Federation, exhibit the most pronounced inequality of income.

Source: *Peters Atlas of the World* (1990); updates by John Macionis from the United Nations Development Programme (1999).

neering in which every individual talent that makes one person different from another has been systematically neutralized by high-handed government agents.

To neutralize differences that make one person "better" than another, the state mandates that physically attractive people wear masks that render them average looking, that intelligent people don earphones that generate distracting noise, and that the legs of the best athletes and dancers be precisely fitted with weights to make their movements just as cumbersome as everyone else's. While we may imagine that social equality would liberate people to make the most of their talents, Vonnegut concludes that a truly egalitarian society could exist only by reducing everyone to a lowest common denominator.

CHAPTER 10 Social Stratification **253**

The Bell Curve Debate: Are Rich People Really Smarter?

It is rare that the publication of a new book in the social sciences captures the attention of the public at large. But *The Bell Curve: Intelligence and Class Structure in American Life* by Richard J. Herrnstein and Charles Murray (1994) did that and more, igniting a firestorm of controversy over why pronounced social stratification divides U.S. society and what to do about it. Note that had Herrnstein and Murray written about Canada, they would have reached very similar conclusions.

The Bell Curve is an 800-page book that addresses many critical issues and resists simple summary. But its basic thesis is captured in the following propositions:

1. There exists something we can describe as "general intelligence"; people with more of it tend to be more successful in their careers than those with less of it.

2. At least half the variation in human intelligence (Herrnstein and Murray use figures of 60 to 70 percent) is transmitted genetically from one generation to another; the remaining variability is due to environmental factors.

3. Over the course of the twentieth century—and especially since the Information Revolution— intelligence has become more necessary to the performance of our society's top occupational positions.

4. Simultaneously, the best U.S. colleges and universities have shifted their admissions policies away from favouring children of inherited wealth to admitting young people who perform best on standardized tests such as the Scholastic Aptitude Test (SAT), American College Testing Program (ACT), and Graduate Record Examination (GRE).

5. As a result of these changes in the workplace and higher education, U.S. society is now coming to be dominated by a "cognitive elite," who are, on average, not only better trained than most people but actually more intelligent.

6. Because more intelligent people are socially segregated on the college campus and in the workplace, it is no surprise that they tend to pair up, marry, and have intelligent children, perpetuating the "cognitive elite."

7. Near the bottom of the social ladder, a similar process is at work. Increasingly, poor people are individuals with lower intelligence, who live segregated from others and who tend to pass along their modest abilities to their children.

Resting on the validity of the seven assertions presented above, Herrnstein and Murray then offer, as an eighth point, a basic approach to public policy:

8. To the extent that membership in the affluent elite or the impoverished underclass is rooted in intelligence and determined mostly by genetic inheritance, programs to assist underprivileged people will have few practical benefits.

This chapter's explanations of social stratification also involve value judgments. The Davis-Moore thesis, which finds social stratification universal, interprets this pattern as evidence that inequality is a necessary element of social organization. Class differences, then, reflect both variation in human abilities and the importance of occupational roles. From this point of view, the spectre of equality is a threat to a society of diverse people, since such uniformity could exist only as the product of the relentless and stifling efforts of officials like Vonnegut's fictitious Handicapper General.

Social-conflict analysis, advocated by Karl Marx, interprets universal social inequality very differently. Rejecting the notion that inequality is necessary, Marx condemned social hierarchy as a product of greed. Guided by egalitarian values, he advocated social arrangements that would enable everyone to share important resources equally.

The "Controversy & Debate" box addresses the link between intelligence and social class. This issue— also a mix of facts and values—is among the most troublesome in social science, not only because it is difficult to define and measure "intelligence," but also because the idea that elites are inherently "better" than others challenges our democratic culture.

The next chapter ("Social Class in Canada") takes a close look at inequality in our own society. But, here again, even people who agree on the basic facts often interpret them quite differently. This lesson is repeated in Chapter 12 ("Global Stratification"), which examines inequality among the world's nations and offers two opposing explanations for it. Thus, the study of social stratification involves a complex, ongoing debate that yields no single or simple truth.

Within weeks of the book's publication, analysts pro and con were squaring off on television news shows, including *Nightline*, and trading charges across the pages of practically every U.S. news magazine. Most social scientists tended to side with *The Bell Curve's* critics. In response to the book's thesis, critics first questioned exactly what is meant by "intelligence," arguing that people's innate abilities can hardly be separated from the effects of socialization. Intelligence tests, they continue, don't measure cognitive *ability;* they measure certain kinds of cognitive *performance*. And we might well expect rich children to perform better on intelligence tests, since they have had the best schooling. Some critics dismiss the concept of "intelligence" outright as phony science. At the very least, we should not think of "intelligence" as a cause of achievement since research indicates that mental abilities and life experiences are *interactive*, each affecting the other.

In addition, while most researchers who study intelligence agree that genetics does play a part in transmitting intelligence, the consensus is that no more than 25 to 40 percent is inherited—only about half what Herrnstein and Murray claim. Therefore, critics conclude, *The Bell Curve* misleads readers into thinking that social elitism is both natural and inevitable. In its assumptions and conclusions, moreover, *The Bell Curve* amounts to little more than a rehash of the social Darwinism popular a century ago, which heralded the success of industrial tycoons as merely "the survival of the fittest."

Perhaps, as one commentator noted, the more society seems like a jungle, the more people think of stratification as a matter of blood rather than upbringing. But, despite its flaws and exaggerations, the book's success suggests that *The Bell Curve* raises many issues we cannot easily ignore. Can democratic systems tolerate the "dangerous knowledge" that elites (including not only rich people but also our political leaders) are at least somewhat more intelligent than the rest of us? What of *The Bell Curve's* description that our society's elites are increasingly insulating themselves from social problems, including crime, homelessness, and poor schools? As such problems have become worse in recent years, how do we counter the easy explanation that poor people are hobbled by their own limited ability? And, most basically, what should be done to ensure that all people have the opportunity to develop their abilities as fully as possible?

Continue the debate . . .

1. *Do you agree that "general intelligence" exists? Why or why not?*

2. *In general, do you think that people of higher social position are more intelligent than those of lower social position? If you think intelligence differs by social standing, which factor is cause and which is effect?*

3. *Do you think sociologists should study controversial issues such as differences in human intelligence? Why or why not?*

Sources: Herrnstein and Murray (1994), Jacoby and Glauberman (1995), and Kohn (1996).

SUMMARY

1. Social stratification refers to categories of people ranked in a hierarchy. Stratification is (1) characteristic of society, not something that merely arises from individual differences; (2) persistent over many generations; (3) universal, yet variable in form; and (4) supported by cultural beliefs.

2. Caste systems, typical of agrarian societies, are based on ascription and permit little or no social mobility. Caste hierarchy, which is supported by strong moral beliefs, shapes a person's entire life, including occupation and marriage.

3. Class systems, common to industrial societies, reflect a greater measure of individual achievement. Because the emphasis on achievement opens the way for social mobility, classes are less clearly defined than castes.

4. Historically, socialist societies have claimed to be classless, based on their public ownership of productive property. While such societies may exhibit far less economic inequality than their capitalist counterparts, they are notably stratified with regard to power.

5. Social stratification persists owing to support from various social institutions and the power of ideology to define certain kinds of inequality as both natural and just.

6. The Davis-Moore thesis states that social stratification is universal because it contributes to the operation of society. In class systems, unequal rewards motivate people to aspire to the occupational roles most important for society.

7. Critics of the Davis-Moore thesis note that (1) it is difficult to assess objectively the functional importance of any occupational position; (2) stratification prevents many people from developing their abilities; and (3) social stratification often generates social conflict—benefiting some at the expense of others.

8. Karl Marx, a key architect of social-conflict analysis, recognized two major social classes in industrial societies. The capitalists, or bourgeoisie, own the means of production in pursuit of profits; the proletariat, in contrast, offer their labour in exchange for wages.

9. The socialist revolution that Marx predicted has not occurred in industrial societies such as Canada and the United States. Some sociologists see this fact as evidence that Marx's analysis was flawed.

10. Max Weber identified three dimensions of social inequality: economic class, social status or prestige, and power. Taken together, they form a complex hierarchy of socioeconomic standing.

11. Gerhard Lenski and Jean Lenski explained that, historically, technological advances have been associated with more pronounced social stratification. A reversal of this trend occurs in advanced, industrial societies, as represented by the Kuznets curve; recently, however, the emergence of a post-industrial economy in some societies has increased economic inequality once again.

12. Social stratification is a complex and controversial area of research because it deals not only with facts but also with values that suggest how society should be organized.

CRITICAL-THINKING QUESTIONS

1. How is social stratification evident on university and college campuses? What categories of people are there? In what respects are they unequal?

2. Why are agrarian societies typically caste systems? Why does industrialization replace castes with classes?

3. According to the Davis-Moore thesis, why should a university president be paid more than a professor? Do you agree with this analysis?

4. In what respects have the predictions of Karl Marx failed? In what respects are they correct?

APPLICATIONS AND EXERCISES

1. Visit the Internet website **www.aflcio.org/corporateamerica/paywatch/** to determine the compensation for chief executive officers of various large American corporations. (Compensation for Canadian CEOs is provided at *The Globe and Mail*'s *Report on Business* website; see **www.theglobeandmail.com/special/robmagazinecover/**). To see how their companies performed, check the corporate stock price for that period (available from Yahoo!; click on the financial news link). What conclusions do you reach?

2. Read Kurt Vonnegut's short story "Harrison Bergeron" (in his collection of stories entitled *Welcome to the Monkey House*). What are Vonnegut's views of social stratification and the prospect of an egalitarian society? Do you agree with him or not? Why?

3. With parents, grandparents, or other relatives, try to assess the social class position of your own family over the last three generations. Have changes taken place? If so, what caused this mobility?

4. Identify the "seven deadly sins," human failings according to the medieval Christian church. These may be deadly to the agrarian caste system, but what about the modern, capitalist class system?

 SITES TO SEE

www.macionis.com
or
www.TheSociologyPage.com
You can find more than fifty weblinks to sociological journals and other sources of data and information by visiting the Links Library at this website.

http://carbon.cudenver.edu/public/sociology/introsoc/topics/topic4a.html
This article defines the *Basic Concepts in Social Stratification*, including social status, power, and systems of stratification. Links are provided to the topic of inequality.

www.anu.edu.au/polsci/marx/marx.html

The *Marxism Page* contains the full text of *The Communist Manifesto*, various introductions to Marxist politics, lyrics and a sound recording of "The Internationale," contemporary Marxist writings, and links to other resources on the Web.

www.worldbank.org/data/wdi2003/index.htm

This site presents samples from the 2003 edition of the World Bank annual publication *World Development Indicators*, including information about the effects of development on people, the economy, markets, and the en-

vironment. Change the date in the URL to access samples from other years.

www.truth.org.za/

The official home page of the *Truth and Reconciliation Committee* (TRC) in South Africa includes statements and press releases, news reports from the South African Press Association, Amnesty decisions and statistics, written submissions to the TRC, transcripts of the Human Rights Violations Hearings and the Amnesty Hearings, background information, recommended reading, and more.

 ## STUDY TOOLS

For more study tools to help you with your next exam, be sure to check out the Companion Website at **www.pearsoned.ca/macionis**, as well as Chapter 10 in your Study Guide.

 ## INVESTIGATE WITH CONTENTSELECT

Follow the instructions found on page 25 of this textbook to access ContentSelect™ at the Research Navigator™ website. Once at the site, enter your LOGINID and Password. Then, enter keywords such as "social class," "meritocracy," "Karl Marx," and "apartheid," and the search engine will supply relevant and recent scholarly and popular press publications.

Beauford Delaney (1901–1979, African-American)
Can Fire in the Park, 1946

Oil on canvas, 61.0 × 76.2 cm.
Smithsonian American Art Museum, Washington, D.C./Art Resource, N.Y.

SOCIAL CLASS IN CANADA

Karen Moss, a twenty-two-year-old single mother, was packing up her belongings to move for the third time in seven months. Her dreams of improving her life with a college education were dashed when the Ontario government cut welfare payments by almost 22 percent in 1996. Moss was now receiving $957 per month—down from $1221—to support her three-year-old son, Cameron, and herself.

Moss had also lost government funding for school. She had been doing very well in a retail management course at a local community college, but bureaucratic mix-ups and problems with getting a work placement forced her to discontinue her studies. "If it wasn't for the welfare cuts," Moss said, "I'd still be living in my old apartment and I'd

be two semesters away from completing my course."

The cuts meant that Moss could no longer afford the $700-a-month rent for her one-bedroom apartment. She tried sharing an apartment with another single mother, but when that didn't work she moved in with her parents. But living in their small condominium was too cramped and stressful for Moss and her son. So once again she found herself looking for another place to live.

Cameron's father, also on welfare, did not help support their son. So Moss decided that the best thing to do was to try a fresh start in a new city. "I just want to get off welfare and get back on my feet. Once that happens, I'll look into trying to finish school," she said (Monsebraaten, 1996).

The story of Karen Moss offers stark evidence of the pervasive power of social stratification to shape the lives of people throughout Canada. Whether individuals easily achieve great success, struggle simply to get by, or collapse with broken spirits is not a simple matter of people's talents and personal ambitions. For all of us, social standing reflects the distribution of wealth, power, and opportunity in our society.

DIMENSIONS OF SOCIAL INEQUALITY

We tend to think of ourselves as a "middle-class society," but in fact Canadian society is highly stratified. The rich not only control most of the money, they also benefit from more schooling, they enjoy better health, and they consume a greater share of almost all goods and services than others do. On the other end of the socioeconomic spectrum, poor families struggle from day to day simply to make ends meet. This chapter

will explain that the popular perception of Canada as a society with a bulging middle class and a uniformly high standard of living does not square with many important facts.

Our egalitarian values suggest that we experience equality of opportunity and widespread upward mobility and that, at the very least, we provide a broad social safety net that catches those who fall through the cracks. We fail to recognize that, in reality, birth confers advantages and opportunities on some people that others who are less fortunate could never imagine.

Social inequality in Canada is not easily recognized because our primary groups—including family, neighbours, and friends—typically have the same social standing as we do. At work, we mix with others like ourselves. In effect, most of our daily interaction involves a narrow stratum of society, with only brief and impersonal encounters with people very different from ourselves. The mass media, even in their ads, project a largely middle-class picture of our social world, and recently governments have quoted statistics

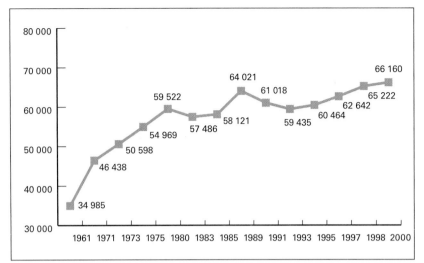

FIGURE 11–1 Average Family Income in Canada in Constant 2000 Dollars, 1961–2000

Sources: Calculations by Gerber based on Statistics Canada, Catalogue No. 13-208, and 2001 Census, www.statcan.ca.

showing that Canadians have one of the highest standards of living in the world. The effect of these images of homogeneity is that the very rich and the very poor are largely invisible to the rest of us.

When people do acknowledge their differences, they often talk of inequality as if it were determined by a single factor such as money. More accurately, however, social class in Canada has several dimensions. *Socioeconomic status* (SES), examined in Chapter 10 ("Social Stratification"), amounts to a composite measure of social position that encompasses not only money but power, occupational prestige, and schooling.

INCOME

One important dimension of inequality involves **income**, *occupational wages or salaries, earnings from investments, and government transfer payments (e.g., welfare)*. As revealed in Figure 11–1, the average family income in Canada in 2000 was $66 160, marking a sustained recovery from a dip in 1993. Note that average family incomes—measured in 2000 dollars—rose from $34 985 to $59 522 through the 1960s and 1970s, dipped in the recession of the early 1980s, climbed to a high in 1989, and dipped again in the recession of the early 1990s. By reporting incomes in constant dollars, Figure 11–1 reveals the fluctuation in buying power of the average family from 1961 to 2000, suggesting that the earlier rate of increase has essentially levelled off since about 1980. Note that an important contributor to rising family income was the increase in dual-income families through the 1960s and 1970s.

Table 11–1, which shows the distribution of income by quintiles (by fifths, or groups of 20 percent) among all Canadian families from 1961 to 2001, suggests stability over time. Taking 2001 as the point of reference, the 20 percent of families with the highest

earnings received 43.6 percent of all income, while the bottom 20 percent made only 5.2 percent. In short, the bulk of the nation's income is earned by a small proportion of families, while the rest of the population makes do with far less. Note as well that the remarkable stability of the 1961–91 period is marred by greater income disparity in 2001.

A glance at the Canadian figures over the 1961–91 period suggests that little changed in terms of the pattern of income distribution. That stability is discouraging considering Canada's economic growth and the firm establishment of our social welfare system over that period. It appears that, despite our efforts, we have failed to redistribute income to those who are less well off. More discouraging is the change between 1991 and 2001, which suggests that the top quintile gained income (40.0 to 43.6 percent of all income) at the expense of the poorest quintile (whose share dropped from 6.4 to 5.2 percent).

A comparison of the Canadian and American figures in 1991/1990 and 2001/2000 (Table 11-1) suggests that although Canada's income is more equitably distributed than that of the United States, our performance has become worse just as the Americans have made advances in income equity. While Canada's income disparity increased in the 1990s, that of the United States increased a decade earlier (in the 1980s) as a result of changes in the economy, new tax polices, and cuts in social programs that assist low-income people (Levy, 1987; Reich, 1989).

World Bank data (Figure 11-2) paint a more positive picture of Canada's current record on income disparities in an unspecified year (countries may differ in the years for which data were collected). With 39.3 percent of income going to the top quintile and 7.5 percent going to the bottom, Canada's performance falls between that of Switzerland and Germany and looks much better than that of the United States.

TABLE 11–1 Distribution of Family Income by Quintile* in Canada, 1961–2000, and in the United States, 1990–2000							
	Canada					**United States**	
Quintile	1961	1971	1981	1991	2001	1990	2000
Lowest	6.6	5.6	6.4	6.4	5.2	3.9	4.3
Second	13.5	12.6	12.9	12.2	11.3	9.6	9.8
Middle	18.3	18.0	18.3	17.6	16.7	15.9	15.5
Fourth	23.4	23.7	24.1	23.9	23.3	24.0	22.3
Highest	38.4	40.0	38.4	40.0	43.6	46.6	47.4
Total**	100.0	100.0	100.0	100.0	100.0	100.0	100.0

*Quintiles divide those with income into five equal categories. The distribution refers to the percentage of total income going to each category.
**Any errors are due to rounding.

Sources: Fréchette (1988); Statistics Canada, Catalogue No. 13-207; U.S. Bureau of the Census (2000), and Statistics Canada, 2001 Census, www.statcan.ca.

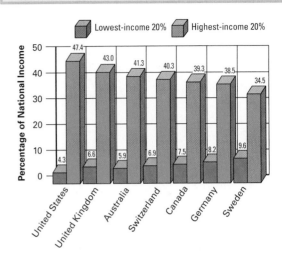

GLOBAL SNAPSHOT

FIGURE 11–2 **Income Disparities for Selected High-Income Countries**

Source: U.S. Census Bureau (2001) and The World Bank (2001).

Regrettably, other economic indicators—which point to increased income disparity in Canada—suggest that the World Bank data are out of line, rather than those of our census.

Canada Map 11-1 shows 2000 median incomes for Canada's census subdivisions, as well as for the country, provinces, and territories. It reveals that incomes are lowest in Newfoundland and Nunavut and highest in the Yukon and Northwest Territories, ranging from $17 270 in Nunavut to $29 030 in the Northwest Territories. Ontario's median income, at $24 816, is the highest of the provinces, but only $2700 above the Canadian median.

WEALTH

Income is but one component of a person's or family's **wealth**, *the total amount of money and other assets, minus outstanding debts.* Wealth in the form of stocks, bonds, real estate, and other privately owned property is distributed even less equally than income. Paul Tellier, CEO of Bombardier, for example, has to declare his "income" to Revenue Canada, but not the value of his mansions or business holdings. It is the control of these kinds of assets that really sets the wealthy apart from the rest of us. When the political left talks of establishing a wealth tax and an inheritance tax, it is this component of wealth that it seeks to redistribute.

POWER

In Canadian society, as elsewhere, wealth stands as an important source of power. Major owners of corporate stock, for example, make decisions that create jobs for ordinary people or scale back operations, throwing people out of work.

More broadly, the "super-rich" families who own most of the nation's wealth have a great deal of say about the national political agenda (Clement, 1975; Francis, 1986). Chapter 17 ("Politics and Government") raises a question that has engaged sociologists for decades: Can a society maintain a political democracy if a small share of the population controls most of the wealth? Some analysts maintain that while the rich may have some advantages, they do not dominate the political process. Others argue, as did Marx, that the political system represents the interests of the wealthy.

OCCUPATIONAL PRESTIGE

Occupation is a major determinant of income, wealth, and power. In addition, it serves as a key source of social prestige, since we commonly evaluate one another according to the kind of work we do, respecting some while looking down on others. Once we learn that Linda Cook is the new CEO of Shell Canada in Calgary, we can make numerous assumptions about her lifestyle, education, and income. We are likely to treat her with respect and listen more closely to her opinions.

For more than half a century, sociologists have measured the relative social prestige of various occupations (Counts, 1925; Blishen, 1958; Hodge et al., 1966; Blishen et al., 1987). Surveys asking respondents to rate occupations in terms of prestige produce a ranking that reflects both income and education. Physicians, lawyers, and engineers (high on income

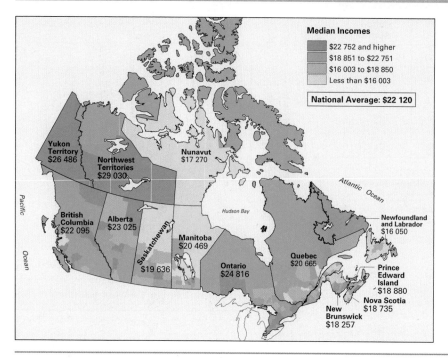

**CANADA MAP 11–1
Median Incomes by Province, Territory, and Census Subdivision, 2000**

Source: Calculations by Gerber based on data retrieved in October, 2003, from Statistics Canada online database, B2020, Profile Series.

and education) are ranked near the top on prestige, while cashiers and janitors are ranked near the bottom. In global perspective, occupational prestige rankings tend to be roughly the same in all industrial societies (Ma, 1987). Almost everywhere, white-collar work that involves mental activity free from extensive supervision confers greater prestige than blue-collar occupations that require supervised, manual labour. There are exceptions to this pattern, however. For example, a blue-collar aircraft mechanic enjoys greater social prestige than a white-collar filing clerk.

Table 11–2 shows the ranking of various occupational categories in Canada in 1986, based on the Blishen scale, which uses income and education to assess socioeconomic status and produces a ranking very similar to the survey-based prestige scales. In a ranking of 514 census occupations, physicians and surgeons come out at the top with a score of 101.3, while newspaper carriers and vendors scored 17.8. Collapsing occupations into broader categories makes certain patterns apparent (Creese et al., 1991). In the middle range of occupations, the Blishen scores are lower for women than for men—particularly in the various white- and blue-collar categories. This is where the *pink ghetto* jobs—lower status and poorly paid—are concentrated. Women and men have similar educational levels across occupational categories, with the few differences usually resulting from higher educational attainment among women. There are, how-

ever, marked differences in the incomes of women and men: in most of the occupational categories, women earn about 60 percent of male income, but in the professional and semi-professional/technical categories, the figures are 72 and 84 percent respectively. Though not apparent in the table, Creese et al. (1991) note that self-employed professional women fare best, earning 88 percent of the income earned by their male counterparts.

The important point here is that social stratification typically involves various dimensions of inequality (based on income and prestige as well as sex and race) *that are superimposed* on each other, forming a complex, and often steep, hierarchy.

SCHOOLING

Education is an important determinant of labour force participation, occupation, and income, so it is highly valued in industrial societies. Although industrial societies generally define schooling as everyone's right, the opportunity for formal education is not always equal. In Canada, traditionally, women did not pursue formal education as far as their male counterparts; however, in recent years, more than half of the undergraduate degrees and community college diplomas have been earned by women (though they have not caught up with men in earning master's and doctoral degrees). Table 11–2 suggests that while educational

TABLE 11–2 Occupational Categories by Average Blishen Scores, Years of Schooling, Income, and Sex, 1986

Occupation	Blishen Scores		Years of Schooling		Income ($)	
	Male	Female	Male	Female	Male	Female
1. High-level management	69	67	14.0	14.0	62 555	36 637
2. Professional	65	65	15.0	15.0	38 226	27 672
3. Middle management	52	52	13.0	13.0	36 935	21 894
4. Semi-professional/technician	52	51	13.6	14.0	30 784	25 732
5. Upper (skilled) white-collar	46	42	12.7	12.9	37 334	18 005
6. Upper (skilled) blue-collar	44	37	11.0	11.6	28 572	18 476
7. Lower (unskilled) white-collar	33	32	12.0	12.0	23 016	13 301
8. Lower (unskilled) blue-collar	32	28	10.5	10.0	22 186	13 444
9. Farmers	28	28	10.0	14.0	26 528	–13 147[*]
10. Farm labourers	24	24	10.0	11.0	14 774	8830

[*]The negative income reflects net losses for some farmers. Since there are relatively few female farmers, a large net loss for a small number of individuals can produce a negative average income for the category as a whole.

Source: Creese et al. (1991:37), based on analysis of data collected for the 1986 General Social Survey.

differences between men and women employed in similar jobs are minimal, overall, women have completed slightly more years of schooling than men.

Schooling not only promotes personal development but also affects an individual's occupation and income. Individuals with higher levels of schooling are more likely to be in the labour force, to be employed rather than unemployed, and to earn higher incomes (Secretary of State Canada, 1992).

ASCRIPTION AND SOCIAL STRATIFICATION

To a large extent, the class system in Canada rewards individual talent and effort. But, as explained in Chapter 10 ("Social Stratification"), class systems still rest on ascription: who we are at birth greatly influences what we become later in life.

ANCESTRY

Nothing affects social standing in Canada as much as our birth into a particular family—an event over which we have no control. Ancestry determines our point of entry into the system of social inequality. Some Canadian families, including the Reichmanns, Blacks, Thomsons, Irvings, Nygards, and Stronachs, are known around the world. On a more modest scale, certain families in practically every Canadian community have wealth and power that have become well established over several generations.

Being born to privilege or poverty sets the stage for our future schooling, occupation, and income. Although there are numerous "rags to riches" stories in Canada, many of the richest individuals—those with hundreds of millions of dollars in wealth—derived their fortunes primarily through inheritance. By

the same token, the "inheritance" of poverty and the lack of opportunity that goes with it just as surely shape the future of those in need. The family, in short, transmits property, power, and possibilities from one generation to the next, contributing to the persistence of social stratification.

GENDER

People of both sexes are born into families at every social level. Women born into families of high social standing, therefore, draw on many more social resources than men born into disadvantaged families. Yet, on average, women earn lower income, accumulate less wealth, enjoy lower occupational prestige, and rank lower in some aspects of educational achievement than men do (Bernard, 1981; Lengermann and Wallace, 1985; Creese et al., 1991).

Later in the chapter, you will discover that women do not "inherit" the social position of their fathers to the extent that men do. You will also learn that households headed by women are many times more likely to be poor than are those headed by men. A full picture of the link between gender and social stratification is found in Chapter 13 ("Gender Stratification").

RACE AND ETHNICITY

Although we think our society is largely egalitarian, race and ethnicity remain important determinants of social position. In Chapter 20 ("Education") we shall see that, in Canada, people of Asian origin have higher levels of educational attainment than those of British and French origin and that Blacks are ahead on some educational measures and labour force participation. The Native population, on the other hand, has not acquired the same levels of education or gained the same

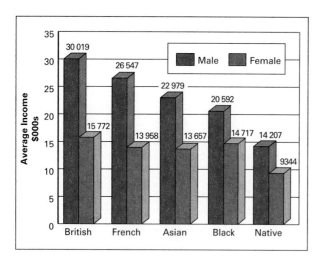

FIGURE 11–3 Average Income* in Canada by Gender for Selected Categories, 1990

*Figures based on populations fifteen years of age and over, including individuals with no income.

Source: Compiled by Gerber from Canada Census 1991, Public Use Microdata.

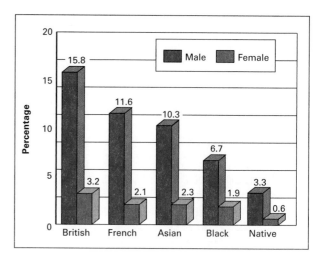

FIGURE 11–4 Percentage* in Canada with Incomes of $50 000 or More, by Gender for Selected Categories, 1990

*These figures refer to percentages of populations fifteen years of age and over.

Source: Compiled by Gerber from Canada Census 1991, Public Use Microdata.

access to employment as have others in Canada. Figures 11–3 and 11–4 suggest that race and ethnicity have a bearing on income as well.

In Figure 11–3, we see that, for men, average incomes decline steadily as we move from the British through the French, Asian, Black, and Native categories. Among men, the three visible minority categories have lower incomes than the British and the French. Among women, the differences are not as clear in that the average income of Black women is greater than those of women of French and Asian origin. This is in part the result of substantial education and high levels of labour force involvement (including full-time employment) among Black women.

Figure 11–4 reveals income differences based on a different measure. The bars in the graph indicate the proportion of the population (fifteen years of age and over) in each category with incomes of $50 000 or more—and on this measure the intercategory differences are much more dramatic. The proportion of British males in this high-income category is almost *five times* that of Native males. Women in each ethnic or racial category have fewer members in the $50 000-plus income category than their male counterparts, but British women, too, are *five times* as likely to be in the high-income category as are Native women. In terms of entry into high income levels, the French are behind the British while the three visible minorities trail behind the French: clearly, Natives are the most disadvantaged in terms of income.

While it is true that income is only one dimension of social class, race and ethnicity are clearly associated with differential placement in the socioeconomic hierarchy of Canada.

SOCIAL CLASSES IN CANADA

As Chapter 10 ("Social Stratification") explained, people living in rigid caste systems can tell anyone's social ranking at a glance. Assessing the social position in a more fluid class system, however, poses a number of challenges.

Consider the joke about the fellow who orders a pizza, asking that it be cut into six slices because he isn't hungry enough to eat eight. While sociologists acknowledge extensive social inequality in Canada, they have long debated precisely how to divide up this social hierarchy. Some who follow Karl Marx's thinking contend that there are two major classes; others suggest that North American society breaks down into as many as six categories (Warner and Lunt, 1941). Still others align themselves with Max Weber, believing that people form a multidimensional status hierarchy, rather than clear-cut classes.

Defining classes in Canada is difficult owing to the relatively low level of status consistency. Especially towards the middle of the hierarchy, an individual's social standing on one dimension often contradicts that person's position on another (Tepperman, 1979; Gilbert and Kahl, 1987). A government official, for example, may control a multi-million-dollar budget yet earn a modest income. Similarly, members of the clergy typically enjoy ample prestige while possessing only moderate power

People often distinguish between the "new rich" and those with "old money." Men and women who suddenly begin to earn high incomes tend to spend on "status symbols" because they enjoy the new thrill of high-roller living and want others to know of their success. Those who grow up surrounded by wealth, on the other hand, are used to a privileged way of life and are quieter about it. Thus, the "conspicuous consumption" of the lower-upper class (left) can differ dramatically from the more private pursuits and understatement of the upper-upper class (right).

and earning low pay. Or consider a lucky professional gambler who may win little respect despite considerable wealth.

The social mobility typical of class systems—again, most pronounced near the middle—means that social position often changes during one's lifetime, further blurring the lines between social classes.

Despite these problems of definition, it is useful to think of four general social classes in Canada: the upper class, the middle class, the working class, and the lower class. As we shall explain, however, some categories are more clear-cut than others.

In a society in which economic development is focused on knowledge-based industries, computer technology is being applied very widely, even in underground mining. Computer literacy is increasingly distinguishing the highly employable from those who face multiple barriers to satisfactory employment. If the children of the affluent have more exposure to computers at school, and that exposure is augmented by the presence of computers in the home, social class position will be perpetuated in the younger generation.

 For more information on Internet use in Canada, see the Canadian Internet Fact Page posted by market research company Angus-Reid at www.ipsos-reid.com/ca/data/dsp_little_cdn_fact_book.cfm

THE UPPER CLASS

The upper class, perhaps 3 to 5 percent of the population, derives much of its income from inherited wealth, in the form of stocks and bonds, real estate, and other investments. And this income may be substantial. In January 1996, the *Financial Post* magazine

profiled fifty of the richest individuals and families in Canada, each of them with a minimum net worth of $145 million and eight of them worth at least $1 billion. On the top is Kenneth R. Thomson with a net worth of $8.2 *billion* (Hamilton, 1996). By 2003, *Forbes* listed Kenneth Thomson as the thirteenth richest person in the world, with an estimated net worth of $14 billion (U.S.)—$18.3 billion Canadian (Forbes, 2003). *The* upper class thus comprises what Karl Marx termed *capitalists*, those who own or control most of the nation's productive property.

Despite this immense wealth, many members of the upper class work as top executives in large corporations—often earning salaries of $5 million or more: in 2002 Frank Stronach and Belinda Stronach of Magna Corporation were rewarded to the tune of $52 million and $12.5 million respectively, while Travis Engen of Alcan made $17 million (*Globe and Mail, Report on Business*, July 2003:147). As corporate executives and as senior government officials, these privileged individuals further enhance their power to shape events in the nation—and the entire world.

Members of the upper class also attain the highest levels of education, typically in the most expensive and highly regarded schools and universities. Historically, though less so today, the upper class has been composed of people of British origin (Porter, 1965; Clement, 1975; Tepperman, 1979). In the mid-1990s, among the fifty most wealthy families or individuals noted above, about half were of British origin and the rest a mix of Jewish, French, other European, and one Asian. Over the next decade or two we can expect to find an increasing number of Asians represented in this highly select group.

Computers and Social Class

In the past decade or so Canada ceased to be an industrial society and moved through to the post-industrial phase. This means that the service sector has expanded to include a high proportion of knowledge-based industries, which in turn means that information technology is increasingly relied on in a wide range of work environments. If computer literacy, in particular, is becoming the key to opportunity in Canada, then the question of who is comfortable with the technology is of considerable importance.

Schools across Canada (in rural or urban, affluent or poor communities) are gradually introducing computers into the classroom from the earliest grades: where available, special school networks and the Internet have expanded horizons and revolutionized the learning process. But the number of computers available is usually limited, so that individual students often have little opportunity to put new skills into practice. The most adept students (often the boys) tend to monopolize the equipment while the more reticent watch from the sidelines. As long as the supply of computers in the classroom is limited, additional exposure to computers in the home environment will play an important role in skill development. It is here that social class background has an impact.

John Goyder (1997) examined patterns of technology diffusion in Canada, comparing the presence of telephones

in 1911 and personal computers (PCs) in 1994 in the homes of people in various occupational categories. Note that both of these technologies started off in offices and were later adopted in homes.

The more affluent homes were more likely to have both telephones and computers. Home telephone subscribers in 1911, in Kingston, Ontario, were overwhelmingly in the professional and managerial categories: 96 percent of professionals had telephones at home, compared with 3 percent of those in skilled and semi-skilled trades. In 1994 PCs were more evenly distributed in the homes of various occupational categories. Among professionals (employed and self-employed), 61 percent had computers at home, compared with 24 percent of unskilled craft and farm labourers. Considering the expense of computers, the fact that about 25 percent of households in the four lowest occupational categories have PCs is remarkable and indicative of the centrality of computers in modern Canadian life. The absence of computers in the homes of 39 percent of professionals may be a function of age: some older professionals have not adopted computers either in the office or at home.

Statistics Canada tracks changes in Internet use by education and age of household head, specifying location of access (e.g., home, work, or school). Between 1997 and 2001, the proportion

of households with home access headed by those with less than high school education increased from 3.9 to 22.8 percent. Among households with heads having university degrees, home access increased from 37.6 to 74.2 percent. The effect of the age of the household head has a similarly dramatic impact. Among households with heads less than thirty-five years of age, Internet access at home increased from 37.3 to 76.2 percent in the same five-year period. Among households with heads sixty-five years of age and over, home access increased from 5.3 to 19.3 percent. Clearly, both education and age of household head have dramatic effects on Internet access at home (Statistics Canada, Canadian Statistics, **www.statcan.ca**).

Upper-Uppers

The *upper-upper class*, often described as "society" or "bluebloods," includes less than 1 percent of the Canadian population. Membership is usually the result of ascription or birth, as suggested by the old quip that the easiest way to break into "society" is to be born there. These families possess enormous wealth, primarily inherited rather than earned. For this rea-

son, members of the upper-upper class are said to have *old money*.

Set apart by their wealth, members of the upper-upper class live in a world of exclusive affiliations. They inhabit elite neighbourhoods, such as Forest Hill in Toronto or Westmount in Montreal. Schools extend this privileged environment. Their children typically attend private schools such as Upper Canada College with others of similar background, complet-

The life of this Newfoundland fisherman has been changed drastically by the moratorium on cod fishing. How do you think different classes are affected by this type of change in the local economy?

ing their formal education at high-prestige universities such as Cambridge, Oxford, or Harvard. In the historical pattern of European aristocrats, they study liberal arts rather than vocationally directed subjects.

Women of the upper-upper class often maintain a full schedule of volunteer work for charitable organizations. For example, women from Toronto's upper-crust neighbourhoods are the backbone of the Toronto Symphony and the National Ballet: old-money families support these organizations, offering their time as well as funds. While helping the larger community, such charitable activities also build networks that put these families at the centre of this nation's power elite (Ostrander, 1980, 1984).

Lower-Uppers $100,000 +

The remaining 2 to 4 percent of the population that makes up the upper class falls into the *lower-upper class*. From the point of view of the average Canadian, such people seem every bit as privileged as the upper-upper class. The major difference, however, is that "lower-uppers" are the "working rich" who depend on earnings rather than wealth as their primary source of income. Few people in this category inherit a vast fortune from their parents, although the majority do inherit some wealth.

Especially in the eyes of members of "society," those in the lower-upper class are merely the "new rich," people who can never savour the highest levels of prestige enjoyed by those with rich and famous grandparents. Thus, while the new rich typically live in expensive homes, they often find themselves excluded from the most prestigious clubs and associations maintained by old-money families.

Historically, the dream of great success has meant joining the ranks of the lower-upper class through exceptional accomplishment. The entrepreneurial individual who makes the right business moves with split-second timing, the athlete who accepts a million-dollar contract to play in the big leagues, the computer whiz who designs a new program that sets a standard for the industry—these are the lucky and talented achievers who reach the level of the lower-upper class. Their success stories fascinate us because this kind of upward social mobility has long stood as a goal that, however unlikely, is still within the realm of the possible. A dual-earner family in which both wife and husband are professionals can make it into this lower-upper stratum of families. Members of the upper-upper class, in contrast, move in rarefied circles far from the everyday reality of the rest of us.

THE MIDDLE CLASS

Encompassing about 40 to 50 percent of the Canadian population, the middle class exerts tremendous influence on patterns of North American culture. Television and other mass media usually portray middle-class people, and most commercial advertising is directed at these "average" consumers. The middle class encompasses far more racial and ethnic diversity than the upper class. While many upper-class people (especially "upper-uppers") know each other personally, such exclusiveness and familiarity do not characterize the middle class.

Upper-Middles $50 – 100,000

The top half of this category is often termed the *upper-middle class*, based on above-average income in the range of $50 000 to $100 000 a year. Such income allows upper-middle-class families gradually to accumulate considerable property—a comfortable house in a fairly expensive area, several automobiles, and some investments. Virtually all upper-middle-class people

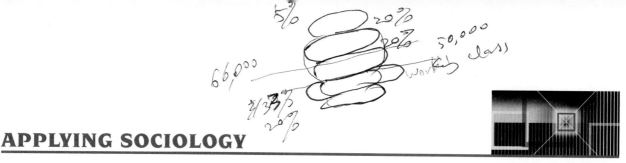

APPLYING SOCIOLOGY

Social Class and Native People

Many scholars and observers of the Canadian scene have characterized Native people as suffering from cultural dislocation, substance abuse, suicide, and poverty. Furthermore, the figures and tables throughout this text comparing people of French, English, Asian, Black, and Native origins suggest that Native people lag behind the larger Canadian population in terms of education, labour force participation, and income. In other words, the general belief is that Natives live in relative poverty.

The above observations deal with Native people in the *aggregate*. Indeed, Aboriginal people—on average—do fare poorly on a wide range of measures of social, economic, and physical health. Yet in an early publication, based on her analysis of 600 First Nations communities, Linda Gerber (1979) pointed out the diversity among them. That diversity led her to develop a typology of reserve-based communities: Inert, Pluralistic, Municipal, and Integrative bands reveal very different responses to changing socioeconomic circumstances. Underlying this diversity are real differences in economic well-being. Where communities have acquired wealth, there is also individual diversity, as some individuals benefit more than others.

Wotherspoon and Satzewich (1993) observe the status of Native people from a Marxist—or rather, neo-Marxist—perspective, noting that race, class, and gender relations enter into the picture. These variables, they argue, "intersect in complex ways to structure the social position of groups." The authors are quick to point out that, collectively, Native peoples "occupy disadvantaged positions within social and economic structures of Canada" and that, because they "share a structurally similar position," the assumption is that race and class converge—in other words, race equals class. While the aggregate statistics support this assumption, Wotherspoon and Satzewich counter it with evidence that, in fact, Aboriginal people "are distributed across the range of class sites" (pp. 42–43). Some of that evidence comes from Gerber (1990), who provides an occupational breakdown of Indian, Métis, and Inuit people.

Native people are to be found in each of the Marxist categories of proletariat, reserve army of labour, working class, petit bourgeoisie, and bourgeoisie. Thus, they span the range from street people to capitalists. However, although the media and the literature provide substantial analysis of Aboriginal communities and populations, they rarely focus on the petit bourgeoisie and the bourgeoisie, "those people who either own large sums of capital privately, or who control large sums of 'communally'—or band-based capital" (Wotherspoon and Satzewich, 1993:64). As expected, some Native-owned businesses are based on crafts, tourism, natural resources, construction, hunting, fishing, and farming; but many others offer services in consulting and multimedia communications. Businesses are located on reserves and in major urban centres. The start-up capital for these ventures comes from land-claim settlements, special funds from Indian and Northern Affairs Canada (INAC), or the banks—some of which specifically serve Aboriginals.

Native businesses are newer and generally smaller than their mainstream counterparts, but many are capitalized at the multimillion-dollar level. In fact, executive incomes put many Aboriginal individuals in Canada's upper-income categories.

The federal government provides services for Aboriginal businesses through INAC as well as through Industry Canada.

 To obtain more information about Native businesses, go to Aboriginal Business Canada at the Industry Canada website at www.ic.gc.ca/, or go directly to www.cbsc.org/english/absn/

receive university educations, and postgraduate degrees are common. Many go on to high-prestige occupations (physicians, engineers, lawyers, accountants, or business executives). Lacking the power of the upper class to influence national or international events, the upper-middle class often plays an important role in local political affairs.

Average-Middles

The rest of the middle class falls near the centre of our class structure. *Average-middles* typically work in less prestigious white-collar occupations (as bank tellers, middle managers, and sales clerks) or in highly skilled blue-collar jobs (including electrical work and carpentry). Family income is sufficient to provide a secure, if modest, standard of living. Middle-class people generally accumulate a small amount of wealth over the course of their working lives, and most will own a house. Middle-class men and women are likely to be high-school graduates themselves. If they do send their children to university, it is more likely to be the one closest to home to save on accommodation expenses.

below National Everage

THE WORKING CLASS

Including about one-third of the population, the *working class* (sometimes called the *lower-middle class*) refers to people who have lower incomes than those in the middle class and little or no accumulated wealth. In Marxist terms, the working class forms the core of the industrial proletariat. The blue-collar occupations of the working class generally yield a family income that is somewhat below the national average, although unionized blue-collar workers can contribute to family incomes that are well above that level.

Many working-class jobs provide little personal satisfaction—requiring discipline but rarely imagination—and subject workers to continual supervision. These jobs also provide fewer benefits, such as dental insurance and pension plans. University is less likely to be part of the experience of children of working-class parents. The many working-class families who own their own homes are likely to own them in lower-cost neighbourhoods.

THE LOWER CLASS

The 20 percent of our population with the lowest family income makes up the *lower class*. A lack of work and little income renders life unstable and insecure. In 1996, over 5 million people (18 percent of our population) were classified by the federal government as poor. While some of these people are supported entirely by social welfare payments, others are among the "working poor"—those whose incomes from full-time jobs fall short of what is required to cover necessities such as food, shelter, and clothing.

The working poor have low-prestige jobs that provide minimal income and little intrinsic satisfaction. Some have managed to complete high school, but university degrees and college diplomas are relatively rare. In fact, many lower-class men and women are functionally illiterate.

Lower-class families find themselves segregated into specific, less-desirable neighbourhoods—some of which are ethnically or racially distinct (Michelson, 1988:93). Although there are many poor people in small towns and rural areas—where resource-based industries have collapsed or plants have closed—physical segregation of the poor is most starkly apparent in cities, where large numbers of poor people live in rental housing that is avoided by others.

Lower-class children quickly learn that many people consider them to be only marginal members of society. Observing their parents and other lower-status adults, they may conclude that their own futures hold little hope for breaking the cycle of poverty. Lower-class life, then, can generate self-defeating resignation among those cut off from the resources of an affluent society: welfare dependency, as a lifestyle, can be passed from one generation to the next. Some of the poor simply give up, but others—the working poor—go to great lengths to avoid going on welfare, often working at two or three jobs to make ends meet.

The policies of the Ralph Klein and Mike Harris/Ernie Eves governments in Alberta and Ontario have led to reductions in welfare payments and tighter eligibility requirements. Fewer people are on welfare but no one yet knows where the missing welfare recipients have gone or how they are managing to survive. Relatively low unemployment rates may account for some of the drop in welfare dependency.

CLASS, FAMILY, AND GENDER

Family life is closely related to social class. Because the typical individual marries someone of comparable social position, distinctive family patterns correspond to each class level. For example, because lower-class people marry earlier in life and make less use of birth control, they have more children than middle-class parents do.

Working-class parents encourage children to conform to conventional norms and remain obedient and respectful to authority figures. In contrast, parents of higher social standing transmit a different "cultural capital" to their children, motivating them to express their individuality and to use their imaginations more freely. This difference reflects parents' expectations about their children's future: the odds are that less-privileged children will take jobs demanding close adherence to specified rules, while most advantaged children will enter fields that call for more creativity (Kohn, 1977; McLeod, 1995).

Of course, it stands to reason that the more social resources a family has, the more parents can develop their children's talents and abilities. An affluent family will spend $300 000 or more in raising a child to the age of eighteen. Ballet, music lessons, summer camp, and (for some) private-school education provide opportunities about which poor families may not even dream. Such differences underline how privilege tends to beget privilege as family life reproduces the class structure in each generation.

Class also shapes the relationship between spouses. Elizabeth Bott (1971; orig. 1957) documented that working-class couples maintain a rigid division of responsibilities according to gender. Middle-class marriages, in contrast, are more egalitarian, sharing more activities as well as greater intimacy. Keeping this insight in mind, we can understand why divorce is more common among disadvantaged couples, who may be overwhelmed by the stress of low-income living (Kitson and Raschke, 1981; National Council of Welfare, 1990:60–61). Lack of love, poor communication, adultery, and alcohol and wife abuse are important contributors to marriage breakdown among the poor.

Middle-Class Stampede?

Who participates in community festivals? Surely the Calgary Stampede, for example, draws a cross-section of the community (and Canadians from a wide geographic area) into a generalized tension-release ritual. Without a doubt "yahoos" and "yippees" will be part of the spontaneous vocabulary of people everywhere. Right?

Richard J. Ossenberg set out to show that while homogeneous communities might give rise to generalized participation, complex urban centres such as Calgary would elicit differentiated or selective participation. His research involved "a systematic pub-crawl on two evenings of the weeklong Stampede" held every July. He expected to find that members of the middle class, who are more "sensitive to legal and other restrictive norms," might be most likely to respond to the relaxation of social controls with "festival-related aggressive/expressive behaviour" (p. 405).

Ossenberg had already carried out extensive analysis of Calgary bar behaviour as a way of discovering the social class structure in Calgary, so he knew which nine of the city's beer parlours and lounges would represent a cross-section of social-class-related drinking establishments. Those chosen for the study were close to the Stampede grounds; two were upper class, three were middle class, and four were lower class. The establishments are described as follows:

The upper-class establishments are usually patronized by the elite oil and ranching group as well as the nouveau riche and the occasional white-collar couple celebrating an anniversary. The middle-class bars are patronized by clerical workers, small businessmen, and generally middle-range employees of the larger local firms, with the occasional labourers drifting in. The lower-class bars are the clearest in definition. They are patronized by service personnel, labourers, winos, and deprived Indians as well as by members of newly arrived immigrant groups (p. 406).

During the two evenings of observation "only about one in ten of the tipplers at the lower-class establishments wore Western cowboy costume, and most of those who did were completely ignored by the other patrons." The noise level was lower than usual, fights broke out less frequently, prostitutes were more in evidence, and patrons stuck to the normal men's parlour and "ladies and escorts" parlour pattern, even though restrictions were lifted during the Stampede. And there were virtually no rodeo-related "yahoos" to be heard.

In the middle-class establishments—two cocktail lounges and one beer parlour in a posh hotel—90 percent or more of the patrons were in cowboy or Western costume. In fact, the researchers were ridiculed for their lack of such attire. The noise levels were intolerable, "yippees" and "yahoos" filled the air, and back slapping and necking were the norm. Executives interacted freely with their secretaries, and tourists or strangers were readily accepted and even invited to house parties. Call girls, rather than streetwalkers, made their appearances.

The two upper-middle-class cocktail lounges in Calgary's plush, reputable hotels presented a very different picture. About 25 percent of patrons were costumed, but the noisy celebration was missing. Here, as in the working-class bars, it was business as usual. The few costumed patrons who tried to liven up the scene soon left in disgust: "Let's blow this joint—it's like a graveyard" (p. 410).

Ossenberg concluded that Stampede week is "functional" for people who are inhibited in their daily lives and "look forward to the 'green light' of tolerated deviance during a community festival." Behaviour during such festivals reflects the social structure of the city but does not reinforce solidarity across class lines. It is, in effect, a "middle-class 'binge.'"

Postscript: In January 1996, Calgary had its first (annual) cowboy convention, in opulent surroundings. Here cowboys and cowgirls—the authentic and the "wannabes"—gathered to share cowboy lore, paraphernalia, and music, or simply to celebrate a way of life. So central is the horse to the cowboy lifestyle that (to the dismay of the hotel staff who had to clean up the plush carpets in their wake), several of the better-known horses were invited to mingle with their fans.

 The official website of the Calgary Stampede at www.calgarystampede.com offers news and FAQs, provides exhibit and event information, and sells souvenirs through the Stampede Store and tickets to the upcoming annual celebration.

Source: Adapted from Ossenberg (1979).

SOCIAL MOBILITY

Ours is a dynamic society marked by a significant measure of social mobility. As we noted in the last chapter, social mobility involves individuals moving upward or downward in the stratification system. Earning a university degree, securing a higher-paying job, or succeeding in a business endeavour contributes to *upward social mobility*, while dropping out of school, losing a job, or having a business enterprise fail may signal the onset of *downward social mobility*.

Over the long term, most social mobility is not a matter of individual decision as much as changes in society itself. During the first half of the past century, for example, industrialization expanded the economy, dramatically raising living standards for the majority of Canadians. Even without being very good swimmers, so to speak, people were able to "ride a rising tide of prosperity." As explained presently, *structural social mobility* in a downward direction has more recently dealt many people economic setbacks.

In studying social mobility, sociologists distinguish between changes within a single generation and shifts between generations of a family. **Intragenerational social mobility** refers to *a change in social position occurring during a person's lifetime*. **Intergenerational social mobility**, *upward or downward social mobility of children in relation to their parents*, has special significance because it reveals long-term changes in society that affect virtually everyone.

MYTH VERSUS REALITY

Although the "American Dream" may be attributed to people south of the border, Canadians share, to some extent, the belief that those who apply themselves can "get ahead" and that each new generation will do better than the last. But how much social mobility is there in Canada?

Data from the 1986 General Social Survey revealed that Canadians have been a little more likely to experience upward than downward mobility (Creese et al., 1991). Compared with their fathers, 48 percent of women moved up, while 40 percent moved down; the comparable figures for men are 39 and 36 percent respectively. Only 12 percent of women and 26 percent of men experienced no mobility at all, meaning that they were in the same occupational category as their fathers.

Occupational inheritance, or "following in Dad's footsteps," occurs most commonly among men whose fathers are in the professional, white-collar, and farming categories. Specific occupational inheritance has been less common for women because of the types of occupations traditionally available to them.

Though overall educational levels are increasing, class background continues to affect educational attainment: the higher the level of education and occupation of one's father, the more years of schooling one is likely to complete. Furthermore, a person's first job is *principally* affected by his or her level of education. Therefore, parental education and occupation have an impact on occupational status, not directly but through their effects on the educational attainment of the younger generation. Thus, a physician passes his

Education is key to occupational mobility in Canada. As many provinces reverse or at least relax policies that improve financial accessibility to post-secondary education for people at lower income levels, will there continue to be an upgrading of educational levels between generations?

occupation on to his child *if* he inspires that child to jump the educational hurdles required to gain admission to and complete medical school.

Education, then, is the key to occupational mobility in Canada. If family background has an impact, it is through its effect on schooling. But, as we saw earlier, francophones, visible minorities, and women have difficulty translating their educational accomplishments into higher-status, well-paid work.

Others have also noted the general lack of occupational inheritance in Canada. In a study of occupational mobility over four generations, Goyder and Curtis (1979) found that the occupations of great-grandfathers had no bearing whatsoever on those of their great-grandsons. Occupationally speaking, the descendants were all over the map. On the basis of their findings and those of others who have studied the extreme upper and lower ends of the spectrum, Goyder and Curtis conclude that the "two types of processes may well occur together: high over-all three-generation mobility in the general population along with low three-generation mobility in poverty and elite groups" (p. 229). In other words, those at the very top and bottom of the socioeconomic ladder may experience substantial occupational inheritance, while those in the middle do not.

Historically, women have had less opportunity for upward mobility than men. As we shall see in Chapter 13 ("Gender Stratification"), the majority of working

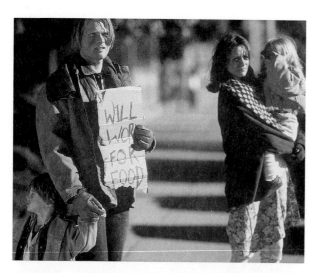

North American culture has long held the idea that, through talent and hard work, people can make their dreams come true. Do you think that social position is more a matter of individual effort or more a matter of the social class into which we are born? Why?

women hold clerical positions (e.g., secretaries) and low-paying service jobs (such as waitresses). These jobs offer little chance for advancement, which effectively limits upward social or economic movement. Divorce also commonly results in downward social mobility for women—but not for men—as Chapter 18 ("Family") explains. Data reflecting income change during the 1980s and early 1990s reveal a narrowing of the gap between the earnings of women and men, with the female-to-male income ratio increasing from about 60 to over 70 percent.

POVERTY IN CANADA

Social stratification simultaneously creates "haves" and "have-nots." Poverty, therefore, inevitably exists within all systems of social inequality. Sociologists employ the concept of poverty in two different ways, however. **Relative poverty**, which is by definition universal and inevitable, refers to *the deprivation of some people in relation to those who have more*. The richest and most egalitarian of societies have some members who live in relative poverty. Much more serious is **absolute poverty**, or *a deprivation of resources that is life-threatening*. Defined in this way, poverty is a pressing, but solvable, human problem.

As the next chapter ("Global Stratification") explains, the global dimensions of absolute poverty place the lives of perhaps 800 million people—one in seven of the earth's entire population—at risk. Even in affluent Canada, with its social welfare safety net, families go hungry, live in inadequate housing, and endure poor health because of wrenching poverty.

THE EXTENT OF CANADIAN POVERTY

Poverty statistics are based on the "poverty line," also known as the "low-income cut-off." People who spend at least 55 percent of their pre-tax income on food, clothing, and shelter are considered to be below the poverty line. Accordingly, there were about 5.5 million Canadians in 1995 who had incomes below the poverty line—19.7 percent of our population. By 2001, the situation had improved somewhat with 4.4 million Canadians, or 14.4 percent, living below the low-income cut-off.

In the past, our lack of progress in eliminating poverty prompted a United Nations committee to sharply criticize the Canadian government "for allowing poverty and homelessness to persist at disturbing levels in one of the world's richest countries" (York, 1993:A1). We were criticized by the UN committee because about half of our single mothers and a million children lived in poverty, and many Canadians depended on voluntary food banks to deal with hunger. While the proportions are now lower, the actual numbers are similar. In 2001, we still have 1.1 million children living in poverty.

Poverty means hunger, and many of the people at lower income levels are forced to rely on food banks and soup kitchens, both of which, in Canada, are run by voluntary organizations. The demand for food banks has increased substantially over the past few years to a point where today there are more than 615 food banks that feed 800 000 different people each month. A 1998 United Nations report criticized Canada for its poor response in dealing with human poverty. Canada placed tenth among seventeen industrialized nations (behind Sweden, the Netherlands, Germany, Norway, Italy, Finland, France, Japan, and Denmark) in "spreading around the wealth," reducing social inequality, and avoiding the immense social costs of impoverishment (Duffy and Mandel, 2001:79). The fact that so many people feel the need to resort to food banks, which function only because some people volunteer to staff them while others donate food, is particularly distressing in a country where we have the resources to alleviate poverty, if only we had the political will.

 For more information about Canada's food banks, see www.cafb-acba.ca

WHO ARE THE POOR?

Although no single description covers all poor people, poverty is pronounced among certain categories of our population. Children, women, certain visible minorities (specifically Natives), and those who live in rural areas are all at higher risk of being poor. Regional disparities in economic development and income are also in evidence in that poverty is a particularly acute problem in the Atlantic provinces, Quebec, and the North. With any combination of the above factors, the problem of poverty is especially serious.

Age

The burden of poverty falls heavily on Canadian children, with 1.1 million children (15.6 percent) living below the low-income cut-off. From another perspective, one in four poor Canadians is a child under the age of eighteen. Our child poverty rates rose from 17.4 percent in 1990 to a high of 21.1 in 1996 before dropping off to 15.6 percent in 2001. As encouraging as the more recent decline might be, we are far from eradicating child poverty despite the Liberal Party's vows to do so in the elections of 1993, 1997, and 2000.

A generation ago, the elderly were at greatest risk of poverty. In 1990, the rates for women and men sixty-five years of age and over were 26.8 and 13.4 percent respectively; by 2001, the rates had dropped to 21.2 and 11.1 percent. Although the situation of our elderly improved over the decade with better pension support from the government and employers, the movement of the baby boomers into the retirement years means that the *numbers* of elderly and poor elderly will increase accordingly. One might expect the poverty rate among elderly women to improve over the next decade as more women who have been employed reach retirement age.

Education

Education is another factor that determines the likelihood of having an income below the poverty line. People who have higher levels of education are less likely to be unemployed and more likely to have higher incomes. Not surprisingly, they are also less likely to fall below the poverty line: the incidence of poverty drops with each added level of education.

Race and Ethnicity

The likelihood of experiencing poverty is related to race and ethnicity in Canada, but the ranking of various categories is not necessarily what we might expect. A study based on 1986 census data offered some surprising results. Those of British origin are not all at the top of the income hierarchy; in fact, in a ranking of sixty ethnic and racial categories by average male income for those employed full time all year, those of English origin rank twenty-fifth (Gerber, 1990:79). The French, too, are near the middle. Canadians of Welsh and Scottish background appear in the top fifteen, along with those of Jewish and Japanese descent.

In the bottom fifteen categories we find Blacks, West Indians, Latin Americans, some of the Asian groups, and Native peoples. The only categories that rank below Natives are groups that tend to be recent immigrants and possibly refugees—Chileans and

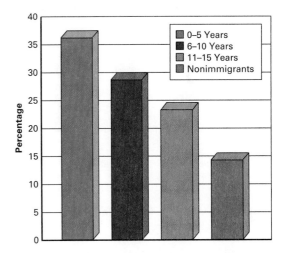

FIGURE 11–5 Low Income Rates of Immigrants, 2001, by Number of Years in Canada

Source: Adapted from Statistics Canada, *The Daily*, June 19, 2003, www.statcan.ca.

"other" Latin Americans, Vietnamese, Haitians, Laotians, and Cambodians. While male income for those employed full time is only one indicator of economic well-being, the rank ordering by race or ethnicity is suggestive. We would expect to find that more of the individuals or families in the bottom fifteen categories have incomes below the poverty line.

Gender and Family Patterns

The disparity in male and female incomes and the fact that lone-parent families tend to be headed by females contribute to higher rates of poverty among women. Statistics Canada provides data that help account for the **feminization of poverty**, *the trend by which women represent an increasing proportion of the poor.* The effects of pay or employment inequity and family structure on the economic well-being of women are clear. Women are less likely to be employed—63 percent of women fifteen to twenty-four years of age are employed, as compared to 74 percent of men. Women who work full time all year are paid only 71.6 percent

 Information about women and the economy is presented at http://unpac.ca/economy/index2.html, a website sponsored by the UN Platform for Action Committee in Manitoba.

of male income. Further, women are more likely than men to be working part time.

Lone-parent families, making up 14.5 percent of all families in 1995, tend to have lower incomes than

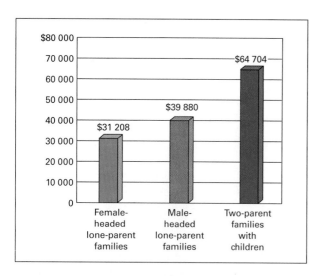

FIGURE 11–6 Average Family Income by Family Structure, 2001

Source: Adapted from Statistics Canada, www.statcan.ca.

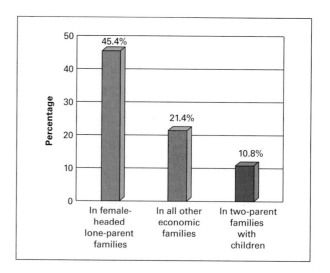

FIGURE 11–7 Percentage of Children Under 18 Years of Age with Low Income by Family Structure, 2001

Source: Adapted from Statistics Canada, www.statcan.ca.

husband-wife families. Female-headed lone-parent families have the lowest average income (see Figure 11–6) and the largest percentage falling below the official low-income cut-off. Of children living in female-headed lone-parent families, 45.4 percent live in poverty (Figure 11–7).

It is clear, then, that lone-parent families have substantially lower incomes than two-parent families, and that female-headed lone-parent families are the most disadvantaged. Issues of pay equity, employment equity, and family structure combine to increase the incidence of poverty among women, thus contributing to the feminization of poverty.

EXPLAINING POVERTY

The presence of 4.4 million poor people in one of the world's most affluent societies raises serious social and moral concerns. It also sparks considerable controversy within Canada—and from abroad. Many Canadians concur with the UN committee mentioned earlier, arguing that our government should take a much more active role in eradicating poverty. Others feel that the poor must bear responsibility for themselves. It is also possible to argue that *both* governments and the poor themselves need to contribute to the solution. The arguments underlying these approaches to the problem of poverty together frame a lively and pressing political debate.

One View: Blame the Poor

Proponents of one side of the issue hold the following view: *the poor are primarily responsible for their own poverty.* In this land of immigration and once seemingly unlimited resources and opportunities, we have embraced the notion that people are largely responsible for their own social standing. This approach assumes that our society offers considerable opportunity for anyone able and willing to take advantage of it. The poor, then, are those with fewer skills, less schooling, lower motivation, or, perhaps, a debilitating drug addiction—in sum, people who are somehow undeserving.

Anthropologist Oscar Lewis (1961) illustrates this approach in his studies of Latin American poverty. Lewis claims that the poor become entrapped in a *culture of poverty* that fosters resignation to one's plight. Socialized in this environment, children come to believe that there is little point in aspiring to a better life. The result is a self-perpetuating cycle of poverty.

Edward Banfield (1974) adds the contention that, where there is intense poverty, there exists a distinctive lower-class subculture that denigrates and erodes personal achievement. One element of this subculture, a present-time orientation, encourages living for the moment, rather than looking towards the future by engaging in hard work, saving, and other behaviour likely to promote upward social mobility. In Banfield's view, poor people who live largely for the moment perpetuate their own poverty; he defines this kind of behaviour as basically irresponsible, and he concludes that the poor reap more or less what they deserve.

Counterpoint: Blame Society

The other view of the issue is the following: *society is primarily responsible for poverty.* This alternative position, argued by William Ryan (1976), holds that soci-

U.S. artist George Tooker captured the humanity and humility of impoverished people in his painting The Laundress. *This message—that the poor are human beings, most doing the best they can to get by—is important to remember in a society that tends to define poor people as morally unworthy and deserving of their bitter plight.*

George Tooker (b. 1920), *The Laundress*, 1952. Oil on masonite, 59.7 × 61 cm. Christie's Images, N.Y. © George Tooker.

ety—not the poor—is responsible for poverty because of the way it distributes resources. In global context, societies that distribute wealth very unequally face a significant poverty problem. Societies that strive for more equality (such as Sweden and Japan) lack such extremes of social stratification.

Poverty, Ryan insists, is not inevitable: the problem is simply a matter of low incomes, not personal deficiencies. Ryan interprets any lack of ambition on the part of poor people as a *consequence* rather than a *cause* of their lack of opportunity. He therefore dismisses Banfield's analysis as little more than "blaming the victims" for their own suffering. In Ryan's view, social policies that empower the poor would give them real economic opportunity, and this should yield greater equality.

Critical evaluation. Each of these explanations of poverty has won its share of public support, and each has advocates among government policymakers. Some, particularly on the right of the political spectrum, believe that society should strive to encourage equality of opportunity, but should otherwise adopt a laissez-faire attitude towards the poor. Others, on the left, hold that society should actively reduce poverty by redistributing income in a more equitable manner through programs such as a comprehensive child-care package that would allow poor mothers to gain skills necessary to maintain jobs, or a guaranteed minimum income for every family. Canada has seriously considered national programs in both of these areas and

might have moved ahead had we not turned our attention to the national debt and deficit reduction.

Since the heads of many low-income families do not have jobs, their poverty is attributed to *not holding a job*. But the reasons that people do not work are a reflection on society as much as the individuals concerned. Middle-class women combine working and child-rearing, but doing so is much harder for poor women who cannot afford child care.

Quebec is the exception with respect to child care—which it makes available at the phenomenal rate of $5 per day. In the rest of Canada, few employers provide child-care programs for their employees, and few low-income workers can afford to buy this service from the private sector. Where child-care subsidies are provided, parents may still find that, when all costs are considered, it is cheaper to stay at home and take care of one's own children. Most poor men report that either there are no jobs to be found, that illness or disability has sidelined them, or, in the case of the elderly, that they have retired. Overall, poor adults are poor not by choice, but because they know of no alternatives.

The Working Poor

But not all poor people are jobless. At various points in this chapter, tables and figures refer to salaries of people who work full time all year. Many of these salaries—for women, for certain occupations, and for specific ethnic and racial categories—are low relative to the official

Social scientists debate the causes of poverty. Some cite the failings of individuals, such as lack of initiative or drug abuse, and others point to flaws of society, including a minimum wage that does not allow a full-time worker to support a family. Here, homeless people gather under a bridge in Hamburg, Germany.

poverty line. If these people, working full time, have incomes that are below the poverty line for individuals, what happens if they are single parents with two or three children? The working poor are the men and women who labour for at least fifty weeks of the year and yet cannot escape poverty; many people who involuntarily work part time are also included among the working poor. Such "working poverty" places the poor in a bind: their jobs provide low wages that barely allow them to make ends meet, but consume the time and energy needed to obtain training or schooling that might open new doors. People in this situation are often reluctant or simply unable to risk the jobs they do have in hopes of finding something better. Even with minimum wages of $5.50 to $7.60 in 2000, depending on the province, a full-time worker could not support a family above the official poverty line.

Clearly, individual ability and initiative play a part in shaping everyone's social position. On balance, though, the weight of sociological evidence points to society—not individual character traits—as the primary cause of poverty. This is because the poor are categories of people who contend with special barriers and limited opportunities.

HOMELESSNESS

Many low-income people in Canada cannot afford even basic housing: as a society, we have failed to ensure an adequate supply of affordable housing. In light of the enormous wealth of our country and its purported commitment to providing opportunity and/or social safety nets for everyone, homelessness may be fairly described as a societal scar that demands an effective response. The scar consists of thousands of

people across the country living on the streets, in various (often temporary) shelters, and even in our jails.

The familiar stereotypes of homeless people—men sleeping in doorways and women carrying everything they own in a shopping bag—have been undermined by the reality of the "new homeless": those thrown out of work by plant closings; people forced out of apartments by rising rents, condominium conversions, or "gentrification" (e.g., converting rooming houses into expensive single-family homes); and others unable to meet mortgage or rent payments because they must work for low wages. Clearly, no stereotype paints a complete picture of the homeless.

But virtually all homeless people have one thing in common: poverty. For that reason, the explanations of poverty already offered also apply to homelessness. One side of the debate places responsibility on personal traits of the homeless themselves. Perhaps one-third of homeless people are mentally ill; others are addicted to alcohol or other drugs. Some, for whatever reason, seem unable to cope in a complex and highly competitive society (Bassuk, 1984; Whitman, 1989).

On the other side, advocates assert that homelessness results from *societal* factors, including a lack of low-income housing and the economic transition towards low-paying jobs (Kozol, 1988; Schutt, 1989). Fully one-third of all homeless people are now entire families, and children are the fastest growing category of the homeless. The closing of a plant, making it necessary for an individual to take a job at McDonald's—at $11 500 per year—makes it impossible to support a family.

No one disputes that a large proportion of homeless people have personal difficulties to some degree, although how much is cause and how much effect is difficult to untangle. But structural changes in the Canadian economy coupled with declining government support for lower-income people have all contributed to homelessness.

In the winter of 1995–96, the Toronto churches that provide emergency overnight accommodation for the homeless were finding that more *families* were appearing on their doorsteps. Some of these families were evicted by landlords when reduced welfare payments could no longer cover the rent. In the same winter (a record cold one for Toronto), at least two homeless people froze to death while huddled in their makeshift shelters. One man, who died under a highway ramp, did not even have shoes on his feet.

A comprehensive response to homelessness must consider both personal and societal dimensions of the problem. Increasing the supply of low-income housing (other than shelters) is one important step. Additionally, low-income people must have the opportunity to earn the income necessary to pay for housing. Homelessness, however, is not only a housing problem—it is also a *human* problem. People who endure months or years of insecure living come to need various types of social services.

CLASS AND WELFARE, POLITICS AND VALUES

This chapter presents a great many facts about social class in Canada. In the end, however, our understanding of what it means to be wealthy and privileged or poor and perhaps homeless also turns on politics and values. Support for the notion that social standing reflects personal merit, effort, and responsibility is strongest among people who are well-off and support the political right. The idea that society should distribute wealth and other resources more equally finds greatest favour among those with relatively few advantages or those on the political left.

Although we may recognize that structural constraints place insurmountable barriers in the paths of some categories of people, we still share a general North American belief in a meritocracy. These cultural values encourage us to see successful people as personally meritorious and the poor as personally deficient. This judgment, applied to the poor, is called "the hidden injury of class" (Sennett and Cobb, 1973). In other words, poverty significantly lowers the self-image of disadvantaged people, while the more fortunate display their affluence as a personal "badge of ability." Values supporting individual responsibility also contribute to negative views of social welfare programs and the people who rely on them. While advocates for the poor defend welfare programs as necessary for millions of people lacking opportunities and advantages, our cultural values promote the view that social welfare programs undermine initiative. Accepting assistance of this kind is personally demeaning, which explains why many people who are eligible for assistance are reluctant to apply for it.

Finally, the drama of social stratification extends far beyond Canada's borders. The most striking social disparities are found not by looking within one country but by comparing living standards in various parts of the world. In Chapter 12 ("Global Stratification"), we broaden our investigation of social stratification, focusing on global inequality.

SUMMARY

1. Social inequality in Canada involves disparities in a host of variables, including income, wealth, education, and power.

2. White-collar occupations generally confer more prestige and higher incomes than blue-collar jobs. The pink-collar occupations typically held by women offer little social prestige or income.

3. Ascription exerts a powerful effect on stratification in Canada; ancestry, race or ethnicity, and gender are all related to social position.

4. The upper class, which is small (perhaps 4 or 5 percent of the population) includes the richest and most powerful families. Members of the upper-upper class, or the old rich, derive their wealth through inheritance over several generations; those in the lower-upper class, or the new rich, depend on earned income as their primary source of wealth.

5. The middle class encompasses 40 to 50 percent of the Canadian population. The upper-middle class may be distinguished on the basis of higher income, higher-prestige occupations, and more schooling.

6. The working class makes up about one-third of our population. With below-average income, working-class families have less financial security than those in the middle class. Few working-class people attain more than a high-school education, and they commonly work in blue-collar or lower-prestige white-collar jobs.

7. About one-fifth of the population belongs to the lower class and lives near or below the official poverty line.

8. Social class affects nearly all aspects of life, beginning with health and life expectancy, and encompassing a wide range of attitudes and patterns of family living.

CONTROVERSY & DEBATE

The Welfare Dilemma

The predicament of Karen Moss, described at the beginning of this chapter, highlights a remarkable consensus in this country regarding "welfare"—nobody likes it. The political left criticizes it as an inadequate response to poverty; conservatives charge that it is hurting the people it allegedly helps and driving the country to bankruptcy; and the poor themselves find welfare a complex, confusing, and often degrading program.

Conservative critics (those to the right of the political spectrum) contend that, rather than alleviating poverty, welfare has actually *worsened* the problem for two reasons. First, it has eroded the traditional family by making living as a single person an attractive alternative to marriage. As conservatives see it, welfare makes it economically beneficial for women to have children outside of marriage and is a key reason for the rapid rise in out-of-wedlock births among poor people.

Second, the conservative critique holds that government assistance undermines self-reliance among the poor and fosters dependency. Dependence on government "handouts," argue critics, is the main reason that so many poor heads of households do not have steady, full-time jobs. Clearly, conservatives say, welfare has strayed far from its original purpose of helping nonworking women with children (typically, after the death or divorce of a husband) make the transition to self-sufficiency. On the contrary, welfare has become a way of life. Once trapped in dependency, poor women most often raise children who will themselves remain poor as adults.

The left charges its opponents with using a double standard for assessing government programs. Why, they ask, is there so much outrage at the thought of the government transferring money to poor mothers and children when most "welfare" actually goes to relatively rich people? The amounts spent on welfare across Canada, while they are not negligible, pale in comparison with the tax write-offs received by more affluent people for the registered retirement savings plans (RRSPs) they buy each year. And what about the billions of dollars in tax write-offs for corporations, many of which are enjoying record profits? As the left sees it, "wealthfare" costs the country a great deal more than "welfare," even though public opinion takes the opposite view.

Critics claim that conservatives (and much public opinion) distort the performance of public assistance. Images of irresponsible "welfare bums" mask the fact that most poor families who turn to public assistance are truly needy. Karen Moss received only $1221 a month for herself and her son before the rates were cut, hardly enough to attract people to a "life of welfare dependency." Across Canada in recent years, the trend has been to slash welfare rates as a deficit-reduction measure. Overall, the left faults public assistance as a Band-Aid approach to the growing social problems of unemployment and poverty in Canada.

As for the charge that public assistance undermines families, the left concedes that the proportion of single-parent families is rising, but disputes the argument that welfare is to blame. Rather, single parenting is a widespread cultural trend found at all class levels in most industrial societies.

Thus, critics conclude, public assistance programs such as welfare are not attacked because they have failed, but because they benefit poor people, a segment of the population long scorned as "undeserving." Our cultural tradition of equating wealth with virtue and poverty with vice allows rich people to display privilege as a "badge of ability" while poverty carries a negative stigma. Sennett and Cobb (1973) call this the "hidden injury of class."

---

9. Social mobility is common in Canada, as it is in other industrial societies. For only 12 percent of women and 26 percent of men is there no intergenerational mobility; typically, however, only small changes (upward or downward) occur from one generation to the next.

10. Since the early 1970s, changes in the Canadian economy have reduced the standard of living for low- and moderate-income families. In one important trend, manufacturing industries have declined in Canada, paralleling growth in low-paying service-sector jobs.

11. Some 4.4 million people in Canada are officially classified as poor. About 1.1 million of the poor are children and young people under the age of eighteen. Increasingly, poor families are headed by women; the elderly, Natives, and certain other racial and ethnic categories are overrepresented among the poor as well.

12. Oscar Lewis and Edward Banfield advanced the "culture of poverty" thesis, suggesting that poverty can be perpetuated by the social patterns of the poor themselves. Opposing this view, William Ryan argues that poverty is caused by the unequal distribu-

Many on the right believe all welfare programs should be abolished. Those on the left, in contrast, want to both improve and expand them. Are there areas of common ground in this debate? The province of Ontario, as part of its welfare reform program, has instituted "workfare," which makes income assistance contingent on able-bodied recipients performing useful work and participating in occupational training. Other provinces are monitoring Ontario's program with great interest.

Continue the debate . . .

1. *Is it fair for provinces across the country to slash their welfare budgets and for the federal government to slash the transfer payments that support those budgets, all in the name of deficit reduction, while at the same time no effort is made to recoup the tax write-offs that middle-class and wealthy people are awarded when they buy RRSPs? Is this just one more case of the poor being exploited because they are politically powerless?*

2. *Do you think public assistance has become a "way of life" for many people, as conservatives charge?*

3. *Do you feel that an expanded public assistance program would lessen the extent of poverty in Canadian society? Why or why not?*

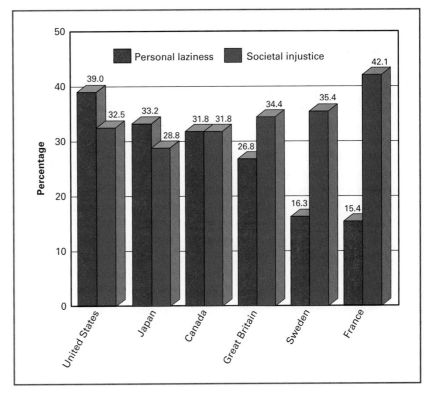

FIGURE 11–8 Assessing the Causes of Poverty

Survey Question: "Why are there people in this country who live in need?" Percentages reflect respondents' identification of either "personal laziness" or "societal injustice" as the primary cause of poverty.

Percentages for each country do not add up to 100 because less frequently identified causes of poverty were omitted from this figure.

Source: World Values Survey (1994).

tion of wealth in society. Although Lewis and Banfield's view is consistent with our society's cultural pattern of personalizing social position, Ryan's view is supported by more evidence.

CRITICAL-THINKING QUESTIONS

1. Assess your own social class. Does your family have consistent standing on various dimensions of social stratification (including income, education, and occupational prestige)? Why do most people find talking about their own social position awkward?

2. Identify some of the effects of Canadian social stratification on health, values, politics, and family patterns.

3. What categories of people are at high risk of poverty in Canada? What evidence supports the assertions (1) that the poor are responsible for their low social position, and (2) that society is primarily responsible for poverty?

APPLICATIONS AND EXERCISES

1. Develop several simple questions that, taken together, would let you measure someone's social class position. Try these questions on several adults, and refine your questions as you proceed.

2. Visit Statistics Canada's website at **www.statcan.ca**. Here you will find income data as well as a host of other statistics about social inequality. See what you

can learn about social standing in your part of the country.

3. During an evening of television viewing, assess the social class level of the characters you see in various shows. In each case, note precisely why you place someone in a particular social position. Do you discern any patterns?

 SITES TO SEE

www.macionis.com
or
www.TheSociologyPage.com

You can find more than fifty weblinks to sociological journals and other sources of data and information by visiting the Links Library at this website.

www.ccsd.ca/facts.html

Maintained by the Canadian Council on Social Development, the *Statistics and Information* page publishes statistical information on family income, poverty lines, child poverty, welfare incomes, the estimated number of Canadians on welfare, and other related topics.

www.nald.ca/lithome.htm

Gimme Shelter: A Resource on Literacy and Homelessness Work is an online book written mostly for people who do, or would like to do, literacy and community development work with people who are transient or homeless. It defines literacy and homelessness, discusses critical issues including outreach, racism, and gender, offers instruction for literacy tutors, and provides resource materials.

www.napo-onap.ca

The National Anti-Poverty Organization is a non-governmental, non-partisan advocacy organization of low-income Canadians and others concerned about issues affecting poor people. The site includes a poverty quiz, NAPO newsletters and research, facts about poverty, and ideas for action.

www.nationalpost.com/
and
www.theglobeandmail.com/business/

The online versions of the *Financial Post* and the *Report on Business* publish daily reports and opinion, technology articles, investment information, profiles of top companies, and other business news.

www21.hrdc-drhc.gc.ca/home/

The National Homelessness Initiative is a Canadian government program that helps governments and community organizations work together to address the problem of homelessness.

 STUDY TOOLS

For more study tools to help you with your next exam, be sure to check out the Companion Website at **www.pearsoned. ca/macionis**, as well as Chapter 11 in your Study Guide.

 INVESTIGATE WITH CONTENTSELECT

Follow the instructions found on page 25 of this textbook to access ContentSelect™ at the Research Navigator™ website. Once at the site, enter your LOGINID and Password. Then, enter keywords such as "social class,"

"wealth," and "poverty," and the search engine will supply relevant and recent scholarly and popular press publications.

CHAPTER

12

José Belon (d. 1927, French)
Famine in India

Illustration from *Le Petit Journal*, c. 1899 (coloured engraving).
Private collection. The Bridgeman Art Gallery.

GLOBAL STRATIFICATION

Standing in the burning sun at the edge of the North African desert, two reporters nervously wait to meet their contacts. They have travelled thousands of miles in pursuit of a stunning story—that, in the 1990s, slavery still exists. To many people, slavery is a vestige of the 1800s, and an evil that has been eradicated from the world. But this is not the case, and Gilbert Lewthwaite and Gregory Kane (1996) are about to prove it. They have travelled from Baltimore to the nation of Sudan to buy a human being.

Two men approach, carrying assault rifles, and exchange words with the interpreter who accompanies the reporters. The interpreter then explains that they will travel on foot to meet the slave trader. The sun climbs higher, and heat rises up from the ground. On their three-hour walk, the reporters drain their canteens, but the men with the rifles never drink at all.

Finally, under a giant mango tree, the group escapes from the pounding sun. Minutes later the slave trader, Adam al Haj, appears. He explains that he is in the business of trying to return to their families women and children seized by tribal raiders. Over the last five years, he claims, he has helped 473 slaves gain their freedom. His price is five cows or $500 per person. The reporters hand over $1000 in cash. From around the tree, associates come forward with a dozen young boys, most showing signs of malnutrition. The trader motions to the reporters: pick any two.

The boys are fearful, imagining that they are being resold to unknown owners. For most such boys—seized in intertribal warfare—life as a slave means tending animals, doing menial labour, and enduring periodic abuse. For girls, sexual assault is commonplace.

The boys have no idea that they are to be returned to their families so they stand expressionless, eyes fixed on the ground. The reporters are paralyzed by the thought of picking out two boys as if they were shirts on a rack. They settle on the boy who seems to be the oldest. Nearby stands a cluster of anxious parents who have heard that children are to be freed. The reporters ask if the boy's parents are there. The interpreter points and a man named Deng Kuot Mayen steps forward towards his son. The father points to a second boy—also his son. The deal is struck. Twelve-year-old Akok Deng Kuot and ten-year-old Garang Deng Kuot stand silently. It has been six years since they were seized: they do not recognize their father or comprehend that their ordeal is over.

While the details vary, this story is far from unique. In fact, experts claim that tens of millions of children across Latin America, Africa, and Asia have been seized by raiders or sold into bondage by their desperately poor families.

The fact that slavery still exists is a powerful sign of the extent of social inequality in the world. As this chapter explains, poverty is a reality in Canada, but the problem is both more widespread and more severe in the poor countries of the world.

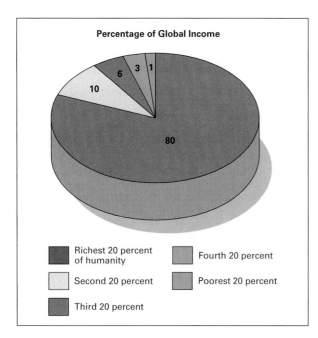

Percentage of Global Income

Richest 20 percent of humanity

Second 20 percent

Third 20 percent

Fourth 20 percent

Poorest 20 percent

FIGURE 12–1 Distribution of World Income

Sources: Calculated by John Macionis based on United Nations Development Programme (2000) and The World Bank (2001).

GLOBAL INEQUALITY: AN OVERVIEW

Chapter 11 ("Social Class in Canada") detailed the income inequality that marks our own society. In global perspective, however, social stratification is even more pronounced. Figure 12–1 divides the world's total income by fifths of the population. Recall that the richest 20 percent of the Canadian population earns about 44 percent of the national income (see Table 11–1 on page 261); the richest 20 percent of the global population, however, receives about 80 percent of all income. At the other end of the social scale, the poorest 20 percent of the Canadian population earns 5.2 percent of our national income; the poorest 20 percent of the world's people, in contrast, struggles to survive on just 1 percent of global income.

Because global income is so concentrated, the average member of a rich society (such as Canada) lives extremely well by world standards. In fact, the living standard of most people below our government's poverty threshold far surpasses that of the majority of the earth's people.

A WORD ABOUT TERMINOLOGY

Most people are familiar with the "Three Worlds" model for describing the unequal distribution of global income. Developed after World War II, this model has been in wide use ever since. Rich, industrialized countries are "First World" nations, less-industrialized socialist countries are the "Second World," and the re-

maining nonindustrialized and poor countries are called the "Third World."

Recently, however, the "Three Worlds" model has lost validity. For one thing, it was a product of Cold War politics by which the capitalist West (the First World) faced off against the socialist East (the Second World), while the rest of the world (the Third World) remained more or less on the sidelines. But the sweeping transformation of Eastern Europe and the former Soviet Union means that a distinctive Second World no longer exists. Even the superpower opposition that defined the Cold War has faded in recent years.

A second problem with the model is that it lumped together in the Third World more than one hundred countries at different levels of development. Some better-off nations of the Third World (such as Chile in South America) have ten times the per-person productivity of the poorest countries of the world (including Ethiopia in eastern Africa).

Today's world calls for a modestly revised system of classification. We will, therefore, use the terms introduced in Chapter 1 ("The Sociological Perspective"): *high-income countries* are the richest forty nations with the most-developed economies and the highest overall standard of living for their people. Next, the world's roughly ninety *middle-income countries* are somewhat poorer nations whose economic development is more or less typical for the world as a whole. Finally, the remaining sixty *low-income countries* are marked by the lowest productivity and the most severe and extensive poverty.

Compared to the older "Three Worlds" system, this new form of classification has two main advantages. First, it focuses on the key issue of economic development rather than highlighting whether societies are capitalist or socialist. Second, this revision provides a more precise picture of the relative economic development of the world's countries because it does not lump together all less-industrialized countries into a single Third World.

Nonetheless, classifying the 192 nations on earth into any three categories (or, even more crudely, dividing them into the "rich North" and the "poor South") ignores pronounced differences in their ways of life. The countries at each of the three levels of economic development have rich and varied histories, speak hundreds of languages, and encompass diverse peoples who are proud of their cultural distinctiveness.

Further, just as the world's nations form an economic hierarchy of very rich to very poor, so every country on earth is also internally stratified. The extent of global inequality is actually greater than national comparisons suggest, since the most well-off people in rich countries (like Canada) live worlds apart from the poorest people in low-income countries (like Sudan and India). This striking contrast helps explain why, despite the affluence familiar to so many Canadians,

When natural disasters strike high-income societies, as in the 1997 floods in southern Manitoba, property loss is great but the loss of life is low. In low-income societies, in contrast, the converse is true; the death toll from Hurricane Mitch's rampage through Honduras in 1998 reached 5000.

millions of the world's children fall victim to life-threatening poverty.

HIGH-INCOME COUNTRIES

High-income nations are rich because theirs were the first economies to be transformed by the Industrial Revolution more than two centuries ago, increasing their productive capacity one hundredfold. To grasp how this development enriched our own region of the world, consider that the small European nation of Holland is more productive than the vast continent of Africa below the Sahara Desert; likewise, tiny Belgium outproduces all of India.

The forty high-income countries of the world include Canada and the United States, Argentina, the nations of Western Europe, Israel, Saudi Arabia, Singapore, Hong Kong (now part of the People's Republic of China), Japan, South Korea, Australia, and New Zealand.

Taken together, countries with the most-developed economies cover roughly 25 percent of the earth's land area—including parts of five continents—while lying mostly in the northern hemisphere. In 2002, the total population of these nations was about 1 billion, or 18 percent of the earth's people. By global standards, rich nations are not densely populated; even so, some countries (such as Japan) are crowded while others (such as Canada) are sparsely settled. Inside their borders, however, about three-quarters of the people in high-income countries congregate in or near cities.

High-income countries reveal significant cultural differences—the nations of Europe, for example, recognize more than thirty official languages. But these wealthy countries share an industrial capacity that generates, on average, a rich material life for their

people. Per capita income in these societies ranges from about $10 000 annually (in Slovakia and Saudi Arabia) to more than $25 000 annually (in the United States and Norway).[1] This prosperity is so great that residents of the most-developed countries enjoy more than half the world's total income.

Finally, just as people in a single society perform specialized work, so various regions form a global division of labour. Generally speaking, high-income countries dominate the world's scientific efforts and employ the most complex and productive technology. Production in rich societies is capital-intensive, meaning high investments in factories and related machinery. High-income countries also stand at the forefront of the Information Revolution; the majority of the largest corporations that design and market computers, as well as most computer users, are found in rich societies. With the lion's share of wealth, high-income countries also control the world's financial markets; ups and downs on the financial exchanges of New York, London, and Tokyo affect people throughout the world.

MIDDLE-INCOME COUNTRIES

Middle-income countries have per capita income ranging between $2500 and $10 000, roughly the median for the world's *nations* (but above that for the world's *people*

---

[1]High-income countries have per capita annual income of at least $10 000. For middle- and low-income countries the comparable figures are $2500 to $10 000, and below $2500, respectively. All data reflect the United Nations' concept of "purchasing power parities," which avoids distortion caused by exchange rates when converting all currencies to U.S. dollars. Instead, the data represent the local purchasing power of each nation's currency.

Japan represents the world's high-income countries, in which industrial technology and economic expansion have produced material prosperity. The presence of market forces is evident in this view of downtown Tokyo (above, left). The Russian Federation represents the middle-income countries of the world. Industrial development has been slower in the former Soviet Union, as socialist economies have performed sluggishly. Residents of Moscow, for example, chafe at having to wait in long lines for their daily needs (above, right). The hope is that the introduction of a market system will raise living standards, although it probably will also increase economic disparity. Bangladesh (left) represents the low-income countries of the world. As the photograph suggests, these nations have limited economic development and rapidly increasing populations. The result is widespread poverty.

because most people live in the poorest countries). Two-thirds of the people live in cities, and industrial jobs are common. The remaining one-third of the people live in rural areas, where most are poor and lack access to schools, medical care, adequate housing, and even safe drinking water.

About ninety of the world's nations fall into the middle-income category. At the high end are Chile (Latin America), South Africa (Africa), and Malaysia (Asia), where annual income is about $8500. At the low end are Ecuador (Latin America), Albania (Europe), Egypt (Africa), and Indonesia (Asia) with roughly $3000 annually in per capita income.

One cluster of middle-income countries includes the former Soviet Union and the nations of Eastern Europe (in the past, known as the Second World). These countries had mostly socialist economies until popular revolts between 1989 and 1991 swept aside their governments. Since then, these nations have begun to introduce market systems, but so far the results have been uneven. Some (including Estonia) have improving economies, whereas living standards in others (including Russia) have fallen.

A second, and larger, category of middle-income nations includes Chile and Brazil in South America, and Algeria and Botswana in Africa. Although South Africa's white minority lives as well as people in the United States, the country is considered less developed because its majority Black population has far less income.

Taken together, middle-income countries span roughly 47 percent of the earth's land area and include about 3.3 billion people, or more than one-half of humanity. Some countries (such as Russia) are far less crowded than others (such as El Salvador), but compared with high-income countries, these societies are densely populated.

LOW-INCOME COUNTRIES

Low-income countries, where most people are very poor, are largely agrarian societies with some industry. Most of these nations are found in Africa and in southern Asia. Low-income countries cover 28 percent of the planet's land area and are home to 28 percent of its people. Population density is generally high, although it is greater in Asian countries (such as Bangladesh and India) than in central African nations (such as Chad and the Democratic Republic of the Congo).

In poor countries, 31 percent of the people live in cities; most inhabit villages and farms, living much as their families have for centuries. In fact, half the

Tens of millions of children fend for themselves on the streets of Latin America, where many fall victim to disease, drug abuse, and outright violence. What do you think must be done to put an end to scenes like this one in San Salvador, the capital city of El Salvador?

world's people are peasants who, by and large, follow cultural traditions. With limited industrial technology, peasants are not very productive, one reason that many endure severe poverty. Hunger, disease, and unsafe housing frame the lives of the world's poorest people.

People living in affluent nations such as Canada find it hard to grasp the scope of human want in much of the world. From time to time, televised pictures of famine in very poor countries such as Ethiopia and Bangladesh give us a shocking glimpse of the poverty that makes every day a life-and-death struggle. Behind these images lie cultural, historical, and economic forces that we explore in the remainder of this chapter.

GLOBAL WEALTH AND POVERTY

To classify a country as "low income" does not mean that only poor people live there. On the contrary, the rich neighbourhoods of Manila (the Philippines) and Madras (India) testify to the high living standards of some. Indeed, the typical well-to-do household is staffed by several servants, a gardener, and a chauffeur. The following journal notes provide a sense of the dramatic inequality that marks poor nations.

October 14, 1994, Smokey Mountain, on the northern side of Manila, the Philippines. What caught my eye was how clean she was—a girl no more than seven or eight years old, hair carefully combed and wearing a freshly laundered dress. Her eyes followed us as we walked past; camera-toting Americans stand out in this, one of the poorest neighbourhoods in the entire world.

Fed by methane from the decomposing garbage, the fires never go out on Smokey Mountain, Manila's vast garbage dump. Smoke envelops the hills of refuse like a thick fog. But Smokey Mountain is more than a dump; it is a neighbourhood that is home to thousands of people. The residents of Smokey Mountain are the poorest of the poor, and one is hard pressed to imagine a setting more hostile to human life. Amid the smoke and the squalor, men and women do what they can to survive, picking plastic bags from the garbage and washing them in the river, stacking flattened cardboard boxes outside a family's plywood shack. And all over Smokey Mountain are children who must already sense the enormous odds against them. What chance do they have, living in families that earn scarcely a few hundred dollars a year? With barely any opportunity for schooling?

And, against this backdrop of human tragedy, one lovely little girl has put on a fresh dress and gone out to play....

With Smokey Mountain behind us, our taxi driver threads his way through heavy traffic towards the other side of Manila. The change is amazing: the forbidding smoke and smells of the dump give way to the polished

TABLE 12–1 Wealth and Well-Being in Global Perspective, 1999

Country	Gross Domestic Products ($ billion)	GDP per Capita (PPP$)*	Quality of Life Index
High Income			
Norway	153	28 433	.939
Australia	404	24 547	.936
Canada	635	26 251	.936
Sweden	239	22 636	.936
United States	9152	31 872	.934
Japan	4347	24 898	.928
France	1432	22 897	.924
United Kingdom	1442	22 093	.923
South Korea	407	15 712	.875
Middle Income			
Eastern Europe			
Poland	155	8450	.828
Lithuania	11	6656	.803
Russian Federation	401	7473	.775
Ukraine	39	3458	.742
Latin America			
Mexico	484	8297	.790
Venezuela	102	5495	.765
Brazil	752	7037	.750
Asia			
Malaysia	79	8209	.774
Thailand	124	6132	.757
China, P.R. of	990	3617	.718
Middle East			
Iran	111	5531	.714
Syria	19	4454	.700
Africa			
Algeria	48	5063	.693
Botswana	6	6872	.577
Low Income			
Latin America			
Honduras	5	2340	.634
Haiti	4	1464	.467
Asia			
India	447	2248	.571
Bangladesh	46	1483	.470
Africa			
Democratic Republic of the Congo	6	801	.429
Guinea	4	1934	.397
Ethiopia	6	628	.321
Sierra Leone	1	448	.258

*These data are the United Nations' purchasing power–parity calculations, which avoid currency rate distortion by showing the local purchasing power of each domestic currency.

Source: United Nations Development Programme (2001).

neighbourhoods that look like Miami or Los Angeles.

In the distance, a cluster of yachts is visible on the bay. No more rutted streets; now we glide quietly along wide tree-lined boulevards filled with expensive Japanese cars. We pass shopping plazas, upscale hotels, high-rise office buildings, and entrances to exclusive residential enclaves set off by gates and protected by armed guards. Here, in large, air-conditioned homes, live the rich of Manila.

Poor nations are home to both rich and poor people, but hardly in equal numbers. Indeed, for most people in the world's poor countries, poverty is the rule. Moreover, with incomes of only several hundred dollars a year, the burden of poverty is greater than it is among the poor of Canada. This does not mean that deprivation here at home is a minor problem. Especially in a rich society, the lack of food, housing, and health care for millions of people—almost half of them children—amounts to a national tragedy. Yet, even after years of recession and government cutbacks in Canada, poverty in poor countries remains both *more severe* and *more extensive* than it is in this country.

THE SEVERITY OF POVERTY

Poverty in poor countries is more severe than it is in rich nations such as Canada. The data in Table 12–1 provide a statistical picture of global stratification. The first column of figures shows the gross domestic product (GDP)[2] for countries at each level of economic development. Industrial societies have a high economic output primarily because of their industrial technology. A large, industrial nation such as the United States had a 1999 GDP of about $9 trillion; Japan's GDP stood at about $4.2 trillion; Canada's was about $0.8 trillion. Comparing GDP figures shows that the world's richest nations are thousands of times more productive than the poorest countries on earth.

The second column of figures in Table 12–1 indicates per capita GDP in terms of what the United Nations (1995) calls "purchasing power parities"—what people can buy using their income in the local economy. The per capita GDP for rich countries such as the United States, France, and Canada is very high—more than $20 000. For middle-income coun-

[2]Gross domestic product refers to all the goods and services on record as produced by a country's economy in a given year. Income earned outside the country by individuals or corporations is excluded from this measure; this is the key difference between GDP and gross national product (GNP), which includes foreign earnings. For countries that invest heavily abroad (Kuwait, for example), GDP is considerably less than GNP; for countries in which other nations invest heavily (Hong Kong), GDP is much higher than GNP.

tries, such as Botswana and Lithuania, the figures are much lower—about $6500. In the world's low-income countries, per capita annual income is just a few hundred dollars. In the Democratic Republic of the Congo or in Ethiopia, for example, a typical person labours all year to make what the average worker in the United States earns in several days.

The last column in Table 12–1 measures quality of life in these nations. This index, calculated by the United Nations, is based on income, education (extent of adult literacy and average years of schooling), and longevity (how long people typically live). Index values are decimals that fall between the hypothetical extremes of 1 (highest) and zero (lowest). By this calculation, Norwegians enjoy the highest quality of life (.939), with the residents of Australia and Canada close behind (.936). At the other extreme, people in the African nation of Sierra Leone have the world's lowest quality of life (.258).

One reason that quality of life differs so much around the world is that economic productivity is lowest in precisely the regions of the globe where population growth is highest. Figure 12–2 shows the division of global population and global income for countries at each level of economic development. High-income countries are by far the most advantaged, with 79 percent of global income supporting just 18 percent of humanity. In middle-income nations, 54 percent of the world's people earn about 18 percent of global income. This leaves 28 percent of the planet's population with just 3 percent of global income. In short, for every dollar received by individuals in a low-income country, someone in a high-income nation takes home $41.

Relative versus Absolute Poverty

The distinction made in the last chapter between relative and absolute poverty has an important application to global inequality. People living in rich societies typically focus on *relative poverty*, meaning that some people lack resources others take for granted. Relative poverty, by definition, cuts across every society, rich or poor.

Especially important in a global context is the concept of *absolute poverty*, a lack of resources that is life threatening. Human beings in absolute poverty commonly lack the nutrition necessary for health and long-term survival. To be sure, some absolute poverty exists in Canada. Inadequate nutrition that leaves children or elderly people vulnerable to illness and even outright starvation is a reality in this nation. But such immediately life-threatening poverty strikes only a small proportion of the Canadian population; in low-income countries, in contrast, one-third or more of the people are in desperate need.

Since absolute poverty threatens people with death, one indicator of the extent of the problem is the

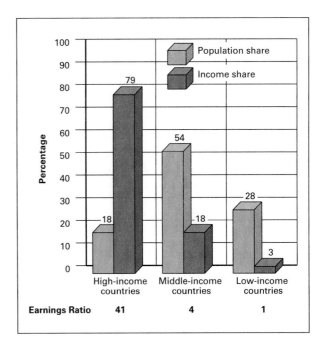

FIGURE 12–2 The Relative Share of Income and Population by Level of Economic Development

Sources: Calculated by John Macionis based on United Nations Development Programme (2000) and The World Bank (2001).

median age at death. Global Map 12–1 identifies the age by which half of all people born in a society die. In rich societies, most people die after reaching the age of seventy-five; in poor countries, however, half of all deaths occur among children who have not yet reached the age of ten.

THE EXTENT OF POVERTY

Poverty in poor countries is more extensive than it is in rich nations such as Canada. Chapter 11 ("Social Class in Canada") noted that the Canadian government officially classifies about one in six or seven people as poor. In low-income countries, however, most people live no better than our poor, and many are far worse off. As Global Map 12–1 shows, the high death rates among children in Africa indicate that absolute poverty is greatest there, where half the population is malnourished. In the world as a whole, at any given time, 15 percent of the people (about 1 billion) suffer from chronic hunger, which leaves them less able to work and puts them at high risk of disease (Kates, 1996; United Nations Development Programme, 2001).

Members of rich societies, such as Canada, tend to be overnourished. On average, a member of a high-income society consumes about 3500 calories daily, an excess that contributes to obesity and related health problems. Most people in low-income countries not only do more physical work than we do, but they rarely consume more than 2000 calories daily. In short,

 Read a report on world hunger by the Food and Agriculture Organization of the United Nations at www.fao.org/NEWS/1999/img/SOFI99-E.PDF

they lack sufficient food or, more precisely, enough of the right kinds of food.

Lack of necessary nutrition makes death a way of life in poor societies. In the ten minutes it takes to read through this section of the chapter, about three hundred people in the world will die from disease because they have been weakened by an inadequate diet. This amounts to about 40 000 people a day, or 15 million people each year. Clearly, easing world hunger is one of the most serious responsibilities facing humanity today.

POVERTY AND CHILDREN

Death often comes early in poor societies, where families lack adequate food, safe water, secure housing, and access to medical care. Organizations combatting child poverty estimate that poverty forces some 75 million city children in poor countries to beg, steal, sell sex, or serve as couriers for drug gangs to provide income for their families. This almost always means dropping out of school and places children at high risk of illness and violence. Many street girls, with little or no access to medical assistance, become pregnant—a case of children who cannot support themselves having still more children.

About 100 million of the world's children leave their families altogether, sleeping and living on the streets as best they can. Roughly half of all street children are found in Latin America. Some 10 000 homeless children move through the streets of Mexico City (Ross, 1996). In Brazil, millions of street children live in makeshift huts, under bridges, or in alleyways. In Rio de Janeiro, known to many of us as Brazil's beautiful seaside resort, police try to keep the number of street children in check; on occasion, death squads may sweep through a neighbourhood in a bloody ritual of "urban cleansing." In Rio, several hundred street children are murdered each year (Larmer, 1992; U.S. House of Representatives, 1992).

POVERTY AND WOMEN

Women in Sikandernagar, one of India's countless rural villages, begin work at 4:00 in the morning, lighting the fires, milking the buffalo, sweeping floors, and walking to the well for water. They care for other family members as they rise. By 8:00, when many people in Canada are just beginning their day, these women move on to their "second shift," working under the hot sun in the fields until 5:00 in the afternoon. Returning home, the women gather wood for their fires, all the time searching for whatever plants they can find to enrich the evening meal. The buffalo, too, are ready for a meal, and the women tend to them.

 Read about a woman who spent six years working in a sweatshop in Saipan producing clothing for sale by the Gap at www.globalexchange.org/getInvolved/speakers/5.html

It is well past dark before their eighteen-hour days are through (Jacobson, 1993:61).

In rich societies, the work women do is typically unrecognized, undervalued, and underpaid; women receive less income for their efforts than men do. In low-income countries, this pattern is even more pronounced. Furthermore, although women do most of the work in poor nations, they are disproportionately the poorest of the poor.

Families in poor societies depend on women's work to provide income. At the same time, tradition bars many women from school, as they have primary responsibility for child-rearing and maintaining the household. The United Nations estimates that in poor societies, men own 90 percent of the land, a far greater gender disparity in wealth than in industrial nations. Multilayered systems of tradition and law subordinate women in poor societies so that about 70 percent of the world's roughly 1 billion people near absolute poverty are women (Hymowitz, 1995).

Women in poor countries have limited access to birth control (which, obviously, raises the birth rate), and they typically give birth without the assistance of any trained health personnel. Figure 12–3 draws a stark contrast between high- and low-income countries in this regard.

Gender inequality is starkest in low-income societies, especially in Asia where cultural traditions favour males. The cultural preference for males is evident in virtually every dimension of life, and has produced a stunning lack of females in some regions (Kishor, 1993).

SLAVERY

Poor societies are vulnerable to a host of related problems: hunger, illiteracy, warfare, and slavery. Anti-Slavery International (ASI) is an organization that helped bring an end to slavery in the British Empire in 1833. Upper Canada (Ontario) was the first to take action when, under Lieutenant-Governor John Graves Simcoe, it took steps to phase out slavery in 1793. The United States banned slavery in 1865 as an outcome of the Civil War. According to ASI, as many as 400 million men, women, and children (almost 7 percent of humanity) currently live in conditions that amount to slavery (Janus, 1996).

ASI distinguishes four types of slavery. The first is *chattel slavery*, in which one person owns another. The number of chattel slaves is difficult to estimate because slavery violates laws almost everywhere. But slave trading—as portrayed in the opening of this chapter—takes place in many countries, mostly in Africa, the

GLOBAL MAP 12–1 Median Age at Death in Global Perspective

This map identifies the age below which half of all deaths occur in any year. In the high-income countries of the world, including Canada, it is the elderly who face death—that is, people aged seventy-five or older. In middle-income countries, including most of Latin America, most people die years or even decades earlier. In low-income countries, especially in Africa and parts of Asia, it is children who die, half of them never reaching their tenth birthdays.

Sources: The World Bank (1993); map projection from *Peters Atlas of the World* (1990).

Middle East, and Asia. The "Global Sociology" box describes the reality of one slave's life in the African nation of Mauritania.

Child slavery refers to children abandoned by their families or boys and girls so poor that they take to the streets in an effort to survive. Perhaps 100 million children—many in poor countries of Latin America—fall into this category. *Debt bondage* refers to the practice, found in dozens of countries around the world, of paying people to work (sometimes as prostitutes), but charging them more than they earn for food and shel-

ter. Never able to pay their debts, these workers are, for practical purposes, enslaved. Lastly, *servile forms of marriage* also amount to slavery. In India, Thailand, and some African nations, families marry off women against their will. Many end up as slaves to their husband's family; some are forced into prostitution.

In 1948, the United Nations issued the Universal Declaration of Human Rights, which states: "No one shall be held in slavery or servitude; slavery and

 Read the United Nations' Universal Declaration of Human Rights at www.un.org/rights/50/decla.htm

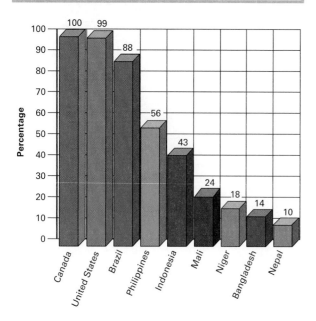

FIGURE 12–3 Percentages of Births Attended by Trained Health Personnel

Source: The World Bank (2001); UN Development Programme (1997); World Health Organization (1998).

the slave trade shall be prohibited in all their forms." Unfortunately, fifty years later, this social evil persists.

CORRELATES OF GLOBAL POVERTY

What accounts for the severe and extensive poverty throughout much of the world? The rest of this chapter weaves together explanations from the following facts about poor societies.

1. **Technology.** Almost two-thirds of people in low-income countries farm the land; the productive power of industrial technology is all but absent in these poorest nations. Energy from human muscles or beasts of burden falls far short of the force unleashed by steam, oil, gas, or nuclear fuels; this technological disparity limits the use of complex machinery. Moreover, poor societies' focus on farming, rather than on specialized production, inhibits development of human skills and abilities.

2. **Population growth.** As Chapter 22 ("Population, Urbanization, and the Environment") explains, countries with the least-developed economies have the world's highest birth rates. Despite the

death toll from poverty, the populations of poor countries in Africa, for example, double every twenty-five years. In these countries, half the people are teenagers or younger. Because they are just entering their childbearing years, a wave of population growth will roll into the future. In recent years, for example, the population of Kenya has swelled by 4 percent; as a result, even with economic development, living standards actually fell.

3. **Cultural patterns.** Poor societies are typically very traditional. Kinship groups pass folkways and mores from generation to generation. Adhering to long-established ways of life, people resist innovations—even those that promise a richer material life.

    The members of poor societies often accept their fate, although it may be bleak, in order to maintain family vitality and cultural heritage. Such attitudes bolster social bonds, but at the cost of discouraging development.

4. **Social stratification.** Low-income societies distribute their wealth very unequally. Chapter 10 ("Social Stratification") explained that social inequality is more pronounced in agrarian societies than in industrial societies. In Brazil, for example, half of all farmland is owned by less than 1 percent of the people (Bergamo and Camarotti, 1996).

5. **Gender inequality.** As we have already explained, poor societies subordinate women even more than industrial societies do. Moreover, women with few opportunities typically have many children, and the needs of a growing population, in turn, restrain economic development. As a result, many analysts conclude that raising living standards in much of the world depends on improving the social standing of women.

6. **Global power relationships.** A final cause of global poverty lies in the relationships among the nations of the world. Historically, wealth flowed from poor societies to rich nations through **colonialism**, *the process by which some nations enrich themselves through political and economic control of other nations.* The countries of Western Europe colonized much of Latin America and Africa beginning roughly 500 years ago. Such global exploitation allowed some nations to develop economically at the expense of other nations.

    Although 130 former colonies gained their independence during the twentieth century, exploitation continues through **neocolonialism** (*neo* is the Greek word for "new"), *a new form of global power relationships that involves not direct political control but economic exploitation by multina-*

"God Made Me to Be a Slave"

Fatma Mint Mamdou is a young woman living in North Africa's Islamic Republic of Mauritania. Asked her age, she pauses and smiles. She has no idea when she was born. Nor can she read or write. What she knows is tending camels, herding sheep, hauling bags of water, sweeping, and serving tea to her owners. This young woman is one of perhaps 90 000 slaves in Mauritania.

In the central region of this nation, having dark brown skin almost always means being a slave to an Arab owner. Fatma accepts her situation; she has known nothing else. She explains in a matter-of-fact voice that she is a slave, as was her mother before her. And her grandmother before that. "Just as God created a camel to be a camel," she shrugs, "he created me to be a slave."

Fatma, her mother, and her brothers and sisters live in a squatter settlement on the edge of Nauakchott, Mauritania's capital city. Their home is a three-by-four-metre hut that they built from wood scraps and other materials taken from construction sites. The roof is nothing more than a piece of cloth; there is no plumbing, not even any furniture. The nearest water comes from a well a mile down the road.

In this region, slavery began five hundred years ago, about the time Columbus sailed west towards the New World. Then, as Arab and Berber tribes moved across the region spreading Islam, they raided local villages and made slaves of the people. So it has been for dozens of generations ever since. In 1905, the French colonial rulers of Mauritania banned slavery. After the nation gained independence in 1961, the new government banned slavery once again. But such proclamations have done little to change strong traditions. Indeed, people like Fatma have no idea what freedom to choose means.

Human slavery continues to exist in the twenty-first century.

The next question is more personal: "Are you and other girls ever raped?" Again, Fatma hesitates. With no hint of emotion, she responds, "Of course, in the night the men come to breed us. Is that what you mean by rape?"

Source: Based on Burkett (1997).

---

tional corporations. **Multinational corporations—** *huge businesses that operate in many countries—* wield tremendous economic power. Corporate decision makers often impose their will on countries where they do business, just as colonizers did in the past.

GLOBAL INEQUALITY: THEORETICAL ANALYSIS

There are two major explanations for the unequal distribution of the world's wealth and power—*modernization theory* and *dependency theory*. Each approach suggests why so many of the world's people are poor and why members of rich societies enjoy such relative advantages.

MODERNIZATION THEORY

Modernization theory is *a model of economic and social development that explains global inequality in terms of technological and cultural differences among societies.*

Modernization theory emerged in the 1950s, a decade of fascination with new technology in North America and a period of hostility towards U.S. interests in many poor societies. Socialist countries—especially the Soviet Union—were gaining influence among low-income nations by asserting that economic progress was impossible under the sway of rich, capitalist countries. In response, policy makers in the industrialized world framed principles of support for a free-market economy that have shaped official foreign policy towards poor nations ever since.[3]

Historical Perspective

Modernization theorists point out that as recently as several centuries ago, the entire world was poor. Because poverty has been the norm throughout human history, it is *affluence* that requires an explanation.

---

[3] The following discussion of modernization theory draws primarily on Rostow (1960, 1978), Bauer (1981), and Berger (1986); see also Firebaugh (1996).

In rich nations such as the United States and Canada, most parents expect their children to enjoy years of childhood, largely free from the responsibilities of adult life. This is not the case in poor nations across Latin America, Africa, and Asia. Poor families depend on whatever income their children can earn, and many children as young as six or seven work full days weaving or performing other kinds of manual labour. Child labour lies behind the low prices of many products imported for sale in North America.

Affluence came within reach of a growing share of people in Western Europe during the late Middle Ages as exploration of other parts of the world expanded trade. Soon, the Industrial Revolution was underway, transforming Western Europe and, shortly thereafter, North America. Industrial technology coupled with entrepreneurial innovation created new wealth on an unprecedented scale. At the outset, this new wealth benefited only a few. But industrial technology was so productive that gradually the standard of living of even the poorest people began to rise. Absolute poverty, which had cast a menacing shadow over society for its entire history, was finally being routed.

During the past century, the standard of living in high-income countries, where the Industrial Revolution began, jumped at least fourfold. Many middle-income nations in Asia and Latin America are now industrializing, and they, too, are becoming wealthier. But without industrial technology, low-income countries have changed little.

The Importance of Culture

Why didn't the Industrial Revolution sweep away poverty the world over? Modernization theory holds that not every society has been eager to seek out and use new technology. Doing so requires a cultural environment that emphasizes the benefits of innovation and materialism.

According to modernization theory, *tradition* is the greatest barrier to economic development. In societies with strong family systems and a reverence for the past, a "cultural inertia" discourages people from adopting new technologies that would improve their living standards. Even today, many people—from Canadian Mennonites to the Islamic people of Iran and the deeply traditional Semai of Malaysia—oppose technological advances as threats to their family relationships, customs, and religious beliefs.

As Max Weber (1958; orig. 1904–05) explained, at the end of the Middle Ages the cultural environment of Western Europe distinctly favoured change. The Protestant Reformation had reshaped traditional Catholicism to create a new progress-oriented way of life (see Chapter 4, "Society"). Material affluence—regarded with suspicion by the Catholic Church—became a personal virtue, and the growing importance of individualism steadily undermined the emphasis on kinship and community. Taken together, these emerging cultural patterns nurtured the Industrial Revolution, which propelled one segment of humanity from poverty to prosperity.

Rostow's Stages of Modernization

Modernization theory holds that the door to affluence remains open to all. Indeed, as technological advances diffuse around the world, all societies are gradually becoming industrialized. According to W.W. Rostow (1960, 1978), the process of modernization occurs in four stages:

1. **Traditional stage.** Initially, cultural traditions are strong, so poor people resist change including new technology. Venerating the past, most people in traditional societies cannot even imagine how life could be very different from what they know. Thus, they build their lives around their families

and local communities, following well-worn paths that allow for little individual freedom and few options to make life better. Life in such communities is often spiritually rich but lacking in material abundance.

A century ago, much of the world was at this initial stage of economic development. And because nations such as Bangladesh, Niger, and Somalia are still at the traditional stage, they remain impoverished to this day.

2. **Take-off stage.** As a society begins to shake off the grip of tradition, people start to use their talents and imagination, sparking economic growth. A market emerges as people produce goods not just for their own consumption but to trade with others for profit. The culture is marked by a developing spirit of individualism and a stronger achievement orientation, often at the expense of family ties and long-standing norms and values.

   Great Britain reached take-off by about 1800, the United States by 1820. Rostow determined that take-off in Canada occurred between 1890 and 1914 (Pomfret, 1981). Thailand, a middle-income country in eastern Asia, is now at this stage. Rich nations can help poor countries reach the take-off stage by supplying foreign aid, advanced technology, investment capital, and opportunities for schooling abroad.

3. **Drive to technological maturity.** By this time, "growth" has become a widely accepted concept that fuels a society's pursuit of higher living standards. An active, diversified economy drives a population eager to enjoy the benefits of industrial technology. At the same time, people begin to realize (and sometimes lament) that industrialization is eroding traditional family and community life. Great Britain reached stage three in about 1840, the United States by 1860, and Canada between 1914 and 1950. Mexico, Puerto Rico, and the Republic of Korea are among the nations now driving to technological maturity.

   By this stage of economic development, absolute poverty has declined. Cities swell with people who stream in from rural areas in search of economic opportunity, occupational specialization renders relationships less personal, and heightened individualism sparks movements pressing for expanded political rights. Societies approaching technological maturity provide basic schooling to all their people, and advanced training for some. The newly educated consider tradition "backwards," opening the door to further change. The social position of women steadily becomes more equal to that of men. Even so, the process of development may subject women to unanticipated problems, as the "Global Sociology" box explains.

4. **High mass consumption.** Economic development driven by industrial technology steadily raises living standards. This rise occurs, Rostow explains, as mass production stimulates mass consumption. Simply put, people soon learn to "need" the expanding array of goods that their society produces.

   The United States moved into this stage of development by 1900, and other high-income countries such as Canada were not far behind. Japan, for example, was sufficiently industrialized to become a military power early in the twentieth century. Then, after recovering from World War II, the Japanese entered an era of high mass consumption, and Japan's economic output is now second only to that of the United States. Now entering this fourth stage of economic development are two of the most prosperous small societies of eastern Asia, Hong Kong, and Singapore. (The long-term economic impact of Hong Kong's 1997 return to Chinese control remains to be seen.)

The Role of Rich Nations

Modernization theory credits high-income countries with a crucial role in global economic development. More specifically, rich societies are the key to alleviating global inequality in the following ways:

1. **Assisting in population control.** As noted above, population growth is greatest in the poorest societies of the world, where rising population easily overtakes economic advances and lowers the standard of living. As rich nations export birth control technology and promote its use, they help curb population growth, a crucial step in combatting poverty. Integral to this process are programs that advance the social standing of women. Once economic development is under-way, birth rates should decline as they have in industrialized societies.

2. **Increasing food production.** Modernization theory asserts that "high-tech" farming methods, exported from rich to poor nations, raise agricultural yields. Such techniques, collectively referred to as the *Green Revolution*, involve the use of new hybrid seeds, modern irrigation, chemical fertilizers, and pesticides.

3. **Introducing industrial technology.** Technological transfers should involve industry as well as agriculture. Rich nations can accelerate economic growth in poor societies by introducing machinery and information technology, which moves

Modernization and Women: A Report from Rural Bangladesh

In Rajshahi, Bangladesh, women meet to address their common problems.

In global perspective, gender inequality is most pronounced where people are poorest. Economic development, then, gives women opportunities for schooling and work outside the home, reduces birth rates, and therefore weakens traditional male domination.

Along the way, however, the process of modernization often impedes women's progress. Investigating the lives of women in a poor, rural district of Bangladesh, Sultana Alam (1985) observed several hazards of development for women.

As economic opportunity draws men from rural areas to cities in search of work, women and children must fend for themselves. Some men sell their land and simply abandon their wives and children.

The waning strength of family and neighbourhood leaves women who are deserted in this way with little assistance. The same holds true for women who become single through divorce or the death of a spouse. In the past, Alam reports, kin or neighbours readily took in a Bangladeshi woman who found herself alone. Today, as Bangladesh struggles to advance economically, the number of poor households headed by women is increasing. Rather than enhancing women's autonomy, a new spirit of individualism has actually eroded the social standing of women.

Economic development—and the growing influence of Western movies and mass media—undermine women's traditional roles as wives, sisters, and mothers, defining them instead as objects of sexual attention. A new cultural emphasis on sexuality now encourages men in poor countries to abandon aging spouses for younger, more physically attractive partners. The same sexual emphasis contributes to the world's rising tide of prostitution.

Modernization, then, does not affect men and women in the same way. In the long run, evidence suggests that modernization gives the sexes more equal standing. But in the short term, the economic position of many women actually declines, and women are also forced to contend with problems previously unknown in traditional societies.

Sources: Based on Alam (1985) and Mink (1989).

---

the labour force to skilled industrial and service jobs.

4. **Instituting programs of foreign aid.** Investment capital from rich nations can boost the prospects of poor societies striving to reach the "take-off" stage. Foreign aid can purchase fertilizers and fund irrigation projects, which raise agricultural productivity, as well as build power plants and factories that improve industrial output.

Critical evaluation. Modernization theory, a sweeping analysis of how and why industrialization transforms societies, has influential supporters among social scientists (Parsons, 1966; W. Moore, 1977, 1979; Bauer, 1981; Berger, 1986; Firebaugh and Beck, 1994). Moreover, this model has guided the foreign policy of Canada and other rich nations for decades. Proponents point to rapid economic development in Asia as proof that the affluence created in Western Europe and North America is within reach of all regions of the world. With the assistance of rich countries, South Korea, Taiwan, and Singapore have made impressive economic gains.

From the outset, however, modernization theory has come under fire from socialist countries (and left-leaning analysts in the West) as a thinly veiled defence of capitalism. According to its critics, modernization simply has not occurred in many poor countries. The United Nations recently reported that living standards in a number of nations—including Haiti and Nicaragua in Latin America, and Sudan, Ghana, and Rwanda in Africa—are actually lower than in 1960 (United Nations Development Programme, 1996).

A second criticism of modernization theory is that it fails to recognize how rich nations, which benefit from the status quo, often block paths to development for poor countries. Critics charge that rich countries industrialized centuries ago from a position of global strength; so how can we expect poor countries today to industrialize from a position of global weakness?

Critics point out that modernization theory treats rich and poor nations as worlds unto themselves and fail to see how international relations historically have affected all nations. It was colonization that boosted the fortunes of Europe to begin with; further, this economic windfall came at the expense of countries in Latin America and Asia that are still reeling from the consequences.

Modernization theory also holds up the world's most-developed countries as the standard by which the rest of humanity should be judged, betraying an ethnocentric bias. As environmentalists point out, our Western conception of "progress" has led us to degrade the physical environment throughout the world. Moreover, not every culture buys into our notions about competitive, materialistic living.

Finally, modernization theory draws criticism for locating the causes of global poverty almost entirely in the poor societies themselves. Critics see this analysis as little more than "blaming the victims" for their own plight. Instead, they argue, an analysis of global inequality should focus as much attention on the behaviour of *rich* nations as on that of poor nations (Wiarda, 1987).

From all these concerns has emerged a second major approach to understanding global inequality. This is dependency theory.

DEPENDENCY THEORY

Dependency theory is *a model of economic and social development that explains global inequality in terms of the historical exploitation of poor societies by rich ones.* Dependency theory places primary responsibility for global poverty on rich nations. It holds that high-income countries have systematically impoverished low-income countries, making poor societies dependent on them. This destructive process extends back for centuries and persists today.

Historical Perspective

Everyone agrees that before the Industrial Revolution there was little affluence in the world. Dependency theory asserts, however, that people living in poor countries were actually better off economically in the past than their descendants are now. André Gunder Frank (1975), a noted proponent of this approach, argues that the colonial process that helped develop today's rich nations simultaneously *underdeveloped* poor societies.

Dependency theory is based on the idea that the economic positions of the rich and poor nations of the world are linked and cannot be understood correctly in isolation from one another. This analysis maintains that poor nations are not simply lagging behind rich ones on a linear "path of progress." Rather, the increasing prosperity of the high-income countries came largely at the expense of low-income societies. In short, then, some nations became rich *only because*

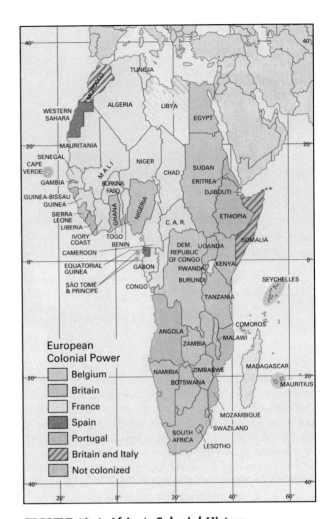

FIGURE 12–4 Africa's Colonial History

Formal colonialism has almost disappeared from the world, but, according to dependency theory, political liberation has not translated into *economic* autonomy. Far from it: the economic relationship between poor and rich nations perpetuates a colonial pattern of domination. This neocolonialism is the essence of a capitalist world economy.

other nations became poor. Both are products of global commerce beginning five centuries ago.

The Importance of Colonialism

Late in the fifteenth century, Europeans began surveying the Americas to the west, the massive continent of Africa to the south, and the vast expanse of Asia to the east. When, for example, Christopher Columbus sailed westward from Spain in 1492 and reached the Americas, Europeans celebrated "the discovery of the New World." From the point of view of people on these shores, however, the arrival of Europeans can be described as the systematic conquest of one region of the world by another (Sale, 1990; Gray, 1991).

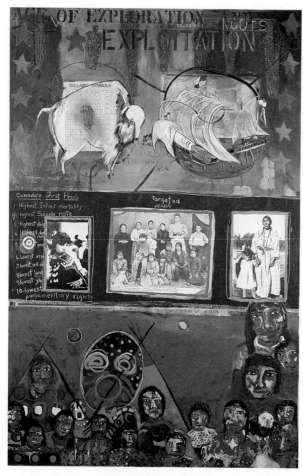

In her mixed-media work Living in the Storm Too Long, *Canadian Native artist Jane Ash Poitras shows Christopher Columbus's flagship, the* Santa Maria, *on a collision course with a buffalo, a symbol of North American Native culture. In Poitras's view, the Age of Exploration meant nothing but exploitation to the indigenous peoples, who were left powerless politically and with a bankrupt culture.*

Jane Ash Poitras, *Living in the Storm Too Long.* Courtesy of Jane Ash Poitras. Photo by Janet Anderson, Thunder Bay Art Gallery.

By the nineteenth century, most of the world had come under the domination of European nations. Spain and Portugal colonized nearly all of Latin America from the sixteenth until the mid-nineteenth century. A century ago, Great Britain controlled about one-fourth of the world's land and people, boasting that "the sun never sets on the British Empire." The United States, itself originally thirteen small British colonies on the eastern seaboard, pushed across the continent, purchased Alaska, and gained control of Haiti, Puerto Rico, Guam, the Philippines, the Hawaiian Islands, and part of Cuba.

Meanwhile, Europeans and Africans engaged in a brutal form of human exploitation—the slave trade—from about 1500 until 1850. But even as the world was rejecting slavery, Europeans gained control of Africa itself, as Figure 12–4 (on page 297) shows. European powers dominated most of the continent until the early 1960s.

Wallerstein's Capitalist World Economy

Immanuel Wallerstein (1974, 1979, 1983, 1984) explains global stratification using a model of the "capitalist world economy."[4] The term *world economy* suggests that the prosperity or poverty of any country is the result of a global economic system. According to Wallerstein, today's global economy is rooted in the colonization that began five hundred years ago when Europeans first saw the wealth of the rest of the world. Since the world economy is based in the most-developed countries, it is capitalist in character.

Wallerstein considers rich nations the *core* of the world economy. Colonialism enriched this core by funnelling raw materials from around the globe to Western Europe. Over the longer term, this wealth helped to ignite the Industrial Revolution. Similarly, today multinational corporations operate worldwide, but channel wealth to North America, Western Europe, Australia, and Japan.

Low-income countries, in contrast, represent the *periphery* of the world economy. Drawn into this system by colonial exploitation, poor nations continue to support rich ones by providing inexpensive labour, easy access to raw materials, and vast markets for industrial products. The remaining countries are considered the *semiperiphery* of the world economy. They include prospering countries such as Portugal and South Korea that have closer ties to the global economic core.

According to Wallerstein, the world economy benefits rich societies (by generating profits) and harms the rest of the world (by perpetuating poverty). In short, the world economy imposes a state of dependency on poor nations, which remain under the control of rich ones. This dependency involves the following three factors:

1. **Narrow, export-oriented economies.** Unlike the diversified economies of core nations, production in poor countries focuses on a few raw materials or crops for export. Examples include coffee and fruits from Latin American nations, oil from Nigeria, hardwoods from the Philippines, and palm oil from Malaysia.

   Replicating colonial-style patterns today, multinational corporations purchase raw materials cheaply in poor societies and transport them to core societies where factories process them for profitable sale. This practice discourages produc-

---

[4]While based on Wallerstein's ideas, this section also reflects the work of Frank (1980, 1981), Delacroix and Ragin (1981), Bergesen (1983), and Dixon and Boswell (1996).

In North America, most affluent people manage to distance themselves from the struggles of the poor. This is far more difficult to do in low-income countries, if only because there are so many more poor people. In the cities in India, for example, people routinely approach foreigners travelling by car in the hopes of receiving money in return.

tion of food or goods needed by local people in poor nations. These corporations also own a great deal of land and have transformed traditional farmers into low-paid farm labourers. Thus, rich nations effectively prevent poor ones from developing industries of their own.

2. **Lack of industrial capacity.** Without an industrial base, poor societies face a double bind. They count on selling their inexpensive raw materials to rich nations, from whom they buy whatever expensive manufactured goods they can afford. In a classic example of this dependency, British colonialists encouraged the people of India to raise cotton, but prohibited them from making their own cloth. Instead, the British shipped Indian cotton to textile mills in Birmingham and Manchester, wove it into cloth, and shipped the finished goods back for profitable sale in India.

   Dependency theorists also blast the Green Revolution, widely praised by modernization theorists. To promote agricultural productivity, poor countries must buy expensive fertilizers, pesticides, and mechanical equipment from core nations. Typically, rich countries profit from this exchange more than the poor nations.

3. **Foreign debt.** Unequal trade patterns have plunged poor countries deeper and deeper into debt to industrialized societies. Collectively, the poor nations of the world owe rich countries more than $1 trillion, including hundreds of billions of dollars to the United States alone. This staggering debt can paralyze a country, causing high unemployment and rampant inflation (Walton and Ragin, 1990; The World Bank, 1997).

The Role of Rich Nations

Nowhere is the difference between modernization theory and dependency theory sharper than in the role they assign to rich nations. Modernization theory maintains that rich societies *produce wealth* through capital investment and technological innovation. From this point of view, as poor nations adopt pro-growth attitudes and policies and seek more productive technology, they, too, will prosper. In contrast, dependency theory sees global inequality in terms of the *distribution of wealth*, arguing that rich countries have *over*developed themselves as they have *under*developed the rest of the world.

Dependency theorists dismiss the idea that strategies proposed by rich countries to control population or to boost agricultural and industrial output will help raise living standards in poor countries. They contend that such programs provide profits to rich countries (through purchases of high technology), while rewarding not the poor majority but the ruling elites, who maintain a favourable "business climate" for multinational corporations (Lappé et al., 1981).

Hunger activists Frances Moore Lappé and Joseph Collins (1986) claim that the capitalist culture of high-income countries encourages people to think of absolute poverty as somehow inevitable. Following this line of reasoning, poverty results from "natural" processes, including having too many children, and from natural disasters such as droughts. Yet global poverty is far from inevitable, they argue; rather, it results from deliberate policies. Lappé and Collins point out that the world produces enough food to allow every person on the planet to grow quite fat. Moreover, India and most of Africa actually *export* food, even though many of their own people go hungry.

According to Lappé and Collins, the contradiction of poverty amid plenty stems from the policy of producing food for profits, not people. That is, corporations in rich nations collaborate with elites in poor countries to grow and export profitable crops such as coffee while simultaneously limiting the production of staples such as corn and beans for local families. Governments of poor countries support the practice of "growing for export" because they need food profits to repay massive foreign debt. At the core of this vicious cycle is the capitalist corporate structure of the global economic system.

Critical evaluation. The main idea of dependency theory—that no nation develops (or fails to develop) in isolation—points out how the global economy shapes the destiny of all nations. Citing Latin America and other poor regions of the world, dependency theorists claim that development simply cannot proceed under the constraints presently imposed by rich countries. Rather, they call for radical reform of the entire world economy so that it operates in the interests of the majority of people.

Critics, however, charge that dependency theory incorrectly treats wealth as a zero-sum commodity, as if no one gets richer without someone else getting poorer. Not so, critics continue, since farmers, small business owners, and industrialists can and do create new wealth through their drive and imaginative use of new technology. After all, they point out, the entire world's wealth has swelled fivefold since 1950.

Critics also contend that dependency theory is wrong in blaming rich nations for global poverty because many of the world's poorest countries (such as Ethiopia) have had little contact with rich nations. Similarly, a long history of trade with rich countries has dramatically improved the economies of nations, including Singapore, South Korea, and Japan. In short, an increasing body of evidence supports the conclusion that foreign investment by rich nations fosters economic growth, as modernization theory claims, not economic decline, as dependency theorists assert (Vogel, 1991; Firebaugh, 1992).

Critics view dependency theory as simplistic for pointing the finger at a single factor—world capitalism—as the cause of global inequality (Worsley, 1990). In doing so, dependency theory casts poor societies as passive victims and ignores factors inside these countries that contribute to their economic plight. Sociologists have long recognized the role of culture in shaping people's willingness to embrace or resist change. Iran's brand of fundamentalist Islam, for example, discourages ties with other countries. Capitalist societies, then, need hardly accept the blame for Iran's stagnation.

Nor can rich societies be saddled with responsibility for the reckless behaviour of some foreign leaders who engage in far-reaching corruption and self-serving military campaigns to enhance their own power (examples include Ferdinand Marcos in the Philippines, François Duvalier in Haiti, Manuel Noriega in Panama, Mobutu Sese Seko in Zaire, and Saddam Hussein in Iraq). Governments have even withheld food supplies for leverage in internal political struggles, a strategy that left the masses starving in the African nations of Ethiopia, Sudan, and Somalia. Other regimes throughout the world have done little to improve the status of women and to control population growth.

Further, critics chide dependency theorists for downplaying the economic dependency fostered by the former Soviet Union. The Soviet army seized control of most of Eastern Europe during World War II and subsequently dominated the Eastern Bloc nations politically and economically. Many consider the uprisings between 1989 and 1991 as a wholesale rejection of a Soviet colonial system by hundreds of millions of people.

Lastly, critics of dependency theory fault this approach for offering only vague solutions to global poverty. Most dependency theorists urge poor societies to sever economic ties to rich countries, and some call for nationalizing foreign-owned industries. Dependency theory implies that the path to ending global poverty begins with the overthrow of international capitalism. At its core, say the critics, dependency theory advocates some sort of world socialism. In light of the difficulties socialist societies have had in meeting the needs of their own people, critics ask, should we really expect such a system to lift the entire world towards prosperity?

Canada and Low-Income Countries

Canada's approach to development in low-income countries reveals tension between the modernization and dependency models on which it is based. In 1995, Canada spent $2.2 billion on aid to developing countries (0.29 percent of our GNP), down from $3.2 billion (0.49 percent of GNP) in 1992. The 2003 federal budget called for increasing aid spending to $3.2 billion (0.26 percent of GDP) in 2003 and set a goal of increasing this to $8 billion (0.40 percent of GDP) by 2015 (Partridge, 2003). Most Canadian aid is distributed through the Canadian International Development Agency (CIDA). In the past, CIDA has concentrated on encouraging industrial development, but it has recently started to emphasize self-sufficiency and improvement of the lives of the poor through enhancement of health care, housing, education, and agricultural methods. The involvement of women in development has also become a priority.

By the mid-1980s, Canada had responded to changing conditions in low-income countries "with increasingly sophisticated social, cultural, and economic

APPLYING SOCIOLOGY

Seeking Livelihood Sustainability for Yucatán Farmers

Canadian rural sociologist Sally Humphries has devoted her career to enhancing sustainable agricultural development in the fragile tropical environments of Latin America. Some of her research has focused on the farmers of Mexico's Yucatán region, who have switched from traditional agriculture to intensive horticultural production for outside markets. Is it possible, Humphries asks, to maintain traditional systems in the face of market integration?

The traditional system, which *was* sustainable, evolved under conditions of low population pressure and, consequently, minimal environmental disruption. Traditional methods came under pressure when transportation links allowed a switch to delicate, perishable crops and tied the northern part of Yucatán to Mexican and world markets; at the same time, *profit* rather than *subsistence* became the goal.

Market integration resulted in more intensive use of the plots of land closest to water supplies (for irrigation); in the past, cutting and burning of bush enriched the soil and prepared new plots for cultivation. To counter the soil depletion resulting from repeated use of the same plots—often with five or six plantings per year—farmers relied increasingly on purchased chemical fertilizers. Crop specialization, primarily in tomatoes, has left farmers vulnerable to losses owing to poor weather, pest attack, and plant diseases.

Agricultural intensification (through irrigated vegetable growing) has forced Yucatán farmers onto the "pesticide treadmill"—administering higher doses of chemicals, which lead to the destruction of natural pest predators, lowered pest resistance, and pest resurgence. The result has been an explosion of an uncontrollable, pesticide-resistant whitefly population—and environmental

damage. Thus, while the decision to adopt vegetable production was rational in economic terms, giving rise to decades of income growth, it was less than rational in environmental terms.

Humphries concludes that, despite its benefits in providing work and incomes above the regional norm, vegetable production in the northern Yucatán is nonsustainable under current technology. Her study points to the "difficulty of achieving the twin goal of economic and environmental sustainability." Those interested in traditional resource management must pay more attention to "the real life activities of producers and the implications of the market for traditional behaviour"—or, more succinctly, to the "decision-making and livelihood strategies" of farmers (p. 100).

Source: Based on Humphries (1993).

---

programs for human development and self-reliance" (Tomlinson, 1991), but tension remains between the goals of eliminating poverty and creating an environment conducive to private-sector development and debt reduction through "economic structural adjustment" (CIDA, 1987). Despite its humanitarian goals, much of Canada's aid continues to be linked to trade or the perceived potential for trade (that is, "tied aid"). Although in this sense Canada's role is similar to that of the United States, some low-income countries are more comfortable accepting aid from Canada, which does not have the superpower status of the United States.

 Information about Canadian foreign aid initiatives is available at the CIDA website at www.acdi-cida.gc.ca/

In addition to its aid and trade involvements with developing countries, Canada plays an active role in the generation and dissemination of knowledge in those societies. Several Canadian universities are involved in overseas research and development and most are involved in teaching foreign students who take their knowledge back home. In 2001, Canada was host to

130 000 foreign students at all levels of education, from elementary to graduate school; 93 000, or 72 percent of these students, are enrolled at the post-secondary level. The overall figure reflects a 79 percent increase over 1995, which is attributable to economic growth in some of the source countries and active recruitment on the part of our government (Canada, 2003). At this point, 55 percent of our foreign students come from South Korea, China, Japan, France, and Malaysia—countries that, one might say, are beneficiaries of Canada's educational activism.

See the "Applying Sociology" box for a further example of Canadian research and activism in the Yucatán.

GLOBAL INEQUALITY: LOOKING AHEAD

Among the most important trends of recent decades is the development of a global economy, which is exacerbating inequality both within our country and around

TABLE 12–2 Modernization Theory and Dependency Theory: A Summary

	Modernization Theory	Dependency Theory
Historical pattern	The entire world was poor just two centuries ago; the Industrial Revolution brought affluence to high-income countries; as industrialization gradually transforms poor societies, all nations are likely to become more equal and alike.	Global parity was disrupted by colonialism, which made some countries rich while simultaneously making other countries poor; barring radical change in the world capitalist system, rich nations will grow richer and poor nations will become poorer.
Primary causes of global poverty	Characteristics of poor societies cause their poverty, including lack of industrial technology, traditional cultural patterns that discourage innovation, and rapid population growth.	Global economic relations—historical colonialism and the operation of multinational corporations—have enriched high-income countries while placing low-income countries in a state of economic dependency.
Role of rich nations	Rich countries can and do assist poor nations through programs of population control, technology transfers that increase food production and stimulate industrial development, and investment capital in the form of foreign aid.	Rich countries have concentrated global resources, conferring advantages on themselves while generating massive foreign debt in low-income countries; rich nations impede the economic development of poor nations.

the world. Profitable investments, many of them in poor nations, and lucrative sales by North American companies to foreign interests have brought greater affluence to those who already have substantial wealth. At the same time, increasing industrial production abroad has cut factory jobs in this country, exerting downward pressure on wages. The net result is gradual economic polarization.

As this chapter has noted, however, social inequality is far more striking in global context. The concentration of wealth among high-income countries, coupled with the grinding poverty typical of low-income nations, may well constitute the most important dilemma facing humanity in the twenty-first century. To some analysts, rich nations hold the keys to ending world poverty; to others, they are the cause of this tragic problem.

Faced with two radically different approaches to understanding global inequality, we might well wonder which one is correct. As with many controversies in sociology, each view has some merit as well as its own limitations. Table 12–2 summarizes important arguments made by advocates of each approach.

In searching for truth, we must consider empirical evidence. According to a world survey conducted by the United Nations Development Programme (1996), people in about one-third of the world's countries enjoy an unprecedented standard of living. These nations—identified in Global Map 12–2—include most of the high-income countries but also dozens of poorer countries, especially in Asia. These developing nations reveal that the market forces endorsed by modernization theory can raise living standards.

In about one-third of the world's countries, living standards are actually *lower* today than they were in 1980. A rising wave of poverty, especially in sub-Saharan Africa, supports the dependency theory assertion that current economic arrangements are leaving hundreds of millions of people behind.

The picture now emerging challenges both modernization and dependency theories. Theorists for both camps are revising their views of the major "paths to development." On the one hand, few societies seeking economic growth now favour a market economy completely free of government control. This view challenges orthodox modernization theory, which endorses a free-market approach to development. On the other hand, recent upheavals in the former Soviet Union and Eastern Europe demonstrate that a global re-evaluation of socialism has been underway. These events, following decades of poor economic performance and political repression, make many poor societies reluctant to consider a government-mandated path to development. Because dependency theory has supported socialist economic systems, changes in world socialism will surely generate new thinking here as well.

Hunger is one critical problem caused by absolute poverty. As the "Controversy & Debate" box explains, many analysts wonder if we have the technological means and political will to address hunger effectively before it overwhelms much of the world.

Despite the uncertainties, we have learned a great deal about global stratification. One key insight, offered by modernization theory, is that world hunger is partly a *problem of technology*. A higher standard of living for a surging world population depends on raising agricultural and industrial productivity. A second insight, derived from dependency theory, is that global inequality is also a *political issue*. Even with higher productivity, the human community must address crucial

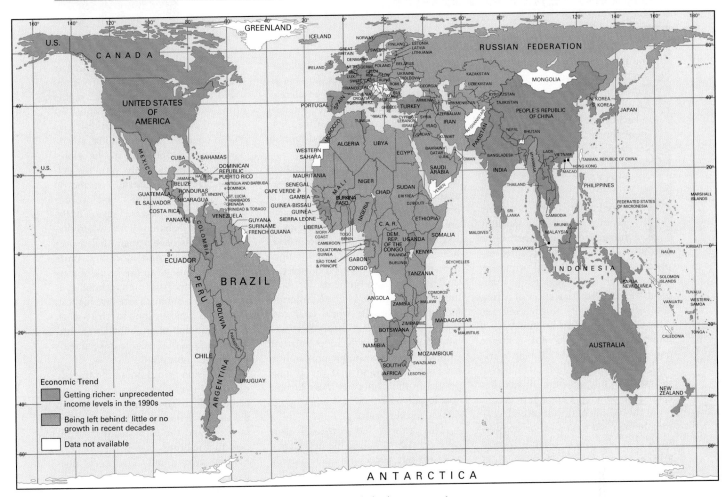

GLOBAL MAP 12–2 Prosperity and Stagnation in Global Perspective

In about sixty nations of the world, people are enjoying a higher standard of living than ever before. These prospering countries are found throughout the world and include some rich nations (such as Canada) and some poor nations (especially in Asia). For most of the world's countries, however, living standards have remained steady or even slipped in recent decades. Especially in Eastern Europe and the Middle East, some nations have experienced economic setbacks since the 1980s. In sub-Saharan Africa, some nations are worse off than they were in 1960.

Source: United Nations Development Programme (1996); updated by John Macionis.

questions about the distributions of resources—both within societies and around the globe.

Note that while economic development increases living standards, it also places greater strains on the natural environment. Imagine, for example, if almost 1 billion people in India were suddenly to become "middle class," with vehicles guzzling gasoline and spewing hydrocarbons into the atmosphere.

Finally, the vast gulf that separates the world's richest and poorest people puts everyone at greater risk of war, as the most impoverished people act to challenge the social arrangements that threaten their very lives. In the long run, we can achieve peace on this planet only by ensuring that all people enjoy a significant measure of dignity and security.

Will the World Starve?

The animals' feet leave their prints
  on the desert's face.
Hunger is so real, so very real,
  that it can make you walk around
  a barren tree looking for
  nourishment.
Not once,
Not twice,
Not thrice

These lines by Indian poet Amit Jayaram describe the appalling hunger found in Rajasthan, in northwest India. As this chapter explains, hunger casts its menacing shadow over large regions of Asia, much of Latin America, most of Africa, and even parts of North America. Throughout the world, hundreds of millions of adults do not consume enough food to enable them to work. And, most tragically, some 10 million of the world's children die each year because they do not get enough to eat.

At the closing of the nineteenth century, humankind took a major step forward by abolishing slavery almost everywhere on the planet. As we enter the twenty-first century, however, what are the prospects for eradicating the wretched misery of human beings enduring daily hunger?

It is easy to be pessimistic: the population of poor countries is currently increasing by 90 million people annually—equivalent to adding another Mexico to the world every year. Poor countries can scarcely feed the people they have now; how will they ever feed *double* their current populations in the near future?

Hunger forces poor people to exploit the earth's resources, using short-term strategies for food production that will lead to long-term disaster. For ex-ample, to feed the swelling populations of poor, tropical countries, farmers are cutting rain forests in order to increase their farmland. Without the protective canopy of trees, it is only a matter of time before much of this land turns to desert.

Taken together, rising populations and ecological approaches that borrow against the future raise the spectre of hunger and outright starvation escalating well beyond current levels. Regarded pessimistically, the world's future is bleak: unprecedented hunger, human misery, and political calamity.

There are also grounds for optimism. Thanks to the Green Revolution, food production the world over rose sharply over the last fifty years, well outpacing the growth in population. Also, the world's economic productivity has risen steadily, so that the average person on the planet has more income now to purchase food and other necessities than ever before.

This growth has increased daily calorie intake as well as life expectancy, access to safe water, and adult literacy, while around the world infant mortality is half of what it was in 1960.

So what are the prospects for eradicating world hunger—especially in low-income nations? Overall, we see less hunger in both rich and poor countries, and a smaller *share* of the world's people faces starvation now than, say, in 1960. But as global population increases, with 90 percent of children born in middle- and low-income countries, the *number* of lives at risk is as great today as ever before. Moreover, as noted earlier, although many low-income countries have made solid gains, many more are stagnating or even losing ground.

Also bear in mind that aggregate data mask different trends in various world regions. The "best-case" region of the world is eastern Asia, where incomes (controlled for inflation) have tripled over the last generation. It is to Asia that the optimists in the global hunger debate typically turn for evidence that poor countries can and do raise living standards and reduce hunger. The "worst-case" region of the world is sub-Saharan Africa, where living standards have actually fallen over the last decade, and more and more people are pushed to the brink of starvation. It is here that high technology is least evident and birth rates are highest. Pessimists typically look to Africa when they argue that poor countries are losing ground in the struggle to keep their people well nourished.

Television brings home the tragedy of hunger every year or so when news cameras focus on starving people in places like Ethiopia and Somalia. But hunger—and the early death from illness that it brings on—is the plight of millions year round. The world does have the technical means to feed everyone; the question is, do we have the moral determination to do so?

Continue the debate . . .

1. *In your opinion, what are the primary causes of global hunger?*
2. *Do you place more responsibility for solving this problem on poor countries or on rich ones? Why?*

Sources: United Nations (1994, 1995).

SUMMARY

1. Elsewhere, social stratification is more pronounced than in Canada. About 18 percent of the world's people live in industrialized, high-income countries such as Canada and take in 79 percent of the earth's total income. Another 54 percent of humanity lives in middle-income countries with limited industrialization, receiving about 18 percent of all income. And 28 percent of the world's population lives in low-income countries that have yet to industrialize, earning only 3 percent of global income.

2. While relative poverty is found everywhere, poor societies contend with widespread, absolute poverty. Worldwide, the lives of some 1 billion people are at risk. About 15 million people, most of them children, die every year from various causes because they lack proper nourishment.

3. Women are more likely than men to be poor nearly everywhere in the world. Gender bias is much greater in poor, agrarian societies than it is in industrial societies such as Canada.

4. The poverty found in much of the world is a complex problem reflecting limited industrial technology, rapid population growth, traditional cultural patterns, internal social stratification, male domination, and global power relationships.

5. Modernization theory maintains that development hinges on acquiring advanced productive technology. This approach views traditional cultural patterns as the key barrier to modernization.

6. Modernization theorist W.W. Rostow identifies four stages of development: traditional, take-off, drive to technological maturity, and high mass consumption.

7. Arguing that rich societies have the keys to creating wealth, modernization theory cites four ways rich nations can assist poor nations: bolstering population-control strategies, providing crop-enhancing technologies, encouraging industrial technology, and providing investment capital and other foreign aid.

8. Critics of modernization theory maintain that this approach has produced limited economic development in the world, while ethnocentrically assuming that poor societies can follow the path to development taken by rich nations centuries ago.

9. Dependency theory claims that global wealth and poverty are directly linked to the historical operation of the capitalist world economy.

10. The dependency of poor countries on rich ones began five centuries ago with colonialism. Furthermore, even though most poor countries have won political independence, neocolonialism persists as a form of exploitation carried out by multinational corporations.

11. Wallerstein views high-income countries as the privileged "core" of the capitalist world economy; middle-income nations as the "semiperiphery," poor societies as the global "periphery."

12. According to dependency theorists, three key factors—export-oriented economies, a lack of industrial capacity, and foreign debt—perpetuate poor countries' dependency on rich nations.

13. Critics of dependency theory argue that this approach overlooks the success of many nations in creating new wealth. Total global wealth, they point out, has increased fivefold since 1950. Furthermore, contrary to the implications of dependency theory, the world's poorest societies are not those with the strongest ties to rich countries.

14. Both modernization and dependency approaches offer useful insights into the development of global inequality. Some evidence supports each view. Less controversial is the urgent need to address the various problems caused by worldwide poverty.

CRITICAL-THINKING QUESTIONS

1. Distinguish between relative and absolute poverty. How do the two concepts apply to social stratification in Canada and the world as a whole?

2. Why do many analysts argue that economic development in low-income countries depends on raising the social standing of women?

3. State the basic tenets of modernization theory and dependency theory, and then spell out several criticisms of each approach.

4. Based on what you have read here and elsewhere, what is your prediction about the extent of global hunger fifty years from now? Will the problem be more or less serious? Why?

APPLICATIONS AND EXERCISES

1. Keep a log book noting any advertising (for coffee from Colombia or exotic vacations to Egypt or India) that you see on television or in other media. What image of life in middle- or low-income countries does this advertising present? Do you think this image is accurate?

2. On most campuses, there are students who have come to Canada from poor countries. Approach one such woman and one such man. Explain that you have been studying global stratification, and ask if they are willing to share their views of life in their countries. You may be able to learn quite a bit from them.

3. Research the extent of slavery in today's world in the university library. Or visit the website of an organization opposing African slavery: the Coalition Against Slavery in Mauritania and Sudan at **www.members.aol.com/casmasalc**.

4. Look over all the global maps in this text. As you examine them, identify the various social traits associated with the world's richest and poorest nations. How do modernization theory and dependency theory help explain the patterns you find?

 SITES TO SEE

www.macionis.com
or
www.TheSociologyPage.com

You can find more than fifty weblinks to sociological journals and other sources of data and information by visiting the Links Library at this website.

www.apc.org/

The Association for Progressive Communications is a global partnership of computer networks that link activists around the world. The mission of APC is to advance and inform movements for peace, economic and social justice, human rights, and environmental sustainability around the world by promoting strategic use of appropriate computer-networking technology.

www.fourmilab.ch/etexts/www/un/udhr.html

Adopted by the General Assembly of the United Nations on December 10, 1948, the *Universal Declaration of Human Rights* declares that "all human beings are born free and equal in dignity and rights," and that everyone is

"entitled to all the rights and freedoms set forth in the Declaration, without distinction of any kind, such as race, colour, sex, language, religion, political or other opinion, national or social origin, property, birth or other status."

www.worldbank.org/data/

Operated by the World Bank, this website provides data about and analysis of world poverty.

www.fh.org/

www.worldconcern.org/

www.worldvision.ca/

http://care.ca/

Here are a number of additional websites that address global inequality. The first is operated by Food for the Hungry International, the second takes you to the home page for World Concern, the third organization is World Vision Canada, and the fourth is CARE Canada. Visit them all and look for differences in their focus and strategies.

 STUDY TOOLS

For more study tools to help you with your next exam, be sure to check out the Companion Website at **www.pearsoned. ca/macionis**, as well as Chapter 12 in your Study Guide.

INVESTIGATE WITH CONTENTSELECT

Follow the instructions found on page 25 of this textbook to access ContentSelect™ at the Research Navigator™ website. Once at the site, enter your LOGINID and Password. Then, enter keywords such as "global poverty," "world hunger," and "slavery," and the search engine will supply relevant and recent scholarly and popular press publications.

CHAPTER
13

Getty Images, Inc.

GENDER STRATIFICATION

At first we traveled quite alone . . . but before we had gone many miles, we came on other wagon-loads of women, bound in the same direction. As we reached different cross-roads, we saw wagons coming from every part of the country and, long before we reached Seneca Falls, we were a procession.

So wrote Charlotte Woodward in her journal as she made her way along the rutted dirt roads to Seneca Falls, a small town in upstate New York. The year was 1848, a time when slavery was legal in much of the United States, and the social standing of all women—regardless of colour—was subordinate in every way to that of men. Back then, in much of the United States, women could not own property or keep their wages if they were married; women could not draft a will; women were barred from filing lawsuits in court, including suits seeking custody of their children; women could not attend college; and husbands could legally beat their wives as long as the stick they used was no thicker than a thumb (the origin of today's phrase "the rule of thumb").

At Wesleyan Chapel in Seneca Falls, some three hundred women gathered to challenge their second-class citizenship. They listened as their leader, Elizabeth Cady Stanton, called for expanding women's rights and opportunities, including the right to vote. To many, such a proposal seemed absurd and outrageous; even many attending the conference were shocked by the idea. Stanton's husband, Henry, rode out of town in protest.

Source: This material is drawn from "On the Forefront of Feminism" by Kate Gurnett (1998:G1, G6).

Much has changed in the century and a half since the Seneca Falls convention, and many of Stanton's proposals are now accepted as a matter of basic fairness—in the United States as well as Canada. But, as this chapter explains, women and men still lead different lives in North America and elsewhere around the world, and in most respects men still dominate. This chapter explores the importance of gender and explains how, like class position, gender is a major dimension of social stratification.

GENDER AND INEQUALITY

Chapter 8 ("Sexuality") discussed the biological differences that divide the human population into categories of female and male. *Gender* refers to the personal traits and social positions that members of a society attach to being female and male. Gender, then, is a dimension of social organization, shaping how we interact with others and how we think about ourselves. Even more importantly, gender involves *hierarchy*, ranking men and women differently in terms of power, wealth, and other resources. This is why sociologists speak of gender stratification, the unequal distribution of wealth, power, and privilege between men and women. Gender, in short, affects the opportunities and constraints each of us faces throughout our lives (Ferree and Hall, 1996; Riley, 1997).

MALE–FEMALE DIFFERENCES

Many people think there is something "natural" about gender distinctions; after all, there are biological differences between the sexes. But we must be careful not to equate social and biological differences. In the 1800s, for example, women were denied the vote because it was assumed that they "naturally" lacked sufficient intelligence and political interest. But such attitudes had nothing to do with biology. Rather, they reflected the cultural conventions of that time and place.

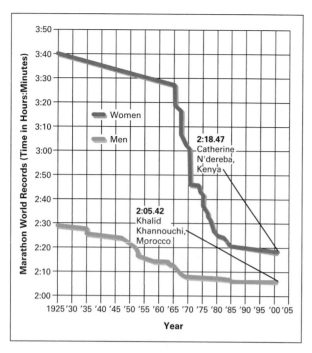

FIGURE 13–1 Men's and Women's Athletic Performance

Do men naturally outperform women in athletic competition? The answer is not obvious. Early in the twentieth century, men outdistanced women by many kilometres in marathon races. But as opportunities for women in athletics increased, women have been closing the performance gap. Thirteen minutes separate the current world marathon records for women (set in 2001) and for men (set in 1999).

Sources: *The Christian Science Monitor* (1995) and Marathon Guide (2001) [online], available at www.marathonguide.com. Adapted with permission of *The Christian Science Monitor*. © 1995 The Christian Science Publishing Society. All rights reserved.

Figure 13–1 presents another example of women's "natural" inferiority—athletics. In 1925, most people doubted that the best women runners could ever finish a marathon in anywhere near the time that men could. Yet, today, as the figure shows, the best women routinely post better times than the fastest men of decades past, and the performance gap between the sexes has greatly narrowed. Again, most of the differences between men and women turn out to be socially created.

 Visit http://archives.cbc.ca// 300c.asp?id=1-41-714 for a multimedia presentation on "Pioneering Canadian Women in Sports" from the CBC's archives.

There are some physical differences between the sexes. On average, males are 10 percent taller, 20 percent heavier, and 30 percent stronger, especially in their upper bodies (Ehrenreich, 1999). On the other hand, Canadian women outperform men in the ultimate game of life itself: whereas life expectancy for men is 77.1 years, women can expect to live 82.2 years.

In adolescence, males show greater mathematical ability, and females excel in verbal skills, a difference that reflects both biology and socialization (Maccoby and Jacklin, 1974; Baker et al., 1980; Lengermann and Wallace, 1985). But there is no overall difference in intelligence between males and females.

Biologically, then, men and women differ in limited ways, with neither one naturally superior. But culture can define the two sexes very differently, as the global study of gender shows.

GENDER IN GLOBAL PERSPECTIVE

The best way to see the cultural foundation of gender is by making global comparisons. Here, we review three studies that highlight how different the ideas of "masculine" and "feminine" can be.

The Israeli Kibbutzim

In Israel, collective Jewish settlements are called *kibbutzim*. The *kibbutz* (singular form) is especially important for gender research because gender equality is one of its goals, with men and women sharing in both work and decision making.

Members of kibbutzim consider sex irrelevant to most of everyday life. Both men and women take care of children, cook and clean, and repair buildings and make decisions about the day-to-day operation of the kibbutz. Girls and boys are raised in the same way, and from the first weeks of life children live together in dormitories. Women and men in kibbutzim have achieved remarkable (although not complete) social equality. Thus, kibbutzim are evidence of the wide latitude cultures have in defining what is feminine and what is masculine.

Margaret Mead's Research

Anthropologist Margaret Mead carried out groundbreaking research on gender. To the extent that gender reflects biological facts of sex, she reasoned, people everywhere should define "feminine" and "masculine" in the same way; if gender is cultural, the two concepts should vary. Mead studied three societies in New Guinea (1963; orig. 1935). In the mountainous home of the Arapesh, Mead observed men and women with remarkably similar attitudes and behaviour. Both sexes, she reported, were cooperative and sensitive to others—in short, what our culture would label "feminine."

Moving south, Mead then studied the Mundugumor, head-hunters and cannibals who stood in striking contrast to the gentle Arapesh. In this culture, both sexes were typically selfish and aggressive, traits we define as more "masculine."

 To learn more about the work of Margaret Mead, visit the U.S. Library of Congress virtual exhibition at www.loc.gov/ exhibits/mead/

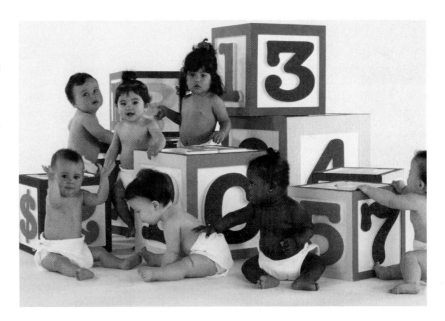

Sex is a biological distinction that develops prior to birth. Gender is the meaning that a society attaches to being female or male. Gender differences are a matter of power, as what is masculine typically has social priority over what is feminine. The importance of gender is not evident among infants, of course, but the ways in which we think of boys and girls set in motion patterns that will continue for a lifetime.

Finally, travelling west to the land of the Tchambuli, Mead discovered a culture that, like our own, defined females and males differently. But the Tchambuli reversed many of our notions of gender: females were dominant and rational, and males were submissive, emotional, and nurturing towards children. Based on her observations, Mead concluded that culture is the key to gender and the definitions of masculine and feminine.

Some critics view Mead's findings as "too neat," as if she saw in these three societies just the patterns she was looking for. Deborah Gewertz (1981) challenged Mead's "reversal hypothesis," claiming that Tchambuli males are really more aggressive and Tchambuli females more submissive than Mead said they were. Gewertz explains that Mead visited the Tchambuli (who actually call themselves the Chambri) during the 1930s, after they had lost much of their property in tribal wars. Working in the home was a temporary domestic role for Chambri men.

George Murdock's Research

In a broader study of more than two hundred pre-industrial societies, George Murdock (1937) found some global agreement about which tasks are feminine and which masculine. Hunting and warfare generally fall to men, while home-centred tasks such as cooking and child care tend to be women's work. With their simple technology, pre-industrial societies apparently assign roles reflecting men's and women's physical attributes. With greater size and strength, men hunt game and protect the group; because women bear children, they assume domestic duties.

But beyond this general pattern, Murdock found significant variation. Consider agriculture: women did the farming in about the same number of societies as men; however, in most societies, the two sexes divided this work. When it came to many other tasks—from building shelters to tattooing the body—Murdock found societies of the world were as likely to turn to one sex as the other.

In Sum: Gender and Culture

Global comparisons show us that, by and large, societies do not consistently define most tasks as either feminine or masculine. As societies industrialize, moreover, the importance of muscle power declines, giving people even more options and further reducing gender differences (Lenski et al., 1995). Thus, gender is simply too variable across cultures to be considered a simple expression of biology. Instead, as with many other elements of culture, what it means to be female and male is mostly a creation of society.

PATRIARCHY AND SEXISM

Although conceptions of gender vary, everywhere in the world we find some degree of **patriarchy** (literally, "the rule of fathers"), a form of social organization in which males dominate females. Despite mythical tales of societies dominated by female "Amazons," **matriarchy**, a form of social organization in which females dominate males, has never been documented in human history (Gough, 1971; Harris, 1977; Lengermann and Wallace, 1985).

But while some degree of patriarchy may be universal, Global Map 13–1 shows significant variation in the relative power and privilege of females and males around the world. According to the United Nations, three Scandinavian countries—Norway, Sweden, and

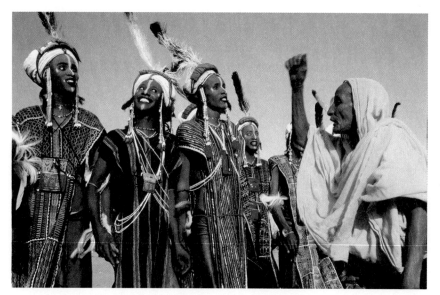

In every society, people assume certain jobs, patterns of behaviour, and ways of dressing are "naturally" feminine while others are just as obviously masculine. But, in global perspective, we see remarkable variety in such social definitions. These men, Wodaabe pastoral nomads who live in the African nation of Niger, are proud to engage in a display of beauty most people in our society would consider feminine.

Finland[1]—afford women the highest social standing; in contrast, women in the Asian nations of Pakistan and Afghanistan and the East African nation of Djibouti have the lowest social standing compared to men. Of 116 countries in the United Nations study, Canada ranked fifth in terms of gender equality (United Nations, 1995).

Sexism, the belief that one sex is innately superior to the other, is the ideological basis of patriarchy. Sexism is not just a matter of individual attitudes; it is built into the institutions of our society. *Institutional sexism* is part of the economy, for example, so that women are highly concentrated in low-paying jobs. Similarly, the legal system has long excused violence against women, especially on the part of boyfriends, husbands, and fathers (Landers, 1990).

The Cost of Sexism

Sexism stunts the talents and limits the ambitions of women, who make up half the population. Although men benefit in some respects from sexism, their privilege comes at a high price. Masculinity in our culture calls for men to engage in many high-risk behaviours, including using tobacco and alcohol, participating in physically dangerous sports, and even driving recklessly, so that motor-vehicle accidents are the leading cause of death among young males. Moreover, as Marilyn French (1985) argues, patriarchy compels men to seek control—not only of women but of themselves and their world. Thus, masculinity is closely linked not only

to accidents but to suicide, violence, and stress-related diseases. The Type A personality—characterized by chronic impatience, driving ambition, competitiveness, and free-floating hostility—is a recipe for heart disease and almost perfectly matches the behaviour that our culture considers masculine (Ehrenreich, 1983).

Finally, insofar as men seek control over others, they lose opportunities for intimacy and trust. As one analyst put it, competition is supposed to separate "the men from the boys." In practice, however, it separates men from men and everyone else (Raphael, 1988).

Is Patriarchy Inevitable?

In pre-industrial societies, women have little control over pregnancy and childbirth, which limits the scope of their lives. Similarly, men's greater height and physical strength are highly valued resources. But industrialization—including birth control technology—gives people choices about how to live. Today, then, in societies like our own, biological differences provide little justification for patriarchy.

But, legitimate or not, male dominance still holds sway in Canada and elsewhere. Does this mean that patriarchy is inevitable? Some sociologists claim that biological factors "wire" the sexes with different motivations and behaviours—specifically, more aggressiveness in males—that make the eradication of patriarchy difficult, perhaps even impossible (Goldberg, 1974, 1987; Rossi, 1985; Popenoe, 1993). Most sociologists, however, believe that gender is primarily a social construction that *can* be changed. Just because no society has yet eliminated patriarchy does not mean that we must remain prisoners of the past.

To understand the persistence of patriarchy, we now examine how gender is rooted and reproduced in society, a process that begins in childhood and continues throughout our lives.

---

[1]For a short time in 2003, Finland had women as both president and prime minister. After a few months in office, the new prime minister was forced to resign. She had lied about a secret communication by which the former prime minister had declared Finland's support for President George W. Bush's war in Iraq—despite its formal neutrality.

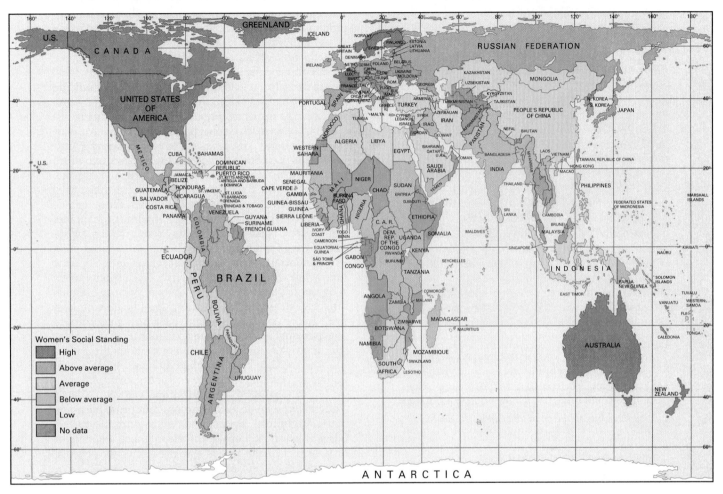

GLOBAL MAP 13–1 Women's Power in Global Perspective

Women's social standing, in relations to men's, varies around the world. In general, women fare better in rich countries than in poor countries. Even so, some nations stand out: In the Nordic nations of Norway, Sweden, and Finland, women come closest to social equality with men.

Source: Data from Seager (2000).

GENDER SOCIALIZATION

From birth to death, human feelings, thoughts, and actions reflect the social definitions that we attach to gender. Children quickly learn that society defines females and males as different kinds of human beings; by about the age of three, they incorporate gender into their identities by applying society's standards to themselves (Bem, 1993). Table 13–1 (on page 315) sketches the traits that North Americans traditionally have used to distinguish "feminine" and "masculine." Such oppositional thinking remains part of our way of

life even though research suggests that most young people do not develop consistently feminine or masculine personalities (L. Bernard, 1980; Bem, 1993).

Just as gender affects how we think of ourselves, so it teaches us to act in normative ways. **Gender roles** (or sex roles) are *attitudes and activities that a society links to each sex.* Insofar as our culture defines males as ambitious and competitive, we expect them to engage in team sports and to aspire to positions of leadership. To the extent that we define females as deferential and emotional, we expect them to be good listeners and supportive observers.

Among the most striking consequences of patriarchy in China is the ancient practice of foot-binding, by which young girls' feet are tightly wrapped as they grow, with predictable results. Although this practice—now rare—produces what people deem "dainty" proportions, what effect would you imagine this deformity has on the physical mobility of women?

GENDER AND THE FAMILY

The first question people usually ask about a newborn—"Is it a boy or a girl?"—looms large because the answer involves not just sex but the likely direction of the child's entire life.

In fact, gender is at work even before the birth of a child, since parents generally hope to have a boy rather than a girl. As we noted in Chapter 12 ("Global Stratification"), in China, India, and other strongly patriarchal societies, female embryos are at risk because parents may abort them, hoping later to produce a boy, whose social value is greater (United Nations Development Programme, 1991).

According to sociologist Jessie Bernard (1981), soon after birth, family members usher infants into the "pink world" of girls or the "blue world" of boys. Parents convey gender messages to children by how they themselves act and even unconsciously in the way they handle daughters and sons. One researcher at an English university presented an infant dressed as either a boy or a girl to a number of women; her subjects handled the "female" child tenderly, with frequent hugs and caresses, while treating the "male" child more aggressively, often lifting him up high in the air or bouncing him on their knees (Bonner, 1984). The lesson is clear: the female world revolves around passivity and emotion, while the male world places a premium on independence and action.

GENDER AND THE PEER GROUP

As children reach school age, their lives spill outside the family as they forge ties with others of the same age. Peer groups further socialize their members according to normative conceptions of gender.

Janet Lever (1978) spent a year observing fifth graders at play. She concluded that boys engage more in team sports—such as baseball and football—that involve many roles, complex rules, and clear objectives such as scoring a run or a touchdown. These games are nearly always competitive, separating winners from losers. Male peer activities reinforce masculine traits of aggression and control.

In contrast, girls play hopscotch or jump rope, or simply talk, sing, or dance together. Such spontaneous activities have few rules, and rarely is "victory" the ultimate goal. Instead of teaching girls to be competitive, Lever explains, female peer groups promote interpersonal skills involving communication and co-operation—presumably the basis for family life.

To explain Lever's observations, recall Carol Gilligan's (1982) gender-based theory of moral reasoning in Chapter 5 ("Socialization"). Boys, Gilligan contends, reason according to abstract principles. For them, "rightness" amounts to "playing by the rules." Girls, in contrast, consider morality more a matter of responsibility to others. Thus, the games we play are preparation for our later lives.

GENDER AND SCHOOLING

Even before children enter school, their reading tends to promote gender distinctions. A generation ago, the Royal Commission on the Status of Women in Canada (1970) analyzed a selection of children's texts and found that "versatile characters who have adventures are invariably males" (Mackie, 1983:185). Even math books represented males and females differently. For example, a problem focusing on the number of words typed per minute in forty-five minutes referred to the typist as female. The commission concluded

 A multimedia presentation on the Royal Commission on the Status of Women is available from the CBC archives at http://archives.cbc.ca// 300c.asp?id=1-73-86

that "a woman's creative and intellectual potential is either underplayed or ignored in the education of children from their earliest years" (Royal Commission on the Status of Women, 1970:175).

More recently, a growing awareness among authors, publishers, and teachers of the limiting effects of gender stereotypes on young people has led to changes. Today's books for children portray females and males in a more balanced way.

Through primary and secondary school, despite many efforts at change, classroom curricula may still encourage children to embrace traditional gender patterns. For example, more young women take instruction in typing and home-centred skills such as nutrition and sewing. Classes in woodworking and auto mechanics, conversely, contain mostly young men.

In university, the pattern continues, with men and women tending towards different majors. Men are disproportionately represented in mathematics and the sciences, including physics, chemistry, and biology. Women cluster in the humanities (such as English), the fine arts (painting, music, dance, and drama), education courses, and the social sciences (including anthropology and sociology). New areas of study are also likely to be gender-typed. Computer science, with its grounding in engineering, logic, and mathematics, enrols mostly men, while courses in gender studies tend to enrol mostly women.

GENDER AND THE MASS MEDIA

Since television first captured the public imagination in the 1950s, white males have held centre stage. Racial and ethnic minorities were all but absent from television until the early 1970s; only in the last few decades have programs featured women in prominent roles.

Even when both sexes appear on camera, men generally play the brilliant detectives, fearless explorers, and skilled surgeons. Women, in contrast, play the less-capable characters and are often important primarily for their sexual attractiveness.

Change came slowly to advertising, which sells products by conforming to widely established cultural norms. Advertising presents the two sexes, more often than not, in stereotypical ways. Historically, ads have shown women in the home, using cleaning products, serving foods, and trying out new appliances. Men, on the other hand, predominate in ads for cars, travel, banking services, industrial companies, and alcoholic beverages. The authoritative "voice-over"—the faceless voice that promotes products on television and radio—is almost always male (Busby, 1975; Courtney and Whipple, 1983; Davis, 1993).

In a systematic study of magazine and newspaper ads, Erving Goffman (1979) found other, more subtle biases. Men, he concluded, are photographed to appear taller than women, implying male superiority. Women are more frequently presented lying down (on sofas and beds) or, like children, seated on the floor. The expressions and gestures of men exude competence and authority, whereas women are more likely to appear in childlike poses. Men focus on the products being advertised; women direct their interest to men, conveying support and submission.

Advertising also actively perpetuates what Naomi Wolf (1990) calls the "beauty myth." The "Diversity: Race, Class, and Gender" box on the next page takes a closer look. And for a discussion of the treatment of minorities—including women—by the media, see the Chapter 5 "Diversity: Race, Class, and Gender" box (page 121).

 "Best and worst" images in current ads are presented at www.mediawatch.ca/

GENDER STRATIFICATION

Gender implies more than how people think and act. The concept of **gender stratification** refers to *a society's unequal distribution of wealth, power, and privilege between the two sexes*. In Canada, the lower social standing of women can be seen in the world of work.

WORKING MEN AND WOMEN

In 1901, women made up 13 percent of Canada's paid workforce and earned one-half of men's income (*Canada's 125th Anniversary Yearbook*, 1992). In 2000, 70 percent of women, compared with 74 percent of men, were active in the Canadian labour force (Statistics Canada, Canadian Statistics, **www.statcan.ca**). So, the traditional view that earning an income is exclusively a "man's role" no longer holds true.

Among the factors at work in the changing Canadian labour force are the decline of farming, the growth of cities, shrinking family size, a rising divorce rate, and the fact that 65 percent of married couples depend on two incomes (*Women in Canada*, 1995:65).

TABLE 13–1 Traditional Notions of Gender Identity	
Feminine Traits	**Masculine Traits**
Submissive	Dominant
Dependent	Independent
Unintelligent and incapable	Intelligent and competent
Emotional	Rational
Receptive	Assertive
Intuitive	Analytical
Weak	Strong
Timid	Brave
Content	Ambitious
Passive	Active
Cooperative	Competitive
Sensitive	Insensitive
Sex object	Sexually aggressive
Attractive because of achievement	Attractive because of physical appearance

Pretty Is as Pretty Does: The Beauty Myth

T he Duchess of Windsor once quipped, "A woman cannot be too rich or too thin." Perhaps the first half of this observation might apply to men as well, but certainly not the second half. It is no surprise that the vast majority of ads placed by the $20-billion-a-year cosmetics industry and the $40-billion-a-year diet industry target women.

Indeed, Naomi Wolf (1990) argues, women in our society are victimized by cultural patterns she terms "the beauty myth." The beauty myth arises, first, because society teaches women to measure themselves in terms of physical appearance (Backman and Adams, 1991). Yet, the standards of beauty (such as the *Playboy* centrefold or the one-hundred-pound fashion model) are unattainable for most women.

The beauty myth also derives from the way society teaches women to prize relationships with men, whom they presumably attract with their beauty. Relentless pursuit of beauty not only drives women towards being highly disciplined, but it also forces them to be highly attuned and responsive to men. Beauty-minded women, in short, try to please men and avoid challenging male power.

The beauty myth affects males as well, as men should want to possess beautiful women. In short, the concept of beauty reduces women to objects and motivates men to possess them as if they were dolls rather than human beings.

As Wolf explains, beauty is really more about behaviour than appearance. It should not be surprising, therefore, that the beauty myth surfaced in our culture during the 1890s, the 1920s, and the 1980s—all decades of heightened debate about the social standing of women.

 Are men starting to buy into the beauty myth too? See www.salon.com/news/feature/1999/11/01/wolf/

Source: Based on Wolf (1990).

In short, Canada and other industrial nations consider women working for income to be the rule rather than the exception. As Global Map 13–2 shows, however, this is not the case in many of the poorer societies of the world.

Gender and Occupations

While the proportions of men and women among the employed have been converging, the work they do remains distinct. Table 13-2 (on page 318) contains occupational statistics for 1982 and 1994: unfortunately, because of differences in the categorization of occupations, it was not possible to update the table with statistics from 2001. Where comparisons with 1982 and/or 1994 are possible, they are noted below.

In 1982 and 1994 respectively, clerical occupations employed 34 and 27 percent of all working women: by 2001, the figure had dropped to 14 percent. In this category are secretaries, typists, stenographers, and others whose efforts typically support the efforts of men. Not surprisingly, while in 1994 more than 80 percent of all such "pink-collar" jobholders were women, by 2001, the figure had dropped to 73 percent. The second largest category is service work, performed by over 17 percent of employed women. These jobs include waiting tables and other food-service work. Both categories of jobs lie at the low end of the pay scale and offer limited opportunities for advancement. A combination of sales and service occupations employed about 28 percent of women in 1982, 1994, and 2001. Teachers were 59 and 63 percent female in 1982 and 1994: when professors and other teachers were combined in 2001, the category was still 64 percent female.

The natural and applied sciences are employing proportionately more women over time—15, 19, and 22 percent in 1982, 1994, and 2001 respectively. The proportion of women in manufacturing has increased from 18 percent in both 1982 and 1994 to 33 percent in 2001. Even construction, the most male of occupations in Table 13–2, has increased its female employment from 1.4 percent in 1982 to 2.4 percent in 2001. It is worth noting that employment in "professional

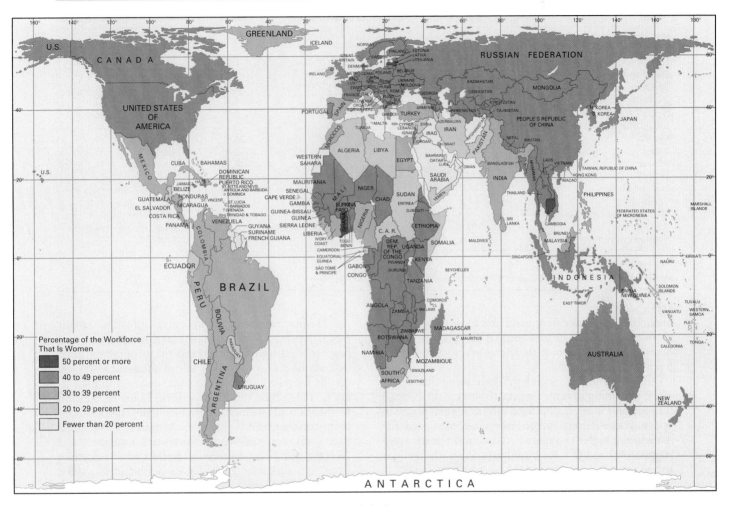

GLOBAL MAP 13–2 Women's Paid Employment in Global Perspective

This map shows the percentage of the labour force made up of women. A country's level of technological development plays an important part here. In 2001, women made up 46.6 percent of the labour force in the Canada—up considerably from the last generation. In high-income nations overall, nearly one-half of the labour force is made up of women. In poor societies, however, women work even harder than in this country, but they are less likely to be paid for their efforts. In Latin America, for example, women represent about one-third of the paid labour force; in Islamic societies of northern Africa and the Middle East, the figure is significantly lower. One exception to this rule is central and southern Africa, where traditionally women make up a large share of farmers.

Source: *Peters Atlas of the World* (1990); updated by the author from The World Bank (2001).

occupations in business and finance" was, by 2001, 49.7 percent female, and that "senior management occupations" are 25 percent female. This suggests that women are making inroads into some high-status occupations that have traditionally been held by males almost entirely (Statistics Canada, B2020 Profile Series).

A history of women's struggles to gain entrance into the legal profession in Ontario is the focus of http://library.lsuc. on.ca/GL/arch_museum.htm: select "Crossing the Bar."

While there remain many occupations that are distinctly male or female, there has been convergence in several occupational categories. Women are moving into business, finance, engineering, the sciences,

TABLE 13–2 **Distribution of Employment, by Occupation, 1982 and 1994**

	1982			1994		
	Women	Men	Women as a % of Occupation	Women	Men	Women as a % of Occupation
Managerial/administrative	6.0	10.2	29.3	12.7	13.8	43.1
Professional:						
Natural sciences/engineering/mathematics	1.3	5.3	14.9	1.7	5.9	19.2
Social sciences/religion	2.0	1.8	42.7	3.3	2.1	56.8
Teaching	6.1	3.0	58.9	6.9	3.3	63.4
Doctors/dentists	0.3	0.8	18.3	0.5	0.9	32.1
Nursing/therapy/other health-related	8.8	1.1	84.7	9.1	1.2	86.1
Artistic/literacy/recreational	1.4	1.6	38.6	2.2	2.1	46.4
Clerical	34.2	6.4	78.8	26.8	5.4	80.2
Sales	10.1	10.8	39.7	10.1	9.9	45.7
Service	18.1	10.7	54.2	17.1	11.0	56.2
Primary	2.8	8.0	19.6	2.1	6.4	21.3
Manufacturing	6.4	19.8	18.4	4.8	17.3	18.5
Construction	0.2	9.3	1.4	0.3	9.3	2.4
Material handling/other crafts	1.8	5.2	19.3	1.6	5.0	21.0
Total*	100.0	100.0	41.2	100.0	100.0	45.2
Total employed (000s)	4544	6491	...	6002	7290	...

*Any errors are due to rounding.

Source: Adapted from *Women in Canada* (1995:76) from Statistics Canada, *Labour Force Survey*.

medicine, and veterinary medicine in unprecedented numbers, while a visit to a hospital or a nursing home reveals the presence of male nurses, who now make up 6 percent of the total.

The "Applying Sociology" box brings us up to 1995, providing average income (based on the census) for men and women employed full time, year-round in selected occupations. As the box reveals, men predominate in the highest paying jobs while women are overrepresented in the lowest paid jobs. Also, the gender gap in income is greatest in the best-paid jobs.

Overall, then, gender stratification permeates the workplace, where men tend to hold occupational positions that confer more wealth and power than those typically held by women. While change is occurring, this gender-based hierarchy is easy to spot in the job setting: most of the time, female nurses assist male physicians, female secretaries serve male executives, and female flight attendants serve male airline pilots. Moreover, in any field, the greater the income and prestige associated with a job, the more likely it is to be held by a man.

HOUSEWORK: WOMEN'S "SECOND SHIFT"

One indicator of the global pattern of patriarchy, shown in Global Map 13–3 (page 320), is the extent to which housework—cleaning, cooking, and caring for children—is the province of women. In North America, housework has always embodied a cultural contradiction: it is touted as essential for family life on the one hand, but it carries little prestige or reward on the other hand (J. Bernard, 1981).

Despite women's rapid entry into the labour force, the amount of housework performed by women has declined only slightly (and the proportion done by men has not changed at all). Although the typical couple shares in disciplining the children and managing finances, men routinely perform home repairs and yardwork while women see to most daily tasks of shopping, cooking, and cleaning. Consuming, on average, twenty-six hours a week, housework amounts to a "second shift" that women undertake after returning from the workplace each day (Schooler et al., 1984; Fuchs, 1986; Hochschild, 1989; Presser, 1993; Keith and Schafer, 1994; Benokraitis and Feagin, 1995).

In sum, men support the idea of women entering the labour force and count on the money women earn but resist modifying their own behaviour to help their partners in their careers by making their home lives more manageable (Komarovsky, 1973; Cowan, 1992; Robinson and Spitze, 1992; Lennon and Rosenfeld, 1994; Heath and Bourne, 1995).

GENDER, INCOME, AND WEALTH

In 2001, women working full time all year earned an average of $34 224, while men working full time earned $49 224. For every dollar earned by men, then, women earned about 71 cents—suggesting no improvement since 1996.

In 1993, the average annual pretax income of women older than age fifteen from all sources was $16 500—only 58 percent of the average income of men at that time. One part of the explanation for this discrepancy is that 11.9 percent of women had no

The Pink Ghetto and the Gender Gap in Income

Among the explanations offered for the gender gap in income are the following: (1) the predominance of women in part-time employment; (2) the predominance of women in poorly paid occupations (the pink ghetto); (3) educational disparities; (4) the tendency among women to interrupt their careers for reasons of child-rearing; and (5) seniority among men.

Women are gradually closing the income gap, in part through educational attainment, but also through reduced fertility, commitment to careers, and fewer and shorter work interruptions (Fast and Da Pont, 2000). Census Canada (www.statcan.ca) provides data on women's employment and income; by analyzing these data, we can determine whether women's employment is concentrated within more poorly paid jobs (the pink ghetto) and the size of the gap between male and female incomes in various occupations.

Table 13–3 reveals that 40 percent of the people involved in full-time, year-round employment are women and that female income is 71 percent of male income. The figures for the highest- and lowest-paying twenty-five occupations reveal some clear contrasts. Women make up 22 percent of those in the top twenty-five occupations and 68 percent of those in the bottom. This confirms that women are overrepresented in the most poorly paid occupations, and they are even more severely underrepresented in the best-paid occupations. Not surprisingly, women earn 68 percent of male income at the top end and 82 percent at the bottom.

In the top half of the table are seven occupations selected from among the twenty-five highest-paying occupations. Among these occupations, women are relatively well represented in one—school principal—at 36 percent. Further, in two highly paid occupations, judge

TABLE 13–3 Income and Distribution of Men and Women in Selected Occupations from the 25 Highest- and 25 Lowest-Paying Occupations,* Canada, 1995

Occupation	% Female	Male Income	Female Income	Female–Male Income Ratio
All occupations	**39.9**	**$42 488**	**30 130**	**70.9**
Highest 25 occupations	**21.8**	**86 139**	**58 943**	**68.4**
Judges	22.9	128 791	117 707	91.4
Specialist physicians	25.6	137 019	86 086	62.8
Family physicians	25.9	116 750	81 512	69.8
Dentists	19.9	109 187	71 587	65.6
University professors	26.1	72 532	55 909	77.1
School principals	36.1	66 837	60 394	90.4
Police officers	9.1	64 865	50 011	77.1
Lowest 25 occupations	**68.3**	**20 238**	**16 564**	**81.8**
Early childhood educators	96.6	25 074	19 586	78.1
Taxi and limousine drivers	5.9	19 845	16 756	84.4
Cooks	80.9	20 224	17 607	87.1
Hairstylists and barbers	74.9	22 867	16 755	73.3
Painters, sculptors, visual artists	41.1	20 421	14 982	73.4
Cashiers	83.9	20 557	16 977	82.6
Babysitters and nannies	97.9	15 106	12 662	83.8

*All of the data refer to people who are employed full time, year-round.

Source: Statistics Canada, www.statcan.ca (Nation Series).

and school principal, women earn over 90 percent of male income.

In the lower half of the table are seven occupations selected from the lowest-income ranks. Five of them, owing to the preponderance of women, can truly be classified as "pink ghetto" jobs; early childhood education and babysitting are the most striking examples, at 97 and 98 percent female respectively. Female incomes in these poorly paid occupations range from 73 to 87 percent of male incomes.

Statistics Canada (*The Daily*, August 8, 2000) provides revealing information on one of the selected occupations in the top income category—university professor. Among full-time faculty in 1998–99, women earned 86 percent of male income. If we control for rank—comparing women and men separately

at assistant, associate, and full professor rank—we find that women earn 95 percent of the income of their male counterparts. Thus, the incomes of male and female *full* professors—or male and female *associate* professors—are very close to equal.

This means that, if we limit our analysis to full-time employees and take into account years of service (seniority) and rank, the income disparity between males and females—within a single occupation—may be greatly reduced or eliminated. Pay equity for a single occupation does not, of course, mean that there is no income disparity between occupations or between full- and part-time workers. It does mean that, in specific circumstances, women have successfully reduced or eliminated the gender gap.

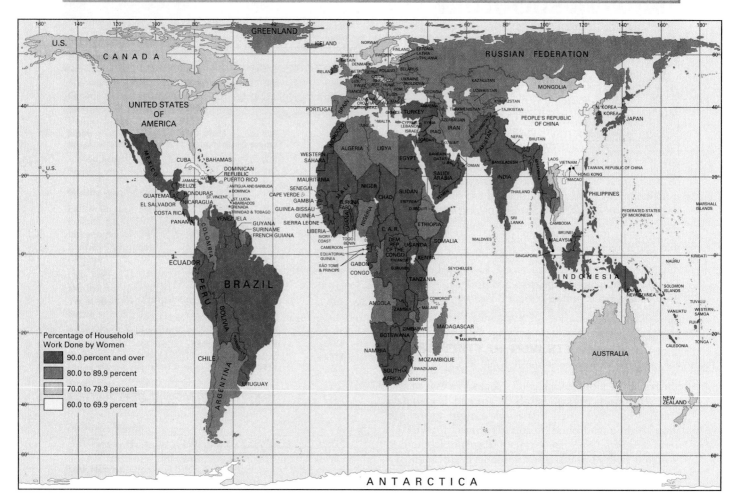

GLOBAL MAP 13–3 Housework in Global Perspective

Throughout the world, housework is a major component of women's routines and identities. This is especially true in poor societies of Latin America, Africa, and Asia, where women are not generally in the paid labour force. But our society also defines housework and child care as "feminine" activities, even though a majority of Canadian women work outside the home. Married women spend almost twice as much time as married men on domestic work.

Sources: *Peters Atlas of the World* (1990), updated by John Macionis; *Women in Canada* (1995:83).

source of personal income at all, compared to 4.5 percent of men (*Women in Canada*, 1995:84). Younger women, those fifty-four and under, have higher incomes than women over fifty-five. Women with university degrees earn more money than those without them: in 1993, women with university degrees had an average annual income of $40 700. Women with non-university but post-secondary graduation earned an average of $28 000, and those who had graduated from high school and had some post-secondary training av-

eraged $25 000. Finally, women without a high-school diploma averaged $20 000 annually.

Furthermore, whatever women's educational levels, men earn more. Female university graduates who worked full time, full year earned three-quarters of the income of their male counterparts (*Women in Canada*, 1995:87). See the "Applying Sociology" box (p. 319) for a refinement of this analysis.

Differences in earnings between men and women in Canada have gradually declined in recent decades.

Some of this change is due to increasing opportunities for working women.

The most important reason for the lower earnings of Canadian working women is the *kind* of work they do: largely clerical and service jobs. In effect, jobs and gender interact. People tend to perceive jobs with less clout as "women's work," and we devalue work simply because it is performed by women (Parcel et al., 1986; Blum, 1991; England, 1992; Bellas, 1994; Huffman et al., 1996).

During the 1980s, proponents of gender equality responded to this mindset by proposing a policy of "comparable worth," which means that people should be paid not according to the historical double standard, but based on the worth of what they actually do. Several nations, including Great Britain and Australia, and provinces such as Ontario adopted such policies, but they have found limited acceptance in the United States.

A second cause of this gender-based income disparity has to do with the family. Both men and women have children, of course, but our culture defines parenting as more a woman's responsibility than a man's. Pregnancy and raising small children keep many younger women out of the labour force altogether at a time when their male peers stand to make significant occupational gains. As a result, women workers have less job seniority than their male counterparts (Fuchs, 1986; Stier, 1996; Waldfogel, 1997).

Moreover, women who choose to have children may be reluctant or unable to maintain fast-paced jobs that tie up their evenings and weekends. Career women with children may resolve this classic case of role strain by favouring jobs that offer a shorter commuting distance, more flexible hours, and employer-sponsored child-care services. Women seeking both a career and a family are torn between their dual responsibilities in ways that men are not. Consider this: among U.S. executives past the age of forty, about 90 percent of men—but only about 35 percent of women—have had a child (F. Schwartz, 1989). Women who do have children, in other words, start to fall behind childless women in terms of earnings.

Felice Schwartz (1989) also points out that corporate women risk their careers by having children. Rather than helping to meet the needs of working mothers, the typical corporation interprets a woman's choice to have a child as evidence that she may leave the company, taking with her a substantial investment in time and training. As an alternative, Schwartz calls on corporations to develop "mommy tracks" that allow women to meet family responsibilities while continuing their careers, with less intensity, for specified periods. This proposal has won praise, but it has also provoked strong criticism. Opponents of the "mommy-track" concept fear that it plays into the hands of corporate men who have long stereotyped

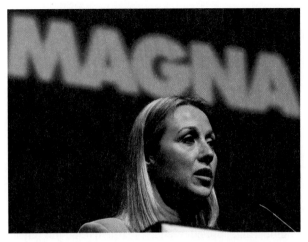

Belinda Stronach, CEO and president of Magna International, the auto-parts titan with over $12 billion (US) in annual revenues, was named by Fortune *as the second most powerful woman in business outside the United States. Given her influence on the international scene, it should have been no surprise to learn that it was Stronach who contacted Brian Mulroney and later Stephen Harper and Peter MacKay to encourage the merger of the Canadian Alliance and the Progressive Conservatives in the fall of 2003. Twice, she got the party leaders back together when talks broke down in a process that will dramatically change Canada's political landscape (Dubé, 2003).*

women as being less attached to careers in the first place. Further, critics add, since companies are unlikely to apply such a plan to men, it can only hurt rather than help the career aspirations of corporate women (Ehrenreich and English, 1995).

The two factors noted so far—type of work and family responsibilities—account for about two-thirds of the earnings disparity between women and men. Researchers conclude that a third factor—discrimination—accounts for most of the remainder (Pear, 1987; Fuller and Schoenberger, 1991).

Because discrimination is illegal, it is often practised in subtle ways (Benokraitis and Feagin, 1995). Corporate women often encounter a *glass ceiling*, a barrier that is hard to see and that is formally denied by high company officials, which effectively prevents women from rising above middle management.

GENDER AND EDUCATION

In the past, our society deemed schooling to be irrelevant for women, whose lives revolved around the home. But times have changed. Each year from 1994 to 1998, more than 57 percent of all university qualifications (undergraduate diplomas through to PhDs) were awarded to women (Statistics Canada, **www.statcan. ca**). In 1988, only 14 percent of those qualifying in engineering and applied sciences and 28 percent of those in the mathematical and physical sciences were women, but by 1998, the figures increased to 21 and 31 percent respectively. On the other hand, in 1988, women received more than half of all qualifications awarded in education (61 percent), fine and applied arts (59 percent), and the humanities (57 percent) (*Women in the Labour Force*, 1990–91). The comparable figures for 1998 are 71, 66, and 63 (Statistics Canada, **www.statcan.ca**). In other words, women are earning proportionally more university qualifications in every discipline.

A growing number of women are pursuing academic programs that until recently were virtually all-male. Women's share of degrees in medicine, engineering, applied sciences, mathematics, and physical sciences has grown steadily since 1975. For instance, in medicine, the percentage of degrees awarded to women rose from 24 percent in 1975 to 41 percent in 1988 (*Women in the Labour Force*, 1990–91) and over 50 percent by 2000. The proportion of women in all these professions is steadily rising. Educators in Canada and the United States have identified a totally new concern in the area of gender and education: as girls surge ahead academically, boys are tuning out and dropping out in large numbers. Before too long, we may be worrying about the failure of boys and men to develop to their full potential.

GENDER AND POLITICS

Before 1918, women could not vote in federal elections. Until 1919, no women were allowed to sit in the House of Commons, and until 1929, no women were allowed to sit in the Senate of Canada (*Canada's 125th Anniversary Yearbook*, 1992). It was not until 1940 that all eligible women in the country could vote in both federal and provincial elections. Table 13–4 cites milestones in women's gradual movement into Canadian political life.

Today, women are involved in all levels of politics in Canada. Still, the largest proportion of women politicians is found in the municipal arena. Women are also well represented on local school boards, where they can, again, act on their normative and institutionalized "responsibility" for their children. Women face many barriers to participation in federal politics, especially if they have young families at home and live in different time zones from Ottawa, where they must spend a major portion of each year, or even most of the year if they are cabinet ministers.

There are, however, signs of change. An increasing proportion of our representatives in the House of Commons are women. The Canadian Advisory Council on the Status of Women stated that if the number of women in the House of Commons continued to increase at the rate it did between the 1984 and 1988 elections, in nine elections, or approximately forty-five years, there would be equal numbers of men and women in the House. But while, by 1997, 20 percent of MPs were women, there was no change in the percentage after the 2000 election, suggesting that the expected increase in female representation had stalled.

In 1989, the NDP became the first of Canada's major federal political parties to elect a woman leader—Audrey McLaughlin. In June 1993, Kim Campbell became Canada's first female prime minister by winning the leadership of the Conservative party when Brian Mulroney stepped down. From 1997 to 2003, Alexa McDonough was the only female party leader in the House of Commons. In the Liberal party, Sheila Copps has been a starring member of the federal cabinet, deputy prime minister for a term, and several times a contender for leadership of her party.

A recent global survey found that while women are half the earth's population, they hold just 11.7 percent of seats in the world's 179 parliaments. While this represents a rise from 3 percent fifty years ago, only in the Nordic nations (Norway, Sweden, Finland, and Denmark) and the Netherlands does the share of parliamentary seats held by women (36.4 percent) even approach their share of the population (Inter-Parliamentary Union, 1997).

ARE WOMEN A MINORITY?

A **minority**[2] is *any category of people, distinguished by physical or cultural difference, that is socially disadvantaged.* Given the clear economic disadvantage of being a woman in our society, it seems reasonable to say that Canadian women are a minority. One can also make the argument that women in specific ethnic and racial categories suffer double or multiple disadvantage based on membership in more than one "minority" category. A First Nations woman, for example, is female, visible minority, and subject to the *Indian Act* (Gerber, 1995).

Subjectively speaking, most white women do not think of themselves as members of a minority (Hacker, 1951; Lengermann and Wallace, 1985). This is partly because, unlike racial and ethnic minorities, white women are well represented at all levels of the class structure, including the very top.

Bear in mind, however, that women at every class level typically have less income, wealth, education, and power than men do. In fact, patriarchy makes women dependent for much of their social standing on men— first their fathers and later their husbands (J. Bernard, 1981).

---

[2]We use the term "minority" rather than "minority group" because, as explained in Chapter 7 ("Groups and Organizations"), a minority is a category, not a group.

MINORITY WOMEN

If women are defined as a minority, what about minority women? Are they doubly handicapped? Generally speaking, the answer is yes. First, there is the disadvantage associated with race and ethnicity. Aboriginal women have both the lowest labour-force participation rate and the second-highest unemployment rate. Their unemployment level, at 28.2 percent, is well over twice that of non-Aboriginal women. Aboriginal women who worked full time in 1990 earned an average of $23 800, compared to the $25 900 earned by non-Aboriginal women. In addition, 33 percent of Aboriginal women—compared to 17 percent of non-Aboriginal women and 28 percent of Aboriginal men—had incomes below Canada's low-income cut-off (Moore 1995:147).

As indicated in Figure 11–3 (p. 264), the average incomes of Asian and Black women are a little lower than that of British women—despite the fact that their levels of education and labour force participation are higher. These disparities reflect minority women's lower positions on the occupational and educational hierarchies in comparison to white women (Bonilla-Santiago, 1990). Further, whenever the economy sags, minority women are especially likely to experience declining income and unemployment.

In short, gender has a powerful effect on our lives, but it never operates alone. Class position, race and ethnicity, and gender form a multilayered system of disadvantage for some and privilege for others (Ginsburg and Tsing, 1990). Minority women, and Native women in particular, suffer "multiple jeopardy" (Gerber, 1990).

VIOLENCE AGAINST WOMEN

Perhaps the most wrenching kind of suffering that our society imposes on women is violence. As Chapter 9 ("Deviance") explained, official statistics paint criminal violence as overwhelmingly the actions of men—hardly surprising since aggressiveness is a trait our culture defines as masculine. Furthermore, a great deal of "manly" violence is directed against women, which we also might expect because North American society devalues what is culturally defined as feminine.

A 1993 Statistics Canada survey found that 51 percent of Canadian women had experienced at least one instance of sexual or physical violence. About 25 percent of women were subject to violence at the hands of an intimate partner (Statistics Canada, 1994b). The most common location for gender-linked violence is the home. Richard Gelles (cited in Roesch, 1984) argues that, with the exception of the police and the military, the family is the most violent organization in the United States. There is no reason, given the statistics cited in the previous paragraph, to think that the picture is any different in Canada. Both

TABLE 13–4 Milestones for Women in Canadian Politics	
Women's Rights	
1916	Women in Manitoba, Alberta, and Saskatchewan gain right to vote in provincial elections.
1917	Women with property permitted to hold office in Saskatchewan. Women in British Columbia and Ontario gain right to vote in provincial elections.
1918	Women gain full federal franchise (right to vote). Women in Nova Scotia gain right to vote in provincial elections.
1919	Women in New Brunswick gain right to vote in provincial elections.
1920	Uniform franchise established through the Dominion Election Act, making permanent the right of women to be elected to Parliament.
1922	Women in Prince Edward Island gain right to vote and to hold elected office.
1925	Women over age twenty-five gain right to vote in Newfoundland.
1929	Women are deemed "persons" and can therefore be appointed to the Senate after the British Privy Council overturns Supreme Court of Canada's 1928 Persons Case decision, which had interpreted the BNA Act to mean women were not "persons" and could therefore not be appointed to the Senate.
1940	Women in Quebec gain right to vote in provincial elections, completing enfranchisement of women in Canada.
1983	Canadian Human Rights Act amended to prohibit sexual harassment and to ban discrimination on basis of pregnancy and family or marital status.
1989	Audrey McLaughlin becomes the first woman to lead a federal Canadian political party.
1993	Kim Campbell becomes Canada's first female prime minister.

Source: *Canada's 125th Anniversary Yearbook (1992), Canadian Global Almanac 2003 (2002).*

 For a United Nations report on violence against women and girls around the world, see www.unicef-icdc.org/publications/pdf/digest6.pdf

sexes suffer from family violence, although, by and large, women sustain more serious injuries than men do (Straus and Gelles, 1986; Shupe et al., 1987; Gelles and Cornell, 1990; Smolowe, 1994; Lupri, 2002). Chapter 18 ("Family") delves more deeply into the problem of family violence.

Violence against women also occurs in casual relationships. As Chapter 8 ("Sexuality") explains, most rapes involve not strangers but men known (and often trusted) by women. Dianne F. Herman (2001) argues that the extent of abuse suggests that sexual violence is built into our way of life. All forms of violence against women—from the wolf whistles that intimidate women on city streets to a pinch in a crowded subway to physical assaults that occur at home—express what

Canadian Women in Hockey: Going for Gold

At the turn of the century, Canadian women were involved in hockey, doing battle in long, flowing skirts that made them look like sisters of the cloth rather than members of hockey teams. The Preston Rivulettes (from what is now part of Cambridge, Ontario) recorded an incredible win-loss record of 348–2 through the 1930s. But World War II intervened, draining attention and energy away from hockey so that by the 1950s, women's hockey had fizzled. The struggle to re-establish women's hockey—to get ice time, good equipment, sponsorships, public acceptance and support, media coverage, the attention of Don Cherry, and Olympic status—consumed the next forty to fifty years. In 1998 in Nagano, Japan, women's hockey was an official Olympic sport for the first time, and the world of Canadian women's hockey changed forever.

The game that originated in Canada had become part of our collective identity, and continues to be our most popular sport, is now played by women—legitimately! Many of the women on Team Canada grew up playing on boys' teams, while at least two, Manon Rheaume and Hayley Wickenheiser, have played in the professional male leagues. As a result of recent publicity (and the decision to prohibit body-checking in women's hockey), parents in large numbers are now willing to enrol their young daughters in girls' hockey leagues. Girls' teams—which often play against boys' teams—are springing up across Canada, and girls' participation in hockey has almost quadrupled in the last decade to 25 000 players nationally.

Without doubt, the image of girls and women as hockey players is inconsistent with our societal expectations of femininity. Off the ice, most of these women conform to our cultural standards of feminine behaviour, dress, and makeup.

However, when they don their protective hockey uniforms and helmets and step out onto the ice, they enter a world in which they exhibit aggression, speed, and impressive skill: power skating, strategic agility, and adroit handling of stick and puck become their tools. This transformation from "woman" to "athlete" (in a traditionally male or macho sport) is not easy for the women themselves, nor is it easy for all members of the general public to accept. There are still people who feel strongly that women should stick to ballet, gymnastics, and synchronized swimming (another Canadian "invention"). Ambivalence is apparent in embarrassment on the part of some Team Canada members about the fact that their first world championship (in Ottawa in 1990) was won in pink and white uniforms.

When the women's and men's hockey teams both won gold at the Salt Lake City Olympics of 2002, celebrations erupted across the country. Olympic publicity has changed the lives of the women who play hockey for Team Canada. The quest for public awareness and support is over. Don Cherry's active support of women's hockey is now part of the public record.

---

she calls a "rape culture" by which men try to dominate women. Sexual violence, then, is fundamentally about power rather than sex, and therefore should be understood as a dimension of gender stratification (Nelson and Fleras, 1998).

Sexual Harassment

Sexual harassment refers to *comments, physical contact, or gestures of a sexual nature that are deliberate, repeated, and unwelcome.* During the 1990s, sexual harassment became an important North American issue that has already significantly redefined the rules for workplace interaction between the sexes.

Most victims of sexual harassment are women. Our culture encourages men to be sexually assertive and to perceive women in sexual terms; social interaction in the workplace, on campus, and elsewhere, then, can readily take on sexual overtones. Furthermore, most individuals in positions of power—including business executives, physicians, bureau chiefs, assembly-line supervisors, professors, and military officers—are men who oversee the work of women. Surveys carried out in widely different work settings confirm that half of women respondents report receiving unwanted sexual attention (Loy and Stewart, 1984; Paul, 1991).

Sexual harassment is sometimes blatant and direct, as when a supervisor solicits sexual favours from a subordinate, coupled with the threat of reprisals if the advances are refused. Courts have declared such *quid pro quo* sexual harassment (the Latin phrase means "one thing in return for another") an illegal violation of human or civil rights.

However, the problem of unwelcome sexual attention often involves subtle behaviour—sexual teasing, off-colour jokes, pinups displayed in the workplace—which an individual may not *intend* as harassment of

Major media in Canada, including *Maclean's*, *The Globe and Mail*, and the CBC, all provided extensive coverage of the exploits and victories of Team Canada, women's style. The team members have agents and contracts for product endorsements. Sports Canada helps cover their expenses, and employers are willing to give the athletes time off to prepare for championship or Olympic competition. These young women are now accustomed to having agents, being recognized on the street, and being the subject of sometimes overwhelming media attention. The dramatic change in the status of women's hockey is exciting for female players across the country and for the Canadian public as a whole. In their own way, these women have stretched the limits of and changed the definition of femininity.

Postscript—On January 16, 1998, as women's hockey was played for the first time at the Olympics, the CBC ran a full-length edition of *The National Magazine* about women's hockey in Canada and our Olympic team. Among

The Canadian women's hockey team won gold at the 2002 Winter Olympic Games in Salt Lake City.

other guests, two of the women who had played for the Preston Rivulettes in the 1930s and who would be watching Team Canada at Nagano, shared their

thoughts on the dramatic changes in the world of women's hockey.

Sources: CBC (1998) and Smith (1997a, 1997b).

---

another person. But, using the *effect* standard favoured by many feminists, such actions create a *hostile environment* (Cohen, 1991; Paul, 1991). Incidents of this kind are far more complex because they involve different perceptions of the same behaviour. For example, a man may think that complimenting a co-worker on her appearance is simply a polite gesture; she, on the other hand, may deem his behaviour offensive and a hindrance to her job performance.

Pornography

Pornography, too, underlies sexual violence. Defining pornography has long challenged scholars and lawmakers alike. Unable to set a single, specific standard to distinguish what is, and what is not, pornographic, the Supreme Court allows provinces, cities, and counties to decide what violates "community standards" of decency and lacks redeeming social value.

But few doubt that pornography (loosely defined) is popular: X-rated videos, 900 telephone numbers offering sexual conversation, and a host of sexually explicit movies, magazines, and Internet websites together constitute a multimillion-dollar-a-year industry.

Traditionally, society has cast pornography as a *moral* issue, involving the expression of sexuality. A more recent view holds that pornography demeans women. That is, pornography is really a *power* issue because it fosters the notion that men should control both sexuality and women (Nelson and Robinson, 1999:355). Catharine MacKinnon (1987) has branded pornography as one foundation of male dominance because it portrays women in dehumanizing fashion as the subservient playthings of men. Worth noting, in this context, is that the term "pornography" is derived from the Greek word *porne*, meaning a harlot who acts as a man's sexual slave.

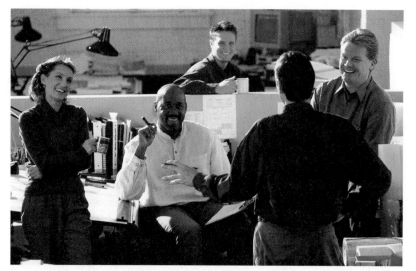

Many private companies and public organizations have adopted policies to discourage forms of behaviour that might create a "hostile or intimidating environment." In practice, such policies seek to remove sexuality from the workplace so that employees can do their jobs while steering clear of traditional notions about female and male relationships. The hope is that sexual harassment policies will develop a comfortable, informal atmosphere in which people can interact freely and easily.

A related charge is that pornography promotes violence against women. While demonstrating a scientific cause-and-effect relationship between what people watch and how they act is difficult, research supports the contention that pornography gives men licence to think of women as objects rather than as people. The public as a whole also voices concern about the effects of pornography, and many people hold the opinion that pornography encourages men to commit rape.

Like sexual harassment, pornography raises complex and sometimes conflicting issues. While everyone objects to material we find offensive, many also endorse the rights of free speech and artistic expression. But pressure to restrict this kind of material is building through the efforts of an unlikely coalition of conservatives (who oppose pornography on moral grounds) and progressives (who condemn it for political reasons). The easy availability of pornography on the Internet complicates the task of those who would restrict access.

THEORETICAL ANALYSIS OF GENDER

Although they come to differing conclusions, the structural-functional and social-conflict paradigms each point out the importance of gender in social organization.

STRUCTURAL-FUNCTIONAL ANALYSIS

The structural-functional paradigm views society as a complex system of many separate but integrated parts. From this point of view, gender functions as a way to organize social life.

As Chapter 4 ("Society") explained, members of hunting-and-gathering societies had little power over the forces of biology. Lacking effective birth control, women experienced frequent pregnancies, and the responsibilities of child care kept them close to home. Likewise, to take advantage of men's greater strength, norms guided men towards the pursuit of game and other tasks away from the home. Over many generations, this sexual division of labour became institutionalized and largely taken for granted (Lengermann and Wallace, 1985).

Industrial technology opens up a vastly greater range of cultural possibilities. Human muscle-power no longer serves as a vital source of energy, so the physical strength of men loses much of its earlier significance. At the same time, the ability to control reproduction gives women greater choice in shaping their lives. Modern societies come to see that traditional gender roles waste an enormous amount of human talent; yet change comes slowly, because gender is deeply embedded in social mores.

Talcott Parsons: Gender and Complementarity

As Talcott Parsons (1942, 1951, 1954) explained, gender differences help to integrate society—at least in its traditional form. Gender, Parsons noted, creates a *complementary* set of roles that link men and women together into family units that carry out various functions vital to the operation of society. Women take charge of family life, assuming primary responsibility for managing the household and raising children. Men, in contrast, connect the family to the larger world, primarily by participating in the labour force.

Parsons further argued that distinctive socialization teaches the two sexes their appropriate gender identities and skills needed for adult life. Thus, society teaches boys—presumably destined for the labour force—to be rational, self-assured, and competitive.

This complex of traits Parsons termed *instrumental*. To prepare girls for child rearing, their socialization stresses what Parsons called *expressive* qualities, such as emotional responsiveness and sensitivity to others.

Society, explains Parsons, promotes gender conformity by instilling in men and women a fear that straying too far from accepted standards of masculinity or femininity courts rejection by members of the opposite sex. In simple terms, women learn to view nonmasculine men as sexually unattractive, while men learn to avoid unfeminine women.

Critical evaluation. Structural-functionalism advances a theory of complementarity by which gender integrates society both structurally (in terms of what people do) and morally (in terms of what they believe). Although influential at mid-century, this approach is rarely used today in exploring the impact of gender.

For one thing, functionalism assumes a singular vision of society that is not shared by everyone. For example, many women have always worked outside the home as a matter of economic necessity, a fact not reflected in Parsons's conventional, middle-class view of family life. Second, critics charge that Parsons's analysis minimizes the personal strains and social costs of rigid, traditional gender roles (Wallace and Wolf, 1995). Third, for those who seek sexual equality, what Parsons describes as gender "complementarity" amounts to little more than male domination.

SOCIAL-CONFLICT ANALYSIS

From a social-conflict point of view, gender involves not just differences in behaviour but disparities in power. Conventional ideas about gender historically have benefited men while subjecting women to prejudice, discrimination, and sometimes outright violence, in a striking parallel to the treatment of racial and ethnic minorities (Hacker, 1951, 1974; Collins, 1971; Lengermann and Wallace, 1985). Thus, conflict theorists claim, conventional ideas about gender promote not cohesion but tension and conflict, with men seeking to protect their privileges while women challenge the status quo.

As earlier chapters noted, the social-conflict paradigm draws heavily on the ideas of Karl Marx. Yet Marx was a product of his time insofar as his writings focused almost exclusively on men. His friend and collaborator Friedrich Engels, however, did develop a theory of gender stratification (1902; orig. 1884).

Friedrich Engels: Gender and Class

Looking back through history, Engels noted that in hunting-and-gathering societies the activities of women and men, although different, had comparable importance. A successful hunt might have brought men great prestige, but the vegetation gathered by

Dorothy Smith is a Canadian sociologist who has influenced a generation of feminist scholarship. Her work involves a radical revision of the way that knowledge, truth, and science are constructed—starting with the actual experiences of women. Her notion of bifurcated consciousness arose out of the discrepancies between her experiences as an academic and as a single mother of two. Combining elements of Marxism, ethnomethodology, and symbolic interaction, hers is a sociology of and for women.

women constituted most of a society's food supply (Leacock, 1978). As technological advances led to a productive surplus, however, social equality and communal sharing gave way to private property and, ultimately, a class hierarchy. At this point, men gained pronounced power over women. With surplus wealth on their hands, upper-class men wanted to be sure of paternity, so they would be able to pass on property to their heirs; they could do this only by controlling women's sexuality. Women were then taught to remain virgins until marriage, to remain faithful to their husbands thereafter, and to build their lives around bearing and raising children.

According to Engels, capitalism intensifies this male domination. First, capitalism creates more wealth, which confers greater power on men as wage earners as well as owners and heirs of property. Second, an expanding capitalist economy depends on defining people—especially women—as consumers and convincing them that personal fulfilment derives from owning and using products. Third, to allow men to work, society assigns women the task of maintaining the home. The double exploitation of capitalism, as Engels saw it, lies in low wages for male labour and no wages for female work (Eisenstein, 1979; Barry, 1983; Jagger, 1983; Vogel, 1983).

Critical evaluation. Social-conflict analysis highlights how society places the two sexes in unequal positions of wealth, power, and privilege. As a result, the con-

FIGURE 13–2 Use of Contraception by Married Women of Childbearing Age

Source: United Nations Development Programme (2001).

flict approach is decidedly critical of conventional ideas about gender, claiming that society would be better off if we minimized or even eliminated this dimension of social structure.

But social-conflict analysis, too, has its critics. One problem, they suggest, is that this approach casts conventional families—defended by traditionalists as morally good—as a social evil. From a more practical standpoint, social-conflict analysis minimizes the extent to which women and men live together cooperatively and often happily. Another problem with this approach is its assertion that capitalism stands at the root of gender stratification. Agrarian countries, in fact, are typically more patriarchal than industrial-capitalist nations. And socialist societies, too—including the People's Republic of China—remain strongly patriarchal (Moore, 1992).

FEMINISM

Feminism is *the advocacy of social equality for the sexes, in opposition to patriarchy and sexism.* The "first wave" of the feminist movement in Canada began in the mid-1800s as Canadian women were influenced by writing such as Mary Wollstonecraft's *A Vindication of the Rights of Women* (1792) and John Stuart Mill's *The Subjection of*

Women (1869). The primary objective of the early women's movement was securing the right to vote, which was achieved for federal elections in Canada by 1918 with the passage of the *Women's Franchise Act.* Ironically, women were not "persons" before the law

 Find out more about the *Persons Case* **by visiting the National Archives of Canada at www.archives.ca/05/0530_e. html**

until 1929, and women living in Quebec could not vote in provincial elections until 1940.

BASIC FEMINIST IDEAS

Feminism views the personal experiences of women and men through the lens of gender. How we think of ourselves (gender identity), how we act (gender roles), and our sex's social standing (gender stratification) are all rooted in the operation of our society.

Although people who consider themselves feminists disagree about many things, most support five general principles:

1. **The importance of change.** Feminist thinking is decidedly political, linking ideas to action. Feminism is critical of the status quo, advocating change towards social equality for women and men.

2. **Expanding human choice.** Feminists maintain that cultural conceptions of gender divide the full range of human qualities into two opposing and limited spheres: the female world of emotion and cooperation and the male world of rationality and competition. As an alternative, feminists pursue a "reintegration of humanity" by which each person develops all human traits (French, 1985).

3. **Eliminating gender stratification.** Feminism opposes laws and cultural norms that limit the education, income, and job opportunities of women.

4. **Ending sexual violence.** Today's women's movement seeks to eliminate sexual violence. Feminists argue that patriarchy distorts the relationships between women and men, and encourages violence against women in the form of rape, domestic abuse, sexual harassment, and pornography (Millet, 1970; J. Bernard, 1982, orig. 1973; Dworkin, 1987).

5. **Promoting sexual autonomy.** Finally, feminism advocates women's control of their sexuality and reproduction. Feminists support the free availability of birth control information. As Figure 13–2 shows, contraceptives are much less available in most of the world than they are in Western nations. In Canada, although information about birth control circulated from the early 1930s on, birth control became legal only in 1969 (Bishop,

As a general rule, patriarchy is strongest in nations with traditional cultures and less economic development. Here we see a husband dragging his wife through the streets of Dhaka, Bangladesh, reportedly because she did not do the cooking on time. But, while violence against women in Canada may not be so public, it remains a serious problem linked to women's subordination here as well.

1988). In addition, most feminists support a woman's right to choose whether to bear children or to terminate a pregnancy, rather than allowing men—as husbands, physicians, and legislators—to regulate sexuality. Many feminists also support gay people's efforts to overcome prejudice and discrimination in a predominantly heterosexual culture (Deckard, 1979; Barry, 1983; Jagger, 1983).

VARIATIONS WITHIN FEMINISM

People pursue the goal of sexual equality in different ways, yielding three general types of feminism: liberal, socialist, and radical (Barry, 1983; Jagger, 1983; Stacey, 1983; Vogel, 1983).

Liberal Feminism

Liberal feminism is grounded in classic liberal thinking that individuals should be free to develop their own talents and pursue their own interests. Liberal feminists accept the basic organization of our society but seek to expand the rights and opportunities of women. Liberal feminists support equal rights and oppose prejudice and discrimination that block the aspirations of women.

Liberal feminists also endorse reproductive freedom for all women. They respect the family as a social institution, but seek changes such as widely available maternity leave and child care for women who wish to work. Moreover, while liberal feminists support the family as a social institution, they contend that families need to change to accommodate the ambitions of both women and men.

With their strong belief in the rights of individuals, liberal feminists do not think that all women need to move collectively towards any one political goal. Both women and men, through their individual achieve-

ment, are capable of improving their lives if society simply ends legal and cultural barriers rooted in gender.

Socialist Feminism

Socialist feminism evolved from Marxist conflict theory, partly as a response to Marx's inattention to gender (Philipson and Hansen, 1992). From this point of view, capitalism intensifies patriarchy by concentrating wealth and power in the hands of a few men.

Socialist feminists view the reforms sought by liberal feminism as inadequate. The bourgeois family fostered by capitalism must change, they argue, to replace "domestic slavery" with some collective means of carrying out housework and child care. This goal can be realized only through a socialist revolution that creates a state-centred economy to meet the needs of all. Such a basic transformation of society requires women and men to pursue their personal liberation together, rather than individually, as liberal feminists maintain.

Radical Feminism

Radical feminism, too, finds the reforms called for by liberal feminism inadequate. Moreover, radical feminists claim that even a socialist revolution would not end patriarchy. Instead, this variant of feminism holds that gender equality can be realized only by eliminating the cultural notion of gender itself.

The foundation of gender, say radical feminists, is the biological fact that only women bear children. Radical feminists, therefore, look towards new reproductive technology (see Chapter 18, "Family") to separate women's bodies from the process of childbearing. With the demise of motherhood, radical feminists reason, the entire family system could be left

Men's Rights! Are Men Really So Privileged?

Anti-male discrimination has become far greater in scope, in degree, and in damage than any which may exist against women.

Richard F. Doyle

It is men, this chapter argues, who dominate society. Men enjoy higher earnings, control wealth, exercise power, do less housework, and get more respect than women do. The controversial assertion above, however, sums up an important counterpoint advanced by the "men's rights movement"—that the male world is not nearly as privileged as most people think.

If men are so privileged in our society, why do they turn to crime more often than women do? Moreover, the operation of the criminal justice system emphasizes the lack of special privileges accorded to men. When police make an arrest for a crime, approximately 85 percent of the time the handcuffs are slapped on a man (*Women in Canada*, 1995:101). Women make up 3 percent of those imprisoned in federal penitentiaries and 9 percent of those admitted to provincial facilities (*Women in Canada*, 1995:102).

Culture, too, is not always generous to men. Our way of life praises as "real men" those males who work and live hard, and who typically drink, smoke, and speed on the highways. Given this view of maleness, is it any wonder that men are twice as likely as women to suffer serious assault, three times more likely to fall victim to homicide, and four times more likely to commit suicide? Even more curious, in light of these statistics, is our national preoccupation with violence against *women*! Perhaps, critics suggest, we are in the grip of a cultural double standard: we expect males to commit self-destructive acts, while lamenting the far fewer cases in which brutality harms women. It is this same double standard, the argument continues, that moves women and children out of harm's way while expecting men to "go down with the ship" or to die defending their country on the battlefield.

There is a great deal of concern about homelessness—especially when the homeless are women and children. Although society produces the marginal men that are homeless, we are unable to recognize their oppression and respond appropriately to their needs. In a similar vein, we have all kinds of mechanisms for dealing with women who are abused by their partners, but fail to recognize that spousal or intimate abuse can go both ways. Men who experience intimate abuse have nowhere to turn for understanding.

Child custody is another sore point from the perspective of many men. Despite decades of consciousness-raising in pursuit of gender fairness, and clear evidence that men earn more income than women, courts across Canada routinely settle custody disputes by awarding primary care of children to mothers. And, to make matters worse, men separated from their children by the courts are then stigmatized as "runaway fathers" or "dead-beat dads."

Many men feel disadvantaged by affirmative action policies. Policies based on these laws give women, all objective criteria being equal, an edge in the workforce (where historic gaps between the sexes are slowly closing).

Even nature seems to have plotted against men by giving women, on average, a 10 percent bonus in longevity. But the controversial question is, when society plays favourites, who is favoured?

Continue the debate . . .

1. Do you think that, overall, our culture benefits men or women? Why?

2. On the campus, do men's organizations (such as fraternities and athletic teams) enjoy special privileges? What about women's organizations?

3. On balance, do you agree or disagree with the "men's rights" perspective? Which specific points do you find convincing or objectionable? Why?

Sources: Based on Doyle (1980), Scanlon (1992), Marin (1995), and Lupri (2002).

---

behind, liberating women, men, and children from the tyranny of family, gender, and sex itself (Dworkin, 1987). Thus, radical feminism envisions a revolution much more far-reaching than that sought by Marx. It seeks an egalitarian and gender-free society.

Nelson and Robinson (1999:101–111) identify several other variants of feminism, which differ from the liberal, socialist, and radical approaches outlined above. Marxist feminism argues that one's position with respect to economic production determines all other aspects of social life: thus, the entire structure of society must be changed to achieve gender equality. Cultural feminism identifies "the suppression of distinctive or different female qualities, experiences, and values as the primary cause of women's subordination." Inclusive feminists reject a privileged white middle-class feminism that ignores the "experiences of differently raced, abled and classed women." And, lastly, postmodern feminism "rejects all statements of claim made by other branches of feminist thought," arguing that any theory "claiming to be fully explanatory is necessarily assuming a dominant and oppressive stance." Clearly, all of the feminist approaches overlap to some extent so that specific authors may move among these approaches or blend them in one way or another.

Opposition to Feminism

Feminism provokes criticism and resistance from both men and women who hold conventional ideas about gender. Some men oppose feminism for the same reasons that many white people have historically opposed social equality for people of colour: they want to preserve their own privileges. Other men and women, including those who are neither rich nor powerful, distrust a social movement (especially its more radical expressions) that attacks the traditional family, rejecting what they see as time-honoured patterns that have guided male–female relationships for centuries.

Further, for some men, feminism threatens the basis of their status and self-respect: their masculinity. Men who have been socialized to value strength and dominance feel uneasy about the feminist notion that they can also be gentle and warm (Doyle, 1983). Similarly, women whose lives centre on their husbands and children may see feminism as trying to deprive them of cherished roles that give meaning to their lives (Marshall, 1985).

Resistance to feminism also comes from within academic circles. Some sociologists charge that feminism wilfully ignores a growing body of evidence that men and women do think and act in somewhat different ways (which may make gender equality impossible). Furthermore, say critics, with its drive to enhance women's presence in the workplace, feminism denigrates the crucial and unique contribution women make to the development of children—especially in the first years of life (Baydar and Brooks-Gunn, 1991; Popenoe, 1993).

Finally, there is the question of how women should go about improving their social standing. Although a large majority of people in Canada believe women should have equal rights, most also believe that women should advance individually, according to their abilities.

Thus, opposition to feminism is primarily directed at its socialist and radical variants; otherwise, there is widespread support for the principles of liberal feminism. Moreover, we are seeing an unmistakable trend towards greater gender equality. In 1942, during World War II, a Gallup poll asked Canadians, "If women take the place of men in industry, should they be paid the same wages as men?" Eighty-nine percent of women and 78 percent of men agreed. By 1995 the idea of equal pay for equal work was supported by 98 percent of a representative sample of Canadians (Bibby, 1995:4).

LOOKING AHEAD: GENDER IN THE TWENTY-FIRST CENTURY

Predictions about the future are, at best, informed speculation. Just as economists disagree about the inflation rate a year from now and political scientists can only guess at the outcome of upcoming elections, sociologists can offer only general observations about the likely future of gender and society.

Certainly, change has been remarkable. A century ago, women in Canada clearly occupied a subordinate position. Husbands controlled property in marriage, and laws barred women from most jobs, from holding political office, and even from voting. Although women today remain socially disadvantaged, the movement towards equality has surged ahead. Note, further, that two-thirds of people entering the workforce during the 1990s have been women. Truly, today's economy *depends* on the earnings of women (Hewlett, 1990).

Many factors have contributed to this transformation. Perhaps most importantly, industrialization has both broadened the range of human activity and shifted the nature of work from physically demanding tasks that favoured male strength to jobs that require human thought and imagination, placing the talents of women and men on an even footing. Additionally, medical technology has afforded us control over reproduction, so women's lives are less constrained by unwanted pregnancies.

Many women and men have also made deliberate efforts in pursuit of social equality. Sexual harassment complaints, for example, now are taken much more seriously in the workplace. And as more women assume positions of power in the corporate and political worlds, social changes in the twenty-first century may turn out to be even greater than those we have already witnessed.

Yet strong opposition to feminism persists. Gender still forms an important foundation of personal identity and family life, and it is deeply woven into the moral fabric of our society. Therefore, efforts at changing cultural ideas about the two sexes will continue to provoke opposition, as the final box illustrates. On balance, however, while change is likely to proceed incrementally, the movement towards a society in which women and men enjoy equal rights and opportunities seems certain to gain strength.

SUMMARY

1. Gender refers to the meaning a culture attaches to being female or male. Because society gives men more power and other resources than women have, gender is an important dimension of social stratification.

2. Although some degree of patriarchy exists everywhere, gender varies historically and across cultures.

3. Gender involves how cultures assign human traits and power to each sex. Gender varies historically and across cultures. Some degree of patriarchy, however, exists in every society.

4. Through the socialization process, people link gender with personality (gender identity) and actions (gender roles). The major agents of socialization—the family, peer groups, schools, and the mass media—reinforce cultural definitions of what is feminine and masculine.

5. Gender stratification entails numerous social disadvantages for women. Although most women are now in the paid labour force, a majority of working women hold low-paying clerical or service jobs. Unpaid housework also remains a task performed predominantly by women.

6. On average, Canadian women earn about 70 percent as much as men do. This disparity stems from differences in jobs and family responsibilities as well as discrimination.

7. Women in Canada now earn a slight majority of all university degrees. Men still receive a majority of all master's degrees, doctorates, and professional degrees.

8. The number of women in politics has increased sharply in recent decades. Still, the vast majority of elected officials nationwide are men.

9. Minority women encounter greater social disadvantages than white women.

10. On the basis of their distinctive identity and social disadvantages, all women represent a social minority, although many do not think of themselves in such terms.

11. Violence against women is a widespread problem in Canada. Our society is also grappling with the issues of sexual harassment and pornography.

12. Structural-functional analysis holds that pre-industrial societies benefit from distinctive roles for males and females reflecting biological differences between the sexes. In industrial societies, marked gender inequality becomes dysfunctional and slowly decreases. Talcott Parsons claimed that complementary gender roles promote the social integration of families and society as a whole.

13. Social-conflict analysis views gender as a dimension of social inequality and conflict. Friedrich Engels tied gender stratification to the development of private property. He claimed that capitalism devalues women and housework.

14. Feminism endorses the social equality of the sexes and actively opposes patriarchy and sexism. Feminism also strives to eliminate violence against women and to give women control over their sexuality (and reproduction).

15. There are three variants of feminist thinking. Liberal feminism seeks equal opportunity for both sexes within current social arrangements; socialist feminism advocates abolishing private property as the means to social equality; radical feminism aims to create a gender-free society.

16. Because gender distinctions stand at the core of our way of life, feminism has encountered strong resistance.

CRITICAL-THINKING QUESTIONS

1. What techniques do the mass media use to "sell" conventional ideas about gender to women and men?

2. Why is gender a dimension of social stratification? How does gender interact with inequality based on race, ethnicity, and class?

3. What do feminists mean by asserting that "the personal is political"? Explain how liberal, socialist, and radical feminism differ from one another in their understanding of this phrase.

APPLICATIONS AND EXERCISES

1. Researchers have found that, when describing the performance of women athletes compared to men athletes, sportscasters are much more likely to use phrases suggesting physical weakness or emotional fragility. Watch a televised tennis match involving men and women and see if you can detect any such pattern.

2. Take a walk through a business area of your local community. Which businesses are frequented almost entirely by women? By men? By both men and women?

3. Several of the research studies noted in this chapter would be easy to replicate on a small scale. Try

spending several hours observing children at play. Do you find that boys and girls play different kinds of games, as Janet Lever's research suggests (see page 314)? Or examine a sample of newspaper or magazine advertisements. Does gender figure in them the way Erving Goffman claims (see page 315)?

 ## SITES TO SEE

www.macionis.com
or
www.TheSociologyPage.com

You can find more than fifty weblinks to sociological journals and other sources of data and information by visiting the Links Library at this website.

www.swc-cfc.gc.ca/

Status of Women Canada is the federal government agency that promotes gender equality and the full participation of women in the economic, social, cultural, and political life of the country. SWC focuses on improving women's economic autonomy and well-being, eliminating systemic violence against women and children, and advancing women's human rights.

www.nac-cca.ca/

The largest feminist organization in Canada, the National Action Committee on the Status of Women en-

gages in grassroots advocacy, lobbying, education, and research and policy development. There is a dedicated page for young women at: **www.nac-cca.ca/young/young_e.htm**

www.feminist.org/

The *Feminist Majority Foundation Online* is a U.S. site that provides a gateway to Internet resources about violence against women, including information networks, research, fact sheets, self-defence, support organizations, and information on global feminism.

www.clga.ca/

Containing more than 300 pages of information, this resource site published by the *Canadian Lesbian and Gay Archives* includes a description of its holdings, many online documents (guides, chronologies, lives, essays, reviews, and monographs), and links to other sites.

 ## STUDY TOOLS

For more study tools to help you with your next exam, be sure to check out the Companion Website at **www.pearsoned.ca/macionis**, as well as Chapter 13 in your Study Guide.

 ## INVESTIGATE WITH CONTENTSELECT

Follow the instructions found on page 25 of this textbook to access ContentSelect™ at the Research Navigator™ website. Once at the site, enter your LOGINID and Password. Then, enter keywords such as "gender," "feminism," and "sexual harassment," and the search engine will supply relevant and recent scholarly and popular press publications.

CHAPTER
14

Claire Carew (Canadian)
Unforgettable, 1993

Oil on canvas, 120 × 90 cm. In honour of the life of Mr. Harry Van Helm Braam.
Courtesy of Claire Carew.

RACE AND ETHNICITY

"When you're brought up with discrimination," says Barbara Carter of Dresden, Ontario, "you know what you can do and what you can't do. So you just abide by the rules and it's not that bad. We knew we couldn't go into the restaurants with our white girlfriends after school, so we just didn't go. I never understood, however, why there were two churches. There were two Baptist churches in town. One for the whites and one for the Blacks."

"It was different for me," says Bruce. "I was a very bitter person when I was a teenager. At one time there was not one restaurant in town where I could get a cup of coffee. Toward the end of the war we had German prisoners of war around here. They were working in the sugar-beet fields under guard. The prisoners of war could go into the restaurants, but a negro soldier in a Canadian army uniform couldn't. It was pretty bad. My aunt taught in a segregated school. The last one closed in the sixties."

"We went to Disney World a while ago," says Bruce. "We went to the Canadian pavilion. They have a movie about Canada there. It's a tremendous movie—all in the round. But do you know what? There is not one Black person in the whole movie. I was watching it and I thought, 'Wait a minute, where am I?' So I sat through it a second time to make sure. It's like we're a non-people. We weren't even in the crowd scenes."

Source: Excerpted from *Welcome Home: Travels in Smalltown Canada* by Stuart McLean (1992:75).

Globally, the pattern of inequality and conflict based on colour and culture is even more pronounced. Ukrainians, Moldavians, Azerbaijanis, and other ethnic peoples in Eastern Europe are struggling to recover their cultural identities after the collapse of the Soviet Union. In the Middle East, deep-rooted friction between Arabs and Jews continues in much the same way that Blacks and whites strive to establish a just society in South Africa. In Rwanda, India, Sri Lanka, and elsewhere, racial and ethnic rifts frequently flare up into violent confrontation.

Surely one of the greatest ironies of the human condition is that colour and culture—traits that are the roots of our greatest pride—are also those that most often foment hatred and violence and propel us into war. This chapter examines the meaning of race and ethnicity, explains how these social constructs have shaped our history, and suggests why they continue to play such a central part—for better or worse—in the world today.

THE SOCIAL SIGNIFICANCE OF RACE AND ETHNICITY

People in Canada and elsewhere in the world frequently use the terms "race" and "ethnicity" imprecisely and interchangeably. For this reason, we begin with important definitions.

RACE

A **race** is *a category composed of people who share biologically transmitted traits that members of a society deem socially significant.* People may classify each other into races based on physical characteristics such as skin colour, facial features, hair texture, and body shape.

Racial diversity appeared among our human ancestors as a result of living in different geographic regions of the world. In regions of intense heat, for example, people developed darker skin (from the natural pigment melanin) that offers protection from the sun; in

July 2000 saw approximately 4000 people of Finnish heritage and their partners descend upon Toronto's Mel Lastman Square. They came from across Canada and the United States as well as from Finland for a celebration of Finnish culture and traditions in the Finn Grand Fest 2000. Here, a young woman of Finn ancestry tries on Lapp hats with her boyfriend.

regions with moderate climates, humans have lighter skin. But such differences are just skin deep because *every* human being the world over is a member of a single biological species.

The striking variety of racial traits found today is the product of migration and intermarriage over the course of human history, so that many genetic characteristics once common to a single place are now evident throughout the world. Especially pronounced is the racial mix found in the Middle East (that is, western Asia), a region that has long served as a crossroads of human migration. Notable racial uniformity, in contrast, characterizes more isolated peoples such as the island-dwelling Japanese. But no society lacks genetic mixture, and increasing contact among the world's peoples will ensure that racial blending will accelerate in the future.

RACIAL TYPOLOGY

Nineteenth-century biologists responded to the world's racial diversity by developing a three-part scheme of racial classifications. They labelled people with relatively light skin and fine hair as *Caucasian*; those with darker skin and coarser, curlier hair *Negroid*; and people with yellow or brown skin and distinctive folds on the eyelids *Mongoloid*.

Sociologists consider such categories misleading, at best, since we now know that no society is composed of biologically pure individuals. In fact, the world traveller notices gradual and subtle racial varia-

tions from region to region. The people conventionally called "Caucasians" or "whites" actually display skin colour that ranges from very light to very dark, and the same variation occurs among "Negroids" and "Mongoloids." Some "whites" (such as the Caucasians of southern India) actually have darker skin and hair than some "Blacks" (including the blond Negroid Aborigines of Australia).

Although we might think that we can readily distinguish between "Black" and "white" people, research confirms that Canadians, like people throughout the world, are genetically mixed. Over many generations, the genetic traits of Negroid Africans, Caucasian Europeans, and Mongoloid Native Americans (whose ancestors came from Asia) have spread widely throughout the Americas. Many "Black" people, therefore, have a large proportion of Caucasian genes, and many "white" people have at least some Negroid genes. Similarly, a significant proportion of the French Canadian population has some—largely unacknowledged—Native ancestry. Some of these people identify themselves as Métis, while others are totally unaware of their biological roots. In short, there is a great deal of racial blending—in North America and elsewhere.

Despite the reality of biological mixing, however, people around the world place each other in racial classifications and rank these categories in systems of social inequality. People sometimes defend racial hierarchy, claiming that one category is inherently "better" or more intelligent than another, although no sound scientific research supports such assertions (see the "Diversity: Race, Class, and Gender" box on page 340). But because so much is at stake, it is no wonder that societies focus on racial labelling more than facts permit. Through much of the twentieth century, for example, many of the southern U.S. states legally defined as "coloured" anyone who had at least one-thirty-second African ancestry (that is, one African-American great-great-great-grandparent or any closer ancestor). Today, with race less of a caste distinction in the United States, the law enables parents to declare the race of a child.

Although Canada has a long-standing interest in its ethnic composition, it was only in the 1996 census that an attempt was made to determine racial identification. In the past, our attempts to determine the size of our visible-minority population were based on declared country of origin (or ancestry) and self-definition. If someone claimed to be of Jamaican origin, for example, it was assumed (often incorrectly) that he or she was Black. Similarly, and equally incorrectly at times, someone who declared British or U.S. origins was assumed to be Caucasian. Even status or treaty Indians, whose precise numbers are known because of registration, are of mixed racial ancestry. Thus, any attempt to describe Canada in terms of racial composition is an approximation only.

One admittedly rough measure of biological mixing is the proportion of people who claim to be of mixed racial origins. By 2001, over half (59 percent) of those claiming Aboriginal origin indicated that they had mixed or multiple origins (Ojibwa and Cree would qualify as multiple origin). This was true of 28 percent who claimed Black origin and an astounding 77 percent of those claiming French origin (Statistics Canada, Census 2001, Highlight Tables, **www.statcan.ca**).

ETHNICITY

Ethnicity is *a shared cultural heritage*. Members of an ethnic category have common ancestors, language, or religion that, together, confer a distinctive social identity. For certain purposes, as in dealing with ethnic categories that are undergoing change, it is important to distinguish between *objective* and *subjective* criteria (Isajiw, 1985). Objective criteria are traits such as ancestry, cultural practices, dress, religion, and language. Subjective criteria involve the internalization of a distinctive social identity, whereby people identify themselves or are perceived by others as belonging to a different group. Subjective ethnic identities may persist beyond cultural assimilation, sometimes over many generations, without perpetuation of traditional ethnic culture (the objective components). Whatever the degree of assimilation, ethnicity remains an important basis of social differentiation in Canada.

Over 5.2 million Canadians (18 percent of the population) claim languages other than French and English as their mother tongues. About half that number still speak those languages at home. There are now more Catholics than Protestants in Canada (see Chapter 19, "Religion"), as Catholic French Canadians have been joined by immigrants from traditionally Catholic areas such as Italy, Poland, and Latin America. Canada's Jewish population (roughly 350 000 people) traces its ancestral ties to various countries, as do the Eastern Orthodox and Muslim people.

Race and ethnicity, then, are quite different: one is biological, the other cultural. But the two sometimes go hand in hand. Japanese Canadians, for example, have distinctive physical traits and—for those who maintain their traditions—cultural attributes as well. But ethnic distinctiveness should not be viewed as racial. Jews may be described as a race but they are distinctive only in their religious beliefs and their history of persecution (Goldsby, 1977).

Finally, people can *change* their ethnicity by adopting a different way of life. Polish immigrants who discard their cultural background over time may cease to have a particular ethnicity. In a similar vein, people of mixed Native and non-Native heritage may have blended into the dominant francophone or anglophone populations of their respective provinces to the point where many are completely unaware of their mixed ancestry. From time to time people actually re-establish ethnic ties and identities after two or three generations, making serious efforts to return to their Polish, Jewish, or Native roots.

MINORITIES

As Chapter 13 ("Gender Stratification") described, a racial or ethnic minority is a category of people, distinguished by physical or cultural traits, that is socially disadvantaged. Distinct from the dominant "majority," in other words, minorities are set apart and subordinated. In recent years, the breadth of the term *minority* has expanded in meaning to include not only people with particular racial and ethnic traits but also people with physical disabilities and, as the previous chapter explained, women.

Minorities have two major characteristics. One trait is that they share a *distinctive identity*. Because race is highly visible (and virtually impossible for a person to change), most minority men and women are keenly aware of their physical differences. The significance of ethnicity (which people can change) is more variable. In Canada, some people have downplayed their historic ethnicity, while others have maintained their cultural traditions and lived in distinctive ethnic neighbourhoods. Some go so far as to insulate themselves from potentially assimilating influences: Hasidic Jews in Montreal have been particularly successful in nurturing a lifestyle that separates them from their neighbours. The Hutterite people of the Prairie provinces, who have the advantage of living in communal agricultural colonies, manage even more effectively to minimize contact with the "outside."

A second characteristic of minorities is *subordination*. Chapter 11 ("Social Class in Canada") explained that minorities in Canada may have lower incomes and less occupational prestige than those of British or French origin, even if, as in the case of Blacks and Asians, their levels of educational attainment are as high or higher. Thus, class, race, and ethnicity, as well as gender, are overlapping and reinforcing dimensions of social stratification.

Of course, not all members of any minority category are disadvantaged. But even the greatest success rarely allows individuals to transcend their minority standing (Benjamin, 1991). That is, race or ethnicity often serves as a *master status* (described in Chapter 6, "Social Interaction in Everyday Life") that overshadows personal accomplishments.

The term *minority* suggests that these categories of people constitute a small proportion of a society's population. But this is not always the case. For example, Blacks form a numerical majority in South Africa although they are grossly deprived of economic and political power by whites. In Canada, women represent slightly more than half the population but are still struggling to gain opportunities and privileges long enjoyed by men.

PREJUDICE

Prejudice is *a rigid and irrational generalization about an entire category of people*. Prejudice is irrational to the extent that people hold inflexible attitudes that are supported by little or no direct evidence. Further, prejudice leads people to characterize an entire category, the vast majority of whom they have never even met. Prejudice may target a particular social class, sex, sexual orientation, age, political affiliation, race, or ethnicity.

Prejudices are *prejudgments* that may be positive or negative. Our positive prejudices tend to exaggerate the virtues of people like ourselves, while our negative prejudices condemn those who differ from us. Negative prejudice runs along a continuum, ranging from mild aversion to outright hostility. Because attitudes are rooted in our culture, everyone has at least some measure of prejudice.

Although some think of racism in Canada as a thing of the past, Fleras (2001:81–2) argues that it is an everyday reality for many Canadians—"a moving target that is difficult to pin down or control." Racism defies definition and is simultaneously elusive and pervasive: it defies definition because whites and minorities do not perceive it in the same way. Whites may think of racism as an "irrational aberration" in an otherwise benevolent society. Minorities, argues Fleras, with a postmodern slant, experience a system in which "patterns of power and privilege are reproduced" so that they perpetuate "a racialized status quo."

STEREOTYPES

Prejudice often involves **stereotypes** (*stereo* is derived from Greek, meaning "hard" or "solid"), *prejudicial views or descriptions of some categories of people*. Because many stereotypes involve emotions such as love and loyalty (generally towards members of ingroups) or hate and fear (towards outgroups), they are hard to change even in the face of contradictory evidence. For example, some people have a stereotypical understanding of the poor as lazy and irresponsible freeloaders who would rather rely on welfare than support themselves (Waxman, 1983). As was explained in Chapter 11 ("Social Class in Canada"), however, this stereotype distorts reality, since more than half of the poor people in Canada are children, working adults (including single mothers), or elderly people.

Stereotypes have been devised for virtually every racial and ethnic minority, and such attitudes can become deeply rooted in a society's culture. In Canada, many white people stereotype Native people and other visible minorities as lacking motivation to improve their own lives. Such attitudes assume that social disadvantage stems from personal deficiency. This stereotypical view ignores some key facts: most poor people in Canada are white, and most members of vis-

ible minorities work as hard as anyone else and are not poor. In this case the bit of truth in the stereotype is that, proportionately, Natives and members of some other visible minorities are more likely than whites to be poor. But by building a rigid attitude out of a few selected facts, stereotypes grossly distort reality.

RACISM

A powerful and destructive form of prejudice, **racism** refers to *the belief that one racial category is innately superior or inferior to another*. Racism has pervaded world history. The ancient Greeks, the peoples of India, and the Chinese were only the first to view people unlike themselves as inferior.

Racism has also been widespread in Canada: at one point, the enslavement of people of African descent or of Native people (called *Panis* in New France) was supported by notions of their innate inferiority—as was the placement of First Nations peoples on reserves under paternalistic administration by an Ottawa-based Indian Affairs department.

Although Canadians are by no means devoid of prejudice, there is evidence that we are more tolerant of racial and ethnic minorities than are our American neighbours (Lipset, 1991:112). The fact that Toronto, in a very short period of time, went from being a largely Anglo-Saxon Protestant city to one with a large immigrant and visible-minority component without major violence or disruption suggests a fair degree of social tolerance (Artibise, 1988:244). Bibby (1995:52–54) reports that between 1980 and 1995, Canadian sensitivity to the fact that minorities are subject to discrimination had increased by about 10 percent. In the meantime, between 1975 and 1995, acceptance of interracial and interfaith marriage had increased by a similar amount: more than 80 percent approve of interracial marriage and 90 percent approve of interfaith marriage—remarkable levels in both cases.

Overt racism in this country has subsided to some extent because of a more egalitarian culture and is "checked by the state in order to preserve social harmony and order" (Li, 1988:49). Racism persists, though in less open and direct forms, and research continues to document the injury and humiliation that racism causes to people of colour (Ramcharan, 1982; Wotherspoon and Satzewich, 1993). As the "Diversity: Race, Class, and Gender" box on page 340 explains, however, racial differences in mental abilities are due to environment rather than to biology.

Historically, the assertion that certain categories of people are *innately* inferior has provided a powerful justification for subjugation. By the end of the nineteenth century, European nations and the United States had forged vast colonial empires. (Canada never acquired external colonies, being one itself, but it has established a system of *internal* colonialism with respect to Aboriginals living on reserves.) Colonial exploitation often took the form of subjugating foreign peoples with the callous claim that they were somehow less human than the explorers who enslaved them.

Stanley Barrett (1987:5–6), an anthropologist who did field research among various white supremacist groups in Canada, notes that

> Racism constitutes an elaborate and systematic ideology; it acts as a conceptual tool to rationalize the division of the world's population into the privileged and the deprived. It is inherently a political phenomenon. It emerged with the advent of the colonization of the Third World by European nations, and thus coincided too with the development of capitalism.

In the twentieth century, racism was central to the Nazi regime in Germany. Nazi racial doctrine proclaimed a so-called Aryan race of blond-haired, blue-eyed Caucasians that was allegedly superior to all others and destined to rule the world. This racist ideology was used to justify the murder of anyone deemed inferior, including some 6 million European Jews and millions of Poles, gypsies, homosexuals, and people with physical and mental disabilities.

More recently, racial conflict has intensified in Britain and Western European societies as whites confront millions of immigrants from former colonies and refugees from strife-torn Eastern Europe. Similarly, in Canada, one can observe signs of increasing racial tensions that are aggravated by tough economic times. Racism—in thought and deed—remains a serious social problem here and elsewhere.

THEORIES OF PREJUDICE

If prejudice does not represent a rational assessment of facts, what are its origins? Social scientists have offered various answers to this vexing question, citing the importance of frustration, personality, culture, and social conflict.

Scapegoat Theory

Scapegoat theory holds that prejudice springs from frustration. Such attitudes, therefore, are common among people who are themselves disadvantaged (Dollard, 1939). A white woman earning low wages in a fish processing plant, for example, might understandably be unhappy about her situation. Directing hostility at the powerful people who operate the factory carries obvious risk; therefore, she may well attribute her low pay to the presence of minority co-workers. Her prejudice may not go far towards improving her situation, but it serves as a relatively safe way to vent anger, and it may give her the comforting feeling that at least she is superior to someone.

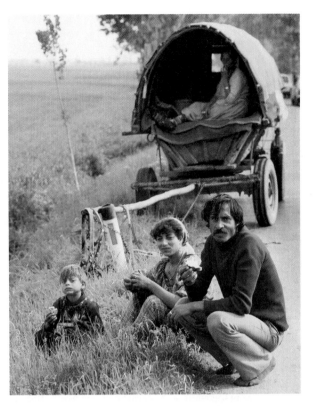

Racial and ethnic stereotypes are deeply embedded in our culture and language. Many people speak of someone "gypping" another without realizing that this word insults European Gypsies, a category of people long pushed to the margins of European societies. What about terms such as "Dutch treat," "French kiss," or "Indian giver"?

A **scapegoat**, then, is *a person or category of people, typically with little power, whom people unfairly blame for their own troubles.* Because they often are "safe targets," minorities are frequently used as scapegoats. The Nazis painted the Jews as responsible for all of Germany's ills in the 1930s. As a less extreme example, while our economy struggles to respond to corporate restructuring, globalization, and national debt, one hears rumblings among Canadians about lax immigration laws and the immigrants and refugees who allegedly contribute to the shortage of jobs and the high costs of social welfare.

Authoritarian Personality Theory

According to T.W. Adorno (1950), extreme prejudice is a personality trait in certain individuals. Research confirms that people who display strong prejudice against one minority are usually intolerant of all minorities. Such people exhibit authoritarian personalities, rigidly conforming to conventional cultural values, envisioning moral issues as clear-cut matters of right and wrong, and advocating strongly ethnocentric views. People with *authoritarian personalities* also look

Does Race Affect Intelligence?

Are Asians more intelligent than Europeans? Is the typical European smarter than the average African? Assertions painting one category of people as more intellectually gifted than another have been common throughout history. Moreover, people have used such thinking to justify the privileges of an allegedly superior category or even to bar supposedly inferior people from entering the country.

The distribution of human intelligence forms a classic "bell curve." By convention, average intelligence is defined as an IQ score of 100 (technically, an IQ score is mental age as measured by a test, divided by age in years, with the result multiplied by one hundred; thus, an eight-year-old who performs like a ten-year-old has an IQ of 10/8 = $1.2 \times 100 = 120$).

Philippe Rushton, a psychology professor at the University of Western Ontario, became the centre of academic controversy in 1989 when he claimed that in terms of intelligence, conformity to the law, and sexual restraint Asians are superior to whites, who, in turn, are superior to Blacks. Other researchers and journalists were quick to point out the methodological flaws in his research, criticizing his basic assumptions, data collection, and causal inferences. So politically incorrect were his assertions in the current Canadian climate that many people across the country demanded that his tenure at Western be revoked.

In a controversial study of intelligence and social inequality, Richard Herrnstein and Charles Murray (1994) argue that research evidence supports the conclusion that race is related to intelligence. Specifically, they place the IQ of people with European ancestry at 100. People of East Asian ancestry exceed that standard slightly, averaging 103; people of African descent fall below that standard, with an average IQ of 90.

Of course, assertions of this kind fly in the face of our democratic and egalitarian beliefs, by implying that people of one racial type are inherently "better" than another. In response, some people charge that intelligence tests are invalid, while others question whether what we call "intelligence" has much real meaning.

Most social scientists acknowledge that IQ tests do measure something important that we think of as "intelligence," and they agree that some *individuals* have more intellectual aptitude than others. But they reject the notion that any *category* of people, on average, is "smarter" than any other. That is, categories of people may show small differences on intelligence tests, but the crucial question is *why*.

Thomas Sowell, an African-American social scientist, has demonstrated that most of the documented racial differences in intelligence are not due to biology but to people's environment. In some skilful sociological detective work, Sowell tracked down IQ scores for various racial and ethnic categories from early in the twentieth century. He found that, on average, immigrants from European nations such as Poland, Lithuania, Italy, and Greece, as well as Asian countries including China and Japan, scored ten to fifteen points below the U.S. average. Sowell's critical discovery came next: people in these same categories *today* have IQ scores that are average or above average.

Among Italian Americans, for example, average IQ jumped almost ten points in fifty years; among Polish and Chinese Americans, the rise was almost twenty points.

Because genetic changes occur over thousands of years and these people largely married among themselves, biological factors simply cannot explain such a rise in IQ scores. Rather, the evidence points to changing cultural patterns. As immigrants settled in the United States, their new surroundings affected them in ways that improved their intellectual performance as measured in intelligence tests.

Sowell found that the same pattern applies to African-Americans. African-Americans living in the northern United States have historically outscored people living in the southern states on IQ tests by about ten points. And among African-Americans who migrated from the south to the north after 1940, IQ scores soon rose as they did among earlier immigrants. Thus, if environmental factors are the same for everyone, racial IQ differences largely disappear.

What IQ test score disparities do tell, according to Sowell, is that *cultural patterns* matter. Asians who score high on tests are no smarter than other people, but they have been raised to value learning and to pursue excellence. For their part, African-Americans are no less intelligent than anyone else, but they carry a legacy of disadvantage that undermines self-confidence and discourages achievement.

Sources: Knowles (1997), Herrnstein and Murray (1994), and Sowell (1994, 1995).

on society as naturally competitive and hierarchical, with "better" people (such as themselves) inevitably dominating those who are weaker.

Adorno also found that people tolerant towards one minority are likely to be accepting of all. They tend to be more flexible in their moral judgments and believe that, ideally, society should be relatively egalitarian. They feel uncomfortable when some people exercise excessive and damaging power over others.

Adorno claimed that people with little education who are raised by cold and demanding parents tend to develop authoritarian personalities. Filled with anger and anxiety as children, they grow into hostile and aggressive adults, seeking scapegoats whom they consider inferior.

Cultural Theory

A third theory contends that, while extreme prejudice may be characteristic of certain people, some prejudice is found in everyone because it is embedded in culture. Belief in the social superiority of some categories of people—the "charter" groups (British and French), the hard-working, reliable people of northern and western European roots—still colours Canadian culture to some extent despite Canada's multicultural policies and programs. Education initiatives aim to broaden the traditionally Eurocentric attitudes by promoting appreciation of the culture and contributions of those of non-European backgrounds.

Emory Bogardus (1968) studied the effects of culturally rooted prejudices on interpersonal relationships for more than forty years. He devised the concept of *social distance* to assess how close or distant people feel in relation to members of various racial and ethnic categories. His research in the United States, which documented widespread agreement, found that Americans held the most positive views towards people of white English, Canadian, and Scottish background, even welcoming marriage with them. Attitudes were less favourable towards the French, Germans, Swedes, and the Dutch, and the most negative prejudices targeted people of African and Asian descent.

When Canadians were asked to rank various racial and ethnic categories on the Bogardus scale (Mackie, 1974), the ranking was very similar—with the British and Americans (white Anglo-Saxon Protestants, or WASPs) ranking first and second. Not only is there consistency within cultures but also between Canadian and American cultures, suggesting that such rankings are indeed normative.

According to Bogardus, then, prejudice is so widespread that we cannot explain it as merely a trait of a handful of people with authoritarian personalities, as Adorno suggests. Rather, Bogardus concludes, almost everyone expresses some bigotry because we live in a "culture of prejudice."

Conflict Theory

A fourth analysis views prejudice as the product of social conflict. According to this theory, powerful people use prejudice to justify their oppression of minorities.

Lincoln MacCauley Alexander was born to immigrant parents in 1922 and grew up in Hamilton, Ontario. With a BA from McMaster University and a law degree from Osgoode Hall, Alexander practised law before entering federal politics as Canada's first Black MP. He was lieutenant-governor of Ontario from 1985 to 1991, and he has been chancellor of the University of Guelph since 1991. He is a Companion of the Order of Canada, and he has received honorary degrees from five universities and numerous outstanding-citizen awards. Hamilton's Lincoln Alexander Expressway is affectionately known as "The Linc." Throughout his career, he has sustained his interest in multicultural affairs.

Canadians certainly did this with the Chinese labourers who were allowed to come to Canada to work—under appalling conditions—on the Canadian Pacific Railway in the 1870s and 1880s. Similarly, all elites benefit when prejudice divides workers along racial and ethnic lines and discourages them from working together to advance their common interests (Geschwender, 1978; Olzak, 1989).

A different conflict-based argument, advanced by Shelby Steele (1990), is that minorities themselves cultivate a climate of race consciousness in order to win greater power and privileges. In raising *race consciousness*, Steele explains, minorities argue that they are victims and that white people are their victimizers. Because of their historic disadvantage, minorities claim that they are entitled to special considerations based on their race. While this strategy may yield short-term gains, Steele cautions that such policies are likely to spark a backlash from white people and others who condemn "special treatment" for anyone on the basis of race or ethnicity.

The Québécois have made precisely that kind of claim on the basis of past injustices and the threat of

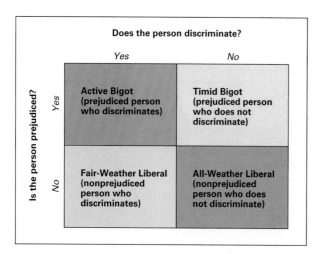

FIGURE 14–1 Patterns of Prejudice and Discrimination

Source: Merton (1976).

assimilation in an English-speaking North America. Some non-Quebecers feel that the wrongs of the past have now been redressed and that entrenching special status (that is, recognition as a "distinct society") in Canada's Constitution is going too far.

DISCRIMINATION

Closely related to prejudice is **discrimination**, *treating various categories of people unequally*. While prejudice refers to attitudes, discrimination is a matter of action. Like prejudice, discrimination can be either positive (providing special advantages) or negative (creating obstacles). Discrimination also varies in intensity, ranging from subtle to blatant.

Prejudice and discrimination often occur together. A personnel manager prejudiced against members of a particular minority may refuse to hire them. Robert Merton (1976) describes such a person as an *active bigot* (see Figure 14–1). But prejudice and discrimination do not always occur together, as in the case of the prejudiced personnel manager who, out of fear of lawsuits, does hire minorities. Merton characterizes this person as a *timid bigot*. What Merton calls *fair-weather liberals* may be generally tolerant of minorities yet discriminate when it is to their advantage to do so, such as when a superior demands it. Finally, Merton's *all-weather liberal* is free of both prejudice and discrimination.

INSTITUTIONAL PREJUDICE AND DISCRIMINATION

We typically think of prejudice and discrimination as the hateful ideas or actions of specific individuals. But back in the 1960s years ago, Stokely Carmichael and

Charles Hamilton (1967) pointed out that far greater harm results from **institutional prejudice or discrimination**, which refers to *bias in attitudes or action inherent in the operation of society's institutions*, including schools, hospitals, the police, or the workplace.

Anderson and Frideres (1981:208) describe this kind of process as follows:

> Bureaucracies have the job of establishing regulations and priorities as well as qualifications for particular positions in our society. Only those individuals able to meet these initial qualifications will be able to participate in the ongoing institutional structure. For example, when Native people suggested that they be hired by the Department of Indian Affairs (with a staff of about 14 000), the response by the Minister of Indian Affairs was that placement was only possible for those belonging to a particular union, and having a particular position and level of seniority in the union. Unless these requirements were met, an Indian could not be hired, and if hired without these qualifications, the union would strike.

There was no need for the authors to point out that Natives were not members of the appropriate union.

PREJUDICE AND DISCRIMINATION: THE VICIOUS CYCLE

Prejudice and discrimination frequently reinforce each other. In the Thomas theorem, W.I. Thomas offered a simple explanation of this fact (see Chapter 6, "Social Interaction in Everyday Life"): *situations defined as real become real in their consequences* (1966:301; orig. 1931).

As Thomas recognized, stereotypes become real to those who believe them, sometimes even to those who are victimized by them. Power also plays a role here, since some categories of people with considerable social power can enforce their prejudices to the detriment of others.

Prejudice on the part of whites towards people of colour, for example, does not produce *innate* inferiority, but it can produce *social* inferiority, consigning minorities to poverty, inferior schooling, low-prestige occupations, and poor housing in racially segregated neighbourhoods. Then, if whites interpret social disadvantage as evidence that minorities do not measure up to their standards, they unleash a new round of prejudice and discrimination, giving rise to a *vicious cycle*, shown in Figure 14–2.

MAJORITY AND MINORITY: PATTERNS OF INTERACTION

Patterns of interaction among racial and ethnic categories are described in terms of four models: pluralism, assimilation, segregation, and genocide.

PLURALISM

Pluralism is *a state in which racial and ethnic minorities are distinct but have social parity.* In a pluralist society, categories of people are different but share resources more or less equally. The relationship between Quebec and the rest of Canada provides an example of pluralism in action. Native peoples, too, would like to acquire social and political parity or equality.

Social diversity has long been a source of pride in Canada. Some argue that our multiculturalism not only acknowledges but actually celebrates our differences and encourages the perpetuation of countless "ethnic villages," communities where people proudly maintain their cultural traditions. These ethnic communities—the components of our cultural mosaic—add variety and colour to our landscape. The viability of these communities is affected by their levels of **institutional completeness**, *the complexity of community organizations that meet the needs of members.* Where communities are institutionally complete, members are able to live, shop, pray, and sometimes work within the boundaries of their groups. They might also have their own welfare and mutual aid societies, credit unions, newspapers, and radio stations. Breton (1964), who coined the term *institutional completeness*, points out that the presence of these formal organizations keeps social relations within group boundaries and minimizes outgroup contacts.

Canada embraces the ideal of multiculturalism, recognition of cultural heterogeneity, and mutual respect among culturally diverse groups. Through policies of multiculturalism, Canada supports the goal of allowing people to participate fully in all aspects of Canadian life without feeling that it is necessary to give up their ethnic identities and cultural practices. The aim of multiculturalism is to promote unity through diversity and to enhance a Canadian identity that embraces differences. We began to use the term *multiculturalism* in the 1960s, in recognition of the diverse backgrounds of Canadians, and adopted multiculturalism as government policy by 1971. The Canadian *Multiculturalism Act* of 1988 sought "to recognize all Canadians as full and equal partners in Canadian society," and in 1991 this goal was given explicit support through the creation of a new Department of Multiculturalism and Citizenship (replaced in 1995 by the Department of Canadian Heritage).

For information about Canadian government programs to encourage multiculturalism and citizenship, see the Canadian Heritage website at www.canadianheritage.gc.ca/

Multicultural programs provide education, consultative support, and funding for a wide range of activities, including heritage-language training, race relations and cross-cultural understanding programs, the ethnic press, ethnic celebrations, policing and justice, and family violence programs.

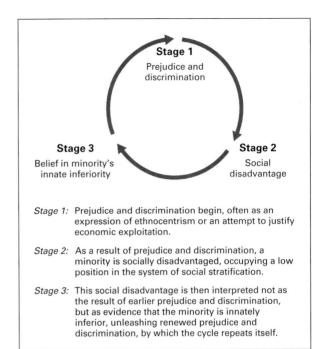

FIGURE 14–2 Prejudice and Discrimination: The Vicious Cycle

Prejudice and discrimination can form a vicious cycle, perpetuating themselves, as explained above.

Stage 1: Prejudice and discrimination begin, often as an expression of ethnocentrism or an attempt to justify economic exploitation.

Stage 2: As a result of prejudice and discrimination, a minority is socially disadvantaged, occupying a low position in the system of social stratification.

Stage 3: This social disadvantage is then interpreted not as the result of earlier prejudice and discrimination, but as evidence that the minority is innately inferior, unleashing renewed prejudice and discrimination, by which the cycle repeats itself.

Not everyone approves of the official goal of multiculturalism. Critics argue that it discourages immigrant adaptation and is divisive and detrimental to a shared and coherent Canadian identity. While Canadians prefer the cultural mosaic to the melting pot—by a slim margin—and over 80 percent approve of interracial marriage (with Natives, Asians, or Blacks), 85 percent feel that immigrants have an obligation to learn Canadian ways (Bibby, 1995). Writer Neil Bissoondath, who feels that continued ethnic identification weakens the social fabric of Canada, met with hostility and caught the attention of the media when he made a plea to be accepted as an unhyphenated Canadian. Criticism of multiculturalism by this "person of colour" led to cries of "traitor" or "sell-out" from minority members and anger from mainstream defenders of the policy. Bissoondath (1994:5) feels that these reactions have "more than a little to do with the psychology of the True Believer, who sees Canada's multicultural policy as the only one possible."

Questions about the impact of multiculturalism can be raised from other perspectives as well. Although they are not necessarily critical of multicultural policy, Reitz and Breton (1994) point out that Canada's "cultural mosaic" and the U.S. "melting pot" result in only minimal differences in assimilation, economic integration, or tolerance of ethnic distinctiveness. Therefore, they argue, the perception that Canada's minorities retain their cultural identities more than minorities in the United States is largely an illusion.

ASSIMILATION

Assimilation is *the process by which minorities gradually adopt patterns of the dominant culture.* Assimilation involves changing modes of dress, values, religion, language, and friends.

Although the United States has been seen as a "melting pot" in which different nationalities fuse into a new way of life, this characterization is misleading. Rather than "melting" into some new cultural pattern, minorities have adopted the traits (the dress, the accent, and sometimes even the names) of the dominant culture established by the earliest settlers. Why? Assimilation is both the avenue to upward social mobility and the way to escape the prejudice and discrimination directed at visible foreigners (Newman, 1973).

The amount of assimilation varies by category. For example, Germans and Irish have "melted" more than Italians, and the Japanese more than the Chinese or Koreans. Multiculturalists, however, criticize the idea of assimilation for painting minorities as "the problem" and defining them (rather than elites) as the ones who need to do all the changing.

Minorities in the United States have adapted to the use of the English language. But recently the rapid growth of the Hispanic population has created areas where Spanish is the dominant language, encouraged the study of Spanish as a second language, and—as a counterforce—inspired a social movement seeking to establish English as the official language of the United States. In fact, as they experience pressure to become officially bilingual—English and Spanish—Americans look to Canada to assess the possible effects of such a policy. Many have concluded that the threat of Quebec separation clearly illustrates its dangers.

The fact that such ethnic enclaves still exist in the United States, where assimilation and the melting pot are the ideals, suggests that race and ethnicity endure as building blocks of American society (Glazer and Moynihan, 1970; Alba, 1985). In Canada, with its claim to be a colourful mosaic in which all the pieces make distinctive contributions, assimilation occurs as well. Immigrants learn to function in English and French, people from different ethnic backgrounds intermarry, ancestral cultural practices fall into disuse, and people acquire a set of shared attitudes and values that can only be called Canadian.

As a cultural process, assimilation involves changes in ethnicity but not in race. For example, many North Americans of Japanese descent have discarded their traditional way of life but still have their racial identity. Even distinctive racial traits may diminish over generations as the result of **miscegenation**, *biological reproduction by partners of different racial categories.* Although resistance to such biological mixing remains strong,

miscegenation (often outside of marriage) has occurred throughout our history.

SEGREGATION

Segregation refers to *the physical and social separation of categories of people.* Some minorities, especially religious orders such as the Hutterites, voluntarily segregate themselves. The concentration of various ethnic and racial groups in Canada's cities results, at least in part, from voluntary action. Mostly, however, majorities segregate minorities involuntarily by excluding them. Various degrees of segregation characterize residential neighbourhoods, schools, workplaces, hospitals, and even cemeteries. While pluralism fosters distinctiveness without disadvantage, segregation enforces separation to the detriment of a minority.

South Africa's system of apartheid (described in Chapter 10, "Social Stratification") illustrates rigid and pervasive racial segregation. Apartheid was created by the European minority it served, and it was historically enforced through the use of brutal power (Fredrickson, 1981). South Africa has now ended official apartheid but, as yet, its basic racial structure has changed little. The nation remains essentially two different societies that touch only when Blacks provide services for whites.

In the United States, too, racial segregation has a long history beginning with slavery and evolving into racially separated lodging, schooling, and transportation. Decisions such as the 1954 *Brown* case have reduced overt and *de jure* (Latin, meaning "by law") discrimination. However, *de facto* ("in fact") segregation continues to this day in the form of countless neighbourhoods that are home to people of a single race. Research points to modest declines in racial segregation in the United States during recent decades (Farley, 1995).

Although Canadians might not want to think of themselves as practising segregation, we have done so historically and still do today. Early Black migrants—Loyalists in Nova Scotia and those brought via the Underground Railroad to Ontario—found themselves living in Africville (part of Halifax) or in small rural communities such as Buxton and Dawn in Ontario. As a general rule, people in these communities did not receive the same kinds of land grants as other immigrants. They often attended segregated schools and

 Multimedia presentations from the CBC's archives document how Africville was uprooted in the 1960s: see http://archives.cbc.ca//300c.asp?id=1-69-96

were denied access to local restaurants. Residential and social segregation were very real.

The clearest example of segregation in Canada is found in our treatment of Native peoples, through the system of reserves for status Indians administered by the Department of Indian and Northern Affairs. Prior to the late 1960s, most of the education of Indian children took place in separate residential schools or on the reserves themselves. The overall effect has been one of extreme physical and social segregation, especially when the reserves are located in remote areas.

GENOCIDE

Genocide is *the systematic annihilation of one category of people by another*. This brutal form of racism and ethnocentrism violates nearly every recognized moral standard; nonetheless, it has recurred time and again in human history.

Genocide figured prominently in centuries of contact between Europeans and the original inhabitants of the Americas. From the sixteenth century on, as the Spanish, Portuguese, English, French, and Dutch forcibly established vast colonial empires, they decimated the Native populations of North and South America. Some Native people fell victim to calculated killing sprees; most succumbed to diseases brought by Europeans to which they had no natural immunities (Cottrell, 1979; Butterworth and Chance, 1981; Matthiessen, 1984; Sale, 1990; Dickason, 1997). The Beothuk of Newfoundland, who experienced the earliest contact with Europeans, had completely disappeared by 1829. Feuding and open hunting season against the Beothuk, as well as tuberculosis, had taken their toll (Dickason, 1997).

 The Newfoundland and Labrador Heritage website looks at the history and culture of the Beothuk: see www.heritage.nf.ca/aboriginal/beothuk.html

Genocide also occurred in the twentieth century. Unimaginable horror befell European Jews in the 1930s and 1940s, as the Nazi regime seized control of much of Europe. During Adolf Hitler's reign of terror, known as the Holocaust, the Nazis exterminated more than 6 million Jewish men, women, and children. Soviet dictator Josef Stalin murdered his country's people on an even greater scale, killing perhaps 30 million real and imagined enemies during his violent rule. Between 1975 and 1980, Pol Pot's Communist regime in Cambodia slaughtered anyone associated in any way with capitalist culture. Men and women able to speak a Western language and even individuals who wore eyeglasses, construed as a symbol of capitalist culture, were cut down. In all, some 2 million people (one-quarter of the population) perished in Cambodian "killing fields" (Shawcross, 1979). More recently, the breakup of Yugoslavia resulted in conflict between ethnic Serbians and Albanians, based on 600 years of feuding. During the spring of 1999, an estimated 10 000 ethnic Albanians were victims of "ethnic cleansing" or mass murder by their Serbian neighbours. Bodies were burned, buried, and reburied in mass graves in attempts to conceal evidence of Serbian crimes. This is one of many troublespots to which Canadian Erin Mooney travelled for her United Nations research into the experience of internal refugees created by ethnic cleansing (Mooney, 1995).

These four patterns of minority–majority interaction co-exist in our society. We proudly point to patterns of pluralism and assimilation but only reluctantly acknowledge that our society has been built on segregation and genocide. The remainder of this chapter examines how these four patterns have shaped the history and present social standing of major racial and ethnic categories in Canada.

RACE AND ETHNICITY IN CANADA

Canada is a land of immigrants. Many thousands of years ago, the people we now call Aboriginal or Native peoples came to North America over a land bridge that once connected Alaska to Siberia across the Bering Strait. The first European explorers and settlers were met by fifty-five founding nations.

The French and then the British established permanent settlements in the 1600s and 1700s, conveniently ignoring the Aboriginal nations, and declared themselves to be the two founding nations. Successive waves of immigration brought northern and then southern and eastern European people to our shores. More recently, in part as a result of changes in immigration laws, new Canadians have come from Asia, Africa, and the Caribbean. In addition, refugees have come to Canada in unprecedented numbers over the last decade. These flows have completely transformed our sociocultural landscape.

Table 14–1 (on page 347) shows the composition of Canada by ethnic origin (2001) for the twenty-five categories that are most heavily represented in Canada, based on responses to census questions about ethnic origin. The "total responses" category includes those who have the same ancestry on both maternal and paternal sides (single origin), as well as those who report mixed heritage (multiple origin). Further columns report the figures for single-origin and multiple-origin individuals separately. As a result of changes in the structure and wording of the census question on ethnic background in 1996, we see a dramatic increase in the number of people claiming "Canadian" ancestry (see the note in Table 14–1). Almost a third of Canada's population claimed Canadian ethnicity or cultural heritage in 1996; by 2001 the figure increased to 39 percent. The significance of this shift will be the subject of considerable debate, especially since between 1991 and 1996, 3.5 million fewer people declared themselves to be single-origin French.

Not surprisingly, considering their early settlement of this country, the largest ethnic categories in Canada (after those reporting Canadian ancestry) are the English and the French. Some 4.2, 3.8, and 2.7 million people are at least partly of Scottish, Irish, and

Black Citizens of Canada: A History Ignored

Harriet Tubman, known as "Moses," had been assisted in her escape from slavery by workers on the Underground Railroad. She returned to Maryland a year later (1850) to free members of her family and then became one of the most active "conductors" on the Railroad, repeatedly risking her life to guide more than three hundred slaves to freedom—many of them to Ontario, where she provided shelter for refugees in a rented house in St. Catharines.

W hen the average Canadian thinks about slavery, the image that comes to mind is likely that of plantation slavery in the Deep South. Few of us are aware that Canada has its own history of slavery and that about 3500 freed slaves came to Nova Scotia and New Brunswick as United Empire Loyalists. They had fought on the side of the British during the American Revolution as members of the Black Pioneers (also known as the Black Loyalists). The 30 000 to 40 000 escaped American slaves who made it to Canada via the Underground Railroad between 1840 and 1865, when

slavery was abolished in the United States, are also unknown.

Slaves were on the scene in the earliest settlements of Canada (then New France). Olivier Le Jeune, who was brought directly from Africa to Canada, was later sold in the first recorded slave sale in Canada, in 1629. By 1759, there were 3604 slaves in New France—1132 Blacks, the rest Natives. In 1793, under the leadership of John Graves Simcoe, Upper Canada became the first British colony to legislate the gradual abolition of slavery.* While slavery remained legal through the rest of Canada until it was abolished throughout the British Empire in 1833, it had effectively died out by about 1810. Slavery was essentially unsuited to Canadian agriculture.

Fugitive slaves arrived in Ontario between the 1790s and 1860s. From about 1840 they used the Underground Railroad, an informal system of people and safe houses bringing escaped slaves to freedom in the northern United States and Canada. These former slaves formed scattered rural settlements from Windsor to Barrie (or across southern Ontario), where some farmed their own land while others hired themselves out as farm labourers. Some Black settlements, such as Buxton and Dawn, were thriving communities with their own schools, blacksmith shops, and other businesses.** Most of the residents of these communities and their descendants eventually abandoned their rural homes and moved to the cities. Some, however, stayed behind. Descendants of the residents of Dawn still live in Dresden, Ontario.

Freed from slavery, Blacks in Canada experienced economic hardship as well as prejudice and discrimination—sug-

gesting that, despite a certain smugness, Canadians are not much more tolerant than Americans. Nevertheless, immigration from many parts of the world, including the West Indies, has added to Canada's Black populations, now comprising 574 000 individuals living mainly in southern Ontario and Montreal.

The Black communities of Montreal are made up of immigrants, and descendants, who come from French-speaking countries such as Algeria and Haiti, but shared language has not meant that social and economic integration have been painless. Racism and discrimination are as likely to appear in Montreal as in Toronto, where many Blacks encounter the combined barriers associated with recent immigration and visible minority status. Despite continued disadvantages, Blacks have made important contributions to Canada's economic and cultural life.

*When Governor Simcoe had dinner at the home of Mohawk leader and Loyalist Joseph Brant (Thayendanegea) in 1793, he was served by Brant's "Black slaves resplendent in scarlet uniforms with white ruffles, and with silver buckles on their shoes" (Walker, 1980:21).

**Dawn was founded in 1842 by Hiram Wilson and Josiah Henson. The latter, a "conductor" on the Underground Railroad who brought about a hundred slaves to freedom, is thought to be the model for Harriet Beecher Stowe's Uncle Tom in her anti-slavery novel *Uncle Tom's Cabin*.

Sources: McClain (1979), Walker (1980), Ducharme (1985), Winks (1988), Nader et al. (1992), and Merrit (1993).

 The National Archives of Canada presents an online exhibition about the anti-slavery movement in Canada at www.archives.ca/05/0531_e.html

German origin, respectively. Those with Aboriginal, Italian, Chinese, or Ukrainian roots also number more than 1 million each. The other ethnic categories

among the top twenty-five drop off quickly in size, down to roughly 212 000 people of Jamaican origin. The results portray Canada as a country dominated by

Ethnic Origin	Total Responses	%	Single Responses	%	Multiple Responses	%
1. Canadian	11 682,680	39.4	6 748 135	36.9	4 934 550	43.5
2. English	5 978 875	20.2	1 479 520	8.1	4 499 355	39.7
3. French	4 668 410	15.8	1 060 755	5.8	3 607 655	31.8
4. Scottish	4 157 210	14.0	607 235	3.3	3 549 975	31.3
5. Irish	3 822 660	12.9	496 865	2.7	3 325 800	29.4
6. German	2 742 765	9.3	705 595	3.9	2 037 170	18.0
7. Aboriginal	1 365 065	4.6	565 040	3.1	800 020	7.1
8. Italian	1 270 370	4.3	726 275	4.0	544 090	4.8
9. Chinese	1 094 700	3.7	936 210	5.1	158 490	1.4
10. Ukrainian	1 071 060	3.6	326 200	1.8	744 860	6.6
11. Dutch (Netherlands)	923 310	3.1	316 220	1.7	607 090	5.4
12. Polish	817 085	2.8	260 415	1.4	556 670	4.9
13. East Indian	713 330	2.4	581 665	3.2	131 665	1.2
14. Norwegian	363 760	1.2	47 230	0.3	316 530	2.8
15. Portuguese	357 690	1.2	252 835	1.4	104 855	0.9
16. Welsh	350 365	1.2	28 445	0.2	321 925	2.8
17. Jewish	348 605	1.2	186 475	1.0	162 130	1.4
18. Russian	337 960	1.1	70 890	0.4	267 070	2.4
19. Filipino	327 545	1.1	266 140	1.5	61 410	0.5
20. Swedish	282 760	1.1	30 440	0.2	252 320	2.2
21. Hungarian (Magyar)	267 255	0.9	91 795	0.5	175 460	1.5
22. American (USA)	250 010	0.8	25 200	0.1	224 805	2.0
23. Greek	215 105	0.7	143 780	0.8	71 320	0.6
24. Spanish	213 100	0.7	66 545	0.4	146 555	1.3
25. Jamaican	211 725	0.7	138 180	0.8	73 545	0.6
Total Population	29 639 035	—	18 307 540	—	11 331 490	—

*The 1996 census asked people to indicate the ethnic or cultural groups to which their ancestors belong. A list of examples, including "Canadian," was provided, and respondents were asked to fill in up to four answers. The structure of this question produced a sevenfold increase in the number of people who identified themselves as single-origin "Canadian"—from 765 095 in 1991 to 5 326 995 in 1996. The number rose to 6 748 135 in 2001.

**The "total responses" column includes those individuals who claim each ethnic background as a single origin or as part of a multiple-origin response. The single-response column includes those individuals whose parents share one ethnic background, while multiple-origin individuals might have, for example, Italian, English, and Scottish ancestry. This hypothetical individual would be counted three times in the "total" or "multiple response" columns.

Source: Adapted by Gerber from Statistics Canada, 2001 Census Highlight Tables, www.statcan.ca.

the British (mainly the English) and the French, but otherwise of remarkable diversity.

Comparing the numbers of people in each ethnic category reveals the extent of integration and inter-marriage in Canada. While 1.5 million people claim English ancestry on both sides, more than three times that number (4.5 million) have some English ancestry. Among German-origin Canadians, three-quarters are of multiple origin; among the Swedish, the figure is 89 percent. The majority of Aboriginal people have multiple origins as well (59 percent). The newer immigrant groups, many of which are visible minorities (Filipino, South Asian, or Jamaican), tend to have much lower proportions claiming multiple origins. However, these proportions are likely to increase over the next few decades. (Note that the choice of "Canadian" ancestry is also an indicator of cultural integration.)

Table 14–2 shows the top ten ethnic origins in the provinces and territories, revealing that ethnic and racial composition vary substantially from one part of the country to another. The proportion claiming

"Canadian" background (either single or multiple origin) varies from 5 percent in Nunavut to 69 percent in Quebec. The frequency of this designation in the 2001 census makes it difficult to observe the traditional predominance of the British categories in the Maritimes and the European influence in the western provinces.

Another dramatic change is in the level of "French" identity in Quebec. In 1991, 75 percent of the Quebec population declared itself to be *single-origin* French. In 1996, only 41 percent declared either full or partial French ancestry—and by 2001, the level had dropped to 30 percent. (Recall that the first change, 1991 to 1996, was due to the suggestion that "Canadian" could be one of the write-in categories. The proportion of Quebecers identifying themselves as Canadian soared to 47.2 percent—the largest of any province or territory—and to 69 percent by 2001. Other former French identifiers seem to have defined themselves as Québécois.) Aboriginal people (combined) appear among the top ten ethnic categories in every province and territory. It is only in Nunavut,

TABLE 14–2 Ethnic Origins for Canada, the Provinces and Territories, 2001 (Rank Order by Percentage of Population*)

	NL	PE	NS	NB	QC	ON	MB	SK	AL	BC	YK	NW	NU
1.	Canadian (53.1)	Canadian (45.0)	Canadian (47.4)	Canadian (57.8)	Canadian (68.7)	Canadian (26.7)	Canadian (22.9)	German (28.6)	Canadian (27.7)	English (29.6)	English (27.1)	NA Indian (36.0)	Inuit (84.8)
2.	English (39.4)	Scottish (38.0)	Scottish (29.3)	French (26.9)	French (29.6)	English (24.0)	English (22.1)	Canadian (25.0)	English (25.6)	Canadian (24.3)	Canadian (26.8)	Canadian (19.6)	English (6.9)
3.	Irish (19.7)	English (28.7)	English (28.1)	English (23)	Irish (4.1)	Scottish (16.3)	German (18.2)	English (24.5)	German (19.6)	Scottish (15.0)	NA Indian (21.9)	English (16.6)	Scottish (5.5)
4.	Scottish	Irish	Irish	Irish	Italian	Irish	Scottish	Scottish	Scottish	Irish	Scottish	Scottish	Canadian
5.	French	French	French	Scottish	English	French	Ukrainian	Irish	Irish	German	Irish	Irish	Irish
6.	NA Indian	German	German	German	Scottish	German	Irish	Ukrainian	French	Chinese	German	Inuit	German
7.	Inuit	Dutch	Dutch	Acadian	NA Indian	Italian	French	French	Ukrainian	French	French	French	NA Indian
8.	German	Acadian	NA Indian	NA Indian	Québécois	Chinese	NA Indian	NA Indian	Dutch	E. Indian	Ukrainian	German	British
9.	Métis	NA Indian	Welsh	Dutch	German	Dutch	Polish	Norwegian	NA Indian	Dutch	Norwegian	Métis	Ukrainian
10.	Welsh	Welsh	Italian	Welsh	Jewish	E. Indian	Métis	Polish	Polish	Ukrainian	Dutch	Ukrainian	Ukrainian

*The first three ethnic categories for Canada and each province and territory include the percentage of population claiming each ethnic background (on the part of both parents, single origin, or just one parent, multiple origin). Categories with more than 25 percent of the population appear in bold, while those with 15 to 25 percent appear in italics. It is important to note that an individual with Scottish and Ukrainian background, for example, would be counted twice. The sum of the percentages therefore would be substantially more than 100.

Source: Adapted by Gerber from Statistics Canada, 2001 Census Highlight Tables, www.statcan.ca.

where the Inuit rank first (85 percent), and the Northwest Territories, where North American Indians rank first (36 percent) and the Inuit sixth (11 percent), that Aboriginal people constitute the largest ethnic group. The Chinese rank eight in Canada, but appear among the top ten only in Ontario and British Columbia. Despite the dramatic shift to "Canadian" identity across the country, diversity and regional variation of backgrounds are still apparent.

Canada's census (1996 and 2001) attempted to measure visible-minority status (as distinct from ethnicity or Aboriginal origins) to assess compliance with employment equity legislation. Respondents were asked to identify themselves as white, Chinese, South Asian, Black, Arab/West Asian, Filipino, Southeast Asian, Latin American, Japanese, Korean, or "Other." Black appeared as a choice among ethnic categories in the 1991 census, but now is part of a more direct question aimed at identifying visible-minority populations. (See the "Applying Sociology" box for further analysis.)

SOCIAL STANDING

A great deal has been written about ethnic and racial inequality in Canada and its causes (Porter, 1965; Ramcharan, 1982; Gerber, 1983, 1990, 1996; Driedger, 1989; McAll, 1990; Frideres, 1998; Wotherspoon and Satzewich, 1993; Li, 2003). The general consensus seems to be that the workings of our capitalist economy, along with racism, prejudice, and discrimination, contribute to socioeconomic inequality, with recent immigrants and visible minorities at the bottom of the scale. For a number of reasons, including a system of internal colonialism, Native peoples are the most

severely disadvantaged in this regard. Table 14–3 (on page 350) compares selected ethnic categories—British, French, Asian, Black, and Native—in a number of socioeconomic dimensions. The observations that we can make based on this table are surprising in some respects and consistent with expectations in others. In 1999, Canadian Asians and Blacks—many of whom were educated elsewhere before coming here as immigrants—had higher levels of post-secondary certification than the British or French. They also had higher levels of labour force participation. However, despite higher levels of educational attainment and labour force participation, Asians and Blacks have lower average incomes than the British and French. Blacks, in particular, are also more likely to be unemployed than the British.

The Native population is disadvantaged on all of the measures in Table 14–3. They have lower levels of educational attainment coupled with both low levels of labour force participation and high unemployment—almost three times the British rate. The average income for Aboriginal individuals is only half the British level.

On the basis of Table 14–3, one can conclude that the British are rewarded on income despite the fact that they have lower levels of post-secondary certification and labour force participation. The French, who are equal to the British on these measures, do not earn the same income—in part, perhaps, because the economy of Quebec had been particularly sluggish. Asians and Blacks, with their high levels of post-secondary education and labour force participation, should have the highest incomes—but do not. This may be the result of racism, prejudice, and discrimination—as many analysts will be quick to point out—but date of

Visible Minorities: Toronto, Vancouver, and Montreal

The 2001 census reveals that 4.0 million people—13.4 percent of Canada's population—identified themselves as members of visible minorities.[*] While the majority of these individuals are immigrants, increasing proportions are Canadian-born.

Three census metropolitan areas (CMAs), namely Toronto, Vancouver, and Montreal, have attracted more than three-quarters of Canada's visible minority population. While visible minorities make up 37, 37, and 14 percent of the three urban populations respectively, the mix is different in each city. Toronto—37 percent visible minority, of which 9 percent is Chinese, 10 percent is South Asian, and 7 percent is Black—is the most diverse of the CMAs. Vancouver's visible minority—37 percent of the total—is almost entirely Asian, half of it Chinese. Montreal, with the smallest visible minority component—14 percent—is 4 percent Black and 10 percent mixed Asian.

The tendency of particular minorities to settle in specific neighbourhoods, where relatives or friends have already located, results in different concentrations in various parts of each CMA. Prior to the amalgamation of a number of municipalities into a larger Toronto (i.e., at the time of the 1991 census), Scarborough had the largest visible minority component—at 52 percent—anywhere in the country. By 2001, with Scarborough no longer in existence, Burnaby (part of the Vancouver CMA) and Markham (in the Toronto CMA) took over as the areas

Toronto is the diversity capital of Canada with 37 percent of the country's visible minority population.

with the largest visible-minority composition. Burnaby, with a population that is 49 percent visible minority, is close to 40 percent Asian. Similarly, Markham—which is 56 percent visible-minority—is at least 45 percent Asian and 4 percent Black. Montreal Nord—24 percent visible minority—is 15 percent Black.

The fact that about 80 percent of our immigrants in recent years have come from Asia, the Middle East, Africa, and the Caribbean has changed our understanding of the term "immigrant" (Li, 2003:44–45). While formally the term refers to anyone who came to Canada from another country, the "folk version" tends to refer to people who appear foreign-looking—or those of different racial and cultural

backgrounds. Even if they are born in Canada, members of visible minorities are likely to be labelled immigrants and assumed to be the cause of urban problems. This social construction of "immigrants" as non-white and the source of problems is most likely to occur in the major cities across Canada that are magnets to our more recent immigrants.

[*]Note that the visible-minority statistics do not include Aboriginal peoples, whose inclusion would change the overall picture substantially. The visible minorities included in these figures are Blacks, South Asians, Filipinos, Arabs and West Asians, Latin Americans, and Pacific Islanders.

Sources: Chard and Renaud (2000), Li (2003), and Statistics Canada, 2001 Census Highlight Tables, www.statcan.ca.

---

entry into Canada also comes into the picture. Immigrants generally enter the Canadian labour market at a lower *entrance status* than they may have occupied in their countries of origin (Porter, 1965; Ujimoto, 1979; Reitz, 1980; Badets and Howatson-Leo, 2000; Li, 2003). Also, recent immigrants are unlikely to have the seniority in their jobs that is associated with higher incomes.

While Blacks and Asians appear to have gained access to higher education and to the labour market (including full-time employment), they appear to face barriers to equity in remuneration. Natives, on the other hand, seem to face a host of barriers—in achieving higher education, in securing employment, and in earning decent wages or salaries. Something is clearly amiss when the First Nations (as some status Indians

	British	French	Asian	Black	Native
Total population	5 618 661	6 145 027	1 452 265	319 300	450 233
Population aged 15+	4 732 962	4 962 228	1 131 899	236 866	294 166
% with less than secondary-school certification	41.0	41.4	32.9	35.9	63.3
% with post-secondary certification	29.7	27.8	38.7	32.6	15.3
% in labour force[*]	62.1	64.4	68.7	72.3	51.8
Unemployment rate[**]	8.5	10.0	10.4	14.5	24.6
Mean income[***]	$22 798	$20 046	$18 216	$17 390	$11 676

[*]Percentages based on populations fifteen years of age or older.
[**]Percentage of the labour force unemployed.
[***]Average income for all people with income.

Source: Calculations by Gerber based on 1991 Census Public Use Microdata Files.

prefer to be called) find themselves systematically excluded from equal participation in our educational and economic institutions.

Although, as Wotherspoon and Satzewich (1993:51) point out, average incomes mask the fact that Native people, as individuals, are distributed across all classes—including the wealthy business or capitalist class—there is socioeconomic stratification in Canada based on race and ethnicity (Porter, 1965; Breton, 1979; Li, 1988; McAll, 1990). It is also clear that, as we saw in Chapter 11 ("Social Class in Canada"), Native peoples are particularly disadvantaged (Gerber, 1990; Frideres, 1993).

SPECIAL-STATUS SOCIETIES

On historical grounds, one might argue that the British have special status within Canada. We have a British parliamentary system, the majority of Canadians speak English, and the dominant culture is Anglo-Saxon. In the past, admission to Canada itself, to the economic elite, and to the most exclusive clubs was controlled, for the most part, by the British. It could also be argued that the policy of multiculturalism gives special status to all of the ethnic and cultural minorities that contribute to the Canadian mosaic. Nonetheless, two categories stand out because they have unique relationships with the federal government and other Canadians—the Native peoples (Indian, Inuit, and Métis) and the Québécois.

NATIVE PEOPLES

The terms *Native* and *Aboriginal* refer to fifty-five or more sovereign peoples who had established themselves on the North American continent thousands of years before the arrival of European explorers and settlers. Native peoples include the Inuit, Indians (such as the Cree, Ojibwa, Micmac, Blackfoot, Iroquois, and Haida) and Métis peoples, among others. The Métis are a sociocultural category of biracial descent—usually French and Indian. Among the Indian peoples

there are numerous categories. Registered Indians (or status Indians), who come under the *Indian Act* and are the responsibility of the Department of Indian and Northern Affairs, may be "treaty" or "non-treaty," depending on whether their ancestors were party to treaties. In addition, there is an undetermined number of people who may be biologically and culturally Indian but are not legally so, because their ancestors, for whatever reasons, did not enter into agreements with the Crown.[1] Many individuals lost or gave up Indian status by acquiring a university education (in the early 1990s), in order to vote (prior to 1960, when status Indians were granted the franchise), or by marriage (when a woman with Indian status married a man without). In 1985, *Bill C-31* allowed people who had lost Indian status to reclaim it. More than 100 000 people—most of them women who had lost status by marrying out—took advantage of this opportunity.

The 2001 census identifies more than 976 000 individuals who claim Aboriginal ancestry: among them are 45 000 Inuit, 292 000 Métis, and 609 000 Indians. Since not all people acknowledge or are aware of their Aboriginal ancestors, these figures probably underestimate the number of people with Native ancestry. It is likely that more than 1.5 million Canadians have Aboriginal roots (Frideres, 1998:27).[2]

Registered Indians who live on reserves or settlements are the special responsibility of the Department of Indian and Northern Affairs. Their relationship with Ottawa over the years could be characterized as

---

[1]Frideres (1998:21–42) provides a detailed explanation of the various Native and Indian categories.

[2]A note about terminology: many of you are aware that use of the term *Indian* may be offensive when applied to Native peoples. Terms like *Native*, *Aboriginal*, and *Indigenous* are good substitutions—except when you need to differentiate between Indian, Métis, and Inuit. The term *First Nation* applies only to those who are status or registered Indians under the *Indian Act*. Likewise, the Assembly of First Nations includes only the chiefs of status Indian communities. Many people who consider themselves to be Indian do not fall under the First Nation definition.

paternalistic and bureaucratic. For example, until the 1980s, Indian children were often removed from the reserves and taken to boarding schools. There they were punished for "talking Indian" among themselves, forced to speak English, and taught that their own languages and cultures were of no value. Removed from their homes and communities for ten months of the year and deprived of parent–child relationships, these children were not prepared to live effectively in either the Native or non-Native world. Christianity was imposed on the communities and on the children in the boarding schools, and education beyond the level required for farming or raising livestock was discouraged. The effect of these measures was an erosion of the social and cultural fabric of community life. In January 1998, Jane Stewart, Canada's Minister of Indian Affairs and Northern Development, took the long overdue step of formally apologizing for the boarding-school experiences of Native youth—which often included physical and sexual abuse.

Because non-status Indians, the Métis, and the Inuit were never confined to reserves, they have escaped some of the negative effects of reserve life. Living in Canada's far North, the Inuit have not felt the same population pressures as Native peoples in the rest of the country. However, they have experienced the same gradual erosion of traditional patterns of life. Oil, gas, and uranium companies have degraded the environment in the North and reduced the game supply. Many Inuit families have moved into permanent settlements, both for employment and to meet the legal requirement of school attendance for their children. Consequently, extended families no longer establish winter camps in traditional hunting grounds or teach their children the old survival skills that used to foster a sense of self-worth.

It is important to realize that there is a great deal of diversity among Native communities (Gerber, 1979), and Native individuals, communities, and organizations have made real strides in dealing with the problems they face today. Where government policy once was based on the assumption that the "Indian problem" would solve itself through urban migration and assimilation, it is now recognized that Native communities on reserves and elsewhere are not only surviving but growing (Gerber, 1984). In addition, high-profile Native leaders such as Ovide Mercredi, Matthew Coon Come, Phil Fontaine, and Paul Okalik have been effective in articulating their demands and thereby have gained public support for greater self-determination. National organizations such as the Assembly of First Nations, Inuit Tapirisat, Native Council of Canada (now the Congress

For information about Canadian Native communities, visit the websites of the Assembly of First Nations at www.afn.ca/, the Inuit Tapirisat at www.tapirisat.ca/, the Congress of Aboriginal Peoples at www.abo-peoples.org/, and the Métis National Council at www.metisnation.ca/

Canada's Native peoples have long been seeking self-determination, a struggle that has been more prominent in the media in recent years but, in fact, has been going on throughout Canada's history. A sign in this protest on Parliament Hill hints at the frustration over another failed attempt at resolution.

of Aboriginal Peoples), and Métis National Council were instrumental in negotiating recognition of the inherent right to self-government through the Charlottetown Accord—which was rejected in the 1992 federal referendum (see the "Diversity: Race, Class, and Gender" box on Native self-government in Chapter 17, "Politics and Government," pp. 420–21).

One dramatic result of the Native quest for self-determination was the creation in 1999 of a new territory, Nunavut, which was carved out of the Northwest Territories. The new territorial government is controlled by the Inuit majority, with support from an established system of cooperatives and the Inuit Broadcasting Corporation (IBC). Political and administrative positions are bringing new employment prospects, potentially stimulating greater educational achievement and enhancing pride. Returning control of Inuit communities to Inuit hands will not alleviate problems overnight; the hope on the part of Native leaders, however, is that it will be one meaningful step towards dealing with a wide range of serious social problems.

Read more about Nunavut at www.gov.nu.ca/Nunavut/

THE QUÉBÉCOIS

From New France to the Quiet Revolution

The French presence in what is now Canada goes back to 1608, when the first permanent settlement in New France was established at Quebec City by Samuel de Champlain with twenty-eight settlers—eight of whom survived the first winter. France claimed a vast territory that extended west of the Thirteen Colonies and down to Louisiana, encompassing most of southern Ontario and the Great Lakes region. But New France grew slowly because of a lack of interest on the part of France in supporting the tiny settlement or in sending more settlers to the area. The population grew from eight in 1609 to just over 3000 in 1663—spread among Quebec City, Trois-Rivières, and Montreal—mainly because of an "extraordinary rate of child bearing" (Beaujot and McQuillan, 1982:4). Two centuries later, at the time of Confederation, the French formed 31 percent of Canada's population of 3.5 million people.

As a result of the size of the French population and its concentration in Quebec, the *British North America Act* of 1867 recognized the province's civil-law tradition, Catholic schools, and language. Confederation was based on bilingualism, and assumed that English- and French-speaking communities would coexist. English and French were to be the legislative and judicial languages in federal and Quebec institutions. Bilingualism was later strengthened and expanded by the *Official Languages Act* of 1969, which declared the equality of the two languages in Parliament and in the Canadian public service.

At the time of Confederation, Quebec encompassed a traditional society based on the seigneurial system of land tenure—in which *habitants*, or tenants, worked the lands of the *seigneurs*, the landowners. In the political vacuum left by an ineffective provincial government, the Catholic Church took upon itself the task of administering many aspects of Quebec society, including education, health care, and social welfare. The Catholic Church, which had long dominated Quebec's major institutions, resisted change:

> Uninterested in questioning the established authorities and the excesses of industrialization, and wary of new ideas, the Quebec church was more concerned with maintaining its privileged position than with helping Quebecers enter the twentieth century. It extolled the virtues of rural life, cautioned against the evils of the city and the dangers of education, and preached the need to accept one's lot in life. (Latouche, 1988:1801)

At this time a British economic and industrial elite based in Montreal dominated the provincial economy. A clear linguistic class structure had developed with the unilingual English at the top, the unilingual French at the bottom, and bilingual people in the middle in supervisory positions. The unilingual French had few opportunities to better their social or financial standing, and even the French-origin bilinguals could rise only so far. Individuals who moved to the cities to seek employment found that a linguistic ceiling restricted upward mobility.

Quebec's "Quiet Revolution" of the 1960s greatly diminished the political power and social influence of the Catholic Church. Newly elected premier Jean Lesage chose to expand the role of the state in the economic, social, and cultural life of the province. The Lesage government established a department of education (encouraging the study of engineering, maths, sciences, and business) and nationalized Hydro-Québec (to attract industry with the promise of cheap electricity). It also took over the administration of Quebec's pension funds. These and other changes served to integrate Quebec into the North American economic structure (Coleman, 1984).

Quebec was now characterized by a rapidly growing working class, a declining birth rate—eliminating "the revenge of the cradle" as a tool for maintaining or improving the linguistic balance in Canada—and a decline in the influence of the church. In other words, French-Canadian society was becoming more like the rest of North America—urban, secular, and industrialized. As a result, language became the primary defining characteristic of Québécois society, and francophone Quebecers became even more aware of the relative numbers of French- and English-speaking people. They also realized that the continued existence of the small francophone minorities outside Quebec was threatened by assimilation. Reaching the conclusion that French language and culture could be protected only in the province of Quebec, many rejected their Canadian or French-Canadian identities and began to think of themselves as Québécois only. The desire to protect their distinct language and culture led them to seek institutional dominance in Quebec, and this in turn had profound implications for federal–provincial relations.

The Growing Demand for Sovereignty

The logical extension of a demand for institutional control was the demand for sovereignty. The late 1960s and 1970s saw an increase in Québécois nationalism and in support for the independence movement. The sentiments that gave rise to the radical terrorist group Front de libération du Québec (FLQ) became more widespread and eventually paved the way for the 1976 election of the separatist Parti Québécois, led by René Lévesque.

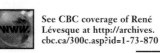 See CBC coverage of René Lévesque at http://archives. cbc.ca/300c.asp?id=1-73-870

One of the first acts of the new Parti Québécois government in Quebec was to introduce Bill 101, making French the only official language of Quebec, including in business and education. Francophones were no longer excluded from the economic elite. In addition, the children of immigrants from other countries or from other provinces would be educated in French and assimilated into francophone society. In response to the election of a separatist government and the language laws, many anglophones and businesses, both large and small, left the province. From 1976 to 1981, Quebec's net loss through interprovincial migration was 156 000 people, double that of the previous five-year period.

In a 1980 referendum on "sovereignty-association," 60 percent of Quebecers voted "No." The debate leading up the referendum was often divisive, especially in the city of Montreal. There, as elsewhere in the province, the referendum revealed a general pattern of increased support for sovereignty the further east one moved from Ontario (Gerber, 1992).

Under the Liberal federal government of Pierre Trudeau, Canada patriated its constitution and incorporated the *Charter of Rights and Freedoms* in 1982. The provincial government of Quebec did not agree to the conditions of patriation and did not sign the constitution at that point. Brian Mulroney and the Progressive Conservative party won the 1984 election with massive support in Quebec, in part because they promised amendments that would overcome Quebec's objections to the constitution.

 The speech in which Brian Mulroney announced the Meech Lake accord to Parliament is available in text and audio form at www.nlc-bnc.ca/primeministers/h4-4022-e.html

For complex political reasons, the Meech Lake Accord of 1987, which included recognition of Quebec as a "distinct society," was not ratified by all the provincial legislatures (specifically Manitoba and Newfoundland) before its 1990 deadline. Among the reasons for public disenchantment with "Meech" was Quebec's 1988 sign law, which banned English from outdoor signs altogether. Anglophone Canadians perceived the sign law as a slap in the face. In turn, Quebecers saw the failure of the Meech Lake Accord as a symbol of rejection by English Canada. Such symbols, as Breton (1992) points out, can have a powerful political impact. Among other things, the failure of Meech spawned the separatist Bloc Québécois—a political party working at the federal level to promote the cause of separation.

The Charlottetown Accord (discussed in Chapter 7, "Groups and Organizations," p. 160) was rejected by Canadians (including 55 percent of Quebecers) in the referendum of October 26, 1992. Support for the separatist Bloc Québécois and Parti Québécois grew, at least in part because of the repeated failures in constitutional accommodation as well as the economic pain associated with a prolonged recession.

The success of the two separatist parties clearly reveals that the politics surrounding the quest for special status and related powers continues to have potentially explosive consequences for Canada. On October 30, 1995, Canadians were stunned by the razor-thin

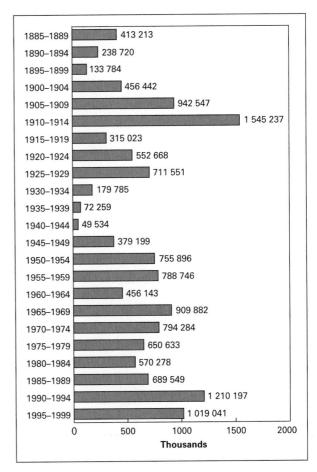

FIGURE 14–3 Immigration to Canada, 1885–1999

Source: Figure by Gerber based on statistics in Knowles (1997:206) and Statistics Canada, www.statca.ca.

victory for the "No" side in Quebec's most recent referendum on sovereignty—50.6 percent voting "No" to 49.4 percent voting "Yes." Quebec came dangerously close to giving its leaders the go-ahead to negotiate separation, which would have had incalculable costs for the country as a whole. The referendum alarm wakened federalist forces in Ottawa and Quebec City, reactivated the "unity" agenda, and, again, raised the question of what can be done to keep Canada whole (see the "Controversy & Debate" box on page 356). The Quebec election of 2003 gave the province a Liberal government under Jean Charest, who reduced tensions substantially because of his willingness to work with the other premiers in a Canadian framework.

IMMIGRATION TO CANADA: A HUNDRED-YEAR PERSPECTIVE

Canada has been—and will remain—a land of immigrants. The ten-year period from 1905 to 1914 saw the arrival of 2.5 million people, making it the peak decade for Canadian immigration. (See Figure 14–3,

TABLE 14-4 Immigrant Population by Region of Birth, 1991–2001		
Region	**Number**	**%**
North, Central, and South America	167 440	9.1
Caribbean and Bermuda	84 005	4.6
Europe	357 845	19.5
Africa	139 770	7.6
Asia	1 066 230	58.2
Other	15 380	0.8
Total	1 830 670	100.0

Source: Adapted from Statistics Canada, www.statcan.ca.

TABLE 14-5 Top 10 Countries of Birth for Immigrants Arriving, 1991–2001		
Country	**Number**	**%**
People's Republic of China	197 360	10.8
India	156 120	8.5
Philippines	122 010	6.7
Hong Kong	118 385	6.5
Sri Lanka	62 590	3.4
Pakistan	57 990	3.2
Taiwan	53 755	2.9
United States	51 440	2.8
Iran	47 080	2.6
Poland	43 370	2.4
Other Countries	920 580	50.2
Total Immigrants	1 830 680	100.0

Source: Adapted from Statistics Canada, www.statcan.ca.

which details our immigration history from 1885 to 1999.) At the height of immigration to Canada, in 1913, one in every seventeen people was a new-comer—not just an immigrant, but someone who had arrived within the past year. In contrast, we now admit about 225 000 immigrants per year into a population of more than 31 million: one in every 140 people today is a newly arrived immigrant of the current year. Knowing the numbers of immigrants absorbed by the tiny Canadian population of the early 1900s should give us encouragement regarding Canada's ability to absorb the numbers arriving in recent years. Immigration increased from 1990–94 and 1995–99, when more than a million individuals arrived in each of these periods.

Race and ethnicity retain their significance in part because of the continuous flow of immigrants into our country. The first wave of immigration after Confederation was driven by the desire to populate the West and to provide workers for the growing economy.

 Canada's advertising campaign to attract immigrants to the West is profiled at www.civilization.ca/hist/advertis/adindexe.html

This trend was encouraged by the controversial policies of Clifford Sifton, Minister of the Interior around the turn of the century (Hiller, 2000).

During the Sifton years, Canada was still trying to promote immigration from Britain—in part out of political necessity. English Canadians assumed that the government would do everything it could to retain the British character of the country (Knowles, 1997). By setting up an immigration office in London, England, Sifton was able to increase the flow from Britain to the point where, by 1905, about a third of our immigrants came from there. But because Sifton was primarily interested in attracting good farmers to populate the West, he also started a trickle of Ukrainian immigration that would peak in 1913, when 22 363 individuals arrived from that country. These Ukrainians, along with a trickle of Doukhobors, Finns, Germans, and Scandinavians, were seen by many politicians and or-

dinary Canadians as ignorant, unassimilable aliens who would do irreparable damage to Canada (Knowles, 1997).

In the early 1900s, policy severely restricted immigration to Canada to white people of Anglo-Saxon origin. Southern and eastern Europeans, as well as the Chinese, the Japanese, and African-Americans, were discouraged from entering. For example, the *Chinese Immigration Act* of 1923 barred all but a select few Chinese from entering Canada. Despite these efforts, immigration soared—in part because politicians and businessmen believed that economic prosperity depended on continued population growth. Immigration fell during World War I (1914–18), the Great Depression (1929–39), and World War II (1939–45). During a short boom in the 1920s, immigrants from Britain and Europe were admitted along with some Jews and Russian Mennonites. By 1931, however, Canada was to close her doors to refugees—especially Jewish refugees, in part because of widespread anti-Semitism.

After World War II there was mounting pressure to open the doors once again and accept large numbers of refugees. Once again, "old" Commonwealth countries and the United States were the initial source of regular (non-refugee) immigrants needed to meet labour needs, settle unpopulated areas, and expand the internal market for goods. But soon, by the 1950s, Germany, Italy, and the Netherlands had become important sources of immigrants and our immigration laws had been liberalized to allow more Asians, as well as Palestinian and Hungarian refugees. Further liberalization would occur under the Conservative government of John Diefenbaker, who foresaw a population of 40 million in the near future and argued that "Canada must populate or perish" (Knowles, 1997:146).

It was not until 1962 that Ellen Fairclough, Canada's first woman federal cabinet minister, put an

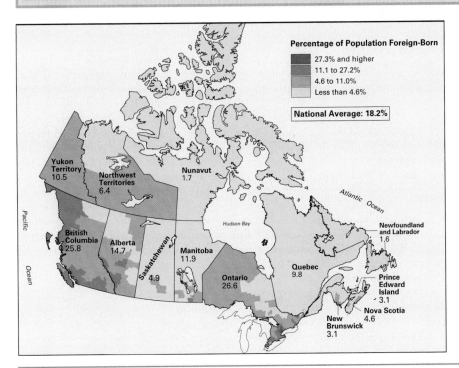

Percentage of Population Foreign-Born

27.3% and higher
11.1 to 27.2%
4.6 to 11.0%
Less than 4.6%

National Average: 18.2%

Yukon Territory 10.5

Northwest Territories 6.4

Nunavut 1.7

Atlantic Ocean

Hudson Bay

British Columbia 25.8

Alberta 14.7

Saskatchewan 4.9

Manitoba 11.9

Ontario 26.6

Quebec 9.8

Newfoundland and Labrador 1.6

Prince Edward Island 3.1

Nova Scotia 4.6

New Brunswick 3.1

Pacific Ocean

CANADA MAP 14–1
Percentage of Population Foreign-Born for Canada, the Provinces, Territories, and Census Subdivision, 2001

Source: Calculations by Gerber based on data retrieved in October 2003 from Statistics Canada, B2020, Profile Series.

---

end to our White Canada immigration policy. Education and occupation and language skills replaced race or national origin as the criteria of admission. After the 1965 election, the Liberals formalized the selection criteria through what we call the *points system*, which allocates points to education, occupation, facility in English or French, age, and the demand for the applicant's skills in the Canadian labour market. The points system reduces reliance on the judgment of the individual immigration officer.

More recently, Canada has experienced waves of immigration from the West Indies and Asia (in the 1970s), from Central and South America (in the 1980s), and from China and India (in the 1990s). As Hiller (1991:173) points out, "these repeated waves of immigration reinvigorated ethnic groups already resident in Canada, and reminded residents of their own ethnicity."

 The experience of Vietnamese refugees who came to Canada in the 1970s is explored through CBC archives at http://archives. cbc.ca/300c.asp?id=1-69-524

The *Immigration Act* of 1976 recognized three classes of people as eligible for landed immigrant status: *family class* (immediate family and dependent children, parents, and grandparents of Canadian citizens or landed immigrants), *humanitarian class* (refugees or persecuted and displaced persons), and *independent class* (those who apply as individuals and are admitted

on the basis of the points system). These changes altered the countries of origin of the applicants, stimulated a greatly expanded flow of refugees, and increased applications by family members, who now outnumber independent applicants. In recent years, Canada has made a concerted effort to attract people who are experienced in business or who have significant amounts of money to invest.

Table 14–4 indicates the sources of our immigrants from 1991 to 2001, by geographic region of birth. Asia is by far the major source region, sending us 58 percent of our immigrants, while Europe—the source of almost all immigration in the first half of the twentieth century—has dropped down to 19.5 percent. Table 14–5 reveals that China and India, which rank first and second, sent us almost 11 and 9 percent of our immigrants, respectively, between 1991 and 2001. Eight out of the top ten birth countries for Canadian immigrants during this period were Asian, including the Philippines, Hong Kong, Sri Lanka, Pakistan, Taiwan, and Iran. The only two non-Asian countries in the top ten were the United States and Poland.

Most of the immigrants who have come to Canada in recent decades have gone to Ontario and British Columbia. As Canada Map 14–1 reveals, Alberta and Manitoba have also attracted immigrants, while the

CONTROVERSY & DEBATE

Distinct Societies and National Unity

Pluralism and diversity are so central to Canadian identity that they are enshrined in our constitution. The French language (official bilingualism and minority language rights), civil law (in Quebec), Catholic or denominational schooling, existing Aboriginal and treaty rights, and the right to preserve and enhance our multicultural heritage are guaranteed by our constitution and the *Charter of Rights and Freedoms*. Freedom from the pressures of assimilation could be taken for granted in this country, yet some of us, anxious to ensure the viability of our own cultures, demand constitutional recognition as distinct societies.

The unwillingness or inability of Canadians across the country to respond positively to demands for such recognition by Quebec threatens the stability of our federation—as we learned so painfully on referendum day in October 1995, when the Québécois came within a hair's breadth of voting for sovereignty and separation. Because distinct-society status is significant for both Quebec and Canada, the debate surrounding it receives a great deal of media attention.

The concept or symbol of a "distinct society" could have explosive consequences for Canada (Breton, 1992). Applying the concept to Quebec, people across Canada say, "But *of course* Quebec is a distinct society. It has its own language, legal system, political parties, and a vibrant French culture." Quebec leaders want to know why, if we accept Quebec's distinctiveness, we cannot agree to include that recognition in our constitution. The answer lies, in part, with the controversy surrounding the label itself.

Let's look at this concept. At one level, it implies that Quebec is *different*— and few would argue with that. (Aboriginal societies are different, too.) The controversy emerges with the argument that different or distinct implies *special* status. The notion that Quebec is not only different, but perhaps *special*, raises the issue of two classes of Canadians, one having special rights. It is this interpretation that raises the hackles of many Canadians and some provinces.

If we assume that the label "distinct society" is purely symbolic and merely implies the recognition of existing social and cultural differences, then putting it into the constitution would not have any significant effect. One way to restrict its potential impact on the constitution would be to define it carefully, so that the distinction implies no new powers, or no powers that substantially differentiate Quebec from the other provinces.

However, to be acceptable to Quebec, "distinct society" must imply special powers, for it is through those that the Québécois hope to become "masters in their own house." To preserve and protect the small island of francophone culture, Quebec sovereigntists want unquestioned control over language (in business, education, social discourse, and government), immigration, employment, trade, natural resources, the economy, population

Atlantic provinces have not. Not surprisingly, the metropolitan areas of Toronto and Vancouver have the largest immigrant components at 44 and 38 percent. Visible minorities made up about 37 percent of the populations of the two metropolitan areas. In Quebec, Montreal has attracted a significant immigrant component, whereas Quebec City has not. Recent immigration has clearly touched some parts of Canada more than others.

RACE AND ETHNICITY: PAST AND FUTURE

Immigration has contributed to the development of a country, which, though it started out Native, British, and French at Confederation, is now quite rightly called multicultural. The characteristics of the newcomers have stimulated the continued, and often uneasy, awareness of race and ethnicity among Canadians. Their geographic distribution has contributed to regional diversity as people with different backgrounds found themselves concentrated in various parts of the country and in different cities, giving substance to the vision of Canada as what former prime minister Joe Clark would call a "community of communities."

Canada is an experiment in multilayered pluralism—multilayered because the British, the French, the Native peoples, and other ethnic and racial minorities have different kinds of relationships with one another and with society as a whole. Each new wave of immigration adds to the complexity of the mosaic. Newly articulated demands and expectations on the part of the Québécois and the various Native peoples will contribute to the definition and redefinition of our unique country. Our survival as a country depends on our success in forging an identity out of diversity.

policy and mobility, social services, and more. Since other provinces do not want all these powers (mainly because of funding concerns), granting them to Quebec would give that province special status.

Another aspect of Quebec's relationship with the rest of the country is threatening to other provinces. Many Québécois see Confederation as joining together *two founding nations*, while other Canadians see it as joining *ten equal provinces*. Is Quebec one of ten equal partners, or one of only two? Clearly, these are serious and potentially catastrophic clashes of vision.

In another attempt to circumvent the "distinct society" problem, Canada's premiers proposed constitutional recognition of Quebec's "unique characteristics" in the Calgary declaration of September 1997. Whatever words are used to describe different, special, or distinct status, implying enhanced autonomy, the impact is not neutral. The process itself is controversial and divisive, and even if we were able to

deliver distinct society status its implementation would generate its own strains. The heated debate that erupts periodically around these powerful concepts is both inevitable and justifiable in the context of Canadian pluralism.

Postscript—In June 2003, Jean Charest, a Liberal, defeated the Parti Québécois government of Bernard Landry to become the new premier of Quebec. This is highly significant for Canada because Jean Charest is willing to help the premiers of the other provinces make the country work better. Ever since the election of 1976, when René Lévesque led the separatist Parti Québécois to its first electoral victory, Quebec has been trying to enhance its sovereignty or increase its clout in Ottawa—even by threatening repeated referenda. When another Liberal, Robert Bourassa, was premier (1985–94), he could not play the role of a committed federalist, but demanded further powers for Quebec and refused to work with the other premiers on shared problems. Jean Charest is deter-

mined to fix Quebec's economic problems by working within the existing Canadian framework. The province's willingness to embrace Charest's vision may be related to the new and surprising tendency of the people to identify their roots as Canadian rather than French or Québécois.

Continue the debate . . .

1. *Francophones outside the province have been abandoned in Quebec's quest for greater autonomy and cultural protections. How might these francophones react to the granting of "distinct society" status to Quebec?*

2. *Native peoples claim distinctiveness and the right to self-government as well. What are the implications of granting "distinct society" status to Quebec for the Aboriginal peoples in the province?*

SUMMARY

1. Race involves a cluster of biological traits that nineteenth-century biologists divided into three broad, overarching categories: Caucasians, Mongoloids, and Negroids. There are, however, no pure races. Ethnicity is based on shared cultural heritage. Minorities are categories of people who are socially distinctive—including those of certain races and ethnicities—who have a subordinate social position.

2. Prejudice is an inflexible and distorted generalization about a category of people. Racism, a destructive form of prejudice, asserts that one race is innately superior or inferior to another.

3. Discrimination is a pattern of action by which a person treats various categories of people differently.

4. Pluralism refers to a state in which racial and ethnic categories, although distinct, have equal social

standing. Assimilation is a process by which minorities gradually adopt the patterns of the dominant culture. Segregation means the physical and social separation of categories of people. Most segregation of minorities is involuntary. Genocide is the annihilation of a category of people.

5. Blacks have a long history in Canada, as free Loyalists, as slaves prior to 1810, and later as escaped slaves coming to Canada via the Underground Railroad. The past two decades have seen increased immigration of Blacks (from Africa, the Caribbean, and elsewhere) who have made their own cultural, economic, and political contributions to Canadian life.

6. The representation of racial and ethnic groups varies substantially from region to region in Canada, as does that of people who claim "Canadian" ancestry.

7. Blacks and Asians have higher levels of education than the British and French, but their incomes tend to be lower. Natives are low on both education and income scales.

8. Native peoples, who face numerous barriers to full participation in the larger society, seek self-government as a potential solution to some of their problems.

9. The Québécois feel that French language and culture can be protected only within Quebec and that they need to have maximum control of their institutions—perhaps through separation—in order to achieve this.

10. Canada, which has historically accepted large numbers of immigrants, is currently receiving most of its immigrants from Asia, especially China and India.

CRITICAL-THINKING QUESTIONS

1. Clearly differentiate between race and ethnicity. Do you think all nonwhite people should be considered minorities, even if they have above-average incomes?

2. In what ways do prejudice and discrimination reinforce each other?

3. Are *all* generalizations about minorities wrong? What distinguishes a fair generalization from an unfair stereotype?

4. Do you think Canadian society is colour-blind? Should we be? Does affirmative action reduce or exacerbate racial conflict?

APPLICATIONS AND EXERCISES

1. Give several of your friends or family members a quick quiz, asking them what share of the Canadian population is white, Black, Aboriginal, or Asian (see Figure 14–3). Do they exaggerate the share of all minorities and understate the white proportion? Does your place of residence affect perceptions?

2. There are probably people on your campus or in your local community who are immigrants. Have you ever thought about asking such people to tell you something about their homelands and their experiences since arriving in Canada? Most immigrants would be pleased to be asked and can provide a wonderful learning experience. If you are an immi-

grant yourself, how does your own experience differ from those of others?

3. Does the ethnic diversity of Canada affect what you eat? Check out your grocery stores, the restaurants in town, your favourite snacks. What is your conclusion?

4. Visit the website of an organization working to improve the social standing of a Canadian minority: B'nai Brith Canada at **www.bnaibrith.ca/**, Canadian Centre on Minority Affairs at **www.ccmacanada.org/**, or the Chinese Canadian National Council at **www.ccnc.ca/**. What are the organization's strategies and goals?

 SITES TO SEE

www.macionis.com
or
www.TheSociologyPage.com
You can find more than fifty weblinks to sociological journals and other sources of data and information by visiting the Links Library at this website.

www.cccj.ca/HomePage.htm
The *Canadian Council of Christians and Jews* is a nonreligious organization dedicated to promoting cultural, racial, and religious harmony among the people of Canada. The council produces a nationwide market research study known as the "Harmony Barometer," which examines the attitudes and behaviours of Canadians to-

wards people of different ethnic, religious, and racial backgrounds.

www.pch.gc.ca/march-21-mars/
Maintained by Canadian Heritage, this site supports International Day for the Elimination of Racial Discrimination (March 21) activities by providing education and information resources.

canada.metropolis.net
Metropolis is a cooperative, international research initiative created to examine immigrant integration and the effects of international migration on urban centres. The project aims to provide all levels of government, community organizations, and businesses with solid information on which to anchor policy ideas and programs.

http://collections.ic.gc.ca/obho/
The Ontario Black History Society is an educational organization that promotes preservation and awareness of Black history in the province. Multimedia presentations on people, places, and events are available at this website.

 ## STUDY TOOLS

For more study tools to help you with your next exam, be sure to check out the Companion Website at **www.pearsoned. ca/macionis**, as well as Chapter 14 in your Study Guide.

 ## INVESTIGATE WITH CONTENTSELECT

Follow the instructions found on page 25 of this textbook to access ContentSelect™ at the Research Navigator™ website. Once at the site, enter your LOGINID and Password. Then, enter keywords such as "race," "ethnicity," and "discrimination," and the search engine will supply relevant and recent scholarly and popular press publications.

Boris Kustodiev (1878–1927, Russian)
Easter Morning, 1911

Regional Gallery of Art, Astrakhan, Russia.
Scala/Art Resource, N.Y.

AGING AND THE ELDERLY

Almost as soon as it was released, the book *Final Exit* shot to the top of the bestseller list in 1991. This is a book about dying—not about the death of a famous person, nor a philosophical treatise on death, but a "how-to" manual explaining how to commit suicide. *Final Exit* gives specific instructions for killing yourself in a host of ways, from swallowing sleeping pills, to self-starvation, to suffocation with a plastic bag.

The author of *Final Exit*, Derek Humphry, is a founder and the executive director of the Hemlock Society, an organization that offers support and practical assistance to people who wish to die. Humphry argues that the time has come for people to have straightforward information about how to end their own lives. The immediate and remarkable popularity of *Final Exit*—especially among the elderly—suggests that millions of people agree with him.

Not surprisingly, *Final Exit* sparked controversy. While supporters view the work as a humane effort to assist people who are painfully and terminally ill, critics worry that it encourages suicide by people who, perhaps, are temporarily depressed (Angelo, 1991). Laws are being tested that prohibit doctors—and others—from assisting in the death of a patient. Sue Rodriguez brought the issue of euthanasia to national attention by fighting, right up to the Supreme Court of Canada, for the right to assisted suicide whenever she decided that her life with ALS was not worth living. She lost the case but was assisted to her chosen death by an anonymous doctor. Sue Rodriguez was supported through her legal battles and her final days by her friend and MP Svend Robinson.

The appearance of *Final Exit* also raises broader questions that are no less disturbing and controversial than the "right to die." As this chapter explains, the ranks of the elderly are swelling rapidly as more and more men and women live longer and longer. As a result, many younger people are uneasy about their responsibilities towards aging parents. For their part, many older people are alarmed at the prospect of losing control of their lives to a medical establishment driven to prolong life at any cost. And people of all ages worry whether the health care system must shortchange the young in order to meet the escalating needs of seniors.

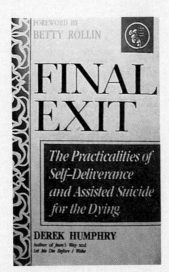

Today, issues related to aging and the elderly command the attention of policymakers as never before. In some respects, growing old in Canada has never been better: people live longer, have better health care, and experience less poverty than they did a generation ago. But stubborn problems persist. Older people, for example, continue to grapple with prejudice and discrimination. And as unprecedented numbers of women and men enter old age, new problems loom on the horizon.

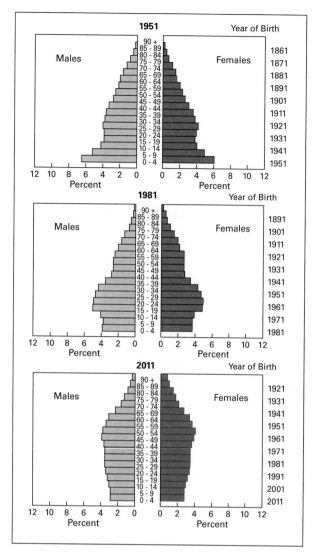

FIGURE 15–1 Age Pyramids of Canada for 1951, 1981, and 2011

Source: Statistics Canada, 1992b.

THE GREYING OF CANADA

A quiet but powerful revolution is reshaping Canada: the number of elderly people—women and men age sixty-five and over—is increasing more than twice as fast as the population as a whole. The effects of this "greying of Canada" promise to be profound.

Some statistics bring this change into sharp focus. The average annual growth of the youth population over the last 120 years has been 1.2 percent, and that of persons over sixty-five has been more than double that rate, at 2.7 percent (Statistics Canada, 1992b). The 2001 census reveals that, in Canada, the population over sixty-five now makes up 13 percent of the whole (Statistics Canada, **www.statcan.ca**).

In just over a century, the life expectancy of Canadians has doubled and their average number of children has declined by a half. The age/sex pyramids for the Canadian population have shown and will continue to demonstrate dramatic shape changes (see Figure 15–1). By 2031, the proportion of the population age sixty-five and over will have increased to almost one-quarter of the whole, or 23.8 percent. The median age of Canadians has risen from 29.6 in 1981 to 37.6 in 2001. Canada Map 15–1 shows the percentage of the population over sixty-five, by province, territory, and census subdivision.

What is prompting the aging of our society? Two factors stand out. The first is the baby boom that began in the late 1940s. After World War II, men and women enthusiastically settled into family life and the bearing of children. The birth rate then took a sharp turn downward after 1965 (the so-called baby bust), so that our population will become increasingly "top-heavy" in the coming decades.

Global Map 15–1 (page 364) shows that it is the rich nations, including Canada, in which the share of elderly people is rapidly increasing. Typically, two factors combine to drive up the elderly population: low birth rates (so there are fewer children) and in-

 This Canadian website offers a portal to services for seniors fifty and over: www.wiredseniors.com/ageofreason/

creasing longevity (so people typically live well into old age).

LIFE EXPECTANCY: GOING UP

The past century has witnessed a remarkable thirty-year increase in life expectancy. Females born in 1900 lived 50.2 years; males lived 47.2 years. In contrast, women now look forward to 81 years of life; men to about 75 years (Colombo, 1997:62).

Our longer life spans are mainly due to medical advances that virtually eliminated infectious diseases such as smallpox, diphtheria, and measles, which killed many young people in the past. More recent medical strides fend off cancer and heart disease, afflictions common to the elderly (Wall, 1980). The decline in mortality rates means that of women born in 1950, only 5 percent will have died before becoming mothers. For every one hundred women born in the 1800s, forty died before giving birth to a child (Statistics Canada, 1992b). In addition, a rising standard of living has promoted the health of people of all ages. One clear indication of this change is that the fastest-growing segment of the entire population is people over eighty-five, who are already more than twenty times more numerous than they were at the beginning of the twentieth century. By 2011, about 20 percent of our elders (people over sixty-five) will be over eighty years of age (Statistics Canada, 1992b).

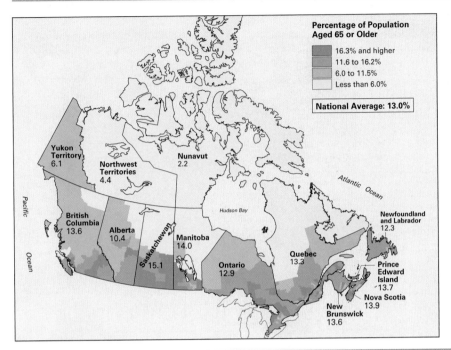

Percentage of Population Aged 65 or Older

- 16.3% and higher
- 11.6 to 16.2%
- 6.0 to 11.5%
- Less than 6.0%

National Average: 13.0%

Yukon Territory 6.1

Northwest Territories 4.4

Nunavut 2.2

British Columbia 13.6

Alberta 10.4

Saskatchewan 15.1

Manitoba 14.0

Ontario 12.9

Quebec 13.3

Newfoundland and Labrador 12.3

Prince Edward Island 13.7

Nova Scotia 13.9

New Brunswick 13.6

Atlantic Ocean

Pacific Ocean

Hudson Bay

CANADA MAP 15–1
Percentage of the Population Age 65 and Over for Canada, the Provinces, Territories, and Census Subdivision, 2001

Source: Calculations by Gerber, October 2003, based on data from Statistics Canada, B2020, Profile Series.

We can only begin to imagine the consequences of this massive increase in the elderly population. As elderly people steadily retire from the labour force, the proportion of nonworking adults—already about ten times greater than in 1900—will generate ever-greater demands for health care and other social resources. And the ratio of elderly people to working-age adults, which analysts call the *old-age dependency ratio*, will almost double in the next fifty years.

However, today's adults, especially women, are considerably different, in many important ways, from previous generations. They will not be entirely like the people who are over sixty-five today. The elderly of the future will tend to have greater levels of education, fewer family responsibilities, better work and better conditions for saving, an improved health care system, and broader access to retirement alternatives. Predicting the use of services on the basis of current use is thus very complicated (Statistics Canada,1992a:144).

At present, the elderly draw heavily on the health care system. One study indicated that health care spending is 4.5 times greater for Canadians over sixty-five and 6.5 times greater for those over seventy-five than for those under sixty-five (*Demographic Aging: The Economic Consequences*, 1991). Older people make the greatest use of physicians, hospitals, and prescription drugs. As Chapter 21 ("Health and Medicine") explains, the costs of medical care have grown in re-

cent years, a trend that shows little evidence of slowing. Unless steps are taken to address the real medical needs of millions of additional older people—at prices that Canadians (or taxpayers) can afford—our society will face a monumental health care crisis in the coming years. While this is a widespread concern, there are analysts who argue that the situation is not as dismal as it seems, pointing out that today's seniors are healthier than any previous generation (Foot, 1998).

AN AGING SOCIETY: CULTURAL CHANGE

As the number of people and the share of the population over sixty-five push upward, our way of life will change. In coming decades, interacting with elderly people will become commonplace. As the proportion of our population over sixty-five increases from 12 percent today to 17 percent by 2020—or one for every six people—younger generations will inevitably have more contact with older people (Foot, 1998). Reduced age segregation, in turn, will lead to greater familiarity and shared understandings.

Will a "culture of aging" ever emerge? Probably not, for one key reason: the elderly are too diverse. After all, the elderly represent an open category in which all of us—if we are lucky—end up. Thus, elderly people in Canada represent not just the two sexes but all cultures, classes, and races.

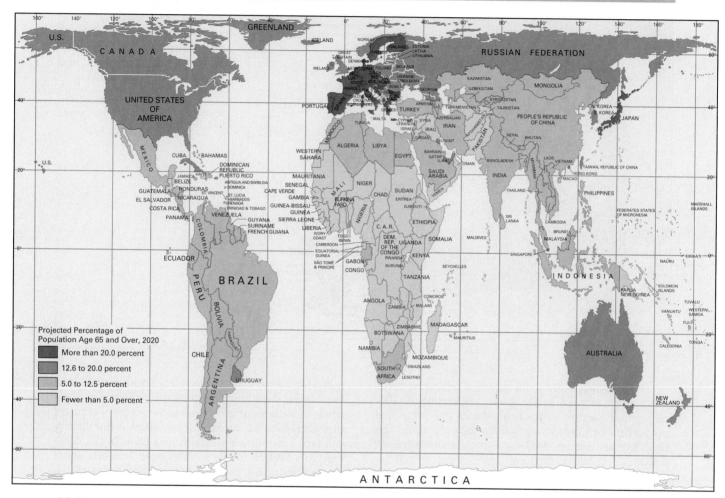

GLOBAL MAP 15–1 The Elderly in Global Perspective, 2020

Here we see projections for the share of population age sixty-five and older in the year 2020, one generation from now. What relationship do you see between a country's income level and its elderly population?

Source: U.S. Census Bureau (2000).

THE "YOUNG OLD" AND THE "OLD OLD"

Analysts sometimes distinguish between two cohorts of the elderly. The "younger elderly," who are between sixty-five and seventy-five years of age, are typically autonomous, enjoy good health and financial security, and are likely to be living as couples. The "older elderly," who have passed age seventy-five, are more likely to be dependent on others because of health and money problems. Women outnumber men in the elderly population (owing to their greater longevity), a discrepancy that increases with advancing age: among the "oldest old"—those over the age of eighty-five—about two-thirds are women.

While there are good reasons to be alert to population aging in Canada, there are scholars who argue that we have pressed the panic button fifteen years too early. The 1996 census suggests that the rate of growth in the elderly population has slowed down and will not pick up substantially until the baby boomers hit retirement age. Susan McDaniel, a demographer at the University of Alberta, and David Foot, co-author of *Boom, Bust and Echo*, agree that we have started worrying too early about the social costs of an elderly population now growing at a rate lower than anticipated (Mitchell, 1997). Foot (1998:275) adds that when "all the surviving boomers are over 65, Canada's elderly as a percentage of its population will be about 22 percent, a level that will match, not exceed, the rest of the developed world." The implication is that other countries—mainly northern European—have already dealt with the issues that are causing panic here in Canada.

GROWING OLD: BIOLOGY AND CULTURE

Tracking the greying of Canada is the special focus of **gerontology** (derived from the Greek word *geron*, meaning "an old person"), *the study of aging and the elderly*. Gerontologists explore the biological processes of aging, ask if personalities change as we grow

 The Canadian Association on Gerontology promotes the study of aging in all its aspects and improvement in the well-being of older people. See www.cagacg.ca/

older, and investigate how cultural assumptions about aging vary around the world.

BIOLOGICAL CHANGES

Aging amounts to a series of gradual, ongoing changes. How we think about life's transitions—whether we cheer our maturity or bemoan our physical decline—depends largely on whether our culture labels such changes as positive or negative. The youth-oriented way of life in Canada hails biological changes that occur early in life as positive. Through childhood and adolescence, we gain responsibility and look forward to expanded legal rights.

But our culture takes a dimmer view of the biological changes that unfold later in life. Few people receive congratulations for getting old. Rather, we commiserate with those entering old age and make jokes about aging to avoid the harsh conclusion that the elderly are on a slippery slope of physical and mental decline. We assume that, by about age forty, people cease growing *up* and begin growing *down*.

Growing old does bring on certain physical problems. Grey hair, wrinkles, loss of height and weight, and an overall decline in strength and vitality all begin in middle age. After the age of fifty, bones become more brittle so that injuries take longer to heal, and the odds of suffering from chronic illnesses (such as arthritis and diabetes) as well as life-threatening conditions (such as heart disease and cancer) rise steadily. The sensory abilities—taste, sight, touch, smell, and especially hearing—also become less keen with age (Treas, 1995; Segall and Chappell, 2000).

One of the most troublesome problems of old age is a group of illnesses called *dementias*, which are characterized by progressive cognitive impairment, including the loss of abilities such as attention span, concentration, orientation, and memory. While dementias can result from several diseases that affect the brain, Alzheimer's is the best known and most

Jackrabbit (Herman Smith) Johannsen was born in Norway in 1875. Along with his skis, he left "an indelible mark on Canada: many kilometres of cross-country ski trails and jumps are directly attributable to him, and so are the thousands of skiers who have been inspired by his spirit of adventure and love for the Canadian winter." He promoted cross-country skiing through Quebec, Ontario, and parts of the United States. He also was responsible for introducing skiing to the Crees in Northern Ontario—from whom he learned their language, his eighth, and who honoured him with the title Chief Jackrabbit. The Jackrabbit part stuck so well that many people never knew his Christian name. When asked, at 105 years of age, about his skiing, he said, "I'm steadier on skis with two poles to hold me up. But I'm not as good a skier as I was 100 years ago." (Norton, 1987)

common form of dementia (about 50 percent of dementia is Alzheimer's). Dementia is a serious and prevalent health problem among elderly Canadians, affecting between 5 and 10 percent of those over

 For more information about Alzheimer's, visit the Alzheimer Society of Canada website at www.alzheimer.ca/

sixty-five and approximately 20 percent of those over eighty.

Without denying that health becomes more fragile with advancing age, the vast majority of older people are neither discouraged nor disabled by their physical condition. Only about one in ten seniors reports trouble walking, and fewer than one in twenty requires intensive care in a hospital or nursing home. No more than 1 percent of the elderly are bedridden. In a 1990 survey, less than 25 percent of people over the age of fifty-five characterized their health as "fair" or "poor," while about 75 percent described their overall condition as "good" or "excellent" (Keith and Landry, 1994:134). Not only are the elderly in better health these days, but they are spending fewer days in the hospital as well. If these trends continue, older people will not be the drain on medical resources suggested by "apocalyptic demography" (Carriére, 2000).

Bear in mind, however, that patterns of well-being vary greatly within the elderly population. More health problems beset the "older elderly" past the age of seventy-five. Moreover, because women typically live longer than men, women spend more of their lives suffering from chronic disabilities such as arthritis. In addition, well-to-do people are likely to live and work in a healthful and safe environment, a fact that pays benefits well into old age. And, of course, richer people can afford much more preventive medical care. As well, happiness level does depend somewhat on income. In one survey, 56 percent of men and 49 percent of women over fifty-five reported being very happy. Very few happy men, only 4 percent, or women, only 9 percent, had incomes of less than $10 000. The greatest proportion of very happy men, 29 percent, fell into the highest income category (Keith and Landry, 1994:134).

PSYCHOLOGICAL CHANGES

Just as we tend to overstate the physical problems of aging, so it is easy to exaggerate the psychological changes that accompany growing old. Looking at intelligence over the life course, the conventional wisdom can be summed up in the simple rule "What goes up must come down" (Baltes and Schaie, 1974).

If we operationalize intelligence to refer to skills such as sensorimotor coordination—the ability to arrange objects to match a drawing—we do find a steady decline as people grow old. The ability to learn new material and to think quickly also appears to diminish, although not until around age seventy. But the ability to apply familiar ideas holds steady with advancing age, and some studies actually show improvement in verbal and mathematical skills (Baltes and Schaie, 1974; Schaie, 1980).

We all wonder if we will think or feel differently as we get older. Gerontologists assure us that, for better or for worse, the answer is usually no. The only common personality change with advancing age is becoming more introspective. That is, people become more engaged with their own thoughts and emotions and less materialistic. Generally, therefore, two elderly people who were childhood friends would recognize in each other many of the same personality traits that distinguished them as youngsters (Neugarten, 1971, 1972, 1977; Wolfe, 1994).

AGING AND CULTURE

<u>November 1, 1994, approaching Kandy, Sri Lanka.</u> Our small van struggles up the steep mountain incline. Breaks in the lush vegetation offer spectacular views that interrupt our conversation about growing old. "Then there are no old-age homes in your country?" I ask. "In Colombo and other cities, I am sure," our driver responds, "but not many; we are not like you North Americans." "And how is that?" I counter. His eyes remain fixed on the road: "We would not leave our fathers and mothers to live alone."

When do people grow old? How do younger people regard society's oldest members? The range of answers to these questions demonstrates that, while aging is universal, the significance of growing old is a variable element of culture.

At one level, how well—and, more basically, how long—people live is closely linked to a society's technology and overall standard of living. Throughout human history, as English philosopher Thomas Hobbes (1588–1679) put it, people's lives were "nasty, brutish, and short" (although Hobbes himself persisted to the ripe old age of ninety-one). In his day, most people married and had children while in their teens, became middle-aged in their twenties, and began to succumb to various illnesses in their thirties and forties. It took several more centuries for a rising standard of living and advancing medical technology to curb deadly infectious diseases. Living to, say, age fifty became commonplace only at the beginning of the twentieth century. Since then, a rising standard of living coupled with medical advances has added more than twenty years to people's longevity in industrial nations.

But living into what we call "old age" is not yet the rule in much of the world. Global Map 15–2 shows that, in the poorest countries, the average life span is less than forty-five years.

Just as significant as longevity is the importance societies attach to their senior members. Most industrial societies push their elderly to the margins, as noted below. Canada, as a whole, is no exception. On the other hand, Native elders are highly respected, as revealed in the "Applying Sociology" box.

AGE STRATIFICATION: A GLOBAL ASSESSMENT

Like race, ethnicity, and gender, age is a basis for socially ranking individuals. **Age stratification**, then, is *the unequal distribution of wealth, power, and privileges among people at different stages in the life course.* As is true of other dimensions of social hierarchy, age stratification varies according to a society's level of technological development.

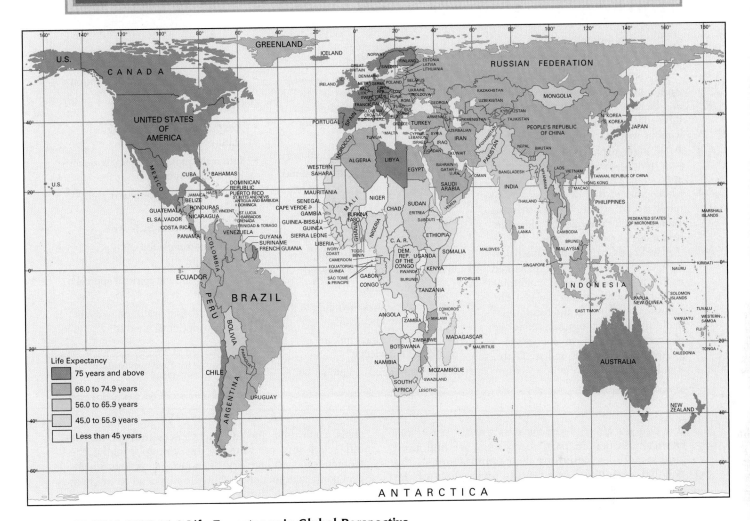

GLOBAL MAP 15–2 Life Expectancy in Global Perspective

Life expectancy has shot upward over the course of the past century in industrial countries including Canada, the United States, the nations of Western Europe, Japan, and Australia. A newborn in Canada can be expected to live about seventy-five years, and our life expectancy would be greater still were it not for the high risk of death among infants born into poverty. Since poverty is the rule in much of the world, lives are correspondingly shorter, especially in parts of Africa where life expectancy may be less than forty years.

Source: Population Reference Bureau (2001).

Hunting-and-Gathering Societies

As Chapter 4 ("Society") explains, without the technology to produce a surplus of food, hunters and gatherers are nomadic. Their survival depends on physical strength and stamina; thus, as members of these societies become elderly (in this case, reaching about age thirty) they become less active, leading others to consider them an economic burden (Sheehan, 1976).

Pastoral, Horticultural, and Agrarian Societies

With control over raising crops and animals, societies gain the capacity to produce a material surplus; consequently, individuals may accumulate considerable wealth over a lifetime. The most privileged members of these societies are typically the elderly, promoting **gerontocracy**, *a form of social organization*

Native Elders: Cultural Custodians

Aboriginal cultures have survived on Turtle Island (the Aboriginal name for North America) for thousands of years, for the most part without written records. Their values, skills, knowledge, laws, and histories have been passed on orally from generation to generation—and elders play a pivotal role in that transmission. The result is that, where Natives strive to maintain cultural traditions, elders are held in high esteem.

The Royal Commission on Aboriginal Peoples, in a massive report, published its findings on the social conditions of Native peoples across Canada. The following are some of the descriptions in the report that together define the position of elders—men and women—in Aboriginal societies and traditions. The Elders or Old Ones:

- Teach the "ancient wisdom about how to live, how to relate to the Creator, and how to coexist" with "brothers and sisters of the plant and animal world"
- Have insight, wisdom, and authority
- Have already walked a great distance on the path of life
- Have received "the gifts of experience and knowledge"
- "Live their lives by example, according to the laws of the Creator"
- Will recount stories and legends
- Are good listeners
- Apply spiritual understanding to community and family life
- Are "a contemporary link to traditional knowledge"
- See life as a sacred ceremony

- "Play a critical role in the retention, renewal and celebration of Aboriginal languages"
- Are the guardians of Aboriginal cultures
- Can make important contributions in the classroom
- Are teachers of the ethics of traditional justice
- Mediate when conflicts arise
- Lead the struggle for self-government
- Take a holistic and spiritual approach to healing
- Help youth find pride and strength in their Aboriginal identity

Source: Based on the Royal Commission on Aboriginal Peoples (1996:107–43).

in which the elderly have the most wealth, power, and prestige. Old people, particularly men, are honoured (and sometimes feared) by their families and, as the "Global Sociology" box reports in the case of the Abkhasians, they remain active leaders of society until they die. This veneration of the elderly also explains the widespread practice of ancestor worship in agrarian societies.

Industrial Societies

Industrialization pushes living standards upward, advances medical technology, and increases life expectancy. These same forces simultaneously erode the power and prestige of the elderly. In part, this decline reflects a shift in the prime source of wealth from land (typically controlled by the oldest members of society) to factories and other goods (often owned or managed by younger people). The peak earning years among Canadian workers, for instance, occur around age fifty; after that, earnings decline.

Modern living also separates the generations physically as children move away to pursue their careers; therefore, they depend less on their parents and more on their own earning power. Furthermore, because industrial, urban societies change rapidly, the

skills, traditions, and life experiences that served the old seem less relevant to the young. Finally, the tremendous productivity of industrial nations means that some members of society do not need to work; as a result, most of the very old and the very young remain in nonproductive roles (Cohn, 1982).

Over the long term, all these factors are transforming *elders* (a term with positive connotations) into the *elderly* (commanding far less prestige). In mature, industrial societies such as Canada and the United States, economic and political leaders are usually middle-aged people who combine seasoned experience with up-to-date skills. In rapidly changing sectors of the economy—especially high-tech fields—many key executives are much younger and sometimes barely out of university or college. Industrial societies often consign older people to marginal participation in the economy because these people lack the knowledge and training demanded by a fast-changing marketplace.

Certainly some elderly men and women remain at the helm of businesses they own but, more commonly, older people predominate in traditional occupations (such as barber and tailor) and jobs that involve minimal activity (night security guard, for instance) (Kaufman and Spilerman, 1982).

Growing (Very) Old: A Report from Abkhasia

Anthropologist Sula Benet was sharing wine and conversation with a man in Tamish, a small village in the Republic of Abkhasia, once part of the Soviet Union. Judging the man to be about seventy, she raised her glass and offered a toast to his long life. "May you live as long as Moses," she exclaimed. The gesture of goodwill fell flat: Moses lived to 120, but Benet's companion was already 119.

An outsider—especially an open-minded anthropologist who studies many of the world's mysteries—should be skeptical of the longevity claims made by some Abkhasians. In one village of 1200 visited by Benet, for example, 200 people declared their age to be over eighty. But government statistics confirm that, even if some Abkhasians exaggerate their longevity, most outlive the average North American.

What accounts for this remarkable life span? The answer certainly is not the advanced medical technology in which North Americans place such

faith; many Abkhasians have never seen a physician nor entered a hospital.

The probable explanation is cultural, including diet and physical activity. Abkhasians eat little saturated fat (which is linked to heart disease), use no sugar, and drink no coffee or tea; few smoke or chew tobacco. They consume large amounts of healthful fruits and vegetables and drink lots of buttermilk and low-alcohol wine. Additionally, Abkhasians maintain active lives built around regular physical work for people of all ages.

Moreover, Abkhasians live according to a well-defined and consistent set of traditional values, which confers on all a strong feeling of belonging and a clear sense of purpose. Here, the elderly remain active and valued members of the community, instead of being pushed to the margins of social life. As Benet explains, "The old [in the United States], when they do not simply vegetate, out of view and out of mind, keep themselves 'busy' with bingo and shuf-

fleboard." For their part, the Abkhasians do not even have a word for old people and have no notion of retiring. Furthermore, younger people accord their senior members great prestige and respect since, in their minds, advanced age confers the greatest wisdom. Elders are indispensable guardians of culture and preside at important ceremonial occasions, where they transmit their knowledge to the young. In Abkhasia, in short, people look to the old, rather than the young, for models of how to live life.

Given their positive approach to growing old, Abkhasians expect to lead long and useful lives. They feel needed because, in their own minds and everyone else's, they are. Far from being a burden, elders stand at the centre of society.

Source: Based on Benet (1971).

Japan: An Exceptional Case

Japan stands out as an exception to the rule: it maintains a traditional culture that elevates the prestige of

older people. Most aged people in Japan live with an adult son or daughter and continue to play a significant role in family life. Elderly men in Japan are also more likely than their counterparts in North America to

TABLE 15–1 Happiness Reported by Senior Men and Women by Health of Self and Spouse, 1996–97

	Percentage Who Are Happy	
	Senior Men	Senior Women
In good health		
Spouse in good health	96%	90%
Spouse in poor health	88	94
In poor health		
Spouse in good health	77	64
Spouse in poor health	64	60

Source: Adapted by Gerber from Crompton and Kemeny (2000:48).

TABLE 15–2 Private Household Living Arrangements among the Elderly,[*] 1991 (Percentages)

	Men	Women
Living with spouse	70%	38%
Living alone	14	34
Living with others[**]	4	8

[*]The majority of the elderly (83.5 percent) maintain their own households.
[**]Includes both relatives and nonrelatives.

Source: Adapted from Che-Alford et al. (1994: Table 3.3).

remain in the labour force, and in many Japanese corporations the oldest employees enjoy the greatest respect. But even Japan is steadily becoming more like other industrial societies, in which growing old means giving up a large measure of social importance (Harlan, 1968; Cowgill and Holmes, 1972; Treas, 1979; Palmore, 1982; Yates, 1986).

TRANSITIONS AND PROBLEMS OF AGING

We confront change at each stage of life. People must unlearn self-concepts and social patterns that no longer apply to their lives and simultaneously learn to cope with new circumstances. Of all stages of the life course, however, old age presents the greatest challenges.

Physical decline in old age is less serious than most younger people think, but even small changes can cause emotional stress. Older people endure more pain, become resigned to limiting their activities, adjust to greater dependence on others, and see in the deaths of friends or relatives frequent reminders of their own mortality. Moreover, because our culture places such a premium on youth, aging often means added frustration, fear, and self-doubt (Hamel, 1990). As one retired psychologist commented about entering old age, "Don't let the current hype about the joys of retirement fool you. They are not the best of times. It's just that the alternative is even worse" (Rubenstein, 1991:13).

FINDING MEANING

Recall from Chapter 5 ("Socialization") Erik Erikson's (1963, orig. 1950; 1980) theory that elderly people must resolve a tension of "integrity versus despair." No matter how much they still may be learning and achieving, older people recognize that their lives are nearing an end. Thus, the elderly spend much time reflecting on their past accomplishments and disappointments. To shore up their personal integrity,

Erikson explains, older women and men must face up to past mistakes as well as savour their successes. Otherwise, this stage of life may turn into a time of despair with little positive meaning.

Research suggests that most people who find satisfaction and meaning in earlier stages of life are likely to achieve personal well-being in old age.

Negative myths about the health, happiness, and sexuality of the elderly abound (McPherson, 1990). Some elderly people share this dim view of their plight, but most have a more positive outlook. As Table 15–1 indicates, a large majority of senior men and women consider themselves to be happy—especially if these men and women and their partners are in good health. Those most likely to report happiness (96 percent) are men in good health with partners in good health. The least likely to report happiness (60 percent) are senior women in poor health with partners in poor health. Married elders have advantages over single ones in a number of areas, including morbidity (their rate of illness), mortality, and psychological well-being. Marriage appears to be particularly advantageous for elderly males because it unites them with a network of other people more easily than singlehood (Nett, 1993).

Overall, research suggests that, while personal adjustments are necessary, the experience of growing old in Canada often provides much cause for joy. However, a person's view does vary based on individual personality, family circumstances, social class, and financial position. People who adapt successfully to changes earlier in life can confidently look forward to deriving satisfaction and meaning from their lives later on (Neugarten, 1971; Palmore, 1979a).

In 2003, at least four new North American books tried to help older people—especially the retired—answer questions about the meaning of life. Some help elders achieve spiritual goals, while others stress making a continuing contribution to society through volunteering or otherwise becoming active and making a positive difference. With the proper outlook, old age provides the opportunity to develop wisdom, balance, gratitude, and self-awareness (Todd, 2003).

SOCIAL ISOLATION

Being alone may provoke anxiety in people of any age; isolation, however, is most common among elderly people. Retirement closes off workplace social interaction, physical problems may limit mobility, and negative stereotypes depicting the elderly as "over the hill" may discourage younger people from close social contact with their elders.

The greatest cause of social isolation, however, is the inevitable death of significant others. Few human experiences affect people as profoundly as the death of a spouse. One study found that almost three-quarters of widows and widowers cited loneliness as their most serious problem (Lund, 1989). Widows and widowers must rebuild their lives in the absence of people with whom they may have spent most of their adult lives. Some survivors choose not to live at all. One study of elderly men noted a sharp increase in mortality, sometimes by suicide, in the months following the deaths of their wives (Benjamin and Wallis, 1963).

Women, who typically outlive their husbands, are more likely to face isolation—as they more often live alone (see Table 15–2). While some studies have found that elderly women suffer more mental health problems as a result of isolation (Nett, 1993), others have found that half of senior widows *choose* to live in the homes they once shared with their husbands. In doing so they rely on a wider range of social supports than men do (McDaniel, 1994). As illustrated in Figure 15–2, the 1995 General Social Survey revealed that senior widows have close emotional ties to neighbours, in particular, as well as friends, other relatives, and their adult children (Bess, 2000). However, living alone—a valued dimension of autonomy—presumes the financial means to do so.

It may surprise you to learn that women who are widowed later in life (i.e., between the ages of 65 and 74) are three times more likely to live by themselves than women who were widowed before they were 65 (Bess, 2000:167). One reason may be that younger widows move in with their children to help raise their grandchildren. Older widows may not be needed in the child-rearing role and may not feel they have the energy. On the other hand, older widows who have grown accustomed to an empty nest and have created new lives for themselves without their adult children might be more reluctant to give up their independence by moving into a three-generation household. The formation of three-generation households is related to ethnicity as well. Recent immigrants, from Asia in particular, are more likely than other Canadians to have their parents or widowed mothers live in their homes (Gerber, 1983; Che-Alford and Hamm, 2000).

RETIREMENT

Work not only provides us with earnings but, it also figures prominently in our personal identities. Retirement

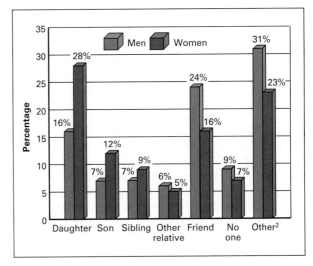

FIGURE 15–2 Sources of Emotional Support for Elderly Men and Women without Spouses,[1] **1990**

[1]Includes persons without sons, daughters, siblings, etc.
[2]Includes neighbours, co-workers, clergy, doctors, professional counsellors, others, and "don't know." None of these specific sources exceeded 5 percent.

Source: Statistics Canada, *General Social Survey, 1990,* cited in McDaniel (1994:130).

from paid work, therefore, generally entails some reduction in income, diminished social prestige, and some loss of purpose in life (Chown, 1977).

Some organizations strive to ease this transition. Universities and colleges, for example, confer the title of "professor emeritus" (from Latin, meaning "fully earned") on retired faculty members, who are permitted to maintain their library privileges, parking spaces, and email accounts.

For many older people, fresh activities and new interests minimize the personal disruption and loss of prestige brought on by retirement. Volunteer work can be personally rewarding, allowing individuals to apply their career skills to new challenges and opportunities. Seventeen percent of men and 16 percent of women report that they engage in volunteer work after retirement. Others return to the labour force after retirement for part-time work, for alternative careers, or as individual entrepreneurs.

Although the idea of retirement is familiar to us, it emerged only within the last century and only in industrial societies (Atchley, 1982). Advancing technology reduces the need for everyone to work and places a premium on up-to-date skills. Retirement permits younger workers, who presumably have the most current knowledge and training, to predominate in the labour force. Then, too, the establishment of private and public pension programs offers the economic foundation for retirement. In poor societies that depend on the labour of everyone, and where no pension programs exist, most people work until they can work no more.

Given how varied the elderly population is, we might wonder exactly when (or even if) we should expect people to retire. Vast differences in the interests and capacities of older people suggest that no one standard will serve the interests of all.

In Canada, retirement at sixty-five is closely tied to the development of pension plans. This is the age, too, when mandatory retirement comes into effect for some workers. There is an ongoing debate about whether mandatory retirement violates the individual's right to work as guaranteed under the *Canadian Charter of Rights and Freedoms*. But while about one-half of the Canadian workforce has been subject to mandatory retirement regulations, only about 1 percent of the workforce would continue to work past sixty-five if given the choice (Tindale, 1991). With Ontario eliminating mandatory retirement in 2003, we will be able to observe the impact on retirement patterns.

Today, with rapid transitions in the Canadian economy resulting from global economic restructuring, new free trade agreements, and a general move to the political right, more and more people are being forced out of work or encouraged to take early retirement. Many of those who have been given the "golden handshake" in this era of unprecedented numbers of employee buyouts are embarking on brand new careers. Severance packages, which may be as high as two years' salary, are often used as the initial investment for the new venture (Lipovenko, 1996).

AGING AND INCOME

On the whole, the image of the elderly as poverty-stricken is unfounded: the poverty rate among the elderly has declined substantially between 1980 and 1998. Among the elderly who live with their spouses or other family members, poverty levels have declined from 18 percent in 1980 to 16.1 percent in 2001. The unattached elderly endured low income at levels of 68 and 42 percent in 1980 and 2001, respectively. Overall, however, 83 percent of the elderly live above the low-income level and some of them are affluent.

For most Canadians, retirement leads to a significant decline in income. For many, home mortgages and children's university expenses are paid off; yet the expenses for medical and dental care, household help, and home utilities typically rise. Many elderly people lack sufficient savings or pension benefits to be self-supporting; for this reason, various pension programs, including the Canada Pension Plan, are their greatest source of income. Because many retirees live with fixed incomes, inflation tends to affect them

 Help the Aged Canada is a nonprofit organization designed to assist elders in Canada and developing countries: see www.helptheaged.ca/

more severely than it does younger working people. Women and people of colour are especially likely to find that growing old means growing poorer.

Gender continues to shape the lives of people as they age. Elderly women are more likely to be poor than elderly men—in 2001, 46 percent of unattached elderly women and 33 percent of elderly men were poor. Income inequality between different ethnic and racial groups is also not blunted by growing old.

What is distinctive about the privation of the elderly, however, is that it is often hidden from view. Because of personal pride and a desire to maintain the dignity of independent living, many elderly people conceal financial problems even from their own families. It is often difficult for people who have supported their children for years to admit that they can no longer provide for themselves, even though it may be through no fault of their own.

ABUSE OF THE ELDERLY

In Canada, we seem to awaken to social problems in stages: we became aware of child abuse during the 1960s, spouse abuse in the 1970s, and elder abuse in the 1980s. Abuse of older people takes many forms, from passive neglect to active torment, and includes verbal, emotional, financial, and physical harm. Most elderly people suffer from none of these, but research suggests that in Canada, Europe, and the United States, the incidence of elder abuse and neglect ranges from 3 to 5 percent. Like other forms of family violence, abuse of the elderly often goes unreported because victims are reluctant to talk about their plight. But as the proportion of elderly people rises, so does the incidence of abuse (Bruno, 1985; Clark, 1986; Pillemer, 1988; Holmstrom, 1994).

What motivates people to abuse the elderly? Often the cause lies in the stress—both financial and emotional—of caregiving. Today's middle-aged adults are a "sandwich generation" who may well spend as much time caring for their aging parents as for their own children. This caregiving responsibility is especially pronounced among adult women who look after parents and children *and* hold down jobs as well.

Even in Japan—where tradition demands that adult children care for aging parents at home—more and more people find themselves unable to cope. Abuse appears to be most common when the stress is greatest: in families with an elder suffering from serious health problems. Here, family life may be grossly distorted by demands and tensions that caregivers simply cannot endure, even if their intentions are good (Douglass, 1983; Gelman, 1985; Yates, 1986).

AGEISM

In earlier chapters, we explained how ideology—including racism and sexism—serves to justify the social disadvantages of minorities. Sociologists use the parallel term **ageism** to designate *prejudice and discrimination against the elderly.*

Like racism and sexism, ageism can be blatant (as when a university decides not to hire a sixty-year-old professor because of her age) or subtle (as when a nurse speaks to elderly patients with a condescending tone, as if they were children) (Kalish, 1979). Also like racism and sexism, ageism builds physical traits into stereotypes; in the case of the elderly, people consider greying hair, wrinkled skin, and stooped posture signs of personal incompetence. Negative stereotypes picture the aged as helpless, confused, resistant to change, and generally unhappy (Butler, 1975). Even sentimental notions of sweet little old ladies and charmingly eccentric old gentlemen gloss over people's individuality and ignore years of experience and accomplishment.

Sometimes, like other expressions of prejudice, ageism has some foundation in reality. Statistically speaking, old people are more likely than young people to be mentally and physically impaired. But we slip into ageism when we make unwarranted generalizations about an entire category of people, most of whom do not conform to the stereotypes.

Betty Friedan (1993), a pioneer of the contemporary feminist movement, believes ageism is central to our culture. Friedan points out that elderly people are still conspicuously absent in the mass media: only a small percentage of television shows, for example, include main characters over sixty. More generally, when most of us do think about older people, it is often in negative terms: this older man lacks a job, that older woman has lost her vitality, and seniors look back to their youth. In short, we tend to think about being old as a disease—marked by decline and deterioration—for which there is no cure.

Rejecting such pessimism, Friedan points out that there are women and men who are discovering that they have far more to contribute than realized. Playing in orchestras, advising small business owners, designing housing for the poor, teaching children to read—there are countless ways in which older people can enhance their own lives and help others.

THE ELDERLY: A MINORITY?

No one doubts that the elderly in Canada do face social disadvantages. But sociologists disagree as to whether the aged form a minority in the same way as, say, Native Canadians or women do.

Leonard Breen (1960) was the first to pronounce the elderly a minority, noting that older people have a clear social identity based on their age and are subject to prejudice and discrimination. Yet, Gordon Streib (1968) countered, minority status is usually both permanent and exclusive. That is, a person is a Native Canadian or a woman *for life* and cannot become part of the dominant category of white males. Being eld-

Sarah Abel, 101 years old, lived in the isolated village of Old Crow above the Arctic Circle in the northern tip of the Yukon until her death in August 1998. Only at 100 years of age did she move out of the home in which she had raised seventeen children—on her own after her husband died of tuberculosis. She drove a dogsled, hunted moose and muskrat, and tanned her own hides: in other words, she did whatever had to be done. She had vivid memories of the past and told stories in person or on the CBC in her native tongue (Gwitchin). As someone who had never touched alcohol, she worried a great deal about the social costs of alcohol abuse in her community (Brend, 1997).

erly, Streib continued, is an *open* status because people are elderly for only part of their lives, and anyone who lives long enough grows old.

Streib made a further point. The social disadvantages faced by the elderly are less substantial than those experienced by the minorities described in earlier chapters. For example, old people have never been deprived of the right to own property, to vote, or to hold office, as Native Canadians and women have. Some elderly people, of course, do suffer economic disadvantages, but these do not stem primarily from old age. Instead, most of the aged poor fall into categories of people likely to be poor at any age. To Streib, it is less true that "the old grow poor" than it is that "the poor grow old."

In light of Streib's arguments and the rising economic fortunes of the elderly in recent decades, it seems reasonable to conclude that old people are not a minority in the same sense as other categories are. Perhaps the best way to describe the elderly is simply as a distinctive segment of our population with characteristic pleasures and challenges.

There may be reasons to disengage elderly people from some critical work roles. But research shows that, for most people, satisfaction in old age (or, for that matter, at any age) depends on maintaining a high level of meaningful activity. A rising number of seniors are finding that they have much to contribute to others.

THEORETICAL ANALYSIS OF AGING

Each of sociology's major theoretical paradigms sheds light on the process of aging in Canada. We examine each in turn.

STRUCTURAL-FUNCTIONAL ANALYSIS: AGING AND DISENGAGEMENT

Drawing on the ideas of Talcott Parsons—an architect of the structural-functional paradigm—Elaine Cumming and William Henry (1961) point out that aging threatens to disrupt society as physical decline and death take their toll. Society's response, they claim, is to disengage the elderly—to gradually transfer statuses and roles from the old to the young so that tasks are performed with minimal interruption.

Disengagement is thus a strategy to promote the orderly functioning of society by easing aging people from productive roles while they are still able to perform them. Such disengagement has an added benefit in a rapidly changing society, since young workers typically bring the most up-to-date skills and training to their work. Formally, then, **disengagement theory** is *the proposition that society enhances its orderly operation by disengaging people from positions of responsibility as they reach old age.*

Disengagement may benefit elderly people as well as society. Aging individuals with diminishing capacities presumably look forward to relinquishing some of the pressures of their jobs in favour of new pursuits of their own choosing (Palmore, 1979b). Society also grants older people greater freedom, so that unusual behaviour on their part is construed as harmless eccentricity rather than dangerous deviance.

Critical evaluation. As a strategy for dealing with human decline, disengagement theory explains why rapidly changing, industrial societies typically define their oldest members as socially marginal. But there are also several limitations to this approach.

Many workers cannot readily disengage from paid work because they do not have sufficient financial resources to fall back on. Furthermore, many elderly people—regardless of their financial circumstances—do not wish to disengage from their productive roles. Disengagement, after all, comes at a high price, including loss of social prestige and social isolation. It is far from clear that the benefits of disengagement outweigh its social costs. There is the loss of human resources on the one hand and, on the other, the costs of increased care for people who might otherwise be able to fend for themselves. Indeed, as the numbers of elderly people swell, finding ways to help seniors remain independent will be a high priority. Lastly, a rigid system of disengagement does not allow for widely differing abilities among the elderly.

SYMBOLIC-INTERACTION ANALYSIS: AGING AND ACTIVITY

One rebuttal to disengagement theory draws heavily on the symbolic-interaction paradigm. **Activity theory** is *the proposition that a high level of activity enhances personal satisfaction in old age.* Because individuals build their social identities from statuses and roles, disengagement is bound to reduce satisfaction and meaning in elderly people's lives. What seniors need, in short, is not to be yanked out of roles, but to be offered a wider range of productive and recreational activities.

Activity theory does not reject the notion of disengagement; rather, it proposes that people substitute new roles and responsibilities for those they leave behind. After all, as members of a society that celebrates productivity, the elderly enjoy active lives as much as younger people do. Research confirms that elderly people who maintain high activity levels derive the most satisfaction from their lives.

Activity theory also recognizes that the elderly are no monolithic category. Older people have highly variable needs, interests, and physical abilities that guide their activities. Therefore, the activities people pursue and the vigour of their pursuit is always an individual matter (Havighurst et al., 1968; Neugarten, 1977; Palmore, 1979a).

Critical evaluation. Activity theory shifts the focus of analysis from the needs of society (as stated in disengagement theory) to the needs of the elderly themselves. It emphasizes the social diversity among elderly people, an important consideration in formulating any government policy.

A limitation of this theory, from a structural-functionalist perspective, is exaggeration of the well-being and competence of the elderly. Critics ask if we really want the elderly actively serving in crucial roles, say, as physicians or airline pilots. Alternatively, activity theory falls short by overlooking the fact that many problems of older people have to do with how society—not the individual—operates. Social conflict theory takes a different approach to the problem.

SOCIAL-CONFLICT ANALYSIS: AGING AND INEQUALITY

A social-conflict analysis is based on the idea that different age categories have different opportunities and different access to social resources, creating a system of age stratification. By and large, middle-aged people in Canada enjoy the greatest power and the most opportunities and privileges, while the elderly (as well as children) contend with less power and prestige and a higher risk of poverty. Employers often replace elderly workers with younger men and women as a way of keeping down wages. Consequently, as conflict theorists see it, older people may well become second-class citizens (Atchley, 1982; Phillipson, 1982).

To conflict theorists, age-based hierarchy is inherent in industrial-capitalist society. Following the ideas of Karl Marx, Steven Spitzer (1980) points out that because our society has an overriding concern with profit, we devalue those categories of people who are economically unproductive. Viewed as mildly deviant because they are less efficient than their younger counterparts, Spitzer reasons, the elderly are destined to be marginal members of a society that is consumed by material gain.

Social-conflict analysis also draws attention to social diversity in the elderly population. Differences of class, race, ethnicity, and gender splinter older people as they do everyone else. The fortunate seniors in higher social classes have more economic security, greater access to top medical care, and more options

Our society has long been concerned with "the good life"; more recently, attention has turned to the idea of a good death. The hospice movement is an important part of this trend. In some cases, terminally ill patients move to a hospice facility, where professional staff provide medical support and emotional comfort. In other cases, hospice workers provide care in the familiar surroundings of a person's home.

for personal satisfaction in old age than others do. Also, the elderly of the dominant group typically enjoy a host of advantages denied to minority elders—recent immigrants, visible minorities, and Aboriginals. And women—who represent an increasing majority of the elderly population with advancing age—suffer the social and economic disadvantages of both sexism and ageism.

Critical evaluation. Social-conflict theory adds to our understanding of the aging process by underscoring age-based inequality and explaining how capitalism devalues elderly people who are less productive. The implication of this analysis is that the aged fare better in noncapitalist societies, a view that has some support in research (Treas, 1979).

One shortcoming of this approach goes right to its core: capitalism is not to blame for the lower social standing of elderly people, say critics; industrialization is the culprit. Socialism might not lessen age stratification. Furthermore, the notion that capitalism dooms the elderly to economic distress is challenged by the steady rise in the income and well-being among the North American elderly in recent decades.

DEATH AND DYING

To every thing there is a season,
And a time to every purpose under the heaven:
A time to be born, and a time to die . . .

These well-known lines from the *Book of Ecclesiastes* in the Bible state two basic truths about human existence: the fact of birth and the inevitability of death. Just as life varies in striking ways throughout history and around the world, so death, too, has many faces. We conclude this chapter with a brief look at the changing character of death—the final stage in the process of growing old.

HISTORICAL PATTERNS OF DEATH

Throughout most of history, confronting death was commonplace. Fearing that a newborn child would not live long led some parents to delay naming children until they survived for a year or two. For those fortunate enough to survive infancy, illness, accident, and natural catastrophe combined to make life uncertain, at best.

At times, societies facing food shortages have protected the majority by sacrificing the least productive members—through infanticide (killing of newborns) and geronticide (killing of the elderly).

If death was routine, it was also readily accepted. Medieval Christianity assured Europeans, for example, that death fit into the divine plan for human existence. To illustrate, historian Philippe Ariès describes how Sir Lancelot, one of King Arthur's fearless Knights of the Round Table, prepared for his own death when he believed himself mortally wounded:

> His gestures were fixed by old customs, ritual gestures which must be carried out when one is about to die. He removed his weapons and lay quietly upon the ground.... He spread his arms out, his body forming a cross ... in such a way that his head faced east toward Jerusalem. (1974:7–8)

As societies gradually gained more knowledge about health, death became less of an everyday experience. Fewer children died in infancy, and accidents and disease took a smaller toll among adults. Except in times of war or catastrophe, people came to view dying as quite extraordinary, except among the very old. In 1900, about one-third of all deaths in Canada occurred before the age of five, another third occurred before the age of fifty-five, and the remaining third of men and women died in what was then defined as old age. By 1995, 85 percent of our population died after the age of fifty-five. Thus, death and old age have become fused in our culture.

THE MODERN SEPARATION OF LIFE AND DEATH

Now removed from everyday experience, death appears as something unnatural. If social conditions prepared our ancestors to accept their deaths, modern society—with its youth culture and aggressive medical technology—has fostered a desire for immortality, or eternal youth. Death is no longer part of life.

Death is also physically removed from everyday activities. The clearest evidence of this is that few of us have seen a person die. While our ancestors typically died at home in the presence of family and friends, most deaths today occur in impersonal settings such as hospitals and nursing homes. Hospitals often relegate dying patients to a special part of the building, and hospital morgues are located out of sight of patients and visitors alike (Sudnow, 1967; Ariès, 1974).

ETHICAL ISSUES: CONFRONTING DEATH

Moral questions are more pressing than ever now that technological advances give humans the power to prolong life and, therefore, to draw the line separating life and death. We now grapple with how to use these new powers, or whether to use them at all.

When Does Death Occur?

Perhaps the most basic question is one of the most difficult: Precisely how do we define death? Common sense suggests that life ceases when breathing and the heartbeat stop. But the ability to revive or replace a heart and artificially sustain breathing renders such notions of death obsolete. Medical and legal experts now define death as an irreversible state involving no response to stimulation, no movement or breathing, no reflexes, and no indication of brain activity (Ladd, 1979; Wall, 1980).

The "Right to Die" Debate

The popularity of the book *Final Exit*, described in the opening to this chapter, suggests that many aging people are less terrified of death than the prospect of being kept alive at all costs. Medical technology now threatens personal autonomy by letting doctors rather than the dying person decide when life is to end. In response, many people now seek control over their deaths just as they seek control over their lives.

Individuals are now taking the initiative and choosing not to employ medical technology to prolong life. After long deliberation, patients, families, and doctors may decide to forgo "heroic measures" to resuscitate a person who is dying. Living wills—statements of which medical procedures an individual wants and does not want under specific conditions—are now widespread.

A more difficult issue involves **euthanasia or mercy killing**, *assisting in the death of a person suffering from an incurable disease*. Euthanasia (from the Greek, meaning "a good death") poses an ethical dilemma since it involves not just refusing life-extending treatment but actively taking steps to end life. Some see euthanasia as an act of kindness, while others find it a form of killing.

Death on Demand: A Report from the Netherlands

Marcus Erich picked up the telephone and dialled his brother Arjen's number. In a quiet voice, thirty-two-year-old Marcus announced, "It's Friday at 5 o'clock." When the time came, Arjen was there, having driven to his brother's farmhouse an hour south of Amsterdam. They said their final goodbyes. Soon afterward, Marcus's physician arrived. Marcus and the doctor spoke for a few moments, and the doctor then prepared a "cocktail" of barbiturates and other drugs. As Marcus drank the mixture, he made a face, joking, "Can't you make this sweeter?"

As the minutes passed, Marcus lay back and his eyes closed. But after half an hour, he was still breathing. At that point, according to their earlier agreement, the doctor administered a lethal injection. In a few minutes, Marcus's life came to an end.

Events like this take us to the heart of the belief that people should have a "right to die." Marcus Erich was dying from the virus that causes AIDS. For five years, his body had wasted away so that he was suffering greatly and had no hope of recovery. It was then that he asked his doctor to end his life.

The Netherlands, a small nation in northwestern Europe, has gone further than any nation in the world in allowing mercy killing or euthanasia. A Dutch law, enacted in 1981, allows a physician to assist in a suicide if the following five conditions are met:

- The patient must take a voluntary, well-considered, and repeated request to the doctor for help in dying.
- The patient's suffering must be unbearable and without prospect of improvement.

- The doctor and the patient must discuss alternatives.
- The doctor must consult with at least one colleague who has access to the patient and the patient's medical records.
- The assisted suicide must be performed in accordance with sound medical practice.

In 1995, according to official records, doctors ended the lives of 3600 people in the Netherlands. Since many such cases are never reported, the actual number is probably at least twice that many. A rough estimate is that, today, about 5 percent of the Dutch people die with the assistance of a physician.

Sources: Based on della Cava (1997) and Mauro (1997).

In Canada and the United States, euthanasia is illegal, including physician-assisted suicide for the elderly and terminally ill, but the issue continues to be hotly debated. The Netherlands, in contrast, has the most permissive euthanasia law in the world. The "Global Sociology" box takes a closer look.

Should Canada hold the line on euthanasia or follow the lead of the Dutch? Supporters of the "right to die" maintain that, faced with unbearable suffering, an individual should be able to choose to live or die. And, if death is the choice, medical assistance can help people achieve a "good death."

For more information about the right-to-die movement, see Derek Humphry's webpage at www.euthanasia.com/

On the other side of the debate, opponents fear that opening the door to physician-assisted suicide invites abuse. Some point to the Netherlands: in about one-third of all cases, critics estimate, the five conditions noted in the box are not strictly met. In 1991, moreover, a Dutch doctor assisted in the death of a woman who was not dying at all, but was simply depressed over the death of her two sons. (The doctor was prosecuted, but not punished.) More generally,

opponents fear that legalization will put society on a "slippery slope" towards more and more euthanasia. Can anyone deny, they ask, that ill people may be pushed into accepting death by doctors who consider suicide the "right" choice for the terminally ill or by family members who are weary of caring for them or who want to avoid the expenses of medical care?

However the debate over the "right to die" turns out in the future, our society has entered a new era when it comes to dying. Individuals, family members, and medical personnel often must face death not as a medical fact but as a negotiated outcome (Flynn, 1991; Humphry, 1991; Markson, 1992).

BEREAVEMENT

Chapter 5 ("Socialization") describes stages by which people usually confront their own death. Elisabeth Kübler-Ross (1969) claims that individuals initially react with denial, then swell with anger, try to negotiate a divine intervention, gradually fall into resignation, and, finally, reach acceptance. Those who will face the loss of a significant person must also adjust to the approaching death.

CONTROVERSY & DEBATE

Setting Limits: Must We "Pull the Plug" on Old Age?

Because death struck at any time, often without warning, our ancestors would have found the question "Can people live too long?" absurd. In recent decades, a surge in the elderly population, widespread support for using technology to prolong life, and a dizzying increase in the costs of life-extending medical technology have prompted people to wonder how much old age we can now afford.

Currently, about half of the total lifetime medical costs of care for an individual are incurred during that individual's final years of life, and this share is projected to increase. Against the spiralling costs of prolonging life, then, we may well have to ask if what is technically possible is necessarily socially desirable. Gerontologist Daniel Callahan warns that a surging elderly population, ready and eager to extend their lives, will eventually force us either to "pull the plug" on old age or to shortchange everyone else.

To even raise this issue, Callahan concedes, smacks of a lack of caring. But consider that the annual bill for elder health care continues to grow substantially. This dramatic boost reflects our current policy of directing more and more medical resources towards studying and treating diseases and disabilities common to old age.

So Callahan makes a bold case for limits. He reasons that to spend more on behalf of the elderly we must spend less on others. With a serious problem of poverty among children, he asks, can we continue to direct more money towards the needs of the oldest members of our society at the expense of those just growing up?

Further, Callahan reminds us, a *longer* life does not necessarily make for a *better* life. Costs aside, does stressful heart surgery that may prolong the life of an eighty-four-year-old woman for a year or two truly improve the quality of her life? Costs considered, would those resources yield more "quality of life" if used, say, to transplant a kidney into a ten-year-old boy?

Callahan urges us to reconsider our notion of death. Today, many people rage against death as an enemy to be conquered at all costs. Yet, he suggests, a sensible health care program for an aging society must acknowledge death as a natural end to the life course. If we cannot make peace with death for our own well-being, limited financial resources demand that we do so for the benefit of others.

A compelling counterpoint, of course, is that those people who have worked all their lives to make our society what it is should, in their final years, enjoy society's generosity. Can we ethically deny an aging individual medical care as our medical care budget is reduced?

What is clear from everyone's point of view is that, in the coming years, we will face questions that few would have imagined even fifty years ago: Is optimum longevity good for everyone? Is it even possible for everyone?

Continue the debate . . .

1. *Should doctors and hospitals devise a double standard, offering complete care to the youngest people but more limited care to society's oldest members?*

2. *Do you think our cultural avoidance of death drives us to extend life at all costs?*

3. *Is the idea of rationing medical care really new? Hasn't our society historically done exactly this by allowing some people to amass more wealth than others?*

Source: Callahan (1987).

According to some researchers, bereavement parallels the stages of dying described by Kübler-Ross. Those close to a dying person, for instance, may initially deny the reality of impending death, reaching the point of acceptance only in time. Other investigators question the validity of any linear "stage theory," arguing that bereavement may not follow a rigid schedule (Lund et al., 1986; Lund, 1989). But all the experts agree that how family and friends view a death influences the attitudes of the person who is dying: acceptance by others of approaching death helps the dying person do the same. Also, denial of impending death may isolate the dying person, who is then unable to share feelings and experiences with others.

One recent development intended to provide emotional and other support to dying people is the hospice. Unlike a hospital, which is designed to cure disease, a hospice helps people have a good death by providing palliative care rather than active treatment. These care centres for dying people work to minimize pain and suffering—either there or at home—and encourage family members to remain close by (Stoddard, 1978). Similar palliative care centres have also been opened within hospitals.

Even under the most favourable circumstances, bereavement may involve profound grief and social disorientation that persist for some time. Research reveals that bereavement is less intense among people

Looking ahead in the twenty-first century, the elderly will represent an increasing share of the Canadian population. How do you think this trend will affect the experiences and attitudes of the young?

who accept the death of a loved one and feel that their relationship with the dying person has reached a satisfactory resolution. By taking the opportunity to bring an appropriate closure to their relationship with a dying person, in other words, family and friends are better able to comfort and support one another after the death has occurred (Atchley, 1983).

LOOKING AHEAD: AGING IN THE TWENTY-FIRST CENTURY

This chapter has explored a remarkable trend: the "greying" of Canada. Indeed, we can predict with confidence that the ranks of the elderly will swell dramatically in the decades to come: by 2050, our elderly population alone will exceed the population of the entire country back in 1900. One in five of these seniors will be over the age of eighty-five. Within the next fifty years, in other words, society's oldest members will gain unprecedented visibility and influence in our everyday lives. As this prediction is realized, gerontology, the study of the elderly, will also grow in stature as part of an expansion of research in all fields directed towards aging and the elderly. The reshaping of the age structure of our society raises many serious concerns. With more people living to increasingly advanced ages, will the support services they need be available? Remember, too, that as the elderly make unprecedented demands, our society will comprise proportionately fewer younger people to meet their needs. And what about the spiralling medical care costs of an aging society? As the baby boomers enter old age, some analysts paint a doomsday picture of their future.

But not all the signs are so ominous. For one thing, the health of tomorrow's elderly people (that is, today's young and middle-aged adults) is better than ever: smoking is decreasing and the consumption of healthy foods is increasing. Such trends probably mean that the elderly of the next generation will be more vigorous and independent than their counterparts are today. Moreover, tomorrow's old people will enjoy the benefits of steadily advancing medical technology although, as the "Controversy & Debate" box explains, seniors require a disproportionate share of our national resources, raising an issue that is already sparking heated debate.

Another positive sign is the surging financial strength of the elderly. Costs of living are certain to rise, but tomorrow's elderly will confront them with unprecedented affluence. Note, too, that the baby boomers will be the first cohort of Canadian seniors in which the vast majority of women have been in the labour force, a fact reflected in their substantial savings and pensions.

On balance, there are reasons for both concern and optimism as we look ahead. But there can be no doubt that younger adults will face a mounting responsibility to care for aging parents. Indeed, as the birth rate drops and the elderly population grows, our society is likely to experience a retargeting of caregiving from the very young to the very old.

Finally, an aging population will almost certainly bring change to the way we view death. In all likelihood, death will become less of a social taboo and more a natural part of the life course as it was in centuries past. Should this come to pass, both young and old alike may benefit.

SUMMARY

1. The proportion of elderly people in Canada has risen from 4 percent in 1900 to about 13 percent today; by the middle of the twenty-first century, 25 percent of our society's members will be elderly.

2. Gerontology, the study of aging and the elderly, focuses on biological and psychological changes in old age, as well as cultural definitions of aging.

3. Growing old is accompanied by a rising incidence of disease and disability. Younger people, however, commonly exaggerate the extent of disability among the elderly.

4. Psychological research confirms that growing old results in neither overall loss of intelligence nor great change in individual personality.

5. The age at which people are defined as old has varied through history: until several centuries ago, old age began as early as thirty. In poor societies today, in which life expectancy is substantially lower than in North America, people become old at fifty or even forty.

6. In global perspective, industrialization fosters a decline in the social standing of elderly people.

7. As people age, they commonly experience social isolation brought on by retirement, physical disability, and the death of friends or spouses. Even so, most elderly people look to family members for social support.

8. Since 1980, poverty among the elderly has dropped sharply. The aged poor are categories of people—including single women and people of colour—who are likely to be poor regardless of age.

9. Ageism—prejudice and discrimination against old people—serves to justify age stratification.

10. Although many seniors are socially disadvantaged, the elderly encompass people of both sexes and all races, ethnicities, and social classes. Thus, older people do not qualify as a minority.

11. Disengagement theory, based on structural-functional analysis, contends that society disengages the elderly from positions of social responsibility before the onset of disability or death. In this way, society accomplishes the orderly transfer of statuses and roles from the older to the younger generation.

12. Activity theory, based on symbolic-interaction analysis, claims that a high level of activity affords people personal satisfaction in old age.

13. Age stratification is a focus of social-conflict analysis. The emphasis on economic output in capitalist societies leads to a devaluing of those who are less productive, including the elderly.

14. Modern society has set death apart from everyday life, prompting a cultural denial of human mortality. In part, this attitude is related to the fact that most people now die after reaching old age. Recent trends suggest that people are confronting death more directly and seeking control over the process of dying.

CRITICAL-THINKING QUESTIONS

1. Why are the populations of industrial societies getting older? What are some of the likely consequences of this demographic shift?

2. Start with common phrases such as "little old lady" and "dirty old man" and identify ways in which our culture devalues old people.

3. Why does industrialization erode the social standing of the elderly?

4. What important insight about growing old is offered by each of sociology's three major theoretical paradigms?

APPLICATIONS AND EXERCISES

1. What practices and policies does your university or college have for helping older faculty pass through the transition of retirement? Ask several faculty nearing retirement—and several already retired—for their views. In what ways does retiring from an academic career seem harder or easier than ending other kinds of work?

2. Flip through an issue of any popular magazine—say, *Maclean's*, *Time*, or *Newsweek*—and note images of men and women featured in stories and pictured in advertising. Are elderly people fairly represented in such publications?

3. Obtain a copy of a living will and try to respond to all the questions it asks. Does filling out such a form help clarify your own thinking about confronting death?

4. Most communities have at least one hospice (check the telephone book). A call to the hospice can provide written material (and, perhaps, even a discussion with someone who works or volunteers there) on how these organizations help dying people.

SITES TO SEE

www.macionis.com
or
www.TheSociologyPage.com

You can find more than fifty weblinks to sociological journals and other sources of data and information by visiting the Links Library at this website.

www.statcan.ca/english/freepub/89-582-XIE/index.htm

Statistics Canada's report on "Caring for an Aging Society" sets out data on elders requiring care and their caregivers.

www.hc-sc.gc.ca/seniors-aines/

Aging and Seniors, a bilingual site maintained by Health Canada, provides resources on aging issues, including health, medication, injury prevention, seniors' programs, government organizations, and various publications.

www.fifty-plus.net

The *Canadian Association of Retired Persons* provides news and information about retirement issues, including finances, health, lifestyles, safety, retirement communities, learning resources, and more.

www.utoronto.ca/lifecourse/

Based at the University of Toronto, the *Institute for Human Development, Life Course and Aging* carries out research into the process of human development, life course and aging, population aging, and the aged, in the social, psychological, and health sciences. This site is also home to the Ontario Network for the Prevention of Elder Abuse (**www.utoronto.ca/lifecourse/onpea.htm**).

http://atlas.gc.ca/site/english/maps/peopleandsociety/age/thegoldenyears

http://atlas.gc.ca/site/english/maps/peopleandsociety/age/theoldestold

The Atlas of Canada, a collection of maps form Natural Resources Canada, show aspects of the age structure of Canada's population based on the 1996 census. "The Golden Years" map shows distribution of elders aged sixty-five to seventy-four, and the "Oldest Old" shows those aged seventy-five or more.

 ## STUDY TOOLS

For more study tools to help you with your next exam, be sure to check out the Companion Website at **www.pearsoned.ca/macionis**, as well as Chapter 15 in your Study Guide.

 ## INVESTIGATE WITH CONTENTSELECT

Follow the instructions found on page 25 of this textbook to access ContentSelect™ at the Research Navigator™ website. Once at the site, enter your LOGINID and Password. Then, enter keywords such as "aging," "retire-ment," and "euthanasia" and the search engine will supply relevant and recent scholarly and popular press publications.

CHAPTER
16

Christopher M. Chinn
Location and Dislocation
Courtesy of Latino/Latina Studies Program,
University of Illinois at Urbana–Champaign

THE ECONOMY AND WORK

"When you compare what my dad looked forward to against what I'm looking forward to, he expected that things would be better for us and that my children would have it better than I have. But there isn't that feeling anymore." Ian Crump, a forty-five-year-old father of three, put three generations of experience in a nutshell as he pondered the situation of the descendants of Kitty and Henry Neville Compton Crump who had gathered at the old prairie homestead south of Regina. The family had felt the effects of the restructured economy, high taxes, and deficits that were contributing to a sense of economic malaise across the country.

Ian's cousin, Tom Crump, went through an experience that clearly illustrates the changing job environment. As a hospital administrator in Vancouver he had been preparing to lay off fifty people when his boss came in and said that it would be fifty-one. A senior position and seventeen years with the same employer proved to be no protection from ongoing economic upheaval and no base for launching his children into middle-class security.

Downsizing and restructuring were leading to layoffs at all levels, including middle management, and breaking the link that once bound company and employee for a much longer period—possibly through the entire working life of the employee. "By the standards of his parents, the job was a brief interlude; by the expectations of his children, an eternity" (Greenspon, 1993).

The experiences of Ian Crump and his extended family were shared by many Canadians: early (forced) retirements, layoffs, part-time employment instead of the desired full-time work, periods of unemployment, a series of jobs rather than a secure long-term career. Factory closings, mergers, downsizing, restructuring, globalization, freelancing, outsourcing, two recessions in the past twenty years, and a jobless recovery have all contributed to economic insecurity. All of these changes, coupled with more working from home (often for multiple employers), mean that, increasingly, people can look forward to finding "work" rather than "jobs." The traditional pattern, in parts of the economy, of working for decades for the same employer has been shaken to its core.

Here, we examine the economy as a social institution, explore the character of work today, and explain some of the consequences of the emerging global marketplace for Canadians. We will see that a good deal of the conventional wisdom about economic life no longer applies in the face of sweeping global changes. Indeed, sociologists debate how the economy ought to work, whose interests it ought to serve, and what companies and workers owe to each other.

THE ECONOMY: HISTORICAL OVERVIEW

The **economy** is *the social institution that organizes the production, distribution, and consumption of goods and services.* To call the economy an "institution" implies that it functions in an established manner that is predictable, at least in its general outlines. This is not to say the economy operates to everyone's liking and, as we shall see, societies the world over organize their economies in various ways with various consequences. *Goods* are commodities ranging from necessities (such as food, clothing, and shelter) to luxury items (such as automobiles, swimming pools, and yachts). *Services* refer to valued activities that benefit others (including the work of bankers, lawyers, physicians, police officers, hairdressers, and telephone operators).

We value goods and services because they ensure survival or because they make life easier, more interesting, or more aesthetically pleasing. The things we produce and consume are also important for our self-concepts and social identities. The distribution of goods and services, then, shapes the lives of everyone in basic ways. In Canada, more than in the United States, governments are involved in the distribution of a number of these services.

The complex economies that mark modern industrial societies are the product of centuries of technological innovation and social change. The following sections highlight three technological revolutions that reorganized the means of production and transformed many other dimensions of social life.

THE AGRICULTURAL REVOLUTION

Technologically simple societies of the past produced only what they immediately consumed. These small nomadic groups lived off the land—hunting game, gathering vegetation, and fashioning rudimentary clothing, tools, and shelters. Production, distribution, and consumption were all part of family life. The development of agriculture about five thousand years ago brought revolutionary change to these societies. Agriculture emerged as people harnessed animals to plows, increasing the productive power of hunting and gathering more than tenfold. The resulting surplus freed certain people in society from the demands of food production. Some people began to adopt specialized economic roles, forging crafts, designing tools, raising animals, and constructing dwellings.

Once agriculture was underway, towns emerged, soon to be linked by networks of traders dealing in food, animals, and other goods (Jacobs, 1970). These four factors—agricultural technology, productive specialization, permanent settlements, and trade—were the keys to a revolutionary expansion of the economy.

In the process, the world of work became distinct from family life, although production still occurred close to home. In medieval Europe, for instance, most people farmed nearby fields. Both country and city dwellers often laboured in their homes—a pattern called *cottage industry*—producing goods sold in frequent outdoor markets.

THE INDUSTRIAL REVOLUTION

By the mid-eighteenth century, a second technological revolution was proceeding apace, first in England and soon afterward elsewhere in Europe and North America. The development of industry was to transform societies even more than agriculture had done thousands of years before. Industrialization introduced five notable changes to the economies of Western societies.

1. **New forms of energy.** Throughout history, people derived energy from their own muscles or those of animals. Then, in 1765, English inventor James Watt pioneered the development of the steam engine. Surpassing muscle power a hundred times over, steam engines soon operated large machinery with unprecedented efficiency.

2. **The centralization of work in factories.** Steam-powered machinery soon rendered cottage industries all but obsolete. Factories—centralized and impersonal workplaces apart from the home—proliferated.

3. **Manufacturing and mass production.** Before the Industrial Revolution, most work involved cultivating and gathering raw materials such as crops, wood, and wool. The industrial economy shifted that focus to manufacturing raw materials into a wide range of saleable products. For example, factories mass-produced lumber into furniture and transformed wool into clothing.

4. **Specialization.** Typically, a single skilled worker in a cottage industry fashioned a product from beginning to end. Factory work, in contrast, demands specialization, so that a labourer repeats a single task over and over, making only a small contribution to the finished product. Thus, as factories raised productivity, they also lowered the skill level of the average worker (Warner and Low, 1947).

5. **Wage labour.** Instead of working for themselves or joining together as households, industrial workers entered factories as wage labourers. They sold their labour to strangers who often cared less for them than for the machines they operated. Supervision became routine and intense.

The impact of the Industrial Revolution gradually rippled outward from the factories to transform all of society. Greater productivity steadily raised the standard of living as countless new products and services filled an expanding marketplace. At the outset, the benefits of industrial technology were shared unequally. Some factory owners made vast fortunes, while most industrial workers hovered perilously close to poverty. Children, too, worked in factories or deep in coal mines for pennies a day.

THE INFORMATION REVOLUTION AND THE POST-INDUSTRIAL SOCIETY

By the middle of the twentieth century, the nature of production itself was changing once again. Canada

DIVERSITY: RACE, CLASS, AND GENDER

The French Canadians of Manchester, New Hampshire

The Amoskeag Manufacturing Company, once the largest textile factory in the world, was the pillar of economic life in Manchester, New Hampshire. From its founding in 1837 to its closing in 1935, the Amoskeag plant provided the major source of employment in Manchester and controlled the development of the city as a whole. The company initially founded a community of young women, from rural New England, who worked and lived together in boarding-houses with 10 p.m. curfews and compulsory church attendance. Irish immigrant families, willing to work for lower wages, eventually replaced the mill girls.

In the 1870s, French-Canadian immigrants who had been forced out of impoverished farming areas by a scarcity of land found their way in substantial numbers from rural Quebec to the Amoskeag mills. The mill owners soon concluded that French Canadians were the ideal labour force, and Amoskeag proceeded to recruit them actively. Mill agents scanned the Quebec countryside for possible recruits, and advertisements in Quebec newspapers extolled the virtues of Amoskeag and Manchester.

French-Canadian workers were ideal in part because they had large families. Entire family groups were brought into the mills (including the children) and could be counted on to draw kinfolk as well as their own large families. So numerous were they, in the end, that the mill bosses were forced to learn a little French. This large group was appreciated by management because it proved to be a "docile," "industrious," and "stable" labour force with a family-based structure that discouraged union involvement. Despite their numbers, however, not one French Canadian was promoted into the supervisory ranks—these positions were filled by native-born Americans or immigrants of British and northern European stock.

Migration from Quebec to Manchester, a convenient stop on the railway linking Montreal and Boston, was so substantial that, by 1910, French Canadians made up 35 percent of the Amoskeag labour force and 38 percent of the population of Manchester. Some of the

families that migrated to Manchester stayed only long enough to save some money before returning to their farms in Quebec. Others put down permanent roots and contributed to life with a French flavour in the section of Manchester that is still called Little Canada.

Source: Based on Hareven and Langenbach (1978).

---

was becoming a **post-industrial economy,** *a productive system based on service work and extensive use of information technology.* Automated machinery (and, more recently, robotics) reduced the role of human labour in factory production, while bureaucracy simultaneously expanded the ranks of clerical workers and managers. Between 1961 and 2002 (Figure 16–1), manufacturing declined from 25 to 22 percent of the labour force; during the same interval, the primary sector labour force (in agriculture, fishing, mining, and the like) declined from 13 to 4 percent. Thus, the dramatic increase in the service sector was due more to the shift in labour from the primary (extraction) sector than from the secondary (manufacturing) sector. Nonetheless, the service industries—such as public relations, health care, advertising, education, and sales—now employ the bulk of Canada's workers (74 percent).

It is commonly argued that Canada's huge service sector—and it is large by world standards (Figure 16–2)—developed at the expense of employment in manufacturing. Even though Canada's secondary sector is small by world standards, it has remained remarkably stable since 1870. While we have lost manufacturing jobs to lower-wage countries in response to globalization, other manufacturing industries have been established to replace those jobs.

Driving this economic change is a third technological transformation: the development of the computer. The Information Revolution is generating new kinds of information, creating new means of communication, and changing the character of work just as factories did two centuries ago. The Information Revolution has unleashed three major trends:

1. **From tangible products to ideas.** As noted in earlier chapters, the industrial era was defined by the production of goods; in the post-industrial era, work involves creating and manipulating symbols. Computer programmers, writers, financial analysts, advertising executives, architects,

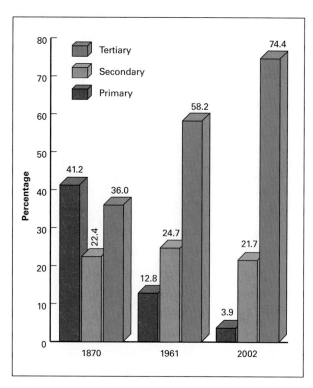

FIGURE 16–1 The Canadian Economic Structure, 1870–2002 (Percentages)

Sources: Adapted from Watson (1988) and Statistics Canada, Canadian Statistics, www.statcan.ca.

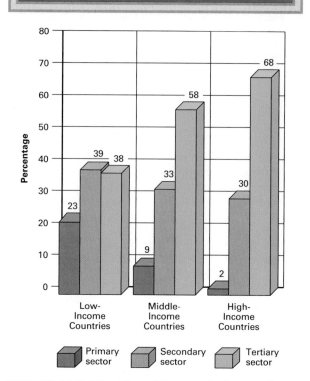

FIGURE 16–2 The Size of Economic Sectors by Income Level of Country

Source: John Macionis's estimates based on United Nations Development Programme (2000) and The World Bank (2000).

educators, editors, and all sorts of consultants make up the labour force of the Information Age.

2. **From mechanical skills to literacy skills.** Just as the Industrial Revolution required mechanical skills, so the Information Revolution requires literacy skills—speaking and writing well and, of course, using computers. People who can communicate effectively enjoy new opportunities; those who cannot face declining prospects.

3. **The decentralization of work away from factories.** Industrial technology drew workers into factories containing the machines and energy sources, but computer technology allows people to work almost anywhere. Indeed, laptop computers, cell phones, and portable fax machines now turn the home, car, or even an airplane into a "virtual office." New information technology, in short, blurs the line between work and home life, bringing about a return of cottage industries in the form of home-based offices and small businesses.

The need for face-to-face communication as well as the availability of supplies and information still keep most workers in the office. But the trend is clear, and many in today's more educated and skilled labour

force no longer require—and often resist—the close supervision of yesterday's factories.

SECTORS OF THE ECONOMY

The three revolutions just described reflect a shifting balance among the three sectors of a society's economy. The **primary sector** is *the part of the economy that generates raw materials directly from the natural environment.* The primary sector, which includes agriculture, animal husbandry, fishing, forestry, and mining, predominates in pre-industrial societies. Figure 16–2 indicates that 23 percent of the economic output of low-income countries is from the primary sector. As a society develops economically, the primary sector becomes less important. Thus, this sector represents 9 percent of economic activity among middle-income nations and just 2 percent of production among high-income countries. Figure 16–1 traces the decline of the primary sector in Canada from 41 percent of the economy in 1870 to less than 4 percent in 2002.

The **secondary sector** is *the part of the economy that transforms raw materials into manufactured goods.*

This sector grows quickly as societies industrialize, just as manufacturing surged in Canada during the 1800s. Secondary sector production includes refining petroleum into gasoline, turning metals into tools and automobiles, and milk into cheese.

The **tertiary sector** is *the part of the economy that generates services rather than goods.* Accounting for just 38 percent of economic output in low-income countries, the tertiary sector grows with industrialization and dominates the economies of high-income nations as they enter the post-industrial era. Today, about three-quarters of the Canadian labour force does some form of service work, including secretarial and clerical work and positions in food service, sales, law, accounting, advertising, teaching, and medicine. Knowledge-based occupations make up an important part of the tertiary or service sector and that component has grown more quickly than predicted. The proportion of the workforce in high-knowledge occupations has increased from 14 to 25 percent between 1971 and 2001 so that one third of the service sector is in that category (Statistics Canada, 2003g).

THE GLOBAL ECONOMY

As technology draws people around the world closer together, another important economic transformation is taking place. Recent decades have witnessed the emergence of a **global economy**, *economic activity spanning many nations of the world with little regard for national borders.*

The development of a global economy has four main consequences. First, we are seeing a global division of labour by which each region of the world specializes in one sector of economic activity. As Global Map 16–1 shows, agriculture occupies more than 70 percent of the workforce in low-income countries. Global Map 16–2 indicates that industrial production is concentrated in the middle- and high-income nations of the world. The economies of the richest nations, including Canada, now specialize in service-sector activity.

Second, an increasing number of products pass through the economies of more than one nation. Consider, for instance, that workers in Taiwan may manufacture shoes, which a Hong Kong distributor sends to Italy, where they receive the stamp of an Italian designer; the distributor in Rome sends the shoes to Vancouver, where they are sold in a store owned by a firm with its headquarters in Tokyo.

Third, national governments no longer control the economic activity that takes place within their borders. In fact, governments cannot even regulate the value of their national currencies, since money is now traded around the clock in the financial centres of Tokyo, London, New York, and Toronto.

Fourth, a small number of businesses, operating internationally, now control a vast share of the world's economic activity. One estimate concludes that the six hundred largest multinational companies account for fully half of the earth's entire total economic output (Kidron and Segal, 1991).

The world is still divided into 192 politically distinct nations—but in light of the proliferation of international economic activity, "nationhood" has lost much of its former significance.

COMPARATIVE ECONOMIC SYSTEMS

Two overarching models—capitalism and socialism—have dominated analysis of economic systems during the past century. No society has an economy that is purely capitalist or purely socialist; these models represent two ends of a continuum on which an actual economy can be placed. Further, societies towards each end of the continuum have undergone extensive change.

CAPITALISM

Capitalism is *an economic system in which natural resources and the means of producing goods and services are privately owned.* Ideally, a capitalist economy has three distinctive features.

1. **Private ownership of property.** In a capitalist economy, individuals can own almost anything. The more capitalist an economy is, the more private ownership there is of wealth-producing property such as factories, real estate, and natural resources.

2. **Pursuit of personal profit.** A capitalist society encourages the accumulation of private property and considers the profit motive natural, simply a matter of "doing business." Further, claimed the Scottish economist Adam Smith (1723–90), the individual pursuit of self-interest helps the entire society prosper (1937:508; orig. 1776).

3. **Free competition and consumer sovereignty.** A purely capitalist economy operates as a free-market system with no government interference (sometimes called a *laissez-faire* economy, from the French words meaning "to leave alone"). Adam Smith contended that a freely competitive economy regulates itself by the "invisible hand" of the laws of supply and demand.

   Smith maintained that a free-market system is dominated by consumers, who select goods and services that provide the greatest value. As producers compete with one another, they provide the highest-quality goods and services at the lowest possible price. Thus, while entrepreneurs and consumers are motivated by personal gain, everyone benefits from more efficient production and ever-increasing value. This is what Smith had

GLOBAL MAP 16–1
Agricultural Employment in Global Perspective

The primary sector of the economy is largest in societies that are least developed. Thus, in the poor countries of Africa and Asia, up to half of the workers are farmers. This picture is altogether different in the world's most economically developed countries—including Canada, the United States, Great Britain, and Australia—which have 2 percent of their workforce in agriculture.

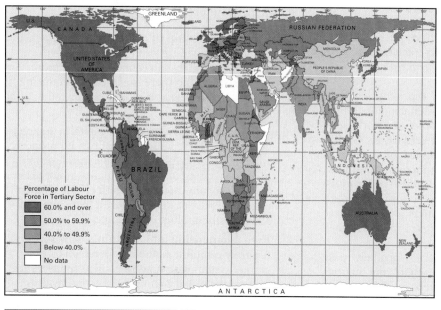

GLOBAL MAP 16–2
Service-Sector Employment in Global Perspective

The tertiary sector of the economy becomes even larger as a nation's income level rises. In Canada, the United States, the countries of Western Europe, Australia, and Japan, about two-thirds of the labour force performs service work.

Source: John Macionis, using data from United Nations Development Programme (2000) and The World Bank (2000, 2001); map projection from *Peters Atlas of the World* (1990).

in mind when he declared that narrow self-interest produces "the greatest good for the greatest number of people." Any government control of the economy, he claimed, distorts market forces, reduces profit motivation, diminishes the quantity and quality of goods produced, and shortchanges consumers.

While Canada is a capitalist society, the guiding hand of government plays an extensive role in eco-nomic affairs. Through taxation and various regulatory agencies, the government influences what companies produce, the quality and cost of merchandise, the products that are imported and exported, and how we consume or conserve natural resources.

The federal and provincial governments own and operate a number of businesses, including the Canadian Broadcasting Corporation, Via Rail, Atomic Energy of Canada, and Hydro-Québec. Governments regulate securities, step in to prevent the collapse of

Capitalism still thrives in Hong Kong (left), evident in streets choked with advertising and shoppers. Socialism is more the rule in China's capital of Beijing (right), a city dominated by government buildings rather than a downtown business district.

businesses (such as Algoma Steel), mandate minimum wages, enforce workplace safety standards, regulate corporate mergers, provide farm price supports, and administer employment insurance, welfare, and pensions. Not surprisingly, federal, provincial, and municipal governments employ 5 percent of Canada's labour force in public administration.

SOCIALISM

Socialism is *an economic system in which natural resources and the means of producing goods and services are collectively owned.* In its ideal form, a socialist economy is the exact opposite of capitalism.

1. **Collective ownership of property.** An economy is socialist to the extent that it limits the right to private property, especially property used to produce goods and services. Laws establish government ownership of property and make housing and other goods available to all, not just to those of some privileged segment of society.

   Karl Marx claimed that private ownership of productive property generates social classes by which an economic elite serves its own interest at the expense of everyone else. Socialism, then, seeks to lessen economic inequality and create a classless society.

2. **Pursuit of collective goals.** The individualistic pursuit of profit is also at odds with the collective orientation of socialism. Socialist values and norms condemn the capitalist entrepreneurial spirit as simple "greed." For this reason, socialist nations outlaw private trading as "black market" activity.

3. **Government control of the economy.** Socialism rejects the idea that a free-market economy regulates itself. Instead of a laissez-faire approach, socialist governments oversee a *centrally controlled* or *command* economy. Socialism also rejects the idea that consumers guide capitalist production. From this point of view, consumers lack the information necessary to evaluate products and are manipulated by advertising to buy what is profitable for factory owners rather than what consumers genuinely need. Commercial advertising thus plays little role in socialist economies.

Socialism and Communism

Most people equate the terms *socialism* and *communism*. More precisely, **communism** is *a hypothetical economic and political system in which all members of a society are socially equal.* Karl Marx viewed socialism as a transitory stage on the path towards the ideal of a communist society devoid of all class divisions. In many socialist societies today, the dominant political party describes itself as communist, but nowhere has the communist goal been achieved.

Why? For one thing, social stratification involves differences of power as well as wealth. In general, socialist societies have succeeded in reducing disparities in wealth only by expanding government bureaucracies and extensively regulating daily life. In the process, government did not "wither away" as Karl Marx imagined. On the contrary, socialist political elites have enormous power and privilege.

Marx might have agreed that a communist society is a *utopia* (from Greek words meaning "not a place"). Yet Marx considered communism a worthy goal, and might well have disparaged reputedly "Marxist" societies such as North Korea, the former Soviet Union, the People's Republic of China, and Cuba for failing to fulfill the promise of communism.

Global comparisons indicate that socialist economies generate the greatest economic equality, although living standards remain relatively low. Capitalist economies, in contrast, engender more income disparity although living standards are typically higher. As the former Soviet Union has moved towards a market system, however, the majority of people have suffered a decline in living standards, while some people have become quite rich.

WELFARE CAPITALISM AND STATE CAPITALISM

Some of the nations of Western Europe—including Sweden and Italy—have combined a market-based economy with extensive social welfare programs. Analysts call this "third way" **welfare capitalism,** *an economic and political system that combines a mostly market-based economy with government programs to provide for people's basic needs.*

Under welfare capitalism, the government owns some of the largest industries and services, such as transportation, the mass media, and health care. In Sweden and Italy, about 12 percent of economic production is "nationalized," or state controlled. That leaves most industry in private hands, although subject to extensive government regulation in the public interest. High taxation (aimed especially at the rich) funds a wide range of social welfare programs, including universal health care and child care (Olsen, 1996).

Another blend of capitalism and socialism is **state capitalism,** *an economic and political system in which companies are privately owned although they cooperate closely with the government.* Systems of state capitalism are common in the rapidly developing Asian countries along the Pacific Rim. Japan, South Korea, and Singapore are all capitalist nations, but their governments work in partnership with large companies, supplying financial assistance and controlling imports of foreign products to help their businesses compete in world markets. Clearly, governments and companies can work cooperatively in many ways (Gerlach, 1992).

RELATIVE ADVANTAGES OF CAPITALISM AND SOCIALISM

Which economic system works best? Comparing economic models is difficult because all countries mix capitalism and socialism to varying degrees. Moreover, nations differ in cultural attitudes towards work, available natural resources, level of technological development, and patterns of trade. Some also carry the burdens of war (Gregory and Stuart, 1985).

Despite these complicating factors, some crude comparisons are revealing. The following sections contrast two categories of countries—those with predominantly capitalist economies and those with predominantly socialist economies. The supporting data reflect economic patterns prior to recent changes in the former Soviet Union and Eastern Europe.

Economic Productivity

One key dimension of economic performance is productivity. A common measure of economic output is gross domestic product (GDP), the total value of all goods and services produced annually by a nation's economy. Per capita (or per person) GDP allows us to compare societies of different population size.

Averaging the economic output of Canada, the United States, and the nations of Western Europe at the end of the 1980s yields a per capita GDP of about $13 500. The comparable figure for the former Soviet Union and the nations of Eastern Europe was about $5000. In other words, capitalist countries outproduced socialist nations by a ratio of 2.7 to 1 (United Nations Development Programme, 1990).

Economic Equality

The distribution of resources within a society is a second crucial test of an economy. A comparative study completed in the mid-1970s calculated income ratios by comparing the earnings of the richest and poorest 5 percent of the population (Wiles, 1977). This research found that societies with predominantly capitalist economies had an income ratio of about 10 to 1; the corresponding figure for socialist countries was 5 to 1.

This comparison of economic performance reveals that capitalist economies support a higher overall standard of living but generate greater income disparity. Or, put otherwise, *socialist economies create less income disparity but offer a lower overall standard of living.*

Personal Freedom

One final consideration in evaluating capitalism and socialism involves the personal freedoms a society accords its people. The capitalist concept of liberty is the *freedom to act* in pursuit of one's self-interest. A capitalist economy, after all, depends on the freedom of producers and consumers to interact without extensive interference from the state.

On the other hand, a socialist conception of liberty is *freedom from basic want.* Providing for the basic needs of everyone means promoting economic equality. This goal requires considerable state intervention in the economy, which limits the personal choices of citizens for the benefit of the public as a whole.

People have yet to devise a social system that expands political freedoms *and* creates economic equality. In a capitalist system that guarantees many personal freedoms, are these freedoms worth as much to the poor as to the rich? Conversely, socialist nations, while more economically equal, restrict the rights of their people to express themselves and move freely inside and outside their borders.

CHANGES IN SOCIALIST COUNTRIES

In 1989 and 1990, the nations of Eastern Europe that were seized by the Soviet Union at the end World War II shook off their socialist regimes. These nations—including the German Democratic Republic, Czechoslovakia, Hungary, Romania, and Bulgaria—have introduced capitalist elements into what were centrally controlled economies. In 1992, the Soviet Union itself formally dissolved and introduced some free-market principles.

The reasons for these sweeping changes were complex. But two factors stand out: first, the mostly socialist economies grossly underproduced their capitalist counterparts. Though they achieved remarkable economic equality, living standards were low by Western European standards. Second, Soviet socialism was heavy-handed, rigidly controlling the media and restricting individual freedom. In short, socialism did away with *economic* elites, as Karl Marx predicted, but increased the clout of *political* elites, as Max Weber said it would.

So far, the market reforms in Eastern Europe are proceeding unevenly. Some nations (Czech Republic, Slovakia, Poland, and the Baltic states of Latvia, Estonia, and Lithuania) are faring well, but others (Romania, Bulgaria, and the former Soviet republics) have been buffeted by price increases and falling living standards. Officials hope that expanding production will eventually bring a turnaround. However, there is already evidence that any improvement in living standards will be accompanied by increasing economic disparity (Pohl, 1996; Buraway, 1997; Specter, 1997a).

WORK IN THE POST-INDUSTRIAL ECONOMY

Change is not restricted to the socialist world; the economy of Canada has also changed dramatically during the last century. The Industrial Revolution transformed the Canadian workforce a century ago; further changes are taking place today.

In 2002, 16.7 million Canadians were in the labour force, representing two-thirds of those over the age of fifteen. As has been the case historically, a larger proportion of men (73.3 percent) than women (60.7 percent) are in the labour force. The gender gap in labour force participation has diminished in recent decades among Canadians. The figure for males has increased very little since 1980, but the female rate is up from 46.7 percent.

Figure 16–3 provides labour force participation rates for selected racial and ethnic categories for the years 1986 and 1991, and reveals some very interesting patterns. For instance, labour force participation rates are very similar for the British and the French—between 62.1 and 64.4 percent for both categories in both 1986 and 1991; the British rate declined slightly, while the French rate rose by one percentage point. Participation among Asians is somewhat higher at almost 71 percent, with a drop of two points by 1991. Blacks are even more likely to be involved in the labour force—75 percent in 1986, and 72 percent in 1991—at a rate roughly ten percentage points higher than the British and French. It is worth noting that Asians and Blacks, with high proportions of immigrants, are the most active in the labour force. (The Public Use Microdata files that would allow comparisons of these ethnic categories, based on Census 2001 data, were not available at the time this book went to press. Partial data, in Statistics Canada B2020 files, suggest that Asians and Blacks are as active in the labour force in 2001 as in 1986 and 1991.)

In contrast, the Native population exhibits markedly lower rates of participation in the labour force in both years—just over 50 percent. The comparison of Native rates with those of Asians and Blacks suggests that race may not be the effective barrier to participation by Natives; instead, it may be the result of a history of internal colonialism, de facto segregation, rural isolation, lower levels of educational attainment, and cultural dislocation (Gerber, 1990; Wotherspoon and Satzewich, 1993; Frideres, 1998).

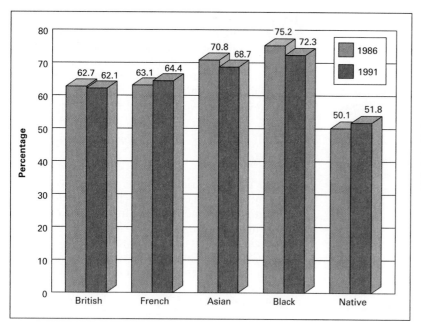

FIGURE 16–3 Labour Force Participation[1] for Selected Categories,[2] 1986 and 1991

[1]Based on population fifteen years of age and older.
[2]Refers to single origin only—that is, those who are of the same origin on both paternal and maternal sides.

Sources: Adapted by Gerber from Statistics Canada, *Profile of Ethnic Groups—Dimensions*, Catalogue No. 95-154, 1989, and 1991 Census, Individual Public Use Microdata.

THE DECLINE OF AGRICULTURAL WORK

At the beginning of the twentieth century, about 35 percent of the Canadian labour force was engaged in farming. By 1961, this proportion had fallen to almost 13 percent, and by 2001 to less than 4 percent. Still, because today's agriculture involves more machinery and fewer people, it is more productive than ever. A century ago, a typical farmer could feed five people; today, one farmer feeds seventy-five. This dramatic rise in productivity also reflects new types of crops, pesticides that promote higher yields, greater energy consumption, and other advances in farming techniques. The average Canadian farm has more than doubled in size from about 250 acres in 1950 to about 600 acres today.

This process signals the eclipse of "family farms," which are declining in number and produce only a small part of our agricultural yield; more and more production is carried out by corporate agribusinesses (Bakker and Winson, 1993). But, more productive or not, this transformation has brought painful adjustments for farming communities across the country, as a way of life is lost. The rest of us are affected indirectly by this change: prices have generally been kept low by the rising productivity of agribusiness, although a growing proportion of people are concerned about the effect of widespread use of pesticides and chemicals on crops. (One of the goals of genetic modification is to limit the need for such chemicals.)

THE DUAL LABOUR MARKET

Sociologists divide the jobs in today's economy into two categories. The **primary labour market** includes *occupations that provide extensive benefits to workers*. This segment of the labour market includes the traditional white-collar professions and upper management positions. These are jobs that people think of as *careers*. Work in the primary labour market provides high income and job security and is usually challenging and satisfying. Such occupations require a broad education rather than specialized training, and they offer solid opportunity for advancement.

But few of these advantages apply to work in the **secondary labour market**, *jobs that provide minimal benefits to workers*. This segment of the labour force is employed in low-skill, blue-collar assembly-line operations and low-level service-sector jobs, including clerical positions. Workers in the secondary labour market receive lower income, have less job security, and find fewer chances to advance. Not surprisingly, then, these workers are more likely to experience alienation and dissatisfaction with their jobs (Mottaz, 1981; Kohn and Schooler, 1982).

Another term used to describe some of these workers is the **reserve army of labour**, *the part of the labour force that is last hired during expansion and first fired when the economy contracts*. These problems are especially serious for women, other minorities, and particularly Natives, who tend to be overrepresented in this segment of the labour force (Kemp and Coverman, 1989; Gerber, 1990; Wotherspoon and Satzewich, 1993).

LABOUR UNIONS

Labour unions are worker organizations that seek to improve wages and working conditions through various strategies, including negotiations and strikes. In

Canada, union membership has been remarkably stable over the last twenty years at just over one-third of the labour force, peaking at 35.1 percent in 1983. The involvement of women increased slightly while that of men decreased to the point where, in 1997, women constituted 45 percent of union membership in Canada. The involvement of Canadian workers in international unions has dropped dramatically, while national unions have grown (Glenday, 2001:18–19). The highest level of union membership is found in government or public administration at over 70 percent; the manufacturing and service sectors are both around the one-third mark, while mining and the trades lag behind. Most of the new service-sector jobs being created today are not unionized.

There is substantial interprovincial variation in levels of unionization. In Newfoundland, 55.1 percent of the labour force is unionized; at the other end of the spectrum is Alberta at 26.6 percent (Statistics Canada, 1990). The other relatively highly unionized provinces are British Columbia, Ontario, and especially Quebec. The differences are not entirely due to the economic structures of the various provinces, for even within the same industry there can be substantial variation: the level of unionization within the construction industry, for example, varies from 81 percent in Quebec to 25 percent in Prince Edward Island. In the years from 1998 to 2002, collective agreements have achieved annual wage increases of 1.7 to 3.3 percent in all industries for Canada as a whole. Some of the largest increases were in federal and provincial administration (Statistics Canada, Canadian Statistics, **www.statscan.ca**).

 The Canadian Labour Congress (CLC) is the national voice of the labour movement, representing 2.5 million unionized workers: go to www.clc-ctc.ca/

In global perspective, union membership in industrialized countries varies substantially—from a low of 16 percent of the workforce in the United States to about one-third in Canada, Switzerland, and Japan, one-half in Great Britain, and a high of more than 90 percent in Denmark and Sweden. Clearly, some cultures are more receptive to unions than others; those with social-democratic values tend to have higher levels of unionization. The United States, with its pro-capitalist values, has never been particularly supportive of the union movement.

In the twenty-first century, Canadian unions face new challenges in the face of flatter organizational structures (less room for promotion), downsizing, and outsourcing as corporations attempt to remain competitive in a global environment. Instead of focusing on wage increases, unions now struggle to ensure job security. Trade unions will negotiate for (1) reductions in working time, (2) restrictions on overtime, (3) voluntary early retirement, (4) improved training for job transfer, and (5) an end to subcontracting (Glenday, 2001:33).

D'Arcy Moses is a Gitskan native who grew up in Alberta. Incorporating aboriginal themes and issues in his creations, Moses has become a popular and highly successful fashion designer working out of Montreal.

PROFESSIONS

A **profession** is *a prestigious white-collar occupation that requires extensive formal education.* As distinct from *amateur* (from Latin meaning "lover," one who acts simply out of love for the activity itself), a professional pursues some task for a living. The term *profession* also suggests a public declaration to abide by certain principles. Traditional professions include the ministry, medicine, law, and academia (Goode, 1960). Today, we recognize more occupations as professions, to the extent that they have the following four characteristics (Ritzer, 1972):

1. **Theoretical knowledge.** Professionals have a theoretical understanding of their fields rather than mere technical training. Anyone can master first-aid skills, but physicians claim a theoretical understanding of human health and illness.

2. **Self-regulated training and practice.** The typical professional is self-employed, "in practice." Professionals oversee their own work and observe a code of ethics.

3. **Authority over clients.** Many jobs—sales, for example—require people to respond directly to

the desires of customers. Based on their extensive training, however, professionals expect their clients to follow their direction and advice.

4. **Orientation to community rather than to self-interest.** The traditional "professing" of faith or duty is a professional's vow to serve the community rather than merely seek income. Some professionals, including physicians, are even barred by professional codes from advertising.

Many new service occupations in the post-industrial economy have also sought to *professionalize* their work. A claim to professional standing often begins by re-naming the work to imply special, theoretical knowledge, which also distances the field from its previously less-distinguished reputation. Government bureaucrats, for example, become "public policy analysts," and stockroom workers are reborn as "inventory supply officials."

Professional associations formally attest to specialized skills, license people who perform the work, and develop codes of ethics that emphasize the occupations' contributions to the community. In its effort to win public acceptance, a professional association may also establish schools or other training facilities and perhaps start a professional journal (Abbott, 1988).

Not all occupations claim full professional status. Some *paraprofessionals*, including paralegals and medical technicians, possess specialized skills but lack the extensive theoretical education required of full professionals.

 The Canada Small Business Centres network provides information and links to federal and provincial programs and services for small businesses at www.csbc.org/

SELF-EMPLOYMENT

Self-employment—earning a living without working for a large organization—was once commonplace in North America. Families owned and operated farms, and self-employed workers in the cities owned shops and other small businesses or sold their skills on the open market. C. Wright Mills (1951) estimated that in the early nineteenth century about 80 percent of the U.S. labour force was self-employed, but with the onset of the Industrial Revolution that picture changed dramatically. Self-employment plummeted to one-third, one-fifth, and even lower in both Canada and the United States.

Canada has experienced increases in self-employment so that by 1998 self-employment accounted for roughly 16 percent of the labour force. The increasing importance of self-employment is illustrated by the fact that, between 1975 and 1987 in Canada, the number of self-employed workers grew by 60 percent, while the rest of the workforce grew by only 26 percent (Neill, 1990). By 2002, 15 percent of Canada's

labour force was self-employed (Statistics Canada, Canadian Statistics, **www.statcan.ca**). The highest levels of self-employment are to be found in fishing, trapping, and agriculture.

Professionals such as lawyers, physicians, and dentists have always been well represented among the self-employed because their schooling and skills have high market value. But most self-employed workers in Canada have been small-business owners, plumbers, carpenters, freelance writers, editors, artists, and long-distance truck drivers. Increasingly, women are joining the ranks of the self-employed—mainly, though not exclusively, in white-collar occupations (Gardner, 2000), but in 2002, 65 percent of self-employed were still men (Statistics Canada, Canadian Statistics, **www.statcan.ca**).

Analysis of enumeration areas in Burlington, Ontario (Gerber, Statistics Canada Microdata, 1991), reveals that in one-quarter of the areas, 15 to 18 percent of men were self-employed; only 6 percent of the areas had similar levels of female self-employment. The areas where larger proportions of men and women are self-employed tend to have higher levels of at-home work, home ownership, university degrees, and incomes—and more people who are currently married. By and large, self-employed people in Burlington are not marginal to the mainstream economy: they are numerous, well educated, and relatively affluent. Undoubtedly, computers have facilitated the move to self-employment from home.

Our society has always painted an appealing picture of working independently: no time clocks to punch and no one looking over your shoulder. For those excluded from organizations by prejudice or discrimination, self-employment has served as a strategy to increase economic opportunity (Evans, 1989). Further, self-employment holds the potential of earning a great deal of money. But for all its advantages, self-employment presents workers with special problems. Many are vulnerable to fluctuations in the economy: during the recession of the early 1990s, small businesses filed for bankruptcy in alarming numbers. Another common problem is that the self-employed lack pension and health care benefits generally provided to employees of large organizations, as well as being ineligible for government programs such as EI and parental leave.

UNDEREMPLOYMENT

Underemployment is *employment at a task that uses less than one's full talents or abilities.* It is a serious problem in Canada that affects many categories of workers and is increasingly recognized as the "gap between usable knowledge and its actual use in employment" (Livingstone, 2001:144). Many part-time workers are in that position involuntarily because full-time employment is unavailable to them. Younger workers, many of whom have university degrees, find themselves underemployed—as "almost 50 percent of university graduates in Canada find themselves in jobs that do not require university-level credentials" (Côté and Allahar, 2001:258; Kelly et al., 2000). Women who hit the "glass ceiling" and immigrants whose credentials are not recognized in Canada are also among the underemployed. For every person who is underemployed, Canada loses the potential value of his or her human capital. As a society, we do not take full advantage of the skills and knowledge of our citizens.

Although people with higher levels of education are, by definition, more susceptible to underemployment, it is important to keep in mind that level of education is a major predictor of employment itself. Table 16–1 shows that with each increase in educational attainment (except some post-secondary), employment goes up for both women and men. In assessing the underemployment of people with university certification, one might ask if, after a period in entry-level positions, those with these credentials are more rapidly promoted.

UNEMPLOYMENT

Some unemployment is found in every society. Few young people entering the labour force find a job immediately; some older workers leave the workforce temporarily while seeking a new job, to have children, or because of a strike; others suffer from long-term illnesses; and others who are illiterate or without skills find themselves locked out of the job market.

Although people may be quick to blame themselves if they find themselves out of work, unemployment is not just a personal problem; it is also a product of the economy itself. Capable and willing workers lose their jobs when economic recession occurs, if occupations become obsolete, or as factories close in the face of rising foreign competition (even Hamilton, Ontario-based Stelco, Canada's largest steel producer, was in danger of collapse in 2003). Mergers and "downsizing" can also lead to the dismissal of employees from all levels of an organization. The emerging post-industrial economy has shattered the job security of workers in many traditional blue-collar occupations as well (Kasarda, 1983).

In capitalist societies such as Canada, the unemployment rate rarely dips below 5 percent of the labour force. Public officials view this level of unemployment as natural, and sometimes even describe it as "full employment." An "unemployment problem" is publicly acknowledged only when the unemployment rate exceeds 7 or 8 percent (Albrecht, 1983). In principle, predominantly socialist societies consider work to be each person's right and obligation, so the government may create jobs to keep the unemployment

Jose Clemente Orozco's painting The Unemployed *is a powerful statement of the personal collapse and private despair that afflicts men and women who are out of work. How does a sociological perspective help us to understand being out of work as more than a personal problem?*

Jose Clemente Orozco, *The Unemployed.* © Orozco Valladares Family. Reproduction authorized by the Istituto Nacional de Bellas Artes.

rate low. In practice, however, unemployment is just as great a problem in these societies.

Canada's unemployment rate rose to over 11 percent in 1992 and 1993, before dropping to 9.5 percent in 1995 and 8.1 percent by December 1997. Through 1997, employment in Canada increased by 363 000 (+2.6 percent); most encouraging is the fact that the number of people working full-time hours increased by 377 000 (+3.4 percent), while the number working part time declined by 14 000 (Statistics Canada, 1998). By 2000, our unemployment rate had dropped further to 7.4 percent (Statistics Canada, B2020 files). While there have been gains in the numbers employed during the 1990s, economic restructuring meant that hundreds of thousands of old jobs were lost as new ones were created. Many people who failed to make the transition from old to new jobs were casualties of this employment shift.

Part-time work currently accounts for 19 percent of all employment. In 1994, 5.4 percent of all workers (compared to 2.3 percent in 1981) were "involuntary

TABLE 16–1 Employment among 25- to 44-Year-Olds by Sex and Educational Attainment, 2002

Level of Education	Both Sexes	Men	Women
Total	80.8	85.7	75.8
Less than grade 9	50.2	59.8	37.6
Some secondary school	68.0	76.5	57.1
High-school graduate	79.6	86.2	73.0
Some post-secondary	77.2	82.4	72.2
Post-secondary certificate or diploma	85.2	89.2	81.2
University degree	85.3	89.1	81.8

Source: Adapted from Statistics Canada, Canadian Statistics, "People Employed, by Educational Attainment, 2002," Cat. No. 89F0133XIE, www.statcan.ca/english/Pgdb/labor62.htm.

part-timers," or people who have been unable to find full-time employment (Wells, 1996). In 2002, 18.7 percent of all workers were employed part-time (10.9 and 27.7 percent of male and female workers, respectively). Some women, even physicians and other professionals, work part-time by choice for a wide range of reasons, including family responsibilities, but others do so involuntarily. Thus, some, but not all, of this part-time work can be classified as underemployment.

The national unemployment rate tells only part of the story, for unemployment in provinces such as Newfoundland and P.E.I. may approach twice the national rate. While Canada Map 16–1 reveals the regional pattern in unemployment rates, it is worth noting that cities or metropolitan areas have widely divergent rates: unemployment in Chicoutimi-Jonquière is roughly three times that of Toronto.

Unemployment rates differ for various segments of the Canadian population. In 1991, those of French origin had a higher unemployment rate (10.0 percent) than those of British origin (8.5 percent). The rate for Asian Canadians was similar to that of the French, while that of Black Canadians was substantially higher (14.5 percent). As has been the case over the past decade, the unemployment rate for Natives is two to three times that of the other categories (24.6 percent). Note that these rates refer to the standard unemployment rates measured as a percentage of the *labour force* that is unemployed and actively looking for work.

Figure 16–4 (on page 398) looks at employment or labour force involvement from a different perspective, indicating the proportion of *people fifteen years of age and over* who are (1) not in the labour force, (2) employed, or (3) unemployed. A comparison of the blue bars reveals that Asians and Black Canadians, at about 30 percent, are least likely to be classified as "not in the labour force." They are most likely to be employed (almost 62 percent of those over fifteen, red bars), but also more likely than the British or French to be unemployed (green bars). Native Canadian "adults"

(that is, fifteen and over) have the highest percentage not in the labour force (48 percent), and are by far the least likely to be employed and most likely to be unemployed. In other words, Aboriginal people face barriers initially in becoming involved in the labour force, and then in finding or retaining employment.

Official unemployment statistics, based on monthly national surveys, generally understate unemployment for two reasons. To be counted among the unemployed, a person must be actively seeking work. Especially during economic recessions, many people become discouraged after failing to find a job and stop looking. These "discouraged workers" are not counted among the unemployed. Further, many people who are unable to find jobs for which they are qualified take "lesser" employment: a former university teacher, for example, may drive a taxi while seeking a new teaching position. Such people are included among the employed, although they too might better be described as underemployed. Official statistics also may overlook the fact that some people who are out of work receive income from odd jobs or illegal activity.

THE UNDERGROUND ECONOMY

Government requires all businesses and individual workers to periodically report on their economic activity, especially earnings. Not reporting income received makes a transaction part of the **underground economy**, *economic activity involving income or the exchange of goods and services that is not reported to the government as required by law.*

On a small scale, evidence of the underground economy can be found everywhere: teenagers baby-sit for neighbours; a family makes some extra money by holding a garage sale without reporting the income to the government. Of course, far more of the underground economy is attributable to criminal activity such as illegal drug sales, prostitution, bribery, theft, illegal gambling, and loan-sharking.

But the single largest segment of the underground economy involves "honest" people who fail to accurately report their legally obtained income on income tax forms. Self-employed people, such as various tradespeople or owners of small businesses, may understate their incomes; waiters, waitresses, and other service workers may not report their full income from tips. Even relatively small omissions and misrepresentations on individual income tax returns add up to billions of dollars in the underground economy (Simon and Witte, 1982; Dalglish, 1993).

In Canada, the underground economy accounted for some 15 to 20 percent of economic activity in 1990, up from about 10 percent a decade earlier (Dalglish, 1993:20). A survey by the Canadian Home Builders' Association estimated that 55 percent of all renovations in 1992 were done on the black market. Statistics Canada suggests that underground activity

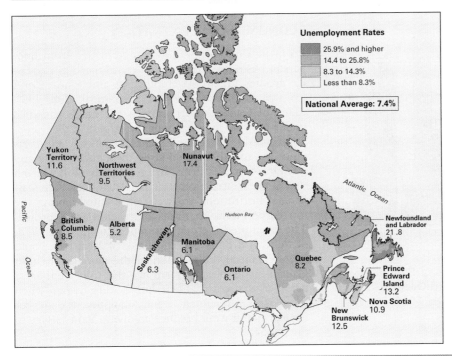

Unemployment Rates

25.9% and higher
14.4 to 25.8%
8.3 to 14.3%
Less than 8.3%

National Average: 7.4%

Yukon Territory 11.6
Northwest Territories 9.5
Nunavut 17.4
British Columbia 8.5
Alberta 5.2
Saskatchewan 6.3
Manitoba 6.1
Ontario 6.1
Quebec 8.2
Newfoundland and Labrador 21.8
Prince Edward Island 13.2
Nova Scotia 10.9
New Brunswick 12.5

Atlantic Ocean
Pacific Ocean
Hudson Bay

CANADA MAP 16–1
Unemployment Rates by Province, Territory, and Census Subdivision, 2000

Source: Calculations by Gerber based on data from Statistics Canada B2020, Profile Series.

accounts for only 3.5 percent of GDP. Although estimates of the magnitude of the problem are all over the map, the existence and growth of the underground economy is not disputed.

A recent increase in underground economic activity is attributed to high tax levels in general and, in particular, to the imposition of the Goods and Services Tax in 1991. The effect of taxing services for the first time was to provide an incentive for under-the-table cash payment. One indication of this trend is a 57 percent increase, between 1991 and 1992, in the use of hard cash rather than credit cards or cheques (Dalglish, 1993).

NEW INFORMATION TECHNOLOGY AND WORK

Another key issue in the workplace of the twenty-first century is the central role of computers and other new information technology. The Information Revolution is changing the kind of work people do, as well as where they do it. Computers are also altering the character of work in four additional ways (Zuboff, 1982; Rule and Brantley, 1992; Vallas and Beck, 1996):

1. **Computers are "deskilling" labour.** Just as industrial machinery "deskilled" the master crafts workers of an earlier era, so computers now threaten the skills of managers. More and more

business decisions are based not on executive decision making but on computer modelling. In other words, a machine determines whether to buy or sell a product, make an investment, or approve or reject a loan.

2. **Computers are making work more abstract.** Industrial workers typically have a "hands-on" relationship with their product. Post-industrial workers manipulate symbols in pursuit of abstract goals such as making a website more attractive, a company more profitable, or software more "user friendly."

3. **Computers limit workplace interaction.** The Information Revolution forces employees to perform most of their work at computer terminals, which isolates workers from one another.

4. **Computers enhance employers' control of workers.** Computers allow supervisors to monitor each worker's output precisely and continuously, whether employees are working at computer terminals or on an assembly line.

The changes wrought by computers remind us that technology is not socially neutral: it shapes the way we work and alters the balance of power between employers and employees. Understandably, then, people welcome some aspects of the Information Revolution while opposing others. See the "Exploring

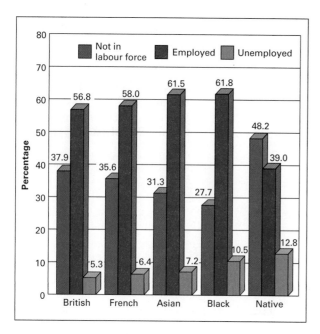

FIGURE 16–4 **Employment Status of Populations 15 Years of Age and Over for Selected Categories, 1991**

Source: Calculations by Linda Gerber based on Statistics Canada, 1991 Census, Individual Public Use Microdata.

Cyber-Society" box for further discussion of the impact of computers on the workplace.

Corporations

At the core of today's capitalist economies lies the **corporation**, *an organization with a legal existence including rights and liabilities apart from those of its members.* By incorporating, an organization becomes an entity unto itself, able to enter into contracts and own property. Incorporation, which arose about a century ago, protects the personal wealth of owners and top executives from lawsuits that might arise from business debts or harm to consumers.

Most large corporations operating in Canada are owned by thousands of stockholders, including other corporations, rather than by single families. This dispersion of corporate ownership has spread wealth by making more people small-scale capitalists. Ralf Dahrendorf (1959) adds that the day-to-day operation of a corporation is the task of white-collar executives who are responsible to the stockholders. Nonetheless, a great deal of corporate stock is owned by a small number of the corporation's top executives and directors, who, in Canada, may be members of a very small number of families (Clement, 1975; Francis, 1986). These major stockholders comprise a small economic elite, which owns and operates the richest and most

powerful Canadian businesses. Thus, the proliferation of corporations has not substantially changed how large businesses operate or affected the distribution of wealth in Canada.

ECONOMIC CONCENTRATION

Profit-making corporations range in size from one-person businesses to veritable giants, such as Loblaw Companies (122 000 employees) and Onex Corp. (98 000 employees) (*Report on Business*, 2003:143). Many of Canada's corporations are small, with less than $100 000 in assets, but the largest of these corporations dominate the Canadian economy and periodically expand their empires through mergers and buyouts of smaller firms. In a pattern that differs from that of the United States, Canada's banks and other financial institutions are well represented among the top corporations in terms of revenues and profits. The attempted merger, announced in January 1998, of the Royal Bank and the Bank of Montreal would have enhanced the position of the new bank within Canada—and placed it among the top twenty-five banks in the world. Their hopes were dashed when the federal government failed to approve the merger for fear that it would reduce competition in service to the public.

Canada's problems of corporate concentration stem from (1) the inordinate wealth and power of specific individuals, families, and corporations; (2) interlocking directorships that bind otherwise diverse corporations; (3) geographic centralization of investment in Ontario and Quebec; and (4) the tendency of corporations to expand or diversify by merging or buying existing firms instead of developing new productive capacity. This last problem was exacerbated by the free trade agreement with the United States, as evidenced by a $20-billion boom in acquisitions and mergers in the first few months of 1989 (Bronson, 1993:204). This trend has been referred to as "paper entrepreneurship," which does nothing to contribute to Canada's wealth: "The pie remains the same size, but the pieces are cut differently" (Francis, 1986:229).

Table 16–2 (on page 401) ranks, by profits, the top thirty companies in Canada. The Royal Bank of Canada, which employs 60 000 people, topped the list with almost $3 billion in profits.

FOREIGN OWNERSHIP

Concern about foreign investment was sparked in the early 1970s when a task force reported that foreign control of Canadian manufacturing had reached 60 percent, and as high as 90 percent in the rubber and petroleum industries. Since then, there has been some form of federal agency in place to review foreign investment, most of which has been American, a fact

Working through Cyberspace

The 1998 Winter Olympic Games in Nagano, Japan, gave IBM an opportunity to showcase its latest technology by transmitting, worldwide, millions of megabytes of data from the games to television viewers, radio listeners, newspaper readers, and Internet surfers. IBM makes the same technology available to business organizations that are involved in "e-business" or Internet-based commerce.

Business has become increasingly dependent on computers linked by intranets, extranets, and the World Wide Web. The number of people connected to the Web is expected to increase to 1.5 billion by 2007 (Computer Industry Almanac Inc., 2002). In Canada alone, private and public sales online increased 27 percent between 2001 and 2002 to reach a total of $13.7 billion (Statistics Canada, 2003b). But the Web is not limited to commercial transactions. Employees of a Vancouver firm can work—on data analysis, design, reports, or problem solving as part of an interactive group— from a home office in Winnipeg, Munich, or Helsinki. Work has invaded cyberspace—the McLuhanesque world

that is free of the limitations of time and space.

Inco's Stobie mine in Sudbury, Ontario, is taking miners out of the underground tunnels and seating them at surface computer terminals from which they run automated drill rigs and scoop trams in various locations. Robo-operator Stan Holloway, who spent fifteen years in Inco's dangerous, dreary, diesel-fumed tunnels, is grateful to be comfortably seated, operating million-dollar scoop trams with a joystick and foot pedals and observing the otherwise back-breaking job through miniature cameras and microphones mounted on the machines.

Inco turned to this kind of high-tech mining in order to remain competitive at this particular mine, which has thirty to forty years' worth of low-grade ore left at the site. To remain in operation, Stobie must compete with mines that have high-grade ore and low labour costs. In Russia, a miner makes about $850 per year; Sudbury miners are employed at $85 000 to $100 000 per year. Robo-trams and drill rigs do a lot of dangerous, dirty work but displace large numbers of highly paid miners. Only a few miners will make the transi-

tion from hard manual labour to robo-operator.

The Department of Finance (**www. fin.gc.ca**) points out that many Canadian industries—beyond software, electronics, and aviation—are leaders in the development and adoption of new technology. New methods of inventory management are changing retailing and the skills needed by personnel, and satellite-generated images are used in resource exploration and development. So pervasive is this change that knowledge-based technology is now the major stimulus to economic growth and job creation. In the past decade, employment growth has been closely linked to intensity of information technology: employment has increased substantially (12 percent) in areas of high information-technology intensity, increased moderately (8 percent) in areas of medium intensity, and declined (–9 percent) in sectors that make minimal use of information technology.

Sources: Canada (1997), IBM (1998), Robinson (1998), Computer Industry Almanac Inc. (2002), and Statistics Canada (2003b) .

---

that has raised questions about Canada's economic and political sovereignty.

A large number of companies, with names familiar to most Canadians, are not traded on Canadian stock exchanges because they are 100 percent American-owned (*National Post Business 500*, June 2000). Among them are General Motors, Ford, DaimlerChrysler, Safeway, Costco, Procter & Gamble, General Electric, McDonald's, Hewlett-Packard, and Motorola. Honda Canada is held by Japanese (50.4 percent) and U.S. investors (49.6 percent). Concerns about these companies, as well as those owned by Japanese, British, Swiss, or other interests, revolve around profits leaving Canada, potential avoidance of Canadian taxes, the lack of research and development or high-level man-

agement functions on Canadian soil, and even political interference.

Concern about the extent of American investment in Canada, and the related processes of "integration, rationalization, and harmonization with the United States economically, socially, and politically" (Hurtig, 1992:4), even spawned a new political party. The National Party of Canada promised, in the 1993 federal election campaign, to end the growth of foreign ownership and control as well as to reverse the growth of excessive corporate concentration (Hurtig, 1992). Failure to win any seats in 1993 and internal dissension led to the demise of the National Party before the next federal election in 1997. In the wake of 9/11, one could argue that the demise of the National Party was

Regional Economic Disparities

Although there is debate about the definition of "region" (Brodie, 1989), there is some justification for defining regions as units with institutional or political boundaries (Breton, 1981; Matthews, 1983). Furthermore, trying to measure regional disparities is easier if data (for example, census data) are collected regularly for the units in question. For these reasons, throughout this text, regions are defined in terms of provinces and territories.

Figure 16–5 shows the variation in the percentage of the labour force employed in manufacturing industries—considered by some to be the real wealth-creating engine of the economy—for Canada's regions or provinces. Despite consistent official efforts to promote regional development and to spread the manufacturing base more evenly across the country, Ontario and Quebec remain the manufacturing core of the Canadian economy, with 23 to 25 percent of their workers involved. Saskatchewan has the weakest manufacturing base of all the provinces, and British Columbia, for all its affluence, is still economically undiversified and overwhelmingly dependent on forestry (Marchak, 1986). Another way of looking at the manufacturing clout of Ontario and Quebec is to note that, with 60 percent of the population, they have 75 percent of the manufacturing jobs.

Brym points out that two explanations have been offered for these regional disparities: the "mainstream" approach

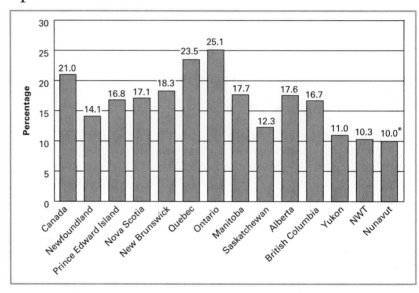

FIGURE 16–5 Percentage of Labour Force Employed in Manufacturing Industries for Canada, the Provinces, and the Territories, 2002

*Estimate due to errors in the data.

Source: Calculations by Gerber, based on Statistics Canada, www.statcan.ca.

and the "radical" or political economy approach. The mainstream approach focuses on the geographic causes of diversity: distance from markets, physical barriers (such as mountains), natural resources (generally in high demand), and population characteristics. From the radical perspective, inequities derive from human actions rather than nature. Confederation allowed "powerful central Canadian economic interests to drain wealth from the weak peripheral or hinterland regions, such as the

prairies and the maritimes" (Brym, 1986:8).

Policies accentuate the disparities by concentrating capital, productive capacity, and jobs in a particular region. Population then flows to that region, which translates into political power (that is, increased representation in Parliament), and eventually into new policies that strengthen the economic centre. With one-half of Canada's population in the Windsor/Quebec City corridor, this trend is difficult to reverse.

---

premature. Since the attack on New York's World Trade Center, Canada has been under severe pressure to increase integration with the United States by harmonizing our policies relating to security, immigration, and the economy. In the absence of the National Party, left-leaning Liberals and the New Democrats are fighting these developments.

CONGLOMERATES AND CORPORATE LINKAGES

The largest businesses are **conglomerates**, *giant corporations composed of many smaller corporations*. Conglomerates emerge as corporations enter new markets, spin off new companies, or take over other companies. Forging

TABLE 16–2 The Top 30 Companies in Canada Ranked by Profits, 2002

Rank by Profit 2002	Company and Province	Profit $000	Revenues $000	No. of Employees	Major Shareholder
1	Royal Bank of Canada ON	2 762 000	23 234 000	59 770	Widely held
2	BCE Inc. QC	2 475 00	19 809 000	66 266	Widely held
3	Bank of Nova Scotia ON	1 797 000	18 310 000	44 633	Widely held
4	Bell Canada ON	1 504 000	15 685 000	54 258	BCE Inc. 100%
5	Bank of Montreal ON	1 417 000	13 059 000	33 912	Widely held
6	Manulife Financial ON	1 378 000	16 532 000	13 000	Widely held
7	EnCana Corp. AB	1 224 000	11 031 000	3646	Widely held
8	Imperial Oil ON	1 210 000	15 821 000	6460	Exxon Mobil Corp. (U.S.) 69.6%
9	Sun Life Financial Services ON	998 000	23 101 000	14 905	Widely held
10	Power Financial QC	988 000	18 700 000	18 300	Power Corp. of Canada 67.4%
11	Petro-Canada AB	974 000	9 917 000	4470	Government of Canada 18.74%
12	Thomson Corp.ON	(US) 615 000	(US) 7 768 000	44 000	Woodbridge Company Ltd. 69%
13	Great-West Lifeco MB	962 000	16 632 000	14 000	Power Financial Corp. 64.99%
14	Magna International ON	(US) 554 000	(US) 13 044 000	70 800	Stronach Trust 66.3%
15	TransCanada PipeLines AB	805 000	5 300 000	2767	Widely held
16	Husky Energy AB	804 000	6 385 000	2753	Li Ka-shing 71.5%
17	Suncor Energy AB	761 000	4 913 000	3422	Widely held
18	Loblaw Companies ON	728 000	23 099 000	122 000	George Weston Ltd. 61%
19	George Weston Ltd. ON	690 000	27 464 000	142 850	W. Galen Weston 62.13%
20	CIBC ON	653 000	17 055 000	42 552	Widely held
21	Power Corp. QC	645 000	19 011 000	19 000	Paul Desmarais & Associates 65%
22	Enbridge Inc. AB	610 100	4 830 600	4000	Widely held
23	Alcan Inc. QC	(US) 374 000	(US) 12 553 000	48 100	Widely held
24	Cdn. Natural Resources AB	574 800	4 114 900	1573	Widely held
25	Canadian Nat'l. Railway Co. QC	571 000	6 173 000	23 190	Widely held
26	Shell Canada AB	561 000	7 314 000	3825	Shell Investments (1996) Ltd. 78%
27	Talisman Energy AB	524 000	5 379 000	1565	Widely held
28	Investors Group MB	511 759	1 940 036	3285	Power Financial Corp. 56.2%
29	Canada Life Financial	499 000	8 598 000	6768	Widely held
30	Cdn. Pacific Railway Ltd. AB	496 000	3 692 600	16 116	Widely held

Source: *Report on Business*, 2003:80.

a conglomerate is also a way to diversify a company, so that new products can provide a hedge against declining profits in the original market. Sometimes these mergers are extremely diverse, as illustrated by the Irving empire, discussed in the "Diversity: Race, Class, and Gender" box on page 402. In the 1980s, Beatrice Foods, then a Canadian company, was another corporate "umbrella," containing more than fifty smaller corporations that manufacture well-known products, including Hunt's foods, Tropicana fruit juices, La Choy foods, Orville Redenbacher popcorn, Max Factor cosmetics, Playtex clothing, and Samsonite luggage—but Beatrice has long since been purchased by Parmalat of Milan, Italy, and lost its diversified umbrella function. Toronto-based George Weston Limited is another corporate umbrella, but it is more clearly in the food sector, owning, among other companies, Loblaws, Zehrs, Provigo, Fortinos, and Interbake Foods (which supplies most of the Girl Guide Cookies to the United States).

Corporations are not only linked in conglomerates, but also by owning each other's stock. For example, in today's global economy, many companies invest heavily in other corporations commonly regarded as their

The Irving Empire

Among the family dynasties Diane Francis examines in *Controlling Interest: Who Owns Canada?* is that of K.C. Irving, based in New Brunswick. "New Brunswick is a company town," claims Francis, "and its proprietor is K.C. Irving." She goes on to describe his empire:

The Irving group of companies is big by anybody's standards. It includes the country's largest shipyard and dry-dock facilities. Irving Oil is one of Canada's ten largest oil companies, with 3000 service stations in Atlantic Canada and the Ottawa Valley, the country's largest refinery, as well as untold holdings in oil and gas discoveries in western Canada. Irving's forestry business is world-scale, including half a dozen pulp and paper mills and sawmills and title to 1.5 million acres of timberlands in New Brunswick and Maine, an area equivalent to the size of Prince Edward Island. These land holdings, which

Irving owns outright, make him the largest private landowner in the Maritimes. He also owns fleets of ships, trucks, buses, and railway cars, most of the media in the province, stores selling cars, food, hardware, drugs, and construction materials, and factories spewing out everything from pre-fab housing to concrete, steel, and hundreds more products. It is hard to get an exact picture of the scope of the Irving empire. None of the companies are publicly owned, and the Irvings fiercely protect their privacy through a complicated and impenetrable corporate structure.

Francis argues that corporate concentration is damaging to the Canadian economy. The Irvings' prosperity has been based, in part, on the ability to lobby politicians, on erecting barriers against competitors, and on a virtual media monopoly. In October 2003, the link between the Irvings and federal politicians suffered an unwelcome bar-

rage of media coverage. One by one, five cabinet ministers admitted to accepting flights and/or salmon-fishing vacations at the Irvings' luxurious lodge. This was acutely embarrassing to Prime Minister Jean Chrétien as he prepared to retire after leading a government that had been repeatedly tainted by scandal.

Since the death of K.C. Irving in 1992, Arthur Irving has taken over as CEO of this vast, privately owned empire. Though its revenues and net income are undisclosed, Arthur Irving is ranked among the two hundred most powerful people in Canada—the Canadian corporate elite. That being said, it is worth noting that the Irving money is now tax-sheltered in Bermuda.

Sources: Francis (1986:16), *Financial Post Magazine* (November 1995:60), and Newman (1998:138).

---

competitors. In the automobile industry, Ford owns a significant share of Mazda, General Motors is a major investor in Isuzu, and DaimlerChrysler is part owner of Mitsubishi.

Besides conglomerates, corporations are also linked by extremely wealthy families who own their stock (Clement, 1975). Among the Canadian families who have had large and varied corporate holdings in Canada (in addition to the Irvings) are the McCains, the Molsons, the Steinbergs, the Eatons, the Desmaraises, the Richardsons, the Mannixes, the Belzbergs, and the Bentleys (Francis, 1986). These families from across Canada know each other, interact socially, and have business interests in common.

Corporations are also linked through *interlocking directorates*, social networks of people serving simultaneously on the boards of directors of many corporations. These connections give corporations access to insider information about each other's products and marketing strategies (Clement, 1975; Marlios, 1975; Herman, 1981; Scott and Griff, 1985). Peter Bentley of

Vancouver-based Canfor Corporation, for example, sits on more than a dozen "blue ribbon boards," has "titled Europeans on his boards and has served on theirs," and has "entered into countless partnerships with English and German firms" (Francis, 1986:193–94).

Not all corporate linkages are formal. Gwen Moore (1979) has described how social networks (discussed in Chapter 7, "Groups and Organizations") informally link members of the corporate elite. In other words, corporate executives travel in many of the same social circles, allowing them to exchange valuable information. Such networks enhance not only the economic clout of big businesses, but also expand the influence of corporate leaders in political, social, and charitable organizations (Clement, 1975; Useem, 1979; Francis, 1986).

Peter C. Newman, columnist and author, argues that the picture outlined above is outdated. Some of the families named are not just old establishment: they go back further to the "Jurassic Canadian Establishment." In his third large volume on the

Canadian establishment, *Titans: How the New Canadian Establishment Seized Power* (1988), Newman argues that Canada's economy is in the hands of a new breed of entrepreneurs. Gone are the days of old family control through family dynasties based on exclusive club memberships, inherited wealth, interlocking directorships, "contacts," and intermarriage. The new establishment, a meritocracy, is based on "what one can do" rather than "whom one knows." The vertical structure of Canadian business has been transformed into a broader one "where nobody really can prevent someone popping up almost anywhere in the scene" (quoting John Evans, p. 18).

Where the old establishment was linked by club membership, the new one is based on networks that are sustained by cell phones, the Internet, and transcontinental flights. The creative spark that gives birth to great enterprises is "hard to define and impossible to reproduce": "the essential life force" that creates and sustains family fortune cannot be passed on to the eldest son through genes" (Newman, 1988:24). The result is that control of Canada's corporate world is slipping away from the old dynasties into the hands of the aggressive, global elite of the new economy.

Corporations: Are They Competitive?

The capitalist model suggests that businesses operate independently in a competitive market. But large corporations are not really competitive because, first, their extensive linkages mean that they do not operate independently; second, a small number of corporations dominate many large markets. In Canada, the competitive sector is made up mostly of small businesses and the self-employed.

From a business point of view, a company establishing a **monopoly**, *domination of a market by a single producer*, could simply dictate prices. A century ago, the U.S. government saw the public danger in this and limited monopolies by law through the *Sherman Anti-Trust Act* of 1890. Canada does not have comparable legislation, but its monopolies have to submit to government regulation. Similarly, Bell Canada and Rogers Cable TV have to apply to the Canadian Radio-television Commission (CRTC) for permission to increase rates.

Although monopolies may be eliminated or at least controlled in North America, the **oligopoly**, or *domination of a market by a few producers*, is a common pattern. Oligopoly arises because the investment needed to enter a major product market, such as the auto industry, is beyond the reach of all but the biggest companies. Moreover, true competition means risk, which big business tries to avoid.

Corporate power is now so great—and competition among corporations so limited—that government regulation is the only way to protect the public interest. Yet the government is the corporate world's single

Corporations are often closely linked, even when they compete in the same market. In the automobile industry, for example, different manufacturers may actually be connected through ownership, as is the case with Ford and Mazda. How might this type of relationship between corporations in the same industry affect the consumer?

biggest customer, and it frequently intervenes to support struggling companies. In truth, corporations and government often work together to make the entire economy more stable and to make businesses more profitable. Paul Martin, as Minister of Finance, had the final say in rejecting the controversial Bank of Montreal/Royal Bank merger.

CORPORATIONS AND THE GLOBAL ECONOMY

Corporations have grown in size and power so fast that they account for most of the world's economic activity. In the process, the largest corporations, centred in the United States, Canada, Japan, and Western Europe, have spilled across national borders and now view the entire world as one vast marketplace.

Multinational corporations produce and market products in many different nations. Canada's Nortel, Magna International, and Alcan are among the huge corporations that earn much—and in some cases, most—of their profits outside their own countries.

Because most of the planet's resources and people are found in less-developed countries, multinationals spread their operations around the world to gain access to raw materials, inexpensive labour, and vast markets. As shown in Figure 16–6, labour costs are far lower in poor countries of the world: a manufacturing worker in Taiwan labours all week to earn what a German worker earns in a single day.

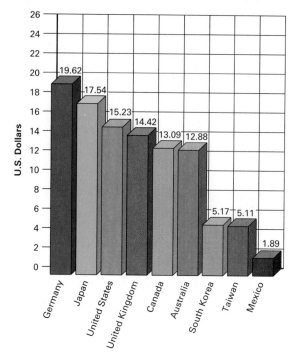

FIGURE 16–6 Average Hourly Wages for Workers in Manufacturing, 1999

Source: Calculations by John Macionis based on U.S. Department of Labor (2000).

The impact of multinationals on poor societies is controversial, as Chapter 12 ("Global Stratification") explains in detail. On one side of the argument, modernization theorists claim that multinationals unleash the great productivity of the capitalist economic system, which will propel poor nations towards a higher standard of living. Specifically, corporations offer poor societies tax revenues, capital investment, new jobs, and advanced technology, which act together to accelerate economic growth (Rostow, 1978; Madsen, 1980; Berger, 1986; Firebaugh and Beck, 1994).

On the other side, dependency theorists argue that multinationals intensify global inequality. Multinational investment, as they see it, actually creates few jobs in poor countries, inhibits the development of local industries, and pushes developing countries to produce goods for export rather than food and other products for local consumption. From this standpoint, multinationals make poor societies poorer and increasingly dependent on rich, capitalist societies (Vaughan, 1978; Wallerstein, 1979; Delacroix and Ragin, 1981; Bergesen, 1983; Walton and Ragin, 1990).

From this perspective, the growth of multinational corporations amounts to little more than an extension of historical colonialism: a neocolonialism now concerned with profit rather than direct political control. As one defender of multinationals asserted, "We are not without cunning. We shall not make Britain's mistake. Too wise to govern the world, we shall simply own it" (cited in Vaughan, 1978:20).

THE ECONOMY OF THE TWENTY-FIRST CENTURY

Social institutions are organizational strategies by which societies meet various needs of their members. But, as we have seen, the Canadian economy only partly succeeds in this respect. Though highly productive, our economy distributes its products in a highly unequal fashion. Moreover, as we move into the new century, economic transformations in our society and the world present us with new opportunities and challenges. One of these challenges, the "brain drain" of Canadian professionals to the United States, is described in the "Applying Sociology" box.

As this chapter highlights, the Information Revolution is driving much of this change. In the post-industrial era, the share of the Canadian labour force involved in the service (or tertiary) sector has increased dramatically to 74 percent. The workers involved in this sector—a broad range, including hairdressers, physicians, researchers, tax consultants, and computer programmers—increasingly are highly skilled and educated people. Most of them (such as teachers from primary to university levels) find that, with each passing year, information technology is more integral to their work.

As we look to the coming years, our society must face up to the fact that millions of men and women lack the language and computer skills needed to participate in a post-industrial economy. Can we afford to consign these workers and their families to the margins of society? How can the government, schools, and families prepare young people to perform the kind of work their society makes available to them?

A second transformation that will define the new century is the emergence of a global economy. Two centuries ago, the ups and downs of a local economy reflected events and trends within a single town. One century ago, local communities throughout the country had become interconnected so that prosperity in once place depended on producing goods demanded by people elsewhere. We have entered the new century with powerful economic connections on the global level. It now makes little sense to speak of a national economy: what Saskatchewan farmers produce and sell may be affected more by what transpires in the wheat-growing region of Russia than by events in

APPLYING SOCIOLOGY

The Brain Drain

Columnist and author Jeffrey Simpson often applies sociological methods to his work, as was the case when he prepared his book, *Star-Spangled Canadians: Canadians Living the American Dream* (2000). His research involved historical and statistical analyses and, most importantly, in-depth interviews with Canadians who live and work in the United States. His book appeared at a time of increasing concern about the "brain drain."

Simpson points out that immigration to the United States is nothing new for Canadians. In fact, historical flows were much larger than the relative trickle today. "Canada's population of 30 million might today be 40 or 50 million had so many Canadians not migrated to the United States, or had so many immigrants to Canada stayed put rather than passing through Canada *en route* to their eventual destination: the United States" (p. 2). The concern about the brain drain stems from the fact that today's minor flow, facilitated by the free trade agreement, consists of highly skilled and educated people lured south by the promise of expanded opportunities and higher incomes: "They are, in a sense, NAFTA's children" (p. 142).

Interviews across the United States revealed that the overwhelming reason for moving to the United States was *opportunity*—not higher income or lower taxes. For some, such as the 2000 to 5000 nurses who have left Canada each

year since 1992, it is simply a matter of finding employment. That many others left for the same reason can be deduced from the fact that for those with university degrees (in 1997), unemployment rates were 2 percent and 4.6 percent for the United States and Canada respectively. With the U.S. economy growing much faster than Canada's, there were simply more and better jobs south of the border. In fact, during the 1990s, many American corporations—most notably Microsoft—began aggressively recruiting on Canadian campuses (especially at the University of Waterloo).

For other Canadian expatriates, opportunity meant better research facilities, state-of-the-art equipment, the ability to work at the "cutting edge" of one's field, greater challenges, larger audiences, a greater critical mass of colleagues, or, more simply, a range and scale of options that cannot be matched in Canada. We are losing our innovators, our creators, and our entrepreneurs in part because American culture celebrates success while ours does not. Those interviewed by Simpson sense "that Americans recognize, honour, and thrive on success, whereas Canadians are more likely to think that a successful person, economically speaking, got there by mysterious means, might have a skeleton or two lurking in the closet, or somehow doesn't quite deserve to be there" (p. 156).

In summary, the numbers are not large when one compares today's brain

drain to historic levels or even to the already reduced levels of the 1950s and 1960s. The important distinction is that recent emigrants do not come from all walks of life, as did their earlier counterparts: the emigrant of the 1990s was more highly skilled and educated, and more likely to be a professional—specifically, part of the knowledge-based economy.

Although 250 000 or more immigrants reach our shores each year—many of them highly educated and holding professional credentials—they cannot necessarily step into the shoes of those who have left. Among recent emigrants are people who were recruited by American companies and universities precisely because they excel in their fields. The ideal, according to Simpson, is to create an environment that continues to attract immigrants (including Americans) while simultaneously slowing the brain drain to the south. In an effort to do just that, our federal government established a program to create up to 2000 Canada Research Chairs that would allow our universities to attract and retain internationally renowned researchers.

 Industry Canada provides links to a number of articles about Canada's brain drain at http://strategis.ic.gc.ca/sc_ecnmy/mera/engdoc/07.html

Source: Based on Simpson (2000).

their own provincial capital. In short, Canadian workers and business owners are not only generating new products and services, but doing so in response to factors and forces that are distant and unseen.

Finally, change is causing analysts around the world to rethink conventional economic models. The emerging global system shows that socialist economies are less productive than their capitalist counterparts,

one important reason for the recent collapse of socialist regimes in Eastern Europe and the former Soviet Union.

But capitalism, too, has seen marked changes, especially an increasing involvement of government in the economy. Moreover, productive enterprises have outgrown national boundaries with the emergence of multinational corporations. The world's societies are

CONTROVERSY & DEBATE

The Market: Does the "Invisible Hand" Serve Our Interests or Pick Our Pockets?

"The market" or "government planning"? Each is a means of economic decision making, determining what products and services companies produce and what people will consume. So important is this process that the degree to which the market or government directs the economy affects how nations define themselves, choose their allies, and identify their enemies.

Historically, the United States has relied on the market—the "invisible hand" of supply and demand—for most economic decisions. Canada has a tradition of greater government involvement in the economy in terms of both control and ownership. (*The North American Free Trade Agreement*, NAFTA, pushes Canada in the direction of reduced government interference in the economy.*

Nevertheless, for the most part, both the United States and Canada allow the market to move prices for products upwards or downwards according to the supply of sellers and the demand of buyers. The market thus co-ordinates the efforts of countless people, each of whom—to return to Adam Smith's insight—is motivated only by self-interest.

Defenders also praise the market for discouraging racial and ethnic prejudice. Though one might restrict one's social contacts, in theory at least, one trades with whomever offers the best deal. Furthermore, as the economists Milton and Rose Friedman (1980) remind us, a more-or-less freely operating market system provides capitalist countries with the highest standards of living. In effect, they argue, the market has produced economic prosperity.

But others point to the contributions government makes to the economy in Canada and, to a lesser extent, in the United States. Government steps in to carry out tasks that no one would do for profit: even Adam Smith, for example, looked to government to defend the country against external enemies. Government also plays a role in constructing and maintaining public projects such as roads and utilities, as well as medical care, education, social security, public housing, and other social services. While Canada is privatizing many of these services, our government still plays a substantial role in the economy—a role that is supported by high levels of taxation.

High taxation and the proliferation of government services and regulation go hand in hand with our widely embraced philosophies of *collectivism* and *egalitarianism*. According to Gairdner (1990:3), these policies allow the central government to "control and engineer the condition of society" in an attempt to ensure *equality of outcome* for all. The effect of this social engineering is to break down traditional values such as "the primacy of honesty, freedom and hard work; respect for society, authority and private property; and all related matters built upon these values." Gairdner and other supporters of free markets believe that minimal state regulation best serves the public interest.

But not everyone views the market as a positive force. For one thing, critics point out, the market has little incentive to produce anything that is not prof-

Although the Information Revolution is centred in high-income countries such as Canada, the effects of high technology are becoming evident even in low income nations. Do you think the expansion of information technology will change the lives of rural people such as these peasants in Vietnam? If so, how?

itable. That is why few private companies set out to meet the needs of poor people since, by definition, they have little money to spend. A number of analysts are critical of a free-wheeling capitalist market economy, which by its nature erodes or threatens essential public services (Barlow and Campbell, 1991; Hurtig, 1991; Shields and McBride, 1994). American ownership of the Canadian economy, corporate power and control, and NAFTA (which pushes us into the embrace of American capitalism) threaten our values, our national identity, and the quality of life of all our citizens. In fact, since Canada is essentially an economic union, diminishing federal involvement in the economy and in the provision of social services even threatens national unity.

Critics look to government to curb what they see as the market system's self-destructive tendencies. Government takes a strong regulatory role, intervening in the market to control inflation (by setting interest rates), protect the well-being of workers (by imposing workplace safety standards), and benefit consumers (by mandating standards for product quality). Even so, advocates of a stronger role for government point out that the power of corporations in Canadian society is so great that the government still cannot effectively challenge the capitalist elite.

Critics also support government's role in curbing the market's tendency to magnify social stratification. Since market economies concentrate income and wealth in the hands of a few, a government system of taxation that applies higher rates to the rich counters this tendency in the name of social justice.

For a number of reasons then, the market operating alone does not serve the public interest. While Canadians are largely supportive of the market, they also see benefits to the public through government involvement in the economy. In fact, government assists not only individual citizens but business itself by providing investment capital, constructing roads and other infrastructure, and shielding companies from foreign competition. Yet in Canada and around the world, people continue to debate the optimal balance of market forces and government decision making.

Continue the debate . . .

1. *How do visions of the market and government intervention in the economy fuel the debate during Canada's federal and provincial elections?*

2. *Why do defenders of the free market assert that "the government that governs best is the government that governs least"?*

3. *In your opinion, does a market system meet the needs of this country's people? Does it serve some better than others?*

4. *Does your family feel that income tax rates in Canada are too high? Too low? Why?*

---

*One notable exception to this trend is the treatment of Canada's poultry, egg, and milk marketing boards, which require trade barriers for their survival. NAFTA's five-member dispute panel—in a "smashing victory" for Canada—voted unanimously to allow Ottawa to maintain high border tariffs indefinitely, in spite of the NAFTA agreement to phase out tariffs between the United States and Canada over eighteen months (Fagan, 1996).

becoming increasingly interconnected, as illustrated by Canada's free trade agreements and the European Economic Community.

What will be the long-term effects of all these changes? Two conclusions seem inescapable: the economic future of Canada and other nations will be played out in a global arena, and we must face up to the issue of global inequality. Whether the world economy ultimately reduces or deepens the disparity between rich and poor societies may well steer our planet towards peace or war.

SUMMARY

1. The economy is a major social institution by which a society produces, distributes, and consumes goods and services.

2. In technologically simple societies, economic activity is subsumed within the family. In agrarian societies, most economic activity takes place apart from the home. Industrialization sparks significant economic expansion built around new sources of energy, factories, mass production, and specialization. In post-industrial economies, the majority of workers provide services rather than contribute to the manufacture of goods.

3. The post-industrial economy is characterized by a productive shift from tangible goods to services. Just

as the Industrial Revolution propelled the industrial economy of the past, so the Information Revolution is now advancing the post-industrial economy.

4. The primary sector of the economy generates raw materials; the secondary sector manufactures various goods; the tertiary sector focuses on providing services. In pre-industrial societies, the primary sector predominates; the secondary sector is of greatest importance in industrial societies; and the tertiary sector prevails in post-industrial societies.

5. The emergence of a global economy means that nations no longer produce and consume products and services within national boundaries. Moreover, the 600 largest corporations, operating internationally, now account for most of the earth's economic output.

6. Social scientists describe the economies of industrial and post-industrial societies in terms of two models. Capitalism is based on private ownership of productive property and the pursuit of profit in a competitive marketplace. Socialism is based on collective ownership of productive property and the pursuit of collective well-being through government control of the economy.

7. Although the Canadian economy is predominantly capitalist, our government is widely involved in economic life. Government plays an even greater economic role in the democratic socialist societies of some Western European nations and the state capitalism of Japan. The former Soviet Union and the nations of Eastern Europe are gradually introducing some market elements into their historically centralized economies.

8. Capitalism is very productive, generally providing a high overall standard of living with extensive civil liberties. Socialism is less productive and restricts civil liberties, but does generate greater economic equality.

9. Agricultural work has declined in Canada during the past century. Blue-collar employment is also reduced and now involves only one-quarter of the labour force. Today, two-thirds of Canadian workers have white-collar service jobs.

10. A profession is a special category of white-collar work based on theoretical knowledge, occupational autonomy, authority over clients, and a claim to serve the community.

11. Work in the primary labour market provides far more rewards than work in the secondary labour market. Most new jobs are in the secondary labour market's service sector.

12. Today, 15 percent of Canada's workers are self-employed. Although many professionals fall into this category, most self-employed workers have blue-collar occupations.

13. Capitalist societies tend to maintain an unemployment rate of at least 5 percent. Socialist societies, too, struggle with high unemployment.

14. The underground economy represents perhaps 15 to 20 percent of the economic activity in Canada, including most criminal business as well as legal income unreported on income tax forms.

15. Corporations form the core of the Canadian economy. The largest corporations, which are conglomerates, account for most corporate assets and profits.

16. The competitive sector of the Canadian economy encompasses smaller businesses. Large corporations dominate the noncompetitive sector.

17. Multinational corporations have grown in number and size during the past century. The consequences for global economic development are a matter of continuing controversy.

CRITICAL-THINKING QUESTIONS

1. What is a social institution? In principle, what is the economy supposed to do? How well do you think our economy does its job?

2. Identify several ways in which the Industrial Revolution reshaped the economy of Canada. How is the Information Revolution transforming the economy once again?

3. What key characteristics distinguish capitalism from socialism? Compare these two systems in terms of productivity, economic inequality, and approach to personal freedom.

APPLICATIONS AND EXERCISES

1. The profile of the Canadian economy—75 percent of output in the tertiary sector, 16.5 in the secondary sector, and less than 4 percent in the primary sector—obscures great variety within this country. A trip to the library and **www.statcan.ca** will allow you to profile your local economy (a city, region, or province).

2. Here are two interesting exercises involving the Internet. Statistics Canada makes available a wide range of data and reports on labour, employment, and unemployment at its website (**www.statcan.ca**). Learn more about Canadian farming at the Canadian Federation of Agriculture's site (**www.cfa-fca.ca**).

3. How are computers changing the character of the university or college campus? Meet with your sociology instructor or an official in the computer centre to find out the various ways computers are used on campus. Is the arrival of new information technology changing professional or personal relationships on campus? How?

4. Visit a discount store such as Zellers or Wal-Mart and select an area of the store of interest to you. Do a little "fieldwork," inspecting products to see where they are made. Does your research support the existence of a global economy?

 ## SITES TO SEE

www.macionis.com
or
www.TheSociologyPage.com

You can find more than fifty weblinks to sociological journals and other sources of data and information by visiting the Links Library at this website.

www.reflection.gc.ca/

This Government of Canada site includes the final report of the Advisory Committee on the Changing Workplace.

www.statcan.ca/english/Pgdb/labour.htm

This site contains Statistics Canada's collection of tables about the Canadian labour market, including information on age and sex, location, commuting, earnings, organized labour, and employment insurance.

www.ilo.org/

Founded in 1919, the International Labour Organization is a UN-specialized agency that seeks the promotion of social justice and internationally recognized human and labour rights.

www.wto.org/

Located in Geneva, Switzerland, the World Trade Organization arranges technical assistance and training for developing countries and provides a forum for international trade negotiations and disputes.

www.fao.org

The Food and Agricultural Organization is a part of the United Nations concerned with how well the global economy meets the needs of the world's people. From their main page, look for their annual report "State of Food Insecurity in the World."

 ## STUDY TOOLS

For more study tools to help you with your next exam, be sure to check out the Companion Website at **www.pearsoned.ca/macionis**, as well as Chapter 16 in your Study Guide.

 ## INVESTIGATE WITH CONTENTSELECT

Follow the instructions found on page 25 of this textbook to access ContentSelect™ at the Research Navigator™ website. Once at the site, enter your LOGINID and Password. Then, enter keywords such as "professions," "monopoly," and "underground economy," and the search engine will supply relevant and recent scholarly and popular press publications.

CHAPTER
17

Christiane Pflug (1936–1972, Canadian)
With the Black Flag, 1971

POLITICS AND GOVERNMENT

In April 1997, a sudden spring thaw and relentless rain brought the crest of a flood north from the United States—where it had already done extensive damage—through the farmlands and small towns of southern Manitoba, right into the city of Winnipeg. As the flood spread, volunteers from across the country and the Canadian Forces arrived to assist with building sandbag dykes and, as was too often necessary, with evacuation.

Intensive television coverage of the "flood of the century" allowed Canadians to monitor the crisis and share the experiences of the victims—as 27 000 people were evacuated and 180 000 hectares of farmland were wiped out. School children across the country engaged in a variety of fundraising activities, contributing to the $12 million raised by Canadians for flood relief.

While the rest of us watched and worried, Jean Chrétien and his Liberal government faced a

dilemma: as the floodwaters rose, Canada was gearing up for a spring election set for June 2. Regulations regarding the length of federal campaigns made it necessary to decide on and call the election date in the week following the declaration of a state of emergency in Manitoba. The prime minister visited the flood site, passed sandbags along the dyke, and worried about the political consequences of calling an election while part of the country was facing disaster. The pressures on him to postpone were considerable, but in the end—since the wheels were already in motion—he decided to go ahead with the election, and make arrangements for people in the flood area to go to the polls at a later date.

The Liberals won a second consecutive majority government in that election, although their total number of seats declined from 177 to 155. In Manitoba, Liberal representation dropped by half—from 12 to 6 seats.

This chapter investigates the dynamics of power within societies and among nations, explaining the rules of the game and noting why people sometimes break them. **Politics**, or, more formally, "the polity," is *the institutionalized system by which a society distributes power, sets the society's agenda, and makes decisions.* Politics, in short, is about power, a topic about which there is considerable disagreement around the world as well as here at home.

POWER AND AUTHORITY

Every society rests on **power**, which sociologist Max Weber (1978; orig. 1921) defined as *the ability to achieve desired ends despite resistance.* To a large degree, the exercise of power is the business of **government**, *a*

formal organization that directs the political life of a society. Yet, as Weber explained, few governments obtain compliance by openly threatening their people. Most of the time, people respect (or, at least, accept) their political system.

Practically speaking, it would be difficult for any large, complex society to persist if power derived only from sheer force, and life in such a society would be a nightmare of terror. Social organization, in contrast, depends on some degree of consensus about proper goals (often in the form of cultural values) and suitable means of pursuing them (cultural norms).

Every society, then, seeks to establish its power as legitimate. Weber therefore focused on the concept of **authority**, *power that people perceive as legitimate rather than coercive.* How is sheer power transformed into stable authority? There are three ways, Weber explained, and the one a society relies on most depends on its level of economic development.

TRADITIONAL AUTHORITY

Pre-industrial societies, Weber explained, rely on **traditional authority**, *power legitimized through respect for long-established cultural patterns*. In ideal terms, traditional authority is power woven into a society's collective memory, so that people consider social arrangements almost sacred. Chinese emperors in antiquity were legitimized by tradition, as were nobles in medieval Europe. The power of tradition was strong enough that people typically viewed members of the hereditary ruling families as godlike.

But traditional authority declines as societies industrialize. Hannah Arendt (1963) pointed out that traditional authority is compelling only as long as everyone shares the same heritage and world view. This form of authority, then, is undermined by the specialization demanded by industrial production, by modern, scientific thinking, and also by the social change and cultural diversity that accompany immigration. Thus, no prime minister of Canada today would claim to rule by the grace of God. However, we still have a monarch, Queen Elizabeth II, as our head of state, although today's more democratic culture has shifted real power to commoners popularly elected to office. On the recommendation of our prime minister, the queen appoints the governor general, who performs largely ceremonial functions such as opening Parliament. Despite this minimal role, many Canadians are uncomfortable with any attachment to the monarchy. The recent decline in prestige suffered by the British monarchy contributed to Canada's move from deference to defiance—the Canadian revolution described by Peter C. Newman (1995).

If traditional authority plays a smaller part in politics, it persists in other aspects of everyday life. Patriarchy, the domination of women by men, is a traditional form of power that remains widespread, even though it is increasingly challenged. Less controversial is the traditional authority parents exert over their children. The fact that traditional authority is linked to a person's status as parent is obvious every time a parent answers a doubting child with "Because I said so!" There is no debating the parent's decision because that would defeat traditional authority by putting parent and child on equal footing.

RATIONAL-LEGAL AUTHORITY

Weber defined **rational-legal authority** (sometimes called *bureaucratic authority*) as *power legitimized by legally enacted rules and regulations*. Rational-legal authority, then, is power legitimized in the operation of lawful government.

As Chapter 7 ("Groups and Organizations") explains, Weber viewed bureaucracy as the organizational backbone of rational-thinking, industrial societies. Moreover, just as a rational world view promotes bureaucracy, so it erodes traditional customs and practices. Instead of venerating the past, members of modern societies look to formally enacted rules—especially law—for principles of justice.

Rationally enacted rules also underlie many power relationships in everyday life. The authority of classroom teachers and deans, for example, rests on the offices they hold in bureaucratic universities and colleges. The police, too, are officers, within the bureaucracy of local government. In contrast to traditional authority, rational-legal authority flows not from family background but from organizational position. Thus, while a queen rules for life, a modern prime minister accepts and relinquishes power according to law; prime ministerial authority lies in the office, not in the person.

CHARISMATIC AUTHORITY

Finally, Max Weber claimed power could be transformed into authority through charisma. **Charismatic authority** is *power legitimized through extraordinary personal abilities that inspire devotion and obedience*. Unlike tradition and rational law, then, charisma has less to do with social organization and is more a mark of an especially forceful and magnetic personality.

Throughout history, some members of societies have been regarded as charismatic. Charisma can enhance the stature of an established leader or strengthen the appeal of an outside challenger. Charismatics turn an audience into followers, often making their own rules and challenging the status quo: Vladimir Lenin guided the overthrow of feudal monarchy in Russia in 1917; Mahatma Gandhi inspired the struggle to free India from British colonialism after World War II; Martin Luther King, Jr., galvanized the civil rights movement in the United States; and, through her work ministering to the Learn more about Martin Luther King and the struggle for civil rights in America at www.stanford.edu/group/King/ poor in Calcutta, India, Mother Teresa asked the world to confront stunning poverty.

The prospects of politicians in Canada rise or fall according to their degree of personal charisma. Among our more charismatic prime ministers, John Diefenbaker (1957–63) and Pierre Elliott Trudeau (1968–79, 1980–84) were able to inspire Canadians with oratory and a vision of Canada. The "Trudeaumania" that accompanied Trudeau into his first term of office is a phenomenon that has not been matched since. René Lévesque and Lucien Bouchard were among our other charismatic leaders.

Because charismatic authority emanates from a single individual, any charismatic movement faces a crisis of survival upon the loss of its leader. Thus, Weber explained, the persistence of a charismatic movement depends on the **routinization of charisma**, *the transformation of charismatic authority into some combination of traditional and bureaucratic authority.* Christianity, for example, began as a cult driven by the personal charisma of Jesus of Nazareth. After his death, the Roman Catholic Church gradually emerged on the twin foundations of tradition and bureaucracy, and it continues to flourish today, two thousand years later.

POLITICS IN GLOBAL PERSPECTIVE

Political systems have taken many forms throughout history. Technologically simple hunting-and-gathering societies, once found all over the planet, operated like one large family. Leadership generally fell to a male with unusual strength, hunting skill, or personal charisma. But these leaders exercised little power, since they lacked the resources to control their own people, much less extend their rule outward. In the simplest societies, then, leaders were barely discernible from everyone else, and government did not exist as a distinct sphere of life (Lenski et al., 1995).

Larger and more complex agrarian societies are characterized by specialized activity and material surplus. These societies become hierarchical, with a small elite gaining control of most wealth and power; politics moves outside the family to become a social institution in its own right. Leaders who manage to pass along their power over several generations may acquire traditional authority, perhaps even claiming divine right to govern. Such leaders also may benefit from Weber's rational-legal authority since they are served by a bureaucratic political administration and system of law.

As societies expand, politics eventually takes the form of a national government or *political state*. But the emergence of a political state depends on technology. Just a few centuries ago, armies moved slowly and communication over even short distances was uncertain. For this reason, early political empires—such as Mesopotamia in the Middle East about five thousand years ago—took the form of many small *city-states*.

More complex technology helped the modern world develop the larger-scale system of *nation-states*. While the world has 192 independent nation-states, each with a somewhat distinctive political system, the world's political systems can be analyzed in terms of four categories: monarchy, democracy, authoritarianism, and totalitarianism.

MONARCHY

Monarchy (with Latin and Greek roots meaning "one ruler") is *a political system in which a single family rules from generation to generation.* Monarchy is typical in the

The death of Pierre Elliott Trudeau (1919–2000), though not unexpected, resulted in an unprecedented outpouring of emotion and tributes from Canadians across the country. No one—not even his sons—could have foreseen the public reaction to the death of our charismatic, infuriating, flamboyant, enigmatic former prime minister. Whatever our individual feelings about this exceptional man, it is clear that he has become part of our collective definition of what it means to be Canadian—on both national and global scales.

history of agrarian societies: the Bible, for example, tells of great kings such as David and Solomon. Today's British monarchy—the Windsor family—traces its lineage back roughly a thousand years. In Weber's terms, then, monarchy is legitimized primarily by tradition.

During the medieval era, *absolute monarchy*, in which hereditary rulers claimed a monopoly of power based on divine right, flourished from England to China and in parts of the Americas. Monarchs in some nations, such as Saudi Arabia, still exercise virtually absolute control over their people.

Over the course of the past century, monarchs have gradually given way to elected officials. Europe's remaining monarchs—in Great Britain, Spain, Norway, Sweden, Belgium, Denmark, and the Netherlands—now preside over *constitutional monarchies*. They serve as symbolic heads of state while elected politicians led by a prime minister govern according to political principles embodied in a constitution. In these nations, then, the nobility may formally reign, but elected officials actually rule.

DEMOCRACY

The historical trend in the modern world is towards **democracy**, *a political system in which power is exercised* *by the people as a whole*. The members of democratic societies rarely participate directly in decision making; numbers alone make this an impossibility. Instead, a system of *representative democracy* places authority in the hands of elected leaders who are accountable to the people.

Most rich countries of the world claim to be democratic. Economic development and democratic government go together because both depend on a literate populace. Moreover, the traditional legitimization of power in a monarchy gives way, with industrialization, to rational-legal authority. A rational election process puts leaders in offices regulated by law. Thus, democracy and rational-legal authority are linked, just as monarchy and traditional authority are.

But countries such as Canada are not truly democratic for two reasons. First, there is the problem of bureaucracy. All democratic political systems rely on the work of large numbers of bureaucratic officials. The actual task of public administration in Canada involves close to 780 000 people as federal, provincial, and municipal employees, making the government Canada's largest employer. The vast majority of these bureaucrats are never elected by anyone and are not directly accountable to the people (Scaff, 1981; Edwards, 1985; Etzioni-Halevy, 1985).

The second problem involves economic inequality. In a highly stratified society, the rich will have far more political clout than the poor. Moreover, given the even greater resources of large organizations (such as multinational corporations), how can we think our "democratic" system responds to—or even hears—the voices of "average people"?

Democracy and Freedom: Capitalist and Socialist Approaches

Despite the problems we have just described, rich capitalist nations such as Canada claim to operate as democracies. Of course, socialist countries such as Cuba and the People's Republic of China make the same claim. This curious fact suggests we need to look more closely at *political economy*: the interplay of politics and economics.

The political life of Canada, the United States, and the nations of Europe is largely shaped by the economic principles of capitalism. The pursuit of profit within a market system requires that "freedom" be defined in terms of people's rights to act in their own self-interest. Thus, the capitalist approach to political freedom translates into personal liberty—to act in whatever ways maximize profits or other forms of income. From this point of view, moreover, "democracy" means that individuals have the right to select their leaders from those running for office.

As we noted earlier, capitalist societies are marked by striking inequality of wealth: if everyone

acts in a self-interested way, the inevitable result is that some people accumulate far more wealth and power than others. It is this elite, then, that dominates the economic and political life of the society.

Socialist systems, in contrast, claim they are democratic because their economies meet everyone's basic needs for housing, schooling, work, and medical care. But critics of socialism counter that the extensive government regulation of social life in these countries can become oppressive. The socialist governments of China and Cuba, for example, do not allow their people to move freely inside or outside their borders and do not tolerate organized political opposition.

These contrasting approaches to democracy and freedom raise an important question: Are economic equality and political liberty compatible? To foster economic equality, socialism constrains the choices of individuals. Capitalism, on the other hand, provides broad political liberties, which, in practice, mean little to the poor. A look back at Global Map 10–1 on page 253 shows the extent of income inequality in the world's nations. Global Map 17–1 shows one organization's assessment of the extent of political freedom around the world.

According to Freedom House, a New York–based organization that tracks global political trends, by 1991 more people in the world were "free" than "not free" for the first time in history. Since then, however, they say the tide has turned against democracy. In 2001, they characterized just 41 percent of the world's people as "free," 24 percent as "partly free," and 35 percent as "not free" (Freedom House, 2001).

AUTHORITARIANISM

As a matter of policy, some nations give their people little voice in politics. **Authoritarianism** refers to *a political system that denies popular participation in government*. An authoritarian government is not only indifferent to people's needs, but it lacks the legal means to remove leaders from office, and provides people with little or no way even to voice their opinions. Polish sociologist Wlodzimierz Wesolowski (1990:435) sums up authoritarianism this way: "the authoritarian philosophy argues for the supremacy of the state [over other] organized social activity."

The absolute monarchies in Saudi Arabia and Kuwait are highly authoritarian, as are the military juntas in Congo and Ethiopia, where political dissatisfaction is widespread. But heavy-handed government does not always breed popular opposition, as we can see in the "Global Sociology" box—a look at the "soft authoritarianism" that thrives in the small Asian nation of Singapore.

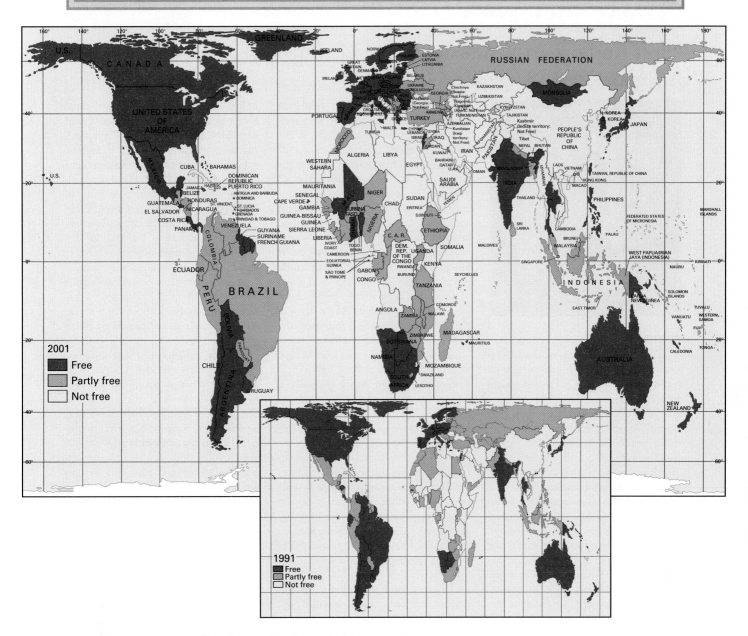

GLOBAL MAP 17–1 Political Freedom in Global Perspective

In 2001, 86 of the world's nations, containing 41 percent of all people, were politically "free"—that is, they offered their citizens extensive political and civil liberties. Another 58 countries, which included 24 percent of the world's people, were "partly free," with more limited rights and liberties. The remaining 48 nations, home to 35 percent of humanity, fall into the category of "not free." In these countries, government sharply restricts individual initiative. Between 1980 and 2000, democracy made significant gains, largely in Latin America and Eastern Europe. In Asia, India (containing 1 billion people) returned to the "free" category in 1999 after falling into the "partly free" category for 7 years. In 2000, Mexico joined the ranks of nations considered "free" for the first time.

Source: Freedom House (2001).

"Soft Authoritarianism" or Planned Prosperity?
A Report from Singapore

To many, Singapore, a tiny nation on the tip of the Malay peninsula with a population of just over 4.6 million, seems an Asian paradise. Surrounded by poor societies grappling with rapidly increasing populations, squalid, sprawling cities, and rising crime rates, Singapore's affluence, cleanliness, and safety make North American visitors think more of a theme park than a country.

In fact, since its independence from Malaysia in 1965, Singapore has startled the world with its economic development; its per capita income now rivals that of the United States. But unlike the United States, Singapore has scarcely any social problems such as crime, slums, unemployment, or children living in poverty. In fact, people in Singapore don't even contend with traffic jams, graffiti on subway cars, or litter in the streets.

The key to Singapore's orderly environment is the omnipresence of government, which actively promotes traditional morality and regulates just about everything. The state owns and manages most of the country's housing and has a hand in many businesses. It provides tax incentives for proper family planning and completing additional years of schooling. To keep traffic under control, the government slaps hefty surcharges on cars, pushing the price of a basic sedan up around $40 000.

Singapore has tough anti-crime laws that mandate death by hanging for drug dealing and permit police to detain a person suspected of a crime without charge or trial. The government has outlawed some religious groups (including Jehovah's Witnesses) and bans pornography outright. Even smoking in public brings a heavy fine. To keep the city streets clean, the state forbids smoking in public, bans eating on the subway, imposes stiff fines for littering, and has even outlawed chewing gum.

In economic terms, Singapore defies familiar categories. Government control of scores of businesses, including television stations, telephone service, airlines, and taxis, seems socialist. Yet, unlike most socialist enterprises, these businesses are operated efficiently and very profitably. Moreover, Singapore's capitalist culture applauds economic growth (although the government cautions people about the evils of excessive materialism), and this nation is home to hundreds of multinational corporations.

Singapore's political climate is as unusual as its economy. Members of this society feel the hand of government far more than their counterparts in Canada. Just as important, one political organization—the People's Action party—has ruled Singapore without opposition since the nation's independence thirty years ago.

Clearly, Singapore is not a democratic country in the conventional sense. But most people in this prospering nation wholeheartedly endorse their way of life. Singapore's political system offers a simple bargain: government demands unflinching loyalty; in return, it provides security and prosperity. Critics charge that this system amounts to a "soft authoritarianism" that stifles dissent and controls people's lives. Most of the people of Singapore, however, know the struggles of living elsewhere and, for now at least, consider the trade-off a good one.

Source: Adapted from Branegan (1993).

TOTALITARIANISM

The most restrictive political form is **totalitarianism**, *a political system that extensively regulates people's lives.* Totalitarian governments emerged only during the past century, with the development of the technological means for rigidly regulating a populace. The Vietnamese government closely monitors the activities of its citizens as well as visitors to the country. Similarly, the government of North Korea uses surveillance equipment and sophisticated computers to store vast amounts of information and thereby manipulate an entire population.

Although some totalitarian governments claim to represent the will of the people, most seek to bend people to the will of the government. As the term itself implies, such governments are *total* concentrations of power, allowing no organized opposition. Denying the populace the right to assemble for political purposes and controlling access to information, these governments thrive in an environment of social atomization and fear. In the former Soviet Union, for example, most citizens could not own telephone directories, copying equipment, fax machines, and even accurate city maps.

Socialization in totalitarian societies is intensely political, seeking not just compliance but personal commitment to the system. In North Korea, one of the world's most totalitarian states, pictures of leaders and political messages broadcast over loudspeakers constantly remind citizens that they owe total allegiance to the state. Government-controlled schools and mass media present only official versions of events.

Government indoctrination is especially intense whenever political opposition surfaces in a totalitarian society (Arendt, 1958; Friedrich and Brzezinski, 1965; Nisbet, 1966; Goldfarb, 1989). After the 1989 pro-democracy movement in the People's Republic of China, for example, officials demanded that citizens report all "unpatriotic" people—even members of their own families—and subjected students at Beijing universities to political "refresher" courses.

Totalitarian governments span the political spectrum from fascist (including Nazi Germany) to communist (North Korea). In some totalitarian states, businesses are privately owned (as was the case in Nazi Germany and, more recently, in Chile); in others, businesses are government-owned (as in North Korea, Cuba, and the former Soviet Union). In all cases, however, one party claims total control of the society and permits no opposition.

A GLOBAL POLITICAL SYSTEM?

Chapter 16 ("The Economy and Work") described the emergence of a global economy, by which more and more companies operate with little regard to national boundaries. Is there a parallel development of a global political system?

On one level, the answer is no. Although most of the world's economic activity now involves more than one nation, the planet remains divided into nation-states, just as it has been for centuries. The United Nations (founded in 1945) might seem like a step towards global government, but, to date, its political role has been limited.

On another level, however, politics has become a global process. In the minds of some analysts, multinational corporations represent a new political order, since they have enormous power to shape social life throughout the world. From this point of view, politics is dissolving into business as corporations grow larger than governments.

Then, too, the Information Revolution has helped move national politics onto the world stage. Hours before the Chinese government sent troops to Tiananmen Square to crush the 1989 pro-democracy movement,

The members of the House of Commons represent the 301 electoral districts distributed across the country according to population. The daily "Question Period" gives members of the opposition parties a chance to grill the prime minister and cabinet ministers in front of the television cameras.

officials "unplugged" the satellite transmitting systems of news agencies to keep the world from watching. Despite their efforts, news of the massacre flashed around the world in minutes via fax machines in universities and private homes.

Finally, several thousand nongovernmental organizations (NGOs) are now in operation, most with global membership and focus. Typically, these organizations seek to advance universal principles, such as human rights (Amnesty International) or an ecologically sustainable world (Greenpeace). In the twenty-first century, NGOs will almost certainly play a key part in forming a global political culture (Boli and Thomas, 1997).

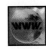 Information about and links to nongovernmental organizations can be found at www.ngo.org/

In short, then, just as the economies of individual nations are linked globally, so are their politics. Today, no nation exists strictly within its own borders.

POLITICS IN CANADA

Canada's national existence comes from the other side of the political upheaval that gave birth to the United States. As Seymour Martin Lipset points out, "The United States is the country of the revolution, Canada of the counterrevolution." The Americans sought "a form of rule derived from the people and stressing individualism," while Canadians desired "free institutions within a strong monarchical state" (1991:1). "Life, liberty, and the pursuit of happiness" are the goals of our neighbours to the south; we chose "peace, order, and good government."

TABLE 17–1 Dates of Entry into Confederation	
Province or Territory	**Date**
New Brunswick	July 1, 1867
Nova Scotia	July 1, 1867
Ontario	July 1, 1867
Quebec	July 1, 1867
Manitoba	July 15, 1870
Northwest Territories*	July 15, 1870
British Columbia	July 20, 1871
Prince Edward Island	July 1, 1873
Yukon Territory	June 13, 1898
Alberta	September 1, 1905
Saskatchewan	September 1, 1905
Newfoundland	March 31, 1949
Nunavut**	April 1, 1999

*Rupert's Land and the North-Western Territories (including central-to-northern Ontario and Quebec and the area west to B.C. and north to the Arctic) was purchased from the Hudson's Bay Company in 1870. A small portion became Manitoba; the remainder, known as the North-West Territories, was governed from Ottawa. Yukon Territory, Alberta, Saskatchewan, and the Northwest Territories were later established from this area.
**Nunavut is a federal territory carved out of lands in the Northwest Territories.

Sources: Adapted from Waite (1988); Hall (1999); and *Canadian Global Almanac 2003* (2003).

Part of the impetus for Confederation was economic, but the leaders in various parts of what was to become Canada were watching nervously over their shoulders, fearing economic and political absorption, if not military conquest, by the increasingly populous and aggressive United States. The various parts of Canada came together somewhat reluctantly: Newfoundlanders initially rejected Confederation in an 1869 election, and the people of Nova Scotia would have done the same had they been asked to vote on the issue. Nowhere did political union occur without vigorous debate and passionate opposition. Table 17–1 reveals that Canada was formed in bits and pieces from 1867 to 1949, when Newfoundland voted "Yes" to Confederation in a referendum.

Because the provinces joined Canada at different times and through various kinds of agreements, they have never had uniform relationships with the federal government. Furthermore, Quebec was seen as unique from the beginning because of its French-speaking Catholic majority. Canada is a rather loose confederation in that important powers were left in provincial hands. Questions of federal–provincial jurisdiction—the centralization or decentralization of power—have been with us since 1867 and may never be fully resolved. The arrival on the scene of the Canadian Alliance (formerly Reform) revitalized that debate: the Alliance wanted to enhance the powers of the provinces.

Canada's provincial structure, its geographic size and diversity, and its immigration and settlement history added an important regional dimension to our collective identity and to Canadian politics. The presence of Quebec, the only entity with a French-speaking majority in North America, adds to our "Canadian" experience in terms of identity, federal–provincial relations, and unity. Our existence as a "fragile federation" (Marsden and Harvey, 1979), ever mindful of the factors that divide and unite us, is expressed in our continuous constitutional navel-gazing.

Canadians are represented in Parliament by the Senate (an appointed body with 105 seats apportioned on a regional basis to the Maritimes, Ontario, Quebec, and the West[1]) and the House of Commons (with 301 seats distributed roughly on the basis of population). Quebec and Ontario together elect 59 percent, or 178, of the 301 members of Parliament, so they have a decisive impact on which party wins the most seats, and who becomes prime minister. Also, the predominance of MPs from Ontario and Quebec reduces the likelihood that Parliament will pass legislation contrary to the interests of central Canada. The unhappiness of the peripheral provinces with the political clout of central Canada at both House of Commons and Senate levels was behind the quest for a *Triple-E Senate* that is equal, effective, and elected.

 The Parliamentary Internet site, created and maintained jointly by the Senate, House of Commons, and Library of Parliament, offers information on the Canadian Parliament, including news updates and back issues of *Hansard*: go to www.parl.gc.ca/

Equal Senate representation for all provinces would counter Quebec/Ontario dominance in the House.

CULTURE, ECONOMICS, AND POLITICS

Unlike Americans, who embrace individualism wholeheartedly, Canadians endorse it with ambivalence. Our individualism is tempered by a sense of communal responsibility, recognition of legitimate group interests, and the realization that we are, in the words of former prime minister Joe Clark, a "community of communities." When the Trudeau government gave us our *Charter of Rights and Freedoms* in 1982, analysts pointed out that we had moved closer to embracing the individualism of the United States:

> The Canadian *Charter of Rights and Freedoms* is not the American *Bill of Rights*. It preserves the principle of parliamentary supremacy and places less emphasis on individual, as distinct from group, rights than does the

[1]There are twenty-four seats in the Senate for each of the regions named, plus six for Newfoundland and one each for the Yukon, Northwest Territories, and Nunavut.

American document. But the Charter brings Canada much closer to the American stress on protection of the individual and acceptance of judicial supremacy with its accompanying encouragement to litigiousness than is true of other parliamentary countries. (Lipset, 1991:3)

In accordance with our emphasis on the collectivity, Canadians endorse a broadly interventionist government. Although in recent years Canadians have been increasingly worried about the costs of government activity, they nonetheless expect government to deal with national defence, law and order, international relations, radio and television broadcasting, stabilization of the economy, regional development, pensions, employment insurance, welfare, transportation, education (right up through university), and medical care. In fact, to the extent that we can articulate a "Canadian" identity, it is based on some of the government services that make us a tolerant and caring society. The widespread anxiety about free trade with the United States arose partly from the fear of job loss, but also from the fear that resulting pressures to harmonize with our powerful neighbour to the south would threaten our social welfare programs and particularly our medicare system.

Government in Canada is more involved in the daily lives of its citizens than in the United States, but this does not mean that Canadians are in complete agreement regarding the appropriateness of that involvement. Some people feel that governments should take a more activist role in areas such as child care, job creation, minority rights, employment or pay equity, and environmental protection. Others feel that government already does far too much, at too great expense, and that it should be withdrawing many of its programs and encouraging privatization of services where feasible. These differences in perspective are in part a function of socioeconomic status and regional subculture, and are reflected in the policies and platforms of Canada's political parties.

The cost of government involvement in the lives of citizens is reflected in the level of taxation. Figure 17–1 shows that Canada falls between some European countries and the United States in terms of tax revenues.

POLITICAL PARTIES

Since about the time of Confederation, Canadians have joined to form **political parties**, *organizations operating within the political system that seek control of the government*. Although we take political parties for granted today as part of a democracy, the party system had tentative beginnings here (and was hotly debated in the United States, where George Washington and Benjamin Franklin, among others, feared that parties would tear their fledgling nation apart).

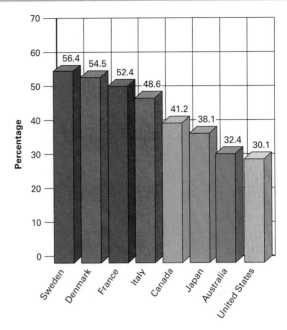

GLOBAL SNAPSHOT

FIGURE 17–1 The Size of Government: Tax Revenues as Share of Gross Domestic Product, 1999

Source: U.S. Census Bureau (2000).

The two political parties that we have known since the 1860s trace their roots to the period after 1840, when the United Provinces of Upper and Lower Canada came into being. In fact, a "Liberal-Conservative" coalition of factions under Sir George-Étienne Cartier and Sir John A. Macdonald provided sufficient political stability to allow for the negotiation of Confederation. The first House of Commons had, among others, "Tory" (Conservative) and "Grit" (Liberal) factions, which, by 1867, were beginning to align themselves with specific sets of policies and supporters. The Tories were "firmly protectionist, expansionist, and pro-business," while the Grits were "anti-railroad, anti-protectionist, and pro-agrarian" (Van Loon and Whittington, 1981:326–27).

After World War I, a number of minor parties appeared on the scene, the most long-lived of which was the anti-capitalist Co-operative Commonwealth Federation (CCF), which became the New Democratic Party (NDP) after 1961.

In recent decades, about twenty different parties have registered at the federal level alone—some of them surviving only long enough to contest one election. Although each of these parties has fielded candidates

Native Self-Government

Canada's Native peoples have never been treated just like other Canadians—for good historical reasons. The first European explorers and settlers encountered fifty-five *founding nations* or *First Nations* (Dickason, 1997), distinct linguistic and cultural groups spread across the continent and north to the Arctic. The groups were self-governing within traditional territories and had formal relationships between tribes. The Iroquois, or Six Nations Confederacy,* had an elaborate constitution and federal structure. Fifty hereditary peace chiefs met yearly to deal with common problems and make new laws. "The laws and decisions of the Confederacy were passed on by word of mouth and recorded in wampum, arguably the world's oldest constitution, predating the American Constitution by 200 years" (Nader et al., 1992). Some aspects of this constitution were incorporated into the federal structures of both the United States and Canada.

The First Nations taught the explorers and early settlers to survive on this harsh continent, introducing them to corn, squash, beans, potatoes, and tobacco. The fur trade would have been impossible without Native expertise, labour, and the canoe, the design of which has not been improved (Nader et al., 1992). If most of the Six Nations, with their widespread reputation for

military prowess, had not sided with the British against the French in the 1750s and with the British and the Loyalists during the American Revolution (1777), Canada might now be either French or part of the United States. As the Americans launched their attack on Canada in 1812, the British concluded that "Amerindian support was vital to the preservation of Britain's remaining North American colonies" (Dickason, 1992:217).

As settlers flowed into Canada, the old fur trade partners and military allies found themselves in conflict as pressures built up over land. To avoid the kind of Native resistance to settlement that had occurred in the United States, a number of treaties were negotiated with some groups, dating from the pre-Confederation period in the Maritimes through to 1921 in the Northwest Territories. The descendants of the Natives who signed treaties are now called *treaty* or *status Indians*.

The terms of the treaties varied over time and across the country (Frideres, 1998), but most commonly they involved the surrender of lands in exchange for reserves and other guarantees. The interpretation of the treaties has been the subject of considerable debate, for the actual wording of the treaties did not usually coincide with the understandings of Native people. More important, in light of the current quest for self-government, is

the debate about whether the existence of treaties implied recognition of Native sovereignty. There are indications that sovereignty was recognized, and many Native peoples believe that they were sovereign prior to the treaties and that the treaties did not extinguish that sovereignty.

Section 35 of Canada's Constitution (patriated in 1982) recognized and affirmed the existing Aboriginal and treaty rights of Aboriginal peoples, including Indian, Inuit, and Métis. Five years later, when the Meech Lake Accord was negotiated in an effort to have Quebec sign on to the Constitution, Native people's request for recognition of their right to self-government was ignored altogether. A technicality in Manitoba allowed a Native member of the Legislative Assembly, Elijah Harper, the historic opportunity to scuttle "Meech" just before its ratification deadline in 1990.

Representatives of four Native organizations participated in the next round of constitutional negotiation, with the result that the Charlottetown Accord of August 1992 recognized the *inherent*** right to self-government of Native people: "The Aboriginal peoples of Canada, being the first peoples to govern this land, have the right to promote their languages, cultures and traditions and to ensure the integrity of their societies, and their governments constitute one of three orders of gov-

---

in ridings across the country, only the Progressive Conservative, Liberal, New Democratic, and Social Credit parties have elected MPs over extended periods of time. The "newest kids on the block" turned Canadian politics upside down in the federal election of 1993, and nothing has been the same since. In that year, the Bloc Québécois and the Reform Party entered Canada's political arena and gave regionalism—in Quebec and the West—a new face. By 2000, after

failing in its attempt to merge with the Progressive Conservatives, Reform changed its name to the Canadian Reform Conservative Alliance (Canadian Alliance, for short). Faced with the prospect of electoral annihilation by a Paul Martin–led Liberal Party, the two parties made a second last-ditch effort to merge in the fall of 2003. The result was a new Conservative Party of Canada, with a new leader and a new constitution, ready to contest Election 2004.

ernment in Canada." The defeat of this accord in the referendum of October 26, 1992, was a bitter disappointment to the Native negotiators. The likelihood is small that a combination of historic conditions, political personalities, and public mood will generate a similar compromise in the foreseeable future.

In the meantime, a number of Native communities have proceeded to manage their own affairs, and the Royal Commission on Aboriginal Peoples (1997) declares that the right of Aboriginal peoples to govern themselves predates Confederation, has a basis in Canadian law, and is already protected in our Constitution. A number of formal self-government agreements have already been negotiated between various Native groups, the federal government, and their respective provinces.

In a dramatic development, the Northwest Territories decided in a 1992 plebiscite to carve a new territory out of its eastern region. Although it is not self-government as the Assembly of First Nations would define it,*** Nunavut, with one-fifth of Canada's land mass and a population that is 80 percent Inuit, became a distinct entity with its own territorial government in 1999. The development of Nunavut will be enhanced by the existence of the Inuit Broadcasting Corporation (IBC), numerous successful cooperatives, and

experienced Inuit businesspeople, but the Inuit people still face formidable challenges as they assume the tasks of territorial government.

In a report on self-determination, the Grand Council of the Crees (1995) concluded that Quebec has no right to secede from Canada nor to forcibly include the Crees and their territories in a sovereign Quebec. When Quebec held its sovereignty referendum in October 1995, the Crees conducted their own referendum in which they almost unanimously chose *not* to be part of an independent Quebec. A Grand Council report based on extensive research into international and Canadian law and precedent, combined with the Crees' referendum, signal that others cannot continue to make decisions for the Crees.

In 2003, Minister of Indian Affairs Robert Nault found himself at loggerheads with the Assembly of First Nations over his attempt to modernize the *Indian Act*. The purpose of the *First Nations Governance Act* is to provide communities with modern tools of governance that would allow them to assume substantial new powers, while remaining accountable to the members of each community. Despite the fact that thousands of Native people and leaders were consulted about the nature of these changes, the Assembly and its leader Matthew Coon Come argue that once again foreign laws and

administrative practices have been forced upon First Nations. If one were to take the principle of inherent right to self-government seriously, First Nations themselves should have designed and implemented the new governance act.

---

*Known as the League of Five Nations (Mohawk, Cayuga, Onondaga, Oneida, and Seneca) until they were joined by the Tuscarora in 1722.

**This terminology is important because it implies that the right to self-government is neither granted by the Canadian government nor subject to repeal. Instead, the right is based on Aboriginal status and granted by their Creator.

***The territorial government of Nunavut is a *public* government serving all of its residents, Inuit and non-Inuit alike. An *ethnic* government, applying to the Inuit peoples (nations) alone, would be more in keeping with the principle of Aboriginal self-determination.

Functions of Political Parties

Political parties in Canada and elsewhere have the following key societal functions:

1. **Promoting political pluralism.** Political parties create centres of power independent of the government. This is why totalitarian governments routinely quash all political parties, save their own.

2. **Increasing political involvement.** Ideally, parties draw people into the political process by articulating various points of view about controversial issues. By encouraging public debate, political campaigns help make government more responsive to the people.

3. **Selection of political candidates.** Political parties nominate candidates to run for office. Through nomination meetings in each constituency, local

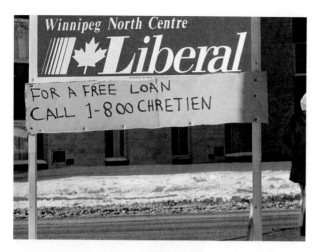

Some Canadian voters vote for particular candidates, but many remain loyal to the same political party from election to election. Party affiliation is often shown through signs on lawns and in windows, and a gathering of signs such as this one is a familiar sight during election campaigns. What effect do these signs have, if any, on the outcome of elections?

party members choose the candidates who will run for office in the next election.[2] Whenever the national or provincial parties are selecting new leaders, the riding associations elect the delegates who go to the leadership conventions.[3]

4. **Forging political coalitions.** While parties can divide a society, they often forge broad coalitions among people interested in various specific issues. Party platforms usually incorporate a wide range of proposals so that the party will appeal to many people, making victory at the polls more likely. Many nations have dozens of narrowly based political parties. Canada has had two dominant federal parties fairly consistently (since Confederation) until the 1993 election introduced its two new challengers.

5. **Maintaining political stability.** By maintaining relatively consistent positions on a number of issues, the major parties promote political stabil-

---

[2]In the 1993 pre-election period, the Liberal party ruffled more than a few feathers by promoting and even appointing certain hand-picked candidates. In some cases, "stars" from outside the ridings were "parachuted" in despite bitter local protest. One of the goals of the Liberal party at that time was to have 25 percent female candidates. The Liberal government of Jean Chrétien was 23 percent female as of 2000. The caucuses of the NDP, Bloc Québécois, Canadian Alliance, and Progressive Conservatives were 38, 26, 11, and 8 percent female, respectively (McDonald, 2001).

[3]Another approach is to have members-at-large, throughout a province, for example, vote for a new leader directly, rather than indirectly by electing delegates to a convention. The Alberta Conservatives used this approach in 1993 to elect Ralph Klein as their leader.

ity. For this reason, of course, those who seek radical change in Canada may criticize political parties in general.

Political Ideology

People commonly label their political views in terms of the political spectrum, a continuum ranging from communism on the left to extreme conservatism on the right. Many Canadians conclude that there are no ideological differences among our major political parties (at least not between the Liberals and Conservatives). William Christian (1983) disagrees, noting that there are some very clear and consistent ideological strains that have characterized our parties over time. Our parties and their ideological orientations are the result of our unique political history and European roots, as evidenced by the fact that they are very different from those in the United States. Furthermore, the ideological *mix* in our parties makes it difficult to accurately place them on a left–right continuum. For example, there were "Red" and "Pink" Tories in the Progressive Conservative party. The stance of the Canadian Alliance was far less ambiguous: it is solidly on the right.

The political left in Canada can be described as anti-capitalist (or anti–big business), egalitarian, collectivist, and interventionist. It supports a broad safety net of social welfare programs, including universal child care, education, and medicare. Government or public ownership and regulation of major industries, unionization, inheritance taxes, and progressive taxation (taxation rates that increase with income) are also part of its policy wish list. The left opposes free trade with the United States and Mexico, because of its presumed negative effects on employment (especially in manufacturing) and social programs.

As one might expect, those on the political right espouse a different set of values and goals. They are in favour of private enterprise, big business, and free markets. Competitiveness, globalization, restructuring, deficit reduction, and privatization of Crown corporations are laudable goals in the eyes of the right, as are private property rights, tax exemptions for capital gains, and free trade. Those on the right generally feel that while government expenditures on social programs are necessary, they should be restricted by our ability to pay for them.

The above package of values is consistent with *fiscal* conservatism. The Canadian Alliance endorsed an additional set of values referred to as *social* conservatism: many of these—including anti-abortion and anti-gay policies—are consistent with the values of fundamentalist Christians. A package referred to as *family values* is the cornerstone of social conservatism, which also embraces some American-style individual rights, such as unfettered gun ownership.

FIGURE 17–2 Selected Canadian Political Parties on a Left–Right Continuum

Parties on the Political Spectrum

Placing Canadian parties on a left–right continuum should be done with some hesitation, since most parties are mixed bags and there is always some movement in party positions. Our major parties moved a little to the right a few years ago, in response to developments in the United States and widespread anxiety about government deficits and debt. Nevertheless, Figure 17–2 suggests

 For a comprehensive set of links to political parties in Canada, go to http://home. ican.net/~alexng/can.html

the approximate location of some of our national parties on this scale.[4]

Party Support

Although some Canadians support one particular political party throughout their lives, and may even come from families that have supported the same party for generations, most of us are considerably more fickle. As a result of changes in party platforms, leaders, dominant issues, or the general economic and political climate, as well as individual social or geographic mobility, there are people who have voted for three or more parties at various points in their lives. It is also common for Canadians to vote for different parties at the federal and provincial levels, even when the elections are only weeks or months apart. Many observers of the Quebec political scene argue that the Québécois hedge their bets by voting for a separatist party (Parti Québécois) at the provincial level and the Liberals or Conservatives federally, or the Bloc Québécois federally and the Liberals provincially. As strange as it might seem to an outside observer, this kind of split voting can be the result of cool calculation rather than confusion on the part of the voter.

Recently there have been dramatic changes in political alignment in this country, as Figure 17–3 reveals. In 1993, we turned away from the three parties with long-term representation across the country to embrace a mix with strong regional bases. In 1997, we confirmed the regionally based pattern of support (Frizzell and Pammett, 1997). As the figure shows, the 1993 election saw the near-collapse of the Conservatives and NDP, coupled with the sudden appearance of the Bloc Québécois and the Reform party. The 1997 results, with minor changes, suggest that Reform and the Bloc had staying power.

The federal election of 1988 (Figure 17–4 on page 425) revealed varying levels of support across the country for the Progressive Conservatives, Liberals, and New Democrats. People in Saskatchewan, British Columbia, and the Yukon were most likely to vote for the NDP, while the Liberals fared well in the Maritimes. Conservative support in Alberta was traditional, while that in Quebec was based on the policies and personal appeal of Prime Minister Brian Mulroney.

The 1993 election results present a very different picture. Half of the votes in Quebec went to the new Bloc Québécois at the expense of the Progressive Conservatives and, to a lesser extent, the NDP. Preston Manning's Reform Party, with roots in Alberta, succeeded there, but also made substantial inroads into B.C., Saskatchewan, Manitoba, and even Ontario. The concentration of Bloc seats in Quebec and Reform seats in B.C. and Alberta accentuates the regional aspect of this pivotal election. Patterns of party support in the elections of 1997 and 2000 were very similar to those of 1993, despite the fact that Preston Manning's Reform Party had reshaped itself into of Stockwell Day's Canadian Alliance.

Just before the 2004 federal election, the Progressive Conservatives and the Canadian Alliance finally merged under the leadership of Stephen Harper, becoming the Conservative Party of Canada. Figure 17-4 reveals that the new party was unable to attract the level of support of the combined PC and CA in 2000.

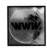 Hillwatch, a government relations firm, offers links to reports on current Canadian polls at www.hillwatch.com/ pollingstation/pollingstation.htm

Nonetheless, its 31.5 percent of the popular vote was enough to give the new CPC twenty-four seats—or that elusive breakthrough—in Ontario.

---

[4]One party that is impossible to place on the left-right continuum is the Rhinoceros Party, which was founded in 1963 with the express purpose of making fun of politicians and the political process. With their outrageous clothes and even more outrageously humorous election platforms, Rhinoceros Party candidates provide an outlet to protest the political process without simply spoiling ballots; at the same time, they add to the entertainment value of Canadian politics for the rest of us. In the 1984 election, 89 Rhino candidates across the country won 99 207 votes, or an astounding 0.8 percent of the national vote. The largest chunk of this support came from a few ridings in the centre of Montreal.

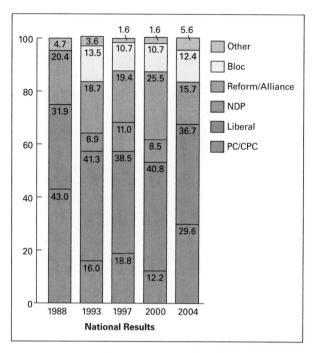

FIGURE 17–3 Support for Canada's Federal Political Parties, Canada, 1988, 1993, 1997, 2000, and 2004 (Percentage of Votes)

Source: Calculated by Gerber from the Report of the Chief Electoral Officer, 1988, 1993, 1997, 2000, and 2004, www.elections.ca.

One of the peculiarities of our political system is the discrepancy between the level of popular support for each party and the number of seats each party wins. One of the more interesting examples appeared in the 1993 election, when the Reform and PC parties had *similar levels of support measured nationally*, but Reform won fifty-two seats to the PC's two. The key to this discrepancy is the existence of over 300 separate races at the constituency or riding level. PC support was spread evenly across the country, while Reform support was concentrated regionally, leading to the high number of wins in local races. Figure 17-5 (on page 427) shows the distribution of popular vote and seats for the 2004 election. The discrepancies in this figure are minor compared to those of the 1993 election.

POLITICS AND THE INDIVIDUAL

The Canadian political system, being democratic, responds, in principle, to the needs and judgments of the electorate. But how do people acquire political attitudes in the first place? And to what extent do we use our right to participate in the political system?

Political Socialization

Pierre Trudeau and Brian Mulroney are among the prime ministers of Canada who raised young children at 24 Sussex Drive and Harrington Lake, the prime minister's official summer residence. Although both of these parents probably shielded their offspring from many aspects of political life, their children undoubtedly learned the basic tenets of liberalism and conservatism from their fathers. These families were unusual in that they were intensely involved in politics; as a result of more intimate exposure, one would expect their children to be very aware of politics and to have clear party affiliations. Justin Trudeau and Ben Mulroney already have public profiles and may well run for office a few years down the road.

Political attitudes, like other elements of culture, are acquired through the socialization process. Of the major agents of socialization shaping our political views—the family, the schools, and the mass media (see Chapter 5, "Socialization")—the family is in a position to exert the earliest influence.

The family is a powerful agent of socialization; not surprisingly, then, children typically come to share many opinions held by their parents. Because neighbourhoods and schools tend to be relatively homogeneous in socioeconomic terms, a child's initial peer groups are likely to reinforce ideas about the world learned at home. In Canada, a large minority of children express a partisan preference by grade 4, and by grade 8 a majority do so (Van Loon and Whittington, 1981:122).

Children are more likely to learn about politics if their families are actively involved, if there is a great deal of political talk in the household, and if their families are of higher socioeconomic status. Also, male children absorb political information and identify political symbols at an earlier age than their female counterparts.

As described in Chapter 20 ("Education"), schools teach the culture's dominant political values, one of them being respect for authority. Our school children also learn to recognize political symbols, such as the flag, the prime minister, and the queen, and like children elsewhere, start off with positive feelings about these political icons. Interestingly, in grades 4 and 5, over 70 percent of children chose the queen as their favourite political figure (over the prime minister or governor general) and not until grade 8 do a majority (53 percent) realize that the prime minister is more powerful than the queen, whose role is entirely ceremonial (Van Loon and Whittington, 1981:121). Very few schools offer anything like the formal civics classes found in American schools. Our political socialization appears to be both more subtle and more informal than that in the United States.

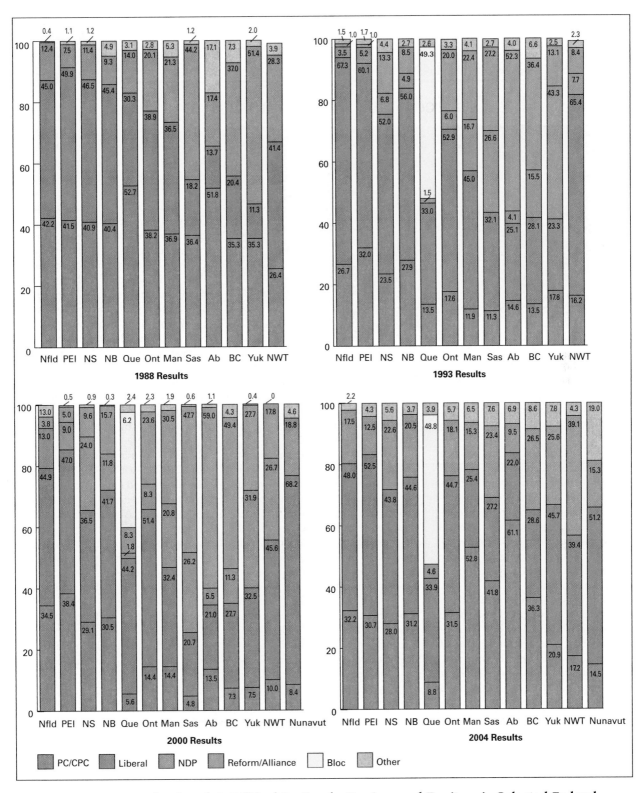

FIGURE 17–4 Support for Canada's Political Parties, by Province and Territory, in Selected Federal Elections (Percentage of Votes in the Elections of 1988, 1993, 2000, and 2004)

Source: Calculated by Gerber from the Report of the Chief Electoral Officer, 1988, 1993, 2000, and 2004, www.elections.ca.

Canada and the United States: Two Snapshots of Politics

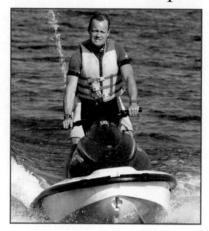

The beauty of comparative analysis is that it teaches you to look at your own society in a completely different light. That being said, what's the point of the two photos in this box?

If we look at any society—and at the process of establishing a political image—we find that certain patterns of behaviour are repeated fairly frequently. When we look at other countries, we again observe repeated behaviour—but it may be very different. Observing image making in Canada and the United States provides us with some sharp contrasts.

Specifically, American politicians in recent elections have tried to outdo one another in their religiosity; ours, in contrast, have tried to create pictures of physical fitness and athleticism.

In the United States, former President Bill Clinton tried to deflect attention from his sexual troubles by providing for photo-ops of the devout family man. He attended church regularly and could be seen (and photographed) emerging from church with the family Bible under his arm and his wife and daughter by his side.

In the 2000 presidential election, George Bush and Al Gore openly claimed to be born-again Christians. Gore's running mate, Joe Lieberman, is a conservative Jew known for his religious ethics. In his acceptance speech, Joe Lieberman told Americans that when Al Gore called to offer him the vice-presidential candidacy, the two men prayed together on the phone.

We do have Canadian politicians who are Christian fundamentalists: Preston Manning (of the former Reform Party) and Stockwell Day (former leader of the Canadian Alliance) are prominent examples. Both Manning and Day believe that religion should colour their political platforms, but when they tried to expand their party bases outside the West, both leaders had to tone down their religiosity. At the national level in Canada, overt religious expression does not play well.

In Canada, our current politicians feel they have to prove that they are healthy, youthful, and athletic. Although not all politicians play the fitness card, Pierre Elliott Trudeau set the precedent. He dazzled us with his skill in diving, skiing, dancing, pirouetting, and, especially, whitewater canoeing.

When Jean Chrétien was preparing for his first election campaign as Liberal leader (in 1993), he needed to counter claims that he was yesterday's man and that he was too old for the job. There were also, for a short time, real concerns about his health. All of these concerns fell by the wayside when Canadians were treated to front-page photos of Chrétien water-skiing—on *one* ski. The vast majority of younger Canadians could not duplicate that feat, so critics fell silent.

As Prime Minister Chrétien, at sixty-six, fought off leadership rivals and prepared for the election of November 2000, he again displayed his physical prowess—this time on the ski slopes. The arrival of Stockwell Day brought an undercurrent of athletic competition into party politics. Day had been seen jet skiing, running, roller-blading, doing karate kicks, and generally showing off his muscular build. Who, one may ask, was fit to be the prime minister?

The mass media, too, convey values and opinions pertaining to politics. Conservatives sometimes charge the Canadian media with having a left-wing agenda, while critics on the left complain that what is packaged as "news" really amounts to support for the status quo. Specific newspapers are frequently identified as having Liberal or Conservative sympathies, and some of the francophone media in Quebec have been labelled as separatist.

Although it is not clear that the media convert their readers at a basic philosophical level, there is little doubt that the media are active players in the day-to-day conduct of politics and that their involvement has changed the way that politics is "done." Good "sound bites" and catchy phrases are gold to the politician, especially when uttered in time for the evening news. Advertising consumes a major part of election campaign budgets, and image takes precedence over substance.

The image projected on nightly television can help to make or break a political career, as our former short-term prime ministers Joe Clark, John Turner, and Kim Campbell learned. Televised debates between the leaders of political parties are almost mandatory in today's political climate and can have a significant impact on the voters' impressions of the party leaders (Widdis-Barr, 1991).

As we saw in Chapter 2 ("Sociological Investigation"), opinion polls are particularly worrisome to some observers of the political scene. Do polls reflect or shape public opinion? If Alliance fortunes seemed to be rising, does the appearance of increasing support, in turn, pull more people onto the newly merged Conservative Party's wagon? Since polls measure change as it is happening, it is difficult to determine cause and effect.

Other agents of political socialization are the many organizations to which people belong. Some of these are professional, ethnic, or voluntary associations, unions, or special-interest organizations such as women's groups. From time to time, churches attempt to mobilize their members behind a particular cause, such as fighting abortion or arranging for the sponsorship of refugees. Seniors clubs, formed initially to encourage social interaction among elders, might find themselves marching on Ottawa to protest the de-indexing of pensions. Political parties themselves would normally recruit people already inclined to be political activists, but, having done so, they may increase participation levels, political knowledge and sophistication, and partisanship. Some of these organizations are founded for political purposes; others with a wide range of nonpolitical goals become political only as a result of circumstances.

Political Participation

Needless to say, socialization does not increase *everyone's* political involvement or enthusiasm for our system of government: significant segments of our population learn that the political system responds little, if at all, to their needs. Indifference or even hostility towards the political system is evident among those who are disadvantaged and feel powerless to remedy the situation. In other cases, those who become committed and actively involved in political action may turn away disillusioned when they see how the political system actually works. In fact, as the Spicer Commission reported in 1991, Canadians have become increasingly cynical about politicians and the political process in general. According to some observers, this is part of a general change in attitude involving Canadians in a move from deference to numerous elites to active defiance (Newman, 1995).

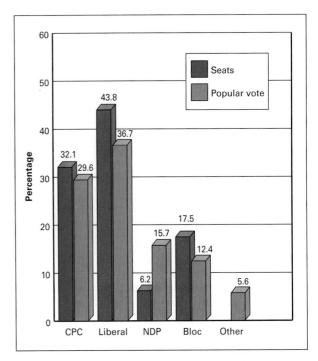

FIGURE 17–5 Distribution of Popular Vote and Seats in the House of Commons by Political Party, 2004 (Percentages)

Source: Calculations by Gerber based on the Report of the Chief Electoral Officer, www.elections.ca.

Lester Milbrath (1966) proposed a typology reflecting a *hierarchy of participation* in electoral politics. He classified individual participation as falling into *gladiatorial*, *transitional*, and *spectator* roles. At the gladiatorial level, participants are actually involved in the political fray, as in attending strategy meetings or running for political office. In a transitional role, one might contact a politician, contribute time to a campaign, or give money to a political party. As a spectator, one might express interest in politics, expose oneself to political information, and vote (and then sit back to watch the returns on television).

According to a 1974 survey, at most 5 percent of Canadians are involved at the gladiatorial level. Another 40 percent participate at the transitional level, most commonly attending a rally or an "all-candidates" meeting and trying to influence the votes of friends or co-workers. Only 5 percent have never voted in a federal election, while 80 to 90 percent engage in informal discussion about elections and follow the campaign to some extent through the media. Although people are a little less inclined to vote in provincial than federal elections, other types of participation seem to be similar at both levels of government (Van Loon and Whittington, 1981).

In any specific federal election about 70 percent or more of the eligible voters come out to the polls

About 70 percent of eligible voters actually vote in Canadian federal elections. Will increasing cynicism about politics and politicians reduce this number?

(compared to roughly 50 to 55 percent in the United States), though turnout in 2000 was an astonishingly low 61 percent. Turnout for provincial elections is generally a little lower and in municipal elections is lower still. To the extent that elections constitute spectator sport, turnout improves if it is a good race.

Canadians participated at every stage of the constitutional negotiations leading to the defeat of the Charlottetown Accord in 1992. After the defeat of the Meech Lake Accord, public demands for wider involvement in constitutional discussions led to the creation of the Spicer Commission in 1990, which conducted town-halls and home meetings and offered a toll-free phone line. In the end more than 400 000 Canadians participated in the sometimes painful, intensely introspective debate about our Constitution.

The Participation of Women

As Chapter 13 ("Gender Stratification") discussed, the women's suffrage movement began in Canada in the 1880s, but since it had to function simultaneously at the provincial and federal levels, it was subject to all "the regional conflicts and divisions that characterized other Canadian social movements" (Bashevkin, 1993:4). Despite divisions that were especially damaging to this movement, women in Canada finally acquired the right to vote at the federal level in 1918. Manitoba was the first province to extend the vote to women (1916), while Quebec was the last (1940).

The extension of the vote to women set the scene for a series of political firsts. Agnes Macphail quickly ran for and won federal political office (1921), but she had to deal with numerous obstacles—including people who said, "We can't have a woman." It was not until 1957 that Canada had its first female federal

cabinet minister, Ellen Fairclough; and it was 1984 before women were given portfolios other than those deemed most "suited" to women, such as health, education, or the status of women. Brian Mulroney broke this pattern at the federal level by appointing Pat Carney to international trade, Barbara McDougall to junior finance, and Kim Campbell to the justice portfolio (Bashevkin, 1993:88). Audrey McLaughlin became the first federal party leader in 1989, and Kim Campbell's leadership win in 1993 automatically made her Canada's first female prime minister. Although, in ideological and practical terms, the NDP has been most persistent in the promotion of women, these firsts involve all three of the major parties.

 The National Library of Canada presents information about Canadian women's achievements in politics; see www.nlc-bnc.ca/2/12/h12-278-e.html

Despite these highly visible firsts, women are still underrepresented in politics. Women still tend to be on the support staff of the political party rather than to be candidates. The higher one goes within the party hierarchy, the smaller the representation of women. Most female candidates run for minor parties or in ridings where wins are unlikely. As well, the proportion of females running for office and winning is greatest at the municipal level, somewhat lower at the provincial level, and lower still at the federal level.

There has been a steady increase in the number of women elected at the federal level in recent years, from 5 percent winning in the 1980 election, to 10 percent in 1984, 13 percent in 1988, 18 percent in 1993, and 21 percent in 1997 and 2000. These figures are high compared with the United States, Britain, and France, which have legislatures that are about 6 percent female, but low when compared with Finland, Sweden, Norway, and Denmark, where 32 to 38 percent of their legislatures are female (Bashevkin, 1993).[5]

Among the barriers to women's participation are socialization, lack of financing or contacts, and the electoral system itself. To the extent that gender stereotypes contribute to resistance on the part of voters and reluctance on the part of potential female candidates, the appearance (even though temporary) of Kim Campbell in the prime minister's office and of Sheila Copps as deputy prime minister may have expanded horizons—but then Agnes Macphail thought that many women would immediately follow in her footsteps.

THEORETICAL ANALYSIS OF POWER IN SOCIETY

Sociologists and political scientists have long debated basic questions about power in society. How is power

---

[5]The NDP government elected in Ontario in 1990 was 27 percent female.

Nellie McClung (left), Manitoba-born teacher, author, and activist, was welcomed in many settings as an effective and humorous speaker. She fought for women's suffrage, prohibition, factory safety, and many other reforms. She was one of the chief activists in the Persons Case, *which involved a court battle to have women legally recognized as persons. Because of her efforts and those of her colleagues, women were given the right to vote, to sit in the House of Commons, and to be appointed to the Senate, in 1918, 1919, and 1929, respectively (Hallett, 1988).*

Agnes Macphail (right) was the only woman elected to the House of Commons in 1921, the first federal election in which women could vote. Like her friend, Nellie McClung, Macphail was a teacher. She was involved in the agricultural cooperative movement of Ontario, various feminist causes, and prison investigation and reform. She founded the Elizabeth Fry Society of Canada and was the first woman appointed to Canada's delegation to the United Nations. Macphail was largely responsible for Ontario's first pay-equity legislation in 1951 (Black, 1988).

distributed? Who makes the decisions? Whose interests does government serve?

Power is among the most difficult topics of scientific research because decision making is complex and often occurs behind closed doors. Moreover, as Plato recognized more than two thousand years ago, it is difficult to separate a theory of power from the theorist's personal beliefs and interests. Nevertheless, three competing models of power have emerged.

THE PLURALIST MODEL

The **pluralist model** is *an analysis of politics that views power as dispersed among many competing interest groups.* This approach is closely tied to structural-functional theory. Pluralists claim that politics is an arena of negotiation. There are thousands of interest groups in Canada, most of which seek narrow goals. The Canadian Association of University Teachers (CAUT), for example, involves itself in issues that affect university faculty, leaving to others debates over health policy, the death penalty, or gun control. But even with limited objectives, no organization holds sufficient power to realize all its goals. The political process, then, relies heavily on negotiating alliances and compromises among various interest groups so that policies gain wide support. In short, pluralists see power as widely dispersed throughout society so that many people have a voice in the political system (Dahl, 1961, 1982).

In *The Vertical Mosaic: An Analysis of Social Class and Power in Canada* (1965), John Porter addresses the question of who makes the major decisions (or exercises power) in Canada. On the basis of extensive research, he concludes that there are competing elites at the top of five major organizational clusters: economic, political, bureaucratic, labour, and ideological (that is, church, education, and the media). Of the five, the economic or corporate elite and the bureaucratic elite are the most powerful. While there is competition among these elites because of the opposing interests of their respective institutions, Porter points out that these powerful and wealthy elites are also highly integrated. To keep the system working, they are willing to accommodate one another. As a result, we have what one might call cooperative pluralism.

THE POWER-ELITE MODEL

The **power-elite model** is *an analysis of politics that views power as concentrated among the rich.* This second approach is closely allied with the social-conflict paradigm in sociology.

The term *power elite* is a lasting contribution of C. Wright Mills (1956), who argued that the upper class holds the bulk of society's wealth, enjoys most of its prestige, and exercises the lion's share of power. Mills claimed that the power elite stands atop the three major sectors of society—the economy, the government, and the military. Thus, the power elite includes the "super-rich" (executives and large stockholders of major corporations), top officials in government, and the highest ranking officers in the military.

Further, Mills explained, these elites move from one sector to another, consolidating their power as they go. It is not unusual for national political leaders

Who Decides? The Impacts of Modern Communications—and Now the Courts

Parliamentary democracy in Canada involves political parties, party discipline, equal representation (in theory, at least), local constituencies (where the candidate with the most votes wins), a prime minister, Cabinet (chosen by the prime minister), and the Senate (appointed by prime ministers, present and past). In the wings, the Prime Minister's Office (PMO) controls physical access as well as the flow of information to the prime minister. The net effect of these interacting components, with imperfections* at each level of representation, is a system in which our prime minister—whom we do not elect directly—has more power in decision making and implementation than the U.S. president.

In the past, newspapers and the radio reported on the activities of our elected officials, undoubtedly affecting future electoral outcomes, but the speed with which news led to opinion change and to effective pressure on parliamentarians and their leaders was limited. Because politicians were "in the know" and we were not, Canadians re-lied on and deferred to the political elite.

Today there is almost constant communication between elected representatives and their constituents. Television, satellite transmission, the telephone, improved transportation, the Internet, email, almost continuous opinion polling, and the potential for electronic voting ensure that the general public can be more quickly and completely informed about what is going on and that politicians can more quickly take the pulse of the public.

Electronic or televised town-halls do not always turn out as expected. The Reform party made an early attempt to establish its platform through an ultra-democratic process of electronic consultation with party members. Preston Manning soon learned that consensus is more difficult to achieve over cyberspace than in a crowded convention, where participants are subject to persuasion. Prime Minister Chrétien had a disappointing experience with a televised town-hall when the situation became confrontational. Both of these experiments in communicative democracy were abandoned.

Politicians are very sensitive to public opinion and wary of offending potential voters. They are still subject to all of the traditional influences and constraints, but their responses to these must be tempered by their new instant and intimate relationship with the public. We know about Oka, the Manitoba flood, the ice storm disaster, helicopter purchases, or the same-sex marriage debate *as events unfold*: we watch our political leaders and judge them—instantly and continually.

Some people applaud this spirit of active citizen participation. After all, in a democratic system government *should* be aware of and responsive to public opinion, even as it changes between elections. Active participation—through discussions, public meetings, electronic town-hall meetings, radio and TV talk shows, letters to the editor, email, referenda, and public opinion polls—serves to keep politicians on their toes. Clearly, they counter the influence of big business, lobbyists, senior bureau-

to enter public life from powerful and highly paid positions in business. For example, Brian Mulroney was a labour lawyer and then vice-president of Iron Ore Company of Canada before becoming prime minister. Since he left political office, he has returned to Montreal to practise corporate law. And prior to his run for prime ministership, Paul Martin was the owner and CEO of Canadian Steamship Lines. In order to avoid future conflict of interest, he passed the company on to his sons.

Wallace Clement (1975) argues that Canada is ruled by an economic or corporate elite that is becoming increasingly powerful. The members of this group are likely to have upper-class origins and to have a vested interest in maintaining the capitalist system. As a result of the dense networks that bind the economic, political, and bureaucratic elites, they are blending into one group dominated by the corporate elite. Clement rejects the pluralist model, noting that the state and private capital are complementary and mutually dependent. In effect, the state and the capitalists act as one.

Power-elite theorists challenge the claim that Canada is a political democracy. They maintain that the concentration of wealth and power is simply too great for the average person's voice to be heard. They reject the pluralist idea that various centres of power serve as checks and balances on one another. Instead, the power-elite model maintains that those at the top encounter no real opposition. Figure 17–6 (on page 432) shows that a majority of Canadians favour the power-elite theory.

On the other hand, even the most powerful members of our society do not always get their way. As long as ordinary people continue to form political associacrats, and others. Conversely, governments are elected by much larger numbers of people on the basis of campaign promises. In that light, should less representative "activists" influence our politicians on an ongoing basis? Should events of the day and shifting public moods divert government action? Some argue that this kind of give and take between politicians and the general public enhances the democratic process. Others argue that the effects, which are increasingly real and immediate, are actually ones of distortion. (Comedian Rick Mercer revealed the frivolous side of constant polling and referenda when more than 1 million Canadians signed his online petition to have Canadian Alliance leader Stockwell Day change his name to Doris.)

Recently, we have looked to the courts to redefine—and even force change in—our laws. Nowhere is this more apparent than in our current debate about same-sex marriage. In British Columbia, Quebec, and, most recently, Ontario, the courts have declared marriage laws that prohibit same-sex marriage are discriminatory and unconstitutional. The federal government had already been told to rewrite its legislation—changing its definition of marriage from the union of a man and a woman—but the Ontario Supreme Court went further, instructing Ontario to start issuing marriage licenses to same-sex couples *immediately*, without waiting for the federal government to act.

The federal government sent draft legislation to the Supreme Court of Canada for approval, wanting assurances that the proposed legislation is constitutional and that it does not impinge upon religious freedom by forcing religious bodies to perform same-sex marriages. Since it will take the court many months to deliver an opinion, the legislation is essentially in limbo. In the meantime, all kinds of groups—including the Roman Catholic Church, led by the Pope himself, and gay rights organizations—are mobilizing to oppose or support change in the definition of marriage. The Canadian public appears to be almost evenly divided on the issue, as are the Liberal MPs who will be participating in the free vote when the time comes. But in an article entitled "Forget the preaching, gay marriage is a done deal," political columnist Jeffrey Simpson argues that the courts have spoken. He says Canada, thanks to the *Charter of Rights and Freedoms*, is a constitutional democracy now, and the courts are the interpreters of the constitution. Members of Parliament, public opinion, or organized opposition—modern communication notwithstanding—cannot turn the tide on the issue (Simpson, 2003).

---

*One complaint about our electoral system—usually voiced by political parties when they lose elections despite substantial support in the popular vote—is that it is possible to win a seat with 35 percent of the vote, while another party loses with 34.9 percent. Repeated across the country, this pattern can result in two parties with almost identical levels of popular support having vastly different numbers of seats in the legislature—as did the PCs and Reform in the 1993 election. Losing parties are bound to question the fairness of democratic representation in Canada.

---

tions or express themselves in the context of various interest groups, our society will retain a substantial degree of pluralism. There are numerous examples of situations where Québécois, Natives, environmentalists, labour unions, or feminists have won concessions and inspired policy changes that are anathema to big business. The Charlottetown Accord was defeated in the 1992 referendum despite support by major political parties, big business, and the media: grassroots opposition and the Reform party spearheaded the "No" forces and staged an upset victory.

THE MARXIST MODEL: BIAS IN THE SYSTEM ITSELF

A third approach to understanding politics is the **Marxist political-economy model**, *an analysis that explains politics in terms of the operation of a society's economic system*. While the power-elite model focuses on the disproportionate wealth and power of certain individuals, the Marxist model highlights bias rooted within this nation's institutions, especially its economy. As noted in Chapter 4 ("Society"), Karl Marx claimed that a society's economic system (capitalist or socialist) goes a long way towards shaping how the political system operates. Power elites, therefore, do not simply appear on the scene; they are creations of capitalism itself.

From this point of view, reforming the political system—say, by limiting the amount of money that rich people can contribute to candidates, as we have recently done—is unlikely to promote true democracy. The problem does not lie in the people who exercise great power or the people who don't vote: the

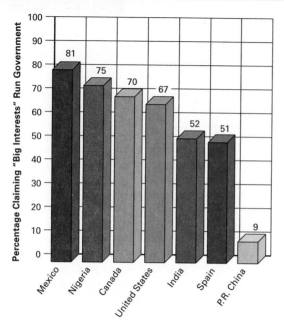

FIGURE 17–6 Who Runs the Government?

Survey Question: "Generally speaking, would you say this country is run by a few big interests looking out for themselves, or is it run for the benefit of all the people?"

Source: World Values Survey (1990).

problem is rooted in the system itself, what Marxists term the *political-economy of capitalism*. In other words, within a capitalist economy, the majority of people will be shut out of politics just as surely as they are exploited in the workplace.

Critical evaluation. Which of the three different models of our political system is correct? Over the years, research has provided support for each model, suggesting that a case can be made for all three. In the end, how one views this country's political system, and how one thinks it ought to operate, turn out to be as much a matter of political values as scientific fact.

Table 17–2 summarizes the three political models. In the end, then, what are we to make of the Canadian political system? At one level, it affords almost everyone the right to participate in the political process through elections. This is an important opportunity, one that is not enjoyed by a majority of the world's people. At the same time, however, the power-elite and Marxist models point out that, at the very least, the Canadian political system is far less democratic than most people think it is.

POWER BEYOND THE RULES

Politics always involves disagreement over a society's goals and the means to achieve them. Political systems, therefore, try to resolve controversy within a system of rules. But political activity sometimes exceeds—or tries to do away with—established practices.

REVOLUTION

Political revolution is *the overthrow of one political system in order to establish another*. In contrast to reform, which involves change *within* a system, revolution involves change *of the system itself*. Thus, even one leader deposing another—called a *coup d'état* (in French, literally, "stroke concerning the state")—falls short of revolution since it involves only a change at the top. And while reform rarely escalates into violence, revolution often does. The revolutions in Eastern Europe beginning in 1989 were surprisingly peaceful, with the exception of Romania, where violence claimed thousands of lives.

Closer to home, one sees revolutionary potential in Quebec's quest for greater autonomy. In the referendum on October 30, 1995, 49.4 percent of the people of Quebec voted "Yes" to Quebec becoming sovereign. Had a few more people voted "Yes," they would have set in motion a process that would dismantle Canada as presently constituted and force the creation of two or more new and very different political entities.

No political system is immune to revolution; nor does revolution invariably produce any one kind of government. The American Revolution ended colonial rule by the British monarchy and produced a democratic government. French revolutionaries in 1789 overthrew a monarch, only to set the stage for the return of another kind of authoritarianism in the person of Napoleon. In 1917, the Russian Revolution replaced the czarist monarchy with a socialist government built on the ideas of Karl Marx. In 1992, the Soviet Union was reborn as the Russian Federation, moving towards a market system and a greater political voice for its people.

Despite their striking variety, analysts claim, revolutions share a number of traits (de Tocqueville, 1955, orig. 1856; also Davies, 1962; Brinton, 1965; Skocpol, 1979; Lewis, 1984; Tilly, 1986).

1. **Rising expectations.** Common sense suggests that revolution would be more likely when people are grossly deprived, but history shows that most revolutions occur when people's lives are improving. Rising expectations, rather than bitter resignation, fuel revolutionary fervour.

2. **Unresponsive government.** Revolutionary zeal gains strength if a government is unable or un-

TABLE 17-2 Three Models of Canadian Politics: A Summary

	Pluralist Model	Power-Elite Model	Marxist Model
How is power distributed in Canadian society?	Highly dispersed	Concentrated	Concentrated
Is Canada basically democratic?	Yes, because voting offers everyone a voice, and no one group or organization dominates society.	No, because a small share of the people dominate the economy, government, and military.	No, because the bias of the capitalist system is to concentrate both wealth and power.
How should we understand voter apathy?	Apathy is indifference; after all, even poor people can organize for a greater voice if they wish.	Apathy is understandable, given how difficult it is for ordinary people to oppose the rich and powerful.	Apathy is alienation generated by a system that leaves most people powerless.

willing to reform, especially when demands for change are made by large numbers of people or powerful segments of society.

3. **Radical leadership by intellectuals.** The English philosopher Thomas Hobbes (1588–1679) observed that intellectuals often provide the justification for revolution, and universities frequently are the centre of sweeping political change. During the 1960s, students were at the forefront of much political unrest in North America and Western Europe. Students also played a critical role in China's recent pro-democracy movement and in the Eastern European uprisings.

4. **Establishing a new legitimacy.** Overthrowing a political system is not easy, but more difficult still is ensuring a revolution's long-term success. Some revolutionary movements are unified mostly by hatred of the past regime and fall apart once new leaders are installed. Revolutionaries must also guard against counterrevolutionary drives led by the deposed leaders. This explains the speed and ruthlessness with which victorious revolutionaries dispose of previous rulers.

Scientific analysis cannot declare that a revolution is good or bad. The full consequences of such an upheaval depend on one's values and, in any case, become evident only after many years. In the wake of recent revolution, for example, the future of the former Soviet Union remains unsettled.

TERRORISM

On September 11, 2001, terrorists hijacked four commercial airliners, and although one airliner crashed in a wooded area the other three were flown into public buildings full of people. The attack, which killed some 3000 innocent people—25 of them Canadian—and injured many thousands more, completely destroyed the World Trade Center in New York City and seriously damaged the Pentagon in Washington, D.C. Not since the attack on Pearl Harbor at the outbreak of World War II had the United States suffered such a blow. Indeed, this event was the most serious terrorist act ever recorded, resulting in greater loss of life than all previous acts of terrorism combined.

Terrorism constitutes *random acts of violence or the threat of such violence employed by an individual or a group as a political strategy.* Like revolution, terrorism is a political act beyond the rules of established political systems. According to Paul Johnson (1981), terrorism has four distinguishing characteristics.

First, terrorists try to paint violence as a legitimate political tactic, despite the fact that such acts are condemned by virtually every nation. Terrorists also bypass (or are excluded from) established channels of political negotiation. Terrorism is therefore a weak organization's strategy to harm a greater foe. The Front de libération du Québec (FLQ), which may have comprised fewer than thirty people, used terrorism to promote its goal of an independent, socialist Quebec. From 1963 to 1971, it was involved in two hundred or more bombings of increasing seriousness, and in 1970 it kidnapped Pierre Laporte (a Quebec cabinet minister) and James Cross (the British trade commissioner) and murdered Laporte. The FLQ clearly caught the attention of the country.

Second, terrorism is employed not just by groups, but also by governments against their own people. **State terrorism** is *the use of violence, generally without support of law, by a government or its agents.* State terrorism may be lawful in some authoritarian and totalitarian states, which survive by inciting fear and intimidation. Saddam Hussein, for example, shored up his power in Iraq through state terrorism.

Third, democratic systems reject terrorism in principle, but they are especially vulnerable to terrorism because they offer extensive civil liberties and have less extensive police networks. This susceptibility helps to explain the tendency of democratic governments to suspend civil liberties if they fear attack, as

After 9/11: Managing Our Relationship with the United States

On the day when two passenger planes crashed into the twin towers of the World Trade Center in New York, ordinary Canadians reacted with horror and compassion. In the immediate aftermath, Canadians across the country—and in tiny Gander, Newfoundland, in particular—opened their hearts and homes to airline passengers diverted from American airports. Three days later, about 100 000 people gathered on Parliament Hill to pay their respects to the victims of terrorism in New York. There seemed to be widespread empathy for our neighbours to the south, along with a sense of shared vulnerability as we faced the unprecedented attack on North American soil.

Before long, a different perspective on the events of 9/11 began to emerge. We feared a loss of sovereignty or independence in the face of pressure to agree to a common perimeter for defence and border control. Pressure to harmonize our immigration policy with that of the Americans gave rise to images of racial profiling, which is not consistent with Canadian values. The latent anti-Americanism that helps us maintain our distinctiveness from our giant neighbour seemed to rise to the surface, manifesting itself as the notion

that the Americans brought 9/11 upon themselves. The attack, it was argued, was a response to provocation—either American foreign policy in the Middle East and elsewhere or Western (i.e., American) indifference to global inequity. The sense that 9/11 was an attack on all of us was replaced with one that—despite the symbolism of the *World* Trade Center—made the United States the villain and the attack understandable, if not justifiable. Prime Minister Chrétien had an opportunity, in his first message of condolence, to influence public opinion and counter this interpretation of events. He did not. It was in this context that President Bush failed to list us among America's friends in his speech to Congress.

It was with reluctance that we joined the "war on terror" in Afghanistan where, tragically, we lost soldiers to American friendly fire. Our role actually expanded after the main conflict was behind us: in late 2003, maintaining a precarious peace in Kabul continued to be the job at hand and the one to which Canada had most recently committed additional resources.

When U.S. president George W. Bush turned his attention to Iraq on the grounds that it produced and used

weapons of mass destruction (against its own people) and allegedly supported suicide bombers (by making payments to their families), he looked to his Canadian friends for support. Canada's leadership dug in its heels and actively resisted direct involvement in Iraq. We had every right to say "no" to participation in Iraq, but there was no need for Canadian officials to insult George Bush (calling him a "moron" and a "failed statesman") or the American people ("Damn Americans! I hate the bastards!"). None of this did anything to heal a relationship with Americans that was fraying at the edges. Sadly, we were aggravating the Americans when, in fact, we *were* contributing to the war in Iraq—albeit indirectly. We had ships patrolling the Gulf in a supportive role, soldiers fighting within British and American units, and senior military personnel involved in the Iraq war at the decision-making level.

There are many Canadians who argue that we must nurture our relationship with the Americans for two very important reasons. Our military strength has been eroded to the point that, more than ever, we are dependent upon the United States for our defence. In addition, the United States is our

was done in 1970 when, in response to the murder of Pierre Laporte by the FLQ, Pierre Trudeau invoked the *War Measures Act* and arrested more than 450 people, many of whom were suspected of being FLQ members and sympathizers. Since 9/11, we have had new civil rights concerns. Individuals, some of them Canadian, have been held without being charged in the United States, and Canadian–Syrian Maher Arar was deported by U.S. authorities to Syria, where he was imprisoned and tortured over a year before being returned to Canada. (We may never know Canada's role, through the RCMP or CSIS, in Arar's story.) Other Canadians of Arab, Muslim, or visible minority background have been subject to what looks like racial profiling as they are singled out for prolonged

searches and questioning *en route* to the United States. Canadian author Rohinton Mistry was one of many to report such hassling.

Hostage-taking and outright killing provoke popular anger, but responding to such acts is difficult. Before taking action, a government must identify those responsible. However, because most terrorist groups, such as al Qaeda, are shadowy organizations with no formal connection to any established state, reprisal may be extremely difficult, if not impossible. Yet, terrorism expert Brian Jenkins warns, the failure to respond "encourages other terrorist groups, who begin to realize that this can be a pretty cheap way to wage war" (quoted in Whitaker, 1985:29).

major trading partner: in excess of 85 percent of our exports go to the United States, with about $2 billion in trade going back and forth across our common border *every day*. Since the implementation of our free trade agreements, our trade *surplus*—exports minus imports—has increased steadily to $133 billion in 2001. In short, we are militarily and economically dependent on our giant neighbour. Events in the summer of 2003 brought home that, normally, our cattle herds and our power grids move back and forth across the border too.

Canadians and Americans shared fallout from 9/11, SARS, West Nile, and mad cow diseases, and the power outage of 2003. We cannot close our borders and effectively isolate ourselves from each other. Social issues, like immigration, border security, same-sex marriage, marijuana use, and prescription drug sales also transcend our border. The Bush administration came under pressure as a result of several decisions that we made in 2003: our steps towards legalization of same-sex marriage, our decriminalization of marijuana use, and our sale of cheaper prescription drugs to Americans have caused it considerable discomfort.

Since the same-sex marriage issue is hotly debated in the United States, our example is hard to ignore. The marijuana issue, in turn, is accentuated by the flow of our homegrown pot to American users. (Lest you think this is a minor concern, take note of the fact that marijuana is big business in Canada—second only to the cattle industry among our agricultural producers. *Conservatively* estimated, our pot production is valued at $7 billion, compared to $7.8 billion in cattle. As with our other exports, 85 percent of our high-grade marijuana is exported to the United States (Turner, 2003).) Recently, more and more American individuals and even municipalities have been buying their prescription drugs from Canada, in most cases for less than half the price in the United States. Some of those drugs are brand-name drugs sold to Canada at lower prices, only to be sold back to Americans; others are generic drugs produced in Canada in defiance of American patent laws. Busloads of Americans cross the border to pick up their prescription drugs while others use the Internet to place their orders.

Some of the most biting criticism of U.S. policy on Iraq comes from Americans themselves—and much of it is aired on CNN. In the eyes of those critics, Canada was right to stay out of the war in Iraq. There are also many Americans who think Canada is "cool" for its stand on same-sex marriage, marijuana, or prescription-drug price controls. Nonetheless, the Bush administration, which faced each of these controversies on its own turf, has been understandably exasperated with those uncooperative Canadians up north.

Continue the debate . . .

1. *How would Canadians and the Canadian government have reacted if the attack on 9/11 had been directed against Toronto's CN Tower and commercial core?*

2. *Should the fact that Canadian and American economies are highly integrated mean that we should work together on security issues? What are the consequences of not cooperating on security?*

3. *If the United States had had a Democratic president, like Bill Clinton, at the time of 9/11, would events have unfolded very differently? Would Canada's reaction have been different?*

And finally, terrorism is always a matter of definition. Governments claim the right to maintain order, even by force, and may brand opposition groups who use violence as "terrorists." Similarly, political differences may explain why one person's "terrorist" is another's "freedom fighter." This is illustrated well in the Palestinian/Israel conflict.

WAR AND PEACE

Perhaps the most critical political issue is **war**, *organized, armed conflict among the peoples of various societies*. War is as old as humanity, of course, but understanding it now takes on greater urgency. Because we have the technological capacity to destroy ourselves, war poses unprecedented danger to the entire planet. Most scholarly investigation of war aims to promote peace, which is the *absence of war* (but not necessarily the lack of all political conflict).

Many people think of war as an extraordinary occurrence; yet for almost all of the twentieth century, nations somewhere on earth were in violent conflict. Most wars are localized, while others, like the two World Wars, are widespread. Canada's involvement in several of these wars cost Canadian lives: 60 661 Canadians were killed in World War I, 42 042 in World War II, and 312 in the Korean War. In the Vietnam War, some Canadian individuals signed up to fight in the American forces, but Canada's official role involved serving on truce commissions and supplying

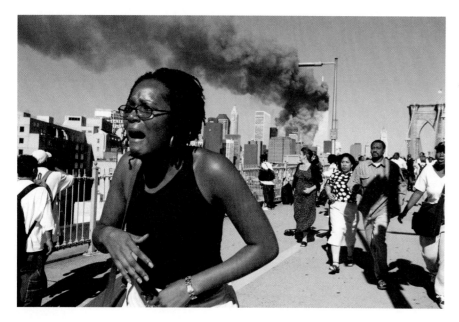

According to many analysts, our way of life changed with the events of September 11, 2001. Why? The power of terror lies in creating fear—fear that the unimaginable can actually happen. Unless we can take basic safety for granted, in short, it is difficult to get on with our lives. How has your life, as a Canadian, been different since that fateful day?

 For information on Canada's contributions to international peacekeeping, go to www. dfait-maeci.gc.ca/peacekeeping/ medical or technical assistance. Since Vietnam, Canada has generally been involved in the world's trouble spots as a peacekeeper.

The Gulf War of 1991 brought war right into our livingrooms through close-up television coverage. At that time, the video-game quality of the images gave rise to intense criticism. The embedded journalists of the Iraq War of 2003 provided very different, more people-oriented coverage, but they also faced criticism for being "too cozy" with the American forces. See the "Controversy & Debate" box for more on terrorism, war, and Canadian/American relations.

THE CAUSES OF WAR

The frequency of war in human affairs might imply that there is something natural about armed confrontation. But while many animals are naturally aggressive, research provides no basis for concluding that human beings inevitably wage war under any particular circumstances. Indeed, governments have to use considerable coercion to mobilize their people for war (Lorenz, 1966; Montagu, 1976).

Like all forms of social behaviour, warfare is a product of *society* that varies in purpose and intensity from culture to culture. The Semai of Malaysia, among the most peace-loving of the world's people, rarely resort to violence. In contrast, the Yąnomamö of Venezuela and Brazil are quick to wage war with others.

If society holds the key to war or peace, under what circumstances *do* humans go to battle? Quincy Wright (1987) identifies five factors that promote war.

1. **Perceived threats.** Societies mobilize in response to a perceived threat to their people, territory, or culture. The danger of armed conflict between the United States and the former Soviet Union, for example, decreased as the two nations became less fearful of each other.

2. **Social problems.** Internal problems that generate widespread frustration may prompt a society's leaders to divert attention by attacking an external "enemy" as a form of scapegoating. Some analysts see problems at home as part of the reason for President Bush's attack on Iraq in 2003.

3. **Political objectives.** Leaders sometimes use war as a political strategy. Poor societies, such as Algeria and Vietnam, have fought wars to end foreign domination. For powerful societies such as the United States, a periodic show of force (recall the recent deployments of troops in Somalia, Haiti, and Bosnia) enhances their global political stature.

4. **Moral objectives.** Rarely do nations claim to fight merely to increase their wealth and power. Leaders infuse military campaigns with moral urgency, rallying their people around visions of "freedom" or the "fatherland." U.S. leaders characterized the recent attack on the Taliban and the al Qaeda network in Afghanistan as a clear case of good against evil.

5. **The absence of alternatives.** A fifth factor promoting war is the absence of alternatives. Although the United Nations has the job of maintaining international peace, it has had limited success in resolving tensions among self-interested societies.

In short, war is rooted in social dynamics on both national and international levels. Moreover, even combat has rules, and breaking them can lead to charges of war crimes.

TERRORISM: A NEW KIND OF WAR?

In the wake of the terrorist attack on September 11, 2001, U.S. government officials spoke of terrorism as a new kind of war. As we have explained, war is usually played out according to at least some rules, the warring parties are known to each other, and they clearly state their objectives, which generally involve control of territory.

Terrorism, however, breaks from these patterns. In cases of terrorism, the identity of terrorist individuals and organizations may not be known, those involved may deny their responsibility, and their goals may be unclear. Indeed, the recent terrorist attacks against the United States were not attempts to defeat the nation's military, nor to secure territory. They were carried out by people representing not a country but a cause—one not well understood in the United States. In short, they were expressions of anger and hate, an effort to destabilize the country and shatter public morale by inciting widespread anger and fear.

Conventional warfare is "symmetrical," with two nations sending their armies into battle. In contrast, terrorism is a new form of war, an "asymmetrical conflict" in which the small number of attackers use terror and their own willingness to die as a means to "level the playing field" against a much more powerful enemy. Furthermore, while the terrorists may be ruthless, the nation under attack must exercise restraint in its response to terror because little may be known about the identity and location of those responsible. It is for this reason that U.S. officials maintain that the reaction to the 2001 attacks is likely to unfold over a period of years.

THE COSTS AND CAUSES OF MILITARISM

The cost of armed conflicts extends far beyond battlefield casualties. Together, the world's nations spend some $1 trillion annually (almost $160 for every person on the planet) for military purposes. Such expenditures, of course, divert resources from the desperate struggle for survival by hundreds of millions of poor people. If the world's nations could muster the will and the political wisdom to redirect their military spending, they could greatly reduce global poverty.

In recent years, defence has been the U.S. government's largest single expenditure, accounting for 16 percent of all federal spending, or $291 billion in 2000. This huge sum is the result of the *arms race*, a mutually reinforcing escalation of military power, between the United States and the former Soviet Union. Canada, which in effect depends on the United States

for its defence, allocates about 8 percent of government spending to defence.

Yet, even after the collapse of the Soviet Union in 1992, U.S. military expenditures remain high. Thus, analysts who support the power-elite theory say that the United States is dominated by a **military-industrial complex**, *the close association between the federal government, the military, and defence industries.* The roots of militarism, then, lie not just in external threats to that nation's security; they also grow from within the institutional structures of U.S. society (Marullo, 1987).

Another reason for persistent militarism in the post–Cold War world is regional conflict. Since the collapse of the Soviet Union, for example, localized wars have broken out in Bosnia, Chechnya, and Zambia, and tensions still run high in a host of other countries, including Northern Ireland, Iraq, and a divided Korea. Even wars of limited scope have the potential to escalate and involve other countries. And as more and more nations acquire nuclear weapons, the risk that regional conflicts will erupt into deadly wars goes up.

NUCLEAR WEAPONS

Despite the easing of superpower tensions, nations still hold almost 25 000 nuclear warheads, a destructive force equivalent to five tons (4 536 kg) of TNT for every person on the planet. Should even a small fraction of this stockpile be used in war, life as we know it might cease on much of the earth. Albert Einstein, whose genius contributed to the development of nuclear weapons, reflected, "The unleashed power of the atom has changed everything *save our modes of thinking,* and we thus drift toward unparalleled catastrophe." In short, nuclear weapons make unrestrained war unthinkable in a world not yet capable of peace.

Great Britain, France, and the People's Republic of China all have a substantial nuclear capability, but the most nuclear weapons are based in the United States and the Russian Federation. The two superpowers agreed to reduce their stockpiles of nuclear warheads by 75 percent by the year 2003. But even as the superpower rivalry winds down, the danger of catastrophic war is increasing along with **nuclear proliferation**, *the acquisition of nuclear-weapons technology by more and more nations.* Israel, India, and Pakistan also possess some nuclear weapons, and other nations (including Iran, North Korea, and Libya) are developing them, while Iraq's presumed readiness to deploy nuclear weapons was the most pressing justification for the U.S. invasion of Iraq. Although some nations have taken steps to limit the development of nuclear weapons—Argentina and Brazil stopped their work in 1990 and South Africa dismantled its arsenal in 1991— by 2010, as many as fifty nations could be capable of fighting a nuclear war. Such a trend makes any regional

In recent years, the world has become aware of the death and mutilation caused by millions of land mines placed in the ground during wartime and left there afterward. Civilians, many of them children, maimed by land mines receive treatment in this Kabul, Afghanistan, clinic.

conflict much more dangerous (McGeary, 1998; Thomas et al., 1998).

INFORMATION WARFARE

As earlier chapters have explained, the Information Revolution is changing almost every dimension of social life. In the coming years, how will computers reshape warfare?

For decades, scientists and military officials have studied how to use computers to defend against missiles and planes. Recently, the military has recognized that new information technology can fundamentally transform warfare itself, replacing rumbling tanks and screaming aircraft with electronic "smart bombs" that would silently penetrate an enemy country's computer system and render it unable to transmit information. In such "virtual wars," soldiers seated at workstation monitors would dispatch computer viruses to shut down the enemy's communication links, causing telephones to fall silent, air traffic control and railroad switching systems to fail, computer systems to feed phony orders to field officers, and televisions to broadcast "morphed" news bulletins urging people to turn against their leaders.

Like the venom of a poisonous snake, the weapons of "information warfare" might quickly paralyze an adversary prior to a conventional military attack. Another more hopeful possibility is that new information technology might not just precede conventional fighting but prevent it entirely. If the "victims" of computer warfare could be limited to a nation's communication links—rather than its citizens and cities—wouldn't we all be more secure?

Yet so-called infowar also poses new dangers, since, presumably, a few highly skilled operators with sophisticated electronic equipment could also wreak communications havoc on Canada or the United States. The United Sates may be militarily without equal in the world, but given its increasing reliance on high technology it is also more vulnerable to cyber-attack than any nation on earth. As a result, in 1996, the Central Intelligence Agency (CIA) began work on a defensive "cyberwar centre" to help prevent what one official termed an "electronic Pearl Harbor" (Waller, 1995; Weiner, 1996).

THE PURSUIT OF PEACE

How can the world reduce the danger of war? Here are the most recent approaches to promoting peace:

1. **Deterrence.** During the Cold War, from the end of World War II in 1945 to the dissolution of the Soviet Union in the early 1990s, the logic of the arms race linked security to a "balance of terror" between the superpowers. Based on the principle of mutually assured destruction (MAD)—meaning that whichever side launched a first-strike nuclear attack against the other would sustain massive retaliation—deterrence has kept the peace for over fifty years. But it has three flaws. First, it has fuelled an exorbitantly expensive arms race. Second, as missiles become capable of delivering their warheads more and more quickly, computers are left with less and less time to react to an apparent attack, thereby increasing the risks of unintended war. Third, deterrence cannot curb nuclear proliferation, which poses a growing threat to peace.

2. **High-technology defence.** If technology created the weapons, some maintain, it can also deliver us from the threat of war. This was the idea behind the *strategic defence initiative* (SDI), proposed by

the U.S. Reagan administration in 1981. Under SDI, satellites and ground installations provide a protective shield or umbrella against enemy missiles. In principle, the system detects enemy missiles soon after launch and destroys them with lasers and particle beams before they re-enter the atmosphere. If perfected, advocates argue, such a "star wars" defence would render nuclearweapons obsolete.

But critics charge that even years of research costing trillions of dollars would yield at best a leaky umbrella. The collapse of the Soviet Union also calls into question the need for such an extensive and costly defence scheme. Furthermore, sophisticated technology raises not only new possibilities for defence, but also new strategies for waging war.

3. **Diplomacy and disarmament.** Still other analysts point out that the best path to peace is diplomacy rather than technology (Dedrick and Yinger, 1990). Diplomacy can enhance security by reducing weapons stockpiles.

But disarmament, too, has limitations. No nation wishes to become vulnerable by reducing its defences. Successful diplomacy, then, depends not on "soft" concession making or "hard" demands, but on everyone involved sharing responsibility for a common problem (Fisher and Ury, 1988).

While the United States and the former Soviet Union have managed to negotiate arms-reduction agreements, the threat from other nations that desire to build a nuclear arsenal (e.g., Libya and North Korea) remains great.

4. **Resolving underlying conflict.** As the United States attacked terrorist targets in Afghanistan, many people were aware that at least one nation bordering this poor country has nuclear weapons. Given the threat that any local conflict may erupt into a regional—and potentially nuclear—confrontation, it may be that the best way to reduce the danger of nuclear war is to resolve underlying conflicts. Some people in the Islamic world, for example, argue that the United States deserves to be attacked because it has stationed military personnel in a number of Islamic nations, enacted sanctions against Iraq, and supported what they see as Israel's oppression of Palestinians. While the vast majority of people in the United States and elsewhere in the world reject such "justifications" for terrorism, it remains true that establishing lasting peace depends on resolving the conflicts that have long divided the Middle East. And, if so, should the world's nations continue to spend thousands of times as much money on militarism as they do on peacekeeping? (Sivard, 1988; Kaplan & Schaffer, 2001).

Ever since Canadian prime minister Lester B. Pearson proposed the creation of a United Nations peacekeeping force in 1956 (for which he was awarded the Nobel Peace Prize in 1957), Canada has seen its international role mainly in terms of mediation and peacekeeping. Although we did participate in the Allied attack on Iraq during the Gulf War, after the war Canadians helped patrol the demilitarized zone. Our role in the former Yugoslavia has been largely limited to peacekeeping and medical assistance. Most recently, we have assumed a more active role in post-war Afghanistan, helping to maintain control of Kabul if not the rest of the country.

LOOKING AHEAD: POLITICS IN THE TWENTY-FIRST CENTURY

Just as economic systems—the focus of the last chapter—are changing, so are political systems. As we enter the twenty-first century, several problems and trends command widespread attention.

Among these trends is the extension of global politics. The Information Revolution is changing politics just as it is reformulating the economy (although political change seems to be somewhat slower). Communications technology now allows news and political analysis to flow instantly from one point in the world to another. But will this global avalanche of information expand democracy by empowering individuals? Or will new information technology provide governments with new tools to manipulate their citizens?

Another major trend is the global rethinking of political models. The Cold War cast political debate in the form of two rigid political alternatives based on capitalism and socialism. Today, in the post–Cold War era, analysts envision a broader range of political systems, linking government to economic production in various ways. "Welfare capitalism" as found in Sweden or "state capitalism" as found in Japan and South Korea are just two possibilities.

Finally, we still face the danger of war in many parts of the world. Even as tensions between the United States and the former Soviet Union have eased, vast stockpiles of weapons remain, and nuclear technology continues to proliferate around the world. New superpowers may arise in the century ahead (the People's Republic of China seems a likely candidate), just as regional conflicts will surely continue to fester. The chronic hostilities between Palestinians and Israelis show no signs of resolution, despite the promise of the "roadmap" to peace. Nevertheless, one can hope that, as the century progresses, world leaders will devise nonviolent solutions to the age-old problems that provoke war.

CONTROVERSY & DEBATE

Reforming Canada's Political System: Throwing Out the Baby with the Bathwater

Our political system can be described as a parliamentary democracy and a constitutional monarchy, with Queen Elizabeth II as our head of state. Prior to Confederation, French Canadians were already resisting our ties to the British Empire and the monarchy. As Canada became more multicultural and less "British," others argued that we should abolish the monarchy—and become a republic with a president. Undercurrents of the monarchy debate are detectable much of the time.

Our Senate is criticized harshly because the prime minister *appoints* senators, who serve until they are seventy-five years of age. Since it is unelected, the Senate lacks the legitimacy to flex its muscles to counter the House of Commons—where 59 percent of the members come from the populous provinces of Ontario and Quebec.

When the Reform party emerged to run in the 1993 federal election, one of the main planks in its platform was senate reform: its Triple-E Senate would be *equal*, *elected*, and *effective*. Each province, regardless of population, would elect the same number of senators. A watered-down version of senate reform was included in the Charlottetown Accord, which was defeated by referendum in 1992.

The third element of our political system that comes under attack is the one by which we elect our members of Parliament (MPs). Under our system of 301 mini-elections at the riding or electoral district level, regional parties win a disproportionate number of seats; conversely, parties with support thinly spread across the country win relatively few seats. A dramatic instance of this occurred in 1993, when 16 and 18.7 percent of Canada's voters, respectively,

supported the Progressive Conservatives and the Reform party. Despite the similarity in popular vote, the Conservatives won two seats while Reform won fifty-two (0.7 and 17.6 percent of the seats). The reason is that Reform was concentrated in the West—in specific ridings—while Conservative support was spread fairly evenly across Canada. In our *first-past-the-post* system, the party with the most votes in any one of our ridings wins the seat. Regional or riding level concentration of party support increases the chances of winning seats.

The most commonly advocated solution is a system of *proportional representation*, in which the number of seats won mirrors the popular vote. In Election 2000, the Liberals won 101 of 103 Ontario seats (98 percent) with 49.5 percent of the popular vote; the Canadian Alliance won 2 seats (1.9 percent) with 19.1 percent of the Ontario

SUMMARY

1. Politics is the major social institution by which a society distributes power and organizes decision making. Max Weber explained that three social contexts transform coercive power into legitimate authority: tradition, rationally enacted rules and regulations, and the personal charisma of a leader.

2. Traditional authority is common to pre-industrial societies; industrial societies, in contrast, legitimize power through bureaucratic organizations and law. Charismatic authority, which arises in every society, sustains itself through routinization into traditional or rational-legal authority.

3. Authoritarian political regimes deny popular participation in government. Totalitarian political systems go even further, tightly regulating people's everyday lives.

4. The world remains divided into 192 politically independent nation-states; one dimension of an emerg-

ing global political system, however, is the growing wealth and power of multinational corporations. Additionally, new technology associated with the Information Revolution means that national governments can no longer control the flow of information across national boundaries.

5. The government of Canada is based on an elected House of Commons and an appointed Senate. Because representation in the House of Commons is based (roughly) on population, Quebec and Ontario together have 59 percent of the seats. This weighting in favour of central Canada is a source of concern for the other provinces.

6. Canada has traditionally had three major political parties at the federal level. The Progressive Conservative party leaned to the right on social and economic issues, the Liberal party is closer to the centre, and the New Democratic party is further to

vote. Proportional representation would have given the Liberals 51 seats and the Alliance 20. If the Alliance had been rewarded with 20 Ontario seats and 2 of the 32 Atlantic seats, Westerners would not be feeling that "their" party, once again, had been shut out in the east. Under proportional representation, the Liberals would have fewer Ontario seats, but more throughout the western provinces, so that the regional bases of political parties would be weakened. Across Canada, the Liberals would have won 123 of 301 seats instead of the 172 that they won in 2000 under the first-past-the-post system. We would not have a majority Liberal government under proportional representation. In fact, majority governments would be less common in a multi-party system like ours.

So what do we lose, apart from majority governments, if we adopt proportional representation? The answer is simple: our local MPs would be the babies thrown out with the bathwater. Our MPs, who usually live in their ridings, are the ones to whom we go with our problems and for whom some of us volunteer during and between elections. MPs are also the ones who act as hosts if their constituents appear in Ottawa, and who watch out for the interests of their ridings as the House of Commons goes about its business. Under proportional representation, we could no longer say that Medicine Hat is an Alliance riding or Joliette is a Bloc Québécois riding—because there would *be* no ridings for which to tally the votes! The relationship between people and their government representatives would be very different.

Some Canadians advocate senate reform, proportional representation, and abolition of the monarchy, but in order to accomplish any one of these we would need to amend our Constitution. Since any of these would constitute major change, consent of the House of Commons, the Senate, and the legislatures of all ten provinces would be required. Furthermore, we would turn to a referendum to seek public approval. The likelihood that any amendment would make it over these hurdles is small. And, think of it: if you were a prime minister doing rather well under the current set of rules, would *you* be eager to initiate constitutional change?

the left. Since each of the parties is a bit of a mixed bag, accurate placement on a left–right continuum is difficult.

7. One of the major political struggles going on in Canada involves the centralization versus the decentralization of power, or provincial versus federal power.

8. Canadian government takes an active role in the daily lives of its citizens. Canadian political culture supports widespread intervention in social and economic spheres.

9. Native self-government is a current issue that has deep historic roots. Many Native groups are currently practising some level of self-government under a wide range of agreements, but constitutional recognition of an inherent right to self-government is still an important goal.

10. The pluralist model holds that political power is widely dispersed; the power-elite model takes an opposing view, arguing that power is concentrated in a small, wealthy segment of the population.

11. Revolution radically transforms a political system. Revolutions aim at different political objectives and meet with various degrees of success.

12. Terrorism is the use of violence in pursuit of political goals. Although attention has long focused on group terrorism, state terrorism is potentially far more powerful.

13. War is armed conflict between governments. The development and proliferation of nuclear weapons have increased the possibility of global catastrophe. Enhancing world peace ultimately depends on resolving social problems and the conflicts that underlie militarism.

CRITICAL-THINKING QUESTIONS

1. What is the difference between authority and power? What forms of authority characterize pre-industrial and industrial societies? Why does democracy gradually replace monarchy as societies industrialize?

2. How would you describe the attitudes of the Canadian population on the political spectrum? How is class position linked to political opinions?

3. Contrast the pluralist, power-elite, and Marxist political-economy models of societal power. Which do you find more convincing?

4. Do you think that the dangers of war in the world are greater or less than in past generations? Why?

APPLICATIONS AND EXERCISES

1. Immediately after every federal election, newspapers publish an analysis of who voted and for whom. Visit the library to obtain a "scorecard" for the 2000 federal election. To what extent do men and women vote for different candidates? What about people of various racial categories? Different ages? Religions? Income levels? In short, what variables affect political attitudes the most?

2. The Internet provides enormous organizational potential, linking people who share an interest in some political issue. The goal of the **www.womennet.ca/** website is to provide a community for women on the Internet. Visit the website. Do you think such sites will make a difference in Canadian politics?

3. Along with several other people, make a list of leaders you think are or were charismatic. Discuss why someone is on the list. Do you think personal charisma is something more than "being good on television"? If so, precisely what is it?

4. Do a little research to trace the increase in the size of the federal government over the last fifty years. Try to discover how organizations at different points along the political spectrum (from socialist organizations on the left through the NDP, Liberal, Conservative, and Alliance parties, to right-wing groups) view the size of the current welfare state.

 SITES TO SEE

www.macionis.com
or
www.TheSociologyPage.com

You can find more than fifty weblinks to sociological journals and other sources of data and information by visiting the Links Library at this website.

www.law-lib.utoronto.ca/law-review/abstract/ultr53-2/53_2_235.htm

"Approaches to Sorting Out Jurisdiction in a Self-Government Context" by John M. Olynyk, published in the *University of Toronto Faculty of Law Review*, examines how First Nations jurisdiction might interact with and be distinguished from that of the federal and provincial governments.

www.statcan.ca/english/Pgdb/govern.htm

This site contains Statistics Canada's collection of tables about Canadian government, including information on elections, revenues and expenditures, and employment.

www.parl.gc.ca/information/library/idb/forsey/index-e.asp

"How Canadians Govern Themselves," by Eugene A. Forsey, is an essay on the Canadian system of government.

www.un.org/

The United Nations is an organization of sovereign nations. It provides the machinery to help find solutions to international problems or disputes, and to deal with pressing concerns that face people everywhere.

www.amnesty.org/

Amnesty International's website offers information about human rights around the world.

www.usis.usemb.se/terror/index.html

This U.S. State Department website provides information on global terrorism.

STUDY TOOLS

For more study tools to help you with your next exam, be sure to check out the Companion Website at **www.pearsoned. ca/macionis**, as well as Chapter 17 in your Study Guide.

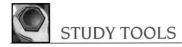

INVESTIGATE WITH CONTENTSELECT

Follow the instructions found on page 25 of this textbook to access ContentSelect™ at the Research Navigator™ website. Once at the site, enter your LOGINID and Password. Then, enter keywords such as "charisma," and "terrorism" and the search engine will supply relevant and recent scholarly and popular press publications.

CHAPTER
18

Daphne Odjig (1928– , Canadian)
Afloat in Memories, 1996
Acrylic/canvas, 50.8 × 61 cm. Courtesy of Daphne Odjig and the Bearclaw Gallery.

FAMILY

When you see a woman pushing a stroller, does it cross your mind that you might be watching a lesbian mother? In an article entitled "We Are Family: Lesbian Mothers in Canada," Katherine Arnup (1995) points out that, by some estimates, 10 percent of women are lesbians—and that 20 to 30 percent of those lesbians are mothers. Among these women, gaining recognition and acceptance as mothers (that is, as legitimate, good mothers) is not easy. The problems become especially apparent for lesbian mothers who leave a heterosexual relationship and try to gain custody of their children.

Many of these women choose not to contest custody in court because they fear defeat by a clearly homophobic legal system. Instead, they hope to get liberal access rights. Despite the obstacles, other lesbian mothers are trying to get custody. In doing so, they have learned that there is an informal distinction between "good" and "bad" lesbian mothers. The "good" ones are those "who live quiet, discreet lives, who promise that they will raise their children to be heterosexual, [and] who appear to the outside world to be heterosexual single parents"—in other words, those who are completely secretive about their identities. The "bad" ones are the women

"who are politically active, who attend gay and lesbian demonstrations, and who view their lesbianism as one aspect of an entire challenge to society" (p. 331)—that is, those who have "come out."

Knowing the criteria the courts consider in determining "the best interests of the child," lesbian mothers face difficult choices. Most try to appear as "straight" as possible in court to increase the chances of gaining custody, rather than being open about their identities. "Such women have met with harsh criticism from some elements of the lesbian community, however, for sustaining an oppressive familial ideology, rather than standing up for their rights as open and proud lesbian mothers" (p. 333).

When they do have custody of their children, lesbian mothers have to decide whether to be open about their "unusual" family situations—in the community, at school, at church. By being forthright, they might find that they share all kinds of common concerns with heterosexual mothers, and, gradually, they might stretch or expand the notion of what is acceptable family life. Changing the formal definition of marriage to allow same-sex marriage, will have profound, though not instant, impacts on our society's acceptance of families with lesbian (or gay) parents.

In Canada, the state of the family is a hot topic. Indeed, a rising chorus of voices charges that families in Canada are fast becoming an endangered species. And some hard facts back up their case. The marriage rate within Canada is decreasing while the divorce rate has increased. The proportion of Canadians 15 years of age and older who are "ever-divorced" doubled between 1975 and 1995—from 7 to 14 percent (Bibby, 1995:6). Marital breakdown, coupled with the increase in the number of children born to unmarried women, means that half of Canadian children born today will live with a single parent for some time before reaching age eighteen. Not surprisingly, the proportion of Canadian children living in poverty has been rising steadily in recent years.

In modern industrial societies, the members of extended families usually pursue their careers independently while living apart from one another. However, various nuclear families may assemble periodically for rituals such as weddings, funerals, and family reunions.

Taken together, these facts suggest a basic truth: families in Canada and in other industrial societies are changing dramatically. Not long ago, the cultural ideal of the family consisted of a working husband, a homemaker wife, and their young children. Today, fewer people embrace this singular vision of the family, and, at any given time, only a minority of Canadian households fit that description.

This chapter highlights important changes in family life, and offers some insights into these trends. Yet, as we shall also point out, changing family patterns are nothing new to this country. A century ago, for example, concern over the decline of the family swept the nation as the Industrial Revolution propelled men from farms to factories. Today, of course, many of the same concerns surround the rising share of women whose careers draw them away from home. In short, changes in other social institutions, especially the economy, are leaving their mark—for better or worse—on marriage and family life.

THE FAMILY: BASIC CONCEPTS

The **family** is *a social institution that unites individuals into cooperative groups that oversee the bearing and raising of children.* These social units are, in turn, built on **kinship**, *a social bond, based on blood, marriage, or adoption, that joins individuals into families.* Although all societies contain families, just who is included under the umbrella of kinship has varied through history, and varies today from one culture to another.

During the twentieth century and today, most members of our society have regarded a **family unit** as *a social group of two or more people, related by blood, marriage, or adoption, who usually live together.* Initially, individuals are born into a family composed of parents and siblings, which is sometimes called the *family of*

orientation because this group is central to socialization. In adulthood, people forge a *family of procreation* to have or adopt children of their own.

Throughout the world, families form around **marriage**, *a legally sanctioned relationship, usually involving economic cooperation as well as normative sexual activity and childbearing, that people expect to be enduring.* Our cultural belief that marriage is the appropriate context for procreation is apparent in the historical use of the term *illegitimate* for children born out of wedlock. While *matrimony*, in Latin, means "the condition of motherhood," the link between childbearing and marriage has weakened, as the proportion of children born to single women has increased and as more couples have remained childless. These definitions of marriage and family will have to be changed to accommodate Canada's redefinition of marriage to allow same-sex unions, since childbearing will be the central focus of fewer marriages.

Just as we have changed our definition of marriage, so we are changing our understanding of "family." Census 2001 defines families as married or common-law couples with or without children, or a lone parent (of any marital status) with at least one child living at home. Most significantly, in 2001 a couple living common-law might be of opposite or same sex. By the time of the next census (2006), a *married* couple might be of opposite or same sex. We have come a long way from the days when only married couples with children were considered "families."

THE FAMILY: GLOBAL VARIETY

Members of pre-industrial societies take a broad view of family ties, recognizing the **extended family** as *a family unit including parents and children, but also other kin.* Extended families are also called *consanguine families,*

GLOBAL SOCIOLOGY

International Adoption

The rate of international adoption is rapidly increasing (Fulton, 1995:34) from ten per year in 1970 to about two thousand per year from forty-two different countries in the 1990s.

In the past, Canadians would adopt the children of unwed mothers. Abortion was illegal and infrequent, and women who bore and raised children outside marriage were stigmatized. Now abortion is legal and relatively available, and women who give birth outside marriage are increasingly likely to keep their babies. Between 1981 and 1990, adoptions of children born in Canada declined almost 50 percent.

In the low-income and war-torn countries of the world, out-of-country adoption of babies represents a potential benefit both to the individuals and to the nations who are unable to pro-vide food, shelter, and schooling for these children. Canadians pay between $10 000 and $25 000 to adopt a child internationally. The money goes to adoption and state agencies for legal, medical, and transportation costs—not to pay for the child.

What does the future hold for these families? Often the adopted child has a different cultural heritage than the adoptive family. For instance, Vietnamese boat-lifts in 1971 unleashed the largest wave of international adoptions since after the Korean War in the 1950s. China's one-child policy, established in the 1980s, has led many Chinese couples to give daughters up for adoption so that they can try again for a son to carry on the family name.

One can only speculate about the adjustments of these children and their adoptive families. A decade ago, 57 per-cent of Canadians said that they would prefer less immigration (Serrill, 1995:22), raising fears that these children would have to struggle with prejudice. On a more optimistic note, research in Canada by Westhues and Cohen (1994) indicates that most of these adoptions have many elements of success. Among the issues they considered are self-esteem, the degree of integration into the adoptive family, peer relations, and the children's comfort with their ethnic backgrounds. The unfolding stories of these adoptions and the children's adjustment to Canadian society will continue to hold great interest for Canadian researchers in the years to come.

Sources: Fulton (1995) and Westhues and Cohen (1994).

---

meaning that they include everyone with "shared blood." With industrialization, however, increasing geographic and social mobility gives rise to the **nuclear family**, *a family unit composed of one or two parents and their children.* Because it is based on marriage, the nuclear family is also known as the *conjugal family.* Although many members of our society live in extended families, the nuclear family has become the predominant family form in Canada.

Many couples go to great lengths to become parents in pursuit of the model of the nuclear family. International adoption, discussed in the "Global Sociology" box, is one of the methods used. Furthermore, when legislation allowing same-sex couples to marry is passed, they will be seeking children to adopt; some of them may turn to international adoption in their attempts to form typical nuclear families.

MARRIAGE PATTERNS

Cultural norms, as well as laws, identify people as desirable or unsuitable marriage partners. Some marital norms promote **endogamy**, *marriage between people of the same social category.* Endogamy limits marriage prospects to others of the same age, race, religion, or social class. In contrast, **exogamy** mandates *marriage between people of different social categories.* In rural India, for example, young people are expected to marry someone of the same caste (endogamy), but from a different village (exogamy). The logic of endogamy is that people of similar social position pass along their standing to offspring, maintaining traditional social patterns, whereas exogamy builds alliances and encourages cultural diffusion.

In industrial societies, laws prescribe **monogamy** (from Greek meaning "one union"), *a form of marriage joining two partners.* Our high level of divorce and remarriage, however, suggests that *serial monogamy* is a more accurate description of Canada's marital practice.

Global Map 18–1 shows that while monogamy is the rule throughout the Americas and in Europe, many lower-income societies—especially in Africa and southern Asia—permit **polygamy** (from Greek, meaning "many unions"), *a form of marriage uniting three or more people.* Polygamy takes two forms. By far the more common is **polygyny** (from Greek, meaning "many women"), *a form of marriage uniting one male and two or more females.* Islamic societies in Africa and southern Asia, for example, allow men up to four

GLOBAL MAP 18–1 Marital Form in Global Perspective

Monogamy is the legally prescribed form of marriage in all industrial societies and throughout the western hemisphere. In most African nations and in southern Asia, however, polygamy is permitted by law. In many cases, this practice reflects the historic influence of Islam, a religion that allows a man to have up to four wives. Even so, most marriages in these traditional societies are monogamous, primarily for financial reasons.

Source: *Peters Atlas of the World* (1990).

wives. Even so, most families in these societies are monogamous because few men have the wealth needed to support several wives and even more children.

Polyandry (from Greek, meaning "many men" or "many husbands") is *a form of marriage uniting one female with two or more males.* This pattern appears only rarely. One example is among people of Tibet, where agriculture is difficult. There, polyandry discourages the division of land into parcels too small to support a family and divides the work of farming among many men. Polyandry has also been linked to

female infanticide—aborting female fetuses or killing female infants—because a decline in the female population forces men to share women.

Historically, most world societies have permitted more than one marital pattern; even so, most actual marriages have been monogamous (Murdock, 1965; orig. 1949). This cultural preference for monogamy reflects two key facts of life: supporting multiple spouses is a heavy financial burden, and the number of men and women in most societies is roughly the same.

RESIDENTIAL PATTERNS

Just as societies regulate mate selection, so they designate where a couple resides. In pre-industrial societies, most newlyweds live with one set of parents, gaining economic assistance and security in the process. Most societies observe a norm of **patrilocality** (Greek for "place of the father"), *a residential pattern in which a married couple lives with or near the husband's family*. But some societies (such as the North American Iroquois) endorse **matrilocality** (meaning "place of the mother"), *a residential pattern in which a married couple lives with or near the wife's family*. Societies that engage in frequent, local warfare tend towards patrilocality since families want their sons close to home for protection. Societies that engage in distant warfare may be patrilocal or matrilocal, depending on whether sons or daughters have greater economic value (Ember and Ember, 1971, 1991).

Industrial societies show another pattern: when finances permit, they favour **neolocality** (Greek meaning "new place"), *a residential pattern in which a married couple lives apart from the parents of both spouses*.

PATTERNS OF DESCENT

Descent refers to *the system by which members of a society trace kinship over generations*. Most pre-industrial societies trace kinship through only one side of the family—the father or the mother. The more prevalent pattern is **patrilineal descent**, *a system tracing kinship through men*. In a patrilineal system, children are related to others only through their fathers, and fathers typically pass property on to their sons. Patrilineal descent characterizes most pastoral and agrarian societies, since men produce the most valued resources. Less common is **matrilineal descent**, *a system tracing kinship through women*. Matrilineal descent, through which mothers pass property to their daughters, is found more frequently in horticultural societies where women are the primary food producers.

Industrial societies with greater gender equality recognize **bilateral descent** ("two-sided descent"), *a system tracing kinship through both men and women*. Here, children recognize as relatives people on the "father's side" *and* the "mother's side" of the family.

PATTERNS OF AUTHORITY

The predominance of polygyny, patrilocality, and patrilineal descent in the world reflects the universal presence of patriarchy. Without denying that wives and mothers exercise considerable power in every society, as Chapter 13 ("Gender Stratification") explains, no truly matriarchal society has ever existed.

In industrial societies such as Canada, more egalitarian family patterns are evolving, especially as increasing numbers of women enter the labour force.

However, even here, men are typically heads of households. Parents in Canada also still prefer boys to girls, and usually give children their father's last name. In Quebec, where married women keep their birth names, some children are given their mothers' surnames.

THEORETICAL ANALYSIS OF THE FAMILY

As in earlier chapters, several theoretical approaches offer a range of insights about the family.

FUNCTIONS OF THE FAMILY: STRUCTURAL-FUNCTIONAL ANALYSIS

The structural-functional paradigm contends that the family performs several vital tasks. From this point of view, the family operates as "the backbone of society."

1. **Socialization.** As explained in Chapter 5 ("Socialization"), the family is the first and most influential setting for socialization. Ideally, parents teach children to be well-integrated and contributing members of society (Parsons and Bales, 1955). Of course, family socialization continues throughout the life cycle. Adults change within marriage, and, as any parent knows, mothers and fathers learn as much from raising their children as their children learn from them.

2. **Regulation of sexual activity.** Every culture regulates sexual activity in the interest of maintaining kinship organization and property rights. One universal regulation is the incest taboo, a cultural norm forbidding sexual relations or marriage between certain kin. Which kin fall within the incest taboo varies from one culture to another. The matrilineal Navajo, for example, forbid marrying any relative of one's mother. Our bilateral society applies the incest taboo to both sides of the family but limits it to close relatives, including parents, grandparents, siblings, aunts, and uncles. But even brother–sister marriages found approval among the ancient Egyptian, Incan, and Hawaiian nobility (Murdock, 1965; orig. 1949).

   Reproduction between close relatives can mentally and physically impair offspring. Yet only human beings observe an incest taboo, suggesting that the real reason for controlling incest is social. Why? First, the incest taboo minimizes sexual competition within families by restricting legitimate sexuality to spouses. Second, it forces people to marry outside their immediate families, integrating the larger society. Third, since kinship defines people's rights and obligations towards each other, reproduction among close relatives would hopelessly confuse kinship ties and threaten social order.

3. **Social placement.** Families are not biologically necessary for people to reproduce, but they do help maintain social organization. Parents confer their own social identity—in terms of race, ethnicity, religion, and social class—on children at birth. This fact explains the long-standing preference for birth to married parents.

4. **Material and emotional security.** People view the family as a "haven in a heartless world," looking to kin for physical protection, emotional support, and financial assistance. To a greater or lesser extent, most families do all these things, although not without periodic conflict. Not surprisingly, then, people living in families tend to be healthier than those living alone.

Critical evaluation. Structural-functional analysis explains why society could not exist without families. But this approach overlooks the great diversity of Canadian family life. Also, it ignores ways in which other social institutions (say, government) could meet some of the same human needs. Finally, structural-functional analysis overlooks negative aspects of family life, including its support of patriarchy and the alarming extent of family violence.

INEQUALITY AND THE FAMILY: SOCIAL-CONFLICT ANALYSIS

Like the structural-functional approach, the social-conflict paradigm considers the family central to the operation of society, but rather than focusing on societal benefits, conflict theorists investigate how the family perpetuates social inequality. Families perpetuate social inequality in several ways:

1. **Property and inheritance.** Friedrich Engels (1902; orig. 1884) traced the origin of the family to the need to identify heirs so that men (especially in the higher classes) could transmit property to their sons. Families thus support the concentration of wealth and reproduce the class structure over generations (Mare, 1991).

2. **Patriarchy.** According to Engels, men determine their heirs by controlling the sexuality of women. Families thus transform women into the sexual and economic property of men. A century ago in Canada, a wife's earnings belonged to her husband. Today, despite striking economic gains, women still bear major responsibility for child care and housework (Nett, 1993) and earn substantially less than men. Statistics Canada indicated that in 1992 employed women with at least one child under age five spent 5.3 hours per day on housework, child care, and shopping, whereas

the average man in this situation spent about 3 hours per day on domestic responsibilities (Steele, 1995:29). If this unpaid work were added to the economy, it would be worth $234 billion dollars (Philp, 1995:A8).

3. **Race and ethnicity.** Racial and ethnic categories will persist over generations only to the degree that people marry others like themselves. Thus, endogamous marriage also shores up the racial and ethnic hierarchy in our own society and elsewhere.

Critical evaluation. Social-conflict analysis reveals another side of family life: its role in maintaining social inequality. Engels condemned the family as part and parcel of capitalism. Yet noncapitalist societies have families (and family problems) all the same. While kinship and social inequality are deeply intertwined, as Engels argued, the family appears to carry out various societal functions that are not easily accomplished by other means.

CONSTRUCTING FAMILY LIFE: MICRO-LEVEL ANALYSIS

Both structural-functional and social-conflict analyses take a broad view of the family as a structural system. Micro-level approaches, in contrast, explore how individuals shape and experience family life day to day.

Symbolic-Interaction Analysis

People experience family life in terms of relationships, and these vary from person to person and change from day to day. In ideal terms, however, family living offers an opportunity for *intimacy*. As a result of sharing a wide range of activities over a long period of time, members of families forge emotional bonds. Of course, the fact that parents act as authority figures often inhibits their communication with younger children. But as young people reach adulthood, kinship ties typically "open up" to include confiding as well as turning to one another for emotional support and assistance with numerous tasks and responsibilities (Macionis, 1978a).

Social-Exchange Analysis

Social-exchange analysis, another micro-level approach, depicts courtship and marriage as forms of negotiation (Blau, 1964). Dating allows each person the chance to assess the likely advantages and disadvantages of taking the other as a spouse, always keeping in mind the value of what one has to offer in return. In essence, exchange analysts contend, individuals seek to make the best "deal" they can in selecting a partner.

Physical attractiveness is one critical element of social exchange. Throughout history, patriarchal societies have made beauty a commodity offered by

The family is a basic building block of society because it performs important functions, such as conferring social position and regulating sexual activity. To most family members, however, the family (at least in ideal terms) is a "haven in a heartless world" in which individuals enjoy the feeling of belonging and find emotional support. Marc Chagall conveyed the promise of marriage in his painting To My Wife. *In this painting, how does the artist characterize marriage?*

Marc Chagall (1887–1985), *To My Wife*, 1933–44. Georges Pompidou Centre, Paris. The Bridgeman Art Library, London.

women on the marriage market. The high value assigned to beauty explains women's traditional concern with physical appearance and their sensitivity about revealing their age. Men, in turn, have traditionally been assessed according to their financial resources. Recently, however, because women are joining the labour force, they are less dependent on men for support. Thus, the terms of exchange have been converging for men and women.

Critical evaluation. Micro-level analysis offers a useful counterpoint to structural-functional and social-conflict visions of the family as an institutional system. Both the interaction and exchange viewpoints give a better sense of the individual's experience of family life and how people shape this reality for themselves.

This approach, however, misses the bigger picture, namely, that family life is similar for people in the same social and economic categories. Canadian families vary in predictable ways according to social class and ethnicity, and, as noted below, typically evolve through distinct stages linked to the life course.

STAGES OF FAMILY LIFE

The family is dynamic, with marked changes across the life course. Typically, family life begins with courtship, followed by settling into the realities of married life. Next, for most couples at least, is raising children, leading to the later years of marriage after children have left home to form their own families. We look briefly at each of these stages.

COURTSHIP

`November 2, 1994, Kandy, Sri Lanka.`
`Winding our way through the rain for-`
`est of this beautiful island, the van`
`driver, Harry, recounts to his audi-`
`ence how he met his wife. Actually, it`
`was more of an arrangement: the two`
`families were both Buddhist and of the`
`same caste group. "We got along well,`
`right from the start," recalls Harry.`
`"We had the same background. I suppose`
`she or I could have said no. But 'love`
`marriages' happen in the city, not in`
`the village where I grew up."`

People in Sri Lanka, and in pre-industrial societies throughout the world, generally consider courtship too important to be left to the young (Stone, 1977). Arranged marriages represent an alliance between two extended families of similar social standing, and usually involve not just an exchange of children, but also of wealth and favours. Romantic love has little to do with it, and parents may make such arrangements when their children are quite young. A century ago in Sri Lanka and India, for example, half of all girls married before reaching the age of fifteen (Mayo, 1927; Mace and Mace, 1960). And, as the "Global Sociology" box explains, in some parts of the world child marriage persists today.

Arranged marriages fit into Emile Durkheim's model of *mechanical solidarity* (see Chapter 4, "Society"). Because traditional societies are culturally homogeneous, almost any member of the opposite sex has been suitably socialized to perform the roles of spouse and parent. Thus, parents can arrange marriages with confidence that virtually any couple will be *culturally* compatible, regardless of whether they are *personally* compatible.

Early to Wed: A Report from Rural India

Sumitra Jogi was crying as her wedding was about to begin. Were they tears of joy? Not exactly: this "bride" is an eleven-month-old squirming in the arms of her mother. The groom? A boy of six.

In a remote, rural village in India's western state of Rajasthan, two families gather at midnight to celebrate a traditional wedding ritual. It is May 2, an especially good day to marry according to Hindu tradition. Sumitra's father smiles as the ceremony begins; her mother

cradles the infant, who, having just finished nursing, has now fallen asleep. The groom, dressed in a special costume with a red-and-gold turban on his head, gently reaches up and grasps the baby's hand. Then, as the ceremony reaches its conclusion, the young boy leads the child and mother three and a half times around the wedding fire—while the audience beams—marking the couple's first steps together as husband and wife.

Child weddings of this kind are illegal in India, but in the rural regions traditions are strong and marriage laws are difficult to enforce. In fact, experts estimate that thousands of children marry each year in ceremonies of this kind. "In rural Rajasthan," explains one social welfare worker, "all the girls are married by age fourteen. These are poor, illiterate families, and they don't want to keep girls past their first menstrual cycle."

For the immediate future, Sumitra Jogi will remain with her parents. But by the time she is eight or ten, a second ceremony will mark the time for her to move to the home of her husband's family, where her married life will begin.

If the responsibilities of marriage lie years in the future, why do families push their children to marry at such an early age? Parents of girls know that the younger the bride, the smaller the dowry offered to the groom's parents. Then, too, when girls marry this young, there is no chance that they will lose their virginity, which would spoil their attractiveness on the marriage market. But, of course, the entire system rests on the assumption that love has nothing to do with it. Marriage is an alliance between families, so no one worries that the children are too young to understand what is taking place.

Source: Based on Anderson (1995).

Industrialization erodes the importance of extended families and weakens traditions while enhancing personal choice in courtship. Young people expect to choose their own mates, and usually delay doing so until they have financial security and the experience to select a suitable partner. Dating sharpens courtship skills and may serve as a period of sexual experimentation.

Romantic Love

Our culture celebrates *romantic love*—the experience of affection and sexual passion for another person—as the basis for marriage. We find it hard to imagine marriage without love, and popular culture—from remakes of traditional fairy tales such as "Cinderella" to today's paperback romance novels—portrays love as the key to a successful marriage.

Our society's emphasis on romance has some useful consequences. Passionate love motivates individuals to "leave the nest" to form new families of their own, and it can help a new couple through the difficult adjustments of living together (Goode, 1959). Yet because feelings wax and wane, romantic love is a less

stable foundation for marriage than social and economic considerations—an assertion supported by Canada's high divorce rate compared to lower rates in societies that allow less choice in partners.

But even in a culture of more choice, sociologists know that Cupid's arrow is aimed by society more than we like to think. Most people fall in love with others of the same race, comparable age, and similar social class. All societies "arrange" marriages to the extent that they encourage **homogamy** (literally, "like marrying like"), *marriage between people with the same social characteristics*.

In short, "falling in love" may be a strong personal feeling, but it is guided by social forces. We exaggerate the importance of romantic love to reassure ourselves that we may control our own lives.

SETTLING IN: IDEAL AND REAL MARRIAGE

Our culture presents marriage to the young in idealized, "happily-ever-after" terms. One consequence of such optimistic thinking is the danger of disappointment, especially for women—who, more than men, are taught to see in marriage the key to future happiness.

People in every society recognize the reality of physical attraction. But the power of romantic love, captured in Christian Pierre's painting I Do *holds surprisingly little importance in traditional societies. In much of the world, it would be less correct to say that individuals marry individuals and more true to say that families marry families. In other words, parents arrange marriages for their children with an eye to the social position of the kin groups involved.*

Christian Pierre, b. 1962, *I Do*, American Private Collection. Superstock, Inc.

Then, too, romantic love involves a good deal of fantasy. We fall in love with others, not necessarily as they are, but as we want them to be (Berscheid and Hatfield, 1983). Only after marriage do many spouses regularly confront each other as they carry out the day-to-day routines of maintaining a household.

Sex can also be a source of disappointment. In the romantic haze of falling in love, people may anticipate marriage as an endless sexual honeymoon, only to face the sobering realization that sex becomes a less than all-consuming passion. Nevertheless, two in three married people report that they are satisfied with the sexual dimension of their relationship (Blumstein and Schwartz, 1983).

Many experts agree that couples with the most fulfilling sexual relationships experience the greatest satisfaction in their marriages. This correlation does not mean that sex is the key to marital bliss, but, more often than not, good sex and good relationships go together (Hunt, 1974; Tavris and Sadd, 1977; Blumstein and Schwartz, 1983). As Figure 18–1 shows, about 60 percent of married couples say that they are having sex weekly (Bibby, 1995:66).

Infidelity—sexual activity outside marriage—is another area in which the reality of marriage does not coincide with our cultural ideal. We strongly support traditional marriage vows "to forsake all others." In a survey, for example, three out of four adults said that extramarital sex is "always wrong" and only 4 percent believed that it was never wrong (Bibby, 1983). Even so, 17 percent of men and 9 percent of women indicated that they had been sexually unfaithful to their partners at least once (*Gallup Sexual Life Style Survey*, 1988). Moreover, increased rates of premarital sex may suggest even greater weakening of the bonds of fidelity within marriage (Herold, 1984:13).

CHILD REARING

Despite the substantial demands children make on the time and energy of parents, sometimes to the point of straining their marriage, almost all Canadians include at least one child in their conception of the ideal family. The smaller families of today represent a marked change from two centuries ago, when eight children was average!

Big families pay off in pre-industrial societies because children perform needed labour. Indeed, people generally regard having children as a wife's duty and, without reliable birth-control technology, childbearing is a regular event. Of course, a high death rate in pre-industrial societies prevents many children from reaching adulthood; as late as 1900, a substantial minority of children born in Canada died in infancy or early childhood (*Canada Year Book*, 1994).

Economically speaking, industrialization transforms children from a vital asset to a burdensome liability. Today, the expense of raising a child is substantial, especially if the child acquires a university education.

 For expert advice, links, and networks for Canadians with questions about parenting, see www.canadianparents.com/ This helps to explain the steady drop in family size during the twentieth century to slightly more than one child per family in Canada today.

The trend towards smaller families also holds for all other industrial societies. But the picture differs sharply in low-income countries in Latin America, Asia, and especially Africa, where many women have few alternatives to bearing and raising children. In such societies, four to six children is the norm.

Not only is parenting expensive, but it is a lifetime commitment. As our society has afforded its members more choice about family life, more adults have opted

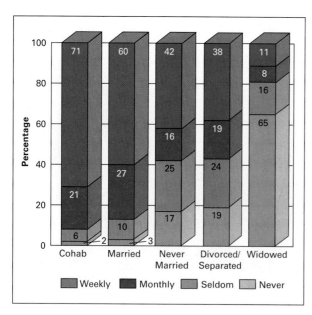

FIGURE 18–1 Sexual Activity by Marital Status

Source: Bibby (1995:66).

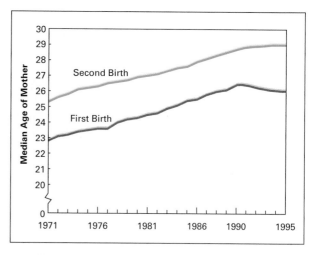

FIGURE 18–2 Median Age of Mothers Giving Birth to First or Second Child, 1971–95

Source: Statistics Canada, *Canadian Centre for Health Information, Health Status Section* (1991); Colombo (1997).

to delay childbirth or to remain childless. As Figure 18–2 shows, the median age of mothers giving birth to their first child rose by three years between 1971 and 1995; the age of mothers giving birth to their second child increased by four years in the same period. About two-thirds of parents in the United States claim they would like to devote more of their time to child rearing (Snell, 1990). The majority of Canadian parents would likely agree. But unless we are willing to accept some decline in our material standard of living, economic realities demand that most parents pursue careers outside the home. Thus, the child-rearing patterns we have described reflect ways of coming to terms with economic change.

As Chapter 13 ("Gender Stratification") explained, most women with young children now work for income. In 1997, 76.6 percent of women aged twenty-five to fifty-four were in the workforce; most mothers with children under eighteen worked for income outside the home. But while women and men share the burden of earning income, women continue to bear the traditional responsibility for raising children and doing housework. Many men in our society are eager parents, but most resist sharing responsibility for household tasks that our culture historically has defined as "women's work" (Hochschild, 1989; Presser, 1993; Keith and Schafer, 1994).

As more women join men in the labour force, parents have less time for parenting. Children of working parents spend most of the day at school. But many school-age youngsters are *latchkey kids* who fend for themselves after school. Traditionalists in the "family values" debate caution that mothers often work at

the expense of children, who receive less parenting. Progressives counter that such criticism ignores the role of fathers in parenting and unfairly faults women for seeking equal opportunity in the world of work.

THE FAMILY IN LATER LIFE

Increasing life expectancy in Canada means that, barring divorce, couples are likely to remain married for a long time. By about age fifty, most have completed the task of raising children. The remaining years of marriage bring a return to living with only one's spouse.

Like the birth of children, their departure (the "empty nest") requires adjustments, although the marital relationship often becomes closer and more satisfying in midlife. Years of living together may diminish a couple's sexual passion for each other, but mutual understanding and companionship are likely to increase.

Personal contact with children usually continues, since most older adults live a short distance from at least one of their children (Nett, 1993). Moreover, many Canadians are grandparents, and many help their daughters and sons with child care and a host of other responsibilities.

Recent developments have created new intergenerational challenges for Canadian families in that the transition to adulthood has been extended. Increasingly, "mid-life parenthood comprises prolonged periods of co-residence with grown young adults" (Mitchell, 2000:80). Mitchell found that, according to the 1995 General Social Survey, 27 percent of adults, aged nineteen to thirty-five, had left home and returned for periods of four months or more. Among the reasons for returning were the termination of jobs or relation-

Child Discipline, Child Abuse?

Is abuse the logical extension of socially acceptable punishment in Canada? Some researchers have found correlations between child abuse and rigid parenting styles, unrealistic expectations of children, a history of abuse in the early lives of the parents, and condoning high levels of physical punishment. A McMaster University study of parenting, based on home interviews, included a series of questions regarding child discipline (Lenton, 1990). Table 18–1 provides a brief overview of the common techniques the respondents used.

Notice how many mothers and fathers reported that they yelled at their children. The next two most frequently used strategies were slapping or spanking, followed by verbal threats. It is important to realize that these numbers may well be underrepresentations because, regardless of whether the practices are normative, the parents surveyed are still likely to be affected by the "social desirability effect" (the tendency to describe oneself in socially desirable terms).

Lenton also examined the extent to which parental discipline of children reflected the type of discipline they had received as children, or current norms favouring certain types of discipline. She found that parents generally used the type of discipline they had received as children, but only when social norms supported that type. However, when parents were particularly stressed, from unemployment or low family income, they were more likely to use violent discipline. Lenton found that unemployment is especially threatening to fathers and that low family income is particularly challenging to mothers.

At the structural level, the privacy of the family, the tradition of absolute parental authority, and the widespread acceptance of physical punishment as legitimate do support violence towards children.

TABLE 18–1 Aggressive Disciplinary Actions Tried by Parents, Ever and in Past Year (Percentages)

Ever Tried			Past Year	
Mothers	Fathers		Mothers	Fathers
99	94	yell	96	94
38	54	ridicule child	35	52
71	73	verbally threaten	65	71
18	33	withdraw emotionally	14	27
61	58	push, grab, shove	55	46
17	6	throw something at child	11	4
88	81	slap or spank with hand	75	58
20	19	hit child with object	15	10
10	10	withhold food	4	8
16	21	beat child	12	15

Source: Lenton (1990:169).

Source: Lenton (1990:169).

ships, financial considerations, or the need to complete schooling. Some of those who returned for financial reasons could afford to live on their own—but not at their parents' standard of living.

The other side of the coin, explained in Chapter 15 ("Aging and the Elderly"), is that more adults in midlife must care for aging parents. The "empty nest" may not be filled by a parent coming to live in the home, but parents living to eighty and beyond require practical, emotional, and financial care that can be more taxing than raising young children. The oldest of the "baby boomers"—now in their fifties—are often called the "sandwich generation" because they will spend as many years caring for their aging parents as they did for their own offspring.

The final, and surely the most difficult, transition in married life comes with the death of a spouse. Wives typically outlive their husbands because of women's longer life expectancy and the fact that wives are usually younger than husbands to begin with. Wives can thus expect to spend a significant period of their lives as widows. The bereavement and loneliness accompanying the death of a spouse are extremely difficult, and the experience may be worse for widowers, who usually have fewer friends than widows and may be unskilled at cooking and housework.

CANADIAN FAMILIES: CLASS, RACE, AND GENDER

Dimensions of inequality—social class, ethnicity and race, and gender—are powerful forces that shape marriage and family life. Here, we address each factor separately, though they overlap in our lives.

Prairie families, particularly those with a strong ethnic identity, traditionally tend to maintain kinship ties. William Kurelek's painting Manitoba Party *depicts a Ukrainian family reunion.*

William Kurelek, *Manitoba Party*, National Gallery of Canada, Ottawa, by permission of the estate of William Kurelek, c/o The Isaacs Gallery of Toronto.

SOCIAL CLASS

Social class frames a family's financial security and range of opportunities. Interviewing working-class women, Lillian Rubin (1976) found that wives deemed a good husband to be one who held a steady job and refrained from excessive drinking and violence. Her middle-class informants never mentioned such things: these women simply *assumed* a husband would provide a safe and secure home. Their ideal husband was someone with whom they could communicate, sharing feelings and experiences.

Such differences reflect the fact that people with higher social standing have more schooling, and most have jobs that emphasize verbal skills. In addition, middle-class couples share a wider range of activities, while working-class life is more divided along gender lines. As Rubin explains, many working-class men hold traditional ideas about masculinity and self-control, so they stifle emotional expressiveness. Women then turn to each other as confidantes.

What women (and men) think they can hope for in marriage—and what they end up with—is linked to their social class. Much the same holds for children: boys and girls lucky enough to be born into more affluent families enjoy better mental and physical health, develop higher self-confidence, and go on to greater achievement than children born to poor parents (Komarovsky, 1967; Bott, 1971, orig. 1957; Rubin, 1976; Fitzpatrick, 1988; McLeod and Shanahan, 1993).

ETHNICITY AND RACE

As Chapter 14 ("Race and Ethnicity") discusses, ethnicity and race are powerful social forces, and the effects of both ripple through family life. Keep in mind, however, that all families are diverse and they conform to no single stereotype.

Native Canadian Families

There are more than seven hundred Native communities in Canada: about six hundred bands live on reserves, and there are dozens of Inuit and Métis villages and settlements as well. Over the past few decades, increasing numbers of First Nations (status Indian) people are living off reserve—to the point where about half are now living off reserve. While Calgary, Edmonton, Saskatoon, and Winnipeg have substantial Native populations, residence in the major cities of Montreal, Vancouver, and Toronto is also increasing (Gerber, 1995). Given this diversity, it is impossible to discuss the family patterns of Native Canadians as a homogeneous group.

Native Canadians are often among the most economically deprived members of our society, and suffer discrimination and prejudice, resulting in high rates of unemployment, inadequate housing, and family instability. As one researcher says, "under these circumstances, identification with traditional cultures suffers, and their central familistic values of kin solidarity, respect for elders, and the welfare of children have been weakened" (Nett, 1993:101). Moreover, because of their political and economic subordination by Europeans, the family norms of many Native people have been threatened.

Throughout the early 1900s, most Native people lived on reserves or with extended families in isolated regions. Child care was the responsibility of the extended family, and highly respected elders taught the young their languages and traditions. Christian missionaries, who had made concerted efforts to assimilate and Christianize Native peoples, took children away from the reserves to church-run residential schools to learn another language, religion, and culture, while also learning to despise their own. Traditional family values began to erode: the elders lost their authority, and the extended families lost their responsibilities for nurturing and caretaking. Young people raised outside normal family settings failed to learn parenting skills to apply later on when raising their own children. In addition, resettlement programs broke up whole communities and diminished family ties even further (Shkilnyk, 1985).

The involvement of the church and the state in Canadian Aboriginal life has been troublesome over the years. From the 1950s until the mid-1970s, under the auspices of social workers employed by various Children's Aid Societies, children were taken away from parents who were no longer functioning as adequate parents because of poverty, unemployment, prejudice, alcohol abuse, and a variety of other social conditions. Many of these children were placed in non-Native foster homes, where they lost contact with their remaining Native traditions and culture; others were adopted by non-Native families in Canada and even in the United States. Having observed the severe adjustment problems of many of these children, authorities now focus on keeping children with their families whenever possible or placing them with other Native Canadian families when it is necessary to remove them (Baker, 1991).

Mixed Marriages

Most spouses have similar social backgrounds with regard to class, race, and ethnicity, but over the course of the past century, ethnicity has mattered less and less. Thus, a man of German/French ancestry might marry a woman of Irish/English background.

Race remains a more formidable consideration, however. Since in 2001 African, Arab, Asian, and Native Canadians represented about 17 percent of the Canadian population, about that share of marriages would be "mixed" if people ignored race altogether in choosing marriage partners. The actual proportion is not as large, attesting to the continuing importance of race in social relations. Even so, the number of racially mixed marriages is rising steadily in the United States and will likely do so in Canada as the populations of "minority" Canadians increase. Table 18–2 shows that attitudes towards intergroup marriage in Canada have become more accepting over time. The vast majority (80 to 92 percent) of Canadian adults approve of intermarriage across various racial and religious lines (Bibby, 1995:54).

GENDER

Among all races, said Jessie Bernard (1982; orig. 1973), every marriage is actually *two* different relationships: a

TABLE 18–2 Approval of Intergroup Marriage, 1975 through 1995

	1975	1980	1985	1990	1995
Whites and Natives	75%	80%	83%	84%	84%
Whites and Asians (Orientals)	66	75	78	82	83
Whites and East Indians/Pakistanis	58	66	72	77	80
Whites and Blacks	57	64	72	79	81
Protestants and Roman Catholics	86	88	89	90	92
Protestants and Jews	80	84	84	86	90
Roman Catholics and Jews	78	81	82	85	89

Source: Bibby (1995:54).

woman's marriage and a man's marriage. Although patriarchy has diminished, even today few marriages are composed of two equal partners. We still expect men to be older as well as taller than their wives and to have more important careers (McRae, 1986).

The persistence of the notion of man-as-breadwinner, wife-as-homemaker was illustrated in a study of steelworkers and their wives in Hamilton, Ontario. When, in 1979–80, the Women Back into Stelco Committee launched a successful discrimination complaint with the Ontario Human Rights Commission, the introduction of female co-workers into the masculine world of dangerous manual labour and big machinery was resisted by the steelworkers. In-depth interviews revealed that steelmaking was seen as men's work, and linked to the notion that men must be breadwinners. This attitude was tied to men's "deeper sense of responsibility to provide for their families" (Livingstone and Luxton, 1995:187).

Such patriarchal values are associated with the persistent notion that marriage is more beneficial to women than to men (Bernard, 1982). The positive stereotype of the carefree bachelor contrasts sharply with the negative image of the lonely spinster. This image is rooted in a traditional view of women as being fulfilled only by being wives and mothers.

But, Bernard claimed, married women have poorer mental health, less happiness, and more passive attitudes towards life than do single women. Married men, however, live longer than single men, have better mental health, and report being happier. It is hardly surprising, then, that after divorce men are more eager than women to find a new partner.

Bernard concluded that there is no better guarantor of long life, health, and happiness for a man than a woman socialized to perform the "duties of a wife" by devoting her life to caring for him and providing the security of a well-ordered home. She adds that marriage *could* be healthful for women if husbands did not dominate wives and expect them to perform virtually all of the housework. Indeed, research confirms that

During her long career conducting sociological research, Jessie Bernard provided evidence that marriage is something of a surprise for women. Taught to see marriage as a solution to life's problems, many women who enter traditional marriages soon face problems they did not expect. Susan Pyzow's painting Bridal Bouquet *illustrates this idea.*

© Susan Pyzow, *Bridal Bouquet*, watercolour on paper, 25.4 × 34.3 cm. Studio SPM Inc.

husbands and wives with the best mental health deliberately share responsibilities for earning income, raising children, and doing housework (Ross et al., 1983; Mirowsky and Ross, 1984).

TRANSITION AND PROBLEMS IN FAMILY LIFE

Ann Landers (1984), a well-known observer of the North American scene, once remarked that "One marriage out of twenty is wonderful, four are good, ten are tolerable, and five are pure hell." Families can be a source of joy, but the reality of family life sometimes falls far short of this ideal.

DIVORCE

Our society strongly supports marriage, and more than nine out of ten people marry at some point, al-

though the marriage rate is declining (Serrill, 1995:23). Moreover, many of today's marriages eventually unravel. Figure 18–3 shows the great increase in the Canadian divorce rate since 1968, followed by fluctuations between 1982 and 1996. Before 1968, divorces were granted only if one of the spouses was proven to have committed adultery; at that time the divorce rate was 40 per 100 000 population. The *Divorce Act* of 1968 allowed for divorce in certain other circumstances: if one of the spouses had committed a matrimonial offence (such as adultery or emotional or physical cruelty), if one spouse had deserted, or if the spouses had lived apart for at least three years. In 1985, the Act was rewritten, making "marriage breakdown" the only reason for divorce. (Marriage breakdown includes separation of at least one year, adultery, and physical and mental cruelty.) The divorce rate peaked in 1987 and has dropped off fairly steadily since then.

The increasing North American divorce rate has many causes (Thornton, 1985; Waite et al., 1985; Weitzman, 1985; Gerstel, 1987; Furstenberg and Cherlin, 1991; Etzioni, 1993):

1. **Individualism is on the rise.** Today, we spend less time together than in the past. We are more individualistic and more concerned with personal happiness and success than with the well-being of families and children.

2. **Romantic love often subsides.** Our culture emphasizes romantic love as a basis for marriage, rendering relationships vulnerable as sexual passion fades. Many people end a marriage in favour of a new relationship that renews excitement and romance.

3. **Women are now less dependent on men.** Increasing participation in the labour force has reduced wives' financial dependence on husbands. As a practical matter, then, women find it easier to walk away from unhappy marriages.

4. **Many of today's marriages are stressful.** With both partners working outside the home in most cases, jobs consume time and energy that in the past were directed towards family life. Under such circumstances (and given the difficulty of securing good, affordable child care), raising children is a particular burden. Children stabilize some marriages, but divorce is most common during the early years of marriage when many couples have young children.

5. **Divorce is more socially acceptable.** Divorce no longer carries the powerful, negative stigma it did a century ago. Family and friends are now less likely to discourage couples in conflict from considering divorce.

6. **Divorce is legally easier to accomplish.** In the past, courts required divorcing couples to

demonstrate that one or both were guilty of behaviour such as adultery or physical abuse. Today, as one law professor notes, "It is easier to walk away from a marriage than from a commitment to purchase a new car" (quoted in Etzioni, 1993).

The divorce rate has eased downwards slightly over the last decade for two reasons. First, the large baby-boomer cohort that was born shortly after World War II is now reaching middle age, when divorce is less common. Second, hard economic times in the mid-1990s discouraged divorce, since living alone typically is more expensive than living in families.

Although our divorce rates have stopped climbing, Canada's rates remain a little higher than those of many European countries. Nonetheless, it is roughly half of that of the United States (Colombo, 1997). Ed Kain (1990) cautions that we commonly exaggerate the stability of marriage in the past, when the early death of a spouse ended as many marriages after a few years as divorce does now.

Who Divorces?

At greatest risk of divorce are young spouses, especially those who marry after a brief courtship, have few financial resources, and have yet to mature emotionally. People of lower social position are also more likely to divorce, usually because of financial strains. At all social levels, the risk of divorce increases if a couple marries in response to an unexpected pregnancy, or if one or both partners have alcohol- or other substance-abuse problems. People who are not religious divorce more readily than those who are.

Divorce is more common if both partners have successful careers. This is partly due to the strains of a two-career marriage, and the fact that financially independent women are less likely to remain in an unhappy marriage. Also, men and women who divorce once are more likely to divorce again, presumably because problems follow them from one marriage to another (Booth and White, 1980; Yoder and Nichols, 1980; Glenn and Shelton, 1985).

Canada Map 18–1 (on page 461) takes a look at divorce levels across the country. For Canada as a whole, 7.9 percent of the population 15 years of age and over was divorced in 2001. Quebec and Yukon have the highest levels, Nunavut and Newfoundland and Labrador, the lowest. Divorce is pronounced where religious values are weaker and where people are more likely to move often, thus distancing themselves from family and friends. The Yukon fits both of those descriptions, having that largest proportion claiming "no religion" and substantial migration into and out of the territory in response to changes in the resource industries. While very few Quebecers claim

FIGURE 18–3 The Divorce Rate in Canada, 1968–2000

Sources: Statistics Canada, Catalogue Nos. 82-003S17 and 84-213, Health Statistics Division, 1991; and Canadian Statistics, www.statcan.ca.

no religion, the province did experience rapid secularization during the Quiet Revolution, so that their attachment to the Catholic Church is relatively weak. The Quiet Revolution also involved rural-urban migration and social mobility, both of which weaken ties to old communities and networks.

Divorce as Process

Divorce is a form of role exit, as described in Chapter 6 ("Social Interaction in Everyday Life"). Paul Bohannan (1970) and others point to six distinct adjustments divorcing people make:

1. **Emotional divorce.** Distancing oneself from the former spouse usually begins before the formal break occurs. A deteriorating marriage can be fraught with indifference, disappointment, or outright hostility.

2. **Legal divorce.** Since marriage is a legal contract, divorce involves a legal change of status. Financial settlements are central to most divorce agreements.

3. **Psychic reorganization.** Many divorced people suffer not just from loneliness but from a sense that ending their marriage represents a personal failure.

4. **Community reorganization.** Ending a marriage requires both partners to reorganize friendships and adjust relations with parents and other family members who are accustomed to seeing them as a couple.

Not all marriages thrive "til death do us part." Canada has one of the highest divorce rates in the world. The breakdown of communication that lies at the heart of failing relationships is clearly shown by Edward Hopper in his 1932 painting Room in New York.

Edward Hopper (1882–1967), *Room in New York*, 1932. Oil on canvas. 73.7 × 91.4. Sheldon Memorial Art Gallery, University of Nebraska– Lincoln. F.M. Hall Collection. 1932. H–166.

5. **Economic reorganization.** Divorce courts often require ex-spouses to sell homes and divide marital assets equally. No-fault divorce laws have reduced the amount of alimony and child support paid by men to their former wives. While divorce raises the living standards of many men (who no longer support wives and children), it can mean financial calamity to women whose earnings are lower than those of their husbands and who may be responsible for supporting children as well (Weitzman, 1985, 1996; Peterson, 1996).

6. **Parental reorganization.** More than half of all divorcing couples face the issue of child custody. Our society's conventional practice is still to award custody of children to mothers, based on the notion that women are more committed parents than men. A recent trend, however, is towards joint custody, whereby children divide their time between both parents. Joint custody is difficult if divorced parents live far apart or do not get along, but it has the advantage of keeping children in regular contact with both parents (Roman and Haddad, 1978; Cherlin and Furstenberg, 1983).

Because mothers usually have custody of children but fathers typically earn more income, the well-being of children often depends on fathers making court-ordered child-support payments. Yet most children of divorced parents do not receive the financial support to which they are entitled by law. What has been called "an epidemic of nonsupport" has led to legislation mandating that employers withhold money from the paycheques of delinquent parents. Still, the legislation has proven very difficult to enforce (Nett, 1993).

In February 1998, British Columbia became the first North American jurisdiction to give gay and lesbian couples "the same privileges and obligations as heterosexuals for child support, custody and access" (Matas, 1998). Assuming that Canada passes legislation allowing gays and lesbians to marry, same-sex couples across the country will soon face the normal consequences of divorce (a situation already confronted by gays in Ontario, where courts granted them the right to marry in the summer of 2003).

Divorce may well be hardest on children. Divorce can tear young people from familiar surroundings, entangle them in bitter feuding, and distance them from a parent they love. And, most seriously of all, in their own minds, many children blame themselves for their parents' breakup. For many children, divorce changes the trajectory of their entire lives, increasing the likelihood of emotional and behavioural problems and the risk of dropping out of school and getting into trouble with the law. Some experts, however, point out that divorce can be better for children than staying in a family torn by tension or violence. In any case, parents must be mindful that, when deciding whether to divorce, much more than their own well-being is at stake (Wallerstein and Blakeslee, 1989; Popenoe, 1992; Adelson, 1996).

REMARRIAGE

Despite the rising divorce rate, marriage—and remarriage—remain as popular as ever. Four out of five people who divorce remarry, and most do so within three

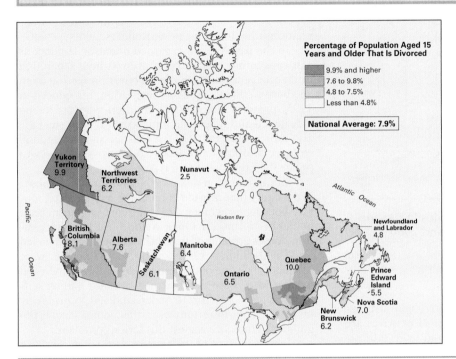

CANADA MAP 18–1
Population Aged 15 Years and Older That Is Divorced (Percentage, by Province and Territory), 2001

Source: Calculation by Gerber based on data from Statistics Canada, B2020, Profile Series (data retrieved in October 2003).

years (Ahlburg and De Vita, 1992). Nationwide, almost half of all marriages are now remarriages for at least one partner. Men, who derive greater benefits from wedlock, are more likely to remarry than women.

Remarriage often creates blended families, composed of children and some combination of biological parents and stepparents. Blended families have to define precisely who is part of the child's nuclear family (Furstenberg, 1984). They also require children to reorient themselves; an only child, for example, may suddenly find she has two older brothers. And, as already noted, the risk of divorce is high in remarriages. But blended families also offer both young and old the opportunity to relax rigid family roles.

FAMILY VIOLENCE

The ideal family serves as a haven from the dangers of the outside world. However, from the Biblical story of Cain's killing of his brother Abel to the Bernardo–Homolka case, the disturbing reality of many homes is **family violence**, *emotional, physical, or sexual abuse of one family member by another*. Sociologist Richard J. Gelles points to a chilling fact:

> The family is the most violent group in society with the exception of the police and the military. You are more likely to get killed, injured, or physically attacked in your home by someone you are related to

than in any other social context. (Quoted in Roesch, 1984:75)

Violence against Women

The common stereotype of a violent partner is a lower-class man who now and then drinks too much, loses control, and beats up his wife. In reality, although financial problems and unemployment do make the problem worse, violence against women in the home is perpetrated by men of all social classes, races, and ethnicities (Lupri, 1988:170). Furthermore, this violence often occurs at random. Family brutality frequently goes unreported to police, but researchers estimate that 20 percent of couples—or one in five—endure at least some violence each year (Lupri, 1988:171). Many of these couples experience serious incidents of violence, including kicking, biting, and punching.

Almost 30 percent of women who are murdered—as opposed to 6 percent of men—are killed by spouses, ex-spouses, or unmarried partners (Lupri, 1988). In 1989, 119 women in Canada were murdered by former husbands or partners (Begin, 1991). Overall, women are more likely to be injured by a family member than they are to be mugged or raped by a stranger or injured in an automobile accident.

Physically abused women have traditionally had few options. They may want to leave home, but

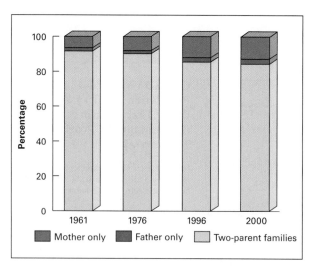

FIGURE 18–4 Single-Parent Families in Canada, 1961, 1976, 1996, and 2000

Sources: Statistics Canada, Household and Family Projections, 1976–2001, Catalogue No. 91-522, 1991; Canadian Statistics, www.statcan.ca.

many—especially those with children and without much money—have nowhere to go. Most wives are also committed to their marriages and believe (however unrealistically) that they can help abusive husbands to change. Some, unable to understand their husbands' violence, blame themselves. Others, raised in violent families, consider assault to be part of family life. Most abused women see no way out of the family violence that makes fear the centre of their lives. In one study, researchers found that one-quarter of women who had entered a metropolitan hospital after attempting suicide had been victims of family violence (Stark and Flitcraft, 1979).

In 1990, Canada's solicitor general attempted to address the problem of crime and abuse against women by producing *Woman Alone*, a book of prevention advice. But this document ignored the situations that most frequently expose women to danger—domestic and private settings where they are threatened by men they know. One reason for this misjudgment is that victimization studies ask about "crime" and "many victims do not perceive their partners' violent actions as crimes in the legal sense" (DeKeseredy et al., 1995:479).

In 1993, Statistics Canada published the results of its *Violence Against Women Survey*, revealing that 29 percent of women had been physically or sexually assaulted by their partners. Rates of violence are higher in new partnerships (under two years), in common-law unions, and following separation. Women were more likely to report violent abuse in their past relationships than in current ones. Since almost half of abused women had been assaulted with weapons, and since the assaults were repeated, it is not surprising that

The National Clearinghouse on Family Violence (NCFV) offers research and resources to address family violence: see www.hc-sc.gc.ca/hppb/familyviolence/

about 30 percent of abused women actually feared for their lives at some point during their relationships (Johnson, 1996; Rodgers, 2000).

In the past, the law regarded domestic violence as a private, family matter. Now, even without separation or divorce, a woman can obtain court protection from an abusive spouse. "Stalker" legislation, introduced in 1993, protects women and children who are being threatened and followed. Some medical personnel are also more aware today of the tell-tale signs of spousal violence and are more likely to report such cases to police than they were in the past.

Communities across North America are establishing shelters that provide counselling as well as temporary housing for women and children driven from their homes by violence. In Ontario alone, in 1989, 78 transition houses accommodated 9838 women, accompanied by 11 000 children. Of these families, 87 percent were in shelters because of domestic violence. Some men and women who abuse their partners are also joining self-help groups in an effort to understand and control their own behaviour. In various ways, then, our society is beginning to mobilize against this serious problem.

It is important to understand that, when men and women are asked how often they engage in a range of violent acts against their partners (as methods of conflict resolution, so that sexual assault is not included)) men are as likely to be the victims (Lupri, 2002) of domestic violence as women. While Canada, quite rightly, has mobilized to assist women and children, there is no attempt to help the male victims who also suffer severe loss of self-esteem.

Violence against Children

Family violence also victimizes children. Perhaps 4 percent of all youngsters suffer abuse each year, including several hundred who die as a result. Child abuse entails more than physical injury because abusive adults misuse power and trust to undermine a child's emotional well-being. Child abuse is most common among the youngest and most vulnerable children (Straus and Gelles, 1986; Van Biema, 1994; Besharov and Laumann, 1996).

In 1996, children were reported missing in Canada at a rate of one every nine minutes—more than 56 000 in that year. An alarming 78 percent of these youngsters are runaways; 57 percent of the runaways are girls; and the runaways are getting younger. Too many of these youngsters leave home because of abuse (psychological, sexual, or physical) and neglect. Recently, more of these children are leaving home because their parents say they can't afford to keep them, thereby repeating a pattern that appeared during the recession of the early 1980s. These numbers are described as an alarming sign of the increasing disintegration of the family (Mitchell, 1998, reporting on Statistics Canada's *Juristat*, February 12, 1998, Catalogue No. 85-002-XIE1998002).

Many abused children suffer in silence, believing that they are to blame for their own victimization. Abuse, compounded by years of guilt, can leave lasting emotional scars that prevent people abused as children from forming healthy relationships as adults.

About 90 percent of child abusers are men, but they conform to no simple stereotype. Most abusers, however, share one trait: having been abused themselves as children. Research shows that violent behaviour in close relationships is learned. In families, then, violence begets violence (Gwartney-Gibbs et al., 1987; Widom, 1996).

Elder Abuse

Another form of family violence that society was slow to recognize is elder abuse. Parents are living longer and the costs, in terms of time and money, of caregiving into old age can be the cause of considerable stress for the "sandwich generation," which is simultaneously caring for parents and children. Of course, the frail elderly are vulnerable to abuse—physical, psychological, and financial—because of failing mental and physical abilities. For more on elder abuse, which is underreported because of shame and dependence, see Chapter 15, "Aging and the Elderly," page 360.

ALTERNATIVE FAMILY FORMS

Most families in Canada are still composed of a married couple who raise children. But in recent decades, our society has displayed greater diversity in family life.

ONE-PARENT FAMILIES

As Figure 18–4 (on page 462) indicates, in 1961, 8.4 percent of Canadian families were headed by a single parent and 91.6 percent were husband-wife families. By 2001, single-parent families had risen to 15.6 percent. Projections are that by 2011, two-parent families will decrease further to 83 percent (*1993 Corpus Almanac and Canadian Sourcebook*). Thus, the proportion of one-parent families is growing, and almost 12 percent of children in Canada now live in these families. One-parent families—about four times more likely to be headed by women than men—may result from divorce, the inability to find a suitable husband, or an unmarried woman's decision to have a child (Kantrowitz, 1985). Figure 18–5 compares the proportion of Canadian births out of wedlock to those of other industrial nations.

Single parenthood increases a woman's risk of poverty because it limits her ability to work and to further her education. The converse is also true:

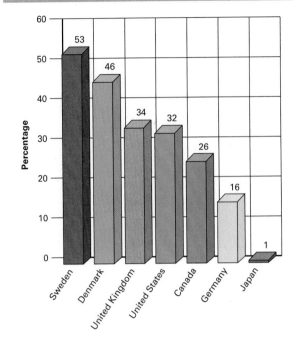

FIGURE 18–5 Percentage of Births to Unmarried Women, 1995

Source: U.S. Census Bureau (1998).

poverty raises the odds that a young woman will become a single mother (Trent, 1994).

Considerable research shows that growing up in a one-parent family usually disadvantages children. Some studies indicate that because a father and a mother each make distinctive contributions to a child's social development, it is unrealistic to expect one parent alone to do as good a job. But the most serious problem among families with one parent—especially if that parent is a woman—is poverty. Female lone-headed families have the highest rate of low income (*Women in Canada*, 1995:86).

On average, children growing up in a single-parent family start out poorer, get less schooling, and end up with lower incomes as adults. Such children are also more likely to be single parents themselves (Mueller and Cooper, 1984; McLanahan, 1985; Weisner and Eiduson, 1986; Wallerstein and Blakeslee, 1989; Astone and McLanahan, 1991; Li and Wojtkiewicz, 1992; Biblarz and Raftery, 1993; Popenoe, 1993; Shapiro and Schrof, 1995; Webster et al., 1995; Wu, 1996).

COHABITATION

Cohabitation is *the sharing of a household by an unmarried couple*. A generation ago, widespread use of terms

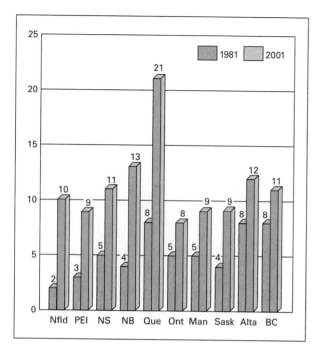

FIGURE 18–6 Couples Living Common Law by
Province, 1981 and 2001
(Percentage of All Couples)*

*Includes married and common-law couples with and without children.

Sources: Statistics Canada, Catalogue Nos. 93-312 and 93-320, cited in
Stout (1994:9); calculations based on Statistics Canada, Census Tables,
www.statcan.ca.

such as "shacking up" and "living in sin" indicated dis-
approval of cohabitations. But as our society has grown
more accepting of premarital sex, the proportion of
couples cohabiting has increased from 8 percent in
1981 to 16.4 percent in 2001. Figure 18-6 shows the
increase in cohabitation over this period by province.
Quebec stands out clearly as the province with the
most dramatic increase in common-law living.

In global perspective, cohabitation is common in
Sweden and other Nordic societies as a long-term
form of family life, with or without children. But it is
rare in more traditional (and Roman Catholic) nations
such as Italy. In the "Applying Sociology" box we

 For research on cohabitation
and other family relationships
with a focus on strengthening
the institution of marriage,
see The Marriage Project at
Rutgers University:
http://marriage.Rutgers.edu

take a closer look
at the phenomenon
in Canada from
a sociological per-
spective.

GAY AND LESBIAN COUPLES

In 1989, Denmark became the first country to legalize
same-sex marriages, thereby extending to gay and lesbian couples the legal advantages for inheritance, taxation, and joint property ownership. Norway (1993)

and Sweden (1995) have followed suit. In Canada,
where gays and lesbians could not marry until courts
in Ontario, British Columbia, and Quebec allowed
same-sex marriage in 2003, there were churches that
would sanctify such unions. The Metropolitan
Community Church in Toronto is an ecumenical denomination that serves gays and lesbians with many of
the rituals of the Christian church. The gay or lesbian
marriage or "commitment" ceremony, for instance, is
based on traditional Christian marriage vows. A number of institutions acknowledge homosexual partnerships in various spousal support and benefit schemes.

Even though they were barred from legal marriage, many gay men and lesbians formed long-term,
committed partnerships and families (Bell et al., 1981;
Gross, 1991). This is especially true of lesbian couples,
who are more likely than gay couples to remain sexually exclusive (Blumstein and Schwartz, 1983). In 1995,
members of gay and lesbian couples in Ontario won
the right to adopt the biological children of their partners under the "stepparent adoption clause" of the
Child and Family Services Act. In 1998, as already mentioned, British Columbia gave separating same-sex
parents equal privileges and obligations with respect

 Kevin Bourassa and Joe Varnell,
the first same-sex couple to
legally marry in Canada,
maintain a webpage with news,
legal updates, and resources
for same-sex partners at
www.samesexmarriage.ca/

to their children.
The right to marry
will institutional-
ize such rights and
obligations.

SINGLEHOOD

Because nine out of ten people in Canada marry, we
tend to see singlehood as a transitory stage of life. In
recent decades, however, more women and men have
deliberately chosen the freedom and independence of
living alone, remaining both single and childless
(Nett, 1993).

Most striking is the rising number of single young
women. In 1960 about one in four women aged twenty
to twenty-four was single; by 1990 the proportion was
nearing two-thirds. Underlying this trend is women's
greater participation in the labour force. Women who
are economically secure consider a husband a matter of
choice rather than a financial necessity.

By midlife, however, women who have not married confront a lack of available men. Because our culture expects a woman to "marry up," the older a
woman is, the more education she has, and the better
her job, the more difficulty she has in finding a suitable husband (Leslie and Korman, 1989).

NEW REPRODUCTIVE
TECHNOLOGY AND THE FAMILY

In 1991, Arlette Schweitzer, a forty-two-year-old li-
brarian living in Aberdeen, South Dakota, became the

APPLYING SOCIOLOGY

Cohabitation among Canadians

Zheng Wu (2000) has used a number of data sources—the Canadian census of various years and the General Social Surveys of 1990 and 1995—to study cohabitation. He assumes that the increase in cohabitation over the past few decades indicates a change in the norms that regulate the behaviour of families and their members.

Normative change tends to occur slowly, over long periods of time, in response to massive social and structural change. These changes challenge established lifestyles and values, forcing the development of normative solutions. Marriage and fertility trends—and ultimately cohabitation, as an alternative to marriage—are affected by economic factors, to be sure, but they also vary by language, religion, and region. Although Quebec was once the most conservative province, it now stands out as the most liberal on social and welfare issues. Despite its Catholic roots, fertility and marriage rates are low—and cohabitation levels are high. Other factors affecting levels of cohabitation are referred to as age, cohort, and period affects—or the effects of being born into a particular age cohort at a specific point in time.

In 1981, 8 percent of all couples were cohabiting. By 2001 the figure had increased to 16.4 percent—representing 1.2 million cohabiting couples. These couples were to be found disproportionately in Quebec and in Aboriginal communities.

In 1981, cohabitation peaked among those twenty to twenty-four years of age (8.2 percent); the next highest level was 7.6 percent among those aged twenty-five to twenty-nine. By 1996, the peak had moved up one age category to those aged twenty-five to twenty-nine (with 16.9 percent cohabiting); for thirty- to thirty-four-year-olds, the figure was 14.1 percent. Throughout the period studied, men had higher cohabitation rates than women.

Wu also looked at the factors that were associated with approval of premarital sex and cohabitation. Among the factors that predicted higher levels of approval of both were education, Catholicism, church attendance, being Canadian-born, being single, and living in Quebec.

Within Canada, actual rates of cohabitation are increasing, as is approval of this alternative family form. Also, people are increasingly likely to have children within such unions. Nonetheless, cohabitation is inherently unstable. About 30 percent of these unions last for no more than three years, and only one in twenty lasts for fifteen years. On the bright side, the reason for dissolving half of all cohabitations is the marriage of the two partners.

Source: Based on Wu (2000).

---

first woman on record to bear her own grandchildren. Because her daughter was unable to carry a baby to term, Schweitzer agreed to have her daughter's fertilized embryos surgically implanted in her own womb. Nine months later, she gave birth to a healthy boy and girl (Kolata, 1991).

Such a case illustrates how *new reproductive technology* has created both new choices for families and new controversies for society as a whole. The benefits of this rapidly developing technology are exciting, but it raises daunting ethical questions about the creation and manipulation of life itself.

A generation ago, England's Louise Joy Brown became the world's first "test-tube" baby; since then, tens of thousands of people have been conceived this way. Early in the twenty-first century, 2 or 3 percent of the children in industrial societies may result from new birth technologies.

Test-tube babies are the product of *in vitro fertilization*, a procedure whereby the male sperm and the female ovum are united "in glass" rather than in a woman's body. When successful, this complex medical procedure, undertaken by several thousand Canadian couples each year, produces embryos, which doctors either implant in the womb of a woman who is to bear the child or freeze for use at a later time.

At present, *in vitro* fertilization helps some couples who cannot conceive normally to have children. Looking ahead, new birth technologies may help reduce the incidence of birth defects. Genetically screening sperm and eggs allows medical specialists to increase the odds for the birth of a healthy baby. At the same time, new reproductive technology raises fascinating questions: Is Arlette Schweitzer the mother of the children she bore? The grandmother? Both? Then, too, we need to consider that, when it comes to manipulating life, what is technically possible may not always be morally desirable (Vines, 1986; Ostling, 1987; Thompson, 1994).

For better or worse, the family is certainly changing. But the fact that young people still find marriage so attractive—even amid the most severe adversity—suggests that families will continue to play a central role in society for centuries to come.

LOOKING AHEAD: FAMILY IN THE TWENTY-FIRST CENTURY

Family life in Canada has changed in recent decades, and this change will continue. Change causes controversy, in this case pitting advocates of "traditional family values" against supporters of new family forms and greater personal choice. Sociologists cannot predict the outcome of this debate, but we can posit five probable future trends.

1. **Divorce rates are likely to remain high.** This trend will continue, even in the face of evidence that marital dissolution harms children. Yet today's marriages are about as durable as they were a century ago, when many were cut short by death (Kain, 1990). The difference is that more couples now *choose* to end marriages that fail to live up to their expectations. Therefore, although the divorce rate has stabilized recently, it is unlikely that marriage will ever again be as durable as in the 1950s. But perhaps we should view the recent trend towards higher divorce rates less as a threat to families than as a sign of change in family form. Since most divorces lead to remarriage, marriage is hardly becoming obsolete.

2. **Family life will be highly variable.** Cohabiting couples, one-parent families, gay and lesbian families, and blended families are all increasing in number. Most families, of course, still are based on marriage, and most married couples still have children. But, taken together, the variety of family forms implies a growing belief that family life is a matter of choice.

3. **Men are likely to continue to play a limited role in child rearing.** In the 1950s, a decade many people see as the "golden age" of families, men began to withdraw from active parenting (Snell, 1990; Stacey, 1990). Since then, the share of children growing up in homes without their fathers has risen steadily. A countertrend is now emerging as some fathers eagerly jump into the parenting role. But, on balance, the high divorce rate and a surge in single motherhood point to more children growing up with weak ties to fathers. At the same time, evidence is building that the absence of fathers harms children, at least because such families are at high risk of being poor.

4. **We will continue to feel the effects of economic changes in our families.** In many families, both household partners now work, making marriage the interaction of weary men and women who try to squeeze in a little "quality time" for themselves and their children (Dizard and Gadlin, 1990). Two-career couples may advance the goal of gender equality, but the long-term effects on families are likely to be mixed (Hochschild, 1989).

5. **The importance of new reproductive technologies will increase.** While ethical concerns surely will slow these developments, new methods of reproduction will continue to alter the traditional meanings of parenthood, as the "Controversy & Debate" box discusses.

Despite the social changes buffeting the family in Canada, most people still report being happy as partners and parents. Marriage and family life today may be more controversial than in the past, but both will likely remain the foundation of our society for some time to come.

The New Reproductive Technologies

Are "traditional families" an arrangement of the past? Singlehood has increased, people often live together without marriage, divorce is on the increase, and a growing number of young women are having and keeping children as single parents. But perhaps the most controversial change to the family is the introduction of new reproductive technologies (NRTs), which have created a revolution in reproduction, in science, and in the family, with the potential for major social repercussions.

The very availability of these technologies raises important ethical questions about what kind of world we want to live in and how much control we want over that world. Among the new reproductive technologies are such alternatives as sex selection techniques, artificial insemination, *in vitro* fertilization, embryo transplants, and surrogate motherhood. At one time, it was not unusual to see ads in university newspapers in Canada in which a young woman would offer her services as a surrogate mother, or a young man would offer his sperm for sale.

NRTs carry with them a host of ethical questions and decisions. They have separated gestational, genetic, and social parenthood; eliminated the need for intercourse between a man and a woman for reproduction; and enabled men and women to purchase the necessities of reproduction (eggs and sperm) without the possibility of identifying the other parent.

Consider the following example. In his book *The Ethics of Genetic Control* (1974), Joseph Fletcher argues for quality control in the creation of children. According to Fletcher, fetuses should be monitored, and those that show evidence of disease should be aborted. "We ought," he says, "to protect our families from the emotional and material burden of such diseased individuals and from the misery of their simply existing (not living) in a nearby 'warehouse' or public institution. . . . Choosing high quality fetuses and rejecting low quality ones is not tragedy; sad, but not agonizing."

The question we face is this: Once we decide to abort "low quality" fetuses, where do we draw the line? For Fletcher, all female fetuses that might carry a gene predisposing their children to hemophilia should automatically be aborted, even though today hemophiliacs can lead long and productive lives.

In Canada, the federal government has taken a hard line on regulating NRTs. In June 1996, legislation was tabled in the House of Commons that effectively banned many procedures. The bill would, however, still allow couples to practise "sex selection" by aborting female fetuses with the hemophilia gene.

But Madeline Boscoe, who works at a women's health clinic in Winnipeg, says that most Canadians support regulation in these areas. "I think it is important that we say as a society that you can't sell your eye to get through medical school. Why is this any different?" (McIlroy, 1996)

Continue the debate . . .

1. *Do you agree that NRTs should be regulated by the government? Should there be fines and jail sentences for men selling their sperm and women selling their eggs? Why or why not?*

2. *Do you agree with Joseph Fletcher that fetuses should be monitored so that society can exercise "quality control" over those allowed to take their place in it? Are there similarities between Fletcher's recommendations and Adolf Hitler's plan to develop a "Master Race"?*

3. *Is the sale of reproductive elements comparable to the sale of body parts? Why or why not?*

SUMMARY

1. All societies are built on kinship, although family forms vary considerably across cultures and over time.

2. In industrial societies such as Canada, marriage is monogamous. Many pre-industrial societies, however, permit polygamy, of which there are two types: polygyny and polyandry.

3. In global perspective, patrilocality is most common, while industrial societies favour neolocality and a few societies have matrilocal residence. Industrial societies use bilateral descent, while pre-industrial societies tend to be either patrilineal or matrilineal.

4. Structural-functional analysis identifies major family functions: socializing the young, regulating sexual activity, transmitting social placement, and providing material and emotional support.

5. Social-conflict theories explore how the family perpetuates social inequality by transmitting divisions based on class, ethnicity, race, and gender.

6. Micro-level analysis highlights the variable nature of family life both over time and as experienced by individual family members.

7. Families originate in the process of courtship. Unlike Canada, few societies base the choice of a mate on romantic love. But even among members of our society, romantic love tends to join people with similar social backgrounds.

8. The vast majority of married couples have children, although family size has decreased over time. The key reason for this decline is industrialization, which transforms children into economic liabilities, encourages women to gain an education and to join the labour force, and reduces infant mortality.

9. Married life changes as children leave home to form families of their own. Many middle-aged couples, however, care for aging parents and are active grandparents. The final stage of this life course begins with the death of one spouse, usually the husband.

10. Families differ according to class position, race, and ethnicity. Some immigrant families, for example, tend to maintain extended kinship ties. Poorer families are more likely than others to be headed by women. Among all categories of people, well-to-do families enjoy the most options and the greatest financial security.

11. Gender affects family dynamics since husbands dominate in most marriages. Research suggests that marriage provides more benefits to men than to women.

12. The divorce rate today is ten times higher than it was a century ago; four in ten current marriages will end in divorce. Most people who divorce—especially men—remarry, often forming blended families that include children from previous marriages.

13. Family violence victimizes women and children and is far more common than official records indicate. Most adults who abuse family members were themselves abused as children.

14. Our society's family life is becoming more varied. One-parent families, cohabitation, gay and lesbian couples, and singlehood have proliferated in recent years. Before courts in Canada ruled in favour of same-sex marriages, many gay men and lesbians were forming long-lasting relationships and, increasingly, becoming parents.

15. Although ethically controversial, new reproductive technology is altering conventional notions of parenthood.

CRITICAL-THINKING QUESTIONS

1. How has the emerging post-industrial economy affected family life? What other factors are changing the family?

2. Why do some analysts describe the family as the "backbone of society"? How do families perpetuate social inequality?

3. Do you think that single-parent households do as good a job as two-parent households of raising children? Why or why not?

4. On balance, are families in Canada becoming weaker or not? What evidence can you cite?

APPLICATIONS AND EXERCISES

1. Parents and grandparents can be wonderful sources of information about changes in marriage and the family. Spend an hour or two with married people of two different generations and ask about when they married, what their married lives have been like, and what changes in today's world stand out to them.

2. Relationships with various family members differ. With which family member—mother, father, brother, sister—do you most readily and least readily share secrets? Why? Which family member would you turn to first in a crisis? Why?

3. Focus on the Family Canada is a conservative organization supporting what they call "traditional family values." Visit their website (**www.fotf.ca**) and find out what they consider to be a "traditional family." Why do they defend "traditional families"? What problems of families do they ignore?

4. Organize a debate for one class period with a team arguing each side of the "family values" controversy. Present arguments for and against the following statement: "Resolved: The traditional family is necessary for the survival of our country's way of life."

SITES TO SEE

www.macionis.com
or
www.TheSociologyPage.com
You can find more than fifty weblinks to sociological journals and other sources of data and information by visiting the Links Library at this website.

www.cfc-efc.ca/
Initiated by the Canadian Child Care Federation, with the cooperation of forty-one nonprofit organizations, *Child & Family Canada* is all about child care, child development, parenting, health, safety, literacy, media influences, nutrition, physical activities, play, family life, adolescence, learning activities, social issues, and special needs.

http://www.vifamily.ca/
The Vanier Institute of the Family provides current news and research to create awareness of the issues and challenges facing Canadian families.

www.trinity.edu/~mkearl/family.html
Michael Kearl's *Guide to the Sociology of the Family* provides a useful sociological overview of family issues, including a survey of family relations across cultures and time; cultural factors (matters of age, gender, sex, and violence) that shape family structures and processes; parenting; genealogy; divorce; and so on.

www.lesbian.org/lesbian-moms/
Lesbian Mothers Support Society is a Canadian, nonprofit group that provides peer support for lesbian parents and their children, as well as for lesbians considering parenthood. The site includes information about adoption, alternative fertilization, children's resources, coming out, legal issues, lesbian health, parenting, pregnancy, and a guide to lesbian babymaking.

www.worklifecanada.ca/
The Centre for Families, Work and Well-Being at Guelph University researches and promotes family well-being and responsive work environments.

STUDY TOOLS

For more study tools to help you with your next exam, be sure to check out the Companion Website at **www.pearsoned.ca/macionis**, as well as Chapter 18 in your Study Guide.

INVESTIGATE WITH CONTENTSELECT

Follow the instructions found on page 25 of this textbook to access ContentSelect™ at the Research Navigator™ website. Once at the site, enter your LOGINID and Password. Then, enter keywords such as "family values," "cohabitation," and "new reproductive technology" and the search engine will supply relevant and recent scholarly and popular press publications.

CHAPTER
19

Blake Debassige (1956– , Canadian)
The Enlightenment, 1983
Acrylic on canvas, 76.3 × 61.0 cm.
Purchase 1984, McMichael Canadian Art Collection. 1984.3

RELIGION

Elisha Hack was elated at the news: highly prestigious Yale University had accepted him for the Class of 2001. But when he arrived on campus in the fall of 1997, his excitement turned to disappointment and confusion. In his dorm, Hack—an Orthodox Jew—was stunned to find only a short staircase separating men's and women's rooms. Copies of the "Safer Sex Menu" were prominently displayed in the lounges alongside bowls of condoms, and orientation that evening was a "safe-sex" seminar complete with a demonstration of how to use dental dams.

Was university life—at least at Yale—consumed by sin like the biblical cities of Sodom and Gomorrah? Hack wanted an education, but not if the living arrangements violated his religious principles. So Hack proposed what he viewed as a reasonable solution: he would enrol at Yale, but live off campus in an environment more to his liking. Yale, however, stuck to its requirement that all first-year students live in dorms, where they learn to interact with others who are different from themselves. The case was destined to end up in court (Cloud, 1999).

Religion has always played a central part in North American society, and conflicts like the one between Elisha Hack and Yale University are nothing new. Indeed, this dispute is merely one example of the long-standing debate over the proper role of religion in social life. This chapter explains what religion is, explores the changing face of religious belief, and examines the vital—yet sometimes controversial—place of religion in today's modern, scientific culture.

RELIGION: BASIC CONCEPTS

For French sociologist Emile Durkheim, whose ideas are discussed in detail in Chapter 4 ("Society"), the focus of religion is "things that surpass the limits of our knowledge" (1965:62; orig. 1915). As human beings, Durkheim explained, we organize our surroundings by defining most objects, events, or experiences as **profane** (from Latin meaning "outside the temple"), *that which is an ordinary element of everyday life*. But we set some things apart, Durkheim continued, by designating them as **sacred**, *that which is defined as extraordinary, inspiring a sense of awe, reverence, and even fear*. Distinguishing the sacred from the profane is the

essence of all religious belief. **Religion**, then, is *a social institution involving beliefs and practices based on a conception of the sacred*.

A global perspective reveals great variety in matters of faith, with no one thing sacred to everyone on earth. Although people regard most books as profane, Jews view the Torah (the first five books of the Hebrew Bible or Old Testament) as sacred, in the same way that Christians revere the Old and New Testaments of the Bible and Muslims exalt the Qur'an (Koran).

But no matter how a community of believers draws religious lines, Durkheim (1965; orig. 1915) explained, people understand profane things in terms of their everyday usefulness: we log onto the Web with our computer or turn the key to start our car. What is sacred, however, we reverently set apart from everyday life and denote as "forbidden." Marking the boundary between the sacred and the profane, for example, Muslims remove their shoes before entering a mosque to avoid defiling a sacred place of worship with soles that have touched the profane ground outside.

The sacred is embodied in **ritual**, *formal, ceremonial behaviour*. Holy communion is the central ritual of Christianity; the wafer and wine consumed during

Religion is founded on the concept of the sacred: that which is set apart as extraordinary and which demands our submission. Bowing, kneeling, or prostrating oneself are all ways of symbolically surrendering to a higher power. This monk is performing an act of prostration circumambulation, a complicated way of saying that he falls flat on the ground every few steps as he moves around a holy shrine. In this way, he expresses his complete surrender to his faith.

communion are sacred symbols of the body and blood of Jesus Christ.

RELIGION AND SOCIOLOGY

Because religion deals with ideas that transcend everyday experience, neither sociology nor any other scientific discipline can verify or disprove religious doctrine. Religion is a matter of **faith**, *belief anchored in conviction rather than scientific evidence.* The New Testament of the Bible, for instance, describes faith as "the assurance of things hoped for, the conviction of things not seen" (Heb. 11:1) and exhorts Christians to "walk by faith, not by sight" (2 Cor. 5:7).

Through most of our history, human beings lived in small societies and attributed birth, death, and whatever happened in between to the operation of supernatural forces. Over the last several hundred years, however, science has emerged as an alternative way of understanding the natural world, and scientific sociology offers various explanations of how and why societies operate the way they do.

Some people with strong faith may be disturbed by the thought of sociologists turning a scientific eye on what they hold as sacred. In truth, however, a sociological study of religion is no threat to anyone's faith. Sociologists recognize that religion is central to virtually every culture on earth, and they seek to understand how religious beliefs and practices guide human societies. As sociologists, they cannot comment on the meaning and purpose of human existence or pass judgment on any religion as right or wrong. Rather, scientific sociology takes a more "worldly" approach by delving into why religions take particular forms in one society or another and how religious activity affects society as a whole.

THEORETICAL ANALYSIS OF RELIGION

Although, as individuals, sociologists may hold any number of religious beliefs—or none at all—they agree that religion plays a major role in the operation of society. Each theoretical paradigm suggests ways in which religion shapes social life.

FUNCTIONS OF RELIGION: STRUCTURAL-FUNCTIONAL ANALYSIS

Emile Durkheim (1965; orig. 1915) maintained that in religious life, people celebrate the awesome power of their society. Doesn't society, he asked, have an awesome power and an existence of its own beyond the life of any individual? Thus, some form of religion is found everywhere because society itself is "godlike." No wonder, too, that people in all societies transform certain everyday objects into sacred symbols of their collective life. Members of technologically simple societies, Durkheim explained, do this with the **totem**, *an object in the natural world collectively defined as sacred.* The totem—perhaps an animal or an elaborate work of art—becomes the centrepiece of ritual, symbolizing the power of collective life over any individual. In our society, the flag is a quasi-sacred totem. It is not to be used in a profane manner (say, as clothing) or allowed to touch the ground.

Why is the religious dimension of social life so important? Durkheim pointed out three major functions of religion:

1. **Providing social cohesion.** The shared symbols, values, and norms of religion unite people. Religious doctrine and ritual establish rules of

Regularly taking part in religious rituals sharpens the distinction between the sacred and the profane. The wafer used in the Christian ritual of holy communion is never thought of in the everyday sense of food; rather, it is a sacred symbol of the body of Christ.

"fair play" that make organized social life possible. Religion also involves *love* and *commitment*, which underscore both our moral and emotional ties to others (Wright and D'Antonio, 1980).

2. **Ensuring social control.** Every society uses religious imagery and rhetoric to promote conformity. Societies infuse many cultural norms—especially mores relating to marriage and reproduction—with religious justification. Religion may even legitimize the political system. In medieval Europe, in fact, monarchs claimed to rule by divine right. Few of today's political leaders invoke religion so explicitly, but many publicly ask for God's blessing, implying to audiences that their efforts are right and just.

3. **Providing meaning and purpose.** Religious beliefs offer the comforting sense that the vulnerable human condition serves some greater purpose. Strengthened by such convictions, people are less likely to despair when confronted by life's calamities. For this reason, major life-course transitions—including birth, marriage, and death—are usually marked by religious observances that enhance our spiritual awareness.

Critical evaluation. In Durkheim's structural-functional analysis, religion represents the collective life of society. The major weakness of this approach, however, is that it downplays religion's dysfunctions—especially the fact that strongly held beliefs can generate social conflict. During the early Middle Ages, for example, religious faith was the driving force behind the Crusades, in which European Christians battled Muslims for the Holy Lands that both religions considered to be sacred. Conflict among Muslims, Jews, and Christians is still a source of political instability in the Middle East today. Similarly, tensions continue to divide Protestants and Catholics in Northern Ireland; Dutch Calvinism historically supported apartheid in South Africa; and religious conflict persists in Algeria, India, Sri Lanka, and elsewhere. In short, many nations have marched to war under the banner of their gods, and few analysts dispute that differences in faith have provoked more violence in the world than have differences of social class.

CONSTRUCTING THE SACRED: SYMBOLIC-INTERACTION ANALYSIS

"Society," asserts Peter Berger (1967:3), "is a human product and nothing but a human product, that yet continuously acts back upon its producer." In other words, from a symbolic-interactionist point of view, religion (like all of society) is socially constructed (although perhaps with divine inspiration). Through various rituals, from daily prayers to annual religious observances such as Easter or Passover, individuals sharpen the distinction between the sacred and profane. Further, Berger explains, by placing everyday events within a "cosmic frame of reference," people give their fallible, transitory creations "the semblance of ultimate security and permanence" (1967:35–36).

Marriage is a good example. If two people look on marriage as merely a legal contract between them, they can end the marriage whenever they want to. But defined as holy matrimony, their relationship makes a far stronger claim on them. This fact, no doubt, explains why the divorce rate is lower among people who are more religious.

Especially when humans confront uncertainty and life-threatening situations—such as illness, war, and natural disaster—we turn to religion. Seeking sacred meaning helps people recover from life's setbacks and even face the prospect of death with strength and courage.

Religion and Patriarchy: Does God Favour Males?

Why do Canadians tend to envision God in male terms? Perhaps we link the "godly" attribute of power to men. Organized religions tend to favour males, a fact evident in passages from many of the sacred writings of major world religions.

The Qur'an (Koran)—the sacred text of Islam—asserts that men are to dominate women:

> Men are in charge of women. . . . Hence good women are obedient. . . . As for those whose rebelliousness you fear, admonish them, banish them from your bed, and scourge them. (quoted in Kaufman, 1976:163)

Christianity—the major religion of the Western world—supports patriarchy. While many Christians revere Mary, the mother of Jesus, the New Testament also includes the following passages:

> A man . . . is the image and glory of God; but woman is the glory of man. For man was not made from woman, but woman from man. Neither was man created for woman, but woman for man. (1 Cor. 11:7–9)

> As in all the churches of the saints, the women should keep silence in the churches. For they are not permitted to speak, but should be subordinate, as even the law says. If there is anything they desire to know, let them ask their husbands at home. For it is shameful for a woman to speak in church. (1 Cor. 14:33–35)

> Wives, be subject to your husbands, as to the Lord. For the husband is the head of the wife as Christ is the head of the church. . . . As the church is subject to Christ, so let wives also be subject in everything to their husbands. (Eph. 5:22–24)

> Let a woman learn in silence with all submissiveness. I permit no woman to teach or to have authority over men; she is to keep silent. For Adam was formed first, then Eve; and Adam was not deceived, but the woman was deceived and became a transgressor. Yet woman will be saved through bearing children, if she continues in faith and love and holiness, with modesty. (1 Tim. 2:11–15)

Judaism, too, traditionally supports patriarchy. Male Orthodox Jews include the following words in daily prayer:

> Blessed art thou, O Lord our God, King of the Universe, that I was not born a gentile.

> Blessed art thou, O Lord our God, King of the Universe, that I was not born a slave.

> Blessed art thou, O Lord our God, King of the Universe, that I was not born a woman.

Major religions are also patriarchal in excluding women from the clergy. Even today, Islam and the Roman Catholic Church ban women from the priesthood. A growing number of Protestant denominations have overturned historical policies and now ordain women—the Anglican Church since 1975 (Bibby, 1995). Orthodox Judaism upholds the traditional prohi-

Critical evaluation. The symbolic-interaction approach views religion as a social construction, placing everyday life under a "sacred canopy" of meaning (Berger, 1967). Of course, Berger adds, the religion's ability to legitimize and stabilize society depends on its constructed character going unrecognized. After all, we would derive little strength from sacred beliefs that we saw as mere devices for coping with tragedy. Then, too, this micro-level view pays scant attention to religion's part in maintaining social inequality, to which we now turn.

INEQUALITY AND RELIGION: SOCIAL-CONFLICT ANALYSIS

The social-conflict paradigm highlights religion's support of social hierarchy. Religion, claimed Karl Marx, serves ruling elites by legitimizing the status quo and diverting people's attention from social inequities.

Even today, the British monarch is the nominal head of the Church of England, illustrating the close alliance between religious and political elites. In practical terms, working for political change may mean opposing the church and, by implication, God. Religion also encourages people to look with hope to a "better world to come," minimizing the social problems of this world. In one of his best-known statements, Marx offered a stinging criticism of religion as "the sigh of the oppressed creature, the sentiment of a heartless world, and the soul of soulless conditions. It is the opium of the people" (1964b:27; orig. 1848).

Religion and social inequality are also linked through gender. Virtually all the world's major religions reflect and encourage male dominance in social life, as the "Diversity: Race, Class, and Gender" box explains.

bition against women serving as rabbis, but Reform and Reconstructionist Judaism have looked to both men and women as spiritual leaders since the early 1970s (and both these denominations ordain gay and lesbian people), and the first woman rabbi in the Conservative denomination of Judaism was ordained in 1985. Of the eighty religious denominations surveyed in Canada in 1986, only twenty-nine ordained women. The United Church of Canada reported the highest number, with 441 female clergy (11 percent of the total); 7 percent of Anglican clergy and 8 percent of Presbyterian clergy were women (Baril and Mori, 1991). The proportion of women among students in seminary schools across Canada has never been higher, evidence that that the ordination of women will increase steadily over time.

Challenges to the patriarchal structure of organized religion—from ordaining women to using gender-neutral language in hymnals and prayers—has sparked heated controversy, delighting progressives while outraging tradition-

alists. Propelling these developments is a lively feminism in many religious communities. According to feminist Christians, for example, patriarchy in the church stands in stark contrast to the largely feminine image of Jesus Christ in the Scriptures as "non-aggressive, noncompetitive, meek and humble of heart, a nurturer of the weak and a friend of the outcast" (Schneiders, quoted in Woodward, 1989:61).

Feminists argue that unless traditional notions of gender are removed from our understanding of God, women will never be equal to men in the church. Theologian Mary Daly puts the matter bluntly: "If God is male, then male is God" (quoted in Woodward, 1989:58).

During Marx's lifetime, powerful Christian nations of Western Europe justified the conquest of Africa, the Americas, and Asia by claiming that they were "converting heathens." In the United States, major churches in the South considered the enslavement of African-Americans to be consistent with God's will, and churches throughout the nation remain segregated to this day. In the words of African-American novelist Maya Angelou, "Sunday at 11:30 a.m., America is more segregated than at any time of the week."

Many would argue that for many years the Catholic Church turned a blind eye to repeated complaints of child sex abuse by its members. According to Bibby (1993), as many as fifteen thousand Canadian children were sexually abused in Quebec orphanages before 1960. Not until the child abuse by priests at Mount Cashel orphanage in Newfoundland came to

light did Canadians see any significant acknowledgment of the problem or the beginnings of restitution.

Critical evaluation. Social-conflict analysis reveals the power of religion to legitimize social inequality. Yet critics of religion, Marx included, minimize the ways religion has promoted both change and equality. Nineteenth-century religious groups in the United States, for example, were at the forefront of the movement to abolish slavery. In Canada, the Social Gospel movement, active from the 1890s through the 1930s, created settlement houses and city missions and was instrumental in the development of Canada's social safety net.

RELIGION AND SOCIAL CHANGE

Religion is not just the conservative force portrayed by Karl Marx. At some points in history, as Max Weber

(1958a; orig. 1904–5) pointed out, religion has promoted dramatic social transformation.

MAX WEBER: PROTESTANTISM AND CAPITALISM

Max Weber contended that new ideas are often the engines of change. It was the religious doctrine of Calvinism, for example, that sparked the Industrial Revolution in Western Europe.

As Chapter 4 ("Society") explains, John Calvin (1509–64), a leader in the Protestant Reformation, advanced the doctrine of predestination. According to Calvin, an all-powerful and all-knowing God predestines some people for salvation while condemning most to eternal damnation. With each individual's fate sealed before birth and known only to God, the only certainty is what hangs in the balance: eternal glory or hellfire.

Understandably anxious about their fate, Calvinists sought signs of God's favour in *this* world and came to regard prosperity as a symbol of divine blessing. This conviction, and a rigid sense of duty, led Calvinists to work all the time, and many amassed great riches. But wealth was never to fuel self-indulgent spending or to be shared with the poor, whose plight Calvinists saw as a mark of God's rejection.

As agents of God's work on earth, Calvinists believed that they best fulfilled their "calling" by reinvesting profits and reaping ever-greater success in the process. All the while, they were thrifty and eagerly embraced technological advances that would enhance their efforts. Driven by religious motives, then, they laid the groundwork for the rise of industrial capitalism. In time, the religious fervour that motivated early Calvinists evaporated, leaving a profane Protestant "work ethic." In this sense, concluded Weber, industrial capitalism amounts to a "disenchanted" religion. Weber's analysis clearly demonstrates the power of religious thinking to alter the basic shape of society.

LIBERATION THEOLOGY

Christianity has a long-standing concern for poor and oppressed people, urging all to strengthen their faith in a better life to come. In recent decades, however, some church leaders and theologians have embraced **liberation theology**, *a fusion of Christian principles with political activism, often Marxist in character.*

This social movement started in the late 1960s in Latin America's Roman Catholic Church. Today, in addition to the church's spiritual work, Christian activists are helping people in the least-developed countries to liberate themselves from abysmal poverty. The message of liberation theology is simple: social oppression runs counter to Christian morality and is

also preventable. Therefore, as a matter of faith and social justice, Christians must promote greater social equality.

A growing number of Catholic men and women have taken up the cause of the poor in the liberation theology movement. The cost of opposing the status quo has been high. Many church members—including Oscar Arnulfo Romero, the archbishop of San Salvador (the capital of El Salvador)—have been killed for seeking political change.

Liberation theology has also divided the Catholic community. Pope John Paul II condemns the movement for distorting traditional church doctrine with left-wing politics. But despite the pontiff's objections, the liberation theology movement has become powerful in Latin America, where many find their Christian faith drives them to improve the condition of the world's poor (Boff, 1984; Neuhouser, 1989).

TYPES OF RELIGIOUS ORGANIZATION

Sociologists categorize the hundreds of different religious organizations that exist in Canada along a continuum, with *churches* at one end and *sects* at the other. We can describe any actual religious organization, then, in relation to these two ideal types by locating it on the church–sect continuum.

CHURCH AND SECT

Drawing on the ideas of his teacher Max Weber, Ernst Troeltsch (1931) defined a **church** as *a type of religious organization well integrated into the larger society.* Churchlike organizations usually persist for centuries and include generations of the same family. Churches have well-established rules and regulations, and their leaders are formally trained and ordained.

While concerned with the sacred, a church accepts the ways of the profane world, which gives it broad appeal. Church doctrine conceives of God in highly intellectualized terms (say, as a force for good), and favours abstract moral standards ("Do unto others as you would have them do unto you") over specific rules for day-to-day living. By teaching morality in safely abstract terms, a church can avoid social controversy. For example, many Christian churches that, in principle, celebrate the unity of all peoples have, in practice, all-white memberships. Such duality minimizes conflict between a church and political life (Troeltsch, 1931).

A church generally takes one of two forms. Islam in Morocco represents an **ecclesia**, *a church formally allied with the state.* Ecclesias have been common in history; for centuries Roman Catholicism was the state religion of the Roman Empire, as was Confucianism in China until early in the twentieth century. Today, the Anglican Church is the official Church of England, as Islam is the official religion of Pakistan and Iran. State churches count everyone in a society as members; tolerance of religious difference, therefore, is severely limited.

A **denomination**, in contrast, is *a church, independent of the state that accepts religious pluralism*. Denominations exist in nations that formally separate church and state, such as ours. Canada has dozens of Christian denominations—including Catholics, Baptists, Methodists, and Lutherans—as well as various branches of Judaism, Islam, and other traditions. While members of a denomination hold to their own beliefs, they recognize the right of others to disagree.

A second general religious form is the **sect**, *a type of religious organization that stands apart from the larger society*. Sect members hold rigidly to their religious convictions and discount the beliefs of others. In extreme cases, members of a sect may withdraw completely from society to practise their religion without interference from outsiders. The Old Order Mennonites are an example of a North American sect that has long isolated itself (Fretz, 1989). Since our culture views religious tolerance as a virtue, members of sects are sometimes accused of being narrow-minded in their insistence that they alone follow the true religion (Stark and Bainbridge, 1979).

In organizational terms, sects are less formal than churches. Their members may be highly spontaneous and emotional in worship, while members of churches tend to listen passively to their leaders. Sects reject the intellectualized religion of churches, stressing instead the personal experience of divine power. Rodney Stark (1985:314) contrasts a church's vision of a distant God—"Our Father, who art in Heaven"—with a sect's more immediate God—"Lord, bless this poor sinner kneeling before you now."

A further distinction between church and sect turns on patterns of leadership. The more churchlike an organization, the more likely are its leaders to be formally trained and ordained. Sectlike organizations, which celebrate the personal presence of God, expect their leaders to exhibit divine inspiration in the form of **charisma** (from Greek meaning "divine favour"), *extraordinary personal qualities that can turn an audience into followers*, infusing them with an emotional experience.

Sects generally form as breakaway groups from established churches or other religious organizations (Stark and Bainbridge, 1979). Their psychic intensity and informal structure render them less stable than churches, and many sects blossom, only to disappear a short time later. The sects that do endure typically become more like churches, losing fervour as they become more bureaucratic and established.

To sustain their membership, many sects actively recruit, or *proselytize*, new members. Sects highly value the experience of *conversion*, a personal transformation

In global perspective, the range of human religious activity is truly astonishing. Members of this Southeast Asian cult show their devotion to God by suspending themselves in the air using ropes and sharp hooks that pierce their skin.

or religious rebirth. Jehovah's Witnesses, for example, eagerly share their faith with others in hopes of attracting new members.

Finally, churches and sects differ in their social composition. Because they are more closely tied to the world, well-established churches tend to include people of high social standing. Sects, in contrast, attract more disadvantaged people. A sect's openness to new members and promise of salvation and personal fulfilment may be especially appealing to people who perceive themselves as social outsiders. However, as we shall explain presently, many established churches in Canada have lost membership in recent decades. For instance, the United Church membership declined from 2 850 000 to 2 521 000 between 1985 and 1990, while the Anglican Church declined from 2 017 000 to 1 892 000. In the process, a number of sects now find themselves with more affluent members (Baril and Mori, 1991:22).

CULT

A **cult** is *a religious organization that is substantially outside a society's cultural traditions*. Whereas a sect breaks off from a conventional religious organization, a cult represents something new. Cults typically form around a highly charismatic leader who offers a compelling message of a new way of life.

Because some cult principles or practices may seem unconventional, the popular view is that they are deviant or even evil. The suicides of fifty-three members of the Order of the Solar Temple in 1994, and of five more members in 1997—in the belief that death on earth would allow transit to another planet where their lives would continue—confirmed the negative image the public holds of most cults. In short, according to some scholars, calling any religious community a "cult" amounts to dismissing its members as crazy (Richardson, 1990; Gleick, 1997).

This view of cults is unfortunate, because there is nothing intrinsically wrong with this kind of religious organization. Many long-standing religions—Christianity, Islam, and Judaism included—began as cults. Of course, not all or even most cults exist for very long. One reason is that they are even more at odds with the larger society than sects. Many cults demand that members not only accept their doctrine but embrace a radically new lifestyle. Such lifestyle changes sometimes prompt others to accuse cults of brainwashing their members, although research suggests that most people who join cults experience no psychological harm (Barker, 1981; Kilbourne, 1983).

RELIGION IN HISTORY

Religion shapes every society of the world. And, like other social institutions, religion shows considerable variation both historically and cross-culturally.

RELIGION IN PRE-INDUSTRIAL SOCIETIES

Religion predates written history. Archaeological evidence indicates that our human ancestors performed religious rituals some forty thousand years ago.

Early hunters and gatherers embraced **animism** (from Latin meaning "the breath of life"), *the belief that elements of the natural world are conscious life forms that affect humanity.* Animistic people view forests, oceans, mountains, and even the wind as spiritual forces. Many Native societies are animistic, which accounts for their historical reverence for the natural environment. Hunters and gatherers conduct their religious life entirely within the family. Members of such societies may single out someone as a shaman with special religious skills, but there are no full-time, specialized religious leaders.

 Visit www.umista.org/masks_story/ to learn more about traditions of the Kwakiutl people of the Northwest Coast, as portrayed through a collection of potlatch masks and stories about the creatures they represent.

Belief in a single divine power responsible for creating the world arose with pastoral and horticultural societies. We can trace our society's conception of God as a "shepherd," directly involved in the world's well-being, to the roots of Christianity, Judaism, and Islam, all of whose original followers were pastoral peoples.

As societies develop more productive capacity, religious life expands beyond the family, and priests take their place among other specialized workers. In agrarian societies, religion becomes more important, evident in the huge medieval cathedrals in town centres throughout Europe.

RELIGION IN INDUSTRIAL SOCIETIES

The Industrial Revolution ushered in science as a way of knowing. Increasingly, people looked to physicians and scientists for the knowledge and comfort they had sought from religious leaders.

Even so, religious thought persists simply because science is powerless to address issues of ultimate meaning in human life. In other words, learning how the world works is a matter for scientists, but why we and the rest of the universe exist is a question about which science has nothing to say. Science may improve our material lives, but religion is uniquely suited to address the spiritual dimension of human existence.

WORLD RELIGIONS

The diversity of religious expression in the world is almost as wide-ranging as the diversity of culture itself. Many of the thousands of different religions are highly localized with few followers. *World religions*, in contrast, are widely known and have millions of adherents. We shall briefly describe six world religions, which together claim as adherents some 4 billion believers—almost three-quarters of humanity.

CHRISTIANITY

Christianity is the most widespread religion, with 2 billion followers, roughly one-third of the world's people. Most Christians live in Europe or the Americas; more than 85 percent of the people in Canada and the United States identify with Christianity. Moreover, as shown in Global Map 19–1 (on page 480), people who are at least nominally Christian represent a significant share of the population in many other world regions, with the notable exceptions of northern Africa and Asia. European colonization spread Christianity throughout much of the world over the last five hundred years. Its dominance in the West is evident in the practice of numbering years on the calendar beginning with the birth of Christ.

Christianity originated as a cult, incorporating elements of its much older predecessor, Judaism. Like many cults, Christianity was propelled by the personal charisma of a leader, Jesus of Nazareth, who preached a message of personal salvation. Jesus did not directly challenge the political powers of his day, calling on his followers to "Render therefore to Caesar the things that are Caesar's" (Matt. 22:21). But his message was revolutionary nonetheless, promising that faith and love would triumph over sin and death.

Christianity is one example of **monotheism**, *belief in a single divine power*. This new religion broke with the Roman Empire's traditional **polytheism**, *belief in many gods*. Yet Christianity has a unique vision of the Supreme Being as a sacred Trinity: God the Creator; Jesus Christ, Son of God and Redeemer; and the Holy Spirit, a Christian's personal experience of God's presence.

The claim that Jesus was divine rests on accounts of his final days on earth. Tried and sentenced to death in Jerusalem on charges that he was a threat to established political leaders, Jesus was executed by crucifixion. The cross therefore became a sacred Christian symbol. According to Christian belief, three days later Jesus rose from the dead, showing that he was the Son of God.

Jesus' apostles spread Christianity throughout the Mediterranean region. Although the Roman Empire initially persecuted Christians, by the fourth century Christianity had become an ecclesia—the official religion of what then became known as the Holy Roman Empire. What had begun as a cult four centuries before was now an established church.

Christianity took various forms, including the Roman Catholic Church and the Orthodox Church, based in Constantinople (now Istanbul, Turkey). Towards the end of the Middle Ages, the Protestant Reformation in Europe created hundreds of denominations, dozens of which now comprise about 31 percent of the adult Canadian population—as compared with the 43 percent that is Roman Catholic.

ISLAM

Islam has some 1.1 billion followers (about 20 percent of humanity); followers of Islam are called Muslims. A majority of people in the Middle East are Muslims, which explains our tendency to associate Islam with Arabs in that region of the world. But most Muslims live elsewhere; Global Map 19–2 shows that most people in northern Africa and western Asia are also Muslims. Moreover, significant concentrations of Muslims are found in Pakistan, India, Bangladesh, Indonesia, and the southern republics of the former Soviet Union. Although representing a small share of the population, North American Muslims number between 5 and 10 million (Roudi, 1988; Weeks, 1988; University of Akron Research Center, 1993).

Islam is the word of God as revealed to the prophet Muhammad, who was born in the city of Mecca (now in Saudi Arabia) in about the year 570. To Muslims, Muhammad is a prophet, not a divine being as Jesus is to Christians. The Qur'an (Koran), sacred

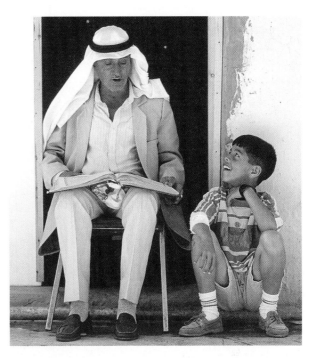

Many religions promote literacy because they demand followers study sacred texts. As part of their upbringing, most Islamic parents teach their children lessons from the Qur'an (Koran); later, the children will do the same to a new generation of believers.

to Muslims, is the word of God (in Arabic, *Allah*) as transmitted through Muhammad, God's messenger. In Arabic, the word *Islam* means both "submission" and "peace," and the Qur'an urges submission to Allah as the path to inner peace. Muslims express this personal devotion in a daily ritual of five prayers.

Islam spread rapidly after the death of Muhammad, although divisions arose, as they did within Christianity. All Muslims, however, accept the Five Pillars of Islam: (1) recognizing Allah as the one true God, and Muhammad as God's messenger; (2) ritual prayer; (3) giving alms to the poor; (4) fasting during the month of Ramadan; and (5) making a pilgrimage at least once to the Sacred House of Allah in Mecca (Weeks, 1988; El-Attar, 1991). Like Christianity, Islam holds people accountable to God for their deeds: those who live obediently will be rewarded in heaven, while evil-doers will suffer unending punishment.

Muslims are also obligated to defend their faith, which has led to holy wars against unbelievers (in roughly the same way that medieval Christians fought in the Crusades). Recently, in Algeria, Egypt, Iran, and elsewhere, some Muslims have sought to rid their society

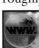 **"The Spirit of Islam"** is an exhibition that brought Muslim communities in the lower mainland of B.C. together with the Museum of Anthropology at the University of British Columbia to explore Islamic spirituality through its exquisite calligraphy. Go to www.moa.ubc.ca/spiritofislam/

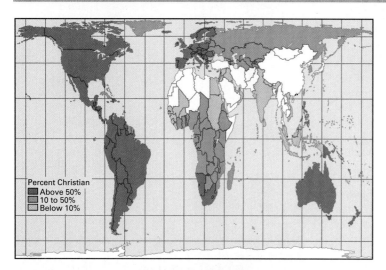

GLOBAL MAP 19–1
Christianity in Global Perspective

Source: *Peters Atlas of the World* (1990).

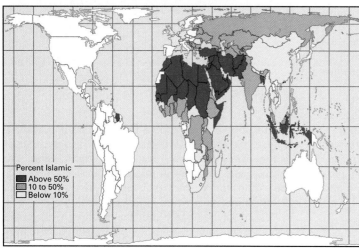

GLOBAL MAP 19–2
Islam in Global Perspective

Source: *Peters Atlas of the World* (1990).

of Western influences that they regard as morally wrong (Martin, 1982; Arjomand, 1988).

To many Westerners, Muslim women are among the most socially oppressed people on earth. Muslim women do lack many of the personal freedoms enjoyed by Muslim men, yet many—and perhaps most—accept the mandates of their religion and find security in a rigid system that guides the behaviour of both women and men (Peterson, 1996). Moreover, patriarchy was well established in the Middle East long before the birth of Muhammad. Some defenders argue that Islam actually improved the social position of women by demanding that husbands deal justly with their wives. While Islam permits a man to have up to four wives, it admonishes men to have only one wife if

having more would encourage him to treat any woman unjustly (Qur'an, "The Women," v. 3).

JUDAISM

In terms of simple numbers, Judaism's 14 million followers worldwide makes it something less than a world religion. Moreover, only in Israel do Jews represent a national majority. But Judaism has special significance in North America because the largest concentration of Jews (6 million people) is found here.

Jews look to the past as a source of guidance in the present and future. Judaism has deep historical roots that extend back some four thousand years before the birth of Christ to the ancient cultures of Mesopotamia.

At this time, Jews were animistic, but this belief changed after Jacob—grandson of Abraham, the earliest great ancestor—led his people to Egypt.

Jews endured centuries of slavery in Egypt. In the thirteenth century B.C.E., a turning point came as Moses, the adopted son of an Egyptian princess, was called by God to lead the Jews from bondage. This exodus (this word's Latin and Greek roots mean "a marching out") from Egypt is commemorated by Jews today in the annual ritual of Passover. Once liberated, Jews became monotheistic, recognizing a single, all-powerful God.

A distinctive concept of Judaism is the *covenant*, a special relationship with God by which Jews became "the chosen people." The covenant also implies a duty to observe God's law, especially the Ten Commandments as revealed to Moses on Mount Sinai. Jews regard the Bible (or, in Christian terms, the Old Testament) as both a record of their history and a statement of the obligations of Jewish life. Of special importance are the Bible's first five books (Genesis, Exodus, Leviticus, Numbers, and Deuteronomy), designated as the *Torah* (a word roughly meaning "teaching" and "law"). In contrast to Christianity's central concern with personal salvation, Judaism emphasizes moral behaviour in this world.

Judaism is composed of four main denominations. Orthodox Jews strictly observe traditional beliefs and practices, wear traditional dress, segregate men and women at religious services, and eat only kosher foods. Such traditional practices set off Orthodox Jews in Canada, notably in Montreal, as the most sectlike. In the mid-nineteenth century, Jews sought greater acceptance by the larger society, leading to the formation of more churchlike Reform Judaism. A third segment—Conservative Judaism—has since established a middle ground between the other two denominations. These were followed in the 1930s by the fourth and smallest denomination, Reconstructionist Judaism, which blends egalitarian and democratic thinking with traditional practices.

Whatever their denomination, Jews share a cultural history of considerable prejudice and discrimination. A collective memory of centuries of slavery in Egypt, conquest by Rome, and persecution in Europe has shaped Jewish identity. Jews in Italy were the first to live in an urban ghetto (derived from the Italian word *borghetto*, meaning "settlement outside the city walls"), and this form of residential segregation soon spread to other parts of Europe.

Jewish immigration to North America began in the mid-1600s. Many early immigrants prospered, and many were also assimilated into largely Christian communities. But as larger numbers entered the country during the final decades of the nineteenth century, prejudice and discrimination against them—commonly termed *anti-Semitism*—increased. Jews were not allowed to work in certain institutions, and others maintained quotas: for instance, there were quotas on the number of Jewish students who were to be admitted to universities (Abella, 1989). During World War II, German Jewish refugees were refused admittance to Canada (Abella and Troper, 1982). And it was during World War II that anti-Semitism reached a vicious peak as the Nazi regime in Germany systematically annihilated 6 million Jews.

 "Open Hearts, Closed Doors" is a virtual museum that tells the stories of Jewish war orphans who came to Canada after World War II: see www.virtualmuseum.ca/ Exhibitions/orphans/english/

The University of Toronto, in its *National Report '97*, announced the endowment of two chairs in Jewish studies, an innovative and comprehensive program that reflects the belief that "the study of Jewish culture and history is critical to the understanding of Western civilization" and highly relevant to a "young, multicultural country like Canada."

HINDUISM

Hinduism is the oldest of all the world religions, originating in the Indus River Valley approximately 4500 years ago. Hindus number some 793 million (14 percent of humanity). Global Map 19–3 shows that Hinduism remains an Eastern religion, predominantly practised in India and Pakistan, but with a significant presence in southern Africa and Indonesia.

Over the centuries, Hinduism and Indian culture have become intertwined, so that now one is not easily described apart from the other. This connection also explains why Hinduism, unlike Christianity, Islam, and Judaism, has not diffused widely to other nations. However, Hindus living in North America make this religion a significant part of the continent's cultural diversity.

Hinduism differs from most other religions by not being linked to the life of any single person. Hinduism also has no sacred writings comparable to the Bible or the Qur'an. Nor does Hinduism envision God as a specific entity. For this reason, Hinduism—like other Eastern religions, as we shall see—is sometimes described as an "ethical religion." Hindu beliefs and practices vary widely, but all Hindus recognize a moral force in the universe that presents everyone with responsibilities, termed *dharma*. Dharma, for example, calls people to observe the traditional caste system described in Chapter 10 ("Social Stratification").

Another Hindu principle, *karma*, refers to the belief in the spiritual progress of the human soul. To a Hindu, all actions have spiritual consequences, and proper living contributes to moral development. Karma works through *reincarnation*, a cycle of death and rebirth, by which the individual is reborn into a

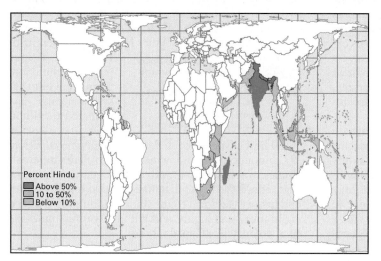

GLOBAL MAP 19–3
Hinduism in Global Perspective

Source: *Peters Atlas of the World* (1990).

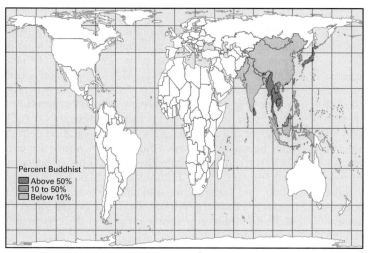

GLOBAL MAP 19–4
Buddhism in Global Perspective

Source: *Peters Atlas of the World* (1990).

spiritual state corresponding to the moral quality of his or her previous life. Unlike Christianity and Islam, Hinduism proclaims no ultimate judgment by a supreme god, although in the cycle of rebirth people reap exactly what they have sown. *Moksha* is the sublime state of spiritual perfection: only when a soul reaches this level is it no longer reborn.

Hinduism stands as evidence that not all religions can be neatly labelled monotheistic or polytheistic. Hinduism is monotheistic insofar as it envisions the universe as a single moral system, yet Hindus see this moral order at work in every element of nature. Many Hindus participate in public rituals, such as the *Kumbh Mela*, which, every twelve years, brings some 20 million pilgrims to the sacred Ganges River to bathe in its purifying waters. At the same time, Hindus practise private devotions, which vary from village to village across the vast nation of India.

While elements of Hindu thought have characterized some cults in North America over the years, Hinduism is still unfamiliar to most Westerners. But like religions better known to us, Hinduism is a powerful force offering both explanation and guidance in life (Pitt, 1955; Sen, 1961; Embree, 1972; Kaufman, 1976; Schmidt, 1980).

BUDDHISM

Some 2500 years ago, the rich culture of India also gave rise to Buddhism. Today, more than 325 million people (6 percent of humanity) embrace Buddhism, and almost all are Asians. As shown in Global Map

19–4, Buddhists make up more than half the population of Myanmar (Burma), Thailand, Cambodia, and Japan; Buddhism is also widespread in India and the People's Republic of China. Of the world religions considered so far, Buddhism most resembles Hinduism in doctrine, but, like Christianity, its inspiration springs from the life of one individual.

Siddhartha Gautama was born to a high-caste family in Nepal in about 563 B.C.E. As a young man, he was preoccupied with spiritual matters. At the age of twenty-nine, he underwent a radical personal transformation, and set off for years of travel and meditation. His journey ended when he achieved what Buddhists describe as *bodhi*, or true wisdom. Understanding the essence of life, Gautama became a Buddha.

Energized by the Buddha's personal charisma, followers spread his teachings—the *dhamma*—across India. During the third century B.C.E., the ruler of India became a Buddhist and sent missionaries throughout Asia, making Buddhism a world religion.

Buddhists believe that much of life involves suffering. This idea is rooted in the Buddha's own travels in a society rife with poverty. But the Buddha rejected wealth as a solution to suffering; on the contrary, he warned that materialism inhibits spiritual development. Instead, Buddha taught that we must transcend our selfish concerns and desires through meditation, with the goal of obtaining *nirvana*, a state of enlightenment and peace.

Buddhism closely parallels Hinduism in recognizing no god of judgment; both proclaim that each daily action has spiritual consequences. Another similarity is a belief in reincarnation. Only enlightenment ends the cycle of death and rebirth and finally liberates a person from the suffering of the world (Schumann, 1974; Thomas, 1975; Van Biema, 1997).

 For information about the Dalai Lama and Tibetan Buddhism, go to www.dalailama.com

CONFUCIANISM

From about 200 B.C.E. until the beginning of the twentieth century, Confucianism was an ecclesia—the official religion of China. Following the 1949 revolution, religion was suppressed by the communist government of the new People's Republic of China. Today, though officials provide no precise count, hundreds of millions of Chinese are still influenced by Confucianism. Almost all Confucianists live in China, although Chinese immigration has spread this religion to other nations in Southeast Asia. Perhaps one hundred thousand followers of Confucius live in North America.

Confucius, or, properly, K'ung-Fu-tzu, lived between 551 and 479 B.C.E. Like Buddha, Confucius was deeply concerned about people's suffering. The Buddha's response was a sectlike spiritual withdrawal from the world; Confucius, in contrast, instructed his

The spiritual leader of Tibetan Buddhism is the Dalai Lama, shown here teaching a large assembly of followers.

followers to engage the world according to a strict code of moral conduct. Thus it was that Confucianism became fused with the traditional culture of China. Here we see a second example of what might be called a "national religion": as Hinduism has remained largely synonymous with Indian culture, Confucianism is enshrined in the Chinese way of life.

A central concept of Confucianism is *jen*, meaning humaneness. In practice, this means that we must always subordinate our self-interest to moral principle. In the family, the individual must be loyal and considerate. Likewise, families must remain mindful of their duties towards the larger community. In this way, layer upon layer of moral obligation integrates society as a whole.

Most of all, Confucianism stands out as lacking a clear sense of the sacred. Recalling Durkheim's analysis, we might view Confucianism as the celebration of the sacred character of society itself. Alternatively, we might argue that Confucianism is less a religion than a model of disciplined living. Certainly the historical dominance of Confucianism helps to explain why Chinese culture is skeptical towards the supernatural. But even as a disciplined way of life, Confucianism shares with religion a body of beliefs and practices that have as their goal goodness, concern for others, and the promotion of social harmony (Kaufman, 1976; Schmidt, 1980; McGuire, 1987).

When Western people perform religious rituals they typically do so collectively and formally as members of specific congregations. Eastern people, in contrast, visit shrines individually and informally, without joining a specific congregation. For this reason, Asian temples such as this one in Hong Kong receive a steady flow of people—families praying, individuals engaging in business, and foreign tourists just watching—that seems somehow inappropriate to the Western visitor.

RELIGION: EAST AND WEST

This overview of world religions reveals two general differences between the belief systems of Eastern and Western societies. First, Western religions (Christianity, Islam, Judaism) are typically deity-based, with a clear focus on God. Eastern religions (Hinduism, Buddhism, Confucianism) tend to be ethical codes; therefore, they make a less clear-cut distinction between the sacred and the secular.

Second, the operational unit of Western religious organization is the congregation, people who worship in formal groups at a specific time and place. Eastern religious organization, in contrast, is informally fused with culture itself. For this reason, a visitor finds a Japanese temple filled with tourists and worshippers alike, who come and go as they please and pay little attention to those around them.

These two distinctions do not overshadow the common element of all religions: a conception of a higher moral force or purpose that transcends the

 For information about various religions, visit www.adherents.com

concerns of every-day life. In their global variety, religious beliefs give people of the world guidance and a sense of purpose in their lives.

RELIGION IN CANADA

In global perspective, Canada is a relatively religious nation. As Figure 19–1 shows, more than six in ten members of our society claim to gain "comfort and strength from religion," a proportion approximately in the middle of other industrial countries.

RELIGIOUS AFFILIATION

On national surveys, nearly 90 percent of Canadian adults claim a religious preference (Baril and Mori, 1991). Traditionally, Canada has been fairly evenly divided between Catholics and Protestants. For more than a century, until about 1971, Protestants outnumbered Catholics; now the reverse is true. Census 2001 shows that approximately 43 percent of respondents embrace Catholicism, Protestants make up almost 31 percent of the population, 1 percent are Jewish, and just over 16 percent claim to have no religious affiliation. Muslims make up 2 percent of our population and Buddhists, Hindus, and Sikhs make up 1 percent each.

Table 19–1 reveals the religious affiliation of Canadians for the fifteen largest religions and "no religion" (Statistics Canada, Census 2001). One does not find a category for Protestant (31 percent of the population) listed in the table: the United Church, Anglican, Baptist, Lutheran, Presbyterian, and Pentecostal affiliations are among those making up the Protestant category. Note that indicating a religious affiliation on one's census return does not mean that the individual attends religious services with any regularity, as noted below.

An intriguing question related to religious affiliation is the effect of interfaith marriage on children. Bibby (2000) found that in interfaith marriages, children are more likely to embrace the religions of their mothers. Similarly, when mothers with no religion marry men of various faiths, the children are most likely to report no religion.

Canadian society has no official religion, and the separation of church and state is enshrined in the constitution. The population of Canada is also more religiously diverse than that of most other countries—one result of our historically high level of immigration.

RELIGIOSITY

Religiosity refers to *the importance of religion in a person's life.* Identifying with a religion is only one measure of religiosity, of course, and a superficial one at that. How religious Canada turns out to be, therefore, depends on how we operationalize the concept.

Years ago, Charles Glock (1959, 1962) proposed five distinct dimensions of religiosity. *Experiential* religiosity refers to the strength of a person's emotional

TABLE 19–1 Religious Affiliation for Canada's Largest Religions: Percentage of the Population in 2001	
Religion	Percentage
Roman Catholic	43.2
No Religion	16.2
United Church	9.6
Anglican	6.9
Baptist	2.5
Lutheran	2.0
Muslim	2.0
Presbyterian	1.4
Pentecostal	1.2
Jewish	1.1
Buddhist	1.0
Hindu	1.0
Sikh	0.9
Greek Orthodox	0.7
Mennonite	0.6
Jehovah's Witnesses	0.5

Source: Adapted from Census 2001, Highlight Tables, www.statcan.ca.

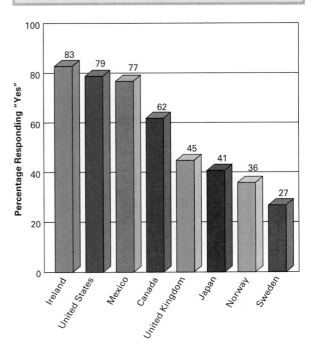

FIGURE 19–1 Religiosity in Global Perspective

Survey Question: "Do you gain comfort and strength from religion?"

Source: World Values Survey (1994).

ties to a religion. *Ritualistic* religiosity refers to frequency of ritual activity such as prayer and church attendance. *Ideological* religiosity describes an individual's degree of belief in religious doctrine. *Consequential* religiosity has to do with how strongly religious beliefs figure in a person's daily behaviour. Finally, *intellectual* religiosity refers to a person's knowledge of the history and doctrines of a particular religion. Any person is likely to be more religious on some dimensions than on others, so assessing religiosity is a difficult task.

How religious, then, are members of our society? Canada Map 19–1 shows the percentage of respondents in each province that stated they had "no religion" on the 2001 census, ranging from a low of 2.5 percent in Newfoundland and Labrador to a high of 38.4 percent in the Yukon. In Canada as a whole, 16.6 percent claimed no religion, compared to 7 percent 2 decades earlier. This increase in the number of Canadians reporting no religion is mirrored by a drop in weekly church attendance, from close to 60 percent in the 1950s to about 25 percent in 1995 (Baril and Mori, 1991; Bibby, 1995). Bibby points out that the decline in attendance accelerated in the 1970s and has affected Catholics in Quebec in particular. The "Applying Sociology" box examines attendance at religious services among children under twelve.

On a comparative note, Canada and the United States are becoming increasingly diverse with respect to religiosity. Americans, with their Puritan roots, continue to be highly religious, while Canada has become increasingly secular over the years. A recent survey revealed that 30 percent of Canadians and 59

percent of Americans indicate that religion is important in their lives: similarly, 21 percent of Canadians say they attend church regularly, compared to twice the number of Americans. Interestingly, American politicians make frequent references to God and their own religious practices, while Canadian politicians almost never do. For example, it was only after the death of Pierre Elliott Trudeau that we learned he was

 For "Religion in Canada: Its Development and Contemporary Situation" see http://are.as.wvu.edu/o'toole.html

a devout Catholic (Krauss, 2003). For more on this difference between Canadian and American politicians, see the "Applying Sociology" box on page 426.

Nevertheless, 81 percent of Canadians believe in God. Further, 74 percent believe in miracle healing, 61 percent believe in angels, and 49 percent believe in hell (Bibby, 1995:131). In terms of experiential religiosity, then, Canadians are still religious, although they tend to believe in the more positive doctrinal aspects, such as God and heaven, rather than the more negative aspects, such as hell. In addition, it seems that

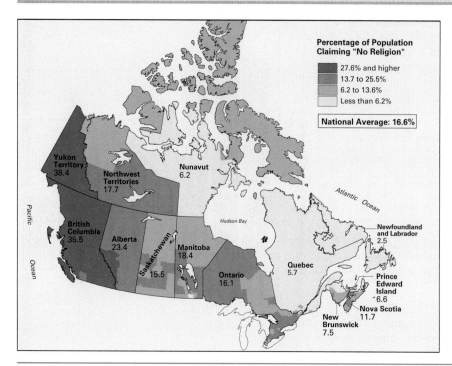

Percentage of Population Claiming "No Religion"

- 27.6% and higher
- 13.7 to 25.5%
- 6.2 to 13.6%
- Less than 6.2%

National Average: 16.6%

CANADA MAP 19–1
Canadians Claiming "No Religion" (by Province, Territory, and Census Subdivision), 2001

Source: Calculations by Gerber based on data from Statistics Canada, B2020 Tables, Census 2001.

"spirituality" is highly valued by 36 percent, religion by 26 percent (Bibby, 1995).

RELIGION AND SOCIAL STRATIFICATION

Sociologists who study religion have found that religious affiliation is related to other familiar social patterns. We shall consider two: social class and ethnicity.

Social Class

Historically, Canada has been stratified along religious lines. By and large, Protestants with high social standing are people of northern European background. Members of the Anglican Church, and later the other establishment Protestant churches, have long been among Canada's most affluent, powerful people. Anglophone political and economic dominance, and traditional Catholic doctrine, kept Catholics in Quebec subordinate and poor. Jews command unexpectedly high social standing considering that they often contend with anti-Semitism. The reason for this achievement is mostly cultural, since Jewish tradition places great value on education and achievement. Although a large proportion of Jews began life in North America in poverty, many—but certainly not all—improved their social position in subsequent generations.

Although income is only one dimension of social class, the ranking of various religious categories by income in Table 19–2 (on page 488) shows that stratification along religious lines is still with us. Jews have the highest average income, while members of the United Church, Anglicans, Presbyterians, and Lutherans also earn above-average incomes. Members of all other religions, including Christian fundamentalists and Roman Catholics, fall below the Canadian average. Despite massive changes in Canada's population after World War II, the old relationship between religion and economic well-being persists.

Ethnicity

Throughout the world, religion is tied to ethnicity. Many religions predominate in a single nation or geographical region. Islam predominates in the Arab societies of the Middle East; Hinduism is fused with the culture of India, as is Confucianism with life in China. Christianity and Judaism, however, do not follow this pattern: while these religions are predominantly Western, Christians and Jews are found all over the world.

Religion and national identity come together in Canada as well. We have, for example, *Anglo-Saxon* Protestants, *Irish* Catholics, *Russian* Jews, and *Greek*

Are Children Going to Religious Services?

Reginald Bibby (1995) points out that for the overall population of Canada, weekly attendance at religious services dropped off dramatically—from 60 to 25 percent—between 1945 and 1995. The decline has been particularly dramatic for Roman Catholics in Quebec and mainline Protestant churches (United, Anglican, Presbyterian, and Lutheran) in the rest of the country. In 1995, weekly attendance was least common in Quebec and B.C.—19 and 21 percent—and highest in the Atlantic region—38 percent. In addition, Bibby notes that attendance remained the highest in Canada's smaller communities.

To project future attendance, one needs to look at the youngest Canadians. Frank Jones (2000) uses data from the National Longitudinal Survey of Children and Youth (1994–95) to do just that; specifically, he addresses questions relating to religious observance among children under age twelve.

Jones found that 23 percent of Canada's children attend religious services weekly—a level that is consistent with that in the total population. Thirty-six percent attend at least once a month. Jones echoes Bibby's observations as he points out that

> Regular attendance (weekly or monthly) varied considerably depending on the child's age, sex, region of residence and religious affiliation. It generally increased until children were eight years old and then began to stabilize. Girls were somewhat more likely to be regular attendees (38%) than boys (34%). Children living in Atlantic Canada had the highest regular attendance rate, 52%, while those in Quebec had the lowest, 19%. (2000:203)

In addition, Jones found that weekly attendance levels were highest among the Jehovah's Witnesses (90 percent) and lowest in the Anglican and United churches (18 percent). Surprisingly, he found that regular attendance increased with the educational attainment of the mother.

On the basis of historical trends, it is unlikely that children of this generation will increase their level of attendance with age. Instead, levels can be expected to continue to decline. In the absence of a major cultural shift, the mainline churches in Canada's larger urban centres—particularly in Quebec and B.C.—have little cause for optimism regarding future levels of attendance.

Sources: Based on Bibby (1995) and Jones (2000).

Orthodox. This linking of nation and creed results from the influx of immigrants from nations with a single major religion, or from societies where large numbers of a particular religious group emigrated to escape persecution. Still, nearly every ethnic category displays some religious diversity. People of English ancestry, for instance, may be Protestants, Roman Catholics, Jews, or followers of other religions.

RELIGION IN A CHANGING SOCIETY

All social institutions evolve over time. Just as the economy, politics, and family life have changed over the course of the past century, so has our society's religious life.

SECULARIZATION

One of the most important patterns of social change is **secularization**, *the historical decline in the importance of the supernatural and the sacred.* For society as a whole, secularization points to the waning influence of religion in everyday life. For religious organizations, be-

coming more secular means that they focus less on otherworldly issues (such as life after death) and more on worldly affairs (such as sheltering the homeless and feeding the hungry). Secularization also means that functions once performed by the church (such as charity) are now primarily the responsibility of businesses and government.

Secularization was at the core of the Quiet Revolution in Quebec during the 1960s. The Catholic Church, which had administered welfare, health care, and education in addition to dealing with the spiritual needs of Quebec society, lost influence on the religious front, while giving up its social service involvement to the provincial government.

With Latin roots meaning "the present age," secularization is commonly associated with modern, technologically advanced societies (Cox, 1971, orig. 1965; O'Dea and O'Dea Aviad, 1983). Conventional wisdom holds that secularization results from the increasing role of science in understanding human affairs. Today, in other words, people perceive birth, illness, and death less as the work of a divine power than as natural stages in the life course. These events

TABLE 19–2 Average Income by Selected Religious Affiliation, 1991

Religion	Average Income
Jewish	$34 488
United	24 096
Anglican	24 088
Presbyterian	23 668
No religion	22 536
Lutheran	22 365
Roman Catholic	20 523
Baptist	20 311
Greek Orthodox	17 863
Mennonite	17 691
Pentecostal	16 756
Jehovah's Witness	15 509
Other religions	16 086–20 237
Canadian average	21 524

Source: Analysis by Gerber from Statistics Canada 1991 Census, Individual Public Use Microdata.

are now more likely to occur in the presence of physicians (scientific specialists) than religious leaders (whose knowledge is based on faith). As Harvey Cox explains,

> The world looks less and less to religious rules and rituals for its morality or its meanings. For some, religion provides a hobby, for others a mark of national or ethnic identification, for still others an aesthetic delight. For fewer and fewer does it provide an inclusive and commanding system of personal and cosmic values and explanations. (1971:3)

If Cox is correct, should we expect that religion will disappear completely someday? The consensus among sociologists is "no." The vast majority of people in Canada still profess a belief in God.

Secularization does not, then, signal the death of religion. More correctly, some dimensions of religiosity (such as belief in life after death) may have declined, but others (such as religious affiliation) have increased. A global perspective shows the same mixed pattern: religion is declining in importance in some regions (the Scandinavian countries, for example), but rising in others (such as Algeria) (Cox, 1990). For a look at religiosity and secularization in Canadian and American politics, see the "Applying Sociology" box in Chapter 17 (p. 426).

Our society is of two minds as to whether secularization is good or bad. Conservatives take any erosion of religion as a mark of moral decline. Progressives, however, think secularization liberates people from the all-encompassing beliefs of the past and allows them to choose what to believe. Secularization has also brought the practices of many religious organiza-

tions (for example, ordaining both men and women) into line with widespread social attitudes.

CIVIL RELIGION

One dimension of secularization is the rise of what Robert Bellah (1975) calls **civil religion**, *a quasi-religious loyalty binding individuals in a basically secular society*. In other words, although some dimensions of formal religion are weakening, our patriotism and citizenship retain many religious qualities.

Canada is a case in point. Just as religion presents a blueprint for leading a good life, a vast majority of people in Canada believe that their political, economic, and medical systems exemplify what is good, and that life in Canada is the best in the world.

Civil religion also involves a wide range of rituals, from rising to sing the national anthem at sporting events to sitting down to watch public parades. At all such events, like the Christian cross or the Jewish Star of David, the Canadian flag serves as a sacred symbol of our national identity that we expect people to treat with reverence.

Civil religion is not a specific religious doctrine. It does, however, incorporate many elements of traditional religion into the political system of a secular society.

RELIGIOUS REVIVAL

A great deal of change is going on in the world of organized religion. Membership in established, "mainstream" churches such as the Anglican and Presbyterian denominations has decreased. Between 1981 and 1991, Presbyterian membership decreased by 22 percent, United by 18 percent, Anglican and Lutheran by 10 percent, and Baptist by 5 percent. In the meantime, most of the smaller denominations—including the Spiritualist, Evangelical, Christian and Missionary Alliance, New Apostolic, and Missionary churches—grew significantly in the same time period. Jewish and Eastern Orthodox congregations grew by 7 percent. Secularization itself may be self-limiting so that as churchlike organizations become more worldly, many people abandon them in favour of more sectlike religious communities that offer a more intense religious experience (Bibby, 1987). Much the same pattern is found in other industrial societies.

RELIGIOUS FUNDAMENTALISM

One of the striking religious trends today is the growth of **fundamentalism**, *a conservative religious doctrine that opposes intellectualism and worldly accommodation in favour of restoring traditional, otherworldly spirituality*. Fundamentalism has made the greatest gains among Protestants, but fundamentalist groups have also proliferated among Roman Catholics and Jews.

In response to what they see as the growing influence of science and the erosion of the conventional family, religious fundamentalists defend what they call "traditional values." As they see it, liberal churches are simply too tolerant of religious pluralism and too open to change. Religious fundamentalism is distinctive in five ways (Hunter, 1983, 1985, 1987).

1. **Fundamentalists interpret sacred texts literally.** Fundamentalists insist on a literal interpretation of the Bible and other sacred texts to counter what they consider excessive intellectualism among more liberal religious organizations. Fundamentalist Christians, for example, believe that God created the world precisely as described in Genesis.

2. **Fundamentalists reject religious pluralism.** Fundamentalists believe that tolerance and relativism diminish personal faith. They maintain, therefore, that their religious beliefs are true while those of others are not.

3. **Fundamentalists pursue the personal experience of God's presence.** In contrast to the worldliness and intellectualism of other religious organizations, fundamentalism seeks a return to "good old-time religion" and spiritual revival. To fundamentalist Christians, being "born again" and having a personal relationship with Jesus Christ should be evident in a person's daily life.

4. **Fundamentalism opposes "secular humanism."** Fundamentalists believe that accommodation to the changing world undermines religious conviction. *Secular humanism* is a general term fundamentalists use to refer to our society's tendency to look to scientific experts (including sociologists) rather than to God for guidance about how to live.

5. **Many fundamentalists endorse conservative political goals.** Although fundamentalism tends to back away from worldly concerns, some fundamentalist leaders have entered politics in recent years to oppose the "liberal agenda" of feminism and gay rights. Fundamentalists oppose abortion, gay marriages, and liberal bias in the media, while supporting the traditional two-parent family and seeking a return of prayer in schools (Viguerie, 1981; Hunter, 1983; Speer, 1984; Ostling, 1985; Ellison and Sherkat, 1993; Green, 1993; Thomma, 1997).

Opponents regard fundamentalism as rigid and self-righteous. But many find in fundamentalism—with its greater religious certainty and emphasis on the emotional experience of God's presence—an appealing alternative to the more intellectual, tolerant, and worldly mainstream denominations (Marquand, 1997).

Which religions are "fundamentalist"? This term is most correctly applied to conservative Christian organizations in the evangelical tradition, including Pentecostals and Seventh-Day Adventists.

The Electronic Church

In contrast to small village congregations of years past, some religious organizations—especially fundamentalist ones—have become electronic churches featuring "prime-time preachers" (Hadden and Swain, 1981). Electronic religion in the United States has propelled Oral Roberts, Pat Robertson, and others to greater prominence than all but a few clergy in the past. Canadian "televangelists" David Mainse and Terry Winter, true to the "Canadian personality," are relatively low-key and have exhibited fewer public "sins" (Bibby, 1987:34–36). About 5 percent of the national television audience regularly tunes in to religious television. Moreover, the majority of people who watch religious programs on TV are also regular churchgoers. Almost 80 percent of them attend church either weekly (68 percent) or monthly (11 percent).

 Visit the website of the Monastery of Christ in the Desert at www.christdesert.org

Recently, an increasing number of religious organizations are using computer technology to spread their message, a trend that Pope John Paul II has termed the "new evangelism." The "Exploring Cyber-Society" box deals with finding God online.

LOOKING AHEAD: RELIGION IN THE TWENTY-FIRST CENTURY

The popularity of media ministries, the rapid growth of religious fundamentalism, and the continuing adherence of millions more people to mainstream churches show that religion will remain a major institution of modern society. Moreover, high levels of immigration from many religious countries (Asia, Africa, the Caribbean, and elsewhere) will intensify and diversify the religious character of Canadian society in the decades to come.

In addition, the pace of social change is accelerating. As the world becomes more complex, rapid change seems to outstrip our capacity to make sense of it all. But rather than undermining religion, this process fires the religious imagination of people who seek a sense of religious community and ultimate meaning in life. Tensions between the spiritual realm of religion and the secular world of science and technology will surely continue—as suggested in the "Controversy & Debate" box.

But science is simply unable to provide answers to the most basic human questions about the purpose of our lives. Moreover, new technology that can begin

The Cyber-Church: Logging On to Religion

It takes only a few minutes on the Internet to discover that religion is alive and well on the World Wide Web, where you can find electronic Bibles for computer-assisted research, a proverb a day, prophecies related to the End of Time (from an online book entitled *In the Light of Biblical Prophecy*), as well as announcements of events, products, publications, and conventions. Chat groups, university or college courses, monthly magazines, and prayer groups provide opportunities for active participation. Internet Evangelism Central is a site designed to inspire Christians to evangelize the Web through the creation of further evangelical sites. New Age is also represented, with sites such as *New Age Web Works* or *The Cyberzine for the Open Minded*.

This is hardly the first time technological innovation has brought change to religion. Six hundred years ago in medieval Europe, face-to-face speaking was the major channel for transmitting religious ideas, as clerics gathered in the universities of the largest cities of the day and people went to services in churches and other houses of worship. At that time, Bibles and other sacred texts were few and far between; monks in monasteries took years to complete the painstaking task of copying them by hand. But religion changed when Johann Gutenberg, a German inventor, built a movable-type press and published the first printed book—a Bible—in 1456. Within fifty years, millions of books were in print across Europe, and most of them were about religious matters. It is no coincidence that the spread of printed books was soon followed by a major religious transformation—the Protestant Reformation—as an expanding market of religious ideas prompted people to rethink established principles and practices.

More and more religious organizations are using the Internet to spread their message. Do you think computer technology will serve to strengthen or weaken religion?

In the twentieth century, radio (beginning in the 1920s) and television (after 1950) extended the reach of religious leaders, who founded "media congregations" no longer confined by the walls of a single building. During the 1990s, the Internet accelerated this trend, as hundreds of thousands of websites offered messages from established churches, obscure cults, and "New Age" organizations.

How will computer technology affect religious life? With more to learn than ever before, some analysts anticipate a new "post-denominational" age in which people's religious ideas are not bound by particular organizations, as in the past. New information technology may also usher in an age of "cyber-churches." Television has already shown it can transmit the personal charisma and spiritual message of religious leaders to ever-larger audiences. Perhaps the Internet will lead to "virtual congregations," both larger in number and broader in background than any before.

Source: Based on Ramo (1996).

and sustain life confronts us with vexing moral dilemmas as never before. Against this backdrop of uncertainty, it is little wonder that many people rely on their faith for assurance and hope.

SUMMARY

1. Religion is a major social institution based on distinguishing the sacred from the profane. Religion is a matter of faith, not scientific evidence, which people express through various rituals.

2. Sociology analyzes the consequences of religion for social life, but no scientific research can assess the truth of any religious belief.

Does Science Threaten Religion?

At the dawning of the modern age, the Italian physicist and astronomer Galileo (1564–1642) made a series of startling discoveries. Dropping objects from the Leaning Tower of Pisa, he discovered some of the laws of gravity; fashioning his own telescope, he surveyed the heavens and found that the earth orbited the sun, not the other way around.

For his discoveries, Galileo was denounced by the Roman Catholic Church, which had preached for centuries that the earth stood motionless at the centre of the universe. In response, Galileo only made matters worse by declaring that religious leaders and Biblical doctrine had no place in the growing wave of science. Before long, he found his work banned and himself condemned to house arrest.

From its beginnings, science has had an uneasy relationship with religion. Indeed, as Galileo's life makes clear, the claims of one sometimes infringe on the other's truth.

Through the twentieth century, too, science and religion had their battles, mostly over the issue of creation. In the wake of Charles Darwin's masterwork, *On the Origin of Species* (1859), scientists concluded that humanity evolved from lower forms of life over the course of a billion years. Yet the theory of evolution seems to fly in the face of the Biblical account of creation found in Genesis, which states that "God created the heaven and the earth," introducing life on the third day and, on the fifth and sixth days, creating animal life, including human beings, who were fashioned in God's own image.

Galileo would certainly have been an eager observer of the famous "Scopes monkey trial" of 1925, in which the state of Tennessee prosecuted science teacher John Thomas Scopes. Scopes taught evolution in violation of a state law that forbade teaching "any theory that denies the story of the Divine Creation of man as taught in the Bible" and especially the idea that "man descended from a lower order of animals." Scopes was found guilty and fined $100. His conviction was reversed on appeal, perhaps to prevent the case from reaching the U.S. Supreme Court, and so the Tennessee law continued to ban the teaching of evolution until 1967. A year later, the U.S. Supreme Court struck down all such laws as an unconstitutional case of government-supported religion.

Today—almost four centuries after the silencing of Galileo—many people still ponder the apparently conflicting claims of science and religion. But a middle ground is emerging, stating that the Bible may be inspired by God and contain important philosophical truth without being literally correct in a scientific sense. That is, science and religion represent two different levels of understanding that respond to different questions. Both Galileo and Darwin devoted their lives to investigating how the natural world operates. Yet only religion can address why humans and the natural world exist in the first place.

This basic difference between science and religion helps explain how our society can be at once actively scientific and devoutly religious. Moreover, the more scientists discover about the origins of the universe, the more awesome creation seems. Indeed, as one scientist recently pointed out, the mathematical odds that some cosmic "Big Bang" 12 billion years ago created the universe and led to the development of life on earth as we know it today are utterly infinitesimal—much smaller than the chance of one person winning a provincial lottery for twenty weeks in a row. Doesn't such a scientific fact allow for an intelligent and purposeful power in our creation? Can't one be both a religious believer and a scientific investigator?

There is another reason to appreciate both scientific and religious thinking: the rapid advances of science continue to present society with ethical dilemmas. We have unleashed the power of atomic energy, yet we struggle to find its rightful use in the world. And discovering secrets of human genetics has brought us to the threshold of being able to manipulate life itself, a power that few have the moral confidence to use.

In 1992, a Vatican commission created by Pope John Paul II conceded that the church had erred in silencing Galileo. Most scientific and religious leaders agree that science and religion represent distinctive truths, and their teachings are complementary. And many believe that, in today's rush to scientific discovery, our world has never been more in need of the moral guidance afforded by religion.

Continue the debate . . .

1. *On what grounds do some scientists completely reject religious accounts of human creation? Why do some religious people reject scientific accounts?*

2. *Do you think the sociological study of religion challenges anyone's faith? Why or why not?*

3. *Does science sometimes develop outside moral constraints? Is science too powerful? Where do science and religion conflict today?*

Sources: Based on Gould (1981), Hutchingson (1994), and Applebome (1996).

3. Emile Durkheim argued that, through religion, individuals experience the power of their society. His structural-functional analysis suggests that religion promotes social cohesion and conformity and confers meaning and purpose on life.

4. Using the symbolic-interaction paradigm, Peter Berger explains that religious beliefs are socially constructed as a means of responding to life's uncertainties and disruptions.

5. Using the social-conflict paradigm, Karl Marx charged that religion promotes social inequality and the status quo. On the other hand, Max Weber's analysis of Calvinism's contribution to the rise of industrial capitalism demonstrates religion's power to promote social change.

6. Churches, which are religious organizations well integrated into their society, fall into two categories—ecclesias and denominations.

7. Sects, the result of religious division, are marked by charismatic leadership and suspicion of the larger society.

8. Cults are religious organizations that embrace new and unconventional beliefs and practices.

9. Technologically simple human societies were generally animistic, with religion just one facet of family life; in more complex societies, religion emerges as a distinct social institution.

10. Followers of six world religions—Christianity, Islam, Judaism, Hinduism, Buddhism, and Confucianism—represent three-quarters of all humanity.

11. Almost all adults in Canada identify with a religion; almost 90 percent claim to have a religious affiliation, with the largest number being Roman Catholic.

12. How religious we conclude our nation is depends on how we operationalize the concept of religiosity. The vast majority of Canadians say they believe in God, but only a minority attend religious services regularly.

13. Secularization refers to the diminishing importance of the supernatural and the sacred. In Canada, while some indicators of religiosity (such as membership in mainstream churches) have declined, others (such as membership in sects) are on the rise. Thus, it is doubtful that secularization will bring on the demise of religion.

14. Civil religion refers to the quasi-religious patriotism that ties people to their society.

15. Fundamentalism opposes religious accommodation to the world, favouring a more otherworldly focus. Fundamentalism advocates a literal interpretation of sacred texts, rejects religious diversity, and pursues the personal experience of God's presence. Some fundamentalist Christian organizations actively support conservative political goals.

16. Some of the continuing appeal of religion lies in the inability of science (including sociology) to address timeless questions about the ultimate meaning of human existence.

CRITICAL-THINKING QUESTIONS

1. Explain the basic distinction between the sacred and the profane that underlies all religious belief.

2. Explain Karl Marx's contention that religion supports the status quo. Develop a counter-argument, based on Max Weber's analysis of Calvinism, that religion can be a major force for social change.

3. Distinguish between churches, sects, and cults. Is one type of religious organization inherently better than another? Why or why not?

4. What evidence points to a decline in religion in Canada? In what ways does religion seem to be getting stronger?

APPLICATIONS AND EXERCISES

1. Investigate the place of religion on your campus. Is your school affiliated with any religious organization? Was it ever? Is there a chaplain or other religious official? See if you can learn from sources on campus what share of students regularly attend any religious service.

2. Assessing people's religious commitment is very difficult. Develop several questions measuring religiosity that might be asked on a questionnaire or in an interview. Present them to several people. How well do they seem to work?

3. At first, only cults used the Internet. But, today, many religious organizations are online, and even the Roman Catholic Church has a webpage. Access Yahoo! Canada or another search engine and generate sites by searching with a keyword such as "religion," "Judaism," "Hindu," or "cult." Visit several sites and see what you can learn about online religion.

4. Is religion getting weaker? To test the secularization thesis, go to the library or local newspaper office and obtain an issue of your local newspaper published fifty years ago and, if possible, one hundred years ago. Compare the attention devoted to religious issues then and now.

 ## SITES TO SEE

www.macionis.com
or
www.TheSociologyPage.com

You can find more than fifty weblinks to sociological journals and other sources of data and information by visiting the Links Library at this website.

www.statcan.ca/english/Pgdb/demo30a.htm

Statistics Canada presents national and provincial data from the 2001 and 1991 Censuses at this webpage.

www.utoronto.ca/stmikes/theobook.htm

The APS Guide to Resources in Theology is a collection of links to theological resources on the Web, maintained by the Faculty of Theology, University of St. Michael's College, Toronto.

www.religioustolerance.org/

The *Ontario Consultants on Religious Tolerance* site includes an extensive library of more than 550 essays on different faiths, from Asatru to Christianity to Zoroastrianism, and controversial religious topics, from abortion to homosexuality to female clergy.

www.escape.ca/~jclong/

Created in conjunction with a 1998 conference at Carleton University School of Journalism, Ottawa, to explore how faith groups and the media can work together to improve faith coverage in Canada, *Faith and the Media* includes media reports about the conference, plenary session addresses, and selected readings.

 ## STUDY TOOLS

For more study tools to help you with your next exam, be sure to check out the Companion Website at **www.pearsoned. ca/macionis**, as well as Chapter 19 in your Study Guide.

 ## INVESTIGATE WITH CONTENTSELECT

Follow the instructions found on page 25 of this textbook to access ContentSelect™ at the Research Navigator™ website. Once at the site, enter your LOGINID and Password. Then, enter keywords such as "religion," "spirituality," "cult," and "liberation theology," and the search engine will supply relevant and recent scholarly and popular press publications.

CHAPTER

20

Jacob Lawrence (1917– , African-American)
The Libraries Are Appreciated, 1943

Gouache and watercolour on paper, 36.2 × 53.9 cm. Louis E. Stern Collection, Philadelphia Museum of Art, Philadelphia, PA, 63-181-40. © Philadelphia Museum of Art/CORBIS. © Jacob Lawrence.

EDUCATION

Thirteen-year-old Naoko Matsuo returns from school to her home in suburban Yokohama, Japan. But instead of dropping off her books to begin an afternoon of fun, she settles in to do her homework. Several hours later, Naoko's mother reminds her that it is time to leave for the *juku*, a "cram school" that Naoko attends for three hours three evenings a week. Mother and daughter take the subway to an office building in downtown Yokohama where Naoko joins dozens of other girls and boys for intensive training in Japanese, English, math, and science.

Attending the *juku* costs the Matsuo family several hundred dollars a month. But the extra classroom hours are a good investment that will pay off when Naoko takes national examinations for high-school placement. Later on, the challenge will be to gain admission to an exclusive national university, a prize earned by just one-third of Japanese students. Given the cutthroat competition for educational success in Japan, the Matsuos know that their daughter cannot work too hard or begin too early (Simons, 1989).

Why do the Japanese pay such attention to schooling? In this modern, industrial society, admission to an elite university all but ensures a high-paying, prestigious career. This chapter spotlights **education**, *the social institution guiding a society's transmission of knowledge—including basic facts, job skills, and cultural norms and values—to its members*. In industrial societies, as we shall see, education is largely a matter of **schooling**, *formal instruction under the direction of specially trained teachers*.

EDUCATION: A GLOBAL SURVEY

Like people in Japan, we in Canada expect children to spend much of their first eighteen years of life in school. A century ago, however, only a small elite enjoyed the privilege of schooling. In the 1830s it is estimated that in Upper Canada about half of the children attended school—and only for an average of twelve months in total (Johnson, 1968:27). In low-income countries, even today, the vast majority of people receive little or no schooling.

SCHOOLING AND ECONOMIC DEVELOPMENT

The extent of schooling in any society is closely tied to its level of economic development. Chapter 4 ("Society") explained that our hunting-and-gathering ancestors lived a simple life in families without govern-

ments, churches, or schools: "schooling" amounted to the knowledge and skills parents transmitted directly to their children (Lenski et al., 1995).

In agrarian societies—in which most of the world's people live today—young people spend several years in school. In contrast, the opportunity to study literature, art, history, and science is a privilege generally available only to people freed by wealth from the need to work. The English word *school*, in fact, comes down to us from the Greek word for "leisure." In ancient Greece, renowned teachers such as Socrates, Plato, and Aristotle concentrated their efforts on aristocratic men to the exclusion of everyone else. Similarly, in ancient China, the famous philosopher K'ung-Fu-tzu (Confucius) shared his wisdom with only a select few. During the Middle Ages, European education took a step forward as the church established the first colleges and universities. But, here again, the privilege of schooling remained largely restricted to ruling elites.

Today, schooling in low-income nations is very diverse, reflecting the local cultures. In Iran, for example, education and religion are intertwined, so Islam figures prominently in schooling there. Elsewhere—including Bangladesh, Zimbabwe, and Nicaragua—distinctive cultural traditions have moulded the process of schooling.

All low-income countries have one trait in common: limited access to schooling. In the poorest nations (including several in central Africa), only half of

GLOBAL MAP 20–1 Illiteracy in Global Perspective

Reading and writing skills are widespread in high-income countries, with illiteracy rates generally below 5 percent. In much of Latin America, however, illiteracy is more common, one consequence of limited economic development. In twenty-seven nations—twenty of them in Africa—illiteracy is the rule rather than the exception; there, people rely on the "oral tradition" of face-to-face communication rather than the written word.

Sources: United Nations Development Programme (2001); map projection from *Peters Atlas of the World* (1990).

all elementary-aged children ever get to school; throughout the world, just half of all children attend secondary school (Najafizadeh and Mennerick, 1992). As a consequence, illiteracy disadvantages one-third of Latin Americans, almost half of Asians, and two-thirds of Africans. Global Map 20–1 displays the extent of illiteracy around the world.

Industrial, high-income societies embrace the principle of schooling for everyone. Industrial production demands that workers gain at least basic skills in

For a history of key moments in twentieth-century education, see http://fcis.oise.utoronto.ca/~daniel_schugurensky/assignment1/

the so-called three Rs—reading, 'riting, and 'rithmetic. For many industrial nations, literacy is also a necessary condition of political democracy.

The following national comparisons show how schooling is linked to economic development. Notice, too, how even industrial nations differ in their approach to educating their populations.

In the past, young children in poor countries such as India were as likely to work as to attend school. In recent decades, however, India has made great strides towards universal schooling. Still, in a nation that is largely rural, about 40 percent of Indian children receive no more than an elementary education.

SCHOOLING IN INDIA

India is a low-income country in which people earn about 5 percent of the income standard in Canada. Consequently, many parents depend on children's earnings. Thus, even though India has outlawed child labour, many Indian children work in factories—weaving rugs or making handicrafts—up to sixty hours a week, which greatly limits their opportunity for schooling.

In recent decades, schooling in India has increased. Most children now receive some primary education, typically in crowded schoolrooms where one teacher attends to perhaps sixty children (more than twice as many as in Canadian classrooms). This is all the schooling most people ever acquire, since fewer than half pursue secondary education and very few enter university or college. The result is that about half of the people in this vast country are literate.

Patriarchy also significantly shapes Indian education. Indian parents are joyful at the birth of a boy, since he and his future wife both will contribute income to the family. Girls are a financial liability, since parents must provide a dowry at the time of marriage, and a daughter's work will then benefit her husband's family. Because Indian society offers little incentive to invest in the schooling of girls, 45 percent of boys but only 30 percent of girls attend secondary school. Along with this cultural denigration of females, a large majority of the children working in Indian factories are girls—a family's way of benefiting from their daughter while they can (United Nations Development Programme, 1995).

SCHOOLING IN JAPAN

Schooling has not always been part of the Japanese way of life. Before industrialization brought mandatory education to this country in 1872, only a privileged few enrolled in school. Today, Japan's educational system is widely praised for generating some of the world's highest achievers.

In the early grades, schools foster the cultural values long central to Japanese life, especially obligation to family. In their early teens, as illustrated by the account of Naoko Matsuo at the beginning of this chapter, students encounter Japan's system of rigorous and competitive examinations. Written evaluations are used to place the brightest students in the best schools. In terms of schooling, Japan is more of a meritocracy than Canada or the United States. Here, university or college admission is not limited to only the best students: a bigger barrier to advanced education is the high cost involved. In Japan, in contrast, government support covers most of the financial cost of higher education; however, without high examination scores, even the richest families cannot place their children in a good university.

More men and women in Japan graduate from high school (about 90 percent) than in Canada or the United States. But because of competitive examinations, only about 40 percent of high-school graduates end up entering university—compared to about 55 percent in Canada and about 67 percent in the United States. Understandably, then, Japanese students view entrance examinations with the utmost seriousness, and about half attend *juku* (cram schools) to prepare for them. Most Japanese women, who are still not in the labour force, tend to devote themselves to the future success of their sons and, to a lesser extent, their daughters.

 See www.indiana.edu/ ~japan/digest9.html for an examination of daily life in Japanese high schools.

Because of the pressure it places on students, Japanese schooling produces impressive results. Especially in mathematics and science, Japanese students outperform students of every other industrial country, including Canada and the United States (Benedict, 1974; Hayneman and Loxley, 1983; Rohlen, 1983; Brinton, 1988; Simons, 1989).

SCHOOLING IN GREAT BRITAIN

During the Middle Ages, schooling was a privilege of the British nobility, who studied classical subjects since they had little need for the practical skills related to earning a living. But as the Industrial Revolution created a need for an educated labour force, and as working-class people demanded access to schools, a rising share of the British population entered the classroom. Law now requires every British child to attend school until age sixteen.

Traditional social distinctions, however, persist in British education. Many wealthy families send their children to what the British call *public schools*, the equivalent of Canadian private boarding schools. Such elite schools not only teach academic subjects, they also convey to children from wealthy (especially newly rich) families the distinctive patterns of speech, mannerisms, and social graces of the British upper class.

To lessen the influence of social background on schooling, the British expanded their university system and use competitive entrance examinations. For those who score the highest, the government pays most university costs. Compared with those in Japan, however, British examinations are less crucial, since many well-to-do children who do not score well still manage to attend Oxford or Cambridge, the most prestigious British universities. "Oxbridge" graduates go on to take their places at the core of the British power elite: more than two-thirds of the top members of the British government have "Oxbridge" degrees (Sampson, 1982; Gamble et al., 1993).

These brief sketches of schooling in India, Japan, and Great Britain show the crucial importance of economic development. In poor countries, many children—especially girls—are more likely to work than to go to school. Rich nations adopt mandatory education laws both to forge an industrial workforce and to satisfy demands for political democracy. But rich nations vary among themselves, as we see in the intense competition of Japanese schools, the traditional social stratification that shapes schools in Great Britain, and the practical emphasis found in the schools of Canada.

SCHOOLING IN CANADA

Initial developments in education in what would later become Canada took place in the early French settlements, where the three Rs (in this case, reading, 'riting, and religion) were taught in church-controlled schools (Johnson, 1968). By 1636, the Jesuits had established a

"college" that eventually became Laval University, which claims to be North America's oldest institution of higher education. By 1668, a trade or vocational school had been established in St. Joachim. In the Maritimes, an Anglican academy established in 1785 became the University of New Brunswick in 1859. The earliest primary schools in Upper Canada, which were established in the 1780s, began receiving government funding in 1792. Elitist boarding schools started in 1807 were the first step in establishing our secondary school system.

Prior to Confederation (1867), governments in Canada had already created separate Catholic and Protestant school systems, embraced universal education and teacher training, and put texts and curricula under control of a department of education. In 1883, Toronto became the second North American city to establish kindergarten within the school system, and by about 1920 Canada had compulsory education to the end of elementary school or the age of sixteen in most provinces. (In the United States, all states had compulsory education by 1918.) In this period, secondary schools were being established and expanded across Canada. The principle of mass education had been firmly entrenched, partly in response to the re-

 Half a century of controversy over the role of religion in Canadian public schools is surveyed at http://archives. cbc.ca/300c.asp?id=1-69-97

quirements of the Industrial Revolution for a literate and skilled workforce.

It is important to note that *official* literacy and *functional* literacy are not the same. Although Canada claims to have minimal illiteracy by international standards, educators and others have long voiced concerns about the extent to which Canadians have the literacy and numeracy skills required to cope with daily living and work—to say nothing of academic pursuits. A 1989 survey carried out by the National Literacy Secretariat concluded that 15 percent of Canada's adult population is not sufficiently literate to deal with normal, everyday situations. More alarming still is the fact that the Economic Council of Canada estimated in 1992 that 28 percent of Canadians aged sixteen to twenty-four could not read a simple newspaper article and that 44 percent were not functionally numerate (*Toronto Star*, August 1, 1992:A1).

A more recent International Adult Literacy Survey, released by Statistics Canada in September 2003, suggests higher levels of functional literacy—perhaps because of the nature of the questions asked. In response, 92 percent report that they never need help reading newspaper articles or instructions on medicine bottles. On the other hand, 88 percent report that their reading skills never limit job opportunities (12 percent feel that they do). Among Canadian adults, 43 percent get information about current events from newspapers, yet 58 percent read the editorial pages. In response to questions relating to numeracy (mathematical skill), 35 percent report that they use mathematics as part of their main jobs every day (Statistics Canada, 2003d).

Further analysis, based on the 1994 International Adult Literacy Survey, looked at francophone/anglophone and provincial variation in literacy scores. Francophones were found to lag behind anglophones in all three measures of literacy—prose, document, and quantitative scales. A comparison of Canada and the provinces reveals that 20 to 22 percent of Canadians function at the highest literacy levels (levels 4–5) on the three scales. This is true for 8 to 13 percent of Quebecers, 23 to 26 percent of Ontarians, and 25 to 35 percent of those in the western provinces (Corbeil, 2000b). Thus, literacy is lowest in Quebec and highest in the western provinces. Levels of educational attainment have increased steadily over the last fifty years, so that over time larger percentages of the adult population have some post-secondary education or university degrees. Between 1961 and 1986, the proportion of Canadians twenty-five to forty-four years of age with some post-secondary education increased from 8 to about 55 percent; between 1971 and 1986—a mere fifteen years—the proportion with a university degree rose from 7 to 15 percent (Secretary of State, 1992:25–27). Clearly, Canadians are becoming aware of the educational requirements of the modern economy.[1]

The percentage of the population age fifteen and over with university degrees rose from 6.4 percent in 1976 to 9.6 and 13.3 percent in 1986 and 1996 respectively. By 2001, 15.4 percent of the population (15 years of age and over) had university degrees. In other words, over a twenty-five-year period, the proportion of people over fifteen with university degrees increased by 141 percent. This doubling parallels the change in educational attainment among those twenty-five to forty-four years of age.

In Canada, the school reformers of the late 1800s were concerned that the "classical curriculum did not reflect the realities of the new economic order. Education, thus, began to be viewed as an essential precondition for national economic growth" (Gilbert, 1989:105). Wide participation and universality were important goals. Canada also has a policy of universal, publicly supported primary and secondary schooling, including that in the "separate," or Catholic, system. Canada has 273 publicly funded post-secondary institutions, sixty-nine of which are classified as universities; tuition fees at our universities cover up to 30

---

[1]The impact of education on unemployment rates is quite apparent. "In March, 1991, the rate of unemployment among those 25 years of age and older with a university degree was only 4.2 percent, compared to 18 percent for those without secondary schooling" (Secretary of State, 1992:27).

GLOBAL SNAPSHOT

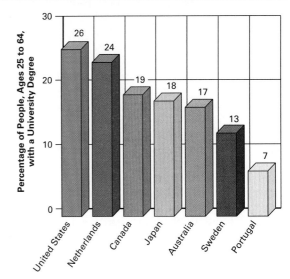

FIGURE 20–1 University Degrees in Global Perspective

Source: U.S. Census Bureau (2000).

percent of the costs, while government subsidies and fundraising account for the rest.

Canada ranks second to the United States and well above the average of fourteen other developed countries in the proportion of twenty- to twenty-four-year-olds enrolled in post-secondary education. We rank above the United States (and below only Sweden) in terms of public expenditures on education—8 percent of our gross national product (Secretary of State, 1992). However, Figure 20–1 indicates that Canada falls substantially behind both the United States and the Netherlands in terms of the proportion of population aged twenty-five to sixty-four with university degrees.

Besides trying to make schooling more widely accessible, Canadian society has long favoured *practical* learning, that is, education that has a direct bearing on people's lives, and especially on their occupations. The educational philosopher John Dewey (1859–1952) advanced the idea that children would readily learn information and skills they found useful. Rejecting the traditional emphasis on teaching a fixed body of knowledge to each generation of students, Dewey (1968; orig. 1938) endorsed progressive education that reflected people's changing concerns and needs. With the Quiet Revolution in Quebec in the 1960s, the classical education favoured by the religious elite was replaced by a system encouraging the study of business, engineering, and science.

Despite the overall trend towards applied or practical fields, Canada lags behind a number of other countries in terms of the proportion of its degrees awarded in engineering. In fact, in Canada the proportion of degrees granted in engineering—to men and women—is less than half that of Belgium, Portugal, Finland, Japan, Sweden, Germany, and Denmark (Oderkirk, 1993:10). The rapid pace of technological change in recent years shows up in a decline in the number of degrees granted in the social sciences, arts, and humanities, coupled with increases in the areas of engineering, mathematics, and science. From 1994 to 1998—a very short period of time—the proportion of degrees granted in engineering and applied sciences increased from 7.1 to 7.5 percent: women earned 18.4 and 21.1 percent of those degrees in the two years respectively. Similarly, the proportion of degrees granted in mathematics and physical sciences increased between 1994 and 1998 from 5.4 to 5.8 percent—with 29.9 and 31.2 percent being earned by women. Thus, there is a clear but gradual shift towards engineering, mathematics, and science, coupled with increased representation of women (Statistics Canada, **www.statcan.ca**).

 Statistics Canada's Canadian Statistics menu provides data on education at www.statcan.ca/ english/Pgdb/educat.htm

THE FUNCTIONS OF SCHOOLING

Structural-functional analysis looks at how formal education enhances the operation and stability of society. Central to the socialization process, schooling serves as one cultural lifeline linking the generations.

SOCIALIZATION

Technologically simple societies transmit their ways of life informally from parents to children. As societies become more technologically complex, young people need rapidly expanding information and new skills, beyond the grasp of family members themselves, so other social institutions play a greater role in socialization. In industrial societies, schooling requires specially trained personnel to convey the knowledge needed for adult roles.

In primary school, children learn basic language and mathematical skills. Secondary school builds on this foundation and, for many, college or university allows further specialization. In addition, schools transmit cultural values and norms. Sometimes the operation of the classroom itself serves to teach important cultural lessons. However, whereas in the United States spelling bees and classroom drills are intended to foster competitive individualism, in Canada there is more emphasis on activities that encourage cooperation, sharing, and team effort. Competitiveness is actually discouraged in many Canadian classrooms because

of potential damaging effects on the self-esteem of those who cannot compete successfully.

Nor is the political component of education as aggressively promoted in Canada as it is in other countries. For example, the American political system and way of doing business are commonly championed in the classroom, and rituals such as saluting the flag and singing "The Star-Spangled Banner" foster patriotism. Although our children do sing "O Canada," we place less emphasis on Canadian history or the workings of our political system than do the Americans—and a consciousness of military purpose or presence is almost completely lacking here. Instead of espousing a unified cultural identity, our classrooms try to encourage respect for the many cultures that make up the Canadian mosaic.

CULTURAL INNOVATION

Educational systems create as well as transmit culture. Schools attempt to stimulate intellectual inquiry and critical thinking, which lead to the development of new ideas. Today, for example, most university professors not only teach but engage in research to expand our knowledge in countless areas. Medical research, carried on mainly at major universities, has helped to increase life expectancy, just as research by sociologists and psychologists has expanded our understanding of human social life and contributed to an improved quality of life.

Marshall McLuhan foresaw the radical cultural transformation and innovation that would accompany incorporating the electronic media into education. Suddenly, there would be classrooms without walls: teaching, educational content, and links with the wider world would change irrevocably.

SOCIAL INTEGRATION

Schooling helps to forge a mass of people into a unified society. This integrative function is especially important in nations characterized by great social diversity, where various cultures know little about—or may even be hostile to—one another. In the past, the Soviet Union and Yugoslavia relied on schools in the attempt to unite their disparate peoples.

As we saw in Chapter 3 ("Culture"), Canada has had a long experience with the challenges of multiculturalism and linguistic dualism and has tried (not always successfully) to foster Canadian nationalism while accommodating a wide variety of interest groups. As a result, our educational policies have been sensitive to the problems of maintaining equality of access and unity in the face of diversity. We have been reluctant to push a national identity because of Quebec's sensitivities and our embrace of the mosaic model (Jaenen, 1981).

One of the latent functions of schooling is to care for children. With a majority of both women and men in the labour force, after-school programs that provide additional hours of supervised activities have become more common across Canada and the United States.

Societies in the Americas, Africa, and Asia similarly strive to foster social integration through schooling. Normally, schools try to meet this challenge by establishing a common language to encourage broad communication and to forge a national identity. Of course, some ethnic minorities resist state-sponsored schooling precisely for this reason. In the former Soviet Union, for example, Lithuanians, Ukrainians, and Azerbaijanis objected to learning Russian because they saw it as emblematic of their domination by outsiders and a threat to their own traditions. For similar reasons, the Hutterites, a culturally distinctive people in our Prairie provinces (mainly in Alberta), teach their children in schools within their own colonies (albeit using the provincial curriculum, and speaking in English for part of the day) and continue to speak a German dialect within their communities. Of course, the Québécois perceive a threat to their distinct culture, resent the need to learn English for economic survival, and insist on full provincial control of education—a recent demand being for control of labour-force training. Quebec has declared itself a unilingual province and only under special circumstances can a child be educated in English there. Native peoples in Canada have been struggling as well to establish greater control of their own schools. In each of the above cases, the peoples in question resist formal schooling in the language of the majority because of very real threats to linguistic and cultural survival.

Although there is understandable resistance to majority-controlled schooling by certain segments of the population, the striking cultural diversity of our country increases the importance of formal education as a path to social integration. The expansion of educational facilities and the enactment of mandatory education laws coincided with the arrival of hundreds of thousands of immigrants from a wide variety of origins who somehow had to be transformed into Canadians. Even today, formal education plays a major role in integrating disparate groups, as immigrants from Asia (roughly 50 percent of recent immigrants), the Caribbean, Eastern Europe, and Latin America—and roughly 30 000 refugees a year—blend their traditions with the existing cultural mix. Although our school systems seek to provide all of them with the linguistic and other skills needed for employment and daily life, Canada has not insisted that they give up their various identities completely.

The retention of other identities is assisted, where there are concentrations of people with shared backgrounds, through our heritage language programs, which provide formal education in traditional languages for ethnic minority children (where numbers warrant it). These programs sometimes attract other students, so that somewhere in Canada, young people of British or Ukrainian ancestry are studying Japanese or Italian. Furthermore, since our country is officially bilingual and since bilingualism is needed for certain types of jobs (that of prime minister or civil servant, for example), the Trudeau government provided funding for French immersion schooling throughout the country. About 3.5 percent of Canada's primary and secondary school students are enrolled in second language—or French—immersion programs. Across the provinces and territories, immersion enrolments vary from 1.6 and 1.8 percent in Nova Scotia and the Northwest Territories to 6.3 and 6.6 percent in New Brunswick and Prince Edward Island (calculations based on Statistics Canada, Canadian Statistics, Education, **www.statcan.ca/english/Pgdb/educ23a.htm**).

From a functionalist point of view, schooling provides children with the knowledge and skills they will need as adults. A conflict analysis adds that schooling differs according to the resources of the local community. When some schools offer children much more than others do, education perpetuates the class structure rather than increasing equality of opportunity.

SOCIAL PLACEMENT

Formal education helps young people assume culturally approved statuses and perform roles that contribute to the ongoing life of society. Ideally, schools accomplish this by identifying and developing each individual's aptitudes and abilities and then evaluating a student's performance in terms of achievement rather than social background.

In principle, teachers encourage the "best and the brightest" to pursue the most challenging and advanced studies, while others are guided into educational programs and occupations suited to their talents. Schooling, in short, enhances meritocracy by making personal merit a foundation of future social position (Hurn, 1978).

Meritocracy has always had special significance to people who begin life with social disadvantages based on ascribed traits such as sex, race, ethnicity, and social class. For this reason, schooling has historically been the major avenue of upward social mobility in Canada.

LATENT FUNCTIONS OF SCHOOLING

Besides these manifest functions of formal education, there are a number of latent functions. One is child care. As the number of one-parent families and two-career couples rises, schools have become vital to relieving parents of some child-care duties.

For teenagers, schooling consumes considerable time and energy, in many cases fostering conformity at a time of life when the likelihood of unlawful behaviour is high. Since many students attend school well into their twenties, education engages thousands of young people for whom jobs may not be available.

Another latent function of schools is to establish social relationships and networks. Many people form lifelong friendships—as well as meet their future spouses—in high school, college, and university. Affiliation with a particular school also can create valuable career opportunities.

Critical evaluation. Structural-functional analysis of formal education identifies both manifest and latent functions of schooling. One key limitation of structural functionalism is that it overlooks how the quality of schooling is far better for some than for others. In the next section, social-conflict analysis places the spotlight on this issue.

SCHOOLING AND SOCIAL INEQUALITY

Social-conflict analysis counters the functionalist view that schooling is a meritocratic strategy for developing people's talents and abilities. Rather, this approach argues that schools routinely provide learning according to students' social background, thereby perpetuating social inequality.

Throughout the world, people traditionally have thought that schooling is more important for males than for females. The education gap between women and men has been closing in recent decades, but many women still study conventionally "feminine" subjects such as literature, while men pursue mathematics and engineering. By stressing the experiences of certain types of people (say, scientists) while ignoring the lives of others (such as farm women), schools reinforce the values and importance of dominant racial, cultural,

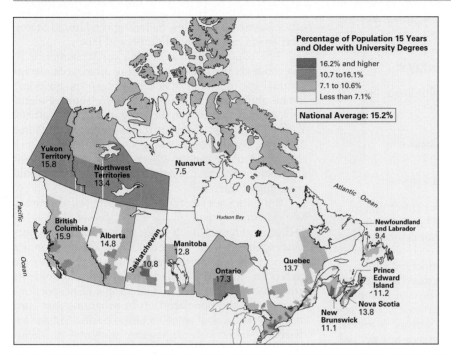

**CANADA MAP 20–1
Population 15 Years or Older with University Degree (Percentages by Province, Territory, and Census Subdivision) 2001**

Source: Calculations by Gerber based on Statistics Canada, B2020 files (accessed October 2003).

and gender categories, to the detriment of minorities. Efforts have been made across Canada to provide gender-neutral texts and library materials and to remove materials that perpetuate negative stereotypes or are offensive to various ethnic, racial, and religious minorities. Schools are also attempting to incorporate multicultural programs and materials into their curricula to increase tolerance and understanding among youngsters of different backgrounds. The intent, in part, is to eradicate stereotypes and to raise the aspiration levels of any people who may have felt themselves to be excluded by the system. Women and francophones are among those who now are spending more time in school and proceeding to university or college (Guppy and Arai, 1993).

It is also the case that affluence affects the extent to which Canadians take advantage of educational opportunities. Along with gender, social class is a strong predictor of aspirations to attend university (Porter et al., 1982): in fact, one is much more likely to attend university or college if one's parents are white-collar with post-secondary education (Guppy and Arai, 1993; Corak, 2000; de Broucker and Lavallée, 2000).

Social class background is also an important determinant of familiarity with computers, which is increasingly vital to education and employment. Home computer ownership rises (from below 30 percent) to well over 60 percent in the homes of those who are university educated, who have incomes of $70 000 or more, and who are professionals (Forcese, 1997:124). Children from these families have an advantage as they progress through the educational system.

Regional variations in affluence and economic structure give rise to marked differences in educational attainment across the country. Canada Map 20–1 indicates the proportions of provincial and territorial populations, fifteen years or older, that have acquired a university degree. The levels range from 7.5 percent in Nunavut to 17.3 percent in Ontario. The Yukon and British Columbia are also above average in educational attainment. Note that the Yukon attracts much of its university-educated population from elsewhere to take jobs in government, natural resources, defence, and research.

SOCIAL CONTROL

Social-conflict analysis asserts that schooling acts as a means of social control, reinforcing acceptance of the status quo. In various, often subtle ways, schools reproduce the status hierarchy, although this process is not always evident to students or even to teachers.

Samuel Bowles and Herbert Gintis (1976) point out that public education grew exponentially in the late nineteenth century when capitalists were seeking a docile, disciplined, and literate workforce. Mandatory education laws ensured that schools would teach immigrants the English language[2] as well as cultural values that support capitalism. Compliance, punctuality, and discipline were—and still are—part of what is called the **hidden curriculum**, *subtle presentations of political or cultural ideas in the classroom.*

TESTING AND SOCIAL INEQUALITY

Here is a question of the kind traditionally used to measure the intelligence and academic ability of school-age children.

Painter is to painting as _____ is to sonnet.

Answers:
(a) driver   (b) poet   (c) priest   (d) carpenter

The correct answer is (b) *poet*: a painter creates a painting as a poet creates a sonnet. This question purports to measure logical reasoning, but demonstrating this skill depends on knowing what each term means. Unless students are familiar with sonnets as a form of written verse, they are unlikely to answer the question correctly. An upper-middle-class student of European descent is likely to have more of the experiences rewarded by such tests. The same person, however, might not score as well on an intelligence test devised by the Ojibwa or the Inuit. Controversy surrounds the use of such tests, for they reflect our society's dominant culture, thereby placing the members of various minorities at a disadvantage. Children from less affluent backgrounds are also at a disadvantage because they face "tests of intelligence and cognitive skills weighted in favour of middle- and upper-class children" (Porter et al., 1982:9). The motivations and attitudes transmitted to children by middle- and upper-class parents also benefit certain students on these tests in the classroom.

Educational specialists claim that bias of this kind has been all but eliminated from standardized tests, since testing organizations carefully study response patterns and drop any question that favours one racial category over another. Critics, however, maintain that some bias based on class, race, or ethnicity is inherent in any formal testing, because questions inevitably reflect our society's dominant culture and thereby put minorities at a disadvantage (Owen, 1985; Crouse and Trusheim, 1988; Putka, 1990).

One of the uses of such tests has been to place students in either a general or an academic (university-bound) stream, another controversial practice that is discussed below.

---

[2]Until Quebec passed Bill 101 in 1977, making French the sole official language in Quebec as well as the language of business, francophones had to be fluently bilingual to succeed economically. Even in Quebec, English was the language of business.

STREAMING AND SOCIAL INEQUALITY

Many Canadian schools practise **streaming**, *the assigning of students to different types of educational programs.* Streaming is also a common practice in many other industrial societies, including the United States, Germany, Great Britain, France, and Japan.

The educational justification for streaming is to give students the kind of schooling appropriate to individual aptitude. For a variety of reasons, including innate ability and level of motivation, some students are capable of more challenging work than others. Young people also differ in their interests, with some drawn to, say, the study of languages, while others seek training in art or science. Given this diversity of talent and focus, no single program for all students would serve any of them well.

But critics see streaming as a thinly veiled strategy to perpetuate privilege. Research shows that social background has as much to do with streaming as personal aptitude does. Students from affluent families generally do well in school and on tests and so are placed in university-bound streams, while students from modest backgrounds (including a disproportionate share of the poor) end up in programs that curb their aspirations and teach technical trades. Streaming, therefore, effectively segregates students—academically and socially—into different worlds.

Furthermore, most schools reserve their best teachers for students in the top streams. These teachers put more effort into teaching, show more respect to students, and expect more from them. In contrast, teachers in lower streams employ more memorization, classroom drill, and other unstimulating techniques. They also emphasize regimentation, punctuality, and respect for authority figures.

In light of these criticisms, many schools are now cautious about streaming. Recent initiatives in Ontario aimed at destreaming were met with opposition from school boards and teachers as well as from parents, who are concerned that their university-bound children will receive lower-quality education in destreamed classrooms.

Without streaming, less academically inclined children may be unable to compete with their classmates, and teachers face the difficult task of teaching students of differing abilities in one class; but these problems are not insurmountable. Rigid streaming, on the other hand, has a powerful impact on student learning and self-concept. Young people in higher streams tend to see themselves as bright and able, whereas those in lower streams end up with less ambition and lower self-esteem (Bowles and Gintis, 1976; Persell, 1977; Oakes, 1982, 1985).

UNEQUAL ACCESS TO HIGHER EDUCATION

In industrial societies, higher education is the main path to occupational achievement. Not surprisingly,

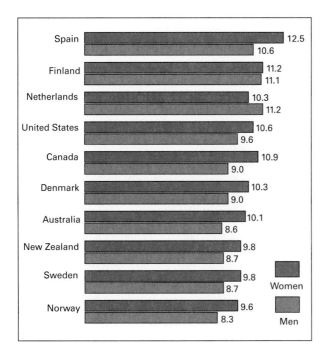

FIGURE 20–2 Ten OECD Countries with the
Highest Percentage of Young
Adults* Enrolled in University, 1995

*Percentage of persons 17 to 34 years of age enrolled at the university level.
The rank order of countries is based on combined male and female figures.

Source: Based on OECD database, Table C5.2a, www.oecd.org/els/stats/
eag97/C5.xls.

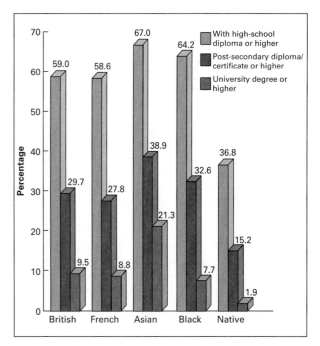

FIGURE 20–3 Educational Attainment for
Selected Categories,* 1991

*Percentages based on populations 15 years of age or older.

Source: Compiled by Gerber from 1991 Census, Individual Public Use
Microdata.

79 percent of Canadians view education as "extremely important to one's future success" (Flower, 1984:27). Despite the decline in the proportion of the population that is eighteen to twenty-four years of age, enrolment in post-secondary education has risen dramatically throughout the postwar period and in recent decades. Between 1988 and 1994, while Canada's population grew by 8.8 percent, full-time post-secondary enrolment grew by 18.1 percent (Statistics Canada, 1996). Figure 20–2 reveals that in 1995 Canada ranked fifth among Organization for Economic Cooperation and Development (OECD) countries in university enrolment of those age seventeen to thirty-four—and ranked third in the enrolment of women. Note that the enrolment of women is ahead of that of men in all but one of these countries.

There are many reasons why most people in Canada do not attend and graduate from university or college. Some high-school students want to enter the labour force right away; others cannot afford to continue their education because of the costs of tuition and deferred income. Vast distances between homes and the nearest university are also major deterrents. In addition, the intellectual demands of the curriculum may dissuade some students with limited talents. Yet most of our young people would like to attend univer-

sity or college, and doing so is certainly within the academic ability of the vast majority.

In one respect at least, we have moved closer to the goal of equal access to higher education in Canada: as noted earlier, women are now more likely than men to attend university. Low or moderate family income, however, remains a formidable barrier to enrolment: young people with lower family incomes or fathers in blue-collar occupations are much less likely to go to university (Wotherspoon, 1991; Corak, 2000). Most universities provide financial assistance to students in the form of bursaries and scholarships, and governments make loans available to those of limited means. Nevertheless, many people cannot afford the remaining costs. The problem has been accentuated in recent years as cutbacks in government funding have forced tuition increases.

Figure 20–3 shows that overall in 1991 the Asian and Black communities in Canada actually had *higher* levels of educational attainment than either the British or the French. However, it is important to note that the arrival of relatively well-educated immigrants in the Asian and Black categories may mean that the high levels of educational achievement are not necessarily characteristic of members of those minorities who are born or schooled in Canada. The figures for the Native

 Go to http://archives.cbc.ca//
300c.asp?id=1-70-692 for a
CBC multimedia presentation
on Canada's residential schools.

"An Education of Oppression": Canada's Indian Residential Schools

Around the turn of the last century, Canada's federal government busily established residential schools for Indian children, run by Christian missionaries and their churches. The intent was to "civilize" and assimilate Native children by stamping out Aboriginal language and culture and replacing them with facility in English or French, rudimentary reading and arithmetic, and agricultural and domestic skills.

Only in the last two decades have we become aware of the damaging consequences of the residential school experience. Removed from their communities and families, Native children were ill prepared for life in the mainstream or for a return to their own communities. Inadequate and, in effect, damaging educational practices were accompanied in many of these schools by verbal, physical, and sexual abuse. By the time the residential schools were phased out in the early 1960s, several generations of Native youngsters had paid a very heavy price.

Vicki English-Currie is one of many Native people to describe her experience in a residential school—in this case, the Roman Catholic Indian Residential School at Brocket, Alberta—to which she was taken at the tender age of seven. Here the missionaries assumed total responsibility for—and total control over—the lives of Indian children.

Because of the different approaches to child rearing and education between the residential school and the community from which she had come, English-Currie experienced the transition as one of total shock, enormous setback, and "the beginning of a lifetime of cultural tragedy." In this setting, her formal education was overshadowed by accumulating "stress, anger, fear and hostility."

Here, English-Currie describes the residential school experience in her own words:

I remember so well the first day of school in September of 1954. I was so excited and eager to get to school, because it meant reading, writing, games, children, and those Grey nuns who I thought were gods. I had wanted to become a nun so I would never sin and go to hell forever. My mother brought me to the door and left. A nun took me to a room and pushed me inside with my bag and closed the door. This was one of the very first times I experienced violence. There was a lot more physical violence later at school, but this was one instance I was never able to forget....

This was the beginning of an education of oppression and the end to family life. We did not realize at that time the oppression and a limited education was an effective way of controlling the Indian people. . . . They

were kept undereducated, in poverty, and dependent upon the false charity of the Indian agent and the mission schools. . . .

What was taught very well in residential school was how to feel guilty and to be grateful to the religious orders for "all they were doing" for us and our people. . . .

The reason for these schools was not the betterment of the Indian child or to give that child an opportunity to excel in a formal educational setting. It was a way for the government to control the Indian people, using a religious order where the church was the instrument of the state. . . .

All of the people in the pictures in our textbooks were white and middle-class; nurses, doctors, dentists, lawyers, and nuns were depicted, creating the impression that those were the only worthwhile persons in life. Native traditional leaders were never used. As a result the students' self-esteem, self-determination, self-worth, pride, and confidence slowly dwindled into a desire to be white. Indian culture taught us to have and to show respect for anyone in an authoritarian position. Indian people were not allowed by law to leave the reserve to attend higher educational institutions unless one joined a religious ministry. What possible point was there to use all these professional white, middle-class

population suggest that we have failed, in a major way, to remove barriers to educational achievement by our first peoples.

Higher education, whether from university or college, expands career opportunities and increases earnings. Figure 20–4 (on page 508) shows that employment among 25- to 44-year-olds increases with educational attainment. This is especially true for

women. Labour-force participation for the population aged 15 and over (not shown) reveals even more dramatic increases. Once again, women experience the greater effect, with labour-force participation increasing fourfold from the lowest to the highest levels of education.

Table 20-1 (on page 509) deals with the average earnings of people aged 15 and older by educational role models with the children during those primary years of schooling if they were to be denied by law ever achieving any of the roles of their models.

We were told outright that not only all Indian religion was heathen and should not be practiced but also that Indian culture and language were savagery. This further oppressed Native people and created a false belief that our culture, language, and religion were degrading and insignificant. (English-Currie, 1993:114–16)

English-Currie goes on to say that Native students were thought to be cognitively deficient and that psychological testing was used to legitimate their treatment. Not surprisingly, then, the core subjects of math, reading, and writing were not the major focus of their education. When the government closed the residential schools in the early 1960s, Native youngsters were unprepared to cope with the integrated provincial schools to which they were sent. Finding themselves two or three grades behind their peers, Native youth were degraded and dehumanized, and thus became inclined to drop out.

The youngsters who were educated in "Indian" residential schools suffered the long-term consequences of being separated from their families and communities and of being wrenched from familiar cultural surroundings and thrust into an alien world where they felt they were unwelcome. These same youngsters, raised outside normal families, were the ones who soon faced parenthood, for which they were ill prepared.

Although 60 percent of on-reserve First Nations children now attend band-operated schools, transition to high school, usually to integrated provincial schools, is still painful. As a result, the majority of Aboriginal youth do not finish high school. The Royal Commission on Aboriginal Peoples points out that these youngsters "leave the school system without the requisite skills for employment [and] without the language and cultural knowledge of their people" (cited in Schissel and Wotherspoon, 2003:59). As a result, they return home to their reserves and find that they do not fit in.

In their recent survey of Aboriginal school children, Schissel and Wotherspoon (2003) found that, while 40 percent of primary-school children are bilingual, the level drops off to 17 percent of high-school students. On the positive side, some 80 to 90 percent of students have had exposure to Aboriginal teachers, and over 90 percent report that they like school (p. 79). Nonetheless, when high-school students are asked about barriers to learning, they mention poverty, housing problems, and violence—but racism tops the list, with over 35 percent of students identifying it as an impediment to learning (p. 82). The authors note that, although both elementary and high-school students express an overwhelming desire to attend university, their aspirations do not translate into reality. All schools—and particularly isolated rural and northern schools—need to help students understand the nature of post-secondary education, the availability of funding and the reality of rural-urban transition (p. 147).

Aboriginal young people have made tremendous advances in recent years, with increasing numbers attending and graduating from universities and other post-secondary institutions. But the legacy of residential schools and high schools that are insensitive to their cultural needs continues to take its toll.

Source: Based on English-Currie (1993), abridged from Jeanne Perreault and Sylvia Vance, eds., *Writing the Circle* (Edmonton: NeWest Press, 1990).

attainment. In Canada and each of the provinces and territories, average incomes rise steadily with higher levels of education (except for the trades certificate/college certificate levels) so that incomes at least double from the lowest to highest educational categories. Across the country, the largest increases show up among those who have earned university certificates, diplomas, or degrees. Among the provinces, university graduates have the highest average earnings in Ontario and Alberta. However, the highest incomes for this category are to be found in the Northwest Territories and Nunavut ($57 000 and $59 000). This is to be expected, since university graduates working in the territories are normally highly paid professionals who often receive isolation pay when they move to the North to work in mining, exploration, and defence.

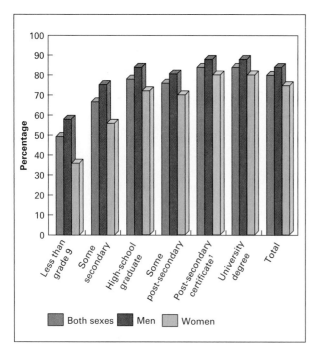

FIGURE 20–4 Employment of 25- to 44-Year-Olds by Educational Attainment and Sex, 2001

¹Post-secondary certificate or diploma includes trades certificates.

Sources: Adapted from Statistics Canada, Catalogue No. 89F0133XIE.

Obtaining a university degree, as opposed to a college diploma, also decreases the likelihood of unemployment two years after graduation; as one progresses from bachelor's through master's and doctoral degrees, the likelihood of being unemployed is further reduced (Secretary of State, 1992:40).

Certainly, many people find schooling to be its own reward, but the income figures shown here indicate that schooling is also a sound investment in financial terms, increasing income by hundreds of thousands of dollars over a person's working life. Bear in mind, of course, that the higher earnings of more educated people may stem from more than schooling. As we have seen, university graduates are likely to come from relatively well-to-do families and to enjoy social and economic advantages—including "old boy" networks, knowledge of how the system works, and a strong desire to achieve.

CREDENTIALISM

Sociologist Randall Collins (1979) calls ours a *credential society* because people view diplomas and degrees as evidence of ability to perform specialized occupational roles. In modern, technologically complex and socially mobile societies, credentials tell "who you are" as much as family background does.

Credentialism, then, is *evaluating a person on the basis of educational degrees*. Structural-functional analysis suggests that credentialism is simply the way our technologically complex society goes about filling jobs with well-trained people. In contrast, social-conflict analysis holds that credentials often bear little relation to the skills and responsibilities of a specific job. Collins argues that degrees serve as a shorthand way to sort out the people with the manners, attitudes, and even skin colour desired by many employers. Credentials, in short, work as a gatekeeping strategy that restricts important occupations to a small segment of the population.

PRIVILEGE AND PERSONAL MERIT

If, as social-conflict analysis suggests, attending university is a rite of passage for affluent men and women, then *schooling transforms social privilege into personal merit*. But given the North American cultural emphasis on individual achievement, we tend to see credentials as "badges of ability," as Sennett and Cobb (1973) put it, rather than as symbols of family affluence. When we congratulate the typical new graduate, we often overlook the social resources that made this achievement possible. In the same way, we are quick to condemn the high-school dropout as personally deficient, with little thought for the social circumstances that surround that person's life (see the "Applying Sociology" box).

Critical evaluation. Social-conflict analysis links formal education and social inequality, and shows how schooling transforms privilege into personal worthiness, and social disadvantage into personal deficiency. However, critics claim that social-conflict analysis minimizes the extent to which schooling provides upward social mobility for talented men and women—especially those from modest backgrounds. Further, despite the claims of many conflict theorists that schooling supports the status quo, "politically correct" educational curricula are challenging patterns of social inequality on many fronts.

PROBLEMS IN THE SCHOOLS

Although Canadians have long debated the quality of education, the debate has intensified over the past decades.

SCHOOL DISCIPLINE

Canadians and Americans alike believe that schools should inculcate personal discipline and that the job is not being done properly. The U.S. government estimates that several hundred thousand students and at least one thousand teachers are physically assaulted on

	Canada	NL	PE	NS	NB	QC	ON	MB	SK	AB	BC	YK	NT	NU
$														
All levels	31 757	24 165	22 303	26 632	24 971	29 385	35 185	27 178	25 691	32 603	31 544	31 526	36 645	28 215
Less than high-school graduation certificate	21 230	15 922	15 058	18 251	17 074	20 553	22 691	19 201	18 288	22 196	21 971	19 265	20 428	14 772
High-school graduation certificate and/or some post-secondary	25 477	16 860	18 236	20 553	20 395	24 071	27 606	22 921	21 780	25 789	25 671	25 753	31 603	26 722
Trades certificate or diploma	32 743	26 118	24 090	27 595	27 694	27 535	36 843	29 357	28 755	37 443	34 196	33 352	42 712	32 454
College certificate or diploma	32 736	28 196	25 613	26 930	27 178	28 742	36 309	29 351	27 742	33 572	33 159	33 817	42 245	39 113
University certificate, diploma, or degree	48 648	41 942	37 063	41 146	40 375	45 834	53 525	41 856	40 279	50 069	44 066	45 982	56 892	58 992

*These figures refer to earned income or employment income.

Source: Statistics Canada, Census 2001, Highlight Tables, www.statcan.ca.

school grounds every year. This violence at school is blamed on poverty-stricken urban environments that breed drug use as well as violence on the street and at home. All too often, violence in U.S. communities and schools involves the use of guns.

Canada's school discipline problems are not of the same type or magnitude, but there have been many instances of assault on students and teachers; students have been found at school with knives—most often in specific violence-prone schools—but very rarely with guns. At the post-secondary level, the 1989 killing of fourteen female engineering students—by Marc Lepine at Montreal's l'Ecole Polytechnique—shocked Canadians across the country, driving home the realization that, even within our schools, we are not immune to deadly violence.

For the results of a survey of school-based violence-prevention programs in Canada, see www.sgc.gc.ca/publications/corrections/199502_e.asp

More commonly, however, the discipline problems in our schools involve students who display disdain for learning, are rude to their teachers or challenge their authority, skip classes, disrupt the classroom, or otherwise interfere with the formal education of themselves and others. "When I was young," parents will say, "we did what the teacher told us." Selective memory notwithstanding, there undoubtedly has been a gradual decline in classroom discipline over the past few decades related to larger societal trends. In teachers' college, discussion of educational theory and the finer points of pedagogy do nothing to prepare would-be teachers for their first field placements, where the most pressing question is how to maintain *control* in

Educators have long debated the proper manner in which to educate children with disabilities. On the one hand, such children may benefit from distinctive facilities and specially trained teachers. On the other hand, they are less likely to be stigmatized as "different" if included in regular classroom settings. What do you consider to be the ramifications of the "special education" versus "inclusive education" debate for the classroom experience of all children, not only those who have disabilities?

the classroom. Teachers, who are trained to teach but find that their energies are diverted into policing students, experience frustration and disillusionment on the job.

Explaining Educational Attainment

Volume 3 of *Canadian Social Trends* (2000) contains several articles dealing with various factors that affect educational attainment, including family structure, parental education/occupation, and Aboriginal status.

Over several decades, Canada has witnessed a marked increase in the number of children raised in lone-parent families. The number of children raised in blended or step-parent families has also increased. Frederick and Boyd (2000) used data from the 1994 General Social Survey to look at the impact of family structure on high-school completion. They found that adults (aged twenty-two to forty-four) who had lived with both biological parents at age fifteen were more likely to have completed high school than those from lone-parent or blended/step-parent families—the rates of completion were 80, 71, and 70 percent respectively.

Looking at the interaction of parental education and family structure, Frederick and Boyd found that 94 percent of those who grew up with two biological parents who had completed high school graduated from secondary school themselves. Where parents had not completed high school, graduation rates dropped off dramatically—to 71 and 59 percent respectively for those

who had lived with both biological parents or a lone parent at age fifteen. Clearly, parental education and family structure both have significant effects.

Using Canadian data from the 1994 International Adult Literacy Survey, de Broucker and Lavallée (2000) assessed the role of "inherited intellectual capital" in the acquisition of post-secondary education. Most adults aged twenty-six to thirty-five have at least as much education as their parents. Not surprisingly, young adults whose parents had post-secondary education were more likely to earn post-secondary diplomas or degrees.

Fathers' occupations also have an effect: fathers with high-status occupations have children with higher educational attainment. The literacy survey suggests that one way of passing on intellectual capital is to provide books and the example of reading to one's children: parents with university degrees (regardless of income) are much more likely to have the habit of reading to their children, contributing to an environment that is conducive to learning.

The importance of education to the employment prospects of Aboriginal people is clear. Tait (2000) notes that in 1996, the unemployment rate for young Native adults without high school was 40 percent; for those with a

university degree, it was 9 percent. Fortunately, there has been considerable improvement in Aboriginal educational achievement over the past decade: the proportions of college and university grads have doubled. By 1996, only 45 percent of young Aboriginal adults had failed to complete high school (compared to 60 percent in 1986); college completion had risen from 15 to 20 percent; and the earning of university degrees increased from 2 to 4 percent. The Métis and Natives living in Canada's largest cities lead the way with respect to educational attainment; reserve-based status Indians trail behind, in part because educational and employment opportunities are severely limited on most reserves.

Tait is optimistic that improved education and employment prospects will lead to further increases in educational achievement. Applying the lessons of the Boyd and the de Broucker and Lavallée articles reported above, one would expect that this improvement will increase the transmission of intellectual capital to future generations, further increasing levels of educational attainment in the Aboriginal population.

DROPPING OUT

If many students are disruptive in class, others are not there at all. The problem of dropping out—quitting school before completing a high-school diploma—leaves young people (many of whom are disadvantaged to begin with) ill-equipped for the world of work and at high risk for poverty.

Numerous Canadian officials, business representatives, and educators have been very concerned about Canada's dropout rate, which seemed to be exceptionally high when compared to those of other countries. In 1970 and 1990, the U.S. rates were 12.2 and 10.7 percent, respectively, indicating a slight decline. Measured

differently,[3] the Canadian rates were 48 and 32 percent in 1970–71 and 1990–91, respectively.

A refined measure suggests that a more realistic dropout rate for Canada in 1991 was 18 percent, with considerable regional variation (see Table 20–2). Many who appear to be dropouts are really only stop-outs,

---

[3]The U.S. rates are based on the proportion of the population between fourteen and twenty-four that left school without a high-school diploma (U.S. Bureau of the Census, 1991). The Statistics Canada figures reflect the number of students who did not enter and graduate from the same high school within four years (Fennell, 1993:49). Therefore, those who changed schools or who left and came back were counted as dropouts.

who leave and return at a later date to complete their secondary-school programs (Fennell, 1993:49). Detailed follow-up of such individuals by several school boards suggests that even the new numbers (in Table 20–2, column 3) are too high. Those numbers—based on Statistics Canada's *School Leavers Survey* (Gilbert et al., 1993)—are more reassuring than the earlier figures, but even at 18 percent or slightly less there is cause for concern.

In the report *Leaving School*, which compares school leavers and high-school graduates, Gilbert et al. (1993) note that leavers are more likely

1. to be from single-parent or no-parent households
2. to have parents with lower educational attainment
3. to be married and to have dependent children (especially the women)
4. to have lower grade averages
5. to have failed a grade in elementary school
6. to have worked more than twenty hours per week during their final school year
7. to use alcohol (regularly) and drugs

Aboriginal people have a very high dropout rate (40 percent), while immigrants have a low level (1 percent). In addition, it is noted that school leavers are currently more likely to be unemployed (34 percent) than are graduates (23 percent).

For young people who drop out of school in a credential-based society, the risks of unemployment or becoming stuck in a low-paying job are easy to imagine. Faced with this reality, many of those who leave school return to the classroom at a later time.

Initial findings from the *School Leavers Follow-up Survey* revealed that one in four students who had left high school as of 1991 had returned to school and earned a diploma by 1995. By then, 85 percent of the cohort—now twenty-two to twenty-four years of age—had graduated from high school. Another 14 percent, who had not returned to obtain a high-school diploma, might be considered the true school leavers. Across Canada, women aged twenty-two to twenty-four are more likely to be high-school graduates than are the men (89.4 and 81.2 percent respectively); graduation levels are highest in Ontario and lowest in Newfoundland. In addition, the follow-up survey revealed that unemployment was highest among those who had not graduated (Statistics Canada, *The Daily*, October 15, 1996).

VALUE FOR OUR MONEY

Canada spends more than 7 percent of its gross national product on education. In terms of per capita spending, this ranks us at the top of the G7 (Group of Seven) leading industrialized countries—and raises questions about the quality of the education we deliver for that

TABLE 20–2 Dropout Rate in Canada (Percentages)			
	1970–71	1990–1991	1991
Canada	48%	32%	18%
British Columbia	46	34	16
Alberta	40	35	14
Saskatchewan	32	24	16
Manitoba	45	27	19
Ontario	38	34	17
Quebec	54	28	22
New Brunswick	38	15	20
Nova Scotia	n/a	25	22
Prince Edward Island	43	24	25
Newfoundland	62	25	24

Sources: Based on Fennell (1993:49) and Gilbert et al. (1993).

money. Demographer David K. Foot, in a book fittingly entitled *Boom, Bust and Echo 2000* (1998), looks at the effects of the baby boom, the subsequent bust, and the smaller "echo boom" (the children of the boomers) on the economy, consumer habits, real estate, and the demand for social services, including education. Since schooling is compulsory to the age of sixteen in most Canadian provinces, we can predict primary and early secondary enrolments with considerable accuracy,[4] simply by keeping tabs on the numbers of babies born each year and watching them age. The baby boom, for example, caused peaks in elementary-school enrolment in the late 1950s and high-school enrolment in the early 1970s. The inflated cost of our educational system, Foot concludes, is the result of the failure to analyze demographic trends to predict demand at various levels and to adjust budgets, personnel, and policy accordingly.

Unfortunately, the inflated budgets left in the wake of the baby-boom cohort helped to raise our per capita spending above that of the other G7 countries without improving the skills of students. As noted (and refuted) below, Canadian students do not fare well in international tests of scholastic achievement.

ACADEMIC STANDARDS

Canada and the United States share a growing concern with the quality of schooling or, more pointedly, with the quality of publicly funded schooling. *A Nation at Risk*, a comprehensive report on the quality of U.S. schools prepared in 1983 by the National Commission on Excellence in Education, noted that "nearly 40 percent of seventeen-year-olds cannot draw inferences

---

[4]The internal migration of young families between districts and immigration, which expands the numbers of children in specific cities or regions, needs to be taken into account to make predictions in some parts of the country.

Welcome to Cyber-School

The wired planet has no boundaries and no monopolies of knowledge. The affairs of the world are now dependent upon the highest information of which man is capable. . . . The boundaries between the world of affairs and the community of learning have ceased to exist. The workaday world now demands encyclopedic wisdom. . . . Under these conditions, the old forms of specialized job has lost meaning. It was meaningful at very low speeds, but it has now been assumed into patterns of electric speeds. This change of pace from production-line to on-line computer programming has been ignored, just as the shift from hardware to software accelerates, making the old categories meaningless. (McLuhan and Nevitt, quoted in Benedetti and DeHart, 1996:172)

Education is responding to the arrival of computer-literate children and the demands of a drastically altered, knowledge-based economy by integrating computers and the Internet throughout the education system—from kindergarten to PhD. The goal at primary and secondary levels is to have computers in every classroom; universities and colleges are placing more emphasis on computer-based, interactive, self-directed learning in the context of global, electronic information flow. Much of the computer access is arranged for the classroom or on-campus labs, but students are also linking up to school or campus,

by modem, from home. (On some campuses in Canada, it is compulsory for each student to have a computer and modem at home; on almost all, students are given email addresses with their registration packages.) Expanded and more technologically sophisticated distance-learning options and even virtual universities are being developed.

At the John D. Bracco School in northeast Edmonton, a third of the student body "skips classes." The students in question are studying from home via the school's home page. "We've pushed the walls of the school into the community," says principal Ron Bradley, who heads up the online programs called LearnNet. The school walls now embrace students from all over Alberta and as far away as Sri Lanka and Holland. The program started in grades 7 to 9 at John D. Bracco (later in grades 10 to 12) and extended down to grade 2 at Kirkness School. The reasons for choosing LearnNet are varied, including the desire for home-schooling, a family move to a remote area, or a student's having attention deficit disorder. Internet-based learning has expanded the reach of John D. Bracco teachers into a geographically unbounded community (Gooderham, 1997).

Examples of computer-based learning and research abound. In Hamilton, Ontario, students of Scott Park High School have created YouthNet, an Internet-based student project, and YouthNet Mail, a homework hotline and a voting system for students to rank their favourite movies, CDs, and com-

puter games. A retired teacher in Summerland, B.C., created an Internet-based project called Global THINK; participants include about 1000 B.C. students along with others from as far away as Ontario and Alaska (Foss, 1997). SchoolNet is available in Ontario. The list is almost endless.

At the university level we see computer conferencing, online courses, multimedia distance education, and more complex virtual universities. Undergraduate and graduate students are relying increasingly on the Internet as a means of communication and a source of information. Statistics Canada data and publications increasingly are available only on the Internet or on CD-ROM: its *Daily*, among many other products, no longer appears on paper at all. Results of the 1997 and 2000 federal elections are available online. Academic journals in the sciences and social sciences are also becoming available online.

Most recently, purely electronic journals (several in the sociology area) have appeared. The researcher conducts computer analysis, writes a paper through word processing, submits the paper electronically, has it sent to reviewers via the Internet, and then sees it published in electronic form. Throughout this process, pen may never be set to paper. Access to information as well as the production and dissemination of knowledge have changed profoundly and irrevocably.

---

from written material; only one-fifth can write a persuasive essay; and only one-third can solve mathematical problems requiring several steps" (1983:9). Furthermore, scores on the Scholastic Aptitude Test (SAT) have declined steadily since the early 1960s. Some of the decline may stem from the increasing share of students taking the standardized test, not all

of whom are well prepared (Owen, 1985). But few observers of the North American scene doubt that schooling has suffered a setback.

A Nation at Risk noted with alarm the extent of **functional illiteracy**, *reading and writing skills insufficient for everyday living*. Roughly one in eight children in the United States completes secondary school with-

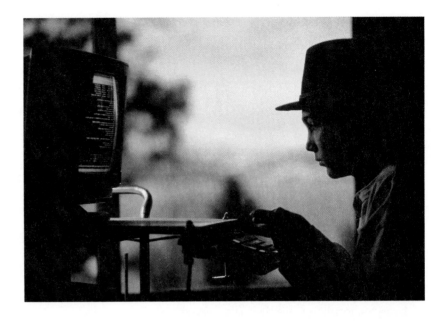

Currently, our society is debating many strategies for improving education. Some parents have kept their children out of formal education altogether, believing their youngsters can learn more at home, using information available not only in books, but also in cyberspace.

out learning to read or write very well; for young African-Americans, this applies to more than a third. As indicated in the "Diversity: Race, Class, and Gender" box, this concern has its Aboriginal parallel in Canada.

Canadians express concerns about the quality of our educational experience, in part because of observations about the skills (or lack thereof) of graduates, but also because of the lack of fit between these skills and the demands of the labour market (as indicated by unemployment levels). Concerns were heightened in 1992 when Canadian students appeared to do poorly in international mathematics tests involving a number of countries (including Japan). The media, special reports, and the business community were quick to criticize our public school system, thereby capitalizing on public disaffection and manipulating public opinion against schools (Barlow and Robertson, 1994). The provincial governments, being responsible for education, were quick to join in the criticism of schools and the search for solutions.

Using test scores in the international study of performance in mathematics—which, according to Barlow and Robertson, were misleading because they compared the performance of elite groups of students in some countries with a more broadly based Canadian cohort—some argued for a radical restructuring of education in Canada. Among the suggested solutions to our problems were many that were consistent with the political right and corporate interests: national testing and standards (to measure the quality of the "product"—that is, students); downsizing for greater efficiency (fewer school boards and teachers); vouchers (to allow students and families to shop for their schools); privatization (schools run by the private sector); partnerships between corporations and schools or universities; corporate sponsorship of various programs (often involving overt advertising within schools); and harmonization with educational practices in the United States.

EDUCATION AND THE WORLD OF WORK

The province of New Brunswick has taken a novel approach to education in its utilitarian role of preparing people to participate in a changing and, it is hoped, expanding labour market. While former premier Frank McKenna actively recruited businesses to establish in or relocate to New Brunswick, some of his province's schools made a special, complementary offer. Their graduates would enter the workforce with "guaranteed" skills: if an employer found them wanting, they could be returned for upgrading at the schools' expense. Strategic spending on education has helped to decrease the overall dropout rate in New Brunswick as well. An appropriately educated, bilingual workforce is one of the factors allowing Moncton, New Brunswick, to entice a wide range of companies to relocate there. Moncton is attracting international attention, and was chosen as one of the top five "Best Cities for Business" by *The Globe and Mail*'s *Report on Business Magazine* (August 1993:55). Advanced telecommunications technology is one of the factors allowing many companies to move to an area without a large population base.

A large study, *Making the Match* (Evers et al., 1993), involving twenty companies and five universities, was designed to assess the skill development experiences of Canadian university students and graduates, as well as the fit between these skills and the needs of corporations. The skills most in demand (and shortest in supply) were not technical skills (such as using a

Functional Illiteracy: Must We Rethink Education?

Imagine being unable to read the labels on cans of food, the instructions for assembling a child's toy, the dosage on a medicine bottle, or even the information on your own paycheque. These are some of the debilitating experiences of functional illiteracy, reading and writing skills inadequate for carrying out everyday responsibilities.

With universal schooling, the Canadian government concluded that illiteracy had been eliminated. The truth of the matter, according to the National Literacy Secretariat, is that only 63 percent of Canadians have sufficient literacy and numeracy skills to deal adequately with everyday tasks; an additional 22 percent have some problems; and about 15 percent have difficulty recognizing familiar words or doing simple addition and subtraction (Montigny, 1994:322). By 1994, another literacy survey revealed that the percentages in the two lower categories had increased to 25 and 22 percent, respectively. Canadians are not alone in this respect, though, for it is estimated that about one in four adults in the United States is functionally illiterate, and that the proportions are higher among the elderly and minorities.

Functional illiteracy is a complex social problem, caused partly by an educational system that passes children from one grade to the next whether they learn or not. Community indifference and parents who offer little encouragement to learn language skills contribute as well.

Functional illiteracy costs the North American economy more than $100 billion a year, through decreased productivity (by workers who perform their jobs improperly) and increased accidents (by people unable to understand written instructions). It also reflects the costs of supporting those unable to read and write well enough to find work who then end up on public assistance or in prison.

Correcting this national problem requires one approach for young people and another for adults. To stop functional illiteracy before it happens, the public must demand that children not be graduated from school until they have learned basic language skills. For adults, the answer begins with diagnosis—a difficult task since many feel shame at their plight and avoid disclosing their need for help. Once such people are identified, however, adult education programs must be provided and used effectively.

It should be noted that in some cases, illiteracy is not an inability to read at all, but an inability to read in English or French. In all the countries participating in the International Adult Literacy Survey, immigrants are disproportionately represented in the lower literacy levels in the languages of the host countries (National Adult Literacy Database, **www.nald.ca**). Canada has an active program teaching English as a second language (ESL) to the constantly replenished body of immigrant schoolchildren and adults.

Our society is one of the most affluent on earth, yet many other countries have more literate populations than we do, as Figure 20–5 illustrates. Functional illiteracy is a personal handicap, and an urgent national problem.

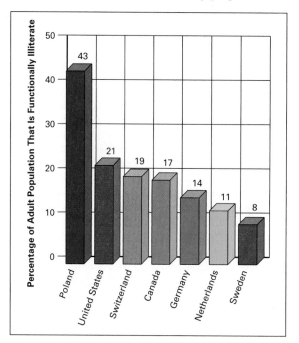

FIGURE 20–5 Functional Illiteracy in Global Perspective

Source: Based on Fiske (1997).

Sources: Based on Kozol (1980, 1985), Colombo (1992:76), Montigny (1994), and National Adult Literacy Database, www.nald.ca.

computer) but a skill composite: the ability to integrate and use information, adapt to change, take reasonable risks, and conceptualize the future. Leadership and conflict management are also scarce skills. The educational system must develop technical skills in its students as well as use innovative approaches to foster the skills needed by industry. Interestingly, there is a link between these skills and the educational "aims and objectives" espoused by many of our universities.

Is Political Correctness Undermining Education?

Are you "PC"? Is your teacher? What about this textbook? The last decade has seen a heightened level of political debate on the university campus. Around 1990, the term *political correctness* entered our language to refer to thinking and acting in accordance with liberal political principles. To be "politically correct," at least as opponents see it, implies that "truth" is less a matter of scientific evidence than having the "correct" politics. Surveying today's campus scene, James Davison Hunter (1991:211) concludes, "The cultural ethos of the modern university clearly favours a progressivist agenda," including support for feminism, gay rights, and various other movements towards social equality.

To some people, political correctness threatens the traditional open-mindedness of the university, at its worst transforming professors into political activists and teaching into indoctrination. Moreover, political correctness may have a chilling effect in the classroom, making students wary of expressing opinions about controversial issues (say, homosexuality or racial differences in measured intelligence) for fear of offending others who might, in turn, charge them with "homophobia" or "racism."

Professors, too, feel the pressure to be politically correct: Douglas Massey

(1995) points out that a number of well-known researchers have been ostracized by their peers for publishing the results of research that is scientifically solid but that advances "unpopular notions" about race and gender.

But not everyone thinks "PC" is a problem. Many students and faculty defend a politically engaged campus on moral grounds. As they see it, there is much injustice in the world that cries out for redress. Richard Rorty (1994), for example, applauds the fact that some academic departments have become "sanctuaries for left-wing political views," because activist colleagues are "doing a great deal of good for people who have gotten a raw deal," namely, women, Blacks, gay men, and lesbians. By focusing on marginalized people, he continues, the politically engaged campus will help to make society "much more decent, more tolerant, and more civilized."

Keep in mind, too, that "political correctness" can be easily exaggerated. While it is probably fair to characterize academia (and sociologists, overall) as politically liberal, virtually every campus includes faculty, administrators, and students who continue to espouse a wide range of political opinions. Furthermore, charges of political correctness in academia are nothing new. Just sixty years ago, for example, a ma-

jority of U.S. states sought to keep teachers in check by requiring that they sign loyalty oaths before permitting them to speak in the classroom (Hunter, 1991).

Quite literally, the perception of political correctness can affect the discussion of Canada–U.S. relations or Middle East issues in the post-9/11 period. Picture someone in a Canadian university classroom arguing that President George Bush was right to invade Iraq, or that Israelis have every right to retaliate against Palestinian suicide bombings. In all likelihood, these opinions will not be expressed at all because those who hold these views have been told they are not "PC."

Continue the debate . . .

1. Overall, do you think that academia has a political bias? What is the bias?

2. Should teachers (or textbooks) take explicit political stands on controversial issues?

3. Have you or other students remained silent during class discussions for fear of sounding "politically incorrect"? Has a course ever led you to change attitudes you came to see as narrow-minded?

EDUCATION FOR TOMORROW

As a society, Canada is undergoing a series of changes with implications for our educational system.

First, we are dealing with increasing diversity as a result of steady immigration, cultural pluralism (partly in response to our policy of multiculturalism), and ethnic nationalism (most visibly among the Québécois and Native peoples), as well as continuing regional and class divisions. In this context, the educational system is required (1) to promote equality of access, participation, and outcome, and (2) to play an integrative

role, in part by fostering a Canadian identity that overrides our differences.

Second, Canada is experiencing technological change involving the expanded use of computers and robots, which in turn has an impact on organizational patterns (for example, the possibility of working at home while "hooked up" to the office). The promise of this new technology goes beyond helping students to learn basic skills: computers actually may improve the overall quality of learning. Interacting with computers prompts students to be more active and allows them to progress at their own pace. For students with disabilities who cannot write using a pencil, computers permit easier self-expression. Using computers in schools—in some cases as early as kindergarten—also appears to increase learning speed and retention of information (Fantini, 1986).

The numerous benefits of computers should not blind us to their limitations, however. Computers will never bring to the educational process the personal insight or imagination of a motivated human teacher. While the jury may be out on whether computers have improved teaching (Skinner, 1997), there is no doubt they have proliferated in the classroom. Computers have become central to the experience of students in many classes, from kindergarten to university. In some Canadian universities, all students are required to have computers and modems, and in some programs they are required to bring lap-top computers to class. This type of requirement presents the danger of a new source of inequity in access to knowledge.

As our society enters the twenty-first century, we should not look to technology to solve many of the problems that plague our schools. What we need is a broad plan for social change that refires this country's early ambition to provide quality universal schooling—a goal that has eluded us so far.

And third, we face a shrinking world of shifting political alliances, economic restructuring, multinational corporations, and global competition—wherein we strive to maintain our quality of life. Insofar as education is responsible for the development of skills relevant to the labour market, our schools must foster in students both technical skills and an ability to be innovative, flexible, and analytical.

Education is intricately involved with change as a catalyst, an adaptive mechanism, and a force for maintaining tradition and continuity. It is simultaneously an explosive irritant and one of the ingredients in the glue that binds us together.

SUMMARY

1. Education is a major social institution for transmitting knowledge and skills, as well as teaching cultural norms and values, to young people. In pre-industrial societies, education occurs informally within the family; industrial societies develop formal systems of schooling.

2. Structural-functional analysis highlights major functions of schooling, including socialization, cultural innovation, social integration, and placing people in the social hierarchy. Latent functions of schooling involve providing child care and building social networks.

3. Social-conflict analysis links schooling to hierarchy involving class, race, and gender. This approach also explains that schooling acts as a means of social control, instilling the value of discipline that produces compliant adult workers.

4. Standardized achievement tests are controversial: some see them as a reasonable measure of academic aptitude and learning, while others say they are culturally biased tools used to label less-privileged students as personally deficient.

5. Streaming, too, is controversial: some see streaming as the way schools provide instruction to students with different interests and aptitudes; others say streaming gives privileged youngsters a richer education.

6. Canada is a "credential society." By requiring degrees for higher-paying occupations, employers ensure that workers have learned norms and attitudes appropriate to the business setting.

7. Many people are critical of public schools. Lack of discipline and questionable standards are seen as problems. In addition, young women and men drop out of high school, thereby placing themselves at high risk of unemployment and poverty.

8. Declining academic standards are reflected in lower than average scores on academic achievement tests and functional illiteracy among a significant proportion of high-school graduates.

9. The Information Revolution is changing schooling through the increasing use of computers. Although computers permit interactive, self-paced learning, they are not suitable for teaching every subject.

CRITICAL-THINKING QUESTIONS

1. Why does industrialization lead societies to expand their system of schooling?

2. Referring to various countries, including Canada, describe ways in which schooling is shaped by economic, political, or cultural factors.

3. From a structural-functional perspective, why is schooling important to the operation of society? From a social-conflict point of view, how does formal education operate to reproduce social inequality in each generation?

APPLICATIONS AND EXERCISES

1. Talk to your peers about their secondary schools. Do the schools have "streaming" policies? How do they work? How much importance does a student's social background have in determining stream assignment?

2. Most people agree that teaching our children is a vital task, yet most teachers earn relatively low salaries. What can you find out at the library about the average salaries of teachers compared to other workers? Can you explain this pattern?

3. To explore how new information technology is reshaping education, visit the website for the first Athabasca University at **www.athabascau.ca**. What do you see as the advantages and disadvantages of this type of schooling?

4. Policies and available funding for providing education to children with physical disabilities vary between provinces. Do some library research, or contact teachers or other officials, to determine the situation in your province.

 ## SITES TO SEE

www.macionis.com
or
www.TheSociologyPage.com

You can find more than fifty weblinks to sociological journals and other sources of data and information by visiting the Links Library at this website.

www.statcan.ca/english/freepub/89-552-MIE/ free.htm

www.nald.ca/nls/ials/introduc.htm

Primarily funded by Human Resources Development Canada, the International Adult Literacy Survey creates comparable literacy profiles across national, linguistic, and cultural boundaries. The survey now encompasses close to thirty countries around the world. Monographs focus on current policy issues and cover topics such as adult training, literacy skill match and mismatch in the workplace, seniors' literacy skills and health, and literacy and economic security.

www.cmec.ca/

Established in 1967, the Council of Ministers of Education, Canada is the national voice for education in Canada. The site includes press releases and reports about education in Canada, as well as international issues.

www.oise.utoronto.ca/~mpress/eduweb/eduweb.html

Maintained by the Ontario Institute for Studies in Education, this site offers a comprehensive list of Canadian education-related resources on the Web.

www.cea-ace.ca/

The Canadian Education Association is a national, bilingual, not-for-profit organization committed to promoting the improvement of education. The association produces a variety of regular and special publications, and serves as a common meeting place for all sectors of education through its activities, special projects, and various committees.

 ## STUDY TOOLS

For more study tools to help you with your next exam, be sure to check out the Companion Website at **www.pearsoned. ca/macionis**, as well as Chapter 20 in your Study Guide.

 ## INVESTIGATE WITH CONTENTSELECT

Follow the instructions found on page 25 of this textbook to access ContentSelect™ at the Research Navigator™ website. Once at the site, enter your LOGINID and Password. Then, enter keywords such as "streaming" and "functional literacy" and the search engine will supply relevant and recent scholarly and popular press publications.

CHAPTER
21

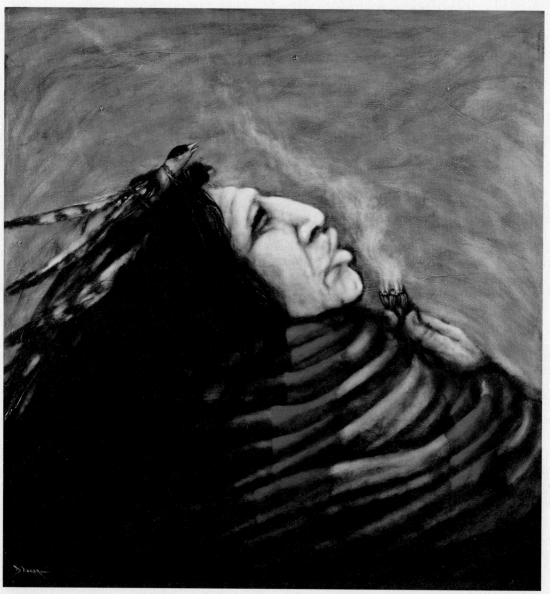

Dale Auger (1958– , Canadian)
Long Time Yellowbird Medicine Calling, 2000
Acrylic on canvas, 91.4 × 91.4 cm. Courtesy of Dale Auger.

HEALTH AND MEDICINE

I n 1995, television came to Fiji, a small island in the South Seas of the Pacific Ocean. A single cable channel carried programming from the United States, Great Britain, and Australia. When Anne Becker, a Harvard researcher specializing in eating disorders, read the news, her sociological imagination led her to wonder what effect watching television would have on young women there.

Becker knew that Fijian culture emphasized good nutrition and looking strong and healthy. Dieting to look very thin had never been common in Figi. Indeed, in 1995, Becker found, just 3 percent of teenage girls reported ever vomiting to control their weight. By 1998, however, a striking change was evident: 15 percent of teenage girls—a five-fold increase—reported this practice. Moreover, Becker found that 62 percent of girls claimed they had dieted during the previous month, and 74 percent reported feeling "too big" or "fat" (Becker, 1999).

The rapid rise in recorded cases of eating disorders in Fiji after television was introduced shows the power of society to shape patterns of health. Eating disorders, including anorexia nervosa (medically, a practice of "severe caloric restriction," commonly understood as compulsive dieting), as well as bulimia (binge eating followed by vomiting) are even more common in North America. This is so in spite of the fact that most of these women, medically speaking, are not overweight.

Consider, too, that 95 percent of people with an eating disorder are female. Why? Because weight control is part of our cultural definition of femininity. As the Duchess of Windsor once put it, "A woman cannot be too rich or too thin." In Canada—and, now, Fiji as well—society teaches young women that they are "never too thin to feel fat" (Wooley et al., 1979; Levine, 1987; Parrott, 1987; Robinson, 1987).

WHAT IS HEALTH?

The World Health Organization defines **health** as *a state of complete physical, mental, and social well-being* (1946:3). This definition underscores the major theme of this chapter: health is as much a social as a biological issue, because well-being and illness have their roots in the organization of society.

For the website of the World Health Organization, go to www.who.int

HEALTH AND SOCIETY

Society shapes people's health in five major ways:

1. **Cultural patterns define health.** Standards of health vary from society to society. Early in the twentieth century, yaws, a contagious skin disease, was so common in sub-Saharan Africa that people there considered it normal (Dubos, 1980; orig. 1965). "Health," therefore, is sometimes a matter of having the same disease as one's neighbours (cf. Pinhey et al., 1997).

2. **People define as "healthy" what they hold to be morally good.** Members of our society (especially men) consider a competitive way of life to be "healthy" because it fits our cultural mores. This is so even though stress contributes to heart disease and many other illnesses. On the other hand, some people who object to homosexuality on moral grounds label this sexual orientation "sick" even though it is quite natural from a biological standpoint. In short, ideas about good health constitute a type of social control that encourages conformity to cultural norms.

3. **Cultural standards of health change over time.** Early in the twentieth century, some physicians condemned women for enrolling in college, claiming that higher education placed an unhealthy strain on the female brain. Others denounced masturbation as a threat to health. Today, on both counts, we know differently.

The profession of surgery has existed only for several centuries. Before that, barbers offered their services to the very sick, often cutting the skin to "bleed" a patient. Of course, this "treatment" was rarely effective, but it did produce plenty of bloody bandages, which practitioners hung out to dry. This practice identifies the origin of the red and white barber poles we see today.

Lucas van Leyden (1494–1533), *The Surgeon and the Peasant*, Rijksmuseum, Amsterdam.

Conversely, few physicians fifty years ago recognized the dangers of cigarette smoking, a practice that we now recognize as a health threat.

4. **A society's technology affects people's health.** In poor societies, infectious diseases are rampant because of malnutrition and poor sanitation. As industrialization raises living standards, people become more healthy. But industrial technology also creates new threats to health. As Chapter 22 ("Population, Urbanization, and the Environment") explains, rich countries threaten human health.

5. **Social inequality affects people's health.** Every society on earth unequally distributes the re-

sources that promote personal well-being. The physical, mental, and social health of wealthier women and men in Canada is far better than that of poor people, as we shall explain presently. This pattern starts at birth, with infant mortality highest among the poor and within the Aboriginal population. Affluent people also live years longer than poor people do.

HEALTH: A GLOBAL SURVEY

Because health is closely linked to social life, we find pronounced change in human well-being over the long course of history. Similarly, we see striking differences in health around the world today.

HEALTH IN HISTORY

With only simple technology, our ancestors could do little to improve health. Among hunters and gatherers, food shortages sometimes forced mothers to abandon children. Children fortunate enough to survive infancy were still vulnerable to a host of injuries and illnesses for which there were few effective treatments, and half died before age twenty. Few lived to forty (Lenski et al., 1995).

The agricultural revolution expanded the supply of food and other resources. Yet because of increasing social inequality, elites enjoyed better health while peasants and slaves faced hunger and endured crowded, unsanitary shelters. Especially in the growing cities of medieval Europe, human waste and other refuse spread infectious diseases, including plagues that periodically wiped out entire towns (Mumford, 1961).

HEALTH IN LOW-INCOME COUNTRIES

Severe poverty in much of the world cuts life expectancy far below the seventy or more years typical of rich societies. Global Map 15–2 (p. 367) shows that average life expectancy among Africans barely reaches fifty, and in the world's poorest nations, such as Ethiopia and Rwanda, the figure falls to forty.

The World Health Organization reports that 1 billion people around the world—one in six—suffer from serious illness due to poverty. Poor sanitation and malnutrition kill people of all ages, especially children. Health is compromised not just by having too little to eat, but also by consuming only one kind of food, as the "Global Sociology" box explains.

In impoverished countries, sanitary drinking water may be as scarce as the chance for a balanced diet. Contaminated water breeds many of the infectious diseases that imperil both adults and children. The leading causes of death in Canada a century ago, including influenza, pneumonia, and tuberculosis, are

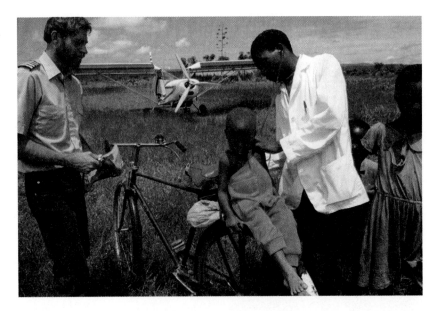

One billion people on the planet suffer from various illnesses due to poverty. For most of these people, medical care is limited or nonexistent. In Tanzania, this physician flies a light plane to reach patients in remote areas, and depends on a computer and satellite links to get the latest information from medical centres around the world.

still widespread killers in poor societies today and, until recently, among Aboriginal peoples in Canada.

To make matters worse, medical personnel are few and far between, so that the world's poorest people—many of whom live in central Africa—never see a physician. Global Map 21–1 (on page 523) illustrates the availability of doctors throughout the world.

In poor nations with minimal medical care, 10 percent of children die within a year of their birth. In some countries, half the children never reach adulthood—a pattern that parallels the death rates seen in Europe more than two centuries ago (George, 1977; Harrison, 1984).

Illness and poverty form a vicious cycle in much of the world: poverty breeds disease, which, in turn, undermines the ability to work. Moreover, when medical technology curbs infectious disease, the populations of poor nations soar. Without resources to ensure the well-being of the people they have now, poor societies can ill afford a larger population. Ultimately, programs to lower death rates in poor countries will succeed only if they can reduce birth rates as well.

HEALTH IN HIGH-INCOME COUNTRIES

Industrialization dramatically changed patterns of human health in Europe, although, at first, not for the better. By 1800, as the Industrial Revolution took hold, factories offered jobs that drew people from all over the countryside. Cities quickly became overcrowded, creating serious sanitation problems. Moreover, factories fouled the air with smoke—a health threat unrecognized until well into the twentieth century. Accidents in the workplace were common.

But industrialization gradually improved health in Western Europe and North America as rising living standards translated into better nutrition and safer housing for the majority of people. After 1850, medical advances also improved health, primarily by controlling infectious diseases. To illustrate, in 1854 John Snow noted the street addresses of London's cholera victims and traced the source of this disease to contaminated drinking water (Rockett, 1994). Soon after, scientists linked cholera to specific bacteria and developed a protective vaccine against the deadly disease. Armed with this knowledge, early environmentalists campaigned against age-old practices such as discharging raw sewage into rivers used for drinking water. As the twentieth century dawned, death rates from infectious diseases had fallen sharply.

Over the long term, industrialization has dramatically improved human health. In 1890, influenza and pneumonia led to one-fourth of all deaths in Canada, and one-fourth of the population died before reaching ten years of age (Roberge et al., 1995:15). Today, these diseases cause fewer than 3 percent of deaths in Canada. Life expectancy has increased and infant mortality rates have decreased, both dramatically, over the last century: we now die of diseases of "affluence," mainly cancer and heart disease, and die in old age. Nothing alters the reality of death, but industrial societies manage to delay death until old age.

 For a look at the physical fitness movement in Canada, see http://archives.cbc.ca/300c.asp?IDCat=41&IDDos=615&IDLan=1&IDMenu=41

HEALTH IN CANADA

Living in an affluent, industrial society, people in Canada are healthy by world standards. Some categories of people, however, enjoy far better health and well-being than others.

Killer Poverty: A Report from Africa

Television images of famine in Africa bring home to people in affluent countries such as Canada the horror of starving children. Some of the children we see appear bloated, while others seem to have shrivelled to little more than skin drawn tightly over bones. Both of these deadly conditions, explains Susan George (1977), are direct consequences of poverty.

Children with bloated bodies are suffering from protein deficiency. In west Africa this condition is known as *kwashiorkor*, literally "one-two." The term derives from the common practice among mothers of abruptly weaning a first child on the birth of a second. Deprived of mother's milk, a baby may receive no protein at all.

Children with shrivelled bodies lack both protein and calories. This deficiency is the result of eating little food of any kind.

Strictly speaking, starvation is rarely what kills children. Their weakened condition makes them vulnerable to stomach ailments such as gastroenteritis or diseases such as measles. The death rate from measles, for example, is a thousand times greater in parts of Africa than in North America.

Eating just a single food also undermines nutrition, causing a deficiency of protein, vitamins, and minerals. Millions of people in low-income countries suffer from goitre, a debilitating, diet-related disease of the thyroid gland. Pellagra, common among people who consume mostly corn, is a serious disease that can lead to insanity. Similarly, people who eat only processed rice are prone to beriberi.

Health is obviously a social issue since diseases virtually unknown to people in rich societies are a common experience of life—and death—in poor nations around the world.

SOCIAL EPIDEMIOLOGY: THE DISTRIBUTION OF HEALTH

Social epidemiology is *the study of how health and disease are distributed throughout a society's population.* Just as early social epidemiologists examined the origin and spread of epidemic diseases, researchers today find links between health and physical and social environments. Such analysis rests on comparing the health of different categories of people.

Age and Sex

Death is now rare among Canadian young people, with two notable exceptions: increases in mortality resulting from accidents and, more recently, from acquired immune deficiency syndrome (AIDS). Nonetheless, sociocultural environments still affect the present and future health of youngsters: in 1998, the CBC's *National Magazine* reported that Canada's children, who are subject to poor diet, lack of exercise, and second-hand smoke, are the obese and the heart patients of tomorrow.

 Go to www.statcan.ca/Daily/ English/031103/d031103a.htm for a report from Statistics Canada on the factors contributing to youth obesity.

Across the life course, women live longer but spend more time without full health. Females have a slight biological advantage that renders them less likely than males to die before or immediately after birth. Then, as socialization takes over, males become more aggressive and individualistic, resulting in higher rates of accidents, violence, and suicide. Our cultural conception of masculinity also pressures adult men to be more competitive, to repress their emotions, and to engage in hazardous behaviours such as smoking cigarettes and drinking alcohol to excess.

Social Class and Race

Infant mortality—the death rate among newborns—is almost twice as high among disadvantaged children as it is among children born to privilege. While the health of the richest children in our nation is the best in the world, our poorest children (especially Aboriginal children) are as vulnerable to disease as those in many low-income countries.

Research by Wilkins and Adams (1983) shows that both life expectancy and life expectancy free of disability vary significantly by income level and by neighbourhood quality. Those at the highest income

GLOBAL MAP 21–1 The Availability of Physicians in Global Perspective

Medical doctors, widely available to people in rich nations, are perilously scarce in poor societies. While traditional forms of healing do improve health, antibiotics and vaccines—vital for controlling infectious diseases—are often in short supply in poor societies. In these countries, therefore, death rates are high, especially among infants.

Source: United Nations Development Programme (2000); map adapted from *Peters Atlas of the World* (1990).

levels live longer than those at the lowest levels, and have more years free of disability. There is some debate about the causal direction in such findings (that is, whether people get sick because they are poor, or people are poor because they are sick). It appears that for the most part class is the independent variable and health is the dependent variable. At times, however, sickness may lead to a decline in income over a long period of time. Also, members of low-income families miss more days of school or work each year owing to illness than do higher-income people.

On the basis of the Health Status Index (HSI), Roberge et al. (1995) concluded that health levels vary with income: the lower the income, the lower the health status. For males and females, low household income has a greater impact with advancing age. In other words, people at all income levels experienced good health while they were young; with advancing age, men and particularly women were less likely to report high levels of health if their incomes were low.

Aboriginal Canadians continue to live shorter lives than their non-Aboriginal counterparts. In 1990,

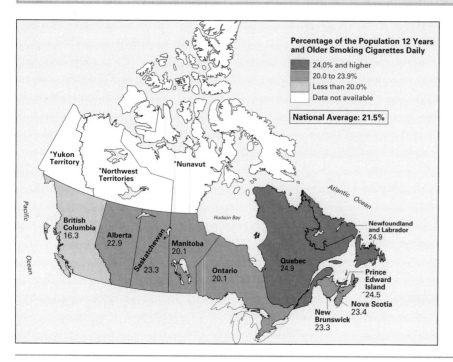

Percentage of the Population 12 Years and Older Smoking Cigarettes Daily

- 24.0% and higher
- 20.0 to 23.9%
- Less than 20.0%
- Data not available

National Average: 21.5%

*Yukon Territory

*Northwest Territories

*Nunavut

Pacific Ocean

British Columbia 16.3

Alberta 22.9

Saskatchewan 23.3

Manitoba 20.1

Hudson Bay

Ontario 20.1

Quebec 24.9

Atlantic Ocean

Newfoundland and Labrador 24.9

Prince Edward Island 24.5

Nova Scotia 23.4

New Brunswick 23.3

CANADA MAP 21–1
Percentage of the Population 12 Years and Over Smoking Cigarettes Daily, 2000–01

*Data not available.

Source: Adapted by Gerber from Statistics Canada, Canadian Statistics, Health (www.statcan.ca).

the life expectancy for a Native male was 67 years (compared to about 73 years for a non-Native male). For a Native female, life expectancy was 74 years (compared to about 81 years for a non-Native female) (Indian and Northern Affairs Canada, 2002).

Causes of death and disease levels also tend to be different for Aboriginal Canadians: infant mortality among Aboriginal people is twice that of Canada as a whole; suicide is eight times higher; tuberculosis seven times higher; and diabetes three times more likely. Furthermore, Aboriginal people are twice as likely to report long-term disabilities. In the 1984–90 period, 1.4 percent of Canada's AIDS cases were Aboriginal, but by 1993–95 that figure had increased to 4.4 per-

 Clips from the CBC's archives examine the history of tuberculosis in Canada, and its new rise: see http://archives.cbc.ca/300c.asp?id=1-75-883

cent (Indian and Northern Affairs Canada, 2002). Clearly, Canada has a long way to go before it can say that its Native people are equal in terms of health and longevity.

Poor people also suffer from nutritional deficiencies. A large percentage of our population tries to get by with a substandard diet and minimal medical care. The results are predictable: while wealthy women and men typically die in old age of chronic illnesses such as heart disease and cancer, poor people are likely to die younger from infectious diseases such as pneumonia.

HEALTH AND SOCIETY: THREE EXAMPLES

Since we all make choices about how to live, we all have some control over our own health. But as the following sections indicate, dangerous behaviours such as cigarette smoking and compulsive dieting are pronounced among certain categories of our population. Sexually transmitted diseases, too, reveal a distinctive social profile.

Cigarette Smoking

Cigarette smoking tops the list of preventable hazards to health. But we can see that smoking has a cultural dimension as well, because it was only after World War I that smoking became popular in Canada. Despite growing evidence of its dangers, smoking remained fashionable even a generation ago. Since then, among adults—but not among young people—smoking has been falling out of favour and is now considered a mild form of social deviance.

As concern about the health effects of smoking has grown, consumption of cigarettes has fallen from its peak in 1960, when almost 45 percent of Canadian adults smoked. By 2000–1, only 21.5 percent were smokers, as illustrated by Canada Map 21–1, which shows levels ranging from 16.3 percent in British Columbia to 24.9 percent in Quebec and Newfoundland and Labrador. These figures represent a drop in smoking from 24.3

in 1994–95 to 21.5 percent for Canada as a whole, and a drop from 29.1 to 24.9 percent in Quebec.

Considering the addictive quality of nicotine and the difficulty of quitting, it is surprising to learn that 24 percent of the people who were smoking in 1994–95 had quit by the 2000–1 follow-up. The percent quitting ranged from 24 to 26 percent in all of the provinces except Prince Edward Island, British Columbia, and Alberta, where the quitting rates were much lower (21, 20, and 16 percent respectively).

Generally speaking, the less education people have, the greater their chances of smoking. Moreover, a larger share of men than women smoke. But cigarettes have taken a growing toll on women's health. Lung cancer now competes with breast cancer as a leading cause of death among Canadian women. Worse yet, smoking is estimated to be responsible for one-quarter of deaths of men and women between thirty-five and eighty-four years of age.

Some 500 000 North American men and women die prematurely each year as a direct result of cigarette smoking, which exceeds the combined death toll from alcohol, cocaine, heroin, homicide, suicide, automobile accidents, and AIDS (Mosley and Cowley, 1991). Smokers also endure frequent minor illnesses such as the flu, and pregnant women who smoke increase the likelihood of spontaneous abortion (miscarriage), prenatal death, and low-birth-weight babies. Even nonsmokers exposed to second-hand cigarette smoke have a higher risk of smoking-related diseases.

The tobacco industry maintained for years that because the precise link between cigarettes and disease has not been specified, the health effects of smoking remained "an open question." Nonetheless, laws mandating smoke-free environments are spreading rapidly. By 1997, the tobacco industry had conceded that cigarette smoking is harmful to health, and agreed to end marketing strategies that target the young. In 1998, Canada took steps to restrict advertising and the sponsorship of sporting and cultural events by the tobacco industry. But by the summer of 2003, organizers of Montreal's Grand Prix were asking the federal government to extend the period during which tobacco companies could sponsor their Formula 1 auto racing event. The fact that several European countries were allowing two more years of tobacco sponsorship for sporting events was putting pressure on Canada and we risked losing the Grand Prix to Europe—or to one of many other countries with no intention of banning sponsorship by the tobacco industry.

Eating Disorders

An **eating disorder** is *an intense form of dieting or other kind of weight control in order to become very thin.* As the opening of this chapter suggests, eating disorders illustrate how cultural pressures shape human health.

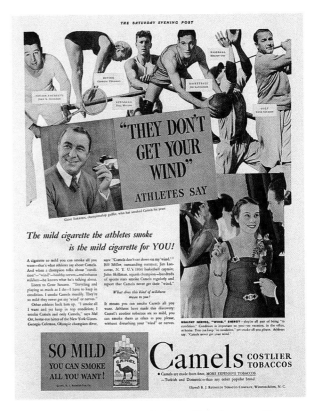

Evidence of the health hazards of smoking cigarettes first appeared in the 1930s. But cigarettes continued to increase in popularity, helped, in part, by celebrity advertising that was, at best, misleading.

Consider, first, that 95 percent of people who suffer from anorexia nervosa or bulimia are women, mostly from white, relatively affluent families. According to Michael Levine (1987), our culture equates slenderness in women with being successful and attractive to men. On the flip side, Levine adds, overweight people tend to be viewed as "lazy," "ugly," "stupid," and "sloppy."

Studies show that most university- and college-age women (1) agree that "guys like thin girls," (2) think that being thin is the most crucial dimension of physical attractiveness, and (3) believe that they are not as thin as men would like them to be. In fact, most university-age women want to be even thinner than university-age men say women should be. For their part, most men describe their actual body shape as just about what they want it to be; thus, compared to women, men display little dissatisfaction over body shape (Fallon and Rozin, 1985).

Chapter 13 ("Gender Stratification") explained that our culture embraces a "beauty myth" that teaches women to exaggerate the importance of physical attractiveness as well as to orient themselves towards pleasing men (Wolf, 1990). Such cultural patterns, Levine continues, pressure women to pursue thinness as a form of perfection. These messages about thinness come from mothers and fathers—especially affluent parents—who pressure a daughter to be "The Best Little Girl in the World." But television and other mass media also play a part in this process, almost exclusively casting actresses and models who are unnaturally thin and unrealistically beautiful. Paradoxically, as the emphasis on thinness has grown, so too has the second wave of the women's movement. This has resulted in a double bind for women, who are faced with an ideal woman who is both successful in the labour market (which often means competition with men) and beautiful and thin enough to be the wife of the very successful man.

The overall result of "gendered" images of women's roles and bodies is low self-image, since few women approach our culture's unrealistic standards of beauty. Just as importantly, those who do are likely to engage compulsively in dieting behaviour to the point of risking their health.

Sexually Transmitted Diseases

Sexual activity, though pleasurable and vital to the perpetuation of our species, can transmit more than fifty illnesses. Sometimes called *venereal diseases* (from Venus, the Roman goddess of love), these ailments date back to humanity's origins. Since our culture has long linked sex to sin, some people regard venereal disease not only as illness but also as a mark of immorality.

Sexually transmitted diseases (STDs) grabbed national attention during the "sexual revolution" of the 1960s, when people began sexual activity earlier and had a greater number of partners. As a result, STDs are an exception to the general decline in infectious diseases during the past century. In recent years, the growing danger of STDs—especially AIDS—has sparked a sexual counterrevolution that has discouraged casual sex, not necessarily for moral reasons, but out of self-interest (Kain, 1987; Kain and Hart, 1987). The following section provides a brief overview of several common STDs.

Gonorrhea. Among the oldest diseases, gonorrhea is caused by microscopic organisms almost always transmitted by sexual contact. Untreated, gonorrhea can cause sterility.

While 7195 cases of gonorrhea were reported in Canada in 2002, the actual number may well be several times greater. Generally speaking, poorer people and particularly visible minorities have higher rates of various STDs. Gonorrhea can easily be cured with antibiotics, such as penicillin, so that it currently presents no serious health threat in Canada.

Genital herpes. An estimated 20 to 30 million adults in the United States (one in seven) are infected with the genital herpes virus. Canadian data are not available (physicians are not required to report cases), but based on differences in the population and in the degrees of inequality between Canadian and U.S. society, the proportion of Canadians infected could be expected to be smaller.

Although far less serious than gonorrhea and syphilis, herpes is incurable. People with genital herpes may exhibit no symptoms, or they may experience periodic, painful blisters on the genitals accompanied by fever and headache. Although not fatal to adults, women with active genital herpes can transmit the disease during vaginal delivery to an infant, to whom it may be deadly. Infected women, therefore, usually give birth by Caesarean section.

AIDS. The most serious of all sexually transmitted diseases is AIDS. Identified in 1981, this disease is incurable and fatal. AIDS is caused by the human immunodeficiency virus (HIV), which attacks white blood cells, the core of the immune system. AIDS thus renders a person vulnerable to a wide range of other diseases that eventually cause death.

The first AIDS case in Canada was reported by the Laboratory Centre for Disease Control (LCDC) in February 1982.

By December 1993 there had been 6187 reported deaths due to AIDS in Canada, and another 2896 people documented as living with AIDS. By December 2002 these numbers had risen to 12 674 reported deaths due to AIDS, 19 213 people diagnosed with AIDS, and 52 640 people diagnosed with HIV. It's important to note that since the late 1990s Canada's widespread education campaign has led to changes in sexual practices and drug and intravenous use, with resulting declines in rates of new HIV infection and deaths due to AIDS. HIV infections reached a high of 1804 in 1994 and deaths due to AIDS reached a high of 1481 in 1995, while corresponding rates in 2001 were 428 and 158 (Health Canada, 2003:61, 40, 11).

Women account for 8 percent of all AIDS cases reported in Canada. From 1982 to 1984, twenty women were diagnosed with AIDS. Between 1988 and 1989, 157 women contracted the disease. By June 2001, 1437 cases of AIDS among women had been reported; 16 percent of all cases reported in 2001 involved females (up from 5.6 percent of cases reported before 1990). As of December 1999, there were 185 children under age fifteen diagnosed with AIDS; 83 percent of them had contracted AIDS from their mothers before or around the time of birth. Another disturbing trend, apart from the increases in HIV/AIDS infection among women and children, is the spread within the Aboriginal community. While the overall increase in AIDS cases has levelled off, the incidence within the Native population has been increasing steadily. Ethnic status is known for only half of AIDS cases, but among these individuals the proportion of Natives increased from 1.5 percent before 1986 to a high of 10 percent in 1999, with fluctuation below that point since then. By 2001, injection drug use was responsible for 64 percent of AIDS cases among Aboriginal women and 28 percent among men (Health Canada, **www.hc-sc.gc.ca**).

In global perspective, HIV infects some 40 million people—half under age twenty-five—and the number is rising rapidly. Africa (more specifically, countries south of the Sahara Desert) has the highest HIV infection rate and currently accounts for two-thirds of all world cases. In central African nations

 Read a dramatic photojournalism account of AIDS in Africa at www.time.com/time/2001/aidsinafrica/

such as Burundi, Rwanda, Uganda, and Kenya, roughly one-fifth of all young adults are infected (Tofani, 1991; Scommegna, 1996). North Americans account for less than 5 percent of global HIV cases.

Upon infection, people with HIV display no symptoms at all, so most are unaware of their condition. Not for a year or longer do symptoms of HIV infection appear. One-third of infected people develop full-blown AIDS within five years, half develop AIDS within ten years, and almost all become sick within twenty years. Even though the number of AIDS deaths began to decline in 1997, the number of deaths so far makes AIDS potentially the most serious epidemic of modern times.

Today, all donated blood is checked for HIV before being transfused. However, the Canadian Hemophilia Society accused the Canadian Red Cross of "bureaucratic foot-dragging" that led to at least 750 hemophiliacs, and potentially many other transfusion recipients, becoming infected with the HIV virus in the mid-1980s. Several high-profile lawsuits were launched against the Red Cross. The Krever Commission, which was established to investigate the issue, found serious mismanagement and negligence and assigned responsibility to specific individuals. As a result, the Red Cross is no longer involved in collecting and managing our blood supplies.

AIDS is infectious but is not contagious. That is, HIV is transmitted through body fluids such as blood, semen, or breast milk but *not* through casual contact such as shaking hands, hugging, sharing towels or dishes, or even coughing and sneezing. The risk of transmitting AIDS through saliva (as in kissing) is extremely low. Infected women can pass HIV to their newborn children, although present evidence indicates that there is less than a 50 percent chance of this occurring. Moreover, the risk of transmitting HIV through sexual activity is greatly reduced by the use of latex condoms. But in the age of AIDS, abstinence or an exclusive relationship with an uninfected person is the only sure way to avoid infection.

Specific behaviours put people at high risk for HIV infection. The first is *anal sex*, which can cause

rectal bleeding that allows easy transmission of HIV from one person to another. While men having sex with men is still the largest risk factor, the proportion of AIDS cases attributable to this factor is decreasing. In 1987, 79 percent of AIDS cases involved men who had sex with men. By 1994, the level had dropped to

69 percent. Because of improvements in blood screening, the proportion of AIDS cases attributable to blood products has also declined over the same period—from 6 to 2 percent (Frank, 2000).

Sharing needles used to inject drugs is a second high-risk behaviour. Casual sex sometimes accompanies drug use; therefore, having sex with an intravenous drug user constitutes high-risk behaviour. The association of this kind of drug use with people of lower socioeconomic levels is another reason that there are class correlates in the incidence of AIDS.

Using any drug, including alcohol, also increases the risk of HIV infection to the extent that it impairs judgment. In other words, even people who under-

 Information on AIDS and HIV is available from Health Canada at www.hc-sc.gc.ca/english/diseases/aids.html

stand what places them at risk of infection may act less responsibly once they are under the influence of alcohol, marijuana, or some other drug.

HIV prevalence among actively homosexual men is probably in the range of 10 to 15 percent. Approximately 22 500 among an estimated 200 000 to 300 000 gay and bisexual men may be infected with HIV in Canada. Some estimate that perhaps 9 percent of infected adults in North America contracted the disease through heterosexual contact (although heterosexuals, infected in various ways, account for more than 30 percent of AIDS cases) (Remis, 1993). But heterosexual activity does transmit AIDS, and the risk rises with the number of sexual partners, especially if they fall into high-risk categories. Worldwide, heterosexual relations are the primary means of HIV transmission, accounting for two-thirds of all infections (Eckholm and Tierney, 1990).

Treating a single person with AIDS costs hundreds of thousands of dollars, and this figure may rise with new therapies. Added to the direct costs of treatment and research are tens of billions of dollars in lost earnings and productivity. Medicare, private insurance, and personal savings rarely cover more than a fraction of the cost of treatment. In addition, there is the mounting cost of caring for children orphaned by AIDS. Overall, AIDS represents both a medical and a social problem of monumental proportions.

It has been suggested that governments responded slowly to the AIDS crisis, largely because gays and intravenous drug users are widely viewed as deviant. More recently, money allocated for AIDS research has

SARS, West Nile, and One Mad Cow

In March 2003, two cases of atypical pneumonia in Toronto were identified as SARS (severe acute respiratory syndrome). Suddenly, Canada was part of a global network that eventually would include thirty-one countries with suspected or probable SARS cases. Controversy regarding the adequacy of federal and provincial responses to this new public health menace will undoubtedly continue for years: we were faced with a two-pronged threat (importation of new cases from abroad and spread from the medical facilities that were caring for active SARS cases), and initially appeared to be coping badly on both fronts.

Tourism in Toronto, and Canada as a whole, was dealt a crippling blow when the World Health Organization (WHO) issued a travel advisory discouraging non-essential visits to Toronto. Conferences were cancelled and individuals from around the world changed their travel plans. Hundreds of people were "voluntarily" quarantined in their homes. Some residents of Toronto began to avoid public places—Chinese restaurants and Chinese-owned businesses in particular. Until it became clear that new cases arose almost exclusively in hospitals—and not from casual contact on the subway—there was a great deal of anxiety about metropolitan Toronto. Six months down the road, with only one active case remaining in the region, people going into doctors' offices, clinics, and hospitals were still washing their hands and signing forms. By August 25, 2003, 438 cases of SARS (251 probable, 187

suspected, 38 deaths) had been identified. At about that time, a milder strain of SARS seemed to infect a number of people in a Vancouver nursing home, but by then people were better educated about SARS and there was neither the same alarm nor a WHO response.

Next, we had to deal with the one mad cow from an Alberta farm. A slaughtered cow had appeared ill when it arrived at the abattoir, but a delay of several months in testing its brain tissues meant that the task of tracking down its bovine contacts, feed sources, and offspring were especially complicated. Thousands of cattle linked in any way to the one identified case were slaughtered and tested for BSE (bovine spongiform encephalopathy). New testing regulations were implemented in Canada's abattoirs, mandating that certain tissues (e.g., brain) be kept out of animal or human foods and diseased carcasses no longer be used for animal feed.

Whereas loyal Canadians (and politicians) continued to eat beef, our cattle industry was devastated by U.S. steps to close its borders to Canadian beef—despite our efforts to ensure its safety. Since beef is our largest agricultural product and since 80 percent of our beef is exported to the United States, the Canadian economy was sent reeling once again. The impact of the closed U.S. border was felt into the fall of 2003, when farmers had to decide what to do with thousands of cattle that had not been slaughtered and/or exported over the spring and summer. Unable to feed those cattle through the coming

winter, farmers were faced with the prospect of burning excess healthy cattle as if they actually were infected with BSE. The partial lifting of the ban (for cattle under 30 months of age and boneless veal from cattle younger than nine months of age) by the United States and Mexico was welcome, but did not solve the problem of how to deal with surplus older cattle through the winter.

The West Nile story for the summer of 2003 came as an unexpected relief. First reported in Canada among Ontario crows and blue jays in 2001, West Nile virus was confirmed in humans only in the summer and fall of 2002, with three confirmed cases, fourteen suspected cases, and one death, all in Ontario. Canadians braced themselves for many more cases in 2003, but perhaps because of mosquito control measures and diligent application of mosquito repellent, the number of Ontario cases in 2003 was limited to two. Elsewhere, the numbers were similarly small—two in the Atlantic provinces, six in Manitoba, and one each in Saskatchewan, Alberta, and British Columbia. Of course, there were many sub-clinical cases of West Nile infection, since the vast majority of infected people are symptom free. Nonetheless, Canada seems to have responded appropriately so as to limit the spread of what can be a debilitating or deadly disease.

Sources: Health Canada (www.hc-sc.gc.ca), and Canada Food Inspection Agency (www.inspection.gc.ca).

---

increased rapidly, and researchers have identified drugs, including recent "protease inhibitors," that dramatically suppress symptoms and prolong life in many patients. Nevertheless, educational programs remain the most effective weapon against AIDS, since prevention is the only way to stop a disease that currently has no cure.

Other Health Issues

In the spring and summer of 2003, Canada experienced three acute health crises that required the response of federal and provincial health authorities. See the "Controversy & Debate" box for details.

ETHICAL ISSUES: CONFRONTING DEATH

Health issues involve ethical considerations, especially now that technological advances have given human beings the power to draw the line separating life and death. Today we grapple with how to use these new powers, or whether to use them at all.

When does death occur? Common sense suggests that life ceases when breathing and the heartbeat stop. But the ability to revive or replace a heart and to artificially sustain respiration have rendered such notions of death obsolete. Medical and legal experts in North America now define death as an *irreversible* state involving no response to stimulation, no movement or breathing, no reflexes, and no indication of brain activity (Ladd, 1979; Wall, 1980).

Do people have a right to die? Today, medical personnel, family members, and patients themselves face the agonizing burden of deciding when a terminally ill person should die. In 1992, Parliament abolished attempted suicide as a crime but retained the prohibition against assisting a suicide. Individuals periodically challenge this law, as did Sue Rodriguez, a British Columbia woman with Lou Gehrig's disease. Rodriguez eventually would have been unable to swallow, to speak, to walk, or even to turn over without assistance. She would have needed a respirator to breathe. As her condition worsened and she expected to lose the desire to live, her ability to end her life would have been reduced. She wanted permission for a doctor, at a given time in the future, to set up an intravenous tube filled with a lethal dose of medication. Her case spawned both widespread support and fervent opposition from churches, anti-abortion activists, and provincial and federal governments (Wood, 1993). On September 30, 1993, the Supreme Court decided, with a vote of 5–4, that Rodriguez's rights were not violated by the federal law against assisting a suicide. The court ruled that the state's interest in protecting the sanctity of life took precedence over the individual's right to a dignified death. In the end, Rodriguez was helped to die by an anonymous physician and a maverick member of Parliament, the long-sitting New Democratic party member Svend Robinson.

Normally, the first responsibility of physicians and hospitals is to protect a patient's life. Even so, a mentally competent person in the process of dying may refuse medical treatment or even nutrition. Moreover, laws require hospitals, nursing homes, and other medical facilities to honour the desires of a patient made earlier in the form of a living will. Thus, most cases of death in Canada now involve a human decision about when and how death will occur.

What about mercy killing? *Mercy killing* is the common term for euthanasia, assisting in the death of a person suffering from an incurable disease. Euthanasia

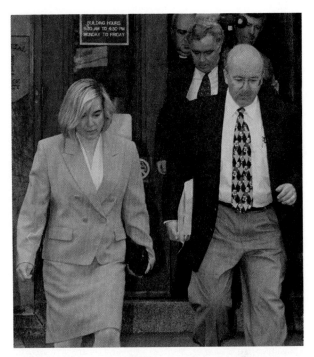

The ability to prolong life has led to increasingly complicated ethical considerations involving death. Nancy Morrison, a Halifax physician, was accused of killing a terminally ill cancer patient in November 1996. Although a judge threw out the charges, the Crown appealed that decision with the intention of proceeding with charges of manslaughter.

(from the Greek, meaning "a good death") poses an ethical dilemma, being at once an act of kindness and a form of killing.

Support for a patient's right to die (that is, *passive* euthanasia) is growing in North America. But assisting in the death of another person (*active* euthanasia) still provokes controversy and may violate the law. When Robert Latimer killed his badly disabled daughter by carbon monoxide poisoning, he was convicted of second-degree murder. He felt that his daughter's life of constant pain was not worth living: he killed her because he loved her. A groundswell of public sentiment, both supportive and hostile, erupted. Though convicted, Latimer was released from prison provided that he remain on his farm. In 1997, the Supreme Court of Canada heard an appeal and convicted Latimer of murder, but gave him a very light sentence owing to the special circumstances of his crime. In January 2001, the Supreme Court turned down his appeal for a new trial and ruled that he should serve at least ten years in prison (Beltrame, 2001).

The debate on euthanasia breaks down roughly as follows. Those who categorically view life—even with suffering and disability—as preferable to death reject both passive and active euthanasia. People who recognize circumstances under which death is preferable to life endorse passive or perhaps active euthanasia, but

The rise of scientific medicine during the nineteenth century resulted in new skills and technology for treating many common ailments that had afflicted humanity for centuries. At the same time, however, scientific medicine pushed forms of health care involving women to the margins, and placed medicine under the control of men living in cities. We see this pattern in the A.F. Seligmann painting General Hospital, *showing an obviously all-male medical school class in Vienna in 1880.*

they face the practical problem of determining just when life should be ended.

THE MEDICAL ESTABLISHMENT

Medicine is *a social institution concerned with combatting disease and improving health.* Through most of human history, health care was the responsibility of individuals and their families. Medicine emerges as a social institution only as societies become more productive, assigning their members formal, specialized roles. As a society industrializes, health care becomes the responsibility of specially schooled and legally licensed healers, from anesthesiologists to X-ray technicians. The medical establishment in Canada took form over the last 155 years—effectively squeezing out the shaman, herbalist, and acupuncturist.

THE RISE OF SCIENTIFIC MEDICINE

In colonial times, doctors, herbalists, druggists, midwives, and ministers all engaged in various forms of

healing arts. But not all did so effectively: unsanitary instruments, lack of anesthesia, and simple ignorance made surgery a terrible ordeal in which doctors probably killed as many patients as they saved.

Gradually, however, specialists learned more about human anatomy, physiology, and biochemistry. Early in the nineteenth century, medical societies appeared in Canada as doctors established themselves as self-regulating professionals (Blishen, 1991). Formal colleges of medicine offered training in the field. The increase in the number of medical schools paralleled the growth in the number of hospitals (Stevens, 1971). Medical societies required those who wished to practise or teach medical skills to obtain licences, and these organizations enforced conformity to specific medical standards.

The standards that lay at the heart of this new profession were established largely through the efforts of the allopathic doctors (Blishen, 1991). The establishment in 1865 of the General Council of Medical Education and Registration in Upper Canada signified acceptance of the scientific model of medicine, and widely publicized the medical successes of its members to further improve its own image. Scientific researchers were touted for tracing the cause of life-threatening illnesses to bacteria and viruses, and also for developing vaccines to prevent disease.

Still, alternative approaches to health care, such as regulating nutrition, also had many defenders. The allopathic (conventional) doctors responded boldly—some thought arrogantly—by criticizing these alternative ideas about health. They established the Canadian Medical Association (CMA) in 1867. With control of the certification process, they were able to define what constituted medical acts and practice. Thus, doctors, through the provincial colleges, could determine what the various "paramedical" occupations could and could not do. Before long, the practice of medicine was limited mainly to those with an MD degree. In the process, both the prestige and income of physicians rose dramatically.

Other practitioners—such as naturopaths, herbal healers, and midwives—held to their traditional roles, but at a high cost: all have been relegated to fringe areas of the medical profession. With far less social prestige and income than physicians, such professionals now have a small, if devoted, following in Canada (Blishen, 1991; Nancarrow Clarke, 1996). Treatment by chiropractors is now partially covered by provincial health insurance, and midwives have recently been legalized as birth attendants in Ontario (Rajhathy and Roulard, 1994:40). Furthermore, more than one-third of North Americans use some form of "complementary medicine" (Eisenberg et al., 1993).

The rise of scientific medicine, taught in expensive, urban medical schools, also changed the social profile of doctors. There is and has long been an overrepresentation of medical students from higher-level social backgrounds. Their fathers have tended to have higher education than average, and to be employed in managerial and professional levels of the labour force (Blishen, 1991). Medicine is also a traditionally male-dominated profession. Women were long considered unfit to practise (Starr, 1982; Huet-Cox, 1984; Nancarrow Clarke, 1996). While in 1992 more than 80 percent of physicians were men and some 97 percent of nurses were women, younger cohorts are changing these male/female ratios dramatically, as noted below.

HOLISTIC MEDICINE

The scientific model of medicine has recently been tempered by the more traditional notion of **holistic medicine**, *an approach to health care that emphasizes the prevention of illness and takes into account a person's entire physical and social environment.*

Some holistic practitioners agree with the use of drugs, surgery, artificial organs, and high technology, but caution that they risk transforming medicine into narrow specialties focusing on symptoms rather than people, on disease instead of health. The following are foundations of holistic health care (Duhl, 1980; Ferguson, 1980; Gordon, 1980):

1. **Patients are people.** Holistic practitioners are concerned not only with symptoms but also with how each person's environment and lifestyle affect health. They extend the bounds of conventional medicine by actively combatting environmental pollution, poverty, and other dangers to public health.

2. **Responsibility, not dependency.** In the scientific model, patients are dependent on physicians. Holistic medicine tries to shift some responsibility for health from physicians to patients themselves by helping them engage in health-promoting behaviour. Holistic medicine favours an *active* approach to *health*, rather than a *reactive* approach to *illness*.

3. **Personal treatment.** Conventional medicine locates medical care in impersonal offices and hospitals, which are disease-centred settings. By contrast, holistic practitioners favour, as much as possible, a personal and relaxed environment such as the home. Holistic medicine seeks to re-establish the personal ties that united healers and patients before the era of specialists. The CMA currently recognizes approximately fifty specialized areas of medical practice, and a growing proportion of MDs are entering these high-paying specialties rather than family practice. Thus, there is a need for practitioners who are concerned with the patient in the holistic sense.

Clearly, holistic care does not oppose scientific medicine, but shifts its emphasis away from narrowly

Traditional healers work to improve people's health throughout the world, especially in low-income nations. Here, a Chinese practitioner treats a patient by burning rolled herbs into his scalp.

treating disease towards the goal of achieving the highest possible level of well-being for everyone.

PAYING FOR HEALTH: A GLOBAL SURVEY

With greater reliance on high technology, the costs of health care in industrial societies have skyrocketed. Countries employ various strategies to meet these costs.

Medicine in Socialist Societies

In societies with predominantly socialist economies, the government provides medical care directly to the people. These nations hold that all citizens have the right to basic medical care. In practice, then, people do not pay physicians and hospitals on their own; rather, the government uses public funds to pay medical costs. The state owns and operates medical facilities and pays salaries to practitioners, who are government employees.

People's Republic of China. As a poor, agrarian society in the process of industrialization, the People's Republic of China faces the daunting task of tending to the health of more than 1 billion people. Traditional healing arts, including acupuncture and the use of medicinal herbs, are still widely practised in China. In addition, a holistic concern with the interplay of mind and body marks the Chinese approach to health (Sidel and Sidel, 1982b; Kaptchuk, 1985).

China has experimented with private medical care, but the government controls most health care. China's famed barefoot doctors, roughly comparable to North American paramedics, have brought some Western methods of medical care to millions of peasants in remote rural villages.

The former Soviet Union. The former Soviet Union is struggling to transform a state-dominated economy into more of a market system. For this reason, medical care is in transition. Nonetheless, the notion that everyone has a right to basic medical care remains widespread.

Currently, the government provides medical care funded from taxes. As is the case in the People's Republic of China, people do not choose a physician but report to a local government health facility.

Physicians in the former Soviet Union have had lower prestige and income than their counterparts in Canada. Surprisingly, they receive about the same salary as skilled industrial workers. Worth noting, too, is that about 70 percent of physicians in the Russian Federation are women, compared with 30 percent in Canada, and as in our society occupations dominated by women yield fewer financial rewards.

In recent years, the new Russian Federation has suffered setbacks in health care, partly owing to a falling standard of living. Rising demand for medical care has strained a bureaucratic system that, at best, provides highly standardized and impersonal care. The optimistic view is that, as market reform proceeds, both living standards and the quality of medical services will improve. What does seem certain is that disparities in medical care among various segments of the population will increase (Specter, 1995).

Medicine in Capitalist Societies

People living in nations with predominantly capitalist economies are more likely to provide for their own health care in accordance with financial resources and personal preferences. However, the high costs of medical care—beyond the reach of many people—mean that government programs underwrite a considerable proportion of health-related expenses.

Sweden. In 1891, Sweden instituted a compulsory, comprehensive system of government medical care. Citizens pay for this program with their taxes, which are among the highest in the world. In most cases, physicians receive salaries from the government rather than fees from patients, and most hospitals are government managed. Because this medical system resembles that of socialist societies, it is often described as **socialized medicine**, *a health care system in which the government owns and operates most medical facilities and employs most physicians.*

Great Britain. In 1948, Great Britain, too, instituted socialized medicine. It did not do away with private care, but created a "dual system" of medical services. All British citizens are entitled to medical care by the National Health Service, but those who can afford to may purchase more extensive care from doctors and hospitals that operate privately.

Japan. Physicians in Japan operate privately, but a combination of government programs and private insurance pays medical costs. As shown in Figure 21–1, the Japanese approach health care much as the Europeans do, with most medical expenses paid through government.

The United States. The United States stands alone among industrialized societies in having no government-sponsored medical system that provides care for every citizen. Called a **direct-fee system**, it is *a medical care system in which patients pay directly for the services of physicians and hospitals.* Thus, while Europeans look to government to fund about 80 percent of their medical costs (paid for through taxation), the U.S. government pays less than half of the country's medical costs (Lohr, 1988; U.S. Census Bureau, 1999).

In the United States, rich people purchase the best medical care in the world. Yet the poor fare worse than their counterparts in Europe. This disparity explains the relatively high death rates among both infants and adults in the United States compared to many European countries (United Nations Development Programme, 1999).

Expenditures for medical care in the United States have increased dramatically from $12 billion in 1950 to more than $1 trillion in 2000. This amounts to about $4000 per person, more than any other industrial society spends for medical care. Who pays the medical bills? The answer is a combination of private and public insurance programs, plus HMOs (health maintenance organizations), which provide medical services and preventive care for subscribers.

In all, 84 percent of the U.S. population has some medical care coverage, either private or public. But most plans do not provide full coverage, so serious illness threatens even middle-class people with financial hardship. Most programs also exclude certain medical services, such as dental care and treatment for mental health problems. Worse, 44 million people (about 16 percent of the population) have no medical insurance at all. Almost as many lose their medical coverage temporarily each year owing to layoffs or job changes. Some people choose to forgo medical coverage (especially young people who take good health for granted), but most are part-time or full-time workers who receive no health care benefits. Most vulnerable are low- and moderate-income people who cannot afford to become ill but cannot afford to pay for the preventive medical care they need to remain healthy (Altman et al., 1989; Hersch and White-Means, 1993; R. Smith, 1993; U.S. Census Bureau, 1999).

MEDICINE IN CANADA

The Canadian government pays doctors and hospitals—who operate privately or independently—for the services they provide according to a schedule of fees set annually by the federal government and provincial governments in consultation with professional medical associations. Thus, Canada has government-funded and -regulated medical care but, because practitioners operate privately, not true socialized medicine. (See the "Controversy & Debate" box on page 538 for further details.)

Canada's system of universal medicare has a long history, with seeds in the pre-Confederation era. By 1884, Canada's *Public Health Act* required health boards and sanitary regulations at the local level. In 1919, Mackenzie King introduced the idea of universal health care as part of the Liberal party platform, but it wasn't until 1972 that all provinces were part of a federal program providing comprehensive medical insurance—eleven years after such a program was first implemented in Saskatchewan by NDP Premier Tommy Douglas. Canada's law was shaped by recommendations of a Royal Commission on Health Services, instituted in 1961 under Supreme Court Justice Emmett Hall. The law was based on four basic premises:

 For a look at NDP stalwart Tommy Douglas and his campaign to establish medicare in Canada, see http://archives. cbc.ca/300c.asp?id=1-74-851

1. **Universality.** All residents of Canada would be eligible on equal terms, regardless of such differences as previous health records, age, income, membership, or other considerations.

2. **Portability.** The benefits were to be portable from province to province.

3. **Comprehensive coverage.** The benefits were to include all necessary medical services and certain surgical services performed by a dental surgeon in hospital.

4. **Administration.** The plan was to be run on a nonprofit basis. (Nancarrow Clarke, 1996:256)

Canada's system has the advantage of providing care for everyone at a total cost that is significantly lower (as a percentage of GDP) than that needed to operate the (nonuniversal) medical system in the United States. Health expenditures, as a percentage of GDP, peaked in 1993 at 9.9 percent, dropping to 8.9 percent by 1997, mainly because of a growing economy. By 2000, Canada's health expenditures had risen to $95 billion or 9.3 percent of GDP. In contrast, American health care expenditures represent at least 13 percent of GDP.

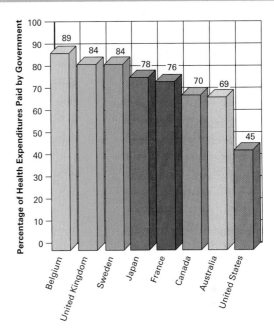

FIGURE 21–1 Extent of Socialized Medicine in Selected Countries

Sources: U.S. Census Bureau (2000) and The World Bank (2001).

However, criticisms of the Canadian system include the claim that it does not make effective use of state-of-the-art technology, as is done south of the border. However, in the United States such technology is available primarily for the wealthy and the well insured. The vast majority of U.S. residents do not reap the benefits of these technological advances, and they do not have access to the medical care that Canadians do. For example, death from cervical cancer is still a major threat in the United States, especially for poor women. In contrast, because of the ready availability of Pap smears, Canada has all but eliminated death from cervical cancer.

Another current criticism of the Canadian system is that it is slower to respond and that people may have to wait long periods of time prior to treatment. Again, the counterargument is that at least people are not denied the possibility of treatment because they are unable to pay for it.

Canadian Women in Medicine

Gone are the days when physicians were almost always male. Today, particularly in the youngest cohort (Table 21–1), women represent half of all physicians, and an astounding 44 percent of specialists. The presence of

TABLE 21-1 The Representation of Canadian Women in Medicine by Age, 2003

Age	Percent Female	
	All Physicians	Specialists
Under 35	50.9	43.6
35–44	40.5	35.4
45–54	31.0	26.8
55–64	17.2	15.3
65 or more	9.8	7.9
Unknown age	27.9	30.0
Total	30.4	25.3

Note: Excludes residents and physicians over 80 years of age.

Source: Calculations by Gerber based on the Canadian Medical Association Masterfile, January 2003 (www.cma.ca).

so many women in specialties means that women are willing to undertake two to six extra years of residency, often postponing child bearing until their thirties, or forgoing it altogether. Table 21–1 does not give the gender breakdown for residents, but the trend suggests that women predominate among residents and especially current medical students, with some medical schools like McMaster graduating classes that are overwhelmingly female (73 percent in 1999).

Of course, many young women doctors—especially residents in emergency and on hospital wards—have to correct the impression that they are nurses. The stereotypical image of doctor as male is still with us (remember "cultural lag"), but young people growing up today are increasingly exposed to women physicians in real life and in the mass media. As a result, twenty or thirty years from now, the stereotypical physician may well be female. (Interestingly, the appearance of male nurses on our hospital wards is not reflected yet in the mass media.)

THEORETICAL ANALYSIS OF HEALTH AND MEDICINE

Each of the major theoretical paradigms in sociology provides a means of organizing and interpreting the facts and issues presented in this chapter.

STRUCTURAL-FUNCTIONAL ANALYSIS

Talcott Parsons (1951) viewed medicine as society's strategy to keep its members healthy. In this scheme, illness is dysfunctional, undermining the performance of social roles and thus impeding the operation of society.

The Sick Role

The normative response to disease, according to Parsons, is for an individual to assume the **sick role**, *patterns of behaviour defined as appropriate for people who are ill.* The sick role has three characteristics.

1. **Illness suspends routine responsibilities.** Serious illness relaxes or suspends normal social obligations, such as going to work or attending school. To prevent abuse of this privilege, however, people do not simply declare themselves ill; they must enlist the support of others—especially a recognized medical expert—before assuming the sick role.

2. **A sick person must want to be well.** We assume that no one wants to be sick. Thus, people suspected of feigning illness to escape responsibility or to receive special attention have no legitimate claim to the sick role.

3. **An ailing person must seek competent help.** People who are ill must seek competent assistance and cooperate with health care practitioners. By failing to accept medical help or to follow doctors' orders, a person gives up any claim to the sick role's exemption from routine responsibilities.

The Physician's Role

The physician's role centres on assessing claims of sickness and restoring sick people to normal routines. This responsibility, Parsons explained, rests on specialized knowledge. Physicians expect patients to follow "doctors' orders" and to provide personal information necessary to assist their efforts.

Although it is inevitably hierarchical, the doctor–patient relationship varies from society to society. Japanese tradition, for example, gives physicians great authority over their patients. Japanese physicians even take it upon themselves to decide how much information about the seriousness of an illness they will share with the patient (Darnton and Hoshia, 1989).

Until about thirty years ago, physicians in Canada acted in much the same way. But the patients' rights movement demands that physicians share more medical information and offer patients a choice of treatment options. A more egalitarian relationship between doctor and patient is also developing in European societies and, gradually, in Japan.

Critical evaluation. Parsons's analysis links illness and medicine to the broader organization of society. Others have extended the concept of the sick role to some nonillness situations such as pregnancy (Myers and Grasmick, 1989).

One limitation of the sick-role concept is that it applies to acute conditions (such as the flu) better than it does to chronic illness (such as heart disease), which may not be reversible. Moreover, a sick person's ability to regain health depends on available resources. Many poor people can ill afford either medical care or time off from work.

Our view of medicine has changed during the last several decades. Television viewers in the 1970s watched doctors like Marcus Welby, M.D., confidently take charge of situations in a fatherly—and almost godlike—manner. By the 1990s, programs like ER *gave a more realistic view of the limitations of medicine to address illness, as well as the violence that wracks society.*

Critics also question the implication of Parsons's analysis that doctors—rather than people themselves—should bear the primary responsibility for health. Treatment-oriented physicians respond to acute illness, of course, but a more prevention-oriented approach makes physicians and patients equal partners in the pursuit of health.

SYMBOLIC-INTERACTION ANALYSIS

According to the symbolic-interaction paradigm, society is less a grand system than a series of complex, ever-changing realities. Both health and medical care are thus human constructions that people perceive subjectively.

The Social Construction of Illness

Since we socially construct our ideas of health and illness, members of a very poor society may view hunger and malnutrition as quite normal. Similarly, people in rich nations, such as our own, may give little thought to the harmful effects of spending leisure time passively watching television or consuming a rich diet.

How we respond to illness, too, is based on social definitions that may or may not square with medical knowledge. For instance, people with AIDS contend with fear and sometimes outright bigotry that has no medical basis.

Furthermore, whether we decide we are "sick" or "well" may rest on a host of nonmedical "contingencies." Canadian university students, for example, have been known to ignore signs of illness on the eve of a vacation, yet dutifully march into the infirmary hours before a difficult examination. Health, in short, is less an objective commodity than a negotiated outcome.

Moreover, how people define a medical situation may actually affect how they feel. Medical experts have long marvelled at *psychosomatic* disorders (a fusion of Greek words meaning "mind" and "body"), in which a state of mind leads to physical sensations (Hamrick et al., 1986). As sociologist W.I. Thomas (1966, orig. 1931) pointed out, a situation defined as real becomes real in its consequences. (See the "Applying Sociology" box for further analysis based on an interpretive approach.)

The Social Construction of Treatment

In Chapter 6 ("Social Interaction in Everyday Life"), we used the dramaturgical approach of Erving Goffman to explain how physicians craft their physical surroundings ("the office") and present themselves to others to foster specific impressions of competence and power.

Sociologist Joan Emerson (1970) further illustrates this process of reality construction by analyzing a situation familiar to women, a gynecological examination carried out by a male doctor. After observing seventy-five such examinations, she explains that this setting is especially precarious, because it is so vulnerable to misinterpretation. The man's touching of a woman's genitals—conventionally viewed as a sexual act and possibly even an assault—must, in this case, be defined as impersonal and professional.

To ensure that people construct reality in this way, doctors and nurses remove sexual connotations as completely as possible. They furnish the examination

"Hi . . . How Are You?"

It is with this question, or a similar one, that we greet almost anyone. While we may not want a detailed or honest answer, we *are* asking about the health or well-being of the individuals we encounter. Medical or health sociologists are interested in a wide range of issues related to health, illness, and medical care and how they relate to society—but underlying it all is an awareness that the "cultural practice of starting conversations with a question about health reflects the fundamental importance that we attach to good health in our society" (Segall and Chappell, 2000:2). Segall and Chappell set out to turn this insight into a comprehensive analysis of health, medicine, and society.

As these researchers point out, the structural-functional paradigm leads the sociologist to look at health and illness as social roles within the context of the social system. Illness places one in a social position that involves performing the sick role, which, in turn, determines the behaviour of those with whom the sick person interacts. In contrast, the conflict paradigm emphasizes the power dimension of social relationships, defining health and illness as professional constructs. The medical profession "defines disease in theory," "identifies it in practice," and supervises the sick in "their efforts to regain good health." The conflict approach "shifts the focus to medical dominance" (2000:23, 26). As always, the symbolic-interaction paradigm turns from emphasis on structured relationships—based on consensus or conflict—and looks at "the ways in which health and illness are personally experienced" (p. 29). It is the *meaning* of health behaviour that is sought through an interpretive approach. How do we perceive health status, and what do we believe we should do to maintain health or manage illness? Segall and Chappell adopt an eclectic approach, recognizing that all three sociological paradigms enhance our understanding of health and illness.

The authors go on to examine health beliefs, health determinants, and the relationship between social structure and health, as well as the creation of our health care system. The result is an enriched analysis of topics that otherwise might be viewed from a single perspective. For example, a look at lay beliefs about health and illness recognizes the impact of structural factors like gender, class, ethnicity, and the Aboriginal experience. The constant negotiation of the meaning or definition of health and illness assumes that a different dynamic is at work in each of these contexts. Likewise, lay definitions of the role of midwives, penicillin, alternative medicine, or physicians themselves challenge the dominant medical model and initiate change.

Community and official responses to gas sniffing among the Innu children of Newfoundland reveal the dynamic negotiation of the definition of illness and of solutions. Medical authorities are responding to the changing beliefs and demands of Innu leaders and families in their efforts to find solutions; beliefs, Aboriginal status, and traditional authority interact in this evolving situation. The rich, multidimensional approach suggested by Segall and Chappell alerts us to the interactions of beliefs, structure, and power—and to the possibility of change.

---

room with nothing but medical equipment; all personnel wear medical uniforms. Staff members act as if such examinations are simply routine, although, from the patient's point of view, they may be quite unusual.

Further, rapport between physician and patient is established before the examination begins. Once underway, the doctor's performance is strictly professional, suggesting to the patient that inspecting the genitals is no different from surveying any other part of the body. A female nurse is usually present during the examination, not only to assist the physician but to dispel any impression that a man and a woman are alone in a room.

The need to manage situational definitions has long been overlooked by medical schools. This omission is unfortunate because, as Emerson's analysis shows, understanding how people construct reality in the examination room is just as crucial as mastering the medical skills required for effective treatment.

Critical evaluation. One strength of the symbolic-interaction paradigm lies in revealing the relativity of sickness and health. What people view as normal or deviant, healthful or harmful, depends on a host of factors, many of which are not, strictly speaking, medical. This approach also shows that all medical procedures involve a subtle process of reality construction between patient and medical staff.

But it seems wrong to deny that there are some objective standards of well-being. Certain physical conditions do indeed cause specific negative changes in human capacities, whether we think so or not. People who lack sufficient nutrition and safe water, for example, suffer from their unhealthy environment, however they define their surroundings.

SOCIAL-CONFLICT ANALYSIS

Social-conflict analysis draws a connection between health and social inequality and, taking a cue from Karl Marx, ties medicine to the operation of capitalism. Researchers have focused on three main issues: access to medical care, the effects of the profit motive, and the politics of medicine.

The Access Issue

Personal health is the foundation of social life. Yet, from a Marxist perspective, capitalist societies make health a commodity, so that health follows wealth. As already noted, this problem is more serious in the United States than in other industrialized societies because it has no universal health care system. However, as Canada's provincial and federal governments continue to wrangle about cost-sharing programs, our heralded medicare scheme is vulnerable to cutbacks and growing inequality among the provinces, as well as among individual Canadians.

Most of the 44 million people in the United States who lack any health care coverage at present have low incomes. Conflict theorists concede that capitalism does provide excellent health care for the rich; it simply does not provide very well for the rest of the population.

The Profit Motive

Some analysts go further, arguing that the real problem is not access to medical care but the character of capitalist medicine itself. The profit motive turns physicians, hospitals, and the pharmaceutical industry into multibillion-dollar corporations. The quest for ever-increasing profits also encourages questionable medical practices, including ordering needless tests, performing unnecessary surgery, and relying overly on drugs (Kaplan et al., 1985).

One example of questionable medical practice involves more than 2 million women in the United States and Canada who have undergone silicone breast-implant surgery, under the assumption that the plastic packets of silicone were safe. Recently, however, it became clear that these implants are not safe enough, a fact apparently known to Dow Corning, their major manufacturer, for decades.

Most surgical operations performed annually in Canada are "elective," meaning that they promote a patient's long-term health rather then being prompted by a medical emergency. Critics charge that the decision to perform surgery often reflects the financial interests of surgeons and hospitals as much as the medical needs of patients (Illich, 1976). Also, drugs or medical procedures prescribed for people subject them to risks, which harm between 5 and 10 percent of patients (Sidel and Sidel, 1982a; Cowley, 1995).

Finally, say social-conflict analysts, our society is all too tolerant of physicians having a direct financial interest in the tests and procedures they order for their patients (Pear and Eckholm, 1991). In short, health care should be motivated by a concern for people, not profits.

Medicine as Politics

Although medicine declares itself to be politically neutral, scientific medicine frequently takes sides on significant social issues. For example, the medical establishment has often opposed government-operated health care programs. The history of medicine, critics contend, is replete with racial and sexual discrimination, defended by "scientific" opinions (Leavitt, 1984). Consider the diagnosis of "hysteria," a term that has its origins in the Greek word *hyster*, meaning uterus. In coining this word, medical professionals called on its resonances to suggest that being a woman was synonymous with being irrational.

Surveying the entire medical field, some critics see political mischief in today's scientific medicine. Scientists explain illness in terms of bacteria and viruses, ignoring the effects of social inequality on health. From a scientific perspective, in other words, poor people get sick because of a lack of sanitation and an unhealthy diet, even though poverty may be the underlying cause of these ills. In this way, critics charge, scientific medicine depoliticizes health by reducing complex political issues to simple matters of biology.

Recently, physicians and politicians have been engaged in an unusual medicalization issue in that the *politicians* are seeking to influence appropriate medical intervention. The issue is that of the medicinal use of marijuana. Along with moves to decriminalize marijuana, our federal government is allowing physicians to prescribe and dispense it to patients for control of pain, nausea, and other symptoms, especially among the terminally ill. Doctors, in turn, are reluctant because marijuana has not gone through the normal, rigorous clinical trials that establish efficacy and safety. In the end, some physicians will cooperate while others will not—just as some refuse to prescribe birth control because of their personal beliefs.

 For information about medical use of marijuana in Canada, see the Health Canada website at www.hc-sc.gc.ca/english/protection/marijuana.html

Critical evaluation. Social-conflict analysis offers another approach to the relationships among health, medicine, and our society. According to this view, social inequality is the reason some people have far better health than others.

The most common objection to the conflict approach is that it minimizes the overall improvement in health through the years and scientific medicine's contribution to our high standard of living today. Even

Two-Tiered Health Care: Threat, Fact, or Fiction?

Emmett M. Hall (1898–1995) had a distinguished legal career leading to his appointment to Canada's Supreme Court, from which he retired in 1973 at the age of seventy-five. Beyond his legal role, Hall helped to develop public medical care in Saskatchewan—before going on to design a system of universal health care for all of Canada, which was implemented in 1967. As the father of medicare, Hall created a national social institution that is dear to our hearts and central to our Canadian identity.

In the fall of 2000, Canadians found themselves involved in a federal election campaign—one that took a number of unexpected turns and resulted with a third majority Liberal government. Central to the Liberal campaign was the attempt to instil fear in eastern Canada of Stockwell Day and his Canadian Alliance. Day and his Alliance candidates, according to the Liberals, were "social conservatives" who, through a "hidden agenda" would force their religious beliefs (about abortion, capital punishment, and homosexuality) on the whole country. Even more damaging was the allegation that they would introduce "two-tiered medicine" resulting in separate systems of medical care for the rich and the poor. They would accomplish this by allowing *private* clinics to deliver health care.

In the weeks that followed, the Liberals, the NDP, and the media refused to acknowledge a reality that Stockwell Day and the Alliance were unable to articulate clearly. The reality is that today, the *funding* of our universal medicare is public, yet its *delivery* is almost entirely private.

In a paper entitled "Getting What We Pay For: Myths and Realities about Financing Canada's Health Care System," Deber (2000) points out the distinction between financing and delivery; she also claims that our failure to distinguish between finance and delivery makes it difficult to diagnose the problems in our system. We call our medicare system *public* because the government ensures its universality by paying most of the bills. Yet Canadians have failed to recognize that almost all of the delivery has been *private*. Most of our hospitals are private, nonprofit organizations, run by independent boards. Physicians are not government employees but rather private practitioners—or people in business. They bill for services rendered, but then have to pay rent, staff salaries, and equipment costs from their revenues. Nursing homes and home care providers are also private organizations.

As long as there is a single payer—the government—and individuals cannot pay to jump the queue, we do not have a two-tier system with superior services for the wealthy. Even if Canadians go to the United States for cancer treatment (in private clinics), we are not dealing with unequal access—because Canadian governments pay all of their expenses. If private clinics, as opposed to hospitals, in Alberta are allowed to do hip surgery and the government picks up the tab, then, once again, this is not two-tiered service.

In Canada, part of the debate about universality revolves around insured and uninsured services. Public funding does not cover all components of medical care: dentistry, cosmetic surgery, eye care (glasses, laser surgery), and drugs are among the services left to private insurance or payment by the individual. In fact, in Canada, public expenditure on health care is only 70 percent of the total cost, compared to 88 and 83 percent in Belgium and the United Kingdom (Deber, 2000). The *Canada Health Act* protects only publicly "insured" services from queue jumping on the part of those willing to pay. Uninsured services are funded and delivered entirely within the private sphere.

Deber argues that Canada's health care costs are not out of control and that part of the reason is that a single payer funds most services. Allowing competition among multiple payers—as in the United States—actually results in escalating health care costs. According to Deber, "the health care system that Canadians have created is already a model for the entire world" (2000:43). Reducing the number of providers or relying on privately funded options (like home care) are false economies that contribute, in the end, to escalating costs. Our best option, in terms of cost effectiveness, is to enhance the funding and delivery of our publicly insured services.

though we could certainly do better, health indicators for our population have risen steadily over the course of the twentieth century and compare fairly well with those of other industrial societies.

In sum, sociology's three major theoretical paradigms convincingly argue that health and medicine are social issues. Indeed, advancing technology is forcing us to confront the social foundations of health and medicine. The famous French scientist Louis Pasteur (1822–95), who spent much of his life studying how bacteria cause disease, said just before he died that health depends much less on bacteria than on the social environment in which bacteria operate (Gordon, 1980:7). Explaining Pasteur's insight is sociology's contribution to human health.

LOOKING AHEAD: HEALTH IN THE TWENTY-FIRST CENTURY

At the beginning of the twentieth century, deaths from infectious disease were widespread, and scientists had yet to develop basic antibiotics such as penicillin. Thus, even common infections represented a deadly threat to health. Today, members of our society take For World Health Organization reports on the health habits of young people in 28 countries, including Canada, see www.hbsc.org/publications/reports.html for granted the good health and long life that was the exception, not the rule, a century ago. There is every reason to expect that our health will continue to improve as we move further into the twenty-first century.

Another encouraging trend is that more people are taking responsibility for their own health (Caplow et al., 1991). Every one of us can live better and longer if we avoid tobacco, eat sensibly and in moderation, and exercise regularly.

Yet certain health problems will continue to plague Canadian society in the decades to come. With no cure in sight, it seems likely that the AIDS epidemic will persist for some time. At this point, the only way to steer clear of contracting HIV is to make a decision to avoid all of the risky behaviours noted in this chapter.

But the changing social profile of people with AIDS—which increasingly afflicts the poor—reminds us that Canada falls short in addressing the health of marginalized members of our society. Even those among us who do not easily embrace the notion of serving as our "brother's keeper" should recognize the moral obligation that we as a people have to ensure that everyone has the security of medical care.

Finally, repeating a pattern seen in earlier chapters, we find that problems of health are far greater in the poor societies of the world than they are in Canada. The good news is that life expectancy for the world as a whole has been rising—from forty-eight years in 1950 to sixty-five years today—and the biggest gains have been in poor countries (Mosley and Cowley, 1991). But in much of Latin America, Asia, and especially Africa, hundreds of millions of adults and children lack adequate food, safe water, and needed medical attention. Improving health in the world's poorest societies remains a critical challenge in the twenty-first century. In 2003, Prime Minister Chrétien and President Bush pledged significant funding to counter HIV and AIDs in Africa. When rock singer Bono appeared at the Liberal convention that was to elect Paul Martin as the party leader (November 14, 2003), he made it clear that he would hold the new prime minister to the promise of his predecessor.

SUMMARY

1. Health is a social and biological issue, and well-being depends on the extent and distribution of a society's resources. Culture shapes both definitions of health and patterns of health care.

2. Through most of human history, health has been poor by today's standards. Health improved dramatically in Western Europe and North America in the nineteenth century, first because industrialization raised living standards and later because medical advances controlled infectious diseases.

3. Infectious diseases were the major killers at the beginning of the twentieth century. Today, most people in Canada die in or near old age of heart disease, cancer, or stroke.

4. Health in low-income countries is undermined by inadequate sanitation and hunger. Average life expectancy is about twenty years less than in Canada; in the poorest nations, half of the children do not survive to adulthood.

5. In Canada, three-quarters of children born today can expect to live to at least age sixty-five. Throughout the life course, however, people of high social position are healthier than the poor.

6. Cigarette smoking increased during the twentieth century to become the greatest preventable cause of death in Canada. Now that the health hazards of smoking are known, social tolerance for the use of tobacco products is declining.

7. The incidence of sexually transmitted diseases has risen since 1960, an exception to the general decline in infectious disease.

8. The ability to prolong the lives of terminally ill people is forcing us to confront a number of ethical issues surrounding death and dying.

9. Historically a family concern, health care is now the responsibility of trained specialists. The model of scientific medicine underlies the Canadian and U.S. medical establishments.

10. Holistic healing encourages people to assume greater responsibility for their own health and well-being, and urges professional healers to gain knowledge of patients and their environments.

11. Socialist societies define medical care as a right that governments offer equally to everyone. Capitalist societies view medical care as a commodity to be purchased, although most capitalist governments support medical care through socialized medicine or national health insurance.

12. Canada's health care system is a source of pride for Canadians and a major source of envy for many in the United States. Yet Canada's system was developed after, and in many ways is more restrictive than, those in Western Europe and Great Britain.

13. Structural-functional analysis links health and medicine to other social structures. A concept central to structural-functional analysis is the sick role, by which the ill person is excused from routine social responsibilities.

14. The symbolic-interaction paradigm views health and medical treatments largely as matters of subjective perception and social definition.

15. Social-conflict analysis focuses on the unequal distribution of health and medical care. It criticizes the North American medical establishment for relying too heavily on drugs and surgery and for emphasizing the biological rather than social causes of illness.

CRITICAL-THINKING QUESTIONS

1. Explain why health is as much a social as a biological issue.

2. In global context, what are the "diseases of poverty" that kill people in poor countries? What are the "diseases of affluence," the leading killers in rich nations?

3. Sexually transmitted diseases represent an exception to the historical decline in infectious illness. What social forces are reflected in the rise in STDs since 1960?

4. Do you think the United States should follow the lead of Canada and other industrial countries by enacting a government program of health care for everyone? Why or why not?

APPLICATIONS AND EXERCISES

1. Ask your friends about their perceptions of the health consequences of smoking, drinking, using drugs, or having unprotected sex. How do their views differ from official or professional ones?

2. Visit the website for Health Canada at **www.hc-sc.gc.ca**. You will find health news, statistical data, and even travellers' health advisories. This site offers considerable evidence of the social dimensions of health.

3. Is there a medical school on or near your campus? If so, obtain a course catalogue and see how much (if any) of the medical curriculum involves the social dimensions of health care.

4. Arrange to speak with a midwife about her work helping women to give birth. How do midwives differ from medical obstetricians in their approach?

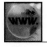 SITES TO SEE

www.macionis.com
or
www.TheSociologyPage.com
You can find more than fifty weblinks to sociological journals and other sources of data and information by visiting the Links Library at this website.

www.who.org/
The World Health Organization is the directing and coordinating authority on international health work. Its responsibilities include assisting governments to strengthen health services; promoting improved nutrition, sanitation, and other living conditions; developing international standards for food and pharmaceutical products; and promoting cooperation among scientific and professional groups.

www.hc-sc.gc.ca/
The Ministry of Health publishes information on health issues, news headlines, advice for travellers, a food guide, reports, government regulations and policies, and more.

www.cihr-irsc.gc.ca/

The Canadian Institutes of Health Research (CIHR) is the major federal funding agency for health research. The website offers information on research, ethics, and strategic initiatives aiming at creating new knowledge that will result in better health care, more effective services, and a stronger Canadian health care system.

www.hc-sc.gc.ca/hppb/hpo/

Developed by Health Canada's Health Promotion and Programs Branch, Health Promotion Online provides health promotion resources, including FAQs and publications about health issues, online discussion forums, a directory of health organizations, and a calendar of events.

www.nlm.nih.gov/

The U.S. National Library of Medicine site offers extensive health and medical information, including access to Medline and other databases, fact sheets and publications, images from the history of medicine, the Visible Human Project, and other resources.

STUDY TOOLS

For more study tools to help you with your next exam, be sure to check out the Companion Website at **www.pearsoned.ca/macionis**, as well as Chapter 21 in your Study Guide.

INVESTIGATE WITH CONTENTSELECT

Follow the instructions found on page 25 of this textbook to access ContentSelect™ at the Research Navigator™ website. Once at the site, enter your LOGINID and Password. Then, enter keywords such as "health," "AIDS," "cigarette smoking," and "right to die," and the search engine will supply relevant and recent scholarly and popular press publications.

CHAPTER
22

W. Louis Sonntag, Jr. (1869–1898, American)
The Bowery at Night, 1895
Copyright Museum of the City of New York.
32.275.2

POPULATION, URBANIZATION, AND THE ENVIRONMENT

"When Water Kills" is the title of a *Maclean's* cover story (Nikiforuk, 2000), written in the aftermath of the deaths and illnesses that followed the contamination of drinking water in Walkerton, Ontario. Eschericia coli 0157, a virulent strain of E. coli, was responsible for the Walkerton deaths, just as it was for the deaths of a dozen children in southern Alberta between 1989 and 1991. Both outbreaks, the article explains, were directly linked to "cattle densities" as mapped by Health Canada.

The global demand for beef and pork has led to the development of a new multibillion-dollar industry in Canada—factory farms, feedlots, or, as our governments call them, "intensive livestock operations." As many as 25 000 cattle may be raised on a plot of land the size of a city block in Alberta's Feedlot Alley (just north of Lethbridge). Hog factories might house as many as 80 000 pigs. Competitive pressures force Canadian producers into these large-scale beef and hog operations, which generate tremendous export revenues and employ hundreds of thousands of workers. Beef and pork are big business in Canada.

The problem with all of this economic activity is that a 25 000-head beef feedlot produces more dung, or fecal matter, than 250 000 Calgarians. Canada lags behind the United States in regulating factory farms—Kansas and Nebraska have banned them altogether—so that almost all of our beef and hog effluent remains untreated and is spread onto fields as fertilizer. From there, runoff takes bacteria and unwanted minerals into our groundwater, lakes, and streams; not surprisingly, E. coli makes its way into our wells. We have the technology to treat this sewage, test water quality, and treat our water. What we do *not* have in any of our provinces, Andrew Nikiforuk explains, is the political will to bring in the regulations that would ensure safe drinking water for all Canadians.

This chapter examines three closely related topics: population increase, urbanization, and the state of the natural environment. As we shall see, population has soared during the past two centuries—not just in Canada but around the world—and cities everywhere have grown rapidly. We shall consider how these changes have altered the shape of societies and what they mean for the future of the planet. We begin with population.

DEMOGRAPHY: THE STUDY OF POPULATION

From the time people first walked the earth, some 250 000 years ago, until just 250 years ago, the earth's population hovered around 500 million—about the number of people in Europe today. Life was brutal and usually short; people fell victim to countless diseases, frequent injury, and periodic natural disasters.

But by about 1750, world population began to spike upward. We now add 77 million people to the planet each year, so that in the fall of 1999, the number of people living on the earth passed the 6 billion mark—reaching 6.2 billion in 2002.

The causes and consequences of these changes are the basis of **demography**, *the study of human population.* Demography (from the Greek, meaning "description of people") is a specialty within sociology that analyzes the size and composition of a population and studies

Birth Rates per 1000 Population

- 15 and higher
- 13 to 14.9
- 10 to 12.9
- Less than 10

National Average: 10.6

Yukon Territory 11.3

Northwest Territories 14.8

Nunavut 25.2

British Columbia 9.8

Alberta 12.3

Saskatchewan 12.0

Manitoba 12.1

Ontario 11.0

Quebec 9.7

Newfoundland and Labrador 8.8

Prince Edward Island 9.9

Nova Scotia 9.4

New Brunswick 9.4

Hudson Bay

Atlantic Ocean

Pacific Ocean

CANADA MAP 22–1
Birth Rates per 1000 Population, by Province and Territory, 2002–2003 (July 1–June 30)

Source: Calculations based on Statistics Canada online database, CANSIM, Births.

---

how people move from place to place. Demographers not only collect statistics, they also pose important

 To find out more about Canadian demography, visit the Statistics Canada website at www.statcan.ca

questions about the effects of population growth and how population might be controlled. The following sections present basic demographic concepts.

FERTILITY

The study of human population begins with how many people are born. **Fertility** is *the incidence of childbearing in a country's population.* Women are capable of childbearing from the onset of menstruation (typically in the early teens) to menopause (usually around fifty). During this time, a well-nourished noncontracepting woman could conceivably bear more than twenty children, but this *fecundity*, or potential childbearing, is sharply reduced for most people by health, financial concerns, cultural norms, and personal choice.

Demographers often measure fertility using the **crude birth rate**, *the number of live births in a given year for every thousand people in a population.* A crude birth rate is calculated by dividing the number of live births in a given year by a society's total population, and multiplying the result by 1000. In Canada in 2000 there were 327 882 live births in a population of 30

million. According to the formula, then, there were 10.9 live births for every thousand people, or a crude birth rate of 10.9.

This birth rate is "crude" because it is based on the entire population, not just women in their childbearing years. Making comparisons using crude birth rates can be misleading because one society may have a higher proportion of women of childbearing age than another. A crude birth rate also tells us nothing about how birth rates differ among people of various races, ethnicities, and religions. But this measure is easy to calculate and serves as a good indicator of a society's overall fertility. Figure 22–1 shows that, in global perspective, the crude birth rate of North Americans is low. Canada Map 22–1 reveals that fertility within Canada varies dramatically, from a low of 8.8 per 1000 population in Newfoundland and Labrador to 25.2 in Nunavut. The low in Newfoundland and Labrador is the result of steady out-migration of young people of childbearing age. Quebec's relatively low fertility rate is the result of the Quiet Revolution of the 1960s, when francophones threw off their poor, rural, Catholic past and embraced a secular, urban future, where educated women entered the labour force. The women of Quebec incurred new opportunity costs (promotion or seniority) if they took time off work to have children; as a result, their birth rate declined and remained low to the present.

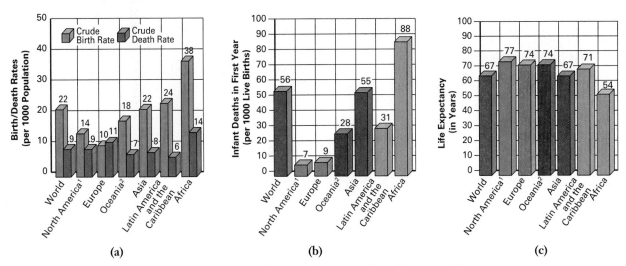

FIGURE 22–1 (a) Crude Birth Rates and Crude Death Rates, (b) Infant Mortality Rates,
(c) Life Expectancy, 2000

[1]United States and Canada
[2]Australia, New Zealand, and South Pacific Islands

Source: Population Reference Bureau (2001).

MORTALITY

Population size is also affected by **mortality**, *the incidence of death in a society's population*. To measure mortality, demographers use a **crude death rate**, *the number of deaths in a given year for every thousand people in a population*. The crude death rate is calculated as the number of deaths in a year divided by the total population and multiplied by 1000. In 2001, Canada's crude death rate was 7.5 per 1000 population. This rate, low by world standards, is even lower than that of the United States (8.7 in 2001).

A third, widely used demographic measure is the **infant mortality rate**, *the number of deaths among infants in the first year of life for each thousand live births in a given year*. This rate is derived from dividing the number of deaths of children under one year of age by the number of live births during the same year and multiplying the result by 1000. In 2001, Canada's infant mortality rate was 5.0 per 1000 live births. This is lower than the U.S. rate (6.8), but above that of most European and Scandinavian countries or Japan (3.9).

Like other demographic variables, this rate conceals considerable variation among segments of the Canadian population. For example, infant mortality rates are higher among the poor, in isolated communities, and among Native peoples. Nonetheless, infant mortality offers a good general measure of overall quality of life and is therefore used as one indicator of socioeconomic development. The second part of Figure 22–1 shows that infant mortality in North America is low by world standards.

Societies with low infant mortality rates have high **life expectancy**, *the average life span of a society's population*. Canadian males born in 1997 can expect to live seventy-six years, while females can expect to live to eighty-one—one or two years longer than their counterparts in the United States. Life expectancy in rich, highly developed countries is about twenty years longer than it is in poor, less-developed societies (see Figure 22–1).

Migration

Population size is also affected by **migration**, *the movement of people into and out of a specified territory*. Migration is sometimes involuntary, as illustrated by the forcible transport of 10 million Africans to the western hemisphere as slaves (Sowell, 1981). Voluntary migration, however, is usually the result of complex "push-pull" factors. Dissatisfaction with life in a poor rural village may "push" people to begin the process of migration. A common "pull" factor is the attraction of a big city, where people assume opportunity is greater. As we shall explain later in this chapter, migration underlies much of rapid urban growth in less-developed countries.

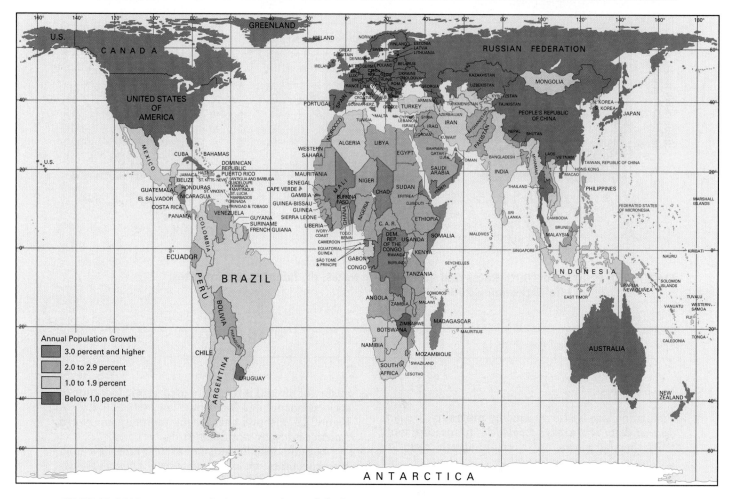

GLOBAL MAP 22–1 Population Growth in Global Perspective

The richest countries of the world—including Canada, the United States, and the nations of Europe—have growth rates below 1 percent. The nations of Latin America and Asia typically have growth rates around 1.6 percent, which doubles a population in forty-four years. Africa has an overall growth rate of 2.4 percent, which cuts the doubling time to twenty-nine years. In global perspective, we see that a society's standard of living is closely related to its rate of population growth: population is rising fastest in the world regions that can least afford to support more people.

Source: Population Reference Bureau (2001); map projection from *Peters Atlas of the World* (1990).

The movement of people into a territory—*immigration*—is measured as an *in-migration rate*, the number entering an area for every thousand people in the population. Movement out of a territory—*emigration*—is measured as an *out-migration rate*, the number leaving for every thousand people. The two types of migration usually occur simultaneously; demographers describe the net result of in-migration and out-migration as the *net-migration rate*.

POPULATION GROWTH

Fertility, mortality, and migration all affect the size of a society's population. In general, rich nations (such as Canada) grow almost as much from immigration as from natural increase; less economically developed societies (such as Mexico) grow almost entirely from natural increase.

Demographers derive the *natural growth rate* of a population by subtracting the crude death rate from

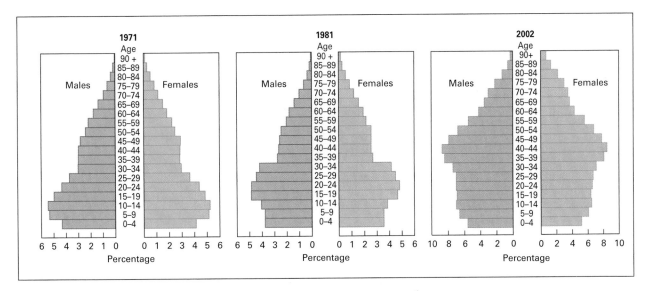

FIGURE 22–2 Age-Sex Population Pyramids for Canada, 1971–2002[*]

[*]Note that, in 1971, the baby boom shows up in the 5-to-19-years-of-age category; by 2002, the baby boom is in the 36-to-50-years-of-age category.

Source: Adapted from Statistics Canada, Catalogue No. 93-310, 1971, 1981, 2002.

the crude birth rate. The natural growth rate of the Canadian population in 2002–3 was 3.3 per thousand (the crude birth rate of 10.5 minus the crude death rate of 7.2), or 0.33 percent annually. Demographers predict that the growth rate of the Canadian population will remain low, but this is not the case for many other regions of the world.

Global Map 22–1 shows that population growth in Canada and other industrialized nations is well below the world average of 1.3 percent. The earth's low-growth continents include Europe (currently posting a slight decline of –0.1 percent annual growth), North America (0.5 percent), and Oceania (1.1 percent). Asia (1.4 percent) and Latin America (1.7 percent) stand slightly above the global average. Africa (2.4 percent) is the high-growth region of the world.

Demographers have a handy rule of thumb for estimating population growth: divide a society's population growth rate into the number seventy to calculate the *doubling time* in years. Thus, annual growth of 2 percent (common in Latin America) doubles a population in thirty-five years, and a 3 percent growth rate (found in some parts of Africa) pares the doubling time to twenty-four years. The rapid population growth of the poorest countries is deeply troubling because they can barely support the populations they have now.

POPULATION COMPOSITION

Demographers also study the composition of a society's population at any point in time. One variable is the **sex ratio**, *the number of males for every hundred females in a given population*. In 2002, the sex ratio in Canada was

98.1, or 98 men for every 100 females. Sex ratios typically fall below 100 because, as was noted in Chapter 21 ("Health and Medicine"), women tend to outlive men. In India, however, the sex ratio is 107. There are more males than females in India because parents value sons more than daughters and may either abort a female fetus or, after birth, give more care to a male infant, raising the odds that a girl child will die.

A more complex measure is the **age-sex pyramid**, *a graphic representation of the age and sex of a population*. Figure 22–2 presents the age-sex pyramids for Canada in 1971, 1981, and 2002. The left side indicates the distribution of males of different ages, while the right side shows the corresponding distribution of females. The rough pyramid shape of these figures results from higher mortality as people age. Also note that after about age thirty, women increasingly outnumber men in Canada. The bulge that moves up the pyramid from 1971–91 represents the *baby boom* from the mid-1940s to 1970. The contraction just below age twenty on the 1981 pyramid shows that the baby boom was followed by a *baby bust* as the birth rate dipped from 28.2 in 1955 to a low of 12.7 in 1996. The bulges in the three pyramids in Figure 22–2 reveal the upward motion of the baby boom generation over a thirty-year period. See Figure 15–1 in Chapter 15 ("Aging and the Elderly") for projections to the year 2011.

By comparing the age-sex pyramids of two different societies, we can predict different demographic trends. Figure 22–3 compares the age-sex pyramids of a rich country, Sweden, and a poor one, Kenya. The age-sex pyramid for Kenya, like that of other low-income nations, is wide at the bottom (reflecting higher

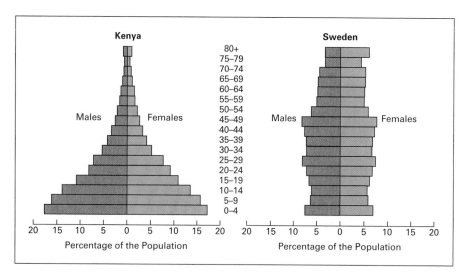

FIGURE 22–3
The Demographic Composition of Sweden and Kenya

Source: Compiled by Gerber from United Nations, *Demographic Yearbook* (1996).

birth rates) and narrows quickly by what we would term middle age (owing to higher mortality). The relatively box-like pyramid for Sweden reveals a birth rate that has long been very low, and that recently has dropped even further. With fewer women entering their childbearing years, population growth is likely to remain low. The Swedish pattern is more or less replicated by other industrial societies.

HISTORY AND THEORY OF POPULATION GROWTH

Through most of human history, people favoured large families since human labour was the key to productivity. Additionally, until the development of rubber condoms 150 years ago, preventing pregnancy was uncertain at best. But high death rates, resulting from widespread infectious diseases, put a constant brake on population growth.

However, as shown in Figure 22–4, a major demographic shift began about 1750 as the world's population turned upward, reaching the 1 billion mark by 1800. This milestone (which took all of human history up to this point) was repeated by 1930—barely a century later—when a second billion people were added to the planet. In other words, not only was population increasing but the *rate* of growth was accelerating. Global population reached 3 billion by 1962 (just thirty-two years later) and 4 billion by 1974 (a scant twelve years later). The rate of world population increase has slowed recently, but our planet passed the 5 billion mark in 1987 and the 6 billion mark late in 1999. In no previous century did the world's population even double. In the twentieth century, it quadrupled.

Currently, the world is gaining 77 million people each year, with 96 percent of the increase in poor countries. Experts predict that the earth's population will reach between 8 billion and 9 billion by 2050 (Wattenberg, 1997; Thirunarayanapuram, 1998). Given the world's troubles in feeding the present population, such an increase is a matter of urgent concern.

MALTHUSIAN THEORY

It was the sudden population growth two centuries ago that sparked the development of demography. Thomas Robert Malthus (1766–1834), an English clergyman and economist, warned that population increase would soon lead to social chaos.

Malthus (1926; orig. 1798) predicted that population would increase by what mathematicians call an *exponential progression*, as in the series of numbers 2, 4, 8, 16, 32, and so on. At such a rate, Malthus concluded, world population would soon soar out of control.

Food production would also increase, Malthus explained, but only in *arithmetical progression* (as in the series 2, 3, 4, 5, 6) because, even with new agricultural technology, farmland is limited. Malthus's analysis yielded a troubling vision of the future: people reproducing beyond what the planet could feed, leading ultimately to catastrophic starvation.

Malthus acknowledged that birth control or abstinence might change the equation. But he found one morally wrong and the other quite unlikely. Thus, famine and war stalked humanity in Malthus's scheme, and he was justly known as "the dismal parson."

Critical evaluation. Fortunately, Malthus's prediction was flawed. By 1850 the birth rate in Europe began to drop, partly b-ecause children were becoming more of an economic liability than an asset, and partly because people *did* use birth control. Also, Malthus underestimated human ingenuity: irrigation, fertilizers, and pesticides have increased farm production far more than he imagined.

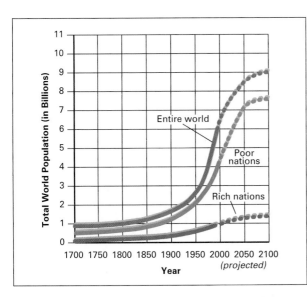

FIGURE 22–4 **The Increase in World Population, 1700–2100**

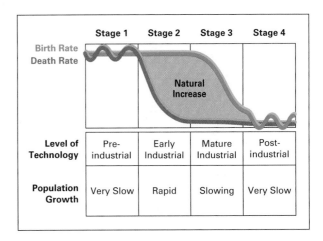

FIGURE 22–5 **Demographic Transition Theory**

Some criticized Malthus for ignoring the role of social inequality in world abundance and famine. For example, Karl Marx (1967; orig. 1867) objected to viewing suffering as a "law of nature" rather than the curse of capitalism.

Still, we should not entirely dismiss Malthus. Habitable land, clean water, and fresh air are finite resources, and greater industrial productivity has taken a toll on the natural environment. In addition, medical advances have lowered death rates, pushing up world population. In principle, of course, no level of population growth is sustainable indefinitely. Thus, people everywhere must become aware of the dangers of population increase.

DEMOGRAPHIC TRANSITION THEORY

Malthusian theory has been superseded by **demographic transition theory**, *a thesis linking demographic changes to a society's level of technological development.* Figure 22–5 shows the demographic consequences at four levels of technological development. Pre-industrial, agrarian societies—those at Stage 1—have high birth rates because of the economic value of children and the lack of birth control. Death rates are also high, owing to low living standards and little medical technology, so that people fall victim to infectious diseases.

Deaths neutralize births, so population rises and falls with only a modest overall increase. This was the case for thousands of years in Europe before the Industrial Revolution.

Stage 2—the onset of industrialization—brings a demographic transition as population surges. Technology expands food supplies and science com-

bats disease. Death rates fall sharply while birth rates remain high, resulting in rapid population growth. It was in a Stage 2 era that Malthus formulated his ideas, which explains his pessimistic view of the future. Most of the world's poorest countries today are in this high-growth stage.

In Stage 3—a mature industrial economy—birth rates drop, finally coming into line with death rates and, once again, curbing population growth. Fertility falls because most children survive to adulthood and rising living standards make raising children expensive. Thus, affluence transforms offspring from economic assets into economic liabilities. Smaller families, made possible by effective birth control, are also favoured by women working outside the home. As birth rates follow death rates downwards, population growth slows further.

Stage 4 corresponds to a post-industrial economy. The birth rate continues to fall, partly because dual-income couples gradually become the norm and partly because the costs of raising children continue to rise. This trend, coupled with steady death rates, means that, at best, population grows only very slowly or even *decreases*. This is the case in Europe currently and may soon be true of Japan as well.

Critical evaluation. Demographic transition theory suggests that the key to population control lies in technology. Instead of the runaway population increase Malthus feared, it sees technology reining in population growth and ensuring material plenty.

Demographic transition theory dovetails with modernization theory, an approach to global development examined in Chapter 12 ("Global Stratification"). Modernization theorists are optimistic that poor countries will solve their population problems as they industrialize. But critics—notably dependency theorists—strongly disagree. Unless there is a significant redistribution of global resources, they maintain, our planet will become increasingly divided into

The Getu family, on the left, lives in the low-income African nation of Ethiopia. The de Frutos family, to the right, lives in the high-income European nation of Spain. Comparing the two photographs, what can you learn about the relationship between a society's level of material affluence and family size? In fact, the fertility rate in Ethiopia is about fives times higher than in Spain. Thus, while population levels are stable or declining in most of the world's richest countries, they are increasing in the world's poorest nations. This is why poor countries now account for 96 percent of global population increase.

industrialized "haves," enjoying low population growth, and nonindustrialized "have-nots," struggling in vain to feed soaring populations.

GLOBAL POPULATION TODAY: A BRIEF SURVEY

What demographic patterns characterize today's world? Drawing on what we have learned so far, we can highlight a number of key trends.

The Low-Growth North

When the Industrial Revolution began, population growth in Western Europe and North America peaked at 3 percent annually, doubling the population in little more than one generation. But, since then, growth rates have eased downwards, dropping below 1 percent by 1970. As our post-industrial society enters Stage 4, the Canadian birth rate has fallen below the replacement level of 2.1 children per woman, a point at which we reach what demographers call **zero population growth**, *the level of reproduction that maintains population at a steady state.* Canada's total fertility rate, which climbed to 3.9 during the baby boom, dropped to 1.64

 To find out more about zero population growth, go to www.populationconnection.org/

by 1996 (Hiller, 2000:32), and to 1.61 by 2001. A fertility rate that low means that, without immigration, Canada's population will begin to decline.

Factors holding down population in these post-industrial societies include a high proportion of men and women in the labour force, the higher costs of

raising children, and the growing number of people choosing to marry at a later age or to remain childless. Contraceptive use and voluntary sterilization have increased dramatically. Catholics, whose religious doctrine prohibits artificial birth control, no longer differ significantly from other Canadians in their contraceptive practices. (In fact, Quebec, which is more than 85 percent Catholic, has one of the lower fertility rates in Canada.)

Abortion has been legal—with "permission" under specified conditions—since 1969, and was effectively decriminalized in 1988, when the Supreme Court declared the earlier restrictions to be unconstitutional. By the 1990s, Canadian women were terminating more than 90 000 pregnancies per year. In 2000, Canadian women obtained 105 427 abortions, yielding a ratio of 32.2 abortions for every 100 live births. This ratio places Canada roughly even with Norway, Sweden, and Denmark, and above Finland, Italy, Iceland, and the United States, which had an abortion-to-birth ratio of 25.6 in 1999 (Health Canada, www.hc-sc.gc.ca; Statistics Canada, 2003a; Centers for Disease Control, 1999). Clearly, abortion now makes a substantial contribution to the arsenal of factors limiting fertility in the industrialized north.

The High-Growth South

Population growth is a critical problem in poor societies of the southern hemisphere. Only a few nations lack industrial technology altogether, placing them at demographic transition theory's Stage 1. Most of Latin America, Africa, and Asia are at Stage 2, with agrarian economies and some industry. In these nations, advanced medical technology (much supplied by

Empowering Women: The Key to Controlling Population Growth

Sohad Ahmad lives with her husband in a farming village eighty kilometres south of Cairo, Egypt's capital city. Ahmad lives a poor life, like hundreds of millions of other women in the world. Yet her situation differs in an important respect: she has had only two children and will have no more.

Why do she and her husband reject the conventional wisdom that children are an economic asset? One part of the answer is that Egypt's rising population has already created such a demand for land that her family could not afford more even if they had the children to farm it. Another part of the answer is that the Ahmads recognize that a bigger family means more bodies to feed, clothe, and house. In other words, if growing more food requires more hungry workers, how is a family better off? But the main reason is that Sohad Ahmad does not want her life defined by childbearing.

Like Sohad Ahmad, more women in Egypt are taking control of their fertility and seeking more opportunities. Indeed, this country has made great

progress in reducing its annual population growth from 3.0 percent in the mid-1980s to 1.7 percent today.

The 1994 Cairo International Conference on Population and Development broke new ground, linking global efforts to control population to raising the standing of women. In the past, population control programs focused on making birth control technology available to women. This is a crucial objective, since only half of the world's married women use birth control. But the larger picture shows that even when birth control is readily available, population continues to increase in societies that define women's primary responsibility as raising children.

Dr. Nafis Sadik, an Egyptian woman who heads the United Nations population control programs, sums up the new approach to lowering birth rates this way: *give women more life choices and they will have fewer children.* In other words, women with access to schooling and jobs, who can decide when and if they wish to marry, and who bear children as a matter of choice, will limit their own

A simple truth: women who have more opportunity for schooling and paid work have fewer children. As more women attend school in traditional societies, the fertility rate in these countries is falling.

fertility. Schooling must be available to older women too, Dr. Sadik adds, since they often exercise great influence in local communities.

Evidence from countries around the world suggests that controlling population and raising the social standing of women are one and the same.

Sources: Linden (1994); Ashford (1995); and *Canadian Global Almanac 2003* (2002).

---

rich societies) has sharply reduced death rates, but birth rates remain high. This is why poor societies now account for two-thirds of the earth's people and 96 percent of global population increase.

In poor countries throughout the world, birth rates have fallen from an average of about six children per woman in 1950 to around four today. But even this fertility level will intensify global poverty if it continues. At a 1994 global population conference in Cairo, delegates from 180 nations agreed on the need for vigorous action to contain population growth. They also pointed out the crucial link between population control and the status of women (see the "Global Sociology" box).

Although few would oppose medical programs that save lives—mostly of children—lower death rates mean population increase. In fact, population growth in most low-income regions of the world is due primarily to declining death rates. Around 1920, Europe and North America began to export advances in scientific

medicine, nutrition, and sanitation around the world. Since then, inoculations against infectious diseases and the use of antibiotics and insecticides have pushed down death rates with stunning effectiveness. For example, in Sri Lanka, malaria caused half of all deaths in the 1930s; a decade later, insecticides used to kill malaria-carrying mosquitoes cut the death toll from this disease in half. With this great medical achievement, Sri Lanka's population soared. Similarly, India's infant mortality rate slid from 130 in 1975 to 74 in 1997, boosting that nation's population to 1 billion.

 Read about efforts to control population increase in South Asia at www.asia-initiative.org/

In short, in much of the world, fertility is falling. But so is mortality, especially among children. Thus, various strategies to control birth are now vital in poor countries where programs to fend off death have worked well in the past.

URBANIZATION: THE GROWTH OF CITIES

For most of human history, the sights and sounds of cities such as Hong Kong, New York, or Montreal were simply unimaginable. The world's people lived in small, nomadic groups, moving as they depleted vegetation or searched for migratory game. The small settlements that marked the emergence of civilization in the Middle East some 12 000 years ago held only a small fraction of the earth's people. Today, the largest three or four cities of the world together are home to as many people as the entire planet was then.

Urbanization is *the concentration of humanity into cities.* Urbanization both redistributes population within a society and transforms many patterns of social life. We will trace these changes in terms of three urban revolutions—the emergence of cities beginning 10 000 years ago, the development of industrial cities after 1750, and the explosive growth of cities in low-income countries today.

THE EVOLUTION OF CITIES

Cities are a relatively new development in human history. Only about 12 000 years ago did our ancestors found permanent settlements, setting the stage for the first urban revolution.

The First Cities

Before humans could build permanent settlements, they had to discover how to domesticate animals and cultivate crops. As explained in Chapter 4 ("Society"), hunting and gathering forced people to move all the time; raising food, however, required people to stay in one place (Lenski et al., 1995). Raising their own food also created a material surplus, which freed some people from food production and allowed them to build shelters, make tools, weave cloth, and take part in religious rituals. The production of surplus food allowed for the gradual emergence of cities, which in turn led to further specialization and higher living standards.

The first city—Jericho, which lies to the north of the Dead Sea and dates back some 10 000 years—was home to only around 600 people. But, as the centuries passed, cities grew to tens of thousands of people and became the centres of vast empires. By 3000 B.C.E., Egyptian cities flourished, as did cities in China by about 2000 B.C.E. and in Central and South America by about 1500 B.C.E. In North America, however, only a few Native American societies formed settlements, so that widespread urbanization had to await the arrival of European settlers in the seventeenth century (Lamberg-Karlovsky and Lamberg-Karlovsky, 1973; Change, 1977; Coe and Diehl, 1980).

Pre-industrial European Cities

European cities date back some 5000 years to the Greeks and, later, the Romans, both of whom created great empires and founded cities across Europe, including Vienna, Paris, and London. With the fall of the Roman Empire, the "Dark Ages" began, as people withdrew within defensive walled settlements and warlords battled for territory. Only in the eleventh century did trade flourish once again, allowing cities to grow.

Medieval cities were very different from today's cities. Beneath towering cathedrals, the narrow and winding streets of London, Brussels, and Florence teemed with merchants, artisans, priests, peddlers, jugglers, nobles, and servants. Occupational groups such as bakers, carpenters, and metalworkers clustered together in distinct sections, or "quarters." Ethnicity also defined communities as residents sought to keep out people who differed from themselves. The term *ghetto* (from the Italian *borghetto*, meaning "outside the city walls") first described the segregation of Jews in Venice.

Industrial European Cities

As the Middle Ages came to a close, steadily increasing commerce enriched a new urban middle class, or *bourgeoisie* (French, meaning "of the town"). With more and more money, the bourgeoisie soon rivalled the hereditary nobility.

By about 1750, the Industrial Revolution triggered a *second urban revolution*, first in Europe and then in North America. Factories unleashed tremendous productive power, causing cities to grow to unprecedented size. London, the largest European city, reached 550 000 people by 1700 and exploded to 6.5 million by 1900 (Weber, 1963, orig. 1899; Chandler and Fox, 1974).

Cities not only grew but changed shape as well. Older winding streets gave way to broad, straight boulevards that held the flow of commercial traffic, the military, and, eventually, motor vehicles. Steam and electric trolleys, too, crisscrossed the expanding cities. Since land was now a commodity to be bought and sold, developers divided cities into regular-sized lots (Mumford, 1961). The centre of the city was no longer the cathedral but a bustling central business district, filled with banks, retail stores, and tall office buildings.

As cities focused on business, they became increasingly crowded and impersonal. Crime rates rose. Especially at the outset, a small number of industrialists lived in grand style, while for most men, women, and children, factory work proved exhausting and provided bare subsistence.

Organized efforts by workers to improve their plight led to legal regulation of the workplace, better housing, and the right to vote. Public services such as water, sewage, and electricity further enhanced urban living. Today some urbanites still live in poverty, but a rising standard of living has partly fulfilled the city's historical promise of a better life.

THE GROWTH OF NORTH AMERICAN CITIES

Most of the Native peoples who inhabited what are now the United States and Canada over tens of thousands of years were migratory peoples, so there were few permanent settlements. Large numbers of villages and towns first sprang up as a product of European colonization. The Spanish made an initial settlement at St. Augustine, Florida, in 1565, and the English founded Jamestown, Virginia, in 1607. Samuel de Champlain founded a trading post in Quebec in 1608. New Amsterdam, later called New York, was established by the Dutch in 1624, Montreal was founded by Maisonneuve in 1642, Halifax was founded in 1749 by the British (to counter the French influence in North America), and York (now Toronto) was founded in 1793.

These tentative intrusions onto Indian lands were accompanied by an expanded fur trade, an invasion of rural settlers, colonial expansion, and a struggle for control over lands involving Natives, the British, and the French—all of which led to massive immigration and gradual urbanization. By 2000, the United States had 200 cities with a population of more than 100 000, while Canada had 40 cities of that size. Now both countries have more than three-quarters of their populations living in urban areas. How we became so urban is explained in the brief history that follows.

Colonial Settlement in North America: 1624–1850

New York and Boston started out as tiny villages in a vast wilderness. Dutch New Amsterdam at the top of Manhattan Island (1624) and English Boston (1630) developed along the lines of medieval towns of Europe, with narrow, winding streets that still curve through lower Manhattan and downtown Boston. New Amsterdam was walled on its north side, the site of New York's Wall Street. Boston, the largest colonial settlement, had a population of only 7000 in 1700. Economic growth soon transformed these quiet villages into thriving towns with wide streets, usually built on a grid pattern.

When Toronto (York) was founded in 1793, by John Graves Simcoe, commander of the Queen's Rangers and later the first lieutenant-governor of Upper Canada, Montreal was already a bustling city of over 5500. In Upper Canada there were only about fifteen settler families between Burlington Bay and the Bay of Quinte—a distance of 200 kilometres (Benn, 1993).

Simcoe's intent was to move the capital from its vulnerable location near Niagara Falls to one from which an American invasion could more easily be repelled. He also wanted to establish a civilian community and a naval base. The map of York Harbour in Figure 22–6 shows the location of "the Garrison" (now called Fort York) and the settlement of York. The gridlike settlement plan is near the area where Toronto's St. Lawrence Market stands today (Benn, 1993). The north–south lines above Queen Street mark the parcels of land that Simcoe granted to some of his regimental comrades and others in an effort to entice them to settle in York as a local aristocracy (the "Family Compact"). The lines separating their land allotments still show up as major north–south arteries on Toronto road maps.

As the first settlements grew, North America remained overwhelmingly rural. In 1790 the first U.S. census counted a national population of 4 million, a scant 5 percent of whom lived in cities. Around the time of Confederation in Canada (1867), the U.S. population of about 40 million was 20 percent urban, while Canada's population of about 3 million was almost as urban at 18 percent. The vast majority of people in both countries lived on farms and small villages. The small Canada–U.S. gap in levels of urbanization essentially disappeared by 1940, and today both Canada and the United States are 80 percent urban. Table 22–1 (on page 555) shows Canada's population growth and levels of urbanization from 1871 to 2001.

Urban Expansion

Early in the nineteenth century, towns sprang up across North America—somewhat later in Canada than in the United States. Waterways, new roads, and railway lines encouraged the growth of these towns and cities. British Columbia agreed to Confederation in 1871 on condition that a transcontinental railway be completed. The last spike was not driven until 1885, but the Canadian Pacific Railway (CPR) gave a powerful boost to settlement and economic development, especially in towns and cities located on the railway line itself. Calgary was incorporated as a town in 1884, and by 1893, with a population of about 4000, it became a city.

By 1920 and 1931, respectively, U.S. and Canadian censuses revealed that more than 50 percent of their populations were living in cities. To some, increased urbanization constituted progress towards better living, but others mourned the gradual passing of traditional agrarian life. Over time, rural–urban tensions grew more pronounced, with adversaries trading negative stereotypes that pitted "ignorant country cousins" against "shady city slickers" (Callow, 1969).

The Metropolitan Era

Dizzying growth and concentration of population by the 1940s marked the coming of the **metropolis**, *a*

FIGURE 22–6 Map of York (Toronto), 1793

York was designed on a grid pattern as a temporary capital for Upper Canada. It was located on a protected bay where it could be shielded from potential attack by Americans.

large city that socially and economically dominates the surrounding area. The current Canadian definition of a Census Metropolitan Area (CMA) involves a population of at least 100 000 spread out among one or more municipalities with economic and commuting ties. These metropolises have become the manufacturing, commercial, and residential centres of North America.

By the 1880s, industrial technology was producing steel girders and mechanical elevators so that builders were raising structures ten stories above the ground. And this, of course, was only the beginning. In 1975, Toronto's CN Tower was completed. At 553.3 metres, it is still the world's tallest free-standing structure. City centres contain these kinds of monuments as well as clusters of soaring buildings of glass, concrete, and steel, while public transit and roadways allow for lower-density city sprawl that stretches for miles.

Canada has twenty-five CMAs, ranging in size from Toronto at more than 5 million population to Thunder Bay, Ontario, at 125 700 (see Table 22–2).

SUBURBS AND CENTRAL CITIES

Just as central cities flourished a century ago, we have recently witnessed the expansion of **suburbs,** *urban areas beyond the political boundaries of a city.* The first

suburbanites were well-to-do, but by the late 1940s, less wealthy people also came to view a single-family house on its own piece of leafy suburban ground as the ideal lifestyle. The mobility provided by increasingly affordable automobiles made this dream come true for more and more people. After World War II, men and women eagerly returned to family life, igniting the baby boom. Since central cities offered little space for new housing construction, suburbs blossomed almost overnight.

Today, more than half of Canada's urbanites live in municipalities outside central cities, or in newer central cities, like those on the Prairies, which are largely suburban in style. As a result of the overall flight to the suburbs by young families and the fact that more people are living alone in their downtown homes, vigorous construction in the central cities has not stopped the decline in some central city populations (Michelson, 1988:86). As population decentralized, businesses also began to migrate to the suburbs. Older people today can recall trips "downtown" to shop, but by the 1970s the suburban mall had replaced "main street" as the centre of retail trade. Manufacturing interests, too, moved to the suburbs, where there was relief from high taxes, escalating property costs, and traffic congestion. The result was financial difficulty for the older central cities owing to reduced tax revenues.

TABLE 22–1 The Urban Population of Canada, 1871–2001

Year	Population (000s)	% Urban
1871	3 689	19.6%
1881	4 325	25.7
1891	4 833	31.8
1901	5 371	37.5
1911	7 207	45.4
1921	8 788	49.5
1931	10 377	52.7
1941	11 507	54.5
1951	14 009	62.9
1961	18 238	69.6
1971	21 568	76.1
1981	24 343	75.7
1991	27 297	76.6
1996	28 847	77.9
2001	30 007	79.7

Sources: Adapted from Artibise and Stelter (1988) and Statistics Canada, www.statcan.ca.

TABLE 22–2 Population of Census Metropolitan Areas* in Canada, 1956 and 2001

	Population (in thousands)	
	1956	2001
Calgary, Alta.	201.0	969.6
Chicoutimi, Que.	90.9	158.8
Edmonton, Alta.	254.8	954.1
Halifax, N.S.	164.2	359.1
Hamilton, Ont.	338.2	680.0
Kitchener, Ont.	128.7	431.2
London, Ont.	154.4	425.2
Montreal, Que.	1745.0	3511.4
Oshawa, Ont.	62.8	304.6
Ottawa–Hull, Ont./Que.	345.4	1108.5
Québec, Que.	311.6	694.0
Regina, Sask.	89.7	198.3
St. Catharines–Niagara, Ont.	85.0	391.9
St. John's, Nfld.	79.1	176.4
Saint John, N.B.	86.0	127.3
Saskatoon, Sask.	72.8	231.5
Sherbrooke, Que.	61.8	155.0
Sudbury, Ont.	97.9	157.0
Thunder Bay, Ont.	N.A.	125.7
Toronto, Ont.	1502.2	4907.0
Trois-Rivières, Que.	75.4	141.2
Vancouver, B.C.	665.0	2099.4
Victoria, B.C.	133.8	319.4
Windsor, Ont.	185.8	313.7
Winnipeg, Man.	412.2	684.3

*Census Metropolitan Areas are defined by Statistics Canada as very large urban areas together with neighbouring urban and rural areas that have a high degree of social and economic integration.

Source: Statistics Canada, *Census of Canada*, www.statcan.ca.

In 1953, in response to this disparity between the core of the city and outlying areas, the Province of Ontario created "Metropolitan Toronto" by combining the central city of Toronto with twelve of its suburbs. The province had to impose the solution initially, as none of the municipalities were exactly enamoured of the prospect. But as a result of the success of Metropolitan Toronto, other urban regions across Canada have followed suit. Note that the creation of the new city of Toronto in 1997 through the amalgamation of six cities—into the GTA or the Greater Toronto Area—is distinct from the creation of metropolitan areas.

The benefits of this model of urban development are clear when we compare Canada's situation to that of the United States. Since American cities rarely adopt a metropolitan-type government, they tend to suffer much more from decaying inner cities. "Canadian metropolitan areas suffer fewer of the glaring contrasts in welfare, infrastructure, and supportive services differentiating American central cities and suburbs" (Michelson, 1988:97).

When several adjacent metropolitan regions get so large that they bump up against each other and form a continuous urban band, they form what is called a **megalopolis**, *a vast urban region containing a number of cities and their surrounding suburbs.* Gottmann (1961) first coined the term *megalopolis* in reference to the area between and including Boston and Washington. In Canada, our closest equivalent is the area known as the Golden Horseshoe, which stretches from Oshawa in the east, through Toronto, and west to St. Catharines; the Windsor–Quebec City corridor forms another, looser version. The political and economic dominance of this region is quite apparent from the fact that the Golden Horseshoe alone contains about one-third of Canada's population, while the larger Windsor–Quebec City corridor contains about one-half.

INTER-REGIONAL POPULATION MOVEMENT

Any country, especially a large country, will experience population shifts from one region to another. In the United States, the major shift is from the cities of the northeast and the midwest to the south. Southern cities such as San Diego, San Antonio, and Phoenix are growing rapidly, while cities in the north such as Detroit, Chicago, and Baltimore are losing population.

Canada—alas—does not have a sunbelt, but that does not stop us from moving from one part of the country to another in search of opportunities. Table 22–3 shows the net gains and losses through inter-provincial migration for each province in each five-year period between 1956 and 2001. When Canadians move from one province to another, it tends to be directly related to economic conditions. This was most apparent from 1977–81, when the resource boom in Alberta caused a large influx there from other provinces. But falling international oil prices in the

The majority of Canada's urban population lives in suburban areas. While subdivisions such as the one pictured here provide desirable single-family dwellings, they can also have negative effects. Declining populations in central cities have reduced the tax base to fund city operations and social programs. As well, new housing construction often takes place at the expense of the environment, including loss of wilderness and agricultural land.

early 1980s led to a temporary reversal of this trend as Canadians moved east, especially to Ontario.

In some parts of the country, the losses are consistent and large: the Atlantic provinces lost population in every five-year period except 1972–76. Quebec lost population in every period, but most dramatically in 1967–71 and 1977–81. The separatist Parti Québécois was elected in 1976 and in 1977 passed Bill 101, making French the language of business and restricting English-language schooling. Several head offices moved out of Montreal, anglophones moved away, and real estate prices plummeted.

As Table 22-3 shows, a number of provinces lost population to interprovincial migration in each of the five-year periods between 1956 and 2001. The consistent losers are Newfoundland and Labrador, New Brunswick, Quebec, Manitoba, and Saskatchewan. Quebec stands out because of the size of the losses and the two peaks in outmigration in the late 1960s and mid-1980s—periods when the Parti Québécois was conceived and Quebec was reeling from the aftereffects of the 1980 referendum on sovereignty. The only province to show consistent gains in every five-year interval (except 1997 to 2001) is British Columbia— the equivalent of our sunbelt as the destination for lifestyle and retirement migration.

URBANISM AS A WAY OF LIFE

As indicated here, early sociologists in Europe and the United States focused a great deal of attention on the rise of cities.

FERDINAND TÖNNIES: *GEMEINSCHAFT* AND *GESELLSCHAFT*

In the late nineteenth century, the German sociologist Ferdinand Tönnies studied how life in the new industrial metropolis differed from life in traditional rural settings. From this contrast, he developed two concepts that have become an established part of sociology's terminology.

Tönnies (1963; orig. 1887) used the German word **Gemeinschaft** (meaning "community") to refer to *a type of social organization in which people are bound closely together by kinship and tradition*. The *Gemeinschaft* of the rural village, he explained, joins people into what amounts to a single primary group.

By and large, argued Tönnies, *Gemeinschaft* is absent in the modern city. On the contrary, urbanization enhances **Gesellschaft** (meaning "association"), *a type of social organization in which people come together only on the basis of individual self-interest*. In *Gesellschaft*, individuals are motivated by their own needs and desires rather than by a desire to advance the well-being of everyone. City dwellers display little sense of community and look to others mostly as the means of achieving their individual goals. Thus, Tönnies saw in urbanization the erosion of close, enduring social relations in favour of the fleeting and temporary ties typical of business.

EMILE DURKHEIM: MECHANICAL AND ORGANIC SOLIDARITY

The French sociologist Emile Durkheim (see Chapter 4, "Society") agreed with much of Tönnies's thinking about cities. But Durkheim did not think urban people lack social bonds: they simply organize social life differently than rural people do.

Durkheim described traditional, rural life as *mechanical solidarity*, social bonds based on common sentiments and shared moral values. Durkheim's concept of mechanical solidarity, with its emphasis on conformity to tradition, bears a striking similarity to Tönnies's *Gemeinschaft*.

Urbanization erodes mechanical solidarity, Durkheim explained, but it also generates a new type of bonding, which he termed *organic solidarity*, social bonds based on specialization and interdependence. This concept parallels Tönnies's *Gesellschaft*, but there is a key difference between the two thinkers. Both thought the expansion of industry and cities would undermine traditional social patterns, but Durkheim took a more optimistic view of this historical transformation. Where societies had been built on *likeness*, Durkheim observed, social organization was now based on *difference*.

For Durkheim, urban society offers more individual choice, moral tolerance, and personal privacy than people find in rural villages. In sum, something is lost in the process of urbanization, but much is gained.

TABLE 22–3 Net Interprovincial Migration* in Canada, 1956–2001

	Nfld	PEI	NS	NB	Que	Ont	Man	Sask	Alta	BC
1957–1961	−4671	−1099	−15 295	−5270	−7756	34 345	−15 957	−33 557	16 787	33 230
1962–1966	−15 213	−2969	−27 124	−25 680	−19 859	85 369	−23 471	−42 094	−1983	77 747
1967–1971	−19 344	−2763	−16 396	−19 599	−122 736	150 712	−40 690	−81 399	32 005	114 964
1972–1976	−1857	3754	11 307	16 801	−77 610	−38 560	−26 827	−40 752	58 571	92 285
1977–1981	−18 983	−829	−7140	−10 351	−156 496	−57 826	−42 218	−9716	186 364	122 625
1982–1986	−15 051	751	6895	−65	−81 254	121 767	−2634	−2974	−31 676	7382
1987–1991	−15 282	−885	−5302	−3798	−39 934	68 730	−35 417	−63 155	−43 282	141 077
1992–1996	−26 937	3045	−6803	−3080	−50 114	−38 440	−19 203	−18 385	3499	157 750
1997–2001	−22 989	−48	−3462	−5700	−53 951	66 183	13 939	−24 673	116 702	−51 812

*The number of persons moving into a province minus the number of persons moving out of that province.

Source: Calculations by Gerber based on Colombo (1992; 1997) and *Canadian Global Almanac, 2003* (2002).

GEORG SIMMEL: THE BLASÉ URBANITE

German sociologist Georg Simmel (1858–1918) offered a microanalysis of cities, studying how urban life shapes people's attitudes and behaviour. According to Simmel, individuals experience the city as a crush of people, objects, and events. To prevent being overwhelmed by all this stimulation, urbanites develop a *blasé attitude*, tuning out much of what goes on around them. Such detachment does not mean that city dwellers lack compassion for others: they simply keep their distance as a survival strategy so that they can devote their time and energy to what really matters to them.

OBSERVING THE CITY: THE CHICAGO SCHOOL

Sociologists in the United States (there were no sociology departments in Canada yet) soon joined their European colleagues in exploring the rapidly growing cities. The first major sociology program in the United States took root at the University of Chicago.

Robert Park, a leader of the Chicago School, sought to give urban studies a street-level perspective by studying real cities. He found the city to be an organized mosaic of distinctive ethnic communities, commercial centres, and industrial districts. Over time, he observed, these "natural areas" develop and change in relation to one another. To Park, then, the city was a living organism—a human kaleidoscope.

Another major figure in the Chicago School of urban sociology was Louis Wirth (1897–1952), best known for blending the ideas of Tönnies, Simmel, and Park into a comprehensive theory of urban life. Wirth began by identifying the city as a setting with a large, dense, and socially diverse population—making urban life impersonal, superficial, and transitory. Sharing the teeming streets, urbanites have contact with many more people than rural residents. Thus, if city residents notice others at all, they know them not in terms of *who they are* but *what they do*: bus driver, florist, or grocery store clerk, for instance. Specialized, urban relationships are sometimes quite pleasant for all concerned. But we should remember that self-interest rather than friendship is the main reason for the interaction.

Critical evaluation. Both in Europe and in the United States, early sociologists presented a mixed view of urban living. On the one hand, rapid urbanization was troubling. Tönnies and Wirth saw personal ties and traditional morality lost in the anonymous rush of the city. On the other hand, Durkheim and Park emphasized urbanism's positive face, pointing to greater personal autonomy and choice.

Another problem is that Wirth and others painted urbanism in broad strokes that overlook the effects of class, race, and gender. There are many kinds of urbanites—rich and poor, white and Black, women and men—all leading distinctive lives (Gans, 1968). In fact, cities often intensify social differences; that is, we see the extent of social diversity most clearly in cities where different categories of people live in close proximity (Macionis and Parrillo, 1998).

URBAN ECOLOGY

Sociologists (especially members of the Chicago School) also developed **urban ecology**, *the study of the link between the physical and social dimensions of cities.* Consider, for example, why cities are located where they are. The first cities emerged in fertile regions where the environment favoured raising crops and, thus, settlement. Pre-industrial societies, concerned with defence, built their cities on mountains (Athens was situated on an outcropping of rock) or surrounded by water (Paris and Mexico City were founded on islands). With the Industrial Revolution, economic considerations led to the founding of cities near rivers and natural harbours that facilitated trade.

Urban ecologists also study the physical design of cities. In 1925, Ernest W. Burgess described land use in Chicago in terms of *concentric zones* that look rather

Peasant Dance *(above, c. 1565), by Pieter Bruegel the Elder, conveys the essential unity of rural life forged by generations of kinship and neighbourhood. In contrast, Ernest Fiene's* Nocturne *(left) communicates the inpersonality common to urban areas. Taken together, these paintings capture Tönnies's distinction between* Gemeinschaft *and* Gesellschaft.

Pieter Bruegel the Elder *(c. 1525/30–69), Peasant Dance, c. 1565, Kunsthistorisches Museum, Vienna/Superstock. Ernest Fiene (1894–1965), Nocturne. Photograph © Christie's Images.*

like a bull's-eye. City centres, Burgess observed, are business districts bordered by a ring of factories, followed by residential rings with housing that becomes more expensive the farther it stands from the noise and pollution of the city's centre.

Chauncy Harris and Edward Ullman (1945) added yet another insight: as cities decentralize, they lose their single-centre form in favour of a *multicentred model*. As cities grow, residential areas, industrial parks, and shopping districts typically push away from one another. Few people wish to live close to industrial areas, for example, so the city becomes a mosaic of distinct districts.

Social area analysis investigates what people in specific neighbourhoods have in common. Three factors seem to explain most of the variation—family patterns, social class, and race and ethnicity (Shevky and Bell, 1955; Johnston, 1976). Families with children gravitate to areas with large apartments or single-family homes and good schools. The rich generally seek high-prestige neighbourhoods, often in the central city near cultural attractions. People with a common social heritage tend to cluster in distinctive communities.

Finally, Brian Berry and Philip Rees (1969) tie together many of these insights. They explain that distinct family types tend to settle in the concentric zones described by Ernest Burgess. Specifically, households with few children tend to cluster towards the city's centre, while those with more children live farther away. Furthermore, racial and ethnic neighbourhoods are found at various points throughout the city, consistent with Harris and Ullman's multicentred model.

Critical evaluation. After almost a century of research, urban ecologists have succeeded in linking the physical and social dimensions of urban life. But, as the researchers themselves concede, their conclusions paint an overly simplified picture of urban life. Critics chime in that urban ecology errs to the extent that it implies that cities take shape simply from the choices ordinary people make. Rather, they assert, urban development responds more to powerful elites than to ordinary citizens (Molotch, 1976; Feagin, 1983).

URBAN POLITICAL ECONOMY

As urban problems—rioting, crime, poverty, and unemployment—proliferated, most visibly in the United States, some analysts turned away from the ecological approach to a social-conflict understanding of city life. *Urban political economy* is influenced by the thinking of Karl Marx, although the scene of social conflict shifts from the workplace to the city (Lindstrom, 1995).

The ecological approach of the Chicago School saw the city as a "natural" organism, with particular districts and neighbourhoods developing according to

FIGURE 22–7 Map of Halifax, 1917

In 1917, Halifax was the scene of Canada's worst disaster: 1600 people were killed, more than 9000 were injured, and thousands left homeless when a French munitions ship and Belgian relief vessel collided in Halifax Harbour—setting off further explosions and multiple fires in the city. Thomas Adams, a British planner then living in Canada, proposed an amazing feat of restoration: a plan for central Halifax that dispensed with the grid pattern and included diagonal and gently curving streets to emphasize vistas and greenery (Sewell, 1993; Kitz, 1989). Robert MacNeil's novel *Burden of Desire* (1992) is a love story based on the Halifax disaster and the inspiration for the Canadian-American feature-length film of the same name.

an internal logic. Political economists disagree, claiming that city life is defined mostly by people with power: corporate leaders and the political elite. In Canada, U.S. multinational corporations, foreign investors, and the global capitalist system are seen as important players as well. These powerholders make the economic and political decisions that determine the location, size, shape, and character of major cities.

For example, deindustrialization of the Maritime provinces and shifts in political and economic clout up the St. Lawrence River to Montreal and then to Toronto caused an inordinate concentration of capital, industry, population, and political power in southern Quebec and Ontario. This relatively small area, and Metropolitan Toronto in particular, emerged as the core to the peripheral areas or hinterland across the rest of the country. The industrialized core dominates weaker areas, rural and urban, that are dependent on natural resources. This relationship accounts for regional inequalities, regionalism, and even threats to national unity (Matthews, 1983; Brym, 1986; Goyder, 1990; Hiller, 2000).

Critical evaluation. The urban-political-economy paradigm has gained much attention in recent years. For one thing, compared to the older urban ecology approach, the political economy view seems better able to address the harsh realities of urban life. But analysis based on the political economy perspective has been largely limited to capitalist societies in the modern era. Capitalism and industrialization are assumed to cause the problems of urban life, while the environment and physical structure of cities are ignored. Jane Jacobs (1984), a highly esteemed expert on urban development and urban life who lives in Toronto, argues that urban social problems are the result of economic stagnation, but sustaining economic development is not a simple function of the availability of capital and political will. Cities are crucial to developing economies, but conditions including environment, population growth, economic differentiation, and a crucial mix of industries are required to sustain economic health.

 For information about the works and influence of Jane Jacobs, go to www.people.virginia.edu/~plan303/

In low-income countries throughout the world, people are migrating from rural areas to cities in hope of a better life. The result is that many cities are overwhelmed with newcomers, who are forced to live wherever they can. Shanty settlements, such as this one in Manila, Philippines, pose obvious dangers to residents (and, especially, children) in terms of accidents and disease. What do you think would happen if heavy rains flooded this neighbourhood?

It is unlikely that any single model of cities can account for the full range of the world's urban diversity.

URBANIZATION IN POOR SOCIETIES

Twice in human history the world has experienced a revolutionary expansion of cities. The first urban revolution began around 8000 B.C.E. with the first urban settlements, and continued as permanent settlements appeared on different continents. The second urban revolution took hold in about 1750 and lasted for two centuries as the Industrial Revolution led to rapid growth of cities in Europe and North America.

A third urban revolution is now underway. Today, 75 percent of people in industrial societies are already city dwellers. But extraordinary urban growth is now occurring in poor societies. In 1950, about 25 percent of the people in low-income countries lived in cities; by 2005, the proportion will exceed 50 percent.

A third urban revolution is taking place because many poor societies have now entered the high-growth Stage 2 of demographic transition. Falling death rates continue to fuel population growth in Latin America, Asia, and, especially, Africa. For urban areas, the rate of population increase is twice as high because, in addition to natural increase, millions of people leave the countryside each year in search of jobs, health care, education, and conveniences such as running water and electricity.

Cities do offer more opportunities than rural areas, but they provide no quick fix for the massive problems of escalating population and grinding poverty. Many cities in less-developed societies—Mexico City is a good example—are simply unable to meet the basic needs of much of their population. Thousands of rural people stream into Mexico City every day, even though more than 10 percent of the current 25 million residents have no running water in their homes, 15 percent lack sewage facilities, and the city can process only half the trash and garbage produced. To make matters worse, exhaust from factories and cars chokes everyone, rich and poor alike (Friedrich, 1984; Gorman, 1991).

ENVIRONMENT AND SOCIETY

Our species has prospered, rapidly increasing the population of the planet. Within the next twenty-five years, most people will live in cities, in hopes of finding a better life than that found in rural villages.

But these developments come at a high price. Never before have human beings placed such demands on the earth. This disturbing development brings us to the final topic of this chapter: the interplay between the natural environment and society. **Ecology** is *the study of the interaction of living organisms and the natural environment*, which rests on the research not only of social scientists but of natural scientists as well. Here, we focus on those aspects of ecology that involve familiar sociological concepts and issues.

The **natural environment** refers to *the earth's surface and atmosphere, including living organisms, as well as the air, water, soil, and other resources necessary to sustain life*. Like every other species, humans depend on the natural environment to live. Yet, with our capacity for culture, humans stand apart from other species. We alone take deliberate action to remake the world according to our own interests and desires—for better *and* for worse.

Why is the environment of interest to sociologists? Simply because environmental problems—from pollution to acid rain to global warming—do not arise from the "natural world" operating on its own. Rather, such problems result from the specific actions of human beings, making them *social* issues (Marx, 1994). Environmental sociology deals with a wide range of issues relating to the interplay of environmental and social factors. It looks at the environmental movement—its values, membership, and actions—as well as the impact of physical environment—especially the natural environment—on social behaviour (Hannigan, 1995).

THE GLOBAL DIMENSION

The study of the natural environment must take a global perspective. The reason is simple: regardless of political divisions among nations, the planet is a single **ecosystem,** *a system composed of the interaction of all living organisms and their natural environment.*

The Greek meaning of *eco* is "house," reminding us that this planet is our home and that all living things and their natural environment are *interrelated.* In practice, change in any part of the natural environment ripples throughout the entire global ecosystem.

Consider, from an ecological point of view, our national love of eating hamburgers. People in North America (and, increasingly, worldwide) have created a huge demand for beef, which has greatly expanded the ranching industry in Brazil, Costa Rica, and other Latin American nations. To produce the lean meat sought by fast-food corporations, cattle in Latin America feed on grass, which uses a great deal of land. Latin American ranchers get the land for grazing by clearing thousands of square kilometres of forests each year. These tropical forests are vital to maintaining the earth's atmosphere. Because of these atmospheric effects, deforestation (for beef production) threatens North America and the rest of the world (Myers, 1984a).

TECHNOLOGY AND THE ENVIRONMENTAL DEFICIT

As humans developed more powerful technology, we increasingly remade the world. Members of societies with simple technology—the hunters and gatherers described in Chapter 4 ("Society")—have scarcely any ability to affect the environment. On the contrary, members of such societies are keenly dependent on nature, so that their lives are defined by the migration of game and the rhythm of the seasons. They are especially vulnerable to natural catastrophes, such as fires, floods, droughts, and storms.

Societies at intermediate stages of sociocultural evolution have a somewhat greater capacity to affect the environment. But the environmental impact of horticulture (small-scale farming), pastoralism (the herding of animals), and even agriculture (the use of animal-drawn plows) is limited because people still rely on muscle power for producing food and other goods.

Human control of the natural environment grew dramatically with the Industrial Revolution. Muscle

Many environmentalists believe that our planet is in danger. The importance of sociology in understanding environmental issues stems from the fact that problems are not caused by the natural world operating on its own. Rather, they result from the way humans organize social life.

power gave way to engines that burn fossil fuels: coal at first and then oil. Such machinery affects the environment in two ways: by consuming natural resources and by releasing pollutants into the atmosphere. Even more importantly, humans armed with industrial technology are able to bend nature to their will, tunnelling through mountains, damming rivers, irrigating deserts, and drilling for oil on the ocean floor. This is why people in rich nations, who represent just 15 percent of humanity, use 80 percent of the world's energy (Connett, 1991; Miller, 1992).

The environmental impact of industrial technology goes beyond energy consumption. Just as important is the fact that members of industrial societies produce and consume 100 times more goods than people in agrarian societies. Higher living standards, in turn, increase the problem of solid waste (since people ultimately throw away most of what they produce) and pollution (since industrial production generates smoke and other toxic substances).

From the start, people recognized the material benefits of industrial technology. But only a century later did they see the long-term effects on the natural environment. Indeed, one trait of the recent postindustrial era is a growing concern for environmental quality (Abrahamson, 1997; Kidd and Lee, 1997): we realize that the technological power to make our lives better can also put the lives of future generations in jeopardy (Voight, cited in Bormann and Kellert, 1991:ix–x).

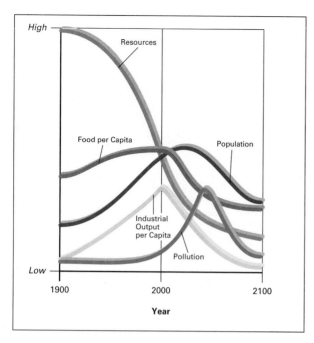

FIGURE 22–8 The Limits to Growth: Projections

Source: Based on Meadows et al. (1972).

Evidence is mounting that we are running up an **environmental deficit,** *profound and negative long-term harm to the natural environment caused by humanity's focus on short-term material affluence* (Bormann, 1990). The concept of environmental deficit is important for three reasons. It reminds us that the state of the environment is a *social issue,* reflecting choices made by people. It also suggests that much environmental damage—to the air, land, and water—is *unintended.* By focusing on the short-term benefits of, say, cutting down forests, strip mining, or using throw-away packaging, we fail to see their long-term environmental effects. Lastly, in some respects, the environmental deficit is *reversible.* Inasmuch as societies have created environmental problems, in other words, societies can undo many of them.

 The history of the environmental activist group Greenpeace is traced from its Vancouver beginnings at http://archives. cbc.ca/300c.asp?id=1-69-867

CULTURE: GROWTH AND LIMITS

Whether we recognize environmental dangers and decide to do something about them is a cultural matter. Along with technology, economics and politics have powerful environmental consequences.

The Logic of Growth

Why does our nation set aside specific areas as "parks" and "conservation areas"? Doing this seems to indicate that, except for these special areas, people can freely use natural resources for their own purposes (Myers, 1991). This aggressive approach to the natural environment has long been central to our way of life.

Chapter 3 ("Culture") described the core values that underlie social life in Canada. One of these is *material comfort,* the belief that money and the things it buys enrich our lives. We also believe in the idea of *progress,* thinking that the future will be better than the present. Moreover, we look to *science* to make our lives easier and more rewarding. Taken together, such cultural values form the *logic of growth.*

The logic of growth is an optimistic view of the world. It holds that more powerful technology has improved our lives and new discoveries will make the future better still. Simply, the logic of growth asserts that "people are clever," "having things is good," and "life gets better." A powerful force throughout the history of Western industrial societies, the logic of growth is the driving force behind settling the wilderness, building towns, and pursuing material affluence.

Even so, "progress" can lead to unexpected problems, including harming the environment. The logic of growth responds by arguing that people (especially scientists and other technology experts) will find a way out of any problem that growth places in our path. If, say, one resource becomes inadequate, we will come up with other, new resources that will do the job just as well. For example, by the time the growing number of cars in the world depletes the planet's oil reserves, scientists will have come up with electric, solar, or nuclear engines or some as yet unknown technology to free us from dependence on oil.

But environmentalists counter that the logic of growth is flawed in assuming that natural resources such as oil, clean air, fresh water, and topsoil will always be plentiful. On the contrary, they claim, these are *finite* resources that we can and will exhaust if we continue to pursue growth at any cost. Echoing Malthus, environmentalists warn that if we call on the earth to support increasing numbers of people, we will surely deplete finite resources, destroying the environment—and ourselves—in the process (Milbrath, 1989; Livernash and Rodenburg, 1998).

The Limits to Growth

If we cannot invent our way out of the problems created by the logic of growth, perhaps we need another way of thinking about the world. Environmentalists, therefore, counter that growth must have limits. Stated simply, the *limits to growth thesis* is that humanity must implement policies to control the growth of population, production, and use of resources in order to avoid environmental collapse.

In *The Limits to Growth,* a controversial book that was influential in launching the environmental movement, Donella Meadows and her colleagues (1972) used a computer model to calculate the planet's available resources, rates of population growth, amount of land available for cultivation, levels of industrial and food production, and amount of pollutants released into the atmosphere. The model reflects changes that have occurred since 1900, and then projects forward to the end of the twenty-first century. The authors concede that such long-range predictions are speculative, and some critics think they are plain wrong (Simon, 1981). But right or wrong, the general conclusions of the study, shown in Figure 22–8, call for serious consideration.

According to the limits to growth thesis, we are quickly consuming the earth's finite resources. Supplies of oil, natural gas, and other energy sources are already falling sharply and will continue to drop—faster or slower depending on conservation policies in rich nations and how quickly other nations industrialize. While food production per person will continue to rise during this century, world hunger will persist because existing food supplies are so unequally distributed. By 2050, the model predicts, hunger will reach a crisis level, first stabilizing population and then sending it back downwards. Eventually, depleted resources will cripple industrial output as well. Only then will pollution rates fall.

Limits to growth theorists are also known as neo-Malthusians because they share Malthus's pessimism about the future. They doubt that current patterns of life are sustainable for even another century. If so, we face a fundamental choice: either we make deliberate changes in how we live, or widespread calamity will force change upon us.

SOLID WASTE: THE DISPOSABLE SOCIETY

As an interesting exercise, carry a trash bag around for a single day and collect everything you throw away. Most people are surprised to find that the average North American discards more than two kilograms of paper, metal, plastic, and other materials daily. For Canada as a whole, this amounts to about 60 000 kilograms of solid waste *each and every day*. Figure 22–9 shows the composition of a normal household's trash.

As a rich nation of people who value convenience, ours has become a *disposable society*. We consume more products than other nations, and many of these products have throw-away packaging. The most familiar case is fast food, served in cardboard, plastic, and Styrofoam that we discard within minutes. And countless other products—from film to fishhooks—are elaborately packaged to make the product more attractive to the customer and to discourage tampering and theft.

Consider, too, that manufacturers market soft drinks, beer, and fruit juices in aluminum cans, glass jars, and plastic containers, which not only consume finite resources but also generate mountains of solid waste. Then there are countless items intentionally

FIGURE 22–9 Composition of Household Trash

Sources: Based on Franklin Associates (1986) and Corley et al. (1993).

designed to be disposable: pens, razors, flashlights, batteries, even cameras. Other products—from light bulbs to automobiles—are designed to have a limited useful life and then become unwanted junk. As Paul Connett (1991) points out, even the words we use to describe what we throw away—*waste, litter, trash, refuse, garbage, rubbish*—show how little we value what we cannot immediately use.

The average person in a rich society consumes 50 times more steel, 170 times more newspaper, 250 times more gasoline, and 300 times more plastic each year than the typical individual in India (Miller, 1992). This high level of consumption means that we not only use a disproportionate share of the planet's natural resources, but we also generate most of the world's refuse.

We like to say that we "throw things away." But 80 percent of our solid waste is not burned or recycled and never "goes away." Rather, it ends up in landfills. One problem with landfills is that, across the country, they are filling up. Furthermore, material in landfills can pollute groundwater. And what goes into landfills all too often stays there—sometimes for centuries. Tens of millions of tires, diapers, and other items that we bury in landfills each year do not decompose and will be an unwelcome legacy for future generations.

Environmentalists argue that we should address the problem of solid waste by doing what many of our grandparents did: turn waste into a resource. One way to do this is through *recycling*, reusing resources we would otherwise discard. Recycling is common practice in Japan and many other nations. In Canada, many cities have recycling programs for glass, cans, and paper. A few cities, like Guelph, Ontario, collect dry and wet waste and convert the wet, organic waste

GLOBAL MAP 22–2 Water Consumption in Global Perspective

This map shows each country's water consumption as a percentage of its internal renewable water resources. Nations near the equator consume only a tiny share of their available resources; indeed, as the map shows, much of this region is covered with rain forest. Northern Africa and the Middle East are a different story, however, with dense populations drawing on very limited water resources. As a result, in countries like Libya, Egypt, and Saudi Arabia, people (especially the poor) do not have as much water as they would like or, often, as they need.

Source: United Nations Development Programme (2000).

into fertile soil. Toronto had to re-evaluate its recycling efforts in the wake of the failure of its controversial plan to take its garbage, by train, to the Adams Mine near Kirkland Lake. Because of concerns about groundwater contamination, politically acceptable landfill sites are becoming increasingly difficult to find. The Adams Mine site is even more controversial because the potential contamination involves First Nations land. Toronto has been sending its waste along the 401 to Michigan for many years; not surpris-ingly, there are periodic protests on the part of communities adjacent to the 401 as well as affected communities in Michigan.

WATER AND AIR

Oceans, lakes, and streams are the lifeblood of the global ecosystem. Humans depend on water for drinking, bathing, cooling, and cooking, for recreation, and for a host of other activities.

According to what scientists call the *hydrological cycle*, the earth naturally recycles water and refreshes the land. The process begins as heat from the sun causes the earth's water, 97 percent of which is in the oceans, to evaporate and form clouds. Because water evaporates at lower temperatures than most pollutants, the water vapour that rises from the seas is relatively pure, leaving various contaminants behind. Water then falls to the earth as rain, which drains into streams and rivers and, finally, returns to the sea. Two major concerns about water, then, are supply and pollution.

Water Supply

For thousands of years, since the time of the ancient civilizations of China, Egypt, and Rome, water rights have figured prominently in codes of law. Today, as Global Map 22–2 shows, some regions of the world, especially the tropics, enjoy a plentiful supply of water. But high demand, coupled with modest reserves, makes water supply a matter of concern in much of North America and Asia, where people look to rivers rather than rainfall for their water. In the Middle East, water supply has already reached a critical level. In Egypt, for instance, an arid region of the world, people depend on the Nile River for most of their water. As the Egyptian population increases, however, shortages are becoming frequent. Egyptians today must make do with one-sixth the amount of water per person from the Nile as in 1900. Experts predict that within thirty years, as many as 1 billion people in northern Africa and the Middle East may lack the water they need for irrigation and drinking (Myers, 1984c; Postel, 1993).

The world over, soaring population and complex technology have greatly increased societies' appetite for water. The global consumption of water (now more than 6 billion cubic feet per year) has tripled since 1950 and is expanding even faster than the world's population. As a result, even in those parts of the world that receive plenty of rainfall, people are using groundwater faster than it can be naturally replenished. In the Tamil Nadu region of southern India, for example, so much groundwater is being used that the water table has fallen thirty metres over the last several decades. Mexico City—which has sprawled to some 3600 square kilometres—has pumped so much water from its underground aquifer that the city has sunk nine metres during the last century and is dropping about five centimetres per year. Farther north in the United States, pumping from the Ogallala aquifer, which lies below seven states from South Dakota to Texas, is now so rapid that some experts fear it could run dry within several decades.

In Canada, where fresh water supplies are adequate—for the time being—we worry that we will become the fresh water supplier for other countries. If we were to export water to the United States for commercial purposes, the North American Free Trade Agreement would require us to keep the tap open, even as our own supplies are threatened.

In light of such developments, we must face the reality that water is a valuable, finite resource. Greater conservation of water by individuals (the average person consumes 45 million litres in a lifetime) is part of the answer. However, households around the world account for just 10 percent of water use. We need to curb water consumption by industry, which uses 25 percent of the global total, and farming, which consumes two-thirds of the total for irrigation.

New irrigation technology may reduce the demand for water in the future. But, here again, we see how population increase, as well as economic growth, strains our ecosystem (Myers, 1984a; Goldfarb, 1991; Falkenmark and Widstrand, 1992; Postel, 1993).

Water Pollution

In large cities—from Mexico City to Cairo to Shanghai—many people have no choice but to drink contaminated water. Infectious diseases like typhoid, cholera, and dysentery—all caused by waterborne micro-organisms—spread rapidly through these populations (Clarke, 1984b; Falkenmark and Widstrand, 1992). Besides ensuring ample *supplies* of water, then, we must protect the *quality* of water.

Water quality in North America is generally good by global standards. However, even here the problem of water pollution is steadily growing. According to the Sierra Club, an environmental activist organization, rivers and streams across the United States alone absorb some 227 million kilograms of toxic waste each year. This pollution results not just from intentional dumping but also from the runoff of industry, agricultural fertilizers, and lawn chemicals.

A special problem is *acid rain*, rain made acidic by air pollution that destroys plant and animal life. Acid rain (or snow) begins with power plants burning fossil fuels (oil and coal) to generate electricity; this burning releases sulphuric and nitrous oxides into the air. As the wind sweeps these gases into the atmosphere, they react with the air to form sulphuric and nitric acids, which turn atmospheric moisture acidic.

This is a clear case of one type of pollution causing another: air pollution (from smoke stacks) ends up contaminating water (in lakes and streams that collect acid rain). Moreover, acid rain is truly a global phenomenon because the regions that suffer the harmful effects may be thousands of kilometres from the original pollution. For instance, British power plants have caused acid rain that has devastated forests and fish in Norway and Sweden, up to 1500 kilometres to the northeast. In Canada, the Inco smokestacks of Sudbury, Ontario, destroyed vegetation for hundreds of kilometres—including the fish habitat of Killarney Provincial Park lakes. Pollution controls in the smokestacks allowed for the gradual revival of Sudbury area

APPLYING SOCIOLOGY

Environmentally Friendly Canada, Eh!

Many Canadians believe that our country and our provinces have come a long way on the environmental front. After all, we have recycling programs; some cities have wet/dry systems that convert organic waste to compost; and Canada turns tires, banned from landfill sites for decades, into an asphalt additive or into the bouncy flooring material for Disney World's *Honey, I Shrunk the Kids* exhibit and Hamilton Harbour's water playground, in Ontario. We have environmental reviews for major resource developments, regulations governing the disposal of pollutants into waterways or the air, international agreements on emission reduction, a wonderful system of national and provincial parks, and an environmentally sensitive public.

We have an environmental movement whose activities are quick to draw public attention to the clear-cutting of forests in B.C. or the slaughter of baby seals in Newfoundland. Our First Nations communities—such as Walpole Island, Ontario—are attempting to achieve sustainable development (Jacobs, 1992; Nin.da.waab.jig, 1992), and organizations such as the Wendaban Stewardship Authority are being created to blend Native and non-Native environmental knowledge and to co-manage timber, land, and resource development in the Temagami area (Shute and Knight, 1995). Surely we can be

forgiven if we are a little smug about our environmental record.

Looks can be deceiving, though! Behind the scenes, Canada and the provinces have been cutting budgets in the environmental protection area. In Ontario, "virtually all of the province's environmental laws have been weakened, enforcement budgets have been cut and regulatory powers are being taken away" (Fine, 1997). So lax is the enforcement of regulations that Ontario ranks fourth among North America's polluters, behind Ohio, Texas, Indiana, and Pennsylvania.

By 1997, Ontario Hydro's nuclear energy program was in serious difficulty and the utility began to deactivate some of its plants amid daunting safety and pollution concerns (Mittelstaedt, 1997). As 1998 rolled in, Toronto was debating the merits of its household recycling program: it is extremely costly and ineffective in ensuring the reuse of materials, and some of the Blue Box deposits actually end up in landfill sites.

Decisions regarding environmental issues are inherently political—and controversial. Having failed to live up to its earlier promises regarding emission targets, Canada was expected to set new ones at the 1997 Kyoto environmental summit to deal with carbon emissions and the threat to global warming. The Vancouver-based David Suzuki Foundation took out full-page newspaper

ads across the country aimed at stopping the global warming plague. In Alberta, fear-mongering reached a fever pitch because the proposed emission targets would reduce the demand for oil and natural gas, which it was claimed would be catastrophic for the province. The rumoured tax on carbon fuels as they come off the wells (to discourage fuel use) would transfer huge amounts of money out of the province. Premier Ralph Klein, the resource industries, and the Alberta public were up in arms and Chrétien felt the heat (Bercuson and Cooper, 1997). The Kyoto agreement was revisited in November 2000. Canada's commitment to reducing global carbon emissions remains in question: in this round, we tried to achieve our reduction goals by "protecting" forests (here and abroad) and buying "credits" from countries that had succeeded in reducing emissions.

In September 2002, Prime Minister Jean Chrétien declared that Canada would ratify the Kyoto Protocol by the end of the year and that Canada would meet its obligations through "domestic action" rather than through the buying and selling of emission credits. If Russia signs on, the Kyoto agreement will be in effect, as 55 of the world's developed (i.e., polluting) nations will be on board. At that point, Canada will have to consider seriously the question of *how* it will meet its commitments.

The politics involved in the fight against acid rain are explored in multimedia clips from the CBC archives: see http://archives.cbc.ca/300c.asp?id=1-75-584

vegetation, in what is now known to be one of Canada's environmental success stories.

Air Pollution

One of the unexpected consequences of industrial technology, especially the factory and the motor vehicle, has been a decline in air quality. Exhaust fumes from automobiles once shrouded cities like Los

Angeles and those of Ontario's Golden Horseshoe (including Hamilton and Toronto). In London, England, factory smokestacks, automobiles, and coal fires used to heat households all added to what was probably the worst urban air quality of the last century. What some British jokingly called "pea soup" was, in reality, a deadly mix of pollution. For five days in 1952, an especially thick haze that hung over London killed 4000 people (Clarke, 1984a).

Air quality improved in the final decades of the twentieth century. Rich nations passed laws that

Canadians have further reason to be concerned. Specifically, the shipment of hazardous or toxic waste from the United States into Canada quintupled between 1993 and 1999 (to 663 000 metric tons), while the reverse flow, from Canada into the United States, remained relatively stable. Ontario and Quebec are the main recipients of this hazardous waste because most U.S. states have increased regulations and restrictions, and Mexico has banned toxic imports altogether—while Canada's regulations remain lax (Hogue, 2000).

Canadian governments, federal and provincial, are engaged in a high-wire act as they deal with environmental issues. Environmentalists, environmentally aware Canadians, and foreign interests exert considerable pressure on our elected leaders to protect our natural environment. Businesses, workers, and agencies in resource-dependent parts of the country (or economy) are equally persuasive. The people who design and implement our environmental policies and programs do so in the face of relentless cross-pressures.

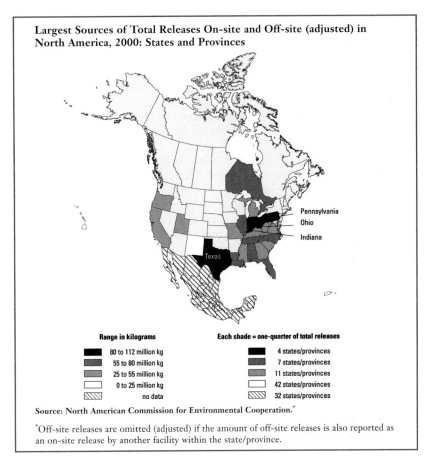

Largest Sources of Total Releases On-site and Off-site (adjusted) in North America, 2000: States and Provinces

Pennsylvania
Ohio
Indiana
Texas

Range in kilograms		Each shade = one-quarter of total releases	
■	80 to 112 million kg	■	4 states/provinces
■	55 to 80 million kg	■	7 states/provinces
■	25 to 55 million kg	■	11 states/provinces
□	0 to 25 million kg	□	42 states/provinces
▨	no data	▨	32 states/provinces

Source: North American Commission for Environmental Cooperation.*

*Off-site releases are omitted (adjusted) if the amount of off-site releases is also reported as an on-site release by another facility within the state/province.

Continue the debate . . .

1. *Are the people around you as concerned about environmental issues as they were five years ago?*

2. *Should we recycle cans, bottles, and newspapers, even if it proves to cost substantially more than other types of waste disposal? Who should bear these costs?*

3. *How much are you willing to give up, in terms of standard of living, to help Canada reach its emission targets?*

---

banned high-pollution heating, including the coal fires that choked London fifty years ago. In addition, scientists devised ways to reduce the noxious output of factories and the growing numbers of automobiles and trucks.

If high-income countries can breathe a bit more easily than they once did, the problem of air pollution in poor societies is becoming more serious. One reason is that people in low-income countries still rely on wood, coal, peat, and other "dirty" fuels for cooking and heating. Nations eager to encourage short-term indus-

trial development may pay little heed to the longer-term dangers of air pollution. As a result, many cities in Latin America, Eastern Europe, and Asia are plagued by air pollution as bad as England's fifty years ago.

THE RAIN FORESTS

Rain forests are *regions of dense forestation, most of which circle the globe close to the equator.* A glance back at Global Map 22–2, on page 564, shows that the largest tropical rain forests are in South America (notably

Brazil), west-central Africa, and Southeast Asia. In all, the world's rain forests cover some 800 million hectares, or 7 percent of the earth's total land surface.

Like other global resources, rain forests are falling victim to the needs and appetites of the surging world population. As noted earlier, to meet the demand for beef, ranchers in Latin America burn forested areas to increase their supply of grazing land. We are also losing rain forests to the hardwood trade. People in rich nations pay high prices for mahogany and other woods because, as environmentalist Norman Myers (1984b:88) puts it, they have "a penchant for parquet floors, fine furniture, fancy paneling, weekend yachts, and high-grade coffins." Under such economic pressure, the world's rain forests are now just half their original size, and they continue to shrink by about 1 percent (168 000 square kilometres) annually. Unless we stop this loss, the rain forests will vanish before the end of the twenty-first century, and with them will go protection for the earth's biodiversity and climate.

Canada has its own rain forest to protect: the Clayoquot Sound area, on the west coast of Vancouver Island, is home to the world's largest remaining coastal lowland temperate rain forest. Friends of Clayoquot Sound (FOCS), a grassroots environmental group founded in 1979, has attempted to force our government to change forest policy and deal with First Nations rights. The Nuu-Chah-Nulth people, who live, hunt, and fish in the Clayoquot area, have dedicated Meares Island as a Tribal Park, hosted festivals and blockades, and worked with the FOCS to change global attitudes to ancient temperate rain forests. The largest civil disobedience action in Canadian history—the protest of July to October 1993—resulted in the arrest of 800 people, the loss of $10 million in European and U.S. contracts by the forest products company MacMillan Bloedel (since taken over by the U.S.-based Weyerhauser), and a government task force on the Clayoquot Sound Sustainable Development Strategy. Also, social justice for First Nations became an integral part of the wilderness and eco-forestry movements (Langer, 1996).

Global Warming

Why are rain forests so important? One reason is that they cleanse the atmosphere of carbon dioxide (CO_2). Since the beginning of the Industrial Revolution, the amount of carbon dioxide produced by humans (mostly from factories and automobiles) has risen tenfold. Much of this carbon dioxide is absorbed by the oceans. But plants take in carbon dioxide and expel oxygen. This is why rain forests are vital to maintaining the chemical balance of the atmosphere.

The problem is that production of carbon dioxide is rising while the amount of plant life on the earth is shrinking. To make matters worse, rain forests are being destroyed mostly by burning, which releases even more carbon dioxide into the atmosphere. Experts estimate the atmospheric concentration of carbon dioxide is now 20 to 30 percent higher than it was 150 years ago.

High above the earth, carbon dioxide acts like the glass roof of a greenhouse, letting heat from the sun pass through to the earth while preventing much of it from radiating away from the planet. The result, say ecologists, is a **greenhouse effect**, *a rise in the earth's average temperature (global warming) due to an increasing concentration of carbon dioxide in the atmosphere.* Over the last century, the global temperature has risen about 0.5°C (to an average of 14.5°C). The Intergovernmental Panel on Climate Change (IPCC) predicts that, over the next century, global temperatures will rise by between 1.4°C and 5.8°C—and claims that most of the increase is attributable to human activities (Clover, 2001).

There are potential advantages to Canada: crops and forests could be grown farther north, and the Arctic Ocean might open up to become a major shipping route. Conversely, the traditional lifestyle of the Inuit, migratory birds, the caribou, and the polar bear would be hard hit as tundra and permafrost disappear. In the summer of 2000, the Inuit reported mud and dripping water along our Arctic shores; these reports and repeated concerns about Canada's receding ice-caps suggest that melting is already well underway. According to the IPCC, melting of the polar icecaps could raise sea levels by 0.09 to 0.88 metres (Clover, 2001); were this to happen, water could cover almost all of Bangladesh and coastal areas—some of them urban—around the world.

Not all scientists share this vision of future global warming. Some point out that global temperature changes have been taking place throughout history, apparently with little or nothing to do with rain forests. Moreover, higher concentrations of carbon dioxide in the atmosphere might speed up plant growth (since plants thrive on this gas), which would correct the imbalance and nudge the earth's temperature downward once again. Still other scientists think global warming might even have benefits, including longer growing seasons and lower food prices (Silverberg, 1991; Begley, 1997; McDonald, 1999).

Declining Biodiversity

Clearing rain forests also reduces the earth's *biodiversity.* This is because rain forests are home to almost half of this planet's living species.

On earth, there are as many as 30 million species of animals, plants, and micro-organisms. Several dozen unique species of plants and animals cease to exist each day, but given the vast number of living species why should we be concerned? Environmentalists give three reasons. First, our planet's biodiversity provides a varied source of human food. Biodiversity, in effect, is needed to feed our planet's rapidly increasing population.

Second, the earth's biodiversity is a vital genetic resource. Medical and pharmaceutical research looks to animal and plant biodiversity for new compounds that cure disease and improve our lives. Children, for example, now have a good chance of surviving leukemia, a disease that was almost a sure killer two generations ago, because of a compound derived from a pretty tropical flower called the rosy periwinkle. The oral birth control pill, used by tens of millions of women, is another product of plant research, this time involving the Mexican forest yam.

Third, with the loss of any species of life—whether it is one variety of ant, the magnificent California condor, or the famed Chinese panda—the beauty and complexity of our natural environment are diminished. And there are clear warning signs of such loss: three-fourths of the world's 9000 species of birds are declining in number.

Finally, note that, unlike pollution, the extinction of any species is irreversible and final. An important ethical question, then, is whether we who live today have the right to impoverish the world for those who live tomorrow (Myers, 1984b, 1991; E. Wilson, 1991; Brown et al., 1993).

ENVIRONMENTAL RACISM

Conflict theory has given rise to the concept of **environmental racism**, *the pattern by which environmental hazards are greatest for poor people, especially minorities.* Historically, factories that spew pollution stand near neighbourhoods of the poor, visible minorities, and Aboriginal people. Why? In part, because the poor themselves were drawn to factories in search of work, and, once hired, their low incomes often meant they could afford housing only in undesirable neighbourhoods. Sometimes the only housing that fit their budgets stood in the very shadow of the plants and mills where they worked.

Nobody wants a factory or dump nearby, but the poor have little power to resist. Through the years, then, the most serious environmental hazards have been located not near the neighbourhoods of the affluent, but near those of the vulnerable and powerless. In Canada, Native communities are frequently affected. Uranium mines across Canada have contaminated ground and water in many of the areas where Native people live and hunt. Clear-cutting of forests and flooding for power generation have contaminated water and destroyed natural habitat in the James Bay region of Quebec, where the Crees, in 1975, had been guaranteed long-term hunting and fishing rights. The Lubicon Crees of north-central Alberta have been fighting since 1930 for recognition of their rights and settlement of their land claim, and to stop the province of Alberta from selling timber rights on their land. The Adams Mine—the initial destination for Toronto's exported garbage in the fall of 2000—is

The earth's rain forests—vital to the planet's ecology—are now half their original size and become smaller every year. Once the lush vegetation of such forests is lost, the soil is at risk of drying out and turning into a desert. Thus, environmental damage is often irreversible.

simply the most recent example of our tendency to dump waste, clear-cut, and contaminate with complete disregard for Aboriginal rights.

LOOKING AHEAD: TOWARDS A SUSTAINABLE WORLD

The demographic analysis presented in this chapter points to some disturbing trends. We see that the earth's population has reached record levels because birth rates remain high in poor nations and death rates have fallen just about everywhere. Lowering fertility will remain a pressing problem for the foreseeable future. Even with some recent decline in population increase, the nightmare Thomas Malthus described is still a real possibility, as the final box explains.

Further, population growth remains greatest in the poorest countries of the world, those without the means to support their present populations, much less their future ones. Supporting 80 million additional people on our planet each year—almost 75 million of whom are in poor societies—will require a global commitment to provide not only food but housing, schools, and employment. The well-being of the entire world may ultimately depend on resolving the economic and social problems of poor, overly populated countries and bridging the widening gulf between "have" and "have-not" societies.

Urbanization, too, is continuing, especially in poor countries. Throughout human history, people have sought out cities with the hope of finding a better life. But the sheer numbers of people who live in the emerging global supercities—Mexico City, São Paulo (Brazil), Kinshasa (Democratic Republic of the

Will People Overwhelm the Earth? The Environmental Challenge

Are you worried about the world's increasing population and the ability of the planet to sustain that growth? Think about this: by the time you finish reading this box, more than 1000 people will be added to our planet. By this time tomorrow, global population will have increased by 209 000: there are about two births for every death on the planet, so the world's population increases by 77 million annually. In effect, global population growth amounts to adding another Egypt to the world every year.

It is no wonder that many demographers and environmentalists are deeply concerned about the future. The earth has an unprecedented population. The 2 billion people we have *added* since 1974 alone exceeds the planet's total in 1900. Might Thomas Robert Malthus—who predicted that population would outstrip the earth's resources and plunge humanity into war and suffering—be right after all?

Lester Brown, a *neo-Malthusian* population and environmental activist, sees a coming apocalypse if we do not change our ways. Brown concedes that Malthus failed to imagine how much technology (especially fertilizers and altering plant genetics) could boost the planet's agricultural output. But he maintains that the earth's burgeoning population is rapidly outstripping its finite resources. Families in many poor countries can find little firewood; members of rich societies are depleting oil reserves; everyone is draining global reserves of clean water.

Just as importantly, according to the neo-Malthusians, humanity is steadily poisoning the planet with waste. There is a limit to the earth's capacity to absorb pollution, they warn, and, as the number of people continues to increase, our quality of life will decline.

But another camp of analysts—the *anti-Malthusians*—sharply disagrees. Asks Julian Simon, "Why the doom and gloom?" Two centuries ago, he points out, Malthus predicted catastrophe. Today, however, there are almost six times as many people on the earth and, on average, they live longer, healthier lives than ever before.

Simon argues that the neo-Malthusians err in assuming that the world has finite resources that are spread more thinly as population increases. Rather, the anti-Malthusians counter, people have the capacity to control population growth and to improve their lives in numerous ways.

Congo), Bombay (India), Manila (the Philippines)—have created urban problems on a massive scale.

Throughout the entire world, humanity is facing a serious environmental challenge. Part of the problem is population increase, which is greatest in poor societies. But part of the problem is also high levels of consumption, which mark rich nations such as our own. By increasing the planet's environmental deficit, our present way of life is borrowing against the well-being of our children and their children. Globally, members of rich societies, who currently consume so much of the earth's resources, are mortgaging the future security of the poor countries of the world.

The answer, in principle, is to form an **ecologically sustainable culture**, *a way of life that meets the needs of the present generation without threatening the environmental legacy of future generations*. Sustainable living depends on three strategies.

A first strategy is *controlling the world's population growth*. The current population of more than 6 billion is already straining the natural environment. Clearly, the higher the world's population climbs, the more difficult environmental problems will become. Even if the recent slow-

Explore the relationship between population increase, global inequality, and the natural environment at www.peopleandplanet.net/

ing of population growth continues, the world will have 8 billion people by 2050. Few analysts think that the earth can support this many people: most argue that we must hold the line at about 7 billion, and some argue that we must *decrease* population in the coming decades.

A second strategy is *conservation of finite resources*. This means meeting our needs with a responsible eye towards the future by using resources efficiently, seeking alternative sources of energy, and, in some cases, learning to live with less.

A third strategy is *reducing waste*. Where possible, simply using less is the best solution. But recycling programs, cost-effective or not, are part of the answer.

In the end, making all these strategies work depends on a more basic change in the way we think about ourselves and our world. Our *egocentric* outlook sets our own interests as standards for how to live, but a sustainable environment demands an *ecocentric* outlook that helps us see how the present is tied to the future and why everyone must work together. Most nations in the southern half of the world are *under-developed*, unable to meet the basic needs of their people. At the same time, most countries in the northern half of the world are *overdeveloped*, using more resources than the earth can sustain over time. Changes needed to create

Furthermore, we do not know how many people the earth can support because humans keep rewriting the rules by developing new fertilizers, new high-yield crops, and new forms of energy. Simon points out that today's global economy makes available more resources and products than ever, at increasingly low prices. He looks optimistically to the future because technology, economic investment, and—above all—human ingenuity have consistently proven the doomsayers wrong. And he is betting they will continue to do so. The assumption here is that substitutes for finite resources (such as oil) will be found, while waste management technology will allow human habitation and industry that do not result in irrevocable contamination or pollution of air, soil, and water.

TABLE 22–4 **Global Population Increase**			
	Births	**Deaths**	**Net Increase**
Per Year	131 577 719	55 001 289	76 540 430
Per Month	10 964 310	4 583 441	6 380 869
Per Day	360 470	150 688	209 782
Per Hour	15 020	6279	8741
Per Minute	250	105	146
Per Second	4.2	1.7	2.4

Continue the debate . . .

1. *Where do you place your bet? Do you think the earth can support 8 or 10 billion people? Why or why not?*

2. *Ninety percent of current population growth is occurring in poor countries. What does this mean for rich nations? For poor ones?*

3. *Does the world population problem affect only people in low-income countries? What must rich societies do to ensure our future?*

4. *How do environment and population interact?*

Sources: Based, in part, on Brown et al. (1993), and Simon (1981).

a sustainable ecosystem will not come easily. But the price of not responding to the growing environmental deficit will certainly be greater (Humphrey and Buttel, 1982; Burke, 1984; Kellert and Bormann, 1991; Brown et al., 1993).

In closing, consider that the great dinosaurs dominated this planet for some 160 million years and then perished forever. Humanity is far younger, having existed for a mere 250 000 years. Compared to the dinosaurs, our species has the gift of great intelligence. But how will we use this ability? What are the chances that our species will continue to flourish 160 million years—or even 1000 years—from now? Our future existence depends on the choices we make today.

SUMMARY

Population

1. Fertility and mortality, measured as crude birth rates and crude death rates, are major components of population growth. In global terms, North American population growth is low.

2. Migration, another key demographic concept, has special importance to the historical growth of cities.

3. Demographers use age-sex pyramids to graphically represent the composition of a population and to project population trends. The sex ratio refers to a society's balance of females and males.

4. Historically, world population grew slowly because high birth rates were largely offset by high death rates. In about 1750, a demographic transition began as world population rose sharply, mostly because of falling death rates.

5. Thomas Robert Malthus warned that population growth would outpace food production, resulting in social calamity. Demographic transition theory, however, contends that technological advances gradually prompt a drop in birth rates.

6. Research shows that lower birth rates and improved economic productivity in poor societies both result from improving the social position of women.

7. World population is expected to reach between 8 and 9 billion by 2050. Such an increase will likely overwhelm many poor societies, where most of the increase will take place.

Urbanization

1. The first urban revolution began with the appearance of cities in about 8000 B.C.E. By the start of the common era, cities had emerged in most regions of the world except in North America.

2. Pre-industrial cities have low-rise buildings, narrow, winding streets, and personal social ties.

3. A second urban revolution began by about 1750 as the Industrial Revolution propelled rapid urban growth in Europe. The physical form of cities changed, as planners created wide, regular streets to facilitate trade. The emphasis on commerce, as well as the increasing size of cities, made urban life more anonymous.

4. Urbanism came to North America with Europeans, who settled in a string of colonial towns along the Atlantic coastline. By 1850, hundreds of new cities were founded from coast to coast.

5. By 1920, a majority of the North American population lived in urban areas, and the largest metropolises were home to millions of people.

6. By about 1950, cities began to decentralize with the growth of suburbs and edge cities.

7. Rapid urbanization in Europe during the nineteenth century led early sociologists to contrast rural and urban life. Tönnies built his analysis on the concepts of *Gemeinschaft* and *Gesellschaft*, while Durkheim proposed parallel concepts of mechanical solidarity and organic solidarity. Georg Simmel claimed that the overstimulation of city life produced a blasé attitude in urbanites.

8. At the University of Chicago, Robert Park believed cities permit greater social freedom. Louis Wirth saw large, dense, heterogeneous populations creating an impersonal and self-interested, though tolerant, way of life. Other researchers have explored urban ecology and urban political economy.

9. A third urban revolution is now occurring in poor countries, where most of the world's largest cities will soon be found.

Environment

1. A key factor affecting the natural environment is the organization of social life. Thus, ecologists study how living organisms interact with their environment.

2. Societies increase the environmental deficit by focusing on short-term benefits and ignoring the long-term consequences of their way of life.

3. Our ability to alter the natural world lies in our capacity for culture. Humanity's effect on the environment has increased along with the development of complex technology.

4. The "logic of growth" thesis supports economic development, claiming that people can solve environmental problems as they arise. The opposing "limits to growth" thesis states that societies must curb development to prevent eventual environmental collapse.

5. Environmental issues include disposing of solid waste, as well as protecting the quality of air and water. The supply of clean water is already low in some parts of the world.

6. Rain forests help remove carbon dioxide from the atmosphere and are home to a large share of this planet's living species. Under pressure from commercial interests, the world's rain forests are now half their original size and are shrinking by about 1 percent annually.

7. Environmental racism refers to the pattern by which the poor, especially minorities, suffer most from environmental hazards.

8. To achieve a sustainable environment that does not threaten the well-being of future generations, we must control world population, conserve finite resources, and reduce waste and pollution.

CRITICAL-THINKING QUESTIONS

1. Explain the meaning of fertility and mortality rates. In which of these two has change been of greater importance in increasing global population? Why?

2. How does demographic transition theory link population patterns to technological development?

3. Over the course of history, how have economic and technological changes transformed the physical shape of cities?

4. According to Ferdinand Tönnies, Emile Durkheim, Georg Simmel, and Louis Wirth, what characterizes urbanism as a way of life?

5. What are the environmental impacts of population growth and urbanization?

6. What *should* Toronto or Vancouver do with its household waste? What are its options?

APPLICATIONS AND EXERCISES

1. Talk to older relatives and acquaintances, asking them to reconstruct the number of siblings several generations back. What has happened to family size over time?

2. Draw a mental map of a city familiar to you with as much detail of specific places, districts, roads, and transportation facilities as you can. Compare your map to a real one, or, better yet, a map drawn by someone else. Try to account for the differences.

3. Carry a plastic trash bag around with you for one full day. Put everything you throw away in the bag. Afterwards, weigh what you have: multiply this amount by 365 to estimate your yearly "trash factor."

Multiply this amount by 31 million to estimate the annual waste of the entire Canadian population.

4. Install the CD-ROM packaged in the back of this new textbook to access a variety of study, review, and applications exercises designed to help you better understand the material covered in this chapter. The CD includes interactive maps, weblinks, and study questions.

 SITES TO SEE

www.macionis.com
or
www.TheSociologyPage.com

You can find more than fifty weblinks to sociological journals and other sources of data and information by visiting the Links Library at this website.

www.eclac.org/

This site, created by the Latin American and Caribbean Demographic Center (part of the United Nations), allows country-by-country analysis of population patterns for this region of the world. Most of the site is available in both English and Spanish.

www.focs.ca/

The Friends of Clayoquot Sound home page provides information about the nonprofit organization's mission, campaigns, and history, as well as a photo gallery.

www.sierraclub.org/

www.greenpeace.org/

These two environmental sites are maintained by the Sierra Club and Greenpeace. Visit the sites and see how these two organizations are similar to one another and how they are different.

www.mccord-museum.qc.ca/

For a fascinating look at how cities have changed over the last hundred years or more, select "Urban Life Through Two Lenses" from the Virtual Exhibitions menu. You'll find photographs and sounds of nineteenth-century Montreal juxtaposed with modern recreations of the same scenes.

www.toronto.com/feature/238/

Watch big-city life from the comfort of your own home. This site uses a Web camera showing the action at Toronto's Bay and Bloor Streets. What does this observation tell you about urban life?

www.info.gov.hk/index_e.htm

This site explores the city of Hong Kong.

http://urban.nyu.edu/

New York University's Taub Urban Research Center is on the Internet. Visit this site to survey recent research on urban issues.

 STUDY TOOLS

For more study tools to help you with your next exam, be sure to check out the Companion Website at **www.pearsoned. ca/macionis**, as well as Chapter 22 in your Study Guide.

 INVESTIGATE WITH CONTENTSELECT

Follow the instructions found on page 25 of this textbook to access ContentSelect™ at the Research Navigator™ website. Once at the site, enter your LOGINID and Password. Then, enter keywords such as "zero population growth," "cities," and "global warming," and the search engine will supply relevant and recent scholarly and popular press publications.

CHAPTER

23

COLLECTIVE BEHAVIOUR AND SOCIAL MOVEMENTS

The summer of 1990 was pivotal for Canada's First Nations: after Elijah Harper and Oka, the relationship between Native peoples and other Canadians would never be the same. The Meech Lake Accord was to have been ratified by each of the provinces by June 23, to allow amendments to the Constitution that would satisfy Quebec—and, thereafter, to block constitutional changes sought by Aboriginal leaders. Newfoundland appeared to be poised to vote and Manitoba was trying to go through the procedural steps required for ratification. The snag came in the form of Elijah Harper, a Native MLA (member of the Legislative Assembly) who, through dramatic delaying tactics, was able to prevent ratification by the Manitoba legislature—thereby "killing" the accord.

In the meantime, the town of Oka, Quebec, was ensuring its international visibility by introducing plans to expand a golf course onto lands that the people of Kanesatake considered to be a sacred burial ground. A barricade erected across a rural road in response to this threat gave rise to a five-month armed confrontation between the residents of Kanesatake (aided by Mohawk Warriors) and the Quebec police—and, later on, the Canadian forces.

The significance of these events lay not in the fact that

Native people and their leaders were taking decisive action to defend their interests—for that had happened many times before—but in the fact that their struggle had captured the attention of both the media (in Canada and abroad) and Native individuals across the country. Suddenly, there was an outpouring of support for Elijah Harper and the people of Kanesatake in the form of letters, donations, marches, a run to bring a peace feather from British Columbia to Oka, a peace camp at Oka, and the barricade of the Mercier Bridge into Montreal. Daily, if not hourly, coverage of the Manitoba legislature and the tense, armed confrontation at Oka hypnotized Canadians across the country and mobilized Native people in support of a cause. A growing sense of solidarity emerged as Native individuals across the country watched events unfold. Many people who had paid little attention to their Aboriginal roots were suddenly intensely interested, proud, and somehow empowered by this new sense of movement and common cause. Consciousness had been raised and bonds had been forged in ways that would have profound effects on relations between Native peoples and other Canadians or their governments. A social movement had gained momentum.

As this chapter explains, a **social movement** is *organized activity that encourages or discourages social change*. Social movements are the most important type of **collective behaviour**, *activity involving a large number of people, often spontaneous, and usually in violation of established norms*. Other forms of collective behaviour— also controversial and sometimes provoking change— are crowds, mobs, and riots, rumour and gossip, public opinion, panic and mass hysteria, and fashions and fads.

For most of the past century, sociologists focused on established social patterns such as the family and social stratification. They paid little attention to collective behaviour, considering most of it unusual or deviant. But numerous social movements that burst on the scene during the tumultuous 1960s ignited sociological interest in the field of collective behaviour (Weller and Quarantelli, 1973; Marx and Wood, 1975; Aguirre and Quarantelli, 1983; Turner and Killian, 1987; McAdam et al., 1988).

STUDYING COLLECTIVE BEHAVIOUR

Despite its importance, collective behaviour is difficult for sociologists to study for three main reasons:

1. **Collective behaviour is wide-ranging.** Collective behaviour encompasses a sometimes bewildering array of human actions. The traits common to fads, rumours, and mob behaviour, for example, are far from obvious.

2. **Collective behaviour is complex.** A rumour seems to come out of nowhere and circulates in countless different settings. For no apparent reason, one new form of dress "catches on" while another does not. Historically speaking, why in the spring of 1998 did Quebecers resist yet another referendum, telling pollsters they were quite comfortable as both Québécois *and* Canadians?

3. **Much collective behaviour is transitory.** Sociologists can readily study the family because it is an enduring element of social life. Since fashions, rumours, and riots tend to arise and dissipate quickly, they are difficult to investigate systematically.

Some researchers point out that these problems apply not just to collective behaviour but to *most* forms of human behaviour (Aguirre and Quarantelli, 1983). Moreover, collective behaviour is not always so elusive: no one is surprised by the crowds that form at sports events and music festivals, and sociologists can study these gatherings firsthand or by reviewing videotapes. Sometimes researchers can even anticipate natural disasters and study the human response they provoke. We know, for example, that tornadoes occur in particular regions of Canada and the United States each year; some sociologists interested in how such disasters affect behaviour can be prepared to initiate research on short notice (Miller, 1985). Researchers can also use historical documents to reconstruct the details of a past natural disaster or riot.

Sociologists now know a great deal about collective behaviour, but they still have much to learn. The most serious shortcoming, according to Benigno Aguirre and E.L. Quarantelli (1983), is that sociologists have no theory that ties together all the diverse actions that fall under the umbrella of "collective behaviour."

At the least, all collective behaviour involves the action of some **collectivity**, *a large number of people whose minimal interaction occurs in the absence of well-defined, conventional norms.* Collectivities are of two kinds. A *localized collectivity* involves physical proximity and is illustrated by crowds and riots. A *dispersed collectivity* or *mass behaviour* involves people who influence one another even though they are separated by great distances; examples here include rumours, public opinion, and fashion (Turner and Killian, 1993).

It is important to distinguish collectivities from the already familiar concept of social groups (see Chapter 7, "Groups and Organizations"). Here are three key differences:

1. **Collectivities are based on limited social interaction.** While group members interact directly and frequently, interaction in localized collectivities such as mobs is limited and temporary. People participating in dispersed collectivities such as a fad typically do not interact at all.

2. **Collectivities have no clear social boundaries.** Group members share a sense of identity that is usually missing among people engaged in collective behaviour. Localized crowds may have a common object of attention (such as someone on a ledge threatening to jump), but they exhibit little sense of unity or coherence. Individuals involved in dispersed collectivities, such as "the public" that turns out to vote in an election, have almost no awareness of shared membership. Of course, some issues divide the public into well-defined factions, but it is often difficult to tell who falls within the ranks of, say, the environmentalist or feminist movements.

3. **Collectivities engender weak and unconventional norms.** Conventional cultural norms usually regulate the behaviour of group members. Some collectivities, such as people travelling on an airplane, observe conventional norms, but these rules usually amount to little more than respecting the privacy of people sitting in nearby seats. Other collectivities—such as emotional soccer fans who destroy property as they leave a stadium—spontaneously develop decidedly unconventional norms (Weller and Quarantelli, 1973; Turner and Killian, 1993).

 A study of soccer fan violence from the Social Issues Research Centre is available at www.sirc.org/publik/football_violence.html

It is easy to understand why ordinary people think they are powerless in the face of entrenched leaders. But when a sense of injustice is strong and widespread (as among these Chilean people seeking a greater voice in government), protest crowds may be effective in bringing about change.

LOCALIZED COLLECTIVITIES: CROWDS

A key form of collective behaviour is the **crowd**, *a temporary gathering of people who share a common focus of attention and who influence one another*. Historian Peter Laslett (1984) points out that crowds are a modern development; in medieval Europe, about the only time large numbers of people assembled in one place was when armies faced off on the battlefield. Today, however, crowds reaching 25 000 or more are common at sporting events, rock concerts, and even the registration halls of large universities.

But all crowds are not alike. Herbert Blumer (1969) identified four categories of crowds. A *casual crowd* is a loose collection of people who interact little, if at all. People at the beach or at the scene of an automobile accident have only a passing awareness of one another.

A *conventional crowd* results from deliberate planning, as with a country auction, a college lecture, or a funeral. In each case, most interaction conforms to norms appropriate to the situation.

An *expressive crowd* forms around an event with emotional appeal, such as World Youth Day 2002, when more than 400 000 Catholic young people from around the world gathered in Toronto to see the Pope. More recently, in Canada's largest concert ever, a similar number gathered to hear the Rolling Stones and other bands to boost Toronto as it recovered from the SARS epidemic. Excitement is the main reason people join expressive crowds, which makes this experience relatively spontaneous and exhilarating for those taking part.

An *acting crowd* is a collectivity motivated by an intense, single-minded purpose, such as an audience rushing the doors of a concert hall or fleeing from a theatre that is on fire. Acting crowds are ignited by powerful emotions, which can reach a feverish intensity and sometimes erupt into mob violence.

Any gathering can change from one type of crowd to another. In 1985, for example, a conventional crowd of 60 000 fans assembled in a soccer stadium to watch the European Cup Finals between Italy and Great Britain. Once the game started, some drunk British fans began taunting the Italians sitting nearby. At this point, the crowd became expressive. The two sides began to throw bottles at each other; then, the British surged in a human wave towards the Italians. An estimated 400 million television viewers watched in horror as what was now an acting crowd trampled hundreds of helpless spectators. In minutes, 38 people were dead and another 400 were injured (Lacayo, 1985).

Deliberate action by a crowd is not simply the product of rising emotions. Participants in *protest crowds*—a fifth category we can add to Blumer's list—may stage strikes, boycotts, sit-ins, and marches for political purposes (McPhail and Wohlstein, 1983). For example, students in a protest crowd vary in emotional intensity; some display the low-level energy characteristic of a conventional crowd, while others are emotional enough to be an acting crowd. Sometimes a protest gathering begins peacefully, but its members become aggressive when confronted with counter-demonstrators. In July 1990, during the Oka crisis, an unexpectedly violent clash occurred between the police and 4000 residents of Quebec's South Shore when the latter came out to protest the Mohawk takeover of the Mercier Bridge into Montreal.

MOBS AND RIOTS

When an acting crowd turns violent, we may witness the birth of a **mob**, *a highly emotional crowd that pursues a violent or destructive goal*. Despite, or perhaps because of, their intense emotion, mobs tend to dissipate quickly. The duration of a mob incident also depends

This picture is a good illustration of a riot that developed from high spirits rather than from a sense of grievance or hatred. In 1993 thousands of hockey fans went on a rampage through the streets of Montreal to celebrate their team's victory over the Los Angeles Kings in the Stanley Cup final.

on whether its leadership tries to inflame or stabilize the crowd, and on the mob's precise objectives.

Lynching is the most notorious example of mob behaviour. This term is derived from Charles Lynch, a Virginia colonist who sought to maintain law and order in his own way before formal courts were established. The word soon became synonymous with violence and murder outside the legal system.

Lynching has always been coloured by race. After the American Civil War, lynch mobs became a terrorist form of social control over emancipated African-Americans. African-Americans who challenged white superiority risked being hanged or burned alive by hateful whites.

Lynch mobs—typically composed of poor whites threatened by competition from freed slaves—reached a peak between 1880 and 1930. About 5000 lynchings were recorded by police in that period; no doubt many more occurred. Most of these crimes were committed in the Deep South, where an agrarian economy still depended on a cheap and docile labour force, but lynchings took place in virtually every state and victimized every minority. For example, on the western frontier, lynch mobs targeted people of Mexican and Asian descent. In only about 25 percent of the cases did whites lynch other whites. Lynchings of women were rare; only about a hundred such instances are known, almost all involving women of colour (White, 1969, orig. 1929; Grant, 1975).

A frenzied crowd without any particular purpose is a **riot**, *a social eruption that is highly emotional, violent, and undirected.* Unlike the action of a mob, a riot usually has no clear goal. Long-standing anger generally fuels riots, which are sparked by some minor incident (Smelser, 1962). Rioters then indulge in seemingly random violence against property or persons. In October 2003, a crowd turned to rioting when a Montreal club announced the cancellation of a con-

cert: the punk rock band that was to appear that night had been turned back at the border. In the few minutes before police arrived, the angry young people smashed store windows, set fire to a number of cars and overturned others. Whereas a mob action usually ends when a specific violent goal has been achieved (or decisively prevented), a riot tends to disperse only as participants run out of steam or as community leaders or the police gradually bring them under control.

Riots often serve as collective expressions of social injustice. Industrial workers, for example, have rioted to vent rage at their working conditions, and race riots have occurred with striking regularity. In Canada, in response to steady migration from China (of what seemed to be unfairly competitive cheap labour) and a sudden influx of over 8000 Japanese in 1907, a riot broke out, during which the people of Vancouver lashed out violently against the Japanese and looted their businesses. In Los Angeles in 1992, an especially destructive riot was triggered by the acquittal of police officers involved in the beating of Rodney King. The turmoil left more than fifty dead and caused thousands of injuries and millions of dollars' worth of property damage. These riots were followed almost immediately by race riots on the streets of Toronto.

Riots are not always fired by hate. They can also stem from positive feelings, such as the celebration of the 1993 Stanley Cup victory in Montreal, which turned into a night of looting and violence. Days later, in anticipation of further violence, the Montreal Canadiens were protected during their victory parade by hundreds of police officers and the riot squad.

CROWDS, MOBS, AND SOCIAL CHANGE

Ordinary people typically gain power only by acting collectively. Historically, because crowds have been able to effect social change, they have also provoked controversy. Defenders of the established social order fear "the mob." In countries around the world, elites know that the masses—when well organized—pose a threat to their power. However, the collective action condemned by some people is supported by others as rightful protest. In 1839, fifty-three Africans rose up and seized the ship *Amistad* off the coast of Cuba to prevent landing in the Americas and being sold into slavery. Were these men a vicious mob? Not according to the U.S. Supreme Court, which, after the ship put in to New York Harbor, ruled that the men were fighting for their freedom and were entitled to be released.

Moreover, crowds share no single political cast: some call for change—others resist it. Judeans rallying to the Sermon on the Mount by Jesus of Nazareth, traditional weavers destroying new industrial machines that were threatening their jobs, masses of marchers carrying banners and shouting slogans for or against abortion—these and countless other cases across the centuries show that crowds can challenge or support their society (Rudé, 1964; Canetti, 1978; Tarrow, 1994).

EXPLAINING CROWD BEHAVIOUR

What accounts for the behaviour of crowds? Social scientists have developed several different explanations.

Contagion Theory

An early explanation of collective behaviour was formulated by French sociologist Gustave Le Bon (1841–1931). According to Le Bon's *contagion theory* (1960; orig. 1895), crowds exert a hypnotic influence over their members. Shielded by the anonymity of a crowd, people evade personal responsibility and surrender to the contagious emotions of the crowd. A crowd thus assumes a life of its own, stirring up emotions and driving people towards irrational, perhaps violent, action.

Critical evaluation. Le Bon's assertion that crowds foster anonymity and sometimes generate emotion is surely true. Yet, as Clark McPhail (1991) points out, systematic research reveals that "the madding crowd" does not take on a life of its own, apart from the thoughts and intentions of members. For example, Norris Johnson (1987), investigating panic at a 1979 Who concert in Cincinnati, identified specific factors that led to the deaths of eleven people, including an inadequate number of entrance doors, an open-seating policy, and insufficient police supervision. Far from an episode of collective insanity, Johnson concluded, that crowd was composed of many small groups of people valiantly trying to help one another.

Convergence Theory

Convergence theory holds that crowd behaviour is not a product of the crowd itself, but is carried into the crowd by individual participants. Thus, crowds amount to a convergence of like-minded individuals. In other words, while contagion theory states that crowds cause people to act in a certain way, convergence theory says the opposite: that people who wish to act in a certain way come together to form crowds.

For example, whites in various U.S. communities have banded together to keep African-Americans from moving into their neighbourhoods. In such instances, convergence theorists contend, the crowd itself does not generate racial hatred or violence; in all likelihood, hostility has been simmering for some time among many local people. A crowd then arises from a convergence of people who oppose the presence of Black residents.

Critical evaluation. By linking crowds to broader social forces, convergence theory claims that crowd behaviour is not irrational, as Le Bon maintained. Rather, people in crowds express existing beliefs and values (Berk, 1974). But in fairness to Le Bon, people sometimes do things in a crowd that they would not have the courage to do alone, because crowds can intensify a sentiment simply by creating a critical mass of like-minded people.

Emergent-Norm Theory

Ralph Turner and Lewis Killian (1993) developed the *emergent-norm theory* of crowd dynamics. These researchers concede that social behaviour is never entirely predictable, but neither are crowds as irrational as Le Bon thought. If similar interests may draw people together, distinctive patterns of behaviour may emerge within a crowd itself.

According to Turner and Killian, crowds begin as collectivities in which people have mixed interests and motives. Especially in the case of less stable crowds—expressive, acting, and protest crowds—norms may be vague and changing, as when, say, one member at a rock concert holds up a lit cigarette lighter to signal praise for the performers, and others follow suit. In short, people in crowds make their own rules as they go along.

Critical evaluation. Emergent-norm theory represents a symbolic-interaction approach to crowd dynamics. Turner and Killian (1972:10) explain that crowd behaviour is neither as irrational as contagion theory suggests, nor as deliberate as convergence theory implies. Certainly, crowd behaviour reflects the desires of participants, but it is also guided by norms that emerge as the situation unfolds.

Decision making, then, plays a significant role in crowd behaviour, even though it may escape the notice of casual observers. For example, frightened people clogging the exits of a burning theatre may appear to be victims of irrational panic, but from their

The Rumour Mill: Paul Is Dead!

Everyone knows the Beatles. The music of John Lennon, Paul McCartney, George Harrison, and Ringo Starr caused a cultural revolution in the 1960s. Not everyone today, however, knows the rumour that circulated about Paul McCartney at the height of the group's popularity.

On October 12, 1969, a young man telephoned a Detroit disc jockey to say that he had discovered "evidence" that Paul McCartney was dead:

1. If you filtered out background music at the end of the song "Strawberry Fields Forever" on the *Magical Mystery Tour* album, you would hear a voice saying, "I buried Paul!"

2. The phrase "Number 9, Number 9, Number 9" from the song "Revolution 9" on the *White Album*, when played backwards, seems to intone, "Turn me on, dead man!"

Two days later, the University of Michigan student newspaper ran a story entitled "McCartney Is Dead: Further Clues Found." It sent millions of Beatles fans scurrying for their albums.

3. A picture inside the *Magical Mystery Tour* album shows John, George, and Ringo wearing red carnations, while Paul is sporting a black flower.

4. The cover of the *Sergeant Pepper's Lonely Hearts Club Band* album shows a grave with yellow flowers arranged in the shape of Paul's bass guitar.

5. On the inside of that album, McCartney wears an arm patch with the letters "OPD." Was this the insignia of some police department, or confirmation that Paul had been "Officially Pronounced Dead"? (Canadians looking closely recognize that the letters are actually "OPP" and the badge is the insignia of the Ontario Provincial Police!)

6. On the back cover of the same album, three Beatles are facing forwards while McCartney has his back to the camera.

7. On the album cover of *Abbey Road*, John Lennon is clothed as a clergyman, Ringo Starr wears an undertaker's black tie, and George Harrison is clad in worker's attire as if ready to dig a grave. For his part, McCartney is barefoot, which is how Tibetan ritual prepares a corpse for burial. Behind Paul, a Volkswagen nearby displays the licence plate "28 IF," indicating that McCartney would have been *28 if* he had not met his demise.

The report in the University of Michigan newspaper provided details of McCartney's alleged death in an automobile accident early in November 1966, and included a photograph allegedly of the musician's bloodied head. After the accident, the story continued, music company executives had secretly replaced Paul with a double.

Of course, Sir Paul McCartney is very much alive and still jokes about the episode. Few doubt that the Beatles intentionally fabricated some of the "clues" to pique the interest of their fans. But the incident has a serious side, revealing how quickly rumours can arise and persist in a climate of distrust. During the late 1960s, many disaffected young people had no trouble believing that the media and other powerful interests would conceal McCartney's death.

McCartney himself denied the rumour in a 1969 *Life* magazine interview. But thousands of suspicious readers also noticed that the back of the page containing McCartney's picture had an advertisement for an automobile: if they held this page up to the light, the car lay across McCartney's chest and blocked his head. Another clue!

Sources: Based on Rosnow and Fine (1976); Kapferer (1992); and BBC (2000).

---

point of view fleeing a life-threatening situation is entirely sensible.

Further, emergent-norm theory points out that people in a crowd take on different roles. Some assume leadership roles, while others become lieutenants, rank-and-file followers, inactive bystanders, or even opponents (Weller and Quarantelli, 1973; Zurcher and Snow, 1981).

DISPERSED COLLECTIVITIES: MASS BEHAVIOUR

It is not just people in physical proximity who participate in collective behaviour. **Mass behaviour** refers to *collective behaviour among people dispersed over a wide geographical area.*

RUMOUR AND GOSSIP

A common type of mass behaviour is **rumour**, *unsubstantiated information spread informally, often by word of mouth*. People pass along rumours through face-to-face communication, of course, but today's modern technology—including telephones, the mass media, and now the Internet—spreads rumours faster and farther than ever before.

Rumour has three essential characteristics:

1. **Rumour thrives in a climate of ambiguity.** Rumours arise among people who lack definitive information about a topic of concern. For example, workers fearing a massive layoff, and hearing little official news from management, will usually find themselves awash in rumours.

2. **Rumour is unstable.** People change a rumour as they pass it along, usually giving it a "spin" that serves their own interests. Before long, many competing variations exist.

3. **Rumour is difficult to stop.** The number of people aware of a rumour increases exponentially as each person relays information to several others. Rumours dissipate with time, but in general the only way to control rumours is for a believable source to issue a clear and convincing statement of the facts.

Rumour can trigger the formation of crowds or other collective behaviour. Thus, authorities often establish rumour-control centres in times of crisis to manage information. Yet some rumours persist for years despite incontrovertible evidence to the contrary; the "Applying Sociology" box provides a notable example.

 To check the truth about recent rumours making the rounds on the Internet, see www.nonprofit.net/hoax

Gossip is *rumour about people's personal affairs*. Charles Horton Cooley (1962; orig. 1909) explained that, while rumour involves issues or events of interest to a large segment of the public, gossip concerns a small circle of people who know a particular person. While rumours spread widely, then, gossip is more localized.

Communities use gossip as a means of social control, praising or scorning someone to encourage conformity to local norms. Moreover, people gossip about others to elevate their own standing as social "insiders." Yet no community wants gossip to get out of control, which may be the reason why people who gossip too much are criticized as "busybodies."

PUBLIC OPINION AND PROPAGANDA

Another form of highly dispersed collective behaviour is **public opinion**, *widespread attitudes about controversial issues*. Exactly who is, or is not, included in any

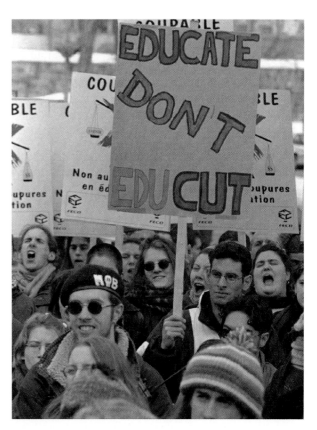

What explains the behaviour of crowds? Although people once thought a crowd takes on a "mind of its own," it is more correct to say that people are brought together by some shared interest. In the case of this protest crowd in Quebec City, the participants are demanding that the province not cut funding to education or raise tuition fees. Exactly what happens next, however, depends on many factors that unfold as the protest proceeds.

"public" depends on the issue involved. Over the years in Canada, "publics" have formed over issues such as water fluoridation, air pollution, the social standing of women, handguns, Quebec separatism, immigration, health care, same-sex marriage, and even the Constitution. As this list indicates, public issues are important matters about which people disagree (Lang and Lang, 1961; Turner and Killian, 1993).

On any given issue, anywhere from 2 to 10 percent of people will offer no opinion because of ignorance or apathy. Moreover, over time, public interest in issues rises and falls. For example, interest in the social position of women in Canada was strong during the decades of the women's suffrage movement but declined after women won the right to vote—federally in 1918 and provincially when Quebec became the last province to extend the vote to women in 1940. Since the 1960s, a second wave of feminism has again created a public with strong opinions on gender issues.

On any issue, not everyone's opinion carries the same clout. Some categories of people have more social influence than others because they are wealthier, more powerful, or better educated. Many special-interest groups shape public policy even though they represent only a small fraction of the population. In general, privileged people make use of their affluence, prestige, and social contacts to promote their opinions more effectively than others.

Political leaders, special-interest groups, and businesses all seek to influence public tastes and attitudes by using **propaganda**, *information presented with the intention of shaping public opinion*. Although the term has negative connotations, propaganda is not necessarily false. A thin line separates information from propaganda: the difference depends mostly on the presenter's intention. We offer *information* to enlighten others; we use *propaganda* to sway an audience towards some viewpoint. Political speeches, commercial advertising, and even some university lectures may disseminate propaganda with the goal of making people think or act in some specific way. Input from Canada's business community during the 1987 debate over free trade with the United States was denounced by opponents as propaganda, as were all of the pronouncements of the three major federal political parties during the 1992 referendum on the Charlottetown Accord.

PANIC AND MASS HYSTERIA

A **panic** is *a form of localized collective behaviour by which people react to a threat or other stimulus with irrational, frantic, and often self-destructive behaviour*. The classic illustration of a panic is people responding to a fire in a crowded theatre. As they flee in fear, they trample one another and block exits so that few actually escape.

Closely related to panic is **mass hysteria**, *a form of dispersed collective behaviour by which people respond to a real or imagined event with irrational, frantic, and often self-destructive behaviour*. Whether the cause of the hysteria is real or not, a large number of people think it is and take it seriously. Parents' fears that their children may become infected with HIV by a schoolmate who has AIDS may stir as much hysteria in a community as the very real danger of an approaching hurricane. Moreover, actions of people in the grip of mass hysteria generally make the situation worse. At the extreme, mass hysteria leads to chaotic flight and sends crowds into panic. People who see others overcome by fear may become more afraid themselves, as hysteria feeds on itself.

During the evening before Hallowe'en in 1938, CBS radio broadcast a dramatization by Orson Welles of H.G. Wells's novel *War of the Worlds* (Cantril et al., 1947; Koch, 1970). It started with a typical program of dance music. Suddenly, a voice interrupted the music with a "special report" of explosions on the surface of the planet Mars and, soon after, the crash landing of a mysterious cylinder near a farmhouse in New Jersey. The program then switched to an "on-the-scene reporter" who presented a chilling account of giant monsters equipped with death-ray weapons emerging from the spaceship. An "eminent astronomer" sombrely informed the audience that Martians had begun a full-scale invasion of Earth. Back then, most people relied on radio for factual news; thus, there was an announcement to clarify that the broadcast was fiction. But about 1 million of the 10 million listeners across the United States and Canada missed the announcement and actually believed the report.

By the time the show was over, thousands were hysterical, gathering in the streets to spread news of the "invasion," while others flooded telephone switchboards with warnings to friends and relatives. Many simply jumped into their cars and fled.

FASHIONS AND FADS

Two additional types of collective behaviour—fashions and fads—affect people dispersed over a large area. A **fashion** is *a social pattern favoured by a large number of people*. Some fashions last for years, while others change after just a few months. The arts (including painting, music, drama, and literature), automobiles, language, architecture, and public opinion all change as ideas go in and out of fashion.

Lyn Lofland (1973) suggests that, in pre-industrial societies, clothing and personal adornment reflect traditional *style*, which changes very little. Categories of people—women and men, and members of various social classes and occupations—wear distinctive clothes and hairstyles that visibly mark their social standing.

In industrial societies, however, style gives way to changing fashion. For one thing, modern people are less tied to tradition and often eagerly embrace new ways of living. Then, too, high social mobility means that people use their "looks" to make a statement about themselves. German sociologist Georg Simmel (1971; orig. 1904) explained that affluent people are typically the trendsetters, since they have the money to spend on luxuries that bespeak privilege. In the lasting phrase of Thorstein Veblen (1953; orig. 1899), fashion involves *conspicuous consumption*, meaning that people buy expensive products simply to display their wealth.

Less affluent people who want to appear wealthy often snap up less expensive copies of what the rich make fashionable. In this way, a fashion moves downwards in society. But the fashion loses its prestige when too many average people now share "the look," so the wealthy move on to something new. Fashions, in short, are born at the top of the social hierarchy, rise to mass popularity in bargain stores across the country, and soon are all but forgotten by everyone.

Because change in industrial societies is so rapid, we can see differences in personal appearance—one important kind of fashion—over short periods of time. The five photographs (beginning with the top left) show hairstyles commonly worn by women in the 1950s, 1960s, 1970s, 1980s, 1990s, and since 2000.

A reversal of this pattern occurs when rich people mimic a fashion found among people of lower social position. In the 1960s, for example, affluent university students began buying blue jeans, or dungarees (from a Hindi word for a coarse fabric). For decades, manual labourers had worn blue jeans, but in the era of civil rights and anti-war movements, jeans became the uniform of political activists and were soon popular on university campuses across the country. Author Tom Wolfe (1970) coined the phrase "radical chic" to satirize the desire of the rich to look fashionably poor.

A **fad** is *an unconventional social pattern that people embrace briefly but enthusiastically.* Fads, sometimes called *crazes*, are commonplace in rich industrial societies where many people have the money to spend on amusing, if often frivolous, products. During the 1950s, two young entrepreneurs in California produced a brightly coloured plastic version of a popular Australian toy, a three-foot-diameter hoop that one swung around the body by gyrating the hips. Dubbed the hula hoop, this odd device soon became a North American craze. But in less than a year, hula hoops vanished from the scene.

Streaking—running naked in public—had an even briefer moment in the sun, lasting only a few months in early 1974. Their fleeting existence suggests that fads happen almost at random, although national fads are usually begun by high-prestige people (Aguirre et al., 1988).

How do fads differ from fashions? Fads are passing fancies that capture the mass imagination but quickly burn out and disappear. Fashions, in contrast, reflect fundamental cultural values such as individuality and sexual attractiveness and tend to evolve over time. Therefore, a fashion—but rarely a fad—is incorporated into a society's culture. The fad of streaking, for instance, came out of nowhere and soon vanished; the fashion of wearing blue jeans, on the other hand, originated in the rough mining camps of Gold Rush California more than a century ago and still influences clothing designs today. This staying power explains the positive connotation of being called *fashionable*, in contrast to the mildly insulting label *faddish* (Blumer, 1968; Turner and Killian, 1987).

SOCIAL MOVEMENTS

Social movements are different from crowds, rumours, and other types of collective behaviour we have examined so far in three ways: they are deliberately organized, they have lasting importance, and they seek to change or defend some social pattern.

Social movements are far more common today than in the past. Pre-industrial societies are tightly integrated by tradition, making the emergence of social movements extremely rare. Industrial societies, however, foster diverse subcultures and countercultures so that social movements develop around a wide range of public issues. In recent decades, for example, homosexual men and women—supported by heterosexuals sympathetic to their political aims—organized to win economic and legal parity with everyone else. With the battle for spousal benefits for same-sex partners behind them, gay rights activists are closing in on the goal of the right to marry. As this book went to press in late 2003, same-sex marriage was legal in Ontario, pending in Quebec and British Columbia, and almost certain to be legislated by the federal government sometime in 2004, changing the definition of marriage from the union of a man and a woman to the union of two people.

 The early history of the gay rights movement in Canada is profiled in film and audio excerpts at http://archives.cbc.ca/300c.asp?id=1-69-599

Yet as recently as 1996, when the Liberal government undertook to add protection against discrimination on the basis of sexual orientation to the *Human Rights Act*, his own party was so bitterly divided on this issue that Prime Minister Chrétien relaxed party discipline and allowed a free vote. Though the bill did pass, more than twenty Liberals joined Reform MPs to vote against it on each of its readings. And twice, since then, the Canadian Alliance introduced a motion to reaffirm the traditional definition of marriage. In the first instance, the definition was reaffirmed overwhelmingly, with the support of a large number of Liberal MPs. In September 2003, the motion was narrowly defeated because many of the same Liberal MPs—despite the fact that this was a free vote—felt they had to vote with Prime Minister Chrétien and his cabinet. The fact that we are now clearing the way for changing the definition of marriage and legalizing same-sex marriage across the country speaks to the powerful impact of the gay rights movement.

However, like any social movement that challenges conventional practices, this one has sparked a countermovement as traditionalists try to block greater social acceptance of homosexuality. Right-wing organizations in Canada, including the Ku Klux Klan and the Western Guard, are opposed to any extension of privileges to Blacks, immigrants, Jews, and homosexuals (Barrett, 1987). In today's society, almost every important public issue gives rise to a social movement favouring change and an opposing countermovement resisting it (Lo, 1982; Meyer and Staggenborg, 1996).

Prior to the 1980s there were three major dynamic sources of social change in Canada: class relations, regional identity, and the bilingual and multicultural nature of our society (Marsden and Harvey, 1979:4). Many of Canada's social movements arose from one of four sources:

1. **Quebec**, as its francophone majority seeks to reshape its relationship with the rest of the country or possibly to establish its sovereignty.

2. **The regions**, as they respond to economic and political inequities and numerous cultural differences.

3. **Native peoples**, as they struggle to gain recognition of an *inherent* right to self-government.

4. **Ethnic and racial minorities**, as they attempt to participate as equals within the larger society without completely losing their identities.

With the patriation of our constitution in 1982 and the incorporation of the Charter of Rights and Freedoms, we have entered a new "post-Charter" era. A number of issues have been brought to the forefront, claiming Charter protection and inspiring social movements and various degrees of social change. Earlier movements, of women or gays and lesbians, gained momentum and reached many goals in this post-Charter period. Others, mobilized around the human rights of refugees, permanent residents (previously called landed immigrants), or Canadian citizens of Middle East origins (post 9/11), are in full force. A smaller movement endorsing euthanasia and the right to die seems to gain momentum periodically in response to the plight of specific individuals, like Sue Rodriguez (see Chapter 21, "Health and Medicine").

TYPES OF SOCIAL MOVEMENTS

Sociologists classify social movements according to several criteria (Aberle, 1966; Cameron, 1966; Blumer, 1969). Since some movements target selected people while others try to change everyone, one variable deals with *who is changed?* A second variable looks at *how much change?* Some movements attempt to foster only superficial changes in how we live, while others pursue a radical transformation of society. Combining these variables, we can identify four types of social movements, shown in Figure 23–1.

Alternative social movements are the least threatening to the status quo because they seek limited change in only some narrow segment of the population. Planned Parenthood, one example of an alternative social movement, encourages individuals of childbearing age to take the consequences of sexual activity more seriously by practising birth control.

Redemptive social movements also have a selective focus, but they seek radical change in those they engage. For example, Alcoholics Anonymous is an organization that helps alcoholics to achieve a sober life.

Reformative social movements, which generally work within the existing political system, seek only limited social change but encompass the entire society. They can be progressive (promoting a new social pattern) or reactionary (countermovements trying to preserve the status quo or to return to past social patterns). In the ongoing debate about abortion in Canada, both the anti-abortion and pro-choice organizations are reformative social movements. The former Canadian Alliance party illustrated the transition of a social conservative, back-to-the-Bible movement into a political party, now an integral part of our political system. Right-wing movements such as the Western Guard, the National Citizens Coalition, and the Ku Klux Klan are examples of reactionary countermovements.

Revolutionary social movements are the most extreme of all. They seek basic transformation of a society. Sometimes pursuing specific goals, sometimes spinning utopian dreams, these social movements reject existing social institutions as flawed while promoting radically new alternatives. The nationalist or sovereigntist (i.e., separatist) movement in Quebec is revolutionary because it seeks, at the very least, a radical restructuring of federal institutions to give Quebec more political and economic autonomy; failing that, Quebec nationalists would argue, the need to protect their distinct society requires the establishment of an independent state and the complete overthrow of existing institutions. As with the social conservative movement, the creation of the Bloc Québécois at the federal level and the Parti Québécois at the provincial level legitimates a revolutionary and potentially separatist movement by incorporating it within Canada's political structure. Few other nations would pass this test of tolerance.

EXPLAINING SOCIAL MOVEMENTS

Because social movements are intentional and long-lasting, sociologists find this form of collective behaviour somewhat easier to explain than fleeting incidents of mob behaviour or mass hysteria. Several theories have come to the fore.

Deprivation Theory

Deprivation theory holds that social movements arise among people who feel deprived. People who feel they lack sufficient income, satisfactory working conditions, important political rights, or basic social dignity may engage in organized collective behaviour to bring about a more just state of affairs (Morrison, 1978; Rose, 1982).

The rise of the Ku Klux Klan and the push for so-called Jim Crow laws to enforce segregation throughout the American South in the wake of the Civil War exemplify deprivation theory. With the end of slavery, white people lost a source of free labour and the claim that they were socially superior to African-Americans. Many whites reacted to this "deprivation" by trying to keep all people of colour "in their place" (Dollard et al., 1939). African-Americans had experienced much greater deprivation, of course, but as slaves they had little opportunity to organize. During the twentieth century, however, African-Americans organized successfully in pursuit of racial equality.

As Chapter 7 ("Groups and Organizations") explains, deprivation is a relative concept. Regardless of how much money and power someone accumulates, people feel either well off or deprived compared to some category of others—a reference group. **Relative**

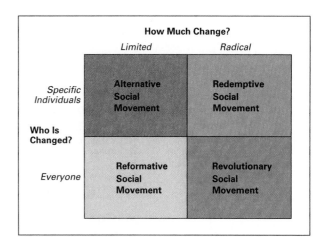

FIGURE 23–1 Four Types of Social Movements

Source: Based on Aberle (1966).

deprivation, then, is *a perceived disadvantage arising from some specific comparison* (Stouffer et al., 1949; Merton, 1968).

More than a century ago, Alexis de Tocqueville (1955; orig. 1856) studied the French Revolution. Why, he asked, did rebellion occur in progressive France rather than in more traditional Germany, where peasants were, by any objective measure, worse off? De Tocqueville's answer was that, as bad as their condition was, German peasants had known nothing but feudal servitude and thus had no basis for feeling deprived. French peasants, in contrast, had seen improvements in their lives that whetted their appetites for more. Thus, the French—not the Germans—felt a keen sense of relative deprivation. In analyzing this apparent paradox, de Tocqueville pinpointed one of the notable ironies of human history: increasing prosperity, far from satisfying the population, is likely to promote a spirit of unrest (1955:175; orig. 1856).

James C. Davies (1962) agrees that as life gets better, people may take their rising fortunes for granted and expect even more. But what happens if the standard of living suddenly stops improving or, worse, begins to drop? As Figure 23–2 illustrates, relative deprivation is the result, generating unrest and social movements aimed at change.

Critical evaluation. Deprivation theory challenges our common-sense assumption that the worse-off people are the most likely to organize for change. People do not organize simply because they are suffering in an absolute sense; rather, they form social movements because of *relative* deprivation. Indeed, both de Tocqueville and Marx—as different as they were in many ways—agreed on the importance of relative deprivation in the formation of social movements.

Since most people experience some discontent all the time, one wonders why social movements emerge

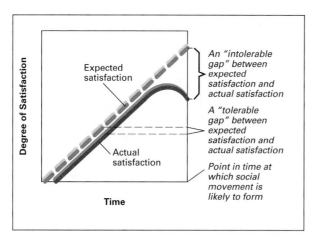

Figure 23–2   Relative Deprivation and Social Movements

In this diagram, the solid line represents a rising standard of living over time. The dotted line indicates the expected standard of living, which is typically somewhat higher. James C. Davies describes the difference between the two as "a tolerable gap between what people want and what they get." If the standard of living suddenly drops in the midst of rising expectations, however, the gap becomes intolerable. At this point, we can expect social movements to form.

Source: Davies (1962).

among certain categories of people and not others. Further, deprivation theory has a tendency towards circular reasoning: we assume that deprivation causes social movements, but often the only evidence of deprivation is the social movement itself (Jenkins and Perrow, 1977). Another limitation of this approach is that it focuses exclusively on the cause of a social movement and tells us little about movements themselves (McAdam et al., 1988). Lastly, some researchers claim that relative deprivation has not turned out to be a very good predictor of social movements (Muller, 1979).

Mass-Society Theory

William Kornhauser's *mass-society theory* (1959) argues that social movements attract socially isolated people who feel personally insignificant. From this point of view, social movements characterize large, complex *mass* societies. Further, social movements are more *personal* than *political*, in that they confer a sense of purpose and belonging on people otherwise adrift in society (Melucci, 1989).

This theory holds that categories of people with weak social ties are most readily mobilized into a social movement. People who have a strong sense of social integration, in contrast, are unlikely to join the ranks of a movement for change.

Like Gustave Le Bon, discussed earlier, Kornhauser offers a conservative view of social movements. He regards activists as psychologically vulnerable individuals who eagerly join groups and are often manipulated by group leaders. Social movements, in Kornhauser's view, are unlikely to be very democratic.

Critical evaluation.   The strength of Kornhauser's theory lies in its explanation of social movements both in terms of the characteristics of the people who join them and the nature of the larger society. However, from a practical standpoint, if we try to evaluate the notion that mass societies foster social movements, we find it extremely difficult to specify what constitutes a "mass society."

A more political criticism holds that placing the roots of social movements in human psychology tends to dismiss the importance of social justice, by suggesting that flawed people, rather than a flawed society, underlie the emergence of social movements.

And what does research show about mass-society theory? The record is mixed. On the down side, some studies conclude that the Nazi movement in Germany did not draw heavily from socially isolated people (Lipset, 1963; Oberschall, 1973). Similarly, urban rioters during the 1960s typically had strong ties to their communities (Sears and McConahay, 1973). Evidence also suggests that young people who join religious cults do not have particularly weak family ties (Wright and Piper, 1986). Finally, researchers who have examined the biographies of 1960s political activists find evidence of deep and continuing commitment to political goals rather than isolation from society (McAdam, 1988, 1989; Whalen and Flacks, 1989).

On the up side, research by Frances Piven and Richard Cloward (1977) supports this approach. Piven and Cloward found that a breakdown of routine social patterns has encouraged poor people to form social movements. Also, in a study of the New Mexico State Penitentiary, Bert Useem (1985) found that when prison programs that promoted social ties among inmates were suspended, inmates displayed higher levels of protest.

Structural-Strain Theory

One of the most influential theories about social movements was developed by Neil Smelser (1962). *Structural-strain theory* identifies six factors that foster social movements. Smelser's theory also offers clues as to which situations spark unorganized mobs or riots and which create highly organized social movements. The prodemocracy movement that transformed Eastern Europe during the late 1980s serves to illustrate Smelser's six factors.

1. **Structural conduciveness.** Social movements arise as people come to think their society has

The mass media often play an important part in guiding public opinion towards or away form change. Media performances do this by providing symbols that mobilize support for some point of view. Soviet-backed governments throughout Eastern Europe were collapsing, one after another, in the early 1990s, when Roger Waters (former member of Pink Floyd) performed "The Wall" at the site of the Berlin Wall, celebrating the fact that this barrier was finally coming down.

some serious problems. In Eastern Europe, these problems included low living standards and political repression by socialist governments.

2. **Structural strain.** People begin to experience relative deprivation when their society fails to meet their expectations. Eastern Europeans joined the prodemocracy movement because they knew their living standards were far lower than living standards in Western Europe and much below what years of propaganda about prosperous socialism had led them to expect.

3. **Growth and spread of an explanation.** Any coherent social movement must formulate a clear statement of a problem, its causes, and likely solutions. If people are confused about their suffering, they are likely to express their dissatisfaction in an unorganized way such as rioting. In Eastern Europe, intellectuals played a key role in the prodemocracy movement by pointing out economic and political flaws in the system and proposing strategies to increase democracy.

4. **Precipitating factors.** Discontent frequently festers for a long time, only to be galvanized into collective action by a specific event. In Eastern Europe, such an event occurred in 1985 when Mikhail Gorbachev came to power in the Soviet Union and implemented his sweeping program of *perestroika* (restructuring). As Moscow relaxed its rigid control over Eastern Europe, people there saw a historic opportunity to reorganize political and economic life.

5. **Mobilization for action.** Widespread concern about a public issue sets the stage for collective action in the form of rallies, distributing leaflets, and building alliances with sympathetic organiza-

tions. The initial success of the Solidarity movement in Poland—covertly aided by the Reagan administration in the United States and by the Vatican—mobilized people throughout Eastern Europe to press for change. The rate of change accelerated as reform movements gained strength: what took a decade in Poland required only months in Hungary and only weeks in other Eastern European nations.

6. **Lack of social control.** The responses of established authorities, such as political officials, police, and the military, largely determine the outcome of any social movement. Firm repression by the state can weaken or even destroy a social movement, as demonstrated by the crushing of prodemocracy forces in the People's Republic of China. In contrast, Gorbachev adopted a policy of nonintervention in Eastern Europe, thereby increasing the possibility for change. Ironically, the forces his program unleashed in these neighbouring nations soon spread to the Soviet Union itself, ending the historic domination of the Communist party and producing a new political confederation in 1992.

Critical evaluation. Smelser's approach—distinctly social, rather than psychological, in focus—recognizes the complexity of social movements and suggests how various factors encourage or inhibit their development. Structural-strain theory also explains how social problems may give rise to either organized social movements or more spontaneous mob action or rioting.

Yet Smelser's theory contains some of the same circularity of argument found in Kornhauser's analysis. A social movement is caused by strain, says Smelser, but the only evidence of this underlying

This photo shows a pro-life demonstration. Mass-society theory suggests that people join social movements in order to gain a sense of meaning and purpose in their lives. How well do you think this theory explains the behaviour of such people? Why?

strain appears to be the social movement itself. Finally, structural-strain theory overlooks the important role that resources such as the mass media or international alliances play in the success or failure of a social movement (Oberschall, 1973; Jenkins and Perrow, 1977; McCarthy and Zald, 1977; Olzak and West, 1991). Canada's Native peoples have been particularly adept at gaining media coverage and winning support for their cause in the United States, Europe, the United Nations, and among the Canadian public.

Resource-Mobilization Theory

Resource-mobilization theory points out that no social movement is likely to succeed—or even get off the ground—without substantial resources, including money, human labour, office and communications facilities, access to the mass media, and a positive public image. In short, any social movement rises or falls on its ability to attract resources, mobilize people, and forge alliances. The collapse of socialism in Eastern Europe was largely the work of dissatisfied people in those countries. But assistance from outside, in the form of fax machines, copiers, telecommunications equipment, money, and moral support, was critical in allowing first the Poles and then people in other countries to successfully oppose their leaders.

In other words, according to resource-mobilization theory, outsiders are as important as insiders to the victory of a social movement, often playing a crucial role in supplying resources. Socially disadvantaged people, by definition, lack the money, contacts, leadership skills, and organizational know-how that a successful movement requires, and it is here that sympathetic outsiders fill the resource gap (Snow et al., 1980; Killian, 1984; Snow et al., 1986; Baron et al., 1991; Burstein, 1991; Meyer and Whitter, 1994; Valocchi,

1996). In Canada, people with all manner of skills, resources, and contacts have been involved in CASNP (the Canadian Alliance[1] in Solidarity with Native Peoples). Well-to-do whites and university students performed a vital service to the Black civil rights movement in the United States in the 1960s.

On the other side of the coin, a lack of resources limits efforts to bring about change. The history of the AIDS epidemic offers a case in point. Initially, the U.S. government made a minimal response as the incidence of AIDS rose in the early 1980s. To a large extent, gay communities in cities such as San Francisco and New York were left to shoulder the responsibility for treatment and educational programs. Gradually, as the general public in both Canada and the United States began to grasp the dimensions of the problem, various levels of government in both countries started to allocate more resources. Galvanizing the public, members of the entertainment industry lent not only money and visibility but their prestige and credibility to the movement to combat the disease. These resources were crucial in transforming a fledgling social movement into a well-organized, global coalition of political leaders, educators, and medical specialists.

Critical evaluation. Resource-mobilization theory recognizes that resources as well as discontent are necessary to the success of a social movement. Research has confirmed that forging alliances to gain resources is especially important, and notes that movements with few resources may, in desperation, turn to violence to call attention to their cause (Grant and Wallace, 1991).

---

[1]There is no relationship between this organization and the federal political party, the former Canadian Reform Conservative Alliance (or Canadian Alliance).

Critics of this theory maintain that even relatively powerless segments of a population can promote change if they are able to organize effectively and have strongly committed members. Research by Aldon Morris (1981) shows that Blacks drew largely on their own skills and resources to fuel the American civil rights movement of the 1950s and 1960s. Further, this theory overstates the extent to which powerful people are willing to challenge the status quo. Some rich white people did provide valuable resources to the civil rights movement but, probably more often, elites were indifferent or opposed to significant change (McAdam, 1982, 1983; Pichardo, 1995).

Overall, the success or failure of a social movement is decided by political struggle. A strong and united establishment, perhaps aided by a countermovement, decreases the chances that any social movement will effect meaningful change. If, however, the established powers are divided, a movement's chances for success multiply as was apparent in the Native struggle for constitutional recognition in Canada. For close to two decades, Aboriginal peoples faced a united front of provincial leaders who were unwilling to give in to demands for Native participation in constitutional negotiations. However, by 1991, the election of several new premiers who were more open to Native involvement set the stage for their active participation in the negotiations leading up to the Charlottetown Accord.

New Social Movements Theory

A final, more recent theoretical approach addresses the changing character of social movements. *New social movements theory* emphasizes the distinctive features of recent social movements in post-industrial societies of North America and Western Europe (Melucci, 1980; McAdam et al., 1988; Kriesi, 1989; Pakulski, 1993).

Most of today's social movements are international, focusing on global ecology, the social standing of women and gay people, reducing the risks of war,

 For information on laws involving animal rights, see www.animal-law.org

and animal rights, among other issues. As the process of globalization connects the world's nations in more and more ways, social movements are becoming global.

While traditional social movements such as labour organizations are concerned primarily with economic issues, new social movements tend to focus on cultural change and improving our social and physical surroundings. The international environmental movement, for example, opposes practices that aggravate global warming and other threats to the environment.

Lastly, whereas most social movements of the past drew strong support from working-class people, new social movements, with their noneconomic agendas, usually draw support from the middle class. Furthermore, in Canada and other rich nations, the number of highly educated professionals—the people who most support "new social movements"—is increasing, which suggests that these movements will grow (Jenkins and Wallace, 1996).

Critical evaluation. One strength of this theory is its recognition that social movements are increasing in scale in response to the development of a global economy and international political connections. This theory also spotlights the power of the mass media to unite people around the world in pursuit of political goals.

Critics, however, claim that this approach exaggerates the differences between past and present social movements. The women's movement, for example, focuses on many of the same issues—workplace conditions and pay—that have concerned labour organizations for decades.

 Each of the five theories we have presented offers some explanation for the emergence of social movements; no single theory, it seems, can stand alone (Kowalewski and Porter, 1992). Table 23–1 summarizes the theories.

GENDER AND SOCIAL MOVEMENTS

Gender figures prominently in the operation of social movements. In keeping with traditional notions about gender in Canada, men more than women tend to take part in public life—including spearheading social movements.

Investigating "Freedom Summer," a 1964 voter registration project in Mississippi, Doug McAdam (1992) found that most people viewed the job of registering African-American voters in the midst of considerable opposition and even hostility from whites to be dangerous, and therefore "men's work" unsuitable for women. Similarly, he discovered, project leaders were likely to assign women volunteers to clerical and teaching positions, leaving the actual field activities to men. This was so even though women who participated in Freedom Summer were more qualified than their male counterparts in terms of years of activism and organizational affiliations. McAdam concluded that only the most committed women were able to overcome the movement's gender barriers. In short, while women have played leading roles in many social movements (including the feminist movement), male dominance has been the norm even in social movements that otherwise oppose the status quo.

STAGES IN SOCIAL MOVEMENTS

Despite the many differences that set one social movement apart from others, all unfold in similar stages. Researchers have identified four phases in the life of the typical social movement (Blumer, 1969; Mauss, 1975; Tilly, 1978).

TABLE 23–1 Theories of Social Movements: A Summary

Deprivation Theory	People experiencing relative deprivation begin social movements. The social movement is a means of seeking change that brings participants greater benefits. Social movements are especially likely when rising expectations are frustrated.
Mass-Society Theory	People who lack established social ties are mobilized into social movements. Periods of social breakdown are likely to spawn social movements. The social movement gives members a sense of belonging and social participation.
Structural-Strain Theory	People come together because of their shared concern about the inability of society to operate as they believe it should. The growth of a social movement reflects many factors, including a belief in its legitimacy and some precipitating event that provokes action.
Resource-Mobilization Theory	People may join for all the reasons noted above and also because of social ties to existing members. The success or failure of a social movement depends largely on the resources available to it. Also important is the extent of opposition within the larger society.
New Social Movements Theory	People who become part of social movements are motivated by "quality of life" issues, not necessarily economic concerns. Mobilization is national or international in scope. New social movements arise in response to the expansion of the mass media and new information technology.

Stage 1: Emergence. Social movements are driven by the perception that all is not well. Some, such as the civil rights and women's movements, are born of widespread dissatisfaction. Others emerge only as a small vanguard group increases public awareness of some issue, as gay activists did with respect to the threat posed by AIDS. As Jean Charest left federal politics to lead the Quebec Liberals, an underlying social movement seemed to be emerging, creating the conditions for effective charismatic leadership on his part. The raising of the Canadian flag in front of city hall in Quebec City in April 1998—for the first time since the failure of the Meech Lake Accord in 1990—was a visible symbol of a growing willingness among francophones to embrace dual Québécois/Canadian identities. Opinion polls at the time suggested a surge of pro-Canadian sentiment and a reluctance to choose between the two identities. Perhaps most significant is the fact that 3 million Québécois who had claimed French origins in the 1991 census called themselves Canadian in 1996 and 2001.

Stage 2: Coalescence. After emerging, a social movement must define itself clearly and develop a strategy for "going public." Leaders must determine policies, select tactics, build morale, and recruit new members. At this stage, the movement may engage in collective action such as rallies or demonstrations to attract media attention and public notice. The movement may also form alliances with other organizations to gain necessary resources.

Stage 3: Bureaucratization. To become an established political force, a social movement must assume bureaucratic traits, described in Chapter 7 ("Groups and Organizations"). As it becomes routinized, a social movement depends less on the charisma and talents of a few leaders and relies more on a capable staff. When social movements do not become established in this

way, they risk dissolving. For example, many activist organizations on university campuses during the late 1960s were energized by a single charismatic leader and, consequently, did not last long. On the other hand, the National Action Committee on the Status of Women (NAC), despite changing leadership, is well established and offers a steady voice on behalf of feminists in Canada. Canada's environmental movement has reached the bureaucratization stage in that we have an envi-

 For more information about the National Action Committee on the Status of Women, go to www.nac-cca.ca/

ronmental ministry and a wide range of environmental organizations.

Stage 4: Decline. Eventually, most social movements lose their influence. Frederick Miller (1983) suggests four reasons why this may occur.

1. If members have met their goals, decline may simply signal success. For example, the women's suffrage movement declined after it won the right to vote for women in Canada and the United States. Such clear-cut successes are rare, since few social movements have a single goal. More commonly, winning one victory leads to new campaigns. Because gender issues extend far beyond voting, the women's movement has recast itself time and again.

2. A social movement may flag owing to organizational factors, such as poor leadership, loss of interest among members, insufficient funds, or repression by authorities. Some people lose interest when the excitement of early efforts is replaced by formal routines. Fragmentation due to internal conflicts over goals and tactics is another common problem. Political parties with radical goals like those of the Parti Québécois (formed in 1968 with sovereignty as its central aim) can lose

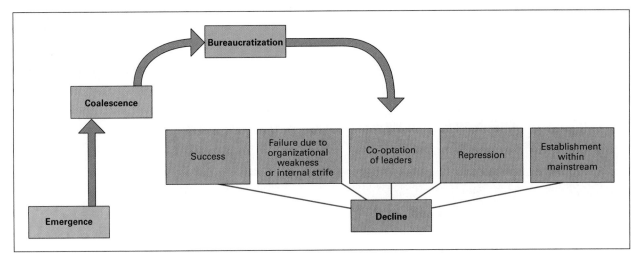

FIGURE 23–3 Stages in the Lives of Social Movements

some of their more committed and activist members when they have to modify their platforms, however temporarily, to govern or to ensure re-election, as the PQ did in 1984.

3. A social movement can fall apart if the established power structure, through offers of money, prestige, and other rewards, diverts leaders from their goals. Co-optation—that is, "selling out"—is one facet of the iron law of oligarchy discussed in Chapter 7 ("Groups and Organizations"). In other words, organizational leaders may use their positions to enrich themselves. For example, the former head of the Daily Bread food bank in Toronto, Gerard Kennedy, may take a different approach to poverty issues now that he is a Liberal cabinet minister in Ontario and a political "insider." But this process can also work the other way: some people leave lucrative, high-prestige occupations to become activists. Cat Stevens, a rock star in the 1970s, became a Muslim, changed his name to Yusuf Islam, and now promotes his religion. Stephen Lewis left Ontario politics, where he was once opposition leader, to be an activist as special UN envoy on AIDS/HIV to Africa.

4. A social movement can collapse because of repression. Officials may crush a social movement by frightening away participants, discouraging new recruits, and even imprisoning leaders. In general, the more revolutionary the social movement, the more officials try to repress it. In the 1960s, the Front de libération du Québec (FLQ)—a revolutionary movement whose aim was an independent socialist Quebec—used bombs, kidnapping, and murder to promote its cause. In 1970, Prime Minister Trudeau invoked the *War Measures Act* in peacetime to suspend civil liberties and facilitate the arrest of FLQ

 See the CBC archives at http://archives.cbc.ca/ 300c.asp?id=1-71-101 for documentary footage on the FLQ crisis.

members and sympathizers. By 1971, the FLQ had folded.

Another reason, beyond those noted by Miller, is that a social movement may "go mainstream." Some movements become an accepted part of the system (typically after realizing some of their goals) to the point that they no longer challenge the status quo. Until 1990, the government of South Africa, for example, banned the African National Congress (ANC), a political organization seeking to overthrow the state-supported system of apartheid. Even suspected members of the ANC were subject to arrest. In 1990, the government lifted the decades-old ban and released ANC leader Nelson Mandela from prison; in 1994, Mandela became president of a country moving away from apartheid.

Figure 23–3 provides a graphic summary of the various stages of social movements.

SOCIAL MOVEMENTS AND SOCIAL CHANGE

Social movements exist to encourage—or to resist—social change. Whatever the intention, their success varies from case to case. Gender equality, still only a partially realized goal, has been advanced by the actions of numerous women's groups in Canada and elsewhere. Environmentalists, as well, have experienced some major successes and changed public awareness dramatically.

Sometimes we overlook the success of past social movements and take for granted the changes that other people struggled so hard to win. Beginning a century ago, workers' movements fought to end child labour in factories, limit working hours, make the

CONTROVERSY & DEBATE

Are You Willing to Take a Stand?

"No" rally in Montreal, October 1995.

Are you satisfied with our society as it is? Surely everyone would change some things about our way of life. Indeed, despite the fact that 92 percent of Canadians claim to be "very happy" or "pretty happy" (Bibby, 1995), there are many things that people would change. Pessimism about our society is widespread. Seventy percent of Canadians believe that, in financial terms, the lot of the average person is getting worse. Only 25 and 22 percent of us have "a great deal" or "quite a bit" of confidence, respectively, in our federal and provincial leaders. We feel that the rich, corporations, and politicians have too much power, and that politicians are paid too much. We fear crime and 85 percent of us believe that the "courts do not deal harshly enough with criminals" (Bibby, 1995).

But are we willing to take a stand to bring about social change? How many of us are willing to serve on the picket lines or barricades, march in protest or in a Gay Pride parade, vote against our own parties in the House of Commons, or tie ourselves to trees to stop clear-cutting?

Certainly, there are good reasons to avoid political controversy. Any time we challenge the system—whether on campus, at work, or in the larger political arena—we risk making enemies, losing a job, or perhaps even sustaining physical injury. Challenging the status quo, by definition, means stepping on powerful toes. For Canadians, who, traditionally, have deferred to authority more readily than Americans, such challenges in themselves may seem to question basic values.

While it may be the case that only a small percentage of Canadians are willing to take a stand, publicly, on specific issues, there have been some highly visible and well-publicized instances of Canadians joining in collective action to address social problems. For example, in October 1995, three days before the referendum on sovereignty in Quebec, an estimated 150 000 Canadians gathered at a massive "No" rally in Montreal, including many thousands from across Canada, to express their solidarity with the people of Quebec. Despite the fact that airlines and buses offered cut rates (fare subsidies, in effect), participation required families to disrupt their routines and people to take time off from work or school. (Some analysts felt that the outpouring of support from the rest of Canada touched Quebecers and may

have helped to bring about the photo finish in favour of the "No" side. In any case, Quebec's chief electoral officer declared that the politicians and corporations who organized the rally acted in contravention of Quebec's referendum laws and, therefore, illegally.)

Some may argue, in light of cultural values emphasizing the responsibility of individuals for their own well-being, that collective action is no remedy for social ills. Sociology, of course, poses a counterpoint to this cultural individualism. As C. Wright Mills (1959) pointed out decades ago, many of the problems we encounter as individuals are caused by the structure of society. Thus, he maintained, solutions to many of life's challenges depend on collective effort—that is, people willing to join together to take a stand for their beliefs.

Continue the debate . . .

1. *Does the reluctance of Canadians to address problems through collective action mean that they are basically satisfied with their lives and their society? Or does it mean that they think individuals acting together can't make a difference?*

2. *Have you ever participated in a political demonstration? What were its goals? What did it accomplish?*

3. *Identify ways that life today has been affected by people who took a stand in the past. Think about race and ethnic relations, the environment, the status of women, and conditions of employment.*

workplace safer, and establish the right to bargain collectively with employers. And women today have greater legal rights and economic opportunities won by earlier generations of women.

Seen one way, major social transformations such as the Industrial Revolution and the rise of capitalism

give rise to social movements, including those involving workers and women. On the other hand, the efforts of workers, women, racial and ethnic minorities, and gay people have sent ripples of change throughout our society. Thus, social change is both the cause and the consequence of social movements.

LOOKING AHEAD: SOCIAL MOVEMENTS IN THE TWENTY-FIRST CENTURY

Especially since the turbulent decade of the 1960s—a decade marked by widespread social protests—Canadian society has been pushed and pulled by many social movements and countermovements. Sometimes tension explodes into violence, as with the Oka standoff described at the beginning of this chapter. In other cases, the struggles are more restrained, as with political debate for and against the free trade agreements. Yet people on all sides of controversial issues agree that many of this nation's most pressing problems—national unity, regionalism, poverty—remain unresolved. In addition, of course, new issues—including the state

 The standoff at Oka is captured in CBC documentary footage at http://archives.cbc.ca/300c.asp?id=1-71-99

of the family and gay rights—have moved to centre stage.

Social movements have always been part of our society, although their focus, tactics, and intensity change with time. There is little doubt, therefore, that social movements will continue to shape our way of life. Indeed, for three reasons, the scope of social movements is likely to increase. Protest should increase as women and other historically excluded categories of people gain a greater political voice. Thus, the twenty-first century should be marked by more social movements here at home. Further, at a global level, the technology of the Information Revolution means that anyone with a satellite dish, personal computer, or fax machine can stay abreast of political events, often as they happen. Finally, new technology and the emerging global economy mean that social movements are now uniting people throughout the entire world—or throughout Marshall McLuhan's *global village*. Moreover, since many problems are global in scope, only international cooperation can solve them.

SUMMARY

1. A collectivity differs from a social group in its limited social interaction, vague social boundaries, and weak and often unconventional norms.

2. Crowds, an important type of collective behaviour, take various forms: casual crowds, conventional crowds, expressive crowds, acting crowds, and protest crowds.

3. Crowds that become emotionally intense and even violent spawn mobs and riots. Mobs pursue a specific goal; rioting involves undirected destructiveness.

4. Crowds have figured heavily in social change throughout history, although the value of their action depends on one's political outlook.

5. Contagion theory views crowds as anonymous, suggestible, and subject to escalating emotions. Convergence theory links crowd behaviour to the traits of participants. Emergent-norm theory holds that crowds may develop their own behavioural norms.

6. One form of mass behaviour is rumour, which thrives in a climate of ambiguity. While rumour involves public issues, gossip deals with personal issues of local interest.

7. Public opinion consists of people's positions on issues of widespread importance. Some people's attitudes carry more weight than others and, on any given issue, a small proportion of the population claims to hold no opinion at all.

8. A panic (in a local area) or mass hysteria (across an entire society) are types of collective behaviour by which people respond to a significant event, real or

imagined, with irrational, frantic, and often self-destructive behaviour.

9. In industrial societies, people adopt fashion to enhance social prestige. A fad, which is more unconventional than a fashion, is of shorter duration but is embraced with greater enthusiasm.

10. Social movements exist to promote or discourage change. Sociologists classify social movements according to the range of people they seek to engage and the extent of change they seek.

11. According to deprivation theory, social movements arise in response to relative deprivation more than the lack of well-being in an absolute sense.

12. Mass-society theory holds that people join social movements to gain a sense of belonging and social significance.

13. Structural-strain theory explains the development of social movements as a cumulative consequence of six factors. Well-formulated grievances and goals encourage the organization of social movements; undirected anger, in contrast, promotes rioting.

14. Resource-mobilization theory ties the success or failure of a social movement to the availability of resources such as money, human labour, and alliances with other organizations.

15. New social movements theory notes that contemporary movements focus on quality-of-life issues that are typically national or international in scope.

16. A typical social movement proceeds through consecutive stages: emergence (defining the public issue),

coalescence (entering the public arena), bureaucratization (becoming formally organized), and decline (brought on by failure or, sometimes, success).

17. Past social movements have shaped society in ways that people now take for granted. Just as movements produce change, so change itself sparks social movements.

CRITICAL-THINKING QUESTIONS

1. The concept of collective behaviour encompasses a broad range of social patterns. What traits do they all have in common?

2. Imagine the aftermath of a hockey game in which the revelry of university students turns into a destructive rampage. What insights into this event do contagion theory, convergence theory, and emergent-norm theory provide?

3. The 1960s was a decade of both great affluence and widespread social protest. What sociological insights help to explain this apparent paradox?

4. In what respects do some recent social movements (those concerned with the environment, animal rights, and gun control) differ from older crusades (focusing on, say, civil rights and gender equality)?

APPLICATIONS AND EXERCISES

1. Visit the website for Hemp Nation at **www.hempnation.com**. What are the goals of this organization? How is it trying to expand the social movement in favour of legalizing marijuana use?

2. With ten friends, try a fascinating experiment: one person writes down a detailed "rumour" about someone important and then whispers it to the second person, who whispers it to a third, and so on. When the rumour comes full circle, the first person writes it down again. Compare the two versions of the rumour.

3. With other members of the class, identify "fad" products, from hula hoops to Beanie Babies. What makes people want them? Why do they drop from favour so quickly?

4. What social movements are represented by organizations on your campus? Your class might invite several leaders to describe their groups' goals and strategies.

 ## SITES TO SEE

www.macionis.com
or
www.TheSociologyPage.com
You can find more than fifty weblinks to sociological journals and other sources of data and information by visiting the Links Library at this website.

www.nathanwolfson.com/scholarship/
From Whence These Rumblings? is a long essay by Nathan Wolfson that examines how particular social structures foster movements for change.

www.ic.org/
The *Intentional Communities* page provides information and access to resources for seekers of community. Intentional Community is an inclusive term for eco-villages, cohousing, residential land trusts, communes, student co-ops, urban housing cooperatives, and other related projects and dreams.

www.webactive.com/
WebActive is a guide to political activism links on the World Wide Web, with a well-organized topic index.

www.propagandacritic.com/
This site contains an extensive analysis of propaganda, with contemporary examples and videos.

www.uni.ca/
The Unity Link is a pro-federalist site for supporters of Canadian national unity, containing news items and anti-separatist documents.

http://erg.environics.net/
www.ipsos-reid.com/ca/
www.legermarketing.com/
Tracking trends in public opinion is the job of various pollsters, including Environics, Ipsos-Reid, and Léger Marketing. Visit their websites to see what they do and read about some of their recent surveys.

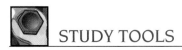

STUDY TOOLS

For more study tools to help you with your next exam, be sure to check out the Companion Website at **www.pearsoned. ca/macionis**, as well as Chapter 23 in your Study Guide.

 INVESTIGATE WITH CONTENTSELECT

Follow the instructions found on page 25 of this textbook to access ContentSelect™ at the Research Navigator™ website. Once at the site, enter your LOGINID and Password. Then, enter keywords such as "lynching," "riots," and "animal rights," and the search engine will supply relevant and recent scholarly and popular press publications.

CHAPTER

24

SOCIAL CHANGE: TRADITIONAL, MODERN, AND POSTMODERN SOCIETIES

The firelight flickers in the gathering darkness as Chief Kanhonk sits, as he has done at the end of the day for many years, ready to begin an evening of animated talk and storytelling (Simons, 2001). This is the hour when the Kaiapo, a small society in Brazil's lush Amazon region, celebrate their heritage. Because the Kaiapo are a traditional people with no written language, the elders rely on evenings by the fire to teach their culture and instruct the grandchildren. (In the past, evenings like this were filled with tales of brave Kaiapo warriors fighting off Portuguese traders in pursuit of slaves and gold.)

As the minutes pass, only a few older villagers assemble for the evening ritual. "It is the Big Ghost," one man grumbles, explaining the poor turnout. The Big Ghost has indeed descended upon them, its bluish glow spilling from windows of homes throughout the village. The Kaiapo children—and many adults as well—are watching television. Installing a satellite dish in the village several years ago has had greater conse-

quences than anyone imagined. In the end, what their enemies failed to do with guns, the Kaiapo may well do to themselves with prime-time programming.

The Kaiapo are among the 230 000 native peoples who inhabit the country we call Brazil. They stand out because of their striking body paint and ornate ceremonial dress. Recently, they have become rich from gold mining and harvesting mahogany trees. Now they must decide if their new-found fortune is a blessing or a curse.

To some, affluence means the opportunity to learn about the outside world through travel and television. Others, like Chief Kanhonk, are not so sure. Sitting by the fire, he thinks aloud, "I have been saying that people must buy useful things like knives and fishing hooks. Television does not fill the stomach. It only shows our children and grandchildren white people's things." Bebtopup, the oldest priest, nods in agreement: "The night is the time the old people teach the young people. Television has stolen the night."

(Simons, 2001:497).

The Kaiapo story raises profound questions about the causes of change and whether change is always for the better. The Kaiapo may be edging towards modernity, but is a higher standard of living necessarily better than their traditional way of life? Moreover, the drama of the Kaiapo is being played out around the globe as more and more traditional cultures are being lured away from their heritage by the materialism and affluence of rich societies.

Within Canada's own boundaries there are people grappling with the same kinds of concerns about the influence of television in particular. In the territory of Nunavut, the Inuit people have long been concerned about the damaging effects of television programming originating in the United States and southern Canada. With financial assistance from the federal government, they created the Inuit Broadcasting Corporation (IBC), which produces news, documentaries, children's programs (including cartoons and puppet shows), and talk shows that deal with issues of relevance to the region—in its own language, Inuktitut. Through the IBC, the Inuit people have been able to mitigate some of the intrusive and damaging impacts of television on their culture. More recently, all Canadians have had access to the Aboriginal Peoples Television Network (APTN) by cable and satellite. In January 2001, APTN increased its international content from 10 to 30 percent to include more programming about Aboriginal peoples around the world.

 See the APTN website at www.aptn.ca/

This chapter examines social change as a process with both positive and negative consequences. Of particular interest to us is what sociologists call *modernity*, changes brought about by the Industrial Revolution, and *postmodernity*, recent transformations sparked by the Information Revolution and the post-industrial economy.

WHAT IS SOCIAL CHANGE?

Earlier chapters have examined relatively *static* social patterns, including status and roles, social stratification, and social institutions. The *dynamic* forces that have shaped our way of life range from innovations in technology to the growth of bureaucracy and the expansion of cities. These are all dimensions of **social change**, *the transformation of culture and social institutions over time*. The process of social change has four key characteristics.

1. **Social change is inevitable.** "Nothing is constant except death and taxes," goes the old saying. Yet even our thoughts about death have changed dramatically as life expectancy in Canada has doubled over the past century. Taxes, meanwhile, were unknown through most of human history, and only emerged with complex social organization several thousand years ago. In short, one is hard-pressed to identify anything that is not subject to the twists and turns of change.

   Still, some societies change more quickly than others. As Chapter 4 ("Society") explained, hunting-and-gathering societies change quite slowly; members of modern, complex societies, on the other hand, experience significant change within a single lifetime.

   Moreover, in a given society, some cultural elements change faster than others. William Ogburn's (1964) theory of *cultural lag* (see Chapter 3, "Culture") states that material culture (that is, things) usually changes faster than nonmaterial culture (ideas

 Information about stem cell research is available at http://stemcells.nih.gov/

and attitudes). For example, medical technology that prolongs life has developed more rapidly than ethical standards for deciding when and how to use it.

2. **Social change is sometimes intentional but often unplanned.** Industrial societies actively promote many kinds of change. For example, scientists seek more efficient forms of energy, and advertisers try to convince consumers that life is incomplete without some new gadget. Yet rarely can anyone envision all the consequences of the changes they set in motion.

   Early automobile manufacturers understood that cars would allow people to travel, in a single day, distances that had previously required weeks or months. But no one foresaw how profoundly the mobility provided by automobiles would reshape our society, scattering family members, threatening the environment, and reshaping cities and suburbs. Nor did anyone foresee the three to four thousand deaths in car accidents in Canada alone each year.

3. **Social change is controversial.** As the history of the automobile demonstrates, most social change yields both positive and negative consequences. Capitalists welcomed the Industrial Revolution because advancing technology increased both productivity and profits. Many workers, however, feared that machines would make their skills obsolete and resisted the push towards "progress."

   Changing patterns of social interaction between white Canadians and Aboriginal peoples or other racial or ethnic minorities, between anglophones and francophones, between women and men, and between gays and heterosexuals give rise to both celebration and backlash as people disagree about how we ought to live.

4. **Some changes matter more than others.** Some social changes (such as clothing fads) have only passing significance, whereas other innovations (such as computers) unleash changes that transform the entire world and resonate for generations. Looking ahead, will the Information Revolution turn out to be as pivotal as the Industrial Revolution? Like the automobile and television, computers will have both beneficial and deleterious effects, providing new kinds of jobs while eliminating old ones, isolating people in offices while joining people together in global electronic networks, offering vast amounts of information while threatening personal privacy.

CAUSES OF SOCIAL CHANGE

Social change has many causes. And in a world linked by sophisticated communication and transportation technology, change in one place often begets change elsewhere.

CULTURE AND CHANGE

Chapter 3 ("Culture") identified three important sources of cultural change. *Invention* produces new objects, ideas, and social patterns. Rocket propulsion research, which began in the 1940s, has produced spacecraft that can reach towards the stars. Today, we take such technology for granted; during the twenty-first century, a significant number of people may well travel in space.

Discovery occurs when people first take note of certain elements or learn to see them in a new way. Medical advances, for example, offer a growing understanding of the human body. Beyond their direct effects on human health, medical discoveries have stretched life expectancy, setting in motion "the greying of Canada" (see Chapter 15, "Aging and the Elderly").

Diffusion creates change as trade, migration, and mass communication spread cultural elements throughout the world. Ralph Linton (1937) recognized that many familiar elements of our culture came from other lands. For example, cloth (developed in Asia), clocks (invented in Europe), and coins (devised in Turkey) have all become part of our way of life. Generally, material things diffuse more readily than nonmaterial cultural traits. The Kaiapo, described at the beginning of this chapter, have been quick to adopt television, but they have been reluctant to embrace the materialism and individualism at the core of Western commercial programming.

During Canada's entire history, immigrants have brought change to the country. In recent decades, people from Southern and Central Europe, Asia, Latin America, and the Caribbean have introduced new cultural patterns, clearly evident in the tastes, sights, smells, and sounds of cities across the country. Little Italies, Chinatowns, Caribana parades, ethnic festivals such as Toronto's Caravan, outdoor cafés, reggae music, pizza, perogies, fajitas, and sushi have become part of the fabric of life for many Canadians.

 See the website for Toronto's Caribana festival, the world's largest celebration of Caribbean culture, at www.caribana.com/

CONFLICT AND CHANGE

Tension and conflict within a society also produce change. Karl Marx saw class conflict as the engine that drives societies from one historical era to another (see Chapter 4, "Society," and Chapter 10, "Social Stratification"). In industrial-capitalist societies, he maintained, struggle between capitalists and workers propels society towards a socialist system of production.

In the century since Marx's death, this model has proven simplistic. Yet he correctly foresaw that social

Today, most of the people with access to computers live in rich countries such as the United States and Canada. But the number of people in agrarian societies going "online" is on the rise. How do you think the introduction of new information technology will change more traditional societies? Are all the changes likely to be for the good?

conflict arising from inequality (involving race and gender as well as social class) would force changes in every society, including our own.

IDEAS AND CHANGE

Max Weber, too, contributed to our understanding of social change. While Weber acknowledged the importance of conflict based on material production, he traced the roots of most social change to ideas. He illustrated his argument by showing how people with charisma can convey a message that sometimes changes the world.

Weber highlighted the importance of ideas by showing how the religious beliefs of early Protestants set the stage for the spread of industrial capitalism (see Chapter 4, "Society"). The fact that industrial capitalism developed primarily in areas of Western Europe where the Protestant work ethic was strong proved to Weber (1958a; orig. 1904–5) the power of ideas to bring about change.

Ideas also direct social movements. Chapter 23 ("Collective Behaviour and Social Movements") explained how change comes from the determination of people acting together to, say, clean up the environment, or make the world more just. The international gay rights movement, for example, draws strength from people who believe that lesbians and gay men should enjoy the same rights and opportunities as the heterosexual majority. Opposition to the gay rights movement, moreover, reveals the power of ideas to inhibit as well as to advance social change.

THE NATURAL ENVIRONMENT AND CHANGE

Human societies are closely connected to their natural environment. For this reason, change in one tends to produce change in the other.

By and large, our culture casts nature as a force to be tamed and reshaped to human purposes. From the outset, European settlers systematically cut down forests to create fields for farming and to make materials for building; they established towns, extended roads in every direction, and dammed rivers as a source of water and energy. Such human construction not only reflects our cultural determination to master the natural environment; it also points up the centrality of the idea of "growth" in our way of life.

But the consequences of this thinking have placed increasing stress on the natural environment. Our society contends with problems of solid waste and air and water pollution, all the while consuming a disproportionate share of global resources. A growing awareness that such patterns are not sustainable in the long term is forcing us to confront the need to change our way of life in some basic respects.

DEMOGRAPHIC CHANGE

Population growth not only places escalating demands on the natural environment, but it alters cultural patterns. In the Netherlands, a high-density nation, homes are small and narrow compared to those in Canada, with extremely steep staircases to make efficient use of space. In Tokyo, bus drivers routinely negotiate city streets that many Canadian drivers would consider dangerously narrow for even a car. Although Canada enjoys a bounty of physical space, urbanization and industrialization have changed our way of life and will continue to do so. Over three-quarters of Canadians live in cities, which cover only a small percentage of the land surface.

Profound change is also taking place as our population, collectively speaking, grows older. As Chapter 15 ("Aging and the Elderly") explained, in 2001, more than 13 percent of Canadians were over sixty-five, more than double the proportion in 1901. Statistics Canada estimates that by the year 2031, seniors will account for almost *one-quarter* of the population. Medical research and health care services will increasingly focus on the elderly, and life will change in countless additional ways as homes and household products are redesigned to meet the needs of older consumers.

Migration within and among societies is another demographic factor that promotes change. Since the early 1800s, tens of millions of immigrants have come to Canada, initially to participate in the fur trade or to establish farming homesteads, but more recently to seek a better life in the growing urban areas. Immigrants to Canada's urban centres were joined by a steady flow of migrants from rural Canada, where high fertility and changes in the structure of agriculture resulted in surplus population. As a result of immigration and rural–urban migration, Canada's urban population grew from 18 to 80 percent of the total population between 1871 and 2001. In a mere 130 years, Canada was transformed from a nation of settlers to an urban-industrial society with one of the world's largest economies.

MODERNITY

A central concept in the study of social change is **modernity**, *social patterns linked to industrialization*. In everyday usage, modernity (its Latin root means "lately") designates the present in relation to the past. Sociologists include within this catch-all concept the many social patterns set in motion by the Industrial Revolution, beginning in Western Europe in the mid–eighteenth century. **Modernization**, then, is *the process of social change initiated by industrialization*. The timeline inside the front cover of this text highlights important events that mark the emergence of modernity.

KEY DIMENSIONS OF MODERNIZATION

Peter Berger (1977) notes four major characteristics of modernization:

1. **The decline of small, traditional communities.** Modernity involves "the progressive weakening, if not destruction, of the concrete and relatively cohesive communities in which human beings have found solidarity and meaning throughout most of history" (Berger 1977:72). For thousands of years, in hunting-and-gathering camps and in the agrarian villages of Europe and North America, people lived in small-scale settlements. Traditional worlds—based on sentiments and beliefs passed from generation to generation—afford each person a well-defined place. These primary groups conferred a limited range of experience with a strong sense of identity, belonging, and purpose.

    Since Canada has a land mass of close to 10 million square kilometres (the second largest in the world) and a population density of only 2.8 persons per square kilometre, and since about

In response to the accelerating pace of change in the nineteenth century, Paul Gauguin left his native France for the South Seas, where he was captivated by a simpler and seemingly timeless way of life. He romanticized this environment in his painting Les trois huttes Tahiti.

Paul Gauguin (1848–1903), *Les trois huttes Tahiti.* Photo © Christie's Images.

80 percent of its population lives within 160 kilometres of the U.S. border, there is a great deal of space through which to scatter isolated communities. Small, isolated communities—many with far fewer than 100 members—still exist in Canada, but they are now home to only a small percentage of our population. Many of these people are Indian, Métis, or Inuit. Even so, cars, telephones, television, and the Internet give most rural families the pulse of the larger society and connect them to the entire world.

2. **The expansion of personal choice.** To people in traditional, pre-industrial societies, life is shaped by forces beyond human control—gods, spirits, or, simply, fate. But as the power of tradition erodes, people come to see their lives as a series of options, a process Berger calls *individualization*. Many people in Canada, for example, adopt one "lifestyle" or another, showing an openness to change.

3. **Increasing social diversity.** In pre-industrial societies, strong family ties and powerful religious beliefs enforce conformity while discouraging diversity and change. Modernization promotes a more rational, scientific world view, in which tradition loses its force and morality becomes a matter of individual attitude. The growth of cities, the expansion of impersonal bureaucracy, and social interaction among people from various backgrounds combine to foster a diversity of beliefs and behaviour. Increasing secularization, or decline in the importance of religion, goes hand in hand with modernization.

4. **Future orientation and growing awareness of time.** While pre-modern people focus on the past, people in modern societies think more about the future. Modern people are not only forward-looking but optimistic that discoveries and new inventions will enhance their lives.

Modern people also organize daily routines according to precise units of time. With the introduction of clocks in the late Middle Ages, Europeans began to think not in terms of sunlight and seasons but in terms of hours and minutes. Preoccupied with personal gain, modern people calculate time to the moment and generally believe that "Time is money!" Berger points out that one key indicator of a society's degree of modernization is the proportion of people wearing wristwatches.

Recall that modernization touched off the development of sociology itself. As Chapter 1 ("The Sociological Perspective") explained, the discipline originated in the wake of the Industrial Revolution in Western Europe, where social change was proceeding most rapidly. Early European and U.S. sociologists tried to analyze and explain modernization and its consequences—good and bad—for human beings.

FERDINAND TÖNNIES: THE LOSS OF COMMUNITY

The German sociologist Ferdinand Tönnies produced a lasting account of modernization in his theory of *Gemeinschaft* and *Gesellschaft* (see Chapter 22, "Population, Urbanization, and the Environment"). Like Peter Berger, whose work he influenced, Tönnies (1963; orig. 1887) viewed modernization as the progressive loss of *Gemeinschaft*, or human community. As Tönnies saw it, the Industrial Revolution weakened the strong social fabric of family and tradition by introducing a businesslike emphasis on facts, efficiency,

TABLE 24–1 Canadian Mobility by Age Group (Percentage Changing Residence over a Five-Year Period)	
Age Group	1996–2001
5–14	45.1
15–29	56.0
30–44	54.2
45–64	29.2
65 and over	19.4
Total	43.3

Source: Calculations by Gerber from Statistics Canada, 2001 Census Tables, www.statcan.ca.

and money. European and North American societies gradually became rootless and impersonal as people came to associate mostly on the basis of self-interest—the condition Tönnies dubbed *Gesellschaft*.

Early in the twentieth century, at least some North American areas approximated Tönnies's concept of *Gemeinschaft*. Families that had lived for generations in small towns and villages were tightly integrated into a hard-working, slow-moving way of life. Telephones (invented in 1876) were rare; the first coast-to-coast call was placed only in 1915 (see the timeline inside the front cover of this book). Before television (introduced in 1939, widespread after 1950), families entertained themselves, often gathering with friends in the evening—much like Brazil's Kaiapo—to share stories, sorrows, or song. Before the onset of rapid transportation (although Henry Ford's assembly line began in 1908, cars became commonplace only after World War II), many people viewed their home town as their entire world.

Inevitable tensions and conflicts—sometimes based on race, ethnicity, and religion—characterized past communities. According to Tönnies, however, because **For a biography of Ferdinand Tönnies, see the Gallery of Sociologists at www.TheSociologyPage.com** of the traditional ties of *Gemeinschaft*, people were "essentially united in spite of all separating factors" (1963:65; orig. 1887).

Modernity turns societies inside out so that, as Tönnies put it, people are "essentially separated in spite of uniting factors" (1963:65). This is the world of *Gesellschaft* where, especially in large cities, most people live among strangers and ignore one another as they pass on the street.

Our high level of geographic mobility is one important cause of a sense of rootlessness. Over one year, about one in six individuals changes his or her place of residence. Close to half of all Canadians move over a five-year interval; 7 percent of the population moves from outside the province or country, while 23 percent moves within the same municipality. Table 24–1 shows that people between the ages of 15 and 29 are the most

mobile, with 56.0 percent having moved within the last five years. The relatively high level of mobility in the youngest age category in the table (5- to 14-year-olds) is probably due to the search for more suitable accommodation by the 30- to 44-year-old parents of these children. In the General Social Survey (1985), the most frequently stated reasons for moving are (1) to purchase or build a home; (2) to live in a larger home; (3) to live in a better neighbourhood; (4) to live near work; and (5) to establish an independent household. Each of these top-ranked reasons is consistent with movement among 30- to 44-year-olds, who are leaving the homes of their parents, getting married, having children, and moving to larger homes to accommodate the children.

Critical evaluation. Tönnies's theory of *Gemeinschaft* and *Gesellschaft* is the most widely cited model of modernization. The theory's strength lies in its synthesis of various dimensions of change—growing population, the rise of cities, and increasing impersonality in social interaction.

One problem with Tönnies's theory, however, is that modern life, while often impersonal, is not completely devoid of *Gemeinschaft*. Even in a world of strangers, modern friendships can be strong and lasting. Traditions are especially pronounced in many ethnic neighbourhoods, where residents maintain close community ties.

Another criticism is that Tönnies's approach says little about which factors (industrialization, urbanization, weakening of families) are cause and which are effect. Critics also assert that Tönnies favoured—perhaps even romanticized—traditional societies while overlooking bonds of family, neighbourhood, and friendship in modern societies.

EMILE DURKHEIM: THE DIVISION OF LABOUR

The French sociologist Emile Durkheim, whose work is examined in Chapter 4 ("Society"), shared Tönnies's interest in the profound social changes wrought by the Industrial Revolution. For Durkheim, modernization is marked by an increasing *division of labour*, or specialized economic activity (1964b; orig. 1893). Whereas every member of a traditional society engages in more or less the same daily round of activities, modern societies rely on people assuming highly distinctive roles.

Durkheim contended that pre-industrial societies are held together by *mechanical solidarity*, or shared moral sentiments. Thus, members of pre-industrial societies view everyone as being basically alike, doing the same kind of work, and belonging together. Durkheim's concept of mechanical solidarity is virtually the same as Tönnies's *Gemeinschaft*.

With modernization, the division of labour becomes more and more pronounced. To Durkheim,

George Tooker's 1950 painting The Subway *depicts a common problem of modern life: weakening social ties and eroding traditions create a generic humanity in which everyone is alike yet each person is an anxious stranger in the midst of others.*

George Tooker, *The Subway*, 1950, egg tempera on gesso panel, $18^{1}/_{8} \times 36^{1}/_{8}$", Whitney Museum of American Art, New York. Purchased with funds from the Julianna Force Purchase Award, 50.23. Photograph © Whitney Museum of American Art.

this change means *less* mechanical solidarity, but *more* of another kind of tie: *organic solidarity*, or the mutual dependency among people who engage in specialized work. Put simply, modern societies are integrated not by likeness but by difference: all of us must depend on others to meet most of our needs. Organic solidarity corresponds to Tönnies's concept of *Gesellschaft*.

 For more on Durkheim, Weber, and Marx, visit the Gallery of Sociologists at www.TheSociologyPage.com

Despite obvious similarities in their thinking, Durkheim and Tönnies interpreted modernity somewhat differently. To Tönnies, the change from *Gemeinschaft* to *Gesellschaft* amounts to the loss of social solidarity because modern people lose the "natural" and "organic" bonds of the rural village, leaving only the "artificial" and "mechanical" ties of the big city. Durkheim had a different take on modernity, even reversing Tönnies's language to bring home the point. Durkheim labelled modern society "organic," arguing that modern society is no less natural than any other, and he described traditional societies as "mechanical" because they are so regimented. Thus, Durkheim viewed modernization not as the loss of community but as a change from community based on bonds of likeness (kinship and neighbourhood) to community based on economic interdependence (the division of labour). Durkheim's perspective on modernity is both more complex and more positive than that of Tönnies.

Critical evaluation. Durkheim's work stands alongside that of Tönnies, which it closely resembles, as a highly influential analysis of modernity. Of the two, Durkheim is the more optimistic; still, he feared that modern societies might become so diverse that they would collapse into a state of *anomie*, a condition in which norms and values are so weak and inconsistent that society provides little moral guidance to individuals. Without strong moral ties to society, modern people tend to be egocentric and find little purpose in life.

Evidence supports Durkheim's contention that anomie plagues modern societies. Suicide rates, which Durkheim considered a prime index of anomie, have risen over the past century in both Canada and the United States; in Canada, the rates have doubled. Suicide rates are especially high in Aboriginal communities, which are still experiencing rapid social change.

Even though modernization is associated with numerous indicators of stress or distress, shared norms and values are still strong enough to give the majority of people a sense of meaning and purpose. Despite the hazards of anomie and atomization, most people seem to value the privacy and personal autonomy that modern society affords.

MAX WEBER: RATIONALIZATION

For Max Weber, whose work is also detailed in Chapter 4 ("Society"), modernity means replacing a traditional world view with a rational way of thinking. In pre-industrial societies, tradition acts as a constant brake on change. Here, Weber explains, "truth" is roughly synonymous with "what has always been" (1978:36; orig. 1921). In modern societies, in contrast, people see truth as the result of rational calculation. Because efficiency is valued more than reverence for the past, individuals adopt whichever social patterns allow them to achieve their goals.

Echoing the claim of Tönnies and Durkheim that industrialization weakens tradition, Weber declared modern society to be "disenchanted." The unquestioned truths of an earlier time have been challenged by rational, scientific thinking: in short, modern society turns away from the gods. Throughout his life, Weber explored various modern "types"—the capitalist, the scientist, the bureaucrat—all of whom share the rational world view that Weber believed was coming to dominate humanity.

Max Weber maintained that the distinctive character of modern society was its rational world view. Virtually all of Weber's work on modernity centred on types of people he considered typical of their age: the scientist, the capitalist, and the bureaucrat. Each is rational to the core: the scientist is committed to the orderly discovery of truth, the capitalist to the orderly pursuit of profit, and the bureaucrat to orderly conformity to a system of rules.

Critical evaluation. Compared with Tönnies, and especially Durkheim, Weber was critical of modern society. He recognized that science could produce technological and organizational wonders, yet worried that it was carrying us away from more basic questions about the meaning and purpose of human existence. Weber feared that rationalization, especially in bureaucracies, would erode the human spirit with endless rules and regulations.

However, some of Weber's critics think that the alienation he attributed to bureaucracy is actually a product of social inequality. That contention leads us to the ideas of Karl Marx.

KARL MARX: CAPITALISM

For Karl Marx, modern society was synonymous with capitalism: he saw the Industrial Revolution primarily as a *capitalist revolution.* Marx traced the emergence of the bourgeoisie in medieval Europe to expanding commerce. The bourgeoisie gradually displaced the feudal aristocracy as the Industrial Revolution placed a powerful new system of production under its control.

Marx agreed that modernity weakened small-scale communities (as described by Tönnies), sharpened the division of labour (as noted by Durkheim), and fostered a rational world view (as asserted by Weber). But he considered these factors simply as conditions necessary for capitalism to flourish. Capitalism, according to Marx, draws people from farms and small towns into an ever-expanding market system centred in cities; specialization is needed for efficient factories;

and rationality is exemplified by the capitalists' relentless quest for profits.

Earlier chapters have painted Marx as a spirited critic of capitalist society, but his vision of modernity also incorporates a considerable measure of optimism. Unlike Weber, who viewed modern society as an "iron cage" of bureaucracy, Marx believed that social conflict within capitalist societies would sow the seeds of revolutionary social change, leading to an egalitarian socialism. Such a society, as he envisioned it, would harness the wonders of industrial technology to enrich people's lives and also rid the world of social classes, the prime source of social conflict and dehumanization. While Marx's evaluation of modern capitalist society was highly negative, then, he imagined a future of human freedom, creativity, and community.

Critical evaluation. Marx's theory of modernization is a complex theory of capitalism. But he underestimated the dominance of bureaucracy in modern societies. In socialist societies, in particular, the stifling effects of bureaucracy turned out to be as bad as—or even worse than—the dehumanizing aspects of capitalism. The recent upheavals in Eastern Europe and the former Soviet Union reveal the depth of popular opposition to oppressive state bureaucracies.

THEORETICAL ANALYSIS OF MODERNITY

The rise of modernity is a complex process involving many dimensions of change, described in previous

TABLE 24–2 Traditional and Modern Societies: The Big Picture

Elements of Society	Traditional Societies	Modern Societies
Cultural Patterns		
Values	Homogeneous; sacred character; few subcultures and countercultures	Heterogeneous; secular character; many subcultures and countercultures
Norms	High moral significance; little tolerance of diversity	Variable moral significance; high tolerance of diversity
Time orientation	Present linked to past	Present linked to future
Technology	Pre-industrial; human and animal energy	Industrial; advanced energy sources
Social Structure		
Status and role	Few statuses, most ascribed; few specialized roles	Many statuses, some ascribed and some achieved; many specialized roles
Relationships	Typically primary; little anonymity and privacy	Typically secondary; considerable anonymity and privacy
Communication	Face-to-face	Face-to-face supplemented by mass media
Social control	Informal gossip	Formal police and legal system
Social stratification	Rigid patterns of social inequality; little mobility	Fluid patterns of social inequality; considerable mobility
Gender patterns	Pronounced patriarchy; women's lives centred in the home	Declining patriarchy; increasing number of women in the paid labour force
Economy	Based on agriculture; some manufacturing in the home; little white-collar work	Based on industrial mass production; factories become centres of production; increasing white-collar work
State	Small-scale government; little state intervention in society	Large-scale government; considerable state intervention in society
Family	Extended family as the primary means of socialization and economic production	Nuclear family retains some socialization functions but is more a unit of consumption than of production
Religion	Religion guides world view; little religious pluralism	Religion weakens with the rise of science; extensive religious pluralism
Education	Formal schooling limited to elites	Basic schooling becomes universal, with growing proportion receiving advanced education
Health	High birth and death rates; brief life expectancy because of low standard of living and simple medical technology	Low birth and death rates; longer life expectancy because of higher standard of living and sophisticated medical technology
Settlement patterns	Small scale; population typically small and widely dispersed in rural villages and small towns	Large scale; population typically large and concentrated in cities
Social Change	Slow; change evident over many generations	Rapid; change evident within a single generation

chapters and summarized in Table 24–2. How can we make sense of so many changes going on all at once? Sociologists have devised two overarching explanations of modern society, one derived from the structural-functional paradigm and one based on the social-conflict approach.

STRUCTURAL-FUNCTIONAL THEORY: MODERNITY AS MASS SOCIETY

One broad approach—drawing on the ideas of Ferdinand Tönnies, Emile Durkheim, and Max Weber—depicts modernization as the emergence of *mass society* (Dahrendorf, 1959; Kornhauser, 1959; Nisbet, 1966, 1969; Stein, 1972; Berger et al., 1974; Pearson, 1993). A **mass society** is *a society in which industry and expanding bureaucracy have eroded traditional social ties.* A mass society is marked by weak kinship

and impersonal neighbourhoods, so that individuals are socially isolated. In their isolation, members of mass societies typically experience feelings of moral uncertainty and personal powerlessness.

The Mass Scale of Modern Life

Mass-society theory argues that the scale of modern life has greatly increased. Before the Industrial Revolution, Europe and North America constituted an intricate mosaic of rural villages and small towns. In these small communities, which inspired Tönnies's concept of *Gemeinschaft*, people lived out their lives surrounded by kin and guided by a shared heritage. Gossip was an informal yet highly effective way to ensure conformity to community standards. These small communities, with their strong moral values, tolerated little social diversity—the state of mechanical solidarity described by Durkheim.

Many people marvelled at new industrial technology that was changing the world a century ago. But some critics pointed out that the social consequences of the Industrial Revolution were not all positive. The painting Trabajadores *(Workers) by Mirta Cerra portrays the exhausting and mind-numbing routines of manual workers.*

Mirta Cerra (1904–86), *Trabajadores,* oil on canvas laid down on panel, 107.3 × 157.5 cm. © Christie's Images.

For example, in England before 1690, both law and local custom demanded that all people regularly participate in the Christian ritual of Holy Communion (Laslett, 1984). On this continent, only Rhode Island among the New England colonies tolerated any religious dissent. Because social differences were repressed, subcultures and countercultures rarely flourished and change proceeded slowly.

Increasing population, the growth of cities, and specialized economic activity driven by the Industrial Revolution gradually altered this pattern. People came to know one another by their jobs (for example, as the "doctor" or the "bank clerk") rather than by their kinship group or home town. People looked on most others simply as strangers. The face-to-face communication of the village was replaced by the mass media—newspapers, radio, television, and, more recently, computer networks. Large organizations assumed more and more responsibility for daily tasks that had once been fulfilled by family, friends, and neighbours; public education drew more and more people to schools; police, lawyers, and formal courts supervised a formal criminal justice system. Even charity became the work of faceless bureaucrats working for various social welfare agencies.

Geographical mobility, mass communication, and exposure to diverse ways of life erode traditional values. People become more tolerant of social diversity, defending individual rights and freedom of choice. Subcultures and countercultures multiply. Treating people differently based on their race, sex, or religion comes to be defined as backward and unjust. In the process, minorities at the margins of society gain greater power and broader participation in public life. Yet, mass-society theorists fear that transforming people of various backgrounds into a generic mass may end up dehumanizing everyone.

The Ever-Expanding State

In the small-scale, pre-industrial societies of Europe, government amounted to little more than a local noble. A royal family formally reigned over an entire nation but, without efficient transportation or communication, the power of monarchs fell far short of that wielded by today's political leaders.

Technological innovation allowed government to expand, and the centralized state grew in size and importance. At the time of Confederation, government, either federal or provincial, had limited functions. Since then, government in Canada has entered more and more areas of social life—establishing publicly owned enterprises in the areas of transportation, communication, and natural resources; regulating wages and working conditions; establishing standards for products of all kinds; educating the population; delivering medical care; protecting the environment; and providing financial assistance to the ill, the aged, and the unemployed. To pay for such programs, taxes have soared, so that today's average worker labours for six months a year just to pay for the broad array of services the government provides.

In a mass society, power resides in large bureaucracies, leaving people in local communities little control over their lives. For example, public officials mandate a standardized educational program for local schools, local products must earn government certification, and every citizen must maintain extensive tax records. While such regulations may protect people and enhance social equality, they force us to deal more and more with nameless officials in distant and often unresponsive bureaucracies, and they undermine the autonomy of families and neighbourhoods.

Critical evaluation. The theory of mass society concedes that the transformation of small-scale communities has positive aspects, but only at the cost of losing our cultural heritage. Modern societies increase individual rights, tolerate greater social differences, and raise standards of living. But they are prone to what Weber feared most—excessive bureaucracy—as well as Tönnies's self-centredness and Durkheim's anomie. Their size, complexity, and tolerance of diversity all but doom traditional values and family patterns, leaving individuals isolated, anxious, and materialistic. Voter apathy is growing in Canada: Should we be surprised that individuals in vast, impersonal societies think no one person can make a difference?

Critics of mass-society theory contend that it romanticizes the past. They remind us that many people in small towns were actually eager to set out for the excitement and higher standard of living found in cities. Moreover, mass-society theory ignores problems of social inequality. Critics say this theory attracts social and economic conservatives who defend conventional morality and are indifferent to the historical plight of women and other minorities.

SOCIAL-CONFLICT THEORY: MODERNITY AS CLASS SOCIETY

The second interpretation of modernity derives largely from the ideas of Karl Marx. From a social-conflict perspective, modernity takes the form of a **class society**, *a capitalist society with pronounced social stratification.* That is, while acknowledging that modern societies have expanded to a mass scale, this approach views the heart of modernization as an expanding capitalist economy, rife with inequality (Miliband, 1969; Habermas, 1970; Clement, 1975; Polenberg, 1980; Blumberg, 1981; Harrington, 1984; Brym, 1985).

Capitalism

Class-society theory follows Marx in claiming that the increasing scale of social life in modern society results from the insatiable appetite of capitalism. Because a capitalist economy pursues ever-increasing profits, both production and consumption steadily rise.

According to Marx and Engels, capitalism rests on "naked self-interest" (1972:337; orig. 1848). This self-centredness erodes the social ties that once cemented small-scale communities. Capitalism also treats people as commodities: as a source of labour and a market for capitalist production.

Capitalism supports science, not just as the key to greater productivity but also as an ideology that justi-fies the status quo. That is, modern societies encourage people to view human well-being as a *technical* puzzle to be solved by engineers and other experts rather than through the pursuit of *social* justice (Habermas, 1970). A capitalist culture, for example, seeks to improve health through scientific medicine rather than by eliminating poverty, which threatens many people's health in the first place.

Business also raises the banner of scientific logic, trying to increase profits through greater efficiency. As Chapter 16 ("The Economy and Work") explains, capitalist corporations have reached enormous size and control almost unimaginable wealth as a result of "going global" as multinationals. From the class-society point of view, then, the expanding scale of life is less a function of *Gesellschaft* than it is the inevitable and destructive consequence of capitalism.

Persistent Inequality

Modernity has gradually eroded the rigid categories that set nobles apart from commoners in pre-industrial societies. But class-society theory maintains that elites persist—albeit now as capitalist millionaires rather than as nobles born to wealth and power. Canada has more billionaire families per capita than the United States: in the early 1980s Canada had six, while the United States, with an economy twelve times larger, had only double that number (Francis, 1986). Furthermore, the distribution of family income is skewed in Canada: from 1951 to 2001, with minor fluctuations, families in the top 20 percent earned about 40 percent of all income while the bottom fifth earned just over 6 percent of all income. When measured in terms of individual income, the pattern is accentuated, with the top quintile earning 46.5 percent of income and the lowest quintile earning 3.4 percent (Statistics Canada, Cat. No. 13-207-XPB).

What of the state? Mass-society theorists contend that the state works to increase equality and combat social problems. Marx was skeptical that the state could accomplish more than minor reforms because, as he saw it, the real power lies in the hands of capitalists who control the economy. Other class-society theorists add that, to the extent that working people and minorities enjoy greater political rights and a higher standard of living today, these changes are the fruits of political struggle, not expressions of government goodwill. Thus, they conclude, despite our pretensions of democracy, power still rests primarily in the hands of those with wealth.

Critical evaluation. Table 24–3 (on page 609) summarizes the interpretations of modernity offered by mass-society theory and class-society theory. While the former focuses on the increasing scale of life and the growth of government, the latter stresses the expansion of capitalism and the persistence of inequality.

Mass-society theory attributes feelings of anxiety, isolation, and lack of meaning in the modern world to rapid social change that washes away tradition. Edvard Munch captured this vision of modern emptiness in his painting The Scream *(left). Class-society theory, in contrast, ties such feelings to social inequality, by which some categories of people are made into second-class citizens (or not made citizens at all). Paul Marcus portrays modern injustice in the painting* Crossing the Rio Grande *(right).*

Class-society theory also dismisses Durkheim's argument that people in modern societies suffer from anomie, claiming instead that they suffer from alienation and powerlessness. Not surprisingly, then, the class-society interpretation of modernity enjoys widespread support among the political left, who call for greater equality and extensive regulation (or abolition) of the capitalist marketplace.

A basic criticism of class-society theory is that it overlooks the many ways in which modern societies have grown more egalitarian. For example, discrimination based on race, ethnicity, gender, or sexual orientation is now illegal and widely regarded as a social problem. Further, most people in Canada favour unequal rewards, at least insofar as they reflect differences in personal talent and effort.

Moreover, few observers think a centralized economy would cure the ills of modernity in light of socialism's failure to generate a high overall standard of living. Many other social problems in Canada—from unemployment, homelessness, and industrial pollution to unresponsive government—have also been commonplace in socialist nations such as the former Soviet Union.

MODERNITY AND THE INDIVIDUAL

Mass- and class-society theories focus on broad patterns of social change since the Industrial Revolution: each "macro-level" approach offers "micro-level" insights into how modernity shapes individual lives.

Mass Society: Problems of Identity

Modernity liberated individuals from the small, tightly knit communities of the past. Most people in modern societies, therefore, have privacy and freedom to express their individuality. Mass-society theory suggests, however, that extensive social diversity, isolation, and rapid social change make it difficult for many people to establish any coherent identity at all (Wheelis, 1958; Riesman, 1970; Berger et al., 1974). Canadians have had considerable difficulty articulating a national identity—and, indirectly, personal identities—to the point where Lipset (1991:42) states that national identity "is the quintessential Canadian issue." Proximity to the United States, regional tensions, ethnic and cultural diversity, bilingualism, and rapid social change make clear self-definition more difficult for Canadians (Taras et al., 1993; Hiller, 1996).

Chapter 5 ("Socialization") explained that people's personalities are largely a product of their social experiences. The small, homogeneous, and slowly changing societies of the past provided a firm (if narrow) foundation for building a meaningful identity. For example, the Hutterite communities that still flourish in Canada's Prairie provinces (especially in Alberta) teach young men and women "correct" ways to think and behave—and most learn to embrace this life as "natural" and right. Everything is shared—property, work, meals—in these tiny communal societies that have perpetuated the Hutterite way of life, largely unchanged, for more than 400 years. Under these circumstances, which contrast sharply with those of modern mass society, it is relatively easy to establish a coherent and secure sense of personal identity.

Mass societies, with their characteristic diversity and rapid change, provide only shifting sands on which to build a personal identity. Left to make their own life decisions, many people—especially those with greater affluence—confront a bewildering range of options. Autonomy has little value without standards for making choices; in a tolerant mass society, people may find one path no more compelling than the next. Not surprisingly, many people shuttle from one identity to another, changing their lifestyle, relationships, and even religion in search of an elusive "true self." Beset by the widespread "relativism" of modern societies, people without a moral compass lack the security and certainty once provided by tradition.

For David Riesman (1970; orig. 1950), modernization brings changes in **social character**, *personality patterns common to members of a particular society*. Preindustrial societies promote what Riesman terms **tradition-directedness**, *rigid conformity to time-honoured ways of living*. Members of traditional societies model their lives on what has gone before so that what is "good" is equivalent to "what has always been."

Tradition-directedness corresponds to Tönnies's *Gemeinschaft* and Durkheim's mechanical solidarity. Culturally conservative, tradition-directed people think and act alike. Unlike the conformity found in modern societies, this uniformity is not an attempt to mimic one another. Instead, people are alike because everyone draws on the same solid cultural foundation. Hutterite women and men exemplify tradition-directedness; in Hutterite culture, tradition ties everyone to ancestors and descendants in an unbroken chain of communal living as ordained by God.

Members of diverse and rapidly changing societies define a tradition-directed personality as deviant because it seems so rigid. Modern people, by and large, prize personal flexibility and sensitivity to others. Riesman calls this type of social character **other-directedness**, *a receptiveness to the latest trends and fashions, often expressed in the practice of imitating others*. Because their socialization occurs within societies that are continuously in flux, other-directed people develop fluid identities marked by superficiality, inconsistency, and change. They try on different roles and identities, sometimes like so many pieces of new clothing, and engage in various "performances" as they move from setting to setting (Goffman, 1959).

TABLE 24–3 Two Interpretations of Modernity: A Summary		
	Process of Modernization	**Effects of Modernization**
Mass-society theory	Industrialization; growth of bureaucracy	Increasing scale of life; rise of the state and other formal organizations
Class-society theory	Rise of capitalism	Expansion of the capitalist economy; persistence of social inequality

In a traditional society, such "shiftiness" marks a person as untrustworthy, but in a modern society, the ability to fit in virtually anywhere is a valued personal trait (Wheelis, 1958).

In societies that value the up-to-date rather than the traditional, people anxiously solicit the approval of others, looking to members of their own generation rather than to elders as significant role models. "Peer pressure" can be irresistible to people with no enduring standards to guide them. Our society urges individuals to be true to themselves. But when social surroundings change so rapidly, how can people develop the self to which they should be true? This problem is at the root of the identity crisis so widespread in industrial societies today. "Who am I?" is a question that many of us struggle to answer. In truth, this problem is not so much psychological as sociological, reflecting the inherent instability of modern mass society.

Class Society: Problems of Powerlessness

Class-society theory paints a different picture of modernity's effects on individuals. This approach maintains that persistent social inequality undermines modern society's promise of individual freedom. For some, modernity delivers great privilege, but for others, modern life means coping every day with economic uncertainty and a gnawing sense of powerlessness (Newman, 1993).

For visible minorities, and Canada's Native population in particular, the problem of relative disadvantage looms even larger. Similarly, although women enjoy increasing participation in modern societies, they continue to run up against traditional barriers of sexism. Elderly people encounter the impediment of *ageism*. In short, this approach rejects mass-society theory's claim that people suffer from too much freedom. Instead, class-society theory holds that our society still denies a majority of people full participation in social life.

On a global scale, as Chapter 12 ("Global Stratification") explained, the expanding scope of world capitalism has placed more of the earth's population in the shadow of multinational corporations. As a result, more than half of the world's income is concentrated in the richest societies, which contain only about 15 percent of its people. Is it any wonder, class-society theorists ask, that people in poor nations seek greater power to shape their own lives?

The problem of widespread powerlessness led Herbert Marcuse (1964) to challenge Max Weber's contention that modern society is rational. Marcuse labels modern society irrational because it fails to meet the basic needs of so many people. While modern capitalist societies produce unparalleled wealth, poverty remains the daily plight of more than a billion people. Moreover, Marcuse argues, technological advances further reduce people's control over their own lives. High technology confers great power on a corps of specialists—not the vast majority of people themselves—who now control events and dominate the public agenda, whether the issue is computing, energy production for communities, or health care. Countering the common view that technology *solves* the world's problems, Marcuse believed that science actually *causes* them. In sum, class-society theory asserts that people suffer because modern, scientific societies concentrate both wealth and power in the hands of a privileged few.

 For more on Herbert Marcuse, see www.marcuse.org/herbert/

MODERNITY AND PROGRESS

In modern societies, most people expect—and applaud—social change. People link modernity to the idea of *progress* (from Latin, meaning "moving forward"), a state of continual improvement. In contrast, we denigrate stability as a form of stagnation.

This chapter began by describing the Kaiapo of Brazil, for whom affluence has broadened opportunities but weakened traditional heritage. In examining the Kaiapo, we notice that social change, with all its beneficial and detrimental consequences, is too complex to simply equate with progress.

More precisely, whether we see a given change as progress depends on our values. A rising standard of living historically among people in Canada has helped to make lives longer and more comfortable, and people in the United States and Canada have considerable confidence in science to improve our lives.

Social change is both complex and controversial. Modern society's recognition of basic human rights is valued by most people. The assertion that individuals have rights simply by virtue of their humanity is a distinctly modern idea that can be found in the Canadian Charter of Rights and Freedoms, the American Declaration of Independence, and the United Nations' Declaration of Human Rights. But, as Chapter 3 ("Culture") explained, we now have something of a "culture of rights" that often overlooks the duties and obligations we have to one another.

In principle, almost everyone in our society supports the idea that individuals should have considerable autonomy in shaping their own lives. Yet, as people exercise their freedom of choice, they inevitably challenge social patterns cherished by those who maintain a more traditional way of life. For example, people may choose not to marry, to live with someone without marrying, perhaps even to form a partnership with someone of their own sex. To those who support individual choice, such changes symbolize progress; to those who value traditional family patterns, however, these developments signal societal decay.

New technology, too, provokes controversy. Rapid transportation and efficient communication have improved our lives in many respects, but complex technology has also weakened traditional attachments to home towns and even to families. Industrial technology has also unleashed an unprecedented threat to the natural environment and, in the form of nuclear weapons, imperilled the future of humanity. In short, we all know that social change comes faster all the time, but we may disagree about whether a particular change is progress or a step backwards.

MODERNITY: GLOBAL VARIATION

October 1, 1994, Kobe, Japan. Riding the computer-controlled monorail high above the streets of Kobe or the 200-mile-per-hour bullet train to Tokyo, we see in Japan the society of the future, in love with high technology. Yet the Japanese remain strikingly traditional in other respects: few corporate executives and almost no senior politicians are women, young people still accord seniors considerable respect, and public orderliness contrasts to the turmoil of North American cities.

Japan is a nation at once traditional and modern. This contradiction reminds us that while it is useful to contrast traditional and modern societies, the old and the new often co-exist in unexpected ways. In the People's Republic of China, ancient Confucian principles are mixed with contemporary socialist thinking. Similarly, in Mexico and much of Latin America, people observe centuries-old Christian rituals even as they struggle valiantly to pursue economic development.

The description of Brazil's Kaiapo that opened this chapter points up the tension that typically accompanies the introduction of modern social patterns in a traditional society. Such combinations of traditional and modern patterns are far from unusual—indeed, they are found around the world.

POSTMODERNITY

If modernity was the product of the Industrial Revolution, is the Information Revolution creating a postmodern era? A number of scholars think so, and use the term **postmodernity** to refer to *social patterns characteristic of a post-industrial society.*

Precisely what postmodernism is remains a matter of debate. The term has been used for decades in literary, philosophical, and even architectural circles. It moved into sociology on a wave of social criticism that has been building since the spread of left-leaning politics in the 1960s. Although there are many variants of postmodern thinking, all share the following five themes (Bernstein, 1992; Borgmann, 1992; Crook et al., 1992; Hall and Neitz, 1993):

1. **In important respects, modernity has failed.** The promise of modernity was a life free from want. As postmodernist critics see it, however, the twentieth century was unsuccessful in eradicating social problems such as poverty or even ensuring financial security for many people.

2. **The bright light of "progress" is fading.** Modern people typically look to the future expecting that their lives will improve in significant ways. Members (even leaders) of a postmodern society, however, have less confidence about what the future holds. Furthermore, the buoyant optimism that swept society into the modern era more than a century ago has given way to stark pessimism; most Canadian adults think that life is getting worse (Bibby, 1995:8).

3. **Science no longer holds the answers.** The defining trait of the modern era was a scientific outlook and a confident belief that technology would make life better. But postmodern critics contend that science has not solved many old problems (such as poor health) and has even created new problems (such as environmental degradation).

   More generally, postmodernist thinkers discredit the foundation of science: that objective reality and truth exist at all. Reality is simply a social construction, they say; moreover, we can "deconstruct" science to show how it has been widely used for political purposes, especially by powerful segments of society.

4. **Cultural debates are intensifying.** Modernity was to be an era of enhanced individuality and expanding tolerance. But it has fallen short here as well. Feminism asserts that patriarchy continues to limit the lives of women, while multicul-turalism seeks to empower minorities who remain at the margins of social life.

5. **Social institutions are changing.** Just as industrialization brought sweeping transformation to social institutions, the rise of a post-industrial society is remaking society once again. For example, just as the Industrial Revolution placed *material things* at the centre of productive life, now the Information Revolution emphasizes *ideas*. Similarly, the postmodern family no longer conforms to a single formula; on the contrary, individuals are choosing among many new family forms.

Critical evaluation. Analysts who claim that Canada and other high-income societies are entering a postmodern era criticize modernity for failing to meet human needs. Yet few think that modernity has failed completely; after all, we have seen marked increases in longevity and living standards over the course of the past century. Moreover, even if we accepted postmodernist criticism that science is bankrupt and traditional notions about progress are a sham, what are the alternatives?

LOOKING AHEAD: MODERNIZATION AND OUR GLOBAL FUTURE

If we imagine the entire world reduced to a village of one thousand people, about 175 residents of this "global village" live in high-income countries, while about half receive less than ideal nourishment. Most seriously, 200 people are so poor that they are at risk for their lives.

Chapter 12 ("Global Stratification") presented two competing views of why 1 billion people the world over are poor. *Modernization theory* claims that in the past the entire world was poor and that technological change, especially the Industrial Revolution, enhanced human productivity and raised living standards. From this point of view, the solution to global poverty is to promote technological development in poor nations.

For reasons suggested earlier, however, global modernization may be difficult. Recall that David Riesman portrayed pre-industrial people as *tradition-directed* and likely to resist change. So modernization theorists advocate that the world's rich societies help poor countries to grow economically. Specifically, industrial nations can export technology to poor regions, welcome students from abroad, and provide foreign aid to stimulate economic growth.

The discussion of modernization theory in Chapter 12 points to some limited success for these policies in Latin America and real success in the small Asian countries of Taiwan, South Korea, and

The United States: A Nation in Decline? Will Canada Follow?

Asked what was his greatest concern about the future of his country, the U.S. novelist Walker Percy responded:

Probably the fear of seeing America, with all its great strength and beauty and freedom . . . gradually subside into decay and be defeated . . . from within by weariness, boredom, cynicism, greed and in the end helplessness before its great problems. . . .

Is the United States, which stood as the world's leading economic and political power during the twentieth century, now a nation in decline? Clearly, by some measures, the United States is thriving. Between 1960 and 1995, for example, the nation's economic output tripled and median family income (controlled for inflation) climbed by more than one-third. During the same time span, the official poverty rate dropped by half.

Nonetheless, William J. Bennett contends, a number of other indicators of well-being paint a very different—and disturbing—picture of life in the United States. Between 1960 and 1995, violent crime shot up fourfold; the number of children born to single mothers as well as the number of children supported by welfare rose more than five-fold; the divorce rate doubled; and teen suicide tripled. Television viewing has increased by 35 percent, and College Board scores have fallen by an average of 75 points.

Government expenditures (in constant dollars) rose fivefold between 1960 and 1995, while the U.S. population increased by just 45 percent. Clearly, then, a wide range of serious social problems continues to plague the United States despite (or, perhaps, because of) government efforts to address them. As a result, Bennett concludes that the nation's decline is primarily

moral—a matter of weakening individual character:

[American] society now places less value than before on what we owe to others as a matter of moral obligation; less value on sacrifice as a moral good; less value on social conformity and respectability; and less value on correctness and restraint in matters of physical pleasure and sexuality.

The current dilemma—that even as governments are made bigger and more powerful, many social problems are getting worse—stems from the fact that government can do little to build individual character. Bennett continues:

[American] social institutions—families, churches, schools, neighbourhoods, and civic associations—have traditionally taken on the responsibility of providing our children with love, order, and discipline—of teach-

Singapore, as well as Hong Kong. But jump-starting development in the poorest countries of the world poses greater challenges. And even where dramatic change has occurred, modernization entails a trade-off. Traditional people, such as Brazil's Kaiapo, may gain wealth through economic development, but they lose their cultural identity and values as they are drawn into global "McCulture," based on Western materialism, pop music, trendy clothes, and fast food. One Brazilian anthropologist expressed hope about the future of the Kaiapo: "At least they quickly understood the consequences of watching television. . . . Now [they] can make a choice" (Simons, 2001:497).

But not everyone thinks that modernization is really an option. According to a second approach to global stratification, *dependency theory*, today's poor societies have little ability to modernize, even if they want to. From this point of view, the major barrier to economic development is not traditionalism but global domination by rich, capitalist societies. Initially, this dominance took the form of colonialism whereby European societies seized much of Latin America,

Africa, and Asia. Trading relationships soon enriched England, Spain, and other colonial powers, and their colonies became poorer and poorer. Almost all societies that were colonized are now politically independent, but economic ties persist in the form of multinational corporations operating throughout the world.

In effect, dependency theory asserts that rich nations achieved their modernization at the expense of poor ones, by plundering poor nations' natural resources and exploiting their human labour. Even today, the world's poorest countries remain locked in a disadvantageous economic relationship with rich nations, dependent on wealthy countries to buy their raw materials and in return sell them whatever manufactured products they can afford. Overall, dependency theorists conclude, continuing ties with rich societies only perpetuate current patterns of global inequality.

Whichever approach is more convincing, we can no longer isolate changes in our own society from those in the rest of the world. At the beginning of the twentieth century, most people in today's high-income countries lived in relatively small settlements with ing self-control, compassion, tolerance, civility, honesty, and respect for authority. . . . The social regression of the past thirty years is due in large part to the enfeebled state of our social institutions and their failure to carry out these critical and time-honoured tasks.

From Bennett's point of view, the primary values of any society are set not by government but by people living in communities and, especially, by families raising their children. In effect, he concludes, we must not assume that affluence is the best—or even the only—measure of a society's well-being. Moreover, we cannot afford to ignore—nor can we hand over to the government—our basic responsibility to sustain civilization.

If asked, many Canadians would raise similar concerns regarding our society. We are not confident about our economy—at least with respect to job creation and job security. Once inflation is taken into account, our average family income is lower, in real terms, than it was in 1989, and about 15 percent of our families continue to fall below the poverty line. Violent crime and homicide rates have declined through the 1990s, yet Canadians are increasingly fearful about the safety of themselves and their children. We are cynical about politicians and worried about the quality of our schools and the survival of the family as we know it. Our political will to ensure universal access to medical care is even in question. To many people, it seems as though we are simply a few steps behind the United States with respect to the growth of social problems.

Despite these changes, which include a decline in church attendance, Canadians seem to have retained certain moral and social values. Honesty and reliability are "very important" to about 90 percent of Canadians, and family life to 86 percent. Intermarriage (cultural, racial, and religious) is approved by 80 to 90 percent, suggesting that we have become quite tolerant. Furthermore, our level of social compassion has remained quite high as evidenced by our beliefs that people who are poor deserve adequate income and medical care (84 and 96 percent, respectively). If ours has become a more cynical and dangerous society, it is clear that we have not rejected many of our basic social values. Of course, professing such beliefs and values is not the same as putting them into action.

Sources: Bennett (1993), Sauvé (1994), and Bibby (1995).

limited awareness of the larger world. In the early twenty-first century, the entire world has become one human village because the lives of all people are increasingly linked.

The twentieth century witnessed unprecedented human achievement. Yet solutions to many problems of human existence—including finding meaning in life, resolving conflicts between nations, and eradicating poverty—have eluded us. To this list of pressing matters new concerns have been added, such as controlling population growth, treating AIDs in Africa, and establishing a sustainable society by living in harmony with the natural environment. The socio-political context of international relations was changed irrevocably by the events of 9/11. Like it or not, Canada was drawn even more tightly into the American sphere of influence—economic, political, and military—to the point where we cannot isolate ourselves from events in Washington, Israel, Afghanistan, Iraq or Europe, or at the United Nations.

SUMMARY

1. Every society changes continuously, although at varying speeds. Social change often generates controversy.

2. Social change results from invention, discovery, and diffusion as well as from social conflict.

3. Modernity refers to the social consequences of industrialization, which, according to Peter Berger, include the erosion of traditional communities, expanding personal choice, increasingly diverse beliefs, and a keen awareness of the future.

The Canadian Revolution through the Information Revolution: The Point of No Return

Journalist and author Jeffrey Simpson opens his book *Faultlines* (1993) with the following passage:

Canada's traditional political culture in the 1980s cracked like river ice in spring. No single current produced the crack-up; it arose from the confluence of powerful new economic, demographic and political factors and the resurgence of older currents. By the early 1990s, a country that had always been at heart a political arrangement—for it had never been a cultural union or a natural economic entity—found its governmental institutions discredited and indebted, its national parties widely reviled, its political leaders mocked, its Constitution the source of division rather than pride, its economy battered by pressures from abroad, its habitual optimism dimmed.

The relative stability of the past, based on elite accommodation, brokerage politics, and deference to authority, had been shattered. Peter C. Newman traced this radical transformation of Canada's political, social, cultural, and economic landscape in *The Canadian Revolution, 1985–1995: From Deference to Defiance* (1995). Political scientist Neil Nevitte used the World Values Survey to reveal changes in Canadian values during the volatile 1980s, in his book *The Decline of Deference* (1996). Both authors agree that Canada and Canadians have changed profoundly.

Through the 1980s and early 1990s, Canadians lost faith in many of the country's major institutions: organized religion, marriage, the Canada Pension Plan, the monarchy, political parties, the Red Cross, the military and peacekeepers, the Grey Cup, Canada Post, the railways, Ontario Hydro, banks, and corporations. Canadians are less inclined to believe in the inevitability of progress, in the ability of governments to solve our problems, or in corporations as the basis for investment or long-term careers. We are confused about our identities and worry that Lucien Bouchard might have been right when he said that "Canada is not a country."

Refusing to defer to traditional leadership and authority, Canadians have turned to themselves as individuals for solutions to their problems, seeking information and making decisions often in defiance of the elite. For example, a majority said "no" to the Charlottetown Accord and "no" to the Conservatives in the 1993 federal election (reducing them from 169 to 2 seats). The Québécois are saying "no" to the separatist leadership of Quebec and to perpetual economic and political turmoil based on the "neverendum referendum." Influential pollster Allan Gregg (1998) notes that over the past fifteen years, Canadians have gone from being perhaps *the* most deferential people in the Western world to the point where we now seek new rights and powers to take decision making away from our leaders.

Marshall McLuhan predicted this kind of radical transformation of Canadian society in the 1960s and early 1970s (Bendetti and DeHart, 1996) as the result of the development of the electronic media. Television was invading homes and classrooms during that period, and computers (room-sized monstrosities) were changing information processing. We moved into a world of instantaneous all-at-onceness:

Time, in a sense, has ceased as space has vanished . . . we now live in a

---

4. Ferdinand Tönnies described modernization as the transition from *Gemeinschaft* to *Gesellschaft*, which signifies the progressive loss of community amid growing individualism.

5. Emile Durkheim saw modernization as a function of a society's expanding division of labour. Mechanical solidarity, based on shared activities and beliefs, gradually gives way to organic solidarity, in which specialization makes people interdependent.

6. According to Max Weber, modernity replaces tradition with a rational world view. Weber feared the dehumanizing effects of rational organization.

7. Karl Marx saw modernity as the triumph of capitalism over feudalism. Viewing capitalist societies as fraught with social conflict, Marx advocated revolutionary change to achieve a more egalitarian, socialist society.

8. According to mass-society theory, modernity increases the scale of life, enlarging the role of government and other formal organizations in carrying out tasks previously performed by family members and neighbours. Cultural diversity and rapid social change make it difficult for people in modern societies to develop stable identities and to find meaning in their lives.

global village of our own making, a simultaneous happening . . . created by instant electronic information movement (p. 40)."

McLuhan foresaw the walls coming down between families, nations, and economies as people became intensely involved in the affairs of everyone else—everywhere. He predicted that electronic data would become indispensable to all decision making in business, politics, and education; education would be completely transformed; students from around the world would develop a sense of unity; people would forge personal identities in the context of the new simultaneous world; violence would escalate in the quest for identity and people (even children) would kill to find out if they are real; privacy would be a thing of the past; and one could be superhuman and nobody simultaneously.

As early as 1971, McLuhan said that the "wired planet has no boundaries and no monopolies of knowledge," that specialized jobs had lost meaning, and that we might return to a "cottage economy" again because one could run the world's largest factory from a kitchen computer. *Individuals* now have instant

access to information, data, or knowledge, at the same time that these are available to the traditional elites—decision makers \and leaders in business, government, education, and religion. Deference to these traditional authorities is difficult to maintain under these conditions. Knowledge is power, and knowledge—through the electronic media—is available to the masses.

Peter C. Newman also sees the electronic media as a central force for social change:

The invisible hand of technology had provided citizens with the ammunition for their Revolution. The advent of saturation television coverage of real-time news events, such as the raw footage of the Aboriginal standoff at Oka, Quebec, left politicians with no place to hide. The new rules expected open covenants be openly negotiated. But by the decade's end television, which had been the dominant technological force at the beginning of the decade, was being supplanted by the computer. A full-scale rout of authority was guaranteed by the advent of the power of the Internet. Unregulated access to unlimited,

cheap information meant the computer channel that was signing up thousands of Canadian recruits daily had changed their world—and ours—by dramatically empowering its users. (1995:xxi)

Information technology is so central to the transformation we have experienced that a new basis for social class appears to be evolving. Control of "the means of production" (using Marxist terms) in the post-industrial world means access to information, primarily through the use of computers. Affluent families are more likely to have computers, and children who grow up using computers have a head start as they further develop their computer skills at school. Growth in employment is taking place almost entirely in the knowledge-based sector. The result is a new privileged class made up of superbly educated, computer literate men and women (Newman, 1995; also Forcese, 1997; Goyder, 1997). The revolution is indeed profound.

9. Class-society theory states that capitalism is central to Western modernization. This approach charges that, by concentrating wealth, capitalism generates widespread feelings of powerlessness.

10. Social change is too complex and controversial simply to be equated with social progress.

11. Postmodernity refers to cultural traits of post-industrial societies. Postmodern criticism centres on the failure of modernity, and specifically science, to fulfil its promise of prosperity and well-being.

12. In a global context, modernization theory links global poverty to the power of tradition. Therefore, some modernization theorists advocate intentional intervention by rich societies to stimulate the economic development of poor nations.

13. Dependency theory explains global poverty as the product of the world economic system. The operation of multinational corporations ensures that poor societies will remain economically dependent on rich nations.

CRITICAL-THINKING QUESTIONS

1. How well do you think Tönnies, Durkheim, Weber, and Marx predicted the character of modern society? How do their visions of modernity differ?

2. What traits render Canada a "mass society"? Do you consider yourself and most of your friends "other-directed"?

3. What is the difference between *anomie* (a trait of mass society) and *alienation* (a characteristic of class society)? Among which categories of Canadians would you expect each to be pronounced?

4. What developments lead some analysts to claim that ours has become a postmodern society?

APPLICATIONS AND EXERCISES

1. Have you an elderly relative or friend? If asked, most older people will be happy to tell you about the social changes they have seen in their lifetimes.

2. Ask people in your class or your friends to make five predictions about Canadian society in the year 2050, when today's twenty-year-olds will be senior citizens. Compare notes. On what issues is there agreement?

3. Talk to friends, extended family, and acquaintances in a wide range of occupations. Ask them about the extent to which they use computers in their work. To what extent do your findings fit your expectations with respect to specific occupations?

4. Finally, on a personal note, we hope this book has helped you and will be a useful resource for courses later on. Please feel free to send an e-mail message (macionis@kenyon.edu and lgerber@uoguelph.ca) with your thoughts and suggestions. And, yes, we *will* write back!

 SITES TO SEE

www.macionis.com
or
www.TheSociologyPage.com

You can find more than fifty weblinks to sociological journals and other sources of data and information by visiting the Links Library at this website.

http://community.web.net/

Web Networks, the Canadian affiliate of the Association for Progressive Communications, hosts a community of several hundred Canadian activists, artists, and nonprofits devoted to social change, including WomensWeb, EcoWeb, UnionNet, the Faith and Justice Network, and more.

www.cprn.com/

Canadian Policy Research Networks is a think-tank that explores ideas for Canada's future through research and debate on issues of social and economic interest.

www.utoronto.ca/utopia/

The Society for Utopian Studies is an international, interdisciplinary association devoted to the study of utopianism in all its forms, with a particular emphasis on literary and experimental utopias. The society publishes the journal *Utopian Studies* and a newsletter.

www.cwis.org/fwdp/fwdp.html

Organized by the Center for World Indigenous Studies, the Fourth World Documentation Archive's mission is to document and make available important documents relating to the social, political, strategic, economic, and human rights situations being faced by developing countries and to create a historical archive of the political struggles waged by indigenous peoples to assert their rights as sovereign nations.

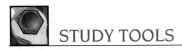

STUDY TOOLS

For more study tools to help you with your next exam, be sure to check out the Companion Website at **www.pearsoned. ca/macionis**, as well as Chapter 24 in your Study Guide.

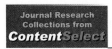

INVESTIGATE WITH CONTENTSELECT

Follow the instructions found on page 25 of this textbook to access ContentSelect™ at the Research Navigator™ website. Once at the site, enter your LOGINID and Password. Then, enter keywords such as "social change," "mass society," and "postmodernity" and the search engine will supply relevant and recent scholarly and popular press publications.

GLOSSARY

abortion the deliberate termination of pregnancy

absolute poverty a deprivation of resources that is life-threatening

achieved status a social position that someone assumes voluntarily and that reflects personal ability and effort

activity theory the proposition that a high level of activity enhances personal satisfaction in old age

ageism prejudice and discrimination against the elderly

age-sex pyramid a graphic representation of the age and sex of a population

age stratification the unequal distribution of wealth, power, and privileges among people at different stages in the life course

agriculture the technology of large-scale farming using plows harnessed to animals or more powerful sources of energy

alienation the experience of isolation resulting from powerlessness

animism the belief that elements of the natural world are conscious life forms that affect humanity

anomie a condition in which society provides little moral guidance to individuals

anticipatory socialization social learning directed towards gaining a desired position

ascribed status a social position that someone receives at birth or assumes involuntarily later in life

asexuality no sexual attraction to people of either sex

assimilation the process by which minorities gradually adopt patterns of the dominant culture

authoritarianism a political system that denies popular participation in government

authority power that people perceive as legitimate rather than coercive

beliefs specific statements that people hold to be true

bilateral descent a system tracing kinship through both men and women

bisexuality sexual attraction to people of both sexes

blue-collar occupations lower-prestige work involving mostly manual labour

bureaucracy an organizational model rationally designed to perform complex tasks efficiently

bureaucratic inertia the tendency of bureaucratic organizations to perpetuate themselves

bureaucratic ritualism a preoccupation with rules and regulations to the point of thwarting an organization's goals

capitalism an economic system in which natural resources and the means of producing goods and services are privately owned

capitalists people who own factories and other productive enterprises

caste system a system of social stratification based on ascription

cause and effect a relationship in which we know that change in one variable causes change in another

charisma extraordinary personal qualities that can turn an audience into followers

charismatic authority power legitimized through extraordinary personal abilities that inspire devotion and obedience

church a type of religious organization well integrated into the larger society

civil religion a quasi-religious loyalty binding individuals in a basically secular society

class conflict (sometimes class struggle) antagonism between entire classes over the distribution of wealth and power in society

class consciousness the recognition by workers of their unity as a social class in opposition to capitalists and, ultimately, to capitalism itself

class society a capitalist society with pronounced social stratification

class system a system of social stratification based on individual achievement

cohabitation the sharing of a household by an unmarried couple

cohort a category of people with a common characteristic, usually age

collective behaviour activity involving a large number of people, often spontaneous, and usually in violation of established norms

collectivity a large number of people whose minimal interaction occurs in the absence of well-defined, conventional norms

colonialism the process by which some nations enrich themselves through political and economic control of other nations

communism a hypothetical economic and political system in which all members of society are socially equal

concept a mental construct that represents some part of the world, inevitably in a simplified form

concrete operational stage the level of human development at which individuals first perceive causal connections in their surroundings

conglomerates giant corporations composed of many smaller corporations

control holding constant all relevant variables except one in order to clearly see its effect

corporation an organization with a legal existence including rights and liabilities apart from those of its members

correlation a relationship by which two (or more) variables change together

counterculture cultural patterns that strongly oppose those widely accepted within a society

credentialism evaluating a person on the basis of educational degrees

crime the violation of norms a society formally enacts into criminal law

criminal justice system a formal response to alleged violations of law on the part of police, courts, and prison officials

criminal recidivism subsequent offences committed by people previously convicted of crimes

critical sociology the study of society that focuses on the need for social change

crowd a temporary gathering of people who share a common focus of attention and who influence one another

crude birth rate the number of live births in a given year for every thousand people in a population

crude death rate the number of deaths in a given year for every thousand people in a population

cult a religious organization that is substantially outside a society's cultural traditions

cultural integration the close relationship among various elements of a cultural system

cultural lag cultural elements changing at different rates, causing various degrees of disruption in cultural systems

cultural materialism (or cultural ecology) a theoretical paradigm that explores the relationship of human culture to the physical environment

cultural relativism the practice of judging a culture by its own standards

cultural transmission the process by which one generation passes culture to the next

cultural universals traits found in every culture of the world

culture the values, beliefs, behaviour, and material objects that constitute a people's way of life

culture shock personal disorientation that comes from encountering an unfamiliar way of life

Davis-Moore thesis the assertion that social stratification has beneficial consequences for the operation of a society

deductive logical thought reasoning that transforms general theory into specific hypotheses suitable for scientific testing

democracy a political system in which power is exercised by the people as a whole

demographic transition theory a thesis linking demographic changes to a society's level of technological development

demography the study of human population

denomination a church, independent of the state, that accepts religious pluralism

dependency theory a model of economic and social development that explains global inequality in terms of the historical exploitation of poor societies by rich ones

dependent variable the variable that changes

descent the system by which members of a society trace kinship over generations

deterrence the attempt to discourage criminality through punishment

deviance the recognized violation of cultural norms

direct-fee system a medical care system in which patients pay directly for the services of physicians and hospitals

discrimination treating various categories of people unequally

disengagement theory the proposition that society enhances its orderly operation by disengaging people from positions of responsibility as they reach old age

division of labour specialized economic activity

dramaturgical analysis the investigation of social interaction in terms of theatrical performance

dyad a social group with two members

eating disorder an intense form of dieting or other kind of weight control in order to become very thin

ecclesia a church formally allied with the state

ecologically sustainable culture a way of life that meets the needs of the present generation without threatening the environmental legacy of future generations

ecology the study of the interaction of living organisms and the natural environment

economy the social institution that organizes the production, distribution, and consumption of goods and services

ecosystem a system composed of the interaction of all living organisms and their natural environment

education the social institution guiding a society's transmission of knowledge—including basic facts, job skills, and cultural norms and values—to its members

ego a person's conscious efforts to balance innate, pleasure-seeking drives with the demands of society

empirical evidence information we can verify with our senses

endogamy marriage between people of the same social category

environmental deficit profound and negative long-term harm to the natural environment caused by humanity's focus on short-term material affluence

environmental racism the pattern by which environmental hazards are greatest for poor people, especially minorities

ethnicity a shared cultural heritage

ethnocentrism the practice of judging another culture by the standards of one's own culture

ethnomethodology the study of the way people make sense of their everyday lives

Eurocentrism the dominance of European cultural patterns

euthanasia (mercy killing) assisting in the death of a person suffering from an incurable disease

exogamy marriage between people of different social categories

experiment a research method for investigating cause and effect under highly controlled conditions

expressive leadership leadership that focuses on collective well-being

extended family (consanguine family) a family unit including parents and children, but also other kin

fad an unconventional social pattern that people embrace briefly but enthusiastically

faith belief anchored in conviction rather than scientific evidence

false consciousness Marx's term for explanations of social problems grounded in the shortcomings of individuals rather than the flaws of society

family a social institution that unites individuals into cooperative groups that oversee the bearing and raising of children

family unit a social group of two or more people, related by blood, marriage, or adoption, who usually live together

family violence emotional, physical, or sexual abuse of one family member by another

fashion a social pattern favoured by a large number of people

feminism the advocacy of social equality for the sexes, in opposition to patriarchy and sexism

feminization of poverty the trend by which women represent an increasing proportion of the poor

fertility the incidence of childbearing in a country's population

folkways a society's customs for routine, casual interaction

formal operational stage the level of human development at which individuals think abstractly and critically

formal organizations large, secondary groups that are organized to achieve their goals efficiently

functional illiteracy reading and writing skills insufficient for everyday living

fundamentalism a conservative religious doctrine that opposes intellectualism and worldly accommodation in favour of restoring traditional, otherworldly spirituality

Gemeinschaft a type of social organization in which people are bound closely together by kinship and tradition

gender the significance members of a society attach to being female or male

gender identity traits that females and males, guided by their culture, incorporate into their personalities

gender roles (sex roles) attitudes and activities that a society links to each sex

gender stratification a society's unequal distribution of wealth, power, and privilege between the two sexes

generalized other widespread cultural norms and values that we use as references in evaluating ourselves

genocide the systematic annihilation of one category of people by another

gerontocracy a form of social organization in which the elderly have the most wealth, power, and prestige

gerontology the study of aging and the elderly

Gesellschaft a type of social organization in which people come together only on the basis of individual self-interest

global economy economic activity spanning many nations of the world with little regard for national borders

global perspective the study of the larger world and our society's place in it

gossip rumour about people's personal affairs

government a formal organization that directs the political life of a society

greenhouse effect a rise in the earth's average temperature (global warming) due to an increasing concentration of carbon dioxide in the atmosphere

groupthink the tendency of group members to conform by adopting a narrow view of some issue

Hawthorne effect a change in a subject's behaviour caused simply by the awareness of being studied

health a state of complete physical, mental, and social well-being

hermaphrodite a human being with some combination of female and male genitalia

heterosexism a view stigmatizing anyone who is not heterosexual as "queer"

heterosexuality sexual attraction to someone of the other sex

hidden curriculum subtle presentations of political or cultural ideas in the classroom

high culture cultural patterns that distinguish a society's elite

high-income countries industrialized nations in which most people enjoy material abundance

holistic medicine an approach to health care that emphasizes prevention of illness and takes into account a person's entire physical and social environment

homogamy marriage between people with the same social characteristics

homophobia the dread of close personal interaction with people thought to be gay, lesbian, or bisexual

homosexuality sexual attraction to someone of the same sex

horticulture technology based on using hand tools to cultivate plants

humanizing organizations fostering a more democratic organizational atmosphere that recognizes and encourages the contributions of everyone

hunting and gathering simple technology for hunting animals and gathering vegetation

hypothesis an unverified statement of a relationship between variables

id the human being's basic drives

ideal culture (as opposed to real culture) social patterns mandated by cultural values and norms

ideal type Weber's term for an abstract statement of the essential characteristics of any social phenomenon

ideology cultural beliefs that serve to justify social stratification

incest taboo a cultural norm forbidding sexual relations or marriage between certain relatives

income occupational wages or salaries, earnings from investments, and government transfer payments (e.g., welfare)

independent variable the variable that causes the change

inductive logical thought reasoning that transforms specific observations into general theory

industrialism technology that powers sophisticated machinery with advanced sources of energy

infant mortality rate the number of deaths among infants in the first year of life for each thousand live births in a given year

ingroup a social group commanding a member's esteem and loyalty

institutional completeness the complexity of community organizations that meet the needs of members

institutional prejudice or discrimination bias in attitudes or action inherent in the operation of society's institutions

instrumental leadership group leadership that emphasizes the completion of tasks

intergenerational social mobility upward or downward social mobility of children in relation to their parents

interpretive sociology the study of society that focuses on the meanings people attach to their social world

interview a series of questions a researcher administers personally to respondents

intragenerational social mobility a change in social position occurring during a person's lifetime

juvenile delinquency the violation of legal standards by the young

kinship a social bond, based on blood, marriage, or adoption, that joins individuals into families

labelling theory the assertion that deviance and conformity result not so much from what people do, as from how others respond to those actions

labour unions worker organizations that seek to improve wages and working conditions through various strategies, including negotiations and strikes

language a system of symbols that allows members of a society to communicate with one another

latent functions consequences that are largely unrecognized and unintended

liberation theology a fusion of Christian principles with political activism, often Marxist in character

life expectancy the average life span of a society's population

looking-glass self the image people have of themselves based on how they believe others perceive them

low-income countries nations with little industrialization in which severe poverty is the rule

macro-level orientation a focus on broad social structures that characterize society as a whole

manifest functions the recognized and intended consequences of any social pattern

marriage a legally sanctioned relationship, involving economic cooperation as well as normative sexual activity and childbearing, that people expect to be enduring

Marxist political-economy model an analysis that explains politics in terms of the operation of a society's economic system

mass behaviour collective behaviour among people dispersed over a wide geographical area

mass hysteria a form of dispersed collective behaviour by which people respond to a real or imagined event with irrational, frantic, and often self-destructive behaviour

mass media impersonal communications directed to a vast audience

mass society a society in which industry and expanding bureaucracy have eroded traditional social ties

master status a status that has exceptional importance for social identity, often shaping a person's entire life

material culture the tangible things created by members of a society

matriarchy a form of social organization in which females dominate males

matrilineal descent a system tracing kinship through women

matrilocality a residential pattern in which a married couple lives with or near the wife's family

measurement the process of determining the value of a variable in a specific case

mechanical solidarity social bonds, based on shared morality, that unite members of pre-industrial societies

medicalization of deviance the transformation of moral and legal issues into medical matters

medicine a social institution concerned with combatting disease and improving health

megalopolis a vast urban region containing a number of cities and their surrounding suburbs

meritocracy a system of social stratification based on personal merit

metropolis a large city that socially and economically dominates the surrounding area

micro-level orientation a focus on social interaction in specific situations

middle-income countries nations characterized by limited industrialization and moderate personal income

migration the movement of people into and out of a specified territory

military-industrial complex the close association among the federal government, the military, and defence industries

minority a category of people, distinguished by physical or cultural traits, that is socially disadvantaged

miscegenation biological reproduction by partners of different racial categories

mob a highly emotional crowd that pursues some violent or destructive goal

modernity social patterns linked to industrialization

modernization the process of social change initiated by industrialization

modernization theory a model of economic and social development that explains global inequality in terms of technological and cultural differences among societies

monarchy a political system in which a single family rules from generation to generation

monogamy a form of marriage joining two partners

monopoly domination of a market by a single producer

monotheism belief in a single divine power

mores a society's standards of proper moral conduct

mortality the incidence of death in a society's population

multiculturalism social policy designed to encourage ethnic or cultural heterogeneity

multinational corporation a large corporation that operates in many countries

natural environment the earth's surface and atmosphere, including living organisms, as well as the air, water, soil, and other resources necessary to sustain life

neocolonialism a new form of global power relationships that involves not direct political control but economic exploitation by multinational corporations

neolocality a residential pattern in which a married couple lives apart from the parents of both spouses

network a web of social ties that links people who identify and interact little with one another

nonmaterial culture the intangible world of ideas created by members of a society

nonverbal communication communication using body movements, gestures, and facial expressions rather than speech

norms rules and expectations by which a society guides the behaviour of its members

nuclear family (conjugal family) a family unit composed of one or two parents and their children

nuclear proliferation the acquisition of nuclear-weapons technology by more and more nations

objectivity a state of personal neutrality in conducting research

oligarchy the rule of the many by the few

oligopoly domination of a market by a few producers

operationalizing a variable specifying exactly what one intends to measure in assigning a value to a variable

organic solidarity social bonds, based on specialization, that unite members of industrial societies

organizational environment a range of factors external to an organization that affects its operation

other-directedness a receptiveness to the latest trends and fashions, often expressed in the practice of imitating others

outgroup a social group towards which one feels competition or opposition

panic a form of localized collective behaviour by which people react to a threat or other stimulus with irrational, frantic, and often self-destructive behaviour

participant observation a method in which researchers systematically observe people while joining in their routine activities

pastoralism technology based on the domestication of animals

patriarchy a form of social organization in which males dominate females

patrilineal descent a system tracing kinship through men

patrilocality a residential pattern in which a married couple lives with or near the husband's family

peer group a social group whose members have interests, social position, and age in common

personality a person's fairly consistent patterns of thinking, feeling, and acting

personal space the surrounding area in which an individual makes some claim to privacy

plea bargaining a legal negotiation in which the prosecution reduces a defendant's charge in exchange for a guilty plea

pluralism a state in which racial and ethnic minorities are distinct but have social parity

pluralist model an analysis of politics that views power as dispersed among many competing interest groups

political parties organizations operating within the political system that seek control of the government

political revolution the overthrow of one political system in order to establish another

politics the institutionalized system by which a society distributes power, sets the society's agenda, and makes decisions

polyandry a form of marriage uniting one female with two or more males

polygamy a form of marriage uniting three or more people

polygyny a form of marriage joining one male and two or more females

polytheism belief in many gods

popular culture cultural patterns that are widespread throughout society

population the people who are the focus of research

pornography sexually explicit material that causes sexual arousal

positivism a means to understand the world based on science

post-industrial economy a productive system based on service work and extensive use of information technology

post-industrialism technology that supports an information-based economy

postmodernity social patterns characteristic of post-industrial societies

power the ability to achieve desired ends despite resistance

power-elite model an analysis of politics that views power as concentrated among the rich

prejudice a rigid and irrational generalization about an entire category of people

preoperational stage the level of human development at which individuals first use language and other symbols

presentation of self an individual's effort to create specific impressions in the minds of others

primary group a small social group whose members share personal and enduring relationships

primary labour market occupations that provide extensive benefits to workers

primary sector the part of the economy that generates raw materials directly from the natural environment

primary sex characteristics the genitals, organs used for reproduction

profane that which is defined as an ordinary element of everyday life

profession a prestigious, white-collar occupation that requires extensive formal education

proletariat people who provide labour necessary to operate factories and other productive enterprises

propaganda information presented with the intention of shaping public opinion

property crimes crimes that involve theft of property belonging to others

prostitution the selling of sexual services

public opinion widespread attitudes about controversial issues

qualitative research investigation in which a researcher gathers impressionistic, not numerical, data

quantitative research investigation in which a researcher collects numerical data

queer theory a growing body of knowledge that challenges an allegedly heterosexual bias in sociology

questionnaire a series of written questions a researcher supplies to subjects requesting their responses

race a category of people who share biologically transmitted traits that members of a society deem socially significant

racism the belief that one racial category is innately superior or inferior to another

rain forests regions of dense forestation, most of which circle the globe close to the equator

rationality deliberate, matter-of-fact calculation of the most efficient means to accomplish a particular goal

rationalization of society the historical change from tradition to rationality as the dominant mode of human thought

rational-legal authority (bureaucratic authority) power legitimized by legally enacted rules and regulations

real culture (as opposed to ideal culture) actual social patterns that only approximate cultural expectations

reference group a social group that serves as a point of reference in making evaluations or decisions

rehabilitation a program for reforming the offender to preclude subsequent offences

relative deprivation a perceived disadvantage arising from some specific comparison

relative poverty the deprivation of some people in relation to those who have more

reliability the quality of consistent measurement

religion a social institution involving beliefs and practices based on a conception of the sacred

religiosity the importance of religion in a person's life

replication repetition of research by other investigators

research method a systematic plan for conducting research

reserve army of labour the part of the labour force that is last hired during expansion and first fired when the economy contracts

resocialization radically altering an inmate's personality through deliberate manipulation of the environment

retribution moral vengeance by which society inflicts suffering on an offender comparable to that caused by the offence

retrospective labelling the interpretation of someone's past consistent with present deviance

riot a social eruption that is highly emotional, violent, and undirected

ritual formal, ceremonial behaviour

role behaviour expected of someone who holds a particular status

role conflict incompatibility among roles corresponding to two or more statuses

role set a number of roles attached to a single status

role strain incompatibility among roles corresponding to a single status

routinization of charisma the transformation of charismatic authority into some combination of traditional and bureaucratic authority

rumour unsubstantiated information spread informally, often by word of mouth

sacred that which is defined as extraordinary, inspiring a sense of awe, reverence, and even fear

sample a part of a population that represents the whole

Sapir-Whorf hypothesis the hypothesis that people perceive the world through the cultural lens of language

scapegoat a person or category of people, typically with little power, whom people unfairly blame for their own troubles

schooling formal instruction under the direction of specially trained teachers

science a logical system that bases knowledge on direct, systematic observation

secondary analysis a research method in which a researcher utilizes data collected by others

secondary group a large and impersonal social group whose members pursue specific interests or activities

secondary labour market jobs that provide minimal benefits to workers

secondary sector the part of the economy that transforms raw materials into manufactured goods

secondary sex characteristics bodily differences, apart from the genitals, that distinguish biologically mature females and males

sect a type of religious organization that stands apart from the larger society

secularization the historical decline in the importance of the supernatural and the sacred

segregation the physical and social separation of categories of people

self a dimension of personality composed of an individual's self-awareness and self-image

sensorimotor stage the level of human development at which individuals experience the world only through sensory contact

sex the biological distinction between females and males

sexism the belief that one sex is innately superior to the other

sex ratio the number of males for every hundred females in a given population

sexual harassment comments, physical contact, or gestures of a sexual nature that are deliberate, repeated, and unwelcome

sexual orientation an individual's preference in terms of sexual partners: same sex, other sex, either sex, neither sex

sick role patterns of behaviour defined as appropriate for people who are ill

social change the transformation of culture and social institutions over time

social character personality patterns common to members of a particular society

social conflict struggle between segments of society over valued resources

social-conflict paradigm a framework for building theory that envisions society as an arena of inequality generating conflict and change

social construction of reality the process by which people creatively shape reality through social interaction

social control various means by which members of a society encourage conformity to norms

social dysfunctions the undesirable consequences of any social pattern for the operation of society

social epidemiology the study of how health and disease are distributed throughout a society's population

social functions consequences for the operation of society

social group two or more people who identify and interact with one another

social institutions major spheres of social life, or society's subsystems, organized to meet basic human needs

social interaction the process by which people act and react in relation to others

socialism an economic system in which natural resources and the means of producing goods and services are collectively owned

socialization the lifelong social experience by which individuals develop their human potential and learn patterns of their culture

socialized medicine a health care system in which the government owns and operates most medical facilities and employs most physicians

social mobility change in a person's position in a social hierarchy

social movement organized activity that encourages or discourages social change

social protection rendering an offender incapable of further offences either temporarily through incarceration or permanently by execution

social stratification a system by which a society ranks categories of people in a hierarchy

social structure relatively stable patterns of social behaviour

society people who interact in a defined territory and share culture

sociobiology a theoretical paradigm that explores ways in which our biology affects how humans create culture

sociocultural evolution the process of change that results from a society's gaining new information, particularly technology

socioeconomic status (SES) a composite ranking based on various dimensions of social inequality

sociology the systematic study of human society

spurious correlation an apparent, although false, association between two (or more) variables caused by some other variable

state capitalism an economic and political system in which companies are privately owned although they cooperate closely with the government

state terrorism the use of violence, generally without support of law, by a government or its agents

status a recognized social position that an individual occupies

status consistency the degree of consistency of a person's social standing across various dimensions of social inequality

status set all the statuses a person holds at a given time

stereotype prejudicial views or descriptions of some categories of people

stigma a powerfully negative social label that radically changes a person's self-concept and social identity

streaming the assigning of students to different types of educational programs

structural-functional paradigm a framework for building theory that envisions society as a complex system whose parts work together to promote solidarity and stability

structural social mobility a shift in the social position of large numbers of people owing more to changes in society itself than to individual efforts

subculture cultural patterns that set apart some segment of a society's population

suburbs urban areas beyond the political boundaries of a city

superego the operation of culture within the individual in the form of internalized values and norms

survey a research method in which subjects respond to a series of items in a questionnaire or an interview

symbol anything that carries a particular meaning recognized by people who share culture

symbolic-interaction paradigm a theoretical framework that envisions society as the product of the everyday interactions of individuals

technology knowledge that a society applies to the task of living in a physical environment

terrorism random acts of violence or the threat of such violence employed by an individual or group as a political strategy

tertiary sector the part of the economy that generates services rather than goods

theoretical paradigm a basic image of society that guides thinking and research

theory a statement of how and why specific facts are related

Thomas theorem situations we define as real become real in their consequences

total institution a setting in which people are isolated from the rest of society and manipulated by an administrative staff

totalitarianism a political system that extensively regulates people's lives

totem an object in the natural world collectively defined as sacred

tradition sentiments and beliefs passed from generation to generation

traditional authority power legitimized through respect for long-established cultural patterns

tradition-directedness rigid conformity to time-honoured ways of living

transsexuals people who feel they are one sex though biologically they are the other

triad a social group with three members

underemployment employment at a task that uses less than one's full talents or abilities

underground economy economic activity involving income or the exchange of goods and services that is not reported to the government as required by law

urban ecology the study of the link between the physical and social dimensions of cities

urbanization the concentration of humanity into cities

validity the quality of measuring precisely what one intends to measure

values culturally defined standards by which people assess desirability, goodness, and beauty, and which serve as broad guidelines for social living

variable a concept whose value changes from case to case

victimless crimes violations of law in which there are no readily apparent victims

violent crimes crimes against people that involve violence or the threat of violence

war organized, armed conflict among the peoples of various societies

wealth the total amount of money and other assets, minus outstanding debts, that a person or family controls

welfare capitalism an economic and political system that combines a mostly market-based economy with government programs to provide for people's basic needs

white-collar crime crimes committed by persons of high social position in the course of their occupations

white-collar occupations higher-prestige work involving mostly mental activity

zero population growth the level of reproduction that maintains population at a steady state

REFERENCES

ABBOTT, ANDREW. *The System of Professions: An Essay on the Division of Expert Labor*. Chicago: University of Chicago Press, 1988.

ABELLA, IRVING. *A Coat of Many Colours: Two Centuries of Jewish Life in Canada*. Toronto: Lester and Orpen Dennys, 1989.

ABELLA, IRVING, and HAROLD TROPER. *None Is Too Many: Canada and the Jews in Europe, 1933–1948*. Toronto: Lester and Orpen Dennys, 1982.

ABERLE, DAVID F. *The Peyote Religion Among the Navaho*. Chicago: Aldine, 1966.

ABRAHAMSON, PAUL R. "Postmaterialism and Environmentalism: A Comment on an Analysis and a Reappraisal." *Social Science Quarterly*. Vol. 78, No. 1 (March 1997):21–23.

ADELSON, JOSEPH. "Splitting Up." *Commentary* (September 1996).

ADORNO, T.W., et al. *The Authoritarian Personality*. New York: Harper & Brothers, 1950.

ADVISORY COUNCIL ON SUICIDE PREVENTION. *Acting on What We Know: Preventing Youth Suicide in First Nations*. Ottawa: Health Canada, 2003 [online]. Available at www.hc-sc.gc.ca/fnihb-dgspni/fnihb/cp/publications/preventing_youth_suicide.htm.

AGUIRRE, BENIGNO E., and E.L. QUARANTELLI. "Methodological, Ideological, and Conceptual-Theoretical Criticisms of Collective Behavior: A Critical Evaluation and Implications for Future Study." *Sociological Focus*. Vol. 16, No. 3 (August 1983):195–216.

AGUIRRE, BENIGNO E., E.L. QUARANTELLI, and JORGE L. MENDOZA. "The Collective Behavior of Fads: Characteristics, Effects, and Career of Streaking." *American Sociological Review*. Vol. 53, No. 4 (August 1988):569–84.

AHLBURG, DENNIS A., and CAROL J. DE VITA. "New Realities of the American Family." *Population Bulletin*. Vol. 47, No. 2 (1992):1–44.

AKERS, RONALD L., MARVIN D. KROHN, LONN LANZA-KADUCE, and MARCIA RADOSEVICH. "Social Learning and Deviant Behavior." *American Sociological Review*. Vol. 44, No. 4 (August 1979):636–55.

ALAM, SULTANA. "Women and Poverty in Bangladesh." *Women's Studies International Forum*. Vol. 8, No. 4 (1985):361–71.

ALBA, RICHARD D. *Italian Americans: Into the Twilight of Ethnicity*. Englewood Cliffs, N.J.: Prentice Hall, 1985.

ALBAS, DANIEL, and CHERYL ALBAS. "Studying Students Studying: Perspectives, Identities and Activities." In Mary Lorenz Dietz, Robert Prus, and William Shaffir, eds., *Doing Everyday Life: Ethnography as Human Lived Experience*. Mississauga, Ont.: Copp Clark Longman, 1994.

ALBRECHT, WILLIAM P., JR. *Economics*. 3d ed. Englewood Cliffs, N.J.: Prentice Hall, 1983.

ALLAN, EMILIE ANDERSEN, and DARRELL J. STEFFENSMEIER. "Youth, Underemployment, and Property Crime: Differential Effects of Job Availability and Job Quality on Juvenile and Young Adult Arrest Rates." *American Sociological Review*. Vol. 54, No. 1 (February 1989):107–23.

ALTMAN, DREW, et al. "Health Care for the Homeless." *Society*. Vol. 26, No. 4 (May–June 1989):4–5.

AMERICAN MEDICAL ASSOCIATION (AMA). Executive Summary of Media Violence Survey Analysis, 1996 [online]. Available www.ama-assn.org/ad-com/releases/1996/mvan1909.htm.

AMNESTY INTERNATIONAL. "The Death Penalty: List of Abolitionist and Retentionist Countries." [online]. Available at www.amnesty.org/ailib/intcam/dp/abrelist.htm, April 3, 2000.

ANDERSON, ALAN B., and JAMES S. FRIDERES. *Ethnicity in Canada: Theoretical Perspectives*. Toronto: Butterworths, 1981.

ANDERSON, DORIS. *The Unfinished Revolution*. Toronto: Doubleday Books, 1991.

ANDERSON, JOHN WARD. "Early to Wed: The Child Brides of India." *Washington Post* (May 24, 1995):A27, A30.

ANDERSON, JOHN WARD, and MOLLY MOORE. "World's Poorest Women Suffer in Common." *Columbus Dispatch* (April 11, 1993):4G.

ANG, IEN. *Watching Dallas: Soap Opera and the Melodramatic Imagination*. London: Methuen, 1985.

ANGELO, BONNIE. "Assigning the Blame for a Young Man's Suicide." *Time*. Vol. 138, No. 2 (November 18, 1991):12–14.

ANGIER, NATALIE. "Scientists, Finding Second Idiosyncracy in Homosexuals' Brains, Suggest Orientation is Physiological." *New York Times* (August 1, 1992):A7.

———. "Sexual identity predominates: Case of boy raised as girl underscores importance of prenatal events, MDs say." *The Globe and Mail* (March 14, 1997):A1.

APA. *Violence and Youth: Psychology's Response*. Washington, D.C.: American Psychological Association, 1993.

APPLEBOME, PETER. "70 Years After Scopes Trial, Creation Debate Lives." *New York Times* (March 10, 1996):1, 10.

ARCHER, DANE, and ROSEMARY GARTNER. *Violence and Crime in Cross-National Perspective*. New Haven, Conn.: Yale University Press, 1987.

ARENDT, HANNAH. *The Origins of Totalitarianism*. Cleveland, Ohio: Meridian Books, 1958.

———. *Between Past and Future: Six Exercises in Political Thought*. Cleveland, Ohio: Meridian Books, 1963.

ARIÈS, PHILIPPE. *Centuries of Childhood: A Social History of Family Life*. New York: Vintage Books, 1965.

ARJOMAND, SAID AMIR. *The Turban for the Crown: The Islamic Revolution in Iran*. New York: Oxford University Press, 1988.

ARMSTRONG, JANE. "RCMP Sour Second Site." *The Globe and Mail* (July 21, 2003):A1.

ARNUP, KATHERINE. "'We Are Family': Lesbian Mothers in Canada." In E.D. Nelson and B.W. Robinson, eds., *Gender in the 1990s: Images, Realities and Issues*. Scarborough, Ont.: Nelson Canada, 1995:330–45.

ARTIBISE, ALAN F.J., and GIL STELTER. "Urbanization." In *The Canadian Encyclopedia*. 2d ed. Edmonton: Hurtig Publishers, 1988:2235–36.

ASCH, SOLOMON. *Social Psychology*. Englewood Cliffs, N.J.: Prentice Hall, 1952.

ASHFORD, LORI S. "New Perspectives on Population: Lessons from Cairo." *Population Bulletin*. Vol. 50, No. 1 (March 1995).

ASTONE, NAN MARIE, and SARA S. MCLANAHAN. "Family Structure, Parental Practices and High School Completion." *American Sociological Review*. Vol. 56, No. 3 (June 1991):309–20.

ATCHLEY, ROBERT C. "Retirement as a Social Institution." *Annual Review of Sociology*. Vol. 8. Palo Alto, Calif.: Annual Reviews, 1982:263–87.

ATWOOD, MARGARET. "True Trash." In *Wilderness Tips*. Toronto: McClelland & Stewart, 1991:1–30.

AXTELL, ROGER E. *Gestures: The DOs and TABOOs of Body Language Around the World*. New York: Wiley, 1991.

BACKMAN, CARL B., and MURRAY C. ADAMS. "Self-Perceived Physical Attractiveness, Self-Esteem, Race, and Gender." *Sociological Focus*. Vol. 24, No. 4 (October 1991):283–90.

BADETS, JANE, and LINDA HOWATSON-LEO. "Recent Immigrants in the Workforce." In Statistics Canada, *Canadian Social Trends*. Vol. 3. Toronto: Thompson Educational Publishing, 2000.

BAHL, VINAY. "Caste and Class in India." Paper presented to the Southern Sociological Society, Atlanta, April 1991.

BAILEY, WILLIAM C. "Murder, Capital Punishment, and Television: Execution Publicity and Homicide Rates." *American Sociological Review*. Vol. 55, No. 5 (October 1990):628–33.

BAILEY, WILLIAM C., and RUTH D. PETERSON. "Murder and Capital Punishment: A Monthly Time-Series Analysis of Execution Publicity." *American Sociological Review*. Vol. 54, No. 5 (October 1989):722–43.

BAKER, MARY ANNE, CATHERINE WHITE BERHEIDE, FAY ROSS GRECKEL, LINDA CARSTARPHEN GUGIN, MARCIA J. LIPETZ, and MARCIA TEXLER SEGAL. *Women Today: A Multidisciplinary Approach to Women's Studies*. Monterey, Calif.: Brooks/Cole, 1980.

BAKER, MAUREEN. In Lorne Tepperman and R. Jack Richardson, eds., *The Social World: An Introduction to Sociology*. Toronto: McGraw Hill Ryerson, 1991:353–81.

BAKKER, J.I. (HANS). "Wilhelm Dilthey: Classical Sociological Theorist." *Quarterly Journal of Ideology: A Critique of Conventional Wisdom*. Vol. 22, No. 1–2 (1999).

BAKKER, J.I. (HANS), and ANTHONY WINSON. "Rural Sociology." In Peter S. Li and B. Singh Bolaria, eds., *Contemporary Sociology: Critical Perspectives*. Toronto: Copp Clark Pitman, 1993:500–17.

BALDUS, BERND, and VERNA TRIBE. "The Development of Perceptions and Evaluations of Social Inequality Among Public School Children." *Canadian Review of Sociology and Anthropology*. Vol. 15, No. 1 (1978):50–60.

BALES, ROBERT F. "The Equilibrium Problem in Small Groups." In Talcott Parsons et al., eds., *Working Papers in the Theory of Action*. New York: Free Press, 1953:111–15.

BALES, ROBERT F., and PHILIP E. SLATER. "Role Differentiation in Small Decision-Making Groups." In Talcott Parsons and Robert F. Bales, eds., *Family, Socialization and Interaction Process*. New York: Free Press, 1955:259–306.

BALTES, PAUL B., and K. WARNER SCHAIE. "The Myth of the Twilight Years." *Psychology Today*. Vol. 7, No. 10 (March 1974):35–39.

BALTZELL, E. DIGBY. *The Protestant Establishment: Aristocracy and Caste in America*. New York: Vintage Books, 1964.

BANFIELD, EDWARD C. *The Unheavenly City Revisited*. Boston: Little, Brown, 1974.

BARASH, DAVID. *The Whispering Within*. New York: Penguin Books, 1981.

BARIL, ALAIN, and GEORGE A. MORI. "Leaving the Fold: Declining Church Attendance." *Canadian Social Trends* (Catalogue No. 11-008E). No. 22 (1991):21–24.

BARKER, EILEEN. "Who'd Be a Moonie? A Comparative Study of Those Who Join the Unification Church in Britain." In Bryan Wilson, ed., *The Social*

Impact of New Religious Movements. New York: The Rose of Sharon Press, 1981:59–96.

BARLOW, MAUDE, and BRUCE CAMPBELL. *Take Back the Nation.* Toronto: Key Porter Books, 1991.

BARLOW, MAUDE, and HEATHER-JANE ROBERTSON. *Class Warfare: The Assault on Canada's Schools.* Toronto: Key Porter, 1994.

BARON, JAMES N., BRIAN S. MITTMAN, and ANDREW E. NEWMAN. "Targets of Opportunity: Organizational and Environmental Determinants of Gender Integration Within the California Civil Service, 1979–1985." *American Journal of Sociology.* Vol. 96, No. 6 (May 1991):1362–401.

BARRETT, STANLEY R. *Is God a Racist? The Right Wing in Canada.* Toronto: University of Toronto Press, 1987.

BARRY, KATHLEEN. "Feminist Theory: The Meaning of Women's Liberation." In Barbara Haber, ed., *The Women's Annual, 1982–1983.* Boston: G.K. Hall, 1983:35–78.

BASHEVKIN, SYLVIA B. *Toeing the Lines: Women and Party Politics in Canada.* 2d ed. Toronto: Oxford University Press, 1993.

BASIC DEPARTMENTAL DATA. Department of Indian Affairs & Northern Development. Ottawa: Statistics Canada, 1992.

BASSETT, ISABEL. *The Bassett Report: Career Success and Canadian Women.* Toronto: Collins, 1985.

BASSUK, ELLEN J. "The Homelessness Problem." *Scientific American.* Vol. 251, No. 1 (July 1984):40–45.

BAUER, P.T. *Equality, the Third World, and Economic Delusion.* Cambridge, Mass.: Harvard University Press, 1981.

BAYDAR, NAZLI, and JEANNE BROOKS-GUNN. "Effect of Maternal Employment and Child-Care Arrangements on Preschoolers' Cognitive and Behavioral Outcomes: Evidence from Children from the National Longitudinal Survey of Youth." *Developmental Psychology.* Vol. 27 (1991):932–35.

BBC. "The Paul McCartney Death Clues," March 9, 2000 [online]. Available at www.bbc.co.uk/h2g2/guide/A277328.

BEAUJOT, RODERIC, and KEVIN McQUILLAN. *Growth and Dualism: The Demographic Development of Canadian Society.* Toronto: Gage, 1982.

BECKER, ANNE. Paper presented at the annual meeting of the American Psychiatric Association, Washington, D.C., May 19, 1999. Reported in "Eating Disorders Jump When Fiji Gets Television." *Toledo Blade* (May 20, 1999):12.

BECKER, HOWARD S. *Outside: Studies in the Sociology of Deviance.* New York: Free Press, 1966.

BEEGHLEY, LEONARD. *The Structure of Social Stratification in the United States.* Needham Heights, Mass.: Allyn & Bacon, 1989.

BEGIN, PATRICIA. *Violence Against Women: Current Response* (Catalogue No. 1391B67). Ottawa: Ministry of Supply and Services, September 1991.

BEGLEY, SHARON. "Gray Matters." *Newsweek* (March 7, 1995):48–54.

———. "How to Beat the Heat." *Newsweek* (December 8, 1997):34–38.

BELL, ALAN P., MARTIN S. WEINBERG, and SUE KIEFER-HAMMERSMITH. *Sexual Preference: Its Development in Men and Women.* Bloomington: Indiana University Press, 1981.

BELL, DANIEL. *The Coming of Post-Industrial Society: A Venture in Social Forecasting.* New York: Basic Books, 1973.

BELLAH, ROBERT N. *The Broken Covenant.* New York: Seabury Press, 1975.

BELLAH, ROBERT N., RICHARD MADSEN, WILLIAM M. SULLIVAN, ANN SWIDLER, and STEVEN M. TIPTON. *Habits of the Heart: Individualism and Commitment in American Life.* New York: Harper & Row, 1985.

BELLAS, MARCIA L. "Comparable Worth in Academia: The Effects on Faculty Salaries of the Sex Composition and Labor-Market Conditions of Academic Disciplines." *American Sociological Review.* Vol. 59, No. 6 (December 1994):807–21.

BELLE, MARILYN, and KEVIN McQUILLAN. "Births Outside Marriage: A Growing Alternative." In Statistics Canada, *Canadian Social Trends.* Vol. 3. Toronto: Thompson Educational Publishing, 2000.

BELSKY, JAY, RICHARD M. LERNER, and GRAHAM B. SPANIER. *The Child in the Family.* Reading, Mass.: Addison-Wesley, 1984.

BELTRAME, JULIAN. "Latimer's Last Chances for Earlier Release Appear Slim." *Maclean's* (January 29, 2001).

BEM, SANDRA LIPSITZ. *The Lenses of Gender: Transforming the Debate on Sexual Inequality.* New Haven, Conn.: Yale University Press, 1993.

BENEDETTI, PAUL, and NANCY DeHART, eds. *On McLuhan: Forward Through the Rearview Mirror.* Scarborough, Ont.: Prentice Hall, 1996.

BENEDICT, RUTH. "Continuities and Discontinuities in Cultural Conditioning." *Psychiatry.* Vol. 1 (May 1938):161–67.

———. *The Chrysanthemum and the Sword: Patterns of Japanese Culture.* New York: New American Library, 1974; orig. 1946.

BENET, SULA. "Why They Live to Be 100, or Even Older, in Abkhasia." *New York Times Magazine* (December 26, 1971):3, 28–29, 31–34.

BENJAMIN, BERNARD, and CHRIS WALLIS. "The Mortality of Widowers." *The Lancet.* Vol. 2 (August 1963):454–56.

BENJAMIN, LOIS. *The Black Elite: Facing the Color Line in the Twilight of the Twentieth Century.* Chicago: Nelson-Hall, 1991.

BENN, CARL. *Historic Fort York, 1793–1993.* Toronto: Natural Heritage, 1993.

BENNETT, WILLIAM J. "Quantifying America's Decline." *Wall Street Journal* (March 15, 1993).

BENOKRAITIS, NIJOLE, and JOE FEAGIN. *Modern Sexism: Blatant, Subtle, and Overt Discrimination.* 2d ed. Englewood Cliffs, N.J.: Prentice Hall, 1995.

BERCUSON, DAVID, and BARRY COOPER. "A New Tax on Energy Is Unacceptable." *The Globe and Mail* (November 8, 1997):D2.

BERESFORD-HOWE, CONSTANCE. *A Serious Widow.* Toronto: McClelland & Stewart, 1991.

BERGAMO, MONICA, and GERSON CAMAROTTI. "Brazil's Landless Millions." *World Press Review.* Vol. 43, No. 7 (July 1996):46–47.

BERGER, PETER L. *Invitation to Sociology.* New York: Anchor Books, 1963.

———. *The Sacred Canopy: Elements of a Sociological Theory of Religion.* Garden City, N.Y.: Doubleday, 1967.

———. *Facing Up to Modernity: Excursions in Society, Politics, and Religion.* New York: Basic Books, 1977.

———. *The Capitalist Revolution: Fifty Propositions About Prosperity, Equality, and Liberty.* New York: Basic Books, 1986.

———. *Redeeming Laughter: The Comic Dimension of Human Experience.* Berlin: Walter de Gruyter, 1997.

BERGER, PETER, BRIGITTE BERGER, and HANSFRIED KELLNER. *The Homeless Mind: Modernization and Consciousness.* New York: Vintage Books, 1974.

BERGER, PETER L., and HANSFRIED KELLNER. *Sociology Reinterpreted: An Essay on Method and Vocation.* Garden City, N.Y.: Anchor Books, 1981.

BERGESEN, ALBERT, ed. *Crises in the World-System.* Beverly Hills, Calif.: Sage, 1983.

BERK, RICHARD A. *Collective Behavior.* Dubuque, Iowa: Wm. C. Brown, 1974.

BERNARD, JESSIE. *The Female World.* New York: Free Press, 1981.

———. *The Future of Marriage.* New Haven, Conn.: Yale University Press, 1982; orig. 1973.

BERNARD, LARRY CRAIG. "Multivariate Analysis of New Sex Role Formulations and Personality." *Journal of Personality and Social Psychology.* Vol. 38, No. 2 (February 1980):323–36.

BERNSTEIN, NINA. "On Frontier of Cyberspace, Data Is Money, and a Threat." *New York Times* (June 12, 1997):A1, B14–15.

BERNSTEIN, RICHARD J. *The New Constellation: The Ethical-Political Horizons of Modernity/Postmodernity.* Cambridge, Mass.: MIT Press, 1992.

BERRY, BRIAN L., and PHILIP H. REES. "The Factorial Ecology of Calcutta." *American Journal of Sociology.* Vol. 74, No. 5 (March 1969):445–91.

BERSCHEID, ELLEN, and ELAINE HATFIELD. *Interpersonal Attraction.* 2d ed. Reading, Mass.: Addison-Wesley, 1983.

BESHAROV, DOUGLAS J., and LISA A. LAUMANN. "Child Abuse Reporting." *Society.* Vol. 34, No. 4 (May/June 1996):40–46.

BESS, IRWIN. "Widows Living Alone." In Statistics Canada, *Canadian Social Trends.* Vol. 3. Toronto: Thompson Educational Publishing, 2000:165–69.

BEST, RAPHAELA. *We've All Got Scars: What Boys and Girls Learn in Elementary School.* Bloomington: Indiana University Press, 1983.

BIBBY, REGINALD W. "The Moral Mosaic: Sexuality in Canada 80s." *Social Indicators Research.* Vol. 13 (1983):171–84.

———. *Fragmented Gods: The Poverty and Potential of Religion in Canada.* Toronto: Irwin, 1987.

———. "Secularization and Change." In W.E. Hewitt, ed., *The Sociology of Religion: A Canadian Focus.* Toronto: Butterworths, 1993.

———. *The Bibby Report: Social Trends Canadian Style.* Toronto: Stoddart, 1995.

———. "The Persistence of Religious Identification in Canada." *Canadian Social Trends* (Spring 1997):24.

———. "The Persistence of Christian Religious Identification in Canada." In Statistics Canada, *Canadian Social Trends.* Vol. 3. Toronto: Thompson Educational Publishing, 2000.

———. *Canada's Teens: Today, Yesterday and Tomorrow.* Toronto: Stoddart, 2001.

BIBBY, REGINALD W., and Donald C. Posterski. *The Emerging Generation: An Inside Look at Canada's Teenagers.* Toronto: Irwin Publishing, 1985.

BIBLARZ, TIMOTHY J., and ADRIAN E. RAFTERY. "The Effects of Family Disruption on Social Mobility." *American Sociological Review.* Vol. 58, No. 1 (February 1993):97–109.

BILLSON, JANET MANCINI, and BETTINA J. HUBER. *Embarking upon a Career with an Undergraduate Degree in Sociology.* 2d ed. Washington, D.C.: American Sociological Association, 1993.

BISHOP, MARY F. "Birth Control." In *The Canadian Encyclopedia.* 2d ed., Vol. 1. Edmonton: Hurtig Publishers, 1988:231–32.

BISSOONDATH, NEIL. *Selling Illusions: The Cult of Multiculturalism in Canada.* Toronto: Penguin Books, 1994.

BLACK, NAOMI. "Agnes MacPhail." In *The Canadian Encyclopedia.* 2d ed., Vol. 2. Edmonton: Hurtig Publishers, 1988:1281.

BLAU, JUDITH R., and PETER M. BLAU. "The Cost of Inequality: Metropolitan Structure and Violent Crime." *American Sociological Review.* Vol. 47, No. 1 (February 1982):114–29.

BLAU, PETER M. *Exchange and Power in Social Life.* New York: Wiley, 1964.

———. *Inequality and Heterogeneity: A Primitive Theory of Social Structure.* New York: Free Press, 1977.

BLISHEN, BERNARD R. "The Construction and Use of an Occupational Class Scale." *Canadian Journal of Economics and Political Science.* Vol. XXIV (1958):519–25.

———. *Doctors in Canada.* Toronto: University of Toronto Press, 1991.

BLISHEN, BERNARD R., W. CARROLL, and C. MOORE. "The 1981 Socio-Economic Index for Occupations in Canada." *Canadian Review of Sociology and Anthropology.* Vol. 24 (1987):465–88.

BLUM, LINDA M. *Between Feminism and Labor: The Significance of the Comparable Worth Movement.* Berkeley: University of California Press, 1991.

BLUMSTEIN, ABRAHAM S. *Criminal Justice.* Chicago: Quadrangle Books, 1970.

BLUMBERG, PAUL. *Inequality in an Age of Decline.* New York: Oxford University Press, 1981.

BLUMER, HERBERT G. "Fashion." In David L. Sills, ed., *International Encyclopedia of the Social Sciences.* Vol. 5. New York: Macmillan and Free Press, 1968:341–45.

———. "Collective Behavior." In Alfred McClung Lee, ed., *Principles of Sociology.* 3d ed. New York: Barnes & Noble Books, 1969:65–121.

BLUMSTEIN, PHILIP, and PEPPER SCHWARTZ. *American Couples.* New York: William Morrow, 1983.

BOFF, LEONARD, and CLODOVIS. *Salvation and Liberation: In Search of a Balance Between Faith and Politics.* Maryknoll, N.Y.: Orbis Books, 1984.

BOGARDUS, EMORY S. "Comparing Racial Distance in Ethiopia, South Africa, and the United States." *Sociology and Social Research.* Vol. 52, No. 2 (January 1968):149–56.

BOHANNAN, PAUL. *Divorce and After.* Garden City, N.Y.: Doubleday, 1970.

BOHM, ROBERT M. "American Death Penalty Opinion, 1936–1986: A Critical Examination of the Gallup Polls." In Robert M. Bohm, ed., *The Death Penalty in America: Current Research.* Cincinnati: Anderson Publishing Co., 1991:113–45.

BOLI, JOHN, and GEORGE M. THOMAS. "World Culture in the World Polity: A Century of International Non-Governmental Organization." *American Sociological Review.* Vol. 62, No. 2 (April 1997):171–90.

BONILLA-SANTIAGO, GLORIA. "A Portrait of Hispanic Women in the United States." In Sara E. Rix, ed., *The American Woman, 1990–91: A Status Report.* New York: Norton, 1990:249–57.

BONNER, JANE. Research presented in "The Two Brains." Public Broadcasting System telecast, 1984.

BOOTH, ALAN, and LYNN WHITE. "Thinking About Divorce." *Journal of Marriage and the Family.* Vol. 42, No. 3 (August 1980):605–16.

BORGMANN, ALBERT. *Crossing the Postmodern Divide.* Chicago: University of Chicago Press, 1992.

BORITCH, HELEN. *Fallen Women: Female Crime and Criminal Justice in Canada.* Toronto: ITP Nelson, 1997.

BORMANN, F. HERBERT. "The Global Environmental Deficit." *BioScience.* Vol. 40 (1990):74.

BORMANN, F. HERBERT, and STEPHEN R. KELLERT. "The Global Environmental Deficit." In F. Herbert Bormann and Stephen R. Kellert, eds., *Ecology, Economics, and Ethics: The Broken Circle.* New Haven, Conn.: Yale University Press, 1991:ix–xviii.

BOSWELL, TERRY E. "A Split Labor Market Analysis of Discrimination Against Chinese Immigrants, 1850–1882." *American Sociological Review.* Vol. 51, No. 3 (June 1986):352–71.

BOTT, ELIZABETH. *Family and Social Network.* New York: Free Press, 1971; orig. 1957.

BOULDING, ELISE. *The Underside of History.* Boulder, Colo.: Westview Press, 1976.

BOWLES, SAMUEL, and HERBERT GINTIS. *Schooling in Capitalist America: Educational Reform and the Contradictions of Economic Life.* New York: Basic Books, 1976.

BOYER, DEBRA. "Male Prostitution and Homosexual Identity." *Journal of Homosexuality.* Vol. 17, Nos. 1–2 (1989):151–84.

BOZINOFF, LORNE, and PETER MACINTOSH. "Vast Majority of Canadians Believe in God and Heaven." Toronto: Gallup Report, August 30, 1990.

BRAITHWAITE, JOHN. "The Myth of Social Class and Criminality Reconsidered." *American Sociological Review.* Vol. 46, No. 1 (February 1981):36–57.

BRANEGAN, JAY. "Is Singapore a Model for the West?" *Time.* Vol. 141, No. 3 (January 18, 1993):36–37.

BREEN, LEONARD Z. "The Aging Individual." In Clark Tibbitts, ed., *Handbook of Social Gerontology.* Chicago: University of Chicago Press, 1960:145–62.

BREND, YVETTE. "Why History Lives in Old Crow." *The Globe and Mail* (November 11, 1997):A2.

BRETON, RAYMOND. "Institutional Completeness of Ethnic Communities and the Personal Relations of Immigrants." *American Journal of Sociology.* Vol. 70 (1964):193–205.

———. "Ethnic Stratification Viewed from Three Theoretical Perspectives." In James E. Curtis and William G. Scott, eds., *Social Stratification: Canada.* 2d ed. Scarborough, Ont.: Prentice Hall, 1979:270–94.

———. "Regionalism in Canada." In David Cameron, ed. *Regionalism and Supranationalism.* Montreal: Institute for Research on Public Policy, 1981.

———. *Why Meech Failed: Lessons for Canadian Constitutionmaking.* Toronto: C.D. Howe Institute, 1992.

BRINTON, CRANE. *The Anatomy of Revolution.* New York: Vintage Books, 1965.

BRINTON, MARY C. "The Social-Institutional Bases of Gender Stratification: Japan as an Illustrative Case." *American Journal of Sociology.* Vol. 94, No. 2 (September 1988):300–34.

BRODIE, JANINE. "The Political Economy of Regionalism." In Wallace Clement and Glen Williams, eds. *The New Canadian Political Economy.* Montreal: McGill-Queen's University Press, 1989:138–59.

BRONSON, HAROLD. "Economic Concentration and Corporate Power." In Peter S. Li and B. Singh Bolaria, eds., *Contemporary Sociology: Critical Perspectives.* Toronto: Copp Clark Pitman, 1993:203–22.

BROWN, LESTER R., et al., eds. *State of the World 1993: A Worldwatch Institute Report on Progress Toward a Sustainable Society.* New York: Norton, 1993.

BROWN, MARY ELLEN, ed. *Television and Women's Culture: The Politics of the Popular.* Newbury Park, Calif.: Sage, 1990.

BRUNO, MARY. "Abusing the Elderly." *Newsweek* (September 23, 1985):75–76.

BRYM, ROBERT J., ed. *Regionalism in Canada.* Toronto: Irwin, 1986.

———. "An Introduction to the Regional Question in Canada." In Robert J. Brym, ed., *Regionalism in Canada.* Toronto: Irwin Publishing, 1986:2–45.

———. "The Canadian Capitalist Class, 1965–1985." In Robert J. Brym, ed., *The Structures of the Canadian Capitalist Class.* Toronto: Garamond, 1985:1–20.

BRYM, ROBERT J., and BONNIE J. FOX. *From Culture to Power: The Sociology of English Canada.* Don Mills, Ont.: Oxford University Press, 1989.

BURAWAY, MICHAEL. "Review Essay: The Soviet Descent into Capitalism." *American Journal of Sociology.* Vol. 102, No. 5 (March 1997):1430–44.

BURKE, TOM. "The Future." In Sir Edmund Hillary, ed., *Ecology 2000: The Changing Face of the Earth.* New York: Beaufort Books, 1984:227–41.

BURSTEIN, PAUL. "Legal Mobilization as a Social Movement Tactic: The Struggle for Equal Employment Opportunity." *American Journal of Sociology.* Vol. 96, No. 5 (March 1991):1201–25.

BUSBY, LINDA J. "Sex Role Research on the Mass Media." *Journal of Communications.* Vol. 25 (Autumn 1975):107–13.

BUTLER, ROBERT N. *Why Survive? Being Old in America.* New York: Harper & Row, 1975.

BUTTERWORTH, DOUGLAS, and JOHN K. CHANCE. *Latin American Urbanization.* Cambridge: Cambridge University Press, 1981.

CALLAHAN, DANIEL. *Setting Limits: Medical Goals in an Aging Society.* New York: Simon & Schuster, 1987.

CALLOW, A.B., JR., ed. *American Urban History.* New York: Oxford University Press, 1969.

CAME, BARRY. "Coming of Age: As He Turns 18, Prince William Is Showing an Independent Streak." *Maclean's* (May 22, 2000):14.

CAMERON, WILLIAM BRUCE. *Modern Social Movements: A Sociological Outline.* New York: Random House, 1966.

CANADA. *The Economic and Fiscal Update.* Ottawa: Department of Finance, October 1997.

———. House of Commons. Standing Committee on Communications and Culture. *Television Violence: Fraying our Social Fabric.* Issue No. 6. Ottawa: Supply and Services Canada, 1993.

———. Royal Commission on Aboriginal Peoples. *Ethical Guidelines for Research.* 8 pp. Ottawa: Supply and Services Canada, 1993.

———. Citizenship and Immigration Canada. Priorities, Planning, and Research Branch. "Foreign Students in Canada, 1980–2001," January 2003 [online]. Available at www.cic.gc.ca/english/srr/research/foreign-students/students.html#_Toc32910764.

Canada's 125th Anniversary Yearbook. Ottawa: Minister of Supply and Services, 1992.

CANADA YEAR BOOK. Ottawa: Statistics Canada, 1994.

CANADIAN BROADCASTING CORPORATION. *The National Magazine.* January 16, 1998.

CANADIAN GLOBAL ALMANAC 2003. Toronto: Wiley & Sons, 2002.

CANADIAN INTERNATIONAL DEVELOPMENT AGENCY (CIDA). *Sharing Our Future: Canadian International Development Assistance.* Ottawa: Ministry of Supply and Services Canada, 1987.

CANADIAN PRESS/LÉGER MARKETING. "Canadian Perceptions of Homosexuality," June 21, 2003 [online]. Available as PDF at www.legermarketing.com/eng/tencan.asp.

CANETTI, ELIAS. *Crowds and Power.* New York: Seabury Press, 1978.

CANTOR, MURIAL G., and SUZANNE PINGREE. *The Soap Opera.* Beverly Hills, Calif.: Sage, 1983.

CANTRIL, HADLEY, HAZEL GAUDET, and HERTA HERZOG. *Invasion from Mars: A Study in the Psychology of Panic.* Princeton, N.J.: Princeton University Press, 1947.

CAPLOW, THEODORE, HOWARD M. BAHR, JOHN MODELL, and BRUCE A. CHADWICK. *Recent Social Trends in the United States, 1960–1990.* Montreal: McGill-Queen's University Press, 1991.

CARLEY, KATHLEEN. "A Theory of Group Stability." *American Sociological Review*. Vol. 56, No. 3 (June 1991):331–54.

CARLSON, MARGARET. "The Real Money Train." *Time*. Vol. 146, No. 24 (December 11, 1995):93.

CARLSON, NORMAN A. "Corrections in the United States Today: A Balance Has Been Struck." *The American Criminal Law Review*. Vol. 13, No. 4 (Spring 1976):615–47.

CARMICHAEL, STOKELY, and CHARLES V. HAMILTON. *Black Power: The Politics of Liberation in America*. New York: Vintage Books, 1967.

CARRIÉRE, YVES. "Population and Hospital Days: Will There Be a Problem?" In Ellen M. Gee and Gloria M. Gutman, *The Overselling of Population Aging: Apocalyptic Demography, Intergenerational Challenges, and Social Policy*. Don Mills, Ont.: Oxford University Press, 2000:26–44.

CARRIGAN, D. OWEN. *Crime and Punishment in Canada: A History*. Toronto: McClelland & Stewart, 1991.

CENTER FOR THE STUDY OF SPORT IN SOCIETY. *1997 Racial Report Card: A Study in the NBA, NFL, and Major League Baseball*. Boston: Northeastern University, 1998.

———. *1998 Racial and Gender Report Card* [online]. Available www.sportinsociety.org, February 19, 2000.

CENTERS FOR DISEASE CONTROL. "Surveillance and Research. Fact Sheet: Abortion Surveillance, 1999" [online]. Available at www.cdc.gov/nccdphp/drh/surv_abort99.htm.

CHANDLER, TERTIUS, and GERALD FOX. *3000 Years of Urban History*. New York: Academic Press, 1974.

CHANGE, KWANG-CHIH. *The Archaeology of Ancient China*. New Haven, Conn.: Yale University Press, 1977.

CHARD, JENNIFER, and VIVIENNE RENAUD. "Visible Minorities in Toronto, Vancouver, and Montréal." In Statistics Canada, *Canadian Social Trends*. Vol. 3. Toronto: Thompson Educational Publishing, 2000.

CHAUNCEY, GEORGE. *Gay New York: Gender, Urban Culture, and the Making of the Gay Male World, 1890–1940*. New York: Basic Books, 1994.

CHERLIN, ANDREW, and FRANK F. FURSTENBERG, JR. "The American Family in the Year 2000." *The Futurist*. Vol. 17, No. 3 (June 1983):7–14.

CHOWN, SHEILA M. "Morale, Careers and Personal Potentials." In James E. Birren and K. Warner Schaie, eds., *Handbook of the Psychology of Aging*. New York: Van Nostrand Reinhold, 1977:672–91.

CHE-ALFORD, JANET, CATHERINE ALLAN, and GEORGE BUTLIN. *Focus on Canada: Families in Canada*, Catalogue No. 96-307E. Scarborough, Ont.: Statistics Canada and Prentice Hall, 1994.

CHE-ALFORD, JANET, and BRIAN HAMM. "Under One Roof: Three Generations Living Together." *Canadian Social Trends*. Vol. 3. Toronto: Thompson Educational Publishing, 2000:161–64.

CHRISTIAN, WILLIAM. "Ideology and Politics in Canada." In John H. Redekop, ed. *Approaches to Canadian Politics*. 2d ed. Scarborough, Ont.: Prentice Hall, 1983.

———. "Innis, Harold Adams." In *The Canadian Encyclopedia*. 2d ed., Vol. 1. Edmonton: Hurtig, 1988:1069.

CLARK, CURTIS B. "Geriatric Abuse: Out of the Closet." In *The Tragedy of Elder Abuse: The Problem and the Response*. Hearings before the Select Committee on Aging, House of Representatives (July 1, 1986):49–50.

CLARK, MARGARET S., ed. *Prosocial Behavior*. Newbury Park, Calif.: Sage, 1991.

CLARK, S.D. *The New Urban Poor*. Toronto: McGraw-Hill Ryerson, 1978.

CLARKE, JAMES W. "Black-on-Black Violence." *Society*. Vol. 33, No. 5 (July/August 1996):46–50.

CLARKE, ROBIN. "Atmospheric Pollution." In Sir Edmund Hillary, ed., *Ecology 2000: The Changing Face of the Earth*. New York: Beaufort Books, 1984a:130–48.

———. "What's Happening to Our Water?" In Sir Edmund Hillary, ed., *Ecology 2000: The Changing Face of the Earth*. New York: Beaufort Books, 1984b:108–29.

CLEMENT, WALLACE. *The Canadian Corporate Elite: Economic Power in Canada*. Toronto: McClelland & Stewart, 1975.

———. "Comparative Class Analysis: Locating Canada in a North American and Nordic Context." *Canadian Review of Sociology and Anthropology*. Vol. 27, No. 4 (1990).

CLINARD, MARSHALL, and DANIEL ABBOTT. *Crime in Developing Countries*. New York: Wiley, 1973.

CLOUD, JOHN. "What Can the Schools Do?" *Time*. Vol. 153, No. 17 (May 3, 1999):38–40.

CLOVER, CHARLES. "Hot, Hot Is the Range." *National Post* (January 24, 2001):A15.

CLOWARD, RICHARD A., and LLOYD E. OHLIN. *Delinquency and Opportunity: A Theory of Delinquent Gangs*. New York: Free Press, 1966.

CLUFF, JULIE, ALISON HUNTER, and RONALD HINCH. "Feminist Perspectives on Serial Murder: A Critical Analysis." *Homicide Studies*. Vol. 1, No. 3:291–308.

COE, MICHAEL D., and RICHARD A. DIEHL. *In the Land of the Olmec*. Austin: University of Texas Press, 1980.

COHEN, ADAM. "A New Push for Blind Justice." *Time*. Vol. 145, No. 7 (February 20, 1995):39–40.

COHEN, ALBERT K. *Delinquent Boys: The Culture of the Gang*. New York: Free Press, 1971; orig. 1955.

COHEN, LLOYD R. "Sexual Harassment and the Law." *Society*. Vol. 28, No. 4 (May–June 1991):8–13.

COHN, RICHARD M. "Economic Development and Status Change of the Aged." *American Journal of Sociology*. Vol. 87, No. 2 (March 1982):1150–61.

COLAPINTO, JOHN. *As Nature Made Him: The Boy Who Was Raised as a Girl*. Toronto: HarperCollins, 2000.

COLEMAN, JAMES S. "Rational Organization." *Rationality and Society*. Vol. 2, (1990):94–105.

COLEMAN, WILLIAM D. *The Independence Movement in Quebec, 1945–1980*. Toronto: University of Toronto Press, 1984.

COLLINS, RANDALL. "A Conflict Theory of Sexual Stratification." *Social Problems*. Vol. 19, No. 1 (Summer 1971):3–21.

———. *The Credential Society: An Historical Sociology of Education and Stratification*. New York: Academic Press, 1979.

COLOMBO, JOHN ROBERT. *Colombo's New Canadian Quotations*. Edmonton: Hurtig Publishers, 1987.

———. *The Canadian Global Almanac 1993: A Book of Facts*. Toronto: Macmillan, 1992.

———. *1998: The Canadian Global Almanac*. Toronto: Macmillan, 1997.

COLTON, HELEN. *The Gift of Touch: How Physical Contact Improves Communication, Pleasure, and Health*. New York: Seaview/Putnam, 1983.

COMMISSION ON SYSTEMIC RACISM IN THE ONTARIO CRIMINAL JUSTICE SYSTEM. *The Report of the Commission on Systemic Racism in the Ontario Criminal Justice System*. Toronto: Queen's Printer for Ontario, 1996.

COMTE, AUGUSTE. *Auguste Comte and Positivism: The Essential Writings*. Gertrud Lenzer, ed. New York: Harper Torchbooks, 1975.

COMPUTER INDUSTRY ALMANAC INC. "Internet Users Will Top 1 Billion in 2005" (press release), March 12, 2002 [online]. Available at www.c-i-a.com.

CONNETT, PAUL H. "The Disposable Society." In F. Herbert Bormann and Stephen R. Kellert, eds., *Ecology, Economics, and Ethics: The Broken Circle*. New Haven, Conn.: Yale University Press, 1991:99–122.

CONTRERAS, JOSEPH. "A New Day Dawns." *Newsweek* (March 30, 1992):40–41.

COOLEY, CHARLES HORTON. *Social Organization*. New York: Schocken Books, 1962; orig. 1909.

———. *Human Nature and the Social Order*. New York: Schocken Books, 1964; orig. 1902.

CORAK, MILES. "Getting Ahead: Does Your Parents' Income Count?" In *Canadian Social Trends: Volume 3*. Toronto: Thompson Educational Publishing, 2000.

CORBEIL, JEAN-PIERRE. "Sport Participation in Canada." In Statistics Canada, *Canadian Social Trends*. Vol. 3. Toronto: Thompson Educational Publishing, 2000a.

———. *Literacy in Canada: Disparity Between Francophones and Anglophones*. Statistics Canada, Catalogue No. 89-573-XIE, 2000b [online]. Available at www.statcan.ca/english/IPS/Data/89-573-XIE.htm.

CORLEY, ROBERT N., O. LEE REED, PETER J. SHEDD, and JERE W. MOREHEAD. *The Legal and Regulatory Environment of Business*. 9th ed. New York: McGraw-Hill, 1993.

CÔTÉ, JAMES E., and ANTON L. ALLAHAR. "Youth: The Disinherited Generation." In Dan Glenday and Ann Duffy, eds. *Canadian Society: Meeting the Challenges of the Twenty-First Century*. Toronto: Oxford University Press, 2001.

COTTRELL, JOHN, and THE EDITORS OF TIME-LIFE. *The Great Cities: Mexico City*. Amsterdam: 1979.

COUNCIL ON FAMILIES IN AMERICA. *Marriage in America: A Report to the Nation*. New York: Institute for American Values, 1995.

COUNTS, G.S. "The Social Status of Occupations: A Problem in Vocational Guidance." *School Review*. Vol. 33 (January 1925):16–27.

COURTNEY, ALICE E., and THOMAS W. WHIPPLE. *Sex Stereotyping in Advertising*. Lexington, Mass.: D.C. Heath, 1983.

COWAN, CAROLYN POPE. *When Partners Become Parents*. New York: Basic Books, 1992.

COWGILL, DONALD, and LOWELL HOLMES. *Aging and Modernization*. New York: Appleton-Century-Crofts, 1972.

COWLEY, GEOFFREY. "The Prescription That Kills." *Newsweek* (July 17, 1995): 54.

COX, HARVEY. *The Secular City*. Rev. ed. New York: Macmillan, 1971; orig. 1965.

———. "Church and Believers: Always Strangers?" In Thomas Robbins and Dick Anthony, *In Gods We Trust: New Patterns of Religious Pluralism in America*. 2d ed. New Brunswick, N.J.: Transaction, 1990:449–62.

COYOTE (CALL OFF YOUR OLD TIRED ETHICS) [online]. Available at www.freedomusa.org/coyotela/what_is.html, April 2, 2000.

CREESE, GILLIAN, NEIL GUPPY, and MARTIN MEISSNER. *Ups and Downs on the Ladder of Success*. Ottawa: Statistics Canada, 1991.

CRISPELL, DIANE. "Speaking in Other Tongues." *American Demographics*. Vol. 19. No. 1 (January 1997):12–15.

CROMPTON, SUSAN, and ANNA KEMENY. "In Sickness and in Health: The Well-Being of Married Seniors." *Canadian Social Trends.* Toronto: Thompson Educational Publishing, 2000:45-50.

CROOK, STEPHAN, JAN PAKULSKI, and MALCOLM WATERS. *Postmodernity: Change in Advanced Society.* Newbury Park, Calif.: Sage, 1992.

CROUSE, JAMES, and DALE TRUSHEIM. *The Case Against the SAT.* Chicago: University of Chicago Press, 1988.

CUFF, E.C., and G.C.F. PAYNE, eds. *Perspectives in Sociology.* London: Allen and Unwin, 1979.

CUMMING, ELAINE, and WILLIAM E. HENRY. *Growing Old: The Process of Disengagement.* New York: Basic Books, 1961.

CURRIE, ELLIOTT. *Confronting Crime: An American Challenge.* New York: Pantheon Books, 1985.

CURTIS, JAMES E., EDWARD G. GRABB, and DOUGLAS BAER. "Voluntary Association Membership in Fifteen Countries: A Comparative Analysis." *American Sociological Review.* Vol. 57, No. 2 (April 1992):139–52.

CURTISS, SUSAN. *Genie: A Psycholinguistic Study of a Modern-Day "Wild Child."* New York: Academic Press, 1977.

CUTRIGHT, PHILLIP. "Occupational Inheritance: A Cross-National Analysis." *American Journal of Sociology.* Vol. 73, No. 4 (January 1968):400–16.

DAHL, ROBERT A. *Who Governs?* New Haven, Conn.: Yale University Press, 1961.

———. *Dilemmas of Pluralist Democracy: Autonomy vs. Control.* New Haven, Conn.: Yale University Press, 1982.

DAHRENDORF, RALF. *Class and Class Conflict in Industrial Society.* Stanford, Calif.: Stanford University Press, 1959.

DALGLISH, BRENDA. "Cheaters." *Maclean's* (August 9, 1993):18–21.

DALY, MARTIN, and MARGO WILSON. *Homicide.* New York: Aldine, 1988.

DANNEFER, DALE. "Adult Development and Social Theory: A Reappraisal." *American Sociological Review.* Vol. 49, No. 1 (February 1984):100–16.

DARNTON, NINA, and YURIKO HOSHIA. "Whose Life Is It, Anyway?" *Newsweek.* Vol. 113, No. 4 (January 13, 1989):61.

DAVIES, CHRISTIE. *Ethnic Humor Around the World: A Comparative Analysis.* Bloomington: Indiana University Press, 1990.

DAVIES, JAMES C. "Toward a Theory of Revolution." *American Sociological Review.* Vol. 27, No. 1 (February 1962):5–19.

DAVIES, MARK, and DENISE B. KANDEL. "Parental and Peer Influences on Adolescents' Educational Plans: Some Further Evidence." *American Journal of Sociology.* Vol. 87, No. 2 (September 1981):363–87.

DAVIS, DONALD M., cited in "T.V. Is a Blonde, Blonde World." *American Demographics,* special issue: Women Change Places. Ithaca, N.Y., 1993.

DAVIS, KINGSLEY. "Extreme Social Isolation of a Child." *American Journal of Sociology.* Vol. 45, No. 4 (January 1940):554–65.

———. "Final Note on a Case of Extreme Isolation." *American Journal of Sociology.* Vol. 52, No. 5 (March 1947):432–37.

———. "Sexual Behavior." In Robert K. Merton and Robert Nisbet, eds., *Contemporary Social Problems.* 3d ed. New York: Harcourt Brace Jovanovich, 1971:313–60.

DAVIS, KINGSLEY, and WILBERT MOORE. "Some Principles of Stratification." *American Sociological Review.* Vol. 10, No. 2 (April 1945):242–49.

DE BROUKER, PATRICE, and LAVAL LAVALLÉE. "Getting Ahead: Does Your Parents' Education Count?" In Statistics Canada, *Canadian Social Trends.* Vol. 3. Toronto: Thompson Educational Publishing, 2000.

DEBER, RAISA. "Getting What We Pay For: Myths and Realities about Financing Canada's Health Care System." *Dialogue on Health Reform.* University of Toronto [online]. Available at www.utoronto.ca/hlthadmin/dhr/.

DECKARD, BARBARA SINCLAIR. *The Women's Movement: Political, Socioeconomic, and Psychological Issues.* 2d ed. New York: Harper & Row, 1979.

DEDRICK, DENNIS K., and RICHARD E. YINGER. "MAD, SDI, and the Nuclear Arms Race." Manuscript in development. Georgetown, Ky.: Georgetown College, 1990.

DEKESEREDY, WALTER S. "Patterns of Family Violence." In Maureen Baker, ed., *Families: Changing Trends in Canada,* 4th edition. Whitby: McGraw-Hill Ryerson, 2001: 238–66.

DEKESEREDY, WALTER S., and RONALD HINCH. *Woman Abuse: Sociological Perspectives.* Toronto: Thompson Educational Publishing, 1991.

DEKESEREDY, WALTER S., RONALD HINCH, HYMAN BURSHTYN, and CHARLES GORDON. "Taking Woman Abuse Seriously: A Critical Response to the Solicitor General of Canada's Crime Prevention Advice." In E.D. Nelson and B.W. Robinson, eds., *Gender in the 1990s: Images, Realities, and Issues.* Scarborough, Ont.: Nelson Canada, 1995:478–89.

DELACROIX, JACQUES, and CHARLES C. RAGIN. "Structural Blockage: A Crossnational Study of Economic Dependency, State Efficacy, and Underdevelopment." *American Journal of Sociology.* Vol. 86, No. 6 (May 1981):1311–47.

DELLA CAVA, MARCO R. "For Dutch, It's as Easy as Asking a Doctor." *USA Today* (January 7, 1997):4A.

DEMERATH, N. J., III. "Who Now Debates Functionalism? From System, Change, and Conflict to 'Culture, Choice, and Praxis.'" *Sociological Forum.* Vol. 11, No. 2 (June 1996):333–45.

Demographic Aging: The Economic Consequences. Ottawa: Ministry of Supply and Services, 1991.

DEPEW, ROBERT. "Policing Native Communities: Some Principles and Issues in Organizational Theory." *Canadian Journal of Criminology.* Vol. 34 (1992).

DE TOCQUEVILLE, ALEXIS. *The Old Regime and the French Revolution.* Stuart Gilbert, trans. Garden City, N.Y.: Anchor/Doubleday Books, 1955; orig. 1856.

———. *Democracy in America.* Garden City, N.Y.: Doubleday Anchor Books, 1969; orig. 1834–40.

DEWEY, JOHN. *Experience and Education.* New York: Collier Books, 1968; orig. 1938.

DIAMOND, MILTON. "Sexual Identity, Monozygotic Twins Reared in Discordant Sex Roles and a BBC Follow-Up." *Archives of Sexual Behavior.* Vol. 11, No. 2 (April 1982):181–86.

DICKASON, OLIVE PATRICIA. *Canada's First Nations: A History of Founding Peoples from the Earliest Times.* Toronto: McClelland & Stewart, 1992.

———. *Canada's First Nations: A History of Founding Peoples from Earliest Times.* 2d ed. Toronto: Oxford University Press, 1997.

DIXON, WILLIAM J., and TERRY BOSWELL. "Dependency, Disarticulation, and Denominator Effects: Another Look at Foreign Capital Penetration." *American Journal of Sociology.* Vol. 102, No. 2 (September 1996):543–62.

DIZARD, JAN E., and HOWARD GADLIN. *The Minimal Family.* Amherst: The University of Massachusetts Press, 1990.

DOLLARD, JOHN, et al. *Frustration and Aggression.* New Haven, Conn.: Yale University Press, 1939.

DONOVAN, VIRGINIA K., and RONNIE LITTENBERG. "Psychology of Women: Feminist Therapy." In Barbara Haber, ed., *The Women's Annual 1981: The Year in Review.* Boston: G.K. Hall, 1982:211–35.

DOUGLASS, RICHARD L. "Domestic Neglect and Abuse of the Elderly: Implications for Research and Service." *Family Relations.* Vol. 32 (July 1983):395–402.

DOWLER, KEVIN. "Cultures, Borders and Free Trade." In Lynne van Luven and Priscilla L. Walton, eds., *Pop Can: Popular Culture in Canada.* Scarborough: Prentice Hall, 1999: 219–23.

DOYLE, JAMES A. *The Male Experience.* Dubuque, Iowa: Wm. C. Brown, 1983.

DOYLE, RICHARD F. *A Manifesto of Men's Liberation.* 2d ed. Forest Lake, Minn.: Men's Rights Association, 1980.

DRIEDGER, LEO, ed. *The Ethnic Factor: Identity in Diversity.* Toronto: McGraw-Hill Ryerson, 1989.

DRYBURGH, HEATHER. "Teenage Pregnancy," *Health Reports,* Vol. 12, No. 1, Statistics Canada, Catalogue 82-003, October 1, 2003 [online]. Available at www.statcan.ca/english/kits/preg/preg3.htm.

DUBÉ, FRANCINE. "Magna's Political Matchmaker." *National Post* (October 18, 2003):A1.

DUBOS, RENÉ. *Man Adapting.* New Haven, Conn.: Yale University Press, 1980; orig. 1965.

DUCHARME, MICHELLE. "The History of Guelph's Black Community." *The Ontarion* (March 26, 1985):7 (Archival Collections: University of Guelph Library).

DUFFY, ANN, and NANCY MANDELL. "The Growth in Poverty and Social Inequality: Losing Faith in Social Justice." In Dan Glenday and Ann Duffy, *Canadian Society: Meeting the Challenges of the Twenty-First Century.* Toronto: Oxford University Press Canada, 2001.

DUHL, LEONARD J. "The Social Context of Health." In Arthur C. Hastings et al., eds., *Health for the Whole Person: The Complete Guide to Holistic Medicine.* Boulder, Colo.: Westview Press, 1980:39–48.

DURKHEIM, EMILE. *The Division of Labor in Society.* New York: Free Press, 1964a; orig. 1895.

———. *The Rules of Sociological Method.* New York: Free Press, 1964b; orig. 1893.

———. *The Elementary Forms of Religious Life.* New York: Free Press, 1965; orig. 1915.

———. *Suicide.* New York: Free Press, 1966; orig. 1897.

———. *Selected Writings.* Anthony Giddens, ed. Cambridge: Cambridge University Press, 1972.

———. *Sociology and Philosophy.* New York: Free Press, 1974; orig. 1924.

DURNING, ALAN THEIN. "Supporting Indigenous Peoples." In Lester R. Brown et al., eds., *State of the World 1993: A Worldwatch Institute Report on Progress Toward a Sustainable Society.* New York: Norton, 1993:80–100.

DWORKIN, ANDREA. *Intercourse.* New York: Free Press, 1987.

Earnings of Men and Women. 1991. Ottawa: Statistics Canada.

EBAUGH, HELEN ROSE FUCHS. *Becoming an EX: The Process of Role Exit.* Chicago: University of Chicago Press, 1988.

ECKHOLM, ERIK. "Malnutrition in Elderly: Widespread Health Threat." *New York Times* (August 13, 1985):19–20.

ECKHOLM, ERIK, and JOHN TIERNEY. "AIDS in Africa: A Killer Rages On." *New York Times* (September 16, 1990):A1, 14.

EDWARDS, DAVID V. *The American Political Experience.* 3d ed. Englewood Cliffs, N.J.: Prentice Hall, 1985.

EDWARDS, PETER. "Boot Campers Get Cool Welcome." *Toronto Star* (August 1, 1997):A1.

EDWARDS, RICHARD. *Contested Terrain: The Transformation of the Workplace in the Twentieth Century*. New York: Basic Books, 1979.

EHRENREICH, BARBARA. *The Hearts of Men: American Dreams and the Flight from Commitment*. Garden City, N.Y.: Anchor Books, 1983.

———. "The Real Truth About the Female Body." *Time*. Vol. 153, No. 9 (March 15, 1999):56–65.

EHRENREICH, BARBARA, and DEIRDRE ENGLISH. "Blowing the Whistle on the 'Mommy Track.'" In E.D. Nelson and B.W. Robinson, *Gender in the 1990s: Images, Realities and Issues*. Toronto: Nelson Canada, 1995.

EICHLER, MARGRIT. *Nonsexist Research Methods: A Practical Guide*. Winchester, Mass.: Unwin Hyman, 1988.

EISENBERG, DAVID M., et al. "Unconventional Medicine in the United States: Prevalence, Costs and Patterns of Use." *New England Journal of Medicine*. Vol. 328, No. 4 (1993):246–52.

EISENSTEIN, ZILLAH R., ed. *Capitalist Patriarchy and the Case for Socialist Feminism*. New York: Monthly Review Press, 1979.

EKMAN, PAUL. "Biological and Cultural Contributions to Body and Facial Movements in the Expression of Emotions." In A. Rorty, ed., *Explaining Emotions*. Berkeley: University of California Press, 1980a:73–101.

———. *Face of Man: Universal Expression in a New Guinea Village*. New York: Garland Press, 1980b.

———. *Telling Lies: Clues to Deceit in the Marketplace, Politics, and Marriage*. New York: Norton, 1985.

EKMAN, PAUL, WALLACE V. FRIESEN, and JOHN BEAR. "The International Language of Gestures." *Psychology Today* (May 1984):64–69.

EL-ATTAR, MOHAMED. Personal communication, 1991.

ELIAS, ROBERT. *The Politics of Victimization: Victims, Victimology and Human Rights*. New York: Oxford University Press, 1986.

ELKIND, DAVID. *The Hurried Child: Growing Up Too Fast Too Soon*. Reading, Mass.: Addison-Wesley, 1981.

ELLIOT, DELBERT S., and SUZANNE S. AGETON. "Reconciling Race and Class Differences in Self-Reported and Official Estimates of Delinquency." *American Sociological Review*. Vol. 45, No. 1 (February 1980):95–110.

ELLISON, CHRISTOPHER G., and DARREN E. SHERKAT. "Conservative Protestantism and Support for Corporal Punishment." *American Sociological Review*. Vol. 58, No. 1 (February 1993):131–44.

ELMER-DEWITT, PHILIP. "First Nation in Cyberspace." *Time*. Vol. 142, No. 24 (December 6, 1993):62–64.

———. "Battle for the Internet." *Time*. Vol. 144, No. 4 (July 25, 1994):50–56.

EMBER, MELVIN, and CAROL R. EMBER. "The Conditions Favoring Matrilocal Versus Patrilocal Residence." *American Anthropologist*. Vol. 73, No. 3 (June 1971):571–94.

———. *Anthropology*. 6th ed. Englewood Cliffs, N.J.: Prentice Hall, 1991.

EMBREE, AINSLIE T. *The Hindu Tradition*. New York: Vintage Books, 1972.

EMERSON, JOAN P. "Behavior in Private Places: Sustaining Definitions of Reality in Gynecological Examinations." In H.P. Dreitzel, ed., *Recent Sociology*. Vol. 2. New York: Collier, 1970:74–97.

ENGELS, FRIEDRICH. *The Origin of the Family*. Chicago: Charles H. Kerr & Company, 1902; orig. 1884.

ENGLAND, PAULA. *Comparable Worth: Theories and Evidence*. Hawthorne, N.Y.: Aldine, 1992.

ENGLISH-CURRIE, VICKIE. "The Need for Re-Evaluation in Native Education." In David Taras, Beverly Rasporich, and Eli Mandel, eds., *A Passion for Identity: An Introduction to Canadian Studies*. 2d ed. Scarborough, Ont.: Nelson Canada, 1993:111–19.

ERIKSON, ERIK H. *Childhood and Society*. New York: Norton, 1963; orig. 1950.

———. *Identity and the Life Cycle*. New York: Norton, 1980.

ERIKSON, KAI T. *Wayward Puritans: A Study in the Sociology of Deviance*. New York: Wiley, 1966.

ETZIONI, AMITAI. *A Comparative Analysis of Complex Organization: On Power, Involvement, and Their Correlates*. Rev. and enlarged ed. New York: Free Press, 1975.

———. "How to Make Marriage Matter." *Time*. Vol. 142, No. 10 (September 6, 1993):76.

ETZIONI-HALEVY, EVA. *Bureaucracy and Democracy: A Political Dilemma*. Rev. ed. Boston: Routledge & Kegan Paul, 1985.

EVANS, M.D.R. "Immigrant Entrepreneurship: Effects of Ethnic Market Size and Isolated Labor Pool." *American Sociological Review*. Vol. 54, No. 6 (December 1989):950–62.

EVERS, FREDERICK T., JAMES C. RUSH, JASNA A. KRMPOTIC, and JOANNE DUNCAN-ROBINSON. *Making the Match: Phase II* (Final Technical Report), Universities of Guelph and Western Ontario, 1993.

FAGAN, DREW. "Canada Triumphs in Tariff Battle." *The Globe and Mail* (July 16, 1996):A1.

FALK, GERHARD. Personal communication, 1987.

FALKENMARK, MALIN, and CARL WIDSTRAND. "Population and Water Resources: A Delicate Balance." *Population Bulletin*. Vol. 47, No. 3 (November 1992). Washington, D.C.: Population Reference Bureau.

FALLON, A.E., and P. ROZIN. "Sex Differences in Perception of Desirable Body Shape." *Journal of Abnormal Psychology*. Vol. 94, No. 1 (1985):100–5.

FANTINI, MARIO D. *Regaining Excellence in Education*. Columbus, Ohio: Merrill, 1986.

FARLEY, CHRISTOPHER JOHN. "Winning the Right to Fly." *Time*. Vol. 146, No. 9 (August 28, 1995):62–64.

FARRELL, MICHAEL P., and STANLEY D. ROSENBERG. *Men at Midlife*. Boston: Auburn House, 1981.

FAST, JANET, and MORENO DA PONT. "Changes in Women's Work Continuity." In Statistics Canada, *Canadian Social Trends*. Vol. 3. Toronto: Thompson Educational Publishing, 2000.

FEAGIN, JOE. *The Urban Real Estate Game*. Englewood Cliffs, N.J.: Prentice Hall, 1983.

FEATHERSTONE, MIKE, ed. *Global Culture: Nationalism, Globalization, and Modernity*. London: Sage, 1990.

FEDERAL, PROVINCIAL AND TERRITORIAL ADVISORY COMMITTEE ON POPULATION HEALTH. *Statistical Report on the Health of Canadians*. Ottawa: Health Canada, 1999.

FELLMAN, BRUCE. "Taking the Measure of Children's T.V." *Yale Alumni Magazine* (April 1995):46–51.

FENNELL, TOM. "A Measure of Hope." *Maclean's* (June 14, 1993):48–49.

FERGUSON, TOM. "Medical Self-Care: Self Responsibility for Health." In Arthur C. Hastings et al., eds., *Health for the Whole Person: The Complete Guide to Holistic Medicine*. Boulder, Colo.: Westview Press, 1980:87–109.

FERREE, MYRA MARX, and ELAINE J. HALL. "Rethinking Stratification from a Feminist Perspective: Gender, Race, and Class in Mainstream Textbooks." *American Sociological Review*. Vol. 61, No. 6 (December 1996):929–50.

FIFE, SANDY. "The Total Quality Muddle." *The Globe and Mail: Report on Business* (November 1992):64–74.

FINKELSTEIN, NEAL W., and RON HASKINS. "Kindergarten Children Prefer Same-Color Peers." *Child Development*. Vol. 54, No. 2 (April 1983):502–8.

FIREBAUGH, GLENN. "Growth Effects of Foreign and Domestic Investment." *American Journal of Sociology*. Vol. 98, No. 1 (July 1992):105–30.

———. "Does Foreign Capital Harm Poor Nations? New Estimates Based on Dixon and Boswell's Measures of Capital Penetration." *American Journal of Sociology*. Vol. 102, No. 2 (September 1996):563–75.

FIREBAUGH, GLENN, and FRANK D. BECK. "Does Economic Growth Benefit the Masses? Growth, Dependence, and Welfare in the Third World." *American Sociological Review*. Vol. 59, No. 5 (October 1994):631–53.

FISCHER, CLAUDE S., et al. *Networks and Places: Social Relations in the Urban Setting*. New York: Free Press, 1977.

FISCHER, CLAUDE W. *The Urban Experience*. 2d ed. New York: Harcourt Brace Jovanovich, 1984.

FISHER, ELIZABETH. *Woman's Creation: Sexual Evolution and the Shaping of Society*. Garden City, N.Y.: Anchor/Doubleday, 1979.

FISHER, ROGER, and WILLIAM URY. "Getting to YES." In William M. Evan and Stephen Hilgartner, eds., *The Arms Race and Nuclear War*. Englewood Cliffs, N.J.: Prentice Hall, 1988:261–68.

FISKE, ALAN PAIGE. "The Cultural Relativity of Selfish Individualism: Anthropological Evidence That Humans Are Inherently Sociable." In Margaret S. Clark, ed., *Prosocial Behavior*. Newbury Park, Calif.: Sage, 1991:176–214.

FISKE, EDWARD B. "Adults: The Forgotten Illiterates." *Christian Science Monitor* (May 30, 1997):18.

FITZPATRICK, MARY ANNE. *Between Husbands and Wives: Communication in Marriage*. Newbury Park, Calif.: Sage, 1988.

FLAHERTY, MICHAEL G. "A Formal Approach to the Study of Amusement in Social Interaction." *Studies in Symbolic Interaction*. Vol. 5. New York: JAI Press, 1984:71–82.

———. "Two Conceptions of the Social Situation: Some Implications of Humor." *The Sociological Quarterly*. Vol. 31, No. 1 (Spring 1990).

FLERAS, AUGIE. *Social Problems in Canada: Conditions, Constructions, and Challenges*. Toronto: Pearson Education Canada, 2001.

FLETCHER, JOSEPH. *The Ethics of Genetic Control: Ending Reproductive Roulette*. Garden City, New York: Anchor/Doubleday, 1974.

FLORIDA, RICHARD, and MARTIN KENNEY. "Transplanted Organizations: The Transfer of Japanese Industrial Organization to the U.S." *American Sociological Review*. Vol. 56, No. 3 (June 1991):381–98.

FLOWER, G.E. *Speaking Out: The 1984 CEA Poll of Canadian Opinion on Education*. Toronto: Canadian Education Association, 1984.

FLYNN, PATRICIA. "The Disciplinary Emergence of Bioethics and Bioethics Committees: Moral Ordering and its Legitimation." *Sociological Focus*. Vol. 24, No. 2 (May 1991):145–56.

FOBES, RICHARD. "Creative Problem Solving." *The Futurist*. Vol. 30, No. 1 (January–February 1996):19–22.

FOOT, DAVID K. *Boom, Bust and Echo 2000: Profiting from the Demographic Shift in the New Millennium*. Toronto: Macfarlane Walter & Ross, 1998.

Forbes. "World's Richest People," February 27, 2003 [online]. Available at www.forbes.com/lists.

FORCESE, DENNIS. *The Canadian Class Structure*. 4th ed. Toronto: McGraw-Hill Ryerson, 1997.

FORD, CLELLAN S., and FRANK A. BEACH. *Patterns of Sexual Behavior*. New York: Harper & Row, 1951.

FOUCAULT, MICHEL. *The History of Sexuality: An Introduction*. Vol. 1. Robert Hurley, trans. London: Penguin Books, 1978.

FRANCIS, DIANE. *Controlling Interest: Who Owns Canada?* Toronto: Macmillan, 1986.

———. *Bre-X: The Inside Story*. Toronto: Key Porter Books, 1997.

FRANK, ANDRÉ GUNDER. *On Capitalist Underdevelopment*. Bombay: Oxford University Press, 1975.

———. *Crisis: In the World Economy*. New York: Holmes & Meier, 1980.

———. *Reflections on the World Economic Crisis*. New York: Monthly Review Press, 1981.

FRANK, JEFFREY. "15 Years of AIDS in Canada." In Statistics Canada, *Canadian Social Trends*. Vol. 3. Toronto: Thompson Educational Publishing, 2000.

FRANKLIN ASSOCIATES. *Characterization of Municipal Solid Waste in the United States, 1960–2000*. Prairie Village, Kans.: Franklin Associates, 1986.

FRASER, SYLVIA. *In My Father's House*. Toronto: Collins Paperback, 1987.

FREDERICK, JUDITH A., and MONICA BOYD. "The Impact of Family Structure on High School Completion." In Statistics Canada, *Canadian Social Trends*. Vol. 3. Toronto: Thompson Educational Publishing, 2000.

FREDRICKSON, GEORGE M. *White Supremacy: A Comparative Study in American and South African History*. New York: Oxford University Press, 1981.

FREE, MARVIN D. "Religious Affiliation, Religiosity, and Impulsive and Intentional Deviance." *Sociological Focus*. Vol. 25, No. 1 (February 1992):77–91.

FREEDOM HOUSE. *Freedom in the World, 2000–2001*. New York: Freedom House, 2001.

FRENCH, MARILYN. *Beyond Power: On Women, Men, and Morals*. New York: Summit Books, 1985.

FRETZ, WINFIELD. *The Waterloo Mennonites: A Community in Paradox*. Waterloo, Ont.: Wilfrid Laurier Press, 1989.

FRIDERES, JAMES S. *Native Peoples in Canada: Contemporary Conflicts*. 4th ed. Scarborough, Ont.: Prentice Hall, 1993.

———. *Aboriginal Peoples in Canada: Contemporary Conflicts*. 5th ed. Scarborough, Ont.: Prentice Hall, Allyn and Bacon Canada, 1998.

FRIEDAN, BETTY. *The Fountain of Age*. New York: Simon and Schuster, 1993.

FRIEDMAN, MILTON, and ROSE FRIEDMAN. *Free to Choose: A Personal Statement*. New York: Harcourt Brace Jovanovich, 1980.

FRIEDRICH, CARL J., and ZBIGNIEW BRZEZINSKI. *Totalitarian Dictatorship and Autocracy*. 2d ed. Cambridge, Mass.: Harvard University Press, 1965.

FRIEDRICH, OTTO. "A Proud Capital's Distress." *Time*. Vol. 124, No. 6 (August 6, 1984):26–30, 33–35.

———. "United No More." *Time*. Vol. 129, No. 18 (May 4, 1987):28–37.

FRIZZELL, ALAN, and JON H. PAMMETT, eds. *The Canadian General Election of 1997*. Toronto: Dundurn Press, 1997.

FUCHS, VICTOR R. "Sex Differences in Economic Well-Being." *Science*. Vol. 232 (April 25, 1986):459–64.

FULLER, REX, and RICHARD SCHOENBERGER. "The Gender Salary Gap: Do Academic Achievement, Intern Experience, and College Major Make a Difference?" *Social Science Quarterly*. Vol. 72, No. 4 (December 1991):715–26.

FULTON, E. KAYE. "Bringing Home Baby." *Maclean's* (May 21, 1995):34–42.

FURSTENBERG, FRANK F., JR. "The New Extended Family: The Experience of Parents and Children After Remarriage." Paper presented to the Changing Family Conference XIII: The Blended Family. University of Iowa, 1984.

FURSTENBERG, FRANK F., JR., and ANDREW CHERLIN. *Divided Families: What Happens to Children When Parents Part*. Cambridge, Mass.: Harvard University Press, 1991.

GAGLIANI, GIORGIO. "How Many Working Classes?" *American Journal of Sociology*. Vol. 87, No. 2 (September 1981):259–85.

GAGNÉ, PATRICIA, RICHARD TEWKSBURY, and DEANNA McGAUGHEY. "Coming Out and Crossing Over: Identity Formation and Proclamation in a Transgender Community." *Gender and Society*. Vol. 11, No. 4 (August 1997):478–508.

Gallup Sexual Life Style Survey. Toronto: Gallup Report, September 3, 1988.

GAMBLE, ANDREW, STEVE LUDLAM, and DAVID BAKER. "Britain's Ruling Class." *The Economist*. Vol. 326, No. 7795 (January 23, 1993):10.

GAMSON, WILLIAM A. "Beyond the Science-versus-Advocacy Distinction." *Contemporary Sociology*. Vol. 28, No. 1 (January 1999):23–26.

GANS, HERBERT J. *People and Plans: Essays on Urban Problems and Solutions*. New York: Basic Books, 1968.

———. *Popular Culture and High Culture*. New York: Basic Books, 1974.

———. *Deciding What's News: A Study of CBS Evening News, NBC Nightly News, Newsweek and Time*. New York: Vintage Books, 1980.

GAIRDNER, WILLIAM D. *The Trouble With Canada*. Toronto: Stoddart Publishing, 1990.

GARDNER, ARTHUR. "Their Own Boss: The Self-Employed in Canada." In Statistics Canada, *Canadian Social Trends*, Vol. 3. Toronto: Thompson Educational Publishing, 2000.

GARFINKEL, HAROLD. "Conditions of Successful Degradation Ceremonies." *American Journal of Sociology*. Vol. 61, No. 2 (March 1956):420–24.

———. *Studies in Ethnomethodology*. Cambridge: Polity Press, 1967.

GEERTZ, CLIFFORD. "Common Sense as a Cultural System." *The Antioch Review*. Vol. 33, No. 1 (Spring 1975):5–26.

GELLES, RICHARD J., and CLAIRE PEDRICK CORNELL. *Intimate Violence in Families*. 2d ed. Newbury Park, Calif.: Sage, 1990.

GELMAN, DAVID. "Who's Taking Care of Our Parents?" *Newsweek* (May 6, 1985):61–64, 67–68.

———. "Born or Bred?" *Newsweek* (February 24, 1992):46–53.

GEORGE, SUSAN. *How the Other Half Dies: The Real Reasons for World Hunger*. Totowa, N.J.: Rowman & Allanheld, 1977.

GERBER, LINDA M. *Minority Survival: Community Characteristics and Out-Migration from Indian Communities Across Canada*. Ph.D. thesis. Toronto: University of Toronto Press, 1976.

———. "The Development of Canadian Indian Communities: A Two-Dimensional Typology Reflecting Strategies of Adaptation to the Outside World." *Canadian Review of Sociology and Anthropology*. Vol. 16, No. 4 (1979):123–50.

———. "Ethnicity Still Matters: Socio-Demographic Profiles of the Ethnic Elderly in Ontario." *Canadian Ethnic Studies*. Vol. XV, No. 3 (1983):60–80.

———. "Community Characteristics and Out-Migration from Canadian Indian Communities: Path Analyses." *Canadian Review of Sociology and Anthropology*. Vol. 21 (1984):145–65.

———. "The Federal Election of 1968: Social Class Composition and Party Support in the Electoral Districts of Ontario." *Canadian Review of Sociology and Anthropology*. Vol. 23, No. 1 (1986):118–35.

———. "Multiple Jeopardy: A Socio-economic Comparison of Men and Women among the Indian, Métis and Inuit Peoples of Canada." *Canadian Ethnic Studies*. Vol. XXII, No. 3 (1990):69–84.

———. "Referendum Results: Defining New Boundaries for an Independent Quebec." *Canadian Ethnic Studies*. Vol. XXIV, No. 2 (1992):22–34.

———. "Indian, Métis, and Inuit Women and Men: Multiple Jeopardy in a Canadian Context." In E.D. Nelson and B.W. Robinson, eds., *Gender in the 1990s: Images, Realities, and Issues*. Scarborough, Ont.: Nelson Canada, 1995:466–77.

GERLACH, MICHAEL L. *The Social Organization of Japanese Business*. Berkeley and Los Angeles: University of California Press, 1992.

GERSTEL, NAOMI. "Divorce and Stigma." *Social Problems*. Vol. 43, No. 2 (April 1987):172–86.

GERTH, H.H., and C. WRIGHT MILLS, eds. *From Max Weber: Essays in Sociology*. New York: Oxford University Press, 1946.

GESCHWENDER, JAMES A. *Racial Stratification in America*. Dubuque, Iowa: Wm. C. Brown, 1978.

GEWERTZ, DEBORAH. "A Historical Reconsideration of Female Dominance Among the Chambri of Papua New Guinea." *American Ethnologist*. Vol. 8, No. 1 (1981):94–106.

GIBBONS, DON C., and MARVIN D. KROHN. *Delinquent Behavior*. 4th ed. Englewood Cliffs, N.J.: Prentice Hall, 1986.

GIBBS, NANCY. "When Is It Rape?" *Time*. Vol. 137, No. 22 (June 3, 1991a):48–54.

———. "The Clamor on Campus." *Time*. Vol. 137, No. 22 (June 3, 1991b):54–55.

———. "How Much Should We Teach Our Children About Sex?" *Time*. Vol. 141, No. 21 (May 24, 1993):60–66.

———. "Cause Celeb." *Time*. Vol. 147, No. 25 (June 17, 1996):28–30.

GIDDENS, ANTHONY. *The Transformation of Intimacy*. Cambridge, UK: Polity Press, 1992.

GIFFEN, P.J. "Official Rates of Crime and Delinquency." In W.T. McGrath, ed., *Crime and Its Treatment in Canada*. Toronto: Macmillan, 1976.

GILBERT, DENNIS, and JOSEPH A. KAHL. *The American Class Structure: A New Synthesis*. 3d ed. Homewood, Ill.: The Dorsey Press, 1987.

GILBERT, NEIL. "Realities and Mythologies of Rape." *Society*. Vol. 29, No. 4 (May–June 1992):4–10.

GILBERT, S.N. "The Forgotten Purpose and Future Promise of University Education." *Canadian Journal of Community Mental Health*. Vol. 8, No. 2 (1989):103–22.

GILBERT, SID, LYNN BARR, WARREN CLARK, MATTHEW BLUE, and DEBORAH SUNTER. *Leaving School: Results from a National Survey Comparing School Leavers and High School Graduates 18 to 20 Years of Age*. Ottawa: Government of Canada (LM-294-07-93CE), 1993.

GILLIGAN, CAROL. *In a Different Voice: Psychological Theory and Women's Development*. Cambridge, Mass.: Harvard University Press, 1982.

———. *Making Connections: The Relational Worlds of Adolescent Girls at Emma Willard School*. Cambridge, Mass.: Harvard University Press, 1990.

GINSBURG, FAYE, and ANNA LOWENHAUPT TSING, eds. *Uncertain Terms: Negotiating Gender in American Culture*. Boston: Beacon Press, 1990.

GIOVANNINI, MAUREEN. "Female Anthropologist and Male Informant: Gender Conflict in a Sicilian Town." In John J. Macionis and Nijole V. Benokraitis, eds., *Seeing Ourselves: Classic, Contemporary, and Cross-Cultural Readings in Sociology.* 2d ed. Englewood Cliffs, N.J.: Prentice Hall, 1992:27–32.

GLADUE, BRIAN A., RICHARD GREEN, and RONALD E. HELLMAN. "Neuroendocrine Response to Estrogen and Sexual Orientation." *Science.* Vol. 225, No. 4669 (September 28, 1984):1496–99.

GLAZER, NATHAN, and DANIEL P. MOYNIHAN. *Beyond the Melting Pot.* 2d ed. Cambridge, Mass.: MIT Press, 1970.

GLEICK, ELIZABETH. "The Marker We've Been Waiting For." *Time.* Vol. 149, No. 14 (April 7, 1997):28–42.

GLENDAY, DAN. "Off the Ropes: New Challenges and Strengths Facing Trade Unions in Canada." In Dan Glenday and Ann Duffy, eds., *Canadian Society: Meeting the Challenges of the Twenty-First Century.* Toronto: Oxford University Press, 2001.

GLENN, NORVAL D., and BETH ANN SHELTON. "Regional Differences in Divorce in the United States." *Journal of Marriage and the Family.* Vol. 47, No. 3 (August 1985):641–52.

GLOCK, CHARLES Y. "The Religious Revival in America." In Jane Zahn, ed., *Religion and the Face of America.* Berkeley: University of California Press, 1959:25–42.

———. "On the Study of Religious Commitment." *Religious Education.* Vol. 62, No. 4 (1962):98–110.

GLUECK, SHELDON, and ELEANOR GLUECK. *Unraveling Juvenile Delinquency.* New York: Commonwealth Fund, 1950.

GOFFMAN, ERVING. *The Presentation of Self in Everyday Life.* Garden City, N.Y.: Anchor Books, 1959.

———. *Asylums: Essays on the Social Situation of Mental Patients and Other Inmates.* Garden City, N.Y.: Anchor Books, 1961.

———. *Stigma: Notes on the Management of Spoiled Identity.* Englewood Cliffs, N.J.: Prentice Hall, 1963.

———. *Interactional Ritual: Essays on Face to Face Behavior.* Garden City, N.Y.: Anchor Books, 1967.

———. *Gender Advertisements.* New York: Harper Colophon, 1979.

GOLDBERG, STEVEN. *The Inevitability of Patriarchy.* New York: William Morrow, 1974.

———. Personal communication, 1987.

GOLDEN, FREDERIC. "Lying Faces Unmasked." *Time.* Vol. 153, No. 13 (April 5, 1999):52.

GOLDFARB, JEFFREY C. *Beyond Glasnost: The Post-Totalitarian Mind.* Chicago: University of Chicago Press, 1989.

GOLDFARB, WILLIAM. "Groundwater: The Buried Life." In F. Herbert Bormann and Stephen R. Kellert, eds., *Ecology, Economics, and Ethics: The Broken Circle.* New Haven, Conn.: Yale University Press, 1991:123–35.

GOLDSBY, RICHARD A. *Race and Races.* 2d ed. New York: Macmillan, 1977.

GOLDSMITH, H.H. "Genetic Influences on Personality from Infancy." *Child Development.* Vol. 54, No. 2 (April 1983):331–35.

GOODE, WILLIAM J. "The Theoretical Importance of Love." *American Sociological Review.* Vol. 24, No. 1 (February 1959):38–47.

———. "Encroachment, Charlatanism, and the Emerging Profession: Psychology, Sociology and Medicine." *American Sociological Review.* Vol. 25, No. 6 (December 1960):902–14.

GORDON, JAMES S. "The Paradigm of Holistic Medicine." In Arthur C. Hastings et al., eds., *Health for the Whole Person: The Complete Guide to Holistic Medicine.* Boulder, Colo.: Westview Press, 1980:3–27.

GORDON, SOL, and CRAIG W. SNYDER. *Personal Issues in Human Sexuality: A Guidebook for Better Sexual Health.* 2d ed. Boston: Allyn & Bacon, 1989.

GORING, CHARLES BUCKMAN. *The English Convict: A Statistical Study.* Montclair, N.J.: Patterson Smith, 1972; orig. 1913.

GORMAN, CHRISTINE. "Mexico City's Menacing Air." *Time.* Vol. 137, No. 13 (April 1, 1991):61.

GOTTFREDSON, MICHAEL R., and TRAVIS HIRSCHI. "National Crime Control Policies." *Society.* Vol. 32, No. 2 (January–February 1995):30–36.

GOTTMANN, JEAN. *Megalopolis.* New York: Twentieth Century Fund, 1961.

GOUGH, KATHLEEN. "The Origin of the Family." *Journal of Marriage and the Family.* Vol. 33, No. 4 (November 1971):760–71.

GOULD, STEPHEN J. "Evolution as Fact and Theory." *Discover* (May 1981):35–37.

GOYDER, JOHN. *Technology and Society: A Canadian Perspective.* Peterborough, Ont.: Broadview Press, 1997.

———. *Essentials of Canadian Sociology.* Toronto: McClelland & Stewart, 1990.

GOYDER, JOHN C., and JAMES E. CURTIS. "Occupational Mobility in Canada over Four Generations." In James E. Curtis and William G. Scott, eds., *Social Stratification: Canada.* 2d ed. Scarborough, Ont.: Prentice Hall, 1979.

GRANDIN, ELAINE, et al. "Couple Violence and Psychological Distress," *Canadian Journal of Public Health,* Vol. 89(1), 1998:43–47.

GRANOVETTER, MARK. "The Strength of Weak Ties." *American Journal of Sociology.* Vol. 78, No. 6 (May 1973):1360–80.

GRANT, DON SHERMAN, II, and MICHAEL WALLACE. "Why Do Strikes Turn Violent?" *American Journal of Sociology.* Vol. 96, No. 5 (March 1991):1117–50.

GRANT, DONALD L. *The Anti-Lynching Movement.* San Francisco: R and E Research Associates, 1975.

GRAY, PAUL. "Whose America?" *Time.* Vol. 137, No. 27 (July 8, 1991):12–17.

GREEN, JOHN C. "Pat Robertson and the Latest Crusade: Resources and the 1988 Presidential Campaign." *Social Sciences Quarterly.* Vol. 74, No. 1 (March 1993):156–68.

GREENBERG, DAVID F. *The Construction of Homosexuality.* Chicago: University of Chicago Press, 1988.

GREENSPON, EDWARD. The Incredible Shrinking Middle Class." *The Globe and Mail* (July 31, 1993):D1.

GREGG, ALLAN R. "Brave New Epoque." *Maclean's* (April 6, 1998):56–60.

GREGORY, PAUL R., and ROBERT C. STUART. *Comparative Economic Systems.* 2d ed. Boston: Houghton Mifflin, 1985.

GREGORY, SOPHFRONIA SCOTT. "The Knife in the Book Bag." *Time.* Vol. 141, No. 6 (February 8, 1993):37.

GROSS, JANE. "New Challenge of Youth: Growing Up in a Gay Home." *New York Times* (February 11, 1991):A1, B7.

GROTH, NICHOLAS A., and H. JEAN BIRNBAUM. *Men Who Rape: The Psychology of the Offender.* New York: Plenum, 1979.

GUPPY, NEIL, and A. BRUCE ARAI. "Who Benefits from Higher Education? Differences by Sex, Social Class, and Ethnic Background." In James E. Curtis, Edward Grabb, and Neil Guppy, eds. *Social Inequality in Canada: Patterns, Problems, Policies.* 2d ed. Scarborough, Ont.: Prentice Hall, 1993: 214–32.

GURNETT, KATE. "On the Forefront of Feminism." *Albany Times Union* (July 5, 1998):G-1, G-6.

GWARTNEY-GIBBS, PATRICIA A., JEAN STOCKARD, and SUSANNE BOHMER. "Learning Courtship Agression: The Influence of Parents, Peers, and Personal Experiences." *Family Relations.* Vol. 36, No. 3 (July 1987):276–82.

GWYNNE, S.C., and JOHN F. DICKERSON. "Lost in the E-Mail." *Time.* Vol. 149, No. 15 (April 21, 1997):88–90.

HABERMAS, JÜRGEN. *Toward a Rational Society: Student Protest, Science, and Politics.* Jeremy J. Shapiro, trans. Boston: Beacon Press, 1970.

HACKER, HELEN MAYER. "Women as a Minority Group." *Social Forces.* Vol. 30 (October 1951):60–69.

———. "Women as a Minority Group: 20 Years Later." In Florence Denmark, ed., *Who Discriminates Against Women?* Beverly Hills, Calif.: Sage, 1974:124–34.

HACKMAN, J.R. "The Design of Work Teams." In J. Lorch, ed., *Handbook of Organizational Behavior.* Englewood Cliffs, N.J.: Prentice Hall, 1988:315–42.

HADDEN, JEFFREY K., and CHARLES E. SWAIN. *Prime Time Preachers: The Rising Power of Televangelism.* Reading, Mass.: Addison-Wesley, 1981.

HAFNER, KATIE. "Making Sense of the Internet." *Newsweek.* (October 24, 1994):46–48.

HAGAN, JOHN, and PATRICIA PARKER. "White-Collar Crime and Punishment: The Class Structure and Legal Sanctioning of Securities Violations." *American Sociological Review.* Vol. 50, No. 3 (June 1985):302–16.

HAIG, ROBIN ANDREW. *The Anatomy of Humor: Biopsychosocial and Therapeutic Perspectives.* Springfield, Ill.: Charles C. Thomas, 1988.

HALBERSTAM, DAVID. *The Reckoning.* New York: Avon Books, 1986.

HALL, DAVID J. "North-West Territories, 1870–1905." In *The Canadian Encyclopedia: Year 2000 Edition.* Toronto: McClelland & Stewart, 1999:1657.

HALL, JOHN R., and MARY JO NEITZ. *Culture: Sociological Perspectives.* Englewood Cliffs, N.J.: Prentice Hall, 1993.

HALLETT, M.E. "Nellie McClung." In *The Canadian Encyclopedia.* 2d ed., Vol. 2. Edmonton: Hurtig Publishers, 1988:1257.

HALLINAN, MAUREEN T. "The Sociological Study of Social Change." *American Sociological Review.* Vol. 62, No. 1 (February 1997):1–11.

HAMEL, RUTH. "Raging Against Aging." *American Demographics.* Vol. 12, No. 3 (March 1990):42–45.

HAMER, DEAN, and PETER COPELAND. *The Science of Desire: The Search for the Gay Gene and the Biology of Behavior.* New York: Simon & Schuster, 1994.

HAMILTON, DWIGHT. "50 Richest Canadians: It's So Much Better to Be Rich." *The Financial Post Magazine* (January 1996):14–28.

HAMRICK, MICHAEL H., DAVID J. ANSPAUGH, and GENE EZELL. *Health.* Columbus, Ohio: Merrill, 1986.

Handgun Control, Inc. Data, 1998 [online]. Available at www.handguncontrol.org.

HANEY, CRAIG, CURTIS BANKS, and PHILIP ZIMBARDO. "Interpersonal Dynamics in a Simulated Prison." *International Journal of Criminology and Penology.* Vol. 1 (1973):69–97.

HANNIGAN, JOHN A. "Sociology and the Environment." In Robert J. Brym, *New Society: Sociology for the 21st Century.* Toronto: Harcourt Brace, 1995.

HAREVEN, TAMARA K. "The Life Course and Aging in Historical Perspective." In Tamara K. Hareven and Kathleen J. Adams, eds., *Aging* and *Life Course Transitions: An Interdisciplinary Perspective.* New York: Guilford Press, 1982:1–26.

HAREVEN, TAMARA K., and RANDOLPH LANGENBACH. *Amoskeag: Life and Work in an American Factory City.* New York: Pantheon Books, 1978.

HARLAN, WILLIAM H. "Social Status of the Aged in Three Indian Villages." In Bernice L. Neugarten, ed., *Middle Age and Aging: A Reader in Social Psychology.* Chicago: University of Chicago Press, 1968:469–75.

HARLOW, HARRY F., and MARGARET KUENNE HARLOW. "Social Deprivation in Monkeys." *Scientific American.* Vol. 207 (November 1962):137–46.

HARRIES, KEITH D. *Serious Violence: Patterns of Homicide and Assault in America.* Springfield, Ill.: Charles C. Thomas, 1990.

HARRINGTON, MICHAEL. *The New American Poverty.* New York: Penguin Books, 1984.

HARRIS, CHAUNCEY D., and EDWARD L. ULLMAN. "The Nature of Cities." *The Annals.* Vol. 242 (November 1945):7–17.

HARRIS, MARVIN. *Cows, Pigs, Wars and Witches: The Riddles of Culture.* New York: Vintage Books, 1975.

———. "Why Men Dominate Women." *New York Times Magazine* (November 13, 1977):46, 115–23.

———. *Cultural Anthropology.* 2d ed. New York: Harper & Row, 1987.

HARRISON, PAUL. *Inside the Third World: The Anatomy of Poverty.* 2d ed. New York: Penguin Books, 1984.

HAVIGHURST, ROBERT J., BERNICE L. NEUGARTEN, and SHELDON S. TOBIN. "Disengagement and Patterns of Aging." In Bernice L. Neugarten, ed., *Middle Age and Aging: A Reader in Social Psychology.* Chicago: University of Chicago Press, 1968:161–72.

HAWTHORNE, PETER. "South Africa's Makeover." *Time.* Vol. 154, No. 2 (July 12, 1999).

HAYNEMAN, STEPHEN P., and WILLIAM A. LOXLEY. "The Effect of Primary-School Quality on Academic Achievement Across Twenty-nine High- and Low-Income Countries." *American Journal of Sociology.* Vol. 88, No. 6 (May 1983):1162–94.

HEALTH CANADA. *HIV and AIDS in Canada: Surveillance Report to December 31, 2002,* Division of HIV/AIDS Epidemiology and Surveillance, Centre for Infectious Disease Prevention and Control, Health Canada, 2003 [online]. Available at www.hc-sc.gc.ca/pphb-dgspsp/publicat/aids-sida/haic-vsac1202/index.html.

HEATH, JULIA A., and W. DAVID BOURNE. "Husbands and Housework: Parity or Parody?" *Social Science Quarterly.* Vol. 76, No. 1 (March 1995):195–202.

HELGESEN, SALLY. *The Female Advantage: Women's Ways of Leadership.* New York: Doubleday, 1990.

HELMES-HAYES, R. *A Quarter-Century of Sociology and the University of Toronto, 1963–1988.* Toronto: Canadian Scholars' Press, 1988.

HENLEY, NANCY, MYKOL HAMILTON, and BARRIE THORNE. "Womanspeak and Manspeak: Sex Differences in Communication, Verbal and Nonverbal." In John J. Macionis and Nijole V. Benokraitis, eds., *Seeing Ourselves: Classic, Contemporary, and Cross-Cultural Readings in Sociology.* 2d ed. Englewood Cliffs, N.J.: Prentice Hall, 1992:10–15.

HERDT, GILBERT H. "Semen Transactions in Sambian Culture." In David N. Suggs and Andrew W. Miracle, eds., *Culture and Human Sexuality.* Pacific Grove, Calif.: Brooks Cole, 1993:298–327.

HEREK, GREGORY M. "Myths about Sexual Orientation: A Lawyer's Guide to Social Science Research." *Law and Sexuality.* No. 1 (1991):133–72.

HERMAN, DIANNE. "The Rape Culture." In John J. Macionis and Nijole V. Benokraitis, eds., *Seeing Ourselves: Classic, Contemporary, and Cross-Cultural Readings in Sociology.* 5th ed. Upper Saddle River, N.J.: Prentice Hall, 2001.

HERMAN, EDWARD S. *Corporate Control, Corporate Power: A Twentieth Century Fund Study.* New York: Cambridge University Press, 1981.

HEROLD, E.S. *Sexual Behaviour of Canadian Young People.* Markham, Ont.: Fitzhenry and Whiteside, 1984.

HERRNSTEIN, RICHARD J. *IQ and the Meritocracy.* Boston: Little, Brown, 1973.

HERRNSTEIN, RICHARD J., and CHARLES MURRAY. *The Bell Curve: Intelligence and Class Structure in American Life.* New York: Free Press, 1994.

HERSCH, JONI, and SHELLY WHITE-MEANS. "Employer-Sponsored Health and Pension Benefits and the Gender/Race Wage Gap." *Social Science Quarterly.* Vol. 74, No. 4 (December 1993):850–66.

HESS, BETH B. "Breaking and Entering the Establishment: Committing Social Change and Confronting the Backlash." *Social Problems.* Vol. 46, No. 1 (February 1999):1–12.

HEWLETT, SYLVIA ANN. "The Feminization of the Work Force." *New Perspectives Quarterly.* Vol. 7, No. 1 (Winter 1990):13–15.

———. *A Lesser Life: The Myth of Women's Liberation in America.* New York: William Morrow, 1986.

HIGHWAY, TOMSON. *Kiss of the Fur Queen.* Toronto: Doubleday, 1999.

HILLER, HARRY H. *Canadian Society: A Macro Analysis.* 2d ed. Scarborough, Ont.: Prentice Hall, 1991.

———. *Canadian Society: A Macro Analysis.* 3d ed. Scarborough, Ont.: Prentice Hall, 1996; 4th ed., 2000.

HIROSHI, MANNARI. *The Japanese Business Leaders.* Tokyo: University of Tokyo Press, 1974.

HIRSCHI, TRAVIS. *Causes of Delinquency.* Berkeley: University of California Press, 1969.

HIRSCHI, TRAVIS, and MICHAEL GOTTFREDSON. "Age and the Explanation of Crime." *American Journal of Sociology.* Vol. 89, No. 3 (November 1983):552–84.

HOCHSCHILD, ARLIE, with ANNE MACHUNG. *The Second Shift: Working Parents and the Revolution at Home.* New York: Viking Books, 1989.

HODGE, ROBERT W., DONALD J. TREIMAN, and PETER H. ROSSI. "A Comparative Study of Occupational Prestige." In Reinhard Bendix and Seymour Martin Lipset, eds., *Class, Status, and Power: Social Stratification in Comparative Perspective.* 2d ed. New York: Free Press, 1966:309–21.

HOERR, JOHN. "The Payoff from Teamwork." *Business Week.* No. 3114 (July 10, 1989):56–62.

HOGUE, CHERYL. "U.S. Exports of Hazardous Waste to Canada Continue to Rise." *Chemical and Engineering News* (November 13, 2000):26.

HOLMSTROM, DAVID. "Abuse of Elderly, Even by Adult Children, Gets More Attention and Official Concern." *Christian Science Monitor* (July 28, 1994):1.

HOWLETT, KAREN, et al. "Enron Deception Aided by CIBC: U.S. Report." *The Globe and Mail* (July 29, 2003):A1.

HUET-COX, ROCIO. "Medical Education: New Wine in Old Wine Skins." In Victor W. Sidel and Ruth Sidel, eds., *Reforming Medicine: Lessons of the Last Quarter Century.* New York: Pantheon Books, 1984:129–49.

HUFFMAN, MATT L., STEVEN C. VELASCO, and WILLIAM T. BIELBY. "Where Sex Composition Matters Most: Comparing the Effects of Job Versus Occupational Sex Composition of Earnings." *Sociological Focus.* Vol. 29, No. 3 (August 1996):189–207.

HULL, JON D. "A Boy and His Gun." *Time* (August 2, 1993):29–35.

HULS, GLENNA. Personal communication, 1987.

HUMPHREY, CRAIG R., and FREDERICK R. BUTTEL. *Environment, Energy, and Society.* Belmont, Calif.: Wadsworth, 1982.

HUMPHREYS, ADRIAN. "First Gay Marriage Legal, for Now." *National Post* (January 15, 2001):A1.

———. "He Is No Longer an Unknown Child." *National Post* (November 7, 2002):3.

HUMPHRIES, SALLY. "The Intensification of Traditional Agriculture among Yucatec Maya Farmers: Facing up to the Dilemma of Livelihood Sustainability." *Human Ecology.* Vol. 21, No. 1 (1993):87–102.

HUMPHRY, DEREK. *Final Exit: The Practicalities of Self-Deliverance and Assisted Suicide for the Dying.* Eugene, Ore.: The Hemlock Society, 1991.

HUNT, MORTON. *Sexual Behavior in the 1970s.* Chicago: Playboy Press, 1974.

HUNTER, JAMES DAVISON. *American Evangelicalism: Conservative Religion and the Quandary of Modernity.* New Brunswick, N.J.: Rutgers University Press, 1983.

———. "Conservative Protestantism." In Philip E. Hammond, ed., *The Sacred in a Secular Age.* Berkeley: University of California Press, 1985:50–66.

———. *Evangelicalism: The Coming Generation.* Chicago: University of Chicago Press, 1987.

———. *Culture Wars: The Struggle to Define America.* New York: Basic Books, 1991.

HURN, CHRISTOPHER. *The Limits and Possibilities of Schooling.* Needham Heights, Mass.: Allyn & Bacon, 1978.

HURST, L. "Tuberculosis Makes a Quiet Return." *Toronto Star* (November 8, 1992):A1, A10.

HURTIG, MEL. *The Betrayal of Canada.* Toronto: Stoddart Publishing, 1991.

———. *A New and Better Canada: Principles and Policies of a New Canadian Political Party.* Toronto: Stoddart, 1992.

HUTCHINGSON, JAMES E. "Science and Religion." *The Herald* (Dade County, Florida) (December 25, 1994):1M, 6M.

HYMOWITZ, CAROL. "World's Poorest Women Advance by Entrepreneurship." *Wall Street Journal* (September 9, 1995):B1.

IBM. "Focus on E-business." *The Globe and Mail* (January 28, 1998):Section C.

IBRAHIM, YOUSSEF. "Finland Suddenly Takes Over as World's Most Wired Country." *The Globe and Mail* (February 1, 1997):A16.

IDE, THOMAS R., and ARTHUR J. CORDELL. "Automating Work." *Society.* Vol. 31, No. 6 (September–October 1994):65–71.

ILLICH, IVAN. *Medical Nemesis: The Expropriation of Health.* New York: Pantheon Books, 1976.

INDIAN AND NORTHERN AFFAIRS CANADA. "Health and Social Indicators," updated December 19, 2002 [online]. Available at www.ainc-inac.gc.ca/gs/soci_e.html.

INTER-PARLIAMENTARY UNION. *Men and Women in Politics: Democracy in the Making.* Geneva: 1997.

IPSOS-REID. "Same-Sex Marriage: The Debate Enjoined." August 8, 2003 [online]. Available at www.ipsos-reid.com/media/dsp_displaypr_cdn.cfm?id_to_view=1877.

IRWIN, JOHN. *Prison in Turmoil.* Boston: Little, Brown, 1980.

ISAJIW, WSEVELOD W. "Definitions of Ethnicity." In Rita M. Bienvenue and Jay E. Goldstein, *Ethnicity and Ethnic Relations in Canada*. 2d ed. Toronto: Butterworths, 1985:5–18.

ISAY, RICHARD A. *Being Homosexual: Gay Men and Their Development*. New York: Farrar, Straus & Giroux, 1989.

JACOBS, DAVID. "Inequality and Police Strength." *American Sociological Review*. Vol. 44, No. 6 (December 1979):913–25.

JACOBS, DEAN. "Walpole Island: Sustainable Development." In Diane Engelstad and John Bird, eds., *Nation to Nation: Aboriginal Sovereignty and the Future of Canada*. Concord, Ont.: House of Anansi Press, 1992:179–85.

JACOBS, JANE. *The Death and Life of Great American Cities*. New York: Random House, 1961.

———. *The Economy of Cities*. New York: Vintage Books, 1970.

———. *Cities and the Wealth of Nations*. Toronto: Random House, 1984.

JACOBSON, JODI L. "Closing the Gender Gap in Development." In Lester R. Brown et al., eds., *State of the World 1993: A Worldwatch Institute Report on Progress Toward a Sustainable Society*. New York: Norton, 1993:61–79.

JACOBY, RUSSELL, and NAOMI GLAUBERMAN, eds. *The Bell Curve Debate*. New York: Random House, 1995.

JAENEN, CORNELIUS. "Mutilated Multiculturalism." In J. Donald Wilson, ed., *Canadian Education in the 1980s*. Calgary: Detselig Enterprises, 1981.

JAGGER, ALISON. "Political Philosophies of Women's Liberation." In Laurel Richardson and Verta Taylor, eds., *Feminist Frontiers: Rethinking Sex, Gender, and Society*. Reading, Mass.: Addison-Wesley, 1983.

JANIS, IRVING. *Victims of Groupthink*. Boston: Houghton Mifflin, 1972.

———. *Crucial Decisions: Leadership in Policymaking and Crisis Management*. New York: Free Press, 1989.

JANUS, CHRISTOPHER G. "Slavery Abolished? Only Officially." *Christian Science Monitor* (May 17, 1996):18.

JENCKS, CHRISTOPHER. "Genes and Crime." *The New York Review* (February 12, 1987):33–41.

JENKINS, J. CRAIG, and CHARLES PERROW. "Insurgency of the Powerless: Farm Worker Movements (1946–1972)." *American Sociological Review*. Vol. 42, No. 2 (April 1977):249–68.

JENKINS, J. CRAIG, and MICHAEL WALLACE. "The Generalized Action Potential of Protest Movements: The New Class, Social Trends, and Political Exclusion Explanations." *Sociological Forum*. Vol. 11, No. 2 (June 1996):183–207.

JOHNSON, CATHRYN. "Gender, Legitimate Authority, and Leader-Subordinate Conversations." *American Sociological Review*. Vol. 59, No. 1 (February 1994):122–35.

JOHNSON, F. HENRY. *A Brief History of Canadian Education*. Toronto: McGraw-Hill, 1968.

JOHNSON, HOLLY. *Dangerous Domains: Violence Against Women in Canada*. Toronto: Nelson Canada, 1996.

JOHNSON, NORRIS R. "Panic at 'The Who Concert Stampede': An Empirical Assessment." *Social Problems*. Vol. 34, No. 4 (October 1987):362–73.

JOHNSON, PAUL. "The Seven Deadly Sins of Terrorism." In Benjamin Netanyahu, ed., *International Terrorism*. New Brunswick, N.J.: Transaction Books, 1981:12–22.

JOHNSTON, R.J. "Residential Area Characteristics." In D. T. Herbert and R. J. Johnston, eds., *Social Areas in Cities. Vol. 1: Spatial Processes and Form*. New York: Wiley, 1976:193–235.

JONES, FRANK. "Are Children Going to Religious Services?" In Statistics Canada, *Canadian Social Trends*. Vol. 3. Toronto: Thompson Educational Publishing, 2000.

KADUSHIN, CHARLES. "Friendship Among the French Financial Elite." *American Sociological Review*. Vol. 60, No. 2 (April 1995):202–21.

KAIN, EDWARD L. "A Note on the Integration of AIDS into the Sociology of Human Sexuality." *Teaching Sociology*. Vol. 15, No. 4 (July 1987):320–23.

———. *The Myth of Family Decline: Understanding Families in a World of Rapid Social Change*. Lexington, Mass.: Lexington Books, 1990.

KAIN, EDWARD L., and SHANNON HART. "AIDS and the Family: A Content Analysis of Media Coverage." Presented to National Council on Family Relations, Atlanta, 1987.

KALISH, CAROL B. "International Crime Rates." Bureau of Justice Statistics Special Report, May. Washington, D.C.: U. S. Government Printing Office, 1988.

KALISH, RICHARD A. "The New Ageism and the Failure Models: A Polemic." *The Gerontologist*. Vol. 19, No. 4 (August 1979):398–402.

———. *Late Adulthood: Perspectives on Human Development*. 2d ed. Monterey, Calif.: Brooks/Cole, 1982.

KALLEBERG, ARNE L., and MARK E. VAN BUREN. "Is Better Better? Explaining the Relationship Between Organization Size and Job Rewards." *American Sociological Review*. Vol. 61, No. 1 (February 1996):47–66.

KALLEN, EVELYN. *Ethnicity and Human Rights in Canada*. Don Mills, Ontario: Oxford University Press, 2003.

KAMINER, WENDY. "Volunteers: Who Knows What's in It for Them." *Ms*. (December 1984):93–94, 96, 126–28.

KANTER, ROSABETH MOSS. *Men and Women of the Corporation*. New York: Basic Books, 1977.

———. *The Change Masters: Innovation and Entrepreneurship in the American Corporation*. New York: Simon & Schuster, 1983.

———. *When Giants Learn to Dance: Mastering the Challenges of Strategy, Management, and Careers in the 1990s*. New York: Simon & Schuster, 1989.

KANTER, ROSABETH MOSS, and BARRY A. STEIN. "The Gender Pioneers: Women in an Industrial Sales Force." In R.M. Kanter and B.A. Stein, eds., *Life in Organizations*. New York: Basic Books, 1979:134–60.

———. *A Tale of "O": On Being Different in an Organization*. New York: Harper & Row, 1980.

KANTROWITZ, BARBARA. "Mothers on Their Own." *Newsweek* (December 23, 1985):66–67.

KAPFERER, JEAN-NOEL. "How Rumors Are Born." *Society*. Vol. 29, No. 5 (July–August 1992):53–60.

KAPLAN, DAVID E., and MICHAEL SCHAFFER. "Losing the Psywar." *U.S. News & World Report* (October 8, 2001):46.

KAPLAN, ERIC B., et al. "The Usefulness of Preoperative Laboratory Screening." *Journal of the American Medical Association*. Vol. 253, No. 24 (June 28, 1985):3576–81.

KAPTCHUK, TED. "The Holistic Logic of Chinese Medicine." In Shepard Bliss et al., eds., *The New Holistic Health Handbook*. Lexington, Mass.: The Steven Greene Press/Penguin Books, 1985:41.

KASARDA, JOHN D. "Entry-Level Jobs, Mobility and Urban Minority Employment." *Urban Affairs Quarterly*. Vol. 19, No. 1 (September 1983):21–40.

KATES, ROBERT W. "Ending Hunger: Current Status and Future Prospects." *Consequences*. Vol. 2, No. 2 (1996):3–11.

KAUFMAN, ROBERT L., and SEYMOUR SPILERMAN. "The Age Structures of Occupations and Jobs." *American Journal of Sociology*. Vol. 87, No. 4 (January 1982):827–51.

KAUFMAN, WALTER. *Religions in Four Dimensions: Existential, Aesthetic, Historical and Comparative*. New York: Reader's Digest Press, 1976.

KEITH, JULIE, and LAURA LANDRY. "Well-being of Older Canadians." In Craig McKie and Keith Thompson, eds. *Canadian Social Trends*. Toronto: Thompson Educational Publishing, 1994.

KEITH, PAT M., and ROBERT B. SCHAFER. "They Hate to Cook: Patterns of Distress in an Ordinary Role." *Sociological Focus*. Vol. 27, No. 4 (October 1994):289–301.

KELLER, HELEN. *The Story of My Life*. New York: Doubleday, Page, 1903.

KELLERT, STEPHEN R., and F. HERBERT BORMANN. "Closing the Circle: Weaving Strands Among Ecology, Economics, and Ethics." In F. Herbert Bormann and Stephen R. Kellert, eds., *Ecology, Economics, and Ethics: The Broken Circle*. New Haven, Conn.: Yale University Press, 1991:205–10.

KEMP, ALICE ABEL, and SHELLEY COVERMAN. "Marginal Jobs or Marginal Workers: Identifying Sex Differences in Low-Skill Occupations." *Sociological Focus*. Vol. 22, No. 1 (February 1989):19–37.

KERCKHOFF, ALAN C., RICHARD T. CAMPBELL, and IDEE WINFIELD-LAIRD. "Social Mobility in Great Britain and the United States." *American Journal of Sociology*. Vol. 91, No. 2 (September 1985):281–308.

KIDD, QUENTIN, and AIE-RIE LEE. "Postmaterialist Values and the Environment: A Critique and Reappraisal." *Social Science Quarterly*. Vol. 78, No. 1 (March 1997):1–15.

KIDRON, MICHAEL, and RONALD SEGAL. *The New State of the World Atlas*. New York: Simon & Schuster, 1991.

KILBOURNE, BROCK K. "The Conway and Siegelman Claims Against Religious Cults: An Assessment of Their Data." *Journal for the Scientific Study of Religion*. Vol. 22, No. 4 (December 1983):380–85.

KING, KATHLEEN PIKER, and DENNIS E. CLAYSON. "The Differential Perceptions of Male and Female Deviants." *Sociological Focus*. Vol. 21, No. 2 (April 1988):153–64.

KINSEY, ALFRED, et al. *Sexual Behavior in the Human Male*. Philadelphia: Saunders, 1948.

———. *Sexual Behavior in the Human Female*. Philadelphia: Saunders, 1953.

KINSMAN, GARY. *The Regulation of Desire: Homo and Hetero Sexualities*. Montreal: Black Rose Books, 1996.

KISER, EDGAR, and JOACHIM SCHNEIDER. "Bureaucracy and Efficiency: An Analysis of Taxation in Early Modern Prussia." *American Sociological Review*. Vol. 59, No. 2 (April 1994):187–204.

KISHOR, SUNITA. "'May God Give Sons to All': Gender and Child Mortality in India." *American Sociological Review*. Vol. 58, No. 2 (April 1993):247–65.

KITSON, GAY C., and HELEN J. RASCHKE. "Divorce Research: What We Know, What We Need to Know." *Journal of Divorce*. Vol. 4, No. 3 (Spring 1981):1–37.

KITTRIE, NICHOLAS N. *The Right to Be Different: Deviance and Enforced Therapy*. Baltimore: Johns Hopkins University Press, 1971.

KITZ, JANET E. *Shattered City: The Halifax Explosion and the Road to Recovery*. Halifax: Nimbus Publishing Limited, 1989.

KLUCKHOHN, CLYDE. "As an Anthropologist Views It." In Albert Deuth, ed., *Sex Habits of American Men*. New York: Prentice Hall, 1948.

KNOWLES, VALERIE. *Strangers at Our Gates: Canadian Immigration and Immigration Policy, 1540–1990*. Toronto: Dundurn, 1997.

KOCH, HOWARD. *The Panic Broadcast: Portrait of an Event*. Boston: Little, Brown, 1970.

KOHLBERG, LAWRENCE. *The Psychology of Moral Development: The Nature and Validity of Moral Stages*. New York: Harper & Row, 1981.

KOHLBERG, LAWRENCE, and CAROL GILLIGAN. "The Adolescent as Philosopher: The Discovery of Self in a Postconventional World." *Daedalus*. Vol. 100 (Fall 1971):1051–86.

KOHN, MELVIN L. *Class and Conformity: A Study in Values*. 2d ed. Homewood, Ill.: Dorsey Press, 1977.

———. "The 'Bell Curve' from the Perspective of Research on Social Structure and Personality." *Sociological Forum*. Vol. 11, No. 2 (1996):395.

KOHN, MELVIN L., and CARMI SCHOOLER. "Job Conditions and Personality: A Longitudinal Assessment of Their Reciprocal Effects." *American Journal of Sociology*. Vol. 87, No. 6 (May 1982):1257–83.

KOLATA, GINA. "When Grandmother Is the Mother, Until Birth." *New York Times* (August 5, 1991):1, 11.

KOMAROVSKY, MIRRA. *Blue Collar Marriage*. New York: Vintage Books, 1967.

———. "Cultural Contradictions and Sex Roles: The Masculine Case." *American Journal of Sociology*. Vol. 78, No. 4 (January 1973):873–84.

KORNHAUSER, WILLIAM. *The Politics of Mass Society*. New York: Free Press, 1959.

KOWALEWSKI, DAVID, and KAREN L. PORTER. "Ecoprotest: Alienation, Deprivation, or Resources." *Social Sciences Quarterly*. Vol. 73, No. 3 (September 1992):523–34.

KOZOL, JONATHAN. *Prisoners of Silence: Breaking the Bonds of Adult Illiteracy in the United States*. New York: Continuum, 1980.

———. *Illiterate America*. Garden City, N.Y.: Doubleday, 1985.

———. *Rachel and Her Children: Homeless Families in America*. New York: Crown Publishers, 1988.

KRAUSS, CLIFFORD. "In God We Trust . . . Canadians Aren't So Sure." *New York Times*, March 26, 2003 [online]. Available at www.nytimes.com/2003/03/26/international/americas/26LETT.html?ex=1049718839&ei=1&en=7b6d16eaa7fa6364.

KRIESI, HANSPETER. "New Social Movements and the New Class in the Netherlands." *American Journal of Sociology*. Vol. 94, No. 5 (March 1989):1078–116.

KRISBERG, BARRY, and IRA SCHWARTZ. "Rethinking Juvenile Justice." *Crime and Delinquency*. Vol. 29, No. 3 (July 1983):333–64.

KRUKS, GABRIEL N. "Gay and Lesbian Homeless/Street Youth: Special Issues and Concerns." *Journal of Adolescent Health*. Special Issue. No. 12 (1991):515–18.

KÜBLER-ROSS, ELISABETH. *On Death and Dying*. New York: Macmillan, 1969.

KUHN, THOMAS. *The Structure of Scientific Revolutions*. 2d ed. Chicago: University of Chicago Press, 1970.

KUZNETS, SIMON. "Economic Growth and Income Inequality." *The American Economic Review*. Vol. XLV, No. 1 (March 1955):1–28.

———. *Modern Economic Growth: Rate, Structure, and Spread*. New Haven, Conn.: Yale University Press, 1966.

LACAYO, RICHARD. "Blood in the Stands." *Time*. Vol. 125, No. 23 (June 10, 1985):38–39, 41.

LADD, JOHN. "The Definition of Death and the Right to Die." In John Ladd, ed., *Ethical Issues Relating to Life and Death*. New York: Oxford University Press, 1979:118–45.

LAMBERG-KARLOVSKY, C.C., and MARTHA LAMBERG-KARLOVSKY. "An Early City in Iran." In *Cities: Their Origin, Growth, and Human Impact*. San Francisco: Freeman, 1973:28–37.

LANDERS, ANN. Syndicated column: *Dallas Morning News* (July 8, 1984):4F.

LANDERS, RENE M. "Gender, Race, and the State Courts." *Radcliffe Quarterly*. Vol. 76, No. 4 (December 1990):6–9.

LANE, DAVID. "Social Stratification and Class." In Erik P. Hoffman and Robbin F. Laird, eds., *The Soviet Polity in the Modern Era*. New York: Aldine, 1984:563–605.

LANG, KURT, and GLADYS ENGEL LANG. *Collective Dynamics*. New York: Thomas Y. Crowell, 1961.

LANGER, VALERIE. "It Happened Suddenly (Over a Long Period of Time): A Clayoquot History." [online] Available at www.ancientrainforest.org/history.htm, 1996.

LAPPÉ, FRANCES MOORE, and JOSEPH COLLINS. *World Hunger: Twelve Myths*. New York: Grove Press/Food First Books, 1986.

LAPPÉ, FRANCES MOORE, JOSEPH COLLINS, and DAVID KINLEY. *Aid as Obstacle: Twenty Questions about Our Foreign Policy and the Hungry*. San Francisco: Institute for Food and Development Policy, 1981.

LAPRAIRIE, CAROL P. "Community Types, Crime and Police Services on Canadian Indian Reserves." *Journal of Research in Crime and Delinquency*. Vol. 25, No. 4 (1988):375–91.

LARMER, BROOK. "Dead End Kids." *Newsweek* (May 25, 1992):38–40.

LASLETT, PETER. *The World We Have Lost: England Before the Industrial Age*. 3d ed. New York: Charles Scribner's Sons, 1984.

LATOUCHE, DANIEL. "Québec." In *The Canadian Encyclopedia*. 2d ed., Vol. 3. Edmonton: Hurtig Publishers, 1988:1793–802.

LAUMANN, EDWARD O., JOHN H. GAGNON, ROBERT T. MICHAEL, and STUART MICHAELS. *The Social Organization of Sexuality: Sexual Practices in the United States*. Chicago: University of Chicago Press, 1994.

LAXER, GORDON. *Open for Business: The Roots of Foreign Ownership in Canada*. Toronto: Oxford University Press, 1989.

LEACOCK, ELEANOR. "Women's Status in Egalitarian Societies: Implications for Social Evolution." *Current Anthropology*. Vol. 19, No. 2 (June 1978):247–75.

LEAVITT, JUDITH WALZER. "Women and Health in America: An Overview." In Judith Walzer Leavitt, ed., *Women and Health in America*. Madison: University of Wisconsin Press, 1984:3–7.

LE BON, GUSTAVE. *The Crowd: A Study of the Popular Mind*. New York: Viking Press, 1960; orig. 1895.

LELAND, JOHN. "Bisexuality." *Newsweek* (July 17, 1995):44–49.

LEMERT, EDWIN M. *Social Pathology*. New York: McGraw-Hill, 1951.

———. *Human Deviance, Social Problems, and Social Control*. 2d ed. Englewood Cliffs, N.J.: Prentice Hall, 1972.

LENGERMANN, PATRICIA MADOO, and RUTH A. WALLACE. *Gender in America: Social Control and Social Change*. Englewood Cliffs, N.J.: Prentice Hall, 1985.

LENNON, MARY CLARE, and SARAH ROSENFELD. "Relative Fairness and the Doctrine of Housework: The Importance of Options." *American Journal of Sociology*. Vol. 100, No. 2 (September 1994):506–31.

LENSKI, GERHARD, PATRICK NOLAN, and JEAN LENSKI. *Human Societies: An Introduction to Macrosociology*. 7th ed. New York: McGraw-Hill, 1995.

LENTON, RHONDA L. "Homicide in Canada and the U.S.A.: A Critique of the Hagan Thesis." In Alexander Himelfarb and James Richardson, eds., *Sociology for Canadians*. 2d ed. Toronto: McGraw-Hill Ryerson, 1989.

———. "Techniques of Child Discipline and Abuse by Parents." *Canadian Review of Sociology and Anthropology*, Vol. 7, No. 2 (1990):157–85.

LEONARD, EILEEN B. *Women, Crime, and Society: A Critique of Theoretical Criminology*. New York: Longman, 1982.

LESLIE, GERALD R., and SHEILA K. KORMAN. *The Family in Social Context*. 7th ed. New York: Oxford University Press, 1989.

LESTER, DAVID. *The Death Penalty: Issues and Answers*. Springfield, Ill.: Charles C. Thomas, 1987.

LeVAY, SIMON. *The Sexual Brain*. Cambridge, Mass.: MIT Press, 1993.

LEVER, JANET. "Sex Differences in the Complexity of Children's Play and Games." *American Sociological Review*. Vol. 43, No. 4 (August 1978):471–83.

LEVIN, B. "Tuition Fees and University Accessibility." *Canadian Public Policy*. Vol. 16, No. 1 (March 1993).

LEVINE, MICHAEL P. *Student Eating Disorders: Anorexia Nervosa and Bulimia*. Washington, D.C.: National Educational Association, 1987.

LEVINSON, DANIEL J., with CHARLOTTE N. DARROW, EDWARD B. KLEIN, MARIA H. LEVINSON, and BRAXTON McKEE. *The Seasons of a Man's Life*. New York: Alfred A. Knopf, 1978.

LEVY, FRANK. *Dollars and Dreams: The Changing American Income Distribution*. New York: Russell Sage Foundation, 1987.

LEWIS, FLORA. "The Roots of Revolution." *New York Times Magazine* (November 11, 1984):70–71, 74, 77–78, 82, 84, 86.

LEWIS, OSCAR. *The Children of Sanchez*. New York: Random House, 1961.

LEWTHWAITE, GILBERT A., and GREGORY KANE. "Bought and Freed." *Baltimore Sun* (June 18, 1996):A1, A8.

LI, JIANG HONG, and ROGER A. WOJTKIEWICZ. "A New Look at the Effects of Family Structure on Status Attainment." *Social Science Quarterly*. Vol. 73, No. 3 (September 1992):581–95.

LI, PETER S. *Ethnic Inequality in a Class Society*. Toronto: Wall and Thompson, 1988.

———. *The Making of Post-War Canada*. Toronto: Oxford University Press, 1996.

———. *Destination Canada: Immigration Debates and Issues*. Toronto: Oxford University Press Canada, 2003.

LIAZOS, ALEXANDER. "The Poverty of the Sociology of Deviance: Nuts, Sluts and Perverts." *Social Problems*. Vol. 20, No. 1 (Summer 1972):103–20.

LICHTER, S. ROBERT, STANLEY ROTHMAN, and LINDA R. ROTHMAN. *The Media Elite: America's New Powerbrokers*. Bethesda, Md.: Adler & Adler, 1986.

LICHTER, S. ROBERT, STANLEY ROTHMAN, and LINDA S. LICHTER. *The Media Elite: America's New Powerbrokers*. New York: Hastings House, 1990.

LINDEN, EUGENE. "Can Animals Think?" *Time*. Vol. 141, No. 12 (March 22, 1993):54–61.

———. "More Power to Women, Fewer Mouths to Feed." *Time*. Vol. 144, No. 13 (September 26, 1994):64–65.

LINDSTROM, BONNIE. "Chicago's Post-Industrial Suburbs." *Sociological Focus*. Vol. 28, No. 4 (October 1995):399–412.

LINTON, RALPH. "One Hundred Percent American." *The American Mercury*. Vol. 40, No. 160 (April 1937):427–29.

————. *The Study of Man*. New York: D. Appleton-Century, 1937.

LIPOVENKO, DOROTHY. "Golden Handshakes Launch New Careers." *The Globe and Mail* (January 29, 1996):A1, A6.

LIPS, HILARY. *Sex and Gender: An Introduction*. 2d ed. Mountain View, Calif.: Mayfield Publishing Co., 1993.

LIPSET, SEYMOUR MARTIN. *Political Man: The Social Bases of Politics*. Garden City, N.Y.: Anchor/Doubleday, 1963.

————. *Canada and the United States*. Charles F. Donan and John H. Sigler, eds., Englewood Cliffs, N.J.: Prentice Hall, 1985.

————. *Continental Divide: The Values and Institutions of the United States and Canada*. New York: Routledge, 1991.

LIPSET, SEYMOUR MARTIN, and REINHARD BENDIX. *Social Mobility in Industrial Society*. Berkeley: University of California Press, 1967.

LISKA, ALLEN E. *Perspectives on Deviance*. 3d ed. Englewood Cliffs, N.J.: Prentice Hall, 1991.

LISKA, ALLEN E., and MARK TAUSIG. "Theoretical Interpretations of Social Class and Racial Differentials in Legal Decision Making for Juveniles." *Sociological Quarterly*. Vol. 20, No. 2 (Spring 1979):197–207.

LISKA, ALLEN E., and BARBARA D. WARNER. "Functions of Crime: A Paradoxical Process." *American Journal of Sociology*. Vol. 96, No. 6 (May 1991):1441–63.

LIVERNASH, ROBERT, and ERIC RODENBURG. "Population Change, Resources, and the Environment." *Population Bulletin*. Vol. 53, No. 1 (March 1998).

LIVINGSTONE, DAVID W. "Public Education at the Crossroads: Confronting Underemployment in a Knowledge Society." In Dan Glenday and Ann Duffy, eds., *Canadian Society: Meeting the Challenges of the Twenty-First Century*. Toronto: Oxford University Press, 2001.

LIVINGSTONE, D.W., and MEG LUXTON. "Gender Consciousness at Work: Modification of the Male Breadwinner Norm Among Steelworkers and Their Spouses." In E.D. Nelson and B.W. Robinson, eds., *Gender in the 1990s: Images, Realities, and Issues*. Scarborough, Ont.: Nelson Canada, 1995:172–200.

LO, CLARENCE Y. H. "Countermovements and Conservative Movements in the Contemporary U.S." *Annual Review of Sociology*. Vol. 8. Palo Alto, Calif.: Annual Reviews, 1982:107–34.

LOFLAND, LYN. *A World of Strangers*. New York: Basic Books, 1973.

LOHR, STEVE. "British Health Service Faces a Crisis in Funds and Delays." *New York Times* (August 7, 1988):1, 12.

LORD, WALTER. *A Night to Remember*. Rev. ed. New York: Holt, Rinehart & Winston, 1976.

LORENZ, KONRAD. *On Aggression*. New York: Harcourt, Brace & World, 1966.

LOY, PAMELA HEWITT, and LEA P. STEWART. "The Extent and Effects of Sexual Harassment of Working Women." *Sociological Focus*. Vol. 17, No. 1 (January 1984):31–43.

LUKER, KRISTEN. *Abortion and the Politics of Motherhood*. Berkeley: University of California Press, 1984.

LUND, DALE A. "Conclusions about Bereavement in Later Life and Implications for Interventions and Future Research." In Dale A. Lund, ed., *Older Bereaved Spouses: Research With Practical Applications*. London: Taylor-Francis-Hemisphere, 1989:217–31.

LUND, DALE A., MICHAEL S. CASERTA, and MARGARET F. DIMOND. "Gender Differences Through Two Years of Bereavement Among the Elderly." *The Gerontologist*. Vol. 26, No. 3 (1986):314–20.

LUNMAN, KIM, "National Response Needed, Cauchon Maintains." *The Globe and Mail* (June 11, 2003):A4.

LUPRI, EUGENE. "Male Violence in the Home." In Craig McKie and K. Thompson, eds., *Social Trends in Canada*. Toronto: Thompson Educational Publishers, 1988:170–72.

————. "Why Does Family Violence Occur?" In Lorne Tepperman and James Curtis, eds., *Everyday Life*. Toronto: McGraw-Hill Ryerson, 1992:289–300.

————. "Intimate Violence: Male Abuse," University of Calgary: unpublished manuscript, 2002.

LUTZ, CATHERINE A. *Unnatural Emotions: Everyday Sentiments on a Micronesia Atoll and Their Challenge to Western Theory*. Chicago: University of Chicago Press, 1988.

LUTZ, CATHERINE A., and GEOFFREY M. WHITE. "The Anthropology of Emotions." In Bernard J. Siegel, Alan R. Beals, and Stephen A. Tyler, eds., *Annual Review of Anthropology*. Palo Alto, Calif.: Annual Reviews, Vol. 15 (1986):405–36.

LUXTON, MEG. *More Than a Labour of Love*. Toronto: Women's Press, 1980.

LYALL, SARAH, and ROBIN POGREBIN. "Desperately Seeking Diana." *The Globe and Mail* (September 11, 1997).

LYND, ROBERT S. *Knowledge For What? The Place of Social Science in American Culture*. Princeton, N.J.: Princeton University Press, 1967.

LYNOTT, PATRICIA PASSUTH, and BARBARA J. LOGUE. "The 'Hurried Child': The Myth of Lost Childhood on Contemporary American Society." *Sociological Forum*. Vol. 8, No. 3 (September 1993):471–91.

MA, LI-CHEN. Personal communication, 1987.

MABRY, MARCUS. "New Hope for Old Unions?" *Newsweek* (February 24, 1992):39.

MABRY, MARCUS, and TOM MASLAND. "The Man after Mandela." *Newsweek* (June 7, 1999):54–55.

MCADAM, DOUG. *Political Process and the Development of Black Insurgency, 1930–1970*. Chicago: University of Chicago Press, 1982.

————. *Freedom Summer*. New York: Oxford University Press, 1988.

————. "The Biographical Consequences of Activism." *American Sociological Review*. Vol. 54, No. 5 (October 1989):744–60.

————. "Gender as a Mediator of the Activist Experience: The Case of Freedom Summer." *American Journal of Sociology*. Vol. 97, No. 5 (March 1992):1211–40.

MCADAM, DOUG, JOHN D. MCCARTHY, and MAYER N. ZALD. "Social Movements." In Neil J. Smelser, ed., *Handbook of Sociology*. Newbury Park, Calif.: Sage, 1988:695–737.

MCALL, CHRISTOPHER. *Class, Ethnicity and Social Inequality*. Montreal and Kingston: McGill-Queen's University Press, 1990.

MCCARTHY, JOHN D., and MAYER N. ZALD. "Resource Mobilization and Social Movements: A Partial Theory." *American Journal of Sociology*. Vol. 82, No. 6 (May 1977):1212–41.

MCCLAIN, PAULA DENISE. *Alienation and Resistance: The Political Behaviour of Afro-Canadians*. Palo Alto, California: R&E Research Associates, 1979.

MACCOBY, ELEANOR EMMONS, and CAROL NAGY JACKLIN. *The Psychology of Sex Differences*. Palo Alto, Calif.: Stanford University Press, 1974.

MCCORMICK, NAOMI B. *Sexual Salvation*. Westport, Conn.: Praeger, 1994.

MCDANIEL, SUSAN. "Emotional Support and Family Contacts of Older Canadians." In Craig McKie and Keith Thompson, eds., *Canadian Social Trends*. Vol. 2. Toronto: Thompson Educational Publishing, 1994:129–32.

MCDONALD, KIM. A. "Debate over How to Gauge Global Warming Heats Up Meeting of Climatologists." *Chronicle of Higher Education*. Vol. XLV, No. 22 (February 5, 1999):A17.

MCDONALD, LYNN. *The Women Founders of the Social Sciences*. Ottawa: Carleton University Press, 1994.

MCDONALD, TERRY. *Hill Times Index of the 37th House of Commons* (January 19, 2001).

MACE, DAVID, and VERA MACE. *Marriage East and West*. Garden City, N.Y.: Doubleday (Dolphin), 1960.

MCGEARY, JOHANNA. "Nukes . . . They're Back." *Time*. Vol. 151, No. 20 (May 25, 1998):34–42.

MCGUIRE, MEREDITH B. *Religion: The Social Context*. 2d ed. Belmont, Calif.: Wadsworth, 1987.

MCILROY, ANNE. "Tough Reproductive Rules Proposed: Legislation Introduced in Commons Would Prohibit Selection of Baby's Sex, Sale of Eggs or Sperm." *The Globe and Mail* (June 15, 1996):A1, A4.

MACIONIS, JOHN J. "Intimacy: Structure and Process in Interpersonal Relationships." *Alternative Lifestyles*. Vol. 1, No. 1 (February 1978a):113–30.

————. "The Search for Community in Modern Society: An Interpretation." *Qualitative Sociology*. Vol. 1, No. 2 (September 1978b):130–43.

————. "A Sociological Analysis of Humor." Presentation to the Texas Junior College Teachers Association, Houston, 1987.

————. "Making Society (and, Increasingly, the World) Visible." In Earl Babbie, ed., *The Spirit of Sociology*. Belmont, Calif.: Wadsworth, 1993:221–24.

————. *Sociology:* 9th Edition. Upper Saddle River, N.J: Prentice Hall, 2003.

MACIONIS, JOHN J., and VINCENT R. PARRILLO. *Cities and Urban Life*. Upper Saddle River, N.J.: Prentice Hall, 1998.

MACKAY, DONALD G. "Prescriptive Grammar and the Pronoun Problem." In Barrie Thorne, Cheris Kramarae, and Nancy Henley, eds., *Language, Gender and Society*. Rowley, Mass.: Newbury House, 1983:38–53.

MACKAY, JUDITH. *The Penguin Atlas of Human Sexual Behavior*. New York: Penguin Group, 2000.

MACKENZIE, BETSY. "Therapeutic Abortion in Canada." In Craig McKie and Keith Thompson, eds., *Canadian Social Trends*. Toronto: Thompson Educational Publishing, 1990.

MACKIE, MARLENE. "Ethnic Stereotypes and Prejudice: Alberta Indians, Hutterites and Ukrainians." *Canadian Ethnic Studies*. Vol. X (1974):118–29.

————. *Exploring Gender Relations: A Canadian Perspective*. Toronto: Butterworths, 1983.

MAKIN, KIRK. "Gay Marriage Is Legalized." *The Globe and Mail* (June 11, 2003):A1

MACKINNON, CATHARINE A. *Feminism Unmodified: Discourses on Life and Law*. Cambridge, Mass.: Harvard University Press, 1987.

MCLANAHAN, SARA. "Family Structure and the Reproduction of Poverty." *American Journal of Sociology*. Vol. 90, No. 4 (January 1985):873–901.

MCLEAN, STUART. *Welcome Home: Travels in Smalltown Canada*. Toronto: Viking, 1992.

Maclean's/CTV Poll, 1994, January 2, 1995. Cited in Rathus, Spencer A., Jeffrey S. Nevid, Lois Fischner-Rathus, and Edward S. Herold, *Human Sexuality in a World of Diversity*, Canadian Edition. Toronto: Pearson Education Canada, 2004:424.

McLEOD, JANE D., and MICHAEL J. SHANAHAN. "Poverty, Parenting, and Children's Mental Health." *American Sociological Review*. Vol. 58, No. 3 (June 1993):351–66.

McLEOD, JAY. *Ain't No Makin' It: Aspirations and Attainment in a Low-Income Neighborhood*. Boulder, Colo.: Westview Press, 1995.

McLUHAN, MARSHALL. *The Gutenberg Galaxy*. New York: New American Library, 1969.

MacNEIL, ROBERT. *Burden of Desire*. New York: Harcourt Brace & Company, 1992.

McPHAIL, CLARK. *The Myth of the Madding Crowd*. New York: Aldine, 1991.

McPHAIL, CLARK, and RONALD T. WOHLSTEIN. "Individual and Collective Behaviors Within Gatherings, Demonstrations, and Riots." *Annual Review of Sociology*. Vol. 9. Palo Alto, Calif.: Annual Reviews, 1983:579–600.

McPHERSON, BARRY D. *Aging as a Social Process: An Introduction to Individual and Population Aging*. 2d ed. Toronto: Butterworths, 1990.

McRAE, SUSAN. *Cross-Class Families: A Study of Wives' Occupational Superiority*. New York: Oxford University Press, 1986.

MADDOX, SETMA. "Organizational Culture and Leadership Style: Factors Affecting Self-Managed Work Team Performance." Paper presented at the annual meeting of the Southwest Social Science Association, Dallas, February 1995.

MADIGAN, NICK. "Cries of Activism and Terror in S.U.V. Torching." *New York Times*, August 31, 2003 [online]. Available at www.nytimes.com/2003/08/31/national/31HUMM.html?ex=1063385291&ei=1&en=aed8e993304c0152.

MADSEN, AXEL. *Private Power: Multinational Corporations for the Survival of Our Planet*. New York: William Morrow, 1980.

MALTHUS, THOMAS ROBERT. *First Essay on Population 1798*. London: Macmillan, 1926; orig. 1798.

MARCHAK, PATRICIA. "The Rise and Fall of the Peripheral State: The Case of British Columbia." In Robert J. Brym, ed., *Regionalism in Canada*. Toronto: Irwin, 1986:123–60.

MARCUSE, HERBERT. *One-Dimensional Man*. Boston: Beacon Press, 1964.

MARE, ROBERT D. "Five Decades of Educational Assortative Mating." *American Sociological Review*. Vol. 56, No. 1 (February 1991):15–32.

MARKOFF, JOHN. "Remember Big Brother? Now He's a Company Man." *New York Times* (March 31, 1991):7.

MARKOVSKY, BARRY, JOHN SKVORETZ, DAVID WILLER, MICHAEL J. LOVAGLIA, and JEFFREY ERGER. "The Seeds of Weak Power: An Extension of Network Exchange Theory." *American Sociological Review*. Vol. 58, No. 2 (April 1993):197–209.

MARKSON, ELIZABETH W. "Moral Dilemmas." *Society*. Vol. 29, No. 5 (July-August 1992):4–6.

MARLIOS, PETER. "Interlocking Directorates and the Control of Corporations: The Theory of Bank Control." *Social Science Quarterly*. Vol. 56, No. 3 (December 1975):425–39.

MARQUAND, ROBERT. "Worship Shift: Americans Seek Feeling of 'Awe.'" *Christian Science Monitor* (May 28, 1997):1, 8.

MARSDEN, LORNA R., and EDWARD B. HARVEY. *Fragile Federation: Social Change in Canada*. Toronto: McGraw-Hill Ryerson, 1979.

MARSDEN, PETER. "Core Discussion Networks of Americans." *American Sociological Review*. Vol. 52, No. 1 (February 1987):122–31.

MARSHALL, SUSAN E. "Ladies Against Women: Mobilization Dilemmas of Antifeminist Movements." *Social Problems*. Vol. 32, No. 4 (April 1985):348–62.

MARTIN, JOHN M., and ANNE T. ROMANO. *Multinational Crime: Terrorism, Espionage, Drug and Arms Trafficking*. Newbury Park, Calif.: Sage, 1992.

MARTIN, RICHARD C. *Islam: A Cultural Perspective*. Englewood Cliffs, N.J.: Prentice Hall, 1982.

MARTIN, SANDRA. "Reining in the Space Cowboys." *The Globe and Mail* (April 19, 2000):R1, R2.

MARULLO, SAM. "The Functions and Dysfunctions of Preparations for Fighting Nuclear War." *Sociological Focus*. Vol. 20, No. 2 (April 1987):135–53.

MARX, GARY T., and JAMES L. WOOD. "Strands of Theory and Research in Collective Behavior." In Alex Inkeles et al., eds., *Annual Review of Sociology*. Vol. 1. Palo Alto, Calif.: Annual Reviews, 1975:363–428.

MARX, KARL. Excerpt from "A Contribution to the Critique of Political Economy." In Karl Marx and Friedrich Engels, *Marx and Engels: Basic Writings on Politics and Philosophy*. Lewis S. Feurer, ed. Garden City, N.Y.: Anchor Books, 1959:42–46.

———. *Karl Marx: Early Writings*. T.B. Bottomore, ed. New York: McGraw-Hill, 1964a.

———. *Karl Marx: Selected Writings in Sociology and Social Philosophy*. T.B. Bottomore, trans. New York: McGraw-Hill, 1964b; orig. 1848.

———. *Capital*. Friedrich Engels, ed. New York: International Publishers, 1967; orig. 1867.

———. "Theses on Feuer." In Robert C. Tucker, ed., *The Marx-Engels Reader*. New York: Norton, 1972:107–9; orig. 1845.

MARX, KARL, and FRIEDRICH ENGELS. "Manifesto of the Communist Party." In Robert C. Tucker, ed., *The Marx-Engels Reader*. New York: Norton, 1972:331–62; orig. 1848.

MARX, LEO. "The Environment and the 'Two Cultures' Divide." In James Rodger Fleming and Henry A. Gemery, eds., *Science, Technology, and the Environment: Multidisciplinary Perspectives*. Akron, Ohio: University of Akron Press, 1994:3–21.

MASSEY, DOUGLAS S. Review of *The Bell Curve: Intelligence and Class Structure in American Life* by Richard J. Herrnstein and Charles Murray. *American Journal of Sociology*. Vol. 101, No. 3 (November 1995):747–53.

MATAS, ROBERT. "B.C. Gay Parents Gain Equality." *The Globe and Mail* (February 5, 1998):A1.

MATTHEWS, RALPH. *"There's No Better Place Than Here": Social Change in Three Newfoundland Communities*. Toronto: Peter Martin Associates, 1976.

———. *The Creation of Regional Dependency*. Toronto: University of Toronto Press, 1983.

———. *Indian Country*. New York: Viking Press, 1984.

MAUER, MARC. "Americans Behind Bars: The International Use of Incarceration, 1995." [online] Available at www.sentencingproject.org/pubs/tsppubs/9030data.html, April 1, 2000.

MAURO, TONY. "Ruling Likely Will Add Fuel to Already Divisive Debate." *USA Today* (January 7, 1997):1A, 2A.

MAUSS, ARMAND L. *Social Problems of Social Movements*. Philadelphia: Lippincott, 1975.

MAXWELL, MARY PERCIVAL, and JAMES D. MAXWELL. "Three Decades of Private School Females' Ambitions: Implications for Canadian Elites." *Canadian Review of Sociology and Anthropology*. Vol. 31, No. 2 (1994):139–68.

MAYO, KATHERINE. *Mother India*. New York: Harcourt, Brace, 1927.

MEAD, GEORGE HERBERT. *Mind, Self, and Society*. Charles W. Morris, ed. Chicago: University of Chicago Press, 1962; orig. 1934.

MEAD, MARGARET. *Coming of Age in Samoa*. New York: Dell, 1961; orig. 1928.

———. *Sex and Temperament in Three Primitive Societies*. New York: William Morrow, 1963; orig. 1935.

MEADOWS, DONELLA H., DENNIS L. MEADOWS, JORGAN RANDERS, and WILLIAM W. BEHRENS, III. *The Limits to Growth: A Report on the Club of Rome's Project on the Predicament of Mankind*. New York: Universe, 1972.

MELTZER, BERNARD N. "Mead's Social Psychology." In Jerome G. Manis and Bernard N. Meltzer, eds., *Symbolic Interaction: A Reader in Social Psychology*. 3d ed. Needham Heights, Mass.: Allyn & Bacon, 1978.

MELUCCI, ALBERTO. "The New Social Movements: A Theoretical Approach." *Social Science Information*. Vol. 19, No. 2 (May 1980):199–226.

———. *Nomads of the Present: Social Movements and Individual Needs in Contemporary Society*. Philadelphia: Temple University Press, 1989.

MENZIES, KEN. *The People-Serving Society*. Manuscript draft.

MERRIT, SUSAN E. *Her Story: Women from Canada's Past*. St. Catharines, Ont.: Vanwell Publishing, 1993.

MERTON, ROBERT K. *Social Theory and Social Structure*. New York: Free Press, 1968.

———. "Discrimination and the American Creed." In *Sociological Ambivalence and Other Essays*. New York: Free Press, 1976:189–216.

MESSING, PHILIP. "City Crime Plummets," *New York Post*, September 5, 2003 [online]. Available at www.nypost.com/news/regionalnews/5020.htm.

MEYER, DAVIS S., and NANCY WHITTIER. "Social Movement Spillover." *Social Problems*. Vol. 41, No. 2 (May 1994):277–98.

MEYER, DAVID S., and SUZANNE STAGGENBORG. "Movements, Counter-movements, and the Structure of Political Opportunity." *American Journal of Sociology*. Vol. 101, No. 6 (May 1996):1628–60.

MICHELS, ROBERT. *Political Parties*. Glencoe, Ill.: Free Press, 1949; orig. 1911.

MICHELSON, WILLIAM. "Urbanization and Urbanism." In James Curtis and Lorne Tepperman, eds., *Understanding Canadian Society*. Toronto: McGraw-Hill Ryerson, 1988:73–104.

MILBRATH, LESTER W. *Political Participation: How and Why Do People Get Involved in Politics*. Chicago: Rand McNally, 1966.

———. *Envisioning a Sustainable Society: Learning Our Way Out*. Albany: State University of New York Press, 1989.

MILGRAM, STANLEY. "Behavioral Study of Obedience." *Journal of Abnormal and Social Psychology*. Vol. 67, No. 4 (1963):371–78.

———. "Group Pressure and Action Against a Person." *Journal of Abnormal and Social Psychology*. Vol. 69, No. 2 (August 1964):137–43.

———. "Some Conditions of Obedience and Disobedience to Authority." *Human Relations*. Vol. 18 (February 1965):57–76.

MILIBAND, RALPH. *The State in Capitalist Society*. London: Weidenfield and Nicolson, 1969.

MILLER, ARTHUR G. *The Obedience Experiments: A Case of Controversy in Social Science*. New York: Praeger, 1986.

MILLER, DAVID L. *Introduction to Collective Behavior*. Belmont, Calif.: Wadsworth, 1985.

MILLER, FREDERICK D. "The End of SDS and the Emergence of Weatherman: Demise Through Success." In Jo Freeman, ed., *Social Movements of the Sixties and Seventies.* New York: Longman, 1983:279–97.

MILLER, G. TYLER, JR. *Living in the Environment: An Introduction to Environmental Science.* Belmont, Calif.: Wadsworth, 1992.

MILLER, MARK. "Under Cover, in the Closet." *Newsweek* (January 14, 1991):25.

MILLER, WALTER B. "Lower Class Culture as a Generating Milieu of Gang Delinquency." In Marvin E. Wolfgang, Leonard Savitz, and Norman Johnston, eds., *The Sociology of Crime and Delinquency.* 2d ed. New York: Wiley, 1970:351–63; orig. 1958.

MILLET, KATE. *Sexual Politics.* Garden City, N.Y.: Doubleday, 1970.

MILLS, C. WRIGHT. *White Collar: The American Middle Classes.* New York: Oxford University Press, 1951.

———. *The Power Elite.* New York: Oxford University Press, 1956.

———. *The Sociological Imagination.* New York: Oxford University Press, 1959.

MINK, BARBARA. "How Modernization Affects Women." *Cornell Alumni News.* Vol. III, No. 3 (April 1989):10–11.

MIROWSKY, JOHN. "The Psycho-Economics of Feeling Underpaid: Distributive Justice and the Earnings of Husbands and Wives." *American Journal of Sociology.* Vol. 92, No. 6 (May 1987):1404–34.

MIROWSKY, JOHN, and CATHERINE ROSS. "Working Wives and Mental Health." Presentation to the American Association for the Advancement of Science, New York, 1984.

———. *The Social Causes of Psychological Distress.* Hawthorne, N.Y.: Aldine, 1989.

MITCHELL, ALANNA. "Greying of Canada Oversold Notion." *The Globe and Mail* (July 30, 1997):A4.

———. "More Children Running Away Younger, Statscan Says." *The Globe and Mail* (February 13, 1998):A3.

MITCHELL, BARBARA A. "The Refilled 'Nest.'" In Ellen M. Gee and Gloria M. Gutman, eds., *The Overselling of Population Aging: Apocalyptic Demography, Intergenerational Challenges, and Social Policy.* Don Mills, Ont.: Oxford University Press, 2000.

MITTELSTAEDT, MARTIN. "Change Unavoidable for Ontario Hydro." *The Globe and Mail* (August 18, 1997):A1.

MOLM, LINDA D. "Risk and Power Use: Constraints on the Use of Coercion in Exchange." *American Sociological Review.* Vol. 62, No. 1 (February 1997):113–33.

MOLOTCH, HARVEY. "The City as a Growth Machine." *American Journal of Sociology.* Vol. 82, No. 2 (September 1976):309–33.

MONSEBRAATEN, LAURIE. "Struggling On in Wake of Cuts." *Toronto Star* (May 5, 1996): F6.

MONTAGU, ASHLEY. *The Nature of Human Aggression.* New York: Oxford University Press, 1976.

MONTIGNY, GILLES. "Reading Skills." In Craig McKie and Keith Thompson, eds., *Canadian Social Trends: A Canadian Studies Reader.* Vol. 2. Toronto: Thompson Educational Publishing, 1994:111–19.

MOONEY, ERIN. "Presence, ergo Protection? UNPROFOR, UNHCR and the ICRC in Croatia and Bosnia and Herzegovina." *International Journal of Refugee Law* 7/3 (1995).

MOORE, GWEN. "The Structure of a National Elite Network." *American Sociological Review.* Vol. 44, No. 5 (October 1979):673–92.

———. "Gender and Informal Networks in State Government." *Social Science Quarterly.* Vol. 73, No. 1 (March 1992):46–61.

MOORE, WILBERT E. "Modernization as Rationalization: Processes and Restraints." In Manning Nash, ed., *Essays on Economic Development and Cultural Change in Honor of Bert F. Hoselitz.* Chicago: University of Chicago Press, 1977:29–42.

———. *World Modernization: The Limits of Convergence.* New York: Elsevier, 1979.

MORRISON, DENTON E. "Some Notes Toward Theory on Relative Deprivation, Social Movements, and Social Change." In Louis E. Genevie, ed., *Collective Behavior and Social Movements.* Itasca, Ill.: Peacock, 1978:202–9.

MORTON, JACKSON. "Census on the Internet." *American Demographics.* Vol. 17, No. 3 (March 1995):52–53.

MOSLEY, W. HENRY, and PETER COWLEY. "The Challenge of World Health." *Population Bulletin.* Vol. 46, No. 4 (December 1991). Washington, D.C.: Population Reference Bureau.

MOTTAZ, CLIFFORD J. "Some Determinants of Work Alienation." *The Sociological Quarterly.* Vol. 22, No. 4 (Autumn 1981):515–29.

MUELLER, DANIEL P., and PHILIP W. COOPER. "Children of Single Parent Families: How Do They Fare as Young Adults?" Presentation to the American Sociological Association, San Antonio, Texas, 1984.

MUHTADIE, LUMA. "The Jewel in Its Crown: CBC Beats Foes at Coronation." *The Globe and Mail* (June 2, 2003):A3.

MULLER, EDWARD N. *Aggressive Political Participation.* Princeton, N.J.: Princeton University Press, 1979.

MUMFORD, LEWIS. *The City in History: Its Origins, Its Transformations, and Its Prospects.* New York: Harcourt, Brace & World, 1961.

MURDOCK, GEORGE PETER. "Comparative Data on the Division of Labor by Sex." *Social Forces.* Vol. 15, No. 4 (May 1937):551–53.

———. "The Common Denominator of Cultures." In Ralph Linton, ed., *The Science of Man in World Crisis.* New York: Columbia University Press, 1945:123–42.

———. *Social Structure.* New York: Free Press, 1965; orig. 1949.

MYERS, NORMAN. "Humanity's Growth." In Sir Edmund Hillary, ed., *Ecology 2000: The Changing Face of the Earth.* New York: Beaufort Books, 1984a:16–35.

———. "The Mega-Extinction of Animals and Plants." In Sir Edmund Hillary, ed., *Ecology 2000: The Changing Face of the Earth.* New York: Beaufort Books, 1984b:82–107.

———. "Disappearing Cultures." In Sir Edmund Hillary, ed., *Ecology 2000: The Changing Face of the Earth.* New York: Beaufort Books, 1984c:162–69.

———. "Biological Diversity and Global Security." In F. Herbert Bormann and Stephen R. Kellert, eds., *Ecology, Economics, and Ethics: The Broken Circle.* New Haven, Conn.: Yale University Press, 1991:11–25.

MYERS, SHEILA, and HAROLD G. GRASMICK. "The Social Rights and Responsibilities of Pregnant Women: An Application of Parsons' Sick Role Model." Paper presented to Southwestern Sociological Association, Little Rock, Arkansas, March 1989.

NADER, RALPH, NADIA MILLERON, and DUFF CONACHER. *Canada Firsts.* Toronto: McClelland & Stewart, 1992.

NAJAFIZADEH, MEHRANGIZ, and LEWIS A. MENNERICK. "Sociology of Education or Sociology of Ethnocentrism: The Portrayal of Education in Introductory Sociology Textbooks." *Teaching Sociology.* Vol. 20, No. 3 (July 1992):215–21.

NANCARROW CLARKE, JUANNE. *It's Cancer: The Personal Experiences of Women Who Have Received a Cancer Diagnosis.* Toronto: IPI, 1985.

———. *Health, Illness & Medicine in Canada.* 2d ed. Toronto: McClelland & Stewart, 1996.

———. "Media Portrayal of Disease from the Medical, Political Economy and Life Style Perspectives." *Qualitative Health Research.* Vol. 1, No. 3 (1991):287–308.

———. "Cancer, Heart Disease and AIDS: What Do the Media Tell Us About These Diseases?" *Health Communication.* Vol. 4, No. 2 (1992):105–20.

———. Unpublished research.

NATIONAL COUNCIL OF WELFARE. *Women and Poverty Revisited.* Ottawa: Supply and Services, 1990.

NATIONAL LITERACY SECRETARIAT. International Adult Literary Survey, 1994 [online]. Available at www.nald.ca/nls/ials/introduc.htm.

NAWAZ, MOHAMED. *Potsmoking and Illegal Conduct: Understanding the Social World of University Students.* Canada: Diliton Publications, 1978.

NEILL, SHIRLEY. "Unionization in Canada." In Craig McKie and Keith Thompson, eds., *Canadian Social Trends.* Toronto: Thompson Educational Publishing, 1990.

NELSON, E.D., and AUGIE FLERAS. *Social Problems in Canada: Issues and Challenges.* 2d ed. Scarborough, Ont.: Prentice Hall, 1998.

NELSON, E.D., and BARRY W. ROBINSON. *Gender in Canada.* Scarborough, Ont.: Prentice Hall, 1999.

NEMETH, MARY. "God Is Alive." *Maclean's* (April 12, 1993).

NETT, EMILY M. *Canadian Families: Past and Present.* 2d ed. Toronto: Butterworths, 1993.

NEUGARTEN, BERNICE L. "Grow Old with Me. The Best Is Yet to Be." *Psychology Today.* Vol. 5 (December 1971):45–48, 79, 81.

———. "Personality and the Aging Process." *The Gerontologist.* Vol. 12, No. 1 (Spring 1972):9–15.

———. "Personality and Aging." In James E. Birren and K. Warner Schaie, eds., *Handbook of the Psychology of Aging.* New York: Van Nostrand Reinhold, 1977:626–49.

NEUHOUSER, KEVIN. "The Radicalization of the Brazilian Catholic Church in Comparative Perspective." *American Sociological Review.* Vol. 54, No. 2 (April 1989):233–44.

NEUMAN, W. LAURENCE. *Social Research Methods: Qualitative and Quantitative Approaches.* 3d ed.; Boston: Allyn & Bacon, 1997;. 4th ed., 2000.

NEVITTE, NEIL. *The Decline of Deference.* Peterborough, Ont.: Broadview Press, 1996.

NEW HAVEN JOURNAL-COURIER. "English Social Structure Changing." November 27, 1986.

NEWMAN, KATHERINE S. *Declining Fortunes: The Withering of the American Dream.* New York: Basic Books, 1993.

NEWMAN, PETER C. *The Canadian Revolution, 1985–1995: From Deference to Defiance.* Toronto: Penguin Books, 1995.

———. *Titans: How the New Canadian Establishment Seized Power.* Toronto: Penguin, 1998.

NEWMAN, WILLIAM M. *American Pluralism: A Study of Minority Groups and Social Theory.* New York: Harper & Row, 1973.

NFO CFGROUP. "Public Divided About Definition of Marriage," September 5, 2003 [online]. Available as a PDF file at www.nfocfgroup.com/news/news.html#news_items.

NIELSEN, FRANCOIS, and ARTHUR S. ALDERSON. "The Kuznets Curve: The Great U-Turn: Income Inequality in U.S. Counties, 1970 to 1990." *American Sociological Review.* Vol. 62, No. 1 (February 1997):12–33.

NIELSEN, JOYCE MCCARL, ed. *Feminist Research Methods: Exemplary Readings in the Social Sciences.* Boulder, Colo.: Westview Press, 1990.

NIKIFORUK, ANDREW. "When Water Kills." *Maclean's* (June 12, 2000).

NIN.DA.WAAB.JIG., WALPOLE ISLAND HERITAGE CENTRE. "Walpole Island in 2005: A View from the Future." In Diane Engelstad and John Bird, eds., *Nation to Nation: Aboriginal Sovereignty and the Future of Canada.* Concord, Ont.: House of Anansi Press, 1992:186–96.

1991 Green Book. U.S. House of Representatives. Washington, D.C.: U.S. Government Printing Office, 1991.

NISBET, ROBERT A. *The Sociological Tradition.* New York: Basic Books, 1966.

———. *The Quest for Community.* New York: Oxford University Press, 1969.

———. "Sociology as an Art Form." *In Tradition and Revolt: Historical and Sociological Essays.* New York: Vintage Books, 1970.

NORBECK, EDWARD. "Class Structure." In *Kodansha Encyclopedia of Japan.* Tokyo: Kodansha, 1983:322–26.

NORC. *General Social Surveys, 1972–1998: Cumulative Codebook.* Chicago: National Opinion Research Center, 1999.

NORTON, PHILLIP. "Jackrabbit Johannsen: The Pioneer of Skiing in Canada." *Canadian Geographic* (April/May 1997):18–23.

OAKES, JEANNIE. "Classroom Social Relationships: Exploring the Bowles and Gintis Hypothesis." *Sociology of Education.* Vol. 55, No. 4 (October 1982):197–212.

———. *Keeping Track: How High Schools Structure Inequality.* New Haven, Conn.: Yale University Press, 1985.

OBERSCHALL, ANTHONY. *Social Conflict and Social Movements.* Englewood Cliffs, N.J.: Prentice Hall, 1973.

O'BRIEN, DAVID J., EDWARD W. HASSINGER, and LARRY DERSHEM. "Size of Place, Residential Stability, and Personal Social Networks." *Sociological Focus.* Vol. 29, No. 1 (February 1996):61–72.

O'DEA, THOMAS F., and JANET O'DEA AVIAD. *The Sociology of Religion.* 2d ed. Englewood Cliffs, N.J.: Prentice Hall, 1983.

ODERKIRK, JILLIAN. "Education Achievement: An International Comparison." *Canadian Social Trends* (Autumn 1993):8–12.

OFFIR, CAROLE WADE. *Human Sexuality.* New York: Harcourt Brace Jovanovich, 1982.

OGBURN, WILLIAM F. *On Culture and Social Change.* Chicago: University of Chicago Press, 1964.

OLSEN, GREGG M. "Re-Modeling Sweden: The Rise and Demise of the Compromise in a Global Economy." *Social Problems.* Vol. 43, No. 1 (February 1996):1–20.

OLZAK, SUSAN. "Labor Unrest, Immigration, and Ethnic Conflict in Urban America, 1880–1914." *American Journal of Sociology.* Vol. 94, No. 6 (May 1989):1303–33.

OLZAK, SUSAN, and ELIZABETH WEST. "Ethnic Conflict and the Rise and Fall of Ethnic Newspapers." *American Sociological Review.* Vol. 56, No. 4 (August 1991):458–74.

ONTARIO WOMEN'S DIRECTORATE. *Words That Count Women Out/In.* Toronto: Ontario Women's Directorate, 1992.

O'REILLY, FINBARR. "Richest in the World? Wal-Mart Women." *National Post* (July 11, 2000):A2.

OSGOOD, D. WAYNE, JANET K. WILSON, PATRICK M. O'MALLEY, JERALD G. BACHMAN, and LLOYD D. JOHNSTON. "Routine Activities and Individual Deviant Behavior." *American Sociological Review.* Vol. 61, No. 4 (August 1996):635–55.

OSSENBERG, RICHARD J. "Social Class and Bar Behavior during an Urban Festival." In James E. Curtis and William G. Scott, eds., *Social Stratification: Canada.* 2d ed. Scarborough, Ont.: Prentice Hall, 1979.

OSTLING, RICHARD N. "Jerry Falwell's Crusade." *Time.* Vol. 126, No. 9 (September 2, 1985):48–52, 55, 57.

———. "Technology and the Womb." *Time.* Vol. 129, No. 12 (March 23, 1987):58–59.

OSTRANDER, SUSAN A. "Upper Class Women: The Feminine Side of Privilege." *Qualitative Sociology.* Vol. 3, No. 1 (Spring 1980):23–44.

———. *Women of the Upper Class.* Philadelphia: Temple University Press, 1984.

OUCHI, WILLIAM. *Theory Z: How American Business Can Meet the Japanese Challenge.* Reading, Mass.: Addison-Wesley, 1981.

OWEN, DAVID. *None of the Above: Behind the Myth of Scholastic Aptitude.* Boston: Houghton Mifflin, 1985.

PAKULSKI, JAN. "Mass Social Movements and Social Class." *International Sociology.* Vol. 8, No. 2 (June 1993):131–58.

PALMORE, ERDMAN. "Predictors of Successful Aging." *The Gerontologist.* Vol. 19, No. 5 (October 1979a):427–31.

———. "Advantages of Aging." *The Gerontologist.* Vol. 19, No. 2 (April 1979b):220–23.

———. "What Can the USA Learn from Japan About Aging?" In Steven H. Zarit, ed., *Readings in Aging and Death: Contemporary Perspectives.* New York: Harper & Row, 1982:166–69.

PARCEL, TOBY L., CHARLES W. MUELLER, and STEVEN CUVELIER. "Comparable Worth and Occupational Labor Market: Explanations of Occupational Earnings Differentials." Paper presented to the American Sociological Association, New York, 1986.

PARENTI, MICHAEL. *Inventing Reality: The Politics of the Mass Media.* New York: St. Martin's Press, 1986.

PARKINSON, C. NORTHCOTE. *Parkinson's Law and Other Studies in Administration.* New York: Ballantine Books, 1957.

PARRILLO, VINCENT N. "Diversity in America: A Sociohistorical Analysis." *Sociological Forum.* Vol. 9, No. 4 (December 1994):42–45.

PARROTT, JULIE. "The Effects of Culture on Eating Disorders." Paper presented to Southwestern Social Science Association, Dallas, Texas, March 1987.

PARSONS, TALCOTT. "Age and Sex in the Social Structure of the United States." *American Sociological Review.* Vol. 7, No. 4 (August 1942):604–16.

———. *Essays in Sociological Theory.* New York: Free Press, 1954.

———. *The Social System.* New York: Free Press, 1964; orig. 1951.

———. *Societies: Evolutionary and Comparative Perspectives.* Englewood Cliffs, N.J.: Prentice Hall, 1966.

PARSONS, TALCOTT, and ROBERT F. BALES, eds. *Family, Socialization and Interaction Process.* New York: Free Press, 1955.

PARTRIDGE, JOHN. "Balanced Foreign Aid Policy Urged." *The Globe and Mail,* October 8, 2003 [online]. Available at www.globeinvestor.com/servlet/ArticleNews/story/LAC/20031008/RCONFERENCE.

PAUL, ELLEN FRANKEL. "Bared Buttocks and Federal Cases." *Society.* Vol. 28, No. 4 (May–June, 1991):4–7.

PEAR, ROBERT. "Women Reduce Lag in Earnings, but Disparities with Men Remain." *New York Times* (September 4, 1987):1, 7.

PEAR, ROBERT, with ERIK ECKHOLM. "When Healers Are Entrepreneurs: A Debate over Costs and Ethics." *New York Times* (June 2, 1991):1, 17.

PEARSON, DAVID E. "Post-Mass Culture." *Society.* Vol. 30, No. 5 (July–August 1993):17–22.

PERITZ, INGRID. "Sex-Change Soldier Hails Canada's Liberal Attitudes." *The Globe and Mail* (February 22, 2000):A1.

PERSELL, CAROLINE HODGES. *Education and Inequality: A Theoretical and Empirical Synthesis.* New York: Free Press, 1977.

PESSEN, EDWARD. *Riches, Class, and Power: America Before the Civil War.* New Brunswick, N.J.: Transaction Books, 1990.

PETER, LAURENCE J., and RAYMOND HULL. *The Peter Principle: Why Things Always Go Wrong.* New York: William Morrow, 1969.

PETERS, THOMAS J., and ROBERT H. WATERMAN, JR. *In Search of Excellence: Lessons from America's Best-Run Companies.* New York: Warner Books, 1982.

Peters Atlas of the World. New York: Harper & Row, 1990.

PETERSON, RICHARD R. "A Re-Evaluation of the Economic Consequences of Divorce." *American Sociological Review.* Vol. 61, No. 3 (June 1996):528–36.

PETERSON, SCOTT. "Women Live on Own Terms behind the Veil." *Christian Science Monitor* (July 31, 1996):1, 10.

PEVERE, GEOFF, and GREIG DYMOND. *Mondo Canuck: A Canadian Pop Culture Odyssey.* Scarborough, Ont.: Prentice Hall Canada, 1996.

PHILIPSON, ILENE J., and KAREN V. HANSEN. "Women, Class, and the Feminist Imagination." In Karen V. Hansen and Ilene J. Philipson, eds., *Women, Class, and the Feminist Imagination: A Socialist-Feminist Reader.* Philadelphia: Temple University Press, 1992:3–40.

PHILLIPSON, CHRIS. *Capitalism and the Construction of Old Age.* London: Macmillan, 1982.

PHILP, MARGARET. "Unpaid Work Worth at Least $234 Billion." *The Globe and Mail* (December 21, 1995):A8.

———. "Aboriginal Languages Nearing Extinction: Expert." *The Globe and Mail* (May 13, 2000):A7.

PICHARDO, NELSON A. "The Power Elite and Elite-Driven Countermovements: The Associated Farmers of California During the 1930s." *Sociological Forum.* Vol. 10, No. 1 (March 1995):21–49.

PILLEMER, KARL. "Maltreatment of the Elderly at Home and in Institutions: Extent, Risk Factors, and Policy Recommendations." In U.S. Congress. House, Select Committee on Aging and Senate, Special Committee on Aging. *Legislative Agenda for an Aging Society: 1988 and Beyond.* Washington, D.C.: U.S. Government Printing Office, 1988.

PINES, MAYA. "The Civilization of Genie." *Psychology Today.* Vol. 15 (September 1981):28–34.

PINHEY, THOMAS K., DONALD H. RUBINSTEIN, and RICHARD S. COLFAX. "Overweight and Happiness: The Reflected Self-Appraisal Hypothesis Reconsidered." *Social Science Quarterly.* Vol. 78, No. 3 (September 1997):747–55.

PITT, MALCOLM. *Introducing Hinduism*. New York: Friendship Press, 1955.

PIVEN, FRANCES FOX, and RICHARD A. CLOWARD. *Poor People's Movements: Why They Succeed, How They Fail*. New York: Pantheon Books, 1977.

PLOMIN, ROBERT, and TERRYL T. FOCH. "A Twin Study of Objectively Assessed Personality in Childhood." *Journal of Personality and Social Psychology*. Vol. 39, No. 4 (October 1980):680–88.

POHL, RUDIGER. "The Transition from Communism to Capitalism in East Germany." *Society*. Vol. 33, No. 4 (June 1996):62–65.

POLENBERG, RICHARD. *One Nation Divisible: Class, Race, and Ethnicity in the United States Since 1938*. New York: Pelican Books, 1980.

POMFRET, RICHARD. *The Economic Development of Canada*. Toronto: Methuen, 1981.

POPENOE, DAVID. "American Family Decline, 1960–1990: A Review and Appraisal." *Journal of Marriage and the Family*. Vol. 55, No. 3 (August 1993):527–55.

POPULATION REFERENCE BUREAU. *2001 World Population Data Sheet*. Washington, D.C.: Population Reference Bureau, 2001.

PORTER, JOHN. *The Vertical Mosaic: An Analysis of Social Class and Power in Canada*. Toronto: University of Toronto Press, 1965.

PORTER, JOHN, MARION PORTER, and BERNARD R. BLISHEN. *Stations and Callings*. Toronto: Methuen, 1982.

A Portrait of Seniors in Canada. Catalogue No. 89–59. Ottawa: Statistics Canada, 1990.

POSTEL, SANDRA. "Facing Water Scarcity." In Lester R. Brown et al., eds., *State of the World 1993: A Worldwatch Institute Report on Progress Toward a Sustainable Society*. New York: Norton, 1993:22–41.

POWELL, CHRIS, and GEORGE E. C. PATON, eds. *Humour in Society: Resistance and Control*. New York: St. Martin's Press, 1988.

PRESS, ANDREA L. Review of *Enlightened Racism: "The Cosby Show," Audiences, and the Myth of the American Dream*, by Sut Jhally and Justin Lewis. *American Journal of Sociology*. Vol. 99, No. 1 (July 1993):219–21.

PRESSER, HARRIET B. "The Housework Gender Gap." *Population Today*. Vol. 21, No. 7/8 (July–August 1993):5.

PRICEWATERHOUSECOOPERS. "Filmed Entertainment Industry in Canada the Fastest Growing in World," September 13, 2003 [online]. Available at www.pwcglobal.com/extweb/ncpressrelease.nsf/docid/B8AC0264872F898085256D9B00634DB6.

PRIMEGGIA, SALVATORE, and JOSEPH A. VARACALLI. "Southern Italian Comedy: Old to New World." In Joseph V. Scelsa, Salvatore J. LaGumina, and Lydio Tomasi, eds., *Italian Americans in Transition*. New York: The American Italian Historical Association, 1990:241–52.

PRINDLE, DAVID F., and JAMES W. ENDERSBY. "Hollywood Liberalism." *Social Science Quarterly*. Vol. 74, No. 1 (March 1993):136–49.

———. "Take Three on Hollywood Liberalism." *Social Science Quarterly*. Vol. 75, No. 2 (June 1994):458–59.

PRUS, ROBERT. "Approaching the Study of Human Group Life: Symbolic Interaction and Ethnographic Inquiry." In Mary Lorenz Dietz, Robert Prus, and William Shaffir, eds., *Doing Everyday Life: Ethnography as Human Lived Experience*. Mississauga, Ont.: Copp Clark Longman, 1994.

PUTERBAUGH, GEOFF, ed. *Twins and Homosexuality: A Casebook*. New York: Garland, 1990.

PUTKA, GARY. "SAT to Become a Better Gauge." *Wall Street Journal* (November 1, 1990):B1.

QUINNEY, RICHARD. *Class, State and Crime: On the Theory and Practice of Criminal Justice*. New York: David McKay, 1977.

RADEMACHER, ERIC W. "The Effect of Question Wording on College Students." *The Pittsburgh Undergraduate Review*. Vol. 8, No. 1 (Spring 1992):45–81.

RAJHATHY, JUDITH, and DAVID ROULARD. "Victory for Health Freedom." *Health Naturally* (June/July 1994).

RAMCHARAN, SUBHAS. *Racism: Nonwhites in Canada*. Toronto: Butterworths, 1982.

RAMO, JOSHUA COOPER. "Finding God on the Web." *Time* (December 16, 1996):60–67.

RAPHAEL, RAY. *The Men from the Boys: Rites of Passage in Male America*. Lincoln and London: University of Nebraska Press, 1988.

RECKLESS, WALTER C., and SIMON DINITZ. "Pioneering with Self-Concept as a Vulnerability Factor in Delinquency." *Journal of Criminal Law, Criminology, and Police Science*. Vol. 58, No. 4 (December 1967):515–23.

REICH, ROBERT B. "As the World Turns." *The New Republic* (May 1, 1989):23, 26–28.

———. *The Work of Nations: Preparing Ourselves for 21st-Century Capitalism*. New York: Alfred A. Knopf, 1991.

REID, C. "Sick to Death: The Health of Aboriginal People in Australia and Canada." In B. Singh Bolaria and Rosemary Bolaria, eds., *Racial Minorities, Medicine and Health*. Halifax: Fernwood Publishing, 1994:297–312.

REID, SUE TITUS. *Crime and Criminology*. 6th ed. Fort Worth, Tex.: Holt, Rinehart & Winston, 1991.

REIMAN, JEFFREY H. *The Rich Get Richer and the Poor Get Prison: Ideology, Class, and Criminal Justice*. 3d ed. New York: John Wiley & Sons, 1990.

REINHARZ, SHULAMIT. *Feminist Methods in Social Research*. New York: Oxford University Press, 1992.

REITZ, JEFFREY G., and RAYMOND BRETON. *The Illusion of Difference: Realities of Ethnicity in Canada and the United States*. Toronto: C.D. Howe Institute, 1994.

REMIS, ROBERT S. "The Epidemiology of HIV and AIDS in Canada: Current Perspectives and Future Needs." *Canadian Journal of Public Health*. Vol. 84, No. 1 (January/February 1993):534, 536.

REMOFF, HEATHER TREXLER. *Sexual Choice: A Woman's Decision*. New York: Dutton/Lewis, 1984.

Report on Business (The Globe and Mail). "The Top 1000: Canada's Power Book." Vol. 20, No. 1 (July 2003):73–154.

Report on the Demographic Situation in Canada. Ottawa: Statistics Canada, 1992.

RICHARDSON, JAMES T. "Definitions of Cult: From Sociological-Technical to Popular Negative." Paper presented to the American Psychological Association, Boston, August 1990.

RIDGEWAY, CECILIA L. *The Dynamics of Small Groups*. New York: St. Martin's Press, 1983.

RIESMAN, DAVID. *The Lonely Crowd: A Study of the Changing American Character*. New Haven, Conn.: Yale University Press, 1970; orig. 1950.

RILEY, MATILDA WHITE, ANNE FONER, and JOAN WARING. "Sociology of Age." In Neil J. Smelser, ed., *Handbook of Sociology*. Newbury Park, Calif.: Sage, 1988:243–90.

RILEY, NANCY E. "Gender, Power, and Population Change." *Population Bulletin*. Vol. 52, No. 1 (May 1997).

RITZER, GEORGE. *Man and His Work: Conflict and Change*. New York: Appleton-Century-Crofts, 1972.

———. *The McDonaldization of Society: An Investigation into the Changing Character of Contemporary Social Life*. Thousand Oaks, Calif.: Pine Forge Press, 1993.

ROBERGE, ROGER, JEAN MARIE BERTHELOT, and MICHAEL WOLFSAN. "Health and Socio-Economic Inequalities." *Canadian Social Trends* (Catalogue No. 11-008E). (Summer 1995):15–19.

ROBINSON, ALLAN. "Inco Sends in the Robo-Miners." *The Globe and Mail* (January 3, 1998):B1.

ROBINSON, DAWN. "Toward a Synthesis of Sociological and Psychological Theories of Eating Disorders." Paper presented to Southwestern Social Science Association, Dallas, Texas, March 1987.

ROBINSON, JOYCE, and GLENNA SPITZE. "Whistle While You Work? The Effect of Household Task Performance on Women's and Men's Well-Being." *Social Science Quarterly*. Vol. 73, No. 4 (December 1992):844–61.

ROBINSON, VERA M. "Humor and Health." In Paul E. McGhee and Jeffrey H. Goldstein, eds., *Handbook of Humor Research*, Vol. II, *Applied Studies*. New York: Springer-Verlag, 1983:109–28.

ROCKETT, IAN R.H. "Population and Health: An Introduction to Epidemiology." *Population Bulletin*. Vol. 49, No. 3 (November 1994). Washington, D.C.: Population Reference Bureau.

RODGERS, KAREN. "Wife Assault in Canada." In Statistics Canada, *Canadian Social Trends*. Vol. 3. Toronto: Thompson Educational Publishing, 2000.

ROESCH, ROBERTA. "Violent Families." *Parents*. Vol. 59, No. 9 (September 1984):74–76, 150–52.

ROETHLISBERGER, F.J., and WILLIAM J. DICKSON. *Management and the Worker*. Cambridge, Mass.: Harvard University Press, 1939.

ROHLEN, THOMAS P. *Japan's High Schools*. Berkeley: University of California Press, 1983.

ROMÁN, MEL, and WILLIAM HADDAD. *The Disposable Parent: The Case for Joint Custody*. New York: Holt, Rinehart & Winston, 1978.

RÓNA-TAS, ÁKOS. "The First Shall Be Last? Entrepreneurship and Communist Cadres in the Transition from Socialism." *American Journal of Sociology*. Vol. 100, No. 1 (July 1994):40–69.

ROOS, PATRICIA. "Marriage and Women's Occupational Attainment in Cross-Cultural Perspective." *American Sociological Review*. Vol. 48, No. 6 (December 1983):852–64.

RORTY, RICHARD. "The Unpatriotic Academy." *New York Times* (February 13, 1994):15.

ROSE, JERRY D. *Outbreaks*. New York: Free Press, 1982.

ROSNOW, RALPH L., and GARY ALAN FINE. *Rumor and Gossip: The Social Psychology of Hearsay*. New York: Elsevier, 1976.

ROSS, CATHERINE E., JOHN MIROWSKY, and JOAN HUBER. "Dividing Work, Sharing Work, and In-Between: Marriage Patterns and Depression." *American Sociological Review*. Vol. 48, No. 6 (December 1983):809–23.

ROSS, JOHN. "To Die in the Street: Mexico City's Homeless Population Boom as Economic Crisis Shakes Social Protections." *SSSP Newsletter*. Vol. 27, No. 2 (Summer 1996):14–15.

ROSSI, ALICE S. "Gender and Parenthood." In Alice S. Rossi, ed., *Gender and the Life Course*. New York: Aldine, 1985:161–91.

ROSTOW, WALT W. *The Stages of Economic Growth: A Non-Communist Manifesto*. Cambridge: Cambridge University Press, 1960.

————. *The World Economy: History and Prospect.* Austin: University of Texas Press, 1978.

ROSZAK, THEODORE. *The Cult of Information: The Folklore of Computers and the True Art of Thinking.* New York: Pantheon Books, 1986.

ROTHMAN, STANLEY, STEPHEN POWERS, and DAVID ROTHMAN. "Feminism in Films." *Society.* Vol. 30, No. 3 (March–April 1993):66–72.

ROUDI, NAZY. "The Demography of Islam." *Population Today.* Vol. 16, No. 3 (March 1988):6–9.

ROWE, DAVID C. "Biometrical Genetic Models of Self-Reported Delinquent Behavior: A Twin Study." *Behavior Genetics.* Vol. 13, No. 5 (1983):473–89.

ROWE, DAVID C., and D. WAYNE OSGOOD. "Heredity and Sociological Theories of Delinquency: A Reconsideration." *American Sociological Review.* Vol. 49, No. 4 (August 1984):526–40.

ROYAL COMMISSION ON ABORIGINAL PEOPLES. *Choosing Life: Special Report on Suicide among Aboriginal People.* Ottawa: Minister of Supply and Services Canada, 1995.

————. *Report of the Royal Commission on Aboriginal Peoples: Perspectives and Realities.* Vol. 4. Ottawa: Minister of Supply and Services Canada, 1996.

ROYAL COMMISSION ON THE STATUS OF WOMEN IN CANADA. *Report of the Royal Commission on the Status of Women in Canada.* Ottawa: Information Canada, 1970.

RUBENSTEIN, ELI A. "The Not So Golden Years." *Newsweek* (October 7, 1991):13.

RUBIN, KEN. "Privacy." In *The Canadian Encyclopedia.* 2d ed., Vol. 3. Edmonton: Hurtig Publishers, 1988:1761.

RUBIN, LILLIAN BRESLOW. *Worlds of Pain: Life in the Working-Class Family.* New York: Basic Books, 1976.

RUDÉ, GEORGE. *The Crowd in History: A Study of Popular Disturbances in France and England, 1730–1848.* New York: Wiley, 1964.

RULE, JAMES, and PETER BRANTLEY. "Computerized Surveillance in the Workplace: Forms and Delusions." *Sociological Forum.* Vol. 7, No. 3 (September 1992):405–23.

RYAN, WILLIAM. *Blaming the Victim.* Rev. ed. New York: Vintage Books, 1976.

SAGAN, CARL. *The Dragons of Eden.* New York: Ballantine, 1977.

SALE, KIRKPATRICK. *The Conquest of Paradise: Christopher Columbus and the Columbian Legacy.* New York: Alfred A. Knopf, 1990.

SAMPSON, ANTHONY. *The Changing Anatomy of Britain.* New York: Random House, 1982.

SAMPSON, ROBERT J., and JOHN H. LAUB. "Crime and Deviance Over the Life Course: The Salience of Adult Social Bonds." *American Sociological Review.* Vol. 55, No. 5 (October 1990):609–27.

SAPIR, EDWARD. "The Status of Linguistics as a Science." *Language.* Vol. 5 (1929):207–14.

————. *Selected Writings of Edward Sapir in Language, Culture, and Personality.* David G. Mandelbaum, ed. Berkeley: University of California Press, 1949.

SAUVÉ, ROGER. *Borderlines: What Canadians and Americans Should—but Don't—Know About Each Other.* Whitby, Ont.: McGraw-Hill Ryerson, 1994.

SCAFF, LAWRENCE A. "Max Weber and Robert Michels." *American Journal of Sociology.* Vol. 86, No. 6 (May 1981):1269–86.

SCANLON, JAMES P. "The Curious Case of Affirmative Action for Women." *Society.* Vol. 29, No. 2 (January–February 1992):36–42.

SCHAIE, I. WARNER. "Intelligence and Problem Solving." In James E. Birren and R. Bruce Sloane, eds., *Handbook of Mental Health and Aging.* Englewood Cliffs, N.J.: Prentice Hall, 1980:262–84.

SCHEFF, THOMAS J. *Being Mentally Ill: A Sociological Theory.* 2d ed. New York: Aldine, 1984.

SCHELLENBERG, KATHRYN. "Policing the Police: Technological Surveillance and the Predilection for Leniency." *Criminal Justice and Behavior* (1995).

————. "Taking It or Leaving It: Instability and Turnover in a High-Tech Firm." *Work and Occupations.* Vol. 23, No. 2 (1996):190–213.

SCHELLENBERG, KATHRYN, and GEORGE A. MILLER. "Turbulence and Bureaucracy." *Journal of Applied Behavioral Science.* Vol. 43, No. 2 (1998):202–21.

SCHMIDT, ROGER. *Exploring Religion.* Belmont, Calif.: Wadsworth, 1980.

SCHOOLER, CARMI, JOANNE MILLER, KAREN A. MILLER, and CAROL N. RICHTAND. "Work for the Household: Its Nature and Consequences for Husbands and Wives." *American Journal of Sociology.* Vol. 90, No. 1 (July 1984):97–124.

SCHUMANN, HANS WOLFGANG. *Buddhism: An Outline of Its Teachings and Schools.* Wheaton, Ill.: The Theosophical Publishing House/Quest Books, 1974.

SCHUTT, RUSSELL K. "Objectivity Versus Outrage." *Society.* Vol. 26, No. 4 (May–June 1989):14–16.

SCHWARTZ, BARRY. "Memory as a Cultural System: Abraham Lincoln in World War II." *American Sociological Review.* Vol. 61, No. 5 (October 1996):908–27.

SCHWARTZ, FELICE N. "Management, Women, and the New Facts of Life." *Harvard Business Review.* Vol. 89, No. 1 (January–February 1989):65–76.

SCHWARTZ, JOE. "Rising Status." *American Demographics.* Vol. 11, No. 1 (January 1989):10.

SCHWARTZ, MARTIN D. "Gender and Injury in Spousal Assault." *Sociological Focus.* Vol. 20, No. 1 (January 1987):61–75.

SCOMMEGNA, PAOLA. "Teens' Risk of AIDS, Unintended Pregnancies Examined." *Population Today.* Vol. 24, No. 8 (August 1996):1–2.

SCOTT, D.B. "Lean Machine." *Report on Business Magazine, The Globe and Mail* (November 1992):90–99.

SCOTT, HANNAH. *The Female Serial Killer: A Well-Kept Secret of the "Gentler Sex."* Master's thesis: University of Guelph, 1992.

SCOTT, JOHN, and CATHERINE GRIFF. *Directors of Industry: The British Corporate Network, 1904–1976.* New York: Blackwell, 1985.

SCOTT, W. RICHARD. *Organizations: Rational, Natural, and Open Systems.* Englewood Cliffs, N.J.: Prentice Hall, 1981.

SEAGER, JONI. *The State of Women in the World Atlas.* New revised 2d ed. New York: Penguin Group, 2000.

SEARS, DAVID O., and JOHN B. MCCONAHAY. *The Politics of Violence: The New Urban Blacks and the Watts Riot.* Boston: Houghton Mifflin, 1973.

SECRETARY OF STATE CANADA. *Profile of Higher Education in Canada* (S2-196/1991). Ottawa: Ministry of Supply and Services, 1992.

SEGALL, ALEXANDER, and NEENA L. CHAPPELL. *Health and Health Care in Canada.* Toronto: Prentice Hall, 2000.

SEKULIC, DUSKO, GARTH MASSEY, and RANDY HODSON. "Who Were the Yugoslavs? Failed Sources of Common Identity in the Former Yugoslavia." *American Sociological Review.* Vol. 59, No. 1 (February 1994):83–97.

SELIMUDDIN, ABU K. "The Selling of America." *USA Today.* Vol. 117, No. 2525 (March 1989):12–14.

SELLIN, THORSTEN. *The Penalty of Death.* Beverly Hills, Calif.: Sage, 1980.

SEN, K.M. *Hinduism.* Baltimore: Penguin Books, 1961.

SENNETT, RICHARD, and JONATHAN COBB. *The Hidden Injuries of Class.* New York: Vintage Books, 1973.

SEWELL, JOHN. *The Shape of the City: Toronto Struggles with Modern Planning.* Toronto: University of Toronto Press, 1993.

SHAPIRO, JOSEPH P., and JOANNIE M. SCHROF. "Honor Thy Children." *U.S. News and World Report.* Vol. 118, No. 8 (February 27, 1995):39–49.

SHAWCROSS, WILLIAM. *Sideshow: Kissinger, Nixon and the Destruction of Cambodia.* New York: Pocket Books, 1979.

SHEEHAN, TOM. "Senior Esteem as a Factor in Socioeconomic Complexity." *The Gerontologist.* Vol. 16, No. 5 (October 1976):433–40.

SHELDON, WILLIAM H., EMIL M. HARTL, and EUGENE MCDERMOTT. *Varieties of Delinquent Youth.* New York: Harper, 1949.

SHELEY, JAMES F., JOSHUA ZHANG, CHARLES J. BRODY, and JAMES D. WRIGHT. "Gang Organization, Gang Criminal Activity, and Individual Gang Members' Criminal Behavior." *Social Science Quarterly.* Vol. 76, No. 1 (March 1995):53–68.

SHERMAN, LAWRENCE W., and DOUGLAS A. SMITH. "Crime, Punishment, and Stake in Conformity: Legal and Informal Control of Domestic Violence." *American Sociological Review.* Vol. 57, No. 5 (October 1992):680–90.

SHEVKY, ESHREF, and WENDELL BELL. *Social Area Analysis.* Stanford, Calif.: Stanford University Press, 1955.

SHIELDS, JOHN, and STEPHEN MCBRIDE. "Dismantling a Nation: The Canadian Political Economy and Continental Free Trade." In Les Samuelson, ed., *Power and Resistance: Critical Thinking About Canadian Social Issues.* Halifax: Fernwood Publishing, 1994:227–60.

SHIPLER, DAVID K. *Russia: Broken Idols, Solemn Dreams.* New York: Penguin Books, 1984.

SHIPLEY, JOSEPH T. *Dictionary of Word Origins.* Totowa, N.J.: Roman & Allanheld, 1985.

SHIVELY, JOELLEN. "Cowboys and Indians: Perceptions of Western Films Among American Indians and Anglos." *American Sociological Review.* Vol. 57, No. 6 (December 1992):725–34.

SHKILNYK, ANASTASIA M. *A Poison Stronger Than Love: The Destruction of an Ojibwa Community.* New Haven: Yale University Press, 1985.

SHUPE, ANSON, WILLIAM A. STACEY, and LONNIE R. HAZLEWOOD. *Violent Men, Violent Couples: The Dynamics of Domestic Violence.* Lexington, Mass.: Lexington Books, 1987.

SHUTE, JEREMY J., and DAVID B. KNIGHT. "Obtaining an Understanding of Environmental Knowledge: Wendaban Stewardship Authority." *The Canadian Geographer.* Vol. 39, No. 2 (1995):101–11.

SIDEL, RUTH, and VICTOR W. SIDEL. *A Healthy State: An International Perspective on the Crisis in United States Medical Care.* Rev. ed. New York: Pantheon Books, 1982a.

————. *The Health Care of China.* Boston: Beacon Press, 1982b.

SILMAN, JANET. *Enough Is Enough: Aboriginal Women Speak Out.* Toronto: Women's Press, 1987.

SILVERBERG, ROBERT. "The Greenhouse Effect: Apocalypse Now or Chicken Little?" *Omni* (July 1991):50–54.

SIMMEL, GEORG. *The Sociology of Georg Simmel.* Kurt Wolff, ed. New York: Free Press, 1950:118–69.

————. "The Metropolis and Mental Life." In Kurt Wolff, ed., *The Sociology of Georg Simmel.* New York: Free Press, 1964:409–24; orig. 1905.

————. "Fashion." In Donald N. Levine, ed., *Georg Simmel: On Individuality and Social Forms.* Chicago: University of Chicago Press, 1971; orig. 1904.

SIMON, CARL P., and ANN D. WITTE. *Beating the System: The Underground Economy.* Boston: Auburn House, 1982.

SIMON, JULIAN. *The Ultimate Resource.* Princeton, N.J.: Princeton University Press, 1981.

SIMON, RITA J., and N. SHARMA. "Women and Crime: Does the American Experience Generalize?" In F. Adler and R.J. Simon, eds., *Criminology of Deviant Women.* Boston: Houghton Mifflin, 1979.

SIMONS, CAROL. "Japan's Kyoiku Mamas." In John J. Macionis and Nijole V. Benokraitis, eds., *Seeing Ourselves: Classic, Contemporary, and Cross-Cultural Readings in Sociology.* Englewood Cliffs, N.J.: Prentice Hall, 1989:281–86.

SIMONS, MARLISE. "The Price of Modernization: The Case of Brazil's Kaiapo Indians." In John J. Macionis and Nijole V. Benokraitis, eds., *Seeing Ourselves: Classic, Contemporary, and Cross-Cultural Readings in Sociology.* 5th ed. Upper Saddle River, N.J.: Prentice Hall, 2001:496–502.

SIMPSON, JEFFREY. *Faultlines: Struggling for a Canadian Vision.* Toronto: HarperCollins, 1993.

————. *Star-Spangled Canadians: Canadians Living the American Dream.* Toronto: Harper Collins, 2000.

————. "Forget the Preaching, Gay Marriage Is a Done Deal." *Globe and Mail* (August 23, 2003):A17.

SINGER, JEROME L., and DOROTHY G. SINGER. "Psychologists Look at Television: Cognitive, Developmental, Personality, and Social Policy Implications." *American Psychologist.* Vol. 38, No. 7 (July 1983):826–34.

SIVARD, RUTH LEGER. *World Military and Social Expenditures, 1987–88.* 12th ed. Washington, D.C.: World Priorities, 1988.

SKELTON, CHAD. "Decide Military's Role, Ottawa Told." *The Globe and Mail* (August 12, 1997):A4.

SKINNER, DAVID. "Computers: Good for Education?" *The Public Interest.* No. 128 (Summer 1997):98–109.

SKOCPOL, THEDA. *States and Social Revolutions: A Comparative Analysis of France, Russia, and China.* Cambridge: Cambridge University Press, 1979.

SKOLNICK, ARLENE. *The Psychology of Human Development.* New York: Harcourt Brace Jovanovich, 1986.

SLATER, PHILIP E. "Contrasting Correlates of Group Size." *Sociometry.* Vol. 21, No. 2 (June 1958):129–39.

————. *The Pursuit of Loneliness.* Boston: Beacon Press, 1976.

SMELSER, NEIL J. *Theory of Collective Behavior.* New York: Free Press, 1962.

SMILGAS, MARTHA. "The Big Chill: Fear of AIDS." *Time.* Vol. 129, No. 7 (February 16, 1987):50–53.

SMITH, ADAM. *An Inquiry into the Nature and Causes of the Wealth of Nations.* New York: The Modern Library, 1937; orig. 1776.

SMITH, DAN. *The Seventh Fire: The Struggle for Aboriginal Self-Government.* Toronto: Key Porter, 1993.

SMITH, DOROTHY E. "Women, the Family and Corporate Capitalism." In M. Stephenson, ed., *Women in Canada.* Don Mills, Ont.: General Publishing, 1977:32–48.

————. "Women's Inequality and the Family." Department of Sociology, Ontario Institute for Studies in Education, Mimeograph, 1979.

————. "Women, Class and the Family." In R. Miliband and J. Saville, eds., *The Socialist Register.* London: Merlin Press, 1983.

————. *The Everyday World as Problematic: A Feminist Sociology.* Toronto: University of Toronto Press, 1987.

SMITH, DOROTHY E., and SARA J. DAVID, eds. *Women Look at Psychiatry.* Vancouver, B.C.: Press Gang Publishers, 1975.

SMITH, DOUGLAS A. "Police Response to Interpersonal Violence: Defining the Parameters of Legal Control." *Social Forces.* Vol. 65, No. 3 (March 1987):767–82.

SMITH, DOUGLAS A., and PATRICK R. GARTIN. "Specifying Specific Deterrence: The Influence of Arrest on Future Criminal Activity." *American Sociological Review.* Vol. 54, No. 1 (February 1989):94–105.

SMITH, DOUGLAS A., and CHRISTY A. VISHER. "Street-Level Justice: Situational Determinants of Police Arrest Decisions." *Social Problems.* Vol. 29, No. 2 (December 1981):167–77.

SMITH, GWEN. "The Home Team." *Maclean's* (April 17, 1997a):68.

————. "She Shoots: She Scores!" *Elm Street* (November/December 1997b):32.

SMITH, ROBERT B. "Health Care Reform Now." *Society.* Vol. 30, No. 3 (March–April 1993):56–65.

SMITH, ROBERT ELLIS. *Privacy: How to Protect What's Left of It.* Garden City, N.Y.: Anchor/Doubleday, 1979.

SMITH-LOVIN, LYNN, and CHARLES BRODY. "Interruptions in Group Discussions: The Effects of Gender and Group Composition." *American Journal of Sociology.* Vol. 54, No. 3 (June 1989):424–35.

SMOLOWE, JILL. "When Violence Hits Home." *Time.* Vol. 144, No. 1 (July 4, 1994):18–25.

SNELL, MARILYN BERLIN. "The Purge of Nurture." *New Perspectives Quarterly.* Vol. 7, No. 1 (Winter 1990):1–2.

SNIDERMAN, PAUL M., DAVID A. NORTHRUP, JOSEPH F. FLETCHER, PETER H. RUSSELL, and PHILIP E. TETLOCK. "Psychological and Cultural Foundations of Prejudice: The Case of Anti-Semitism in Quebec." *Canadian Review of Sociology and Anthropology.* Vol. 30, No. 2 (May 1993):242–70.

SNOW, DAVID A., E. BURKE ROCHFORD, JR., STEVEN K. WORDEN, and ROBERT D. BENFORD. "Frame Alignment Processes, Micromobilization, and Movement Participation." *American Sociological Review.* Vol. 51, No. 4 (August 1986):464–81.

SNOW, DAVID A., LOUIS A. ZURCHER, JR., and SHELDON EKLAND-OLSON. "Social Networks and Social Movements: A Macrostructural Approach to Differential Recruitment." *American Sociological Review.* Vol. 45, No. 5 (October 1980):787–801.

SNOWMAN, DANIEL. *Britain and America: An Interpretation of Their Culture, 1945–1975.* New York: Harper Torchbooks, 1977.

SOUTH, SCOTT J., and STEVEN F. MESSNER. "Structural Determinants of Intergroup Association: Interracial Marriage and Crime." *American Journal of Sociology.* Vol. 91, No. 6 (May 1986):1409–30.

SOUTHWORTH, NATALIE. "Judge Refuses to Ban Spanking of Children." *The Globe and Mail* (July 6, 2000):A1.

SOWELL, THOMAS. *Ethnic America.* New York: Basic Books, 1981.

————. *Race and Culture.* New York: Basic Books, 1994.

————. "Ethnicity and IQ." In Steven Fraser, ed., *The Bell Curve Wars: Race, Intelligence and the Future of America.* New York: Basic Books, 1995:70–79.

————. *Migrations and Cultures: A World View.* New York: Basic Books, 1996.

SPATES, JAMES L. "Sociological Overview." In Alan Milberg, ed., *Street Games.* New York: McGraw-Hill, 1976a:286–90.

————. "Counterculture and Dominant Culture Values: A Cross-National Analysis of the Underground Press and Dominant Culture Magazines." *American Sociological Review.* Vol. 41, No. 5 (October 1976b):868–83.

————. "The Sociology of Values." In Ralph Turner, ed., *Annual Review of Sociology.* Vol. 9. Palo Alto, Calif.: Annual Reviews, 1983:27–49.

SPATES, JAMES L., and JOHN J. MACIONIS. *The Sociology of Cities.* 2d ed. Belmont, Calif.: Wadsworth, 1987.

SPATES, JAMES L., and H. WESLEY PERKINS. "American and English Student Values." *Comparative Social Research.* Vol. 5. Greenwich, Conn.: JAI Press, 1982:245–68.

SPECTER, MICHAEL. "Plunging Life Expectancy Puzzles Russia." *New York Times* (August 2, 1995):A1, A2.

————. "Moscow on the Make." *New York Times Magazine* (June 1, 1997):48–55, 72, 75, 80, 84.

SPEER, JAMES A. "The New Christian Right and Its Parent Company: A Study in Political Contrasts." In David G. Bromley and Anson Shupe, eds., *New Christian Politics.* Macon, Ga.: Mercer University Press, 1984:19–40.

SPITZER, STEVEN. "Toward a Marxian Theory of Deviance." In Delos H. Kelly, ed., *Criminal Behavior: Readings in Criminology.* New York: St. Martin's Press, 1980:175–91.

STACEY, JUDITH. *Patriarchy and Socialist Revolution in China.* Berkeley: University of California Press, 1983.

STANLEY, LIZ, ed. *Feminist Praxis: Research, Theory, and Epistemology in Feminist Sociology.* London: Routledge & Kegan Paul, 1990.

STANLEY, LIZ, and SUE WISE. *Breaking Out: Feminist Consciousness and Feminist Research.* London: Routledge & Kegan Paul, 1983.

STARK, EVAN, and ANN FLITCRAFT. "Domestic Violence and Female Suicide Attempts." Presentation to American Public Health Association, New York, 1979.

STARK, RODNEY. *Sociology.* Belmont, Calif.: Wadsworth, 1985.

STARK, RODNEY, and WILLIAM SIMS BAINBRIDGE. "Of Churches, Sects, and Cults: Preliminary Concepts for a Theory of Religious Movements." *Journal for the Scientific Study of Religion.* Vol. 18, No. 2 (June 1979):117–31.

STARR, PAUL. *The Social Transformation of American Medicine.* New York: Basic Books, 1982.

STATISTICS CANADA. *1881, 1921, and 1961 Censuses of Canada and Projections.* Catalogue No. 91-520. Ottawa: Statistics Canada, 1989a.

————. *Profile of Ethnic Groups—Dimensions.* Ottawa: Statistics Canada, 1989b.

————. *Perspectives on Labour and Income.* Catalogue No. 71-202. Ottawa: Statistics Canada, 1990.

————. *Lone-Parent Families in Canada.* Catalogue No. 89-522E. Ottawa: Statistics Canada, 1992a.

————. *Report on the Demographic Situation in Canada,* Catalogue No. 91-209. Ottawa: Statistics Canada, 1992b.

————. *Juristat Service Bulletin.* Catalogue No. 85-002. Ottawa: Statistics Canada, 1994a.

————. *Violence Against Women Survey.* Ottawa: Minister of Industry, Science and Technology, 1994b.

————. "Social Indicators." *Canadian Social Trends* (Spring 1996).

———. "Labour Force Survey, December 1997." *The Daily*, January 9, 1998 [online]. Available at www.statcan.ca/Daily/English/980109/d980109.htm.

———. "Suicide by Age Group, 1961–97." *Health Statistics at a Glance*. CD-ROM. Ottawa: Minister of Supply and Services Canada, 1999.

———. "2001 Census: Age and Sex," *The Daily*, July 16, 2002a [online]. Available at www.statcan.ca/Daily/English/020716/td020716.htm.

———. "Selected Dwelling Characteristics and Household Equipment," Canadian Statistics, November 27, 2002b [online]. Available at www.statcan.ca/english/Pgdb/famil09c.htm.

———. "Profile of Canadian Families and Households: Diversification Continues," 2001 Census Analysis Series, Catalogue no. 96F0030XIE2001003, October 22, 2002c [online]. Available at www12.statcan.ca/english/census01/products/analytic/companion/fam/contents.cfm?

———. "Average Hours per Week of Television Watching, Fall 2001," Canadian Statistics, December 2, 2002d [online]. Available at www.statcan.ca/english/Pgdb/arts23.htm.

———. "Television Viewing," *The Daily*, December 2, 2002e [online]. Available at www.statcan.ca/Daily/English/021202/d021202a.htm.

———. "Induced (Therapeutic) Abortions, 2000." *The Daily*, March 23, 2003a [online]. Available at www.statcan.ca/Daily/English/030328/d030328e.htm.

———. "Electronic Commerce and Technology," *The Daily*, April 2, 2003b [online]. Available at www.statcan.ca/Daily/English/030402/td030402.htm.

———. "Sexual Assault, 2002." *The Daily*, July 25, 2003c [online]. Available at www.statcan.ca/Daily/English/030725/d030725a.htm.

———. "International Adult Literacy Database," Catalogue No. 89-588-XIE, September 8, 2003d [online]. Available at www.statcan.ca/english/IPS/Data/89-588-XIE.htm.

———. "Homicides, 2002." *The Daily*, October 1, 2003e [online]. Available at www.statcan.ca/Daily/English/031001/d031001a.htm.

———. "Family Income and Participation in Postsecondary Education, 1998 to 2000," *The Daily*, October 3, 2003f [online]. Available at www.statcan.ca/Daily/English/031003/d031003b.htm.

———. "Study: Knowledge Workers in Canada's Workforce, 1971–2001," *The Daily*, October 30, 2003g [online]. Available at www.statcan.ca/Daily/English/031030/td031030.htm.

STAVRIANOS, L.S. *A Global History: The Human Heritage*. 3d ed. Englewood Cliffs, N.J.: Prentice Hall, 1983.

STEELE, SCOTT. "Women at Work: Room to Improve." *Maclean's* (August 21, 1995):28–29.

STEELE, SHELBY. *The Content of Our Character: A New Vision of Race in America*. New York: St. Martin's Press, 1990.

STEIN, MAURICE R. *The Eclipse of Community: An Interpretation of American Studies*. Princeton, N.J.: Princeton University Press, 1972.

STEVENS, ROSEMARY. *American Medicine and the Public Interest*. New Haven, Conn.: Yale University Press, 1971.

STIER, HAYA. "Continuity and Change in Women's Occupations Following First Childbirth." *Social Science Quarterly*. Vol. 77, No. 1 (March 1996):60–75.

STINCHCOMBE, ARTHUR L. "Some Empirical Consequences of the Davis-Moore Theory of Stratification," *American Sociological Review*. Vol. 28, No. 5 (October 1963).

STODDARD, SANDOL. *The Hospice Movement: A Better Way to Care for the Dying*. Briarcliff Manor, N.Y.: Stein and Day, 1978.

STONE, LAWRENCE. *The Family, Sex and Marriage in England, 1500–1800*. New York: Harper & Row, 1977.

STOUFFER, SAMUEL A., et al. *The American Soldier: Adjustment During Army Life*. Princeton, N.J.: Princeton University Press, 1949.

STOUT, CAM. "Common-law: A Growing Alternative." *Canadian Social Trends* (Summer 1994):9.

STRAUS, MURRAY A., and RICHARD J. GELLES. "Societal Change and Change in Family Violence from 1975 to 1985 as Revealed by Two National Surveys." *Journal of Marriage and the Family*. Vol. 48, No. 4 (August 1986):465–79.

STREIB, GORDON F. "Are the Aged a Minority Group?" In Bernice L. Neugarten, ed., *Middle Age and Aging: A Reader in Social Psychology*. Chicago: University of Chicago Press, 1968:35–46.

SUDNOW, DAVID N. *Passing On: The Social Organization of Dying*. Englewood Cliffs, N.J.: Prentice Hall, 1967.

SUMNER, WILLIAM GRAHAM. *Folkways*. New York: Dover, 1959; orig. 1906.

SURTEES, LAWRENCE. "Northern Telecom: The Morning After." *The Globe and Mail* (July 5, 1993): B1, B4.

SUTHERLAND, EDWIN H. "White Collar Criminality." *American Sociological Review*. Vol. 5, No. 1 (February 1940):1–12.

SUTHERLAND, EDWIN H., and DONALD R. CRESSEY. *Criminology*. 10th ed. Philadelphia: J.B. Lippincott, 1978.

SZASZ, THOMAS S. *The Manufacturer of Madness: A Comparative Study of the Inquisition and the Mental Health Movement*. New York: Dell, 1961.

———. *The Myth of Mental Illness: Foundations of a Theory of Personal Conduct*. New York: Harper & Row, 1970; orig. 1961.

———. "Mental Illness Is Still a Myth." *Society*. Vol. 31, No. 4 (May–June 1994):34–39.

———. "Idleness and Lawlessness in the Therapeutic State." *Society*. Vol. 32, No. 4 (May–June 1995):30–35.

TAIT, HEATHER. "Educational Achievement of Young Aboriginal Adults." In Statistics Canada, *Canadian Social Trends*. Vol. 3. Toronto: Thompson Educational Publishing, 2000.

TAJFEL, HENRI. "Social Psychology of Intergroup Relations." *Annual Review of Psychology*. Palo Alto, Calif.: Annual Reviews, 1982:1–39.

TANNAHILL, REAY. *Sex in History*. Chelsea, Mich.: Scarborough House Publishers, 1992.

TANNEN, DEBORAH. *You Just Don't Understand Me: Women and Men in Conversation*. New York: Wm. Morrow, 1990.

———. *Talking from 9 to 5: How Women's and Men's Conversational Styles Affect Who Gets Heard, Who Gets Credit, and What Gets Done at Work*. New York: Wm. Morrow, 1994.

TARAS, DAVID, BEVERLY RASPORICH, and ELI MANDEL. *A Passion for Identity: An Introduction to Canadian Studies*. Scarborough, Ont.: Nelson, 1993.

TARROW, SIDNEY. *Social Movements, Collective Action and Politics*. New York: Cambridge University Press, 1994.

TAVRIS, CAROL, and SUSAN SADD. *The Redbook Report on Female Sexuality*. New York: Delacorte Press, 1977.

TEPPERMAN, LORNE. "Status Inconsistency in the Toronto Elite of the 1920s." In James Curtis and William G. Scott. *Social Stratification: Canada*. 2d ed. Scarborough, Ont.: Prentice Hall, 1979.

TEPPERMAN, LORNE, and JENNY BLAIN. *Think Twice: Sociology Looks at Current Issues*. Scarborough, Ont.: Prentice-Hall, 1999.

THEEN, ROLF H.W. "Party and Bureaucracy." In Erik P. Hoffmann and Robbin F. Laird, eds., *The Soviet Polity in the Modern Era*. New York: Aldine, 1984:131–65.

THIRUNARAYANAPURAM, DESIKAN. "Population Explosion Is Far from Over." *Popline*. Vol. 20 (January–February, 1998):1, 4.

THOMAS, EDWARD J. *The Life of Buddha as Legend and History*. London: Routledge & Kegan Paul, 1975.

THOMAS, EVAN, JOHN BARRY, and MELINDA LIU. "Ground Zero." *Newsweek* (May 25, 1998):28–32A.

THOMAS, W.I. "The Relation of Research to the Social Process." In Morris Janowitz, ed., *W.I. Thomas on Social Organization and Social Personality*. Chicago: University of Chicago Press, 1966:289–305; orig. 1931.

THOMAS, W.I., and F. ZNANIECKI. *The Polish Peasant in Europe and America*. New York: Octagon Books, 1971; orig 1919.

THOMMA, STEVEN. "Christian Coalition Demands Action from GOP." *Philadelphia Inquirer* (September 14, 1997):A2.

THOMPSON, LARRY. "The Breast Cancer Gene: A Woman's Dilemma." *Time*. Vol. 143, No. 3 (January 17, 1994):52.

———. "Fertility with Less Fuss." *Time*. Vol. 144, No. 20 (November 14, 1994):79.

THORNBERRY, TERRANCE, and MARGARET FARNSWORTH. "Social Correlates of Criminal Involvement: Further Evidence on the Relationship Between Social Status and Criminal Behavior." *American Sociological Review*. Vol. 47, No. 4 (August 1982):505–18.

THORNE, BARRIE, CHERIS KRAMARAE, and NANCY HENLEY, eds. *Language, Gender and Society*. Rowley, Mass.: Newbury House, 1983.

THORNTON, ARLAND. "Changing Attitudes Toward Separation and Divorce: Causes and Consequences." *American Journal of Sociology*. Vol. 90, No. 4 (January 1985):856–72.

TILLY, CHARLES. *From Mobilization to Revolution*. Reading, Mass.: Addison-Wesley, 1978.

———. "Does Modernization Breed Revolution?" In Jack A. Goldstone, ed., *Revolutions: Theoretical, Comparative, and Historical Studies*. New York: Harcourt Brace Jovanovich, 1986:47–57.

TINDALE, JOSEPH A. N.A.C.A. "Older Workers in an Aging Workforce." Ottawa: Statistics Canada, 1991.

TITTLE, CHARLES R., and WAYNE J. VILLEMEZ. "Social Class and Criminality." *Social Forces*. Vol. 56, No. 22 (December 1977):474–502.

TITTLE, CHARLES R., WAYNE J. VILLEMEZ, and DOUGLAS A. SMITH. "The Myth of Social Class and Criminality: An Empirical Assessment of the Empirical Evidence." *American Sociological Review*. Vol. 43, No. 5 (October 1978):643–56.

TODD, DOUGLAS. "Giving Old Age Meaning." *National Post* (July 28, 2003): A11.

TÖNNIES, FERDINAND. *Community and Society (Gemeinschaft und Gesellschaft)*. New York: Harper & Row, 1963; orig. 1887.

TOFANI, LORETTA. "AIDS Ravages a Continent, and Sweeps a Family." *Philadelphia Inquirer* (March 24, 1991):1, 15–A.

TOLSON, JAY. "The Trouble with Elites." *The Wilson Quarterly*. Vol. XIX, No. 1 (Winter 1995):6–8.

TOMLINSON, BRIAN. "Development in the 1990s: Critical Reflections on Canada's Economic Relations with the Third World." In Jamie Swift and

Brian Tomlinson, eds., *Conflicts of Interest: Canada and the Third World.* Toronto: Between the Lines, 1991.

TREAS, JUDITH. "Socialist Organization and Economic Development in China: Latent Consequences for the Aged." *The Gerontologist.* Vol. 19, No. 1 (February 1979):34–43.

———. "Older Americans in the 1990s and Beyond." *Population Bulletin.* Vol. 50, No. 2 (May 1995). Washington, D.C.: Population Reference Bureau.

TREIMAN, DONALD J. "Industrialization and Social Stratification." In Edward O. Laumann, ed., *Social Stratification: Research and Theory for the 1970s.* Indianapolis, Ind.: Bobbs-Merrill, 1970.

TRENT, KATHERINE. "Family Context and Adolescents' Expectations About Marriage, Fertility, and Nonmarital Childbearing." *Social Science Quarterly.* Vol. 75, No. 2 (June 1994):319–39.

TROELTSCH, ERNST. *The Social Teaching of the Christian Churches.* New York: Macmillan, 1931.

TROIDEN, RICHARD R. *Gay and Lesbian Identity: A Sociological Analysis.* Dix Hills, N.Y.: General Hall, 1988.

TUMIN, MELVIN M. "Some Principles of Stratification: A Critical Analysis." *American Sociological Review.* Vol. 18, No. 4 (August 1953):387–94.

———. *Social Stratification: The Forms and Functions of Inequality.* 2d ed. Englewood Cliffs, N.J.: Prentice Hall, 1985.

TURCOTTE, PIERRE, and ALAIN BÉLANGER. "Moving in Together: The Formation of First Common-Law Unions." In *Canadian Social Trends: Volume 3.* Toronto: Thompson Educational Publishing, 2000:105–8.

TURNER, RALPH H., and LEWIS M. KILLIAN. *Collective Behavior.* 2d ed. Englewood Cliffs, N.J.: Prentice Hall, 1972; 3d ed., 1987; 4th ed., 1993.

TYGIEL, JULES. *Baseball's Great Experiment: Jackie Robinson and His Legacy.* New York: Oxford University Press, 1983.

TYREE, ANDREA, MOSHE SEMYONOV, and ROBERT W. HODGE. "Gaps and Glissandos: Inequality, Economic Development, and Social Mobility in 24 Countries." *American Sociological Review.* Vol. 44, No. 3 (June 1979):410–24.

UCHITELLE, LOUIS. "But Just Who is That Fairy Godmother?" *New York Times* (September 29,1991):Section 4, p. 1.

UJIMOTO, K. VICTOR. "Postwar Japanese Immigrants in British Columbia: Japanese Culture and Job Transferability." In Jean Leonard Elliott, ed., *Two Nations, Many Cultures: Ethnic Groups in Canada.* Scarborough, Ont.: Prentice Hall, 1979.

UNITED NATIONS. *Demographic Yearbook, 1996.*

UNITED NATIONS DEVELOPMENT PROGRAMME. *Human Development Report 1990.* New York: Oxford University Press, 1990.

———. *Human Development Report 1991.* New York: Oxford University Press, 1991.

———. *Human Development Report 1993.* New York: Oxford University Press, 1993.

———. *Human Development Report 1994.* New York: Oxford University Press, 1994.

———. *Human Development Report 1995.* New York: Oxford University Press, 1995.

———. *Human Development Report 1996.* New York: Oxford University Press, 1996.

———. *Human Development Report 1997.* New York: Oxford University Press, 1997.

———. *Human Development Report 1999.* New York: Oxford University Press, 1999.

———. *Human Development Report 2000.* New York: Oxford University Press, 2000.

———. *Human Development Report 2001.* New York: Oxford University Press, 2001.

———. *Human Development Report 2003.* "Human Development Index," Human Development Report 2003 [online]. Available at www.undp.org.

UNIVERSITY OF AKRON RESEARCH CENTER. *National Survey of Religion and Politics 1992.* Akron, Ohio: University of Akron Research Center, 1993.

UNNEVER, JAMES D., CHARLES E. FRAZIER, and JOHN C. HENRETTA. "Race Differences in Criminal Sentencing." *The Sociological Quarterly.* Vol. 21, No. 2 (Spring 1980):197–205.

U.S. BUREAU OF JUSTICE STATISTICS. *Criminal Victimization 1998: Changes 1997–98 with Trends 1993–98.* Washington, D.C.: The Bureau, 1999.

———. *Sourcebook of Criminal Justice Statistics 1998.* Washington, D.C.: The Bureau, 1999.

U.S. CENSUS BUREAU. Press release on homeless count (CB91–117). Washington, D.C.: U.S. Government Printing Office, 1991.

———. *Health Insurance Coverage* (P60-208). Washington, D.C.: The Bureau, 1999.

———. *International Data Base.* [online]. Available at www.census.gov/ipc/www/idbprint.html, February 24, 2000.

U.S. DEPARTMENT OF LABOR. *International Comparisons of Hourly Compensation Costs for Production Workers in Manufacturing, 1975–1998.* Supplementary tables for BLS News Release USDL 00–07, January 11, 2000. Washington, D.C.: The Bureau, 2000.

———. *International Comparisons of Hourly Compensation Costs for Production Workers in Manufacturing, 1975–1999.* Supplementary tables for BLS News Release USDL 00-254, September 7, 2000. Washington, D.C.: The Bureau, 2000.

USEEM, BERT. "Disorganization and the New Mexico Prison Riot of 1980." *American Sociological Review.* Vol. 50, No. 5 (October 1985):677–88.

USEEM, MICHAEL. "The Social Organization of the Corporate Business Elite and Participation of Corporate Directors in the Governance of American Institutions." *American Sociological Review.* Vol. 44, No. 4 (August 1979):553–72.

U.S. HOUSE OF REPRESENTATIVES. "Street Children: A Global Disgrace." Hearing on November 7, 1991. Washington, D.C.: U.S. Government Printing Office, 1992.

VALLAS, STEPHEN P., and JOHN P. BECK. "The Transformation of Work Revisited: The Limits of Flexibility in American Manufacturing." *Social Problems.* Vol. 43, No. 3 (August 1996):339–61.

VALLEE, F.G. "Porter, John Arthur." In *The Canadian Encyclopedia.* 2d ed. Edmonton: Hurtig Publishers, 1988: 1726.

VALOCCHI, STEVE. "The Emergence of the Integrationist Ideology in the Civil Rights Movement." *Social Problems.* Vol. 43, No. 1 (February 1996):116–30.

VAN BIEMA, DAVID. "Parents Who Kill." *Time.* Vol. 144, No. 20 (November 14, 1994):50–51.

———. "Buddhism in America." *Time.* Vol. 150, No. 15 (October 13, 1997):71–81.

VAN DEN HAAG, ERNEST, and JOHN P. CONRAD. *The Death Penalty: A Debate.* New York: Plenum Press, 1983.

VAN LOON, RICHARD J., and MICHAEL S. WHITTINGTON. *The Canadian Political System: Environment, Structure and Process.* 3d ed. Toronto: McGraw-Hill Ryerson, 1981.

VARDY, JILL. "Job Hopes Take Sharp Nosedive." *The Financial Post* (August 7, 1993):1.

VAUGHAN, MARY KAY. "Multinational Corporations: The World as a Company Town." In Ahamed Idris-Soven et al., eds., *The World as a Company Town: Multinational Corporations and Social Change.* The Hague: Mouton Publishers, 1978:15–35.

VEBLEN, THORSTEIN. *The Theory of the Leisure Class.* New York: The New American Library, 1953; orig. 1899.

VIGUERIE, RICHARD A. *The New Right: We're Ready to Lead.* Falls Church, Va.: The Viguerie Company, 1981.

VINES, GAIL. "Whose Baby Is It Anyway?" *New Scientist.* No. 1515 (July 3, 1986):26–27.

VOGEL, EZRA F. *The Four Little Dragons: The Spread of Industrialization in East Asia.* Cambridge, Mass.: Harvard University Press, 1991.

VOGEL, LISE. *Marxism and the Oppression of Women: Toward a Unitary Theory.* New Brunswick, N.J.: Rutgers University Press, 1983.

VOLD, GEORGE B., and THOMAS J. BERNARD. *Theoretical Criminology.* 3d ed. New York: Oxford University Press, 1986.

VON HIRSH, ANDREW. *Past or Future Crimes: Deservedness and Dangerousness in the Sentencing of Criminals.* New Brunswick, N.J.: Rutgers University Press, 1986.

VONNEGUT, KURT, JR. "Harrison Bergeron." In *Welcome to the Monkey House.* New York: Delacorte Press/Seymour Lawrence, 1968:7–13; orig. 1961.

VOWELL, SARAH. "Canuck Yuks." *Salon,* January 27, 1999 [online]. Available www.salon.com/ent/music/vowe/1999/01/27vowe.html.

WAITE, LINDA J., GUS W. HAGGSTROM, and DAVID I. KANOUSE. "The Consequences of Parenthood for the Marital Stability of Young Adults." *American Sociological Review.* Vol. 50, No. 6 (December 1985):850–57.

WAITE, P.B. "Confederation." In *The Canadian Encyclopedia.* 2d ed. Edmonton: Hurtig Publishers, 1988:488–89.

WALDFOGEL, JANE. "The Effect of Children on Women's Wages." *American Sociological Review.* Vol. 62, No. 2 (April 1997):209–17.

WALDIE, PAUL. "Report Deepens Bre-X Fiasco." *The Globe and Mail* (February 19, 1998).

WALDIE, PAUL, and KAREN HOWLETT. "Reports Reveal Tight Grip of Ebbers on WorldCom." *The Globe and Mail* (June 11, 2003):B1, B7.

WALKER, JAMES W. ST. G. *A History of Blacks in Canada.* Ottawa: Ministry of Supply and Services Canada, 1980.

WALL, THOMAS F. *Medical Ethics: Basic Moral Issues.* Washington, D.C.: University Press of America, 1980.

WALLACE, RUTH A., and ALISON WOLF. *Contemporary Sociological Theory: Continuing the Classic Tradition.* 4th ed. Englewood Cliffs, N.J.: Prentice Hall, 1995.

WALLER, DOUGLAS. "Onward Cyber Soldiers." *Time.* Vol. 146, No. 8 (August 21, 1995):38–44.

WALLERSTEIN, IMMANUEL. *The Modern World-System: Capitalist Agriculture and the Origins of the European World-Economy in the Sixteenth Century.* New York: Academic Press, 1974.

———. *The Capitalist World-Economy.* New York: Cambridge University Press, 1979.

———. "Crises: The World Economy, the Movements, and the Ideologies." In Albert Bergesen, ed., *Crises in the World-System*. Beverly Hills, Calif.: Sage, 1983:21–36.

———. *The Politics of the World Economy: The States, the Movements, and the Civilizations*. Cambridge: Cambridge University Press, 1984.

WALLERSTEIN, JUDITH S., and SANDRA BLAKESLEE. *Second Chances: Men, Women, and Children a Decade After Divorce*. New York: Ticknor & Fields, 1989.

WALTON, JOHN, and CHARLES RAGIN. "Global and National Sources of Political Protest: Third World Responses to the Debt Crisis." *American Sociological Review*. Vol. 55, No. 6 (December 1990):876–90.

WARNER, W. LLOYD, and J.O. LOW. *The Social System of the Modern Factory*. Yankee City Series, Vol. 4. New Haven, Conn.: Yale University Press, 1947.

WARNER, W. LLOYD, and PAUL S. LUNT. *The Social Life of a Modern Community*. New Haven, Conn.: Yale University Press, 1941.

WATSON, JOHN B. *Behaviorism*. Rev. ed. New York: Norton, 1930.

WATSON, WILLIAM. "Economy." In *The Canadian Encyclopedia*. 2d ed. Edmonton: Hurtig Publishers. 1988: 652–56.

WAXMAN, CHAIM I. *The Stigma of Poverty: A Critique of Poverty Theories and Policies*. 2d ed. New York: Pergamon Press, 1983.

WATTENBERG, BEN J. "The Population Explosion Is Over." *New York Times Magazine* (November 23, 1997):60–63.

We Need to Know About AIDS. Ottawa: Minister of National Health and Welfare, 1994.

WEBER, ADNA FERRIN. *The Growth of Cities*. New York: Columbia University Press, 1963; orig. 1899.

WEBER, MAX. *The Protestant Ethic and the Spirit of Capitalism*. New York: Charles Scribner's Sons, 1958a; orig. 1904–5.

———. "Science as a Vocation." In H.H. Gerth and C. Wright Mills, *From Max Weber: Essays in Sociology*. New York: Oxford University Press, 1958b:129–56; orig. 1918.

———. *Economy and Society*. G. Roth and C. Wittich, eds. Berkeley: University of California Press, 1978; orig. 1921.

WEBSTER, MURRAY, JR., and STUART J. HYSOM. "Creating Status Characteristics." *American Sociological Review*. Vol. 63, No. 3 (June 1998):351–78.

WEBSTER, PAMELA S., TERRI ORBUCH, and JAMES S. HOUSE. "Effects of Childhood Family Background on Adult Marital Quality and Perceived Stability." *American Journal of Sociology*. Vol. 101, No. 2 (September 1995):404–32.

WEEKS, JOHN R. "The Demography of Islamic Nations." *Population Bulletin*. Vol. 43, No. 4 (December 1988). Washington, D.C.: Population Reference Bureau.

WEINBERG, GEORGE. *Society and the Healthy Homosexual*. Garden City, N.Y.: Anchor Books, 1973.

WEINER, TIM. "Head of C.I.A. Plans Center to Protect U.S. Cyberspace." *New York Times* (June 26, 1996):B7.

WEINRICH, JAMES D. *Sexual Landscapes: Why We Are What We Are, Why We Love Whom We Love*. New York: Charles Scribner's Sons, 1987.

WEISBERG, D. KELLY. *Children of the Night: A Study of Adolescent Prostitution*. Lexington, Mass.: D.C. Heath, 1985.

WEISNER, THOMAS S., and BERNICE T. EIDUSON. "The Children of the '60s as Parents." *Psychology Today* (January 1986):60–66.

WEITZMAN, LENORE J. *The Divorce Revolution: The Unexpected Social and Economic Consequences for Women and Children in America*. New York: Free Press, 1985.

———. "The Economic Consequences of Divorce Are Still Unequal: Comment on Peterson." *American Sociological Review*. Vol. 61, No. 3 (June 1996):537–38.

WELLER, JACK M., and E.L. QUARANTELLI. "Neglected Characteristics of Collective Behavior." *American Journal of Sociology*. Vol. 79, No. 3 (November 1973):665–85.

WELLFORD, CHARLES. "Labeling Theory and Criminology: An Assessment." In Delos H. Kelly, ed., *Criminal Behavior: Readings in Criminology*. New York: St. Martin's Press, 1980:234–47.

WELLMAN, BARRY. "The Community Question: Intimate Networks of East Yorkers." *American Journal of Sociology*. Vol. 84, No. 5 (March 1979):1201–31.

WELLMAN, BARRY, and MILENA GULIA. "Net-Surfers Don't Ride Alone: Virtual Communities as Communities." In Barry Wellman, ed., *Networks in the Global Village: Life in Contemporary Communities*. Boulder, Colo.: Westview Press, 1999:331–66.

WELLS, JENNIFER. "Jobs." *Maclean's* (March 11, 1996):12–16.

WENDELL, SUSAN. "Toward a Feminist Theory of Disability." In E.D. Nelson and B.W. Robinson, eds., *Gender in the 1990's: Images, Realities, and Issues*. Toronto: Nelson Canada, 1995:455–56.

WENKE, ROBERT J. *Patterns of Prehistory*. New York: Oxford University Press, 1980.

WESOLOWSKI, WLODZIMIERZ. "Transition from Authoritarianism to Democracy." *Social Research*. Vol. 57, No. 2 (Summer 1990):435–61.

WESTHUES, ANNE, and JOYCE S. COHEN. "International Adoption in Canada: Predictions of Well-Being." In *Child Welfare in Canada: Research and Policy Implications*, ed. Joe Hudson and Burt Galaway. Toronto: Thompson Educational Publishing, 1994.

WHALEN, JACK, and RICHARD FLACKS. *Beyond the Barricades: The Sixties Generation Grows Up*. Philadelphia: Temple University Press, 1989.

WHEELIS, ALLEN. *The Quest for Identity*. New York: Norton, 1958.

WHITAKER, MARK. "Ten Ways to Fight Terrorism." *Newsweek* (July 1, 1985):26–29.

WHITE, RALPH, and RONALD LIPPITT. "Leader Behavior and Member Reaction in Three 'Social Climates.'" In Dorwin Cartwright and Alvin Zander, eds., *Group Dynamics*. Evanston, Ill.: Row, Peterson, 1953:586–611.

WHITE, WALTER. *Rope and Faggot*. New York: Arno Press and New York Times, 1969; orig. 1929.

WHITMAN, DAVID. "Shattering Myths About the Homeless." *U.S. News & World Report* (March 20, 1989):26, 28.

WHITNELL, TIM. "MD Wants Tabloids Banned." *The Burlington Post* (September 7, 1997):1.

WHYTE, DONALD R., and FRANK G. VALLEE. "Sociology." In *The Canadian Encyclopedia*. 2d ed. Edmonton: Hurtig Publishers, 1988:2035–36.

WHYTE, WILLIAM FOOTE. *Street Corner Society*. 3d ed. Chicago: University of Chicago Press, 1981; orig. 1943.

WHYTE, WILLIAM H., JR. *The Organization Man*. Garden City, N.Y.: Anchor Books, 1957.

WIARDA, HOWARD J. "Ethnocentrism and Third World Development." *Society*. Vol. 24, No. 6 (September–October 1987):55–64.

WIATROWSKI, MICHAEL A., DAVID B. GRISWOLD, and MARY K. ROBERTS. "Social Control Theory and Delinquency." *American Sociological Review*. Vol. 46, No. 5 (October 1981):525–41.

WIDDIS-BARR, CATHY. "The Importance and Potential of Leaders' Debates." In Frederick J. Fletcher, ed., *Media and Voters in Canadian Election Campaigns*, Vol. 18 of the Research Papers of the Royal Commission on Electoral Reform and Party Finance. Ottawa and Toronto: RCERPF/Dundurn, 1991.

WIDOM, CATHY SPATZ. "Childhood Sexual Abuse and Its Criminal Consequences." *Society*. Vol. 33, No. 4 (May/June 1996):47–53.

WILES, P.J.D. *Economic Institutions Compared*. New York: Halsted Press, 1977.

WILKINS, R., and O.B. ADAMS. *Healthfulness of Life: A Unified View of Mortality, Institutionalization, and Non-institutionalized Disability in Canada*. Montreal: The Institute for Research on Public Policy, 1983:126.

WILLIAMS, T. *The Impact of Television: A Natural Experiment in Three Communities*. New York: Academic Press, 1986.

WILLIAMSON, JEFFREY G., and PETER H. LINDERT. *American Inequality: A Macroeconomic History*. New York: Academic Press, 1980.

WILSON, BRYAN. *Religion in Sociological Perspective*. New York: Oxford University Press, 1982.

WILSON, EDWARD O. *Sociobiology: The New Synthesis*. Cambridge, Mass.: Belknap Press of the Harvard University Press, 1975.

———. *On Human Nature*. New York: Bantam Books, 1978.

———. "Biodiversity, Prosperity, and Value." In F. Herbert Bormann and Stephen R. Kellert, eds., *Ecology, Economics, and Ethics: The Broken Circle*. New Haven, Conn.: Yale University Press, 1991:3–10.

WILSON, JAMES Q. *Bureaucracy: What Government Agencies Do and Why They Do It*. New York: Basic Books, 1991.

———. "Crime, Race, and Values." *Society*. Vol. 30, No. 1 (November–December 1992):90–93.

WILSON, JAMES Q., and RICHARD J. HERRNSTEIN. *Crime and Human Nature*. New York: Simon and Schuster, 1985.

WILSON, LOGAN. *American Academics Then and Now*. New York: Oxford University Press, 1979.

WILSON, ROBERT R. "Playing and Being Played: Experiencing West Edmonton Mall." In Lynne van Luven and Priscilla L. Walton, eds., *Pop Can: Popular Culture in Canada*. Scarborough: Prentice Hall, 1999:82–90.

WINN, MARIE. *Children Without Childhood*. New York: Pantheon Books, 1983.

WINSLOW, DONNA. *The Canadian Airborne Regiment in Somalia. A Socio-cultural Inquiry*. Ottawa: Commission of Inquiry into the Deployment of Canadian Forces to Somalia, 1997.

WIRTH, LOUIS. "Urbanism as a Way of Life." *American Journal of Sociology*. Vol. 44, No. 1 (July 1938):1–24.

WITKIN-LANOIL, GEORGIA. *The Female Stress Syndrome: How to Recognize and Live With It*. New York: Newmarket Press, 1984.

WOLF, DIANE L., ed. *Feminist Dilemma of Fieldwork*. Boulder, Colo.: Westview Press, 1996.

WOLF, NAOMI. *The Beauty Myth: How Images of Beauty Are Used Against Women*. New York: William Morrow, 1990.

WOLFE, DAVID B. "Targeting the Mature Mind." *American Demographics*. Vol. 16, No. 3 (March 1994):32–36.

WOLFE, TOM. *Radical Chic*. New York: Bantam, 1970.

WOLFF, LEE, and DOROTA GEISSEL. "Street Prostitution in Canada." In Statistics Canada, *Canadian Social Trends*. Vol. 3. Toronto: Thompson Educational Publishing, 2000.

WOLFGANG, MARVIN E., ROBERT M. FIGLIO, and THORSTEN SELLIN. *Delinquency in a Birth Cohort*. Chicago: University of Chicago Press, 1972.

WOLFGANG, MARVIN E., TERRENCE P. THORNBERRY, and ROBERT M. FIGLIO. *From Boy to Man, From Delinquency to Crime*. Chicago: University of Chicago Press, 1987.

Women in Canada: A Statistical Report. 3d ed. Catalogue No. 89-503E. Ottawa: Statistics Canada, 1995.

Women in the Labour Force. Ottawa: Statistics Canada, 1990–91.

WOOD, DANIELL. "Death Wish: Would You Choose an Assisted Suicide?" *Chatelaine* (July 25–29, 1993):94.

WOODWARD, KENNETH L. "Feminism and the Churches." *Newsweek*. Vol. 13, No. 7 (February 13, 1989):58–61.

———. "The Elite, and How to Avoid It." *Newsweek* (July 20, 1992):55.

WOOLEY, ORLAND W., SUSAN C. WOOLEY, and SUE R. DYRENFORTH. "Obesity and Women—II: A Neglected Feminist Topic." *Women's Studies International Quarterly*. Vol. 2 (1979):81–92.

THE WORLD BANK. *World Development Report 1991: The Challenge of Development*. New York: Oxford University Press, 1991.

———. *World Development Report 1993*. New York: Oxford University Press, 1993.

———. *World Development Report 1995: Workers in an Integrating World*. New York: Oxford University Press, 1995.

———. *World Development Report 1997: The State in a Changing World*. New York: Oxford University Press, 1997.

———. *Entering the 21st Century: World Development Report 1999/2000*. New York: Oxford University Press, 2000.

———. *World Development Report 2000/2001*. Washington, D.C.: The World Bank, 2001.

———. *World Development Indicators 2001*. Washington, D.C.: The World Bank, 2001.

———. *World Bank Atlas 2001*. Washington, D.C.: The World Bank, 2001.

WORLD HEALTH ORGANIZATION. *Constitution of the World Health Organization*. New York: World Health Organization Interim Commission, 1946.

World Values Survey, 1990–1993. Ann Arbor, Mich.: Inter-university Consortium for Political and Social Research, 1994.

WORSLEY, PETER. "Models of the World System." In Mike Featherstone, ed., *Global Culture: Nationalism, Globalization, and Modernity*. Newbury Park, Calif.: Sage, 1990:83–95.

WOTHERSPOON, TERRY. "Transforming Canada's Education System: The Impact on Educational Inequalities, Opportunities and Benefits." In B. Singh Bolaria, ed., *Social Issues and Contradictions in Canadian Society*. Toronto: Harcourt Brace Jovanovich, 1991:448–63.

WOTHERSPOON, TERRY, and VIC SATZEWICH. *First Nations: Race, Class, and Gender Relations*. Scarborough, Ont.: Nelson, 1993.

WREN, CHRISTOPHER S. "In Soweto-by-the-Sea, Misery Lives on as Apartheid Fades." *New York Times* (June 9, 1991):1, 7.

WRIGHT, ERIK OLIN. *Classes*. London: Verso, 1985.

WRIGHT, ERIK OLIN, ANDREW LEVINE, and ELLIOTT SOBER. *Reconstructing Marxism: Essays on Explanation and the Theory of History*. London: Verso, 1992.

WRIGHT, ERIK OLIN, and BILL MARTIN. "The Transformation of the American Class Structure, 1960–1980." *American Journal of Sociology*. Vol. 93, No. 1 (July 1987):1–29.

WRIGHT, JAMES D. "Ten Essential Observations on Guns in America." *Society*. Vol. 32, No. 3 (March–April 1995):63–68.

WRIGHT, QUINCY. "Causes of War in the Atomic Age." In William M. Evan and Stephen Hilgartner, eds., *The Arms Race and Nuclear War*. Englewood Cliffs, N.J.: Prentice Hall, 1987:7–10.

WRIGHT, RICHARD A. *In Defense of Prisons*. Westport, Conn.: Greenwood Press, 1994.

WRIGHT, ROBERT. "The Man Who Invented the Web." *Time*, Canadian Edition (May 19, 1997):44.

WRIGHT, STUART A., and WILLIAM V. D'ANTONIO. "The Substructure of Religion: A Further Study." *Journal for the Scientific Study of Religion*. Vol. 19, No. 3 (September 1980):292–98.

WRIGHT, STUART A., and ELIZABETH S. PIPER. "Families and Cults: Familial Factors Related to Youth Leaving or Remaining in Deviant Religious Groups." *Journal of Marriage and the Family*. Vol. 48, No. 1 (February 1986):15–25.

WU, LAWRENCE L. "Effects of Family Instability, Income, and Income Instability on the Risk of a Premarital Birth." *American Sociological Review*. Vol. 61, No. 3 (June 1996):386–406.

WU, ZHENG. *Cohabitation: An Alternative Form of Family Living*. Don Mills, Ont.: Oxford University Press, 2000.

YATES, RONALD E. "Growing Old in Japan: They Ask Gods for a Way Out." *Philadelphia Inquirer* (August 14, 1986):3A.

YEATTS, DALE E. "Self-Managed Work Teams: Innovation in Progress." *Business and Economic Quarterly* (Fall–Winter 1991):2–6.

———. "Creating the High Performance Self-Managed Work Team: A Review of Theoretical Perspectives." Paper presented at the annual meeting of the Social Science Association, Dallas, February 1995.

YODER, JAN D., and Robert C. Nichols. "A Life Perspective: Comparison of Married and Divorced Persons." *Journal of Marriage and the Family*. Vol. 42, No. 2 (May 1980):413–19.

YOELS, WILLIAM C., and JEFFREY MICHAEL CLAIR. "Laughter in the Clinic: Humor in Social Organization." *Symbolic Interaction*. Vol. 18, No. 1 (1995):39–58.

YORK, GEOFFREY. "UN Body Chastises Canada on Poverty." *The Globe and Mail* (June 25, 1993):A1–2.

ZASLAVSKY, VICTOR. *The Neo-Stalinist State: Class, Ethnicity, and Consensus in Soviet Society*. Armonk, N.Y.: M.E. Sharpe, 1982.

ZEITLIN, IRVING M. *The Social Condition of Humanity*. New York: Oxford University Press, 1981.

ZIMBARDO, PHILIP G. "Pathology of Imprisonment." *Society*. Vol. 9 (April 1972):4–8.

ZUBOFF, SHOSHANA. "New Worlds of Computer-Mediated Work." *Harvard Business Review*. Vol. 60, No. 5 (September–October 1982):142–52.

ZURCHER, LOUIS A., and DAVID A. SNOW. "Collective Behavior and Social Movements." In Morris Rosenberg and Ralph Turner, eds., *Social Psychology: Sociological Perspectives*. New York: Basic Books, 1981:447–82.

CREDITS

PHOTO CREDITS

Paul W. Liebhardt, *ii*; George Breithaupt, *xxxi*.

CHAPTER 1: Smithsonian American Art Museum/Art Resource, N.Y., *2*; Linda Gerber, *3*; Caroline Penn/Corbis, *4 (top, left)*; Paul W. Liebhardt, *4 (top, centre; bottom, left; bottom, centre; bottom, right)*; Minh-Thu Pham, *4 (top, right)*; Paul W. Liebhardt, *5*; Lineair/Peter Arnold, Inc., *7*; Private Collection/The Stapleton Collection/The Bridgeman Art Library International Ltd., *11*; Simon Bening, *April: Farmyard with Woman Milking Cow*, from *Da Costa Book of Hours*. Bruges, c. 1515. © The Pierpont Morgan Library, New York. M.399, F.5V/Art Resource, N.Y., *13 (left)*; Getty Images, Inc., *13 (right)*; National Archives of Canada PA 19694, *15 (left)*; Carleton University, *15 (centre left)*; Canadian Press/CP, *15 (right)*; American Sociological Association, *15 (right)*; Janet Marqusee Fine Arts Ltd., *16*; Paul Marcus/Studio SPM Inc., *17*; Christie's Images/The Bridgeman Art Library International Ltd., *19*; CP Photo/Hamilton Spectator-Sheryl Nadler, *22*.

CHAPTER 2: Alex Colville, *To Prince Edward Island*, 1965, acrylic emulsion on masonite, 61.9 × 92.5 cm, National Gallery of Canada, Ottawa, © NGC/MBAC, *26*; Mike Appleton, Jennifer Becker, Kevin Bucknor, Ryan Daniels, Ryan Genoe, Amanda Ono/photo by Linda Gerber, *27*; Index/The Bridgeman Art Library. ©2003 Banco de Mexico Diego Rivera & Frida Kahlo Museums Trust. Av. Cinco de Mayo No., 2, Col. Centro, Del. Cuauhtemoc 06059, Mexico, D.F., *29*; John Eastcott/Yva Momatiuk/The Image Works, *30*; Bob Daemmrich/Stock Boston, *32*; Argas/Getty Images, *34 (right)*; Steve McCurry/Magnum Photos, Inc., *34 (left)*; Mark Richards/PhotoEdit, *38*; Corbis, *39 (left)*; The Library of Congress, *39 (right)*; Fred Cattroll, *40*; Canadian Press CP, *41*; Bill Keay/Vancouver Sun, *43*; David Bradnum/Robert Estall Photo Agency, *46*; Eugene Fisher Photography Worldwide, *49*.

CHAPTER 3: Emily Carr (1871–1945), *Gitwangak, Queen Charlotte Islands*, 1912, oil on canvas, 33 × 35 inches. Courtesy of Kenneth R. Thomson, personal collection. Associated Press AP, *54*; Tomas Friedmann/Photo Researchers, Inc., *56*; Paul W. Liebhardt, *57 (top, left; middle, left)*; Carlos Humberto/TDC/Contact/Corbis/Stock Market, *57 (top, centre)*; Doranne Jacobson/International Images, *57 (top, right)*; David Austen/Stock Boston, *57 (middle, centre)*; Getty Images, Inc., *57 (middle, right)*; Doranne Jacobson/International Images, *57 (bottom, left)*; Jack Fields/Photo Researchers, Inc., *57 (bottom, right)*; Dimitri Lovetsky/AP/Wide World Photos, *59*; *Mrs. Picasso Dusts the Mantelpiece*, from *Great Housewives of Art* by Sally Swain. Copyright ©1988, 1989 by Sally Swain. Used by permission of Viking Penguin, a division of Penguin Putnam, Inc., *62*; Margaret Courtney-Clarke/Tom Keller and Associates LLC, *64*; Canapress/E.J. Flynn, *69*; J. P. Laffont/Corbis/Sygma, *71*; Jeff Greenberg/Picture Cube Inc., *74 (left)*; Alex Webb/Magnum Photo Inc., *74 (centre)*; Pedrick/The Image Works, *74 (right)*; Sabina Doweell *75 (left)*; CLEO Photo/Jeroboam, Inc., *75 (centre)*; David Young-Wolff/PhotoEdit, *75 (right)*; Copyright 1952, 1980 Ruth Orkin/Getty Images, Inc., *77*; Esther Konigsberg/photo by Linda Gerber, *78*.

CHAPTER 4: Arnaudet/Art Resource, N.Y., *82*; S.S.C. Photo Centre A.S.C. All rights reserved, *83*; Patrick Bordes/Photo Researchers, Inc., *84*; Victor Englebert/Photo Researchers, Inc., *85*; Robert Frerck/Woodfin Camp & Associates, *86*; Getty Images, Inc., *88 (left)*; Corbis/Sygma, *88 (right)*; Corbis, *94*; Norbert Goeneutte *The Paupers' Meal on a Winter Day in Paris*. Waterhouse and Dodd, London. Fine Art Photographic Library, London/Art Resource, N.Y., *95*; Charles Steiner/The Image Works, *96*; The Granger Collection, *98*; D.C. Moore Gallery, *99*; Elliot Landy/Magnum Photos, Inc., *100 (left; centre, left; centre right)*; Robert Sorbo/AP/Wide World Photos, *100 (right)*.

CHAPTER 5: The Bridgeman Art Library International Ltd., *106*; Stanford News Service, *107*; Ted Horowitz/Corbis/Stock Market, *108 (left)*; Henley & Savage/Corbis/Stock Market, *108 (centre)*; Tom Pollack, *108 (right)*; William Kurelek, *Prairie Childhood*, by permission of the Estate of William Kurelek, courtesy of the Isaacs Gallery of Toronto, *109*; Elizabeth Crews/Elizabeth Crews Photography, *112*; Rimma Gerlovina and Valeriy Gerlovin, *115*; Linda Gerber, *118*; Mary Ellen Mark, *122*; G.G. Kopliak (b.1942), *Still Life*, private collection, SuperStock, Inc., *125*; Danny Lyon/Magnum Photos, Inc., *126*; *Toronto Star*/P. Edwards, *127*.

CHAPTER 6: *The Game of Fox and Geese* taken from *They Sought a New World*, © 1985 the estate of William Kurelek, published by Tundra Books, *130*; John Macionis, *131*; Prentice Hall Archives, *132*; CP Photo/Frank Gunn, *133*; DiMaggio/Kalish/Corbis/Stock Market, *136*; Wesley Bocxce/Photo Researchers, Inc., *137*; Comstock, *139*; David Cooper/Getty Images, Inc., *141 (top, left)*; Alan Weiner/Getty Images, Inc., *141 (top, centre)*; Lynn McLaren/Index Stock Imagery, Inc., *141 (top, right)*; Guido Rossi/Getty Images, Inc., *141 (bottom, left)*; Richard Pan, *141 (bottom, centre)*; Costa Manos/Magnum Photos, Inc., *141 (bottom, right)*; Paul Ekman, Ph.D. Professor of Psychology, University of California, San Francisco, *142 (left and right)*; Paul W. Liebhardt, *143 (left; centre; right)*; Angela Maynard/Getty Images, Inc./PhotoDisc, Inc., *145*; Courtesy of Alliance Atlantis Communications Inc., *148*.

CHAPTER 7: The Bridgeman Art Library International Ltd, *154*; Nik Wheeler/Corbis, *155*; CP Photo/Paul Chiasson, *156*; Alex Charlton. Andrew Edelman, Noah Forster, Martin Gerber, Chris Golda/photo by Linda Gerber, *157*; Jonathan Green Studios, Inc., *162*; Dick Hemingway, *163*; Martin Gerber/photo by Linda Gerber, *164*; The Cartoon Bank, *166*; Jonathan Cliché Bibliotheque nationale de France, Paris. From *The Horizon History of China* by the editors of *Horizon Magazine*, The Horizon Publishing Co., Inc., 551 5th Avenue, New York, N.Y. 10017. ©1969, *169*; Paul W. Liebhardt, *170*; The Metropolitan Museum of Art, *172*; Gabe Palmer/The Stock Market, *174*; Saleh Rifai/AP/Wide World Photos, *175*.

CHAPTER 8: Andy Warhol, *Marilyn*, 1967, © 2001 Andy Warhol Foundation for the Visual Arts/Artist Rights Society (ARS), New York Tate Gallery, London, Art Resource, NY, *182*; © 2000 Allen McInnis, all rights reserved, *183*; Andre Gallant/The Image Bank, *184 (top, left)*; Pete Turner/The Image Bank, *184 (top, centre)*; Brun/Photo Researchers, Inc., *184 (top, right)*; Bruno Hadjih/Liaison Agency, Inc., *184 (bottom, left)*; Elliot Erwitt/Magnum Photos, Inc. *184 (bottom, centre)*; George Holton/Photo Researchers, Inc., *184 (bottom, right)*; David McCoy/Rainbow, *186*; Ted Grant/CP Archives, *187*; Robert Noonan/Photo Researchers, Inc., *189(a)*; Biophoto Associates/Science Source/Photo Researchers Inc., *189(b)*; SIU/Photo Researchers, Inc., *189(c)*; Ray Ellis/Science Source/Photo Researchers, Inc., *189(d)*; SIU/Photo Researchers, Inc., *189(e)*; Scott Camazine/Sue Trainor/Photo Researchers, Inc., *189(f, g)*; Canadian Press MACLEANS, *193*; Linda Gerber, *195*; Mark Peterson/SABA Press Photos, Inc., *199*; AKG London Ltd, *200*.

CHAPTER 9: Noah's Ark Fine Art, *206*; Associated Press AP, *207*; SIPA Press, *208*; Dick Hemingway, *209*; Paul W. Liebhardt, *211*; Canapress/Kevin Frayer, *213*; Canapress/Paul Chiasson, *215*; Danny Hellman, *216*; Rich Pedroncelli/AP/Wide World Photos, *222*.

CHAPTER 10: Paul Marcus/Studio SPM Inc., *234*; Illustration by Ken Marshall ©1992 from *Titanic: An Illustrated History*, a Viking Studio/Madison Press Book, *235*; Sebastiao Selgado/Contact Press Images Inc., *236*; Doranne Jacobson/International Images, *237*; Linda Gerber, *238*; Per-Anders Pettersson/Black Star, *239*; John Launois/Black Star, *241*; Francisco Conde/Impact Visuals Photo & Graphics, Inc., *242*; Bridgeman Art Library/London/SuperStock, Inc., *243*; Agence-France Press/Corbis-Bettman, *247*; Doranne Jacobson/International Images, *251*.

CHAPTER 11: Smithsonian American Art Museum/Art Resource, N.Y., *258*; Bob Carroll, *259*; Grapes/Michaud/Photo Researchers, *265 (left)*; Burt Glinn/Magnum Photos, Inc., *265 (right)*; First Light/P. Barton, *266*; Greg Locke, *267*; Dick Hemingway, *271*; Tony Stone Images/Bruce Ayres, *272*; Christie's Images, Inc., *275*; Argus Fotoarchiv/Peter Arnold, Inc., *276*.

CHAPTER 12: The Bridgeman Art Library International Ltd, *282*; Photo by Gregory Kane, Baltimore Sun, *283*; Tony Arruza/Corbis, *285 (left)*; Reuters/Juan Carlos Ulate/Getty Images Inc., *285 (right)*; Martin Benjamin/The Image Works, *286 (top, left)*; Peter Turnley/Corbis, *286 (top, right)*; Pablo Bartholomew/Getty Images, Inc., *286 (bottom)*; Yuri Cortez/AFP Photo/Corbis, *287*; Malcolm Linton/Getty Images, Inc., *293*; Joe McDonald/Corbis, *294 (left)*; Robert van der Hilst/Corbis, *294 (centre)*; Wolfgang Kaehler/Corbis, *294 (right)*; Sean Sprague, *296*; Jane Ash Poitras, *Living in the Storm Too Long*, courtesy of Jane Ash Poitras, photo by Janet Anderson, Thunder Bay Art Gallery, *298*; Steve McCurry/Magnum Photos, Inc., *299*.

CHAPTER 13: Getty Images, Inc., *308*; Archive Photos, *309*; Jon Feingersh/Corbis/Stock Market, *311*; Angela Fisher/Carol Beckwith/Robert Estall Photo Agency, *312*; Underwood & Underwood/Corbis, *314*; Ed Malitsky/Index Stock Imagery, Inc., *316*; CP Photo/Kevin Frayer, *321*; Photo PC/AOC/Mike Ridewood, *325*; R.W. Jones/Corbis, *326*; Liza McCoy, *327*; UNICEF/HQ96-1041/Tapas Barua, *329*.

CHAPTER 14: Claire Carew, *Unforgettable*, 1993, oil on canvas, 120 cm × 90 cm. In honour of the life of Mr. Harry Van Helm Braam. Courtesy of Claire Carew, *334*; Black Cultural Centre for Nova Scotia, *335*; Linda Gerber, *336*; Peter Turnley/Corbis, *339*; Culver Pictures Inc., *346*; EPA Photo/EPA/Warren Toda, *349*; Canapress/Ryan Remiorz, *351*.

CHAPTER 15: Scala/Art Resource, N.Y., *360*; Rob Crandall/Rob Crandall Photographer, *361*; Michael Drummond, Photographer, *365*; Eve Arnold/Magnum Photos, *369*; *The Whitehorse Star*/Cathie Archbould, *373*; Robin Sachs/PhotoEdit, *374*; Ira Wyman/Corbis Sygma, *375*; Alan Oddie/PhotoEdit, *379*.

CHAPTER 16: Latina/Latino Studies Program, University of Illinois at Urbana-Champaign, *382*; Marko Shark, *383*; American Textile History Museum, Lowell, MA, *385*; Bellavia/REA/Corbis/SABA Press Photos, Inc., *389 (left)*; John Bryson/Corbis/Sygma, *389 (right)*; Patrick Ward/Stock Boston, *390*; Christopher Morris, *393*; Fundacion Jose Clemente Orozco, *395*; Dick Hemingway, *403*; Chris Brown/Corbis/SABA Press Photos, Inc., *406*.

CHAPTER 17: Christiane Pflug, *With the Black Flag*, 1971, oil on canvas, 137.2 × 142.2 cm. Art Gallery of Ontario, Toronto, gift of Dr. Michael Pflug, Toronto, 1975, donated by the Ontario Heritage Foundation, 1988 © Dr. Michael Pflug, *410*; Canapress/Jeff McIntosh, *411*; Robert Cooper/National Archives of Canada. Copyright: National Archives of Canada/PA-142647, *413*; David Ball/Index Stock Imagery, Inc., *416*; Government of Canada, *417*; Fred Cattroll, *421*; Canadian Press WFP, *422*; CP/Clement Allard, *426 (left)*; CP/Adrian Wyld, *426 (right)*; Elections Canada, *428*; National Archives of Canada, *429 (left & right)*; Andrade Patrick/Gamma Press, *436*; Joe McNally, Life Magazine ©TimePix, *438*.

CHAPTER 18: Courtesy of Daphne Odjig and the Bearclaw Gallery, *444*; Toronto Sun/Craig Robertson, *445*; G. Stephen/*Toronto Star*, *446*; The Bridgeman Art Library International Ltd, *451*; Barbara Walton/AP/Wide World Images, *452*; Christian Pierre, B. 1962, *I Do*. American Private Collection, Superstock, Inc., *453*; William Kurelek, *Manitoba Party*, National Gallery of Canada, Ottawa, by permission of the estate of William Kurelek, c/o The Isaacs Gallery of Toronto, *456*; Paul Marcus/Studio SPM Inc., *458*; Sheldon Memorial Art Gallery, *460*; Stern (Ullah)/Black Star, *466*.

CHAPTER 19: McMichael Canadian Art Collection, *470*; Mark Peterson/SABA Press Photos, Inc., *471*; Michael Freeman/Corbis, *472*; Owen Franken/Corbis, *473*; Mathieu Polak/Corbis/Sygma, *475*; Doranne Jacobson/International Images, *477*; Annie Griffiths Belt/NGS Image Collection, *479*; Thomas Caplain/Corbis/Sygma, *483*; Hans Kemp/Sygma, *484*; Nick Kelsh/Kelsh Wilson Design Inc., *490*.

CHAPTER 20: Philadelphia Museum of Art/Corbis, *494*; Richard Kalvar/Magnum Photos, Inc., *495*; Doranne Jacobson/International Images, *497*; Bob Daemmrich Photography, Inc., *501*; Tom McCarthy/Corbis/Stock Market, *502 (left)*; Michael Newman/PhotoEdit, *502 (right)*; Mugshots/Corbis/Stock Market, *509*; First Light, *513*.

CHAPTER 21: Courtesy of Dale Auger, *518*; Reuters/Fred Prouser/Getty Images, Inc., *519*; Rijksmuseum, *520*; Mark Peters/Arthur Berry, *521*; Lehman/SABA Press Photos, Inc., *522*; John Coletti/Picture Cube, Inc., *525*; Canapress/Andrew Vaughan, *529*; Adalbert Franz Seligmann, *Allgemeines Krankenhaus* (*General Hospital*) 19th Century Painting, canvas. Professor Theodor Billroth lectures at the General Hospital, Vienna. 1880. Erich Lessing/Art Resource, N.Y., *530*; Galen Rowell/Mountain Light Photography, Inc., *531*; ABC Television/Globe Photos, Inc., *535 (left)*; NBC/Everett Collection, Inc., *535 (right)*; Copyright The Supreme Court of Canada, The Supreme Court of Canada Collection, *538*.

CHAPTER 22: Museum of the City of New York, *542*; Ontario Ministry of Agriculture and Food, *543*; Shawn G. Henry/Material World, *550 (left)*; Jose Manuel Navia/Material World, *550 (right)*; Lauren Goodsmith/The Image Works, *551*; First Light/Craig Hammell; *556*; Christie's Images, *558 (left)*; SuperStock, *558 (right)*; John Wang/PhotoDisc, Inc., *560*; Chip Simons/Getty Images, Inc., *561*; Gregory G. Dimijian/Photo Researchers, Inc., *569*.

CHAPTER 23: © Franklin McMahon/Corbis, *574*; Canapress/S. Komulainen, *575*; Alexis Duclos/Liaison Agency, Inc., *577*; Canapress/J. Boissinot, *578*; Sabina Dowell, *580*; Canapress, CP Photo, *581*; Tom Kelley/Getty Images, Inc., *583 (top, left)*; Inge Morath/Magnum Photos, Inc., *583 (top, centre, left)*; Kimberly Maier, *583 (top, centre, right)*; Willie L. Hill, Jr./Stock Boston, *583 (top, right)*; Michael Grecco/Stock Boston, *583 (bottom, left)*; © Mike Blake/Reuters NewMedia Inc./Corbis, *583 (bottom, right)*; Steve Weinberg/Corbis/Sygma, *587*; CP Photo/Tom Hanson, *588*; Reuters/Peter Jones, *592*.

CHAPTER 24: © Forrest J. Ackerman Collection/Corbis, *596*; Mauri Rautkari/World Wide Fund for Nature, *597*; Mark Peters, *599*; Christie's Images, Inc., *601*; Whitney Museum of American Art, *603*; Simon & Schuster/PH College, *604*; Christie's Images, Inc., *606*; Scala/Art Resource, N.Y., *608 (left)*; Paul Marcus/Studio SPM Inc., *608 (right)*.

LITERARY CREDITS

CHAPTER 1: Table 1-1 The Ten Best Places to Live in the World According to the UN Human Development Index. United Nations Development Program, Human Development Index from Human Development Report 1997, 2001, 2003 available at www.undp.org, *10*.

CHAPTER 2: Table 2-1 Correlates of Piercing and Tattoos. From *Canada's Teens: Yesterday, Today and Tomorrow*, by Reginald Biddy, Stoddart, p. 73. With permission of Reginald Bibby, *28*.

CHAPTER 3: Opening vignette extracted form *Kiss of the Fur Queen* by Tomson Highway. Copyright © Thomson Highway 1988. Reprinted by permission of Doubleday Canada, *55*.

CHAPTER 4: Opening vignette from *Canadian Society: A Macro Analysis*, 4th Edition, by Hiller, Harry H., 2000, Pearson Education Canada. Reprinted with permission by Pearson Canada, *83*.

CHAPTER 5: Opening vignette excerpt from *A Serious Widow*, by Constance Beresford Howe, published by McClelland & Stewart, *107*; Opening vignette from *My Father's House* by Sylvia Fraser, copyright 1987 by Sylvia Fraser. Published by Doubleday Canada, *116*; Figure 5-2 Television Viewing by Province, 1998. Adapted from the Statistics Canada CANSIM database <http://cansim2.statcan.ca>, Table 502-0002, *119*; Figure 5-3 Television Viewing by Age and Sex, 1998 adapted from the Statistics Canada CANSIM database <http://cansim2.statcan.ca>, Table 502-0002, *119*.

CHAPTER 6: Opening vignette excerpt from *Wilderness Tips*, by Margaret Atwood. Used by permission, McClelland & Stewart, Ltd. *The Canadian Publishers*, *131*; Figure 6-2 Common-Law Unions as Proportion of First Unions: Canada, Quebec, and Other Provinces from the article *Moving in Together: The Formation of First Common-Law Unions* by Turcotte, Pierre and Alain Bélanger, published in the Statistics Canada publication *Canadian Social Trends*, Catalogue 11-008, Summer 1997, No. 47, *135*.

CHAPTER 7: Canada Map 7-1 Employment in Government Service, 2001: Percent by Census Division from the Statistics Canada CANSIM database <http://cansim2.statcan.ca>, Table 183-003, *171*.

CHAPTER 8: Table 8-1 Measuring Changing Attitudes towards Nonmarital Sex, Extramarital Sex, and Homosexuality, 1975 to 1995. Material from *The Biddy Report*. Copyright © 1995 by Reginald W. Biddy. Reprinted with permission, *188*.

CHAPTER 9: Canada Map 9-1 Homicide Rates for Canada, Provinces, and Territories, 1997–2001 (Five Year Averages, Rates Per 100 000 People) adapted from the Statistics Canada website http://www.statcan.ca/english/Pgdb/legal12a.htm, *221*; Figure 9-4 Firearm Homicide Rates by Type of Firearm in Canada 1988–1998. Adapted from the Statistics Canada publication *Juristat*, Catalogue 85-002 Vol. 19, No.10, October 1999, *225*.

CHAPTER 11: Canada Map 11-1 Median Incomes by Province, Territory, and Census Subdivision, 2000; Data complied from Statistics Canada online data base, B2020 Profile Series, *262*; Table 11-2 Occupational Categories by Average Blishen Scores, Years of Schooling, Income, and Sex, 1986; adapted from the Statistics Canada publication *General Social Survey Analysis Series*, Catalogue 11-612, 1992 no.7, *263*.

CHAPTER 13: Table 13-4 Milestones for Women in Canadian Politics adapted from the Statistics Canada publication *Canada Yearbook*, Catalogue 11-402, 1992, *323*.

CHAPTER 14: Opening vignette from *Welcome Home: Travels in Smalltown Canada* by Stuart McLean. Copyright © Stuart McLean, permission of Penguin Group (Canada), a Division of Pearson Penguin Canada Inc., *335*; excerpt from Anderson, Alan B. and James S. Frideres. *Ethnicity in Canada: Theoretical Perspectives*. Toronto: Butterworths, 1981:208, *342*; Table 14-1 The Top 25 Ethnic Origins in Canada, Showing Single- and Multiple-Origin Response, 2001 adapted from the Statistics Canada Website http://www12.statcan.ca/english/census01/products/hightlights/ETO/Table1.cfm?Lang=E&T=501&GV=1&GID=0, *347*; Table 14-2 Ethnic Origins for Canada adapted from the Statistics Canada Website http://www12.statcan.ca/english/census01/products/hightlights/ETO/Table1.cfm?Lang=E&T=501&GV=1&GID=0, *348*; Canada Map 14-1 Percentage of Population Foreign-Born for Canada, the Provinces, Territories, and Census Subdivision, 2001. Adapted from the Statistics Canada Website http://statcan.ca/english/Pgdb/demo46a.htm, *355*.

CHAPTER 15: Figure 15-1 Age Pyramids of Canada for 1951, 1981, and 2011 adapted from the Statistics Canada publication *Report on the Demographic Situations in Canada*, Catalogue 91-209, 1992, *362*; Table 15-1 Happiness Reported by Senior Men and Women by Health of Self and Spouse, 1996–1997 from the Statistics Canada publication *Canadian Social Trends*, Catalogue 11-008, Summer 1992, No. 25, *370*; Figure 15.2 Sources of Emotional Support for Elderly Men and Women without Spouses, 1990 adapted form the Statistics Canada publication *General Social Survey Analysis Series*, Catalogue 89F00133, May 2003, *371*.

CHAPTER 16: Table 16-1 Employment among 25- to 44-Year-Olds by Sex and Educational Attainment, 2002 adapted from the Statistics Canada publication *Women in Canada: Work Chapter Updates*, Catalogue 89F00133, May

2003; *396*; Canada Map 16-1 Unemployment Rate by province, Territory, and Census Subdivision, 2000 adapted from the Statistics Canada CANSIM database <http://cansim2.statcan.ca>, Table 183-0003, *397*; Table 16-2 The Top 30 Companies in Canada Ranked by Profits, 2002 reprinted with permission from *The Globe and Mail*, *401*.

CHAPTER 18: Table 18-2 Approval of Intergroup Marriage, 1975 through 1995 from *The Biddy Report* copyright © 1995 by Reginald W. Biddy. Reprinted with permission, *457*; Canada Map 18-1 Population Aged 15 Years and Older That Is Divorced (Percentage, by Province and Territory), 2001 From the Statistics Canada Website http://www.statcan.ca/english/census96/oct14/mar1.htm, *461*.

CHAPTER 19: Table 19-1 Religious Affiliation for Canada's Largest Religions: Percentage of the Population in 2001 created from the Statistics Canada 1991 Census of Canada data Individual Public Use Microdata Files; *485*; Canada Map 19-1 Canadians Claiming "No Religion" (by Province, Territory, and Census Subdivision), 2001 adapted from *Religions in Canada*, Catalogue No. 93-319, *486*; Table 19-2 Average Income by Selected Religious Affiliation, 1991 created from the Statistics Canada 1991 Census of Canada data Individual Public Use Microdata Files, *488*.

CHAPTER 20: Canada Map 20-1 Population 15 Years or Older with University Degree (Percentages by Province, Territory, and Census Subdivision) 2001 from the Statistics Canada Website: http://www.statcan.ca/english/Pgdb/educ41a.htm, *503*; Figure 20-3 Educational Attainment for Selected Categories, 1991 created from the Statistics Canada 1991 Census of Canada data Individual Public Use Microdata Files, *505*; Figure 20-4 Employment among 25- to 44-Year-Olds by Educational Attainment and Sex, 2001 adapted from the Statistics Canada publication *Women in Canada: Work Chapter Updates*, Catalogue 89F00133, May 2003, *508*; Table 20-1 Average Earnings of the Population 15 Years and Over by Highest Level of Schooling, Provinces and Territories, 2001 adapted from the Statistics Canada Website http://www.statcan.ca/english/Pgdb/demo46a.htm, *509*.

CHAPTER 21: Canada Map 21-1 Percentage of Population 12 Years and Over Smoking Cigarettes Daily, 2000–2001 from the Statistics Canada Website http://www.statcan.ca/english/Pgdb/health07a.htm, *524*.

CHAPTER 22: Canada Map 22-1 Birth Rates per 1000 Population, by Province and Territory, 2001-2003 (July1–June 30) adapted from the Statistics Canada publication *Annual Demographic Statistic*s, 1996, Catalogue 91-213, April 1997, *544*; Figure 22-2 Age-Sex Population Pyramids for Canada, 1971–2002 adapted from the Statistics Canada publication *Age, Sex and Marital Status (data products: nation series: 1991 Census of Population*, 1991, Catalogue 93-310, July 1992, *547*; Figure 22-3 The Demographic Composition of Sweden and Kenya data complied from the Demographic Yearbook, *548*; Table 22-1 The Urban Population of Canada, 1871–2001 adapted from the Statistics Canada publication *Population and Dwelling Counts-Urban Areas (data products; population and dwelling counts: 1991 Census of Population)*, 1991, Catalogue 93-305, June 1992, *555*; Table 22-2 Population of Census Metropolitan Areas in Canada, 1956 and 2001 adapted from the Statistics Canada publication *Population and Dwelling Counts–Urban Areas 1991 Census of Population*, 1991, Catalogue 93-305, June 1992, *555*; Table 22-3 Net Interprovincial Migration in Canada, 1956–2001 adapted from the Statistics Canada publication *Population and Dwelling Counts—Urban Areas (data products: population and dwelling counts: 1991 Census of Population)*, 1991, Catalogue 93-305, June 1992, *557*; map titled "Largest Sources of Total Releases On-site and Off-site (adjusted) in North America, 2000: States and Provinces" North American Commission for Environmental Cooperation, *567*.

CHAPTER 24: Table 24-1 Canadian Mobility by Age Group (Percentage Changing Residence over a Five-Year Period) data calculated from the Statistics Canada 1996 National Tables, *602*.

NAME INDEX

A

Abbott, A., 394
Abbott, D., 222
Abbott, S., 198
Abel, S., 373
Abella, I., 481
Aberle, D. F., 584, 585
Aboriginal Peoples Television
  Network, 121, 150
About Turn, 127
Abrahamson, P. R., 561
Access to Justice Network, 232
Ackerman, F. J., 596
Action Group for Violence on
  Television, 120
Adams, O. B., 523
Addams, J., 14, 15
Adelson, J., 460
Adorno, T. W., 340, 341
Advisory Council on Suicide
  Prevention, 6
Ageton, S. S., 222, 223
Aglukark, S., 121
Aguirre, B. E., 576, 583
Ahlburg, D. A., 461
Ahmad, S., 551
Akers, R. L., 214
Alam, S., 296
Alan Guttmacher Institute, 194
Alba, R. D., 344
Albas, C., 35
Albas, D., 35
Albrecht, W. P. Jr., 395
Alderson, A., 252
Alexander, L. M., 341
Allahar, A. L., 395
Allan, E. A., 212
Allen, F., 119
Altman, D., 533
American Medical
  Association, 120
American Psychological
  Assocation, 119
American Sociological
  Association, 39
Amnesty International, 225,
  226
Anderson, A. B., 342
Anderson, D., 36
Anderson, J. W., 452
Ang, I., 120
Angelou, M., 475
Angier, N., 185, 191
Applebome, P., 491
Aquinas, T., 12
Arai, A. B., 5, 503
Arar, M., 434
Archer, D., 230
Arendt, H., 412, 417
Aries, P., 122
Ariès, P., 376
Aristotle, 12, 244, 495
Arjomand, S. A., 480
Armstrong, J., 196
Arnaz, D., 121
Arnup, K., 445
Artibise, A. F. J., 338, 555
Asch, S., 159

Ashford, L. S., 551
Astone, N. M., 463
Atchley, R. C., 371, 375, 379
Atwood, M., 135
Auger, D., 518
Aurelius, M., 12
Axtell, R. E., 75

B

Badets, J., 349
Bahl, V., 237
Bailey, D., 22
Bailey, W. C., 230
Bainbridge, W. S., 477
Baker, M., 457
Baker, M. A., 310
Bakker, J. I. (Hans), 35, 392
Baldus, B., 117
Bales, R. F., 158, 449
Baltes, P. B., 366
Baltzell, E. D., 248
Banfield, E., 274, 275, 279
Banting, 71
Barash, D., 76, 77
Baril, A., 475, 477, 484, 485
Barker, E., 478
Barlow, M., 407, 513
Baron, J. N., 588
Barrett, S. R., 339, 584
Barry, K., 327, 329
Bashevkin, S. B., 428
Bassett, I., 172
Bassuk, E. J., 276
Bauer, P. T., 293, 296
Baydar, N., 331
BBC, 580
Beach, F. A., 191
Beaujot, R., 352
Beck, F. D., 296, 404
Beck, J. P., 397
Becker, A., 519
Becker, H. S., 208, 213
Beckwith, C., 46
Beeghley, L., 252
Begin, P., 461
Begley, S., 109, 568
Bélanger, A., 135
Bell, A. G., 71, 151
Bell, A. P., 464
Bell, D., 88
Bell, W., 558
Bellah, R. N., 63, 77, 488
Bellas, M. L., 321
Belle, M., 194
Belon, J., 282
Belsky, J., 117, 118
Beltrame, J., 529
Bem, S. L., 313
Bendix, R., 238
Benedetti, P., 16, 144, 512, 614
Benedict, R., 201, 498
Benet, S., 369
Benjamin, B., 371
Benjamin, L., 337
Benn, C., 553
Bennett, W. J., 612, 613
Benokraitis, N. V., 150, 318,
  321

Bercuson, D., 566
Beresford-Howe, C., 124, 125
Bergamo, M., 292
Berger, P. L., 35, 150, 293, 296,
  404, 473, 474, 492, 600, 601,
  605, 608
Berger , P. L., 3
Bergesen, A., 298, 404
Berk, R. A., 579
Bernard, J., 263, 314, 318, 322,
  328, 457
Bernard, L. C., 313
Bernard, T. J., 215, 217
Bernstein, N., 179
Bernstein, R. J., 611
Berry, B., 558
Berscheid, E., 453
Besharov, D. J., 462
Bess, I., 371
Best, R., 71, 118
Bibby, R. W., 27, 28, 103, 113,
  138, 187, 188, 189, 190, 192,
  193, 200, 202, 331, 338, 343,
  445, 453, 454, 457, 475, 484,
  485, 486–487, 488, 489, 592,
  611, 613
Biblarz, T. J., 463
Billson, J. M., 11
Birnbaum, J. H., 196
Bishop, M. F., 328
Bissoondath, N., 343
Bisttram, E., 19
Black, N., 429
Blain, J., 228
Blakeslee, S., 460, 463
Blau, J., 223
Blau, P. M., 20, 162, 163, 223,
  450
Blishen, B. R., 262, 263, 530,
  531
Blum, L. M., 321
Blumberg, A., 228
Blumberg, P., 607
Blumer, H. G., 577, 583, 584,
  589
Blumstein, P., 453, 464
Boff, L., 476
Bogardus, E., 341
Bohannan, P., 459
Bohm, R. M., 230
Boli, J., 417
Bonilla-Santiago, G., 323
Bonner, J., 314
Booth, A., 459
Borgmann, A., 611
Boritch, H., 222
Bormann, F. H., 561, 562, 571
Boswell, T., 298
Bott, E., 269, 456
Bouchard, L., 423
Boulding, E., 87
Bourassa, K., 194, 195, 464
Bourassa, R., 357
Bourne, W. D., 318
Bowles, S., 504
Boyd, M., 510
Boyer, D., 196
Brady Bill, 224

Braithwaite, J., 222, 223
Branegan, J., 416
Brant, J., 346
Brantley, P., 397
Breen, L., 373
Brend, Y., 373
Breton, R., 11, 162, 343, 344,
  350, 353, 356, 400
Brinton, C., 432
Brinton, M. C., 242, 498
Brodie, J., 400
Brody, C., 141
Bronson, H., 398
Brooks-Gunn, J., 331
Brown, L. J., 465
Brown, L. R., 569, 570, 571
Brown, M. E., 120
Bruegel, P., 558
Bruno, M., 372
Brym, R. J., 16, 249, 400, 559,
  607
Brzezinski, Z., 417
Buraway, M., 391
Burden of Desire, 559
Burke, T., 571
Burkett, E., 293
Burstein, P., 588
Busby, L. J., 315
Bush, G. W., 426, 434, 436, 539
Butler, R. N., 373
Butterworth, D., 345

C

Cahill, K., 245
Callahan, D., 378
Callow, A. B. Jr., 553
Calvin, J., 96
Camarotti, G., 292
Came, B., 79
Cameron, W. B., 584
Campbell, B., 407
Campbell, K., 427, 428
Canada Census, 264
Canada Year book, 453
Canada's 125th Anniversary
  Yearbook, 315, 322
Canadian Advisory Council on
  the Status of Women, 322
Canadian Association of
  Broadcasters, 120
Canadian Broadcasting
  Company, 150
Canadian Crime Statistics, 220,
  221
Canadian Global Almanac, 418,
  551, 557
Canadian Medical
  Association, 530
Canadian Medical Association
  Masterfile, 534
Canadian Press/Léger
  Marketing, 192
Canadian Radio-television and
  Telecommunications
  Commission, 120
Canadian Social Trends, 510
Canetti, E., 579
Cantor, M. G., 120

Cantril, H., 582
Caplow, T., 539
Capone, A., 211
Carew, C., 334
Carley, K., 162
Carlson, N. A., 231
Carmichael, S., 342
Carr, E., 54
Carriére, Y., 366
Carrigan, O. D., 211, 212, 217
CBC, 325
Census 2001, 485
Census Canada, 319
Centre for Addiction and
  Mental Health, 232
Cerra, M., 606
Chagall, M., 451, 453
Chance, J. K., 345
Chandler, T., 552
Change, K.-C., 552
Chappell, N. L., 365, 536
Chard, J., 349
Charest, J., 353, 357
Chauncey, G., 193
Che-Alford, J. 370, 371
Cherlin, A., 458, 460
Chown, S. M., 371
Christian, W., 422
Clair, J. M., 150
Clark, C. B., 372
Clark, J., 145, 356, 427
Clark, M. S., 163, 248
Clark, S. D., 238
Clarke, R., 565, 566
Clayson, D. E., 219
Clement, W., 249, 261, 265,
  398, 402, 430, 607
Clinard, M., 222
Clinton, B., 426
Cloud, J., 471
Clover, C., 568
Cloward, R., 212, 586
Cluff, J., 222
Cobb, J., 277, 278, 508
Coe, M. D., 552
Cohen, A., 212
Cohen, J. S., 447
Cohen, L. R., 325
Cohn, R. M., 368
Colapinto, J., 185
Coleman, J. S., 170
Coleman, W. D., 352
Collins, J., 299, 300
Collins, R., 327, 508
Colombo, J. R. 362, 454, 459,
  514, 557
Colton, H., 186
Colville, A., 26
Commission on Systemic
  Racism in the Ontario
  Criminal Justice System, 223,
  226
Comte, A., 11–12, 14, 17, 24,
  30, 35
Connett, P., 563
Connett, P. H., 561
Conrad, J. P., 230
Contreras, J., 245
Cooley, C. H., 115, 128, 156,
  581
Cooper, B., 566

Cooper, P. W., 463
Copeland, P., 191
Copernicus, 12
Copps, S., 428
Corak, M., 503, 505
Corbeil, J.-P., 499
Corbeil, Jean-Pierre., 21
Cordell, A. J., 176
Corley, R. N., 563
Cornell, C. P., 323
Correctional Service Canada,
  223
Côté, J. E., 395
Cottrell, J., 345
Counts, G. S., 37, 262
Courtney, A. E., 315
Cousens, P., 183, 185
Coverman, S., 392
Cowan, C. P., 318
Cowgill, D., 370
Cowley, G., 537
Cowley, P., 525, 539
Cox, H., 488
COYOTE, 201
Creese, G., 262, 263, 271
Cressey, D. R., 217
Crispell, D., 58
Crompton, S. 370
Crook, S., 611
Cross, J., 217
Crouse, J., 504
Cuff, E. C., 90, 94
Cumming, E., 374
Curie, M., 71
Currie, E., 224
Curtis, J. E., 167, 271
Curtiss, S., 110
Cutright, P., 238

D
Da Pont, M., 319
Dahl, R. A., 429
Dahrendorf, R., 248, 398, 605
Dalgish, B., 396, 397
Daly, M., 208, 475
Dannefer, D., 123
D'Antonio, W. V., 473
Darnton, N., 534
Darwin, C., 76, 108, 129, 244,
  491
Davies, C., 150
Davies, J. C., 432, 585, 586
Davies, M., 118
Davis, D. M., 315
Davis, K., 107, 110, 200,
  245–248, 246, 254, 255, 256
Day, S., 426, 538
de Broucker, P., 503, 510
De Pisa, C., 12
De Vita, C. J., 461
Deber, R., 538
Deckard, B. S., 329
Dedrick, D. K., 439
DeHart, N., 16, 144, 512, 614
DeKeseredy, W. S., 114, 198,
  199, 462
Delacroix, J., 298, 404
Delaney, B., 258
della Cava, M. R., 377
Demerath, N. J. III., 33
Depew, R., 227

DeVilliers, P., 230
Dewey, J., 499
Diamond, M., 185
Dickason, O. P., 345, 420
Dickerson, J. F., 169
Dickson, W. J., 41
Diefenbaker, J., 354, 412
Diehl, R. A., 552
Dilthey, W., 35
Dinitz, S., 209
Disraeli, B., 50
Dixon, W. J., 298
Dizard, J. E., 466
Dollard, J., 339, 585
Donovan, V. K., 111
Douglas, T., 533
Douglass, R. L., 372
Dowler, K., 63
Doyle, J. A., 331
Doyle, R. F., 330
Driedger, L., 348
Dryburgh, H. 194
Du Bois, W. E. B., 14, 15
Dubé, F. 321
Dubos, R., 519
Ducharme, M., 346
Duffy, A., 272
Duhl, L. J., 531
Durkheim, É., 6, 12, 16, 17, 24,
  30, 39, 47, 52, 83, 99–100,
  101–102, 102, 103, 104,
  210–211, 212, 218, 219, 230,
  231, 451, 471, 472–473, 492,
  556–557, 572, 602, 603, 604,
  605, 607, 608, 609, 614, 616
Durning, A. T., 58
Dworkin, A., 201, 328, 330
Dymond, G., 67

E
Ebaugh, H. R. F., 134, 135
Eckholm, E., 62, 527, 537
Edwards, D. V., 414
Edwards, P., 127
Edwards, R., 249
Ehrenreich, B., 310, 312, 321
Ehrhardt, 185
Eichler, M., 37
Eiduson, B. T., 463
Eisenberg, D. M. 530
Eisenstein, Z. R., 327
Ekman, P., 75, 140, 142, 153
El-Attar, M., 479
Elias, R., 222
Elkind, D., 122
Elliot, D. S., 222, 223
Ellison, C. G., 489
Elmer-De Witt, P., 166
Ember, C. R., 449
Ember, M., 449
Embree, A. T., 482
Emerson, J., 535, 536
Endersby, J. W., 120
Engels, F., 91, 92, 94, 104, 248,
  327, 332, 450, 607
Engen, T., 265
England, P., 321
English, D., 321
English-Currie, V., 506, 507
Erikson, E., 116, 117, 128, 370
Erikson, K., 210, 211

Etzioni, A., 165, 167, 458, 459
Etzioni-Halevy, E., 414
EuroBusiness Magazine, 245
Evans, J. P., 403
Evans, M. D. R., 394
Evers, F. T., 514

F
Fairclough, E., 355, 428
Falk, G., 62
Falkenmark, M., 546, 565
Fallon, A. E., 525
Fantini, M. D., 516
Farnsworth, M., 222
Farrell, M. P., 123
Fast, J., 319
Feagin, J., 150, 318, 321, 558
Featherstone, M., 73
Fellini, F., 78
Fellman, B., 119
Fennell, T., 510, 511
Ferguson, T., 531
Ferree, M. M., 309
Fife, S., 177
Fifth Estate, 185
Financial Post, 175, 252, 265
Fine, G. A., 566, 580
Finkelstein, N. W., 117
Firebaugh, G., 293, 296, 300,
  404
Fischer, C. S., 163
Fischer, C. W., 32
Fisher, A., 46
Fisher, E., 85, 87
Fisher, R., 439
Fiske, A. P., 248
Fiske, E. B., 514
Fitzpatrick, M. A., 456
Flacks, R., 586
Flaherty, M. G., 150
Flemish, D., 243
Fleras, A., 195, 324, 338
Fletcher, J., 467
Fletcher, K., 149
Flitcraft, A., 462
Florida, R., 177
Flower, G. E., 505
Fobes, R., 129
Foch, T. T., 109
Foot, D. K., 363, 364, 365, 511
Forbes, 249, 265
Forcese, D., 503, 615
Ford, C. S., 191
Foss, 512
Foucault, M., 21, 191
Fox, B. J., 16
Fox, G., 552
Fox, M. J., 150
Francis, D., 217, 247, 249, 252,
  261, 398, 402, 607
Frank, A. G., 297, 298
Frank, J., 527
Franklin, B., 98
Franklin Associates, 563
Fraser, S., 116
Frederick, J. A., 510
Fredrickson, G. M., 239, 344
Free, M. D., 215
Freedom House, 414, 415
French, M., 312, 328
Fretz, W., 73, 477

Freud, S., 110–111, 112, 116, 128, 209
Frideres, J. S., 139, 342, 348, 350, 391, 420
Friedan, B., 373
Friedman, M., 406
Friedman, R., 406
Friedrich, C. J., 417
Friedrich, O., 245, 560
Frizzell, A., 423
Fuchs, V. R., 318, 321
Fuller, R., 321
Fulton, E. K., 447
Furstenberg, F. F. Jr., 458, 460, 461

G
Gadlin, H., 466
Gagliani, G., 249
Gagné, P., 185
Gairdner, W. D., 406
Galileo Galilei, 12, 491
Gamble, A., 498
Gamson, W. A., 37
Gans, H. J., 67, 120, 557
Gardner, A., 394
Garfinkel, H., 20, 136, 137, 213
Gartin, P. R., 215
Gartner, R., 230
Gates, B., 169
Gauguin, P., 601, 603
Geertz, C., 185
Geissel, D., 196
Gelles, R. J., 323, 461, 462
Gelman, D., 191, 372
General Social Survey, 227, 263
George, D., 121
George, S., 521, 522
Gerber, L. M., 27, 49, 135, 144, 172, 173, 188, 221, 224, 238, 268, 273, 322, 323, 348, 350, 351, 353, 355, 371, 391, 392, 456
Gerlach, M. L., 390
Gerlovin, V., 115
Gerlovina, R., 115
Gerstel, N., 458
Gerth, H. H., 95
Geschwender, J. A., 341
Gewertz, D., 311
Gibbons, D. C., 209
Gibbs, N., 123, 196, 198, 199
Giddens, A., 200
Giffen, P. J., 222
Gilbert, D., 265
Gilbert, N., 199
Gilbert, S., 511
Gilbert, S. N., 499
Gilligan, C., 112, 113, 115, 128, 314
Ginsburg, F., 323
Gintis, H., 504
Giovannini, M., 38
Gladue, B. A., 191
Glauberman, N., 255
Glazer, N., 344
Gleick, E., 478
Glenday, D., 393
Glenn, N. D., 459
Globe and Mail, 147
Glock, C., 485

Glueck, E., 208
Glueck, S., 208
Goenette, N., 95
Goffman, E., 15, 20, 126, 127, 138, 143, 144, 145, 152, 153, 167, 213, 214, 315, 333, 535, 609
Goldberg, S., 312
Golden, F., 142
Goldfarb, J. C., 417
Goldfarb, W., 565
Golding, W., 129
Goldsby, R. A., 337
Goldsmith, H. H., 109
Goode, W. J., 393, 452
Gooderham, 512
Gorbachev, M., 243
Gordon, J. S., 531, 539
Gordon, S., 196
Gore, A., 426
Gorman, C., 560
Gottfredson, M., 222
Gottfredson, M. R., 227
Gottman, J., 555
Gough, K., 311
Gould, S. J., 491
Goyder, J., 16, 144, 559, 615
Goyder, J. C., 266, 271
Grandin, E., 114
Granovetter, M., 163
Grant, D. L., 578
Grant, D. S. II, 588
Grasmick, H. G., 534
Gray, P., 297
Green, J., 162
Green, J. C., 489
Greenberg, D. F., 191
Greene, G., 121
Greenspon, E., 383
Gregg, A., 614
Gregory, P. R., 390
Griff, C., 402
Gross, J., 464
Groth, N. A., 196
Gulia, M., 164
Gurnett, K., 309
Gutenberg, J., 490
Gwartney-Gibbs, P. A., 463
Gwynne, S. C., 169

H
Habermas, J., 607
Hacker, H. M., 322, 327
Hackman, J. R., 174
Haddad, W., 460
Hadden, J. K., 489
Hafner, K. 166
Hagan, J., 217
Haig, R. A., 149
Halberstam, D., 169
Hall, 418
Hall, E. J., 309
Hall, E. M., 538
Hall, J. R., 67, 73, 611
Hamblin, D. J., 57
Hamel, R., 370
Hamer, D., 191
Hamilton, C., 342
Hamilton, D., 252, 265
Hamilton, M., 141

Hamm, B. 371
Hamrick, M. H., 535
Haney, C., 41, 42
Hannigan, J. A., 561
Hansen, K. V., 329
Hanzlick, R., 147
Hareven, T. K., 125, 385
Harlan, W. H., 370
Harlow, H., 109, 110
Harlow, M., 109, 110
Harries, K. D., 223
Harrington, M., 607
Harris, C., 558
Harris, M., 56, 76, 311
Harrison, P., 521
Hart, S., 526
Harvey, E. B., 418, 584
Haskins, R., 117
Hatfield, E., 453
Havighurst, R. J., 375
Hawthorne, P., 239
Hayneman, S. P., 498
Health Canada, 526, 527, 528
Heath, J. A., 318
Helgesen, S., 173
Helmes-Hayes, R. A., 16
Henderson, W. P., 470
Henley, N., 141, 142, 143, 145
Henry, W., 374
Herdt, G. H., 191
Herek, G. M., 191
Herman, D. F., 323
Herman, E. S., 402
Herold, E. S., 453
Herrnstein, R., 340
Herrnstein, R. J., 109, 208, 254, 255
Hersch, J., 533
Hess, B. B., 37
Hewlett, S. A., 331
Highway, T., 55
Hiller, H. H., 83, 354, 355, 550, 559, 608
Hinch, R., 198, 199
Hiroshi, M., 242
Hirschi, T., 214–222, 227, 231
Hobbes, T., 12, 14, 366, 433
Hochschild, A., 123, 318, 454, 466
Hodge, R. W., 37, 262
Hoerr, J., 177
Hogue, C., 567
Holmes, L., 370
Holmstrom, D., 372
Homans, G., 20
Hopper, E., 460
Hoshia, Y., 534
Howard, R., 121
Howatson-Leo, L., 349
Howlett, K., 217
Huber, B. J., 11
Huet-Cox, R., 531
Huffman, M. L., 321
Hull, R., 172
Huls, G., 208
Human Resources Development Canada, 179
Humphrey, C. R., 571
Humphreys, A., 194, 238
Humphries, S., 301
Humphry, D., 361, 377

Hunt, M., 453
Hunter, J. D., 489, 515
Hurn, C., 502
Hurtig, M., 399, 407
Hutchingson, J. E., 491
Hymowitz, C., 290
Hysom, S. J., 132

I
Ibrahim, Y., 166
Ide, T. R., 176
Igali, D., 22
Iginla, J., 22
Ignace, M., 61
Ignace, R., 61
Illich, I., 537
Indian and Northern Affairs Canada, 524
Innis, H. A., 15
Ipsos-Reid, 195
Irving, K. C., 402
Irwin, J., 128
Isajiw, W. W., 337
Isay, R. A., 191

J
Jacklin, C. N., 310
Jacobs, D., 226, 566
Jacobs, J., 384, 559
Jacobson, J. L., 290
Jaenen, C., 500
Jagger, A., 327, 329
Janis, I. L., 160
Janus, C. G., 290
Jayaram, A., 304
Jencks, C., 208
Jenkins, J. C., 586, 588, 589
Jogi, S., 452
Johannes, H. S., 365
Johnson, C., 141
Johnson, D., 160
Johnson, F. H., 495, 498
Johnson, H., 196, 199
Johnson, N., 579
Johnston, R. J., 558
Jones, A., 16
Jones, F., 487
Jordan, M., 122

K
Kadushin, C., 164
Kahl, J. A., 265
Kain, E., 459
Kain, E. L., 466, 526
Kalish, C. B., 223
Kalish, R. A., 373
Kalleberg, A. L., 168
Kallen, E. 223
Kaminer, W., 163
Kandel, D. B., 118
Kane, G., 283
Kanter, R. M., 172, 173
Kantrowitz, B., 463
Kapferer, J.-N., 580
Kaplan, D. E., 439
Kaplan, E. B., 537
Kaptchuk, T., 532
Kasarda, J. D., 395
Kaufman, R. L., 368
Kaufman, W., 474, 482, 483
Kazaz, E., 206

Keith, J., 366
Keith, P. M., 318, 454
Keller, H., 59
Kellert, S. R., 561, 571
Kellner, H., 35
Kelly, K., 395
Kemeny, A. 370
Kemp, A. A., 392
Kenny, M., 177
Kerckhoff, A. C., 241
Kidd, Q., 561
Kidron, M., 387
Kilbourne, B. K., 478
Killian, L. M., 576, 579, 581, 583, 588
King, K. P., 219
King, M., 533
Kinsey, A., 76, 186, 187, 191, 192, 203
Kinsman, G., 187, 193
Kiser, E., 170
Kishor, S., 290
Kitson, G. C., 269
Kittrie, N. N., 228, 230
Kitz, J. E. 559
Kluckhohn, C., 191
Knight, D. B., 566
Knowles, V., 340, 353, 354
Koch, H., 582
Kohlberg, L., 112, 113
Kohn, M. L., 255, 269, 392
Kolata, G., 465
Komarovsky, M., 318, 456
Konigsberg, E., 78
Kopliak, G. G., 125
Korman, S. K., 464
Kornhauser, W., 586, 588, 605
Kowalewski, D., 589
Kozol, J., 276, 514
Krauss, C. 485
Kriesi, H., 589
Krisberg, B., 222
Kroc, R., 155, 175
Krohn, M. D., 209
Kruks, G. N., 196
Kruse, M., 229
Kübler-Ross, E., 377, 378
Kuhn, T., 16
Kurelek, W., 109, 130
Kustodiev, B., 360
Kuznets, S., 252

L
Lacayo, R., 577
Ladd, J., 376, 529
Lamberg-Karlovsky, C. C., 552
Lamberg-Karlovsky, M., 552
Landers, A., 458
Landers, R. M., 312
Landry, L., 366
Lane, D., 242
Lang, G. E., 581
Lang, K., 581
Langenbach, R. 385
Langer, V., 568
Lapierre, J., 18
Laporte, P., 217, 433, 434
Lappé, F. M., 299, 300
LaPrairie, C. P., 227
Larmer, B., 290
Laslett, P., 240, 577, 606

LaTouche, D., 352
Laub, J. H., 215
Laumann, E. O., 188, 189, 190, 192
Laumann, L. A., 462
Lavallée, L., 503, 510
Lawrence, J., 494
Laxer, G., 47, 48
Le Bon, G., 579
Leacock, E., 84, 327
Leavitt, J. W., 537
Lee, A.-R., 561
Leland, J., 192
Lemert, E., 213
Lengermann, P. M., 263, 310, 311, 322, 326, 327
Lennon, M. C., 318
Lenski, G. E., 83, 84, 85, 86, 87, 88, 90, 91, 102, 103, 251, 256, 311, 413, 495, 520, 552
Lenski, J., 83–84, 85, 86, 88, 90, 91, 102, 103, 251, 256
Lenton, R. L. 455
Lenton, R. L., 230
Leonard, E. B., 218
Lepine, M., 509
Lesage, J., 352
Leslie, G. R., 464
Lester, D., 230
LeVay, S., 191
Lever, J., 117, 314, 333
Levin, B., 5
Levine, M., 525, 526
Levine, M. P., 519
Levinson, D. J., 123
Levy, F., 260
Lewis, F., 432
Lewis, O., 274, 279
Lewthwaite, G., 283
Li, J. H., 463
Li, P. S., 223, 338, 348, 349, 350
Liazos, A., 216
Lichter, R. S., 120
Lieberman, J., 426
Linden, E., 62, 551
Lindert, P. H., 252
Lindstrom, B., 558
Linton, R., 71, 133, 599
Lipovenko, D., 372
Lippitt, R., 158
Lips, H., 190
Lipset, S. M., 63, 238, 338, 417, 419, 586
Liska, A. E., 209, 212, 223
Littenberg, R., 111
Livernash, R., 562
Livingstone, D. W., 395, 457
Lo, C. Y. H., 584
Locke, J., 14
Lofland, J., 582
Logue, B. J., 122
Lohr, S., 532
Lombroso, C., 208, 231
Lord, W., 235
Lorenz, K., 436
Low, J. O., 384
Loxley, W. A., 498
Loy, P. H., 324
Luker, K., 202
Lund, D. A., 371, 378
Lunman, K., 195

Lunt, P. S., 264
Lupri, E., 114, 221, 323, 330, 461, 462
Lutz, C. A., 140
Luxton, M., 36, 457
Lyall, S., 78
Lynd, R. S., 63
Lynott, P. P., 122

M
Ma, L.-C., 262
Mabry, M., 239
Macara, A., 106
Maccoby, E. E., 310
Mace, D., 451
Mace, V., 451
Macionis, J. J., 8, 11, 56, 72, 124, 148, 158, 175, 207, 224, 252, 253, 284, 289, 303, 320, 366, 386, 388, 404, 450, 452, 557, 610
Mackay, D. G., 146
Mackay, J., 9
MacKenzie, B., 202
Mackie, M., 47, 314, 341
MacKinnon, C., 325
Macleans, 65, 79, 150, 249, 543
Macphail, A., 428
Maddox, S., 174
Madigan, N. 70
Madsen, A., 404
Mainse, D., 489
Makin, K., 194
Malthus, T. R., 548, 549, 569, 570, 571
Mamdou, F. M., 293
Mandel, N., 272
Mandela, N., 239
Manning, P., 169, 426, 430
Marathon Guide, 310
Marchak, P., 400
Marconi, G., 151
Marcus, P., 17, 234
Marcuse, H., 610
Mare, R. D., 450
Marin, P., 330
Markoff, J., 174
Markovsky, B., 164
Markson, E. W., 377
Marlios, P., 402
Marquand, R., 489
Marsden, L. R., 418, 584
Marsden, P., 164
Marshall, S. E., 331
Martin, B., 249
Martin, J. M, 224
Martin, R. C., 480
Martin, S., 18
Martineau, H., 14, 15, 38, 39
Martinez, A., 208
Marullo, S., 437
Marx, G. T., 576
Marx, K., 14, 19, 35–36, 52, 74, 83, 89, 90–91, 91–94, 92, 95, 96, 98, 99, 100, 101–102, 102, 103, 104, 210, 216, 231, 243, 244, 248–254, 249, 250, 251, 256, 264, 265, 327, 375, 389, 391, 432, 474–476, 492, 537, 549, 558, 599, 603, 604, 607, 614, 616

Marx, L., 561
Masland, T., 239
Massey, D., 515
Matas, R., 460
Matthews, R., 37, 249, 400, 559
Matthiessen, P., 345
Mauer, M., 230
Mauro, T., 377
Mauss, A. L., 589
Maxwell, J. D., 19
Maxwell, M. P., 19
Mayo, K., 451
McAdam, D., 576, 586, 589
McAll, C., 348, 350
McBride, S., 407
McCarthy, J. D., 588
McClain, P. D., 346
McClung, N., 429
McConahay, J. B., 586
McCormick, N. B., 196
McDaniel, S., 371
McDonald, K. A., 568
McDonald, L., 14, 38, 39
McDonald, T., 422
McGeary, J., 438
McGuire, M. B., 483
McIlroy, A., 467
McLanahan, S. S., 463
McLaughlin, A., 428, 429
McLean, S., 335
McLeod, J., 269
McLeod, J. D., 456
McLuhan, M., 15, 16, 49, 73, 78, 79, 89, 144, 151, 500, 512, 593, 614, 615
McMahon, F., 574
McPhail, C., 577, 579
McPherson, B. D., 370
McQuillan, K., 194, 352
McRae, S., 457
McTeer, M., 145, 146
Mead, G. H., 20, 35, 113–114, 115, 116, 128
Mead, M., 108, 123, 310–311
Meadows, D. H., 562, 563
Meltzer, B. N., 116
Melucci, A., 586, 589
Mennerick, L. A., 496
Menzies, K., 92
Merrit, S. E., 346
Merton, R. K., 17, 133, 160, 170, 211, 212, 217, 218, 342, 585
Messing, P. 223
Messner, S. F., 162
Meyer, D. S., 584, 588
Michels, R., 170
Michelson, W., 269, 554, 555
Milbrath, L. W., 427, 562
Milgram, S., 159, 160
Miliband, R., 607
Mill, J. S., 328
Miller, D. L., 576
Miller, F., 590
Miller, G. A., 174
Miller, G. T. Jr., 561, 563
Miller, M., 179
Miller, W. B., 212
Millet, K., 328
Mills, C. W., 95, 394, 429, 430
Mirowsky, J., 160, 458

Mistry, R., 434
Mitchell, A., 365, 463
Mitchell, B. A., 454
Mittelstaedt, M., 566
Molm, L. D., 20
Molotch, H., 558
Money, J., 185
Monsebraaten, L., 259
Montagu, A., 436
Montigny, G., 514
Mooney, E., 345
Moore, G., 323, 328, 402
Moore, M., 224
Moore, W., 245–248, 246, 254, 255, 256
Moore, W. E., 296
Morgentaler, H., 202
Mori, G. A., 475, 477, 484, 485
Morris, A., 589
Morrison, D. E., 585
Morrison, N., 529
Morton, J., 49
Moses, D., 393
Mosley, W. H., 525, 539
Moss, C. W., 154
Mottaz, C. J., 392
Moynihan, D. P., 344
Mueller, D. P., 463
Muhtadie, L., 79
Muller, E. N., 586
Mulroney, B., 353, 423, 424, 428
Mumford, L., 520, 552
Munch, E., 608
Murdoch, I., 36
Murdock, G., 73, 311
Murdock, G. P., 186, 311, 448, 449
Murphy, E., 121
Murray, C., 254, 255, 340
Myers, N., 561, 562, 565, 568, 569
Myers, S., 534

N
Nader, R., 346, 420
Najafizadeh, M., 496
Nancarrow Clarke, J., 47, 134, 530, 531, 533
Nathan, G. J., 152
National Adult Literacy Database, 514
National Campaign to Prevent Teen Pregnancy, 204
National Crime Prevention Council, 232
National Post Business 500, 399
Nault, R., 421
Nawaz, M., 214
Neill, S., 394
Neitz, M. J., 67, 73, 611
Nelson, E. D., 189, 195, 200, 202, 324, 325, 330
Nett, E. M., 370, 371, 450, 454, 456, 460, 464
Neugarten, B. L., 366, 370, 375
Neuhouser, K., 476
Neuman, L. W., 35
Nevitt, N., 512
Newman, K. C., 402
Newman, K. S., 609

Newman, P. C., 247, 403, 412, 427, 614, 615
Newman, W. M., 344
Newton, I., 12
NFO Cfgroup, 192
Nichols, R. C., 459
Nielsen, F., 252
Nielsen, J. M., 38
Nightingale, F., 39
Nikiforuk, A., 543
Nin.da.waab.jig, 566
Numbers/Symbols
1991 Green Book, 252
Nisbet, R. A., 417, 605
Norbeck, E., 242
NORC, 192, 193, 195

O
Oakes, J., 504
Oberschall, A., 586, 588
O'Brien, D. J., 164
O'Dea, T. F., 488
O'Dea Aviad, J., 488
Oderkirk, J., 500
Offir, C. W., 185
Ogburn, W., 70
Ohlin, L., 212
O'Keefe, P., 147
Olsen, G. M., 390
Olson, C., 230
Olzak, S., 341, 588
Ontario Women's Directorate, 146, 147
O'Reilly, F., 245
Orozco, J. C., 395
Osgood, W. D., 208, 215
Ossenberg, R. J., 270
Ostling, R. N., 465, 489
Ostrander, S. A., 267
Ouchi, W., 176
Owen, D., 504, 512

P
Pakulski, J., 589
Palmore, E., 370, 374, 375
Pammett, J. H., 423
Panula, M., 238
Parcel, T. L., 321
Parenti, M., 120
Park, R., 557, 572
Parker, P., 217
Parkinson, C. N., 171, 172
Parr, R., 238
Parrillo, V. R., 557
Parrott, J., 519
Parsons, T., 17, 73, 158, 296, 326–327, 374, 449, 534, 535
Partridge, J. 300
Pasteur, L., 539
Paton, G. E. C., 150
Paul, E. F., 324, 325
Payne, G. C. F., 90, 94
Pear, R., 321, 537
Pearson, D. E., 605
Pearson, L. B., 439
Percy, W., 612
Peritz, I., 183
Perkins, W. H., 70
Perreault, J., 507
Perri, R., 211, 212

Perrow, C., 586, 588
Persell, C. H., 504
Pessen, E., 248
Peter, L. J., 171, 172
Peters, T. J., 173
Peters Atlas of the World, 60, 197, 253, 291, 317, 320, 388, 448, 480, 482, 496, 523, 546
Peterson, R. D., 230
Peterson, R. R., 460
Peterson, S., 480
Pevere, G., 67
Pflug, C., 410
Pflug, M., 410
Philipson, I. L., 329
Phillipson, C., 375
Philp, M., 61, 450
Piaget, J., 111–112, 128
Pichardo, N. A., 589
Pickton, R., 196
Pillemer, K., 372
Pines, M., 110
Pingree, S., 120
Pinhey, T. K., 519
Piper, E. S., 586
Pitt, M., 482
Piven, F., 586
Plato, 12, 244, 429, 495
Plomin, R., 109
Pogrebin, R., 78
Pohl, R., 391
Poitras, J. A., 298
Polenberg, R., 607
Pomfret, R., 295
Popenoe, D., 312, 331, 460, 463
Population Reference Bureau, 367, 545, 546
Porter, J., 15, 16, 265, 348, 349, 350, 429, 503, 504
Porter, K. L., 589
Postel, S., 565
Posterski, D. C., 113
Powell, C., 150
Press, A. L., 121
Presser, H. B., 318, 454
Primeggia, S., 150
Prindle, D. F., 120
Prus, R., 35
Puterbaugh, G., 191
Putka, G., 504
Pyzow, S., 458

Q
Quarantelli, E. L., 576, 580
Queer Resource Directory, 204
Quinney, R., 216

R
Rademacher, E. W., 43
Raftery, A. E., 463
Ragin, C. C., 404
Ragin, C. R., 298, 299
Rajhathy, J., 530
Ramcharan, S., 338, 348
Ramo, J. C., 490
Raphael, R., 312
Raschke, H. J., 269
Reckless, W. C., 209
Rees, P., 558
Reich, R. B., 260
Reid, S. T., 228

Reiman, J. H., 217
Reimer, D., 185
Reinharz, S., 37, 38
Reitz, J. G., 344, 349
Remis, R. S., 527
Remoff, H. T., 76
Renaud, V., 349
Report on Business, 246, 247, 265, 398, 513
Richardson, J. T., 478
Richler, M., 43
Ridgeway, C. L., 158, 162
Riesman, D., 608, 609, 611
Riley, M. W., 126
Riley, N. E., 309
Ritzer, G., 175, 176, 181, 393
Rivera, D., 29
Roach, H., 147
Roberge, R., 521, 523
Roberts, O., 489
Robertson, H. J., 513
Robertson, P., 489
Robinson, A., 399
Robinson, B. W., 189, 200, 202, 325, 330
Robinson, D., 519
Robinson, J., 318
Robinson, S., 361, 529
Robinson, V. M., 149
Rockefeller, J. D., 244
Rockett, I. R. H., 521
Rodenburg, E., 562
Rodgers, K., 462
Rodriguez, S., 361, 529
Roesch, R., 323, 461
Roethlisberger, F. J., 41
Rohlen, T. P., 498
Roman, M., 460
Romano, A. T., 224
Romero, O. A., 476
Róna-Tas, A., 243
Rorty, R., 515
Rose, J. D., 585
Rosenberg, S. D., 123
Rosenfeld, S., 318
Rosnow, R. L., 580
Ross, C. E., 458
Ross, J., 290
Rossi, A. S., 312
Rostow, W. W., 293, 294, 295, 305, 404
Rothman, S., 120
Roudi, N., 479
Roulard, D., 530
Rowe, D. C., 208
Royal Commission on Aboriginal Peoples, 219, 368
Royal Commission on Health Services, 11
Royal Commission on the Status of Women in Canada, 314
Rozin, P., 525
Rubenstein, E. A., 370
Rubin, K., 179
Rubin, L. B., 456
Rudé, G., 579
Ruffman, A., 238
Rule, J., 397
Rushton, P., 109, 340
Ryan, W., 275, 279

S

Sadd, S., 453
Sadik, N., 551
Sagan, C., 56, 57, 80
Saint-Marie, B., 121
Sale, K., 297, 345
Salgado, S., 236
Sampson, A., 498
Sampson, R. J., 215
Sansom, W., 139
Sapir, E., 62
Satzewich, V., 139, 249, 268, 338, 348, 350, 391, 392
Sauvé, R., 63, 613
Savage-Rumbaugh, E. S., 61, 62
Scaff, L. A., 414
Scanlon, J. P., 330
Schafer, R. B., 318, 454
Schaffer, M., 439
Schaie, K. W., 366
Scheff, T. J., 213, 214
Schellenberg, K., 174, 225
Schissel, B., 507
Schmidt, R., 482, 483
Schneider, J., 170
Schoenberger, R., 321
Schooler, C., 318, 392
Schrof, J. M., 463
Schumann, H. W., 483
Schutt, R. K., 276
Schwartz, B., 67
Schwartz, F., 321
Schwartz, I., 222
Schwartz, P., 453, 464
Schweitzer, A., 465
Scott, D. B., 177, 222
Scott, J., 402
Scott, R. W., 168
Seager, J., 313
Sears, D. O., 586
Secretary of State, 499, 508
Secretary of State Canada, 263
Segal, R., 387
Segall, A., 365, 536
Seiner, P., 166
Sekulic, D., 68
Seligmann, A. F., 530
Sellin, T., 230
Sen, K. M., 482
Sennett, R., 277, 278, 508
Serrill, M. S., 64, 447, 458
Sewell, J., 559
Shakespeare, W., 12, 145
Shanahan, M. J., 456
Shapiro, J. P., 463
Sharma, N., 222
Shawcross, W., 345
Sheehan, T., 125, 367
Sheldon, W., 208
Sheley, J. F., 212
Shelton, B. A., 459
Sherkat, D. E., 489
Sherman, L. W., 215
Shevky, E., 558
Shields, J., 407
Shipler, D. K., 243
Shipley, J. T., 170
Shively, J., 137
Shkilnyk, A. M., 457
Shupe, A., 323
Shute, J. J., 566

Siddhartha, G., 483
Sidel, R., 532, 537
Sidel, V. W., 532, 537
Sifton, C., 354
Silverberg, R., 568
Simcoe, J. G., 290, 346, 553
Simmel, G., 161–162, 557, 572, 582
Simon, C. P., 396
Simon, J., 563, 571
Simon, R. J., 222
Simons, C., 495, 498
Simons, M., 597, 612
Simpson, J., 405, 431, 614
Singer, D. G., 119
Singer, J. L., 119
Sivard, R. L., 439
Skelton , C., 4
Skinner, D., 516
Skocpol, T., 432
Skolnick, A., 112
Slater, P. E., 77, 158, 162
Sloan, J., 2
Smelser, N., 586, 587, 588
Smelser, N. J., 578
Smilgas, M., 64
Smith, A., 14, 387, 388, 406
Smith, D., 36, 327
Smith, D. A., 215, 223, 225
Smith, D. E., 249
Smith, G., 325
Smith, R., 533
Smith, R. E., 179
Smith-Lovin, L., 141
Smolowe, J., 323
Snell, M. B., 454, 466
Sniderman, P. M., 43, 44, 45
Snow, D. A., 580, 588
Snowman, D., 241
Snyder, C. W., 196
Social Sciences and Humanities Research Council, 39
Solheim, O., 43
South, S. J., 162
Southworth, N., 228
Sowell, T., 62, 340, 545
Spates, J. L., 70
Specter, M., 243, 391, 532
Speer, J. A., 489
Spencer, H., 17, 244
Spilerman, S., 368
Spitze, G., 318
Spitzer, S., 216, 217, 375
Stacey, J., 329, 466
Staggenborg, S., 584
Stalin, J., 96
Stanley, L., 38
Stanton, E. C., 309
Stark, E., 462
Stark, R., 477
Starr, P., 531
Statistics Canada, 5, 52, 68, 70, 119, 120, 125, 166, 171, 173, 192, 196, 220, 221, 225, 227, 260, 261, 262, 266, 273, 274, 315, 316, 318, 319, 322, 323, 337, 347, 348, 349, 353, 354, 355, 362, 363, 371, 381, 387, 391, 392, 393, 394, 395, 396, 397, 398, 399, 400, 454, 459, 461, 462, 463, 464, 486, 488,

499, 500, 501, 503, 505, 508, 509, 510, 511, 522, 524, 544, 547, 555, 602, 607
Stavrianos, L. S., 86
Steele, S., 450
Steffensmeier, D. J., 212
Stein, B. A., 172, 173
Stein, M. R., 605
Stelter, G., 555
Stevens, R., 530
Stewart, L. P., 324
Stewart, M., 217
Stier, H., 321
Stinchcombe, A. L., 250
Stone, L., 451
Stouffer, S. A., 160, 585
Straus, M. A., 323, 462
Streib. G., 373
Stronach, B., 265, 321
Stronach, F., 265
Stuart, R. C., 390
Stuckless, N., 229
Sudnow, D. N., 376
Sumner, W. G., 64
Surtees, L., 247
Sutherland, E. H., 214, 215, 217, 218, 231
Sutton, W., 147
Swain, C. E., 489
Swain, S., 62
Szasz, T., 214

T

Tait, H., 510
Tajfel, H., 161
Tannahill, R., 202
Tannen, D., 173, 181
Taras, B. R., 608
Tarrow, S., 579
Tausig, M., 223
Tavris, C., 453
Tepperman, L., 228, 265
Thatcher, M., 241
Theen, R. H. W., 243
Thirunarayanapuram, D., 548
Thomas, E., 438
Thomas, E. J., 483
Thomas, G. M., 417
Thomas, W. I., 47, 136, 342, 535
Thomma, S., 489
Thompson, K. R., 265
Thompson, L., 465
Thornberry, T., 222
Thorne, B., 141, 145
Thornton, A., 458
Tierney, J., 527
Tilly, C., 432, 589
Tindale, J., 372
Tittle, C. R., 222
Tocqueville, A. De, 14, 432, 585
Todd, D., 370
Tolson, J., 171
Tönnies, F., 556, 572, 601–603, 604, 605, 607, 614, 616
Tooker, G., 99, 172, 275, 603
Toronto Star, 498
Treas, J., 365, 370, 375
Treiman, D. J., 238
Trent, K., 463
Tribe, V., 117
Troeltsch, E., 476

Troiden, R. R., 191
Troper, H., 481
Trudeau, J., 424
Trudeau, P. E., 187, 412, 413, 424, 426, 485
Trusheim, D., 504
Tsing, A. L., 323
Tumin, M. M., 236, 247, 248
Turcotte, P., 135
Turner, C., 435
Turner, J., 427
Turner, R. H., 576, 579, 581, 583
Twain, M., 65
Twain, S., 121
Tygiel, J., 23
Tyree, A., 238

U

Uchitelle, L., 250
Ujimoto, K. V., 349
Ullman, E., 558
United Nations, 304, 312, 548
United Nations Development Programme, 10, 253, 284, 288, 289, 296, 302, 303, 314, 328, 386, 388, 390, 496, 497, 523, 532, 564
United Nations Human Development Index, 10
University of Akron Research Center, 479
Unnever, J. D., 223
Ury, W., 439
U.S. Census Bureau, 261, 364, 419, 463, 499, 510, 532, 533
Useem, B., 586
Useem, M., 402

V

Vallas, S. P., 397
Vallee, F. G., 15, 16
Valocchi, S., 588
Van Biema, D., 462, 483
Van Buren, M. E., 168
Van Den Haag, E., 230
Van-Loon, R. J., 419, 424, 427
Vance, S., 507
Vantour, A., 194
Vantour, E., 194
Varacalli, J. A., 150
Varnell, J., 194, 195, 464
Vaughan, M. K., 404
Veblen, T., 582
Viguerie, R. A., 489
Villemez, W. J., 222
Vines, G., 465
Visher, C. A., 223, 225
Vogel, E. F., 300
Vogel, L., 327, 329
Vold, G. B., 215, 217
Von Hirsh, A., 214
Vonnegut, K. Jr., 253, 254, 256
Vowell, S., 150

W

Waddell, D. E., 181
Waite, L. J., 458
Waite, P. B., 418
Waksal, S., 217
Waldfogel, J., 321

Waldie, P., 217
Walker, J. W. St. G., 346
Wall, T. F., 362, 376, 529
Wallace, M., 588, 589
Wallace, R. A., 263, 310, 311, 322, 326, 327
Waller, D., 438
Wallerstein, I., 298, 404
Wallerstein, J. S., 460, 463
Wallis, C., 371
Walton, J., 299, 404
Ward, L., 13
Warner, B. D., 212
Warner, W. L, 264, 384
Waterman, R. H. Jr., 173
Watson, W. 386
Watson, J. B., 108
Wattenberg, B. J., 548
Waxman, C. I., 338
Weber, A. F., 552
Weber, M., 20, 33, 35, 52, 94–99, 100–101, 102, 103, 104, 167–168, 170, 171, 176, 250–251, 256, 264, 294, 391, 411–412, 413, 440, 476, 492, 599, 603, 604, 605, 607, 614, 616
Webster, M. Jr., 132
Webster, P. S., 463
Weeks, J. R., 479
Weinberg, G., 193
Weiner, T., 438
Weinrich, J. D., 191
Weisberg, K. D., 196
Weisner, T. S., 463
Weitzman, L. J., 123, 458, 460

Weller, J. M., 576, 580
Wellford, C., 215
Wellman, B., 164
Wells, J., 396
Wendell, S., 36
Wenke, R. J., 57
Wesolowski, W., 414
West, E., 588
Westhues, A., 447
Whalen, J., 586
Wheelis, A., 608, 609
Whipple, T. W., 315
Whitaker, M., 434
White, G. M., 140
White, L., 459
White, R., 158
White, W., 578
White-Means, S., 533
Whitman, D., 276
Whitnell, T., 78
Whitter, N., 588
Whittington, M. S., 419, 424, 427
Whitton, C., 172
Whorf, B., 62
Whyte, D. R., 16
Whyte, W. F., 45, 46, 47
Whyte, W. H. Jr., 170
Wiarda, H. J., 297
Wiatrowski, M. A., 215
Widdis-Barr, C., 427
Widom, C. S., 463
Widstrand, C., 546, 565
Wiles, P. J. D., 391
Wilkins, R., 523
Williams, T., 120

Williamson, J. G., 252
Wilson, A., 79
Wilson, E. O., 77, 569
Wilson, J. Q., 208
Wilson, L., 33
Wilson, M., 208
Wilson, R. R., 176
Winks, R. W., 346
Winn, M., 122
Winson, A., 392
Winter, T., 489
Wirth, L., 157, 557, 572
Wise, S., 38
Witkin-Lanoil, G., 108
Wohlstein, R. T., 577
Wojtkiewicz, R. A., 463
Wolf, A., 327
Wolf, D. L., 37
Wolf, N., 315, 316, 526
Wolfe, D. B., 366
Wolfe, T., 583
Wolff, L., 196
Wolfgang, M. E., 222, 223
Wolfson, N., 594
Wollstonecraft, M., 328
Women in Canada, 315, 318, 320, 330, 463
Women in the Labour Force, 322
Wood, D., 529
Wood, J. L., 576
Woodward, C., 309
Woodward, K. L., 120, 475
Wooley, O. W., 519
World Bank, 65, 97, 120, 124, 165, 261, 284, 291, 292, 299, 386, 388

World Health Organization, 519, 520, 528
World Values Survey, 138, 167, 279, 432, 485
Worsley, P., 300
Worthington, P., 230
Wotherspoon, T., 139, 249, 268, 338, 348, 350, 391, 392, 505, 507
Wren, C. S., 239
Wright, E. O., 249
Wright, E. R., 224
Wright, Q., 436
Wright, R., 166
Wright, R. A., 230, 231
Wright, S. A., 473, 586
Wu, L. L., 463
Wu, Z., 465

Y
Yates, R. E., 370, 372
Yeatts, D. E., 174
Yeltsin, B., 243
Yinger, R. E., 439
Yoder, J. D., 459
Yoels, W. C., 150
York, G., 272

Z
Zald, M. N., 588
Zaslavsky, V., 243
Zimbardo, P., 41–42, 50
Znaniecki, F., 47
Zuboff, S., 397
Zurcher, L. A., 580

SUBJECT INDEX

A

the Abkhasians, 369
Aboriginal people
  Aboriginal languages, 61
  in Canada, 350
  and Canadian justice system,
    139–140
  disadvantaged status, 348
  diversity among, 351
  dropout rate, 511
  elders, 368
  families, 456–457
  the Inuit, 351
  life expectancy, 524
  media portrayal of
    Aboriginal people, 121
  the Métis, 351
  Nunavut, 351
  registered Indians, 351
  research, 40
  residential schools, 506–507
  self-government, 420–421
  social class, 268
  social movements, 584
  as special-status society,
    350–351
  suicide rates, 6, 219
abortion, 202, 203, 550
absolute monarchy, 413
absolute poverty, 272, 289
academic standards, 511–513
achieved status, 132
active bigot, 342
activity theory, 374–375
Addams, Jane, 14
adolescence
  socialization, 123
  stages of development, 116
  teen pregnancy, 193–194
  as young offenders, 228
adoption, international, 447
adulthood
  early adulthood, 123
  late adulthood. See the elderly
  middle adulthood, 123–125
  socialization, 123–125
  stages of development, 117
affluence. See wealth
Africa, poverty in, 522
Africville, 344
age
  and health, 522–523
  median age at death, global
    perspective, 291
  and poverty, 273
age cohorts, 126
age-sex pyramid, 547–548
age stratification
  agrarian societies, 367–368
  defined, 366
  horticultural societies,
    367–368
  hunting and gathering
    societies, 367
  industrial societies, 368–370
  pastoral societies, 367–368
ageism, 373
agents of socialization

the family, 117
  mass media, 119–122
  peer group, 118–119
  school, 117–118
aging
  see also the elderly
  the Abkhasians, 369
  activity theory, 374–375
  age stratification, 366–370
  biological changes, 365–366
  conflict theory, 375
  cultural change, 363
  and culture, 366
  death and dying, 375–379
  disengagement theory, 374
  elder abuse, 372
  finding meaning, 370
  gender, and income, 372
  gerontology, 365
  greying of Canada, 362
  and income, 372
  life expectancy, 362–365
  problems, 370–372
  psychological changes, 366
  retirement, 371–372
  social-conflict analysis, 375
  social isolation, 371
  structural-functional analysis,
    374
  symbolic-interaction analysis,
    374–375
  theoretical analysis of,
    374–375
  transition, 370–372
  in twenty-first century, 379
agrarian societies
  age stratification, 367–368
  caste systems, 237
  described, 86–87
  health, 520
  and social inequality, 86
  social stratification, 244
  technical advances, 251
agricultural employment,
  388, 392
agricultural revolution, 384
agriculture, 86
  see also agrarian societies
AIDS, 526–528
air pollution, 566–567
alienation
  bureaucracy, 169–170
  and capitalism, 93–94
  defined, 93
  and rationality, 98–99
all-weather liberal, 342
alternative approaches to health,
  530
American Sociological
  Association, 39
androcentricity, 37
animals, and language, 61–62
animism, 478
Anna's case, 107, 110
anomie, 100
anti-Semitism, 43–45
Anti-Slavery International,
  290–291

anticipatory socialization, 119
apartheid, 237, 239
applied sociology, 11
arithmetical progression, 548
arms race, 437
arranged marriages, 451
artifacts, 65
Asch's conformity experiment,
  158–159
ascribed status, 132
ascription
  ancestry, 263
  ethnicity, 263–264
  gender, 263
  race, 263–264
asexuality, 190
assimilation, 344
attachment, 215
attitudes
  blasé attitude, 557
  Canadian teens, 28
  sexual attitudes, 187–190
attraction, vs. sexual
  behaviour, 190
authoritarian leadership, 158
authoritarian personality
  theory, 339–341
authoritarianism, 414
authority
  charismatic authority,
    412–413
  defined, 25
  family, patterns in, 449
  rational-legal authority,
    412
  traditional authority, 412
autonomy (versus doubt and
  shame), 116
average-middle class, 268

B

Bangladesh, and
  modernization, 296
bargain-counter justice, 228
beauty myth, 316
behaviourism, 108
beliefs
  and conformity, 215
  defined, 62
  and social stratification, 236
Bell Curve debate, 254–255
bereavement, 377–379
bias
  described, 34
  in economic system, 431–432
  in research, 33–34
  testing in schools, 504
bilateral descent, 449
biodiversity, 568–569
biological mixing, 336–337,
  344, 457
biological perspective
  aging, 365–366
  deviance, 208–209
  gender differences, 309–310
  incest taboo, 186
  sex, 184
  sexual orientation, 191

biology. See sociobiology
bisexuality, 190
Black Canadians, 346
blasé attitude, 557
Bloc Québécois, 420, 423
blue-collar occupations, 249
"bluebloods," 266
body language, 139, 140–141
boot camp, 127
Bre-X case, 217
British North America Act, 352
Buddhism, 483
bureaucracy
  alienation, 169–170
  bureaucratic bloat, 171
  characteristics of, 167–168
  defined, 167
  formal, written communica-
    tions, 168
  hierarchy of offices, 168
  impersonality, 168
  inefficiency, 170
  inertia, 170
  informal side of, 168–169
  oligarchy, 170–171
  origins of, 167
  Parkinson's law, 171
  Peter Principle, 172
  problems of, 169–172
  rationality of, 98
  ritualism, 170
  rules and regulations, 168
  specialization, 168
  technical competence, 168
bureaucratic bloat, 171
bureaucratic inertia, 170
bureaucratic ritualism, 170

C

Calgary Stampede, 270
Calvinism, 95–96
Canada
  abortion, 202
  academic standards, 511–513
  age pyramids, 362
  American investment in,
    399–400
  ascription, 263–264
  average family income, 260
  average income by gender,
    264
  average-middle class, 268
  Black Canadians, 346
  boot camp, 127
  Canadian society, 83
  Canadian vs. American
    values, 63
  census metropolitan areas,
    population of, 555
  child care, 275
  common-law unions, 135
  Confederation, dates of
    entry into, 418
  criminal statistics, 220–221
  cultural diversity in, 66
  as cultural mosaic, 66, 68
  divorce in, 458, 459
  education in, 262–263

and the environment,
566–567
ethnic origins, 347
ethnicity in, 345–350
euthanasia in, 377
families in. *See* Canadian
families
foreign-born population,
355
frequency of sexual
activity, 189–190
government service
employment, 171
greying of, 362
gun control, 224
health care system, 533
health crises in, 528
high mass consumption
stage, 295
hockey, women in, 324–325
homelessness, 276–277
homicide rates, 221
immigrants, low income
rates of, 273
immigration patterns, 66,
353–356
income in, 260–261
Information Revolution,
impact of, 614–615
interprovincial migration,
557
Kyoto Protocol, 566–567
labour force participation,
392
literacy, 498–499
and low-income countries,
300–301
lower class, 269
lower-middle class, 268–269
lower-upper class, 267
medicine in, 533
middle class, 267–269
mobility by age group, 602
mother tongues in, 70
multiculturalism in, 68–70,
343–344
national unity, 356–357
occupation prestige,
261–262
occupational inheritance, 271
optimism, 103
politics in. *See* Canadian
politics
post-secondary education
in, 499
poverty, 272–277
power, 261
race in, 345–350
racial identification, 336
rain forest in, 568
regional economic disparities,
400
religion in, 484–487
religiosity, 484–486
religious affiliation, 484
residential schools, 506–507
same-sex marriage, 194–195
schooling in, 498–500
sexual attitudes, 188
social classes in, 264–269
social inequality, 259–263

social mobility in, 271–272
social stratification, 263–264
spanking in, 228
special-status societies,
350–353
"super-rich" families, 261
taking a stand, 592
teen pregnancy, 194
television viewing in, 119
top 30 companies in, 401
top ten wants, 138
two-tiered health care, 538
unemployment rate, 395
and United States relations,
after September
11, 434–435
upper class, 265–267
upper-middle class, 267–268
upper-upper class, 266–267
urban population of, 555
visible minority
population, 349
wealth, 261
working class, 268–269
Canadian Alliance Party, 420,
423
Canadian Constitution, 14
Canadian families
child discipline, 455
ethnicity, 456–457
gender and, 457–458
mixed marriages, 457
Native Canadian families,
456–457
race, 456–457
and social class, 456
Canadian peacekeepers, 4
Canadian Political Science
Association, 15
Canadian politics
see also politics
vs. American politics, 426
and culture, 418–419
economics and, 418–419
and the individual, 424–428
interventionist government,
419
Native self-government,
420–421
political participation,
427–428
political parties, 419–424
reform of, 440–441
regional dimension, 418
representation, 418
women in politics, 428
Canadian sociology, 15–16
Canadian *vs.* American values, 63
capital punishment, 225, 226,
228
capitalism
and alienation, 93–94
backbone of capitalism, 218
in Canada, 388–389
and class conflict, 92–93
concentrated wealth, 249
corporations. *See* corporations
defined, 387
democracy, approach to, 414
and deviance, 216–217
elite deviance, 217–218

features of, 387
fragmentation of capitalist
class, 249
health care in, 532–533
and legal protections, 249
and Marxist revolution,
248–249
and modernity, 604
political economy of
capitalism, 432
and Protestantism, 95–96,
476
rationality of, 95
and revolution, 94
and rising standard of
living, 249
vs. socialism, 390–391
state capitalism, 390
struggle, lack of, 249
welfare capitalism, 390
white-collar crime, 217–218
white-collar occupations, 249
and worker organization, 249
capitalists, 89
case studies, 45
caste system
and agrarian life, 237
cultural beliefs, 237
defined, 236
described, 237
India, 237
South Africa, 236, 239
category, 156
cause and effect, 31–32
central cities, 554–555
change. *See* social change
charismatic authority, 412–413
*Charter of Rights and
Freedoms*, 14, 353, 419
chattel slavery, 290
Chicago School, 557
child abuse, 462–463
child care, 275
child discipline, 455
child labour, 124
child rearing, 453–454
child slavery, 291
childbearing in global
perspective, 9
childhood, 122
children
child abuse, 462–463
child care, 275
child labour, 124
childhood, 122
and divorce, 460
global poverty, 290
latchkey kids, 454
lower-class children, 269
marriage of, 452
play, 115
and poverty, 273
religious service
attendance, 487
social isolation, effect of, 110
spanking, 228
stages of development, 116
China, health care in, 532
Chinese Immigration Act, 354
Chinese language, 59
Christianity, 478–479

church, 476–477
cigarette smoking, 524–525
cities
see also urbanization
central cities, 554–555
concentric zones, 558
evolution of, 552–553
first cities, 552
growth of, 13
industrial European cities,
552–553
metropolis, 554
multicentred model, 558
North American cities,
growth of, 553–554
pre-industrial European
cities, 552
social area analysis, 558
civil religion, 488
civilization, 57
class. *See* social class
class conflict, 92–93, 248
class consciousness, 93
class-society theory, 609–610
class system
see also social stratification
defined, 237
status consistency, 239
Clayoquot Sound area, 568
coercive organizations, 167
cognitive development
concrete operational stage,
112
formal operational
stage, 112
preoperational
stage, 111–112
sensorimotor stage, 111
cohabitation, 464
cohort, 126
collective behaviour
collectivities, 576
crowds and crowd
behaviour, 577–580
defined, 576
mass behaviour, 580–583
riots, 578
social movements. *See* social
movements
study of, 576
collective conscience, 100
collectivities
crowds, 577–580
defined, 576
dispersed collectivity, 576,
580–583
localized collectivity, 576,
577–580
mass behaviour, 576,
580–583
vs. social groups, 576
colonial settlement in North
America, 553
colonialism, 292, 297–298
common-law unions, 135
common sense, 29–30
communication
in organizations, 169
in politics, 430–431
communism, 91, 389
community, loss of, 601–602

complementarity, and gender, 326–327
computers
 and social class, 266
 social class and, 503
 work, impact on, 397–402
Comte, Auguste, 12, 14, 17, 35
concrete operational stage, 112
conflict
 and cultural diversity, 68
 and humour, 150
 role conflict, 133
 and social change, 599
conflict analysis. *See* social-
 conflict analysis
conflict subcultures, 212
conflict theory
 of aging, 375
 environmental racism, 569
 of prejudice, 341–342
conformity
 nonconformity. *See* deviance
 and social control, 215
Confucianism, 483
conglomerates, 400–402
conjugal family, 447
Conservative Party. *See*
 Progressive Conservative
 Party
constitutional monarchy, 413
contagion theory, 579
content analysis, 47
Continuous Improvement (CI),
 177
contraception, 188, 328
control, 32
control group, 41
control theory, 214–215
conventional reality, 146
convergence theory, 579
Cooley, Charles Horton, 115
Cornerville, 45–47
corporations
 and competition, 403
 conglomerates, 400–402
 corporate linkages, 400–403
 defined, 398
 economic concentration, 398
 foreign ownership, 398–400
 and global economy,
  403–404
 interlocking directorates,
  402
 Irving empire, 402
 ownership of, in
  Canada, 398
 social networks, and corporate elite, 402–403
 top 30 in Canada, 401
 wealthy family linkages, 402
correlation, 32
cottage industry, 384
counterculture, 70
courts, 227–228
courts, and same-sex
 marriages, 431
courtship, 452
cowboy stereotypes, 18
credentialism, 508
crime
 capital punishment, 225, 226

community approach, 227
components of, 220
defined, 207, 219
gated communities, 227
globalization of, 224
homicide rates in Canada,
 221
illegal drug trade, 225
juvenile delinquency, 207
mens rea, 220
property crimes, 220
self-control and, 227
spanking in Canada, 228
"street" criminal, profile
 of, 221–223
types of crimes, 220–221
victimization survey, 221
victimless crimes, 220
violent crimes, 220
white-collar crime, 217–218
criminal. *See* "street" criminal
Criminal Code, 219
criminal justice system
 courts, 227–228
 defined, 208
 described, 225
 overrepresentation of
  minorities, 226
 plea bargaining, 227–228
 police, 225–227
 punishment, 228–231
criminal recidivism, 230
criminal statistics, 220–221
criminal subcultures, 212
critical sociology, 35–37
crowd behaviour
 contagion theory, 579
 convergence theory, 579
 emergent-norm theory,
  579–580
 lynching, 578
 riot, 578
crowds
 acting crowd, 577
 casual crowd, 577
 conventional crowd, 577
 defined, 577
 described, 156
 expressive crowd, 579
 mob, 577–579
 protest crowds, 577
 and social change, 578–579
crude death rate, 545
cult, 478
cultural analysis
 cultural materialism, 75–76
 social-conflict analysis, 74–75
 sociobiology, 76–77
 structural-functional analysis,
  73–74
cultural changes, 70–71
cultural differences
 see also culture
 cultural relativism, 72
 and culture shock, 56
 gestures, 74–75
 perspective on, 72
 role, 133
 sexual practices, 186
 sexuality, 201
 status, 133

cultural diversity
 in Canada, 66
 and conflict, 68
 counterculture, 70
 cultural change, 70–71
 cultural integration, 70
 cultural lag, 70
 cultural relativism, 72
 ethnocentrism, 71–72
 global culture, 72–73
 high culture, 66–67
 multiculturalism, 68–70
 popular culture, 66–67
 social class, roots in, 66
 subculture, 67–68
cultural ecology, 75–76
cultural innovation, 500
cultural integration, 70
cultural lag, 70, 89
cultural materialism, 75–76
cultural relativism, 72
cultural theory of prejudice, 341
cultural transmission, 59
cultural universals, 73
culture
 see also cultural differences;
  global perspective
 and aging, 366
 artifacts, 65
 beliefs, 62–63
 and Canadian politics,
  418–419
 components of, 58–66
 as constraint, 77
 defined, 55–56
 and emotions, 140
 and environment, 562–563
 evolution of, 58
 folkways, 64
 as freedom, 77
 and global poverty, 292
 and health, 519, 520
 high culture, 66–67
 and human intelligence,
  56–58
 and humour, 148
 ideal culture, 65
 incest taboo, 186
 and information
  technology, 66
 and language, 59–62
 material culture, 56
 material culture, and
  technology, 65–66
 and modernization theory,
  294
 mores, 64
 vs. nation, 58
 nonmaterial culture, 56
 norms, 64
 number of cultures, 58
 popular culture, 66–67
 real culture, 65
 reality construction, 137
 repression, 111
 and sex, 185–186
 sexuality, restriction of, 186
 and social change, 599
 social control, 65
 vs. society, 58
 vs. state, 58

symbols, 58–59
values, 62–64
virtual culture, 67
culture shock, 56, 58

D
Darwin, Charles, 108
date rape, 196–197, 198–199,
 219
Davis-Moore thesis, 245–246
death and dying
 bereavement, 377–379
 defining death, 376, 529
 ethical issues, 376–377,
  529–530
 euthanasia, 376–377,
  529–530
 historical patterns of
  death, 376
 hospice, 378
 life course perspective, 125
 life-extending medical
  technology, 378
 mercy killing, 376–377,
  529–530
 modern separation of life
  and death, 376
 right to die, 376–377, 529
death instinct, 111
death penalty, 225, 226, 228
debt bondage, 291
deception, 140–141, 142
deductive logical thought,
 49–50
degradation ceremony, 213
demeanour, 141–142
democracy, 414
democratic leadership, 158
demographic change, 600
demographic transition
 theory, 549–550
demography
 defined, 544
 fertility, 544
 migration, 545–546
 mortality, 545
 population composition,
  547–548
 population growth, 546–547
denomination, 477
dependency theory
 capitalist world economy,
  298–299
 colonialism, 297–298
 critical evaluation, 300
 defined, 297
 foreign debt, 299
 high-income countries, role
  of, 299–300
 historical perspective, 297
 industrial capacity, lack
  of, 299
 narrow, export-oriented
  economies, 298–299
dependent variable, 31
deprivation theory, 585–586
descent, 449
deterrence
 and peace, 438
 and punishment, 229
development stages, 116–117

deviance
  biological context, 208–209
  and capitalism, 216–217
  control theory, 214–215
  crime. *See* crime
  and cultural norms, 209–210
  defined, 207
  differential association theory, 214
  elite deviance, 217–218
  functions of deviance, 210–221
  and gender, 218–219
  global perspective, 210
  innovation, 211
  labelling theory, 213–214
  labels, significance of, 214
  medicalization of, 214
  moral boundaries, 210
  others' definitions, 210
  personality factors, 209
  and power, 210, 216
  primary deviance, 213
  psychological approach, 209
  Puritans of Massachusetts Bay, 210–211
  rebellion, 212
  retreatism, 211
  ritualism, 211
  secondary deviance, 213
  social change, 210
  social-conflict analysis, 215–218
  and social control, 208
  and social diversity, 218–219
  social foundations of, 209–210
  social unity, 210
  stigma, 213
  strain theory, 211–212
  structural-functional analysis, 210–212
  subcultures, 212
  symbolic-interaction analysis, 213–215
deviant career, 213
differential association theory, 214
diffusion, 71, 599
Dilthey, Wilhelm, 35
diplomacy, 439
direct-fee system, 532
disability, as master status, 133, 134
disarmament, 439
discovery, 71, 599
discrimination
  see also prejudice
  ageism, 373
  defined, 342
  institutional discrimination, 342
  and prejudice, 342
disease, as master status, 133
disengagement theory, 374
dispersed collectivity, 576, 580–583
disposable society, 563–564
distinct societies, 356–357
diversity
  and deviance, 218–219

and group dynamics, 162–163
minorities, media portrayal of, 121
overrepresentation of minorities in justice system, 226
division of labour, 100, 602–603
divorce
  adjustments, 459–460
  in Canada, 458, 459
  causes of, 458–459
  and children, 460
  as process, 459–460
  risk of, 459
domestic violence, 114
double standards
  date rape, 219
  described, 38
  sexual revolution and, 189
  sociobiology and, 76
dramaturgical analysis
  defined, 138
  embarrassment, 144
  gender and personal performances, 141–143
  idealization, 143
  nonverbal communication, 139–141
  performances, 138–139
  tact, 144–145
dropping out, 510–511
Du Bois, William Edward Bughardt, 14
Durkheim, Émile
  anomie, 100
  collective conscience, 100
  division of labour, 100–101, 602–603
  evolving societies, 100–101
  function, 99
  functional interdependence, 100
  functions of deviance, 210–221
  and Information Revolution, 101
  mechanical solidarity, 100, 556, 602
  organic solidarity, 100, 556, 603
  personality, society as, 99–100
  religion, 471, 472–473
  social solidarity, 17, 83
  society as system, 99
  society beyond ourselves, 99
  structure, human behaviour as, 99
  suicide, study of, 6
  totem, 472
dyad, 161–162
dying. *See* death and dying

E
e-business, 399
early adulthood, 123
eating disorders, 525–526
ecclesia, 477
ecologically sustainable culture, 569–571

economic equality, 390–391
economic productivity, 390
economic systems
  bias in, 431–432
  capitalism, 387–389
  comparison of, 390–391
  economic equality, 390–391
  economic productivity, 390
  Marxist view of, 90
  personal freedom, 391
  socialism, 389
  state capitalism, 390
  welfare capitalism, 390
the economy
  agricultural revolution, 384
  corporations. *See* corporations
  defined, 384
  global economy, 387
  goods, 384
  government, role of, 406–407
  historical overview, 383–386
  Industrial Revolution, 384
  Information Revolution, 385–386
  "invisible hand," 406–407
  the market, 406–407
  post-industrial economy, 385
  primary sector, 386
  secondary sector, 387
  services, 384
  tertiary sector, 387
ecosystem, 561
education
  see also schooling
  in Canada, 262–263
  computers, and social class, 266
  defined, 495
  explanations of educational attainment, 510
  and gender, 321–322
  global perspective, 495–500
  and labour market, 513–514
  and occupational mobility, 271
  and political correctness, 515
  and poverty, 273
  practical learning, 499–500
  problems in, 508–513
efficiency
  bureaucracy, 170
  McDonaldization, 175
ego, 111
elder abuse, 372, 463
the elderly
  see also aging
  in Aboriginal culture, 368
  abuse of, 372
  death and dying, 375–379
  dementias, 365
  emotional support, sources of, 371
  global perspective, 364
  greying of Canada, 362
  happiness, 370
  health issues, 365–366
  as a minority, 373
  negative myths, 370
  "older elderly," 364
  private household living arrangements, 370

socialization, 125
stages of development, 117
"younger elderly," 364
electronic church, 489, 490
electronic mail, 169
embarrassment, 144
emergent-norm theory, 579–580
emigration, 546
emotions, 140
empirical evidence, 29
employment. *See* work
endogamous marriage, 237
endogamy, 447
Engels, Friedrich, 327
English language, 59
Enron, 217
environment
  air pollution, 566–567
  biodiversity, 568–569
  challenge, 570–571
  and culture, 562–563
  disposable society, 563–564
  ecologically sustainable culture, 569–571
  environmental deficit, 562
  global perspective, 561
  global warming, 568
  greenhouse effect, 568
  Kyoto Protocol, 566–567
  limits to growth thesis, 562–563
  logic of growth view, 562
  natural environment, 560
  rain forests, 567–568
  recycling, 564
  and social change, 600
  and society, 560–569
  solid waste, 563–564
  sustainability, 569–571
  and technology, 561–562
  water pollution, 565–566
  water supply, 565
environmental deficit, 562
environmental racism, 569
Erikson, Erik H., 116–117
eros, 111
estate system, 240
ethics
  death and dying, 376–377
  and life-extending medical technology, 378
  of research, 39
  "right to die" debate, 376–377, 529
ethnicity
  ascription, 263–264
  and assimilation, 344
  in Canada, 337, 345–350
  and Canadian families, 456–457
  and criminality, 223
  defined, 337
  genocide, 345
  and inequality in Canada, 348–350
  and multiculturalism, 343–344
  and pluralism, 343–344
  poverty, 273
  and religion, 486–487
  and segregation, 344–345

social movements, 584
social significance of, 337
social standing, 348–350
ethnocentrism, 71–72
ethnographies, 45
ethnomethodology, 20, 136–137
Eurocentrism, 68
euthanasia, 376–377, 529–530
exogamy, 447
experiment
control group, 41
defined, 40
experimental group, 41
Hawthorne effect, 41
hypothesis, 40
ideal experiment, 40
illustration of, 41–42
placebo, 41
experimental group, 41
exponential progression, 548
expressive leadership, 158
extended family, 447
extramarital sex, 190, 453
eye contact, 139, 142

F
fad, 583
fair-weather liberals, 342
faith, 472
false consciousness, 91
family
alternative forms of, 463–464
authority, patterns of, 449
basic concepts, 446–449
in Canada. *See* Canadian
families
cohabitation, 464
conjugal family, 447
defined, 446
definitions of, 446
descent, patterns of, 449
extended family, 447
vs. formal organization, 165
formation of, 135
and gender socialization,
314
global variety, 446–447
and homelessness, 277
intergenerational social
mobility, 271
intragenerational social
mobility, 271
kinship, 446
in later life, 454–455
leadership, and gender, 158
lesbian mothers, 445
lone-parent families, 274,
463
micro-level analysis, 450–451
and new reproductive
technology, 464–465,
467
nuclear family, 447
of orientation, 412
and patriarchy, 450
poverty, and family
patterns, 273–274
problems. *See* family transitions and problems
of procreation, 412
property and inheritance, 450

residential patterns, 449
security, 450
sexual activity, regulation
of, 449
and social class, 269
social-conflict analysis, 450
social-exchange analysis,
450–451
social placement, 450
and socialization, 117, 449
structural-functional analysis,
449–450
symbolic-interaction analysis,
450
theoretical analysis, 449–451
transitions. *See* family transitions and problems
family life stages
child rearing, 453–454
courtship, 452
marriage, 452–453
family transitions and problems
divorce, 458–460
elder abuse, 463
remarriage, 461
violence, 461
violence against children,
462–463
violence against
women, 461–462
family unit, 446
family violence, 114, 461
fashion, 582–583
feminism
basic ideas of, 328–329
defined, 328
"first wave" in Canada, 328
liberal feminism, 329
opposition to, 331
Persons Case, 328
radical feminism, 329–331
socialist feminism, 329
variations within, 329–331
feminist paradigm, 20
feminist research
critical and interpretive
examples, 36
gender, and research, 37–38
and mainstream methodology,
38
women as methodologists,
38–39
feminization of poverty, 273
fertility, 544
fieldwork, 45
Final Exit (Humphry), 361
first cities, 552
First Nation people, 350
see also Aboriginal people
folkways, 64
foreign aid programs, 296
foreign debt, 299
formal operational stage, 112
formal organizations
bureaucracy. *See* bureaucracy
coercive organizations, 167
communication in, 169
defined, 164
vs. families and neighbourhoods, 165
gender and, 172–173

global perspective, 178–179
humanizing organizations,
173–174
Japanese model, 176–178,
177, 179
leadership, 169
McDonaldization, 174–176
normative organizations, 167
organizational environment,
174
power, 169
privacy, threats to, 178–179
race and, 172–173
self-managed work teams,
174
size, 168
vs. small groups, 168
social inequality, 172–173
types of, 165–167
utilitarian organiza-
tions, 166
voluntary associations, 167
former Soviet Union, 242–243,
532
Foucault, Michel, 21
Freud, Sigmund, 110–111
Front de libération du Québec
(FLQ), 433
function, and society, 99–101
functional illiteracy, 513, 514
functional interdependence, 100
fundamentalism, 488–489

G
Galileo Galilei, 491
gated communities, 227
gay rights movement, 192–193
gays and lesbians
child custody, 460
gay rights movement,
192–193
lesbian mothers, 445
same-sex couples, 464
same-sex marriage,
194–195, 464
Gemeinschaft, 556, 601–602, 605
gender
see also gender stratification;
women
androcentricity, 37
and ascription, 263
and Canadian families,
457–458
care and responsibility
perspective, 113
and class, 327
and complementarity,
326–327
cultural foundation of,
310–311
defined, 37
demeanour, 141–142
and deviance, 218–219
double standards. *See* double
standards
eye contact, 142
in global perspective,
310–311
interference in research, 38
justice perspective, 113
kibbutzim, 310

and language, 145–146
Mead's research, 310–311
Murdock's research, 311
and organizations, 172–173
and personal performances,
141–143
personal space, 142
and poverty, 273–274
and research, 37–38
smiling, 143
and social class, 269
social-conflict analysis,
327–328
and social movements, 589
and socialization, 113, 114
and "street" criminal, 222
structural-functional analysis,
326–327
theoretical analysis of,
326–328
touching, 143
in twenty-first century, 331
gender blindness, 37
gender differences
athletic performance, 310
biological perspective,
309–310
education, 263
life expectancy, 522
primary sex
characteristics, 184
secondary sex
characteristics, 184
sex, meaning attached to, 189
suicide, 6
gender gap in income, 318–321,
319
gender identity
defined, 185
Joan/John case, 185
traditional notions of, 315
gender inequality
and gender socialization,
313–315
gender stratification. *See*
gender stratification
global perspective, 290, 292
male-female differences,
309–310
matriarchy, 311
patriarchy, 311–312
and poverty, 296
and sexism, 311–312
gender roles, 313
gender socialization
education, 314–315
the family, 314
gender roles, 313
mass media, 315
and patriarchy, 312
peer group, 314
sexism, 312
gender stratification
see also gender
beauty myth, 316
defined, 315
education, 321–322
gender gap in income,
318–321, 319
housework, 318
occupations, 315–318

pink ghetto jobs, 319
politics, 322
violence against women,
323–326
gendered language
attention, 146
control, 145–146
value, 146
general deterrence, 229
generalized other, 115
genetics. *See* biological
perspective
Genie's case, 110
genital herpes, 526
genocide, 345
gerontocracy, 368
gerontology, 365
Gesellschaft, 556, 601–602
gestures, cultural differences in,
74–75
Gilligan, Carol, 113
global communications, 73
global culture, 72–73
global economy
and corporations, 403–404
described, 387
and flow of goods, 72
global inequality
dependency theory, 297–300
extent of, 285
future trends, 301–303
high-income countries, 285
low-income countries,
286–287
middle-income countries,
285–286
modernization theory,
293–297
overview, 284–287
poverty. *See* global poverty
slavery, 283
terminology, 284–285
theoretical analysis,
293–301
"Three Worlds" model,
invalidity of, 284
wealth, 287–288
global migration, 73
global perspective
see also culture
age stratification, 366–370
agricultural employment,
388
Buddhism, 482
capital punishment, 226
car ownership, 65
child labour, 124
Christianity, 480
crime, globalization of, 224
crude birth rates, 545
crude death rates, 545
defined, 6
deviance, 210
the elderly, 364
emotions, 140
environment, 561
euthanasia, 377
formal organizations,
178–179
functional illiteracy, 514
gender, 310–311

global connections, 72–73
global population, 550–551
global village, 7, 8
handgun deaths, 224
happiness, 138
health, 520–521
high-income countries, 7
high technology, 97
Hinduism, 482
housework, 320
illiteracy, 496
importance of, 6–9
incarceration rates, 230
income disparity, 253, 261
infant mortality rates, 545
interconnection, increase in,
7–8
international adoption, 447
Internet access, 165
Islam, 480
life expectancy, 367, 545
low-income countries, 7
manufacturing wages, 404
marital form, 448
median age at death, 291
middle-income countries, 7
most widely spoken languages,
59–60
physicians, availability of,
523
political freedom, 415
politics, 413–417
population growth, 546
poverty, 8
prosperity and stagnation,
303
prostitution, 197
quality of life, 7
reality construction, 137
sacred, 471
and self-knowledge, 8–9
service-sector employment,
388
social groups, 178–179
social stratification. *See*
global inequality
television ownership, 120
union membership, 393
water consumption, 564
wealth and well-being, 288
women, and population
growth control, 551
women's childbearing, 9
women's paid
employment, 317
women's power, 313
women's status, 8
global political system,
possibility of, 417
global population
high-growth south, 551
low-grow north, 550
global poverty
absolute poverty, 289
and children, 290
correlates of, 292–293
extent of, 289–290
hunger, 302–303, 304
relative poverty, 289
severity of poverty, 288–289
slavery, 283, 290–292

Smoky Mountain,
Philippines, 287–288
and women, 290
global power relationships,
292–293
global stratification. *See* global
inequality
global village, 7, 8
global warming, 568
goal orientation, 157
Goffman, Erving, 15, 20
gonorrhea, 526
gossip, 581
government
defined, 411
and the economy, 406–407
interventionist government
in Canada, 419
Great Britain. *See* United
Kingdom
Great Depression, 10
Green revolution, 295
greenhouse effect, 568
group conformity
Asch's research, 158–159
groupthink, 160
Janis's research, 160
Milgram's research,
159–160
group leadership. *See* leadership
groups. *See* social groups
groupthink, 160
gun control, 224
gynocentricity, 37

H
happiness, global perspective,
138
Hawthorne effect, 41
health
access issue, 537
and age, 522–523
alternative approaches, 530
in Canada, 521–524
Canadian health crises, 528
cigarette smoking, 524–525
costs of health care,
531–533
and cultural patterns, 519
cultural standards of health,
520
defined, 519
disease, as master status, 133
eating disorders, 525–526
ethical issues, 529–530
global survey, 520–521
in high-income countries,
521
in history, 520
killer poverty in Africa, 522
in low-income countries,
520–521
mad cow disease, 528
medicine, 530–534
and the moral good, 519
physician's role, 534
profit motive, 537
and race, 522–524
SARS (severe acute respiratory syndrome), 528
and sex, 522–523

sexually transmitted
diseases, 526–528
sick role, 534
and social class, 522–524
social-conflict analysis,
537–539
social epidemiology,
522–524
and social inequality, 520
and society, 519–520,
524–528
starting conversations
with, 536
structural-functional analysis,
534–535
symbolic-interaction analysis,
535–536
and technology, 520
theoretical analysis of,
534–539
two-tiered health care, 538
West Nile virus, 528
WHO definition, 519
Health Status Index, 523
hermaphrodites, 184–185
heterosexism, 201
heterosexuality, 190
hidden curriculum, 118, 504
hierarchy of offices, 168
high culture, 66–67
high-income countries
core of world economy, 298
defined, 7
dependency theory, 299–300
described, 7, 285
health, 521
and modernization theory,
295–296
schooling, 496
higher education, unequal access
to, 504–508
Hinduism, 481–482
Hirschi's control theory,
214–215
historical research, 47–48
HIV infection, 527
Hobbes, Thomas, 14
hockey, women in, 324–325
holistic medicine, 531
homelessness, 276–277
Homo sapiens, 57
homogamy, 452
homophobia, 193
homosexuality
see also gays and lesbians
defined, 190
statistics, 192
horticultural societies
age stratification, 367–368
described, 85–86
and social inequality, 251
horticulture, 85–86
hospice, 378
houses of correction, 229
housework, 318, 320
human development
nature, role of, 108
nurture, role of, 108–109
social isolation, 109–110
social sciences and, 108–109
socialization. *See* socialization

Human Development Index (UN), 7, 10
human nature, 108
humanizing organizations
    critical evaluation, 173–174
    defined, 173
    expanded advancement opportunities, 173
    responsibilities, sharing of, 173
    social inclusiveness, 173
humour
    and conflict, 150
    and controversy, 148–149
    culture and, 148
    dynamics of, 147–148
    foundations of, 146–147
    functions of, 149–150
    in headlines, 149
    "put-down" jokes, 150
    sensitivity and, 149
    topics of, 148–149
hunger
    global poverty, 302–303, 304
    poverty, 272
hunting and gathering societies
    age stratification and, 367
    animism, 478
    described, 84–85
    health, 520
    and social stratification, 251
hydrological cycle, 565
hypothesis, 40

I
ideal culture, 65, 111
ideal type, 94
idealism
    described, 8
    rationality, 95
    rationalization of society, 94–99
    tradition, 95
idealization, 143
ideas
    power of, 83
    and social change, 599–600
    and social movements, 600
    and society, 83, 94–99
identity problems, and modernity, 608–609
identity (versus confusion), 116
ideology
    and Canadian political parties, 422
    defined, 244
    historical patterns of, 244–245
    Karl Marx, 244
    Plato, 244
illegal drug trade, 225
illiteracy, 496, 514
ImClone, 217
immigration, 66, 353–356, 546
Immigration Act, 355
impression management, 135–136
in-migration rate, 546
incest taboo, 186, 449–450
income
    and aging, 372
    in Canada, 260–261

and educational attainment, 507
    gender gap, 319
    gender gap in income, 318–321
    immigrants, 273
    social inequality, 260–261
independent variable, 31
India
    caste system in, 237
    child weddings in, 452
    schooling in, 497
Indian Act, 354
Indigenous people. See Aboriginal people
individual liberty, 14
individual rights, 14
individualization, 601
inductive logical thought, 49
industrial European cities, 552–553
Industrial Revolution, 384
industrial societies
    age stratification, 368–370
    described, 87–88
    religion, 478
    and social stratification, 251–252
industrialism, 87–88
industriousness (versus inferiority), 116
inefficiency, and bureaucracy, 170
infant mortality rates, 545
infants
    imitation, 115
    stages of development, 116
infidelity. See extramarital sex
Information Revolution
    and Canadian revolution, 614–615
    described, 87
    economic polarization, 252
    Émile Durkheim, 101
    impact of, 88
    Karl Marx, 101
    Max Weber, 101
    trends of, 385–386
    work, impact on, 385–386
information technology
    and culture, 66
    e-business, 399
    and research, 49
    virtual culture, 67
    work, impact on, 397–398
information warfare, 438
ingroups, 161
initiative (versus guilt), 116
Innis, Harold A., 15
innovation, 211
institutional completeness, 162–163, 343
institutional prejudice or discrimination, 342
institutionalized personalities, 128
instrumental leadership, 158
integrity (versus despair), 117, 370
intelligence
    Bell Curve debate, 254–255
    and culture, 56–58

race and, 340
inter-regional population movement, 555–556
interaction. See symbolic-interaction paradigm
intergenerational social mobility, 271
international adoption, 447
Internet
    churches, online, 490
    described, 166
    e-business, 399
    education and, 512
    electronic democracy, 166
    electronic mail, 169
    global access, 165
    and global interconnection, 7–8
    origins of, 166
    and research, 48–49
    social interaction, 144
    virtual community, 164
interpretive sociology
    defined, 35
    described, 35
    founder of, 35
    interviews, 35
    observation, 35
    participant-observation, 35
    vs. scientific sociology, 35
    symbolic interaction, 35
interviews, 43
intimacy (versus isolation), 117
intimate networks, 164
intragenerational social mobility, 271
invention, 71, 599
"invisible hand," 406–407
involuntary part-timers, 396
involvement, 215
Irving empire, 402
Isabelle's case, 110
Islam, 479–480
Israeli kibbutzim, 310

J
Janis's conformity research, 160
Japan
    age stratification in, 370
    class system today, 242
    cram school in, 495
    feudal Japan, 241
    formal organizations in, 176–178, 177, 179
    health care in, 532
    high mass consumption stage, 295
    outcast, 241
    schooling in, 497–498
    social stratification in, 241–242
    traditional and modern nature of, 610–611
    women in, 242
Joan/John case, 185
jokes. See humour
Judaism, 480–481
juvenile delinquency, 207

K
the Kaiapo, 597

kaizen, 177
kibbutzim, 310
kinship, 446
Kohlberg, Lawrence, 113
Kuznets curve, 252
Kyoto Protocol, 566–567

L
labelling theory
    defined, 213
    gender, and deviance, 219
    medicalization of deviance, 214
    and mental illness, 214
    primary deviance, 213
    projective labelling, 213
    retrospective labelling, 213
    secondary deviance, 213
    significance of labels, 214
    stigma, 213
labour market, 392
labour unions, 392–393
laissez-faire economy, 387
laissez-faire leadership, 158
landed immigrant status, 355
language
    Aboriginal languages, 61
    animals and, 61–62
    and attention, 146
    and control, 145–146
    cultural transmission, 59
    and culture, 59–62
    defined, 59
    and gender, 145–146
    and human imagination, 61
    most widely spoken languages, 59–60
    mother tongues in Canada, 70
    oral cultural traditions, 61
    and reality, 62
    Sapir-Whorf hypothesis, 62
    of sexuality, 201
    and value, 146
latchkey kids, 454
latent functions
    described, 17
    prostitution, 200
    of schooling, 502
leadership
    authoritarian leadership, 158
    democratic leadership, 158
    expressive leadership, 158
    in formal organizations, 169
    and gender, 158
    instrumental leadership, 158
    laissez-faire leadership, 158
Lenski, Gerhard, 83–89
Lenski, Jean, 83–89
lesbian mothers, 445
liberal feminism, 329
Liberal Party, 420, 423
liberation theology, 476
life course
    adolescence, 123
    adulthood, 123–125
    childhood, 122
    dying, 125
    early adulthood, 123
    middle adulthood, 123–125

old age, 125
overview, 126
life expectancy
 Aboriginal people, 524
 and aging, 362–365
 in Canada, 545
 defined, 545
 gender differences, 522
 global perspective, 367, 545
life instinct, 111
limits to growth thesis, 562–563
literacy, 498–499
localized collectivity, 576,
 577–580
Locke, John, 14
logic of growth view, 562
lone-parent families, 274, 463
looking-glass self, 115
low-income countries
 and Canada, 300–301
 described, 7, 286–287
 health, 520–521
 periphery of world economy,
 298
 schooling, limited access to,
 496
low-income cut-off, 272
lower class, 269
lower-middle class, 268–269
lower-upper class, 267
lynching, 578

M
macro-level orientation, 19
mad cow disease, 528
making a difference (*versus*
 self-absorption), 117
malls, as postmodern
 phenomenon, 176
Malthus, Thomas Robert, 548
Malthusian theory, 548–549
Manchester, New
 Hampshire, 385
manifest functions, 17
marginal voices, 14–15
the market, 406–407
marriage
 arranged marriages, 451
 child weddings, 452
 and childbearing, 446
 defined, 446
 and dyad, 162
 endogamous marriage, 237,
 447
 exogamy, 447
 global perspective, 448
 homogamy, 452
 matrilocality, 449
 mixed marriages, 457
 monogamy, 447–448
 neolocality, 449
 patrilocality, 449
 patterns of, 447–448
 polyandry, 448
 polygamy, 447
 polygyny, 447–448
 real *vs.* ideal, 452–453
 and religion, 473
 same-sex marriage,
 194–195, 431, 464
 servile forms of marriage, 291

two-career marriage, 459
marriage brokers, 17
Martineau, Harriet, 14, 38
Marx, Karl
 see also social-conflict analysis
 alienation, 93–94
 capitalists, 89
 class conflict, 92–93, 248
 class consciousness, 93
 false consciousness, 91
 goal of, 19
 ideas of, 14
 on ideology, 244
 influence of, 74
 and Information
 Revolution, 101
 modernity, and capitalism,
 604
 production, 89–91
 proletariat, 90
 religion, 474
 revolution, 94
 social conflict, 83
 social institutions, 90
 socialist revolution, 248–249
 society and conflict, 89–94
 urban political economy,
 558
Marxist political-economy
 model, 431–432
Marxist revolution, 248–249
mass behaviour
 defined, 580
 described, 576
 fad, 583
 fashion, 582–583
 gossip, 581
 mass hysteria, 582
 panic, 582
 propaganda, 582
 public opinion, 581–582
 rumours, 580, 581
mass hysteria, 582
mass media
 defined, 119
 gender socialization, 315
 minorities, portrayal of, 121
 and socialization, 119–122
 and violence, 120
mass society, 605–607
mass-society theory, 586,
 608–609
master status
 described, 132–133
 disability as, 133, 134
 disease as, 133
 stigma as, 213
material culture, 56
material surplus, 85
materialism, 74
matriarchy, 311
matrilineal descent, 449
matrilocality, 449
McCartney, Paul, 580
McDonaldization
 calculability, 175–176
 control through automation,
 176
 described, 174–175
 efficiency, 175
 expanding scope, 176

organizational principles of,
 175–176
 predictability, 176
 rationality of, 176
 society, 174–176
 uniformity, 176
McLuhan, Marshall, 15, 16, 73
Mead, George Herbert, 20, 35,
 113–116
Mead, Margaret, 310–311
measurement
 defined, 30–31
 operationalizing a variable,
 31
 reliability of, 31
 socioeconomic status, 31
 statistical measures, 31
 validity of, 31
mechanical solidarity, 100, 556,
 602
media. *See* mass media
medicalization of deviance, 214
medicare, 533
medicine
 access issue, 537
 in Canada, 533
 in capitalist societies,
 532–533
 costs of health
 care, 531–533
 defined, 530
 direct-fee system, 532
 holistic medicine, 531
 physician's role, 534
 as politics, 537
 profit motive, 537
 rise of scientific medicine,
 530–531
 sick role, 534
 social-conflict analysis,
 537–539
 in socialist societies, 531–532
 structural-functional analysis,
 534–535
 symbolic-interaction analysis,
 535–536
 theoretical analysis of,
 534–539
 women in, 533–534
megalopolis, 555
men, and privilege, 330
mens rea, 220
mental illness, and labelling, 214
mercy killing, 376–377,
 529–530
meritocracy, 247–248, 502
Merton, Robert K., 17
Merton's strain theory, 211–212
metaphysical stage, 12
metropolis, 554
micro-level orientation, 19
middle adulthood, 123–125
middle class, 267–269
middle-income countries
 described, 7, 285–286
 semiperiphery of world
 economy, 298
migration, 545–546
Milgram's conformity experiment,
 159–160
militarism, 437

military-industrial complex, 437
minorities
 characteristics, 337
 defined, 322
 distinctive identity, 337
 and the elderly, 373
 media portrayal of, 121
 minority women, 323
 subordination, 337
 visible minorities in
 Canada, 349
 women as, 322
minority-majority interaction
 patterns
 assimilation, 344
 genocide, 345
 pluralism, 343–344
 segregation, 344–345
miscegenation, 344
mixed marriages, 457
mob, 577–579
modernity
 see also modernization
 and anomie, 100
 and capitalism, 604, 607
 class-society theory,
 609–610
 defined, 600
 division of labour, 602–603
 ever-expanding state,
 606–607
 Gemeinschaft, 601–602
 Gesellschaft, 601–602
 global variations in,
 610–611
 identity, problems of,
 608–609
 and the individual, 608–610
 loss of community, 601–602
 mass scale of modern
 life, 1605–606
 mass-society theory,
 605–607, 608–609
 organic solidarity, 603
 persistent inequality, 607
 powerlessness, problems of,
 609–610
 and progress, 610
 rationalization, 603–604
 social-conflict analysis,
 607–608
 structural-functional analysis,
 605–607
 theoretical analysis of,
 604–608
modernization
 see also modernity
 characteristics of, 600–601
 decline of small, traditional
 communities, 600–601
 defined, 600
 future orientation, 601
 and global future, 611–613
 personal choice, expansion
 of, 601
 social character, changes in,
 609
 social diversity, increased,
 601
 time, awareness of, 601
modernization theory

critical evaluation, 296–297
culture, importance of, 294
defined, 293
high-income countries, role of, 295–296
high mass consumption, 295
historical perspective, 293–294
Rostow's stages of modernization, 294–295
take-off stage, 295
technological maturity, 295
traditional stage, 295
monarchy, 413
monogamy, 447–448
monopoly, 403
monotheism, 479
moral development, 113
mores, 64
mortality, 545
multiculturalism, 68–70, 343–344
see also cultural diversity
multinational corporations, 293, 404
Murdock, George, 311
Muslims, 479–480

N

nation, 58
nation-states, 413
Native people. *See* Aboriginal people
natural environment, 560
see also environment
natural selection, 76
nature, 108
neo-Malthusians, 570–571
neocolonialism, 293
neolocality, 449
the Netherlands, euthanasia in, 377
networks, 163–164
New Democratic Party, 420, 423
new reproductive technology, 464–465, 467
new social movements theory, 589
Nightingale, Florence, 39
nonconformity, 207–208
see also deviance
nonmaterial culture, 56
nonverbal communication
body language, 139, 140–141
deception, 140–141
defined, 139
described, 139–140
eye contact, 139
normative organizations, 167
norms
described, 64
and deviance, 209–210
North American cities, growth of, 553–554
Northern Health Research Bulletin, 40
nuclear family, 447
nuclear weapons, 437–438
Nunavut, 351
nurture, 108–109

O

objectivity, 32–34
obscenity, 194
occupation prestige, 261–262
occupational inheritance, 271
occupational specialization, 87
occupations
blue-collar occupations, 249
gender stratification, 315–318
white-collar occupations, 249
Official Languages Act, 352
Oka, 575
old age. *See* the elderly
old money, 266
oligarchy, 170–171
oligopoly, 403
operationalizing a variable, 31
opportunity, 215
optimism, 103
oral cultural traditions, 61
organic solidarity, 100, 556, 603
organizational environment
defined, 174
economic trends, 174
other organizations, 174
political trends, 174
population patterns, 174
and technology, 174
organizational size, 168
organizations. *See* formal organizations
other-directedness, 609
out-migration rate, 546
outgroups, 161
overgeneralization, 37

P

panic, 582
paparazzi, 78–79
paraprofessionals, 394
Park, Robert, 557
Parkinson's law, 171
Parsons, Talcott, 17, 326–327, 534
part-time work, 396
Parti Québécois, 423
participant observation
case studies, 45
defined, 45
described, 45
descriptive research, 45
ethnographies, 45
exploratory research, 45
fieldwork, 45
illustration of, 45–47
qualitative research, 45
quantitative research, 45
use of, 45
pastoral societies
age stratification, 367–368
described, 85–86
religion, 86
and social inequality, 251
pastoralism, 85–86
patriarchy
defined, 311
described, 311–312
and family, 450
Indian education, 497

justification, lack of, 312
and religion, 474–475
patrilineal descent, 449
patrilocality, 449
peace, pursuit of, 438–439
peer group
anticipatory socialization, 119
defined, 118
gender socialization, 314
and socialization, 118–119
performances
demeanour, 141–142
described, 138
eye contact, 142
and gender, 141–143
personal space, 142
physician's office illustration, 138–139
smiling, 143
touching, 143
personal freedom, 391
personal orientation, 157
personal space, 142
personality
defined, 107
development, 111
and deviance, 209
ego, 111
elements of, 110–111
Freud's model of, 111
ideal culture, 111
and social experience, 107
and socialization, 110–111
superego, 111
Persons Case, 328
Peter Principle, 172
physician's role, 534
Piaget, Jean, 111–112
the pill, 188
pink ghetto jobs, 262, 319
placebo, 41
Plato, 244
plea bargaining, 227–228
pluralism, 343–344
pluralist model, 429
points system, 355
police, 225–227
political change, 13–14
political correctness, 515
political economy, 414
political-economy of capitalism, 432
political freedom, 415
political parties
in Canada, 419–420
defined, 419
functions of, 421–422
and ideology, 422
on political spectrum, 422–423
support for, 423–424, 425
political revolution, 432–433
political socialization, 424–427
political state, 413
political systems
authoritarianism, 414
Canadian reform, 440–441
democracy, 414
global political system, possibility of, 417

monarchy, 413
in Singapore, 416
totalitarianism, 416–417
politics
see also power
in Canada. *See* Canadian politics
Canadian *vs.* American, 426
global perspective, 413–417
and the individual, 424–428
Marxist political-economy model, 431–432
peace, pursuit of, 438–439
pluralist model, 429
political participation, 427–428
political revolution, 432–433
political socialization, 424–427
power-elite model, 429–431
terrorism, 433–435
war, 435–438
women in politics, 322, 428
pollution, 565–567
polyandry, 448
polygamy, 447
polygyny, 447–448
polytheism, 479
popular culture, 66–67
population
age-sex pyramid, 547–548
composition, 547–548
global population today, 550–551
inter-regional population movement, 555–556
sex ratio, 547
size. *See* demography
study of. *See* demography
population growth
control of, and high-income countries, 295
demographic transition theory, 549–550
described, 546–547
exponential progression, 548
global perspective, 546
and global poverty, 292
history of, 548
Malthusian theory, 548–549
natural growth rate, 547
neo-Malthusians, 570–571
and social change, 600
theory of, 548–550
zero population growth, 550
pornography, 194–195, 325–326
Porter, John, 15, 16
positivism
see also scientific sociology
defined, 12
limitations of, 12
post-industrial economy, 385, 391
post-industrialism, 88–89
postmodernist paradigm, 20–21
postmodernity
defined, 611
themes of, 611

United States, as nation in
  decline, 612–613
poverty
  absolute poverty, 272, 289
  in Africa, 522
  age, 273
  assessment of causes, 279
  blaming society, 274–275
  blaming the poor, 274
  in Canada, 272
  and children, 273
  education, 273
  ethnicity, 273
  explanations for, 274–276
  and family patterns, 273–274
  feminization of poverty, 273
  and gender, 273–274
  global perspective, 8
    see also global poverty
  homelessness, 276–277
  and hunger, 272
  lone-parent families, 274
  low-income cut-off, 272
  poor, described, 272–274
  poverty line, 272
  race, 273
  relative poverty, 272, 289
  statistics, 272
  welfare dilemma, 278–279
  working poor, 275–276
power
  see also politics
  and authority, 411–413
  beyond the rules, 432–435
  in bureaucracies, 169
  in Canada, 261
  defined, 411
  and deviance, 210, 216
  global power relationships,
    292–293
  Marxist political-economy
    model, 431–432
  pluralist model, 429
  political revolution, 432–433
  power-elite model, 429–431
  terrorism, 433–435
  theoretical analysis, 428–432
power elite, 429–430
power-elite model, 429–431
powerlessness, problems
  of, 609–610
pre-industrial European cities,
  552
prejudice
  authoritarian personality
    theory, 339–341
  conflict theory, 341–342
  cultural theory, 341
  defined, 338
  described, 338
  and discrimination, 342
  institutional prejudice, 342
  racism, 338, 339
  scapegoat theory, 339
  stereotypes, 338, 342
  theories of, 339–342
premarital sex, 189
preoperational stage, 111–112
presentation of self
  defined, 138
  demeanour, 141–142

embarrassment, 144
eye contact, 142
gender and personal per-
  formances, 141–143
idealization, 143
nonverbal communication,
  139–141
performances, 138–139
personal space, 142
smiling, 143
tact, 144–145
touching, 143
primary deviance, 213
primary groups, 156–157
primary labour market, 392
primary sector of the economy,
  386
primary sex characteristics, 184
prison violence, 41–42
prisons, 231
privacy, and large
  organizations, 178–179
professional associations, 394
professions, 393–394
Progressive Conservative
  Party, 420, 423
projective labelling, 213
proletariat, 90
propaganda, 582
property crimes, 220
prostitution
  call girls, 196
  defined, 195
  gay prostitutes, 196
  global perspective, 197
  latent functions, 200
  the law and, 196
  massage parlous, 196
  street walkers, 196
  types of, 196
  as victimless crime, 196
  and women's status, 197
Protestantism, 95–96, 476
psychological approach
  aging, 366
  deviance, 209
public opinion, 581–582
punishment
  criminal recidivism, 230
  deterrence, 229
  global incarceration rates,
    230
  houses of correction, 229
  prisons, 231
  reformatories, 229
  rehabilitation, 229
  retribution, 229, 230
  social protection, 229–230
  summary of justifications, 229
Puritans of Massachusetts
  Bay, 210–211

Q
qualitative research, 45
quality of life, 7, 289
quantitative research, 45
Quebec
  anti-Semitism in, 43–45
  Bill 101, 59–61, 353
  Charlottetown accord, 160,
    353

child care in, 275
cohabitation in, 465
distinct society, 356–357
habitants, 86
language issues in, 59–61
Meech Lake accord, 353
migration to Manchester,
  New Hampshire, 385
New France, 352
the Québécois, 352–353
Quiet Revolution, 352
social movements in, 584
sovereignty, growing
  demand for, 352–353
sovereignty-association
  referendum, 353
the Québécois, 352–353
queer theory, 201–203
questionnaires, 42–43

R
race
  ascription, 263–264
  and assimilation, 344
  biological mixing, 336–337
  in Canada, 345–350
  and Canadian families,
    456–457
  as caste, in South Africa, 239
  and criminality, 223
  defined, 335
  genocide, 345
  and health, 522–524
  and inequality in Canada,
    348–350
  and intelligence, 340
  mixed marriages, 457
  and multiculturalism,
    343–344
  and organizations, 172–173
  and pluralism, 343–344
  poverty, 273
  and segregation, 344–345
  social movements, 584
  social significance of,
    335–336
  social standing, 348–350
race consciousness, 341
racial conflict, 339
racial diversity, 336
racial typology, 336–337
racism
  see also prejudice
  in Canada, 338
  defined, 338
  environmental racism, 569
  as everyday reality, 338
  in Nazi regime, 339
  overt racism, 338
radical feminism, 329–331
rain forests, 567–568
random digit dialing, 43
random sampling, 42
rape, 196
rape culture, 324
rape myths, 198–199
rational-legal authority, 412
rational social organization,
  96–98
rationality
  and alienation, 98–99

and bureaucracy, 98
of capitalism, 95
defined, 95
McDonaldization, 176
rationalization, and
  modernity, 603–604
rationalization of society, 95
real culture, 65
reality construction
  broader view of reality
    construction, 137
  and culture, 137
  global perspective, 137
  humour, 146–150
  social construction of reality.
    See social construction of
    reality
rebellion, 212
recycling, 564
reference groups
  defined, 160
  ingroups, 161
  outgroups, 161
  Stouffer's research, 160
Reform Party, 420, 423
reformatories, 229
regional economic disparities,
  400, 503, 584
rehabilitation, 229
Reimer case, 185
relative deprivation, 585
relative poverty, 272, 289
reliability, 31
religion
  agricultural elites, power
    of, 87
  animism, 478
  basic concepts, 471–472
  in Canada, 484–487
  civil religion, 488
  defined, 471
  electronic church,
    489, 490
  and ethnicity, 486–487
  and faith, 472
  fundamentalism, 488–489
  global perspective, 471
  in history, 478
  industrial societies, 478
  liberation theology, 476
  monotheism, 479
  and patriarchy, 474–475
  polytheism, 479
  Protestantism and capitalism,
    476
  religiosity, 484–486
  religious affiliation in Canada,
    484
  religious revival, 488
  ritualism, 472
  sacred, 471
  and science, 491
  secularization, 487–488
  and social change, 475–476,
    487–489
  and social class, 486
  social-conflict analysis,
    474–475
  and social stratification,
    486–487
  and sociology, 472

structural-functional analysis, 472–473
symbolic-interaction analysis, 473–474
theoretical analysis, 472–475
totem, 472
world religions. *See* world religions
religiosity, 484–486
religious fundamentalism, 488–489
religious organization
    church, 476–477
    cult, 478
    denomination, 477
    ecclesia, 477
    sect, 477
religious revival, 488
remarriage, 461
replication, 34
repression, 111
research
    see also sociological investigation
    with Aboriginal peoples, 40
    bias in, 33–34
    cause and effect, 31–32
    control, 32
    correlation, 32
    dependent variable, 31
    ethics, 39
    feminist research, 36, 38–39
    and gender, 37–38
    independent variable, 31
    and Internet, 48–49
    interviews, 35
    measurement, 31
    methods of. *See* research methods
    observation, 35
    participant-observation, 35
    qualitative research, 45
    quantitative research, 45
    replication, 34
    and technology, 48–49
    theory and method, interplay of, 49–50
    value-free research, 33–34
    variables, 30
research methods
    defined, 40
    experiment, 40–42
    hypothesis testing, 40–42
    participant observation, 45–47
    secondary analysis, 47–48
    summary of, 48
    survey research, 42–45
reserve army of labour, 392
residential schools, 506–507
resocialization, 126–128
resource-mobilization theory, 588–589
retirement, 371–372
retreatism, 211
retreatist subcultures, 212
retribution, 229, 230
retrospective labelling, 213
revolution, 432–433
rich nations. *See* high-income countries

right to die, 376–377, 529
riots, 578
ritualism, 170, 211, 472
role
    cultural differences in, 133
    defined, 133
    "exes," 134–135
    exit, 134–135
role conflict, 133
role set, 133
role strain, 133
romantic love, 451, 452, 453
Rostow's stages of modernization, 294–295
rumours, 580, 581

S
sacred, 471
salaries, 246–247
same-sex couples, 464
    see also gays and lesbians
same-sex marriage, 194–195, 431, 464
sample, 42
samurai, 241
sanctions, 65
Sapir-Whorf hypothesis, 62
SARS (severe acute respiratory syndrome), 528
scapegoat, 339
scapegoat theory, 339
school problems
    academic standards, 511–513
    discipline, 508–509
    dropping out, 510–511
    educational costs, and quality, 511
    functional illiteracy, 513, 514
schooling
    see also education
    in Canada, 498–500
    credentialism, 508
    cultural innovation, 500
    defined, 495
    and economic development, 495–496
    gender socialization, 314–315
    in Great Britain, 498
    hidden curriculum, 118, 504
    in high-income societies, 496
    in India, 497
    in Japan, 497–498
    latent functions of, 502
    in low-income countries, 496
    national comparisons, 496–500
    privilege and personal merit, 508
    social-conflict analysis, 502–508
    and social control, 503–504
    and social inequality, 502–508
    social integration, 500–501
    and social placement, 502
    and socialization, 117–118, 500
    streaming, 504

structural-functional analysis, 500–502
    testing, 504
    unequal access to higher education, 504–508
science
    see also scientific sociology
    vs. common sense, 29–30
    defined, 29
    as fourth way of knowing, 29
    objectivity, 32–34
    as one form of "truth," 28–29
    and religion, 491
    and sociology, 12–13
scientific sociology
    see also research
    cause and effect, 31–32
    concepts, 30
    control, 32
    correlation, 32
    dependent variable, 31
    empirical evidence, 29
    independent variable, 31
    vs. interpretative sociology, 35
    limitations of, 34–35
    measurement, 31
    operationalizing a variable, 31
    relationships among variables, 31–32
    reliability of measurement, 31
    replication, 34
    spurious correlation, 32
    validity of measurement, 31
    value-free research, 33–34
    variables, 30
Scopes monkey trial, 491
"second shift," 318
secondary analysis
    content analysis, 47
    defined, 47
    historical research, 47–48
    problems with, 47
secondary deviance, 213
secondary group, 157
secondary labour market, 392
secondary sector of the economy, 387
secondary sex characteristics, 184
secular humanism, 489
secularization, 487–488
segregation, 344–345
self
    defined, 114
    development of, 115–116
    dramaturgical analysis. *See* dramaturgical analysis
    generalized other, 115
    the *I*, 115
    looking-glass self, 115
    the *me*, 115
    objective element, 115
    presentation of. *See* presentation of self
    and social experience, 114–115
    subjective element, 115
self-employment, 394

self-esteem, 113
self-managed work teams, 174
sensorimotor stage, 111
servile forms of marriage, 291
sex
    biological perspective, 184
    and the body, 184–185
    culture and, 185–186
    defined, 184
    and health, 522–523
    hermaphrodites, 184–185
    incest taboo, 186
    primary sex characteristics, 184
    secondary sex characteristics, 184
    transsexuals, 185
sex ratio, 547
sex workers. *See* prostitution
sexism
    cost of, 312
    defined, 312
    and patriarchy, 311–312
sexist language, 145–146
sexual assault, 196
sexual attitudes
    in Canada, 188
    extramarital sex, 190
    frequency of sexual activity, 189–190
    premarital sex, 189
    sexual counterrevolution, 188–189
    sexual revolution, 187–188
sexual behaviour, *vs.* attraction, 190
sexual controversies
    abortion, 202, 203
    pornography, 194–195
    prostitution, 195–196
    sexual violence, 196–197
    teen pregnancy, 193–194
sexual counterrevolution, 188–189
sexual harassment, 18, 324–325
sexual orientation
    asexuality, 190
    biology, product of, 191
    bisexuality, 190
    cultural acceptance of, 191
    defined, 190
    heterosexuality, 190
    homophobia, 193
    homosexuality. *See* gays and lesbians; homosexuality
    society, product of, 191
    statistics, 192
sexual revolution, 187–188
sexual violence
    date rape, 196–197, 198–199
    and pornography, 325–326
    rape, 196
    rape myths, 198–199
    sexual assault, 196
    sexual harassment, 324–325
sexuality
    abortion, 202, 203
    controversies. *See* sexual controversies
    cultural differences, 201

heterosexism, 201
importance of, 183
latent functions, 200
premarital sex, 189
queer theory, 201–203
regulation of, 198–200
restriction of, 186
sexual attitudes, 187–190
sexual orientation, 190–193
social-conflict analysis, 201–203
social construction, 200
and social inequality, 201
structural-functional analysis, 198–200
symbolic-interaction analysis, 200–201
theoretical analysis of, 197–203
understanding, 183–186
sexually transmitted diseases (STDs)
AIDS, 526–528
genital herpes, 526
gonorrhea, 526
HIV infection, 527
and sexual counterrevolution, 526
shaman, 85
shelters, 462
shoguns, 241
sick role, 534
significant others, 115
Simmel, Georg, 557
Singapore, 416
singlehood, 464
slavery, 86, 283, 290–292, 346
smiling, 143
Smith, Adam, 14, 387–388, 406
social behaviourism, 113
social bonds, 100
social change
causes of, 598–600
characteristics of, 598
cities, growth of, 13
civil religion, 488
conflict and, 599
controversial nature of, 598
and crowds, 578–579
and culture, 599
defined, 598
demographic change, 600
and deviance, 210
diffusion, 599
discovery, 599
and ideas, 599–600
industrial economy, 13
inevitability of, 598
intentional, 598
invention, 599
liberation theology, 476
and mobs, 578–579
modernity. See modernity
and natural environment, 600
political change, 13–14
and religion, 475–476, 487–489
secularization, 487–488
significance of, 598
and social movements, 591–592

and sociology, 13–14
taking a stand, 592
unplanned, 598
social character, 609
social class
see also social inequality; social stratification
and Aboriginal people, 268
ascription, 263–264
average-middle class, 268
and Calgary Stampede, 270
in Canada, 264–269
and Canadian families, 456
and computers, 266
computers, familiarity with, 503
and family, 269
and gender, 269, 327
and health, 522–524
lower class, 269
lower-middle class, 268–269
lower-upper class, 267
middle class, 267–269
and religion, 486
and "street" criminal, 222–223
upper class, 265–267
upper-middle class, 267–268
upper-upper class, 266–267
working class, 268–269
social conflict
alienation, 93–94
capitalists, 89
class conflict, 92–93
class consciousness, 93
defined, 89
economic system, 90
false consciousness, 91
history of, 91–92
production, 89–91
proletariat, 90
and revolution, 94
social institutions, 90
and society, 83, 89–94
social-conflict analysis
aging, 375
cultural analysis, 74–75
deviance, 215–218
family, 450
gender, 327–328
health and medicine, 537–539
modernity, 607–608
religion, 474–475
schooling, 502–508
social stratification, 248–251
sports, 22
social-conflict paradigm
critical evaluation of, 19
defined, 18
described, 18–19
Karl Marx, 19
social construction
of deviance, 218
of illness, 535
of reality. See social construction of reality
of sexuality, 200
of treatment, 535–536
social construction of reality
defined, 135

ethnomethodology, 136–137
examples of, 135–136
Thomas theorem, 136
social control
attachment, 215
belief, 215
and conformity, 215
defined, 65
and deviance, 208
Hirschi's control theory, 214–215
involvement, 215
opportunity, 215
religion, 473
and schooling, 503–504
Social Credit Party, 420
social crisis, 10
social diversity. See diversity
social dysfunctions, 17
social epidemiology
age, 522–523
defined, 522
race, 522–524
sex, 522–523
social class, 522–524
social-exchange analysis of family, 450–451
social experience. See socialization
social facts, 99
social functions, 17
social groups
vs. category, 156
vs. collectivities, 576
vs. crowd, 156
defined, 156
dyad, 161–162
formal organizations. See formal organizations
global perspective, 178–179
goal orientation, 157
group conformity, 158–160
group size, 161–162
groupthink, 160
heterogeneous groups, 163
ideal size, and purpose, 162
institutional completeness, 162–163
large groups, 162–163
leadership, 157–158
networks, 163–164
personal orientation, 157
and physical boundaries, 163
primary groups, 156–157
reference group, 160–161
secondary group, 157
social diversity, 162–163
social parity, 163
triad, 162
virtual community, 164
social identity, and status, 131
social inequality
see also social stratification
agrarian societies, 86–87
in Canada, 259–263
conflict analysis, 91–92
dimensions of, 259–263
and education, 262–263, 502–508
ethnicity and, 348–350
formal organizations, 172–173

global perspective. See global inequality
and health, 520
higher education, unequal access to, 504–508
in history, 250–251
horticultural and pastoral societies, 86
hunting and gathering societies, 84
and Kuznets curve, 252
and modernity, 607
occupation prestige, 261–262
power, 261
race and, 348–350
sexuality, 201
and streaming, 504
and testing, 504
wealth, 261
social inferiority, 342
social institutions
defined, 90
distinctive, 96
social integration, and schooling, 500–501
social interaction
defined, 131
dramaturgical analysis, 138–145
in everyday life, 145–150
humour, 146–150
Internet, 144
language and gender, 145–146
presentation of self, 138–145
role, 133–135
social construction of reality, 135–137
social structure, 131–133
social isolation
Anna's case, 107, 110
children, effects on, 110
and the elderly, 371
ethics and, 109
Genie's case, 110
Isabelle's case, 110
nonhuman primates, effects on, 109–110
social marginality, 10
social mobility
described, 236
downward social mobility, 271
intergenerational social mobility, 271
intragenerational social mobility, 271
myth vs. reality, 271–272
occupational inheritance, 271
structural social mobility, 243, 271
upward social mobility, 271
and women, 272
social movements
Aboriginal people, 584
alternative social movements, 584
bureaucratization stage, 590
coalescence stage, 590

decline stage, 590–591
defined, 576
deprivation theory, 585–586
emergence stage, 590
ethnicity and race, 584
and gender, 589
history of, 584
and ideas, 600
mass-society theory, 586
new social movements
    theory, 589
vs. other types of collective
    behaviour, 583
Quebec, 584
redemptive social movements,
    584
reformative social movements,
    584–585
regional disparities, 584
resource-mobilization theory,
    588–589
revolutionary social move-
    ments, 585
and social change, 591–592
sources of, 584
stages in, 589–591
structural-strain theory,
    586–588
types of, 584–585
social parity, 163
social placement
    family, 450
    schooling, 502
social protection, 229–230
social solidarity, 83
social stratification
    see also social inequality
    age stratification, 366–370
    ascription, 263–264
    and beliefs, 236
    Bell Curve debate, 254–255
    caste system, 237
    as characteristic of society,
        236
    class conflict, 248
    class system, 237–243
    combined caste and class
        systems, 239–243
    Davis-Moore thesis, 245–246
    defined, 235
    estate system, 240
    facts, 252–254
    former Soviet
        Union, 242–243
    functions of, 245–248
    gender stratification. *See*
        gender stratification
    global perspective. *See* global
        inequality
    and global poverty, 292
    ideology, 244–245
    income disparity, 253
    Japan, 241–242
    Kuznets curve, 252
    Marx's perspective, 248–250
    meritocracy, 247–248
    persistence over generations,
        236
    poverty, 272–277
    principles of, 236
    and religion, 486–487

social-conflict analysis,
    248–251
structural social mobility, 243
and technology, 251–252
in United
    Kingdom, 239–241
universality of, 236
values, 252–254
Weber's perspective, 250–251
social structure
    achieved status, 132
    ascribed status, 132
    defined, 16–17
    master status, 132–133
    status, 131
    status set, 132
socialism
    vs. capitalism, 390–391
    changes in socialist countries,
        391
    and communism, 389
    defined, 389
    democracy, approach to, 414
    described, 94
    failure of, 250
    features of, 389
    health care in, 531–532
socialist feminism, 329
socialist revolution, 248–249
socialization
    adolescence, 123
    adulthood, 123–125
    agents of socialization,
        117–121
    anticipatory socialization,
        119
    basic human needs, 110–111
    childhood, 122
    and cognitive development,
        111–112
    defined, 107
    dying, 125
    early adulthood, 123
    family-based socialization,
        117
    gender and, 113, 114,
        313–315
        see also gender socialization
    and life course, 122–126
    media-based socialization,
        119–122
    middle adulthood, 123–125
    and moral development, 113
    old age, 125
    and peer group, 118–119
    and personality, 110–111
    political socialization,
        424–427
    resocialization, 126–128
    school-based socialization,
        117–118, 500
    social isolation, effect of,
        109–110
    social self, 113–116
    stages of development,
        116–117
    total institutions, 126–128
society
    agrarian societies, 86–87
    anomie, 100
    better society, design of, 92

beyond ourselves, 99
changes and, 102
vs. culture, 58
defined, 58, 83
division of labour, 100–101
and environment, 560–569
evolving, 100–101
false consciousness, 91
and function, 99–101
functional
    interdependence, 100
health, impact on, 519–520,
    524–528
horticultural societies,
    85–86, 251
hunting and gathering
    societies, 84–85, 86, 251
ideal type, 94
and ideas, 83, 94–99
industrial societies, 87–88
Marx's model of society, 93
McDonaldization, 174–176
mechanical solidarity, 100
organic solidarity, 100
pastoral societies, 85–86
and personality, 99–100
postindustrial societies,
    88–89
and production, 89–91
rationality, 95
rationalization of society, 95
sexual orientation as product
    of, 191
and social conflict, 83, 89–94
social institutions, 90
social solidarity, 83
structure, 99
as system, 99
and technology, 83, 89
tradition, 95
union within, 101–102
"society," 266
sociobiology
    critical evaluation of, 76–77
    and cultural analysis, 76–77
    defined, 76
    double standard, insights
        into, 76
    and evolution, 76
sociocultural evolution
    agriculture, 86–87
    defined, 84
    horticulture, 85–86
    hunting and gathering,
        84–85, 86
    industrialism, 87–88
    limits of technology, 89
    material surplus, 85
    pastoralism, 85–86
    post-industrialism, 88–89
    shaman, 85
    summary of, 90–91
socioeconomic status (SES)
    defined, 250, 260
    as single composite
        assessment, 31
sociological investigation
    see also research
    basics of, 28–30
    common sense, 29–30
    critical sociology, 35–37

deductive logical
    thought, 49–50
gender, and research, 37–38
inductive logical thought, 49
interpretive sociology, 35
positivist sociology, 30–35
science, as "truth," 28–29
scientific evidence, 29–30
scientific sociology, 30–35
steps in, 50–51
sociological perspective
    application of, 9–11
    assessment of opportunities
        and constraints, 10
    benefits of, 10–11
    challenging assumptions, 10
    diversity, recognition of, 11
    general in the particular, 3–5
    individuality in social
        context, 6
    self-empowerment, 10–11
    strange in the familiar, 5
sociological theory
    feminist paradigm, 20
    macro-level orientation, 19
    micro-level orientation, 19
    postmodernist paradigm,
        20–21
    social-conflict paradigm,
        18–19
    structural-functional
        paradigm, 16–18
    summary of, 21
    symbolic-interaction
        paradigm, 19–20
    theoretical paradigm, 16
    theory, defined, 16
sociology
    as academic discipline, 12–13
    applied sociology, 11
    Canadian social policy,
        development of, 11
    Canadian sociology, 15–16
    defined, 3
    marginal voices, 14–15
    origins of, 12–16
    and science, 12–13
        see also science
    and social change, 13–14
    and social crisis, 10
    and social marginality, 10
solid waste, 563–564
South Africa
    apartheid in, 237, 344
    social stratification in, 239
Soviet Union, 242–243
Spanish language, 59
spanking, 228
special-status societies
    Aboriginal peoples, 350–351
    the British, 350
    the Québécois, 352–353
specialization, 168
specialized economic activity,
    100
specific deterrence, 229
Spencer, Herbert, 17
sports
    functions of, 21–22
    as interaction, 22–23
    males, orientation towards, 22

people of colour, 22
social-conflict analysis, 22
structural-function approach to, 21–22
spurious correlation, 32
"stalker" legislation, 462
Stanford County Prison, 41–42
state, 58
state capitalism, 390
state terrorism, 433
statistical measures, 31, 50
status
    achieved status, 132
    ascribed status, 132
    cultural differences in, 133
    defined, 131
    described, 131
    master status, 132–133
status consistency, 239
status set, 132
stereotypes, 338, 342
stigma, 213
Stouffer's reference group research, 160
strain theory, 211–212
streaking, 583
streaming, 504
"street" criminal
    age, 222
    ethnicity, 223
    gender, 222
    race, 223
    social class, 222–223
structural-functional analysis
    aging, 374
    credentialism, 508
    cultural analysis, 73–74
    Davis-Moore thesis, 245–246
    deviance, 210–212
    deviant subcultures, 212
    disengagement theory, 374
    family, 449–450
    gender, 326–327
    health and medicine, 534–535
    mass society, 605–607
    meritocracy, 247–248
    modernity, 605–607
    physician's role, 534
    Puritans of Massachusetts Bay, 210–211
    religion, 472–473
    schooling, 500–502
    sexuality, 198–200
    sick role, 534
    social stratification, 245–248
    sports, 21–22
    strain theory, 211–212
structural-functional paradigm
    Auguste Comte, 17
    critical evaluation of, 17–18
    defined, 16
    Émile Durkheim, 17
    Herbert Spencer, 17
    latent functions, 17
    manifest functions, 17
    Robert K. Merton, 17
    social dysfunctions, 17
    social functions, 17
    social structure, 16–17

Talcott Parsons, 17
structural social mobility, 243, 271
structural-strain theory, 586–588
subculture
    conflict subcultures, 212
    criminal subcultures, 212
    described, 67–68
    deviant subcultures, 212
    retreatist subcultures, 212
sublimation, 111
suburbs, 554
suicide
    in Aboriginal communities, 6, 219
    gender differences, 6
superego, 111
surveys
    close-ended format, 42
    defined, 42
    illustration of, 43–45
    interview, 43
    open-ended format, 42
    population, 42
    questionnaire, 42–43
    random sampling, 42
    sample, 42
    self-administered survey, 42
sustainable agricultural development, 301
sustainable world, 569–571
Sutherland's differential association theory, 214
Sweden, health care in, 532
symbolic-interaction analysis
    activity theory, 374–375
    aging, 374–375
    control theory, 214–215
    deviance, 213–215
    differential association theory, 214
    family, 450
    health and medicine, 535–536
    labelling theory, 213–214
    religion, 473–474
    sexuality, 200–201
    sports, 22–23
symbolic-interaction paradigm
    contemporary sociologists, 20
    critical evaluation of, 20
    defined, 19
    described, 20
    interpretive tradition of, 35
    Max Weber, 20
symbols, 58–59

T
tact, 144–145
taking a stand, 592
technology
    computers, and social class, 266
    defined, 65
    and environmental deficit, 561–562
    and global interconnection, 7–8
    and global poverty, 292
    and health, 520

information technology. See information technology
life-extending medical technology, 378
limits of, 89
and material culture, 65–66
organizational environment, 174
and peace, 439
politics, impact on, 430–431
and research, 48–49
and sexual revolution, 188
and society, 83, 89
    see also sociocultural evolution
strategic defence initiative (SDI), 439
technological innovations, 87
transfers, 296
teen pregnancy, 193–194
television violence, 120
terrorism, 433–435, 437
tertiary sector of the economy, 387
thanatos, 111
theological stage, 12
theoretical paradigm, 16
    see also sociological theory
theory, 16
    see also sociological theory
Thomas theorem, 136
"Three Worlds" model, invalidity of, 284
timid bigot, 342
Titanic, 238
tobacco industry, 525
Tocqueville, Alexis de, 14
Tönnies, Ferdinand, 556, 601–602
total institutions, 126–128
Total Quality Management (TQM), 177
totalitarianism, 416–417
totem, 472
touching, 143
tradition, 95
tradition-directedness, 609
traditional authority, 412
traditional societies
    see also social change
    the Kaiapo, 597
    vs. modern societies, 610
transsexuals, 185
triad, 162
trust (versus mistrust), 116
two-career marriage, 459

U
unconventional reality, 146
underemployment, 395
underground economy, 396–397
unemployment, 395–396
unemployment rate, 395, 396
United Kingdom
    estate system, 240
    health care in, 532
    schooling in, 498
    social stratification today, 240–241
United States

academic standards, 511–513
American politics vs. Canadian politics, 426
and Canada relations, after September 11, 434–435
crime rates, 223–224
direct-fee system, 532
euthanasia in, 377
functional illiteracy, 513
health care in, 532–533
high mass consumption stage, 295
income in, 260
investment in Canada, 399–400
"melting pot" characterization, 344
as nation in decline, 612–613
racial segregation, 344
religiosity, 485
Universal Declaration of Human Rights, 292
upper class, 265–267
upper-middle class, 267–268
upper-upper class, 266–267
urban ecology, 557–558
urban political economy, 558–560
urbanism
    blasé urbanite, 557
    Chicago School, 557
    Gemeinschaft, 556
    Gesellschaft, 556
    organic solidarity, 556
    urban ecology, 557–558
    urban political economy, 558–560
    as way of life, 556–560
urbanization
    see also cities
    defined, 552
    megalopolis, 555
    metropolitan era, 553–554
    in North America, 553
    in poor societies, 560
    suburbs, 554
utilitarian organizations, 166

V
validity, 31
value-free research, 33–34
values
    Canadian vs. American, 63
    defined, 62
    inconsistency and conflict, 63–64
variables
    cause and effect, 31–32
    correlation, 32
    defined, 30
    dependent variable, 31
    independent variable, 31
    measurement, 31
    operationalizing a variable, 31
    relationships among, 31–32
venereal diseases. See sexually transmitted diseases (STDs)
Verstehen, 35

victimization survey, 221
victimless crimes, 196, 220
violence
    child abuse, 462–463
    domestic violence, 114
    elder abuse, 372, 463
    family violence, 461
    and pornography, 325–326
    rape culture, 324
    sexual harassment, 324–325
    sexual violence, 196–197
    "stalker" legislation, 462
    television violence, 120
    against women, 323–326,
      461–462
Violence Against Women Survey,
  221, 462
violent crimes, 220
virtual community, 164
virtual culture, 67
voluntary associations, 167
voluntary migration, 545

W
Wallerstein's capitalist world
  economy, 298–299
war
    arms race, 437
    causes of, 436–437
    defined, 435
    Gulf War, 436
    information warfare, 438
    militarism, costs and causes
      of, 437
    nuclear weapons, 437–438
    regional conflict, 437
    terrorism and, 437
    in twentieth century,
      435–436
water pollution, 565–566
water supply, 565
wealth
    in Canada, 261, 266

concentration of, 249
explanation of, 293–294
global perspective, 288
global wealth, 287–288
Weber, Max
    alienation, and rationality,
      98–99
    authority, 412–413
    bureaucracy, 98
    Calvinism, 95–96
    capitalism, and rationality, 95
    ideal bureaucratic organiza-
      tion, 168
    ideas of, 20
    and Information
      Revolution, 101
    power, definition of, 411
    power of ideas, 83
    Protestantism and capitalism,
      95–96, 476
    rational social
      organization, 96–98
    rationalization, and
      modernity, 603–604
    rationalization of society,
      94–99
    social change, 599–600
    social stratification, 250–251
    technological innovation, 95
    value-free research, 33–34
    Verstehen, 35
    work ethic, 96
welfare capitalism, 390
welfare dilemma, 278–279
West Nile virus, 528
white-collar crime, 217–218
white-collar occupations, 249
Wirth, Louis, 557
women
    see also gender
    and AIDS, 526–527
    beauty myth, 316
    caste-like expectations,

subjection to, 244
childbearing in global
    perspective, 9
in estate system, 240
feminization of poverty, 273
gender gap in income,
    318–321, 319
global poverty, 290
global status of, 8
in hockey, 324–325
housework, 318
in Japanese society, 242
in labour force, 316–318
in medicine, 533–534
as minority, 322
minority women, 323
and modernization, 296
pink ghetto jobs, 262
in politics, 323, 428
population growth, control
    of, 551
pornography and, 325–326
prostitution, and women's
    status, 197
"second shift," 318
self-esteem, 113
sexual harassment, 324–325
and sexual revolution, 188
and social mobility, 272
and violence, 114
violence against women,
    323–326, 461–462
in workplace, 172–173
world's richest, 245
women's studies, 20
work
    agricultural employment in
      global perspective, 388
    agricultural work, decline
      in, 392
    decentralization of work, 386
    dual labour market, 392
    education and, 513–514

Information Revolution,
    impact of, 385–386
and information
    technology, 397–398
labour unions, 392–393
part-time work, 396
in post-industrial
    economy, 391
primary labour market, 392
professions, 393–394
reserve army of labour, 392
secondary labour market,
    392
self-employment, 394
service-sector employment
    in global perspective,
    388
underemployment, 395
underground economy,
    396–397
unemployment, 395–396
work ethic, 96
working class, 268–269
working poor, 275–276
world economy, 298–299
World Health
  Organization, 519, 520
world religions
    Buddhism, 483
    Christianity, 478–479
    Confucianism, 483
    East-West differences, 484
    Hinduism, 481–482
    Islam, 479–480
    Judaism, 480–481
WorldCom, 217

Y
Yucatán farmers, 301

Z
zero population growth, 55